Edison Motion Pictures, 1890-1900

16th Pordenone Silent Film Festival
October 11-18, 1997

Thomas A. Edison in his laboratory at West Orange (ca. 1890).

Charles Musser

Edison Motion Pictures, 1890-1900

An Annotated Filmography

LE GIORNATE
DEL CINEMA
MUTO

Smithsonian Institution Press

This project was made possible by grants from the New York State Council on the Arts, the New Jersey Historical Commission, and the A. Whitney Griswold Faculty Research Fund at Yale University. The publication of this book was facilitated by a grant from the Hilles Publication Fund.

The author expresses appreciation to the University Seminars at Columbia University for assistance in the preparation of the manuscript for publication. The ideas presented have benefited from discussions in the University Seminar on Cinema and Interdisciplinary Interpretation.

Italian publisher and distributor: Le Giornate del Cinema Muto
ISBN 88-86155-07-7

U.S. publisher and international distributor: Smithsonian Institution Press
ISBN 1-56098-567-4
Library of Congress Catalog Number 97-75484

Printed in Italy

04 03 02 01 00 99 98 97   5 4 3 2 1

The other day a tall, lean, lank professor, with a wise and learned air, walked in to see the kinetoscope. He had come in from town where he was teaching school and decided to take advantage of the opportunity to see the wonderful machine, being of a scholarly and investigative turn of mind. He wanted to learn the most possible from his investigation so that he might impart the knowledge to his students and he carried a notebook in his hand so as to jot down facts concerning the instrument while he looked. He paid his quarter and took his stand. "Just wait a minute," he said to the operator, "let me get my notebook." He pulled it out and placing it in position gave the signal to go ahead. The remarks jotted down by the professor strongly resemble the diary of a man on a Christmas drunk. (Clipping, unidentified New York City newspaper, ca. 1894, MH-BA.)

A party of Indians in full war paint invaded the Edison laboratory at West Orange yesterday and faced unflinchingly the unerring rapid fire of the kinetograph. It was indeed a memorable engagement, no less so than the battle of Wounded Knee, still fresh in the minds of the warriors.
It was probably more effective in demonstrating to the red men the power and supremacy of the white man, for savagery and the most advanced science stood face to face, and there was an absolute triumph for one without the spilling of a single drop of blood. (*New York Herald*, 25 September 1894.)

...historical knowledge proceeds from our narrative understanding without losing anything of its scientific ambition. (Paul Ricoeur, *Time and Narrative.*)

Contents

Acknowledgements

We initially conceived of this book as a part of a project that would celebrate the centennial of cinema. It and the accompanying exhibition of Edison motion pictures were intended to have had their debut at Pordenone's Giornate del Cinema Muto in October 1995, at the height of the anniversary hoopla. Although we missed our opening night by two years, this delay was perhaps best for Pordenone regulars as well as the Giornate organizers, the cooperating archives, and myself—all of whom were badly overextended. In fact, this catalog now benefits from some important new information that has emerged in the interim. The delay has also allowed David Francis and Patrick Loughney at the Library of Congress to complete the 35mm refilming of all relevant subjects in the Paper Print Collection and to sequence the films into chronological order. Projects such as this one have a way of getting done at their own pace, at least if they are going to be done right. As David Robinson remarked in a speech at the "Celebrating 1895" conference in Bradford, England: "We only get one chance to celebrate a centennial, so if we do it badly or not at all, we don't get a second opportunity." This project is one effort to do it well, albeit with somewhat belated results.

Begun in the late 1980s, about the time Americans were marking the 100th anniversary of Edison's submission of his first motion picture caveat to the U.S. Patent Office, *Edison Motion Pictures, 1890-1900* came to fruition due to the international support that the centennial of cinema fostered, in particular that of the Cineteca del Friuli (Gemona, Italy), the Library of Congress (Washington, D.C.), the Museum of Modern Art (New York, New York), the George Eastman House (Rochester, New York), the Academy of Motion Picture Arts and Sciences (Beverly Hills, California), and the Thomas A. Edison Papers at Rutgers University (New Brunswick, New Jersey). As this project moved forward, we decided not only to link publication of this catalog with a retrospective but to make available some relatively complete version of the Pordenone program on video cassettes through Smithsonian Video. The logic of this, therefore, pointed toward this catalog's co-publication by the Smithsonian Institution Press, of which Smithsonian Video is a part.

While this project was made possible by the contributions of several large institutions and numerous individuals, it nonetheless has a quite personal dimension. Despite the importance of the centennial, I have often felt myself to be obsessive, foolish and obviously stuck to produce yet another book on the early years of American cinema, particularly on the film activities of Thomas A. Edison and the Edison Manufacturing Company. Certainly it has wrecked havoc with my eagerness to explore new topics, new issues, and new time frames in film and cultural history. And yet, I have told myself, it is only by going deeper—by somehow exhausting the subject—that I can escape this particular area of early cinema research. Unfortunately, working on this book neither exhausted the subject nor my interest. Rather, my interest has been renewed while the topic remains unfinished. I have simply been forced to stop because of an arbitrary but necessary deadline—one that my friends at the Giornate del Cinema Muto could postpone only so many times. Having emerged from this latest ordeal, I hope that a partial escape from the specific field of inquiry will finally be possible. Yet an expanded and corrected version of this project is already anticipated on CD-ROM. The study of early cinema is proving to be a tar baby, from which I find it is extremely difficult to fight free.

In truth, this present work emerged as I tried to free myself from a previous book. When I was revising *Before the Nickelodeon: Edwin S. Porter and the Edison Manufacturing Company* for publication, I felt that the manuscript fell short in several respects. First, I had much more information than I could convey within the framework of a readable if still lengthy study of the film activities of Edwin Porter and the Edison Manufacturing Company. Although that data needed to be presented, I concluded that a filmography was a more suitable format. Second, I knew that in many areas my research could go further. There were many unanswered questions, particularly when it came to Edison-related filmmaking activities in the 1890s. Although I was reaching for answers in some areas, there was just too much minutiae to absorb and fully integrate in others. Publication of *Before the Nickelodeon* represented a consolidation of information and knowledge, not a final statement in all areas. I, at least, knew the questions and the areas where the analyses and chronologies were most speculative—or so I told myself. Third, I finally felt ready to research and analyze the era of kinetoscope production (1893-1895) in ways that I had previously avoided. I was prepared to investigate these earliest films and filmmaking practices without being overly beholden to the impressive but still problematic work of Gordon Hendricks. Thus the essay in this catalog, "Before the Rapid Firing Kinetograph: Edison Film Production, Representation and Exploitation in the 1890s," focuses on this initial period of commercial production. In the end, I could let go of my manuscript *Before the Nickelodeon* because this one was in the process of being formulated.

Creating a systematic, detailed filmography proved to be something more than a simple extension of the questions and problems posed by my efforts to write a thorough history of the Edison Manufacturing Company and its films. This new project produced a series of questions that were new and quite different from what I initial expected. In my previous work, I was interested primarily in constructing a personal, company and industry-wide history; in changing methods of production and representation; in placing cinema in a larger social and cultural framework; and in an interpretive analysis of selected films. A filmography enabled me to get at some of these issues in a new way, but also encouraged a more even study of all films as well as a greater focus on performers and events that were filmed. This was particularly true for the 1890s when so many short films were made and the problems of identification are now particularly complex. Distinguishing the different versions of the *Black Diamond Express* and of *Annabelle Serpentine Dance*, for example, became unexpected challenging—and important.

Filmographies are one of the crucial underpinnings of any serious historical scholarship in film. Perhaps, I sometimes muse, *Edison Motion Pictures* should have been my initial endeavor rather than a final swan song. Yet research aids of this type already existed albeit in skeletal form. One of the first filmographies that I encountered as a young graduate student was a simple chronological listing of Edison films in the Library of Congress Paper Print Collection, arranged by copyright date from 1897 through 1900. For many years I frequently consulted and annotated this inventory, which was compiled by Eileen Bowser, and added to it by covering the 1901-1905 period. Paul Spehr did the same for Edison's pre-paper print copyrighted material, deposited between 1894 and mid-1897.[1] These chronological listings were particularly revealing from a historian's viewpoint because they often suggested how films were shot in related groups and also revealed certain progressions and shifts in genre, subject matter, and production activity over time. One of the few published catalogs of early motion pictures was written by Kemp Niver. Niver's *Early Motion Pictures: The Paper Print Collection in the Library of Congress* listed the pictures in alphabetical order and attempted to provide some production information and a description.[2] If Niver's book was extremely useful, it also contained many inaccuracies and problematic descriptions. Once a trusting reader, I quickly learned to use the information in that catalog cautiously.[3]

Like others interested in early cinema, I increasingly asked myself: "Why could there not be a reliable filmography?" Paul Spehr spurred this search by introducing me to several Edison film catalogs. Such items provided a second kind of filmographic information—detailed descriptions of films that were usually more informative and more accurate than those appearing in Niver's book. Through the good graces of Reese Jenkins and the Thomas A. Edison Papers, I soon became involved in the systematic collection of these crucial documents—gathered from archives, museums, libraries, court records, and private collectors—and their microfilming.[4] These immensely useful materials were crucial to the construction of a more extensive filmography, even though they had significant limitations. Jay Leyda sent me to trade journals where

Edison advertisements often provided the names of films that are neither copyrighted nor appear in surviving catalogs.

Of course, my desire for a reliable filmography was shared with many others working in the field, some of whom were either pursuing or had pursued similar projects. When Gordon Hendricks' papers became available at the Smithsonian Institution, I discovered that he had been working on a filmography of Edison kinetoscope films before his death. His files provided me with much helpful information for this present undertaking. George Pratt had generated many chronological listings of films by production companies, which he kept in his wonderful notebooks. Not only did George give me access to this material, we discussed the present project extensively in the years before his death. George's documentary history of American silent film, *Spellbound in Darkness*, also serves as one obvious model for this present effort.[5] The effort to combine historical rigor with high bibliographic standards was a shared goal.

Edison Motion Pictures, 1890-1900 has come to fruition in parallel with three other somewhat related undertakings. Ray Phillips has been working on a filmography of Edison films from the first kinetoscope motion pictures until the end of 1896. Ray has become a friend whom I admire for his diligence, generosity and thoughtfulness. In many respects our interests and research talents are complimentary: he possesses a sensitivity to technology that exceeds my own—even to the point of constructing replicas of Edison kinetoscopes. And he has located and identified many films in European and American archives. We have been able to share at least some of our respective discoveries, providing each other with appreciative encouragement for the research victories that have been won. At various points I suggested that we combine forces. In the end, our projects were different enough so that Ray's decision to pursue separate but parallel courses was probably the correct one. But this project is a better one, and has been a more enjoyable one, because of Ray. I can only hope that the exchange has not been too one-sided.

More recently I have learned that the Archives du film at Bois d'Arcy, France, has been constructing a detailed Lumière filmography under the direction of Michelle Aubert. From several brief discussions, it seems remarkably similar in format to this one. Our interests in reconstructing the context in which films were shot and exhibited, for example, led us to include extensive quotations of relevant newspaper articles. Because Edison and the Lumières played somewhat similar roles during the formative moments of commercial motion pictures, a comparison between the two catalogs should be rewarding.[6] Moreover, the study of early cinema has now reached a stage in which the comparison between national cinemas can be unusually fruitful. I have made a small effort in this direction with the essay in this volume.

The third project is the American Film Institute's filmography of motion pictures distributed in the United States through 1910: *The American Film Institute Catalog of Motion Pictures Produced in the United States. Film Beginnings 1893-1910: A Work in Progress*.[7] In the last six or seven years I made a number of efforts at coordination and mutual assistance with the AFI, loaning their compiler for that volume, Elias Savada, my personal microfilm copy of *Motion Picture Catalogs by American Producers and Distributors, 1894-1908* when the AFI concluded it could not afford to purchase its own. As I sought funding from the National Endowment for the Humanities for a filmography of Edison films covering the 1890-1908 period, Michael Friend, then acting co-director of the AFI National Center for Film and Video Preservation, arranged for that project to receive the AFI's sponsorship. The NEH unfortunately did not provide the ambitious funding I had hoped (in fact, no funding at all), requiring me to proceed with a more limited time frame, with a different structure, and on a more *ad hoc* basis. At least some of the ideas that make this present filmography distinctive and particularly useful were, I later learned, subsequently incorporated into the AFI's pre-1910 catalog—including the systematic reprinting of contemporaneous descriptions of motion picture subjects, not a feature of previous AFI publications of this kind. Although ideas are not copyrightable, these descriptions were also lifted en mass (and so far as I can tell unacknowledged) from the microfilm edition of catalogs that I had compiled over many years. But then my relationship with the AFI National Center for Film and Video Preservation has been troubled ever since the departure of Michael Friend and the publication of my sometimes critical (though generally enthusiastic) review of the AFI 1910s feature film catalog.[8]

More generally I have been blessed by the assistance of people who share an interest if not a passion for early film. Often contributing in small ways that have ultimately accumulated, they have made a profound difference. Andy Lazes, the computer programmer for this project, has always been there when I needed him—usually when something had to be done yesterday. He deserves special thanks. Harriet Harrison and Wendy White-Hensen have provided crucial bibliographic advise, though it must be emphasized that the shortfalls of this filmography should in no respect be considered their responsibility. Ben Singer was the designated Associate Editor when I was looking for substantial funding for this project and was the first person to help with the research on this project.

A group of scholars lent their names to the project as members of an editorial board. Since this filmography never gained sufficient funding, I could not employ them in the ways we had envisioned. Nonetheless, they were consistently supportive and deserve my deepest thanks: Eileen Bowser, curator emeritus, Department of Film and Video, Museum of Modern Art; Michael Friend, now curator at the Academy of Motion Picture Arts and Sciences; Miriam Hansen, professor, Department of English, University of Chicago; Steven Higgins, collections manager, Department of Film and Video, Museum of Modern Art; Reese Jenkins, professor, Department of History, Rutgers University and former director and general editor of the Thomas A. Edison Papers; Patrick Loughney, assistant head of the Motion Picture, Broadcasting, Recorded Sound Division, Library of Congress; Brooks McNamara, professor, Department of Performance Studies, NYU, and director of the Shubert Archives; Robert Rosen, professor and chair of the Department Film and Television and director, UCLA Film and Television Archives; Robert Sklar, professor, Department of Cinema Studies, NYU; Paul Spehr, former assistant head of the Motion Picture, Broadcasting, Recorded Sound Division, Library of Congress.

Often patient colleagues at the Department of Film and Video, Museum of Modern Art have been consistently supportive of this project—including Mary Lea Bandy, Peter Williamson, Charles Silver, Ron Magliozzi, Mary Corliss, John Johnson and Ann Morra. Assistance from the Department of Cinema Studies—particularly from chair William Simon, Richard Allen, Antonia Lant and the late William K. Everson—has been invaluable in different ways and at different stages. In conjunction with the Department of Cinema Studies at NYU, the Museum of Modern Art co-sponsored the June 1994 Domitor Conference "Cinema Turns 100," and screened numerous pre-1900 films from different archives over a several day period, fostering fruitful comparisons of film titles and variant prints of the same subject. *Filmmaking for Edison's Kinetoscope, 1890-1895: A Filmography with Documentation* was also distributed to participants at that event. That filmography was a preliminary (and now embarrassingly outdated) publication of the first approximately 150 entries in the present undertaking. It created an invaluable framework for subsequently refinements.

Archives and archivists from around the world have contributed to this catalog, notably Luke McKernan of the British Film Institute (London), Jan-Christopher Horak while at the George Eastman House (Rochester, New York), D.J. Turner at the National Film Archive of Canada (Ottawa), Richard Koszarski at the American Museum of the Moving Image (Astoria, New York), and Michelle Aubert at the Archives du film, Centre national de la cinématographie. George Tselos and Nancy Waters at the Edison National Historic Site were long-time allies. Collectors Charles Hummel, Alan Konigsberg, and Lawrence Schlick supplied catalogs and other early materials. Peter DeCherney volunteered to play the role of chief research assistant for several months and without remuneration. Tim Muir, a pen pal, has provided invaluable information about Edison's filmmaking activities in the Northwest, particularly related to the Klondike Gold Rush. John Cloud, a rope performance artist, and Lorena Chambers, have helped with information about Buffalo Bill's Wild West. Richard Brown and Barry Anthony, experts on the kinetoscope and British Mutoscope & Biograph Company in Great Britain have also been helpful. Tom Gunning kindly commented on the essay in this volume. A rapidly expanding community of early film scholars has provided assistance both spiritual and practical: among those not otherwise mentioned: André Gaudreault, Roberta Pearson, William Uricchio, Ansje van

Beusekom, Richard Abel, Don Crafton, Kristin Thompson, Ben Brewster, Lea Jacobs, Matthew Solomon, Thomas Elsaesser, Yuri Tsivian, Janet Staiger, Hiroshi Komatsu, Gregory Waller, Marta Braun, Dan Streible, Noël Burch, Laurent Mannoni and Christian Delage should be thanked. Michael Kerbel at the Yale Film Study Center has always been an active and understanding supporter. Ralph McKay and Patricia Leonardi assisted with the time-consuming task of inputting documents.

This project was made possible by the financial assistance of a number of institutions and organizations. These include the New York State Council for the Arts, the New Jersey Historical Commission, the University Seminars at Columbia University, the Griswold Faculty Research Fund and the Hilles Publication Fund at Yale University. J. Paul Getty, Jr. also helped to support the actual publication of this work. I performed much of the initial work on this project while on a NEH Fellowship during the 1990-91 academic year. The catalog was essential completed while I was on a Morse Fellowship during the 1994-95 academic year.

When this catalog was in its early stages, I discussed it at considerable length with George Pratt. George was not on the advisory board because, as he knew, I planned to dedicate *Edison Motion Pictures, 1890-1900* to him. He approved of, or at least graciously accepted, this role. Unfortunately he died before this project could be completed. George was a feisty guy; he either liked you and was an immensely generous friend, or he did not have much use for you. I was one of the lucky ones: as a young scholar he taught me a great deal about various kinds of primary source research. We remained close and had many wonderful meals together. But this dedication is more than a former apprentice's homage to one of his masters. Pratt's writings on the cinema stand up today, thirty to forty years after they were published, in a way that is almost unique among his contemporaries. Because most of his work was published in the Eastman House journal *Image*, it is less well-known to the present generation of scholars than it should be.[9]

As I worked intensively on this project for the last several years, Hisami Kuroiwa has provided the everyday pleasures and support that make life worth living. Forging a post-modern, bi-cultural household has been our happy adventure—one in which our children Kai and Hannah have taken part. During this period Hisami worked as a producer on such films as Wayne Wang's and Paul Auster's *Smoke* and *Blue in the Face* as well as Hal Hartley's *Flirt* and Frank Grow's *Love God*. Our fax machine, which seems to operate around the clock, has thus transmitted and received correspondence about both the cinema's beginnings and its most current productions. Thomas Edison would, I think, approve. In truth this everyday merging of rapid communication and moving image culture has made me appreciate the inventor's overarching vision and contribution to our world in a deeper way than ever before.

Charles Musser
May 1997

1. Bowser's list and my own were placed in files at the Museum of Modern Art Film Study Center. Paul Spehr published his more polished list as part of an article, "Edison Films in the Library of Congress," in Iris Newsom, ed., *Wonderful Inventions: Motion Pictures, Broadcasting, and Recorded Sound at the Library of Congress* (Washington, D.C.: Library of Congress, 1985), 34-50.

2. Kemp R. Niver with Bebe Bergsten, *Motion Pictures from the Library of Congress Paper Print Collection, 1894-1912* (Berkeley: University of California Press, 1967), subsequently revised and reorganized as *Early Motion Pictures: The Paper Print Collection in the Library of Congress* (Washington, D.C.: Library of Congress, 1985). Two other catalogs worth noting: Rita Horwitz and Harriet Harrison with Wendy White, *The George Kleine Collection of Early Motion Pictures in the Library of Congress: A Catalog* (Washington, D.C.: Library of Congress, 1980) and Wendy White-Hensen and Veronica M. Gillespie, *The Theodore Roosevelt Association Film Collection* (Washington, D.C.: Library of Congress, 1986). Both compare favorably to Niver's effort but unfortunately deal with smaller and more eclectic groups of films.

3. Niver inappropriately attributes various films made in 1899 and 1900 to Edwin S. Porter. This was consistent with the account of Lewis Jacobs, who wrote that Porter worked as a cameraman for the Edison Manufacturing Company during the 1890s (*The Rise of the American Film* [New York: Harcourt, Brace, 1939], 35). Soon I learned that Terry Ramsaye's account of Porter's activities in this period—during which

he was an exhibitor and "operator" (i.e., a projectionist)—was much closer to the mark (*A Million and One Nights* [New York: Simon and Shuster, 1926], 341-348, 399-400, 414-421).

4. Charles Musser et al., *Motion Picture Catalogs by American Producers and Distributors, 1894-1908: A Microfilm Edition* (Frederick, Md.: University Publications of America, 1985).

5. George Pratt, *Spellbound in Darkness: A History of the Silent Film* (Greenwich, Ct: New York Graphic Society, 1966).

6. Michelle Aubert's Lumière project had not been published at the time of this writing.

7. Elias Savada, compiler, *The American Film Institute Catalog of Motion Pictures Produced in the United States. Film Beginnings 1893-1910: A Work in Progress* (Metuchen, N.J.: Scarecrow Press, 1995).

8. Charles Musser, "Patricia King Hanson, executive editor, *The American Film Institute Catalog of Motion Pictures Produced in the United States, Feature Films, 1911-1920,*" *Cineaste* 17, no. 3 (1990), 64. I outlined my main criticisms and kudos for this volume with acting director Michael Friend, who encouraged me to publish the review.

9. Many of George Pratt's articles on early film were reprinted in Marshall Deutelbaum, ed., *"Image": On the Art and Evolution of the Film* (New York: Dover, 1979).

Before the Rapid Firing Kinetograph:
Edison Film Production, Representation and Exploitation in the 1890s

This essay re-examines the beginnings of modern motion pictures, focusing on those films intended for exhibition in the peep-hole kinetoscope and produced at the Edison Laboratory in West Orange, New Jersey, between 1893 and 1895. It also comments on the shift to projection (to the cinema) in the United States and briefly considers aspects of Edison production through the end of the nineteenth century in light of these earlier activities. Finally it compares the emergence of a representational system in Edison kinetoscope films to its equivalent in the first Lumière productions. Though returning to subject matter I have previously analyzed in sections of at least two books, this re-examination has been necessitated by the new research performed for this filmography as well as the opportunity to reflect on this material in light of the present state of film studies. The kinetoscope era, I am increasingly convinced, involved important histori-cal conjunctions that merit intensive analysis. The exhibition of motion pictures in Edison's kinetoscope did more than inspire several inventors to develop viable systems for projection; these first films—more than 135 were taken between 1893 and 1895— also had their own cultural impact. This impact was extended and in many respects transformed by subsequent cinema, which is another way of saying that kinetoscope practices had a profound influence on cinema's subsequent formation.

We could say that the dialectical interaction of screen practices (the magic lantern, stereopticon, and so forth) with motion picture production for peep-hole exhibition yielded the cinema.[1] A number of historians have looked at cinema as part of the larg-er history of screen practice.[2] Certainly this approach has enabled scholars to stop conceiving of the pre-cinema as a process of technological gestation that resulted in the birth of cinema, of a new cultural form that would mature and eventually achieve eloquence and greatness. From this perspective, which is primarily *a perspective based on exhibition*, the cinema is conceived both as part of a longer, ongoing cultural prac-tice and as something that was new, a departure from past practices. The history of projected images had already gone through at least three major transformations—the introduction of the magic lantern itself, Étienne-Gaspard Robertson's Fantasmagorie, and the adoption of photographic images for projection. Moreover, showmen had grad-ually developed a vast array of mechanisms which, when placed in the lantern, pro-duced movement on the screen—from panoramic and slip slides to narrow aquariums filled with sea life. Cinema, the fourth transformation, found a way to encompass the impetus behind almost all of these eclectic moving-image devices in a way that was much more systematic, efficient and scientific.

Scholarship published in the last thirty years has generally ignored the second part of this dialectic—that of pre-cinema motion picture practices. Here I am particularly concerned with kinetoscope practices *from the perspective of film production*—kineto-graph practices to use the name that Edison gave to his motion picture camera— though here as elsewhere it is impossible to completely separate production and exhi-bition. There are many reasons for this comparative absence of attention, including the kinetoscope's own brief history. As Yuri Tsivian has noted, newspaper coverage of the kinetoscope's introduction and initial reception was very slight in comparison to the comments, reviews and advertisement that hailed the cinema's arrival.[3] This neglect has made the historian's task much more difficult, even as it suggests that the kinetoscope's immediate cultural significance was slight—perhaps slight enough to justify scholarly disinterest. Indeed, the kinetoscope was in many respects a novelty item, a kind of optical toy which enjoyed a brief fad.

Historiography and Gordon Hendricks

Our recent neglect of the kinetoscope period has yet another reason, one that has been largely forgotten—the caustic historiography of Gordon Hendricks: *The Edison Motion*

Picture Myth, *The Kinetoscope* and *The Beginnings of the Biograph*.[4] Although Hendricks' pioneering work defined the field, he presented his exhaustive research in ways that verged on the impenetrable. Underneath his convoluted, elusive and intimidating style, he presented a convincing chronology of Edison's experiments and clearly demonstrated the historiographic shortcomings of Terry Ramsaye, Matthew Josephson, and others. When film studies was being formed as a discipline, Hendricks' work stood out for its seriousness of purpose and research. Even its opaque writing style meant that history was not "simple"; it could be "difficult" in ways that an Althussarian Marxist might have appreciated. It was not history for the layman, but a teasing out and questioning of specific documents. It set standards for historiographic rigor and served as a model for those coming up in the emergent discipline of film studies.

Behind Hendricks' claims to historical objectivity and meticulousness lurked a powerful anti-Edison, anti-establishment stance. Thomas Alva Edison—embodiment of the American work ethic, symbol of American ingenuity and can-do creativity—was nothing more than the Machiavellian creator of his own fraudulent legend. Certainly this irreverent questioning of iconographic figures bound up with American identity was in keeping with emerging leftist attitudes of the 1960s. His approach thus appealed to the young turks taking on the film studies establishment in the late-1960s and 1970s: scholars such as Jacques Deslandes and Noël Burch in France, Douglas Gomery, Robert C. Allen, Janet Staiger, André Gaudreault and (why not) myself. For numerous reasons Hendricks garnered our admiration and respect. His iconoclasm refused politesse and easy language. His writings were a syncretic meshing of quotes, reflections, and analyses that lay bare the process of historical writing. They had a heavily ironic tone and yet claimed to offer truth. They spoke truth to power, confronting the cultural elite and implicitly a larger political establishment. For, if Edison could lie about when and how he "invented" the motion picture camera, then—well, then American Presidents could lie about just about anything, including the overthrow of dictators in South Vietnam and North Vietnamese actions used to justify U.S. military intervention in Southeast Asia.

Hendricks did much to invigorate film history in the United States. He demonstrated that important issues were at stake in the field. If platitudes about the invention of cinema proved false, then unknown truths potentially lurked underneath every piece of received wisdom. Hendricks broke with a consensus history in which sustained, in-depth research had seemed almost unnecessary.[5] His fundamental and important influence on contemporary historiography has been quite different from that of other prominent historians who wrote about silent film: archivist scholars such as Iris Barry, Jay Leyda, George Pratt, Eileen Bowser and Paul Spehr.[6] These five also believed in research and revision but spoke with a quieter, more reflective voice. They were mature in a way that we admired but also (as products of 1960s youth culture) were not then always prepared to emulate.

If Hendricks' somewhat obsessive examination of a small area of American motion picture practice opened up the entire history of American cinema for re-examination, it made his own particular domain—the invention and initial exploitation of motion pictures—somewhat off limits. One did not take on a topic that had been detailed so magnificently when other areas were less studied and seemed certain to need substantial revision. It made much more sense for would-be revisionists to take on the work of Lewis Jacobs, Arthur Knight and other old chestnuts rather than the great revisionist himself. Hendricks' knowledge and erudition were not only indisputable, they were virtually unfathomable. He often boasted, for example, a firm knowledge of weather patterns in the Newark area during the mid-1890s. Hendricks had erected fence posts that marked out his terrain, then metaphorically pissed on them. He claimed, for example, to have found 130 to 140 mistakes of fact and opinion in the chapter Matthew Josephson devoted to the invention of motion pictures in his Edison biography. Of these Hendricks detailed a "representative" sixty six.[7] Young upstarts entered his domain at their peril. If a Pulitzer prize-winning historian such as Josephson proved to be sucker-x, then one did not want to wake up some morning and find oneself labeled "sucker-y." Assuming Hendricks even deigned to recognize one's own paltry efforts. In short, the kinetoscope area was too highly charged to pursue. It seemed better (wiser, safer, etc.) to develop one's skills as a film historian with some other, perhaps related topic.

People used and cited Hendricks when it seemed appropriate, principally to evoke W.K.L. Dickson as the "real" inventor of modern motion pictures and to dismiss Edison as a fraud. But there was a funny way in which Hendricks not only defined the field, he made it a sterile one. In books dedicated to art gallery owner Leo Castelli, he limited his concerns primarily to those of chronology, technology and true authorship. The films' cultural significance was pushed aside; the Edison mythology, the biographical legend, was Hendricks' preoccupation. Moreover, there was a peculiar way in which Hendricks' anti-Edison diatribes meshed with the French-Lumièriste position that has seen the cinématographe in Lyons as the beginnings of, and embodiment of, an entirely new expressive form. For it was in regard to the beginnings of projection in the United States that Hendricks was unexpectedly silent. To be "anti-Edison" was not only to be anti-American in the midst of the Vietnam War but pro-French in a way that 1) was consonant with the autobiography of Lumière cameraman Félix Mesguich and 2) made a certain kind of sense in the era of the glorious French Nouvelle Vague.[8] From Edison came Hollywood, from the Lumières—Jean-Luc Godard.

As one might expect, Hendricks has not been a very beloved figure at the Edison National Historic Site—nor at the Thomas A. Edison Papers. As former Edison Papers director Reese Jenkins has astutely remarked, Hendricks just wanted to replace Edison with *his* own hero, William Kennedy Laurie Dickson. Dickson is, after all, the common thread that links together Hendricks' trilogy of books on the beginnings of American film. The Edison Papers thus provided a space where a "young historian" such as myself could begin to rethink the historical landscape mapped out by Hendricks. While holding on to Hendricks' chronology (which I continue to find fundamentally correct) and his iconoclasm (for better or worse), I was able to think about the invention of the kinetograph-kinetoscope motion picture system within the larger context of Edison's work and his laboratory practices. But if this framework pointed the way beyond Hendricks and the demonization of Edison, the focus of the Edison Papers project has necessarily been on the history of technology, on the process of invention, and to a lesser extent commercial exploitation.

Our ability and need to return to the kinetoscope era has diverse sources. The substantial body of historical writings on early film has made Hendricks' contribution less overwhelming in today's context. Moreover, film scholars have utilized an array of theoretical insights and interpretive strategies that were not available to Hendricks, even if he had been prepared to use them. The concept of cinema of attractions, articulated by Tom Gunning, can readily be adapted to the films of this pre-cinematic era.[9] André Bazin, psycho-analytic and feminist film theory, and cultural studies: all are essentially post-Hendricks movements in relation to American film studies.[10] But once again, we can ask why many of these theoretical perspectives were not applied sooner.

Hendricks never participated in or contributed actively to the interest in early cinema that came out of the Brighton (England) Conference of 1978.[11] He was a loner, a man of particular obsessions with few ties to the larger film studies community. Paul Spehr, who worked in the Motion Picture section of the Library of Congress (its assistant chief for many years and often its acting director), recalls having a short and somewhat confrontational exchange with Hendricks when the historian was in Washington, D.C.[12] The revisionist was looking for documentation that could prove his conviction that Edison had not invented the motion picture camera. I had only one brief phone conversation with Hendricks, during which he informed me that he had no pre-1908 motion picture catalogs for a microfilm project on which I was then working. Although he may have already been ill (and I was too awed to speak freely), he expressed no curiosity about what I was then doing. Remoteness may have contributed to his mystique and turned him into a legend of his own, for it is my impression that Hendricks' death somehow made it easier for historians to reconsider the subject area that he had mastered. The more recent availability of his personal archive at the Smithsonian Institution and his film collection at the Library of Congress has simultaneously provided valuable documentation and revealed the limits of his actual research. This is not to suggest that the Emperor had no clothes—Hendricks' research was truly pioneering *and* impressive, though it did have distinct limitations. He left behind materials that demystify the great demystifier—himself. In light of this volume's principal undertaking, it was personally interesting to learn that Hendricks had also been working on a filmography of early Edison films (specifically for the kinetoscope era). Although his filmography was still in its early stages, Hendricks' files for this project contain information that proved useful to the present project in a number of instances. If Hendricks as a figure helps to explain the dearth of research and writing in this area over the past thirty years, he perhaps now facilitates the process of reinvestigation.[13]

Starting from Edison's earliest 35mm motion pictures, this essay seeks to return to certain basic questions. What can the kinetoscope films tell us about movie-making at this formative moment (1893-1895)? How might we characterize the repertoire of representational strategies appearing in these films? What kinds of meanings were attached to these images and how did they imagine the world? Why and how did these films come into existence? What functions did they perform within the framework of an ascendant commercial popular culture? What was their relationship to the larger culture and society? And what impact did they have on subsequent motion picture practice and American life? I want to use these films to make a series of points in ten distinct but related areas, moving forward in a loose historical progression.[14] In examining these early stages of Edison filmmaking, it has proved illuminating to contrast these practices to comparable developments at the Lumière factory. Lumière production came at a slightly later time period; and while not entirely free of Edison influence in terms of subject matter and representational methods, fundamental differences as well as some unexpected parallels exist between the two.

Films for Demonstration Purposes: Spaces, Real and Constructed

One area in which this present filmography departs from Hendricks' chronology (and my own account in *The Emergence of Cinema* and *Before the Nickelodeon*) has to do with the extent of Edison motion picture production during 1893, the year before motion pictures were introduced on a commercial basis. After the experimental process has been completed but before the onset of commercial production, Dickson and Heise made several demonstration films that included *Blacksmithing Scene* (film no. 16), *Horse Shoeing* (no. 17), and *The Barber Shop* (no. 18). A news article in the *Brooklyn Eagle*, which Hendricks and I both somehow managed to overlook, describes

Blacksmithing Scene (film no. 16, 1893).

the showing of *Horse Shoeing* at the Brooklyn Institute of Arts & Sciences on 9 May 1893.[15]At least two films were thus presented on that occasion: *Blacksmithing Scene* (mentioned in an article appearing in *Scientific American*) and *Horse Shoeing* (which Hendricks had "definitely" excluded from this period).[16]

What kinds of spaces were depicted in Edison's demonstration films, made in 1893? In contrast to the experimental subjects made before this trilogy and the vast majority of kinetoscope pictures made afterwards, Edison filmmakers chose to construct simple if meticulous sets that represented well-developed and self-consciously chosen spaces. These locations were not taken from life: the camera was not moved outdoors to shoot the local blacksmith shop that did, in fact, exist at the Edison Laboratory and continued to serve its needs. Nor was an exhaustive replica assembled inside the Black Maria itself. These locales are rendered schematically; they are suggested by the inclusion of carefully chosen props—an anvil and forge, or a barber's chair, a barber's pole and sign. The self-conscious rendering of these spaces was, in fact, foregrounded by their placement against the simple black walls of the studio interior. These were not casual, quickly-done productions. If their running time was brief (about 15 seconds) and quite simple, their forum and place in the Edison production chronology requires us to take them seriously.

Horse Shoeing (film no. 17, 1893).

What is the relationship among 1) these mock spaces (blacksmith shop and barber shop), 2) the more substantive studio space in which they had been constructed (the Black Maria), and 3) the enclosing and essential milieu of the Edison Laboratory itself? Like Russian wooden folk dolls, the depicted spaces are contained within the studio space which is set neatly within the large laboratory. Yet these overlapping spaces have many similarities. Edison employees appearing in the films were simultaneously performing work in the real spaces of the Black Maria and the Edison Laboratory as well as in the mock space of the black smith shop where they worked by pretending to work, in short by acting. The world of the Edison Laboratory—perhaps the ultimate center for modern, innovative technology in 1893—was humorously transfigured in ye olde fashioned blacksmith shoppe. The fictive work carried on with anvil and forge became a kind of play.

For Edison and his employees the newly built Black Maria enabled play to be considered work, and work to become a kind of play. In many respects this is the subject of *Blacksmithing Scene,* the more revealing of the two films that premiered at the Brooklyn Institute. Three blacksmiths work together, shaping a piece of metal in a single work cycle that includes not only hammering the iron but passing around and imbibing from a beer bottle. Work, pleasure, and socializing are again integrated within this view that can accurately be described as nostalgic. Roy Rosenzweig has remarked that work and socializing were increasingly separated by the late nineteenth century, with drinking on the job considered part of a bygone era.[17] This film already reveals a kind of historical impulse, a looking backwards that feeds the ultimate technological novelty—a taste of things to come. Nostalgia continued to be rampant in Edison film production: whether filming Buffalo Bill, Annie Oakley and Sioux Indians (nos. 61-64, 86) after the close of the frontier; ritual ceremonies that eulogized America's heroes such as Ulysses S. Grant (nos. 325-337) and George Dewey (nos. 731-754); or short bad boy comedies which were designed to recall the carefree days of male youth (e.g. *Wringing Good Joke,* no. 679). With *Blacksmithing Scene,* the newest and most modern technology is used to prop up and document a past that it is quickly making obsolete. As André Bazin has remarked film embalms time. Cinematic examples of salvage anthropology, such as *Nanook of the North* (1922), would later reach back and recreate early points of time—then capture them on film. While one does not want to over-read short films such as these, *Blacksmithing Scene* might be considered an initial foray in this direction.

If *Blacksmithing Scene* points to a receding past, it also suggests that the interpenetration of work and leisure still characterized the Edison Laboratory, depicting it in some respects as a utopic, non-alienated space. More accurately filmmaking was a break from the everyday demands of work and experimentation. This shifted form during the following year when professional entertainers began to perform at the studio. The Black Maria became a profitable distraction from Edison's financially disastrous and ultimately unsuccessful efforts at iron ore milling—a project that exhausted the inventor and demoralized his staff. Edison, Dickson and other employees soon found themselves socializing with stars of the variety stage—and "Wizard Edison" was a vaudeville fan. The famed inventor also apparently attended at least some of the boxing exhibitions staged in the Black Maria, a throw back to his youth when he had attended fights in the rougher spots of Manhattan's night life. *Blacksmithing Scene* and *Horse Shoeing* hint at the complex interrelationships—perhaps impossible to pin down either in these films or in the culture of the Edison Laboratory—among work, play and creativity.

Blacksmithing Scene can be contrasted to the Lumières' "first film," *Sortie d'usine*, known in English as *Employees Leaving the Lumière Factory*. In its single shot, the Lumières filmed a complex, transitional space that encompasses both the space of work (the factory) and the space of leisure (the space outside).[18] It is a film that focuses on the boundary between work and play, rather than on their interpenetrations. As Noël Burch has pointed out, the Lumières filmed *their* employees leaving *their* factory after a day of productive toil.[19] Serious work is not interrupted so the Lumière employees might play with this newest novelty. Nor is labor treated in an ironic, mocking way. There is the world of work inside, and the realm of rest and relaxation outside. The two realms, though dependent on each other, are carefully separated. It is a well-regulated and apparently happy world—testimony to the beneficence of Lumière paternalism. Employment by the Lumières does not appear unduly burdensome and there is a certain esprit that is generated by the very act of filming, one that is communicated by the gestures and movements of the employees as they head home (indeed, as Alan Williams has suggested, this scene was probably carefully staged).[20] *Sortie d'usine* is a film made by a self-consciously "enlightened" owner of a large business enterprise. Designed for demonstration purposes (it was shown at various lectures prior to the cinématographe's official premiere), the film served the practical role of self-promotion. *Blacksmithing Scene* was created by Edison's employees working independently of their boss' supervision. However, it was not made by the poorly paid wage earners who labored in Edison's factories (the inventor-entrepreneur would soon break the strike of their fledgling union),[21] but by the cherished members of his laboratory staff—employees who enjoyed considerable latitude to strike a more independent, anarchic attitude.

This then is the first point about *Blacksmithing Scene* and *Horse Shoeing*: as representations they are at once nostalgic and modern, serious and self-mocking, ambiguous and finally contradictory. They are about spaces, particularly that eccentric, almost carnivalesque space that very early on was called the Black Maria, named after the black paddy wagons that brought prisoners to jail. Yet in this topsy turvy world of representations and naming, this Black Maria offered escape into nostalgia and play rather than the likelihood of imprisonment.

Representations of Production, Methods of Invention

Blacksmithing Scene and *Horse Shoeing*, films of symbolic weight, can be analyzed from a perspective that reposes questions about the organization of work (including film production) and the processes of invention at the Edison Laboratory (particularly that of Edison's motion picture system). Recall that there has been many arguments over who should get credit for the invention of the kinetograph-kinetoscope motion picture system. Was it Thomas Alva Edison as Terry Ramsaye and others have maintained or was it William Kennedy Laurie Dickson as Gordon Hendricks has contended?[22] This now sterile debate needs to be framed in different terms—from whom to how. Evidence suggests that it was Edison working with Dickson, as well as Dickson working with William Heise (assigned to the project by Edison), that produced this motion picture system. Evidence not only comes from diverse written documentation pertinent to motion picture experimentation, which can be found at the Edison National Historic Site. The early motion pictures offer key visual evidence as well.

Horse Shoeing shows two men at work, one shaping horseshoes at the forge and the other shoeing the hooves (a third holds the horse's reins). Custom might suggest who is in charge, but both execute essential tasks in a collaborative working method. Their behavior suggests a kind of partnership rather than an employer-employee relationship. Likewise the fictionalized work space of *Blacksmithing Scene* has someone "in charge"—the head blacksmith—but lines of authority are attenuated by egalitarianism and informality. Both films, made in the Black Maria, speak to the way work was performed at the Edison Laboratory more generally. They mime the approach to invention used by Edison—with electric light and other technologies, including film. Despite his nickname ("the Wizard"), the inventor leaned more toward collaboration and partnership than hierarchy and solitary genius when in the laboratory.

Neither *Blacksmithing Scene* nor *Horse Shoeing* shows a solitary blacksmith working alone. This is hardy coincidence. These films, moreover, have an important precursor, the experimental film entitled *A Hand Shake*, made in 1892. It shows Dickson and William Heise congratulating each other on a successful effort—the invention of modern motion pictures. The frames exist self-reflexively, as evidence to substantiate the cause of their jubilation. Who deserves credit for this achievement? Read narrow-

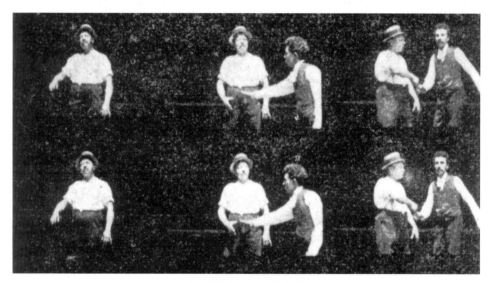

A Hand Shake (film no. 15, 1892).

ly, the film itself suggests that it was neither Edison nor Dickson but Dickson and a third person—Heise, who had been assigned to the project in the fall of 1890. Heise's expertise in advancing rolls of paper tape through an automatic telegraph made him a valuable new member of the motion picture team.[23] In fact, the invention of the Edison motion picture system involved two collaborative pairings—Edison/Dickson and Dickson/Heise. *Horse Shoeing* thus recapitulates the symmetry of *A Hand Shake*. But once again, *Blacksmithing Scene* seems the richer of these two films, for the three blacksmiths would seem to have their counterparts in the three inventors. This is not an effort to split the difference between Ramsaye and Hendricks but to understand the process of invention within the historically specific conditions of production.

Collaborations, based on partnership practices, seem to have been crucial to the development of motion picture technology. Many of the weighty debates about these inventions are disputes over which member of a collaborative pair deserves credit. This seems counterproductive, insensitive to the nature of collaboration itself. Thomas Armat and C. Francis Jenkins, partners on the phantoscope venture, developed modern projection utilizing an intermittent mechanism. When the two had a falling out, they each claimed chief responsibility for something that was a joint effort. In

England, the partnership between Robert W. Paul and Birt Acres has likewise left lingering disputes. Auguste and Louis Lumière, in contrast, claimed joint responsibility for the cinématographe. Only with Louis' death did Auguste reveal that his brother deserved the real credit (or did he?).[24] It was a generous attribution that Louis was hardly in a position to protest. (But then, as Alan Williams and Thomas Elsaesser have noted, the brothers did many things together, including marry sisters of the Winckler family.)[25]

Likewise, filmmaking in late nineteenth and early twentieth century America was primarily collaborative in nature: during most of the kinetoscope era (1893-1895), Dickson acted as producer and Heise as cameraman. Indeed, there was remarkable continuity as the Edison motion picture system moved from the stage of invention to that of commercial production. When the kinetograph was shifted from the accounts of the Edison Laboratory (development of the technology) to those of Edison Manufacturing Company (business exploitation), Dickson and Heise followed. Rather than continuing to work on other inventive projects such as iron ore milling, Edison's two key collaborators helped to develop the commercial end of the new motion picture business. As I have shown elsewhere, this pattern of collaborative pairings remained characteristic of Edison filmmaking until 1908-1909 and was typical of American film production in the pre-nickelodeon era.[26]

The continuity in personnel as Edison moved from invention to full-scale commercial production can be contrasted to the Lumières. Although Louis Lumière took the first cinématographe films, he soon trained young men such as Alexandre Promio, François Doublier, Constant Girel and Gabriel Veyre to become professional cameramen traveling the world to take films.[27] The Lumières could then put many more production units into the field, allowing for a much larger output of films. Moreover, the process of collaboration, to the extent it had any substance in the Lumières' case, was not carried over to the production process. Films were typically made by solitary, traveling cameramen—sometimes working in association with local concessionaires but ultimately accountable to the Lumières, who decided whether or not their productions were of sufficient quality to be added to the company's catalog of film subjects. The Lumières thus established a clear hierarchy in their organization, in contrast to the Edison firm where horizontal structures of work were clearly retained, at least in the area of negative film production (i.e. filmmaking).[28]

Lobsters, or the Joke Is on You

The year 1893 was one of more active production than we had once realized. *The Barber Shop* was taken sometime late in that year, not in 1894 as has previously been assumed. It was a film that visiting dignitaries and the press saw when passing through the Edison Laboratory during the winter of 1893-94. Once again Edison employees appear in the film. Supposedly "working," they are shown quite literally lounging about on the job. At least one fellow is apparently performing his task—the barber. Like *Blacksmithing Scene, The Barber Shop* depicts one complete cycle of a work process. The shave is shown in its entirety.[29] The cyclical structures of work activities that Marshall Deutelbaum has seen as a distinctly Lumière phenomena are already evident in these early Edison films (Eadweard Muybridge, among others, provides the obvious antecedents).[30] But in contrast to the Lumières' earnest films of work activities, *The Barber Shop* mocks the very notion of "process." Truly one would not want to be under this barber's razor!

These short films may appear to be only a necessary artifact, the software required to display what is really important—the new technology; but in an indirect, yet profound way they suggest how that technology works. What Neil Harris calls the operational aesthetic is functioning in quite sophisticated ways.[31] With *The Barber Shop*, the parallel is not between the depicted work process and film production but between exhibition and the shave. A sign appearing in the mise-en-scène emphasizes their affinity by calling this shave "the latest wonder"—a label routinely applied to the kinetoscope.[32] Like the viewing of the film, the shave costs 5 cents. As the film itself demonstrates, both take about the same amount of time. And the voyeuristic pleasures of peep-hole viewing are matched by the pleasures normally associated with the barbershop. Yet if the man has been relieved of his whiskers, the viewer has also been relieved of his cash.

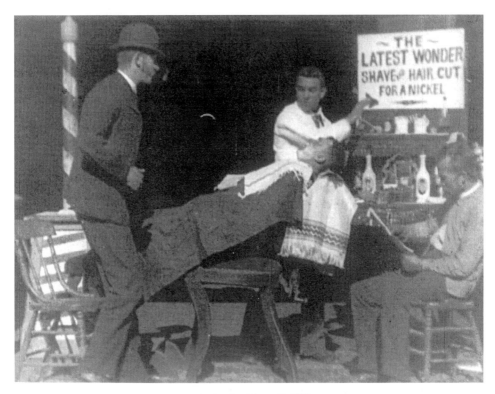

The Barber Shop (film no. 18, 1893).

The viewer can recognizes himself as a kind of "lobster"—that is he has been "burned" or outwitted in a P.T. Barnum kind of way. What did he get for his five cents, for peering into this little hole? Perhaps the suggestion that he has been fooled.

As an analysis of *Blacksmithing Scene* has already suggested, these earliest Edison films offer a subtle self-reflexive humor that has little relationship to the gag structure subsequently found in *Arroseur et arrosé* or later slapstick comedy.[33] In *The Barber Shop* the spectator can find pleasure in the very recognition of being made a lobster and doffs his cap to the cleverness of this playful scam.[34] That is, the viewer need not be entirely fooled. He has matched wits with the famed inventor and grasped the essential situation. Being in the know, he can also urge others to look in the machines only to find themselves similarly outsmarted. Or worse. In truth, the knowing spectator might hope for the absence of recognition by others. The joke is sufficiently subtle so that spectators might need to have it explained before they understand. What does this new venture do? What is the kinetoscope's function? Its principle purpose is to extract cash from the customer. The film's consumer pays for the honor of being fooled (taken to the cleaners, so to speak)—and then finds pleasure in it.

Is there a Lumière counterpart to this film? If so, it might be *Débarquement des congressistes*, the film that Louis Lumière took of a delegation of photographers disembarking at Neuville-sur-Saône on 11 June 1895 and that was projected for them the next day. Here is a film that is also self-reflexive and at least initially addressed its viewers as privileged customers. Here the operational aesthetic was explicit: it was designed to demonstrate what the cinématographe could do—its ability to capture an unfolding event and re-present that event with relative immediacy. But the film did more than impress its first spectators (those attending the Congrès) by displaying the cinématographe's technological achievements, it encouraged them to become consumers of the new technology (either as users or as viewers). It flattered these delegates by letting them see themselves on the screen and making them the honored first subjects of this new technology. In this respect the film was more straight forward and earnest—less cynical than its Edison counterpart.

If these wise men are apparently allowed to keep their whiskers, in fact show them off, there are more subtle ways in which they have been outwitted and made subservient to the Lumières own ambitions. In turning these photographers into evidence of and witnesses to a new era, the cinématographe makes their own achievements somewhat antiquated; from our present day perspective we can say it reduces them quite literally to men of the pre-cinema. Like *The Barber Shop*, it is a subtle kind of one-up-man's-ship. Moreover, the disembarking of the delegates from the boat is similar in its composition to *Sortie d'usine* (though these French bourgeois gentlemen amble down a narrow plank one at a time while the workers exit the factory as a mass). In this parallel between Lumière workers and Lumière customers, the delegates become objects of the Lumière gaze, their metaphoric possessions. Both become unwitting subjects in films that advertise, in effect, the Lumière company as well as the Lumières' new invention, the cinématographe. *The Barber Shop* and *Débarquement des congressistes* thus engaged viewers as consumers in ways that were aggressive and ambivalent. The first emphasized that the motion pictures might offer pleasure (like the barbershop) but leaves the viewer with nothing of substance. Like a shave, the viewing of a film is here today, gone tomorrow. It is ephemeral. In a playful, mocking way it comments on film's failed relation to a producer culture where products are expected to be utilitarian. *The Barber Shop* makes clear that motion pictures do something else. The Lumière film, in contrast, shows how cinema can provide a permanent record of an important event. It tries to reconcile cinema to the established order by showing how the cinématographe works and provides society with concrete benefits. It leaves them with something tangible—a record of an event.

Connecting Theater to Film

Until March 1894, the Edison Laboratory was not only the site of motion picture experimentation and production, it was also the films' subject. Low level employees such as G. Sacco Albanese, James Duncan (a day laborer), and Fred C. Devonald (who worked in the supply room) as well as Dickson and Heise served as subjects for the early experiments. Edison employees continued to serve as performers in the demonstration films of 1893. The making of *Sandow* on 6 March 1894 represented an important break from past efforts; it initiated commercial production with a new kind of subject matter and the introduction of a relationship between the world of performance culture and the motion picture world that has continued in some form to this day.[35]

Eugen Sandow first appeared in the United States at New York City's Casino Theatre in June 1893, then went on to become one of the stars of the 1893 World's Columbian Exposition in Chicago, with assistance from his manager Florenz Ziegfeld.[36] During the winter of 1893-94, he had become a headline attraction at the nation's foremost vaudeville house, Koster & Bial's Music Hall, located on 34th Street and Herald Square just a short distance from the place where the first kinetoscope parlor would be opened.[37] How did Dickson and Heise decide what to film? Not surprisingly they selected a portion of Sandow's act, since it was a well-established and successful routine. At Sandow's New York debut:

> The curtain went up, revealing the stage steeped in gloom. Then, suddenly, two curtains at the back of the stage were drawn aside, in a blaze of light stood the "Strong Man," with his mighty muscles standing out in bold relief in the white glare of an electric light. After performing a number of "tableaux vivants," to the accompaniment of slow music and much perspiration, Mr. Sandow left his cabinet, the lights were turned up, and the show began in earnest.[38]

Sandow began the earnest part of his act by lifting a large dumb bell: the spheres at each end were then opened to reveal two men curled up in tight balls. After demonstrating a few additional feats of strength, he did several somersaults with his eyes blindfolded and his legs tied. Then two horses were led in and played see-saw, using his chest as a pivot.

Despite the possibilities of filming Sandow's more entertaining shenanigans, Dickson chose to film the introductory moment of Sandow's stage act—in which the

Sandow (film no. 26, 1894).

strong man moves through a sequence of held poses. We can only speculate about the reasons for this choice. Posing allowed the strong man to show off his body with a variety of angles and postures while the camera could be moved closer to capture a more intimate view. Weight lifting would have kept the camera at a distant. Perhaps also the film's credibility as an objective recorder of a spectacular feat of this kind would have been undermined in the absence of direct physical verification by the spectator. But Sandow's introductory series of "tableaux vivants" is echoed by the experience of watching the first motion pictures as a series of still images become animated as the familiar static photograph comes to life. As Sandow moves from one pose to the next, alternating back and forth between arrested motion and fluid movement, the film indulges the viewer in a game of fort-da. The viewer's experience when peering into the peep-hole parallels the story of Pygmalion and his statue of Galatea which is brought to life.[39] With this film, Dickson plays Pygmalion to Sandow's Galatea. Indeed, the ways in which motion pictures brings the static or death-like photographic image to life became a virtual cliché in nineteenth-century discussions of the motion pictures. It also became the subject of various early films: not only Georges Méliès' own film of the Pygmalion and Galatea story, but the Edison film *An Artist's Dream* (no. 795).

Sandow offers a nonnarrative moment in which the emphasis is on the body as a spectacle. The rapid succession of poses has no particular order and no tension or climactic moment, which would have been the case if Sandow had chosen to execute a feat of strength. The film's presentational methods, with a powerful emphasis on erotic display, yielded an example of what Tom Gunning has called "the cinema of attractions." And cinema was still almost two years in the future. Yet at the same time, as Brigitte Peucker has suggested in her remarks on tableaux vivant artist Emma Hart, "by framing the body as an aesthetic object and placing it against a funeral backdrop of black velvet, [s]he conversely played on the body's death into representation."[40] Indeed filmmakers displayed an only slightly later fascination with the extinguishing of life in such films as *Rat Killing* and *The Hanging of William Carr* (no. 462). In these instances, the trajectory is in the opposite direction—from moving bodies to dead ones. Yet in both cases the life-like and death-like quality of images collide in ways that are troublesome. With *The Hanging of William Carr*, the spectator witnesses Carr's final moments of life, even as the same film demonstrates that he has been dead for some time. The act of extinguishing life is re-enacted, potentially obsessively, in the most life-like of representational modes. Sandow's poses repeatedly burst forth into life, resulting in a film that suggests cinema's triumph over stasis and death. At the same time, Sandow's perfect body cannot be perfect for very long. Indeed, it will soon cease to exist except as representation. The ways in which Edison's motion picture system thus acts as a time machine—to evoke the title of H.G. Wells' book, published in 1895—becomes foregrounded.[41]

Sandow was a carefully selected and staged example of "filmed theater," an approach to subject matter that proved common in the kinetoscope period and beyond. However, it was filmed theater of a particular kind. If the filmed sequence of poses corresponded in some loose way to the opening of Sandow's routine, the strong man did not bring his posing cabinet. In this instance the Black Maria's dark background focused attention on the star's body much as the cabinet was intended to do. For this production and many that followed, Dickson and Heise dispensed with the sets and backdrops, concentrating viewer attention on performance and movement instead.

Filmed theater (or more accurately filmed performance) as an approach to representation was only a starting point for the development of a multi-faceted relationship between the amusement world and film in this period. *Sandow* inaugurated an impressive mapping of American performance-based popular culture during the 1894-95 theatrical season. It encompasses everything from Hoyt's musical farce *A Milk White Flag* to African-American buck and wing dancers in *The South Before the War*, from Buffalo Bill's Wild West and Barnum & Bailey's Circus to boxing matches, female duelists, and a dog performing a skirt dance. This focus should not be seen as the negative result of a lack of ideas for subject matter. Rather Dickson was tapping into a rich vein of material; and his exploration had its own logic and momentum. Kinetographic practices were re-presenting popular amusements—using them as raw material for this new technology-based form of popular amusement. While this redundancy may seem reductive and lacking in "originality," the social and cultural impact of this approach would be profound.

If a Lumière counterpart to Edison's *Sandow* exists, it involves a very different trajectory. In the Edison imaginary, the world of commercial amusements stood in opposition to the world of work. It filled the leisure realm. For the Lumières, in contrast, family and domestic life were offered as complements to the work-a-day world. In this respect, *Repas de bébé* (July 1895), for which Louis filmed Auguste and his wife feeding their young child, is emblematic.[42] It is the perfect expression of the numerous domestic scenes made in this early period including *Pêche aux poissons rouges* in which a Lumière toddler tries to catch a gold fish in a small aquarium; *Partie d'écarté*, which features Antoine Lumière and Louis' father-in-law; and even *Arroseur et arrosé*. The Lumières generally avoided filming performance culture à la Edison until quite late, while the family unit is not really shown in an Edison film until the summer of 1896, well after the Lumières' impact was felt on American production.[43]

The presence or absence of theater in early motion picture production has been noted by historians in various ways. Georges Sadoul has seen the filmed theater of Edison leading to the fantasy trick films of Méliès and the sterile productions of Pathé Frères. In ways that have been widely celebrated by commentators of documentary film, the Lumières were said to engage the world more directly, rather than retreating to the studio.[44] Although scenes in early Lumière films are frequently staged, there is little acting in the sense that those people in front of the camera do not create fictional personae or play roles: they do not *dissemble*. The Lumières' avoidance of theater, traditionally seen as a positive *aesthetic* choice by many historians, was also an expression of their anti-theatrical prejudice that came out of well-established uses of the stereopticon, illustrated lecture, and amateur photography.[45] Perhaps then, this provides some insight into the Lumières withdrawal from film exhibition early in 1897: it required them to pursue the film-theater connection in ways that made them uncomfortable. Faced with a similar kinds of crisis about 1900, Edison finally decided to open a glass-enclosed studio in the heart of New York City's theater district.

Commercially Corrupt from the Beginning

The extent to which the earliest motion pictures were self-consciously used for purposes of advertising and promotion has never been properly recognized. The assertion that such functions were the predominant commercial feature of the kinetoscope era and beyond might be debated, but it is not obviously wrong. A film's amusement value, its ability to induce potential patrons to spend five cents for a quick look, might be seen only as the necessary pre-condition for the achievement of this underlying goal. The demonstration films helped to draw attention to Edison's newest technology and thus promote it. But *Sandow* went further. The filming of Eugen Sandow at the Edison Laboratory was nothing more than a carefully orchestrated media event. All the major New York newspapers covered the story, either sending reporters to the scene or making up what transpired for their columns. The story had several possible angles. According to the *New York Herald*:

> The strongest man on earth, to quote the play bills, and the greatest inventor of the age met yesterday at Menlo Park [sic], New Jersey. The meeting was an interesting one, and the giant of brain and the giant of muscle found much to admire in each other. Sandow marveled at Edison's inventions, and the Wizard gazed longingly and enviously at the prodigious muscles of the strong man.[46]

The *Herald* had Edison greeting Sandow at the train station, a complete fabrication but one that provided its account with some extra punch.

As the symmetry of the above quote suggests, the event was staged for the benefit of both parties as a criss-cross of mutual endorsements. Certainly it brought attention to Edison's new commercial venture—the kinetoscope, which would debut in little more than a month. This encouraged orders for machines and whetted the interest of potential spectators. At the same time, it was part of Sandow's efforts at self-promotion, for his stage career but more specifically for a book on physical fitness that would appear just one or two weeks later, entitled *Sandow on Physical Training*.[47] Eleven days after its article on Sandow's visit to the Black Maria, the *New York Herald* published a lengthy and glowing review of the strongman's book. Edison's endorsement was thus followed by another. "A great many books have treated the same topic, but they have not equaled this in perspicuity," the reviewer remarked.[48] As an extra boost, on the very day of this *Herald* review, the *New York World* published an article on the kinetograph featuring frames of Sandow.[49] This attention sold books, and it sold kinetoscopes. It also sold the myth of Edison at a time when he faced financial and legal difficulties. Whatever anxieties the inventor must have felt privately, publicly he seemed self-confident, relaxed and carefree.[50]

If Edison faced challenges to his patents, Sandow was being kept in the limelight by challenges to his claim as "the strongest man in the world" from Louis Cyr and other strong men.[51] The Edison association certainly gave the aura of authenticity to Sandow's titles, which were fundamentally promotional and commercial in nature. This media event also inaugurated a relationship between newspapers and filmmaking that was used many times in that first year of commercial production.[52] The visit of heavy weight champion James J. Corbett to the Black Maria on September 7th produced even more copy. Though Edison may have been present, he had to play a more discrete role, given the illegality of the boxing contest that occurred between Corbett and Peter Courtney at the studio.[53] Nonetheless, the affinities between the world champion of the ring and the world champion of invention were potential subtexts of this event as well.[54] Anticipating a relationship that would become much more common in the twentieth century, reports of filming became a periodic source of news (which sold newspapers) and publicity for stars and producers (which sold films and built careers).

One reason so many vaudevillians were eager to appear before Edison's kinetoscope had to do with the promotional nature of such exhibitions. The location of the first kinetoscope parlor was not coincidental. By peering into the kinetoscopes at 1155 Broadway, spectators could see the small images of theatrical stars performing just a few blocks away. If, after such a glimpse, they were not inspired to go to the theater immediately, then perhaps they would go to see "the real thing" later in the week. Or, correspondingly patrons who had gone to Koster & Bial's might have their memory of that night stimulated by these life-like if tiny images. Moreover, as the kinetoscope films were dispersed throughout the country, these films promoted their subjects, encouraging potential visitors to New York to go and see the performers in the flesh. Or, as was the case with some of the musicals and plays, to await the arrival of the touring production with heightened expectation. A careful perusing of news items in theatrical journals and elsewhere indicates that business managers in the amusement field took this promotional value very seriously. Theatrical columns reported:

> W.D. Mann, manager of Hoey's new farce, "The Flams," has conceived an advertising device for next season. Edison's kinetoscope and phonograph are to be combined in a reproduction of the principal spectacular and vocal features of the new performance, the instrument to be publicly exhibited in the principal cities weeks prior to the play's appearance.[55]

Mann's advertising scheme was hardly original; it merely articulated the kinetoscope's imagined impact on the careers of performers.

If Edison's motion picture venture had not been so obviously profitable, it may not have been necessary for Raff & Gammon and Maguire & Baucus to pay performers the respectable sums of money they often received for appearing before the kinetograph. Those headline attractions who were filmed frequently went on to enjoy long and prosperous careers. Many of the less well-known figures became more prominent. The extent to which these films contributed to their success is, of course, speculative. Robetta and Doretto gave what was just one of many "Fun in a Chinese Laundry" routines during the 1894-95 season. Two years later they were still going strong and were being called "old favorites" and "the two cleverest Chinese impersonators on the stage."[56] Welton's Cat Circus seemed to enjoy better billing after it appeared before Edison's camera. But when Welton's act faltered, at least one exhibitor attributed the act to Professor Félicien Trewey, the variety performer and concessionaire for the Lumière cinématographe in England.[57] Wilson & Waring and Frank Lawton went on to be successes in England where they may have been seen first in Edison's peep-hole machine. Annabelle Whitford eventually became the Gibson girl and a star in Ziegfeld's Follies. Hadj Tahar (*Sheik Hadji Tahar*, no. 74) remained an active performer until July 1926, when he appeared at the Palace Theater, New York's premiere vaudeville house.[58] This pattern continued in the era of projected motion pictures. Blackton moved up to top-of-the-line vaudeville after the success of *Blackton Sketches, no. 1* (no. 199, August 1896), more popularly known as *Inventor Edison Sketched by World Artist*.

Kinetoscope films did not promote Edison directly. Rather they served either as evidence of his technological wizardry or as the basis for glowing news items about their production.[59] Only somewhat later did Edison motion pictures become overtly self-promotional in nature and even then only occasionally. These include *Edison Laboratory* (no. 188, August-September 1896), *Inventor Edison Sketched by World Artist*; and *Mr. Edison at Work in His Chemical Laboratory* (no. 334, May 1897). Such direct forms of self-promotion were indebted to the more numerous Lumière films that featured the brothers, their family, their customers, and their factory. *Sortie d'usine* (1895) and its two remakes filled this role most explicitly. But most early cinématographe programs had at least one picture that featured members of the Lumière family and they were often identified in ads and newspaper copy about the programs. And since Louis was behind the camera for most of these, Auguste generally became the media star. Edison tried to appear more reticent, less obvious in the way he presented his own mythic figure to the world. It is noteworthy that the only motion picture featuring the inventor from this period was taken at his laboratory (significantly a mock laboratory constructed inside the Black Maria) in which Edison either showed himself to be an awkward actor or chose to burlesque a popular photograph showing him carefully mixing chemicals (in the tradition of *Blacksmithing Scene* or *The Barber Shop*). The Lumière mixture of amateur cinematography (films of the family) with advertising was potent but avoided by Edison for reasons that seem quite consistent with the kinds of subject matter fostered by each organization.

Given these early experiences, it is not surprising that advertising films made up one of the most popular genres of pre-nickelodeon cinema. *Admiral Cigarette* (no. 362, July 1897) and *Crawford Shoe Store* (no. 362.1) are among the most obvious examples in the following filmography. *Lickmann's Cigar and Photo Store* (no. 549) and *North Side Dental Rooms* (no. 550) were both made for the Commercial Advertising Bureau, owned by J. Stuart Blackton and Albert E. Smith. These two founders of the Vitagraph Company of America—the largest motion picture producer in the United States between 1906 and 1914—all but began their motion picture careers by showing advertising films.

As motion picture subjects in the Paper Print Collection at the Library of Congress have been put back onto 35mm film, the resulting upgrade in quality has often revealed an advertising component. In *Corner Madison and State Streets, Chicago* (no. 354), a stream of signs for various attractions at Electric Park are paraded in front of the camera. *Sutro Baths, no. 1* (no. 392) displays a large banner proclaiming its hours of operations that would seem an unlikely part of the regular decor. *South Spring Street, Los Angeles* (no. 470) discretely includes a sign for Tally's Kinetoscope Parlor on the left side of the screen. For *Freight Train* (no. 479), Horst Brothers went to considerable trouble to put large signs on a series of freight cars which advertised their special hops. What is striking is the ways in which such signage went unacknowledged in catalog descriptions. The inclusion of placards for Electric Park and the well-framed banner at Sutro Baths would appear to be chance occurrences. Or so the unsuspecting viewer (or exhibitor) was led to believe.

Just as notably something approaching half of the Edison films made between the fall of 1896 and the end of 1900 were subsidized by transportation companies or other organizations seeking publicity. James White and William Heise made films of the onrushing Black Diamond Express with the active participation of the Lehigh Valley Railroad, whose executives were eager to present such images of power and speed as an alternative to those of the Empire State Express, then being shown on the biograph to the benefit of the New York Central Railroad. (Signs identifying the train and railroad were usually included in the films as well.) Scenes of Niagara Falls were likewise taken with the assistance of railroad corporations because the site was a favored tourist destination. The films made on James White and Frederick Blechynden's tour of the Far West, Mexico and Asia were all made with the co-operation of railroad and steamship companies, which included free transportation and possibly some financial subsidies. They fully recognized that such films promoted tourism. These promotional schemes were, however, more or less covert. The often stated claim that such films were a cheap *alternative* to travel deflected attention away from the fact that the films were to a considerable extent made and shown precisely to encourage tourism. In various ways, many of these early films were shown to spectators who were unaware that the makers, if not always the exhibitors, had ulterior purposes. One could say that in this gap between overt and covert purposes, the films were made to dissemble. The cinema was never innocent. Within these images there was a dialectical tension between the ways they acted as new forms of commodities and the way they were promoting other kinds of commodities in the era of an emergent consumer society. In complex ways, motion pictures were engaged in the commodification of culture from their earliest years.[60]

Homosocial Space, Affirmed Yet Upended

The earliest Edison films were shot in the male, homosocial world of the Edison Laboratory.[61] When Dickson and Heise began to create imaginary spaces that were both located in and counterparts to the Edison Laboratory, they chose spaces that men exclusively occupied—a smithy and a barber shop. The Edison Laboratory was a bastion of masculinist culture. When work was done by women, it was often done by wives, at home and then brought to the Laboratory (for example, Fred Devonald's wife made a screen or Edmund Kuhn's wife hand tinted kinetoscope films). When men were working on a project, they were expected to put in long hours, perhaps like their boss catching naps in the lab rather than going home. The Edison Laboratory was an alternative to the family as much as or more than its complement. Women were not so much excluded from these earliest Edison films: they were simply not present in the larger space from which the casts was drawn.

Carmencita (film no. 28, 1894).

Throughout 1894-1895 Dickson, Heise and their colleagues continued to make a wide range of films that appealed to this culture of rugged masculinity. In the months immediately after *Sandow* was filmed, light-weight boxing champion Jack McAuliffe visited the Black Maria (*Boxing,* no. 39).[62] Known to be a brawler who was as ready to fight outside the ring as in it, McAuliffe nonetheless declined to participate in a serious exchange of blows in the limited space of the enclosed studio. "Mike" Leonard and Jack Cushing had fewer qualms and fought a bout of six abbreviated rounds in June (*Leonard-Cushing Fight,* no. 40). Additional fights followed. Other films involving man-to-man combats included *Mexican Knife Duel* (no. 72) and *Gladiatorial Combat* (no. 114). In addition there were depictions of blood sports such as *Cock Fight* (no. 27); *Rat Killing* (no. 56), in which a terrier kills six or so rats; and *Dogs Fighting* (no. 109).[63]

Women did eventually find their way into Edison films. One works behind the counter as a barmaid in *Bar Room Scene* (no. 37), made shortly after the opening of the New York kinetoscope parlor and the fourth Edison film to present an elaborated space. This bar room may no longer be an all-male preserve, but it unquestionably remained a homosocial one dominated and regulated by men—one in which the nineteenth-century masculine values were firmly entrenched. Not surprisingly, kinetoscopes showing fight films were sometimes located in bar rooms.[64]

The female bartender was not the first woman to appear in an Edison film, however. This honor belonged to Spanish dancer Carmencita, who was filmed at the Black Maria in mid-March 1894, approximately two weeks after Sandow (*Carmencita,* no. 28). Carmencita debuted on the New York stage in 1889, performing Spanish dances between acts of a musical. She rose to fame under the management of John Koster and Albert Bial, who put her in their original music hall on 23rd Street, commencing

10 February 1890. Carmencita communicated an intense sexuality across the footlights that led male reporters to write long, exuberant columns about her performance (several such articles appear in the document section for this entry).

Following *Carmencita*, Dickson and Heise made numerous pictures featuring women engaged in performances that had an erotic component. Women were often scantily dressed and executed sexually suggestive poses or movements. *Trapeze* (no. 32) featured a female trapeze artist. *Bertoldi (Table Contortion)* (no. 30) presented contortionist Ena Bertoldi who displayed her body in ways that could readily trigger male fantasies of sexual availability. The sexually explicit danse du ventre and the slightly more refined Serpentine dance, particularly as rendered by Annabelle Whitford who cavorted before Edison's kinetograph many times between 1894 and 1898, were mainstays of Edison production throughout this period. When women appeared before the camera it was typically to appeal to male voyeurism, to the interests of the men behind the camera and the men assumed to be looking into the kinetoscope—men like those making the films. In short these films of sex and violence had a strong commercial sense, but the filmmakers tended to imagine an audience consisting of men like themselves.

As Dickson and Heise prepared for the kinetoscope's debut, they belatedly recognized that the kinetoscope's audiences would often be mixed sex ones that included middle-class women who typically saw the burlesque show, music hall, or boxing ring as inimical to their domestic values. Edison's "scientific experiments" would interest these women—as it had interested the heads of women's clubs who had been the first members of the public to see Edison's experimental kinetoscope in May 1891. But what could they see that might be considered acceptable? When the first kinetoscope parlor opened in New York, the only film in those ten machines which was designed to appeal to this more general public was *Highland Dance* (no. 33). Significantly it also served as an exemplary film for an article on Edison's new motion picture system appearing in a journal for adolescents, *Harper's Young People*.[65] Other films such as *Organ Grinder* (no. 36) and *Trained Bears* (no. 38) were soon made to address this shortage. Films of trained animals, bronco busting, and a fire rescue appealed to a more heterosocial audience that included children. Nor is this an esoteric point. Films of Annabelle were banned from exhibition in Asbury Park and other locales.[66] But even though scenes of fire rescues and broncho busting appealed to a mixed sex audience, they came out of the quintessentially masculinist culture of fire companies and the wild west shows.

As should already be evident, the Lumière imaginary was gendered in quite different ways. If Edison's earliest films depicted a homosocial world, theirs was resolutely heterosocial, even feminine in its emphasis on the domestic sphere. As Tom Gunning has suggested they had strong ties to amateur photography, which emphasized the family.[67] Even the factory, located immediately behind the Lumière mansion, was in many ways an extension of this filmic universe. In any case, the departing Lumière employees included women as well as men. Dickson and Heise did move toward gender diversity, first by filming women who performed in these homosocial spaces and then by filming scenes of commercial amusement that included women and were intended to appeal to a more general public. The depiction of heterosocial space, however, remained a weaker impulse throughout the kinetoscope era.

If Edison production expanded from depicting an all-male world to include women, a comparable parallel can be found in the expansion of Lumière filmmaking, in their move from the private realm to incorporation of the public sphere. This had two related trajectories. First the Lumières began to shoot public places such as *Place des Cordeliers* in Lyons, which gradually expanded to include scenes of symbolic spaces associated with different nations: Hyde Park in London, the Brooklyn Bridge in New York, and the Geneva Exposition in Switzerland. Public space was still heterosocial space. Somewhat later, the Lumières expanded their repertoire in a second direction by filming scenes involving the armies of France and then other nations. Their movement backwards into the all-male world of soldiering resulted from the decision to film the military and other representatives of state power. The Lumières came to depict a world in which family, nation and state were among the most prominent features. All three were largely ignored if they were not actively lampooned in Edison pictures of the kinetoscope period. (Dickson took many films of Charles Hoyt's *The Milk White Flag*, a musical comedy which mocked the state militias.)

By some standards, the Lumière films can appear more progressive and enlightened. In Edison kinetoscope films, women are on display. Their status as objects of the male gaze is further heightened by the process of peep-hole viewing itself. Screen entertainment, which the Lumières pioneered, was a form of public viewing that was more proper and allowed for other kinds of subject positions for its spectators. In the world constructed by the Lumière camera, women may not be objects of salacious male voyeurism, but they also have little definition outside the family. As Alan Williams has observed, the Lumières depict an orderly, contented world where bourgeois values have triumphed and are made permanent as representations.[68] The world on screen and the refined, mixed-sexed audiences who came to see these representations were more comfortably matched.

If Edison films were cruder and more shocking than their Lumière counterparts, they were also more disruptive and dynamic, often in ways that were not anticipated. The disjunctions between the semi-illegal, hidden, masculine world of blood sports and heterosocial spectatorship were powerful. Because this performance culture had been reduced to representations, women could, for instance, more freely view Sandow's almost naked body. And they were allowed to see two perfectly conditioned male fighters, stripped down to their togs. Female voyeurism was unexpectedly mobilized, within a socially acceptable framework, in ways that have been discussed by Miriam Hansen.[69] They gained access, however limited, to the male homosocial world from which they had been either excluded or kept at the periphery. Motion pictures thus contributed to the breakdown of two discrete and complimentary realms—that of rugged masculinity and feminine domesticity—by pulling the veil from the former and exposing it to the latter. Kinetoscope films and their exhibition were involved in a breakdown and curtailment of an older homosocial world and the emergence and expansion of a newer heterosocial culture, along the lines discussed by Kathy Peiss in her illuminating study, *Cheap Amusements*.

The Absence of Presence and the Transformation of Culture

Motion pictures as a form of re-presentation contributed to the break down or circumvention of a vast array of taboos from the very outset.[70] Here, the absence of presence liberated these images designed for the kinetoscope. In the 1890s, it would have been impossible to imagine an actual cock fight occurring in Herald Square and for women to attend such an event, perhaps unescorted. Yet motion pictures made this possible. Prize fighting, though common enough in the early 1890s, existed outside the law in every state and territory of the United States. Fights were generally arranged clandestinely and conducted in out of the way places. With film, the opportunity to watch at least the simulacrum of a fistic encounter changed: because the boxers were not present as the fight unfurled, motion pictures of boxing matches were permitted to be shown almost everywhere. When the Corbett-Courtney fight was staged for the kinetograph, a grand jury was asked to see if a law might not have been broken. It was obvious to all that one had. But the all-male jury refused to acknowledge that this fight was anything more than a demonstration or performance, rescuing the fighters and perhaps Edison from likely conviction.[71] These films then enjoyed wide circulation and doubtlessly generated the most income of any motion picture subject made during the kinetoscope era. The decisive moment came with the Corbett-Fitzsimmons fight in March 1897, once the state of Nevada had legalized prize fighting. Because of this legislative act, boxing films shot there no longer served as evidence of illegal activities. With the exhibitions of such films widely tolerated by the authorities even though the sport itself continued to be illegal, the contradictions or hypocrisy was such that other states gradually legalized the sport as well.[72]

Films of boxing and other blood sports were only one aspect of this breakdown of taboos. Police were constantly interfering with performances of the danse du ventre—otherwise known as the muscle or coochee-coochee dance (in short, the belly dance). These women were often arrested or allowed to continue only if their dress and movements were laughably restrained.[73] On film, such performances posed far fewer problems. Again there was a circuit between stage and screen. Performances were more readily accepted on film due to the absence of presence, which then made it increasingly difficult not to accept the performance itself—on stage. This was one aspect of popular culture's dynamism at the turn of the century.

The circumventions of long-established prohibitions involved more than depictions of sex and violence. When three young sisters—La Regaloncita (Mildred Ewer), La Graciosa (Florence Ewer), La Preciosa (Lenora Ewer)—were scheduled to appear in E.E. Rice's burlesque *1492*, the Gerry Society tried to prevent these children—like others—from performing on the stage. Producer E.E. Rice, however, claimed that the girls would not be dancing (and so neither performing nor acting)—just posing. Moreover, the young girls and their widowed mother desperately needed the $100 a week they could earn by these appearances. This dispute was mediated by New York City's Acting Mayor, George B. McClellan, Jr. (then president of the city's board of aldermen).[74] The girls came to his office and "posed." A representative for the Gerry Society insisted they were dancing. E.E. Rice then asked the girls to dance. "See the difference?" he asked the mayor. After receiving a kiss and a heartfelt plea from La Regaloncita, McClellan did indeed see the difference and sided with Rice. The girls could appear—provided they did not dance. But they danced before Edison's kinetograph (*Cupid's Dance*, no. 51) and patrons could see their performance in the nearby kinetoscope parlor.[75]

Similar developments continued in the era of projection. Any effort to present the Passion play, whether on the commercial stage or at a local Catholic church, raised a storm of protest in the United States. When shown via motion pictures projected onto a screen, the results were applauded by the very clergy who condemned the stage-bound rendering of the play. As I have discussed in relationship to the exhibition practices of Lyman Howe, in the era before the proliferation of storefront motion picture houses or nickelodeons (prior to 1906-1907), the powers of photographic mediation took the "curse of presence" off many types of amusements when shown via motion pictures.[76] Here the religious right was active on an array of fronts. Methodist and Baptist groups not only embraced the Passion play in cinematic form but sponsored film exhibitions that re-presented condensed vaudeville acts and excerpted theatrical farces—performances their members were not suppose to see in the flesh. Cinema became a weapon that enabled these groups to offer their own forms of sanitized popular culture as a way to hold the straying faithful. Film, its absence of presence, made the profane if not sacred at least no longer blasphemous, contributing to the secularization of American culture and the upending of an illusory cultural stability. This process, which became most dramatically evident in the late 1890s, was begun in a substantive way during the kinetoscope era.

As Christian Metz has told us, the absence of presence is an essential feature of motion picture representation. Yet it need not always have the kind of profound impact evident in American film practices of the 1890s. The Lumières appear to have been much more conservative in this regard, though some of this may be attributed to French culture. Although the Lumières filmed an early version of the Passion play, its stagings were not a controversial subject in the context of French religious life. The Lumières, in contrast to Méliès and Pathé, avoided depictions of a salacious nature—though in this area French standards were generally looser than in the United States. And boxing did not have the same kind of role or importance in French life.[77] The Lumière programs, which showed life-like representations of the world on a single screen in a theater, produced pleasure and excitement in audiences. But this achievement essentially recapitulated what had already been done with travel lectures using projected magic lantern slides. Photographs of news events had also been projected onto the screen for audiences in various venues. Certainly the addition of life-like movement was an important innovation, but the Lumières' choice of subject matter did not challenge cultural conventions in the way that was true for Edison film production. This does not mean that Lumière filmmaking lacked a sense of play and pleasure. Quite the contrary. Lumière use of reverse motion and films such as *Arroseur et arrosé* indicate that the French brothers had a fine appreciation for film's comic potential. But they were much more disposed to use film to extend bourgeois cultural practices rather than upend them.

Due in large part to the absence of presence inherent in motion pictures, Dickson and Heise began a process that quickly transformed many aspects of performance culture in the United States. They were particularly ready to undermine established boundaries for the presentation of sex and violence, but this shattering of taboos were not limited to these areas. In a period of economic depression, a full array of such filmic dislocations ensured the greatest financial return for this new product. Because of the status of motion pictures in the pre-1908 period, before cinema became a form of mass entertainment and systematic censorship was introduced, the presentation of forbidden subjects did not result in the suppression of such images but in disruptions of established patterns of viewing and social control which were themselves part of a larger socio-cultural transformation.[78]

Art and Science, Eroticism and Ethnography

Although Edison and his associates were using film in a way that disrupted the cultural status quo, the inventor nevertheless appropriated familiar and reassuring discourses about science and art when talking about his new invention. Edison often promised to bring opera, the epitome of high art, to the masses for a reasonable price.[79] Motion pictures, it was promised, would preserve great performances of Shakespeare.[80] In truth, the gap between promise and practice was great: the actual subject matter was of a much more popular kind. Science helped to bridge the gap. Sandow, it was asserted, was taking part in a disinterested scientific experiment. Edison was said to be perfecting his invention—"the latest development of Edison's genius in the line of photography, on which he had been working for the past five years."[81] The *New York World* and *Harper's Weekly* both published sequences of Edison motion pictures which analyzed actions—the successful and unsuccessful somersaults of an amateur gymnast and the sneeze of Edison employee Fred Ott. Black backgrounds focused attention on the isolated events which were themselves reduced to single cycles of action.

In their approach to representation, Dickson and Heise were evoking and reworking aspects of Eadweard Muybridge's serial photography, which also depicted subjects against plain black backgrounds and showed complete cycles of actions, such as walking, jumping, or pouring a bucket of water. Muybridge, who often photographed his subjects in a state of partial or complete undress, claimed the right to take and exhibit (life-size via projection) his highly eroticized photographs of naked or semi-naked men and women because he was doing so for scientific purposes. He was teaching people about human and animal locomotion, or so he claimed. When Muybridge came to lecture on serial photography in Orange, New Jersey, in October 1888, these images scandalized some members of the audience who found them to be pornographic in character.[82] Scientific purpose provide sufficient justification for many but not all patrons.

In the Edison film of Eugen Sandow, the strong man is all but naked; and like many films that followed, it is erotic in its content. Dickson and Heise, like Muybridge, combined a reputedly scientific approach with eroticism. If people were aware that this evocation of science was self-serving, however, Edison's subject matter was finally less controversial.[83] Dickson and Heise played with the periphery of acceptable commercial entertainment, with scantily clothed dancers rather than naked bodies. The staging of so-called scientific experiments, however, also provided opportunities for concealing or at least minimizing the commercial nature of Edison's latest venture into the amusement world, one that would complement the phonograph. Contra Edison's public statements, not science and art but technology and amusement were being forged into a new, explosive combination that would provide the foundation for what has generally come to be called the culture industry.

There was always a certain comic potential in applying the kinetograph's "scientific" method or attitude to an inappropriate object. The *New York World* did this, no doubt intentionally, in April 1896, when it published a sequential series of photographs showing a kiss by John C. Rice and May Irwin. The first film kiss (and the first depiction of a kiss to be published in a newspaper, according to the *World*) was analyzed with a scientific eye. "The first section was devoted to what apparently was a kiss, but was really only the preparation for one. These pictures show very distinctly how easily a person watching a couple might think they kissed when they didn't," observed Mrs. McGuirk of the *World*. When she examined the next and final section of the film, the journalist concluded that "the real kiss is a revelation."[84] This mocking of the scientific stance toward films of sex and violence apparently brought this particular strand of scientific discourse to a halt, though it would re-emerge somewhat later in slightly altered form.

Another way in which Edison's kinetoscope films could be taken seriously in their "scientific" aspirations was as ethnographic "documents." In many respects these films extended the emphasis on displaying cultures offered at the 1893 World Columbian Exposition of Chicago, both in the Anthropological Building and on the Midway Plaisance.[85] In many cases these World's Fair exhibitions involved the presentation of ethnic types "in situ." There was Franz Boas' Skidgate village of Kwakiutl Indians, a Samoan village, and the Street of Cairo. As Barbara Kirshenblatt-Gimblett has observed in relation to ethnographic displays of human beings:

> Human displays teeter-totter on a kind of semiotic seesaw, equipoised between the animate and inanimate, the living and the dead. The semiotic complexity of exhibits of people, particularly those of an ethnographic character, may be seen in reciprocities between exhibiting the dead as if alive and the living as if they are dead, reciprocities that hold as well for the art of the undertaker as they do for the art of the museum preparator.[86]

As already suggested, motion pictures were ideally suited for playing this seesaw between living and dead. The images were "life-like" and yet the people appearing in the films were not actually present. In fact, shot at some earlier point in time, they could be and perhaps might as well be dead. Film more or less quickly became a form for presenting ethnographic information; in fact, it was one of the first uses to which Dickson and Heise put the new medium.

The early kinetoscope films offered a "gallery of nations," similar to the one being employed by Charles Willson Peale as early as 1797 using wax works. Peale's museum presented "a group of contrasting races of mankind" which featured peoples from China, the Pacific Islands, and North and South America.[87] When shown in a battery

Short Stick Dance (film no. 132, 1895).

of kinetoscopes, Edison's early films encouraged patrons to compare people from different nations, cultures and races. Such analyses could proceed along gender lines as men and women engaged in characteristic actions in the area of dance, feats of strength, and combat. With the proper scientific attitude, a spectator might contrast the American Serpentine dance to the danse du ventre of the Middle East, the English pas seul of Lucy Murray, or the Sarachi dance of the Japanese *mako*. Different notions of feminine beauty could also be compared. The same held true for the films of male combats: Mexican knife duels, Irish-American boxing, Buffalo Bill's rifle shooting and Romanesque gladiatorial jousting could be contrasted to each other and to the animal combats of cock fights and rat baiting. Certainly these films as a group conform to a hierarchy of types that was consistent with popular prejudices of the period.

The display of peoples involved a series of tensions or a range of possibilities. Showmen-exhibitors might rely either on theatrical venues or zoological recreations of habitats (for instance the recreation of villages in museums or at international expositions). They could also offer either cultural performances (which might include displays of marital prowess or dances) or what Kirshenblatt-Gimblett has called the drama of the quotidian (cooking, weaving, washing and so forth). Barnum and Bailey's Circus, for example, tended to combine both possibilities in the Ethnographic Congress it toured in 1894 and 1895.[88] Dickson and Heise clearly favored the filming of cultural performances in theater-like settings. When Fiji Islanders from Barnum and Bailey's Circus appeared before the kinetograph, it was not quotidian activities that were filmed but the performative, for instance *Paddle Dance* (no. 130). These distinctions were further complicated by the method in which they were exhibited: the individual kinetoscope may appear to act as a kind of miniature theater, while the machines as a group could become a kind of museum with a succession of displays.

Dickson's and Heise's approach differed, once again, from that of the Lumières who likewise produced a large number of motion pictures with an ethnographic impulse. Lumière subjects were sometimes shot at world's fairs and expositions but were increasingly taken in the countries or territories of their subjects. Correspondingly, their cameramen favored street scenes and quotidian events rather than performances (except the independently generated performances of parades and ceremonies). Indeed, Edison films made after the Lumière impact often tended in this direction as well. *Wash Day in Mexico* (no. 450) or *Japanese Sampans* (no. 525)—films taken by James White and Fred Blechynden in Mexico and the Far East during 1897-1898—are exemplary. Current trends in ethnographic film theory would suggest that the Lumière's "observational" approach is not necessarily to be preferred to the Edison one. There was a much greater level of interaction and exchange between many of Edison's subjects and the filmmakers than was the case with the Lumières. As entertainers, they were on a more equal footing with the Europeans appearing before the kinetograph. That is, they had a much firmer understanding of themselves as "representative types" and cultural performers. In short, kinetoscope films could be understood utilizing ethnographic categories, but their reception was not entirely limited to this paradigm. Performers who might be classified as "ethnographic" when viewed from one perspective might be considered vaudevillians from another.

The Body as the Camera's Subject

The bodies of performers are the foregrounded subject of most kinetoscope pictures. Dickson and Heise isolated the bodies of strong man Sandow, contortionist Ena Bertoldi, trapezist Alcide Capitaine, and acrobat Luis Martinetti, against a black background in ways that encourage the spectator's scrutiny. The absence of a painted backdrop or set gives the spectator only one place to look. Clothing is likewise either minimal or contoured to the body. The absence of presence and claims to a scientific attitude allowed for a much closer examination of bodies than would have otherwise been comfortable for the spectator. By depicting bodies performing a series of related, comparable activities, the filmmakers encouraged viewers to compare and assess their operations (not only in their ability to generate sexual desire or to function as human fighting machines but in terms of their flexibility, dexterity and training).

In many respects, these films continue Muybridge's earlier interest in analyzing human and animal locomotion, though such efforts took a decidedly new form.

The erotics of the trained body. Photo of Eugen Sandow from W.K.L. Dickson and Antonia Dickson, *History of the Kinetograph, Kinetoscope and Kineto-Phonograph*.

Muybridge often employed background grids that provided units of measurement against which movements could be plotted, even if their true utility may be questioned. As has been often noted, Muybridge's serial photography paralleled, if it did not precede, the regime of scientific management, in which work no longer unfurled at a pace considered natural or appropriate but at speed increasing controlled by management. Both were part of the efforts to discipline the actions and activities of people in ways discussed by Michel Foucault. What was the relationship of bodies in these films and those being disciplined in the work place?

Foucault explores the ways in which the body was subject to new forms of discipline in the late eighteenth and nineteenth centuries.[89] In many areas of life, but particularly in the arena of work, the body was subjected to more and more systematic and minute forms of control. Amusement and leisure became a refuge from, and inevitably a reaction to, these new forms of intrusion. The cult of masculinity, epitomized by the bar room, the barbershop and the boxing ring were areas of excess. John L. Sullivan, the first modern heavy-weight boxing champion, was an alcoholic even during his championship years. His brawls and binges were the mark of an undisciplined life made possible by natural talents and physique.[90] Such bodies appeared in these early Edison films with some frequency. Jack McAuliffe, the first well-known fighter to appear before the kinetograph, had this taste for extreme indulgence. His drunken brawls seemed to have been virtually routine events.[91] Tight-rope walker Juan A. Caicedo likewise boasted that he never practiced. His abilities on the wire came naturally, though he had an ugly facial scar and heavily taped wrists from a serious fall that complemented this approach to performance.[92] These personalities thus rejected the discipline of the new regime; and while their sometimes outlandish behavior was routinely reported in the papers, it did not seem to harm their popularity—indeed, it may have enhanced it.

But films like those of McAuliffe and Caicedo were not characteristic of the performance culture being captured by Edison's kinetograph. Many other films engaged with the disciplining of the body in the unexpected area of amusements. In Edison films of Sandow and Ena Bertoldi, the bodies are both disciplined and eroticized. Theirs are bodies that have been trained to exceed the normal human limits for the pleasure of the spectator (but also for the performer's sense of self and the pleasure of being looked at). The forms of discipline that made these bodies possible were comparatively new. Sandow had relied on an innovative system of progressive weight training advocated by his teacher Louis Attila.[93] Like most contortionist, Bertoldi engaged in the training of her flexible body from an early age.[94] The regimentation required of women aerialists such as Alcide Capitaine was much commented on by the press.

> The elegant poise of her body when in motion as well as at rest, her calm, confident manner, the apparent ease with which she executes the most difficult movements, the delicate precision with which her supple limbs move, all prove the attention given to her early training and the fact that she was an apt and intelligent pupil.
>
> Nor is the placidity of her finely chiselled features disturbed by those fearful grimaces and contortions which generally mar the performances of the professional. With business-like exactness of detail, as though exercising alone in her private gymnasium, she goes through her performance, only waving her hand occasionally in response to the applause of the audience.

A journalist visiting Koster & Bial's declared, "The traditional system of child training is played out."[95] Regular, serious athletic work, a good diet, and knowledge of geometry and mathematics were now considered the crucial elements in training young acrobats. Eight-year old Nellie Jordan was a product of this approach. According to her father, "she just loves the business. It is not work to her, it is play. Why she laughs over it all the time and only gets angry when she fails to do some feat she has tried."[96] Alcoholic consumption, of course, had to be avoided. These developments were not simply a perceived change in the way acrobats disciplined their bodies; acrobatics itself tended to require a severe regime of consistent bodily discipline and training.

The fascination with acrobats and aerialists—in vaudeville, by the press and by Edison filmmakers—is noteworthy because their attitudes contrasted significantly with the attitudes expressed by the older Caicedo and many boxers.[97] These differences paralleled those between the "scientific" boxing and self-discipline of James Corbett and the bare knuckle boxing and physical indulgence which characterized the career of boxer John L. Sullivan. Some of this was, as the *New York Herald* reporter recognized, changes in perception as much as substance. If the contrast between Sullivan and Corbett has sometimes been exaggerated, as Michael Isenberg suggests, perhaps it has been due, in part, to Corbett's association with motion pictures in the 1890s, which allied him with scientific discourse, modernity, and even the idea of hard work and self-discipline.[98] Nevertheless, both the rejection of rigorous bodily discipline and the pleasure found in its more systematic application within the realm of performance are opposite but finally complementary responses to an ascendant regime of factory work. Each can be found in these kinetoscope films.

Sandow, Capitaine and Bertoldi disciplined their bodies as a way to foster personality—to liberate the body from its normal constraints.[99] These vaudeville performers created a space (on stage, before the kinetograph) where the effects of discipline were reversed. Long hours of repetition and practice yield brief moments of exhilaration. The regimentation and discipline that makes such feats possible is kept off-stage, off-screen. Pain is said to be replaced by business-like, "scientific" workouts or else it becomes a form of pleasure. Performance provides a sense of identity—and affirmation of self—rather than its loss through subservience to work: it is performance "without purpose" rather than a form of productive labor. The body, however, has reached a new stage in its commodification for cultural consumption.

The Lumières' early films differ from Edison's in their approach to the body. Lumière films focus much more on landscapes and cityscapes. When people are subjects, they are seen in relationship to their background—situated in their world rather than extracted from it. More than bodies, Lumière films commodify landscapes and foreign locales within an imperialist culture. People are heavily clothed and usually stout—these are the bourgeoisie whose bodies are not subject to the discipline of factory labor. Lumière production, which comes out of a tradition of travel slides and amateur photography, differed from the work being done in France by Étienne-Jules Marey and Demenÿ—work which had more in common with Edison production for the kinetoscope.

Edison filmmakers did not entirely abandon their fascination with bodies after they began to make films for projection and in response to the impact of Lumière production. The black background remained common in 1896 and into the first months of 1897: when Annabelle returned to the Black Maria (*Serpentine Dance—Annabelle*, no. 339; *Sun Dance—Annabelle*, no. 340) and for films such as *Seminary Girls* (no. 311). In September 1898 Ella Lola appeared against a black background in two dance films— *Ella Lola, a la Trilby* (no. 631) and *Turkish Dance, Ella Lola* (no. 632). There the practice came to a close; by early 1899 the use of simple theatrical backdrops had become standard, as with *Bicycle Trick Riding, no. 2* (no. 671) and *Arabian Gun Twirler* (no. 672). This was true even when a voyeuristic impulse was in strong evidence—as with *Trapeze Disrobing Act* (© 11 November 1901). Interestingly, plain backgrounds reappeared with the introduction of POV shots and close-ups—for instance, one was used for the close view of a woman's ankle in *The Gay Shoe Clerk* (1903).

From Cosmopolitan Internationalism to Jingoistic Nationalism

Kinetoscope films were often ambiguous in their meanings and genres. Although many were ethnographic in their impulse, most depicted a self-confident commercial popular culture that was international in its scope and orientation. Dickson and cameraman William Heise filmed a vast array of theatrical performers whose geographic, racial and cultural diversity is striking: German strong men Eugen Sandow and Louis Attila; Italian acrobat Luis Martinetti, Columbian tightrope walker Juan Caicedo, French trapezist Alcide Capitaine, Japanese tumbler Toyou Kichi, English dancers Lucy Murray and May Lucas, Arab gun twirler Sheik Hadj Tahar, and Mexican rope performer Vincente Oropeza. And the silent nature of early motion pictures, which effaced the barrier of language, helped to forge this sense of a shared, fluid world. Motion pictures from their earliest moments, whether in the peep-hole kinetoscope or projected onto the screen, provided this sense of a world that could transcend national identity but also a world where performers and viewers could play with, and enjoy cultural particularity.

This international cast was balanced by an American one—Annie Oakley, Buffalo Bill, scenes from Hoyt's musical farce *The Milk White Flag*, Irish-American boxers James Corbett and Peter Courtney, African-American dancers such as James Grundy, and Sioux Indians.[100] Although these 135 kinetoscope films hardly functioned independently of racist and culturally elitist preconception, they display a consistency in depiction that marks this as a remarkable moment. They offered a cosmopolitan vision that admittedly embraced stereotyping but generally avoided demeaning depictions (Robetta and Doretto in *Chinese Laundry Scene* perhaps being an exception). Like the vaudeville stage (notably Koster & Bial's) from which many of these performers came, these films articulated a vision of American identity which was polyglot, self-confident and, within limits, fluid.[101]

43

These kinetoscope films offered a space apart, a fantastic space removed from daily life and its constraints. People of all cultures and races appeared on the same vaudeville stage, enjoying the same basic forms of compensation and attention. At the Black Maria, the camera also treated these subjects approximately the same: camera distance was one of the few variables and it operated within the pragmatic goals of best capturing a performance.[102] As performers who construct their own image (admittedly constrained by performance categories and cultural preconceptions) and compete in the marketplace, they could destabilize established hierarchies of culture and what were often considered scientific categories of race. Each had his or her own specialty or talent which demanded fascination and respect. Here was an alternative rather than an obviously oppositional vision of a world. Racial and economic hierarchies may not have been upended but they were potentially effaced, flattened out or otherwise subverted.

There is a noticeable shift in these representations with the onset of projection in the United States. The Edison group moved from a cultural stance that was cosmopolitan to another that could be, and was probably intended to be, constructed as "American" in a much more narrow sense. Raff & Gammon's choice of films for the vitascope's Koster & Bial premiere in April 1896 was hardly random. Of the three or four films that had been made for the kinetoscope in 1894-1895, all were of white, American performers: the Leigh sisters in *Umbrella Dance*; *Band Drill* from *The Milk White Flag*; and *Walton & Slavin*, showing a burlesque boxing match from *Little Christopher Columbus*. New subjects within the familiar genre of dance films included films of toe dancer Amy Muller and a skirt dance by an unidentified performer (the film may well have been an old one): here again the performers were white, native-born Americans. The two most novel films were *The Monroe Doctrine* (no. 154) and Robert Paul's film *Sea Waves at Dover*—duly credited as an English subject but without acknowledging its true author. Both explored the new potentials of projection. The wave crashing on the shore seemed to threaten the audience by penetrating beyond the proscenium and flooding the spectators. It also seemed to have asserted the geographic mobility of the American machine. *The Monroe Doctrine* was a political cartoon on film, one that asserted U.S. dominance in the western hemisphere, mobilizing and uniting the audience through its jingoistic assertion. This assertion of dominance was at English expense—the victory of Uncle Sam over John Bull. In this context *Sea Waves at Dover* suggests that British waves should best stay on British rather than Latin American shores. Given the repertoire of selected films, this program strongly suggests that Raff & Gammon were preparing to fight the expected influx of international machines (English as well as French) on the basis of patriotic nationalism—even as they had marketed the kinetoscope on the basis of a cosmopolitan internationalism.

The Lumières certainly played a unique and crucial role in the cultural landscape of cinema's novelty year. Edison's camera crew emulated their subject matter and began to take scenes on location with a portable camera on 11 May 1896. By the time the cinématographe had its New York City debut in late June, the Kinetograph Department had a reasonably large selection of outdoor scenes—including pictures of New York, Brooklyn, Coney Island, and Niagara Falls. Edison cameramen had also filmed horse races and parades well before the cinématographe's premiere at Keith's. The erasure of the Edison/stage versus Lumière/outdoor difference, however, meant the creation of another that was at least as profound. Because the Edison crew took its films in the New York area, the vitascope inevitably showed essentially American subjects (views of American cities and tourist landmarks, and of American performers such as May Irwin and John C. Rice in *The Kiss*). The Lumière cinématographe showed foreign, essentially European views (not only of France, but of Italy, Switzerland, Russia and other distant locales). The differences in terms of subject matter were Edison/American versus Lumière/International even as "authorship" distinctions, both of films and the respective technological systems, were Edison/American versus Lumière/French.

If the Lumière cinématographe ran counter to the American nationalism of the vitascope, it also provided the necessary term that made such opposition clear cut and vital. Once unleashed, this jingoism proved powerful. Two years after making *The Monroe Doctrine*, the Edison Manufacturing Company was providing a war-inducing array of films showing the sunken battleship "Maine," Spanish fortresses in Cuba, and

American armament ready to acquire an overseas empire. And to the extent that the cinématographe featured a rich array of military scenes, its internationalism was of a very particular kind—one that easily fostered national rivalries. In these films, the absence of presence suggested power (the cavalry charging the screen) without consequence—the clash of real armies off-screen. The move from peep-hole to projection brought with it new kinds of subject matter and a greater visceral impact on audiences, but this achievement was not without its costs. It also produced a new dialectic: between a patriotic even jingoistic nationalism, which saw American identity in narrow nativist terms; and a cosmopolitanism with a fluid, easy going sense of American identity. These were poles around which United States and even European cinemas fluctuated in the 1890s and beyond. It was a tension strikingly absent from the films of the kinetoscope period.

The debut of motion pictures in Edison's kinetoscope, which occurred just over 100 years ago, produced a complex phenomena. In many instances the films themselves were quite conservative, retaining features of the Edison Laboratory that spawned it. Yet even these conservative qualities often fostered an unexpected cultural dynamism in the process of exhibition and reception. This phenomenon was buttressed by Dickson and Heise's embrace of the most untamed elements of American performance culture. In reflecting on the subversive pleasures which they provided, the work and ideas of Mikhail Bakhtin often come to mind. His view of the carnivalesque can be appropriately applied to many features of the kinetoscope films.[103] As with carnival, the kinetoscope parlors brought marginal, vulgar and illegitimate subjects to the center of people's attention—and to the geographic heart of cities such as New York. Raff & Gammon's catalogs of kinetoscope films offer a virtual inventory of amusements beyond the pale of official or decorous social life. If, as Robert Stam suggests, "carnival represented an alternative cosmovision characterized by the ludic undermining of all norms,"[104] the world envisioned by the kinetoscope was similarly transgressive. Racial and gender hierarchies break down. Discourses about film as an aid to science and high art are shown to be aids to something quite different—to low culture and the mocking of seriousness of purpose. Bodies are celebrated for their excesses—of self-indulgence and violence, for their extreme dexterity, openness and sexual suggestiveness. The Edison name as well as the absence of presence offered unusual protection to these violations of genteel sensibilities.

Although this article has focused on the impact of these films as they were exhibited at 1155 Broadway, New York City, we must not forget that one of their most striking and ludic features was the generation of multiple copies. Simulacrums of these transgressive acts were popping up across the country, transported to towns and cities of all sizes in small metal tins. As a result, motion pictures had a profound impact on American culture right from the beginning—an impact that may have been more extreme and far reaching than their comparable dissemination in Europe. In any case, the concerns and ideological orientations of these early Edison films were surprisingly different from those of the Lumières. The Lumière cinématographe, which at first glance seems to engage the world in a direct way that had considerable radical potential, in fact had many conservative features. Indeed, as the Edison group moved into the era of projection the utopic, carnivalesque quality of these early kinetoscope films was often undermined. Not only jingoistic nationalism but established hierarchies re-emerged. To kinetoscope scenes of African-American dancers, Edison filmmakers soon added scenes of black men eating watermelon with demeaning gusto and another of a black woman scrubbing her baby in the naive hope of ridding the child of his undesired color. Racist stereotypes were thus quickly reasserted. But even at the very outset, Edison, Dickson, and Heise were eagerly pursuing the commodification of culture, which would seem to circumscribe at least some of the films' radical potential.

We have traditionally thought of the beginnings of a new media such as motion pictures as one necessitating experimentation. At the very beginning its representational techniques had not yet had time to achieve coherence and effectiveness. Movies were little more than charming snippets of reality or canned performances. Considered within a latter day framework, this would appear to be a logical conclusion. If properly understood within their historical context, however, Edison's kinetoscope films were rich in meaning and displayed a coherent if limited repertoire of representational techniques. The beginnings of motion picture practices were not only significant as a starting point in relation to the century long history of cinema which followed but intensified a process of rapid, general change within American culture as a whole. It is this framework that I hope readers will bring to an examination of this filmography.

This essay was presented at a number of conferences and symposiums including "Celebrating 1895: An International Conference on Cinema Before 1920 at the National Museum of Photography, Film and Television (Bradford, England), 16 June 1995; the annual meeting of the Japanese Society of Image Arts and Science," Kobe, Japan, 2 June 1995; the American Center (Paris, France) in conjunction with its opening of the show *Before Hollywood: Turn-of-the-Century Films from American Archives*, October 1994, and the Williams Center for the Arts, Rutherford, N.J., 23 April 1994. These forums and the discussion that resulted were essential to the development of this piece. It also benefited immensely from a critical reading by Tom Gunning.

1. In referring to this pre-cinema motion picture work, I certainly do not want to limit our concerns to activities at the Edison Laboratory. The work of Robert Paul and Birt Acres is equally relevant and of considerable international significance. In the United States and possibly Australia, production for peep-hole machines was pursued quite independently of Edison. Nor is this an effort to marginalize the impact of other cultural influences on the beginnings of cinema. Newspapers, popular theater, photography and other cultural forms had profound influences on cinema's initial formation, but we must adequately conceptualize the structure of influence that produced this new but hardly unformed phenomenon. John Fell suggests the array of cultural influences on early cinema in *Film and the Narrative Tradition* (Norman: University of Oklahoma Press, 1974). See also Erwin Panofsky, "Style and Medium in the Moving Pictures," *Bulletin of the Department of Art and Archeology,* Princeton University, 1934, revised version in Daniel Talbot, ed., *Film: An Anthology* (New York: Simon and Schuster, 1959), 15-32.

2. Deac Rossell, "Double-Think: The Cinema and Magic Lantern Culture," presented 16 June 1995, at the Celebrating 1895 Conference (National Museum of Photography, Film and Television, Bradford, England); Charles Musser, "Toward a History of Screen Practice," *Quarterly Review of Cinema Studies* 9, no. 1 (Winter 1984), 59-69; Olive Cook, *Movement in Two Dimensions* (London: Huchinson, 1963). David Francis has given a series of lectures on the magic lantern and cinema at the 1994 Domitor Conference (Museum of Modern Art, New York) and elsewhere.

3. Yuri Tsivian, "The Rorschach Test for Cultures: On Some Parallels between Early Film Reception in Russia and the United States," *Yale Journal of Criticism* 7, no. 2 (1995), 177-178.

4. Gordon Hendricks, *The Edison Motion Picture Myth* (Berkeley: University of California, 1961); Gordon Hendricks, *The Kinetoscope: America's First Commercially Successful Motion Picture Examiner* (New York: The Beginnings of the American Film, 1966); Gordon Hendricks, *Beginnings of the Biograph: The Story of the Invention of the Mutoscope and Biograph and Their Supply Camera* (New York: The Beginnings of the American Film, 1964).

5. A break with historical consensus and the need for new, serious research were points made by Robert C. Allen in "Contra the Chaser Theory," in John Fell, ed., *Film Before Griffith* (Berkeley: University of California Press, 1983), 105-115.

6. Iris Barry wrote numerous film notes for screenings at the Museum of Modern Art. See also Iris Barry, *D.W. Griffith: American Film Master* (1940; New York, Museum of Modern Art, 1965); Jay Leyda's impact on the history of early film was felt most strongly in his teaching, though his historiographic approach and interests are evident in Leyda, *Kino: A History of Russian and Soviet Film* (London: Allen and Unwin, 1960). See also Jay Leyda and Charles Musser, eds., *Before Hollywood: Turn of the Century Films from American Archives* (New York: American Federation of the Arts, 1986); George C. Pratt, *Spellbound in Darkness: A History of the Silent Film* (Greenwich, Conn.: New York Graphic Society, 1966); Paul C. Spehr, *The Movies Begin: Making Movies in New Jersey, 1887-1920* (Newark: Newark Museum and Morgan and Morgan, 1977); Eileen Bowser, ed., *Biograph Bulletins, 1908-1912* (New York: Farrar, Straus and Giroux, 1973) and more recently Bowser, *The Transformation of Cinema, 1907-1915* (New York: Scribners, 1990).

7. Matthew Josephson, *Edison* (New York: McGraw-Hill, 1959); Hendricks, *Edison Motion Picture Myth*, 190-197.

8. Félix Mesguich, *Tours de manivelle: Souvenirs d'un chasseur d'images* (Paris: Bernard Grassett, 1933). The intersection of an anti-Edison, pro-Lumière position is most strongly evident in Robert C. Allen, "Vitascope/Cinematographe: Initial Patterns of Film Industrial Practice," in Fell, ed., *Film Before Griffith*, 144-152.

9. Tom Gunning, "The Cinema of Attraction[s]," *Wide Angle* 8, no. 3-4 (1986), 64; revised version in Thomas Elsaesser, *Early Cinema: Space, Frame, Narrative* (London: BFI Publishing, 1990); Tom Gunning, "Now You See it, Now You Don't: The Temporality of the Cinema of Attractions," *Velvet Light Trap* 32 (Fall 1993); Gunning, "An Aesthetic of Astonishment: Film and the Early (In)credulous Spectator," *Art & Text* (Fall 1989), 34.

10. André Bazin's writings were available only in French until after Hendricks' books were published. English translations did not appear until the late 1960s. See André Bazin, *What Is Cinema?* (Berkeley: University of California Press, 1967), edited and translated by Hugh Gray.

11. Documentation from this conference can be found in *Cinema 1900-1906: An Analytical Study*, 2 vols. (Brussels: FIAF, 1982). Vol. 1: *Brighton Symposium, 1978*. Vol. 2: *Analytical Filmography (Fiction Films), 1900-1906*.

12. Paul Spehr to Charles Musser, June 1995. The Motion Picture Section was for many years part of the Prints and Photograph Division; in an organizational restructuring it became part of the Motion Picture, Broadcasting and Recorded Sound Division.

13. Paul Spehr has recently presented work on W.K.L. Dickson using the Hendricks Collections at the Smithsonian Institution and the Library of Congress. Ray Phillips has written a book on the kinetoscope which Flick Books is scheduled to publish this fall.

14. Although I have presented some of these ideas in earlier work, even those analyses that may be familiar to attentive readers have been pushed further, and often in new directions.

15. "Department of Physics," *Brooklyn Daily Eagle*, 10 May 1893.

16. Hendricks, *The Kinetoscope*, 38.

17. Roy Rosenzweig, *Eight Hours for What We Will: Workers and Leisure in an Industrial City, 1870-1920* (Cambridge: Cambridge University Press, 1983).

18. Edison's motion pictures not only required the development of a new technology and new equipment, it required the construction of new spaces to house them. There was the Photographic Building constructed in August 1889 to house motion picture experiments, the Black Maria studio built in late 1892-early 1893 to support commercial production, and the kinetoscope parlor at 1155 Broadway, in New York City, which opened on 14 April 1894. Yet it was not strictly necessary to create these spaces in the way it was necessary to built the technology. The Lumières, for instance, not only made do with simpler technology—a single piece of equipment that served as camera, printer, and projector—but they were much more efficient in their film-related architectonics. They shot outdoors and located their first commercial exhibitions in a cafe that needed little renovations. (It seems that Lumière père was more interested in building homes, the brothers in building factories.)

19. Noël Burch, *Life to Those Shadows* (Berkeley: University of California Press, 1990).

20. Alan Williams, *Republic of Images* (Cambridge, Ma.: Harvard University Press, 1992), 28-29.

21. "Striking at Edison," *New York Journal*, 18 July 1893, clipping, NjWOE.

22. Terry Ramsaye, *A Million and One Nights* (New York: Simon and Shuster, 1926), caption for frontispiece; Gordon Hendricks, *The Edison Motion Picture Myth*.

23. André Millard, *Edison and the Business of Invention* (Baltimore: Johns Hopkins University Press, 1990), chap. 7.

24. Laurent Mannoni has found evidence that suggests Louis may have been indebted to something more than a sleepless night's thinking. In particular, Léon Gaumont may have offered the key conceptual solutions.

25. Williams, *Republic of Images*, 22; Thomas Elsaesser, "After Lumière/D'après Lumière," Congrès Lumière, Lyons, France, June 1995.

26. Charles Musser, *Before the Nickelodeon: Edwin S. Porter and the Edison Manufacturing Company* (Berkeley: University of California Press, 1991).

27. For information on Constant Girel and Gabriel Veyre, see Futoshi Koga, ed., *Lumière: Les Lumières et le Japon* (Tokyo: Asahi Shimbun, 1995).

28. We know much less about the organization of work for the manufacturing of kinetoscopes and projectors and the making of positive prints.

29. *Edison Kinetoscopic Record of a Sneeze*, made in the first days of 1894, might be considered a fourth film made for demonstration purposes. Extremely short, it nonetheless shows a complete cycle of action.

30. Marshall Deutelbaum, "Structural Patterning in the Lumière Films," in John Fell, ed., *Film Before Griffith*, 299-310. Since kinetoscope films were sometimes shown more than once, and in any case were shown as loops in the kinetoscopes that did not necessarily turn on and off at the beginning, filming a single complete action and the cyclical nature of these films were intertwined in a way that was not the case with Lumière productions.

31. Neil Harris, *Humbug!: The Art of P.T. Barnum* (Boston: Little, Brown & Co., 1973), 72-89. The operational aesthetic fosters a level of skepticism in the spectator who must assess how a technology or some display actually works. Is the viewer being fooled in a game of wits with the showman?

32. "Another of Edison's Wonders," *Orange Chronicle*, 1 February 1890, 5. The motion picture system was described as "the most wonderful of all his wonderful inventions" in "The Kinetograph," *New York Sun,* 28 May 1891, 1-2. See also The Kinetoscope Company, *Edison's Latest Wonders: The Kinetograph, The Kinetoscope* [October 1894].

33. Though on some level *Arroseur et arrosé* is also about how something works and the costs associated with not realizing why a piece of equipment, for example a hose, has stopped doing its job.

34. A showing of *The Barber Shop* is not unlike a con game. The successful con artist not only pulls off the scam but leaves his victim humbled *and* impressed. To jump forward a few years, consider the Lobsterscope that was popular in 1897. Patrons went to the theater knowing they were going to be fooled (i.e. they would see a fake film exhibition).

35. My analysis has admittedly ignored a number of films using members of the Newark Turverein. These films were made, most likely, to simulate subsequent commercial production with its need to accommodate outside performers with reasonable speed and reliability. In short, the German-American athletes, who can be understood as modest counterparts to Sandow, were being used for a dry run. These films represent a transitional moment.

36. David L. Chapman, *Sandow the Magnificent: Eugen Sandow and the Beginnings of Bodybuilding* (Urbana: University of Illinois Press, 1994).

37. Many of the performers in Edison's kinetoscope films had their American vaudeville debut at Koster & Bial's Music Hall and later appeared in houses with "popular prices" such as Keith's Union Square Theatre and Proctor's 23rd Street Theatre. Although Terry Ramsaye suggests that the early 1890s was still a period when variety reigned supreme, newspapers of the period suggest vaudeville was already the appropriate term to be applied to these theaters. See, for example, "Variety to Vaudeville," *New York Herald*, 21 October 1894, 4F.

38. "The Strong Man Appears," *New York Times*, 12 June 1893, 5. The complete text of this review appears in the filmography.

39. My colleague Brigitte Peucker links the tableaux vivant to the Pygmalion and Galatea story on one hand, and to the cinema on the other in *Incorporating Images: Film and the Rival Arts* (Princeton: Princeton University Press, 1995).

40. Brigitte Peucker, "Looking and Touching: Spectacle and Collection in Sontag's *Volcano Lover,*" unpublished paper given at the Modern Language Association Conference, December 1994.

41. Ramsaye discusses the relationship between cinema and Wells' time machine in *A Million and One Nights*, 152-162.

42. The Lumières' *Repas de bébé* is open to a somewhat similar symptomatic interpretation as *Sandow*—as an allegory of regeneration and life.

43. The Lumières, particularly the father, did have some ties to performance culture, for example, Félicien Trewey. In this respect, the films of Trewey's performance must also be seen as the filming of a family friend. Likewise one might argue that some early Edison films do depict families—for instance *Cupid's Dance* of the Ewer sisters—but they occur within the framework of performance culture.

44. Erik Barnouw, *Documentary: A Short History of the Non-Fiction Film,* rev. ed. (1974; New York: Oxford University Press, 1983), 2-22.

45. Jonas Barish, *The Antitheatrical Prejudice* (Berkeley: University of California Press, 1981).

46. "Edison Perfects His Kinetoscope," *New York Herald*, 7 March 1894, 9.

47. *Sandow on Physical Training* (New York: J. Selwin Tait & Sons, 1894).

48. "Development of a Strong Man," *New York Herald*, 18 March 1894, 8E.

49. "Wizard Edison's Kinetograph" *New York World*, 18 March 1894, 21.

50. Hendricks was, of course, right in claiming that Edison effectively managed an adoring press to build an image that did not neatly correspond to reality.

51. "The Chance of Sandow's Life," *New York Herald*, 9 April 1894, 8; "Sandow Would Rather Pose," and "Cyr is the Champion," *New York Herald*, 11 April 1894, 12.

52. This relationship of promoting motion pictures while selling newspapers was similar to that relationship between the press and the sporting world. It was quite different from the ways in which cinema was said to function as a visual newspaper.

53. Edison's presence at the filming of the Corbett-Courtney fight went unreported in the press, but Gordon Hendricks located a reminiscence of James Corbett, which suggests the boxer did meet the inventor on this occasion (*The Kinetoscope*, 109).

54. The affinity between the world champion of boxing and the world champion of invention would become explicit in James Corbett's next play, *The Naval Cadet*, in which he plays a young inventor, not unlike Edison.

55. "In the Breezy Roof Gardens," *New York Tribune,* 24 June 1894, 11.

56. *Providence Journal*, 16 February 1897, 8; *Cincinnati Commercial Tribune*, 20 December 1896, 11.

57. The exhibitor who later attributed Welton's act to Trewey was Englishman William Rock. *New Orleans Picayune*, 25 May 1897, 14, cited in Sylvester Quinn Breard, "A History of Motion Pictures in New Orleans, 1896-1908" (M.A. thesis; Louisiana State University, 1951), 31, published in microfiche in *Historical Journal of Film, Radio and Television* 15, no. 4 (Fall 1995).

58. "Acrobat Dies After Act," *New York Times*, 13 July 1926, 19.

59. It was in some sense unnecessary for Edison to be the frequent or overt subject of his films given that the technology was tied to his name so explicitly: "Edison's latest wonder, the Kinetoscope"; "Edison's Vitascope" and so forth.

60. The use of entertainment for promotional or advertising purposes, of course, continues. Banc One has recently been "the financial services sponsor" of the feature film *Selena*, released by Warner Brothers in March 1997 ("Advertising," *New York Times,* 21 March 1997, D6).

61. Kathy Peiss developed and popularized the concept of homosocial space in *Cheap Amusements: Working Women and Leisure in Turn of the Century New York* (Philadelphia: Temple University Press, 1986).

62. "Griffo and M'Auliffe Fight," *New York Herald,* 17 May 1894, 9.

63. For a study that situates the world of boxing within the context of "the cult of masculinity," see Michael T. Isenberg, *John L. Sullivan and His America* (Urbana: University of Illinois Press, 1988).

64. For a photograph of kinetoscopes in a bar room, see Musser, *The Emergence of Cinema,* 85.

65. *Harper's Young People* 15 (22 May 1894), 500. I am grateful to Ray Phillips for bringing this article to my attention.

66. Hendricks, *The Kinetoscope*, 78-79.

67. Tom Gunning, "A Mischievous and Knowing Gaze: The Films of the Lumière Company and the Culture of Amateur Photography," Congrès Lumière, Lyons, France, 7-10 June 1995.

68. Williams, *Republic of Images*, 32.

69. I first discussed this idea at the May 1987 Society for Cinema Studies conference in Montreal, in relation to the exhibition of Corbett-Fitzsimmons fight films. Several of these types of disjunctions are also analyzed in *The Emergence of Cinema*. The idea of a public sphere where the dynamics of a new media generate unexpected contradictions of this kind has been theorized within a Frankfurt School perspective by Miriam Hansen in *Babel and Babylon: Spectatorship in American Silent Film* (Cambridge: Harvard University Press, 1991). I have been trying to grasp the depth and diversity of this phenomenon both here and in essays such as "Passions and the Passion Play: Theater, Film and Religion, 1880-1900," *Film History* 5, no. 4 (1993), 419-456.

70. The theoretical discussion of the absence of presence in cinema has a long history, which includes Walter Benjamin, André Bazin, and Christian Metz.

71. "Charged the Grand Jury," *Newark Daily Advertiser,* 11 September 1894, 1-2; "Not Regarded as a Fight," *Newark Daily Advertiser,* 12 September 1894, 1. Both are reprinted in the document section for *The Corbett-Courtney Fight* (no. 54).

72. Musser, *The Emergence of Cinema*, 193-208. After film became a form of mass entertainment (ca. 1908), the process gradually reversed itself: boxing films became essentially illegal even though the sport itself remained lawful. See Daniel Gene Streible, "A History of the Prize Fight Film, 1894-1915" (Ph.D. diss., University of Texas, 1994).

73. See, for example, "New Danse du Ventre," *New York Herald*, 14 April 1894, 10, reprinted in document section for *Hadj Cheriff* (no. 75) and "Coochee Coochee Stopped at Coney Island," *New York Herald,* 8 June 1896, 11, in document section for *Streets of Cairo* (no. 241).

74. George B. McClellan, Jr. (23 November 1865-30 November 1940) would eventually become mayor of New York City, serving from 1904-1909.

75. "She Coaxed the Mayor," *New York Herald*, 25 August 1894, 10, reprinted in document section for *Cupid's Dance*, no. 51.

76. Charles Musser with Carol Nelson, *High-Class Moving Pictures: Lyman H. Howe and the Forgotten Era of Traveling Exhibition, 1880-1920* (Princeton, N.J.: Princeton University Press, 1991), 69-84.

77. Streible, "A History of the Prize Fight Film, 1894-1915."

78. John Higham, "The Reorientation of American Culture in the 1890s," in *Writing American History: Essays on Modern Scholarship* (Bloomington: Indiana University Press, 1970), 73-102, 187-192; Warren Susman, *Culture as History* (New York: Pantheon, 1984), 271-285; Alan Trachtenberg, *The Incorporation of America* (New York: Hill & Wang, 1982); T.J. Jackson Lears, "From Salvation to Self-Realization: Advertising and the Therapeutic Roots of the Consumer Culture, 1880-1930," in Richard Wightman Fox and T.J. Jackson Lears, eds., *The Culture of Consumption: Critical Essays in American History, 1880-1980* (New York: Pantheon, 1983), 1-38.

79. "The Kinetograph," *New York Sun,* 28 May 1891, 1-2, reprinted after entry for *[Men Boxing]* (no. 10).

80. *New York World*, 3 June 1888, 16.

81. "Edison Perfects His Kinetoscope," *New York Herald*, 7 March 1894, 9. The idea that Sandow was participating in an "experiment" is mentioned in almost every news report.

82. *Orange Journal*, 3 March 1888, 2. The day following his controversial exhibition in Orange, N.J., Muybridge met with Edison at the inventor's near-by laboratory. In the course of their discussions, the two promised to collaborate by combining Edison's phonograph with Muybridge's serial photography. Muybridge thus spurred Edison to develop his motion picture system. But his work also influenced the subject matter and representational strategies adopted for these early films.

83. The sexual proclivities of both Muybridge and Dickson merit further study. Dickson's fascination with Sandow goes beyond the depiction of a homosocial space to one that is homoerotic. This becomes quite obvious when one looks at the highly charged photographs of Sandow, which Dickson included in his *History of the Kinetograph, Kinetoscope and Kineto-Phonograph*. In fact, it is tempting to see a homoerotic circuit of desire at play here, one that involves Hendricks as well as Dickson and Sandow. Desire intertwined with "scientific method," whether of photography or history.

84. "Anatomy of a Kiss," *New York World*, 26 April 1896, 21, reprinted in document section for *May Irwin Kiss* (no. 155).

85. Curtis M. Hinsley, "The World as Marketplace: Commodification of the Exotic at the World's Columbian Exposition, 1893," in Ivan Karp and Steven D. Lavine, eds., *Exhibiting Cultures: The Poetics and Politics of Museum Display* (Washington, D.C.: Smithsonian Institution Press, 1991), 344-365.

86. Barbara Kirshenblatt-Gimblett, "Objects of Ethnography," in Karp and Lavine, eds., *Exhibiting Cultures*, 398.

87. Kirshenblatt-Gimblett, "Objects of Ethnography," 399.

88. "Strange People from Far Away," *New York Herald*, 18 February 1894, 10, reprinted in document section after *Princess Ali* (no. 134).

89. Michel Foucault, *Discipline and Punish: The Birth of the Prison* (New York: Pantheon, 1978), particularly 154-156.

90. Isenberg, *John L. Sullivan and His America*.

91. "Griffo and M'auliffe Fight," *New York Herald*, 17 May 1894, 9, reprinted in document section for *Boxing* (no. 39).

92. "Caicedo, King of Wire Walkers," New York Herald, 20 May 1894, 8E.

93. Chapman, *Sandow the Magnificent*, 9.

94. "Ena Bertoldi," *New York Clipper*, 5 May 1894, 129, reprinted in document section for *Bertoldi (Mouth Support)* (no. 31).

95. "From Cradle to Trapeze," *New York Herald,* 6 September 1896, 16D.

96. Ibid.

97. "Caicedo, King of Wire Walkers," *New York Herald*, 20 May 1894, 8E, reprinted in document section for *Caicedo (with pole)* (no. 46) and *Caicedo (with spurs)* (no. 47).

98. Michael Isenberg has argued that the differences of attitude that Sullivan and Corbett represent are not as clear cut as historians have sometimes suggested. Comparisons between old and new, for example, might not be symmetrical (a comparison between Sullivan's training and his body at the end of his career with Corbett's when he was a challenger preparing for his first championship bout). As Isenberg points out, other boxers in the style of Sullivan would become heavy-weight champions in the future—for example Jack Johnson. Isenberg, *John L. Sullivan and His America*.

99. Warren Susman, *Culture as History* (New York: Pantheon, 1984), 271-285. Susman focuses on a shift from a concern with character to that of personality. This change begins in the 1890s, while the idea of personality reaches a level of dominance in the 1910s and 1920s when the movie star had become a pervasive feature of American life.

100. A certain amount of more or less intentional confusion accompanies any effort to identify the ethnic and national identity of vaudevillians. Despite her Italian sounding stage name, Ena Bertoldi was English. Likewise, despite their Italian stage names, Robetta and Doretto (Phil Lauter) were of British descent. In playing an Irish cop and Chinese laundryman, they were playing somewhat anarchically across racial and ethnic lines.

101. Alan Trachtenberg, "Conceivable Aliens," *The Yale Review* 82, no. 4 (October 1994), 42-64; Werner Sollors, *Beyond Ethnicity* (New York: Oxford University Press), 149-173.

102. So far as we know, Dickson and Heise employed closer views (camera framings approaching a medium shot in today's terminology) only with European and European-American performers.

103. Mikhail Bakhtin, *Rabelais and His World* (Cambridge, Ma.: MIT Press, 1968). See also Robert Stam, *Subversive Pleasures: Bakhtin, Cultural Criticism and Film* (Baltimore: Johns Hopkins University Press, 1989).

104. Stam, *Subversive Pleasures*, 86.

How to Use This Filmography—and Why

Beginnings always have a privileged place in a given practice—whether for disciplines such as psychology and history, a cultural form such as theater, or for film. With the cinema, an investigation of the 1890s can provide us with a fresh perspective on more recent moving images—and new moving image technologies—which have become a pervasive and extremely influential part of our everyday life. Possibilities that were novel and exciting as cinema began are now taken for granted. Other practices from this period were subsequently marginalized but now serve as a touchstone for film-makers seeking opportunities for renewal. More generally, an exploration of the first decade of motion pictures can provide scholars and ordinary Americans with new insights into a period that is increasingly recognized as a formative one for modern, industrial America.

As we approached the cinema's 100th anniversary, the need for detailed filmo-graphic information about an array of early films became increasingly evident. Turn-of-the-century motion pictures already constituted a rich resource around which schol-ars and cinephiles showed a lively interest. Nonetheless, significant barriers contin-ued to impede a basic appreciation and effective use of these materials. Nonfiction images, routinely stripped of their historical specificity, often seemed banal. Many films that document significant moments in America's cultural, social and political life still waited to be effectively identified—flotsam of America's past. Likewise, motion pictures of performers and short fiction films were meant to be seen within an inter-textual context that had been lost. The inclusion of information and documentation in this catalog is designed to help reclaim this historical heritage.

Throughout the nineteenth century, producers and showmen alike routinely con-ceived of films intended for projection as building blocks for larger programs rather than as self-sufficient texts. Motion pictures that were taken at a particular event or on a given filming trip were frequently exhibited in groups and were often structured into multi-shot/multi-film narratives. Exhibitors sequenced films showing—among other topics—President William McKinley's inauguration (1897), the Spanish-American War (1898), Admiral George Dewey's triumphal return to the United States (1899) and the Paris Exposition (1900). A chronological organization thus becomes essential if today's scholars and researchers are to make effective use of these materials. The affinity between these short subjects (many only a single shot) is obscured when they are ordered alphabetically. And yet without significant excep-tion, existing catalogs of early motion pictures organize their entries synchronically (alphabetically) rather than a diachronically (chronologically). *Edison Motion Pictures, 1890-1900*, in contrast, makes the historical framework predominant while retaining traditional cataloging features.

Cataloging Edison Motion Pictures: Scope, Definition, Rationale

This scholarly finding aid restricts its focus to providing essential documentation of all known Edison films made between 1890 and 1900. Thomas Edison and his asso-ciates at the Edison Laboratory in West Orange, New Jersey, invented the first system of commercial motion pictures. The inventor's production entity, the Edison Manufacturing Company, was the only motion picture producer in the world before 1895 and the leading American producer and distributor of 35mm films through 1900 and beyond. The first eleven years were chosen because 1) they cover Edison produc-tion throughout the nineteenth century and 2) the period runs from Edison's first surviving motion picture experiments through the effective closing of the Black Maria Studio in January or early February 1901, when Edison opened a glass-enclosed, roof-top studio on East 21st Street in Manhattan. This new facility not only involved the move to a new locale but shifts in commercial strategies. This moment provides a convenient stopping point because the intervening eleven-year period embraces a large but manageable number of films. Depending on the way in which one counts, employees and affiliates made approximately 1,000 films for the Edison organization during this eleven year period—almost all between 1894 and 1900. The vast majority were between 50 and 150 feet. None was more than 1,000 feet in length—unless pre-packaged groupings of individual films, the case with passion play subjects for instance, are included. An extraordinary number of these pictures survives: approximately 60 per cent, in contrast to the general survival rate for films of the silent period which is closer to 15 per cent.

For purposes of this filmography an Edison film is:

1) Any film made within an entity owned and controlled by Thomas A. Edison. This includes both films made within the framework of the Edison Laboratory before 1 April 1894 and those produced by the Edison Manufacturing Company and its employees after that date. Most of these films were copyrighted in the name of Thomas A. Edison, though a few were copyrighted in the name of others, notably James White and W.K.L. Dickson.

2) Any film made by licensed cameramen such as William Paley, J. Stuart Blackton and Albert E. Smith *and* distributed by the Edison Manufacturing Company. Not all films made by these licensees found their way into Edison distribution: a filmography of Vitagraph productions for the 1890s would encompass many pictures not appearing in this Edison filmography as well as numerous films that do.

3) Other films made independently of any direct Edison influence but subsequently acquired for distribution by the Edison Manufacturing Company with the (not always happy) agreement of the original producer. For example, *The Passion Play of Oberammergau* was made through the Eden Musee, a New York amusement center, but was turned over to the Edison Manufacturing Company for distribution as part of the settlement for a patent infringement case. For commercial purposes this was marketed as an Edison film.

Edison films are those made within an Edison organization or contractually distributed by the Edison Manufacturing Company and its affiliates. However, this filmography does not treat all films appearing in Edison catalogs and advertisements as Edison films. The Edison Manufacturing Company often marketed duplicate prints of films without the permission of their creators. This was particularly true for pictures made by European producers such as Georges Méliès, but to a lesser extent this practice was also applied to the work American rivals such as Sigmund Lubin. Although the selling of such dupes was not strictly illegal (since the films had not been copyrighted), it was, as even Edison executives recognized, unethical. Such "pirated" films were excluded from this filmography for reasons that should be largely self-evident. Most of these films—particularly European productions—were duplicated and distributed by other American firms at approximately the same time. Any claims to these films as being of Edison authorship were greeted with skepticism. In most instances, knowledgeable exhibitors doubtlessly knew their true provenance.

There are arguments for including even pirated films in an Edison filmography, but such a decision would significantly expand the number of entries for the years 1899 and 1900. Other information would have to be excluded. And since my intention has been to extend this work in a subsequent volume to approximately 1908, such inclusiveness would probably become burdensome. (Nonetheless, a handful of titles that currently appear to be pirated subjects could subsequently prove to be Edison films when additional information comes to light.) If including pirated Méliès films in an Edison filmography seems too all-inclusive, simply limiting the filmography to films made at the Edison Laboratory or by Edison employees must be deemed too narrow. The reliance on freelance cameraman operating under Edison license was a fundamental commercial strategy in the 1897-1900 period. Moreover, the authorship of certain films copyrighted by Thomas A. Edison is still uncertain. Whether they were made by Edison employees or Edison licensees regretfully remains to be determined.

Distinctive Features of the Filmography
The decision to catalog all Edison films made within the designated period is an important feature of this filmography. Most previous efforts have focused on catalog-

ing copyrighted or surviving films. This assumes that the catalog is a tool meant primarily to access the films rather than a collection of documents with their own integrity. Such cataloging strategies inevitably affect historical research. Much has been made by film historians, for example, of data derived from copyright information on the number of fiction films compared to the number of actualities. Yet during certain periods, fiction films were copyrighted but news films and other actualities were not. It is an almost insurmountable task for historians to overcome biases built into scholarly aids. To minimize these kinds of problems, this filmography is as complete as possible. While records are not available for every Edison film, it is possible to come close to achieving this goal by using a variety of overlapping sources: copyright information, catalogs, trade journals, correspondence, business records, newspapers, and so forth.

This cataloging of Edison films involves a fundamentally different way of thinking about, organizing and researching early motion pictures. In keeping with recent trends in historiography, it seeks to apply bibliographic techniques to a broader conception of motion picture practice rather than to a body of discrete film texts. This is appropriate, perhaps essential for the pre-1904 period. As already suggested, before this date films were rarely conceived as self-sufficient texts but rather as units that functioned within larger programs. The Edison Manufacturing Company encouraged exhibitors to select films from James White's world tour and use them to construct an evening-length travelogue, or buy films of the Spanish-American War to create a twenty-minute vaudeville program. Organization by chronology has become essential if today's scholars are to make effective use of these materials. In the past, a chronological approach has been urged by such historians and archivists as Jay Leyda and George Pratt. What has been in doubt perhaps has been our ability to create an adequate chronology for this early period, when documentation has appeared so fragmentary. Extensive searches in newspapers, particularly the examination of rarely used information such as the "Hotel Arrivals" and "Shipping" columns, has made it possible to construct a chronology of film production that was previously assumed to be impossible. Areas of uncertainty remain, but they generally occur within reasonable parameters.

When treating subjects historically, previous scholarly aids have usually relied on the copyright date. Research has found this to be a serious problem. Films were often copyrighted many months—and in some cases several years—after they were made and first shown. The decision to provide a chronological listing by production date can be demonstrated by S.S. "Coptic" Running Before a Gale, entry no. 500. A film copyrighted in December 1898 was made at the same time as other films copyrighted nine months earlier. Motion pictures made on distant filming trips were typical copyrighted in large batches and the copyright date thus lacks sufficient specificity. Moreover, since we are listing many films that were not copyrighted, the production date—even when not known precisely—is the only consistent feature available for chronological organization.

To appreciate the value of this approach, the reader might briefly peruse the entries which cover the first five months of 1898 (entry no. 471 through roughly no. 589). This section demonstrates the viability of presenting an Edison filmography chronologically by date of production rather than in alphabetical order. Here is a challenging group of films to document, one for which no production records are available. Previous catalogers have made little headway in identifying the specific contents and production contexts of these films. Nevertheless, these historiographic challenges were effectively overcome. This selection also suggests the diversity of topics filmed by Edison personnel, and the ways in which this chronological approach enables the reader to look at groups of related entries. Moreover, it illustrates the way information, such as the date a cameraman arrived in a particular location, can help the reader better understand the chronology of entries and the process of film production. With the Edison Manufacturing Company operating three production units by early 1898, this section also shows how entries are grouped by production unit, in a rough but overlapping chronology. The way several entries (for example, no. 574 through no. 577) were shot in groups, sometimes over several days, demonstrates how events—parades, ship launching and even winter sleigh rides—can be illuminated by a staggered chronology.

Research Uses

Edison Motion Pictures, 1890-1900 should be of value to a wide range of scholars interested in American life at the turn of the century—those working in performance studies, film and media studies, cultural history, ethnic studies, and social and political history. Edison films from the 1894-1900 period offer a unique visual record of American entertainment and popular culture—moving images that become much more interesting and useful when they can be examined in conjunction with pertinent descriptions and relevant production information. Research on the 1894-1895 period makes clear that the Edison Manufacturing Company was systematically recording various forms of commercial, urban amusement at a crucial moment in their histories. For example, *Sandow* (film no. 26), Edison's first official commercial subject, was of a celebrated and controversial strong man who was more interested in posing than in simply executing feats of strength. Documentation indicates that Edison's camera recorded an abbreviated version of his opening act. A brief but illuminating account of Prof. Ivan Tschernoff's visit to Edison's Black Maria studio illuminates the two films made of his trained dogs—as do reports of Tschernoff's initial appearance in the United States at Koster & Bial's Music Hall. Although neither *Skirt Dance Dog* (no. 81) nor *Summersault Dog* (no. 82) is known to survive, frame enlargements for the second of these films were published and are reproduced in this catalog. The accumulation of information—for example, the several kinetoscope films of skirt dances by renowned performers such as Annabelle Whitford—gives texture and a framework for understanding *Skirt Dance Dog* as a burlesque.

Comedy Set-to (no. 578) "shows Curtis and Gordon in one of their cleverest acts." As was often the case, the description identifies the performers (who remain unidentified in previous catalogs such as Kemp Niver's *Early Motion Pictures*) and characterizes their act. A series of documents reprinted in the document section sketches the history of this act, which broke up at the turn of the century. One half of the act, Billy Curtis, remained in the entertainment industry long enough for his obit to appear in *Variety*, which is reprinted. Such information, when available, suggests the place of the film in a given performer's overall career. Another short comedy (*The Burglar*, no. 579) was adapted from "the well-known scene in 'The Parlor Match,' made famous by Evans and Hoey." Here the "pre-note" provides the date and location of the premiere of this theatrical piece—revealing that it occurred almost thirty years before the film was made. A review of its revival in 1896 provides an almost contemporaneous perception of the farce and the assumptions viewers might have brought to a viewing of the film. Likewise two other entries (nos. 583 and 584) identify the date and location of a parade by Buffalo Bill's Wild troupe, accompanying the brief catalog descriptions with a news account of the event.

Entries for the spring of 1898 provide revealing information about the Spanish-American War. They suggest ways that motion pictures were used to provide Americans with information and propaganda about the Cuban crisis. A simple viewing of the films might suggest a comparatively "value free" depiction of events. The catalog descriptions, however, indicate that this was not the case. Such texts were often adapted for a lecture to accompany the films' screening. In any case, they articulate the framework within which contemporaneous spectators were viewing the films. From this perspective we see that the film *experience* was anything but value free (see entries nos. 537 through 547). While offering immensely useful details about the films' subjects, these descriptions display an underlying jingoism that should surprise no one. An obituary of Hearst journalist Karl Decker, who appeared in at least two of these films and helped to produce the others, recalls the romantic escapades of this figure and suggests the kind of drama many must have associated with these films. A newspaper article from the *New York Journal*, which concludes this section, also reveals the ways that William Randolph Hearst utilized motion pictures to extend his "yellow journalism" and promote his jingoistic views. Thus it underscores the early, intimate relationship between press and film.

Scholars interested in ethnic studies and African-American history will find a new and unexpected source of information. Although Thomas Cripps in *Slow Fade to Black* sees these early films as relatively free of offensive stereotyping in their depiction of African Americans, the catalog descriptions help to show how racial prejudices were assumed and perpetuated. Cripps's assessment of entry no. 559, *Colored Troops Disembarking* ("black men with weapons in hand marched down a gangplank on their way to Cuba"), as affirming black dignity is contradicted by the catalog description which sees their behavior as "laughable."[1] Several catalog descriptions, moreover, are noteworthy precisely because racial stereotypes were imposed and highlighted in situations that seem both inappropriate and unexpected. The description for *10th U.S. Infantry, 2nd Battalion, Leaving Cars* (no. 552) goes out of its way to refer to a "comical looking 'nigger dude' with sun umbrella." *Parade of Chinese* (no. 487) might likewise appear to be a fairly banal image, but the accompanying news article details an earlier incident in which Chinese paraders "were set upon by a crowd of toughs, who sought to destroy their banner and clamber on their floats." In many such instances, this annotated filmography raises questions about the relationship between image and subjective interpretation that could bear further exploration.

The entries in this catalog can illuminate attitudes toward the world beyond American shores. James White's tour through the Far East and his images of the British and American empires reflect European and U.S. self-confidence, as well as a burgeoning tourist industry. Many entries from the 1898-1900 period address the issue of imperialism and Japan's unusual position as an Asian power already challenging western interests. Scholars interested in the portrayal of war, depictions of the American presidency, or many other topics in American political history will find much useful information. For example, Edison personnel filmed events surrounding William McKinley's election as President, including such anti-Bryan comedies as *Pat and the Populist* (no. 233). This film shows "the Populist endeavoring to convert Pat to his own political views" but Pat demonstrates "his displeasure by dropping bricks on the politician." Films of President McKinley's inauguration, of his first visit to a Washington church as President, and his speech on Grant's Day are among those shot in March and April 1897.

In cinema studies, historians have begun to recognize that the first years of motion pictures are much richer and more complex than previously assumed. Increasingly they are returning in their analyses to this early, formative period. Yet if scholars see and then write about these films without a better understanding of their historically specific content as well as their conditions of production and reception, the resulting analyses will often yield dubious insights. (The preceding essay is only an initial effort to utilize newly available documentation gathered for this volume.) This scholarly aid enables historians of American culture and film, film programmers, and documentary filmmakers to use or discuss these films with greater accuracy and sensitivity.

The accumulation of filmographic information provides a new and more thorough understanding of Edison production practices. For example, the annual output at Edison is possible to estimate with greater accuracy than in the past.

Year	# of films	# of surviving films§	# of copyrighted films
1890-92	15	3 (20%)	0
1893	3	2 (67%)	0
1894	94	28 (30%)	3 (03%)
1895	42	9 (21%)	0
1896	133	25 (19%)	39 (29%)
1897	188	132 (70%)	180 (96%)
1898	173	165 (95%)	164 (95%)
1899	135	97 (72%)	95 (70%)
1900	159	78 (49%)	73 (46%)
Totals	942	539 (57%)	554 (59%)

§ Does not include short fragments such as still sequences published in books and journals.

Completion of this filmography, moreover, opens up a new stage of inquiry, one that will allow for a more accurate quantification of selected historical trends. Computing the number of films actually produced by the Edison Manufacturing Company versus those produced by licensees but acquired by Edison for distribution will indicate the commercial orientation of the Kinetograph Department during the late nineteenth century. Seasonal fluctuations, the number of acted films versus nonacted films produced and/or distributed under Edison auspices can all be traced with greater accuracy. Number crunching can refine previous historical observations, serve as a check and make possible more concrete and reliable assessments. At the same time, it is important to acknowledge that these are always approximation. The limits of our knowledge are real, and different methods of tabulation would produce somewhat different figures.[2]

Schematic of Catalog Entries

This filmography is organized by individual films, listed with a control number in staggered chronological order by production date. Each entry provides the title, alternate titles, the advertised lengths at which the film was sold (in 35mm), the copyright date, listings of key production personnel (including actors and people appearing in the films, directors, cameramen), the date and location of production, and the sources for the film. This information is followed by one or more contemporaneous description of the film, usually taken from Edison catalogs, and the corresponding citations. Each entry also provides subject headings used for purposes of indexing, and a listing of archives where a print of the film can be seen, assuming it survives. A "citation" rubric lists references to other documentation such as 1) newspaper articles of the event being filmed, accounts of the actual filming, and items involving the personalities appearing in the film as well as 2) advertisements and additional catalogs listing the film—materials that could supplement what has otherwise been reprinted in the filmography. A "note" section conveys, when necessary, additional information about the film. To give readers a more tangible sense of these films, a frame enlargement or related photographic evidence accompanies each entry whenever possible.

Groups of related entries are typically contextualized by introductory commentary or pre-notes, which provide pertinent production information such as dates for the departures or arrivals of personnel on filming trips, as well as information about performers or events being filmed. Grouped entries are also often followed by selected documentation, for instance newspaper accounts of a film's production, a description of the event being filmed, reviews of the play being excerpted, or advertisements about the relevant performers.

To enhance the utility and accessibility of this filmography with documentation, there are six indexes. The first index gives an alphabetical listing of titles and alternate titles. Since many films were assigned different titles over the course of their commercial life, this will enable readers to access a film, irrespective of the title they are using. In addition, there are indexes for personal and corporate names of subjects, cast and production personnel; topic subjects; geographic location; sources for adaptation such as plays, short stories, vaudeville acts, novels, popular songs and other films; and archival holdings. The indexes are described in greater detail later in this essay.

This filmography uses a MARC-compatible format (similar to one being employed by the National Moving Image Database) for its filmography and follows national standards (AACR 2) for cataloging. An entry can thus be shown with appropriate MARC tags:

001$a (control number): **480**
245$a (title): **Launch of Japanese Man-of-War "Chitosa" [sic]**
740$a (alternate title): **Launching Japanese Man-of-War "Chitose"**
740$a (alternate title): **Launching of Japanese Man-of-War "Chitose"**
300$a (length): 50 ft.
260$a (copyright holder and date): © Thomas A. Edison, 10 March 1898.
508$a (producer): James White.
508$a (camera): Fred Blechynden.
511$a and 600$a (cast):
518$a (production date): 22 January 1898.
518$a (location): San Francisco, Calif.
500$a (source):
520$a (description): Taken at the docks of the Union Iron Works, San Francisco,

Cal., and shows the launching of this mammoth modern war vessel. The scene opens with a group of three people in the immediate foreground and another group of three just behind them in small row-boats. The large ship slides slowly down the ways, stern first, and the water line showing high up, even exposing the keel under the bow. As the boat floats out of sight another row-boat comes slowly into focus in the left foreground. The small boats rise and fall over the swells created by the launching. Immediately the ship has passed out of sight two of the occupants of the row-boat in the right background are seen to plunge into the water, while more boats come into focus. This is a scene which very few people have an opportunity to witness, and as the picture is very true to life it should prove a subject of great interest to the public. This film is very sharp, with the figures well defined.

510$a (source of description): (*Edison Films*, 15 March 1898, 14.)

650$a (subject headings A): Ships–launchings. Navies–Japan. Japanese. Boats and boating. Piers.

610$a (subject headings B): Union Iron Works. Southern Pacific Railroad.

535$3$ (archive): DLC-pp.

500$a (citations): "Two Cruisers for Japan," *Washington Post*, 1 January 1897, 2; "Chitose in Old Ocean's Arms," *San Francisco Chronicle*, 23 January 1898, 40. *Edison Films*, March 1900, 22.

500$a (note):

These different fields are explicated in greater detail in the following section.

Control number (001$a)

Many catalogs assign each entry a control number, but they play a crucial role in this filmography. Accessing an entry must be done either by production date or via the indexes by control number. A reader who knows the title of a film might feel that this has certain disadvantages and that an alphabetical listing is preferable. However, because films from the 1890s were often given several titles, access by title may be misleading or completely inaccurate. An alphabetical listing of entries cannot include alternate titles without a plethora of "see ——". In the case of the sample above, these title variations might possibly have been grouped on the same page. But this is obviously not the case for other entries. Entry no. 537 has two titles: *Morro Castle, Havana Harbor* and *Panoramic View, Showing Entrance to Havana Harbor and Morro Castle*. Both titles appear in the index of alphabetical listing of film titles, followed by the same control number. The control number thus accesses the entry for the film. Control numbers are generally whole integers, but a handful of recently located Edison films were inserted into the filmography using a decimal system—for reasons explained in the "Use of Automated Technology Section" at the end of this essay. Thus, a final review of Raff & Gammon correspondence revealed a reference to an uncataloged film, *French Dancers*. This was inserted in proper chronological order between film no. 53 and film no. 54 and assigned the control number 53.1.

Titles and alternate titles (245$a and 740$a)

Unlike other catalogs which usually handle alternative titles with analytic notes and added entries, this work treats a film's "first" or "original release" title and its alternate titles in similar ways. Indeed, for reasons that should quickly become clear, the first title is not necessarily the preferred title. The historian might prefer to use the alternative title *Launching Japanese Man-of-War "Chitose"* to either the first title, which is misspelled, or a silently corrected first title (as I did in *Before the Nickelodeon*).[3] Indeed the lack of standardized titles is a fact of early film historiography, and the resulting title variation will not be easy to resolve. The process of verifying and, in some cases, designating titles for a particular films is complicated and necessarily elaborate in some instances.

When the copyright title is available, it is listed first and treated as the original release title. If a film was not copyrighted, the earliest available published title will be treated as the first or principal title. Although AACR-2 guidelines would use the "original release" title rather than the copyright title, this designation is, in truth, difficult if not impossible to determine in the pre-1900 period. Because the Edison

Manufacturing Company did not attach head titles to its films until mid-1903 and did not do so on a regular basis for another year or two, the naming of a film was much more fluid in the nineteenth century than it subsequently became. The "original release title" does not therefore have the same weight that it would later assume, even when we such a title can be reasonably determined.

Listing the copyrighted title, when it is available, as the first title seems justified for the following reasons. Since Edison films were systematically copyrighted before they were sold, the copyright title is generally the earliest available title. Since such catalogs as Kemp Niver's *Early Motion Pictures* and Howard Lamarr Walls's *Motion Pictures 1894-1912* offer alphabetical listings of these films by copyright titles, this assures maximum compatibility with these complementary resources. In addition, historians generally refer to these films by their copyright title (roughly 1,000 films survive in Paper Print Collection) and so these titles have become the ones most commonly used. For several practical reasons, therefore, the copyright title should appear first.

A user can easily determine if a film was copyrighted or not by a quick glance at the relevant entry. Thus its place as the first listed title leaves no doubt that this is the title under which it was copyrighted. Any other system that included the copyright title would require some additional designation. Moreover, there is no guarantee that the original Edison release title, as indicated by trade journal advertising or catalogs, is currently available since many of these sources are lost and sources from the same period may conflict. Furthermore, in some situations the earliest available title is through a non-Edison source and this differs from the title given by a later Edison source. The copyright title, however, remains a stable reference point for a substantial majority of these films and has value as an Edison designated name.

In a few cases, almost exclusively in the period before October 1896 (after which Edison began to copyright its pictures on a routine basis), the titles of films come from newspapers or business correspondence. In these instances, there is neither a catalog nor a copyright title. For instance, entry no. 175 has the title *The Ferris Wheel*, which is derived from a *Boston Herald* newspaper advertisement. In other instances, particularly for kinetoscope films, the Edison Manufacturing Company or its agents referred to a particular film by a title in invoices and correspondence. Because so little catalog documentation survives from this period, these titles are treated as release titles. Indeed, they are also included as alternate titles for other entries.

In various instances it has been necessary to assign a title to a film. Such titles are placed in brackets. This occurred for several reasons. In some cases a film was shot but it was either not sold commercially or its commercial title does not survive in any form (at least in English). In some cases the same basic picture was made several times and an identical or similar title was used in various forms on different occasions. It has proved very useful to assign a name, along with a numerical designation in these instances. For example, *New Black Diamond Express* (no. 817) was also assigned the title *[Black Diamond Express, no. 4]*. In some instances, a number in brackets has been added after the copyright or published title for purposes of clarity and specificity. In these instances, a film was assigned a title that has been previous used or would be used again. Thus Annabelle's first filmed performance of the butterfly dance is labeled *Annabelle, [no. 1]*, while the first film of Annabelle Whitford doing a serpentine dance is listed as *Annabelle, [no. 2]*, *Annabelle Serpentine Dance,* and *[Annabelle Serpentine Dance, no. 1]*. The clear and consistent use of titles is obviously a challenge. Particularly as one chooses a "prefered title," an application of rigid rules can produce unsatisfactory results: misspelled, ambiguous or unilluminating titles.

Length (300$a)

For all entries this field lists the footage published in catalogs and Edison advertisements. It is for the original 35mm. Because all films were in 35mm and black and white, gauge and color status are not included as elements of the physical description. The published length is not necessarily the actual length of the film being sold. Kinetoscope films were consistently listed as 50 feet in length even though they were approximately 42 feet. A picture tended to be slightly shorter than its advertised length, though a few Paper Prints are longer than this length because the print that was submitted to the Library of Congress had not yet been fully "trimmed" (i.e., edited).

With many subjects, purchasers were given a choice of two or more lengths. All the different advertised lengths are provided, in ascending order. The length for *Football Game Between Orange Athletic and Newark Athletic Clubs* (no. 770) is listed as 50, 100, 200, and 550 ft. We should remember, however, that exhibitors had considerable latitude in determining the length of a picture that they wished to purchase and the Edison Manufacturing Company would have almost certainly sold a given film in other lengths if an exhibitor insisted. In some cases, a film either became damaged and its advertised length was shortened or the initial figure proved an inflated estimate that was subsequently reduced. *Uncle Josh in a Spooky Hotel* (no. 796) is thus listed as 80 *or* 100 ft. These two different listings appeared in two different places at different times. Purchasers were therefore not given a choice of lengths.

One 35mm foot of film contains 16 different images or frames. Although projection speed varied, one foot of film equaled approximately half a second of running time in 1894-1896 (when Edison films were taken and shown roughly between 30 and 36 frames per second) and closer to one second in 1898-1900 (when Edison films were taken and shown at roughly between 18 and 20 frames per second).

Copyright holder and date (260$a)

Copyright holder and date are crucial pieces of information related to a film's "publication." In almost all instances, Edison films were copyrighted in the name of Thomas A. Edison—even those made by non-Edison employees; in a few isolated cases, films were copyrighted by the producer (W.K.L. Dickson, James H. White) or contracting individuals in the entertainment industry (Margaret May, probably the actress Margaret M. Fish). Because there is some variation we decided to provide the name, followed by the copyright date.

Although the copyright date was not used when creating the chronological listing of film titles, it remains an important piece of information that usually indicates the approximate date that a film became available for sale via the Edison Manufacturing Company. Thus *Launching of Japanese Man-of-War "Chitose"* was shot on 22 January 1898 but the first prints were not made off the negative until shortly before March 10th, the date it was copyrighted.

Copyright information is often very helpful in estimating the approximate date of filming. When Edison personnel (or licensees on assignment) made a film at the Black Maria or in the New York area, it was typically copyrighted one week to six weeks after its production. News films were generally copyrighted more quickly than acted films (or else the news films were not copyrighted at all). Films were often copyrighted in blocks rather than immediately after they had been taken and processed. Films copyrighted at the same time were generally offered for sale at the same time.

This catalog does not include the copyright number, since this is rarely used by researchers and can be found elsewhere (in Howard Lamarr Walls's *Motion Pictures 1894-1912* as well as Niver's *Early Motion Pictures*).

Producer (508$a)

Terminology that is now used routinely for film production was not in place during the 1890s. Information on the precise roles of production personnel is also hard to establish. Only very rarely can an individual be characterized or identified as the director. This catalog assigns the role of producer to those individuals who organized and supervised these productions. This includes Edison employees such as W.K.L. Dickson and James H. White, who headed Edison's Kinetograph Department, and agents such as Raff & Gammon or Maguire & Baucus, who were responsible for selecting subjects and paying the cost of production. In the case of Edison licensees, individuals rather than companies are listed: J. Stuart Blackton and Albert E. Smith rather than the American Vitagraph Company. The Edison organization generally insisted on licensing individuals rather than business entities.

Camera (508$a)

The cameraman, who typically set up the shot and operated the equipment, generally had a large degree of authority and usually worked as the producer's partner or collaborator rather than as a simple employee. As a rule, the cameraman also developed the film negative and was responsible for "trimming" or editing this material prior to marketing. In some cases the cameraman had one or more assistants, but these are generally unknown and so cannot be listed.

Cast (511$a and 600$a)

Under the rubric of "cast," we include both cast members and name subject entries. This includes all people known to be appearing before the camera in a particular film. Although this category is thus used for nonfiction as well as fiction productions, the distinction is often blurred in this period. Is *Sandow* a nonfiction film of the vaudeville performer Eugen Sandow or a fictional film of Friedrich Müller playing the role of Sandow who is performing as a strong man? Perhaps we could agree that *Sandow* and *Annabelle, [no.1]* are nonfiction even though they are staged while *The Barber Shop* is fiction. But is not *Pas Seul, no. 1* (no. 88) "fiction" because it is based on *The Gaiety Girl* and the actress plays some role, even if a name is not assigned to her portrayal? And yet two of the titles for *Pas Seul, no. 1* are *Miss Lucy Murray* and *Lucy Murray*—suggesting a filmographic treatment similar to that of the Annabelle films. Such distinctions in this period are illusive, making it expedient to include both categories in a single heading.

A note on other personnel and name authority

Other production personnel (e.g., director, scenarist, or art director) are listed in the note section for each entry, though such additional information is rare. Many present day job categories were assumed by the producer. Thus J. Stuart Blackton generally painted the backdrops and sets for those films that he made with Albert E. Smith of American Vitagraph. In other cases, the information is not known.

Information for cast and production personnel has been gathered from an array of sources. Where the person is a known individual, the filmography has generally relied on the Library of Congress Name Authority File (NACO), *Who Was Who* (vols. 1-3), and an array of other reference books listed in the bibliography. We have also developed our own name authority file, using obituaries and a variety of other sources. Documentation from the period is crucial, though often contradictory. To offer an extreme case, Frederick W. Blechynden had his name spelled many different ways in "Hotel Arrivals" columns. Only after building a name authority file were we able to determine the proper spelling of his last name. For American sources, we rely on legal documents when possible. In such circumstances a person has to give his correct name. Thus the first name of Edison cameraman James Blair Smith became Jacob for purposes of depositions. Often however we are dealing with stage names that are more or less stable. Rather than assert a correct name, the catalog includes variants, often through the use of brackets. Eugen[e] Sandow was the stage name for Friedrich Müller and while Sandow generally spelled his first name without the final *e*, the extra letter appeared so frequently that to consider it incorrect and deserving a [sic] would be inaccurate and counter productive. Indeed variations in spelling and naming were far more acceptable in the 1890s than they are today.

Production date (518$a)

The exact date of production is provided whenever possible. Newspaper articles, correspondence, financial accounts and other documents often provide this precise information. When dates are not known precisely, a somewhat broader time frame can be reasonably established based on availability of performers or other information. In some cases these parameters can be reasonably deduced. Copyright information is often helpful in this regard. It is usually safe to assume that if one group of films was copyrighted in early February and a second group in late February then this second group was shot in the month of February (assuming they were shot by Edison personnel in the New York area rather than by licensees). In other instances, large numbers of films were taken on a filmmaking expedition and because certain moments in that itinerary have been precisely dated it has become possible to date other films with considerable precision. The "Hotel Arrival" listing in newspapers as well as shipping news have proved extremely useful in this regard.

Location (518$a)

The location where a picture was shot provides essential information about the film as well as the commercial and production practices of the Edison Manufacturing Company. In this regard catalog descriptions are helpful but not always accurate. Films of American warships taken near Key West were later said to have been shot in the Dry Tortugas, where the warships were when the films were being offered for sale. At earlier stages of this project, such discrepancies encouraged a rampant skepticism about all catalog information, which has gradually receded. Inaccuracies, when they occur, were not gratuitous.

Source (500$a)

The source listing enables the reader to connect a particular picture to other cultural forms: plays, operas, burlesques, paintings, short stories, and earlier films made by the Edison Manufacturing Company or its competitors. These connections are often elaborated in the notes (for example, film no. 579, *The Burglar, [no. 1]*). Performances in which the act is identified by the name of a specific performer or group, for example by vaudevillians, are not provided in this section. They can be ascertained through subject headings (under Vaudeville–performances) and by the name of individuals under cast.

Description (520$a)

The description of a film is always taken from period documents. In the vast majority of cases, we took the description from a catalog or trade journal advertisement offered by either the Edison Manufacturing Company or an affiliated distributor. In a few instances, newspaper descriptions of the film are used, most commonly for the 1893-1896 period. If two catalog descriptions are sufficiently different so that their mutual inclusion would enhance the reader's knowledge about the film, both are included. Catalog descriptions for the same film vary in length and detail but generally the earliest catalog description is the most complete and subsequent entries are shortened.

The decision to quote contemporaneous Edison-derived descriptions of these films is an essential feature of this undertaking, one that complements our chronological approach. When no appropriate documentation survives, this filmography does not provide a description. When modern day catalogers such as Kemp Niver have tried to describe a film, the results have proved to be so inaccurate and counterproductive that this approach is best avoided. We are seeking to create a scholarly aid of maximum utility for a wide variety of potential users. At the same time we are seeking to lay bare the limits of our knowledge and to avoid subjective or print-specific judgments. In the past, for example, modernized versions of early films have been accepted as authentic. Many summary descriptions must still be made based on incomplete prints (lacking head, tail or internal sections). Even two authenticated, "complete" prints of the same subject may be quite different (*Life of an American Fireman* and *Tom, Tom, the Piper's Son* are but two examples). Whatever rules are established for describing a film, a description is never completely objective. The subjective description of the producer, however, has historic value and can avoid certain interpretive pitfalls. Moreover, once viewers have seen a given film, the value of the typical catalog description is reduced since they now have their own mental or written experience of the film. Yet a viewing of the film can subsequently be enhanced by a contemporaneous trade description because the text shows how the film may have been understood (or how the company hoped it would be understood) at the time the film was released. This creates a powerful, historical dialectic between the film as viewed today and the description offered at the time of its release. Trade descriptions also provide much specific information that would never be available to today's viewers—no matter how many times they screen the film. When a description of a film is not available, other forms of documentation—for example news articles of the event being filmed—may be more helpful.

Source of description (510$a)

A complete citation for the source of the description is included in parentheses following the description.

Subject (650$a, 610$a and 600$a)

There are two types of subject headings that are handled separately in the data base but merged into a single "subject" field in this catalog. The first type of subject headings are descriptive (650$a). The second type of subject headings are reserved for the proper names of organizations and corporations (610$a) and for individuals who are the subject of the film but do not necessarily appear in it (600$a). For the descriptive or topic headings, Library of Congress subject headings are utilized with only a few minor exceptions which are by way of variation. The principal variations are as follows: the term "Social elites" is employed rather than Elite (social sciences) and "Working classes" for "Working class." The category "Hotels, taverns, etc." has been broken down into 1) Hotels and 2) Taverns, etc. The second category also includes bars and saloons. The term "Doves" has been used for "Columbidae and Pigeons" and the heading "United States–National Guard" was reduced to "National Guard" and then broken down by states. The more recent and popular term "African Americans" was considered as a substitute for "Afro-Americans" but the decision finally favored the maintenance of established cataloging terms. Films are normally indexed with at least three topic subject headings but rarely more than six. Considerable attention was devoted to the consistent employment of headings, though discrepancies doubtlessly crept in (particularly those of omission).

The second type of subject headings includes the names of theatrical companies whose members appear in the cast lists. The entry for *Annie Oakley* (no. 86), for example, has an organization name heading (610$a) of Buffalo Bill's Wild West but also a descriptive subject heading (650$a) of "wild west shows." Annie Oakley's name, of course, appears under cast. Among the many corporate names appearing in the catalog are those associated with a particular film. Thus *Hotel Del Monte* (no. 405) was taken as part of a series of films designed to promote the Southern Pacific Railroad (and with that railroad's active cooperation). Even though the railroad does not appear in the film, its name appears as a corporate subject heading. The names of specific military units are also listed here. Thus Ninth U.S. Cavalry appears as the proper name of an organization for *U.S. Cavalry Supplies Unloading at Tampa, Florida* (no. 554) and *9th U.S. Cavalry Watering Horses* (no. 555). Cavalry is a topic heading as well. In merging these two categories of subject headings in the catalog, the proper names always follow the descriptive headings.

Personal name subject headings are relatively infrequent for they involve people who are in some sense the subject of the film yet do not generally appear in it. A dozen films (nos. 325 through 337) were taken of the ceremonies dedicating Grant's Tomb in New York City, 27 April 1897. Grant's body and even his tomb do not appear in these films. Nevertheless, Ulysses S. Grant is listed in the proper name subject headings. Mary, Queen of Scots is a personal name subject heading for *The Execution of Mary, Queen of Scots* (no. 142), an historical reenactment. E.J. "Lucky" Baldwin owned the ranch that served as the background for *California, Ltd., A.T. & S.F.R.R.* Because Baldwin was a legend in his own time, the Edison Manufacturing Company used him as an important selling point in its descriptive summary of the film and he is therefore listed in the subject headings. Both topic headings and the names of corporations and organizations are listed in the Subject Index, while the personal name subject headings are listed in the Name Index.

Archive (535$3$)

If a film is known to survive in an institution that is a member of FIAF (Fédération Internationale des Archives du Film), the USMARC symbol is listed here. In a few instances, though less systematically, private collections are also indicated. These do not represent all the relevant materials held by these archives. Commercially available 16mm film and video are generally not included. And more materials continue to be acquired or made available. Nor are all archives necessarily covered. A list of abbreviations and archives is presented at the beginning of the filmography.

The majority of surviving Edison films are at the Library of Congress, and the designations for this institution are generally subdivided by collection. One reason for this is that provenance is significant in terms of the source material. "DLC-Hendricks" indicates that a film is at the Library of Congress in the Gordon Hendricks Collection.

While these films are now available in 35mm, these materials were all made from 16mm reduction prints. "DLC-pp" means prints are from the Paper Print Collection, a fact which also affects image quality. DLC-AFI indicates a film in the AFI Collection at the Library and generally comes from original 35mm exhibition prints.

Database versions of this filmography are eventually expected to include the "shelf number" or location designation of available viewing prints at different institutions. These call numbers will be added in parentheses after the symbol designating the archive holding materials. It was not possible to include this information for this catalog because many of the paper print films were still being reshot in 35mm when we went to press. Since this information could not be included in a systematic manner, it was excluded. Researchers must search other appropriate databases or contact the institutions listed in order to identify actual holdings and accompanying materials.

Citations (500$a)

This section cites various documents that provide relevant information for the film. The reference source citations are broken into two fields in the database which are merged for this catalog. The first lists books, correspondence, newspaper articles, and trade journal information about the performer(s), the subject or event that was filmed. Among other things, the documents cited in this section provided the information appearing in other entry fields (production date, location, cast and so forth). These citations are not intended to be exhaustive. Indeed a researcher could easily expand the number of citations for any given entry. Those provided are a starting point, and also suggest the kinds of news articles that feature or mention a performer or event. Articles reprinted in the document section following the entry or group of related entries are not listed in the citation section.

The second type of citation field, appearing at the end of the "citations" section, is for catalog and trade journal listings of the film itself. The listing of catalogs promoting the film is useful because it suggests a film's longevity, that is, the period of time that a film was available for purchase. These are also the source for most of the alternate titles.

When a particular entry is part of a larger series of films featuring a particular performer or event, the redundant citations are not repeated (i.e., those of the first type; the second group of citations is specific to each entry). Thus two articles about the launching of the Japanese Man-of-War "Chitose" are cited under *Launching Japanese Man-of-War "Chitose"* but not listed again for the two subsequent entries which covered the same event. The catalog reference—*Edison Films*, March 1900, 22—indicates that this film was still being promoted and offered for sale two years after the event. Such citations of Edison catalogs do not appear in the entries for three subsequent films of this event (nos. 481-483) because those films were not listed in later catalogs or trade journals.

Note (500$a)

The "note" section brings various kinds of pertinent information to the reader's attention. This section provides an array of information about the film, its source or performers that could be of value to a researcher but not provided in the other fields. The history of a play or the career of a performer often appears here though it may be found in the introductory note to the entry as well. Information about the film—for instance, some aspect of its exhibition history—may appear here. The note section is the place to address ambiguities or potential confusions. Entry no. 498, *S.S. "Coptic" Running Against the Storm*, for example, includes a note about a possible alternative title and description.

Documents

An entry or group of related entries is typically followed by a document section (which may be lengthy) that reprints news articles or related written information that illuminate the film(s) under consideration. These range from newspaper articles and trade journal advertisements to letters.

Frame enlargements

Frame enlargements complement catalog descriptions and/or newspaper information about the individual film. There is a tension between the image and the text that the two in combination will illuminate. Illustrations are also helpful for archival identification and as a way for readers to recall a film.

Indexes
There are six different indexes which access pertinent films through their control number:

1. Title Index. Since films from this period have many different titles (as many as seven titles for a single film), the catalog provides an alphabetical listing of titles and alternate titles followed by the control number assigned to that title. This allows users coming from a range of different sources (paper prints, catalog information, etc.) to locate the relevant entry quickly and easily.

2. Personal and Corporate Name Index. This includes all production people credited with working on a picture as well as anyone listed as appearing in the picture. Individuals not appearing in the films but connected with the subject matter as established through news articles or catalog descriptions are also listed. The birth and death dates of these individuals, when known and established through the Name Authority File, are indicated here. A brief characterization of the individual's occupation is also provided as a way to facilitate identification. Corporations and organizations appearing in or connected with the films are also indexed here. This includes the names of railroads, shipping lines, theatrical companies, political parties and military units.

3. Subject Index. This compiles information from descriptive or subject headings. Films are normally indexed by three topic subject headings and rarely more than six.

4. Geographic Index. This lists all films according to the location where they were shot. When a film is shot in one place but said to represent another, it is listed twice, in bold for the place it is said to represent.

5. Index of Cultural Sources for Films. This lists literary and nonliterary sources—plays, songs, books, previous films, and so forth and indicates the films which utilized them.

6. Index of Holdings in FIAF Archives and Selected Private Collections. This suggests the holdings of the different archives for a given film. It does not represent all the relevant material held by these archives. Commercially available 16mm film and video are generally not included. Nor are all archives covered.

Use of Automation Technology
This filmography was generated from a database in Hypercard on the Macintosh and was then produced in Microsoft Word. This book is considered version 2.1 of the data base. A portion of the database was published in June 1994 as *Filmmaking for Edison's Kinetoscope*. This is considered version 1.0 of the filmography. Version 2.0 was completed in March 1995. The database was spit out into a word processing program (from Hypercard to Microsoft Word). The control numbers for 1.0 and 2.0 generally differ as new films were found and inserted or additional information changed the ordering of the titles. The process of moving the database into a word processing program requires substantial refinement of the files. Subsequent changes to version 2.0 were made both in the database and the word processing files. During the last two years a few additional films were uncovered, as the process of gathering photographs was completed and as the filmography was reviewed by others (notably Ray Phillips and Tim Muir). Since the discovery of a new Edison film should, in principle, alter all control numbers after its insertion, the way in which this has been handled needs to be explained. New films were inserted using a decimal system. It turned out, for example, that there were at least three different negatives taken of Eugen Sandow on 6 March 1894. *Sandow* remained entry no 26 while *[Sandow, no. 2]* and *[Sandow, no. 3]* became 26.1 and 26.2 respectively. Future refinements of this database will be signaled by changes in the numerical designation of the version. A version 2.2 would keep all numerical designations for control numbers but include corrections and, potentially, additional films using this type of insertion. At some point, it may be appropriate to renumber all entries so that each film has a simple integer for a control number. This would become version 3.0.

There are a number of documents that were entered into the database but are not included in the catalog after readability and length were considered. Also some citations appear in the database that were not entered in the catalog.

At present there are two fields that appear in the database that are not in the catalog. The first is a "Code Word" field. When ordering a film by telegraph, exhibitors were able to identify a film by its short code word rather than its more lengthy title. In some instances the code word can help scholars to identify the approximate date when a film entered a company's catalog and so the rough time of production. For the Edison Manufacturing Company, code words are as likely to be deceptive as helpful. The lag between a film's production and its entry into the catalog is often significant—several years in some cases. Moreover, the code words are not applied consistently and are often simply confusing. Many films received different code words over the course of their commercial life. At this point the code word was excluded as a distraction. The second excluded field is for genres. Much work still needs to be done on genres in early film. It remains an important topic for film scholars; but in the case of this filmography, the genre field was not ready for publication.

The database as a database will be helpful for researchers because they will be able to cross-reference their searches; for instance, they will be able to find all films that were assigned both "Railroad" and "Japan" as topic subject headings.

Corrections and additions will be made to the database as appropriate information comes to light. Readers who have contributions, questions or corrections are encouraged to contact the author at Box 820, Times Square Stat., New York, N.Y. 10108.

1. Thomas Cripps, *Slow Fade to Black: The Negro in American Film* (London: Oxford University Press, 1977), 10.

2. If this filmography had treated the surviving twenty-three scenes of the *The Passion Play of Oberammergau* as twenty-three individual films and the sixteen nonextant films of the New York Public Schools made for the Paris Exposition of 1900 (nos. 818-833) as a single subject, the figure of surviving films would have been between 59% and 60%.

3. My "silent" correction of this film title to *Launch of Japanese Man-of-War "Chitose"* was based on the fact that the misspelled name ("Chitosa") was almost certainly due to an error in transcription.

Filmography

Key to Abbreviations and Symbols

CaOOANF	Canada, Ontario, Ottawa, National Archives of Canada, Visual and Sound Archives (David Flaherty Collection)
CLAc	California, Los Angeles, Academy of Motion Picture Arts and Sciences (Ray Phillips Collection)
CL-UC	California, Los Angeles, University of California at Los Angeles, Film and Television Archive
DLC	District of Columbia, Washington, Library of Congress
DLC-AFI	District of Columbia, Washington, Library of Congress (American Film Institute Collection)
DLC-Hendricks	District of Columbia, Washington, Library of Congress (Collection Hendricks)
DLC-pp	District of Columbia, Washington, Library of Congress (Paper Print Collection)
DLC-Roosevelt	District of Columbia, Washington, Library of Congress (Theodore Roosevelt Association Film Collection)
DNA	District of Columbia, Washington, National Archives
FPA	Film Preservation Associates (David Shepard)
FrBaADF	France, Bois d'Arcy, Archives du film du Centre national de la cinématographie
Killiam	Paul Killiam, New York, N.Y.
MH-BA	Massachusetts, Harvard Business School, Archive (Raff & Gammon Collection)
NjWOE	New Jersey, West Orange, Edison National Historic Site
NN	New York Public Library
NNMoMA	New York, Museum of Modern Art
NR-GE	New York, Rochester, George Eastman House
TAEP	*Thomas A. Edison Papers: A Selective Microfilm Edition* Part I (1850-1878); Part II (1878-1886); Part III (1886-1898) (Frederick, Md.: University Publications of America, 1985-1994)
UkLNFA	United Kingdom, London, National Film Archive

√ (before film title)	Indicates that frames or very short fragments of the picture survive.
* (before film title)	Indicates that the picture survives.

Thomas A. Edison and his associates, notably William Kennedy Laurie Dickson and William Heise, developed a technological system of motion picture production and exhibition over a five year period. The process of invention was initially spurred by a meeting between Edison and serial photographer Eadweard Muybridge at his new laboratory in West Orange, New Jersey, on 27 February 1888. During their discussions, Muybridge proposed that they combine Edison's phonograph with his own zoopraxiscope, which projected a series of painted images (based on his sequences of photographs) onto the screen, thus creating the illusion of "life-like" motion. Edison was receptive, for he was seeking to improve his phonograph and one way of doing this, he thought, was to combine it with a motion picture device.

Eight months after his meeting with Muybridge, in October of 1888, Edison wrote his first motion picture caveat, which outlined his initial ideas for developing "an instrument which does for the Eye what the phonograph does for the Ear, which is the recording and reproduction of things in motion, in such a form as to be both Cheap practical and convenient." The inventor had concluded, upon further reflection, that Muybridge's zoopraxiscope was neither practical nor convenient. And the per image cost was hardly inexpensive. Edison's first formulation bears considerable resemblance to today's movies on laser disks. He imagined approximately 42,000 microscopic images, each about 1/32 of an inch wide, on a cylinder that was the size and shape of his phonograph records. These were to be taken on a continuous spiral with 180 images per turn. The spectator would look at the pictures through a microscope while also listening to sound from a phonograph. Each cylinder could contain twenty-eight minutes of pictures.

Edison wrote a second and then a third caveat in March and August 1889; the ideas articulated in these documents tried to solve some of the problems inherent in his initial formulation. The inventor's fourth and last motion picture caveat, of November 1889, was heavily indebted to the serial photographic work of Étienne-Jules Marey, whom Edison met in Paris while attending the 1889 Paris Exposition. This document outlined a contrivance that passed a tape-like band of film past a camera lens, halting and then exposing a single frame of film for a brief fraction of a second, after which the strip was again moved forward, until the next frame of film was halted in front of the lens and likewise exposed. Despite the promising direction of this last formulation, Edison pursued his cylinder experiments, from the time he opened a kinetoscope account in February 1889 until sometime in late 1890. As Dickson explained the progression of experiments in his History of the Kinetograph, Kinetoscope and Kineto-Phonograph *(1895, written with his sister Antonia Dickson):*

The initial experiments took the form of microscopic pin-point photographs, placed on a cylinder shell, corresponding in size to the ordinary phonograph cylinder. These two cylinders were then placed side by side on a shaft, and the sound record was taken as near as possible synchronously with the photographic image, impressed on the sensitive surface of the shell. The photographic portion of the undertaking was seriously hampered by the materials at hand, which, however excellent in themselves, offered no substance sufficiently sensitive. How to secure clear-cut outlines, or indeed any outlines at all, together with phenomenal speed, was the problem which puzzled the experimenters. The Daguerre, albumen and kindred processes met the first requirements, but failed when subjected to the later test. These methods were therefore regretfully abandoned, a certain precipitate of knowledge being retained, and a bold leap was made to the Maddox gelatine bromide of silver emulsion, with which the cylinders were coated. This process gave rise to a new and serious difficulty. The bromide of silver haloids, held in suspension with the emulsion, showed themselves in an exaggerated coarseness when it became a question of enlarging the pin-point photographs to the dignity of one-eighth of an inch, projecting them upon a screen, or viewing them through a binocular microscope. Each accession of size augmented the difficulty, and it was resolved to abandon that line of experiment and revolutionize the whole nature of the proceedings by discarding these small photographs and substituting a series of very much larger impressions, affixed to the outer edge of a swiftly moving rotating wheel or disk and supplied with a number of pins, so arranged as to project under the centre of each picture. On the rear disk, upon a stand, a Geissler tube was placed, connected with an induction coil, the primary wire of which, operated by the pins, produced a rupture of the primary current, which in its turn, through the medium of the secondary current, lighted up the Geissler tube at the precise moment when a picture crossed its range of view. This electrical discharge was performed in such an inappreciable fraction of time, the succession of pictures was so rapid and the whole mechanism so nearly perfect that the goal of the inventor seemed almost reached. "We needs must love the highest," however, an axiom which holds good in science as well as in character, and the methods still pointed to possible improvements. (8-11.)

None of the physical materials from these experiments survive, and it seems unnecessary to attempt to include them in the present filmography. In any case, Dickson's enthusiasm for the Edison Laboratory's limited achievements in motion picture technology at this stage in the invention process helps to explain the fanciful though vague reports appearing in various newspapers, including the local Orange Chronicle:

Another of Edison's Wonders.

For many months past Mr. Edison has been at work on a series of experiments in instantaneous photography which have been at last successfully concluded. The point desired was to devise a mechanical camera so arranged that instantaneous photographs, with an exposure of from the 250th to the 1000th of a second, could be taken in a series following one another at the rate of from 8 to 20 per second. It was found that the slight imperceptible tremor of the buildings caused by the vibration of the machinery was sufficient to interfere materially with the experiments and hence it became necessary to erect a special building in which to conduct the experiments. This was done and a solid pier was built on rock foundation, on which the camera was placed. The experiments were then begun and were at last crowned with complete success. The idea Mr. Edison had in mind was to take a public speaker and photograph him successfully eight or twelve times a second throughout his entire speech, the subject matter being at the same time recorded by the telephone. By an ingeniously constructed mechanism the reproduction of the audible speech by the phonograph and the personal appearance, gesticulations and facial changes as thrown on a screen by the stereopticon are so exactly timed as to be synchronous. The photographic pictures following one another at the rate of eight to twenty a second produce a constantly moving picture, exactly simulating the appearance of the speaker, while the speech as reproduced by the phonograph will apparently come from the lips of the orator. The experiments were perfectly successful and are now concluded, the next stage being the development of the commercial side of the invention and the creation for a demand for new products. (*Orange Chronicle*, 1 February 1890, 5.)

A cylinder drum used for Edison's early motion picture experiments (circa 1890).

But, as Dickson makes clear in his History of the Kinetograph, Kinetoscope, and Kineto-Phonograph, *the inventors once again returned to the cylinder experiments:*

Then followed some experiments with drums, over which sheets of sensitized celluloid film were drawn, the edges being pressed into a narrow slot in the surface, similar in construction to the old tinfoil phonograph. A starting and stopping device was also applied, identical with the one used and in a later experiment explained in these pages. The pictures were then taken spirally to the number of two hundred or so, but were limited in size owing to the rotundity of surface, which only brought the centre of the picture into focus. The sheet of celluloid was then developed, etc., and placed upon a transparent drum, bristling at its outer edge with brass pins. When the brass was rapidly turned these came in contact with the primary current of an induction coil, and each image was lighted up in the same manner as described in the previous disk experiment, with this difference only, that the inside of the drum was illumined. (11-12.)

In October 1890 Edison assigned a new associate to work with Dickson on the motion picture project—William Heise.

The first surviving examples of Edison's motion picture work are dated convincingly by Gordon Hendricks as November 1890. These are sheets of celluloid film that were wrapped around the cylinders.

1   *[Monkeyshines, no. 1]
LENGTH : 21/2"x135/8".   © No reg.
PRODUCER: W.K.L. Dickson.
CAMERA: W.K.L. Dickson, William Heise.
CAST: [G. Sacco Albanese.]
PRODUCTION DATE: 21-27 November 1890.
LOCATION: Edison Laboratory, West Orange, N.J.
SOURCE:
DESCRIPTION:
SUBJECT: Motion pictures–experiments.
ARCHIVE: DNA, NjWOE.
CITATIONS: W.K. Laurie Dickson, "A Brief History of the Kinetograph, The Kinetoscope and the Kinetophonograph," *Journal of the Society of Motion Picture Engineers*, December 1933, 444.

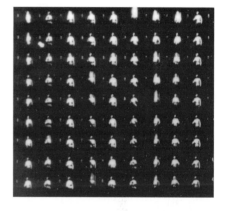

NOTE: A surviving example of Edison's early cylinder experiments, taken outside the ore-milling outhouse (Building 4).

2   √[Monkeyshines, no. 2]
LENGTH: © No reg.
PRODUCER: W.K.L. Dickson.
CAMERA: W.K.L. Dickson, William Heise.
CAST: [G. Sacco Albanese.]
PRODUCTION DATE: 21-27 November 1890.
LOCATION: Edison Laboratory, West Orange, N.J.
SOURCE:
DESCRIPTION:
SUBJECT: Motion pictures–experiments.
ARCHIVE: NjWOE.
CITATIONS: W.K. Laurie Dickson, "A Brief History of the Kinetograph, The Kinetoscope and the Kinetophonograph," *Journal of the Society of Motion Picture Engineers*, December 1933, 444.

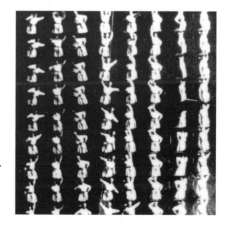

NOTE: A surviving fragment of Edison's cylinder experiments, taken outside the ore-milling outhouse (Building 4).

3 √**[Monkeyshines, no. 3]**

LENGTH: © No reg.

PRODUCER: W.K.L. Dickson.

CAMERA: W.K.L. Dickson, William Heise.

CAST: [G. Sacco Albanese.]

PRODUCTION DATE: 21-27 November 1890.

LOCATION: Edison Laboratory, West Orange, N.J.

SOURCE:

DESCRIPTION:

SUBJECT: Motion pictures–experiments.

ARCHIVE: NjWOE.

CITATIONS: W.K. Laurie Dickson, "A Brief History of the Kinetograph, The Kinetoscope and the Kinetophonograph," *Journal of the Society of Motion Picture Engineers*, December 1933, 444.

NOTE: A surviving fragment of Edison's cylinder experiments, taken outside the ore-milling outhouse (Building 4).

After the cylinder experiments Dickson and Heise began to explore the possibilities inherent in the fourth, Marey-inspired caveat, in which a narrow band of photographic film was passed through the camera. Heise had been brought onto the project, in part, because he was expert in devising ways to move tape-like strips of paper (or other materials) through a machine. The Edison-Dickson-Heise experimental horizontal-feed kinetograph camera and kinetoscope viewer, which used 3/4" wide film, were completed in the spring of 1891. At least seven films are known to have been made with this camera:

4 √[Dickson Greeting]
LENGTH: © No reg.
PRODUCER: W.K.L. Dickson, William Heise.
CAMERA: William Heise.
CAST: W.K.L. Dickson.
PRODUCTION DATE: By 20 May 1891.
LOCATION: Photographic Building, Edison Laboratory, West Orange, N.J.
SOURCE:
DESCRIPTION:
SUBJECT: Motion pictures–experiments.
ARCHIVE: NjWOE.
CITATIONS: "Edison's Visit to Chicago," *Western Electrician,* 23 May 1891; "Mr. Edison's Latest," *Orange Chronicle,* 23 May 1891; "Wizard Edison Weds Light to Sound," *New York Herald,* 28 May 1891, 3; "Pictured on the Run," *New York Morning Journal,* 29 May 1891; "Work of the Kinetograph," *New York Herald,* 1 June 1891, 3 (with illustrations); "Edison's Latest Invention," *Photographic News,* 5 June 1891, 418-419; George Parsons Lathrop, "Edison's Kinetograph," *Harper's Weekly,* 13 June 1891, 446; "Edison's Kinetograph and Cosmical Telephone," *Scientific American,* 20 June 1891, 393 (with illustrations); "Punch and the Kinetograph," *Illustrated American,* 20 June 1891, 224.
NOTE: Shot on 3/4" film. Fragment survives in the Charles Batchelor notebook at NjWOE.

5 [Duncan and Another, Blacksmith Shop]
LENGTH: © No reg.
PRODUCER: W.K.L. Dickson, William Heise.
CAMERA: W.K.L. Dickson, William Heise.
CAST: James Duncan.
PRODUCTION DATE: May-June 1891.
LOCATION: Photographic Building, Edison Laboratory, West Orange, N.J.
SOURCE: Muybridge's sequential photographs of work processes.
DESCRIPTION:
SUBJECT: Motion pictures–experiments. Blacksmithing.
ARCHIVE:
CITATIONS: Notes, legal files, NjWOE.
NOTE: Shot on 3/4" film. James Duncan was a day laborer at the Edison Laboratory.

6 [Monkey and Another, Boxing]
LENGTH: © No reg.
PRODUCER: W.K.L. Dickson, William Heise.

CAMERA: W.K.L. Dickson, William Heise.
CAST:
PRODUCTION DATE: May-June 1891.
LOCATION: Photographic Building, Edison Laboratory, West Orange, N.J.
SOURCE:
DESCRIPTION:
SUBJECT: Motion pictures–experiments. Boxing. Monkeys. Animal fighting.
ARCHIVE:
CITATIONS: Notes, legal files, NjWOE.
NOTE: Shot on 3/4" film.

7 [Duncan or Devonal with Muslin Cloud] [sic] / [Duncan or Devonald with Muslin Cloud]
LENGTH: © No reg.
PRODUCER: W.K.L. Dickson, William Heise.
CAMERA: W.K.L. Dickson, William Heise.
CAST: James Duncan, or Fred C. Devonald.
PRODUCTION DATE: May-June 1891.
LOCATION: Photographic Building, Edison Laboratory, West Orange, N.J.
SOURCE:
DESCRIPTION:
SUBJECT: Motion pictures–experiments.
ARCHIVE:
CITATIONS: Notes, legal files, NjWOE.
NOTE: Shot on 3/4" film. Fred C. Devonald was an Edison employee who worked in the stock shop, sometimes ordering materials for Dickson and the motion picture experiments.

8 √[Duncan Smoking]
LENGTH: © No reg.
PRODUCER: W.K.L. Dickson, William Heise.
CAMERA: W.K.L. Dickson, William Heise.
CAST: James Duncan.
PRODUCTION DATE: May-June 1891.
LOCATION: Photographic Building, Edison Laboratory, West Orange, N.J.
SOURCE:
DESCRIPTION:
SUBJECT: Motion pictures–experiments.
ARCHIVE: NjWOE.
CITATIONS: Notes, legal files, NjWOE.
NOTE: Shot on 3/4" film.

9 √[Newark Athlete] / [Club Swinger, no. 1] / [Indian Club Swinger]
LENGTH: © No reg.
PRODUCER: W.K.L. Dickson, William Heise.
CAMERA: W.K.L. Dickson, William Heise.
CAST:
PRODUCTION DATE: May-June 1891.
LOCATION: Photographic Building, Edison Laboratory, West Orange, N.J.
SOURCE:
DESCRIPTION:
SUBJECT: Motion pictures–experiments. Sports. Gymnastics.
ARCHIVE: NjWOE, NNMoMA, DLC-Hendricks.
CITATIONS: Notes, legal files, NjWOE.

NOTE: Shot on 3/4" film. Fragment in the Charles Batchelor notebook at NjWOE was reanimated on the Hendricks reel, Library of Congress.

10 √[Men Boxing]
LENGTH: © No reg.
PRODUCER: W.K.L. Dickson, William Heise.
CAMERA: W.K.L. Dickson, William Heise.
CAST:
PRODUCTION DATE: May-June 1891.
LOCATION: Photographic Building, Edison Laboratory, West Orange, N.J.
SOURCE:
DESCRIPTION:
SUBJECT: Motion pictures–experiments. Boxing. Sports.
ARCHIVE: NjWOE.
CITATIONS: Notes, legal files, NjWOE.
NOTE: Shot on 3/4" film. Fragment in the Charles Batchelor notebook at NjWOE.

On 20 May 1891 members of the Federation of Women's Clubs, attending a meeting at the Edison home in Glenmont, walked down the hill to Edison's laboratory, peered into the peep-hole viewer and saw a film of Dickson waving his hat (no. 4). The New York press appeared a few days later. According to a reporter from the New York Sun:

THE KINETOGRAPH.
Edison's Latest and Most Surprising Device.
PURE MOTION RECORDED AND REPRODUCED
Voice and Action Being Caught in His Compound Machine.
Some One Said the Wizard Talked Too Much, and Now He Has Justified His Talk–The Scenes, Characters, Movements, and Voices of an Act of the Opera May be Reproduced in One's Own Parlor by This Marvellous Machine, Which Takes Continuous Photographs at the Rate of Forty-Six a Second, as the Phonograph Records Sound Waves, and Throws the Moving Pictures on a Screen While the Phonograph Repeats the Songs and Dialogue–Edison's Cosmical Telephone to Hear Sunspots Roar.
Three or four years ago, in a magazine article, Edison, the electric wizard, wrote that he would produce a machine which should record and reproduce motion as the phonograph recorded and reproduced sound. Other electrical periodicals scouted the idea and irreverent newspapers told Edison that he talked too much. That made Mr. Edison angry, and he registered a vow that he would accomplish all he had said and more. He would reproduce the image of a living, moving, speaking human being, and not only one image but a dozen images together, or forty of them: a whole opera company if you like, and the ballet girls should dance and the stars sing while the full orchestra performed and the leader swung his baton in proud consciousness of his importance.
People laughed for a while, but Edison kept still and they forgot the wizard's "wild scheme." He did not forget it, however. He went to work on his idea, and no one but the assistants in his big laboratory at Orange knew anything about what was going on. He worked for more than three years, and at last was successful, in so far as to correctly establish his "germ" or "base principle." Then Edison laughed. He sat in the big armchair in his laboratory and watched a crude model of the machine, and thought of what a lot of fun he would have with the people who had told him he talked too much. For he knew that when he had found his "base principle" the completion of

the work was a mere question of time and details. Every invention he had ever made proved that fact to him. So he watched the model and chuckled at his success.

A little while ago there was a great convention of the women's clubs of America. Mrs. Edison is interested in women's clubs and their work and she decided to entertain the Presidents of the various clubs at the Convention. Edison entered into the plan, and when 147 club women visited his workshop he showed them a working model of his new Kinetograph, for that is the name he has given to the most wonderful of all his wonderful inventions.

The surprised and pleased club women saw a small pine box standing on the floor. There were some wheels and belts near the box, and a workman who had them in charge. In the top of the box was a hole perhaps an inch in diameter. As they looked through this hole they saw the picture of a man. It was a most marvellous picture. It bowed and smiled and waved its hands and took off its hat with the most perfect naturalness and grace. Every motion was perfect. There was not a hitch or a jerk. No wonder Edison chuckled at the effect he produced with his Kinetograph.

Recently he went to Chicago. While there some one who was interested in the World's Fair asked him if he was going to get up some electric novelty to place on exhibition at the big exposition.

"I have a machine projected," replied Edison, "but the details are not perfected yet. My intention is to have such a happy combination of electricity and photography that a man can sit in his own parlor and see reproduced on a screen the forms of the players in an opera produced on a distant stage, and, as he sees their movements, he will hear the sound of their voices as they talk or sing or laugh. When the machine is perfected, which it will be long before it can be exhibited at the fair, each little muscle of the singer's face will be seen to work, his facial expression with its every change will be exactly reproduced, and the stride and positions will be natural and will vary as do those of the person himself.

"That is only one part of what the machine will do. To the sporting fraternity I can say that before long it will be possible to apply this system to prize fights and boxing exhibitions. The whole scene with the comments of the spectators, the talk of the seconds, the noise of the blows, and so on will be faithfully transferred."

When this interview was published here a couple of weeks ago people laughed again and said Edison had been having fun with some Chicago reporter. Edison sat in court all day on Tuesday during the argument of his counsel for an injunction to restrain the United States Electric Light Company from making incandescent lamps. A SUN reporter asked him about this phenomenal machine and was invited to go out to the laboratory at Orange and see the model of the machine work. Yesterday morning the reporter found Mr. Edison at the laboratory, and showed him a copy of the Chicago interview. Edison read it and laughed.

"Yes, it's true," he said. "You can sit in your parlor and look at a big screen and see Chauncey Depew come out just as if he was introducing Stanley at the Metropolitan Opera House. He will walk up to the front of the stage and bow and smile and take a drink of water and start off with his oration. Every time your eyes see him open his mouth your ears will hear what he says, that is if he says anything.

"Just the same way with an opera. You watch the screen, and see a picture of the stage, fullsize. Maria Jansen comes out and sings, and the band will play a charming waltzing minuet, and then she dances around and the audience applauds. Maybe DeWolf Hopper comes in and cracks a joke or Digby Bell wakes up from his twenty-five years' sleep and asks if the New Yorks have won a game yet."

"How do you expect to do all that, Mr. Edison?"

"If it is desired to reproduce an opera or a play I will get the company to give a dress rehearsal for me. I place back of the orchestra on a table a compound machine consisting of a phonograph and a kinetograph, with a capacity of thirty minutes continuous work. The orchestra plays, the curtain rises, and the opera begins. Both machines work simultaneously, one recording sound and the other taking photographs, recording motion at the rate of forty-six photographs per second. Afterward the photographic strip is developed and replaced in the machine, a projecting lens is substituted for the photographic lens, and the reproducing part of the phonograph is adjusted. Then by means of a calcium light, the effect is reproduced life-size on a white curtain, reproducing to the audience the original scene with all the sounds and all the motions of the actors exactly as in the original scene."

The phonograph which Mr. Edison will use in his compound motion and sound reproducer will be an improvement on the phonographs now in common use. He said yesterday that he had now in use about 500 phonographs, of which he was taking constant observations. The result of all these observations he will embody in the improved phonograph to be used with the kinetograph.

The accompanying sketch is from a drawing of the compound machine made by Mr. Edison himself at his laboratory yesterday. It represents the table on which the two machines are placed. The phonograph B is connected to the kinetograph C by a shaft seen in the sketch just over the letter B. This shaft is attached to the cylinder of the phonograph at one end and to the apparatus which operates the shutter of the kinetograph at the other. It thus insures exactly simultaneous action on the part of the two machines. So when the phonograph hears a sound and records it the kinetograph sees the exact motion which accompanied that sound and fixes it. If the machine had been placed on the floor of the Metropolitan Opera House at the Stanley reception, at the exact instant when the phonograph heard Dr. Depew exclaim: "It is the glorious privilege of few men to become so completely the property of the world," the kinetograph would have seen Dr. Depew's smile and his lips move in articulations, while his right arm completed a swinging gesture toward the man of whom he was talking.

The kinetograph is nothing more nor less than a photograph camera arranged in a new way to do new work. Its name implies its use. The name is derived from the Greek words meaning "to move" and "to write," and the machine literally furnishes a complete record of all the motions made before it. It photographs action. As Edison says, "The kinetograph does for the eye what the phonograph does for the ear." In this small box camera Mr. Edison places a roll of gelatine film about three fourths of an inch wide and of any length desired. The interior of the camera is of course arranged on a plan similar to that on which the ordinary roll cameras are made. The gelatine strip is unrolled from one spindle and rerolled on another, and in passing from the first spindle to the second is carried before the lens of the camera. The shutters of the camera are arranged to be worked by the shaft attached to the cylinder of the phonograph. This shaft also works the spindles which carry the rolls of film.

The mechanism of this camera is so arranged that when the shutters open the spindles stop and the gelatine film is fixed before the lens. In less than the forty-sixth part of a second the photograph is taken, the shutters snap, the spindles turn, and the gelatine slip moves on for a new photograph. The arrangement is so complete that forty-six perfect photographs are taken in one second.

"The trouble with all attempts heretofore made to reproduce action and motion by photographs," said Edison, "was that the photographs could not be taken in series with an efficient rapidity to catch accurately the motion it was desired to reproduce. Hemment, the man who photographs running horses in the thousandth part of one second, had the idea, but he failed because he could take only half a dozen photographs at a time. All these photographs, if reproduced in a series, would have shown a jerky and imperfect motion. My idea was to take a series of instantaneous photographs of motions so rapidly that in the reproduction the photographic representatives become resolved into a pure motion, instead of a series of jerks. The kinetograph takes a series of forty-six photographs in one second and keeps it up as long as desired. It starts, moves, stops, uncloses the shutter, takes a photograph, closes the shutter, and starts on, forty-six times a second. The result when reproduced is a pure motion."

To illustrate what he had said, Mr. Edison took one of the rolls of gelatine film which had been through the kinetograph and showed it to the reporter. On it was photographed one of the boys in his laboratory. The photographs were about half an inch square and were taken in the film at intervals of about one inch. They represented the boy in the act of taking off his hat and bowing. Between the first view and the last of the series the complete motion of removing the hat and making the bow was clearly discernible, but between any two consecutive views there was no apparent change in the position of the boy's arm or head. In the first view the boy's hand was at his side, gradually it was raised toward his head, and his head inclined forward. Then the hat was removed and the bow completed after which the hat was replaced.

"To reproduce perfectly a complete record of a pure motion," continued Mr. Edison, "it is necessary that the photographs should be taken at the rate of forty-six per second. Any smaller number would show irregularities and a break in the motion. There was a machine made a while ago to print pictures of an object in motion, but it would not work fast enough. It reproduced an imperfect and jerky motion, like this," he illustrated by raising his arms in a series of short jerks to his shoulder.

"How did I find out that forty-six photographs must be taken every second? Well, I've been experimenting with this thing for a long time. Now I've got it. That is, I've got the germ or base principle. When you get your base principle right, then it's only a question of time and a matter of details about completing the machine. The details can all be worked out after you get the germs. Come up stairs and see the germ work."

He ran up stairs with the step of a boy and easily headed the procession to the spot where the "germ" was expected to prove that the reproduction of motion by photography was an established fact. It is a question which part of the kinetograph Edison himself regards as the greatest part of his invention, the arrangement for taking the photographs or the contrivance for reproducing them. It was the reproducing contrivance which he showed to the reporter as the "germ."

To outward appearance the "germ" is nothing but a pine box which looks very much as if it might have been originally intended as a packing case for shoes or boots. It stood on end in front of a lathe, and the open top was nearest to the lathe. In the upper end was cut a hole about an inch in diameter and [in] the hole was set a lens. On the bottom of the box was arranged a series of wheels and spindles. A roll of gelatine film was placed on a spindle on one side of the bottom. The end of the gelatine strip was then carried over one of the wheels and past the legs in the pole in the top of the box to another spindle on the other side of the box bottom and fastened. A small belt ran from the lathe to the shaft on which was set the spindle to which the end of the gelatine strip was fastened. When the motor was turned so the roll of gelatine strip was transferred from the first spindle to the second, and in the transfer passed under the lens. The photographs on the strip came out perfectly. As the "germ" was worked fast or slow the reproduction showed a pure motion or a series of jerks. When it was run at the highest speed the reporter saw a young fellow waving his hands and touching his hat. Sometimes he laughed or shook his head or twisted his body and wriggled around. The slip could be seen to be in rapid motion, but the figure was always in front of the lens, tossing his arms and shaking his head and laughing. Every motion was natural and perfect, and it needed but the projecting lens and the larger screen to see the whole figure accurately produced, and to be able to distinguish every feature and to recognize the action of all the muscles of the face.

After running the "germ" for a while at full speed Edison had it slowed down a little. At once the difference became apparent, and the reason of the failure of the machine to which Edison had referred were quite evident. Instead of reproducing a smooth pure motion, the strip showed under the lens a lazy, indifferent young fellow, who moved himself by jerks, and whose actions were abrupt and unsteady. As the strip moved more slowly this became more and more clearly seen until the machine was stopped altogether.

In a few weeks Mr. Edison will be ready to make a test of the practical powers of the "germ" on a much larger scale. In the office of the laboratory he has had an immense screen put up such as is used for stereopticon exhibitions. The screen hangs over the big fire place, and covers the whole side of the wall. As soon as he can perfect some little details of the kinetograph, he will make a trial at life-size reproduction on this big success. He hopes to get around to this trial in the course of a few weeks. But all the work and time which he gives to the kinetograph he counts as his amusement. He took up the idea for amusement, and now that he has so far succeeded as to have gotten over being angry at the people who insinuated that he talked too much when he first spoke of his idea, he only works at the "germ" for amusement's sake.

The idea which has actuated our Edison in his work on the kinetograph is the reproduction of opera. He does not mean to show on his white screen simply a lot of silhouettes but to represent the stage with the actors on it, "moving around and speaking, or singing, exactly as you see them and hear them if you have a seat in the orchestra." To produce this effect the reproduction will be a gigantic photograph not merely of the actors but of the whole stage, with its scenery and all the furniture and other settings used in making up any scene it is desired to reproduce. In order to obtain this result it is necessary to make a phonograph large enough to have a cylinder which will record every sound made in thirty minutes, which is about the duration of the average act at the theatre. It will of course be impossible to change the cylinders of the phonograph or stop the kinetograph during the act, even for a single second, without making a serious break in the reproduction. Mr. Edison says the kinetograph can be made to run for any desired length of time.

"I can put a roll of gelatine strip a mile long into it if I like," said the inventor yesterday. "The work it will do in half an hour is something astonishing." Taking 46 photographs per second, in half an hour there would be 82,800 photographs on the gelatine strip. If the photographs were half an inch square and half an inch apart, the strip of film used in taking a thirty minute act of opera would be 6,900 feet long, and Mr. Edison would need something more than his "mile of gelatine."

It does not seem likely that the kinetograph will ever be put to a practical use, that is, for commercial purposes. At the first blush the thought seems to be that Mr. Edison has found a scheme for telegraphing the representation of action. This is not the case. The method of using the kinetograph will be exactly similar to that of using the phonograph except that the phonograph has been put to practical use to some extent by stenographers and lawyers. Invented and built for the amusement of its creator, it will always be an object of amusement. But in that way is seems likely to be a tremendous success. It will be operated exactly as the phonograph is by the use of duplicates. From the roll of gelatine film on which the negatives of the original scene were made, Edison expects to be able to print any number of duplicates. These duplicates will be sold to the owners of kinetographs as cylinders are now sold to the owners of phonographs. So when the machine is perfected if a man desires to reproduced for his private benefit or amusement any opera which the compound phonograph-kinetograph has been heard and seen, he has only to secure the duplicate cylinders and gelatine roles for that opera and invite in his friends and neighbors while he has an opera of his own in his own house on his own screen.

This practical arc, Mr. Edison suggested could be much of the invention. It can be arranged for nickel-in-the-slot machines, and the wizard electrician said that he would probably rig up a lot of these machines to take the place of the nickel-in-the-slot phonographs which are scattered around so plentifully. When this is accomplished it will be the proper thing to step into a drug store and, dropping a nickel to the slot, see Madame Patti trip across the stage and watch her white throat swell as you hear again the notes of her "Home, Sweet Home." And when you have done that for five cents you can walk away and dream of the time when you paid five dollars to hear the same thing.

The kinetograph is bound to be a most faithful reproducer, as is the phonograph. It will catch every motion made. With out-of-door athletic exhibitions and prize fights its work will be just as perfect, and Luther Carey's stride will be measured as carefully and reproduced as distinctly as the terrible blows by which Fitzsimmons disposed of Dempsey.

Now that the thing is done the first remark is the usual one of "How simple." There is not one of us who has not seen the idea in use hundreds of times. The children in the streets have for playthings little windmills whose painted arms embody the very idea which Edison has used in the Kinetograph. One arm will have part of a [figure] painted on it, the next will have another part, and the next another, and so on, and as the arms whirl rapidly around one looking on sees only the perfect picture. That is the whole scheme....(*New York Sun,* 28 May 1891, 1-2.)

Edison Photographic Building, built September-October 1889.

Although the 3/4" horizontal feed camera worked in principle, significant improvements in overall design were necessary before the invention would be ready for commercial use. Following the successful presentation of the horizontal-feed system to the press, Edison, Dickson and Heise constructed a sturdier, vertical-feed camera that utilized a 1 and 1/2" strip of celluloid film. Although the results were similar to the system that Edison would subsequently commercialize, the format and camera design had not yet achieved their final form. According to notes in Edison's legal files, at least one film reflected this intermediate phase.

11 [Man on Parallel Bars]
LENGTH: © No reg.
PRODUCER: W.K.L. Dickson.
CAMERA: William Heise.
CAST:
PRODUCTION DATE: 1892.
LOCATION: Photographic Building, Edison Laboratory, West Orange, N.J.
SOURCE:
DESCRIPTION:
SUBJECT: Motion pictures–experiments. Sports. Gymnastics.
ARCHIVE:
CITATIONS: Notes, legal files, NjWOE.
NOTE:

During 1892, Dickson and Heise refined the design of their motion picture camera. They took a number of films with this improved camera in the late summer and early fall of 1892. Among other things, film width was adjusted at about this time to 1 and 9/16ths of an inch (approximately 35mm). If format is considered, these films can be called the first modern motion pictures—though they were not shot with commercial use in mind. Selected frames from several of these subjects were subsequently published in The Phonogram.

12 √Boxing

LENGTH: © No reg.
PRODUCER: W.K.L. Dickson.
CAMERA: William Heise.
CAST:
PRODUCTION DATE: By October 1892.
LOCATION: Photographic Building, Edison Laboratory, West Orange, N.J.
SOURCE:
DESCRIPTION:
SUBJECT: Motion pictures–experiments. Sports. Boxing.
ARCHIVE:
CITATIONS: "The Kinetograph," *The Phonogram*, October 1892, 217 (with illustrations).
NOTE:

13 √Fencing / Fencers

LENGTH: © No reg.
PRODUCER: W.K.L. Dickson.
CAMERA: William Heise.
CAST:
PRODUCTION DATE: By October 1892.
LOCATION: Photographic Building, Edison Laboratory, West Orange, N.J.
SOURCE:
DESCRIPTION:
SUBJECT: Motion pictures–experiments. Sports. Fencing.
ARCHIVE:
CITATIONS: "The Kinetograph," *The Phonogram*, October 1892, 218 (with illustrations); W.K.L. Dickson and Antonia Dickson, *History of the Kinetograph, Kinetoscope and Kineto-Phonograph*, 37 (with illustrations).
NOTE:

14 √Wrestling

LENGTH: © No reg.
PRODUCER: W.K.L. Dickson.
CAMERA: William Heise.
CAST:
PRODUCTION DATE: By October 1892.
LOCATION: Photographic Building, Edison Laboratory, West Orange, N.J.
SOURCE:
DESCRIPTION:
SUBJECT: Motion pictures–experiments. Sports. Wrestling.

ARCHIVE:
CITATIONS: "The Kinetograph," *The Phonogram*, October 1892, 219 (with illustrations).
NOTE:

15 √**A Hand Shake**
LENGTH: © No reg.
PRODUCER: W.K.L. Dickson.
CAMERA: William Heise.
CAST: W.K.L. Dickson, William Heise.
PRODUCTION DATE: By October 1892.
LOCATION: Photographic Building, Edison Laboratory, West Orange, N.J.
SOURCE:
DESCRIPTION:
SUBJECT: Publicity. Motion pictures–experiments.
ARCHIVE:
CITATIONS: "The Kinetograph," *The Phonogram*, October 1892, 220 (with illustrations).
NOTE:

Selected frames from the previous four films illustrated the following article.

THE KINETOGRAPH.
A NEW INDUSTRY HERALDED.

It is difficult for those not familiar with the phonograph to conceive the extent of its field of operations, or the diversity, one might almost say the inconsistency, of the functions it fills. It is like the "harp of a thousand strings" of which we read.

Its latest role is by no means the least wonderful, and though this instrument has already achieved conquests in the sphere of industry that may be denominated vast, the greatest is yet to come; and when it stands forth before the world, will make such gigantic strides as were never previously witnessed.

At the opening of the Columbian Exposition there will appear a dual instrument, two steeds of almost infinite capacity in their special powers, whose performances it will tax the human eye and ear to follow.

The Edison Kinetograph is an instrument intended to reproduce motion and sound simultaneously, being a combination of a specially constructed camera and phonograph. The camera used in connection with this instrument will take forty-six pictures a second, which is 2,760 pictures a minute, or 165,600 in an hour. The rapid photographing of these pictures upon a long band of extremely light sensitive film creates the illusory spectacle of real motion of the figures, and when to this visual impression The Phonograph is called to join its voice, we have a combination of effects upon both auditory and optic nerves. This specially constructed camera is attached electrically to a phonograph and their combined movements are simultaneously registered, and thus we have the duplex sensation of vision and sound.

Now the advantages of the kinetograph are, that we may enjoy the eloquence of a great orator, hear his voice, see his face and form and every movement he makes at one time while in our own homes; celebrated actors, singers, etc., may in like manner be called before us while we sit in our drawing rooms; we need not resort to seats in the open air, situated miles away from our dwellings, to see military processions or civic parades; those who are interested in swift-running horses can see a race going on at Sheepshead Bay or Monmouth, without leaving New York, and just here let it be remembered that this instrument may play a most useful part, for in a close race where a few inches of space turns the scales, it will take down just what happened, faithfully; and the kinetograph will also record with fidelity all that takes place at prize fights, baseball contests and the noise, stir and progress of games.

It would be impossible at the present stage of this invention to enumerate all the uses to which the phono-camera or kinetograph is applicable. Suffice it to say that its capacities are apparently unlimited; especially does this view of it apply to its powers as a source of amusement. (*The Phonogram*, October 1892, 217-218.)

In December 1892, with the camera technology in place, the kinetograph team com-menced construction of the world's first specially-designed motion picture studio, located on the grounds of the Edison Laboratory. The Dickson-designed studio, com-pleted in early 1893, was affectionately known as the "Black Maria" after the police paddy wagons it was said to resemble. Over the course of 1893, Dickson and Heise made at least three films that were subsequently presented in the kinetoscope. These were shot on film purchased from the Blair Camera Company, initially at the cost of $2.20 per roll, 505" x 19/16". (Blair Camera Company to Thomas A. Edison, 29 April 1893, NjWOE.) The subjects were also the first instances of commercial modern motion picture production in the world.

If the new motion picture studio was affectionately named after a vehicle for impris-oned criminals, these first motion pictures designed for public consumption playfully transposed and refigured the activities and concerns of the Edison Laboratory with its all-male staff. Dickson and Heise were working at the center of technological innova-tion—inside a celebrated symbol of American ingenuity. Yet films taken within this mythic place showed ye olde blacksmithy and the small-town barbershop.

16 *Blacksmithing Scene / Blacksmiths

LENGTH: 50 ft.   © No reg.

PRODUCER: W.K.L. Dickson.

CAMERA: William Heise.

CAST: [Charles Kayser, John Ott.]

PRODUCTION DATE: Mid-April to early May 1893.

LOCATION: Black Maria, West Orange, N.J.

SOURCE: *[Duncan and An-other, Blacksmith Shop]* (Edison film no. 5, May-June 1891).

DESCRIPTION: The picture rep-resented a blacksmith and two helpers forging a piece of iron. Before beginning the job a bottle was passed from one to the other, each imbibing his portion. The blacksmith then removed his white hot iron from the forge with a pair of tongs and gave directions to his helpers with the small hand hammer, when they immediately began to pound the hot iron while the sparks flew in all directions, the blacksmith at the same time making intermediate strokes with his hand hammer. At a signal from the smith, the helpers put down their sledge hammers, when the iron was returned to the forge and another piece substituted for it, and the operation was repeated. ("First Public Exhibition of Edison's Kinetograph," *Scientific American*, 20 May 1893, 310.)

SUBJECT: Blacksmithing. Alcoholic beverages.

ARCHIVE: NNMoMA.

CITATIONS: "Edison and the Kinetoscope," *Photographic Times*, 6 April 1894, 209-212; Continental Commerce Company to W.E. Gilmore, 18 September 1894 (TAEP, 135:389).

NOTE:

17 √**Horse Shoeing**

LENGTH: 50 ft.   © No reg.
PRODUCER: W.K.L. Dickson.
CAMERA: William Heise.
CAST: W.K.L. Dickson (with hand on horse's rump).
PRODUCTION DATE: By early May 1893.
LOCATION: Black Maria, West Orange, N.J.
SOURCE:
DESCRIPTION: One of the pictures to be seen in the machine, for example, was that of a blacksmith shop in which two men were working, one shoeing a horse, the other heating iron at the forge. The one would be seen to drive the nail into the shoe on the horse's hoof, to change his position and every movement needed in the work was clearly shown as if the object was in real [life]. In fact, the whole routine of the two men's labor and their movements for the day was presented to the view of the observer. (*Brooklyn Daily Eagle*, 10 May 1893.)
SUBJECT: Blacksmithing. Horseshoeing.
ARCHIVE:
CITATIONS: Continental Commerce Company to W.E. Gilmore, 18 September 1894 (TAEP, 135:389).
NOTE:

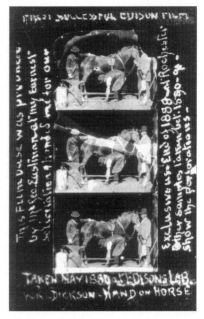

On 9 May 1893, the Brooklyn Institute of Arts and Sciences, gave the first public exhibition of Edison's 1 and 9/16", vertical-feed, peep-hole kinetoscope, showing both Blacksmithing Scene *and* Horse Shoeing.

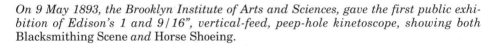

DEPARTMENT OF PHYSICS
Annual Election in an Important Branch of the Institute.
The Business Meeting Was Followed by an Exhibition of Edison's New Instrument, the Kinetograph, Which Throws a Picture on a Screen Simultaneously With the Production by Phonograph of the Description of the Scene Presented and the Movements Pictured.

The Annual Election for officers in the department of physics, Brooklyn Institute, followed by an exhibition of Edison's new instrument, the kinetograph, was held at 502 Fulton street last evening. The following new officers were unanimously elected: President, Professor Samuel Sheldon; vice president, Professor W. Gould Levison; secretary, James R. Priddy; treasurer, P.H. Van Evern. After a few words from the new officers, Mr. George M. Hopkins addressed the audience. In his desire to get something to interest the department he had written to Mr. Edison, who had replied in substance: "How would the kinetograph do?" He immediately visited Mr. Edison's laboratory to investigate, and found that the kinetograph he had hoped to secure was beyond his reach. The instrument of that name, about which so much appeared in the papers a few years ago, is an optical lantern and a mechanical device by which a moving image is projected on the screen simultaneously with the production by a phonograph of the words or song which accompany the movements pictured. For example: The photograph of a prima donna would be shown on the screen, with the movements of the lips, the head and the body, together with the changes of facial expression, while the phonograph would produce the song. To arrange this apparatus for this evening was impracticable, he said, and the audience would have to be satisfied with the small instrument designed for individual observation, which simply shows the movements without the accompanying words. This apparatus is the refinement of Plateau's phenakistoscope or the zootrope, and is carried to great perfection. The principle can be readily understood by anyone who has ever examined the instrument. Persistence of vision is depended upon to blend the successive images into one continuous ever-changing photographic picture. In addition to Plateau's experiments he referred to the work accomplished by Muybridge and Anschuetz, who very successfully photographed animals in motion, and Demeny, who produced an instrument called the phonoscope, which gave the facial expression while words were being spoken, so that deaf and dumb people could readily understand. But Mr. Edison, Mr. Hopkins said, has produced a machine by means of which far more perfect results are secured. The fundamental feature in his experiments is the camera, by means of which the pictures are taken. This camera starts, moves and stops the sensitive strip which receives the photographic image, forty-six times a second, and the exposure of the plate takes place in one-eighth of this time, or in about one-fifty-seventh of a second. The lens for producing these pictures was made to order at an enormous expense, and every detail at this end of the experiment was carefully looked after. There are 700 impressions on each strip, and when these pictures are shown in succession in the kinetograph the light is intercepted 700 times during one revolution of the strip. The duration of each image is 1-92 of a second and the entire strip passes through the instrument in about thirty seconds. In this instrument each image dwells upon the retina until it is replaced by the succeeding one, and the difference between any picture and the succeeding one or preceding one is so slight as to render it impossible to observe the intermittent character of the picture. He explained the manner in which the photographs were produced by presenting the familiar dancing skeleton on the screen. A zootrope, adapted to the lantern shows the principle of the Kinetograph. In this instrument a disk having a radial slit is revolved rapidly in front of a disk bearing a series of images in different positions, which are arranged radially upon rapidly revolving disk. The relative speeds of these disks are such that when they are revolved in the lantern the radial slit causes the images to [be] seen in regular succession, so that they replace each other and appear to really be in motion, but this instrument on exhibition, as compared with the kinetograph, is a very crude affair.

At the conclusion of Mr. Hopkins' address every one was accorded an opportunity of looking into the new machine, which was for the first time exhibited publicly. It is one of many Mr. Edison has made for the world fair and was exhibited last night by one of his assistants, Mr. W. Kennedy Laurie Dickson. It can be compared to the phonograph, that is, it pictorially presents every object brought within its view. As described above, it shows living subjects portrayed in a manner to excite wonderment. One of the pictures to be seen in the machine, for example, was that of a blacksmith shop in which two men were working, one shoeing a horse, the other heating iron at the forge. The one would be seen to drive the nail into the shoe on the horse's hoof, to change his position and every movement needed in the work was clearly shown as if the object was in real [life]. In fact, the whole routine of the two men's labor and their movements for the day was presented to the view of the observer. At the conclusion of the exhibition a vote of thanks was passed to Mr. Hopkins. (*Brooklyn Daily Eagle*, 10 May 1893, 9.)

18 *The Barber Shop / Barber Shop / The Barbershop

LENGTH: 50 ft.   © No reg.
PRODUCER: W.K.L. Dickson.
CAMERA: William Heise.
CAST:
PRODUCTION DATE: By late 1893.
LOCATION: Black Maria, West Orange, N.J.
SOURCE:
DESCRIPTION: Interior of Barber Shop. Man comes in, takes off his coat; sits down, smokes; is handed a paper by attendant, who points out a joke; both laugh. Meantime the man in the chair is shaved and has his hair cut. Very funny. (The Kinetoscope Company, *Edison's Latest Wonders: The Kinetograph, The Kinetoscope,* [October 1894].)

The kinetoscope which is in Mr. Edison's workshop, contains a picture of a barbershop. Looking into it one sees the barber and three men waiting to be shaved. One of the men rises and walks across the picture to the chair, sits down and the barber goes through all the customary operations of shaving a man. Every motion of the barber from the stropping of the razor to the brushing of the man's hair, is reproduced, and the actions of the men who are waiting to be shaved are also reproduced. ("Thomas Edison's Latest Contrivance," *New York Herald*, 11 March 1894, 2.)

"A Lightning Shave." (The Kinetoscope Company, *Bulletin No. 1*, [December 1894].)
SUBJECT: Barbershops. Shaving.
ARCHIVE: NNMoMA, CLAc.
CITATIONS: "Edison and the Kinetoscope," *Photographic Times*, 6 April 1894, 211-212; W.K.L. Dickson and Antonia Dickson, "Edison's Invention of the Kineto-Phonograph," *Century Magazine*, June 1894, 206-214 (with illustrations); Continental Commerce Company to W.E. Gilmore, 18 September 1894 (TAEP, 135:389).
NOTE:

SOME OF EDISON'S LATEST.
SEE THE LIVING SUBJECTS.

For the edification of a party of sightseers, at the Orange laboratory, in St. Louis [sic], recently, an improvised barbershop was fitted up, and the services of a nearby tonsorial artist were secured. An attendant at the laboratory took a seat in the chair, and the machine was set in motion. The barber lathered his man and then proceeded to shave him in regulation style. While the barber was at work, several pretended customers entered, and one showed the barber a humorous paragraph in a newspaper. When the strip of gelatine was again passed through the kinetograph, every detail of the shave, every motion of the barber's hands, each expression of the men's faces were produced so perfectly and so well-timed that the spectators could see the scenes repeated in the machine. As yet the new instrument has no commercial value, but the parties interested believe that its possibilities as a means of furnishing amusement are unlimited....(*Albany [N.Y.] Telegram*, 7 January 1894, TAEP, 146:0895.)

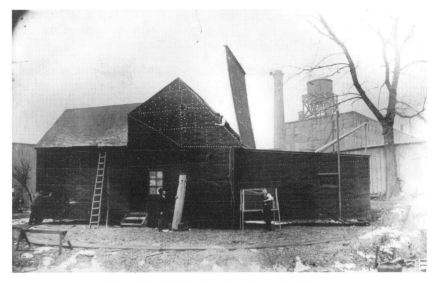

Exterior of the Black Maria studio (November 1893-March 1894).

In the first year of commercial production, W.K.L. Dickson and William Heise filmed a remarkable sampling of entertainment—everything from rat-killing terriers and boxing cats to opera singers—from a Turkish couchee couchee dancer and a South American tight rope walker to selected scenes from Broadway's top musicals. These films—typically shown first in a kinetoscope parlor on Broadway just north of Herald Square in New York City, the nation's entertainment capital—offered a collection of moving snap shots, ephemeral images that surveyed the city's eclectic entertainments.

As the new year began and preparations for the commercial exploitation of Edison's motion pictures moved forward, publicity became of increasingly importance. One or two films were therefore shot specifically to appear in Harper's Weekly.

19 ***Edison Kinetoscopic Record of a Sneeze, January 7, 1894 / Fred Ott's Sneeze**

LENGTH: © William K.L. Dickson, 9 January 1894.

PRODUCER: W.K.L. Dickson.

CAMERA: William Heise.

CAST: Fred Ott.

PRODUCTION DATE: 2-7 January 1894.

LOCATION: Black Maria, West Orange, N.J.

SOURCE:

DESCRIPTION:

SUBJECT: Publicity. Sneeze.

ARCHIVE: DLC-pp, DLC-Hendricks.

CITATIONS: "The Kineto-Phonograph," *Electrical World,* 16 June 1894, 799-801 (with illustrations).

NOTE: This film was made for publicity purposes, as a series of sequential still photographs to illustrate an article appearing in *Harper's Weekly.*

THE RECORD OF A SNEEZE.

Expressed in simplest terms, sneezing is caused by a stimulus applied to the lining membrane of the nose. An impulse is carried to the respiratory center by the nasal and other branches of the fifth nerves. The business (so to speak) of the sneeze consists of a deep inspiration, then a closing of the glottis, followed by an explosive expiration; then the forced opening of the glottis and posterior nares. The facial distortion is the farce of the sneeze. It is a purely reflex action, and you may not sneeze at will. To produce it, however, in good style, you may use a stimulant, and then nature makes a determined effort to drive off the irritating substance. Perhaps there is more in sneezing than physiologists can account for. Sternutation in the beginning of man's animal life might have been of vital importance.

I would not discuss that difficult subject of pleasure and pain, and how they are not so far apart, for both are in a measure combined in a sneeze. There is, however, a curious phenomenon in the sneeze, and that is that there exists, if but for the fractional portion of a second, something like a collapse. Might it not be accounted for? By the sudden closing of the glottis the pent-up air becomes over-saturated with carbonic acid gas, and then comes to the brain the oblivious condition. May that not allay what might be a really painful sensation, the outburst of a large volume of air through that delicate organ the nose? Somebody versed in human dynamics ought to measure the force of a regulation sneeze, and the power of it would be found to be surprising. Without, then, this half-comatose condition, which is the prelude to the sneeze, the muscular effect might be painful.

A heavy volume might be compiled devoted to sneeze-lore. What we know is this—that a sneeze is kindly greeted all over the world, and that if in parts of Europe and America snuff-taking is no longer in vogue, among savage tribes the use of tobacco introduced into the nose is rapidly increasing as a habit. There is only one Irish story Mr. Le Fanu tells about the sneeze which struck me as novel. When an Irishman hears a natural unpremeditated sneeze he says "God bless you!" If he believes, however, that the sneeze has been induced by tobacco, he modifies his congratulations, "God bless you," he says, "barring the snuff!"

The Edison kinetoscope gives the entire record of a sneeze from the first taking of a pinch of snuff to the recovery. As seen in this wonderful mechanical device of Mr. Edison's invention, when he exhibits the series of photographs the figure actually sneezes, and the phonograph as an accompanist sounds the precise "as-shew." The illusion is so perfect that you involuntarily say, "Bless you!" Looking at the eighty-one prints taken in about two seconds—or, to be exactly correct, forty pictures to the second—the gradual changes are seen.

For the purposes of study the numerals from 1 to 9 have been put on the top of the print, and the letters from A to I on the side. Any point particularly mentioned in the eight-one may be found at the intersection of the numeral and letter lines. In this way the marked differences of the sneeze are observable. I might designate A 1 as the priming; C 2, the nascent sensation; G 2, the first distortion; G 3, expectancy; E 4, pre-meditation; I 5, preparation; C 6, beatitude; A 8, oblivion; A 9, explosion; I 9, recovery. This curious gamut of grimace and sound the kinetoscope has exactly scored.

We know that in the workings of nature our eyes and our ears only take heed of what are the salient impressions, because the minutiae escape us. As there is the partially unseen; so there is undoubtedly the partially unheard. I am not going to argue as to the advantages of mechanical devices in an art sense, but in a scientific way their benefits we barely appreciate to-day. Take this kinetoscopic record of a sneeze, a topic inclined to excite a smile, and let us try and rise higher.

Within the last ten years the one great thing which has put us in closer touch with the heavens has been photography. It is not the lense working alone to-day which satisfies our requirements; it must be in partnership with the sensitive film. We are certain to demand greater delicacy, a larger accumulation of minute facts in our observatories, and so the time must come when we will ask for more than the varied expressions of a star. Some day, then, the heavens will have star phases kinetoscopically recorded. Barnet Phillips. (*Harper's Weekly*, 24 March 1894, 280.)

20 *[Fred Ott Holding a Bird]

LENGTH: © No reg.

PRODUCER: W.K.L. Dickson.

CAMERA: William Heise.

CAST: Fred Ott.

PRODUCTION DATE: [January 1894?]

LOCATION: Edison Laboratory, West Orange, N.J.

SOURCE:

DESCRIPTION:

SUBJECT: Publicity. Birds.

ARCHIVE: CL-UC, FPA.

CITATIONS:

NOTE: This short film may have been made as a possible alternative to *Edison Kinetoscopic Record of a Sneeze*, intended to illustrate an article by Barnet Phillips appearing in *Harper's Weekly*.

Dickson and Heise made a series of films, using athletes from the local Newark Turnverein as cooperative subjects. These may have been made as Dickson and Heise prepared to begin serious production. These films, however, were generally not sold or shown commercially and could have been made the previous year.

21 ***[Athlete with Wand] / [Leçon de Baton]**
LENGTH: 50 ft.   © No reg.
PRODUCER: W.K.L. Dickson.
CAMERA: William Heise.
CAST:
PRODUCTION DATE: February 1894.
LOCATION: Black Maria, West Orange, N.J.
SOURCE:
DESCRIPTION:
SUBJECT: Motion pictures–experiments. Sports. Gymnastics. Newark Turnverein.
ARCHIVE: FrBaADF, NNMoMA, DLC-Hendricks.
CITATIONS:
NOTE:

22 **√[Unsuccessful Somersault] / [Amateur Gymnast, no. 1]**
LENGTH: 50 ft.   © No reg.
PRODUCER: W.K.L. Dickson.
CAMERA: William Heise.
CAST:
PRODUCTION DATE: By mid-March 1894.
LOCATION: Black Maria, West Orange, N.J.
SOURCE:
DESCRIPTION: One of the series gives successive pictures of an athlete in an unsuccessful attempt to turn a somersault. Everybody who has seen a boy perform this act knows the brief space of time it takes him to throw himself upon his hands, with his feet in the air, and how quickly he recovers himself if he fails to go over. Yet it will be seen that the kinetograph photographed the athlete forty-four times between the beginning and the end of the act, aside from the numerous pictures taken when he was bending down to the ground and coming back to an erect position. ("Wizard Edison's Kinetograph," *New York World*, 18 March 1894, 21, with illustrations.)
SUBJECT: Motion pictures–experiments. Sports. Gymnastics. Newark Turnverein.
ARCHIVE:
CITATIONS:
NOTE:

23 **√[Successful Somersault] / [Amateur Gymnast, no. 2]**
LENGTH: 50 ft.   © No reg.
PRODUCER: W.K.L. Dickson.
CAMERA: William Heise.
CAST:
PRODUCTION DATE: By mid-March 1894.
LOCATION: Black Maria, West Orange, N.J.
SOURCE:
DESCRIPTION: It will be seen in the second series which illustrates the successful attempt to throw the somersault that the athlete in twenty-six pictures was carried from the place where he was about to put

his hands upon the ground to that where the body was completely in the air, and that six pictures were afterwards taken while he was in this position well on his way towards the completion of the somesault. ("Wizard Edison's Kinetograph," *New York World*, 18 March 1894, 21, with illustrations.)
SUBJECT: Motion pictures–experiments. Sports. Gymnastics. Newark Turnverein.
ARCHIVE:
CITATIONS: "Edison and the Kinetoscope," *Photographic Times*, 6 April 1894, 211 (with illustrations); Thomas Maguire, "The Kinetograph," *Frank Leslie's Weekly*, 5 April 1894, 223-226 (with illustrations).
NOTE:

24 [Men on Parallel Bars]
LENGTH: 50 ft.   © No reg.
PRODUCER: W.K.L. Dickson.
CAMERA: William Heise.
CAST:
PRODUCTION DATE: By mid-March 1894.
LOCATION: Black Maria, West Orange, N.J.
SOURCE:
DESCRIPTION:
SUBJECT: Motion pictures–experiments. Sports. Gymnastics. Newark Turnverein.
ARCHIVE:
CITATIONS: "Wizard Edison's Kinetograph," *New York World*, 18 March 1894, 21.
NOTE:

25 [Boxing Match]
LENGTH: 50 ft.   © No reg.
PRODUCER: W.K.L. Dickson.
CAMERA: William Heise.
CAST:
PRODUCTION DATE: By mid-March 1894.
LOCATION: Black Maria, West Orange, N.J.
SOURCE:
DESCRIPTION:
SUBJECT: Sports. Boxing. Newark Turnverein.
ARCHIVE:
CITATIONS: "Wizard Edison's Kinetograph," *New York World*, 18 March 1894, 21; "The Kineto-Phonograph," *The Electrical World*, 16 June 1894, 799 (with illustrations).
NOTE:

Eugen Sandow, the strong man, was enjoying extraordinary attention in the American press (only rivaled by heavy-weight boxing champ James J. Corbett and Buffalo Bill Cody), when he became the first important theatrical star to appear before Edison's kinetograph. Promoted as "the perfect man" and "the strongest man in the world," this predecessor to Arnold Schwarzenegger helped to launch the new commercial phase of Edison's motion picture endeavor. Many of the variety stars who subsequently performed at the Black Maria were, like Sandow, appearing at Koster & Bial's Music Hall and/or were under long-term contract to theater managers John Koster & Albert Bial. Articles document his American debut at the Casino Theatre in June, his enormously successful engagement at Koster & Bial's Music Hall, lasting from 11 December 1893 to 17 March 1894, and his well-publicized appearances at Edison's laboratory.

26 *Sandow / Eugen Sandow / [Sandow, no. 1]
LENGTH: 50 ft.   © William K.L. Dickson, 18 May 1894.
PRODUCER: W.K.L. Dickson.
CAMERA: William Heise.
CAST: Eugen[e] Sandow (Friedrich Müller).

PRODUCTION DATE: 6 March 1894.

LOCATION: Black Maria, West Orange, N.J.

SOURCE:

DESCRIPTION: The strongest man in the world, in his act, showing muscular movement, development, etc. (The Kinetoscope Company, *Edison's Latest Wonders: The Kinetograph, The Kinetoscope*, [October 1894].) "The Modern Hercules." (The Kinetoscope Company, *Bulletin No. 2*, January 1895.)

SUBJECT: Vaudeville–performances. Strong men. Germans.

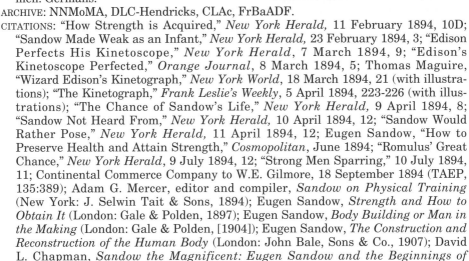

ARCHIVE: NNMoMA, DLC-Hendricks, CLAc, FrBaADF.

CITATIONS: "How Strength is Acquired," *New York Herald,* 11 February 1894, 10D; "Sandow Made Weak as an Infant," *New York Herald,* 23 February 1894, 3; "Edison Perfects His Kinetoscope," *New York Herald*, 7 March 1894, 9; "Edison's Kinetoscope Perfected," *Orange Journal*, 8 March 1894, 5; Thomas Maguire, "Wizard Edison's Kinetograph," *New York World*, 18 March 1894, 21 (with illustrations); "The Kinetograph," *Frank Leslie's Weekly*, 5 April 1894, 223-226 (with illustrations); "The Chance of Sandow's Life," *New York Herald,* 9 April 1894, 8; "Sandow Not Heard From," *New York Herald,* 10 April 1894, 12; "Sandow Would Rather Pose," *New York Herald,* 11 April 1894, 12; Eugen Sandow, "How to Preserve Health and Attain Strength," *Cosmopolitan*, June 1894; "Romulus' Great Chance," *New York Herald*, 9 July 1894, 12; "Strong Men Sparring," 10 July 1894, 11; Continental Commerce Company to W.E. Gilmore, 18 September 1894 (TAEP, 135:389); Adam G. Mercer, editor and compiler, *Sandow on Physical Training* (New York: J. Selwin Tait & Sons, 1894); Eugen Sandow, *Strength and How to Obtain It* (London: Gale & Polden, 1897); Eugen Sandow, *Body Building or Man in the Making* (London: Gale & Polden, [1904]); Eugen Sandow, *The Construction and Reconstruction of the Human Body* (London: John Bale, Sons & Co., 1907); David L. Chapman, *Sandow the Magnificent: Eugen Sandow and the Beginnings of Bodybuilding* (Urbana: University of Illinois Press, 1994).

NOTE: In his initial U.S. performance, Sandow began his show by posing under electric lights in a way that was closely duplicated in this motion picture. A portion of the film was copyrighted as *Souvenir Strip of the Edison Kinetoscope* on 18 May 1894.

26.1 √[**Sandow, no. 2**]

LENGTH: [50 ft.]   © No reg.

PRODUCER: W.K.L. Dickson.

CAMERA: William Heise.

CAST: Eugen[e] Sandow (Friedrich Müller).

PRODUCTION DATE: 6 March 1894.

LOCATION: Black Maria, West Orange, N.J.

SOURCE:

DESCRIPTION:

SUBJECT: Vaudeville–performances. Strong men. Germans.

ARCHIVE:

CITATIONS: *American Photography* (with illustrations), 1895, in Gordon Hendricks Papers.

NOTE:

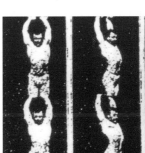

26.2 √[**Sandow, no. 3**]

LENGTH: [50 ft.]   © No reg.

PRODUCER: W.K.L. Dickson.

CAMERA: William Heise.

CAST: Eugen[e] Sandow (Friedrich Müller).

PRODUCTION DATE: 6 March 1894.
LOCATION: Black Maria, West Orange, N.J.
SOURCE:
DESCRIPTION:
SUBJECT: Vaudeville–performances. Strong men. Germans.
ARCHIVE:
CITATIONS: W.K.L. Dickson and Antonia Dickson, *History of the Kinetograph, Kinetoscope and Kineto-Phonograph*, 36 (with illustrations).
NOTE: Sandow used black hand weights for this film.

THE "STRONG MAN" APPEARS
Sandow Gives a Private Exhibition at the Casino.

Over 500 people were in the auditorium of the Casino last night to see a private entertainment given by Sandow, the "Strong Man." The invitations announced that a number of prominent physicians and surgeons would be present, and they probably were, but they were not conspicuous.

The curtain went up, revealing the stage steeped in gloom. Then, suddenly, two curtains at the back of the stage were drawn aside, in a blaze of light stood the "Strong Man," with his mighty muscles standing out in bold relief in the white glare of an electric light. After performing a number of "tableaux vivants," to the accompaniment of slow music and much perspiration, Mr. Sandow left his cabinet, the lights were turned up, and the show began in earnest. First Mr. Sandow toyed with fifty-six-pound dumbbells, which he tossed as if they were feathers, and then he turned his attention to an unfortunate "supe," and used him for a dumbbell for some moments.

An immense dumbbell 9 feet long, each bell being 4 feet in diameter, was carried on by four men and dropped on the stage. The men retired, mopping their foreheads. Then the "Strong Man" set the big dumbbell on end, essayed thrice to "put it up," and failed each time. Then he rested, tried again, and was successful. While the audience rapturously applauded, the bells at each end of the connecting bar were opened, and two warm and disheveled young men were dragged out. Mr. Sandow hung by his feet from an upright iron pole and made a right angle with it, with his body for a base, while he held two fifty-six-pound weights in his hands. Then he grabbed two unwary "supes" and again made a right angle, which he destroyed by suddenly letting his victims fall upon the stage.

As it was rather warm, Mr. Sandow refreshed himself by turning a few somersaults with his eyes bandaged and his legs tied, and then three horses were led in. "The audience is requested not to applaud while these animals are on the stage, as it scares 'em," announced a man who suddenly appeared from the wings and again disappeared like Kellar's "Vanishing Lady." Mr. Sandow had placed on his chest, as he got down on the floor, supported only by his legs and arms, a long and wide platform, and on this the horses–small, but heavy–played at see-saw. When it was over there was great applause. (*New York Times*, 12 June 1893, 5.)

SANDOW AT KOSTER AND BIAL'S.
A Remarkable Musico-Athletic Feat That Astonished the Spectators.

The bill presented at Koster and Bial's last evening was a capital one from end to end, and although the "chappies" did not have the pleasure of gazing on and listening to that well known London music hall singer, Miss Bessie Belwood, whose appearance has been postponed for a week, they were abundantly pleased with what the management provided them. The programme was too long to repeat here in detail, it can be dismissed with one fell swoop, as it were, as excellent; a much better congregation of entertainers than one finds on a single variety stage now-a-days.

The pièce-de-resistance of the evening was the muscular phenomenon Sandow, who accomplished several of his familiar feats of strength and introduced some new ones. The most astonishing was his final effort, an elaborate performance in which the cast of characters included Sandow, a Steinway grand piano, half a dozen stage hands, a Hungarian band, a stepladder, a pianist and a large wooden platform. This is how they worked the performance out. Sandow bent backwards till his hands and feet touched the floor; while in that position a large wooden platform about 5 by 10 feet was placed on his chest, steadied there by partly resting on his knees; six men place heavy wooden bars under a grand piano, lifted it above the platform, on which they then placed it carefully; a stepladder was placed alongside and the Hungarian Band, with most of their music scared out of them, ascended gingerly and stood on top of the piano, and incidentally on Sandow's chest; a pianist then crawled up into place and seating himself at the piano, the band accompanied by the pianist burst forth into the music of "Yankee Doodle" in a wild Hungarian way calculated to increase the difficulty of Herr Sandow's task and the terror of their own position. The men who had thus far been supporting the main weight with their poles withdrew them, leaving the combined burden of the piano, band, the pianist and "Yankee Doodle" on Sandow's mighty chest. He sustained it for a moment, while the house rang with cheers, and the curtain descended slowly on undoubtedly the greatest musico-athletic feat of its kind that has ever been witnessed in this city. A moment later he came before the curtain as fresh as ever and acknowledged the long continued applause in a delighted manner. What became of the band and the grand piano heaven and the management only know—when Sandow is though with the latter, to judge from last night's performance, it will probably be in condition to be sold cheap by "a widow unexpectedly obliged to leave for Europe." (*New York Herald*, 12 December 1893, 12.)

SANDOW PERFORMS NEW FEATS.

Two new feats were performed by Sandow at Koster & Bial's last night. The public have become familiar with his bearing upon his chest a platform upon which are three horses. This feat, while also on the programme, was supplemented by a similar though much more difficult performance. Resting his neck and heels upon two trestles, which were his only supports, he upheld upon his abdomen a platform and horse weighing 950 pounds. At the same time he held at arm's length two fifty-six pound dumb bells. The act seems the more wonderful from the fact that all the weight was sustained by the centre of his outstretched body while the support was by the extremities. The other new feature was barrel jumping and turning somersaults with fifty-six pounds in each hand.

The other attractions were Valican, Clown Jigg, Bonnie Thornton, Wood and Shepard, Mlle. Bertoldi, "Unthan." Mlle. Alcide Capitaine, Mlle. Arman d'Arcy, Mario and Dunham, and Les Frères Deltorelli. (*New York Herald*, 27 February 1894, 10.)

Sandow at the Edison Laboratory

A remarkable test of the kinetoscope was made on Wednesday at the Edison Laboratory, when the world-renowned Sandow, the strong man, came out from New York, and was photographed in a number of poses. He also went through various of his characteristic motions. Mr. Sandow was accompanied by Mr. Koster, of Koster & Bial's; C.B. Cline, the business manager of Koster & Bial, and Richard T. Haines, of the North American Phonograph Company. The party arrived at the Phonograph Works about 11 o'clock and were there met by William K.L. Dickson, head of the photo-kinetographic department of the laboratory, and head of the electric ore milling department as well. Extensive preparations had been made for the visit.

The exhibitions were all made in the new building which Mr. Dickson invented and built for the kinetoscopic experiments. This is a building 50x13, entirely lined with black tarred paper, giving the effect of a dead black tunnel behind the subject to be photographed. The building is poised on a graphite center so skillfully that it can be rotated on a turntable and keep the full sunlight turned on the subject. Mr. Edison was not present when the party arrived, having worked all night and lain down at 7:30 in the morning for needed rest. He reached the building soon after 12 o'clock and was introduced to Mr. Sandow. Sandow had previously stated that he would charge $250 for coming out to give the exhibition, but would gladly come for nothing for the privilege of shaking the hand of Edison, the greatest man of the age. Sandow was stripped to the waist so as to show the wonderful play of his muscles and his marvelous chest expansion. This was fourteen inches.

In addition to the kinetoscope, with which over three thousand pictures were taken in less than a minute and a half, an average of nearly forty-six a second, there was a battery of cameras on each side of the kinetoscope, with which special pictures of various poses were taken. These pictures varied from 4x5 to 14x17. One of the large pictures was one of Mr. Edison feeling Sandow's muscles with a curiously comical expression on his face. A funny scene was when Sandow asked Mr. Cline if he would mind being "chucked" out of the door for the benefit of the kinetoscope. Mr. Cline demurred but quicker than a flash Sandow caught him with one hand and sent him sailing through the air and out of the door. Unfortunately the whole thing was done so quickly that it could not be caught by the cameras. Sandow expressed his regret and said that he would have to bring out next time some man that liked to be "chucked." After the experiments were over Mr. Dickson made a group photograph of Mr. Edison, Sandow, Mr. Koster, Mr. Cline and Mr. Haines. The party were then driven to Davis's restaurant where a fine dinner had been served by Mr. Edison's orders. The latter could not accompany them, but Mr. Dickson did so as the personal representative of Mr. Edison. The dinner was a fine one and reflected great credit on Davis. Sandow gave an account of his life and how he had developed his phenomenal strength and Mr. Dickson gave a history of Mr. Edison's life and personality and his wonderful achievements.

The kinetograph has now been thoroughly perfected and placed on the market. This has been one of the chief objects at which Mr. Dickson has been at work for the past five years. He has succeeded in producing a light and portable instrument which can be readily taken around and catch novel objects everywhere over the world. Some of the details about the wonderful machine are interesting. The film is a sensitized one and tears along through the field of exposure at the rate of twenty-six miles an hour. The motion is not continuous but the film is at absolute rest during each exposure. When it is considered that these follow one another as above stated at the rate of forty-six in a second, and when it is further remembered that the film is at absolute rest nine-tenths of the time, the jump from one exposure to the next being in one-tenth of the time of the actual exposure, the marvelous accuracy of the machine and the lightning-like speed of the film can be appreciated.

Sandow and Mr. Cline came out again yesterday and were met by Mr. Dickson. They were driven to the home of Mr. Edison in Llewellyn Park, where they spent an hour or more. After taking a dinner at Davis's they went out for a drive.

Mr. Dickson then took his guests to his home on Cleveland street where the remainder of the afternoon was spent, Miss Antonia Dickson assisting her brother in entertaining and playing several selections on the piano. Last night Sandow was the guest of the Orange Camera Club at its dinner at Davis's and returned to New York on the 8:14 train. Mr. Dickson and his sister, Miss Antonia Dickson, have just finished a life of Mr. Edison, which will soon be given to the public. They are well qualified for the undertaking, Mr. Dickson having been associated with Mr. Edison for some thirteen years, ever since he was superintendent of his electrical works in New York, and during that time has been brought into close personal intimacy with him. (*Orange Chronicle*, 10 March 1894, 5.)

Dickson and Heise filmed blood sports of all kinds—boxing, dog fights, rat killing and cock fighting—during the first year of commercial production. Cockfights, a favorite subject, were shot several times between 1894 and 1896.

27 The Cock Fight / Cock Fight, no. 1 / Roosters
LENGTH: 50 ft.   © No reg.
PRODUCER: W.K.L. Dickson.
CAMERA: William Heise.
CAST:
PRODUCTION DATE: Early March 1894.
LOCATION: Black Maria, West Orange, N.J.
SOURCE:
DESCRIPTION:
SUBJECT: Cockfighting.
ARCHIVE:
CITATIONS: The Kinetoscope Company, *Bulletin No. 2*, January 1895.
NOTE:

Carmencita was the first woman to appear before Edison's motion picture camera. She first performed on the New York stage at Niblo's Garden on 17 August 1889, dancing in the ballet of Antiope. *She rose to fame under the management of Koster & Bial, who put her in their 23rd Street music hall commencing 10 February 1890. She had not danced on the New York stage for six months when she pirouetted in front of Edison's motion picture camera. During at least some of the 1893-94, season she toured with the Carmencita Royal Star Specialty Co. (Auditorium Theatre, Philadelphia: 14-19 May; Holliday Theatre, Baltimore: 21-16 May). She danced at the American Theatre Roof Garden in August, and returned to Koster & Bial's for the month of November 1894, before selling her furniture and moving back to Europe.*

28 *Carmencita
LENGTH: 50 ft.   © No reg.
PRODUCER: W.K.L. Dickson.
CAMERA: William Heise.
CAST: Carmencita.
PRODUCTION DATE: 10-16 March 1894.
LOCATION: Black Maria, West Orange, N.J.
SOURCE:
DESCRIPTION: The noted dancer, who goes through her grace-ful act exactly as she does at Koster & Bial's, New York. (The Kinetoscope Company, *Edison's Latest Wonders: The Kinetograph, The Kinetoscope*, [October 1894].)
Carmencita, the Spanish dancer, sways her graceful fig-ure and pirouettes with a whirl of flying skirts. (*London Daily Graphic*, 18 October 1894, TAEP, 146:195.)
The Spanish "Queen of Dancers." (The Kinetoscope Company, *Bulletin No. 1*, [December 1894].)
SUBJECT: Vaudeville–performances. Dancing. Spaniards.
ARCHIVE: DNA, DLC-Hendricks.
CITATIONS: "'Antiope' at Niblo's Garden," *New York Tribune*, 18 August 1889, 7; "Carmencita Reappears on the Stage," *New York Herald*, 14 August 1894, 12; Continental Com-

merce Company to W.E. Gilmore, 18 September 1894 (TAEP, 135:389); "Carmencita's Goods Went Cheap," *New York Herald,* 20 December 1894, 11.
NOTE:

Concerning Carmencita

Blacker than ever as to her hair and with her waist supple and springy as a split bamboo rod, Carmencita returned last evening to Koster & Bial's concert hall. She received a clamorous welcome that lasted till she had used every one of her smiles, half a dozen times over. Then she danced. Much nonsense has been written about this young Spaniard since the night, memorable to her, when a bald-headed newspaper man discovered her there and wrote a lyric composed all of adjectives ending in "est." Since then numberless columns have followed, some of hysterical commendation, others absurdly derisive—both undeserved.

The fact remains that Carmencita is curiously interesting. She replaces grace with an apparently untaught abandon rarer than grace. Possibly she likes to dance; she gives that impression, and therein lies the secret of her popularity. Nobody is like her, so she has no rivals. She suggests the Spain of old novels; she is impossible and admirable. (*New York Times*, 26 January 1892, 4.)

Carmencita will visit Orange next week and have her picture taken while she dances. (*Orange Journal*, 8 March 1894, 5.)

THE VAUDEVILLE FAD.

Carver B. Cline, owing to his former connection with the business department of Koster & Bial's Music Hall, is somewhat of an authority on the progress of the vaudeville fad in New York. Consequently he was hunted up recently by a Mirror representative and requested to hold forth on the subject.

"The vaudeville fad," said Mr. Cline, "so far as New York is concerned, may be said to date from Carmencita's first engagement at Koster & Bial's. Previous to that engagement society people never dreamed of patronizing a vaudeville performance. The only variety specialties they ever saw were those that were introduced in farce comedy productions. When Carmencita came to this country she first appeared under the Kiralfy's management at Niblo's as one of the premiere danseuses in the ballet of a spectacular production called *Antiope*. She attracted very little attention, but Koster & Bial's offered her an engagement.

"One evening a prominent journalist occupied a box at Koster & Bial's former music hall in Twenty-third Street, and was very much surprised at Carmencita's dancing. The following Sunday two columns about the new dancer appeared in a Sunday paper. Then the other papers took her up, and in less than a month she was the best advertised vaudeville star in America, and, mind you, without any attempt whatever to obtain press work in her behalf. Her popularity finally penetrated the exclusive circles of New York society, when she was invited to a swell reception at the studio of Chase, the artist. It became a fad to have Carmencita dance at the receptions of the Four Hundred, and society people made up parties to go and see her at Koster & Bial's. (*New York Dramatic Mirror*, 27 June 1896, 11.)

29 Wrestling Match
LENGTH: 50 ft.   © No reg.
PRODUCER: W.K.L. Dickson.
CAMERA: William Heise.
CAST: Petit, Kessler.
PRODUCTION DATE: By 1 April 1894.
LOCATION: Black Maria, West Orange, N.J.
SOURCE:
DESCRIPTION: Two men engaged in wrestling are shown in one of the series of illustrations that accompany the kinetoscope. They were photographed in the "Black Maria" by the kinetograph and the kinetoscope portrays the whole bout from beginning to end with every move that the wrestlers made. As the struggle carried them about over considerable space they were placed at quite a distance from the camera, and their figures are smaller than those of Sandow, which form another series of illustrations. ("Edison's Latest Invention," *Newark Daily Advertiser*, 7 April 1894, 7.)
  By Petit and Kessler. (F.Z. Maguire & Co., *Catalogue*, [March 1898], 33.)
SUBJECT: Sports. Wrestling.
ARCHIVE:
CITATIONS: Continental Commerce Company to W.E. Gilmore, 18 September 1894 (TAEP, 135:389). The Kinetoscope Company, *Bulletin No. 1*, [December 1894]; The Kinetoscope Company, *Price List of Films*, [May 1895], 2; Maguire & Baucus,

Edison and International Photographic Films, April 1897, 16; Maguire & Baucus, *Fall Catalogue*, 1897, 13.
NOTE: The wrestling film of Petit and Kessler may have been taken subsequent to the film described in the *Newark Daily Advertiser*.

Ena Bertoldi performed her contortions at Koster & Bial's Music Hall from 19 February until 12 May 1894, during which time she appeared before Edison's camera. She reappeared at the same venue for another long engagement, from 8 October to 1 December 1894. Despite her renown, she was never a headline attraction at Koster & Bial's theater—a level of recognition she received when at Keith's Union Square Theatre for the week of 10 December 1894.

30 Bertoldi (Table Contortion) / Bertoldi

LENGTH: 50 ft.   © No reg.
PRODUCER: W.K.L. Dickson.
CAMERA: William Heise.
CAST: Ena Bertoldi.
PRODUCTION DATE: Early March to early April 1894.
LOCATION: Black Maria, West Orange, N.J.
SOURCE:
DESCRIPTION: The Marvelous Lady Contortionist and Acrobat. (The Kinetoscope Company, *Bulletin No. 1*, [December 1894].)
SUBJECT: Vaudeville–performances. Acrobats.
ARCHIVE:

CITATIONS: Edison Phonograph Works to Continental Commerce Company, shipping order, 29 September 1894 (TAEP, 135:391); W.K.L. Dickson and Antonia Dickson, *History of the Kinetograph, Kinetoscope and Kineto-Phonograph*, 13 (with illustrations); H.J. Holmes, "A Queen of Contortionists," *Royal Magazine*, May 1899, 77-80. The Kinetoscope Company, *Price List of Films*, [May 1895], 2; Maguire & Baucus, *Edison and International Photographic Films*, April 1897, 5; Maguire & Baucus, *Fall Catalogue*, 1897, 11; F.Z. Maguire & Co., *Catalogue*, [March 1898], 27.
NOTE:

31 Bertoldi (Mouth Support)

LENGTH: 50 ft.   © No reg.
PRODUCER: W.K.L. Dickson.
CAMERA: William Heise.
CAST: Ena Bertoldi.
PRODUCTION DATE: Early March to early April 1894.
LOCATION: Black Maria, West Orange, N.J.
SOURCE:
DESCRIPTION:
SUBJECT: Vaudeville–performances. Aerialists. Acrobats.
ARCHIVE:
CITATIONS: Edison Phonograph Works to Continental Commerce Company, shipping order, 29 September 1894 (TAEP, 135:391); W.K.L. Dickson and Antonia Dickson, A *History of the Kinetograph, Kinetoscope and Kineto-Phonograph*, 13 (with illustrations).
NOTE:

ENA BERTOLDI.

This graceful littlest contortionist, whose equal in point of neatness, refinement, and finish of her act is hardly to be found, was born in Sheffield, Eng., in 1876. Her father is Thomas Claxton, a noted gymnast and trainer. Little Ena showed a remarkable liking for the work performed by her father and practiced all sorts of body twists and close bends at an early age.

Under her father's tuition she advanced so rapidly that in 1882 she made her professional debut at the Royal Amphitheatre, Portsmouth, doing the most difficult tricks with perfect ease. She subsequently appeared at Hengler's Grand Circus, Ginnett's Circus, Sanger's Circus, Meyer's Circus, the Crystal Palace and in the leading music and exhibition halls of London and the provinces. In 1891 John D. Hopkins engaged her through Mr. Claxton, now acting as her manager, for the Howard Athenaeum Specialty Co., and she made her first appearance in America at Stamford, Ct., Aug. 29, 1891, with that company. The following Monday, Aug. 31, she opened with the company at Tony Pastor's Theatre, New York, and created a sensation. She traveled with Mr. Hopkins' organization for two seasons, filling in dates at the leading variety theatres in and around New York during the summer. Miss Bertoldi is at present filling a twelve weeks' engagement at Koster & Bial's, New York, which fact attests the value of her act in pleasing the patrons of that resort. Many new tricks are introduced by the industrious performer, all of the difficult hand and teeth balancing being executed by her with the utmost ease. The apparatus she employs is of the most attractive kind, and the act in its entirety is a bright feature of the programme. The present engagement will shortly close, and will be followed by one at B.F. Keith's Philadelphia and Boston houses. Personally Miss Bertoldi is slightly built, with a fine, expressive face and well proportioned figure. She is a charming conversationalist and an accomplished musician. (*New York Clipper*, 5 May 1894, 129.)

32 Trapeze

LENGTH: 50 ft. © No reg.
PRODUCER: W.K.L. Dickson.
CAMERA: William Heise.
CAST: [Alcide Capitaine?]
PRODUCTION DATE: Early March to early April 1894.
LOCATION: Black Maria, West Orange, N.J.
SOURCE:
DESCRIPTION:
SUBJECT: Vaudeville–performances. Aerialists.
ARCHIVE:
CITATIONS:
NOTE: It is possible that Alcide Capitaine was the performer appearing in *Trapeze*, given her association with Koster & Bial's. If this had been the case, however, the film would probably have been identified by her name—as was the case with *Sandow* and *Carmencita* (see *Mlle Capitaine*, no. 87).

33 √Highland Dance / Scotch Reel

LENGTH: 50 ft. © No reg.
PRODUCER: W.K.L. Dickson.
CAMERA: William Heise.
CAST:
PRODUCTION DATE: Early March to early April 1894.
LOCATION: Black Maria, West Orange, N.J.
SOURCE:

DESCRIPTION: Shows Laddie and Lassie Dancing, in Costume. (The Kinetoscope Company, *Edison's Latest Wonders: The Kinetograph, The Kinetoscope,* [October 1894].)
The pictures, sixty-five of them, show a Scotch lad and lassie dancing a reel. In the No. 1 there is the beginning of it. Both figures are on their feet. They are not dancing yet. The introductory bars of the music, the bagpipes, have just started. Look at No. 3. The man has his left foot a trifle raised from the floor, but the woman has not. Her arms begin to rise in the No. 2, 5, 6, and 7, and the man is about turning. In the No. 10 he has struck his dancing gait. Necessarily he can't hop around on the same foot all the time, and so he is putting that foot on the floor, so as to get another spring. That foot comes to the floor in the No. 13.
The dancer is ready now to take his partner and to spin her round, and she shows that she is preparing

for that. In No. 18, you will see what was at first but a slight bending of her knee becomes more marked than in No. 16. In Nos. 17 and 18 she is jigging it. No. 19 shows the turning round of the figures at its commencement. The scarf of the man in No. 18, as the movement is getting to be more rapid, is beginning to stream out. Do not forget to watch the shadows, because they vary all the time with the position of the figures.

In the No. 20 the positive change of place is marked. It is the man in No. 25 who has now his back to you. The lassie is hidden, all but her hand and wrist, where she has them on his shoulder.

From Nos. 27 to 40 the lady is coming more and more to the front. The man is now entirely to the right, and the woman to the left. They have changed places after 42. They are to resume their first positions. In the whirl, see the movement of the scarf of both the dancers. They dance faster and faster, until in No. 61 they are about as when they started. The spin is rapid, because the woman's skirt indicates that. What the prints do not show are the shuffle of the feet of the dancers, and how they mark the time; the graceful sway of the figures, or how they rise and fall, following the musical rhythm; or how the feathers in the man's bonnet bob up and down; or the changing expressions on the faces of the lad and lassie.

Place the pictures in the Edison box, however; start the machinery, and the actual movement is all there. Man and woman caper away, heel and toe, and there is no flagging. It is just as vivid as if it were a performance on the stage and you saw it from the boxes. (*Harper's Young People* 15, 22 May 1894, 500.)

SUBJECT: Dancing. Scots.

ARCHIVE:

CITATIONS: Edison Phonograph Works to Continental Commerce Company, shipping order, 29 September 1894 (TAEP, 135:391). The Kinetoscope Company, *Bulletin No. 1*, [December 1894].

NOTE:

The first kinetoscope parlor opened on 14 April 1894 at 1155 Broadway, New York City. Films sent to be shown in the storefront's ten machines were listed as follows: "Sandow," "Horse Shoeing," "Barber Shop," "Bertoldi (Mouth Support)," "Wrestling," "Bertoldi (Table Contortion)," "Blacksmiths," "Highland Dance," "Trapeze," and "Roosters." (Bill for first films, 14 April 1894, in Gordon Hendricks, The Kinetoscope, 56.)

34 √Organ Grinder, [no. 1]

LENGTH: 50 ft.   © No reg.

PRODUCER: W.K.L. Dickson.

CAMERA: William Heise.

CAST:

PRODUCTION DATE: By May 1894.

LOCATION: Black Maria, West Orange, N.J.

SOURCE:

DESCRIPTION:

SUBJECT: Street music and musicians. Organ grinders. Monkeys. Italians.

ARCHIVE:

CITATIONS: W.K.L. Dickson and Antonia Dickson, "Edison's Invention of the Kineto-Phonograph," *Century Magazine*, June 1894, 211 (with illustrations).

NOTE:

35 √Organ Grinder, [no. 2]

LENGTH: 50 ft.   © No reg.

PRODUCER: W.K.L. Dickson.

CAMERA: William Heise.

CAST:

PRODUCTION DATE: By May 1894.

LOCATION: Black Maria, West Orange, N.J.

SOURCE:

DESCRIPTION:

SUBJECT: Street music and musicians. Organ grinders. Monkeys. Italians.

ARCHIVE:

CITATIONS: W.K.L. Dickson and Antonia Dickson, "Edison's Invention of the Kineto-Phonograph," *Century Magazine*, June 1894, 211 (with illustrations).

NOTE:

36 [Trained Bears]

LENGTH: 50 ft.   © No reg.

PRODUCER: W.K.L. Dickson.

CAMERA: William Heise.

CAST:

PRODUCTION DATE: By 25 May 1894.

LOCATION: Black Maria, West Orange, N.J.

SOURCE:

DESCRIPTION:

SUBJECT: Circus animals. Bears. Animal trainers. Hungarians.

ARCHIVE:

CITATIONS:

NOTE: This film was sold in Italy as *Orsi ammaestrati*. (Continental Phonograph Kinetoscope Company, *Kinetoscenes*, [March 1895].)

One day chronicled the engagement of a troupe of trained bears and their Hungarian leaders. The bears were divided between surly discontent and a comfortable desire to follow the bent of their own inclinations. It was only after much persuasion that they could be induced to subserve the interests of science. One furry-monster waddled up a telegraph pole to the soliloquy of his own indignant growls; another settled himself comfortably in a deep arm-chair, with the air of a post-graduate in social science; a third rose solemnly on his hind legs and described the measures of some dance, to the weird strains of his keeper's music. Another licked his master's swarthy face, another accepted his keeper's challenge, and engaged him in a wrestling match, struggling, hugging, and rolling on the ground. (W.K.L. Dickson and Antonia Dickson, "Edison's Invention of the Kineto-Phonograph," *Century Magazine*, June 1894, 212.)

37 *A Bar Room Scene / [Bar Room Scene, no. 1]

LENGTH: 50 ft.   © No reg.

PRODUCER: W.K.L. Dickson.

CAMERA: William Heise.

CAST:

PRODUCTION DATE: By May 1894.

LOCATION: Black Maria, West Orange, N.J.

SOURCE:

DESCRIPTION: The only thing unusual about the bar was that the bar-tender was a girl—an unusual thing in the States. A loafer is hanging over the bar, drinking (not so unusual), and making a movement to help himself. The girl's mouth opens to

remonstrate, her hand flies to the glasses—which are falling onto the ground. In a second a stalwart potman appears on the scene and closes with the loafer; there is a struggle, joined presently by a police-constable, and the loafer is thrown out of the bar with the promptitude and energy of a Maxim gun. The potman returns with a smile on his face and turning down his sleeves. The girl behind the bar replaces the glasses. (*London Daily Graphic*, 18 October 1894, TAEP, 146:195.)

Showing the wind-up of a political discussion. Dramatis Personae: A Democrat, a Republican, a Bar Maid, and a Policeman. (The Kinetoscope Company, *Bulletin No. 1*, [December 1894].)

SUBJECT: Taverns, etc. Alcoholic beverages. Politics, practical. Police. Violence.

ARCHIVE: CLAc.

CITATIONS: Edison Phonograph Works, to Maguire & Baucus, shipping order, 13 August 1894 (TAEP, 135:378); *The Photographic Times*, January 1895, 23 (with illustrations).

NOTE: The illustration appearing in *The Photographic Times* is flipped.

French chanteuse Armand 'Ary had her American debut at Koster & Bial's Music Hall on 19 February 1894 (after a week's delay due to illness). She was received enthusiastically and performed there through 14 April. During this time, or shortly thereafter, she appeared before Edison's camera.

38 Armand D'Ary [sic] / Armand 'Arry [sic] / Armand 'Ary

LENGTH: 50 ft.   © No reg.

PRODUCER: W.K.L. Dickson.

CAMERA: William Heise.

CAST: Armand 'Ary or Arman D'Ary (stage name for Marthe Armandary or Mme du Plessy).

PRODUCTION DATE: Mid-March to May 1894.

LOCATION: Black Maria, West Orange, N.J.

SOURCE:

DESCRIPTION: French Danseuse and Chanteuse. Pantomine, Song, etc. (The Kinetoscope Company, *Edison's Latest Wonder: The Kinetograph, The Kinetoscope*, [October 1894].)

SUBJECT: Vaudeville–performances. Dancing. French.

ARCHIVE:

CITATIONS: Edison Phonograph Works, to Maguire & Baucus, shipping order, 13 August 1894 (TAEP, 135:378). The Kinetoscope Company, *Bulletin No. 1*, [December 1894].

NOTE:

MLLE. D'ARY AT KOSTER & BIAL'S.

Yet another "chanteuse Parisienne" appeared at Koster & Bial's last evening. This débutante was Mlle. Armand Ary, from Les Folies Bergères. She is one of the daintiest little chansonnette singers imaginable. Her four selections were remarkably bright, gayly rhythmical, full of subtle humor and–mirabile dictu!–entirely free from vulgarity. Mlle. Ary is a miniature Vanoni and has an exceedingly captivating style that is as chic as she is pretty, and that is saying a great deal. After Mlle. Ary's last chanson two superb baskets of roses and several enormous bouquets artistically arranged and decorated with the French colors were handed across the footlights to the clever young singer, who received them with the prettiest little gesture of thanks to the audience....(*New York Herald*, 20 February 1894, 10.)

The costumes and effects of Armand 'Ary were held under writ of attachment, Feb. 27, at Koster & Bial's, and were only released in time for her to make her appearance at the evening's performance. The difficulty grows out of a suit brought by Rudolph Aronson against Mlle. 'Ary, or Mme. du Plessy, as she is known in private life, in the City Court to recover 2,000f. Mr. Aronson engaged Mlle. 'Ary to sing at the Casino roof garden during last July. He was to pay her 3,000f in advance, but he sent only 2,000f. Of this Rosinsky, the Paris agent through whom the engagement was made, took 800f., his commission for the whole engagement. The remaining 1,200f Mlle. 'Ary put in her own pocket, and then cabled Mr. Aronson she could not come to this country unless he sent the other 1,000f. When Mlle. 'Ary arrived here a few weeks ago, Mr. Aronson made a formal demand upon her for a return of his money, and offered to settle the matter for 1,200f. Mlle. 'Ary declined to pay and claimed that Mr. Aronson had broken the contract by not advancing the whole 3,000f and had forfeited the 2,000f. The case has not yet been settled. (*New York Clipper*, 10 March 1894, 7.)

ARMAND' ARY'S CHANSONS.
The Clever Little Frenchwoman Gives Capital Burlesques of Well Known Variety Singers.

Mimetic as a dainty little monkey is Armand' Ary! This latest addition to the long list of "chanteuses Parisiennes" who have sung–Heaven save the mark!–danced and kicked their way into popularity at Koster & Bial's is one of the drollest, the most characteristic, the most original of them all. You see arrive upon the stage a tiney, svelte figure. There is about her something of a bashful air, as of a schoolgirl. And yet there is such an odd look of good natured malice which flashes from the pretty brown eyes from time to time that you are undecided whether Mlle. Armand' Ary is only a novice or a very cunning little actress. But you are not long in doubt. When you hear her mimic Paulus–for not even the "creator of 'le brav' Général'" is sacred to this comical little creature–when you have seen her burlesque the coquettish manner of "les belles Americaines," when you have watched her walk like Paquerette, kick like Fougere, dance like Carmencita, talk like an Englishman and make love like an Italian you are quite satisfied that Armand' Ary is a type that reunites all other types in this line.

ALWAYS IMITATIVE.

"I have sung ever since I was so high," said she the other day, holding her hand a couple of feet above the floor. "I have always been imitative and fond of mimicking every one who had any distinctive features. It was this faculty that suggested my chanson 'Les Universels Gestes,' which I 'create' at the Eldorado de Paris," and with the unctuous accent characteristic of "une Bordelaise," Mlle Armand' Ary began to sing:–

> Puisqu'l'on met tout en chanson,
> Je vais vous peindre sans façon
> De Paris toutes les allures.
> Et de ses phrases les tournures.
> J'ai pendant l'Exposition
> Croqué les types de chaque nation.
> Et comme j'avais des aptitudes
> Voici l'résultat d'mes études!

Then followed a series of the most laughable burlesque salutations. There was the courtly greeting, the form of salutation common in Turkey, in Armenia, in China. The "gommeux" was gayly satirized. Even Grossmith might have learned a thing or two if he had seen Mlle. Armand' Ary's version of the greeting extended by a New York "dude" to one of his fellows, and the series wound up with an imitation of the salutation given by a "gamin de Paris" that was the apotheosis of Rue St. Antoine drollery. Then comes the turn of the popular singers in Paris. Listen!

> Anna Thibant chante com[m]e ceci:
> "Vite son mari lui pose
> Un petit rigolo."
> Puis aux danseurs on crie ainsi,
> Paula Brebion chante comme ça:
> "C'est à Chaton qu'c'est arrivé.
> Gniouf! gniouf! Petif, petaf!
> C'est à Chaton qu'c'est arrivé
> Petif, petaf! la brigue don! dal!"
> L'élégant Kam Bill chante comme ça:
> "Car la lune éclairait au loin
> Le tricorne du garde champêtre."
> Le gommeux de Libert chante ainsi:
> "Elle m'envoie des postillons!
> En toutes les saisons."

With a mischievous twinkle in her eye, as though the imitation carried with it some subtle joke, Armand' Ary closes with a charicature of Paulus that is perfect–even the famous handkerchief is not forgotten, nor the good service to which it is put by the perspiring "comique" after each verse.

LIKE QUICKSILVER.

Such a volatile creature is this Armand' Ary, who, in her native Bordeaux is Mlle. Marthe Armandary. She is like quicksilver. Every phrase is illustrated by a gesture that is full of meaning, almost every word is accentuated with a toss of the head, a wicked little wink or a delicious grimace. There is the suggestion of an impudent tilt to the nose that adds a most piquant look of *gaminerie* to what is a remarkably pretty face. Her stay in London has taught her a few scraps of English, which she drags in at the most inopportune moments with the greatest air of naiveté. And how Armand' Ary talks! What a frank little chatterbox she is! "I hate costumes that don't display 'la forme,'" she said, pointing to a photograph of La Carmencita in a loose, voluminous robe. "Such a dress would make me feel as though I were a mummy." And then she laughed merrily at the idea of a mummy singing some of the sparkling little chansonnettes she sings every night. (*New York Herald*, 4 March 1894, 7D.)

Jack McAuliffe was the light-weight boxing champion of the world, and his activities were frequently reported in the sports pages of city newspapers. His appearance before Edison's camera was never shown commercially.

39 √**Boxing**
LENGTH: 50 ft.   © No reg.

PRODUCER: W.K.L. Dickson.
CAMERA: William Heise.
CAST: Jack McAuliffe.
PRODUCTION DATE: By May 1894.
LOCATION: Black Maria, West Orange, N.J.
SOURCE:
DESCRIPTION:
SUBJECT: Sports. Boxing.
ARCHIVE:
CITATIONS: "The Kineto-Phonograph," *Electrical World,*
16 June 1894, 799; "M'Auliffe Writes a Letter," *New
York Herald,* 30 August 1894, 10; "Talking of the
Match," *New York Herald,* 5 October 1894, 10.
NOTE:

JACK McAULIFFE.

GRIFFO AND M'AULIFFE FIGHT.

If the statements of turfmen who were detained at the Gravesend race
track until after eight o'clock on Tuesday evening are true, "Jack"
McAuliffe and Young Griffo, the pugilists, had an exciting rally there at
close quarters. The stories told by those who claim to have witnessed
the fight is that McAuliffe and the Australian feather weight champion
met in the barroom under the grand stand and pounded each other very hard before friends interfered and separated them. It is said that McAuliffe had been drinking heavily and was in a fighting mood when the last race was over. Somebody told "Mac" that Griffo was on the track and was looking for him, as the story goes, and "Jack" started out to find Griffo. When they met each made a pass and then they "mixed it," in a lively fashion. Griffo was finally taken off the track and McAuliffe and his friends retired to the wineroom, where another free-for-all fight took place before the party broke up. McAuliffe was pretty badly used up it is said. (*New York Herald,* 17 May 1894, 9.)

*The carefully orchestrated encounter between Michael Leonard and Jack Cushing
yielded the first boxing films produced for commercial exhibition. The six-round affair
was made for presentation in specially constructed, oversized kinetoscopes designed to
handle almost 150 feet of film (in comparison to the regular kinetoscopes which handled strips of less than 50 feet). These fight films were made for the Kinetoscope
Exhibiting Company controlled and operated by Samuel Tilden, Jr., Enoch Rector, and
the Latham family (Otway, Gray and their father Woodville).*

40 ***Leonard-Cushing Fight**
LENGTH: 6 films of 150 ft. each.   © No reg.
PRODUCER: W.K.L. Dickson, Kinetoscope Exhibiting Company.
CAMERA: William Heise.
CAST: Michael "Mike" Wellington Leonard, Jack Cushing.
PRODUCTION DATE: 14 June 1894.
LOCATION: Black Maria, West Orange, N.J.
SOURCE:
DESCRIPTION: This fight consists of six rounds between Mike Leonard, the very popular
and well-known pugilist, commonly called the "Beau Brummel" of pugilism, and
Jack Cushing. It was an actual contest,
and is full of hard fighting. It has proved
a popular and interesting subject. It is
sold by rounds, and the titles are 1st
round, 2d round, 3d round, 4th round,
5th round and 6th round. 150 feet only.
(F.Z. Maguire & Co., *Catalogue,* [March
1898], 15.)
SUBJECT: Sports. Boxing.
ARCHIVE: CLAc, UkLNFA, Big Fights, Inc.
CITATIONS: "Fight for Edison," *New York
Journal,* 16 June 1894 (TAEP, 146:0903).

Maguire & Baucus, *Edison and International Photographic Films*, April 1897, 19; Maguire & Baucus, *Fall Catalogue*, 1897, 15; *Edison Films*, March 1900, 27; *Edison Films*, July 1901, 51.

NOTE: CLAc and UkLNFA each have only one round of this match, but they appear to be different rounds.

JACK CUSHING'S WATERLOO
Michael Wellington Leonard Dallies with His Corpus That Posterity May Learn What Action's Like.
EDISON WAS THE FRAME-HOLDER.
'Twas a Rattling Bout, the Kinetoscope Will Have It, at Ten Cents a Round, and All Will Be Edified.

Thomas A. Edison weighs about 185 pounds and has invented a machine called the kinetograph, which takes forty-six photographs in a second. Michael Leonard and Jack Cushing weigh 130 pound each and are prize-fighters. Yesterday morning while they fought a prize-fight in real, solemn, bloody earnest, Thomas A. Edison photographed them with his machine while he and six scientific friends looked on.

It was a very strange and unusual fight. The ring only 12 feet square, was arranged in Edison's laboratory. It had to be a small ring so that the photographing machine might be able to take it all in. Such a fight has rarely been seen. Mr. Mike Leonard, the same who paid $60 for his paddock coat, said that he would not fight for $35, which was offered to him originally, but that he would fight for $150 and all his expenses. He insisted that any unfortunate who should be put up against him should receive $50 for his pluck and endurance.

The rounds were to last one minute only. That was necessary, as the kinetograph could not be arranged to work more than one minute at a time. There were to be six rounds, and between each round the men were to rest seven minutes while the men in charge of the kinetograph prepared it to receive new impressions.

In every second of every sixty-second round the marvellous kinetograph made forty-six photographs. It made a series of 16,560 photographs, in all measuring 900 feet in length. These photographs will be put into the kineto-scope, which will be divided off into separate rounds. The man who wishes to look will pay ten cents for each round, beginning with the first. The theory is that when in the first round he sees Mr. Leonard, to use his own language, "pushing Mr. Cushing in the face," he will want to see the next round and the next four. Thus he will pay 60 cents for the complete kinetograph of the strange and unheard of fight.

It began very early in the morning. Since Monday Mr. Leonard, whose fame is world wide, has been walking about in his paddock coat, and Mr. Cushing, who is brave but unknown, had been eyeing him from a distance. They were waiting for a good day with such light and atmosphere as would best suit the kinetograph. The fighting began in earnest from the start. Mr. Leonard, who had put his paddock coat with the velvet cuffs on a chair where he could see it, felt that he of all the world's prize-fighters was to be the first to be made immortal and Mr. Cushing, proud and ambitious as all young men should be, hoped that fame and the kinetograph would hand him down as a knock-er-out of Mr. Leonard. If such a thing could be.

Each noble fighter had a trusty friend to act as second. Mr. Edison, in the good old days when he had very little money and a great deal of health, used to sit in the "mule pen" in Harry Hill's place in Houston street to hear ladies sing and watch fighters fight. There he saw John L. Sullivan as a mere boy break the proud spirits of sea-soned fighters and beheld Paddy Ryan of the weak knees and shining locks starring as well as he could. Mr. Edison was well fitted to supervise a prize-fight and see that all was fair and right.

The most interesting thing was the automatic time keeper. The kinetograph was selected to fill that office. It could go on taking pictures for just one minute and no longer. When the minute was ended the kinetograph man was to announce the fact and the round was to stop. Mr. Leonard, whose full name, Michael Wellington Leonard, was embroidered on his shirts and socks and stamped on his underclothes, remarked that it was a weird and unheard of fight and had many strange points about it: he doubted whether his new Brooklyn backer would like to see him in it, be he worried especially on account of young Mr. Cushing, against whom he had nothing, but whom he must severely punish in the interest of science and future ages.

Mr. Cushing, a man of few words and a very plain face, remarked: "Mike, if you could fight like you can talk, Corbett and Sullivan would be dead [and] you'd be tried for murder."

The story as it proceeds will show why Mr. Cushing rued these words.

Mr. Edison and the six wise men whom he had invited had comfortable chairs, and at first discussed only the kine-tograph, pretending that the fight was nothing to them. But as the battle went on they left those chairs, and their scientific manners vanished. Mr. Edison tossed his long locks out of his eyes and imitated every movement of the fighters. Sometimes he dashed his forehead forward as Mr. Leonard reached for Mr. Cushing's ear, and sometimes he twitched his mouth to one side as Mr. Leonard ducked to avoid Cushing's vengeance. All the six wise men did the same, and their excitement was proper and natural. The result of this kinetographic battle showed that a rest of seven minutes between one-minute rounds was a great and glorious idea. Instead of being only six rounds, it was six fights of one-minute each.

The seven minutes between rounds enabled the heroic gladiators to recover their breath and start to work each time fresh and nimble as though nothing had happened. The ignorant should not despise the six fights because they only lasted a minute. Whoever has fought knows that one minute is a long time to keep at it.

Until the kinetoscope is in working order the true story of this night will not be known, for Mr. Edison and the six wise men were too excited to remember just what happened, and the accounts of the two fighters vary. Mr. Leonard, whose word in Brooklyn is considered as valuable as that of Mr. Schleren, said only this: "I hit him when I liked and where I liked. I'd hit him oftener, only Mr. Edison treated me right, and I didn't want to be too quick for his machine."

"I generally hit 'im in the face, because I felt sorry for his family and thought I would select the only place that couldn't be disfigured. It's lucky the rounds lasted only a minute, for while I tried to spare him, of course I couldn't keep all my strength in."

Mr. Cushing, who has no paddock coat, but whose language is as simple and direct as that of Robinson Crusoe, said that in his opinion fighting in front of a photographing machine was no fight at all.

"I've got so in the habit of being tin-typed at Coney Island," he said, "that I felt as if I ought to keep a pleasant expression all the time. Once or twice while I was trying to get that expression on I went into a trance and Mike hit me, but he is not very strong. His tailor in Williamsburg charges him $3 extra for padding his shoulders, and that's what enables him to get a backer. But he's not muscular enough to fold towels in a Turkish bath."

The six fights of one minute each were full of movement but free from gore. When they were done the six wise men decided that Mr. Leonard had won the fight, but there was no knock out. It is only fair to Mr. Cushing to remark that before the judgment was given to Mr. Leonard he had put on his paddock coat with the velvet cuffs. Mr. Cushing, whose mind runs largely to persiflage, accepted his humble remuneration and said only this:

"Mike had this job put up, and I've no doubt the photograph machine was fixed, but if it takes pictures like they say, everybody that looks at it will think it's a statue of me with my fist in the pit of Mike's stomach.

"Say, Mike had his stage name in red painted on the pit of his shirt. You can put it down that he'll need a nail brush to wash that name off his stomach. I bet I hit it often enough to print it there. I took it as my mark."

Mr. Leonard and Mr. Cushing went back to Brooklyn together. (*New York World*, 16 June 1894, 1.)

JACK CUSHING KNOCKED OUT.

SIOUX FALLS, S.D., OCT. 9, 1894.–Teddy Gallagher of Sioux Falls, knocked out Jack Cushing, of Brooklyn, in three rounds at an early hour this morning. The fight took place on the open prairie in Lincoln county, eight miles from here, in the presence of two hundred persons. The fight was for $250, with two ounce gloves. Gallagher had the best of it from the start. (*New York Herald*, 10 October 1894, 11.)

Numerous acts featured trained dogs and cats on the vaudeville circuit in the 1890s. In New York City, Prof. J.W. Hampton's Boxing Cats, "James Corbett" and "Charles Mitchell," appeared at Proctor's in December 1893. Hampton's cats "Corbett" and "Jackson" (named for Corbett's newest challenger) boxed at Pastor's vaudeville house for the week beginning 11 June 1894 and Keith's Union Square Theatre for the week of 26 August 1894. Prof. Henry Welton and his cat circus appeared at Huber's 14th Street Museum in May and June, about the time they traveled to Orange to perform for Edison's camera. After appearing before Edison's kinetograph, Prof. Welton's Trained Cat Circus appeared at the Terrace Roof Garden for week beginning 23 July 1894, Proctor's Theatre for the week beginning 17 September 1894, and at Tony Pastor's for week beginning 8 October 1894. Welton was thus engaged by a higher class of theater after his motion picture appearance.

41 *The Boxing Cats (Prof. Welton's)

LENGTH: 50 ft.   © No reg.

PRODUCER: W.K.L. Dickson.

CAMERA: William Heise.

CAST: Henry Welton.

PRODUCTION DATE: By mid-July 1894.

LOCATION: Black Maria, West Orange, N.J.

SOURCE:

DESCRIPTION: An interesting film for children. (Maguire & Baucus, *Edison and International Photographic Films*, April 1897, 4.)

A glove contest between trained cats. A very comical and amusing subject, and is

sure to create a great laugh. (*Edison Films*, March 1900, 26.)

SUBJECT: Vaudeville–performances. Boxing. Circus animals. Animal trainers. Cats. Animal fighting. Burlesque. Prof. Henry Welton's Cat Circus.

ARCHIVE: FrBaADF, NNMoMA, DLC-Hendricks, CLAc.

CITATIONS: *Newark Evening News*, 17 July 1894; Continental Commerce Company to W.E. Gilmore, 18 September 1894 (TAEP, 135:389). The Kinetoscope Company, *Bulletin No. 1*, [December 1894]; Maguire & Baucus, *Edison Films*, 20 January 1897, 6; Maguire & Baucus, *Fall Catalogue*, 1897, 11; F.Z. Maguire & Co., *Catalogue*, [March 1898], 33.

NOTE:

42 The Wrestling Dog

LENGTH: 50 ft.   © No reg.

PRODUCER: W.K.L. Dickson.

CAMERA: William Heise.

CAST: Henry Welton.

PRODUCTION DATE: By mid-July 1894.

LOCATION: Black Maria, West Orange, N.J.

SOURCE:

DESCRIPTION: Wrestles with his trainer. (The Kinetoscope Company, *Bulletin No. 1*, [December 1894].)

SUBJECT: Vaudeville–performances. Wrestling. Circus animals. Animal trainers. Dogs. Burlesque. Prof. Henry Welton's Cat Circus.

ARCHIVE:

CITATIONS: *Newark Evening News*, 17 July 1894; Edison Phonograph Works to Maguire & Baucus, shipping order, 13 August 1894 (TAEP, 135:378).

NOTE: See also filmographic entries for Ivan Tschernoff's Trained Dogs (nos. 81 and 82).

TERRACE GARDEN. Welton's cat circus was the feature of the entertainment and a large audience enjoyed the antics of the intelligent felines. (*New York Herald*, 24 July 1894, 7.)

Central Opera House–Henry Welten [sic] presented a troupe of well-trained cats, and their curious exhibitions of sagacity were accorded good applause. (*New York Clipper*, 29 September 1894, 472.)

Prof. Welton's Trained Cats
Cats Who Ride Bicycles
Cats Who Turn Somersaults
Cats Who Walk Through Fire
Cats Who Box Like Men

(Advertisement for Tony Pastor's Theatre, *New York Herald*, 7 October 1894, 8C.)

Tony Pastor's....Prof. Henry Welton's trained cats closed the evening's entertainment in clever style. (*New York Clipper*, 13 October 1894.)

Ruth Dennis, billed as the "Graceful Dancer and Wonderful High Kicker," appeared at Keith's Union Square Theatre for the week beginning 25 June 1894. Generally going by the simple stage name of "Ruth," she apparently performed at Madison Square Roof Garden for the following two weeks and then at the American Theatre (as "Ruth, acrobatic dancer") for a week. Sometime during the summer, the youthful vaudevillian, who was born in Newark, N.J., traveled to Orange and danced for Edison's kinetograph. Ten years later, at the behest of David Belasco, she would change her name to Ruth St. Denis and eventually went on to become an important figure in the American modern dance movement.

43 Ruth Dennis

LENGTH: 50 ft.   © No reg.

PRODUCER: W.K.L. Dickson.

CAMERA: William Heise.

CAST: Ruth Dennis (Ruth St. Denis).

PRODUCTION DATE: [Mid-July 1894.]

LOCATION: Black Maria, West Orange, N.J.

SOURCE:

DESCRIPTION: Said to be the Champion High Kicker of the World. (The Kinetoscope Company, *Bulletin No. 1*, [December 1894].)

SUBJECT: Vaudeville–performances. Dancing.

ARCHIVE:

CITATIONS: Edison Phonograph Works to Continental Commerce Company, shipping order, 29 September 1894 (TAEP, 135:391).

NOTE:

Frank Kissell, the lightning drillist who subsequently adopted the stage name of Hadj Lessik, performed at Keith's Union Square Theatre for the week beginning 11 December 1893 and on the American Roof Garden for the week beginning 9 July 1894. It is possible that he traveled to Orange and performed for the kinetograph at the time of this second engagement.

44 Whirlwind Gun Spinning / [Kissell]

LENGTH: 50 ft.   © No reg.

PRODUCER: W.K.L. Dickson.

CAMERA: William Heise.

CAST: Hadj L[l]essik (Frank Kissell).

PRODUCTION DATE: [Mid-July 1894.]

LOCATION: Black Maria, West Orange, N.J.

SOURCE:

DESCRIPTION:

SUBJECT: Vaudeville–performances. Juggling. Arabs.

ARCHIVE:

CITATIONS: "Notes of the Stage," *New York Herald*, 8 July 1894, 4D; Dickson to Raff & Gammon, 8 January 1895, MH-BA.

NOTE: Kissell started with the old Sig Sautelle circus, later playing with a couple of minstrel shows and Barnum and Bailey's Circus. ("Hadj Llessik," *Variety*, 15 November 1939.)

Kissell, expert gun juggler, informs that there is but one Mrs. Frank Kissell, professionally known as Sultana. While playing in Troy, N.Y. recently Sultana met with an injury to one of her ankles. (*New York Clipper*, 4 January 1896, 694.)

WHAT HAS BECOME OF THE LIVE, PROGRESSIVE MANAGER. CAN ANYONE TELL?
HADJ LESSIK (KISSELL)
THE MARVELOUS ARAB WHIRLWIND GUN SPINNING WONDER.

Backed with a Magnificent Special Drop–20x30–of the Sphinx and Pyramids of Egypt, with Beautiful Mechanical Rising Moon Effect, Etc., Etc., asks the above question, and makes the following statement: To constantly ask of the artist something new, only to ignore it when presented, strikes me as a strange anomaly. That novelty artists and skilled manipulators in this country are rated all the way from next to nothing down to absolute nothing, is notorious the world over, but an exception is always made of this most marvelous and meritorious creation since the affinity between the present war scare and the juggling of fire arms. Patriotic tableaux, Etc., has made this act a red hot howling sensation. Up to date managers who are prepared to deal with a $1,000 Attraction that impresses the intelligent class of people as being Distinctly and Emphatically **New**, will do well to address:

108 FOURTH AVE., N.Y. (Advertisement, *New York Clipper*, 5 March 1898, 12.)

The Greatest Novelty Success Seen In England During the Past 20 Years.
HADJ LESSIK (Kissell)
THE ACKNOWLEDGED KING OF HIGH PRICED SENSATIONAL AND SKILLFUL
WHIRLWIND ARAB GUN SPINNERS AND JUGGLERS OF FIRE ARMS.

As a result of trial weeks I am booked, commencing Nov. 12 next, over the entire MOSS & THORNTON tour, through the courtesy of MR. FRANK ALLEN, the Manager. Have also booked the Livermore tour, the Sparrow tour, the Stoll tour, and, in fact, every tour in England that would pay the price. Will not be at liberty, or have an open date, until July 1901, and the jumps are so close together that I can, from the town I am in, whisper in the next manager's ear. Communications of every kind sent to my agents reach me promptly.

HADJ LESSIK, ANGER & BAUER, AGENTS, 50 Rupert St. Conventry St., West London, England. MR. JOHN HAYMAN, London Representative. (Advertisement, *New York Clipper*, 29 September 1900, 676.)

Edison Kinetoscope Parlor, 1155 Broadway, New York City.

*If newspapers provided frequent accounts of film production at the Black Maria, partic-
ularly when celebrities were involved, they paid little attention to the actual exhibition
of the resulting films. Comment on this topic was limited almost entirely to brief notes,
such as the following, which appeared in the theatrical columns.*

The exhibition of the kinetoscope at No 1155 Broadway has become one of the recognized sights of the town. It is
a wonderful invention that is as astonishing as it is amusing. With the aid of instantaneous photography and
electricity one is able to see Carmencita dance, just as she does in real life, and other continuous actions accurately depicted. (*New York Herald*, 17 June 1894, 21.)

*When Dickson and Heise shot an Edison employee picnic, it was, as Gordon Hendricks
has suggested, almost certainly a test for the filming of Caicedo, who would soon have
to perform his slack wire act outside the Black Maria.*

45 √[**Edison Employee Picnic**]
LENGTH: © No reg.
PRODUCER: W.K.L. Dickson.
CAMERA: William Heise.
CAST:
PRODUCTION DATE: By mid-July 1894.
LOCATION: Edison Laboratory, West Orange, N.J.
SOURCE:
DESCRIPTION:
SUBJECT: Motion pictures–experiments.
   Picnicking. Edison Laboratory.
ARCHIVE:
CITATIONS: W.K.L. Dickson and Antonia
   Dickson, *History of the Kinetograph, Kine-
   toscope, and Kineto-Phonograph*; Gordon
   Hendricks, *The Edison Motion Picture Myth*, 55 and 76.
NOTE:

*Juan A. Caicedo, Venezuelan rope and slack wire performer, established his reputation
in Australia. He first appeared at Koster & Bial's Music Hall on 14 May 1894 and performed there throughout the summer, until 8 September 1894, when he joined the
Boston Howard Athenaeum Star Specialty Co. He returned to Europe, only to reappear
in the United States at the end of the century.*

46 *Caicedo (with pole) / Caicedo, no. 1 / Caciedo [sic] / Caceido [sic]

LENGTH: 50 ft.   © No reg.
PRODUCER: W.K.L. Dickson.
CAMERA: William Heise.
CAST: Juan A. Caicedo.
PRODUCTION DATE: 25 July 1894.
LOCATION: Edison Laboratory, West Orange, N.J.
SOURCE:
DESCRIPTION: King of the slack wire. His daring feats of balancing as he performs his thrilling feats in midair show that he is perfectly at home. (*Edison Films*, March 1900, 24.)
SUBJECT: Vaudeville–performances. Aerialists. South Americans.
ARCHIVE: DLC-Hendricks, CLAc, FrBaADF.
CITATIONS: *Brooklyn Citizen*, 16 August 1894; Edison Phonograph Works to Continental Commerce Company, shipping order, 29 September 1894 (TAEP, 135:391); W.K.L. Dickson and Antonia Dickson, *History of the Kinetograph, Kinetoscope and Kineto-Phonograph*, 40; advertisements, *New York Clipper,* 15 September 1894, 448; 10 October 1896, 515; 20 January 1900, 991; 7 April 1900, 138; 14 July 1900, 444; 11 August 1900, 535. The Kinetoscope Company, *Edison's Latest Wonders: The Kinetograph, The Kinetoscope,* [October 1894]; The Kinetoscope Company, *Bulletin No. 1,* [December 1894]; Maguire & Baucus, *Edison and International Photographic Films*, April 1897, 6; Maguire & Baucus, *Fall Catalogue*, 1897, 11; F.Z. Maguire & Co., *Catalogue*, [March 1898], 33.
NOTE:

47 *Caicedo (with spurs) / Caicedo, no. 2

LENGTH: 50 ft.   © No reg.
PRODUCER: W.K.L. Dickson.
CAMERA: William Heise.
CAST: Juan A. Caicedo.
PRODUCTION DATE: 25 July 1894.
LOCATION: Edison Laboratory, West Orange, N.J.
SOURCE:
DESCRIPTION:
SUBJECT: Vaudeville–performances. Aerialists. South Americans.
ARCHIVE: FrBaADF.
CITATIONS: W.K.L. Dickson and Antonia Dickson, *History of the Kinetograph, Kinetoscope and Kineto-Phonograph*, 40.
NOTE:

BACKWARD TURN WITHOUT POLE.

KOSTER & BIAL'S...Caicedo, who titles himself "king of the wire," made his first appearance at this house after an absence of five years from this country. His feats on the high wire are little less than marvelous. He seems as much at home on the slender thread as the ordinary being is on *terra firma*, and performs with as much ease, without the balancing pole as with it, turning sommersaults in rapid succession and landing firmly on his feet. He first appeared with sandals, but soon replaced them with top riding boots. (*New York Clipper,* 19 May 1894, 166.)

KOSTER & BIAL'S...Caicedo, "the king of the wire," made something of a stir by making his way to the stage over the orchestra from the front of the house, and doing his turn in ordinary street attire. It was stated by the manager that the wire walker had not arrived at the theatre until late, and had no time to change his clothes. When he had finished his performance he climbed back over the orchestra and left the house by the same way he had come. (*New York Herald,* 10 July 1894, 3.)

CAICEDO, KING OF WIRE WALKERS.
He Turns Somersets in the Air with Heavy Riding Boots and Spurs On.
BALANCING POLE UNNECESSARY.
In Some Way he Stops the Oscillation of the Wire and Keeps It Perfectly Still.
THE CZAR WAS IN DANGER.

Every inch an athlete is Don Juan A. Caicedo. To be sure there are not many inches of him, but they all count, and furnish muscle and agility enough to stock four or five ordinary men. Caicedo, as every one calls him, or to be more polite, Senor Caicedo, is quite a wonder in his way. He is claimed to be, and nobody has yet come forward to dispute the claim, the most daring and accomplished wire-walker in the world. "King of the Wire," he calls himself, and he has a good right to the title if anybody has.

For fifteen years Caicedo has been balancing himself on ropes and wires until now he is as much at home up in the air as the ordinary mortal is on a solid bluestone pavement.

Ten days ago he landed from a transatlantic steamer, five weeks from Australia, via London. He began his engagement at Koster & Bial's the next day, where he is to appear for several months, and although he still had on his sea legs, and had not practised for several weeks, he was as much at home on the wire as ever.

For that matter he never practises. "My only rehearsing is before the audience," he told me.

A TYPE.

A typical South American he is in appearance, as he trips out and makes a smiling bow under the wire drawn tightly across the stage, twelve feet above the floor. He is short, well proportioned, but not stocky. You first notice a thick crop of jet black hair, and a jet black curling mustache, made all the more pronounced by the powder put on thick to cover up the freckles and the sunburn. The eyes are bright, black, snappy and fearless. His costume is a rather gaudy get up, unmistakably denoting his Spanish blood, with it predominance of yellow and red, and the toreador velvet jacket lavishly embroidered with gold lace.

As soon as he mounts the pole and steps on the wire it is evident that his claim to be the champion in his line is not an idle one. He tries the wire once with his foot to see if it is properly stretched, and then picking up the balancing pole runs nimbly along the thirty feet of its length.

STOPPING THE WIRE.

Then he stops, abruptly. The wire does not move. He bounces up and down, going high up in the air, and, when he stops again he does it with a peculiar trick of straightening the back so that the wire again comes to a perfect standstill from its violent oscillations.

Of course the audience cheer wildly at this trick and Caicedo smiles at them in a self-satisfied Spanish way.

He does not keep in constant motion on the wire in the manner of most tight rope walkers to preserve their equilibrium, but stands still between each act, sometimes on one foot only. His most effective act—and for that matter the most difficult—is turning somersets on the wire, both forward and backward, a dozen times in succession. A little spring throws him up in the air, where he turns and lands as he pleases, either astride, with a leg on each side of the wire, or both on the same side.

WITHOUT A POLE.

All this is done with a balancing pole. On his second appearance, however, he does the same acts without a pole and seems to rather enjoy the way he has fooled the audience, who thought that the pole was a necessary adjunct. They hardly get over wondering how he can skip around so unconcernedly on the wire, with nothing for a balance—not even holding out his arms in lieu of a pole, when Caicedo comes out again and caps his performance with his crowning effort.

This time he not only does not use a pole but on his feet are heavy Austrian cavalry boots, with [big] and ugly looking Mexican spurs attached to them. It seems almost impossible that he can manipulate his feet deftly enough thus encumbered to even walk across the wire, much less perform on it. However, the boots and spurs don't seem to bother him in the least. He danced about with just as much grace, turned somersets with just as much agility, shot up in the air just as high, landing in all sorts of positions, and did just as many breakneck feats as though he were dressed in the easiest of costumes.

OFF THE STAGE.

I had an interesting half hour's chat with this "king of the wire" after he has pulled off his gaudy tights and bespangled jersey and donned a rather "sporty" looking check suit and a red necktie. He talks English fairly well, is a man of quick perception, bright ideas and large experience with all kinds of humanity all over the world.

It is very seldom that a native South American is to be found in the show business. Caicedo is perhaps the only one in this country at the present time. He says himself that in all his travels he has never met one anywhere in the world outside of his native land and that he feels quite a curiosity on that account.

A COLOMBIAN.

Caicedo was born on June 13, 1861, in the city of Popayau, State of Cauca, Columbia, South America. When he was seven years old his father died. Then a circus manager, who had been a friend of the father, took the boy to bring him up, and as Juan was small for his age, light and agile, the manager commenced a systematic training to make him an acrobat. So apt a pupil was Juan that in six months he appeared in the ring and did an act on a single trapeze. "Then," said Caicedo, "when once the cheers of the audience to me had been heard I grew to love it, and nothing could make me want to be in business or learn trades."

CHAMPION RIDER.

He stayed with the circus until he was a young man. Meanwhile he had become the champion bareback rider in South America and an expert trapeze performer and wire walker. Then he became ambitious and wanted to have a circus of his own. Finally he raised money enough to start one, and for three years made money with it travelling through South America. Then some evil genius tempted him to go to Cuba. After six months he had lost everything—money, horses, paraphernalia and all—and had to sell his watch to go to Mexico, where he joined a circus again on a salary. From that time (fifteen years ago) he began to wander, and since then he has performed in nearly every civilized country in the world.

His first meeting with the late P.T. Barnum was a characteristic one. "Mr. Barnum," said Caicedo in describing it, "came to my dressing room, running, so soon as I had left the ring. 'You Spanish man,' he said, 'why is it you not speak English. You are great.' Then he, what do you say it, hugged me, and I was engaged."

SLACK AND TIGHT WIRE.

"Which is the more difficult to perform on," I asked—"a tight wire or a slack wire?" "Ah," with a shrug of the shoulders and a significant gesture with the hands, "the tight wire, to be sure. I can teach a boy in two weeks to perform on the slack wire. It is nothing."

"Is the feat of undressing on a wire difficult?" "No, no, not very much. I can undress just as I am, street costume and shoes, on a tight wire with my eyes covered so, a blindfold. It is not needed to see to do that, only to feel and calculate."

"What do you consider to be the most difficult feat on a wire?" I asked again. "The forward somerset is the most difficult of all. You do not see the wire at all in turning forward and you must go all by calculation. In turning the backward somerset it is much easier. Then you can see the wire and guide yourself."

MIGHT HAVE HURT THE CZAR.

Once when giving a private performance before the Czar, or the "Caesar of the Russia," as Caicedo calls him, and the imperial household, the "Great White Father" persisted in standing under the wire to satisfy himself that there was no trick about the balancing. This made Caicedo so afraid of falling on his royal spectator and seriously injuring the head of the Russian Empire that he lost all his nerve and gave a very bad performance.

The Prince of Wales saw Caicedo first in Vienna. After the performance the Prince sent for him and inquired if he was going to appear in London. When answered in the affirmative the Prince said, "When you come there I will help you."

"That surprised me." said Caicedo. "I could not see how he could help me. He was not a manager, I was sure. I thought him a funny man and paid no attention. I went to London. After a week or two a letter came from the Prince asking me to go to his palace and perform. My manager was very glad for me to go, so of course I went. The next day the Prince sent me £200. I did not want to take it. I felt paid by the honor, but they told me it would not do to send it back. I did not like it. If he had sent me a medal, something to cost ten, fifteen or twenty pounds, I would have then been pleased, for I could have shown it."

OBJECTS TO NETS AND MATS.

I had noticed that there was no mattress or netting stretched under the wire while he was on it, nothing to save him from the hard boards of the stage floor should he fall. Caicedo told me that he never allows anything to be put down, because when he sees it there it looks like an invitation to fall, and he feels tempted to accept the invitation. Then again, he thinks it spoils the effect of the act with the audience.

To pay for his fad, however, he occasionally gets bad tumbles. The worst he ever had was the very last night of a six months engagement in London. Just as he was closing his performance he became dizzy and fell. Both wrists were broken and his nose torn away from the cheek. It has left an ugly scar. His wrists, too, are far from recovered. He has to wear leather bandages around them, and after each performance they swell up alarmingly.

UNDER DIFFICULTIES.

The most difficult performance he ever gave, he told me, was on board ship coming to this country, about two weeks ago. The passengers teased him and finally he gave it, although it was impossible for him to keep on the wire owing to the motion of the vessel.

Although he never smokes, which is in itself singular for a Spaniard, nor indulges in strong drink, he takes no systematic exercise and never rehearses or practises. (*New York Herald*, 20 May 1894, 8E.)

Signor Caicedo's Fine Exhibition.

A remarkable exhibition was given at the Edison laboratory on Wednesday morning, when Signor Caicedo, the king of the tight rope dancers, who has been exhibiting at Koster & Bial's, came out and was photographed by Professor W.K.L. Dickson. The kinetographic pictures were the principal ones taken, although several large pictures were also made. Those who have seen Signor Caicedo perform his marvelous acts need no description of them. The Kinetographic "Black Maria," as it is called, in which the pictures are usually made, was of course not available for the purpose, as it would have been impossible to stretch a tight rope in the limited space of the building. The tight rope of wire was therefore stretched in the open air directly north of the building. It is the first time that any kinetographic pictures have been taken in the open air, and the results were looked forward to with interest. Heretofore, the success of the pictures has depended largely on the intense inky blackness of the tunnel behind the figure or figures, and hence the development of the films was looked forward to with no little interest. Signor Caicedo went through all his well known feats on the tight wire, jumping, dancing, posturing, turning sommer-saults forward and backward, springing in the air and facing in the opposite direction before he settled on the wire again, and making effective poses on the wire at intervals. When he had gone through this series of feats he discarded the balance pole and with a big pair of boots and a huge pair of Mexican spurs on went through the same wonderful series of performances. There were present at the exhibition, besides Mr. Dickson and his assist-ants, only three or four ladies, friends of Professor Dickson, and a representative of the CHRONICLE. Signore Caicedo was loudly applauded. He was engaged in conversation between the feats and gave many interesting anec-dotes of his experiences. (*Orange Chronicle*, 28 July 1894, 5.)

Annabelle Whitford had her debut at the 1893 Columbian Exposition in Chicago. Her stage name was "Peerless Annabelle." She danced before Edison's Black Maria came-ra more often than any other performer, appearing repeatedly in three different sub-jects for which she executed the Serpentine, Sun and Butterfly dances (returning each time the negatives wore out). Whitford became famous well-after her career in early motion pictures: Charles Dana Gibson chose her as the original Gibson girl for the Ziegfeld Follies of 1907. ("Left Ziegfeld in 1910," New York Herald Tribune, *2 December 1961.)*

48 ***Annabelle, [no. 1] / Annabelle Butterfly Dance / [Annabelle Butterfly Dance, no. 1]**
LENGTH: 50 ft.   © No reg.
PRODUCER: W.K.L. Dickson.
CAMERA: William Heise.
CAST: Annabelle Whitford.
PRODUCTION DATE: By 10 August 1894.
LOCATION: Black Maria, West Orange, N.J.
SOURCE:
DESCRIPTION: In her famous "Butterfly Dance."
 (The Kinetoscope Company, *Bulletin No. 1*,
 [December 1894].)
SUBJECT: Vaudeville–performances. Dancing.
ARCHIVE: NNMoMA.
CITATIONS: *Brooklyn Citizen*, 16 August 1894;
 Continental Commerce Company to W.E.
 Gilmore, 18 September 1894 (TAEP, 135:389).
NOTE: Ray Phillips reports a copy of this film in the DLC collection.

49 ***Annabelle, [no. 2] / Annabelle Serpentine Dance / [Annabelle Serpentine Dance, no. 1]**
LENGTH: 50 ft.   © No reg.
PRODUCER: W.K.L. Dickson.
CAMERA: William Heise.
CAST: Annabelle Whitford.
PRODUCTION DATE: By 10 August 1894.
LOCATION: Black Maria, West Orange, N.J.
SOURCE:
DESCRIPTION: Serpentine Dancer. Beautiful effect. (The
 Kinetoscope Company, *Edison's Latest Wonders:
 The Kinetograph, The Kinetoscope*, [October 1894]).
SUBJECT: Vaudeville–performances. Dancing.
ARCHIVE: DLC.
CITATIONS: *Brooklyn Citizen*, 16 August 1894;
 Continental Commerce Company to W.E. Gilmore,
 18 September 1894 (TAEP, 135:389).
NOTE: Negative was replaced by *Annabelle Serpentine
 Dance, [no. 2]*, made early in 1895.

50   Annabelle, [no. 3] / Annabelle Sun Dance / [Annabelle Sun Dance, no. 1]

LENGTH: 50 ft.   © No reg.
PRODUCER: W.K.L. Dickson.
CAMERA: William Heise.
CAST: Annabelle Whitford.
PRODUCTION DATE: By 10 August 1894.
LOCATION: Black Maria, West Orange, N.J.
SOURCE:
DESCRIPTION: In the "Sun Dance." (The Kinetoscope Company, *Bulletin No. 1*, [December 1894].)
SUBJECT: Vaudeville–performances. Dancing.
ARCHIVE:
CITATIONS: *Brooklyn Citizen*, 16 August 1894; Edison Phonograph Works to Continental Commerce Company, shipping order, 29 September 1894 (TAEP, 135:391).
NOTE:

Raff & Gammon, as managers of the Kinetoscope Company, acquired the North American rights to exploit the kinetoscope on 18 August 1894. Only the special over-sized kinetoscopes designed for the exhibition of fight films are excluded. Before this date kinetoscopes were being sold to showmen and entrepreneurs on an ad-hoc, disorganized basis. (Thomas A Edison with Norman C. Raff and Frank R. Gammon, agreement, 18 August 1894, NjWOE.)

The Ewer sisters—La Regaloncita, La Graciosa, La Preciosa—were prohibited from dancing in New York theaters through the efforts of the Gerry Society. Acting Mayor George B. McClellan, Jr., however, did permit them to "pose" on stage, in E.E. Rice's burlesque 1492. Soon New Yorkers could see them dance by visiting the kinetoscope parlor.

51   Cupid's Dance / The Fairies' Dance / Children Dancing / 3 Little Girls / Cupid Dance

LENGTH: 50 ft.   © No reg.
PRODUCER: W.K.L. Dickson.
CAMERA: William Heise.
CAST: La Regaloncita (Mildred Ewer), La Graciosa (Florence Ewer), La Preciosa (Lenora Ewer).
PRODUCTION DATE: August 1894.
LOCATION: Black Maria, West Orange, N.J.
SOURCE: *1492* (musical farce).
DESCRIPTION: Three beautiful little girls—La Regloncita, La Graciosa and La Preciosa—in a charming dance. (The Kinetoscope Company, *Edison's Latest Wonders: The Kinetograph, The Kinetoscope*, [October 1894]).
SUBJECT: Musicals–performances. Dancing. Children. Edward E. Rice.
ARCHIVE: FrBaADF.
CITATIONS: "Notes of Music and Drama," *New York Herald*, 24 August 1894, 10; Raff & Gammon to Chicago Office, invoice, 10 September 1894, 1:8, MH-BA; Edison Manufacturing Co., requisition no. 151, 9 November 1894, NjWOE; Edison Phonograph Works to Continental Commerce Company, shipping order, 29 September 1894 (TAEP, 135:391). The Kinetoscope Company, *Bulletin No. 1*, [December 1894].
NOTE: *1492* premiered in Boston on 3 September 1892 and opened at New York City's Garden Theatre on 15 May 1893 to positive reviews. The burlesque reopened on Saturday, August 25th, with new specialties including these three young girls. It had its 400th performance on Friday, August 31st and ended its New York run at the Garden Theatre on 13 October 1893, making way for *Little Christopher Columbus*. For more information on *1492*, see *Walton and Slavin—From Rice's 1492 Co.* (film no. 70).

La Regaloncita, the child dancer, and her two little sisters are at present in London. They are expected to return on Saturday, being under engagement of E.E. Rice for the next three years. (*New York Herald*, 29 July 1894, 6D.)

Manager E.E. Rice is busy preparing for the revival of "1492" at the Garden Theatre on Saturday night. The burlesque, it is announced, has been brought still further "up to date." There will be entirely new costumes and scenery and a realistic ship scene. The "Daily Hints from Paris" will, it is said, foreshadow the very latest novelties in fall gowns. Theresa Vaughn, Yolande Wallace, Mabel Clark, Edward Favor, Walter Jones, Richard Harlow, John Peachey, Walton and Slavin and H.H. Keefe will all be seen again in their familiar roles. The music will be directed by Gustave Kerker and there will be a new series of Kilanyi's living pictures. The postponed 400th performance falls due on a week from Friday and the souvenirs will again be the Columbus clocks of carved wood. (*New York Herald,* 19 August 1894, 7D.)

She Coaxed the Mayor.
La Regaloncita and Her Little Sisters May Pose in "1492" for a Week at Least.

Acting Mayor McClellan decided yesterday that La Regaloncita and her two little sisters, La Graciosa and La Preciosa, might appear for a week in "1492" at the Garden Theatre. Manager E.E. Rice asked for this permit several days ago but Mr. McClellan, having learned that Mr. Gerry opposed the appearance of the children on the stage, refused to grant it until he had seen exactly what La Regaloncita and her sisters were expected to do. Yesterday was the day set for the hearing, and the Mayor's office in the City Hall was crowded with spectators when the three little girls appeared with Manager Rice. Superintendent Jenkins was there to represent Mr. Gerry.

The children went into the Mayor's private office and in a few minutes reappeared dressed in boys' costumes. Then at Mr. Rice's direction, they began to go through a series of poses, La Regaloncita humming a little tune the while. "Now dance," said Mr. Rice, when this was over, and the children did dance–danced as if they thoroughly enjoyed it, too.

"See the difference?" queried the manager. "We only want them to pose."

"But they will pose to music," objected Mr. Jenkins, "and that is the same as dancing." "No, it isn't," retorted Mr. Rice hotly, and then he went on to say that the Gerry society was persecuting Mrs. Ewer, the mother of the little girls; that he was willing to pay them $100 a week for doing something that wouldn't hurt them any more than play, and the society for some reason wanted to prevent their mother from making this money.

The children meantime had resumed their street clothes, and Mr. McClellan said he would think the matter over and decide later. Just as La Regaloncita was leaving the room she ran up to the Mayor and putting on her prettiest smile, said coaxingly:–

"Now, please be nice and let us go on."

That evidently settled it, for it wasn't long after that Mr. McClellan ordered that the children should be permitted to pose for a week, and if during that time they did not dance nor sing a longer permit should be granted them. (*New York Herald*, 25 August 1894, 10.)

An intriguing image on the cover of W.K.L. and Antonia Dicksons' A History of the Kinetograph, Kinetoscope and Kineto-Phonograph shows two boxing monkeys. Most of the images on the cover illustrate specific motion picture subjects. If this illustration has a corresponding film, then its subject was almost certainly Alleni's Boxing Monkeys. They were appearing at Huber's 14th Street Museum in New York City for a five week period from late July to early September 1894.

52   [Alleni's Boxing Monkeys]
LENGTH: 50 ft.   © No reg.
PRODUCER: W.K.L. Dickson.
CAMERA: William Heise.
CAST:
PRODUCTION DATE: [August 1894.]
LOCATION: Black Maria, West Orange, N.J.
SOURCE:
DESCRIPTION:
SUBJECT: Monkeys. Animal fighting. Burlesque.
ARCHIVE:
CITATIONS:
NOTE:

53   *Cock Fight, no. 2 / The Chicken Fight
LENGTH: 50 ft.   © No reg.
PRODUCER: W.K.L. Dickson.
CAMERA: William Heise.

CAST:
PRODUCTION DATE: By early September 1894.
LOCATION: Black Maria, West Orange, N.J.
SOURCE: *The Cock Fight* (Edison film no. 27, March 1894).
DESCRIPTION: Most popular of all. Shows two cocks fighting, and spectators betting. Perfectly true to life. (The Kinetoscope Company, *Edison's Latest Wonders: The Kinetograph, The Kinetoscope*, [October 1894].)
SUBJECT: Cockfighting. Gambling.
ARCHIVE: NNMoMA.
CITATIONS: Continental Commerce Company to W.E. Gilmore, 18 September 1894 (TAEP, 135:389); Holland Brothers to Raff & Gammon, 13 February 1895, 1:302, MH-BA.

NOTE: This film was sold in Italy as *Combattimento di galli N. 2.* (Continental Phonograph Kinetoscope Company, *Kinetoscenes,* [March 1895].) The identification of this print is not certain. Given the white background, it could have been shot in the summer of 1896. However, knowledge gained from making *The Cock Fight* (film no. 27) and other films of animal fighting might well have encouraged the Edison crew to move the camera closer and lighten the background even at this early date.

53.1 French Dancers
LENGTH: 50 ft.   © No reg.
PRODUCER: W.K.L. Dickson.
CAMERA: William Heise.
CAST:
PRODUCTION DATE: By early September 1894.
LOCATION: Black Maria, West Orange, N.J.
SOURCE:
DESCRIPTION:
SUBJECT: Vaudeville–performances. Dancing. French.
ARCHIVE:
CITATIONS: Continental Commerce Company to W.E. Gilmore, 18 September 1894 (TAEP, 135:389).
NOTE: Probably women performing the French Can-Can. May have sometimes been referred to as *Frog Dance* (see film no. 181). See also *Parisian Dance* (Edison film no. 285).

On 3 September 1894 Thomas A. Edison assigned the rights to manage his kinetoscope business in Europe to Maguire & Baucus, as long as they did so to his satisfaction. (Thomas A. Edison to Maguire & Baucus, 3 September 1894, NjWOE.) This territory was later expanded to include parts of Asia and South America.

On the anniversary of his victory over John L. Sullivan, world heavy-weight boxing champion James J. Corbett knocked out another opponent, this time for the benefit of Edison's camera. To visit Edison's Laboratory he took the ferry and train from Manhattan where he was then starring in the play Gentleman Jack, *which had reopened earlier in the week at the American Theatre.*

54 *Corbett and Courtney Before the Kinetograph / The Corbett-Courtney Fight
LENGTH: 6 films of 150 ft. each.   © William K.L. Dickson, 17 November 1894.
PRODUCER: W.K.L. Dickson, Kinetoscope Exhibiting Company.
CAMERA: William Heise.
CAST: James J. Corbett, Peter Courtney.
PRODUCTION DATE: 7 September 1894.
LOCATION: Black Maria, West Orange, N.J.
SOURCE:

DESCRIPTION: This fight consists of six rounds, each round shown on a film 150 feet long. This is not a facsimile or a fake of any description: it is an actual contest between James J. Corbett, former champion of the world, and Peter Courtney. The films are listed as 1st round, 2d round, 3d round, 4th round, 5th round, and 6th round. (F.Z. Maguire & Co., *Catalogue,* [March 1898], 15.)

SUBJECT: Sports. Boxing.

ARCHIVE: DLC, NNMoMA, Big Fights, Inc.

CITATIONS: "Corbett the Victor," *Newark Daily Advertiser,* 7 September 1894, 1; "Corbett Visits Orange and Takes Part in a Six Round Fight Before the Kinetoscope," *Orange Chronicle,* 8 September 1894, 7; "Corbett Before the Kinetoscope," *New York Herald,* 8 September 1894, 11; "Edison Defended," *Boston Advertiser,* 18 September 1894, clippings, NjWOE. Maguire & Baucus, *Edison and International Photographic Films,* April 1897, 19; Maguire & Baucus, *Fall Catalogue,* 1897, 15; *Edison Films,* March 1900, 27; *Edison Films,* July 1901, 51.

NOTE: DLC and NNMoMA each possess only one round and it appears to be the same.

American Theatre–James J. Corbett in "Gentleman Jack" was greeted by a packed house last evening. The piece has undergone few changes since last seen here. The champion sparred three lively rounds with Steve O'Donnell. (*New York Herald*, 4 September 1894, 7.)

KNOCKED OUT BY CORBETT.
The Champion Beats Peter Courtney in Six Rounds.
FOR THE EDISON KINETOSCOPE.
In the Interests of Science and for a Price of $5,000 Champion Jim Stops a Trenton Heavy Weight After a Fierce Battle–Each Round Lasted a Fraction Over a Minute and Five-Ounce Gloves Were Used so that Corbett's Task Was Not an Easy One–Courtney is Game to the End.

Champion James J. Corbett knocked out Peter Courtney, a clever Trenton heavy weight in six rounds at Edison's laboratory, Llewellan Park, yesterday morning. The fight was in the interests of science, as it took place in the Black Maria before the kinetograph, and was for a purse of $5,000 of which the loser received $250.

Everything had been arranged to have the battle on Thursday, and the principals and seconds were on hand at the Christopher Street Ferry early in the morning, but as the sky was overcast, word was telephoned from the scene of action that nothing could be done without clear weather and a bright sun. It was then agreed to meet again yesterday morning at the same time and place, providing the elements were propitious.

Accordingly at 8:15 o'clock yesterday morning the select party of sports began to arrive at the ferry entrance. A heavy fog hung over the North River, but as the sun's rays were slowly but surely burning through the mist, a successful trip was anticipated. THE SUN reporter found John P. Eckhardt, who refereed the fight, first upon the scene. Soon after Champion Corbett and his retainers [came] in sight, followed by the usual curious crowd. The big pugilist was attired in a well-fitting suit of light checked cloth, an immaculate white shirt, standing collar, and black necktie in which nestled a cluster of diamonds, while a broad-brimmed straw hat shaded his sunburned features. He carried a massive cane, and on the little finger of his right hand three big gold rings set with diamonds and rubies attracted the attention of the onlookers. Corbett was in a pleasant frame of mind, and cordially received the complimentary remarks and salutations hurled at him from all sides. Close beside him walked big John McVey, who has assisted in the champion's training in his fights with Sullivan and Mitchell. Little Bud Woodthorpe, his private secretary, ran along behind, lugging a suspicious-looking valise, and Frank Belcher, another attendant, carried several paper bundles. Several intimate friends were also in the champion's party, but Manager W.A. Brady was among the missing.

"Where's Courtney?" queried Corbett, when he stopped in front of the Delaware, Lackawanna and Western Railroad ticket office and lighted a black cigar.

"Oh, he's gone on ahead!" came the reply from a stout individual who seemed to be on the inside. "He took an early train, so as to get a good breakfast before facing the music."

"All right," said Corbett, "we'll wait a few minutes for Brady." By this time it had been noised about that the famous prize fighter was inside the ferry house, and hundreds of persons flocked down the dock to catch a glimpse of him. A policeman came up and extended his hand to Mitchell's conqueror, at the same time asking:

"Where are you going, Mr. Corbett? Out on the road?"

"Oh, I'm just taking a little run out into the country," rejoined the big fellow, "and my friends here are going along, too, to see that I don't get lost."

"Ah, I see," mused the copper. "Well, I'm awful glad to see you looking so well, and I wish you luck." Then the blue-coat chased the small boys away with renewed vigor.

"Whew!" whistled Corbett. "That was a narrow escape. If that fellow had known I was going out in Jersey to knock out a stiff, he'd have made trouble, perhaps."

OFF FOR THE FIGHTING GROUND.

At this moment the managers of the concern which has charge of the kinetograph came into the ferry house and said that a start should be made at once for the battle ground. Bags and satchels were picked up, and the whole party swung onto the ferryboat Secaucus, bound for Hoboken. Manager Brady had been left behind at which Corbett seemed to feel a bit nervous. On the boat the champion was surrounded by a crowd of gaping men and boys, all of whom asked the question: "Where's he going, any how?"

But Corbett never opened his mouth except to chat with THE SUN man about the prospects of his battle.

"This fellow Courtney," said he, "is big and lusty, although unknown to the sporting world. I never saw him before yesterday, and know nothing about him. These kinetograph people secured him and have offered a purse of $5,000 for a finish fight. It is stipulated that I must put the guy out in six rounds or I get nothing for, as I understand it, the machine is so arranged that a longer fight is undesirable. If I put the man out I get $4,750 and he will take the balance for his trouble. You can bet I'll do the trick, too, for it's too much money to let slip out of one's grasp."

By the time Corbett finished the above statement the boat had run into her slip and the short walk to the cars began. It seemed as if Corbett's coming had already been announced, for the crowd was waiting for him as he entered the depot. The party was just in time for the 8:45 train for the Oranges, and seats in the smoking car where the sports rode were at a premium.

The handlers of the affair were most mysterious. They told Corbett on the quiet that the utmost secrecy must prevail or the whole crowd would be "pinched" for aiding and abetting a prize fight, a violation of the New Jersey State laws. Exposure, they explained, meant an almost certain sojourn behind the bars, and nobody relished that they were sure. Then [   ] in order to divert suspicion they suggested that the party divide into two sections and each leave the train at different stations. Corbett readily agreed to this, so when the Brick Church was reached, the Californian, accompanied by McVey, Belcher, and two friends left the cars and boarded a trolley car. At the next station, Johnny Eckhardt, Woodthorpe, the manager of the affair, and THE SUN reporter jumped upon the platform and at once repaired to a neighboring restaurant to get a bite to eat.

CORBETT'S OPPONENT.

It was here that Pugilist Peter Courtney was discovered. He was a rather tough-looking citizen, with a bull neck, big shoulders, immense hands, and the proverbial thin legs. His eyes were small and set well back under his low brow. His jaws were square, and his nose looked as if it had taken many a good punch. Courtney was attired in an ill-fitting light suit with a neglige shirt and a straw hat, the brim of which looked as if it had been doing business with a poll parrot. He carried a small black handbag and smoked a fat cigar. As the critics sized him up, they united in declaring him a "pretty hard-looking nut to crack," and one man ventured the opinion that a mallet blow squarely delivered on the top of his head would never phase him. Peter was as cool and unconcerned when THE SUN reporter approached him as if he had been on his way to a country picnic.

"I ain't no spring chicken," he declared, "and I don't think this here champion will have such a picnic with me as he thinks. I was born in Pennsylvania and am 26 years old. A year and a half ago I went to Trenton to get a job, and that's how I got in the fighting business. There was a duck there named E. Warner, and they said he was the champeen of Jersey. Well, Jack McNally, a boxing instructor in Trenton, give me a few lessons, and I just put this here Warner to sleep in just one round. Soon after that I did up Jim Glynn in two rounds, Jim Dwyer in three, Jack Welch in four, and recently I went agin Bob Fitzsimmons, who couldn't put me out in four rounds. These people made it an object for me to stack up agin Corbett, and here I am, ready for business."

COURTNEY IS FIRST AT THE FIGHTING GROUNDS.

Courtney had with him several friends who were constantly telling him to keep a stiff upper lip, but such advice was unnecessary, as a cooler, more confident fighter could hardly be found. After breakfast a trolley car was boarded, and after an invigorating ride the brick buildings and tall chimneys of the famous electrical works were seen straight ahead. At the entrance to the laboratory the party was confronted by a high picket fence, through which a watchman scrutinized all hands. The managers of the fight soon explained matters, so that a big gate was swung back and the battle ground had been reached. Corbett and those who had left the train at Brick Church had not yet arrived: neither had Brady. But that cut no figure with Courtney. He walked around the grounds looking at everything in open-mouthed wonder, apparently oblivious to the fact that he was about to face a human cyclone that meant insensibility to him before the jig was up. Peter soon took a chair in the photographer's office and chatted quietly with his seconds. The man from Trenton was still in good spirits and the small crowd of persons who were there to see the fun marvelled at his self-control.

"Ain't you afraid Corbett will knock your head off?" asked one of the workmen who stood around the fighters.

"Naw!" said Courtney. "He's got to hit hard to do that, for me nut is well set."

CORBETT ARRIVES.

"Here he comes," shouted a small boy when the creaking of the big gate announced the arrival of the champion. Everybody shook hands with Corbett as he sauntered down the gravel walk to the place where his opponent was sitting.

"How do you do?" exclaimed Corbett, extending his hand to Trenton's pride.

"Howdy?" replied Peter in turn, as he looked the tall fighter full in the face.

"It's a nice day for this little affair of ours," remarked Jim, smiling grimly.

"Ain't it!" was the slow rejoinder, and Courtney turned on his heel.

"He looks like a tough customer," said Corbett, "and I think he'll take quite a punching."

The sun was now shining brightly, and the heat became so oppressive that everybody hunted for shady spots, while the fighters took chairs in a small wooden building where greasy workmen were pottering over all sorts of things electric.

THE BLACK MARIA.

Over at the Black Maria, which has been full described in THE SUN, several attendants were busy fixing the kinetograph, so that there might be no slips or mistakes in photographing the impending struggle. The Maria, as the building in which Edison's wonderful machine is located, is called, reminded everybody of a huge coffin. It was covered with black tar paper, secured to the woodwork by big metal-topped nails, and was the most dismal-looking affair the sports had ever seen. Inside the walls were painted black, and there wasn't a window of any description, barring a little slide which was directly beside the kinetograph and could be opened or closed at the will of the operator. Half of the roof, however, could be raised or lowered like a drawbridge by means of ropes, pulleys, and weights, so that the sunlight could strike squarely on the space before the machine.

The ring was 14 feet square. It was roped on two sides, the other two being the heavily padded walls of the building. The floor was planed smooth and covered with rosin. All battles in this arena must be fought under a special set of rules. A round lasts a little over one minute, with a rest of a minute and a half to two minutes between the rounds. Consequently, the smallness of the ring and the shortness of the rounds, necessitate hot fighting all the time.

GETTING READY FOR THE BATTLE.

It was nearly 11 o'clock when the managers told the pugilists to get ready. Corbett prepared for the battle in the photographer's private room, while Courtney disrobed in a shanty just beyond. Corbett stripped in a jiffy, Woodthorpe untying his shoes for him and arranging his clothes over the back of a chair. When he was in the nude the champion presented a magnificent spectacle. Though a trifle fat, his long, sinewy arms showed that he was in pretty good trim. His legs were rather thin, as they always have been, but he showed there was great strength in them by the up-and-down movement of the muscles when he walked across the floor. He didn't put on his flesh-colored Jersey, or his blue trunks, such as he wears when he gives his sparring exhibitions, but he simply pulled on a red elastic breech-clout and slipped his feet into black fighting shoes. In other words, he made careful preparation for a fight and not a boxing bout for points. He was in excellent spirits, although he worried considerably over Brady's absence. But when the hustling manager arrived later, with the excuse that he didn't wake up in time to catch the early train, Corbett evidently felt relieved.

Courtney, meanwhile, was getting ready, with the assistance of his friends. He showed that he was in the finest possible shape, for his flesh was clear, his muscles flexible, and his body as hard as nails. He put on a pair of black trunks and the regulation fighting shoes. As he sat on a canvas cot bed, slapping the knuckles of his left hand with the fingers of his right, he looked like a typical prize fighter. His hair was cut close with the exception of a small pompadour that made Corbett laugh when he saw it. Peter was still self-possessed, and to all questions as to how he felt he had but one reply: "First rate!" Some of the spectators thought he looked pale around the gills, but big McVey, after talking with him, said: "He's a dead game fellow and fears nothing."

FIVE OUNCE GLOVES.

Woodthorpe's suspicious looking valise was now opened in Corbett's quarters and two sets of gloves were produced. One set were two ounces and the other five. Corbett put on a pair of the big gloves and playfully punched McVey in the chin to try them. Then he sat down and pondered:

"What's the matter?" asked the ever anxious Brady.

"Why," answered Corbett, "I'm in a quandary. You see, each round only lasts a minute, and with these big bags on my hands I might not be able to put this fellow out. I'm thinking it might be well to put the small gloves on and be sure of doing the job clean."

At this a messenger was despatched to Courtney to ask him which gloves he preferred. The Trenton boy replied that it made no difference to him, that whatever suited Corbett was agreeable.

"I'm here to fight," said he, "and I'll put on big or small gloves, just as the champeen says."

Corbett then nearly made up his mind to wear the two-ounce gloves, but McVey dissuaded him from it. He said: "You will cut this man up awful, Jim, and then people would say it was brutal. Better wear the big mitts, and if

Jim Corbett and Peter Courtney pose for a Dickson photograph before the filming of their fistic encounter (7 September 1894).

you find you can't do him, why you can shift with his consent to the small ones. But you can do him as it is, for you can make the pillows hurt."

Still Corbett didn't know what to do. He argued that, as the rounds were so short and the rests so long, Courtney would have plenty of time to recover from heavy blows. He also explained that if Courtney succeeded in staying five rounds he (Corbett) would have to work unusually hard in the sixth round to put him out in order to win the purse. Jim had a strong leaning toward the small gloves up to within a short time before entering the ring, but Brady and McVey finally succeeded in driving the idea out of his mind.

INTO THE RING THEY GO.

There was a half hour's delay now over some defect in the kinetograph, and the fighters sat restlessly in the quarters, while the sports wandered about the grounds waiting for the fun to begin. But at 11:40 o'clock the chief operator said all was ready, and the march to the Black Maria began. Corbett and Courtney walked from their dressing rooms fully fifty yards across the yard to the entrance to the fighting house, while their seconds followed carrying towels, bottles, sponges, and pails of water. It was so warm that nearly everybody carried his coat over his arm and fanned himself with his hat.

The moment Corbett stepped into the ring, he stopped short and exclaimed: "My, but this is small. There's no chance to bring any foot movement into play here, that's sure. A fellow has got to stand right up and fight for his life." Then he examined the ropes and padding very carefully and tried the flooring with his feet, before taking a chair in the corner. Courtney came into the building a moment or two later. He looked calmly at the arrangements, but made no comments. He smiled and nodded to those around him, as much as to say, "Watch me!" As he sat down he looked hastily at Corbett, and meeting the champion's steady gaze, he grinned a second or two and then scowled. There was still something the matter with the machine, and as the roof had been raised so as to let in the sunlight, the heat was overpowering. Both men began to perspire, and finally Corbett jumped up and drew his chair back into a shady place. Courtney, who never did anything until Corbett took the initiative, also changed his seat, and the seconds were kept busy fanning the men with towels.

EVERYTHING READY AT LAST.

At 11:45 o'clock everything was ready. The men were first requested to pose in fighting attitudes for an ordinary photograph. Then the chief operator told them to get ready for the fight. John P. Eckhardt of this city was the referee and W.A. Brady held the watch. In Corbett's corner were his seconds, John McVey and Frank Belcher, with Bub Woodthrope, bottle holder. In Courtney's corner were John Tracey and Edward Allen, seconds, and Sam Lash, bottle holder. Corbett weighed 195 pounds, he said, and Courtney 190. The men were ordered to shake hands and received instructions as to clinching. Then they went to their corners and waited for the signal to begin the battle. The operators were all ready now, and when the word was given the kinetograph began to buzz.

FIRST ROUND.

Courtney evidently thought that his play was to force the fighting, for he rushed savagely at Corbett and swung a heavy right for the jaw. Corbett dodged the blow and laughed. Peter, however, rushed again, and it was swing and punch for several seconds. Corbett avoided nearly every one of Courtney's heavy swings by the cleverest kind of ducking and when the Trenton man rushed for a third time, but found nothing in front of him but the ropes, the champion gave a hoarse laugh. Now, it was Jim's turn to be aggressive and he rushed fiercely at his man, jabbing him repeatedly in the face with straight lefts and knocking Peter's head back with every blow. Try as hard as he might, Courtney could not ward off the hail storm of punches that landed all over his face and body. But he never for a moment winced. On the contrary, Courtney seemed to like to mix it with the champion, and when Jim landed a wicked upper cut on the chin, just as the round closed, Courtney grinned. Time of the round, 1 minute and 16 seconds.

SECOND ROUND.

It was clearly a case of science versus slugging. Courtney began rushing, and swung some terrible blows, but Corbett avoided them all. Courtney finally landed a pretty stiff one on the champion's head, and got a terrific right-hand swing on the jaw in return. Corbett followed this up with a vicious upper cut that made Peter see stars. Then Courtney rushed madly and blindly at Corbett, swinging right and left handers that never landed, but made Jim keep well out of harm's way. Corbett was not hitting hard at all, evidently waiting for an opening to put in a sockdolager when Peter least expected it. Courtney got two smashing lefts in the face and a right hand ripper in the wind, but he was still in the game, and continued to [tilt?] at Jim for all he was worth. Corbett kept well out of the way of the vicious blows, however, and laughed good naturedly at the efforts of his rival to do him an injury. Time of this round, one minute and twenty-four seconds.

When Corbett went to his corner he said to McVey: "This fellow is taking some awful punches without wincing, and I'm afraid the big gloves are going to make trouble for me. He is getting a good rest after each round and comes up like a new man." To this McVey replied: "Well, try him hard this next round and find out if you can hurt him with the pillows. Then if you can't, it's time to worry." Corbett readily agreed to this, and looked determined when the third round was ordered.

THIRD ROUND.

Corbett planned to try a left-hook punch, a right-hand swing, and a cross counter. Courtney at once rushed at Jim like a wild man. He swung his arms around his head like a windmill and aimed blow after blow for Corbett's face. Finally he landed a hot right on Corbett's wind, and Jim went at him with blood in his eye. Courtney was fighting desperately at the time, but when Corbett landed his left-hook punch flush on the jaw, Peter was knocked flat onto the floor. He was game as a pebble, however, and after being down seven seconds, he arose and went on with the battle. Corbett showered a dozen blows on his neck and face, but he showed remarkable nerve and pluck. Time of the round, 1 minute and 12 seconds.

Corbett's quickness in this round was wonderful. When he feinted Courtney always jumped five feet away, but when Jim really let fly a hard blow it came so quickly that Courtney couldn't avoid it. Peter's heavy swings were generally wasted for Jim's judge of distance was simply perfect, and he escaped many a blow by pulling himself just far enough away to let Peter's fists fly just one or two inches from him. When Courtney went to his corner, Corbett called across the ring: "Did I hurt you?" "Naw," answered Peter. "There's a buzzing sound in me head, but I guess it's the heat." Everybody had to laugh, including Corbett, while Peter sponged his face off and got ready for the next set-to.

FOURTH ROUND.

Corbett knew that the big gloves would work all right now, but concluded not to take any chances, as Courtney was very strong and still full of fight. So when Peter rushed, Corbett clinched him and then laughingly threw him off. They mixed it up a bit, with Courtney landing more blows than in all of the previous rounds combined. Suddenly, just as time was about to be called, the Trenton fighter land a heavy swing behind Corbett's left ear, and Jim retaliated with a body blow that doubled Courtney up so he was glad to sit down to catch his breath. Time of the round, 1 minute and 20 seconds.

It was now a certainty that Courtney would not last the six rounds, but his gameness was incomprehensible. He was taking some fierce punching on the neck and jaw, but he seemed to be made of iron. True, the rounds were not long enough to well demonstrate his staying powers, but it must be remembered that Corbett's heavy blows were enough to take all the fight out of an ordinary boxer.

FIFTH ROUND.

Courtney was still game when he toed the mark. He knew very well that Corbett would sooner or later knock him out, but he didn't flinch a particle, and faced the music like a man. He tried his old rushing tactics, and swung wildly for the jaw, but, as before, Corbett ducked and was never touched. Then Peter tried for the wind, but Corbett banged him on the mouth with a hot right, drawing blood. Jim followed this up with two terrific body blows, and a heavy cross-counter on the jaw that sent Courtney up against the wall with a bump. But Peter came back with a tremendous right that just grazed Corbett's jaw and went over his shoulder. Corbett then punched his man when and where he pleased until time was up, finally doubling him up again with a punch in the wind. Time of the round, 1 minute and 23 seconds.

The moment Corbett sat down he whispered to McVey:

"Now I'll put him out. I'm going to rush him and sing his jaws with both hands. His defence is weak and I can easily beat down his guard. I've got to do it quick, though, for there's only a little over a minute, and that's a precious short time in which to knock a man out. He is dead game and will take some frightful smashes before he goes to sleep."

McVey told Corbett he had a cinch, and when the men jumped up to the centre of the ring again Billy Brady smiled as he thought of the fun he'd have counting the $4,750 after the battle.

SIXTH ROUND.

Corbett cut loose at once. He rushed at his antagonist like an infuriated wild beast and began to beat down his guard. Jim was no longer "Corbett, the actor and gentleman," but "Corbett, the prize fighter," who had no mercy. He swung a pile-driving left that landed squarely on the jaw. Courtney staggering from the force of the blow. Then Jim sent his right square on the chin and knocked Peter to the floor in the champion's corner. But Courtney was game to the end, instead of quitting, as many other fighters would have done under the circumstances, he struggled to his feet still swinging fiercely at the elusive Corbett, who followed him closely to land the knock-out blow. Along one side of the ring Courtney reeled, fighting back with all his might, although he was too dazed to know where to direct his blows. His pluck and sand were remarkable, and even Corbett's seconds felt for the poor fellow. Jim had to finish him, however, as a matter of business, so he nailed him one on the jaw with his left, and then felled him like an ox with his right on the same place. Courtney rolled over gasping and then half crawled to his knees, but his strength had left him, and he pitched foreward on his face insensible. Referee Eckhardt counted off ten seconds, and declared Peter out.

CORBETT CARRIES COURTNEY TO HIS CORNER.

Corbett immediately rushed across the ring, picked Courtney up in his arms and carried him to his corner, where he helped bring him to his senses by pinching his ears and slapping his hands. A few moments later, when Trenton's Pride opened his eyes, he smiled faintly and said:

"I was all right until I struck the floor. Then I couldn't quite place myself. This Corbett is much stronger and a harder hitter than Fitzsimmons, and can lick him, sure. I've tackled both and I know what it is."

Corbett shook him warmly by the hand and exclaimed:

"Say, my boy, I give you credit for being one of the pluckiest men I ever faced. You put up a great fight and did wonderfully well. You took an awful punching, and I want to congratulate you."

AFTER THE FIGHT WAS OVER.

Then the fighters, their seconds, and friends hurried out of the Black Maria and were soon ready for the trip back to New York. Before leaving the laboratory Corbett was introduced to Edison's two sons, who seemed delighted to grasp the hand that did up Courtney.

Corbett was elated over his success, but he said that Courtney had really faced him but two rounds under Queensberry rules, or six minutes in all. He said he knew the public would give credit to Courtney for staying six rounds, but they would not consider that each round was of a minute's duration. Courtney at once claimed that he stayed longer than Charley Mitchell, as the Englishman was knocked out by Corbett in three rounds, but he soon changed his mind on that point.

Two year ago yesterday Corbett beat Sullivan at New Orleans, so that Jim's latest triumph can be regarded as a sort of anniversary. When the party reached the railroad station, a crowd of 2,000 or more men, women, and children covered the platform and filled the waiting rooms.

The fact that there had been a fight at the laboratory was known by everybody, but the particulars were lacking. Corbett took a seat in the waiting room and was immediately surrounded. One man walked coolly forward and touched Corbett on the lapel of his coat. Then he walked back just as coolly, while the crowd couldn't understand his audacity. The fellow, as Corbett explained, simply wanted to tell his friends that he had touched Corbett, but not financially, of course. Finally a young man with glasses perched close to the tip of his nose pucked up courage enough to say:

"Are you Mr. Corbett?"

"Yes," was Jim's reply. "What can I do for you?"

"Well, you had a fight up at Edison's to-day, and I want to know did you knock anybody out?"

"No! No!" laughed Corbett, "I just had a friendly boxing match with my trainer, McVey over there, so that Mr. Edison could work his new-fangled machine."

"Oh, that was it, eh? Well, you must be very clever. That McVey is an awful big man." Then the young man walked away, while Corbett longed for the arrival of the 2 o'clock train. When it finally did roll into the station, Jim and his followers, together with Courtney, jumped into the smoking car and were soon on the ferryboat. They all gave a sigh of relief when they landed at the foot of Barkley street, out of the reach of Jersey Justice. All hands repaired to Johnny Eckhardt's place, where lunch was served, and Corbett opened wine. Courtney by this time had recovered his former equilibrium, and after drinking several glasses of fizz as if it were beer he exclaimed:

"I tell you what it is, boys, this here stuff is liable to change your color if you take enough of it." Then he took another gulp, and at a late hour last night he had no idea of returning to Trenton.

It was the original intention of the producers of the affair to have John L. Sullivan stand up before Corbett for six rounds, but Sullivan wanted $25,000 for his services. (*New York Sun*, 8 September 1894, 1-2.)

CHARGED THE GRAND JURY.
JUDGE DEPUE WANTS THE CORBETT FIGHT INVESTIGATED.
Touches Upon the Killing of Hugh Drain, and the cases of Albert Turton, Mary Russo,
Harry Kohl and Others—Sheriff's Constables Appointed—No Supreme Court Cases this Week.

The County Courts got down to their regular business to-day, for the September term. In the Circuit Court the morning was taken up in setting down the days for calling causes. There was a fair sprinkling of lawyers in Judge Depue's Court when the new Grand Jury came in and heard the Judge's charge.

There was a smell of fresh paint and varnish in the atmosphere. The usual formalities were gone through by Court Crier Ougheltree and the accumulation of six weeks of dust was shaken from the old court-house bell a few minutes before 10 o'clock.

The names of the Grand Jurors have already been given. Judges Kirkpatrick, Ledwith, and Schalk sat with Judge Depue during the delivery of the charge. Cyrus Currier, the twenty-fourth man on the jury was excused from duty according to custom, and the County Clerk swore the jurors, after which Judge Depue delivered the charge.

Matters of intense local interest were touched upon and the homicide cases that have shocked the community since the last term—the Hugh Drain case, that of Albert Turton, Mary Russo and Harry Kohl. The deaths of John Curley and Isaac Bartl were reviewed and the Grand Jury was instructed to look into the Corbett fight in West Orange, before Edison's kinetoscope, and find an indictment if the law has been violated.

The charge is as follows:

Gentlemen of the Grand Jury: A brief reference to such matters as have come to my knowledge is all I propose this morning. If occasion shall arise during your sittings, I will be ready at any time to communicate with the Grand Jury. A number of inquisitions have been returned to this court, a brief notice of which is all that is necessary at this time....

I have also had sent to me from several sources newspaper accounts and descriptions of an alleged violation of the criminal law in West Orange under the pretext of "scientific experiments." If the reports that are contained in the newspapers represent these facts truly, there has undoubtedly been a violation of the law. It will be your duty to take notice of it, no matter what collateral purpose, what incidental motive, parties may have had in view in conducting these violations of law. The criminal laws apply to all classes of the community and a man may as well do murder for the sake of scientific investigation as to violate any other laws for inquiries and experiments of this character. I really hope that these reports were exaggerated but I will ask you, gentlemen, to investigate them, and if, as appears very probable, there has been a violation of the law, the Court will certainly expect from this Grand Jury that it will be followed by indictment, no matter who are the parties concerned. (*Newark Daily Advertiser*, 11 September 1894, 1-2.)

NOT REGARDED AS A FIGHT.
EDISON'S IDEA OF THE CORBETT-COURTNEY MILL.
Rumors that a Deputy Sheriff is at the Laboratory at West Orange Awaiting an Opportunity
to Serve a Summons on Those Implicated—The Report Denied at the Wizard's Workshop.

It is rumored that a Deputy Sheriff is at the Edison laboratory in West Orange this afternoon, to serve summonses on the persons implicated in the recent Corbett-Courtney fight before the kinetoscope.

At the laboratory this afternoon, the rumor was emphatically denied. None of those who were present at the fight were in the laboratory when the reporter called. It was the talk around the Court House to-day that the principals and witnesses in the fight would be brought before the Grand Jury, in conformity with the charge made by Judge Depue yesterday. In fact, it is said that the subpoenas are out. None of the court officials would deny or affirm the report.

OGDENSBURG, N.J., Sept. 12.—Thomas A. Edison said yesterday in speaking of Judge Depue's charge to the Grand Jury in the matter of the Corbett-Courtney prize fight before the kinetoscope:

"I don't see how there could be any trouble about that fight. Those kinetograph people take pictures of anything that comes along. They have to do it, and we don't interfere with them.

"Certainly, I did not understand that a prize-fight was to take place, and it was not a prize-fight in any sense of the word, as I understand it. It was one of such boxing exhibitions as are given at athletic clubs in New York and other cities. I have been told that the men wore five-ounce gloves, and that it was a contest similar to others that have been given for reproduction by the kinetograph.

"I was not there, I have my business to attend to up here, but I have seen some of my men who were there and they say that the contest was similar to others, except that Corbett being one of the principals there was more interest in it.

"There was no knocking out done. It was simply a boxing match for a show for which these men were paid, and nothing more. The people who are making a fuss about it have not been correctly informed as to the facts. I don't anticipate any trouble for I don't see how they can prove it to be anything more than a boxing match. I should certainly not permit any fight to a finish in my place under any consideration." (*Newark Daily Advertiser,* 12 September 1894, 1.)

SOME CITY VIEWS AFOOT.

...A tall, red haired man leaned over the kinetoscope in a Broadway establishment a few days ago looking at Champion Corbett polish off that aspiring young pugilist Peter Courtney. As he looked, his big shoulders hitched convulsively and his hands were clinched, as though he were countering every blow. When the knockout came, a sneer overspread his countenance.

"Well, what do you think of him?" asked a burley looking individual near the box office window. "I think he is quite rude," was the reply, "but if he ever goes up against me he won't have the snap he had in you, Courtney."

"That's all right, Fitz," said the burly man, "but don't go into the fight thinking you are going to have a kindergarten. He can hit like a mule kicking." "Well all I got to say is this, that if he makes some of the moves with me he makes in that looking glass there I'll punch his head off."

Then Fitz buttoned up his long frock coat, threw back his shoulders and walked away. (*New York Herald*, 14 October 1894, 5D.)

After the success of The Corbett-Courtney Fight, *there was considerable interest in staging a bona fide championship bout for the kinetograph. This failed to materialize for a number of reasons, however, including technological limitations.*

KINETOSCOPE WON'T DO.
Its Impracticability for the Corbett-Fitzsimmons Fight as Shown by Manager Brady.
SPEAKS FROM EXPERIENCE.
He Suggests That "Fitz," Perhaps, Is Not Over Eager To Do Battle with the Champion.
SAYS FLORIDA'S ALL RIGHT.

Of late rumors have been circulated to the effect that Corbett and Fitzsimmons would never fight in Florida. Sporting men, however, who are close to the officials of the Florida Athletic Club do not hesitate to say that it is their belief that the big battle will take place in Florida, as per agreement. In speaking of this matter, and of Fitzsimmons' anxiety to have the battle decided before the kinetoscope, Manager William A. Brady said yesterday:–

"If the Florida Athletic Club is unable to pull off the fight we are willing to accept any reasonable offer the kinetoscope people may make for a fight in America, but I understand Mr. Edison says he does not want the fight. Therefore I can't see why Fitzsimmons keeps harping about the kinetoscope. Fitzsimmons has never had any experience with kinetoscopes, while Corbett and I have.

KINETOSCOPE NOT PRACTICAL.

"Furthermore, in its present condition, the kinetoscope would be absolutely useless for a finish fight. A kinetoscope round is limited to a minute and a half. Under the Marquis of Queensbury rules a round lasts three minutes. Mr. Edison hopes to perfect the kinetoscope so that it can be regulated to suit any time, but it may take him a long time to do so, and Fitzsimmons and Corbett might be grayheaded before he succeeded.

"When Corbett fought Courtney before the kinetoscope the machine got out of order, causing a delay of fifteen minutes. If such an accident should happen in a big fight the man having the worse of it up to that time would have a fine chance to recuperate. In this way the men might fight until the Judgement Day and neither be able to knock the other out. I mention this merely to show Fitzsimmons' absurd position in the matter.

FOR "FITZ" TO THINK ABOUT.

"If Fitzsimmons really wants to fight Corbett he had better live up to his agreement with the Florida Athletic Club, whose sincerity of purpose is shown by the business like manner in which it has arranged the preliminaries for the fight. Mitchell did not want to fight Corbett, and his talk before the battle was not unlike Fitzsimmons' at the present time.

"Perhaps Fitzsimmons is trying to crawl out of his match with Corbett. Mitchell said his fight with Jim would not take place in Florida, but it did. Now, Fitzsimmons makes a similar declaration. With him as with Mitchell the wish may be father to the thought. I see no reason why Corbett and Fitzsimmons should not fight in Florida, providing Fitzsimmons is sincere." (*New York Herald*, 28 December 1894, 13.)

The Glenroy Brothers appeared in New York vaudeville houses with some frequency during 1894. At Tony Pastor's for the week beginning 18 June 1894, they offered "The Comic View of Boxing, The Tramp and Athlete." They also performed at Keith's Union Square Theatre for the week beginning 16 July 1894.

55   **[Glenroy Brothers, no. 1]**
LENGTH: 50 ft.   © No reg.
PRODUCER: W.K.L. Dickson, Raff & Gammon.
CAMERA: William Heise.
CAST: Glenroy Brothers.
PRODUCTION DATE: 13 September 1894.
LOCATION: Black Maria, West Orange, N.J.
SOURCE:
DESCRIPTION:
SUBJECT: Vaudeville–performances. Boxing.
ARCHIVE:
CITATIONS: "Kinetoscope Company in Acct. with Holland Brothers, 13 September 1894," MH-BA.
NOTE: Raff & Gammon paid the Glenroy Brothers $26 to appear in this film. See also *[Glenroy Brothers, no. 2]*, *[Glenroy Brothers, no. 3]*, and *[Glenroy Brothers, no. 4]*.

At Liberty–Glenroy Brothers
A Good Strong Act
This week Koster & Bial's.
(Advertisement, *New York Clipper*, 15 September 1894, 449.)

Rat killing was one of several blood sports filmed at the Edison laboratory in 1894-1895 (others being cock fighting, dog fighting, and boxing). It was the least successful, "the rats being too small." (Kinetoscope Company to Kansas Phonograph Company, 29 December 1894, 1:172, MH-BA.)

56   **Rat Killing / Rat Catcher / [Rats and Terrier, no. 1]**
LENGTH: 150 ft.   © No reg.
PRODUCER: W.K.L. Dickson, Raff & Gammon.
CAMERA: William Heise.
CAST:
PRODUCTION DATE: 20 September 1894.
LOCATION: Black Maria, West Orange, N.J.
SOURCE:
DESCRIPTION: "Dick the Rat" and his rat-terrier. The dog is turned loose among a lot of big, live rats, and kills them in lightning order. (The Kinetoscope Company, *Edison's Latest Wonders: The Kinetograph, The Kinetoscope*, [October 1894]).
SUBJECT: Animal fighting. Rats. Dogs.
ARCHIVE:
CITATIONS: "Kinetoscope Company in Acct. with Holland Brothers, 22 September 1894," MH-BA; Kinetoscope Co. to Kansas Phonograph Co., invoice, 29 December 1894, 1:172, MH-BA.
NOTE: W.A. Heitler was paid $32.30 to provide rats and possibly the weasel for the "rat catching" subjects. The length of time needed for the killing of the six rats required a 150-foot load of film. It is unclear which of the three *Rats and Terrier* negatives was used to generate prints. The negative for at least one of the *Rats and Terrier* subjects, probably the only reasonably successful one, was ruined in late 1894. (W.K.L. Dickson to Raff & Gammon, 8 January 1895, MH-BA.)

57   **[Rats and Terrier, no. 2]**
LENGTH: [150 ft.]   © No reg.

PRODUCER: W.K.L. Dickson, Raff & Gammon.
CAMERA: William Heise.
CAST:
PRODUCTION DATE: 20 September 1894.
LOCATION: Black Maria, West Orange, N.J.
SOURCE:
DESCRIPTION:
SUBJECT: Animal fighting. Rats. Dogs.
ARCHIVE:
CITATIONS:
NOTE: See note for film no. 56.

58 [Rats and Terrier, no. 3]
LENGTH: [150 ft.]   © No reg.
PRODUCER: W.K.L. Dickson, Raff & Gammon.
CAMERA: William Heise.
CAST:
PRODUCTION DATE: 20 September 1894.
LOCATION: Black Maria, West Orange, N.J.
SOURCE:
DESCRIPTION:
SUBJECT: Animal fighting. Rats. Dogs.
ARCHIVE:
CITATIONS:
NOTE: See note for film no. 56.

59 [Rats and Weasel]
LENGTH: 50 ft.   © No reg.
PRODUCER: W.K.L. Dickson, Raff & Gammon.
CAMERA: William Heise.
CAST:
PRODUCTION DATE: 20 September 1894.
LOCATION: Black Maria, West Orange, N.J.
SOURCE:
DESCRIPTION:
SUBJECT: Animal fighting. Rats. Weasels.
ARCHIVE:
CITATIONS:
NOTE: This unsuccessful film was never sold commercially.

In the Edison laboratory, on Valley road, West Orange, Professor W.K.L. Dickson, one of the leading spirits in the development of the kinetograph, had great success last Thursday in taking a rat-killing exhibition. Through a New York professional rat-catcher, he secured a large cage full of dock rats, and he has had at the laboratory for some time two pretty little full-blooded rat terriers. It was an extremely difficult task to arrange the ring, which, on account of the limitations of the kinetograph, could be only four feet square. The first contest was with six rats turned loose in the pit at once, and in fifty-two and one-half seconds all had been killed by one of the terriers. A second and a third trial were made with equally good results. A trial was made with a weasel and the same number of rats, but this was not a success as one of the rats fastened its teeth in the weasel's lip and the weasel squealed and fled in terror to the corner of the ring. There were no spectators, except a few of the employees of the laboratory. ("Before the Kinetograph," *Newark Daily Advertiser*, 24 September 1894, 3.)

The Glenroy Brothers visited the Edison Laboratory at least three times: previously on 13 September 1894 and subsequently on 6 October 1894; the reasons for their repeated trips are not known, although the first two dates probably produced unacceptable negatives.

60 [Glenroy Brothers, no. 2]
LENGTH: 50 ft.   © No reg.
PRODUCER: W.K.L. Dickson, Raff & Gammon.

CAMERA: William Heise.
CAST: Glenroy Brothers.
PRODUCTION DATE: 22 September 1894.
LOCATION: Black Maria, West Orange, N.J.
SOURCE:
DESCRIPTION:
SUBJECT: Vaudeville–performances. Boxing. Burlesque.
ARCHIVE:
CITATIONS: "Kinetoscope Company in Acct. with Holland, Brothers, NY," MH-BA.
NOTE: See also *[Glenroy Brothers, no. 1]*, *[Glenroy Brothers, no. 3]*, and *[Glenroy Brothers, no. 4]*.

Buffalo Bill's Wild West was based at Ambrose Park in Brooklyn, New York, from 12 May to 6 October 1894. Numerous performers associated with the show appeared in front of Edison's camera in September and October. Buffalo Bill led the first expedition on Monday morning, September 24th, less than two weeks before his organization departed for Europe. He brought with him a large group of American Indians, the first time these stalwarts of the western appeared before a motion picture camera.

61 √Buffalo Bill

LENGTH: 50 ft.   © No reg.
PRODUCER: W.K.L. Dickson, Maguire & Baucus.
CAMERA: William Heise.
CAST: William Frederick Cody.
PRODUCTION DATE: 24 September 1894.
LOCATION: Black Maria, West Orange, N.J.
SOURCE:

DESCRIPTION: The noted proprietor of "The Wild West." (The Kinetoscope Company, *Price List of Films*, [May 1895], 3.)
The famous army scout in an exhibition of rifle shooting. A fine picture of the principal, and beautiful smoke effects. (F.Z. Maguire & Co., *Catalogue*, [March 1898], 30.)
SUBJECT: Wild west shows. Shooting. Rifles and rifle practice. Buffalo Bill's Wild West.
ARCHIVE:
CITATIONS: "The Wild West," *New York Clipper*, 19 May 1894, 166; "Two Famous War Chiefs," *New York Herald,* 1 July 1894, 7; "The Wonderful Wild West," *New York Times*, 2 September 1894, 11; "Indians Before the Kinetograph," *Orange Journal*, 27 September 1894, 5; "Indians Before the Kinetoscope," *Orange Chronicle*, 29 September 1894, 4; W.K.L. Dickson and Antonia Dickson, *History of the Kinetograph, Kinetoscope and Kineto-Phonograph*, 20 (with illustration). Ohio Phonograph Co., *The Edison Kinetoscope. Price List*, August 1895, 8; Maguire & Baucus, *Edison and International Photographic Films*, April 1897, 5; Maguire & Baucus, *Fall Catalogue*, 1897, 11.
NOTE: Among Buffalo Bill's numerous imitators and competitors at this time were Pawnee Bill's Wild West Show (then in Europe), Lucky Bill's Historical Wild West and Texas Hippodrome, and Mexican Billy's Wild West Fair Ground Show. (*New York Clipper*, 8 September 1894, 422.)

62 *Sioux Ghost Dance / Ghost Dance / Ghost

LENGTH: 50 ft.   © No reg.
PRODUCER: W.K.L. Dickson, Maguire & Baucus.
CAMERA: William Heise.
CAST:
PRODUCTION DATE: 24 September 1894.
LOCATION: Black Maria, West Orange, N.J.
SOURCE:

DESCRIPTION: One of the most peculiar customs of the Sioux Tribe is here shown, the dancers being genuine Sioux Indians in full war paint and war costumes. (*Edison Films*, March 1900, 19.)

SUBJECT: Wild west shows. Dancing. Indians of North America. Buffalo Bill's Wild West.

ARCHIVE: FrBaADF, NNMoMA, CLAc.

CITATIONS: The Kinetoscope Company, *Price List of Films*, [May 1895], 3; Ohio Phonograph Co., *The Edison Kinetoscope. Price List*, August 1895, 7; Maguire & Baucus, *Edison Films*, 20 January 1897, 6; Maguire & Baucus, *Edison and International Photographic Films*, April 1897, 8; Maguire & Baucus, *Fall Catalogue*, 1897, 12; F.Z. Maguire & Co., *Catalogue*, [March 1898], 31; *Edison Films*, July 1901, 41.

NOTE:

63 √Indian War Council / War Council

LENGTH: 50 ft.   © No reg.

PRODUCER: W.K.L. Dickson.

CAMERA: William Heise.

CAST: William Frederick Cody.

PRODUCTION DATE: 24 September 1894.

LOCATION: Black Maria, West Orange, N.J.

SOURCE:

DESCRIPTION: Showing seventeen different persons—Indian warriors and white men—in Council. (The Kinetoscope Company, *Price List of Films*, [May 1895], 3.) Here is a group of genuine Sioux Indians sitting around in war council, deliberating. Buffalo Bill is addressing them. (*Edison Films*, March 1900, 19.)

SUBJECT: Wild west shows. Indians of North America. Buffalo Bill's Wild West.

ARCHIVE:

CITATIONS: W.K.L. Dickson and Antonia Dickson, *History of the Kinetograph, Kinetoscope and Kineto-Phonograph*, 21 (with illustration). Ohio Phonograph Co., *The Edison Kinetoscope. Price List*, August 1895, 9; Maguire & Baucus, *Edison and International Photographic Films*, April 1897, 10; Maguire & Baucus, *Fall Catalogue*, 1897, 12; F.Z. Maguire & Co., *Catalogue*, [March 1898], 31.

NOTE:

64 *Buffalo Dance

LENGTH: 50 ft.   © No reg.

PRODUCER: W.K.L. Dickson, Maguire & Baucus.

CAMERA: William Heise.

CAST: Last Horse, Parts His Hair, Hair Coat.

PRODUCTION DATE: 24 September 1894.

LOCATION: Black Maria, West Orange, N.J.

SOURCE:

DESCRIPTION:

SUBJECT: Wild west shows. Indians of North America. Dancing. Buffalo Bill's Wild West.

ARCHIVE: CaOOANF, FrBaADF, NNMoMA, DLC-Hendricks, CLAc.

CITATIONS:

NOTE: This film was incorrectly identified as *Sioux Indian Ghost Dance* in W.K.L. Dickson and Antonia Dickson, *History of the Kinetograph, Kinetoscope and Kineto-Phonograph*, 23 (with illustration). The symbol "MB" was written in ink on the negative at the top of the frame to identify the company as financing the film.

A production still for *Indian War Council* featuring Buffalo Bill negotiating with the Indians.
The photograph was shot on the stage of the Black Maria (24 September 1894).

INDIANS AT WAR ON LONG ISLAND.
Mayor Schieren Witnesses the Annihilation of United States Troops.
BUFFALO BILL DIRECTED IT.
Wild West Up to Date Receives its Initial Production Amid Powder and Applause.
CONGRESS OF ROUGH RIDERS.

That medley of the heroic life sports of various nationalities, a-foot and a-horse, known as the "Wild West," had its initial production for the season at Ambrose Park, at the foot of Thirty-ninth street, South Brooklyn, yesterday afternoon. It was carried through with a dash and daring that impelled continuous applause.

The accessories of the representation were of the best. Ambrose Park has been converted into a tented encampment, with streets laid out and turf and flower gardens galore along their edges. In the middle of the enclosure is the four and half acre arena surrounded on three sides by a huge covered stand with twenty thousand seats.

There was the inspiration of a vast audience of probably fifteen thousand to spur on the performers yesterday.

Mayor Schieren with several members of his Cabinet had the central box. Private Secretary and Mrs. Holly represented Mayor Gilroy. George Gould had another box with a party of friends, and many other well known persons were in the audience which was of a representative character.

Buffalo Bill himself received an ovation. It was his first appearance here since his European tour of several years' duration and his welcome was very warm.

FEATURES OF THE SHOW.

The entertainment opened with a grand entry of the whole company, the various troops of cavalry, Indians, rough riders and others galloping into position to the sound of continuous applause on the part of the big audience. Buffalo Bill, on a spirited animal, made a sensational appearance at the last, and then with well executed evolutions the arena was cleared. More than four hundred persons made up this brilliant procession.

Then followed in quick succession the features of the exhibition. Four troops of cavalry, representing the Seventh United States Cavalry, the Fifth Royal Irish Lancers, a detachment from the Garde Cuirassiers of Emperor William of Germany and the Dragoons of France, executed a series of manoeuvres appertaining to the regulations of these countries, that served to make, with the variegated uniforms of the men, a very attractive series of pictures.

Scenes of life in the West, that really made up the entire show when the Wild West was originally launched, "took" with the audience. There was a dash and apparent danger about it that proved entertaining. The Indians comprise representatives of the Sioux, Cheyennes, Shoshones and Ogalallas. There are 135 of them, including a sprinkling of squaws and lively youths.

They came upon the grounds, chiefs mounted and braves and squaws on foot. Tepees were set up, an encampment laid out, and then the tribes went through councils of war, war dances in which the predominating features were horrible shrieking and the noise of half a dozen drums. Indian sports on foot and mounted were exhibited.

A rude interruption to these noisy but peaceful scenes followed upon the approach of Custer's famous Seventh cavalry, whose scouts came upon the Indian village.

The action that followed was extremely realistic. The background of the arena, beyond rolling turf at its far end, is a huge representation in oils on canvas, showing in its perspective the valley of the Little Big Horn where General Custer, at the head of the Seventh cavalry, met his death at the hands of Indians, some of whom are now in the Wild West. Some of the troopers were also in the Seventh at the time.

REALISTIC INDIAN WARFARE.

Upon this scene came the Seventh on a run, and there was a sharp engagement between the troop and the Indians. Horses and men went down as in true warfare, and the cavalry was apparently annihilated. There was the regulation attack by Indians on the famous old Deadwood coach, rusty and battle scarred, groaning with its weight of years, and drawn by six mules. "Old Man" Nelson was on top, armed to the teeth. With a reckless use of blank cartridges the cowboys beat off the red men and rescued the half dozen guests from the grand stand who had taken the ride.

Other features of Western life were given with good results. There was a great deal of skillful riding by the congress of Rough Riders of the World. These included our own cowboys, Russian Cossacks, Mexicans, Arabs and Indians, each of whom presented the characteristic rough outdoor sports of their countries.

Miss Annie Oakley exhibited her prowess as a rifle shot, and Johnnie Baker cracked glass balls while standing on his head. The rifle shooting however was brought to a climax by Buffalo Bill himself, who, mounted on a swift bronco, gave some examples of his skill with firearms. He only missed three or four of a couple of baskets of glass balls thrown into the air while he encircled the arena. During the grand review at the outset one of the Irish Lancers who had before been troubled with a weak heart fell from his charger. He was attended in the arena by a surgeon, who said he would be all right to-day. (*New York Herald,* 13 May 1894, 5B.)

BEFORE THE KINETOGRAPH
EXHIBITION BY BUFFALO BILL AND HIS INDIANS
Last Horse and His Band Perform as the Machine Revolves—Colonel Cody's Shooting
Feats Recorded—Mrs. Edison and Miss Stella Edison Present—Battle Between Rats and a Terrier

Buffalo Bill and his troupe of Indians from the Wild West Show came out to Orange this morning to give an exhibition in front of the kinetograph. The took the steam road to Orange station, and from there took the cars of the Consolidated Traction Company to the Laboratory. In the party were Major Jack Stillwell, the celebrated scout, whose wonderful feat of carrying dispatches four days and four nights through the centre of the Indian lines in 1867 is still fresh in the minds of the public; John Shangren, the interpreter; Major John M. Burke, manager of the Wild West Show and F. Madden, the advertising manager of the show.

The Indians were all of the Brule and Ogalalla tribes and the big chief was Last Horse. The other Indians were Parts His Hair, Black Cat, Hair Coat, Charging Crow, Dull Knife, Holy Bear, Crazy Bull, Strong Talker, Pine, Little Eagle Horse, Young Bear, Johnny No Neck Burke, Seven Up and Runs About.

Mrs. Edison and Miss Stella Edison were present to see the exhibition, which was under the management of Professor W.K.L. Dickson.

The pow-wow opened with an exhibition of rapid firing in a circle by Mr. Cody. Then came the Indian war dance, in which the entire band, in their warpaint and feathers, to the music of the native drums, danced a howling war dance, brandishing their tomahawks and scalping knives. This was followed by a war council between Buffalo Bill and the chiefs, where the wampum belt was passed around and the pipe of peace smoked to the ejaculations of "how, how."

Next came a group picture of all the party arranged in artistic shape. The morning closed with a buffalo dance, given to the music of the two drummers, by the three great chiefs, Last Horse, Parts His Hair and Hair Coat. The party took the 12:58 train back to New York. (*Newark Daily Advertiser*, 24 September 1894, 3.)

RED MEN AGAIN CONQUERED
Easily Subdued Before the Rapid Fire of the Kinetoscope at Edison's Laboratory.
MORE EFFECTIVE THAN GUNPOWDER.
Holy Bear of an Investigative Turn, Became Unwittingly Attached to a Live Wire.
WONDER OF THE SAVAGES.

A party of Indians in full war paint invaded the Edison laboratory at West Orange yesterday and faced unflinchingly the unerring rapid fire of the kinetograph. It was indeed a memorable engagement, no less so than the battle of Wounded Knee, still fresh in the minds of the warriors.

It was probably more effective in demonstrating to the red men the power and supremacy of the white man, for savagery and the most advanced science stood face to face, and there was an absolute triumph for one without the spilling of a single drop of blood.

Holy Bear will, more than any of the visitors, bear the lesson to heart, for in endeavoring to grasp the situation, he included a live wire as one of the details, and perforce executed a war dance which threatened to dismember himself. He was a very meek, docile and fearful Indian when at last rescued from the current.

"Buffalo Bill" was at the head of the party, which arrived at the Orange station of the Delaware, Lackawanna and Western railroad at nine o'clock. Trolley cars conveyed them to the laboratory, a mile distant. Besides Major "Jack" Burke, there was Major "Jack" Stillwell, of El Reno, Oklahoma, whose feat of carrying despatches for four days and nights through hostile country in 1867 is stilled recalled along the frontier.

HOLY BEAR'S MISHAP.

The fifteen Indians were big chief Last Horse, and braves Parts His Hair, Black Cat, Hair Coat, Charging Crow, Dull Knife, Holy Bear, Crazy Bull, Strong Talker, Pine, Little Eagle Horse, Young Bear, Seven Up, Runs About and Johnny-No-Neck-Burke, the little lad who was the sole survivor of the fight at Wounded Knee.

While preparations were being made for the kinetographic pictures the Indians manifested the liveliest interest in the wonderful things about them. They peeped into the kinetoscope containing a strip of the Corbett-Courtney fight and yelled in surprise. Crazy Bull took only a brief glance and when he saw the figures moving as though in life, he sprang quickly from the machine. "It is bewitched!" he exclaimed. "It is bad medicine!"

Holy Bear, as much as an Indian's stoicism would admit, smiled derisively, and uttering a Sioux epigram at his companion's expense, looked at the mimic fight with the composure of a person who witnessed the same sort of thing every day. Holy Bear has a bent for investigation and generally wants to know the reason why concerning everything that is new to his ken.

Parts His Hair, who is an up to date red man, is just a little jealous of the progressive spirit of Holy Bear, and when he looked into the kinetoscope and beheld its wonders he did not even emit the suspicion of a grunt. Thirteen other Indians did, however, and not only grunted but said "How!" "How!" This indicates wonder and surprise. But Holy Bear and Parts His Hair showed no evidence of either.

Then Holy Bear started an investigation on his own account and strode past Parts His Hair with an expression of superior intelligence in his face. It was not apparent to the ordinary observer, for it was hidden under a good layer of war paint, but it was there just the same and Parts His Hair knew it. But he said nothing, only waited.

PARTS HIS HAIR'S TRIUMPH.

He was soon rewarded, for it was not a minute later that Holy Bear began to examine the big cable that carries the electric current from the dynamos in the laboratory to the phonographic works, half a mile away.

He got hold of it just at the spot where the insulation was a little worn. Howls and shrieks rent the air as the luckless Indian's hands were firmly glued to the cable. It is said that when Parts His Hair saw this he broke into something that resembled a laugh. At last the current was shut off and Holy Bear released from his predicament. It was fortunate for him that the current was weak and used to run some of the incandescent lamps about the place.

Mrs. Edison and her stepdaughter, Miss Stella Edison, as well as Thomas A. Edison, Jr., drove into the yard shortly after the arranged show opened and viewed it with great interest. Colonel Cody first gave a fine exhibition of his rapid firing, discharging his Winchester sixteen times at imaginary objects all around a circle within twenty seconds. Then came the war dance of the Indians. The two native drummers pounded away on their curious drums and the braves whooped and howled, brandished their tomahawks and scalping knives, attitudinized and showed off their talent to the best advantage. Last Horse, clad only in a breech cloth, gave a pas de guerre in what appeared a most comical way, and called forth shouts of laughter.

Next came a war council of all the braves in a circle with "Buffalo Bill" in the centre. The argument was gone through with dumb show, the string of wampum duly delivered and the pipe of peace smoked, all shaking hands at the close and grunting out numerous "Hows!" After a group picture had been taken of the entire party, the show closed with the characteristic buffalo dance by Last Horse, Parts His Hair and Hair Coat. (*New York Herald*, 25 September 1894, 12.)

Aunty (showing Bible pictures to four-year-old niece)–And now, Maggie, who is the man in the lions' den?
Maggie–Buffalo Bill, Aunt Jennie. (*New York Herald*, 18 November 1894, 4E.)

George Layman, "the expressionist," appeared at Proctor's Theatre for the week commencing 7 May 1894. The performer, who was known as "the man with 1,000 faces," appeared at Pastor's Theatre in early December 1899: a month later he was dead at the age of 36.

65 **"The Man of a Thousand Faces" / Layman**
LENGTH: 50 ft.   © No reg.
PRODUCER: W.K.L. Dickson, Raff & Gammon.
CAMERA: William Heise.
CAST: George Layman.

PRODUCTION DATE: 24 September 1894.
LOCATION: Black Maria, West Orange, N.J.
SOURCE:
DESCRIPTION: A great act. (The Kinetoscope Company, *Edison's Latest Wonders: The Kinetograph, The Kinetoscope*, [October 1894].)
Man of thousand faces; facial changes. (F.Z. Maguire & Co., *Catalogue*, [March 1898], 31.)
SUBJECT: Vaudeville–performances. Facial expression.
ARCHIVE:
CITATIONS: "Kinetoscope Company in Acct. with Holland Brothers," 24 September 1894, MH-BA; Raff & Gammon to J.L. Andem, invoice, 12 November 1894, 1:34, MH-BA. The Kinetoscope Company, *Price List of Films*, [May 1895], 3; Maguire & Baucus, *Edison and International Photographic Films*, April 1897, 11; Maguire & Baucus, *Fall Catalogue*, 1897, 12.
NOTE: Layman received only $6 to appear in this film, which may be at the origins of the "facial expression film," a genre that was popular in the late 1890s and early 1900s. Sigmund Lubin made a subsequent facial expression film of Layman, which survives at CL-UC. A still from the Lubin picture illustrates this entry.

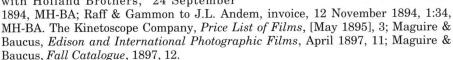

OPEN FOR SPRING AND SUMMER ENGAGEMENTS.
LAYMAN,
MAN OF ONE THOUSAND FACES. Can be engaged for the season of 1896-97 for Vaudeville, Comedy, Dramatic, or Concerts. Will add many new novelties with my Regular Specialty. N.B.–Can open or close my act in (one) if required. Permanent address, 117 East Ninety-Second Street, New York City, or all agents. (Advertisement, *New York Clipper*, 2 May 1896, 142.)

George Layman, a vaudeville performer, died at his home in New York City on January 18, of heart failure. He was known as "the man with 1,000 faces," and his specialty won favor with audiences both in America and Europe. He was thirty-six years of age, and had been on the stage for eighteen years. The remains were interred on Jan. 19 in the Washington Cemetary, Brooklyn, N.Y. (*New York Dramatic Mirror*, 3 February 1900, 13.)

Helen Englehart, like other sports figures, made much of her living on the stage, as half of various vaudeville duos. Englehart and Blanchard, billed as "lady fencers and sharpshooters," performed at Proctor's 23rd Street Theatre for the week beginning 1 October 1894—one week after they appeared before the kinetograph.

66 Lady Fencers (With Foils)
LENGTH: 50 ft.   © No reg.
PRODUCER: W.K.L. Dickson.
CAMERA: William Heise.
CAST: Helen Englehart, Louise Blanchard (Englehart Sisters).
PRODUCTION DATE: 26 September 1894.
LOCATION: Black Maria, West Orange, N.J.
SOURCE:
DESCRIPTION:
SUBJECT: Sports. Fencing.
ARCHIVE:
CITATIONS: Raff & Gammon, receipts, MH-BA; Raff & Gammon to Columbia Phonograph Parlor, 27 October 1894, MH-BA; "Sporting News," *New York Herald*, 24 July 1894, 7. The Kinetoscope Company, *Bulletin No. 1*, [December 1894].
NOTE: Englehart and Blanchard received $10 for appearing before the kinetograph.

67 Lady Fencers (With Broadswords) / Broadsword Combat / Broadswords
LENGTH: 50 ft.   © No reg.
PRODUCER: W.K.L. Dickson.
CAMERA: William Heise.

CAST: Helen Englehart, Louise Blanchard (Englehart Sisters).
PRODUCTION DATE: 26 September 1894.
LOCATION: Black Maria, West Orange, N.J.
SOURCE:
DESCRIPTION: By two famous lady fencers. (Maguire & Baucus, *Edison and International Photographic Films*, April 1897, 4.)
SUBJECT: Sports. Fencing.
ARCHIVE:
CITATIONS: Maguire & Baucus, *Fall Catalogue*, 1897, 12; F.Z. Maguire & Co., *Catalogue*, [March 1898], 32.
NOTE:

Englehart and Raymond, female fencers, has dissolved partnership. (*New York Clipper*, 19 May 1894, 165.)

Helen Englehart, lady fencer, has joined hands with her old partner Louise Blanchard. (*New York Clipper*, 26 May 1894, 180.)

The challenge of Madeline de Morna, the professional woman fencer of France, has been accepted by Helen Englehart, who says she will fence the French woman in New York, Chicago, Philadelphia or Boston for $1,000 a side. (*New York Herald*, 25 July 1894, 11.)

Englehart and Raymond, lady fencers, have closed their northwestern engagements. (*New York Clipper*, 18 April 1896, 102.)

68 ***Hornbacker-Murphy Fight / Hornbacker and Murphy**
LENGTH: 5 films of 50 ft. each.   © No reg.
PRODUCER: W.K.L. Dickson, Raff & Gammon.
CAMERA: William Heise.
CAST: Eugene Hornbacker.
PRODUCTION DATE: 2 October 1894.
LOCATION: Black Maria, West Orange, N.J.
SOURCE:
DESCRIPTION: The noted pugilists in a five-round contest. Lively infighting. Hard and rapid blows, and scientific sparring from first to last. (The Kinetoscope Company, *Edison's Latest Wonders: The Kinetograph, The Kinetoscope*, [October 1894].)
"Five Round Glove Contest to a finish." (The Kinetoscope Company, *Price List of Films*, [May 1895], 3.)

SUBJECT: Sports. Boxing.
ARCHIVE: NNMoMA.
CITATIONS: "Kinetoscope Company in Acct. with Holland Brothers," 29 September 1894 and 2 October 1894, MH-BA; Raff & Gammon to J.L.Andem, invoice, 24 October 1894, 1:18, MH-BA. Maguire & Baucus, *Edison and International Photographic Films*, April 1897, 10; Maguire & Baucus, *Fall Catalogue*, 1897, 12; F.Z. Maguire & Co., *Catalogue*, [March 1898], 33.
NOTE: Raff & Gammon paid Hornbacker and Murphy $68.30 on 29 September 1894 and $41.70 on 2 October 1894 for appearing in this five-part subject (a total of $110). Only one round survives at NNMoMA. It is one of the first films to have a placard in the scene with an "R" to indicate that it was financed by Raff & Gammon. In "Hard Fight with Gloves," the *New York Herald* mentions Hornbacker and a Dan Murphy (21 March 1894, 12). By 1898 F.Z. Maguire & Co. was advertising this subject as a four-round glove contest.

The danse du ventre, French for the belly dance, was also known as the "coochee coochee dance," "oriental dance" or the "muscle dance." In the wake of the World's Columbian Exposition, numerous women performed the highly erotic danse du ventre on the stage. Not infrequently, these performances were halted by the police. ("New Danse du

Ventre," New York Herald, 14 April 1894, 10.) Perhaps because the absence of presence offered by motion pictures provided a certain degree of protection from state censorship, the Edison staff often filmed coochee coochee dancers. Significantly, few of these films were ever listed in Edison catalogs—and then only long after their production. This suggests that a body of Edison films were circulated more or less clandestinely.

69 Danse du Ventre
LENGTH: 50 ft.   © No reg.
PRODUCER: W.K.L. Dickson, Raff & Gammon.
CAMERA: William Heise.
CAST: Madame Ruth or Rita.
PRODUCTION DATE: 2 October 1894.
LOCATION: Black Maria, West Orange, N.J.
SOURCE:
DESCRIPTION:
SUBJECT: Vaudeville–performances. Dancing. Danse du ventre.
ARCHIVE:
CITATIONS: "Kinetoscope Company in Acct. with Holland, Brothers," 2 October 1894, MH-BA.
NOTE: Madame Ruth or Rita was paid $25 to appear in this film.

Saturday, October 6th, was the day before Buffalo Bill's Wild West departed for Europe, and it was a busy one at the Black Maria. Many performers were filmed. As one newspaper reported (in a short article that misspelled most of their names):

Before the Kinetograph.

A party of Wild West performers under the guidance of F. Madden, advertising manager of Buffalo Bill's Wild West Show, accompanied by a number of the star players of Lucy Daly's Pickaninnies from the Casino Theatre, New York, visited the Edison laboratory about 11:30 o'clock this morning and performed before the Edison kinetograph. Lucy Daly's pickaninnies, Walter Wilkins, Denny Tolliver and Joe Rastus, gave a funny performance of dancing and tumbling. A Mexican duel with knives was fought by Dionisius Ramon and Pedro Esquibel, in which both participants were carved up in true Mexican style. Vincenti Orapazza gave an exhibition of lasso throwing, jumping through the loop of the lasso as it circled in the air. Sheik Habjtahaor gave an exhibition of tumbling and posturing with his gun, which he fired from all sorts of positions. A farcical pugilistic act was performed by Walton and Slevin, of Rice's "1492" Company. (*Newark Daily Advertiser*, 6 October 1894, 2.)

Walton and Slavin were the first to perform for the kinetograph on October 6th. They were then appearing on Broadway in the musical farce 1492, which had premiered in Boston on 3 September 1892 and opened in New York City on 15 May 1893 to positive reviews. After a brief summer break it resumed at the Garden Theatre on 27 August 1894 and completed its New York run on October 13th, one week after the duo's visit to the Black Maria.

70 √Walton and Slavin—From Rice's 1492 Co. / Walton and Slavin
LENGTH: 4 films of 50 ft. each.   © No reg.
PRODUCER: W.K.L. Dickson, Raff & Gammon.
CAMERA: William Heise.
CAST: Charles F. Walton (Captain Pinzon),
    John C. Slavin (Don Pedro Magerite).
PRODUCTION DATE: 6 October 1894.
LOCATION: Black Maria, West Orange, N.J.
SOURCE: *1492* (musical farce).
DESCRIPTION: "The Long and the Short of it."
    Comical and mirth exciting burlesque
    Boxing Contest from Rice's 1492. (The
    Kinetoscope Company, *Price List of
    Films*, [May 1895], 2.)
    A burlesque boxing bout in which the con-
    testants were a very tall, thin man and a
    very short, stout one. The little fellow was

knocked down several times and the movements of the boxers were well represented. (*New York Daily News,* 24 April 1896, clipping, MH-BA.)
SUBJECT: Musicals–performances. Boxing. Burlesque. Edward E. Rice.
ARCHIVE:
CITATIONS: "Kinetoscope Company in Acct. with Holland Brothers," 6 October 1894, MH-BA; Raff & Gammon to J.L. Andem, invoice, 12 November 1894, 1:34, MH-BA; "Before the Kinetograph," *Orange Chronicle,* 13 October 1894, 5; W.K.L. Dickson and Antonia Dickson, *History of the Kinetograph, Kinetoscope and Kineto-Phonograph,* 45 (with illustrations). The Kinetoscope Company, *Edison's Latest Wonders: The Kinetograph, The Kinetoscope,* [October 1894]).
NOTE: Raff & Gammon paid Walton & Slavin $26.75 to appear in these films. Charles F. Walton should not be confused with George Walton, who was appearing on the New York stage at this time in similar roles. George was a recent arrival from Australia, whose first appearance in America was in *Little Christopher Columbus.* For more information, see *Cupid's Dance* (film no. 51).

Walton & Slevin [sic], the "long and short of it," of Rice's "1492" company, gave a burlesque four round sparring bout before the Edison kinetoscope at East Orange, N.J., Oct. 5 [sic]. They were the first actors to appear before the machine. The short end won the bout. (*New York Clipper,* 13 October 1894, 506.)

TO MANAGERS
CHAS F.   JOHN
WALTON AND **MAYON**
PAST THREE SEASONS WITH   PAST FOUR SEASONS WITH
RICE'S "1492" CO.   **EDW. HARRIGAN'S CO.**
(THE TALL CONSPIRATOR)   (THE FUNNY LITTLE TAYLOR)

Have formed a partnership and would like to arrange with A1 Farce Comedy, Burlesque or Vaudeville Combination. Have one of the strongest and most novel Specialties on the Vaudeville Stage. Address: WALTON AND SLAVIN 473 Fourth Street, Jersey City, N.J. (Advertisement, *New York Clipper,* 3 August 1895, 352.)

A native of N.Y., [John C. Slavin] started his career at the age of 10 in San Francisco minstrels. Slavin appeared in such musicals as 'The Wizard of Oz,' 'Singing Girl,' 'The Belle of New York,' 'A Knight for a Day,' and 'When Dreams Come True.' With Charles Walton he formed a vaude act known as Walton and Slavin, a prominent turn a generation ago. A member of the original cast of 'Jack and the Beanstalk,' he also was seen with the Lillian Russell Opera Co. His last part was in a production of 'His Honor the Mayor.' (*Variety,* 4 September 1940, 54.)

Lucy Daly's "Pickaninnies" were the first African Americans to appear before a motion picture camera. Lucy Daly, who does not appear in this film, had been in Miss Lillian Russell's theatrical entertainment Girolfle-Girofla. *After the show concluded its New York run, she remained in the city to appear in* The Passing Show *and teamed with a group of black dancers. Such acts, featuring a white woman and several black men, were not uncommon in this period. The* New York Herald *of 22 July 1894 announced that at the American Roof Garden "some pickaninnies who are said to come directly from the South will appear with Miss Chadwell in a plantation sketch, introducing negro wing and buck dancing." Such acts were among the few integrated performances (along with* Uncle Tom's Cabin) *on the American stage. These black men were, however, infantalized and desexualized by the label "pickaninnies."* The Passing Show *opened on Saturday, 13 May 1894 and ran until 11 August on the Casino Roof Garden. It toured briefly and then returned and reopened for three weeks at the Casino beginning on 29 October 1894. Managers of* The Passing Show *regularly changed its specialties, keeping the revue fresh, and toured the nation's theaters into the early twentieth century.*

71 ***The Pickaninny Dance—From the "Passing Show" / The Pickaninnies / Pickanninies [sic]**
LENGTH: 50 ft.   © No reg.
PRODUCER: W.K.L. Dickson, Raff & Gammon.
CAMERA: William Heise.
CAST: Joe Rastus, Denny Tolliver, Walter Wilkins.
PRODUCTION DATE: 6 October 1894.

LOCATION: Black Maria, West Orange, N.J.

SOURCE: *The Passing Show* (revue).

DESCRIPTION: A lot of comical little darkies in a variety of tricks. (The Kinetoscope Company, *Edison's Latest Wonders: The Kinetograph, The Kinetoscope*, [October 1894].)

A scene representing Southern plantation life before the war. A jig and a breakdown by three colored boys. (F.Z. Maguire & Co., Catalogue, [March 1898], 27.)

SUBJECT: Revues–performances. Dancing. Afro-Americans. Lucy Daly.

ARCHIVE: CLAc, UkLNFA.

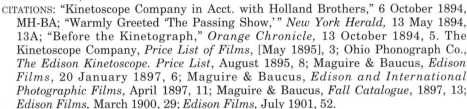

CITATIONS: "Kinetoscope Company in Acct. with Holland Brothers," 6 October 1894, MH-BA; "Warmly Greeted 'The Passing Show,'" *New York Herald,* 13 May 1894, 13A; "Before the Kinetograph," *Orange Chronicle,* 13 October 1894, 5. The Kinetoscope Company, *Price List of Films,* [May 1895], 3; Ohio Phonograph Co., *The Edison Kinetoscope. Price List,* August 1895, 8; Maguire & Baucus, *Edison Films,* 20 January 1897, 6; Maguire & Baucus, *Edison and International Photographic Films,* April 1897, 11; Maguire & Baucus, *Fall Catalogue,* 1897, 13; *Edison Films,* March 1900, 29; *Edison Films,* July 1901, 52.

NOTE: Raff & Gammon paid $15 to "Harvey for Pickaninny subjects," giving these black performers less compensation than many of their white counterparts. Notations in Kinetoscope Company accounts also suggest that these African Americans performed for more than one set of negatives. The "R" in the frame indicates that the film was financed by Raff & Gammon.

"The Passing Show."
A Novel Kind of Entertainment Tested Satisfactorily at the Casino.

What in the theatrical business is miscalled "farce-comedy" is badly worn out and broken down as a vehicle to carry mixed loads of farce, vaudeville, and burlesque. Something similarly serviceable, but refreshingly different, has been needed. At the Casino last night an experiment was made with "The Passing Show," described in the bills as an extravaganza and intended to roll lightly along under a freight of miscellaneous diversions. In the way of burlesque it contained first-rate imitation and ridicule of "Sowing the Wind," and paid some attention to other recent dramas. Sydney Rosenfeld had written the original words spoken and sung, and, in the uneven manner usual in his work, they went from witticism to stupidity and back again every minute. Paul Arthur and Adele Ritchie did well with Mr. Rosenfeld's matter, and Jefferson D'Angelis and John E. Henshaw fairly. Grace Filkins undertook to mimic well-known actresses, but her impersonations were barely recognizable. This first section of the entertainment ranged from very good to very bad, but it should improve with repetition, and no doubt it will.

The second act represented a show at a vaudeville club, and, besides several old things in it, there were some new ones. A lot of "living pictures" had the women modestly screened by comic contrivances, such as enormous fig leaves for Adam and Eve, and a tub that exposed only the head, arms, and feet of Venus at the bath. Tamale boys sang and danced, and a Coxey army of tramps was grotesque. Then came a quarter of an hour of operatic medley, in which vocalists lately at the Metropolitan were caricatured, selections from grand operas were intermixed with current ditties, and the most effective and showy burlesquing of the evening was done. Alfred Thompson and Ludwig Englander had arranged the action and music for this affair, and had done it cleverly. The end of the show was a resplendent march and a spectacular climax.

There should be success for "The Passing Show" and other shows prepared on the same plan, but much needs to be done at the Casino in quickening and condensing the matter. Of course, improvements will be made without delay. The company contains a great deal of ability, but it was not fully utilized. Capable persons stood idle while incapable ones were busy. One lesson was taught in a way that could hardly have failed to impress the management. A flagrant and shameful exploit in nudity spoiled all the value of what otherwise would have been the best sight in the whole exhibition. Four *Pierrots* and four *Phyrnettes* were introduced in a pantomime and dance based on "L'Infant Prodigue." The women were French, and they performed their parts so well that their little play would have been applauded enthusiastically but for a disgraceful achievement in the costuming of the *Phyrnettes,* who wore black stockings up to their knees, and black skirts down to their knees, but the skirts were made of gauze so thin that the upper halves of their legs and lower halves of their bodies were plainly exposed in skin-tight, flesh-colored silk webbing. The spectators could scarcely believe their eyes. Women averted their gaze, and most of the men were ashamed to look. No opera glasses were used. Hardly a score of desultory hand-claps followed this astounding offence, and there was no encore for the most costly and artistic feature of the evening. New York does not like Parisian nastiness. (*New York Sun*, 13 May 1894, 4.)

The eleven colored boys who form Lucy Daly's Pickaninny troupe in "The Passing Show" at the Casino were discharged last night by Messrs. Canary and Lederer. They refused to do their turn on the roof garden without extra compensation, which the management refused to give. ("Notes on Music and Drama," *New York Herald*, 19 July 1894, 11.)

Buffalo Bill's Wild West gave its last performance at Ambrose Park on October 6th; the following day a scaled-down version of the troupe embarked for Europe. On the their last day in the United States, several members visited the Black Maria to appear in films. Significantly these motion pictures were taken for Maguire & Baucus, who controlled the European rights to the kinetoscope.

72 ***Pedro Esquirel and Dionecio Gonzales / Mexican Knife Duel / Mexican Duel**
LENGTH: 50 ft.   © No reg.
PRODUCER: W.K.L. Dickson, Maguire & Baucus.
CAMERA: William Heise.
CAST: Pedro Esquivel, Dionecio Gonzales (Gonzallo).
PRODUCTION DATE: 6 October 1894.
LOCATION: Black Maria, West Orange, N.J.
SOURCE:
DESCRIPTION: Mexican Knife Duel (Full of action, exciting and interesting). (The Kinetoscope Company, *Price List of Films*, [May 1895], 3.)
SUBJECT: Wild west shows. Dueling. Mexicans. Buffalo Bill's Wild West.
ARCHIVE: FrBaADF, CLAc.

CITATIONS: "Before the Kinetograph," *Orange Chronicle,* 13 October 1894, 5; W.K.L. Dickson and Antonia Dickson, *History of the Kinetograph, Kinetoscope and Kineto-Phonograph*, 32 (with illustration). Maguire & Baucus, *Edison and International Photographic Films*, April 1897, 12; Maguire & Baucus, *Fall Catalogue*, 1897, 12; F.Z. Maguire & Co., *Catalogue*, [March 1898], 33.
NOTE: This film was sold in Italy as *Duello Messicano a coltelli.* (Continental Phonograph Kinetoscope Company, *Kinetoscenes,* [March 1895].)

73 **√Vincente Ore Passo / Lasso Thrower**
LENGTH: 50 ft.   © No reg.
PRODUCER: W.K.L. Dickson, [Maguire & Baucus].
CAMERA: William Heise.
CAST: Vi[n]cente Oropeza.
PRODUCTION DATE: 6 October 1894.
LOCATION: Black Maria, West Orange, N.J.
SOURCE:
DESCRIPTION: Champion Lasso Thrower. This shows the wonderful skill attained by the subject and is exceedingly interesting and popular. (The Kinetoscope Company, *Price List of Films*, [May 1895], 3.)
SUBJECT: Wild west shows. Lasso. Mexicans. Buffalo Bill's Wild West.
ARCHIVE:
CITATIONS: "Before the Kinetograph," *Orange Chronicle,* 13 October 1894, 5; W.K.L. Dickson and Antonia Dickson, *History of the Kinetograph, Kinetoscope and Kineto-Phonograph,* 25 (with illustration); Frank Dean, *Will Rogers Rope Tricks* (Colorado Springs, Colo.: Western Horseman, 1969); Marv "Slim" Girard, *Makin' Circles with a Rope: The Lore of the Lasso Wizards* (Francestown, N.H.: Marshall Jones Company, 1985). Maguire & Baucus, *Edison*

W.K.L. Dickson's portrait of performers who had been appearing with Buffalo Bill's Wild West Show (6 October 1894). Seated (left to right): Sheik Hadj Tahar, Vincente Oropeza. Standing: Hadj L. Cheriff, Pedro Esquivel and Dionecio Gonzales.

and International Photographic Films, April 1897, 11; Maguire & Baucus, *Fall Catalogue*, 1897, 12; F.Z. Maguire & Co., *Catalogue*, [March 1898], 31.

NOTE: Vicente Oropeza's name was spelled in various ways while he worked in the United States. Born in the state of Puebla, Mexico, he first appeared as part of the Mexican *charro* troupe with Buffalo Bill's Wild West in 1893 at the Columbian World's Exposition. He worked with the maguey rope: a stiff, laid rope with hard and tight spin, which is extremely difficult to control. He turned roping into a performance art. One of his best known tricks was to use the rope to form a series of letters that spelt his name (Vicente)—including the dotting of the *i*. Will Rogers reportedly saw Oropeza in 1901 and promptly set about mastering the Mexican's repertoire.

The Wonderful Wild West.

...In addition to the tableaus presented by the Indians, Gauchos from the Argentine Republic, for the first time seen in North America, give fine exhibitions of horsemanship, lassoing and throwing the bolas. Bisento Orapeso, the champion lasso thrower of Mexico, with a troop of experts, does some very fine work that is always appreciated. (*New York Times*, 2 September 1894, 11.)

Although Sheik Hadj Tahar was attached to Buffalo Bill's Wild West during its lengthy 1894 engagement in Brooklyn, this was an association of mutual benefit and convenience. Tahar and his troupe remained in the United States after the Wild West embarked for Europe and immediately joined Primrose's and West's Minstrels in Philadelphia. On Saturday, October 6th, quite possibly on their way to join the Minstrel show, they stopped off in Orange, New Jersey, and performed before the Edison kinetograph. Tahar's troupe continued to appear with Buffalo Bill in subsequent seasons—1898 being the sixth of their association.

74 Sheik Hadji Tahar / [Sheik Hadj Tahar] / [Arab Gun Juggler]
LENGTH: 50 ft.   © No reg.
PRODUCER: W.K.L. Dickson.
CAMERA: William Heise.
CAST: Sheik Hadj Tahar (Sie Tahar Ben Belhassan).
PRODUCTION DATE: 6 October 1894.

LOCATION: Black Maria, West Orange, N.J.

SOURCE:

DESCRIPTION:

SUBJECT: Wild west shows. Jugglers. Arabs. Rifles and rifle practice. Buffalo Bill's Wild West.

ARCHIVE:

CITATIONS: Advertisements, *New York Clipper*, 10 March 1894, 11; 13 October 1894, 518; "Before the Kinetograph," *Orange Chronicle*, 13 October 1894, 5; advertisements, *New York Clipper*, 27 October 1894, 549; 30 May 1896, 210; 5 December 1896, 645; 30 October 1897, 587; 30 September 1899, 639; 5 January 1901, 1007.

NOTE: Dickson apparently confused Sheik Hadj Tahar with Hadj Cheriff in his book on the beginnings of the motion picture. (W.K.L. Dickson and Antonia Dickson, *History of the Kinetograph, Kinetoscope and Kineto-Phonograph*, 44 [with illustrations].) He thus incorrectly identifies Sheik Hadj Tahar with knife juggling. But Tahar not only claimed to be the world champion gun twirler, he was photographed with a gun during his visit to the Black Maria. Finally Tahar has a mustache and this man, like Cheriff, does not. (Hendricks suggests that Dickson confused Hadj Tahar with Toyou Kichi but this does not appear to be the case.) Sold in Italian as *Giocoliere Arabo di fucile*. (Continental Phonograph Kinetoscope Co., *Kinetoscenes* [March 1895].)

SHEIK HADJ TAHAR,
And His Troupe of Reffian All Round Athletes and the Whirlwinds of the Desert

In their wonderful Gun Spinning, Balancing, Tumbling and Human Pyramids, in which Black Samson, the modern Hercules, will display his marvelous strength by holding twelve men. He is without equal, and stands alone, like the Pyramid of Cheops. This wonderful troupe has just closed its second successful year with Buffalo Bill's Wild West, and have joined Messrs. PRIMROSE & WEST'S MINSTRELS, opening at Empire Theatre, Philadelphia, October 8th. I wish to return thanks to Messrs. CODY and SALSBURY for courtesies extended to me during my engagement with their Company and Congress of Nations of the Rough Riders of the World. I am sincerely yours, SHEIK HADJ TAHAR, Manager of Oriental Companies, with Primrose & West, as per route. Kind regards to all friends. (Advertisement, *New York Clipper*, 13 October 1894, 518.)

ACROBAT DIES AFTER ACT.
Sie Tahar Ben Belhassan Found in Dressing Room at Palace Theatre.

Shortly after he had finished his act, the opening number at the Palace Theatre this week, Sie Tahar Ben Belhassen [sic], head of the Sie Tahar troupe of acrobats and tumblers, died in his dressing room yesterday afternoon from heart trouble caused by his strenuous exertions on the stage. His body was discovered by Elmer E. Rogers, manager of the theatre, about half an hour after the performance. Sie Tahar, as he was known to vaudeville and circus performers, was an Algerian. He had played for a number of years at the head of his troupes, but for several months he had been suffering from ill-health and had been away from the stage. He had not intended to appear yesterday, but at the last minute he went in. His heart could not stand the strain, according to Dr. Wallace E. Brown of 135 West Forty-Seventh Street, who was summoned by Mr. Rogers. The matinee at the Palace went on as usual, and many of the performers were not aware of the death. Sie Tahar, who was about 46 [sic] years old, is survived by a widow. His body was taken in charge by the National Vaudeville Artists, Inc. (*New York Times*, 13 July 1926, 19.)

Hadj Cheriff had been touring with his own small troupe when he encountered difficulties with law enforcement officials for the risque nature of the belly dance performed by his wife, Cheriffa. After these difficulties and as the 1893-94 theatrical season came to a close, his troupe joined Buffalo Bill's Wild West.

75 ***Hadj Cheriff / [Arab Knife Juggler]**

LENGTH: 50 ft.   © No reg.

PRODUCER: W.K.L. Dickson.

CAMERA: William Heise.

CAST: Hadj L. Cheriff.

PRODUCTION DATE: 6 October 1894.

LOCATION: Black Maria, West Orange, N.J.

SOURCE:

DESCRIPTION:

SUBJECT: Wild west shows. Jugglers. Arabs. Buffalo Bill's Wild West.
ARCHIVE: FrBaADF, NNMoMA, DLC-Hendricks, CLAc.
CITATIONS: W.K.L. Dickson and Antonia Dickson, *History of the Kinetograph, Kinetoscope and Kineto-Phonograph*, 44 (with illustrations).
NOTE: Sold in Italian as *Giocoliere Arabo di coltelli*. (Continental Phonograph Kinetoscope Co., *Kinetoscenes*.) See note for film no. 74.

Hadj Cheriff and his troupe are playing a special engagement this week at Miner's Bowery Theatre with the City Sports Co. Their exhibition of gun drilling, dervish dancing, feats of strength and the contortion act of one of the ladies are enthusiastically received. The danse du ventre performed by La Belle Cheriffa, who danced at the Midway Plaisance, is a sensation. (*New York Clipper*, 14 April 1894, 83.)

Miner's Bowery Theatre...Two Moorish Muscle Dancers, claimed to be the original from the Midway Plaisance, are a sensational feature. (*New York Clipper*, 14 April 1894, 86.)

NEW DANSE DU VENTRE.
How the Oriental Dance Should be Performed to Avoid Police Interference.

The Cheriff troupe of Arabs, playing with "The City Sports" company at Miner's Bowery Theatre, have been giving an exhibition of the danse du ventre which, it is alleged, was a vulgar and indecent performance. A halt was called yesterday, however, by the police and the dance was done at the matinee performance in a manner calculated to suit the most puritanical ideas. The attention of Inspector Williams was called to the matter yesterday. The inspector not long ago stopped a similar performance at the Grand Central Palace. The thing was vulgar and indecent, he said. Yesterday he sent for Captain Cortright, of the Eldridge street station, in whose district Miner's Theatre is located, and asked him about it. Captain Cortright declared that he had witnessed the performance several times and had seen nothing wrong or indecent in it. The inspector, however, said that the dance should be stopped, and at yesterday's matinee performance Captain Cortright and his men were on hand to carry out the Inspector's instructions. The Captain first, however, saw Manager Flynn before the show. "I want you to cut out the whole of that danse du ventre business," said he. Mr. Flynn began to argue, but the Captain wouldn't have it.

The Cheriff Troupe, of two men and two women of uncertain ages, came on the stage toward the end of the performance. Their attire would have sent a truly Oriental audience into convulsions. The dancers looked sad and unhappy. The women was clad in loose fitting vari-colored garments that covered their forms entirely from their ankles to their necks. The old blue laws of Connecticut could not have demanded more. Their costumes reminded one in the makeup, if not in color, of the regulation Asbury Park Bathing suit. One of the men wore long flowing robes, after the fashion of a dervish. The other was arrayed like a circus acrobat. Then the orchestra struck up a funeral air and the "dance" began. There was not a single wriggle or contortion. The dance in fact resembled a minuet. The Arab in the flowing robes gave a slight wriggle and looked startled, as if he expected the hand of the law to punish him for it. After about two minutes of this sort of thing the audience began to get demonstrative. There were yells of "Get a move on you!" "What are you giving us?" and the like. But the curtain dropped at this point and the audience filed out of the place, making remarks that were more forcible than elegant. (*New York Herald*, 14 April 1894, 10.)

The Glenroy Brothers returned to the Black Maria for the third time on 6 October 1894. The Glenroy boxing subjects that entered Edison's catalog presumably date from this final visit.

76 Glenroy Bros., Boxers / Glenroy Bros., [no 1] / Burlesque Boxing / [Glenroy Brothers, no. 3]

LENGTH: 50 ft.   © No reg.
PRODUCER: W.K.L. Dickson, Raff & Gammon.
CAMERA: William Heise.
CAST: Glenroy Brothers.
PRODUCTION DATE: 6 October 1894.
LOCATION: Black Maria, West Orange, N.J.
SOURCE:
DESCRIPTION: A burlesque Prize Fight. One of the funniest subjects ever taken. (The Kinetoscope Company, *Edison's Latest Wonders: The Kinetograph, The Kinetoscope*, [October 1894].)
  Boxing Bout (Burlesque). (The Kinetoscope Company, *Price List of Films*, [May 1895], 2.)
SUBJECT: Vaudeville–performances. Boxing. Burlesque.
ARCHIVE:

CITATIONS: "Kinetoscope Company in Acct. with Holland Brothers," 6 October 1894, MH-BA; Raff & Gammon to Columbia Phonograph Parlor, 27 October 1894, MH-BA. Maguire & Baucus, *Edison and International Photographic Films*, April 1897, 4; Maguire & Baucus, *Fall Catalogue*, 1897, 11; F.Z. Maguire & Co., *Catalogue*, [March 1898], 32.

NOTE: See film no. 55, *[Glenroy Brothers, no. 1]*, shot on 13 September 1894, for documents. See also film no. 60, *[Glenroy Brothers, no. 2]*, which was shot on 22 September 1894.

77 *****Glenroy Bros., [no. 2] / [Glenroy Brothers, no. 4]**

LENGTH: 50 ft.   © No reg.

PRODUCER: W.K.L. Dickson, Raff & Gammon.

CAMERA: William Heise.

CAST: Glenroy Brothers.

PRODUCTION DATE: 6 October 1894.

LOCATION: Black Maria, West Orange, N.J.

SOURCE:

DESCRIPTION: Farcical pugilist in costume. (The Kinetoscope Company, *Price List of Films*, [May 1895], 2.)

SUBJECT: Vaudeville–performances. Boxing. Burlesque.

ARCHIVE: DLC-Hendricks, CLAc.

CITATIONS:

NOTE: See also *[Glenroy Brothers, no. 1]* and *[Glenroy Brothers, no. 2]* shot previously on 13 and 22 September 1894. This scene seems to correspond to their vaudeville routine.

Many observers of the cultural scene noted the potential affinities between Edison's kinetoscope and Alexander Black's "picture plays." Miss Jerry, the first of Black's programs in this genre, debuted on 9 October 1894.

SAW A PICTURE PLAY
Mr. Alexander Black's "Miss Jerry" Produced for the First Time Last Evening.

The idea is original. It has been cleverly worked out, and if the principle of Edison's latest invention could only be applied to the figures, so that they would move, the "picture play," given for the first time last evening at Mr. James L. Breese's studio, in West Sixteenth street, would furnish a more than usually pleasant way of spending an hour. "Miss Jerry," as the work is called, is from the pen of Mr. Alexander Black. If you can imagine yourself in a luxuriously appointed room, staring at a white sheet spread on a wall, on which illustration after illustration appears, picturing a story read aloud by the author, you will have some idea of "Miss Jerry."

The story tells how a young lady, imagining that her father is financially embarrassed, secures a position as a reporter on the New York Daily Dynamo, and finally marries the city editor. There are many touches of humor in the novelette–it is rather that than a play in the usual acceptance of the word–and the interest is well-sustained, though some extraneous matter might be cut out with advantage. The pictures, of which there are about 250, follow the story very closely, and allow the incidents of Miss Jerry's daily life, her interviews, amusements, reveries, courtship; a number of New York scenes, such as Madison Square, Washington Square, the Fifth Avenue Hotel, Brooklyn Bridge, the interior of Mr. Depew's private office in the Grand Central Depot, with an admirable series of the genial Chauncey being "interviewed" by Miss Jerry, and a host of interesting sketches and views.

The photographs were all taken from life by the carbon process and reproduced on the screen by the aid of the stereopticon. Musical illustrations were played on the piano and organ by Mr. John Hyatt Brewer. As a whole, it is a very charming and successful effort to amplify and adapt the illustrated magazine for the purpose of a reading and was warmly received by an audience that completely filled the studio and included among its numbers President Seth Low, of Columbia; Mr. William Dean Howells, Mr. James Herbert Morse, Mrs. Edmund Clarence Stedman, Miss Christine Terhune Herrick, Mr. John D. Champlin, Mr. C.C. Buell, Dr. John Coleman Adams, Mr. Henry Abbey, Mr. Henry Marquand and Mr. Arthur Stedman. (*New York Herald*, 10 October 1894, 6.)

Luis Martinetti was almost certainly one half of the Martinetti Brothers who had their American debut at Koster & Bial's Music Hall on 10 September 1894—effectively replacing Caicedo. They remained until 24 November 1894 and then, after a week's absence from New York's theaters, appeared briefly at Keith's Union Square Theatre. Mid-way through their appearance at Koster & Bial's, Luis performed for the kinetograph.

78 *Luis Martinetti / Luis Martinetti, Contortionist / Louis Martinetti / Louis Martinelli [sic]

LENGTH: 50 ft.   © No reg.
PRODUCER: W.K.L. Dickson.
CAMERA: William Heise.
CAST: L[o]uis Martinetti.
PRODUCTION DATE: 11 October 1894.
LOCATION: Black Maria, West Orange, N.J.
SOURCE:
DESCRIPTION: Gymnast and Contortionist, performing on the Flying Rings. (The Kinetoscope Company, *Price List of Films*, [May 1895], 3.) Spanish contortion act in rings. (F.Z. Maguire & Co., *Catalogue*, [March 1898], 33.)
SUBJECT: Vaudeville–performances. Aerialists. Acrobats. Spaniards.

ARCHIVE: NR-GE, DLC-Hendricks, CLAc.
CITATIONS: The Kinetoscope Company, *Bulletin No. 1*, [December 1894]; Maguire & Baucus, *Edison and International Photographic Films*, April 1897, 11; Maguire & Baucus, *Fall Catalogue*, 1897, 12; F.Z. Maguire & Co., *Catalogue*, [March 1898], 33.
NOTE: Luis Martinetti was paid $14.10 to perform on the grounds of the Edison grounds. The Three Martinetti Brothers, acrobats, performed at Proctor's Theatre for the first week in April 1894. The relation between this trio, the duo that subsequently appeared at Koster & Bial's, and Luis Martinetti is unclear.

Koster & Bial's...The two Martinetti Brothers, acrobats, made their first bow to an American audience and found immediate favor. They seem to possess unlimited strength and skill, and performed several feats new to this side of the water. They were recalled several times and made a most pronounced hit. (*New York Clipper,* 15 September 1894, 440.)

Louis Martineli [sic], a flying ring contortionist, came out to the Edison laboratory on Thursday noon and was kinetographed in his characteristic poses. ("Before the Kinetograph," *Orange Chronicle*, 13 October 1894, 5.)

Les Freres Martinetti. The Famous Italian Hand to Hand Acrobats conceded to be without equal for daring, agility, skill and strength, creating a sensation wherever they appear. (*New York Herald*, 2 December 1894, 2C.)

Martinetti, formerly a contortionist, is now one of the best theatrical agents here [Paris, France]....In one year he has built up a wonderful business. (*New York Clipper*, 10 March 1900, 27.)

Cowboy stars Frank Hammitt and Lee Martin did not make the European trip with Buffalo Bill. Nine days after the Wild West's departure, the broncho busters came to the Edison Laboratory.

79 *Bucking Broncho / Bucking Bronchos

LENGTH: 50 ft.   © No reg.
PRODUCER: W.K.L. Dickson, Maguire & Baucus.
CAMERA: William Heise.
CAST: Lee Martin (on "Sunfish"), Frank Hammitt.
PRODUCTION DATE: 16 October 1894.
LOCATION: Edison Laboratory, West Orange, N.J.
SOURCE:
DESCRIPTION: From Buffalo Bill's Wild West Show. A lively, rattling subject. True to nature on the Western plains. Plenty of action. (The Kinetoscope Company, *Edison's Latest Wonders: The Kinetograph, The Kinetoscope*, [October 1894].)
An out-of-door Scene. The men and horse of this subject are from "Buffalo Bill's Wild

West." (The Kinetoscope Company, *Price List of Films*, [May 1895], 2.)

A fine exhibition of horsemanship by Lee Martin, a genuine cowboy. This particular broncho is an unusually wicked one. (*Edison Films*, March 1900, 26.)

SUBJECT: Wild west shows. Horsemanship. Cowboys. Buffalo Bill's Wild West.

ARCHIVE: NR-GE, DLC-Hendricks.

CITATIONS: Raff & Gammon to J.L. Andem, invoice, 12 November 1894, 1:34, MH-BA. The Kinetoscope Company, *Bulletin No. 1*, [December 1894]; Ohio Phonograph Co., *The Edison Kinetoscope. Price List*, August 1895, 8; Maguire & Baucus, *Edison Films*, 20 January 1897, 6; Maguire & Baucus, *Edison and International Photographic Films*, April 1897, 3; Maguire & Baucus, *Fall Catalogue*, 1897, 11; F.Z. Maguire & Co., *Catalogue*, [March 1898], 28; *Edison Films,* July 1901, 49.

NOTE:

80 [Lasso Exhibition]

LENGTH: 50 ft.   © No reg.

PRODUCER: W.K.L. Dickson.

CAMERA: William Heise.

CAST: Lee Martin, Frank Hammitt.

PRODUCTION DATE: 16 October 1894.

LOCATION: Edison Laboratory, West Orange, N.J.

SOURCE:

DESCRIPTION:

SUBJECT: Wild west shows. Lasso. Cowboys. Buffalo Bill's Wild West.

ARCHIVE:

CITATIONS:

NOTE: This film was apparently never offered for sale.

All Americans know what the cowboys are and what they can do. Their riding is simply superb, and their daring acts on bucking bronchos are among the most interesting features of the exhibition. ("The Wonderful Wild West," *New York Times*, 2 September 1894, 11.)

Before the Kinetograph.

Edward Madden, the genial press manager for the Buffalo Bill Wild West exhibition was in this city on Tuesday. He was accompanied by Frank Hammitt and Lee Martin, two of the world's greatest riders of bucking bronchos. Both are members of the Wild West Combination and are prominent cowboys. Mr. Hammitt, who is the equestrian manager of the Wild West show is native of the plains of Colorado, and Mr. Martin hails from Wyoming. They are both men of nerve, finely built and for men accustomed to rough and ready living they are gentlemanly sort of fellows.

The three came to Orange on invitation of Professor William K.L. Dickson, the manager of the photo-kinetographic department and chief of the electro-mining at the Edison Laboratory, and the two cowboys brought with them their favorite horses to appear before the kinetograph. Mr. Martin rode Sunfish in an area arranged for the occasion in the rear of the "Black Maria," wherein Mr. Corbett and Mr. Courtney had a "fake" bout with the gloves not long ago. The interior of the "Maria" was not large enough to allow any broncho busting, therefore Mr. Dickson had fenced in a place in the open. Mr. Hammitt was to have mounted his horse El Diablo, but he deemed it advisable not to attempt the act as the place was not large enough, the animal being an extraordinarily dangerous one. While Mr. Martin handled Sunfish, Mr. Hammitt sat on the fence surrounding the pen and fired off his prize revolver a number of times, thereby adding much excitement and realism to the scene. The revolver was presented to Mr. Hammitt by a number of New York reporters who were detailed at the Wild West show at Ambrose Park on special duty. While there the newspaper men were extended many courtesies by Mr. Hammitt, who, by the way, is chief of the Wild West cow boys, and the revolver was given him as a testimonial of the esteem in which he was held by the scribes. At the conclusion of the broncho bucking Mr. Martin and Mr. Hammitt displayed their abilities before the great kinetograph with the lasso. Professor Dickson was highly pleased with the exhibition as a whole and feels confident that the reproduction in the kinetoscope will prove a big success. In taking the saddle off Sunfish, the little kicker got away and for a time it was the sole owner of the Edison yard. Mr. Hammit, however, pluckily gave chase and caught the animal.

The following were the guests of Mr. Dickson who views the bronco bucking from "improved" reserved seats located in the "Black Maria;" Mrs. John L. Seward, of Maint street and her sister, Miss Kember, of Leadville, Col., and Dr. Perry, of San Francisco. Among the newspaper men present was Morris E. Moses of Pittsburg, who is on the staff of the New York Dramatic News.

Toyou Kichi, of Kisto, Japan, the Japanese contortionist and acrobat exhibited before the kinetograph this morning. Miss Annie Oakley, the celebrated rifle shot, will exhibit to-morrow. (*Orange Journal*, 18 October 1894, 5.)

Maguire & Baucus opened the first kinetoscope parlor in England on 17 October 1894. ("Mr. Edison's Living Pictures," London Daily Graphic, 18 October 1894, TAEP, 146:195.)

Numerous trained animal acts appeared in New York theaters during 1894. In late September Mlle Carlini and her performing dogs and monkeys performed at Proctor's Theatre and Professor Wormwood's Dog and Monkey's Circus was at Huber's Museum. That fall Hagenbeck's Trained Animals had a long and successful run at Madison Square Garden. Of these acts, Tschernoff's Trained Dogs was arguably the most successful. According to the New York Dramatic Mirror *of 9 June 1894, "the funniest thing [Albert Bial] saw on the European concert hall stage was the spectacle of two dogs executing a serpentine dance. They wore the regulation skirts, were illuminated by the calcium, and gyrated with much skill and considerable grace." Three months later, on 9 September, Ivan Tschernoff's trained dogs had their American debut at Koster & Bial's Music Hall in New York City. Their run at that theater lasted into the following year— long even by Koster & Bial's standards. Five weeks into their stay, Tschernoff and his dogs became motion picture subjects.*

81 Wonderful Performing Dog / Skirt Dance Dog / Dancing Dog
LENGTH: 50 ft.   © No reg.
PRODUCER: W.K.L. Dickson.
CAMERA: William Heise.
CAST: Ivan Tschernoff, Lucy (dog).
PRODUCTION DATE: 17 October 1894.
LOCATION: Black Maria, West Orange, N.J.
SOURCE:
DESCRIPTION: In the "Skirt Dance." (The Kinetoscope Company, *Edison's Latest Wonders: The Kinetograph, The Kinetoscope*, [October 1894].)
   A serpentine dance in costume, performed by one of Prof. Tschernoff's marvelous trained dogs. (Ohio Phonograph Co., *The Edison Kinetoscope. Price List*, August 1895, 8.)
   Skirt dance by a trained dog. A film for children. (Maguire & Baucus, *Edison and International Photographic Films*, April 1897, 6.)
SUBJECT: Vaudeville–performances. Animal trainers. Circus animals. Dogs. Dancing. Burlesque. Prof. Ivan Tschernoff's Trained Dogs.
ARCHIVE:
CITATIONS: The Kinetoscope Company, *Bulletin No. 1*, [December 1894]; The Kinetoscope Company, *Price List of Films*, [May 1895], 2; Maguire & Baucus, *Fall Catalogue*, 1897, 11.
NOTE:

82 √Summersault Dog
LENGTH: 50 ft.   © No reg.
PRODUCER: W.K.L. Dickson.
CAMERA: William Heise.
CAST: Ivan Tschernoff, Leo (dog).
PRODUCTION DATE: 17 October 1894.
LOCATION: Black Maria, West Orange, N.J.
SOURCE:
DESCRIPTION:
SUBJECT: Vaudeville–performances. Animal trainers. Circus animals. Dogs. Gymnastics. Prof. Ivan Tschernoff's Trained Dogs.
ARCHIVE:
CITATIONS: Raff & Gammon to T. Mavro, 6 December 1894, 1:103, MH-BA; W.K.L. Dickson and Antonia Dickson, *History of the Kinetograph, Kinetoscope and Kineto-Phonograph*, 12 (with illustrations). The Kinetoscope Company, *Bulletin No. 1*, [December 1894]; The Kinetoscope Company, *Price List of Films*, [May 1895], 2.
NOTE:

DANCED THE SERPENTINE
A FIN-DE-SIECLE CANINE BEFORE THE KINETOGRAPH
Ivan Tschernoff's Pupils' Remarkable Feats Recorded by the Wizard's Revolving Wonder—Leo and
Lucy Were to Have Been Married, but Had to Postpone the Happy Day—News of the Oranges.

A novel exhibition took place yesterday at the Edison laboratory, in West Orange, when Ivan Tschernoff, from Koster & Bial's, came out with the trained dogs Leo and Lucy, and gave an exhibition in front of the kinetograph. Leo turned somersaults forward and backward and Lucy created a scene by being dressed as a danseuse and giving a most clever serpentine dance. There had been arrangements made to have a real, bona-fide marriage take place in front of the kinetograph and all the paraphernalia of organ, altar, etc., were in place, but at the last moment word was received that there was some hitch about the matter and that the wedding had been postponed. It is probable that it will yet be held. (*Newark Daily Advertiser*, 18 October 1894, 3.)

Sie Hassan Ben Ali's troupe of Beni Zoug Zoug Arabs performed for Buffalo Bill during the summer of 1894. When Cody's Wild West closed on 6 October and embarked for Europe, they remained behind, appearing for three weeks at Koster & Bial's Music Hall, from the 15 October to 3 November 1894. During their first week at that theater, the troupe probably visited the Black Maria en mass, though the appearance of only one member, Toyo Kichi, was reported in the press.

83 Human Pyramid

LENGTH: 50 ft.   © No reg.
PRODUCER: W.K.L. Dickson.
CAMERA: William Heise.
CAST: Saleem Nassar.
PRODUCTION DATE: [18 October 1894.]
LOCATION: Black Maria, West Orange, N.J.
SOURCE:
DESCRIPTION:
SUBJECT: Wild west shows. Vaudeville—performances. Acrobats. Arabs. Buffalo Bill's Wild West. Sie Hassan Ben Ali.
ARCHIVE:
CITATIONS: Raff & Gammon to F.D. Higbee, invoice, 8 March 1895, 1:349, MH-BA; advertisements, *New York Clipper*, 25 July 1896, 335; 29 August 1896, 418; 24 December 1898, 733.
NOTE: Sie Hassan Ben Ali's troupe of Beni Zoug Zoug Arabs was a rival of Sheik Hadj Tahar and his troupe of Reffian All Round Athletes, also filmed by Dickson and Heise. Sie Hassan Ben Ali subsequently brought other groups of Arab performers to the United States. This film was sold in Italy as *Salim Nassar e truppa Araba, piramidi umane*. (Continental Phonograph Kinetoscope Company, *Kinetoscenes*, [March 1895].)

من بعد عناية سليم نصر
SALEEM NASSAR.

84 Sword Combat

LENGTH: 50 ft.   © No reg.
PRODUCER: W.K.L. Dickson.
CAMERA: William Heise.
CAST: Saleem Nassar, Najid.
PRODUCTION DATE: [18 October 1894.]
LOCATION: Black Maria, West Orange, N.J.
SOURCE:
DESCRIPTION:
SUBJECT: Wild west shows. Vaudeville—performances. Dueling. Arabs. Buffalo Bill's Wild West. Sie Hassan Ben Ali.
ARCHIVE:
CITATIONS: Raff & Gammon to R.T. Haines, invoice, 18 December 1894, 1:119, MH-BA; Dickson to Raff & Gammon, 8 January 1895, MH-BA.
NOTE:

85 Toyou Kichi
LENGTH: 50 ft.   © No reg.
PRODUCER: W.K.L. Dickson.
CAMERA: William Heise.
CAST: Toyo[u] Kichi.
PRODUCTION DATE: 18 October 1894.
LOCATION: Black Maria, West Orange, N.J.
SOURCE:
DESCRIPTION: The Marvellous and Artistic Japanese Twirler and Juggler. (The Kinetoscope Company, *Bulletin No. 1*, [December 1894].)
SUBJECT: Vaudeville–performances. Wild West shows. Gymnastics. Tumbling. Japanese. Buffalo Bill's Wild West. Sie Hassan Ben Ali.
ARCHIVE:
CITATIONS: "The Wonderful Wild West," *New York Times,* 2 September 1894, 11.
NOTE: In Japanese, Toyo means either Eastern Hemisphere (literally Eastern Sea) or wealth. Kichi was a popular nickname for an entertainer and means "luck." His name, therefore, can be translated either as Eastern Luck or Wealth and Luck.

KOSTER & BIAL'S.–The bill presented Oct. 15 for week was unusually attractive and won hearty applause from the crowded house present....The Sie Hassen [sic] Ben Ali troupe of Arabian acrobats appeared at this house for the first time and received the approval of the audience for their many difficult acrobatic feats. (*New York Clipper*, 20 October 1894, 524.)

On Thursday Tovin Kichi came out and gave a remarkable exhibition of somersaults on one hand backwards and forwards. ("In the Kinetoscopic Theatre," *Orange Chronicle*, 20 October 1894, 4.)

Special Notice.
THE STRONGEST AND MOST POWERFUL ARAB IN THE WORLD.
SALEEM NASSAR
The Human Pyramid, Understander, and Expert Swordsman with Sie Hassan Ben Ali's celebrated troupe of Beni Zoug Zoug Arab Athletes now performing with Buffalo Bill's Wild West Show.
SALEEM NASSAR CHALLENGES THE WORLD FOR $5,000 TO PRODUCE HIS ACTS.
THE NEW YORK SUNDAY TIMES of Sept 2, 1894 says: "It is a conceded fact, by all managers, that the best acrobats who have ever been in America are the Arabs and little Jap Toyo, members of Beni Zoug Zoug Troupe. The greatest picture of Saleem Nassar, holding aloft in the form of a pyramid and moving around with twelve men, whom he supports by means of strength, must be seen to be thoroughly understood." Saleem Nassar is a native of Huran, Arabia; his unlimited strength is gained by drinking many gallons of camel's milk and eating dates while traveling across the deserts of Arabia. This remarkable Arab was brought over to this country by Sie Hassan Ben Ali for his troupe of Beni Zoug Zoug Arabs. Address all communications to Saleem Nassar, care of Beni Zoug Zoug Troupe, with Buffalo Bill's Wild West Show, South Brooklyn, N.Y. (Advertisement, *New York Clipper,* 15 September 1894, 446.)

Saleem Nassar, Arabian acrobat, died June 11, in Chicago, Ill., from typhoid pneumonia. The deceased was a member of Sheik Hadji Tahar's [sic] Troupe of Arabs, of which he was understander and strong man. He leaves a widow and one child in Arabia. (*New York Clipper*, 20 June 1896, 248.)

A bevy of stars appeared before Edison's Kinetograph on 1 November 1894. As one local paper reported:

In the Kinetograph Theatre.
Thursday was a red letter day at the kinetograph theatre in the Edison laboratory. First Miss Annie Oakley, the champion shot of the world, gave a wonderful exhibition of her abilities. Signorina Alcide Capitaine, the trapeze artist, from the Union Square Theatre, gave a marvelous exhibition of her powers. Then came the "Gaiety Girls," Miss Madge Crossland, Miss Lucy Murray and Miss May Lucas, from Daly's theatre, in their clever high kicking dance from the second act. A number of the other members of the company came out, among them Miss Decima Moore, the prima donna of the company; Miss Grace Palotte and Miss Florence Lloyd, two of the "Gaiety Girls." At the close of the exhibition at the laboratory the party was taken to Davis' where they were dined by Mr. Tate as representative of the Kinetographic Exhibition Company [sic]. (*Orange Chronicle*, 3 November 1894, 7.)

Annie Oakley did not travel with Buffalo Bill, who had departed for Europe three weeks earlier. Seeking ways to develop her career on a more independent basis, she toured the British provinces during the winter of 1894-95 in the comedy drama Miss Rora, *in which she displayed her shooting, riding and acting skills. She then rejoined Buffalo Bill in the spring of 1895, when he too had returned to the United States.*

86 ***Annie Oakley**

LENGTH: 50 ft.   © No reg.
PRODUCER: W.K.L. Dickson, Raff & Gammon.
CAMERA: William Heise.
CAST: Annie Oakley (Phoebe Ann Moses, Mrs. Frank E. Butler).
PRODUCTION DATE: 1 November 1894.
LOCATION: Black Maria, West Orange, N.J.
SOURCE:
DESCRIPTION: The 'Little Sure Shot' of the 'Wild West.' Exhibition of Rifle Shooting at Glass Balls, etc. (The Kinetoscope Company, *Bulletin No 1*, [December 1894].)
Champion lady shot of the world, in an exhibition of rifle shooting. Fine smoke effects. (F.Z. Maguire & Co., *Catalogue*, [March 1898], 28.)
SUBJECT: Wild west shows. Shooting. Rifles and rifle practice. Buffalo Bill's Wild West.
ARCHIVE: FrBaADF, NNMoMA, DLC-Hendricks, CLAc.
CITATIONS: Advertisement, *New York Clipper,* 20 April 1895, 112; Isabelle S. Sayers, *Annie Oakley and Buffalo Bill's Wild West Show* (New York: Dover Publications, 1981). Ohio Phonograph Co., *The Edison Kinetoscope. Price List*, August 1895, 8; Maguire & Baucus, *Edison and International Photographic Films*, April 1897, 3; Maguire & Baucus, *Fall Catalogue*, 1897, 11; *Edison Films*, March 1900, 45.
NOTE:

Annie Oakley, the rifle shot, will tour the British Provinces next Winter in Ullie Akerstrom's play "Miss Roarer" [sic], in which she will use the trained horse, Gyp, and carry a pack of foxhounds. (*New York Clipper*, 22 September 1894, 454.)

Trapezist Alcide Capitaine had her American debut in The Voyage of Suzette *at the American Theatre on 23 December 1893. By the end of the month, the "queen of the air" had been hailed as the female Sandow and "the perfect woman" by the* New York Herald—*a label that stuck and was used in subsequent newspaper advertisements. She performed for the first time at Koster & Bial's Music Hall on 19 January 1894 and remained there until 17 March 1894. She then moved to Proctor's Theatre, appearing there as a headliner for four weeks, after which she sailed for Europe. She returned to New York aboard the "Fuida" on 20 August 1894. Initially engaged by the Boston Howard Specialty Star Company for the 1894-95 theatrical season, she soon left that troupe and appeared for two weeks as an independent headline attraction at Keith's Union Square Theatre, beginning 22 October 1894. During this time she visited the Black Maria and performed before the kinetograph, possibly for the second time (see* Trapeze, *film no. 32). She continued to appear on the vaudeville circuit—a headline attraction at Keith's Union Square Theatre for two weeks, commencing 7 October 1895, and at Proctor's 23rd Street Theatre for the week of 5 November 1900.*

87 √**Mlle. Capitaine / Capitaine / Alciede Capitaine**

LENGTH: 50 ft.   © No reg.
PRODUCER: W.K.L. Dickson, Raff & Gammon.
CAMERA: William Heise.
CAST: Alci[e]de Capitaine.
PRODUCTION DATE: 1 November 1894.
LOCATION: Black Maria, West Orange, N.J.
SOURCE: *Trapeze* (Edison film no. 32, spring 1894).
DESCRIPTION: The great Lady Trapezist. Her daring acts on the flying bar command breathless attention. Her graceful figure warrants her billed description, The

Perfect Woman. (*Edison Films*, March 1900, 24.)

SUBJECT: Vaudeville–performances. Aerialists. Italians.

ARCHIVE:

CITATIONS: *New York Herald*, 21 August 1894, 9; 26 August 1894, 6D; 21 October 1894, 8C; Raff & Gammon to Peter Bacigalupi, invoice, 12 November 1894, 1:32, MH-BA; W.K.L. Dickson and Antonia Dickson, *History of the Kinetograph, Kinetoscope and Kineto-Phonograph*, 31 (with illustrations). The Kinetoscope Company, *Bulletin No. 1*, [December 1894]; The Kinetoscope Company, *Price List of Films*, [May 1895], 3; Maguire & Baucus, *Edison and International Photographic Films*, April 1897, 6; Maguire & Baucus, *Fall Catalogue*, 1897, 11; F.Z. Maguire & Co., *Catalogue*, [March 1898], 33.

NOTE: Mlle. Capitaine's first name was generally given as Alcide but sometimes appeared as "Alciede."

ALCIDE CAPITAINE, A FEMALE SANDOW.
Remarkable Feats of Strength of a Pretty Girl of Nineteen.
VERY HIGH ART IN GYMNASTICS.
Her First Public Appearance Was Made in Messina Before She was Three Years Old.
WALKING HEAD DOWNWARD.

The blasé New Yorker, surfeited with the alluringly suggestive visions of feminine loveliness in the theatres, may now turn his admiring glances toward a dark haired girl who unites strength with grace, who does the most wonderful gymnastic feats with the greatest possible ease, and who takes evident delight in her perilous mid-air evolutions. Mlle. Alcide Capitaine (from the Empire Theatre, London), the queen of the air, is the pompous announcement of the American Theatre programme. It would, perhaps, suggest more nearly the actual facts to the average playgoer to call her the female Sandow, and to paraphrase the strong man's claim by adding "the perfect woman." Capitaine's act is not at all like that of Sandow, however; his exhibitions of strength are made on the level stage; hers are made far above on the flying trapeze. Muscles that stand out in ridges from his arms and torso as the result of lifting heavy weights do not show under her more delicate skin, while, on the other hand, she has developed to an extraordinary extent those muscles that constant work on the trapeze brings into play.

PRETTY, AND ONLY NINETEEN.

Capitaine is very young. One look at her face is enough to prove that. Her father, Enrico Capitaine Magnago, places her age at nineteen. Her features are regular, her hair is black, her merry, roguish eyes are very dark. Her red lips disclose a perfect row of white teeth, powerful and even. She is of slightly less than average height and admirably proportioned. Concealed under the ordinary bodice, with fashionably wide sleeves, there would be nothing about her body to suggest great strength, though the width of her shoulders is most unusual in a woman.

With her arms and neck bared, her appearance becomes extraordinary. As she moves her head, great bunches of muscle appear on her white throat, extending down toward her shoulders. Her powerful arms taper gracefully down to her slender wrists. Her hands are not exceptionally large, while her feet are really noticeably small.

Her first appearance in this city a week ago last night in the circus scene of "The Voyage of Suzette" was most successful. As she remarked after the act, it was surprising who recognized the true character of her performance. It is the greenroom of the circus. Suzette, rescued from the Pacha's palace, has found a refuge there, and thither she is followed by the Pacha and his myrmidons. Unable to find her the Pacha decides to delay his pursuit long enough to enjoy the novel spectacle of a rehearsal.

HER FIRST APPEARANCE HERE.

Out of the wings walks a little woman, enveloped in a long wrap of velvet. The centre of the stage reached, she throws aside the wrap, and there is Capitaine ready for her marvellous performance.

Somewhat below the average height of woman, she gives no hint of her remarkable strength as she stands for a moment, smiling, with her arms at her side. You see she is a very pretty woman, very young, as well, and her symmetrical form is a delight to the eye.

But when she grasps a rope and begins her hand over hand ascent the swelling muscles of her arms and shoulders assert themselves, and it is seen at once that her one hundred and twenty-eight pounds are safe when controlled by those two arms, which are those of a giant.

She is at the trapeze and seizing the bar in one small hand she hangs for a moment. Then both hands clutch the bar, and by the movement which small boys delight to call "skinning the cat" she seats herself on the bar.

A breathing spell of a second and she throws herself backward. But so securely are her legs wrapped around the bar that there is no danger of a fall, and she swings gracefully and idly. Again she is hanging at full length by her hands, and then she does what is technically known as a "breast up," which, for ease of execution and faultless style, is the very poetry of motion. The "breast up" is a sudden pull by which the body is brought up until the hands holding the bar are at the hips. Around and around she circles, until the spectator is dizzy.

STRENGTH, SKILL AND GRACE.

These evolutions have been enough to tell the initiated, and those, as well, who have no knowledge of gymnastics that the little woman is, indeed, a mistress of her art. The elegant poise of her body when in motion as well as at rest, her calm, confident manner, the apparent ease with which she executes the most difficult movements, the delicate precision with which her supple limbs move, all prove the attention given to her early training and the fact that she was an apt and intelligent pupil.

Nor is the placidity of her finely chiselled features disturbed by those fearful grimaces and contortions which generally mar the performances of the professional. With business-like exactness of detail, as though exercising alone in her private gymnasium, she goes through her performance, only waving her hand occasionally in response to the applause of the audience.

From a sitting position on the bar she straightens out until she is rigid, and then balances. Grasping the bar she falls backward, but not to sag down; her iron muscles keep the bar against her back, and slowly she revolves until she regains her original position. When done properly—and her execution could not be improved—this is an extremely difficult manoeuvre, much more so than the next, in which she revolves rapidly, feet foremost.

WALKING HEAD DOWNWARD.

Capitaine then does her head downward walk. Extending from one trapeze to the other, a distance of twelve feet, is a stout pole, from each side of which, at alternating intervals, extend stout rings. By the aid of the trapeze ropes she places one arched instep on the first rung, and then treads—if that expression may be used—her fearless way across to the other trapeze. As she goes her hands are clasped at her back, are held close to her sides or are gracefully waving, as her fancy dictates.

It is on this trapeze that her most difficult feats are performed. Most difficult they certainly are, but they are of that quiet, undemonstrative order, that sometimes they fail to appeal to the lay mind as much as a dashing feat of the most simple description.

How many women are there, or men either, for that matter, who can kneel on the floor and bending forward can pick up with their teeth a handkerchief placed between the knees? Not many, you think. Yet Capitaine does this very act, and she is kneeling on the slender bar of the swaying trapeze and not on a carpeted floor.

As she slowly bows forward it looks every second as if she must plunge head first into the net slung underneath. But no, she is not of that class of performers—and every one knows there are many in the class—who try to impress an audience with the difficulty of a trick by failing in it once or twice before succeeding. She, on the other hand, makes no such byplays, but seems to find a delight in doing everything at the first trial, and doing it cleverly and apparently easily.

THE HANDKERCHIEF TRICK.

Noting the swing of the trapeze, she waits until the proper moment, and then, with a pretty inclination of the head, she seizes the delicate piece of lace with her lips, straightens up, and still balancing on her knees places the handkerchief in her corsage.

An exhibition of truly wonderful strength and one which demonstrates that she places as much reliance in one arm as the other, came next. It is called "La Plance," and few outside the very best in the profession ever attempt it.

Hanging from the bar by one hand, she gives her body a little turn and gradually pulls herself up until she rests at right angles with her arm, which is still behind her, and upon which her body reclines. Maintaining this attitude for a few seconds, she allows her body to drop slowly. Then she repeats the trick with her other hand.

Probably to give the muscles of her arms a little rest, she then places the back of her neck against the bar, and, removing her hands, hangs suspended, gazing up into the flies. Next she hangs from the bar by her toes, and taking away one foot places it in her hand, after the style made familiar by circus riders and skirt dancers, only that she is inverted and hangs by one foot rather that stands on it.

A GREAT FEAT.

A trick which has rarely been seen in this country, and when seen has been done in such a bungling manner as to warrant no praise, is the next. It is what is known as "dislocating" the shoulder joints. It is frequently and easily performed on the flying rings, where one throws his feet over his head, allows his body to drop down, and then, by a sudden twist, allows his joints to revolve in the sockets so that the original position is assumed. It will readily be understood that the ropes of the rings twist as this is done, making it a comparatively simple trick. Not so on a bar, however, for there is no give there, and all the twist must be borne in the arms.

Grasping the bar in such a manner that her finger nails are toward her face, she throws her feet through and lets her body fall down as far as it will go without "dislocating." Then slowly and gently, without any sideway, ungraceful squirm, but both shoulders together in time and action, she "dislocates" and hangs just as she did before beginning the trick, except that there is a fearful strain on the arms and fingers.

"DISLOCATE" AGAIN.

As if to show it is of no moment, however, she swings for a time, and then gradually but surely she reverses the operation of "dislocating." Raising her body slightly, she bends her head forward, the joints revolve and she is just as she was a second before the first "dislocation." It is a remarkable feat and artistically executed, but, as said above, it is not one of those which will appeal to a miscellaneous audience, inasmuch as its intricacy and difficulty are not readily appreciated. Capitaine then does a few "horizontals," as they are called, holding the body rigid in air at right angles to the arms, and either before or behind them. She does these easily and prettily, as though her previous tricks have not taxed her strength in the slightest.

Then she grasps a rope, and twining one leg around allows herself to slide gracefully to the stage. Then she has only to wait until the applause of the audience subsides, must walk forth once or twice to satisfy the most enthusiastic of her admirers, and then she can retire to her dressing room to rest and receive the congratulations of her happy father.

IN HER DRESSING ROOM.

Under the guidance of Manager T. Henry French I found my way to Capitaine's dressing room behind the scenes. It was a difficult trip, as the circus procession had begun to move around the stage, and the wings were filled with strange animals in various degrees of excitement. We dodged by llamas, zebus, mules and ponies. Horses snorted, whinnied and tugged on their bits. The camel stalked by, lazily chewing his cud, while the elephant which obeys commands before the audience with almost human intelligence showed symptoms of uneasiness, and the stage supernumeraries crowded back, fearful lest he should try dancing on his hind legs and then suddenly return to all fours and pull down the bystanders with him.

Mr. French dodged in and out and I kept close at his heels. On the way he told me about the amusing effect of Capitaine's first appearance on one of the first nighters. Mr. French's partner in the American Theatre enterprise is Mr. Zborowaki, who lives in Belgium, and whose interest here are looked after by Lawyer D.H. Ogden. Capitaine's exhibition made a great impression on Mr. Ogden, who subsequently tried to explain to his friends what she had done. He wrote to Mr. French to say his friends told him that he must have been dreaming, and he wished to know if he had actually seen what he thought he had.

Capitaine was resting when I reached her dressing room. She was flushed and breathing rapidly after her final efforts, and her father and a maid were hovering round her. Stray slippers ornamented the dressing table, and there were little stacks of clothes here and there, for other women use the same room.

The very idea of an interview was most amusing to the young gymnast. She laughed merrily, and declared she didn't know how to talk about herself. By dint of questions, however, I drew out her story.

BEGAN VERY YOUNG.

She made her first public appearance at the age when most children are toddling around and lisping cute sentences to the delectation of their parents. Her father, Mr. Magnago, had been a trapeze performer for many years, and an Instructor of gymnastics in Italian schools. Alcide Capitaine was born in Trieste. From her earliest infancy she showed her predilection for a gymnastic career by utilizing her bed curtains and the furniture for swinging and suspending herself from at every opportunity. Her father was so much impressed by this that he fixed up a small trapeze over her cot, and so she grew up with a trapeze constantly by her. To make sure that he was not injuring her health by allowing her to take the gymnastic exercise, Mr. Magnago consulted a medical expert, who assured him that the child was so strong that trapeze work in moderation would be beneficial. Her progress was wonderful, and when she was two years and eight months old she was ready to appear before the public. She made her debut in Messina, and soon won a reputation throughout Southern Europe as "the marvellous infant."

She has been constantly before the public since then, and has appeared everywhere in Europe and in most South American countries. She has incidentally picked up the most important of modern languages, and speaks English, French, Spanish and German as fluently as she does her native Italian. She played for a long time in London, in the Aquarium, Crystal Palace, Covent Garden and Empire, and her English shows a slight trace of Cockney surroundings.

NOT DOING ALL HER TRICKS.

"No," she exclaimed in response to my queries. "I don't know any woman in Europe who does just the same work that I do, although, of course, the number of woman gymnasts is legion. I am not doing here nearly as much as I did in London. In the first place I have not the space I require. I should have three trapezes instead of two, and forty-eight feet between the ends, not twelve or fourteen. In large places abroad I used to slide down wires, holding by my teeth. That takes lots of room, though. My wire was 500 feet long, with descent of 150 feet. It is a peculiar experience to whirl over thousands of persons, with every face looking up at you.

"I arrived in the city late Saturday afternoon, only a few hours before my opening performance, and had very little time for making arrangements." "Oh, dear, no!" she answered. "I had not touched a trapeze or done any work since my last appearance in Birmingham, the Saturday before I sailed from Southampton. I did nothing more until I opened in this city, and then I found that everything was crooked."

Capitaine showed me that the neat satin shoes she wore were not padded. I had asked her about them, wondering if the pressure on her high instep as she hangs from the rungs was not painful, and if some padding was not required to avoid the danger of slipping. The only precaution she makes is by rubbing the shoes well with rosin to prevent slipping.

SITS FOR A HERALD ARTIST.

To obtain a sketch of her remarkable shoulders, I called with a HERALD artist at the Forty-second street hotel where she is living. It was not without serious hesitation that she consented to bare her shoulders for the artist, but finally, at her father's urgent request, she did so, and sat patiently with her arms stretched out and her great muscles extended while she was sketched. It was a difficult position to maintain for a number of minutes, but she proved an excellent model and sat without a murmur of complaint.

She has received instruction in various forms of stage dancing, as well as tumbling, she told me, but she has practically given up both. She does not wish to do anything which might possibly sprain one of her ankles.

A measurement of her biceps while she was sitting showed that it took fourteen inches to encircle her arm. The sitting over, Capitaine sat down at the piano and played her own accompaniment, while she sang a Spanish ditty in a rich contralto voice. Among the accomplishments of which this pretty, young gymnast boast is that she can cook as well. (*New York Herald,* 31 December 1893, 8C.)

The musical comedy A Gaiety Girl *featured a cast of English show girls who became the preoccupation of New York "dudedom" even as they provided American women with much toted fashion cues. Since these "Gaiety Girls" were the source of numerous articles and much speculation, it was perhaps inevitable that they became motion picture subjects. The women who performed before Edison's kinetograph however, were hardly the stars of the show.*

88 Pas Seul, no. 1 / Miss Lucy Murray / Lucy Murray
LENGTH: 50 ft.   © No reg.
PRODUCER: W.K.L. Dickson, [Raff & Gammon].
CAMERA: William Heise.
CAST: Lucy Murray.
PRODUCTION DATE: 1 November 1894.
LOCATION: Black Maria, West Orange, N.J.
SOURCE: *A Gaiety Girl* (musical comedy).
DESCRIPTION: Leading lady of The Gaiety Girls, in an up-to-date skirt dance. Very spectacular indeed, and especially so when colored. (*Edison Films*, March 1900, 28.)
SUBJECT: Musicals–performances. Dancing. English. Motion pictures–colored. London "Gaiety Girl" Company.
ARCHIVE:
CITATIONS: "A Gaiety Girl is Here," *New York Herald*, 12 September 1894, 6; "Gaiety Girls Saw Red Men," *New York Herald*, 3 October 1894, 14; "A Gaiety Girls Feast," *New York Herald,* 28 December 1894, 7. The Kinetoscope Company, *Bulletin No. 1*, [December 1894]; The Kinetoscope Company, *Price List of Films*, [May 1895], 3; Ohio Phonograph Co., *The Edison Kinetoscope. Price List*, August 1895, 7; Maguire & Baucus, *Edison and International Photographic Films*, April 1897, 11; Maguire & Baucus, *Fall Catalogue*, 1897, 12; F.Z. Maguire & Co., *Catalogue*, [March 1898], 27.
NOTE:

89 Pas Seul, no. 2 / May Lucas
LENGTH: 50 ft.   © No reg.
PRODUCER: W.K.L. Dickson, [Raff & Gammon].
CAMERA: William Heise.
CAST: May Lucas.
PRODUCTION DATE: 1 November 1894.
LOCATION: Black Maria, West Orange, N.J.
SOURCE: *A Gaiety Girl* (musical comedy).
DESCRIPTION: Dance by Miss Lucas, of the "Gaiety Girl" Company. (The Kinetoscope Company, *Bulletin No. 1*, [December 1894].)
SUBJECT: Musicals–performances. Dancing. English. London "Gaiety Girl" Company.
ARCHIVE:
CITATIONS: Raff & Gammon to Exhibition Department, NYC, invoice, 23 November 1894, 1:62, MH-BA. Ohio Phonograph Co., *The Edison Kinetoscope. Price List*, August 1895, 8.
NOTE:

90 √The Carnival Dance / Carnival / Gaiety Girls

LENGTH: 50 ft.   © No reg.

PRODUCER: W.K.L. Dickson, [Raff & Gammon].

CAMERA: William Heise.

CAST: May Lucas, Lucy Murray, Madge Crossland.

PRODUCTION DATE: 1 November 1894.

LOCATION: Black Maria, West Orange, N.J.

SOURCE: *A Gaiety Girl* (musical comedy).

DESCRIPTION: A very fascinating dance by three of the London "Gaiety Girls." Full of grace and abandon. Coloring adds greatly to the charm of the picture. (*Edison Films*, March 1900, 28.)

SUBJECT: Musicals–performances. English. Dancing. Motion pictures–colored. London "Gaiety Girl" Company.

ARCHIVE:

CITATIONS: Raff & Gammon to Peter Bacigalupi, invoice, 12 November 1894, 1:32, MH-BA; W.K.L. Dickson and Antonia Dickson, *History of the Kinetograph, Kinetoscope and Kineto-Phonograph*, 18 (with illustrations). The Kinetoscope Company, *Bulletin No. 1*, [December 1894]; Ohio Phonograph Co., *The Edison Kinetoscope. Price List*, August 1895, 7; Maguire & Baucus, *Edison Films*, 20 January 1897, 6; Maguire & Baucus, *Edison and International Photographic Films*, April 1897, 5; Maguire & Baucus, *Fall Catalogue*, 1897, 11; F.Z. Maguire & Co., *Catalogue*, [March 1898], 27; *Edison Films*, July 1901, 53.

NOTE:

GAIETY GIRLS IN TOWN.
And All Dudedom Is in a State of Deliriously Happy Anticipation.
SCANTY BUT VERY STUNNING COSTUMES.
Their Appetites Are Good, They Travel in Hansoms and Like Cold Bottles and Birds.

Ever since the thirty odd pretty Gaiety Girls got to town a week or so ago, New York "Johnnies" have been in a tremendous state of excitement. Nothing less than new evening suits would, they were sure, make them acceptable to the stunning goddesses from Albion's Isle. They had heard their elder brothers talk of the Gaiety girls of years gone by–the Nellie Farrens, the Sylvia Greys and the Letty Linds–but with the usual progressiveness of the American youth they have decided in solid conclave to give these gallus English girls a few surprises. Just what they will comprise the Johnnies have not made public, but one thing is certain, and that is that Mr. George Edwardes' young women will not be allowed to suffer from ennui during their seven weeks' stay in New York.

INFORMATION FOR THE JOHNNIES

Through exceptional advantages furnished the Herald, I was allowed to percolate about Daly's Theatre the other morning during a thorough rehearsal of the Gaiety company. For the benefit of uninformed dudes, I will state that the back door–the sacred portal through which the British beauties will pass–is located in West Twenty-ninth street in a commonplace brown stone house which might be taken for a private residence.

As I strolled timidly up the steps and presented my card to the grim faced, gray mustached man seated in the lobby, my heart was sent into my boots when, as the door leading into the long hall opened, I saw a laughing crowd of nattily attired girls, the eldest of whom couldn't have been more than twenty-one years of age.

My card proved the open sesame and I was at once ushered up to Stage Manager Malone's private office. Ten feet from the door was the stage, ablaze with bunch lights, footlights and electric lights. Flying about in all kinds of brilliant costumes were the pretty girls who have made "A Gaiety Girl" such a howling success. In a group near the first entrance stood Miss Palotta, Miss Florrie Lloyd and Cissy Fitzgerald. They are the three naughty Gaiety girls, who throw such consternation into the ranks of conservative English society at the garden party which is in the play. They were in their French bathing suits.

QUALITY NOT QUANTITY

It was a warm day, but they looked cool enough. Down in front, leaning confidently over the footlights, was dainty Decima Moore, a second edition of Nellie Farren, and the prima donna of the company, chatting with the leader of the orchestra preparatory to trying one of her most fetching songs. These bathing suits by the way, will carry the average New York youth so far out of his sober senses that he won't know where he is at. They are daintiness personified, and the girls say they make up in quality what they lack in quantity. Imagine three shapely girls gotten up in pink tights, white silk knickerbockers, sandals and gauzy peignoirs through which the contour of necks and arms are just seen enough to be mysteriously fascinating. Long silk cloaks of different shades are provided to throw about them in going and coming from the water, but, as one charming girl put it, "We are supposed to cover ourselves up a bit, only we don't."

"These suits made an awful hit in London," said Cissy Fitzgerald, as she swung around on her right foot, with her arms bowed above her head. "This is our first visit to American in just this way, but, so far, I am delighted with what you call your 'Johnnie' verdure." "Johnnies!" This in a chorus from the girls that had gathered around. At the magic word every eye had brightened, and every rosy mouth had posed itself, so to speak.

FAVORABLE COMPARISONS

The difference between the youth in America who spends time and admiration upon the charming goddess of the stage and the young English swell who prostrates himself at their shrine is vast, indeed, according to those who ought to know—namely these Gaiety girls. They are loyal enough to their own kinsmen to compliment them upon being very nice, but the absolute freshness and verve of our New York boy transfixes them with admiration.

There is quite a kennel of valuable dogs at the back door of this particular theatre, and it is whispered that the grand mogul who waits there in state has clearly described the youth who waits too long and too often, but these particular Gaiety girls laugh merrily in serene complaisance at all these preparations as they mildly suggest to you that they "know a thing or two."

THEY ARE FETCHING GIRLS

And they do. They are the brightest, healthiest, prettiest crew of young British maidens that ever came over to conquer the American heart and pocketbooks. Most of them are of the race of famous English blondes. Statuesque Miss Moore is glorious in nut brown tresses. Besides those tantalizing bathing dresses which they smooth with a tender, affectionate touch as they talk of the pleasant times they anticipate having in America, they exhibited exquisite garden party gowns and bal masque costumes by the dozens. It is said that when one young millionaire in town heard of Miss Fitzgerald's dancing gown of green and white silk, combined with violets, he immediately ordered a barrelful of choicest Parma violets for the first night's appearance.

The youths with the fat pocketbooks and head[s] filled already with bright visions of blond Gaiety girls and myriads of silken skirts, are even now picking out their particular seats for the season's campaign, both in front of the house and at the rear entrance. When the natty girls came trooping in yesterday for letters from old England, it wasn't five minutes by the clock across the way before several swell Calumet Club youths strolled by with that look of strained indifference only acquired after much practice, their hands drifted up to their hat brims in an involuntary gesture of true admiration. A word to them all. The Gaiety girl is a beauty and a joy forever. She loves the good things of life. She rides in cabs and must have them. She has a good appetite, and enjoys an excellent supper, from an English chop to champagne and truffles. (*New York Herald*, 18 September 1894, 10.)

"A GAIETY GIRL" ON DECK.
Hearty Welcome to the London Musical Comedy and Mr. Edwardes' Company at Daly's Theatre.
BEVY OF BEAUTIES, GALAXY OF GOWNS.
The New and Gay Production Is Greeted by a Very Large and Notable Gathering.
IN BOX AND ORCHESTRA.

DALY'S THEATRE.—A Gaiety Girl, a musical comedy in two acts by Owen Hall and Sidney Jones.

Charles Goldfield	Mr. Charles Ryley.
Major Barclay	Mr. Fred Kaye.
Bobbie Rivers	W. Louis Bradfield.
Harry Fitz Warren	Mr. Cecil Hope.
Ronney Farquhar	Mr. Compton Taylor.
Sir Lewis Grey	Mr. Leedham Bantock.
Lance	Mr. E.G. Woodhouse.
Auguste	Mr. Fritz Rimma.
Dr. Montague Brierly	Mr. Harry Monkhouse.
Rose Brierly	Miss Decima Moore.
Lady Edytha Aldwyn	Miss Marie Yorke.
Miss Gladys Stourton	Miss Sophie Elliott.
Hon. Daisy Ormsbury	Miss Ethel Selwyn.
Lady Grey	Mrs. Edmund Phelps.
Alma Somerset	Miss Blanche Massey.
Cissy Verner	Miss Florence Lloyd.
Haidee Walton	Miss Grace Palotta.
Ethel Hawthorne	Miss Cissy Fitzgerald.
Lady Virginia Forrest	Miss Maud Hobson.
Mina	Miss Juliette Nesville.

Hail, all hail to that most charming and unconventional of British Institutions—the Gaiety Girl. The sweet creature was received at Daly's Theatre last evening a bras ouverts. She was petted, admired, flattered, spoiled and applauded to such an extent that when she returns to her native soil—if she ever does—it will be found that her head has been sadly turned by those dear, warm hearted Americans. Rarely have I noted such a consensus of opinion as could be heard on all sides while leaving the theatre.

Your haughty society woman observed to her escort, "Thank heaven, we have something interesting at lawst," while your bookmaker, who never misses a first night (have you ever noticed what an ardent critic he is?), voted "A Gaiety Girl" "a ripping good show." A sweeping, generous gesture accompanied the word "ripping," just as if he were marking up even money against the favorite.

All these encomiums, let it be said, were fully deserved. Even the man whose artistic ideals are high, who hates bad comic operas and all that sort of thing was moved to genuine admiration by the work itself, by the actors, and by the exquisite manner in which the whole matter was bodied forth.

It was seen, moreover, that a good burlesque—and this is a good one—is deserving of the same care and artistic nicety which Mr. Irving brings to the production of the poetic drama.

The plot of the "Gaiety Girl" may be dismissed in a few words. Some of the girls of that theatre are asked to a garden party in order to contribute to the amusement of the guests. There the leading Gaiety girl is falsely accused of annexing Lady Thingamy's diamond comb. Complications and disguises there are, fortunately, next to none in this travesty, but the manner is really delightful, the text fairly bristling with witty lines and the interest never flagging for an instant.

Nothing that has been said of the charm and loveliness of the ladies of this organization is at all exaggerated. They are not voluptuous Aphrodites, but sweet, beautiful English girls, exceedingly lovable and modest, even while saying and doing the most risque things—which is as much as saying that they are not only beautiful but also artistic. They dance to a miracle, they sing acceptably and they are exquisitely dressed—not like queens of the stage but like gentlewomen, one and all.

And what melodious, beautiful diction; what grace, ease and savoire faire generally. Miss Massey in the title role, in a Directoire dress, was a thing of beauty and of joy forever, while Miss Hobson, as Lady Virginia, looked stunning, no matter what she wore. And for the first time we heard Miss Nesville, a French maid with a genuine Gallic accent, and Miss Cissy Fitzgerald's marvelous dance I am sure will be one of the sights of the town.

The men, too, are superb, for they are men who have splendid humor, who know how to act and to sing so well that our own comedians will have to look very sharply to their laurels. Mr. Monkhouse and Mr. Kaye kept the audience in splendid good humor throughout the evening. Mr. Riley has a most sympathetic barytone voice and there seems to be nothing that young Mr. Bradford can't do. As for the performance as a whole, I have never seen anything in the line that could boast of the same cachet, the same fine artistic feeling.

Act I.—Pleasant grounds with a view of Windsor. The audience thinking that they were to look to the chorus for the much heralded beauty contained in the "Gaiety Girl," was a trifle disappointed. But when Lady Virginia's charge were trotted out, and a few minutes later the three genuine girls came on, then all ill-suppressed ejaculation of delight could be heard all over the house. Beautiful scenery, the most fetching of dresses, intoxicating dances and a wealth of funny lines ingratiated the "Gaiety Girl" with everybody in the house.

Act II.—Nice, with a view of Monte Carlo. What with women being carried by big, hulking Italians to their baths, a kaleidoscopic carnival scene, and copious allusions to the dangers of bucking the tiger, there was at no time a lack of couleur locale. And people remained seated to applaud after it was all over. As much has not happened here at a lighter entertainment in a long, long time.

GOWNS AND STALLS

An old friend "The Gaiety Girl" proved, and she brought wither an atmosphere of London, Piccadilly Circus by day and night, the Burlington Arcade, Whitehall and Knightbridge, and not least important, the "currant bun," that distinctive style of coiffure now as much a part of London as her fogs. And then, too, there was a decided smack of the garden party element: fresh girls, pretty gowns—all so "very English, you know," and so easily recognized by the annual globe trotters, and even by the stay at homes.

As for the gowns, they might well be copied, for warm weather is not quite over. Lady Virginia's (Miss Maud Hobson) first gown would do excellent service at a Lenox archery party. It was a broche silk, checked and flowered, of light colors, with a bodice of coral colored velvet, over which were Van Dykes of yak lace, and round the waist a full belt of black satin, with long narrow ends. A tiny bonnet, which seemed but a golden butterfly, and a few velvet bows were perched on top of Lady Virginia's "currant bun" coiffure. Alma Somerset (Miss Blanche Massey) was a Gainsborough in effect, in a gown of white satin brocaded with garlands of pink flowers, and a huge white hat and plumes. Ethel Hawthorne (Miss Cissy Fitzgerald), in a bewilderment of seafoam green skirts, which were, in fact, multitudinous, with here and there clusters of mauve flowers, brought to mind the early triumphs of Letty Lind and Sylvia Grey. Miss Sophie Elliott, as Miss Gladys Stourton, was the type of much photographed English beauty, in her gown of delicate pink crepon, with belt and shoulder knots of ruby velvet and a big picture hat of white lace trimmed with bows of ruby velvet. (*New York Herald*, 19 September 1894, 14.)

DANCING FOR THE KINETOGRAPH.
A Party of the Gayety Girls Visit Edison's Laboratory at Orange.

The "Gayety Girls" went out to Orange, N.J. yesterday afternoon and gave an exhibition of high kicking before the Edison Kinetograph. On account of the limited space in the exhibition room only three dancers in the second act appeared in costume, Miss Madge Crossland, Miss Lucy Murray and Miss May Lucas. They gave their high kicking act with great spirit. Miss Cissy Fitzgerald, who was to have accompanied the party and executed her serpentine dance, was ill and could not go. Along with the dancers went Miss Decima Moore, the prima donna of the company, and Miss Florence Lloyd. Mr. Malone, the manager of the company, also went, together with Major Kay and Cecil Hope. The girls entered into the spirit of the occasion and kicked up their heels with refreshing frankness and freedom. Miss Annie Oakley, the "Wild West" shot, also appeared and gave an exhibition of her shooting. There was also present at the laboratory Signorina Alcide Capitaine, the trapeze performer. Her performance called out loud applause. After the close of the exhibition the entire party were entertained at lunch by Mr. Tate. (*New York Herald*, 2 November 1894, 11.)

Japanese performers, almost exclusively male acrobats and female dancers, were a significant presence on the New York stage in the mid 1890s.

91 *Imperial Japanese Dance / Japanese Dance / Jap Dance

LENGTH: 50 ft.   © No reg.

PRODUCER: W.K.L. Dickson, Raff & Gammon.

CAMERA: William Heise.

CAST: Sarashe Sisters (Imperial Dancing Girls?).

PRODUCTION DATE: Mid-October to mid-November 1894.

LOCATION: Black Maria, West Orange, N.J.

SOURCE:

DESCRIPTION: Three Japanese Ladies in the Costumes of their Country. (The Kinetoscope Company, *Price List of Films*, [May 1895], 3.) A charming representation of The Mikado dance by three beautiful Japanese ladies in full costume. Very effective when colored. (*Edison Films,* July 1901, 53.)

SUBJECT: Musicals–performances. Dancing. Japanese. Motion pictures–colored.

ARCHIVE: NR-GE, CLAc, DLC-Hendricks.

CITATIONS: Raff and Gammon to Exhibition Department, Chicago, invoice, 30 November 1894, 1:73, MH-BA; Kinetoscope Co. to Holland Brothers, 29 December 1894, 1:161, MH-BA; W.K.L. Dickson and Antonia Dickson, *History of the Kinetograph, Kinetoscope and Kineto-Phonograph*, 46 (with illustrations). Ohio Phonograph Co., *The Edison Kinetoscope. Price List*, August 1895, 8; Maguire & Baucus, *Edison and International Photographic Films*, April 1897, 5; Maguire & Baucus, *Fall Catalogue*, 1897, 12; F.Z. Maguire & Co., *Catalogue*, [March 1898], 27; *Edison Films*, March 1900, 29.

NOTE: According to Kenji Iwamoto and Hiroshi Komatsu, this film was part of the first group of pictures shown in Japan, on a peep-hole kinetoscope in Kobe, on 17 November 1896. Its title was *Nippon Maiko Nuno Sarashi* (Japanese Dancing Girls [maidens] Waving Streamers). This dance is a Kyoto dance. Sarashee Sisters thus refers to the act of waving the cloth banners and was, at most, a stage name.

JAPANESE DANCERS IN "THE MIKADO."

Pulp of pomegranate and spice of chrysanthemum: The scarlet and sun of Japan glowed at the Fifth Avenue Theatre last night, where five little Japanese girls came and danced before the "Mikado."

It was in the second act of the opera, and Mr. Stevens didn't have anything to do at all, for the five little Japanese girls danced a court dance and a pleasant dance and a flower dance just as though the comedian was the Mikado and all was "dead serious." And all the while another little Japanese girl thrummed a fiddle and a little old Japanese woman crooned as though it hurt her, and the audience was very much delighted.

No, it cannot exactly be called graceful, but it was cute. It was just as though little Alice had got into a Japanese wonderland and wanted to stay there. Of course, the serving of tea in the theatre lobby just before the little Japanese girls danced brought the audience to a realization of the genuineness of the dancers, for didn't we all take a cup of tea and get a paper napkin? (*New York Herald*, 21 June 1894, 11.)

5th AVENUE THEATRE. Two new dances were introduced into the second act of "The Mikado" by the Imperial Dancing Girls. Both were graceful and characteristic of different phases of social life in Japan, the first being a figure peculiar to Niegata, and the other–called Shi chi fu kugin, or dance of the seven gods–being an allegorical sacred dance. (*New York Herald*, 24 July 1894, 7.)

Rosa made her American debut at the Turkish village at the Chicago World Columbian Exposition in 1893. Touring with the Boston Howard Athenaeum Company, Rosa was at Waldmann's Opera House in Newark for the week beginning 11 November 1894. (Newark Evening News, 12 November 1894.) She was almost certainly kinetographed sometime during this week.

92 Oriental Dance / Mlle Rosa
LENGTH: 50 ft.   © No reg.
PRODUCER: W.K.L. Dickson.
CAMERA: William Heise.
CAST: Rosa.
PRODUCTION DATE: Mid-November 1894.
LOCATION: Black Maria, West Orange, N.J.
SOURCE:
DESCRIPTION:
SUBJECT: Vaudeville–performances. Dancing. Turks. Danse du ventre.
ARCHIVE:
CITATIONS: Kinetoscope Company to Holland, 29 December 1894, 1:161; Dickson to Raff & Gammon, 8 January 1895, MH-BA.
NOTE: The negative for this film was destroyed during printing in late 1894.

Rosa's Wonderful Feat

In the Turkish Village they have a dancer whom they think a great star. She can whirl rapidly like a top for five minutes, and then walk off the stage without deviating a particle from a straight line. That is a great accomplishment, and entitles her to precedence. It is about as much as some of the French eccentric dancers now before the public can do. Rosa is short and plump and rather nice looking. She was born at Thessalonica, in Turkey. She has visited all the great towns of the Sultan's dominions, and, as the playbills would say, she had them all at her feet. ("Dancing in Midway Plaisance," *New York World*, 23 July 1893, 17.)

A revival of the Midway entertainment on a larger scale than has been attempted before will be the feature of the State Street Globe Museum this week. Kohl & Middleton claim they have secured the services of Rosa, the dancer of the Turkish Theater at the World's Fair, and Sultana of the Cairo Street Theater, and a dozen others, including Ali Ben Dib's troupe of Bedouins, Turks, and Armenians. The theater has been altered to resemble a Turkish playhouse, with new scenery and appointments. (*Chicago Tribune*, 3 February 1895, 38.)

ROSA, ROSA, ROSA
**The Peerless Star of the Midway, Turkish Dancing and Whirling
Wonder, Making 145 Revolutions a Minute.**
AT LIBERTY
Has just concluded a marvelously successful engagement of one year and a half with Kohl & Middleton, Chicago. Address **THE GREAT ROSA, 292 State St., Chicago, Ill.** (Advertisement, *New York Clipper*, 28 March 1896, 58.)

The Black Maria studio was almost certainly bustling with activity on 26 November 1894. The Rixfords, at least, performed their acrobatic feats before the kinetograph on that day. Other vaudevillians probably executed their routines then as well, though the evidence is less definitive. Films were typically delivered to the Kinetoscope Company's store front exhibition rooms in New York and Chicago about three weeks after the subjects were taken. A group of motion picture subjects were sent to these venues on 18 December 1894. These included films of Robetta and Doretto, Elsie Jones, Topack and Steel, and Frank Lawton (of The Milk White Flag*).*
The Rixfords had been performing in San Francisco before traveling to the East Coast in late spring 1894 They had engagements at Keith's Union Square Theatre for the week beginning 18 June 1894 and at Proctor's for the week of 12 November 1894.

93 **The Rixfords, [no. 1]**
LENGTH: 50 and 150 ft.   © No reg.
PRODUCER: W.K.L. Dickson.
CAMERA: William Heise.
CAST: John L. Rixford (P.B. Ryan) and "brother."
PRODUCTION DATE: 26 November 1894.
LOCATION: Black Maria, West Orange, N.J.
SOURCE:
DESCRIPTION: Acrobatic Feats. (The Kinetoscope Company, *Price List of Films*, [May 1895], 3.)
 Lifting with hands only. A difficult feat of strength. (F.Z. Maguire & Co., *Catalogue*, [March 1898], 33.)
SUBJECT: Vaudeville–performances. Acrobats.
ARCHIVE:
CITATIONS: *Richmond [Va.] Times-Dispatch*, clippings, NN. Maguire & Baucus, *Edison and International Photographic Films*, April 1897, 18; Maguire & Baucus, *Fall Catalogue*, 1897, 13 and 14.
NOTE: Although this title was only sold in 50-foot lengths in 1894-95, the same subject—apparently from the same negative—was later offered for sale as a 150-foot film.

94 **The Rixfords, [no. 2]**
LENGTH: 50 ft.   © No reg.
PRODUCER: W.K.L. Dickson.
CAMERA: William Heise.
CAST: John L. Rixford (P.B. Ryan) and "brother."
PRODUCTION DATE: 26 November 1894.
LOCATION: Black Maria, West Orange, N.J.
SOURCE:
DESCRIPTION: Acrobatic Feats (Head Balancing, a difficult and interesting feat). (The Kinetoscope Company, *Price List of Films*, [May 1895], 3.)
 Head balancing, showing one man balancing another on his head, and both disrobing while in that position. (F.Z. Maguire & Co., *Catalogue*, [March 1898], 33.)
SUBJECT: Vaudeville–performances. Acrobats.
ARCHIVE:
CITATIONS: Raff & Gammon to Exhibition Department, NYC, invoice, 18 December 1894, 1:135, MH-BA. Maguire & Baucus, *Fall Catalogue*, 1897, 13.
NOTE:

The Rixfords are closing the olio with Spring and Welty's "Black Crook" Co. in San Francisco, Cal. They write of success for themselves and the old time specialties. (*New York Clipper*, 14 April 1894, 83.)

THE RIXFORDS, ACROBATS, gave a successful performance before Edison's Kinetoscope, in the laboratory in Orange, N.J., Nov. 26th. (*New York Clipper*, 8 December 1894, 636.)

THE RIXFORDS. These famous Acrobats were first seen here in 1881, with John H. Murray's Circus, and later with Barnum's, Forepaugh's and other shows. Their great experience, both in Europe and America brought them conspicuously to the front. In 1889-90 they produced the original Donizetti Troupe, seven in number, in Columbus, O., with Miller Bros.' Kajanka Co. Their success being so pronounced, were immediately engaged the following season, and with an eye to uptodateness, put on at Niblo's Garden the wonderful Mariani Troupe, nine in number; this was Aug. 16, 1891. Returning to Europe in 1893 they met with warm receptions in their various acts with Circus Renz, Berlin; Wulff, Budapest; Cinizelli, St. Petersburg; Noveaux Cirque, Paris, etc. In 1894-5, they were seen with Tompkins' "Black Cook Co." touring the States. 1896 found them in London, where they succeeded in signing contracts with Mr. Geo. Andey Paine, for the Syndicate Halls, London–38 weeks every year, the balance of the time being filled in Paris, Vienna, Berlin. The success of the Rixfords is a just tribute to the true artistic instincts they bring to bear on everything they undertake, and they are to be congratulated on their latest acrobatic novelty. (Advertisement, *New York Clipper*, 5 November 1898, 616.)

The Rexfords [sic], John and Connie, Lena, La Couvier and Jack and "Ray Gram" arrived from London, Eng., March 3, after a stormy passage. Miss La Couvier, while on her way from the dining room, was thrown down the stairs by the rolling of the ship, and hurt herself very severely. (*New York Clipper*, 10 March 1900, 28.)

There were many all-white comedy duos who impersonated Chinese characters for their vaudeville skits during 1894. Harding and Ah Sid presented a skit "illustrating Contemporaneous Chinese Life" at Keith's Union Square Theatre for two weeks in January 1894, which was retitled "Fun in a Chinese Laundry" on their return engagement in mid-August. At that same venue, Robetta and Doretto appeared as "the Chinese comiques" for the week beginning 29 January 1894. The duo, now billed as "Robetta and Doreto," staged "Heap Fun Laundry" at Tony Pastor's 14th Street Theatre for the week beginning 26 November 1894, about the time they performed for Edison's camera. For the next several years, they appeared in vaudeville with the same basic act, often billed as "the Chinese Emperors." They were still presenting their "Fun in a Chinese Laundry" act at J.D. Hopkins's St. Charles Theater in New Orleans for the week beginning 28 March 1898. (New Orleans Picayune, 27 March 1898, 7.)

95 √Robetta and Doretto, [no. 1] / Opium Den / Opium Joint / Opium Scene
LENGTH: 50 ft.   © No reg.
PRODUCER: W.K.L. Dickson.
CAMERA: William Heise.
CAST: Phil Doret[t]o (Phil Lauter), Robetta.
PRODUCTION DATE: [26 November 1894.]
LOCATION: Black Maria, West Orange, N.J.
SOURCE:
DESCRIPTION: Scene represents section of the interior of a Chinese Opium Den. (Ohio Phonograph Co., *The Edison Kinetoscope. Price List*, August 1895, 9.)
SUBJECT: Vaudeville–performances. Police. Narcotics. Chinese.
ARCHIVE:
CITATIONS: Raff & Gammon to Exhibition Department, Chicago, invoice, 21 December 1894, 1:136, MH-BA; W.K.L. Dickson and Antonia Dickson, *History of the Kinetograph, Kinetoscope and Kineto-Phonograph*, 47 (with illustration). The Kinetoscope Company, *Price List of Films*, [May 1895], 3; Maguire & Baucus, *Edison and International Photographic Films*, April 1897, 13; Maguire & Baucus, *Fall Catalogue*, 1897, 12; F.Z. Maguire & Co., *Catalogue*, [March 1898], 87.
NOTE: Robetta and Doret[t]o were stage names, making it difficult to trace the background of these performers. The identification of Phil Doreto as the stage name for Phil Lauter, based on a brief obituary of his father, which appeared in *Variety* in 1907, is hopefully a start.

96 *Robetta and Doretto, [no. 2] / Chinese Laundry Scene
LENGTH: 50 ft.   © No reg.
PRODUCER: W.K.L. Dickson.
CAMERA: William Heise.
CAST: Phil Doret[t]o (Phil Lauter), Robetta.
PRODUCTION DATE: [26 November 1894.]
LOCATION: Black Maria, West Orange, N.J.
SOURCE:
DESCRIPTION: The pursuit of Hop Lee by an irate policeman. (Maguire & Baucus, *Fall Catalogue*, 1897, 11.)
SUBJECT: Vaudeville–performances. Police. Chinese. Irish.
ARCHIVE: NNMoMA, DLC-Hendricks.
CITATIONS: Raff & Gammon to Exhibition Department, NYC, invoice, 18 December 1894, 1:135, MH-BA. The Kinetoscope Company, *Price List of Films*, [May 1895], 3; Maguire & Baucus, *Edison Films*, 20

January 1897, 6; Maguire & Baucus, *Edison and International Photographic Films*, April 1897, 6; F.Z. Maguire & Co., *Catalogue*, [March 1898], 28.
NOTE:

97 [Robetta and Doretto, no. 3]

LENGTH: 50 ft.   © No reg.
PRODUCER: W.K.L. Dickson.
CAMERA: William Heise.
CAST: Phil Doret[t]o (Phil Lauter), Robetta.
PRODUCTION DATE: [26 November 1894.]
LOCATION: Black Maria, West Orange, N.J.
SOURCE:
DESCRIPTION:
SUBJECT: Vaudeville–performances. Police. Chinese. Irish.
ARCHIVE:
CITATIONS: W.K.L. Dickson and Antonia Dickson, *History of the Kinetograph, Kinetoscope and Kineto-Phonograph*, 48 (with illustration).

NOTE: The Continental Commerce Company listed three films featuring Robetta and Doreto in its Italian catalog. Two were very similar subjects: *Robetto e Doretto, scene del lavatoio* and *Hip Lee inseguito dai poliziotti*. (Continental Phonograph Kinetoscope Company, *Kinetoscenes*, [March 1895].) Despite the assertion that the photograph in the Dicksons' *History of the Kinetograph* is a frame enlargement, it is a production still.

OPIUM SMOKERS ARRESTED.
Chinese Prisoners Declare They Were in Their Own Clubroom.

Detective Downing and six policemen of the Elizabeth street station raided an alleged opium den at No 18 Mott street last night. Twenty-four prisoners, all Chinamen, were captured. The premises raided have been occupied lately by several Celestials, who have designated the place the "Chinese Laundry Club." Complaints had been made that the men assembled there for the purpose of smoking opium. Detective Downing looked in last night and saw several Chinamen lying about on settees, smoking opium. He secured assistance at the station and the raid was made. The prisoners protested loudly against the arrest. They said the place was in no sense a "joint," but a "private club," and that the members had a right to smoke opium if they saw fit. Their protests, however, were of no avail. They were locked up and will be arraigned in the Essex Market Police Court this morning. (*New York Herald*, 19 November 1894, 3.)

Robetta and Doreto, in their sketch heap fun laundry, closed the show in good style. (*New York Clipper*, 1 December 1894, 622.)

People's...the two cleverest Chinese impersonators on the stage, Robetta and Doreto, will be seen in a funny laundry scene, showing the effect of opium or how a Chinaman will act while under the influence. (*Cincinnati Commercial Tribune*, 20 December 1896, 11.)

Columbia Theatre...Robetta and Doreto, with their Chinese laundry act, introducing grotesque tumbling, are old favorites. (*Providence Journal*, 16 February 1897, 8.)

Elsie Jones was one of several performers appearing in New York City music halls during the fall of 1894, who were called "magnets." That is, despite their often diminutive look, they were said to have some special power or skill that made it difficult or impossible even for strong men to lift them off the ground.

98 Elsie Jones, no. 1 / Elsie Jones / Elsie Sones [sic]

LENGTH: 50 ft.   © No reg.
PRODUCER: W.K.L. Dickson.
CAMERA: William Heise.
CAST: Elsie Jones.

PRODUCTION DATE: [26 November 1894.]

LOCATION: Black Maria, West Orange, N.J.

SOURCE:

DESCRIPTION: "The Little Magnet," Buck Dance. (The Kinetoscope Company, *Price List of Films*, [May 1895], 3.)

America's greatest "Buck" dancer. (Maguire & Baucus, *Fall Catalogue*, 1897, 11.)

SUBJECT: Vaudeville–performances. Dancing. Afro-Americans.

ARCHIVE:

CITATIONS: Raff & Gammon to Exhibition Department, NYC, invoice, 18 December 1894, 1:135, MH-BA. Ohio Phonograph Co., *The Edison Kinetoscope. Price List*, August 1895, 8; Maguire & Baucus, *Edison Films*, 20 January 1897, 6; Maguire & Baucus, *Edison and International Photographic Films*, April 1897, 7; F.Z. Maguire & Co., *Catalogue*, [March 1898], 27.

NOTE:

99 Elsie Jones, no. 2

LENGTH: 50 ft.   © No reg.

PRODUCER: W.K.L. Dickson.

CAMERA: William Heise.

CAST: Elsie Jones.

PRODUCTION DATE: [26 November 1894.]

LOCATION: Black Maria, West Orange, N.J.

SOURCE:

DESCRIPTION:

SUBJECT: Vaudeville–performances. Dancing. Afro-Americans.

ARCHIVE:

CITATIONS: Raff & Gammon to Rudolph Maquer, 5 March 1895, 1:341, MH-BA.

NOTE:

Topack and Steel first appeared together in "Humpty Dumpty" during the 1881-82 season. After that season they performed as a duo in variety and vaudeville, playing the Bowery Theatre and other locations. During 1894, Keith's Union Square Theatre engaged the burlesquers to spoof one former and one current president in their Cleveland and Harrison routine (titled "Grover and Ben") for the weeks beginning 1 January and 28 May. They subsequently returned to the Union Square "in their newest political satire" for the week of 22 October. They remained a popular combination through the end of the century.

100 Topack and Steele / Cleveland and Harrison / [Topack and Steel]

LENGTH: 50 ft.   © No reg.

PRODUCER: W.K.L. Dickson.

CAMERA: William Heise.

CAST: George Topack, George W. Steel[e].

PRODUCTION DATE: [26 November 1894.]

LOCATION: Black Maria, West Orange, N.J.

SOURCE:

DESCRIPTION: Lively Political Debate, Representing Cleveland and Harrison. (The Kinetoscope Company, *Bulletin No. 1*, [December 1894].)

SUBJECT: Vaudeville–performances. Politics, practical. Burlesque. Grover Cleveland. Benjamin Harrison.

ARCHIVE:

CITATIONS: Raff & Gammon to Exhibition Department, NYC, invoice, 18 December 1894, 1:135, MH-BA. The Kinetoscope Company, *Price List of Films*, [May 1895], 3.

NOTE:

1,000 ACES

An enormous success and one of the best laughing acts in the business, pronounced by managers and press the best comedy act we ever did; fifteen minutes' solid laughter: no talk; all action; just finished ORPHEUM AND CASTLE CIRCUIT. Can be engaged for next season. Our address for few weeks only, **Topack & Steel, 2344 Ingersoll St., Philadelphia, Pa.** (Advertisement, *New York Clipper*, 4 February 1899, 833.)

Howard Athenaeum...Topack and Steel also presented a new skit that puts their famous "Judge & Major" act in the shade. (*Boston Herald*, 18 April 1899, 8.)

GEORGE TOPACK

George Topack (68[?]) of the once well-known blackface knockabout song and dance team, Topack and Steele, passed away June 3 at the Coney Island (N.Y.) Hospital of pneumonia. George Topack started his career in the show business in the late '70s, with George L. Fox (called the world's greatest clown) in the latter's production of "Humpty Dumpty," with which he remained for several seasons. The deceased then went into vaude, working with several partners, as Topack and Long, Topack and Horner, Topack and Moore (Yankee Moore relative of John and Harry Kernell) until in 1922 [1892?] he joined with George Steele. Topack and Steele became recognized as a standard in vaudeville attraction, and featured comedians in burlesque years ago. Steele bought a cigar store in Philadelphia, which he is still running. After a short retirement, following the dissolution, Topack, too old to take the bumps which the act formerly were noted for, became doorman of the Gaiety, St. Louis, later accepting the same position at the Casino, Brooklyn, N.Y. During the summer seasons, he has acted as ticket man for the Sam Gumpert attractions at Coney Island, N.Y., and was so engaged when taken ill. Internment was June 6, in Evergreen Cemetery. He leaves a widow and two sons Charles and Frank. (*Variety*, 11 June 1924.)

GEORGE W. STEEL

George W. Steel, 76, vaudeville actor, died suddenly Feb. 19 in Philadelphia. Mr. Steel was of the vaude team of Topack and Steel, which was a standard and well known act 35 years ago. For years Topack and Steel specialized in blackface, although in later years they appeared in whiteface. Interment in Philadelphia. (*Variety*, 25 February 1931, 69.)

Charles Hoyt's musical farce A Milk White Flag *had its New York premiere at Hoyt's Theatre in New York City on 8 October 1894. The burlesque, however, was still being put into shape, and at the end of the month Hoyt interpolated the role of the tramp, played by Lew Bloom, into the performance. Sometime after this date, the cast of* A Milk White Flag *traveled to the Edison Laboratory and appeared in at least five films. The musical remained at Hoyt's Theatre until February 1895, when it was replaced by* The Foundling, *starring Cissy Fitzgerald.*

101 √**Finale of 1st Act, Hoyt's "Milk White Flag" / Milk White Flag**
LENGTH: 50 ft.   © No reg.
PRODUCER: W.K.L. Dickson.
CAMERA: William Heise.
CAST:
PRODUCTION DATE: Late November 1894.
LOCATION: Black Maria, West Orange, N.J.
SOURCE: *A Milk White Flag* (burlesque).
DESCRIPTION: Showing 34 Persons in Costume.

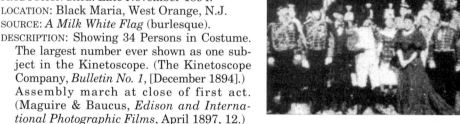

The largest number ever shown as one subject in the Kinetoscope. (The Kinetoscope Company, *Bulletin No. 1*, [December 1894].) Assembly march at close of first act. (Maguire & Baucus, *Edison and International Photographic Films*, April 1897, 12.)
SUBJECT: Musicals–performances. Bands (Music).
ARCHIVE:
CITATIONS: "New Bills at the Theatres," *New York Times*, 9 October 1894, 4; Raff & Gammon to Exhibition Department, NYC, invoice, 20 December 1894, 1:136, MH-BA; W.K.L. Dickson and Antonia Dickson, *History of the Kinetograph, Kinetoscope and Kineto-Phonograph*, 50 (with illustrations). Ohio Phonograph Co., *The Edison Kinetoscope. Price List*, August 1895, 9; Maguire & Baucus, *Edison Films*, 20 January 1897, 7; Maguire & Baucus, *Fall Catalogue*, 1897, 12; F.Z. Maguire & Co., *Catalogue*, [March 1898], 28.
NOTE:

.02 ***Band Drill**
LENGTH: 50 ft.   © No reg.
PRODUCER: W.K.L. Dickson, Raff & Gammon.

CAMERA: William Heise.

CAST: Frank Baldwin (Steele Ayers, the band-master), Fred W. Boardman, William Cushing, Ad. Dorsch, E.P. Brown, J.F. Boardman, George Goddard, E.F. Balch, Paul Pfarr.

PRODUCTION DATE: Late November 1894.

LOCATION: Black Maria, West Orange, N.J.

SOURCE: *A Milk White Flag* (burlesque).

DESCRIPTION: From "Milk White Flag," Marching band with leader at the head. (The Kinetoscope Company, *Bulletin No. 1*, [December 1894].)

SUBJECT: Musicals–performances. Bands (Music).

ARCHIVE: NR-GE, CLAc, DLC-Hendricks.

CITATIONS: Ohio Phonograph Co., *The Edison Kinetoscope. Price List*, August 1895, 9; Maguire & Baucus, *Edison and International Photographic Films*, 3; Maguire & Baucus, *Fall Catalogue*, 1897, 14; Maguire & Baucus, *Fall Catalogue*, 1897, 11; F.Z. Maguire & Co., *Catalogue*, [March 1898], 28.

NOTE:

103 Dance / Frank Lawton / Trio Dance / Trio

LENGTH: 50 ft.   © No reg.

PRODUCER: W.K.L. Dickson.

CAMERA: William Heise.

CAST: Frank Lawton (Gideon Foote, the dance master), Etta Williamson and Rosa France (as vivandieres).

PRODUCTION DATE: Late November 1894.

LOCATION: Black Maria, West Orange, N.J.

SOURCE: *A Milk White Flag* (burlesque).

DESCRIPTION: A lively, eccentric dance by Frank Lawton and Misses Williamson and France of Hoyt's "Milk White Flag." Attractive costumes. (Ohio Phonograph Co., *The Edison Kinetoscope. Price List*, August 1895, 7.)

SUBJECT: Musicals–performances. Dancing.

ARCHIVE:

CITATIONS: Raff & Gammon to Exhibition Department, NYC, invoice, 18 December 1894, 1:135, MH-BA; "Dramatic Notes," *Chicago Tribune*, 20 January 1895, 39. The Kinetoscope Company, *Bulletin No. 1*, [December 1894]; Maguire & Baucus, *Edison and International Photographic Films*, April 1897, 15; Maguire & Baucus, *Fall Catalogue*, 1897, 13; F.Z. Maguire & Co., *Catalogue*, [March 1898], 28.

NOTE:

Rosa France Is Very Ill

BOSTON, March 1.–Rosa France, well known here as a comic actress and singer, is lying seriously ill at the Hoffman House in this city. Her malady is neuritis, or inflammation of the nerves. She has been ill since Christmas, and for seven weeks has been confined to her bed. Miss France has just completed her thirtieth year. She was recently a member of the company presenting "A Milk White Flag" at Hoyt's Theatre, New York. She belongs to an old theatrical family. Her mother, Rachel Noah, who is attending her in her illness, is a well-known actress. (*New York Times*, 2 March 1895, 1.)

London, England–Frank Lawton is a decided success at the syndicate halls, and uses a special set of scenery at each of the three houses. He has been offered a good engagement in Berlin. (*New York Clipper*, 7 April 1900, 124.)

FRANK LAWTON STRANDED.
Whistling Comedian Hard Hit by Collapse of a Show in London.
By Marconi Transatlantic Wireless Telegraph to The New York Times.

LONDON, Jan. 19.–One of the victims of the recent collapse of the plans for a big Indian spectacle at Earl's Court is a man who shared the talk of the town with Edna May when "The Belle of New York" was the rage. He is Frank Lawton, the famous whistling comedian, who took the part of Blinkey Bill in the production.

His photograph then was featured in the illustrated magazines and the audiences at the Shaftsbury Theatre were enthusiastic over his performance. To-day he is among the stranded artists who are receiving relief from a fund established on their behalf in consequence of the non-production of the spectacle. (*New York Times*, 20 January 1914, 4.)

Frank Lawton, the whistler, died in London, April 16. He had not been very prosperous of late and leaves a family in poor circumstances. Lawton went over from America as a member of the original "Belle of New York" company. (*Variety*, 24 April 1914, 18.)

104 The Tramp–Milk White Flag
LENGTH: 50 ft.   © No reg.
PRODUCER: W.K.L. Dickson.
CAMERA: William Heise.
CAST: Lew Bloom (Capt. Dodge Shotwell).
PRODUCTION DATE: Late November 1894.
LOCATION: Black Maria, West Orange, N.J.
SOURCE: *A Milk White Flag* (burlesque).
DESCRIPTION:
SUBJECT: Musicals–performances. Tramps.
ARCHIVE:
CITATIONS: W.K.L. Dickson to Raff & Gammon, 8 January 1895, MH-BA; advertisements, *New York Clipper*, 3 October 1896, 497; 8 July 1899, 379.
NOTE: The negative for this film was destroyed during printing in late 1894. After his appearance in *A Milk White Flag*, Lew Bloom moved on to play his tramp speciality in vaudeville, his first appearance coming at Keith's Union Square Theatre on 14 October 1894. When appearing at Tony Pastor's in July 1896, he "caused hearty laughter by his genteel tramp make-up." (*New York Clipper,* 18 July 1896, 312.) By the fall, he had teamed up with Jane Cooper in the vaudeville sketch "The Tramp's Visit," a duo which was still together three years later. In 1926, he had a horse in the Kentucky Derby.

105 The Widder / [The Widow]
LENGTH: 50 ft.   © No reg.
PRODUCER: W.K.L. Dickson.
CAMERA: William Heise.
CAST: Isabelle Coe (Aurora Luce).
PRODUCTION DATE: Late November 1894.
LOCATION: Black Maria, West Orange, N.J.
SOURCE: *A Milk White Flag* (burlesque).
DESCRIPTION:
SUBJECT: Musicals–performances.
ARCHIVE:
CITATIONS: W.K.L. Dickson to Raff & Gammon, 8 January 1895, MH-BA.
NOTE: The negative for this film was destroyed during printing in late 1894.

ISABELLE COE
AS THE WIDOW
IN "A MILK WHITE FLAG"

WITH "A MILK WHITE FLAG."
Hoyt's Theatre, Late the Madison Square, Christened by the Satire on the Militia.
CLEVERLY WRITTEN, BRIGHTLY PLAYED.
A BRILLIANT "MILK WHITE FLAG."

HOYT'S THEATRE. *A Milk White Flag*, a musical farce-comedy in three acts by Charles A. Hoyt.

The Colonel (Christian Berriel)	Chas. Stanely
The Major (Paul Baring)	Lloyd Wilson
The Judge Advocate (Howland Hooper)	Arthur Pacie
The Surgeon (Mark Tombs)	Ed Garvie
The Bandmaster (Steele Ayres)	Frank Baldwin
The Private (Willing Singer)	Sam Weston
The Dancing Master (Gideon Foote)	Frank Lawton
The Lieutenant (Phil Graves)	John S. Marble

A .... Toma Hanlon
B .... Lillian Markham
C .... Rosa France
D .... Etta Williamson
The Standard Bearer (Carrie Flagg) .... Maguerite Benford
The General (Hurley Burleigh) .... Frank J. Keenan
The Dear Departed (Piggott Luce) .... R.A. Roberts
The Orphan (Pony Luce) .... Lottie Moore
The Particular Friend of the Bereaved Wife ("Lize" Dugro) .... Lillie Deaves
The Bereaved (Aurora Luce) .... Isabelle Coe

In Mr. Hoyt's latest contribution to stage entertainments he has unmercifully satirized the National Guard, but he has not been unkind about it, however. The entertainment, or farce comedy, or what you please, is called "A Milk White Flag." It was given last night for the first time in this city at Hoyt's Theatre, before an audience which was largely made up of well known New Yorkers, who were enthusiastic in their praise of the performance.

Well they might be, for "A Milk White Flag" is witty in dialogue and situations, musically attractive, brilliantly costumed and handsomely staged.

It was also the occasion of the opening of Hoyt's Theatre, as the Madison Square Theatre is henceforth to be known, with Messrs. Hoyt and McKee as managers. During the summer the house has been redecorated and refurnished in buff and gold. The new coloring has vastly improved the appearance of the auditorium. It is bright and attractive, while the absence of any attempt at gaudiness is a charming novelty. The new curtain, the walls and the uniforms of the attendants were all in harmony.

The new work of Mr. Hoyt differs from the general style of his previous comedies in the introduction of a spectacular effect and the use of a ballet. The gorgeous uniforms of the "guards" and the girls who are vivandlers and drummers keep the stage in a constant glitter. Songs are numerous. They are sung on the slightest provocation and well sung, too, for the company is musically quite capable of rendering a comic opera. Most of the music was composed by Mr. Percy Gaunt, who, it is announced, made it as original as he dared to.

The idea of the story is to set forth the weakness of human kind in wanting to strut around in military uniforms, without any of a soldier's spirit to warrant it. In this case there were supposed to be two rival organizations, whose members were all officers. Their efforts to out-do each other furnish the humor. The Ransome Guards was the name of the organization whose members appeared. The old members of the Ransome Guards and the Barlow Grays, of St. Albans, Vt., formerly the crack military organizations in the State, may take Mr. Hoyt's satire a little to heart.

ACT I.–The scene is in the Guards' armory. General Burleigh,–of the regular army, is the guest of the regiment. In doing him the honors, the members show how thoroughly witty they can be. One instance is a member rushing in, and, putting on his uniform just to get a drink, taking it off and rushing out again. There is only one private. He is the waiter, Sam Weston. There is a band, who, when not playing, are kept at the bar drinking, as it makes no difference whether a band is drunk or sober. The Colonel (Charles Stanley) has been made so because he looks like Napoleon. The rival organization have had a military funeral, and the Guards resolve to have one also.

ACT II.–Is in the home of a speculator who has arranged with an undertaker to feign death to get an insurance policy. He is brought, supposedly dead, and his sufferings in the box packed with ice, while the officers are making love to his wife, furnish opportunity for clever though broad humor. Quite too broad it is in spots, as when a young lady is constantly being tempted to put a pair of trousers on the supposed corpse. Mr. Hoyt should certainly cut this out. It rather shocked the audience, and certainly Mr. Hoyt does not need to resort to any such device to create fun.

ACT III.–In their brilliantly lighted armory there is the presentation of the milk white flag, as it is the only one the regiment would stand by in battle. The corpse comes to life and all is straightened out.

Miss Isabelle Coe was charming in the leading female role and Miss Lottie Moore made a vivacious soubrette and danced prettily.

SOME GALA GOWNS

While the play does not call for many modern costumes, the burlesque order being carried out in the main, two of the gowns are well worthy of mention.

In the first act Miss Isabelle Coe (Aurora Luce) wears a superb reception gown of salmon pink satin, brocaded with silver ostrich plumes, made with a very full skirt just clearing the ground. The body is of a brocade, with puffed sleeves and front of tucked chiffon to correspond and bands of silver. A high collar of chiffon, with rhinestone buckles, finishes the waist. A stunning "picture" hat of salmon pink velvet, with ostrich plumes, silver aigrettes and rhinestone buckles, and a long parasol of pink moire with silver handle, completed this very striking costume.

That worn in the same act by Miss Rillie Deaves ("Lize" Dugro) is of the latest corn flower shades, the skirt of moire and long coat of deeper shade velvet, lined with cream colored satin, and waistcoat the same color as lining, embroidered in gold. The hat is of the lighter corn flower shades....(*New York Herald,* 9 October 1894, 8.)

106 *****Fire Rescue Scene / Fire Rescue**
LENGTH: 50 ft.　© No reg.
PRODUCER: W.K.L. Dickson, Raff & Gammon.
CAMERA: William Heise.
CAST:
PRODUCTION DATE: Late November to early December 1894.
LOCATION: Black Maria, West Orange, N.J.
SOURCE:
DESCRIPTION: Showing Fine Smoke Effects and Uniformed Firemen in Action. (The Kinetoscope Company, *Bulletin No. 1*, [December 1894].)
Uniformed firemen rescuing people from a burning building. Fine smoke effects. (F.Z. Maguire & Co., *Catalogue*, [March 1898], 28.)
SUBJECT: Fire fighters. Fires.
ARCHIVE: NR-GE, CLAc, DLC-Hendricks.
CITATIONS: Raff & Gammon to Exhibition Department, NYC, invoice, 20 December 1894, MH-BA; W.K.L. Dickson and Antonia Dickson, *History of the Kinetograph, Kinetoscope and Kineto-Phonograph*, 49 (with illustrations). The Kinetoscope Company, *Price List of Films*, [May 1895], 3; Ohio Phonograph Co., *The Edison Kinetoscope. Price List*, August 1895, 9; Maguire & Baucus, *Edison Films*, 20 January 1897, 6; Maguire & Baucus, *Edison and International Photographic Films*, April 1897, 8; Maguire & Baucus, *Fall Catalogue*, 1897, 12; *Edison Films*, March 1900, 30.
NOTE:

Wilson and Waring, after touring with McCarthy Mishaps, *found themselves with unbooked time in May 1894. For the week beginning 7 May 1894, "Wilson and Wareing" [sic] performed at Keith's Union Square Theatre, billed as "first appearance of this popular comedy duo." (New York Herald, 6 May 1894, 8C.) The pair subsequently became part of the* Little Christopher Columbus *cast, and when the musical comedy opened to mix reviews, Edward E. Rice introduced their speciality to strengthen the show (quite like Hoyt's belated introduction of the tramp character in* A Milk White Flag*). In fact, the introduction of new specialties over the course of a show's run was characteristic of theatrical production in this period. The film of Wilson and Waring thus had only a tenuous relation to* Little Christopher Columbus, *although the association doubtlessly helped to promote the film.*

107 **John W. Wilson and Bertha Waring / Waring and Wilson / Wilson and Waring**
LENGTH: 50 ft.　© No reg.
PRODUCER: W.K.L. Dickson.
CAMERA: William Heise.
CAST: Bertha Waring, John W. Wilson.
PRODUCTION DATE: Late October 1894 to mid-December 1894.
LOCATION: Black Maria, West Orange, N.J.
SOURCE: *Little Christopher Columbus* (burlesque).
DESCRIPTION: An eccentric dance from "Little Christopher Columbus," by John Wilson, the famous "Tramp," and Bertha Waring. (F.Z. Maguire & Co., *Catalogue*, [March 1898], 28.)
SUBJECT: Musicals–performances. Dancing. Tramps. Edward E. Rice.
ARCHIVE:
CITATIONS: W.K.L. Dickson and Antonia Dickson, *History of the Kinetograph, Kinetoscope, and Kineto-Phonograph*, 40 (with illustration); Raff & Gammon to F.D. Higbee, invoice, 18 March 1895, 1:369, MH-BA; advertisement, *New York Clipper*, 26 January 1901, 1070. The Kinetoscope Company, *Price List of Films*, [May 1895], 4; Ohio Phonograph Co.,

The Edison Kinetoscope. Price List, August 1895, 7; Maguire & Baucus, *Edison Films*, 20 January 1897, 6; Maguire & Baucus, *Edison and International Photographic Films*, April 1897, 16; Maguire & Baucus, *Fall Catalogue*, 1897, 13. NOTE: From Act II of *Little Christopher Columbus*.

THE HIT OF THE SEASON
J.W. **WILSON** AND **WARING** BERTHA
WITH "McCARTHY'S MISHAPS" CO.
P.S.-NOTHING BUT CURTAIN CALLS EACH EVENING.
Managers come and see this act at H.R. Jacobs' this week.
7th, 14th, and 21 OF MAY OPEN, and Next Season.
P.S.–Specially engaged at Schlitz's Park, Milwaukee, Wis., for the month of June.
Address 325 E. 14th Street, N.Y. City.
(Advertisement, *New York Clipper,* 21 April 1894, 112.)

Wilson & Waring close the second act of "McCarthy's Mishaps" with their speciality and are obliged to respond with an encore. (*New York Clipper*, 28 April 1894, 116.)

John W. Wilson and Bertha Waring have been engaged by Edward E. Rice for next season. (*New York Clipper*, 19 May 1894, 165.)

JOHN W. WILSON.
John W. Wilson, whose grotesqueries as Weary Raggles, the Midway Plaisance tramp of "Little Christopher," has brought him into prominence and popularity, is a genuinely comic performer. He was born in Sutter Creek, Amador County, Cal., March 7, 1864. At the age of fifteen he made his first appearance at the Bella Union, San Francisco, then under the management of Tetlow & Skentlebury. His partner was Mitchell Ford, and under the name of Wilson and Ford they were billed as "a pocket edition of Johnson and Bruno," in songs and dances. They separated early in 1881, and a few months later Wilson doubled up with William Cameron. For the next eleven years the song and dance team of Wilson and Cameron was well known throughout the country. They opened for Ned Buckley at the Adelphi, San Francisco, played there an entire year, and changing their act every week. They were engaged for two weeks with Billy Emerson's Minstrels, at the Standard Theatre, and remained two years and a half; then followed a long and popular engagement with Charley Reed's Minstrels, at the same house. Their first appearance in white face was in 1885, at the old California Theatre, then under the direction of E.D. Price, who is business manager of the company in which Wilson in now performing. They appeared as the two Parisian street gamins in an eccentric dance in "The Pavements of Paris," and made a hit. After that season Wilson and Cameron joined Haverley's Minstrels, in black face, and subsequently took their own minstrel company through California. In 1887 they went to the Antipodes with the All Star Specialty Co., under the management of Frank Clark, and played all through Australia and New Zealand, returning to San Francisco in 1890. They came East for the first time with Weber and Field's Own Company, and played at the principal vaudeville houses. Mr. Wilson dissolved partnership with Cameron in the later part of 1891, and played the janitor in John H. Russell's "City Directory" with much success. He next impersonated a tramp in "McCarthy's Mishaps," where he was seen by Manager Edward E. Rice and engaged for "Little Christopher," produced at the Garden Theatre in October last, and still the current attraction. Mr. Wilson's tramp is a thoroughly original and humorous creation, with a nimble wit and grotesque personality. In this specialty Mr. Wilson has capital assistance from Bertha Waring, a dainty little singer and dancer who appears as an Irish villager. (*New York Clipper,* 13 April 1895, 81.)

BERTHA WARING.
Was born in New York City, and made her professional debut in 1881, in Madison, Ind., playing Topsy with the World's "Uncle Tom's Cabin" Co. She remained with this company for one year, and then went West, playing vaudeville engagements. At this time she met Kitty O'Neill, from whom she received dancing lessons, which inured so greatly to her benefit that she is now considered one of the best soft shoe and general dancers in the profession. In 1883 she joined the "Fun in Bristol" Co., and played the role of Bella during a long run at the Tivoli Theatre, in San Francisco, Cal. She then came East with Devene's Allied Attractions, with which she remained one season. From 1885 to 1890 she played vaudeville engagements. In 1891 she joined "McCarthy's Mishaps," and successfully played the part of Mrs. Mulligan. She afterwards joined Rice's "Little Christopher" Co., playing the role of Zuelika, the dancing girl, and the soubrette part of Kitty Conners, doing moreover, a specialty in conjunction with John W. Wilson. She was with this company during the run of the piece at the Garden Theatre, this city, and, in fact, remained with it two seasons. She is at the present time doing a strong specialty with Mr. Wilson, having recently concluded an engagement with "Jack and the Beanstalk," at the Casino, this city. (*New York Clipper*, 12 December 1896, 650.)

HOME AGAIN

WILSON AND WARING

AFTER THEIR EUROPEAN TRIUMPHS. FOUR YEARS OF UNINTERRUPTED SUCCESS.

Will play Twenty weeks for the Association-managers of U.S.A. THEN BACK TO THE MINES,
to work out Two Years' Contract. (Advertisement, *New York Clipper*, 27 October 1900, 784.)

"LITTLE CHRISTOPHER COLUMBUS."
An Americanized Version of the London Burlesque To Be Seen at the Garden Theatre.

"Little Christopher Columbus" will be presented by Manager E.E. Rice for the first time in this country at the Garden Theatre to-morrow night. The original burlesque, by George R. Sims and Cecil Raleigh, with music by Ivan Carlyll [sic], which was produced at the Lyric Theatre, in London, and is still running there, has been considerably changed to adapt it to the American stage, and Mr. Gustave Kerber has written several new musical numbers.

The opening scene is in the great square of Cadiz, upon the anniversary of the Columbus fetes. Here are assembled Spanish soldiers, fisher lads, flower sellers, street vendors, and American sailors, bent upon a holiday recreation. Little Christopher Columbus, a cabin boy, has deserted from an American liner—the Choctow—being deeply enamored of Guinivere, a beautiful American girl, the daughter of the Second Mrs. Tanqueray Block, an eccentric widow, whose husband was a rich Chicago pork packer. The widow has a private detective, O'Hoolegan, whose mission is to assume quaint disguises and investigate the antecedents of fortune hunting suitors, but he is unscrupulous, and is at the command of the longest purse. Little Christopher Columbus is arrested, changes costumes and identities with Pepita, a Spanish dancing girl, and is finally released through the bribery of the detective.

In the second act the tourists, with a party of performers bound for the World's Fair, are captured by the Bey of Barataria, before whom they give an improvised entertainment. The Bey is captivated by the bogus Pepita, whose identity is revealed by the detective in self defence. He has posed as Pepita's oldest brother until he learns that the laws of Barataria condemn to death the eldest brother of the Bey's bride. Existing complications are straightened out at the World's Fair, where the principal characters, with other foreign visitors from strange lands are assembled in the Midway Plaisance, represented in the third act. Little Christopher Columbus proves to be the last lineal descendant of the great explorer, and all ends merrily.

More than one hundred people are seen upon the stage and among the characters are Little Christopher Columbus, a cabin boy: Miss Helen Bertram; O'Hoolegan, private detective: Mr. George Walton, an Australian actor who will make his first appearance in America on this occasion; Captain Slammer, of the steamship Choctaw, Mr. Herman Blakemore; Mayor of Cadiz, Mr. Edward Chapman; Diego, his clerk, Mr. John W. Wilson; Don Juan of the Spanish police, Mr. Edgar Temple; Squire Hemingway, from Maine, Mr. James P. Gentry; the Bey of Barataria, Mr. Alexander Clark; his Grand Vizier, Mr. Henry Leoni; the Second Mrs. Tanqueray Block of Chicago, Mr. Harry Mcdonough; Guinivere, her daughter, Miss Yolande Wallace; Pepita the dancing girl, Miss Mabel Bouton.

A number of specialties will be introduced in the second and third acts, and a quartet of dancing girls from London have come over to present the dance which was one of the features of the English production. (*New York Herald*, 14 October 1894, 4D.)

"Little Christopher Columbus" Arrives.

GARDEN THEATRE. *LITTLE CHRISTOPHER COLUMBUS,* burlesque by George R. Sims and Cecil Raleigh; music by Ivan Caryll and Gustave Kerber....

There was a stage full of pretty girls, all magnificently and becomingly costumed, at the Garden Theatre last night, when "Little Christopher Columbus" was produced for the first time in this city.

As a spectacle it was a great and attractive success. Musically it was only mediocre. And as a laughter provoker it was entirely inadequate.

This successor to "1492," which Mr. Rice made a conspicuous feature of New York amusements, is in much the same line as its predecessor, except, unfortunately, it has very few of the features that made "1492" so pronounced a success. It was written by George R. Sims and Cecil Raleigh. The music was composed by Ivan Caryll and Gustave Kerker. While there are several pretty airs in it, and one or two that have the elements of popularity and will be whistled, there is not one that is conspicuous by its excellence.

The dialogue was of course written with the air of being witty. It is tiresome, instead. The humor is poor, and the comedy situations are rather strained and uninteresting. More than all that, the production was drawn out to a somewhat tiresome length. It was evident that the audience was inclined to be favorably disposed, for when there was the slightest warrant for applause it was given liberally. Generally, however, there was a painful silence.

Miss Helen Bertram and Miss Yolande Wallace were seen to excellent advantage. The former's work lent the piece spirit that was sadly needed. The leading comedian, Mr. George Walton, an English importation, was rather a disappointment.

ACT I.–In Cadiz, where the characters are all introduced, with little attempt at rhyme or reason. The start for Chicago.

ACT II.–En route to Chicago they are captured and brought to the throne room of the Bey of Barataria, when they all do some variety hall specialties.

ACT III.–They are released, and all meet again in the Midway Plaisance, at the World's Fair. (*New York Herald*, 16 October 1894, 7.)

108 **Fancy Club Swinger / Club Swinger / [Club Swinger, no. 2]**

LENGTH: 50 ft.   © No reg.

PRODUCER: W.K.L. Dickson.

CAMERA: William Heise.

CAST: John R. Abell.

PRODUCTION DATE: By early December 1894.

LOCATION: Black Maria, West Orange, N.J.

SOURCE:

DESCRIPTION:

SUBJECT: Juggling. Gymnastics.

ARCHIVE:

CITATIONS: Kinetoscope Company to Maguire & Baucus, invoice, 22 December 1894, 1:145, MH-BA; Dickson to Raff & Gammon, 8 January 1895, MH-BA.

NOTE: The negative for this film was destroyed during the printing process in late December 1894.

109 **[Dogs Fighting] / [Dog Fight]**

LENGTH: 50 ft.   © No reg.

PRODUCER: W.K.L. Dickson.

CAMERA: William Heise.

CAST:

PRODUCTION DATE: By March 1895 (but probably much earlier).

LOCATION: Black Maria, West Orange, N.J.

SOURCE:

DESCRIPTION:

SUBJECT: Animal fighting. Dogs.

ARCHIVE:

CITATIONS:

NOTE: This film was sold in Italy as *Zuffa di cani*. (Continental Phonograph Kinetoscope Company, *Kinetoscenes,* [March 1895].) It has been suggested that this film might actually be *Wrestling Dog* (Edison film no. 42, 1894).

Exterior of the Black Maria (winter 1894-95).

The kinetoscope novelty had begun to fall off by the spring of 1895. Attempts to revive interest, either through new types of subject matter or technological gimmicks such as the combination of kinetoscope and phonograph, failed. By the end of the year, sales of machines had virtually stopped.

As the 1895 year began, the Edison Manufacturing Company needed to replace many of its worn-out or damaged negatives. Dickson had supplied Raff & Gammon and Maguire & Baucus with a lengthy list of n.g. (i.e., no good) printing elements early in the year. (Dickson to Raff & Gammon, 8 January 1895, MH-BA.) The most successful subjects were to be redone when possible.

110 New Bar Room [Scene] / Barroom / Barroom Scene / [Bar Room Scene, no. 2]
LENGTH: 50 ft.   © No reg.
PRODUCER: W.K.L. Dickson.
CAMERA: William Heise.
CAST:
PRODUCTION DATE: 17 January 1895.
LOCATION: Black Maria, West Orange, N.J.
SOURCE: *A Bar Room Scene* (Edison film no. 37, spring 1894).
DESCRIPTION: Showing a Quarrel in a Bar Room and a Policeman Taking a Glass of Beer on the Sly. (The Kinetoscope Company, *Price List of Films*, [May 1895], 4.)
Presents a barroom, with all the accessories, including a barmaid, who serves a policeman with a glass of beer at the side entrance. Two men are smoking and having a quiet game of "draw," when a couple of "toughs" lounge in and a quarrel arises, in which the policeman takes a hand and forcibly expels the crowd. A very popular and realistic subject of this kind. (Ohio Phonograph Co., *The Edison Kinetoscope. Price List*, August 1895, 9.)

SUBJECT: Taverns, etc. Police. Alcoholic beverages. Gambling. Violence.
ARCHIVE:
CITATIONS: W.K.L. Dickson to Raff & Gammon, 17 January 1895, MH-BA; Raff & Gammon to Holland Bros., invoice, 9 February 1895, 1:292, MH-BA; Raff & Gammon, "Statement: Costs of Film Subjects from January 25th to Date," 18 April 1895, 1:434, MH-BA. Maguire & Baucus, *Edison Films*, 20 January 1897, 6; Maguire & Baucus, *Edison and International Photographic Films*, April 1897, 4; Maguire and Baucus, *Fall Catalogue*, 1897, 11; F.Z. Maguire & Co., *Catalogue*, [March 1898], 29; *Edison Films*, March 1900, 43.
NOTE:

111   *New Barber's Shop / Barber Shop / Barber Shop Scene / [Barber Shop, no. 2]
LENGTH: 50 ft.   © No reg.
PRODUCER: W.K.L. Dickson, Raff & Gammon.
CAMERA: William Heise.
CAST:
PRODUCTION DATE: 17 January 1895.
LOCATION: Black Maria, West Orange, N.J.
SOURCE: *The Barber Shop* (Edison film no. 18, fall 1893).
DESCRIPTION: The old negative having worn out, we have had a new one taken which is superior to the old. (The Kinetoscope Company, *Price List of Films*, [May 1895], 3.)

Represents the interior of a "Tonsorial Palace." A good subject. *With customer getting a "shave"*; meanwhile "next" is having his shoes polished by the usual darky attendant. This is one of the most popular films ever produced. (Ohio Phonograph Co., *The Edison Kinetoscope. Price List*, August 1895, 9.)
SUBJECT: Barbershops. Afro-Americans. Shaving.
ARCHIVE: CLAc, UkLNFA.
CITATIONS: Dickson to Raff & Gammon, 17 January 1895, MH-BA; Raff & Gammon to Holland Bros., invoice, 9 February 1895, 1:292, MH-BA; Raff & Gammon, "Statement: Costs of Film Subjects from January 25th to Date," 18 April 1895, 1:434, MH-BA. Maguire & Baucus, *Edison Films*, 20 January 1897, 6; Maguire & Baucus, *Edison and International Photographic Films*, April 1897, 4; Maguire & Baucus, *Fall Catalogue*, 1897, 11; Maguire and Baucus, *Edison and International Photographic Films*, April 1897; F.Z. Maguire & Co., *Catalogue*, [March 1898], 29.
NOTE: It is possible that this description represents a third barber shop scene, since the shoeblack in the film used here as an illustration is white.

112   *New Blacksmith Shop / Blacksmith Shop / Blacksmith Shop Scene / [Blacksmith Shop, no. 2]
LENGTH: 50 ft.   © No reg.
PRODUCER: W.K.L. Dickson.
CAMERA: William Heise.
CAST:
PRODUCTION DATE: Late January 1895.
LOCATION: Black Maria, West Orange, N.J.
SOURCE: *Blacksmithing Scene* (Edison film no. 16, fall 1893).
DESCRIPTION: Shows two men at anvil. A third is repairing a wagon wheel. Incidentally a little liquid refreshment is passed around as the work progresses. (Ohio Phonograph Co., *The Edison Kinetoscope. Price List*, August 1895, 9.)
SUBJECT: Blacksmithing. Alcoholic beverages.
ARCHIVE: UkLNFA.

CITATIONS: Raff & Gammon to Holland Bros., invoice, 9 February 1895, 1: 292, MH-BA; Raff & Gammon, "Statement: Costs of Film Subjects from January 25th to Date," 18 April 1895, 1:434, MH-BA. The Kinetoscope Company, *Price List of Films*, [May 1895], 4; Maguire & Baucus, *Edison Films*, 20 January 1897, 6; Maguire & Baucus, *Edison and International Photographic Films*, April 1897, 5; Maguire & Baucus, *Fall Catalogue*, 1897, 11; Maguire and Baucus, *Edison and International Films*, April 1897; F.Z. Maguire & Co., *Catalogue*, [March 1898], 29.

NOTE:

113 √**In the Dentist's Chair / The Dentist's Chair / Dental Scene**

LENGTH: 50 ft.   © No reg.

PRODUCER: W.K.L. Dickson, Raff & Gammon.

CAMERA: William Heise.

CAST: Dr. Gardner Quincy Colton.

PRODUCTION DATE: Late January 1895.

LOCATION: Black Maria, West Orange, N.J.

SOURCE:

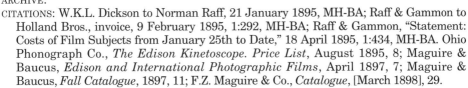

DESCRIPTION: Administering Gas and Extracting a Tooth. Dr. Colton, who first used gas for extracting teeth, is shown administering the gas in this film. (The Kinetoscope Company, *Price List of Films*, [May 1895], 3.)

SUBJECT: Dentistry.

ARCHIVE:

CITATIONS: W.K.L. Dickson to Norman Raff, 21 January 1895, MH-BA; Raff & Gammon to Holland Bros., invoice, 9 February 1895, 1:292, MH-BA; Raff & Gammon, "Statement: Costs of Film Subjects from January 25th to Date," 18 April 1895, 1:434, MH-BA. Ohio Phonograph Co., *The Edison Kinetoscope. Price List*, August 1895, 8; Maguire & Baucus, *Edison and International Photographic Films*, April 1897, 7; Maguire & Baucus, *Fall Catalogue*, 1897, 11; F.Z. Maguire & Co., *Catalogue*, [March 1898], 29.

NOTE: This film was sold in Italy as *Scena del dentista*. (Continental Phonograph Kinetoscope Company, *Kinetoscenes,* [March 1895].)

Sir Humphrey Davy in 1801 observed that nitrous oxide produced insensibility on prolonged inhalation and suggested its use in surgery. It was more than forty years later that Dr. Horace Wells, a dentist in Hartford, Conn., employed nitrous oxide as an anaesthetic in dental surgery. (*The Encyclopedia Americana*, 1989, s.v. "nitrogen compounds.")

GARDNER Q. COLTON DEAD
The Dentist Responsible for the Discovery of Anaesthesia Passes Away in Europe.
RECORD FOR PULLING TEETH
Estimated that Nearly a Million Teeth Were Removed by Himself or His Assistants—Recognition for Dr. Horace Wells.

News reached this city yesterday of the death of Dr. Gardner Quincy Colton, the dentist of this city who after a three months' visit to Europe was about to return home from Rotterdam. Death followed paralysis traceable to old age and its complications. Dr. Colton was eighty-four years old. He was the proprietor of the Colton Dental Association at 19 Cooper Union, and had a town residence at 141 East Thirty-ninth Street. The house in East Thirty-ninth Street was found boarded up last night, and inquiry in the neighborhood failed to reveal where any of the relatives reside.

For two reasons, one pertaining only to local residents, and the other touching each human being, Dr. Colton will be long remembered. So long as man suffers from toothache, it will be called to mind that Dr. Colton was the occasion of the discovery of anaesthesia. In local regions Dr. Colton will be remembered as holding the record for extracting the greatest number of molars on record. So far as is known, no dentist of this country or any other has himself or through assistants drawn so many teeth.

A Million Teeth, Perhaps

Twenty years ago, it is related by friends of the doctor, he estimated his aggregate benefaction on New Yorkers at 300,000 teeth. As his practice grew rapidly year by year, the latest estimate gives a number approaching a million teeth estopped from agonizing their owners through Dr. Colton's efforts and those of his assistants.

Not only in this city, but throughout the country, Dr. Colton had a large circle of friends. He had traveled extensively about the United States, and formed friends readily, to hold them attached to him firmly. For over thirty years he had been in Cooper Union, where his office was known probably to seven out of every ten New Yorkers who ever lost their sleep from troublesome grinders. Dr. Colton also gained considerable repute from devising the first application of electricity as motive power. He was a fine Shakespearean scholar, and had written a brochure, called "Shakespeare and the Bible," that created quite a stir of interest in literary circles several years ago at the time of its publication.

Walter Colton, one of the pioneer settlers of the State of Vermont, was the doctor's father. The doctor was born in Georgia, Vt., February 7, 1814, and was the twelfth child of his parents. After receiving a common school education, he learned the trade of chair making, at the age of sixteen, continuing at this vocation until he was twenty-one years old. He then came to this city, where, while maintaining himself by means of his trade, he neglected no opportunity for culture. He contributed to the newspaper of the day, and in numerous other ways sought to raise himself out of the sphere of artisan labor.

He Studies Medicine.

Progress was slow, but by 1842 he was able to enter the College of Physicians and Surgeons, and later to study in the office of the late Willard Parker, M.D. Two years later he began to deliver lectures on philosophical subjects and chemical phenomena, also giving exhibitions of electric demonstrations and possibilities, and of effects of nitrous oxide gas, which he was the first to call "laughing gas." It was during one of these lectures that he stumbled into the discovery of anaesthetic effects. When he was thirty-four years old, Dr. Colton was still lecturing, and to illustrate the practicability of electricity at one of his lectures he introduced the first electric motor. It was made from his plans by an instrument maker named Lilly, and was the prototype of the electric locomotives common to-day.

In 1849 Dr. Colton went to California, and for several months worked in the newly discovered gold fields, and practiced medicine among the miners. Returning to San Francisco late in the year, he engaged in various enterprises, and was appointed Justice of the Peace by Gov. Riley. It was the first appointment to that office in California. Through his efforts in the extreme West he gained a competence, and returned East to resume his lecture tours. Roaming from city to city and from town to village in this way until 1860, he then became interested in the publication of a series of war maps that bore his name. In 1863 he established the Colton Dental Association, with headquarters in New York and branches in the large cities of this State. Subsequently he introduced the anaesthetic use of nitrous oxide gas in Paris and London. He was also the author of many tracts and pamphlets relating to philosophical and theological subjects.

How Anaesthesia Was Discovered.

It was chiefly due to his part in the discovery of the use of nitrous oxide as an anesthetic and his defense in recent years of Dr. Horace Wells as the one to whom belongs the credit of suggestion the use of the gas, that Dr. Colton was so extensively known. By means of numerous letters to the public through the press and otherwise Dr. Colton succeeded in shaking public belief in Dr. W.T.G. Morton, who claimed to have been the discoverer, and it is now generally acknowledged that Dr. Wells deserves all credit for this discovery.

This was the way the discovery of anaesthesia was made: Dr. Colton, at Hartford. Conn., Dec., 10, 1844, was lecturing on the amusing effects of nitrous oxide gas and illustrating his words by the antics of persons affected with the gas. Among those who inhaled the gas was a young man named Cooley, who, under its influence, ran violently against some settees on the stage and bruised his shins badly. On taking his seat next to Dr. Wells, the doctor remarked that the young man must be painfully hurt. Cooley was astonished to find his legs bloody, and said he felt no pain whatever until the effects of the gas had worn off. Dr. Colton claimed that, as the spectators were leaving, Dr. Wells said to him: "Why cannot a man have a tooth extracted under the influence of the gas and not feel it?" Further Dr. Wells said he believed it could be done and determined to try it. Dr. Colton the next day took a bag of nitrous oxide gas to Dr. Wells's office, and Dr. Riggs, a neighboring dentist, was called in. Dr. Wells had a decayed molar, and he was put under the influence of the gas and the tooth extracted.

A Great Discovery.

When he recovered and found his tooth gone, Dr. Wells cried out excitedly. "It is the greatest discovery ever made! I did not feel so much as the prick of a pin." "This," Dr. Colton claimed, "was the discovery of anaesthesia. He admits a doctor named Long made two operations with ether in 1842, but claims he did not follow them up nor make publication of the results. At the request of Dr. Wells, Dr. Colton taught him to make the gas, and Dr. Wells three weeks later went to Boston and made known the discovery. He called on this dentist and that, and among others on Dr. W.T.G. Morton, his former pupil and partner. All scoffed at it and would not use it. Discouraged Mr. Wells returned to Hartford, where he continued to practice dentistry, using the anaesthetic. Bishop Brownell and forty prominent citizens of Hartford afterward gave their depositions that Dr. Wells extracted teeth from them without causing pain.

It was claimed by Dr. Colton that Dr. Wells's discovery suggested to Dr. Morton the use of sulphuric ether as a anaesthetic, and he tried it with success. A Boston doctor named Jackson also put in a claim to being the true discoverer of anaesthesia, on the ground that he suggested its use to Dr. Morton. Dr. Wells went to Europe for two years, and on his return found that Dr. Morton had got a patent, and claimed to be the true discoverer. A discussion among the three claimants followed, and it was carried on so hotly that all three became deranged. Dr. Wells succumbed first. He committed suicide in January 1848. Dr. Morton also committed suicide, and Dr. Jackson was put in an asylum and died soon after coming out.

Defends Dr. Wells.

No one used nitrous oxide as an anaesthetic, excepting Dr. Wells, from the time he went to Europe in 1845 until 1863, when Dr. Colton revived its use and demonstrated that it was an anaesthetic, and the best anaesthetic for short operations. It was during these seventeen years that the public allowed the claim of Dr. Morton as the discoverer, but when Dr. Colton revived the use of the gas, the medical and surgical journals of this country investigated, and became converts to Dr. Colton's assertion of the right of Dr. Wells to be called the real discoverer.

On the occasion of the fiftieth anniversary of Dr. Wells discovery a grand celebration in his honor was held at Philadelphia, under the auspices of the United States Dental Association. There were 2,000 persons present, and before them Prof. Garetson, the presiding officer, did Dr. Colton the signal honor of saying, "Had there been no Colton, there would have been no Wells." A chance meeting and conversation in 1896 reminded Colton of his electrical motor, which he had completely forgotten. Lawyers engaged in suits involving electrical patents had long before found that a man named Colton had exhibited and lectured on an electrical locomotive nearly half a century before, but they had never found the lecturer. At least one of the suits was pending and Dr. Colton was called in to testify. A large amount was involved, the diversion of which depended considerably on the doctor's testimony. After his recollection was pricked up, the doctor's was still unable to locate the original motor. While visiting relatives in Vermont, he was told an old trunk of his was stored in their garret, and when it was opened the original model was found. With a few repairs, it ran smoothly as fifty years before.

The doctor brought his invention to New York and set up a small track in his office, where it pleased him greatly to show it to visitors. As originally made, it ran on a wooden track about 8 feet in diameter. The rails were formed of iron bands rising on each side of the circular wooden hoop. When first shown, it ran a train of cars with dolls at the windows as passengers. Photographs were taken of it for the Smithsonian Institution at Washington, to illustrate the development of electrical propulsion. (*New York Times*, 12 August 1898, 7.)

Duncan C. Ross, who promoted himself as "Champion All-Round Athlete of the World" (New York Herald, 10 June 1894, 8B), was a local sports figure and celebrity. He was involved in a wide range of manly sports activities, at one point serving as referee for a local boxing match that was broken up by police. He was perhaps best at displaying a certain type of rugged male bravado.

114   Gladiatorial Combat

LENGTH: 50 ft.   © No reg.

PRODUCER: W.K.L. Dickson, Raff & Gammon.

CAMERA: William Heise.

CAST: Capt. Duncan C. Ross, Lieut. Hartung, Capt. Martin.

PRODUCTION DATE: 23 January 1895.

LOCATION: Orange, N.J.

SOURCE:

DESCRIPTION: By Captain Duncan Ross and Lieut. Hartung, with broadswords. (Maguire & Baucus, *Fall Catalogue*, 1897, 12.)
   By Duncan Ross, Lieut. Hartung and Capt. Martin. A spirited and exciting subject. (F.Z. Maguire & Co., *Catalogue*, [March 1898], 33.)

SUBJECT: Dueling. Horsemanship.

ARCHIVE:

CITATIONS: W.K.L. Dickson to Norman C. Raff, 21 January 1895, MH-BA; W.K.L. Dickson to Raff & Gammon, 23 January 1895, MH-BA; Raff & Gammon, "Statement: Costs of Film Subjects from January 25th to Date," 18 April 1895, 1:434, MH-BA. Maguire & Baucus, *Edison and International Photographic Films*, April 1897, 9.

NOTE: Raff & Gammon paid Capt. Ross $125 to appear in this film. It was sold in Italy as *Lotta di gladiatori*. (Continental Phonograph Kinetoscope Company, *Kinetoscenes*, [March 1895].)

N. Finoni, Chevalier Greco's backer and Captain Duncan C. Ross met at the Police Gazette office yesterday and deposited $400, making a total stake of $2,400 in the match for the swordsman's championship of the world. Both men are in training and the contest promises to be one of the greatest ever fought in this country. There was considerable trouble in agreeing on a referee but finally they decided to ask General Fitz Hugh Lee, Governor of

Virginia to act. The swordsmen will meet on Tuesday evening, January 9, on the stage of Lenox Lyceum and decide the championship. (*New York Herald*, 5 January 1894, 14.)

ROEBER THE VICTOR.
He Won the Wrestling Match in Three Straight Falls from Ross.

MORE than one thousand enthusiasts braved the oppressive heat to see the wrestling match between Duncan Ross and Ernest Roeber at the Academy of Music last evening. It was anything but wrestling weather, but the sports didn't seem to mind. It was announced that the principals would wrestle best three out of five falls for a purse and side bet. The style of wrestling adopted by the combatants consisted of catch-as-catch-can and Greco-Roman. For the choice of style in the first bout the men tossed, and Ross won. He selected catch-as-catch-can. As this is his favorite style everybody expected to see him win easily, but he failed to come up to expectations. He was very fat and was puffing like a porpoise after wrestling a moment. It was plain to all that he was far from being in good condition. He executed some very clever moves in avoiding a fall, but at the end of ten and one-half minutes Roeber secured a half Nelson hold, and Ross succumbed.

In the second bout the men wrestled Greco-Roman style. Roeber, who is an expert at this kind of wrestling, tossed Ross about for five minutes and then turned the Scotchman flat on his back. Ross, realizing that he had no chance of winning, declined to wrestle the third bout, but after considerable persuasion changed his mind. For a second time the men wrestled catch-as-catch-can. Ross made a desperate attempt to throw Roeber, but the latter was too quick and clever for him. Roeber scored a fall after four minutes, thus winning the match. (*New York Herald*, 12 June 1894, 10.)

Messers. Raff & Gammon   [23 January 1895]
Dear Sirs—
At the request of Capt. Ross, wd say that the contest of today we hope to be O.K. & will immediately inform you when developed which we will do tomorrow—the last time Capt. Ross was here, the day was not suitable for the purpose. W.K.L. Dickson (Handwritten, MH-BA.)

Duncan C. Ross, the well-known horse back broadsword athlete, came out to Orange on Wednesday and appeared before the Edison kinetograph. He gave a fine exhibition of his abilities and used three fine saddle horses with military equipments sent for his use by Richard Coyne, of East Orange. (*Orange Chronicle*, 26 January 1895, 5.)

Duncan Ross, Dies at 90 Years.
Special to the New York Times.

BALTIMORE, Md., Sept. 8.—Duncan Ross, 90 years old, former champion broad swordsman of the world, wrestling champion of the United States, and hero of the Ashanti and Zulu wars, in which he won the Victoria Cross, was found dead here this afternoon. He was formerly a Captain in the British arny. He had made his home for several years in a little shop here, the sign on the building stating that he sold "everything from a needle to a British tank." (*New York Times*, 9 September 1919, 17.)

Billy Edwards was a middle-aged boxing instructor in 1895. The boxer "Warwick" bears a striking resemblance to Edwards, one reason the film has often been identified (incorrectly) as a Glenroy Brothers subject.

115 ***Billy Edwards and the Unknown (5 rounds) / Billy Edwards Boxing / Billy Edwards and Warwick / Boxing**

LENGTH: 5 films of 50 ft. each.   © No reg.
PRODUCER: W.K.L. Dickson, Maguire & Baucus.
CAMERA: William Heise.
CAST: Billy Edwards, Warwick.
PRODUCTION DATE: Late January to early February 1895.
LOCATION: Black Maria, West Orange, N.J.
SOURCE:
DESCRIPTION: This well-known and prominent pugilist, with an antagonist scienced and skillful, gives one of the most if not the most spirited and exciting exhibitions of sparring ever taken for the Kinetoscope. (The Kinetoscope Company, *Price List of Films*, [May 1895], 4.)

SUBJECT: Sports. Boxing.

ARCHIVE: NR-GE, DLC-Hendricks.

CITATIONS: Raff & Gammon to Peter Bacigalupi, invoice, 16 February 1895, 1:321, MH-BA. Maguire & Baucus, *Edison Films*, 20 January 1897, 7; Maguire & Baucus, *Edison and International Photographic Films*, April 1897, 4; Maguire & Baucus, *Fall Catalogue*, 1897, 11; F.Z. Maguire & Co., *Catalogue*, [March 1898], 33; *Edison Films*, March 1900, 27.

NOTE: The "MB" appearing in this film indicates it was made for Maguire & Baucus. The film was sold in Italy as *Combattimento di Billy Edwards collo ignoto, 5 pugilati a fondo.* (Continental Phonograph Kinetoscope Company, *Kinetoscenes,* [March 1895].)

The Peerless Annabelle appeared before the kinetograph for the second time (at least) in January or February 1895, part of a process of replacing damaged negatives. The "MB" logo was used for these productions in at least some instances, but the expenses for these films were apparently shared with Raff & Gammon. (Raff & Gammon, "Statement: Costs of Film Subjects from January 25th to Date," 18 April 1895, 1:434, MH-BA.)

116 [Annabelle Serpentine Dance, no. 2]

LENGTH: 50 ft.   © No reg.

PRODUCER: W.K.L. Dickson, Maguire & Baucus.

CAMERA: William Heise.

CAST: Annabelle Whitford.

PRODUCTION DATE: By February 1895.

LOCATION: Black Maria, West Orange, N.J.

SOURCE: *Annabelle Serpentine Dance* (Edison film no. 49, summer 1894).

DESCRIPTION:

SUBJECT: Vaudeville–performances. Dancing.

ARCHIVE:

CITATIONS: *Frank Leslie's Popular Monthly*, February 1895 (with illustration).

NOTE: For unknown reasons, no Annabelle subjects were listed in The Kinetoscope Company, *Price List of Films* [May 1895].

117 [Annabelle Butterfly Dance, no. 2]

LENGTH: 50 ft.   © No reg.

PRODUCER: W.K.L. Dickson, Maguire & Baucus.

CAMERA: William Heise.

CAST: Annabelle Whitford.

PRODUCTION DATE: By February 1895.

LOCATION: Black Maria, West Orange, N.J.

SOURCE: *Annabelle Butterfly Dance* (Edison film no. 48, summer 1894).

DESCRIPTION:

SUBJECT: Vaudeville–performances. Dancing.

ARCHIVE:

CITATIONS:

NOTE:

118 [Annabelle Sun Dance, no. 2]

LENGTH: 50 ft.   © No reg.

PRODUCER: W.K.L. Dickson, Maguire & Baucus.

CAMERA: William Heise.

CAST: Annabelle Whitford.

PRODUCTION DATE: By February 1895.

LOCATION: Black Maria, West Orange, N.J.

SOURCE: *Annabelle Sun Dance* (Edison film no. 50, summer 1894).

DESCRIPTION:

SUBJECT: Vaudeville–performances. Dancing.

ARCHIVE:

CITATIONS:

NOTE:

Charles Guyer was part of the team of Guyer & Goodwin, billed as "everybody's favorite in their funny act, 'The Kids,'" when he played at Keith's Union Square Theatre for the weeks beginning 26 March and 28 May 1894.

119 Grotesque Tumbling / Guyer

LENGTH: 50 ft.   © No reg.

PRODUCER: W.K.L. Dickson.

CAMERA: William Heise.

CAST: Charles Guyer.

PRODUCTION DATE: Late January 1895.

LOCATION: Black Maria, West Orange, N.J.

SOURCE:

DESCRIPTION: By Guyer, the famous clown. (Maguire & Baucus, *Edison and International Photographic Films*, April 1897, 9.)

SUBJECT: Vaudeville–performances. Clowns. Acrobats. Tumbling.

ARCHIVE:

CITATIONS: Raff & Gammon to Exhibition Department, invoice, 12 February 1895, 1:300, MH-BA. Maguire & Baucus, *Fall Catalogue,* 1897, 12; F.Z. Maguire & Co., *Catalogue,* [March 1898], 33.

NOTE: Charles Guyer was not part of song and dance team Guyer (Mabel) and Huested (Effie), traveling as part of Sam Devere's Own Company at this time.

During the 1890s, African-American music and dance found a niche within dominant theatrical practices. Such performances, however, were frequently situated in a pre-Civil War framework of slavery. Harry Martell's "South Before the War" Co., which employed Grundy and Frint, was one of the most successful and long-lived.

120 James Grundy, [no. 1] / Buck and Wing Dance

LENGTH: 50 ft.   © No reg.

PRODUCER: W.K.L. Dickson.

CAMERA: William Heise.

CAST: James Grundy.

PRODUCTION DATE: By late January 1895.

LOCATION: Black Maria, West Orange, N.J.

SOURCE: *The South Before the War* (revue).

DESCRIPTION: Buck and Wing Dance. From "South Before the War." These are the best negro subjects yet taken and are amusing and entertaining. (The Kinetoscope Company, *Price List of Films,* [May 1895], 4.)

SUBJECT: Revues–performances. Dancing. Afro-Americans. South Before the War Company.

ARCHIVE:

CITATIONS: "Colored Folks at the Bijou," *New York Times,* 20 November 1894, 5; Raff & Gammon to Exhibition Department, invoice, 18 March 1895, 1:369, MH-BA; advertisement, *New York Clipper,* 12 September 1896, 447. Ohio Phonograph Co., *The Edison Kinetoscope. Price List,* August 1895, 8; Maguire & Baucus, *Edison and International Photographic Films*, April 1897, 3; Maguire & Baucus, *Fall Catalogue*, 1897, 11; Maguire & Co., Catalogue, [March 1898], 28.

NOTE:

121 James Grundy, [no. 2] / Cake Walk

LENGTH: 50 ft.   © No reg.

PRODUCER: W.K.L. Dickson.

CAMERA: William Heise.

CAST: James Grundy.

PRODUCTION DATE: By late January 1895.

LOCATION: Black Maria, West Orange, N.J.

SOURCE: *The South Before the War* (revue).

DESCRIPTION: Cake Walk. These are the best negro subjects yet taken and are amusing and entertaining. (The Kinetoscope Company, *Price List of Films,* [May 1895], 4.)

SUBJECT: Revues–performances. Dancing. Afro-Americans. South Before the War Company.

ARCHIVE:

CITATIONS: "Raff & Gammon to Exhibition Department, invoice, 12 February 1895, 1:300, MH-BA.

NOTE:

122 Grundy and Frint

LENGTH: 50 ft.   © No reg.

PRODUCER: W.K.L. Dickson.

CAMERA: William Heise.

CAST: James Grundy, Frint.

PRODUCTION DATE: By late January 1895.

LOCATION: Black Maria, West Orange, N.J.

SOURCE: *The South Before the War* (revue).

DESCRIPTION: Breakdown from "South Before the War." (The Kinetoscope Company, *Price List of Films*, [May 1895], 3.)

SUBJECT: Revues–performances. Dancing. Afro-Americans. South Before the War Company.

ARCHIVE:

CITATIONS: Ohio Phonograph Co., *The Edison Kinetoscope. Price List*, August 1895, 8.

NOTE:

"THE SOUTH BEFORE THE WAR."

A conglomeration of negro dialect melodies, pastimes on the levee, camp meetings on Frog Island, etc., made up the programme of the performance at Niblo's Garden last evening, and it was witnessed and appreciated by an enormous audience.

The production bears the title of "The South Before the War," and included a number of specialty acts and an old time cake walk in which sixteen couples engaged. The Buckingham Quartet, the Twilight Quartet, the Standard Quartet, Billy Williams, Kathy Carter, etc., made up the speciality bill. Altogether the performance was good. The production is original and novel. (*New York Herald*, 24 April 1894, 6.)

Rob Roy premiered at the Detroit Opera House on 1 October 1894. It opened in New York City at the Herald Square Theatre on 29 October 1894 to enthusiastic reviews. Former President Benjamin Harrison saw the operetta twice. Richard F. Carroll, who appeared in the role of the Mayor of Perth, was filmed near the end of its original New York engagement, which ended 23 March 1895.

123 √Rob Roy / Jamies / The Jamies / Burlesque Scotch Dance

LENGTH: 50 ft.   © No reg.

PRODUCER: W.K.L. Dickson, Continental Commerce Company.

CAMERA: William Heise.

CAST: Richard F. Carroll (Dugald Mac-Wheeble, Mayor of Perth), the Jamies.

PRODUCTION DATE: [March 1895.]

LOCATION: Black Maria, West Orange, N.J.

SOURCE: *Rob Roy* (operetta) and *Highland Dance* (Edison film no. 33, spring 1894).

DESCRIPTION: A Burlesque Scotch Dance by Richard Carroll and the Jamies from the Whitney Opera Co. A success. Full of life and action. (The Kinetoscope Company, *Price List of Films*, [May 1895], 4.)

SUBJECT: Musicals–performances. Dancing. Scots. Burlesque. Whitney Opera Co.

ARCHIVE:

CITATIONS: "Songs From 'Rob Roy,'" *New York Herald*, 28 October 1894, 3D; Raff & Gammon to F. D. Higbee, [23] April 1895, 1:443, MH-BA; List of Films Shipped to Atlanta, Sept. 4, 1895, MH-BA. Ohio Phonograph Co., *The Edison Kinetoscope.*

Price List, August 1895, 7; Maguire & Baucus, *Edison Films*, 20 January 1897, 6; Maguire & Baucus, *Edison and International Photographic Films*, April 1897, 10; Maguire & Baucus, *Fall Catalogue*, 1897, 12; F.Z. Maguire & Co., *Catalogue*, [March 1898], 28.

NOTE: By this date a "C" (for Continental Commerce Company) had replaced the "MB" (for Maguire & Baucus) to indicate the owner of the original negative.

HAIL TO BOLD "ROB ROY."
De Koven and Smith's New Opera Presented with Success at the Herald Square Theatre.

...HERALD SQUARE THEATRE.—*Rob Roy*, a comic opera in three acts by Harry B. Smith and Reginald De Koven.

Rob Roy MacGregor	William Pruette
Janet	Juliette Corden
Prince Charles Edward Stuart	Barron Berthald
Flora MacDonald	Lizzie Macnichol
Dugald MacWheeble	Richard F. Carroll
Louchiel	W.H. McLaughlin
Captain Ralph Sheridan	Anna O'Keefe
Sandy MacSherry	Joseph Herbert
Thomas MacSorlie	Harry Parker
Lieutenant Cornwallis	Mittie Atheron
Lieutenant Clinton	Louise Crane
Angus MacAllister	Jeanette Perie
Duncan Campbell	Julie Senac
Stuart MacPherson	Frankie Leonard
Donald MacAlpine	Carrie Rieger
Nelly	Anita Austin

National types certainly bring success in their train to De Koven & Smith. "Rob Roy" will not, indeed, cause "Robin Hood" to be forgotten, but our affection for it will be divided by these two writers' latest born, which saw the light of New York for the first time last evening at the Herald Square Theatre. Another theatrical work has been created that is neither opera buffoonery nor unmusical farce comedy. It is a great pity that the librettist of so charming a work had not taken a little more trouble over the denouement. Even in opera-comique—and I use the word in its original significance—there is no earthly reason why you should get your characters into a box and then phlegmatically get them out by the prosaic process of merely opening the lid. There is a logic of unreason—look at Labiche—a perverted mode of reasoning, if you will, that the successful vaudevillist must master in order to make the peripatetics of his characters seem natural, be they ever so widely improbable. And with men, who, like Smith and De Koven, write a work that from every point of view is not only worthy of serious attention, but is also worthy of high praise, this should particularly be the case. The one weak point, then in the libretto, is the tame finale, which simply consists of the English captain's turning traitor, for no earthly reason—either comic operatic or otherwise—and hands being given all round.

The dialogue is bright enough. "What!" says Janet, "marry that apology for a man!" "I know," answers the father, "but do, my dear girl, be polite and accept the apology." As to the music I do not know whether I am most astounded by De Koven's musical science or his musical memory. He has without question the faculty of writing phrases of extreme melodic beauty. Certain of the numbers throb with passion, as for instance, Flora's romance, "Dear Heart of My Heart," in the second act, or the equally charming "Roses" duet, tempo de valse, in the first act, with its sprightly introduction sung while Janet stirs the batter and tames the Scottish Hercules into an obedient housewife. The orchestral writing is excellent, often indeed, exquisite, the one objection being that it is in general too heavy. Surely no barytone on the light opera stage has a more resonant organ than Mr. Pruette—nor be it remarked, en passant, one who uses it better—but in his first air he almost shouted himself hoarse in trying to dominate the orchestra.

The finales to both first and second act are wonderfully effective. There is just the right proportion of local color, which might so easily have degenerated into a reminiscence of the bagpipe and thistle, and one of the daintiest fancies in the whole world of comic opera music is a duet and ensemble in the last act with a whistling refrain. What a picture of almost barbaric strength was presented by Mr. Pruette! And how effective he was in the role. Musically his part does not come up to his level, but that he carried off his measures with artistic ease it is needless to say. In splendor of physique and sonority of voice he was hard pressed by Mr. W. McLaughlin, whose Scottish accent sounded strangely Celtic. He was twice encored for his "In Dungeon Deep" solo, and merited every bit of it.

Miss Juliette Corden was a sufficient reason for the worship she aroused and vocally was admirable. I thought Miss Macnicholl did not let out that warm voice she certainly possesses, but she was remarkably effective in the role of Flora MacDonald. Mr. Richard F. Carroll and Mr. J.W. Herbert were droll enough in the last act to make up for the lacking vis comica in the other parts of the work. The former is so funnily pathetic and the latter so pathetically funny that [not] to laugh was an impossibility. Mr. Barron Berthald was vigorous enough in the part of Prince Charlie, and Miss Anna O'Keefe both looked charmingly, acted gracefully and sang with great chic.

Scenically the production was admirable and the costumes were very beautiful. The second act was singularly effective with the entry of the defeated Highlanders over the bridge, while the assembled clans at the end of the first act presented a wonderfully romantic and harmonious picture.

Act I.–An open square in Perth. Janet, the Mayor's daughter, is secretly married to Rob Roy, but her father makes her marry the town crier and an English captain. It is the eve of Culloden, and Rob and his men are marching to the help of Prince Charlie. Janet goes with them disguised in Highland costume.

Act II.–A mountain pass. The Stuart troops are defeated and Charles disguises himself as a miller's boy. A very droll catch is sung in this act that is a worthy pendant to its fellow in "Robin Hood." The English troops arrive, the Prince is denounced by the Mayor, but Flora gives herself up as Charlie, and is carried off to Stirling Castle.

Act III–Stirling Castle. Flora is liberated by Cameron, disguised as a jailor. She is recaptured, the real Charlie turns up, and after a little discussion, the whole party is liberated by the English captain.

AMID PLAIDS AND TARTANS.

The audience was the most brilliant thus far of this dramatic season. Boxes and stalls were all filled....(*New York Herald*, 30 October 1894, 12.)

RICHARD F. CARROLL

was born in Boston, Mass., on Oct. 27, 1864, and made his first appearance on the stage at the age of five years. From 1870 to 1876, in conjunction with his father, R.M. Carroll and his brothers, known as the Carroll Family, he appeared in most of the principal vaudeville theatres of this country among them being Tony Pastor's, and Josh Hart's Theatre Comique. During this time he appeared with G.L. Fox's "Humpty Dumpty," at the old Globe Theatre, Wood's Museum and the old Bowery Theatre. During the season of 1876-77 they starred in Bartley Campbell's "Orphans," a play especially written for the Carroll Family. In 1880 the subject of this sketch made his first venture alone when he joined the Hanlon Bros.' "Voyage en Suisse," replacing Alfred Hanlon, who had been taken sick. He remained four years with this company, and in 1885 was a member of the stock company of the Union Square Theatre, appearing as the dumb idiot in "The Prisoner for Life." During the season of 1886-1887 he was with Lydia Thompson in "Oxygen," with Patti Rosa and in Tony Hart's last venture, "Donnybrook," joined David Henderson's Burlesque Company at the Chicago Opera House for the Summer, playing in "The Arabian Nights." In 1887-88-89 he was at the Casino, New York, taking James T. Powers' place in "Nadjy" and afterwards appearing in "The Brigands," "The Grand Duchess" and "The Brazilian." In 1890 he opened with Marie Tempest in "The Red Huzzar," at Palmer's Theatre, this city, and remained with the company until the end of the New York run. He joined the Pauline Hall Opera Co. for the Summer and for the following season, playing the leading comedy roles in "The Mikado," "The Pirates of Penzance," "Pinafore," "Patience," "The Gondoliers," "The Queen's Mate," "A Trip to Africa," "Paoloa" and other operas. During the season of 1892-93 he appeared as "Charles Favart," and afterwards joined Fred C. Whitney's company, to play the Duke in the "The Fencing Master." Mr. Carroll is still under engagement to Mr. Whitney, and, at present is playing the role of Dugald MacWheeble, the very entertaining Mayor of Perth, in Smith and De Koven's opera, "Rob Roy," now running at the Herald Square in this city, in which he is doing excellent work, which has deservedly won unanimous praise. In addition to his successful labors as a comedian, Mr. Carroll has other professional claims worthy of consideration. He has found time to indulge in dramatic authorship, and among the plays he has written are "Where Can It Be," produced at Tony Pastor's Fourteenth Street Theatre, and "The Dago," played last season by the Carrolls, his father and brothers. He also claims a portion of the responsibility for the creation of Nellie McHenry's play, "Lady Peggy," and "U and I," produced by John T. Kelly and Gus Williams. (*New York Clipper*, 12 January 1895, 714.)

Few films were made specifically for Edison's kinetophone, the inventor's combination of the phonograph and kinetoscope. None of these were distributed commercially, at least in the United States. Even Opera Scene, which was sold in Italy, may not have been shot with synchronous sound firmly in mind.

124 **[Opera Scene]**
LENGTH: 50 ft.   © No reg.
PRODUCER: W.K.L. Dickson.
CAMERA: William Heise.
CAST:
PRODUCTION DATE: By March 1895 (but quite possibly much earlier).
LOCATION: Black Maria, West Orange, N.J.

Efforts of combining phonograph recording and kinetograph filming proved unsuccessful.
E.J. Meeker's fanciful drawing represents the interior of the Black Maria (1894-1895).

SOURCE:
DESCRIPTION:
SUBJECT: Opera–performances. Motion pictures–sound.
ARCHIVE:
CITATIONS:
NOTE: This film was sold in Italy as *Scene d'opera*. (Continental Phonograph Kineto-scope Company, *Kinetoscenes*, [March 1895].)

125 *[Dickson Experimental Sound Film] / [Dickson Violin]**

LENGTH: 50 ft.   © No reg.
PRODUCER: W.K.L. Dickson, Raff & Gammon.
CAMERA: William Heise.
CAST: W.K.L. Dickson or Charles D'Almaine (on the violin).
PRODUCTION DATE: September 1894 to 2 April 1895.
LOCATION: Black Maria, West Orange, N.J.
SOURCE:
DESCRIPTION:
SUBJECT: Motion pictures–experiments. Dancing. Violin. Motion pictures–sound.
ARCHIVE: NNMoMA, CLAc, DLC.
CITATIONS:

NOTE: Charles D'Almaine was an Edison pho-nograph violinist and, according to Paolo Cherchi Usai, a Dickson look-alike. This film looks toward the commercial introduction of the peep-hole kinetophone in April 1895, but could have been made almost anytime in the previous six months. The "R" appearing in the lower right corner suggests that this film was made with commercial purposes in mind and was perhaps less of an "experiment" than we might think. Nevertheless, it was apparently never offered for sale.

Combining the Phonograph and the Kinetoscope.

Within a short time the public will have another novelty shown them from the fertile brain of Thomas A. Edison and his gifted lieutenant, William K.L. Dickson. The novelty is not a new thing in invention, for it has been known and perfected in the Edison Laboratory for several years. It is the connection of the kinetoscope with the phono-graph in such a way that the two will work synchronously and the vocal expression exactly keep pace and follow the visible expression as delineated on the kinetoscope. During the time of experimentation with the kinetoscope and the perfection of its details, experiments were carried on with the connection of the phonograph and the problem effectually solved. Once this was completed the kinetoscope was put on the market and the demand created for these curious and remarkable reproductions of action. Now that they have been fully established in popular favor the added attraction is to be introduced. The apparatus bears little external difference from the kinetoscope, the only change being the protrusion from the top of the well-known rubber ear tubes of the phono-graph. The synchronization of the two instruments is attained in the simplest possible way, the connection being made by a belt from one to the other. With this combination wonderful possibilities are opened out before the public. An entire change will be made in the character of the objects and scenes taken by the kinetograph. Previously only scenes were taken in which there was a great variety of action, the element of sound being entire-ly disregarded. Hence such scenes as prize fights, skirt dances, clog dances, and the like were taken. With the new combination, the eye and ear being both concerned, the range of subjects is largely increased, and many things that could not have been effectively taken under the principle of the kinetograph alone will now become available. It will for instance be possible to take a reproduction of an entire opera with all the action and the music, by the use of a number of instruments operating one after another. In this way the "Opera at Home" will become more than a travesty on the name and instead will be a living reality in the homes of thousands. A fuller and more scientific description of the invention can be found in the book published by W.K.L. Dickson and Miss Antonia Dickson. (*Orange Chronicle,* 16 March 1895, 7.)

W.K.L. Dickson resigned his position at the Edison Laboratory on 2 April 1895 and began to work more closely with two of Edison rivals: the Lathams with their eidolo-scope projector, and the group that was organizing the American Mutoscope Company, for which he became one of the original partners.

Mr. Dickson to Leave the Laboratory

W.K.L. Dickson has resigned his position of electrical engineer at the laboratory of Thomas A. Edison in order to go into business for himself, his company being the Electric Light and Power Co., lately incorporated in the State of New Jersey with Llewellyn H. Johnson as President; W.K.L. Dickson as Electrical engineer, H.C. Douglas as Secretary. Mr. Dickson has made many friends in Orange and all join in good wishes for his success in his new field. (*Orange Chronicle,* 27 April 1895, 7.)

After his departure, W.K.L. Dickson was not immediately replaced. William Heise con-tinued to act as cameraman, shooting a number of films on his own or with guidance from selling agents such as Raff & Gammon.

In the mid-1890s, aging strong man Prof. Attila drew attention to himself by challeng-ing Sandow, the first star to be kinetographed, to competitive feats of strength both directly and increasingly through his students. Indeed, Sandow had once been a stu-dent of Attila, who, according to David L. Chapman, introduced him to the technique of progressive weight training. The two had also often performed together. Even though their competitive exchanges occurred primarily through the newspapers, it is hardly surprising that such forms of self-promotion eventually extended into motion pictures as the Edison company filmed Attila and his student, Young Weimer.

126 **Professor Attilla [sic] / Prof. Attila**

LENGTH: 50 ft.   © No reg.

PRODUCER: William Heise.

CAMERA: William Heise.

CAST: Louis Attila (stage name for Louis Durlacher).

PRODUCTION DATE: April to early May 1895.

LOCATION: Black Maria, West Orange, N.J.

SOURCE:

DESCRIPTION: The World Famous Athlete and Strong Man Trainer. (The Kinetoscope Com-pany, *Price List of Films,* May 1895, 4.)

SUBJECT: Strong men. Germans.

ARCHIVE:

CITATIONS: "How Strength is Acquired," *New*

York Herald, 11 February 1894, 10D (with illustration, and written statement by Attila); "Romulus' Great Chance," *New York Herald,* 9 July 1894, 12; David L. Chapman, *Sandow the Magnificent: Eugen Sandow and the Beginnings of Bodybuilding* (Urbana: University of Illinois Press, 1994).

NOTE: Louis Durlacher and Rosa Sander were married 8 April 1896 by Mayor William Strong of New York. (*New York Clipper,* 18 April 1896, 102.) Attila occasionally appeared in vaudeville, playing Proctor's 23rd Street Theatre for the week beginning 21 October 1895. Gordon Hendricks has suggested that Attila was performing for Barnum & Bailey's Circus.

127 Attila, no. 2

ATTILA AND SANDOW WHEN TWENTY-ONE YEARS OLD.

LENGTH: 50 ft.   © No reg.

PRODUCER: William Heise.

CAMERA: William Heise.

CAST: Louis Attila (stage name for Louis Durlacher).

PRODUCTION DATE: April to early May 1895.

LOCATION: Black Maria, West Orange, N.J.

SOURCE:

DESCRIPTION:

SUBJECT: Strong men. Germans.

ARCHIVE:

CITATIONS: List of Films Shipped to Atlanta, Sept. 4, 1895, MH-BA.

NOTE: The accompanying illustration, from a newspaper, is from an old photograph of Attila and his young pupil—Sandow.

FIGHTING AT THE LYCEUM.
Glove Battles Amuse a Big Crowd at Professor Donovan's Benefit.

Mike Donovan, the instructor in the manly art of self-defense at the New York Athletic Club, had a benefit at Lenox Lyceum last night at which a number of prominent clubmen and lovers of boxing congregated....

Professor Attila, the man of wonderful strength and many medals, opened the show with an exhibition that pleased the spectators. He lifted and juggled all sorts and sizes of weights and concluded with a grand effort in which he withstood the strain on his chest of 1,500 pounds of iron. Then he spoke a few words to the people between gasps. The burden of his speech was that he stood ready to compete against any strong man in the world for the championship or a purse....(*New York Herald,* 18 February 1894, 11.)

STRONG MEN SPARRING.
Romulus Willing to Meet Sandow if the Conditions of the Contest are Changed.
HE WISHES TO NAME TWO JUDGES.
Believes He Can Duplicate Sandow's Feats of Strength if Permitted to Prepare.
WANTS DEAD WEIGHT USED.

Sandow's proposition to Romulus, published in yesterday's HERALD, and his apparent good faith in risking the $10,0000 which he has deposited with the HERALD, was the subject of general discussion yesterday among persons interested in athletics.

Among the most interested readers of the Herald's story of what Sandow was willing to do were Romulus himself and Professor Attila, his manager. Romulus had already prepared this letter when I saw him yesterday:–

TO THE EDITOR OF THE HERALD:

In reading your article of July 9, it occurred to me that the general impression to the casual reader must be that this is the easiest kind of trial necessary to earn the title of better man in a contest of this first description. You cannot call it a contest, even, because in this coming trial of strength the contesting is only being done by myself–namely to duplicate feats of strength which my adversary has been in the habit of practising and performing, perhaps for six to seven years. No feats of which I am special master will be taken into consideration.

Apart from this I do not even know at present what feats will be chosen by Sandow. Notwithstanding I feel that I can most certainly demonstrate on any occasion where only pure physical feats of strength are required my ability to duplicate anything Sandow will be able to show me.

I am willing to agree to the proposed scheme of giving the entire receipts to the Herald's Free Ice Fund but I feel that in justice to myself and to my reputation as a strong man I must make the condition that we have the right to name two judges of the contest while Sandow may name two, the four gentlemen named being instructed to name a fifth, who shall act as referee. Furthermore, I desire to stipulate that Sandow must name the feats to be performed at least a few days before the date fixed upon for the contest, so that I can come properly prepared with paraphernalia adapted to the difference in my dimensions and those of Sandow.

On these conditions, which I have only tried to make fair and just to both contestants, I am willing to prepare for the contest, which may take place in either public or private at an hour's notice. ROMULUS.

HE WANTS FAIR TERMS.

"You see," said Attila, as he read me Romulus' ultimatum, "that we are ready to meet Sandow the moment he agrees to our perfectly reasonable proposition. Why should he name all the judges?

"He risks his $10,000 to boom him in his business and with his own judges and the right to spring any feat he may choose at a moment's notice after getting on the stage he would not be risking a penny.

"I know Sandow better than any one else, for I taught him, and I want to protect Romulus as far as possible.

"If Sandow raises a 200 pound dumbbell we want to have another dumbbell on hand, if we wish, also weighing 200 pounds which we may be allowed to use. The reason for this is that Romulus' hands are as small as a girl's and he can not grasp a handle which would just suit Sandow.

WON'T TAKE ANY CHANCES.

"Then again all the weight lifted should be dead weight. We are not going to have Sandow lift his dumbbell with the two men in the baskets at either end. That would be manifestly unfair, for the slightest movement on the part of the men would make it impossible even for the Hercules of mythology to raise the weight.

"In any case, win or lose, in the coming trial of strength Romulus' backer will on the night of the contest bet Sandow or his representative $1,000 that Romulus will then and there perform three feats of strength no one of which Sandow can repeat successfully. That offer is certainly direct and unequivocal, and shows that we mean business.

"We ask for nothing but a fair representation among the judges and an enumeration of the feats to be performed. With that conceded we will walk into any hall or theatre and met Sandow at a moment's notice, and will be pleased to have all the proceeds go to the Herald's great charity.

"As for giving a bond that Romulus will be on hand when the arrangement is perfected, that seems a trifle absurd since he came to this country from Europe for that very purpose." (*New York Herald*, 10 July 1894, 11.)

TO MAKE A TEST CASE OF SANDOW'S
Proceedings to Ascertain Whether Mr. Shields Is Legally a United States Commissioner.

The case of Sandow, the strong man, against Professor Attila, otherwise Louis Durlacher, his rival, before United States Commissioner Shields in the Federal Building for sending him a scurrillous letter was to have been heard yesterday, but Mr. Shields declined to go on with it. He says the question has not yet been determined whether he is Commissioner or not, according to the law passed by Congress last August.

Ex-Assistant United States District Attorney Abraham Rose, counsel for Sandow, appeared before the Commissioner yesterday morning. Sandow and Attila did not meet. Attila and his counsel said they were anxious to meet Sandow's accusations.

Mr. Rose declared that he wanted to press the charges against Attila, and he would make a test case of Sandow vs. Attila to determine whether Mr. Shields is still a United States Commissioner or not.

A mandamus was drawn up by Mr. Rose to compel Mr. Shields to act as Commissioner on the matter. It was brought before Judge Lacombe in the United States Circuit Court.

Judge Lacombe made the order returnable in the United States Circuit Court at eleven o'clock this morning. (*New York Herald*, 28 September 1894, 7.)

128 Young Weimer

LENGTH: 50 ft.   © No reg.

PRODUCER: William Heise.

CAMERA: William Heise.

CAST: Henry Weimer.

PRODUCTION DATE: April to early May 1895.

LOCATION: Black Maria, West Orange, N.J.

SOURCE:

DESCRIPTION: The Champion Light-weight Dumb Bell Lifter of the World—pupil of Attilla [sic]. (The Kinetoscope Company, *Price List of Films*, [May 1895], 4.)

SUBJECT: Strong men. Germans.

ARCHIVE:

CITATIONS: F.Z. Maguire & Co., *Catalogue*, [March 1898], 33.

NOTE:

A YOUTHFUL "STRONG MAN."

Henry Weimer, the young strong man whom Professor Attila offers to back against any lad his weight, entertained a party of athletes with exhibitions of his strength yesterday. Weimer is only eighteen years old, and weighs but 115 pounds. Those who witnessed Weimer go through his performance agreed that he is an exceedingly fine athlete. Among the feats Weimer performed was lifting the 56-pound weight above his head three times in succession without any apparent effort; lifting the 125 pound dumb-bell above his head seven consecutive times with his right hand and three consecutive times with his left hand; lifting the 145 pound dumb-bell from the floor above his head. His star performance was placing over his shoulders leather straps with six hook attachments. Each hook held a 50 pound weight. He placed the 125 pound dumb-bell across his back and, with a man weighing 150 pounds each on either side of the dumb bell, walked leisurely around. (*New York Herald*, 3 December 1894, 11.)

One important series of subjects taken by William Heise was of Barnum and Bailey's Circus, which performed in Orange, New Jersey, on 9 May 1895. The circus, which had begun its new season in New York City on March 28th, was then advertising its "Grand New Ethnological Congress With Strange and Savage living Races from every clime. Together with their wives, families, implements, huts, musical instruments and domestic utensils." (Advertisement, New York World, *24 March 1895, 13.)*

129 **Dance of Rejoicing**

LENGTH: 50 ft.   © No reg.
PRODUCER: William Heise.
CAMERA: William Heise.
CAST:
PRODUCTION DATE: [9 May 1895.]
LOCATION: Black Maria, West Orange, N.J.
SOURCE:
DESCRIPTION: By Samoan Islanders, with Barnum and Bailey's Greatest Show on Earth. (The Kinetoscope Company, *Price List of Films*, [May 1895], 4.)
SUBJECT: Circus performers. Dancing. Samoan Islanders. Barnum & Bailey's Circus.
ARCHIVE:
CITATIONS: Ohio Phonograph Co., *The Edison Kinetoscope. Price List*, August 1895, 7; Maguire & Baucus, *Edison and International Photographic Films*, April 1897, 6; Maguire & Baucus, *Fall Catalogue*, 1897, 11.
NOTE: Gordon Hendricks' hypothesis, that the Samoans and other circus people were filmed on May 9th, the morning that they were in Orange, New Jersey, seems logical. It is possible (if unlikely) that performers from Barnum & Bailey's Circus appeared before Edison's kinetograph at a somewhat earlier date. That is, they could have traveled from New York City, where they were performing in March and April, to the Black Maria studio.

130 **Paddle Dance**

LENGTH: 50 ft.   © No reg.
PRODUCER: William Heise.
CAMERA: William Heise.
CAST:
PRODUCTION DATE: [9 May 1895.]
LOCATION: Black Maria, West Orange, N.J.
SOURCE:
DESCRIPTION: By Fiji Islanders. A peculiar dance by genuine savages, dressed or rather undressed, in their native garb. The revel takes its name from the paddles they hold in their hands. (*Edison Films*, March 1900, 28.)
SUBJECT: Circus performers. Dancing. Fiji Islanders. Barnum & Bailey's Circus.
ARCHIVE:

CITATIONS: The Kinetoscope Company, *Price List of Films*, [May 1895], 4; Ohio Phono-graph Co., *The Edison Kinetoscope. Price List*, August 1895, 7; Maguire & Baucus, *Edison and International Photographic Films*, April 1897, 13; Maguire & Baucus, *Fall Catalogue*, 1897, 14; F.Z. Maguire & Co., *Catalogue*, [March 1898], 27.

NOTE:

THE SAMOAN WAR CLUB DANCE

If you want vigor without any of the repellent features of the Algerian torture dance go to the Samoan village. There is a war club dance there that calls for more work in a short space of time than almost any other species of human gyration.

The war club dance is that of the Fiji Islands. It is done by about a dozen men standing in three rows. Few Europeans or Americans can rival these men in physical development. They are not tall, but the girth of their chests is tremendous, and their shoulders and arms look like those of some modern Samson. Their bodies are bare to the waist and you can see the play of the great muscles of their dusky arms and shoulders as they swing their heavy war clubs.

The clubs look less like clubs than oars. About half their length is shaped into a kind of two-edged wooden sword.

A gigantic Fiji Islander in the center of the first rank begins a song. The others join in. It is a chant of war, victory and death. It has a well-defined time and tune and is musical. The men swing their heavy clubs from right to left and from left to right. They swing faster and swing their clubs higher. A man in the third rank springs about three feet into the air and utters a yell that would make a Sioux Indian turn green and weak with envy. It is long-drawn and is something like this: "Whee-oo-oo-oo-oop-ee-ee. Kee-ee-ee-ee. Yo-o-o-ow-wow-wow."

Then the men brandish their clubs with all their vigor. They leap as high as they can. They deal blows at imaginary enemies. Their chant is broken into a series of ejaculations and the man in the rear rank makes his mighty springs, and utters his ear splitting shriek about once a minute.

Through it all the men keep perfect time. They leap together. Their feet strike the floor together and the clubs are swung in the same motion. They handle their clubs with real skill. They whirl them around their waists and around their necks and twirls them on their elbows and ankles. Their brown bodies flash across the stage, and their lips part with the force of muscular exertion, showing perfect white teeth.

All the time they are increasing their speed until the limit is reached. Then the man in the rear rank leaps just a little higher than ever, and utters his loudest yell, which he has saved for the last. Then the curtail drops on the exhausted warriors. ("Dancing in Midway Plaisance," *New York World*, 23 July 1893, 17.)

131 Hindoostan Fakir and Cotta Dwarf / Fakir & Dwarf

LENGTH: 50 ft.   © No reg.
PRODUCER: William Heise.
CAMERA: William Heise.
CAST:
PRODUCTION DATE: [9 May 1895.]
LOCATION: Black Maria, West Orange, N.J.
SOURCE:
DESCRIPTION: From Barnum & Bailey's Greatest Show on Earth. (The Kinetoscope Com-pany, *Price List of Films*, [May 1895], 4.)
SUBJECT: Circus performers. East Indians. Barnum & Bailey's Circus.
ARCHIVE:
CITATIONS: List of Films Shipped to Atlanta, Sept. 4, 1895, MH-BA.
NOTE:

132 √Short Stick Dance

LENGTH: 50 ft.   © No reg.
PRODUCER: William Heise, Raff & Gammon.
CAMERA: William Heise.
CAST:
PRODUCTION DATE: [9 May 1895.]
LOCATION: Black Maria, West Orange, N.J.
SOURCE:
DESCRIPTION: A native dance peculiar to India. Very odd and interesting. Strange cos-tumes and stranger motions. (*Edison Films*, March 1900, 29.)

SUBJECT: Circus performers. Dancing. East Indians. Barnum & Bailey's Circus.

ARCHIVE:

CITATIONS: The Kinetoscope Company, *Price List of Films*, [May 1895], 4; Maguire & Baucus, *Edison and International Photographic Films*, April 1897, 14; Maguire & Baucus, *Fall Catalogue*, 1897, 13; F.Z. Maguire & Co., *Catalogue*, [March 1898], 27.

NOTE:

133 Silver Dance

LENGTH: 50 ft.   © No reg.

PRODUCER: William Heise.

CAMERA: William Heise.

CAST:

PRODUCTION DATE: [9 May 1895.]

LOCATION: Black Maria, West Orange, N.J.

SOURCE:

DESCRIPTION: The participants are natives of Ceylon. Their dance is very interesting being so different from Western ideas of harmonies of motion. (*Edison Films*, March 1900, 28.)

SUBJECT: Circus performers. Dancing. Sri Lankans. Barnum & Bailey's Circus.

ARCHIVE:

CITATIONS: The Kinetoscope Company, *Price List of Films*, [May 1895], 4; Maguire & Baucus, *Edison and international Photographic Films*, April 1897, 14; Maguire & Baucus, *Fall Catalogue*, 1897, 13; F.Z. Maguire & Co., Catalogue, [March 1898], 27.

NOTE:

134 *Princess Ali / Egyptian Dance

LENGTH: 50 ft.   © No reg.

PRODUCER: William Heise, Continental Commerce Company.

CAMERA: William Heise.

CAST: Princess Ali.

PRODUCTION DATE: [9 May 1895.]

LOCATION: Black Maria, West Orange, N.J.

SOURCE:

DESCRIPTION: By "Princess Ali." The star of the Midway Plaisance, in her famous Dance du Ventre. (F.Z. Maguire & Co., *Catalogue,* [March 1898], 24.)

SUBJECT: Circus performers. Dancing. Arabs. Danse du ventre. Barnum & Bailey's Circus.

ARCHIVE: NR-GE, DLC-Hendricks.

CITATIONS: Maguire & Baucus, *Edison Films*, 20 January 1897, 6; Maguire & Baucus, *Edison and International Photographic Films*, April 1897, 7; Maguire & Baucus, *Fall Catalogue*, 1897, 11.

NOTE: Gordon Hendricks has established that Princess Ali was affiliated with Barnum & Bailey's Circus at this time.

STRANGE PEOPLE FROM FAR AWAY.
An Ethnological Congress Will Take the Place of the Circus Spectacle This Year.
GETTING THE REPRESENTATIVES.
Difficulties Under Which the Agents in the Far East Labor in Engaging the Natives.
TO OUTDO THE MIDWAY SHOW.

THERE is now on the way to this country a curious company of people who are to compose a grand ethnological congress which will be exhibited at the Madison Square Garden in connection with the Barnum & Bailey show when it opens its season there in the spring. Of course an ethnological congress is no new thing. It has been done in the "Greatest Show on Earth" before, it was, perhaps, the greatest attraction in its line at the World's Fair in the shape of the Midway Plaisance, but all those collections, if what Mr. Bailey says he expects to do, materializes, will be as nothing much in comparison with the exhibition New York will be treated to.

The congress will consist only of representatives of uncivilized peoples from foreign countries. At least thirty, and probably forty, different nations and tribes will be represented. Just how many it is impossible to state at present, as the members of the coming congress have a very disagreeable habit of running away or dying before they can be fairly started on their way to America.

Mr. Bailey has had this congress in contemplation for two years, although it has been a profound state secret in circus circles all the time, and not a word has been made public about it until Mr. Bailey informed me of the project the other day.

IN PLACE OF SPECTACLE.

It is designed to take the place of the spectacle which for several years has been such a prominent feature of the show. This statement will come as a big surprise to many who have come to look upon the glittering array of the ballet as a legitimate part of the circus. All that is done with for this season at least, however. No more grand pageants, no more platoons of dancing girls, no more waving of gayly colored cloths and flashing of colored lights and no more chanting of weird music to tell the story of some mythological event, which no one in the audience tries to understand, or if he does, gets hopelessly confused.

I asked why the spectacles were to be abandoned.

"Because they are too far above the heads of the people and are not, any way, a proper adjunct to a circus," was the answer. "In New York they are all very well. Here they pay and are understood in the Madison Square Garden, but when they are given anywhere else under canvas they are, to put it mildly, unadvisable."

And that is why there will be no more spectacles connected with the Greatest Show on Earth.

ALWAYS SEARCHING.

Agents are despatched to all parts of the world every year by Barnum & Bailey. One makes London a headquarters, another St. Petersburg and still another Ceylon, India. The London and St. Petersburg agents visit the capitals of Europe in the winter season in search of novel and attractive performers who may appear in the theatre or other places of amusement, and if found to be suitable for the circus negotiations are entered into and the "act" secured; or the agents may discover rare animals or curiosities—anything, in fact, that may prove valuable in the circus line that they see or hear about they endeavor to secure, sometimes taking long journeys to different countries.

Mr. J.B. Gaylord is always selected to go to India and has been with Mr. Bailey on and off for twenty years past. He is an experienced man in animal lore and the needs and requirements of the show.

ANTEDATES THE MIDWAY.

An idea was conceived in the year 1887 by Mr. Bailey, long before the Midway Plaisance was thought of, that it would be both an instructive and valuable sight to add such a congress to the circus, and so it proved. The exhibition was so meritorious that, stimulated by its success, he determined upon doing it again for this year, but upon a broader, wider and more colossal scale and make it take the place of the spectacle.

To prepare it for this year, Mr. J.B. Gaylord was sent to India last March, as it would take fully a year to secure representatives from the strange and savage tribes necessary, and Mr. George Starr was sent to Africa and Asia for others.

The manner of securing these people is curious. Making some city a place of rendezvous, the agent proceeds on horseback to the part of the country he desires to go, then selecting some of the tribe, generally a married man with his family, as they are more easily handled, he opens up negotiations, tells his mission, what he proposes to pay them and what they will have to do.

This may turn out all right, but when they are told they are to come thousands of miles to this country—which they have never heard of—they almost run away with fright.

RISKY WORK.

Other tribes, not so timid, sometimes show fight, thinking the agent's intentions are to carry them into slavery. All kind of evil things are attributed to the unfortunate agent, who in many cases goes in quest of those people at the risk of his life.

However, succeeding in getting a few of them, he returns to his base of supplies and intrusting the natives to the care of one of his assistants, he starts again the next week or month to another distant country in search of other tribes, bringing the people back and placing them in charge with his assistants as with the others. Frequently by the time he has returned with the second or third contingent, the first will have become frightened by absurd stories they have heard and taken flight, so that another trip will have to be made to the country from where they were procured.

Time and again has this thing occurred, so that it was thought almost impossible to secure enough people to make a congress of them. But after exactly twelve months a large number have been secured.

A CURIOUS ASSEMBLAGE.

There are Cossacks from the Czar's dominions, Amazons from Dahomey, Siamese, Mongolian and Tartar of the Buddhist religion; Singhalese, from the Island of Ceylon, of the Aryan race; Javanese, both Malay and aboriginal, who are Mohammedans; pure Malays, from the Island of Singapore; Klings, from Madras, India; Hindoos, who are low caste; Sikhs, from Panjaub, India; high caste Hindoos, and Burmese, both Tartars and Aryans.

Other nations and tribes represented will include Nubians, Algerians, Syrians, Esquimaux, Papuans, Australians, Samoans, Dyaks, New Zealanders, Todas, Afghans, Soudanese, Matabeles, Japanese, Sandwich Islanders, Polynesians, Polyandrous people, cannibals and boomerang casters.

IN NATIVE HOUSES.

The natives will live in houses similar to those in their respective native lands. In some cases where it is practicable the houses will be brought along entire, and when that is out of the question the material only will be brought and the houses built here. There will also be shown the agricultural and household implements and the weapons of war and for the hunt peculiar to each tribe.

The following extracts from a letter written recently by Mr. Gaylord, in Singapore, to Mr. Bailey may prove interesting in that it shows just how the work of gathering the congress has been carried on:

OF MANY BELIEFS.

"Enclosed find photos of some of the natives who are engaged for the 'Congress.' They will also constitute a 'Religious Congress,' for they represent Buddhism, Hindooism, Mohammedans and Pagans. They are all couples, with some children. You will have the best collection of the different divisions of the Aryan, Mongolian, Tartar, Malayan and Papuan races ever seen.

"We also have secured material for houses all ready to put up; also agricultural and domestic utensils, tools, b[e]ats, &c., and two jinrikshas. We are almost certain of getting the Australians and Dyaks, as we have made contracts with responsible and reliable parties who are sure to get them, as we pay them liberally if they succeed.

TRANSPORTATION PROBLEMS.

"I may be obliged to land them in New York before you need them, as the steamers direct to New York are so irregular and not all of them will carry the natives. I shall try and have them at New York in ample time to open.

"The small elephant[s] and ponies will go by the first safe steamer. I think the Hankow will take them, and furnish safe and warm accommodations. You know enough about ocean travel to know that it would be simply suicide to ship them on the open deck across the Atlantic in midwinter.

"We now have three small elephants, five pairs Bali buffaloes, one Indian gaur (tame), one axis cow antelope (tame), four axis deer, four cassowaries, thirty black baboons or tailless monkeys and twenty small ponies. The young rhinoceros we lost. They could not get him down to the sea shore, so shot him. We are expecting another soon. The steamer we expected to ship by came in late at night and left at once. The captain refused to remain long enough to get the animals on board. The steamer that followed had no safe place to put them.

"REST EASY"

"You can rest easy regarding the natives. You will have a much better lot than has ever been seen. The houses in some case will have to be built, as the kind of houses, in some places could not be moved. We have got different kinds of bamboo and atap houses [enough] to have one house for each group of four. The houses will be small, six by eight feet and six feet high. They can easily be put up and taken down and will not occupy much space and not be heavy." (*New York Herald,* 18 February 1894, 10D.)

THE BARNUM AND BAILEY SHOW.

The great Barnum and Bailey circus has come and gone and it will be a year before the youngsters of Orange will again see it. The show, while in the main the same as those of the past, had new features. Everything passed off with clock-like precision, and there was the same systematic organization and perfection of discipline which has characterized the show in past years. The street parade came off within a short time of the advertised hour, and the people and children were spared the long and tedious waits on the street incident to smaller shows. The street parade was longer and finer than ever before and contained many new features. Some idea of it can be obtained from the statement that 258 horses were used in it. The usual two entertainments were given. A matinee at 2 o'clock and the evening performance at 8 o'clock. At both the tent was well filled. At the evening performance the huge tent, which has a seating capacity of 14,000, was nearly full. The attractions in the shape of the natives from rare and strange tribes of people is much larger this year than ever before and these were objects of universal interest. The menagerie and all the other departments were unusually full and interesting. But the interest centered in the circus proper, where the performances in three rings and two stages between them were kept going without waits. The features of the great show, the hippodrome races, the equestrian performances in the rings, the wonderful trapeze work and the juggling and acrobatic acts were all of the best, while the aquatic act with which the performance closed was a wonderful exhibition of daring. The dive into the tank of water only about six feet deep was from the extreme top of the tent, an actual distance of thirty-eight feet from the ground, and it was thrilling in the extreme. The riding of Miss Josie Ashton, the principal equestrian rider, was exceptionally good.

She is an Orange woman, and her name was Miss Josephine Gulder. Her mother resides on Lakeside avenue. She is now the wife of Frank Melville, the well known rider. Clarence E. Dean is the advance agent of the show, and W.J. Rouse accompanies the show as the press agent. Both were more than usually polite and courteous in the discharge of their duties. (*Orange Chronicle*, 11 May 1895, 6.)

David Henderson's burlesque Aladdin, Jr. *premiered in Chicago on 7 June 1894 and later toured the West Coast before returning East to St. Louis, Detroit, Buffalo and Boston. It opened in New York at the Broadway Theatre on 8 April 1895. One week later, the play* Trilby *had its New York debut and was a tremendous success. To keep his burlesque up-to-date, Henderson incorporated some additional scenes into his show that lampooned the new hit. These were filmed in late April at the earliest, when these scenes were introduced, and almost certainly after May 9th, the day Barnum & Bailey's Circus performed before Edison's kinetograph. Correspondingly, these films were made before the show's return to Chicago on May 19th.*

135 Trilby Hypnotic Scene / Hypnotic Scene (burlesque)
LENGTH: 50 ft.   © No reg.
PRODUCER: William Heise.
CAMERA: William Heise.
CAST:
PRODUCTION DATE: [10-19 May 1895.]
LOCATION: Black Maria, West Orange, N.J.
SOURCE: *Aladdin, Jr.* (burlesque).
DESCRIPTION: Svengali hypnotizes every one in sight, and causes them to go through sundry burlesque performances. Very popular. (Ohio Phonograph Co., *The Edison Kinetoscope. Price List*, August 1895, 9.)
SUBJECT: Burlesque–performances. Hypnoticism. David Henderson.
ARCHIVE:
CITATIONS: *New York Herald*, 10 May 1896, 6F; Raff & Gammon to Exhibition Department, invoice, 20 June 1895, 1:540, MH-BA. Maguire & Baucus, *Edison Films*, 20 January 1897, 7; Maguire & Baucus, *Edison and International Photographic Films*, April 1897, 10; Maguire & Baucus, *Fall Catalogue*, 1897, 14.
NOTE:

136 Trilby Death Scene / Death Scene (comic)
LENGTH: 50 ft.   © No reg.
PRODUCER: William Heise.
CAMERA: William Heise.
CAST:
PRODUCTION DATE: [10-19 May 1895.]
LOCATION: Black Maria, West Orange, N.J.
SOURCE: *Aladdin, Jr.* (burlesque).
DESCRIPTION: From David Henderson's Burlesque. Representing Trilby, Svengali and the Laird. Svengali hypnotizes Trilby and the Laird, then falls dead across a table. Very funny. The dramatis personae of this act are made up in exact imitation of the illustrations given in Du Maurier's book. (Ohio Phonograph Co., *The Edison Kinetoscope. Price List*, August 1895, 8.)
From the dramatization of the famous "Trilby." (F.Z. Maguire & Co., *Catalogue*, [March 1898], 31.)
SUBJECT: Burlesque–performances. Dancing. David Henderson.
ARCHIVE:
CITATIONS: Raff & Gammon to Michigan Electric Co., invoice, 6 September 1895, 1:614, MH-BA. Maguire & Baucus, *Edison Films*, 20 January 1897, 6; Maguire & Baucus, *Edison and International Photographic Films*, April 1897, 6; Maguire & Baucus, *Fall Catalogue*, 1897, 11.
NOTE:

137 Quartette / Trilby Quartette
LENGTH: 50 ft.   © No reg.

PRODUCER: William Heise.
CAMERA: William Heise.
CAST:
PRODUCTION DATE: [10-19 May 1895.]
LOCATION: Black Maria, West Orange, N.J.
SOURCE: *Aladdin, Jr.* (burlesque).
DESCRIPTION: The latest. Burlesque from David Henderson's "Aladdin, Jr." A decided hit. (Ohio Phonograph Co., *The Edison Kinetoscope. Price List*, August 1895, 7.)
SUBJECT: Burlesque–performances. David Henderson.
ARCHIVE:
CITATIONS: *New York Clipper*, 4 May 1895, 134; Raff & Gammon to Exhibition Department, invoice, 20 June 1895, 1:540, MH-BA; List of Films Shipped to Atlanta, Sept. 4, 1895, MH-BA.
NOTE:

Broadway Theatre–*Aladdin, Jr.* entered on May 6, upon the fifth week and last fortnight of its run. Among the many new features added to it during its stay here the Trilby quadrille has proven the most attractive. The burlesque has evidently found many admirers here, for its business has been satisfactory. (*New York Clipper*, 11 May 1895, 150.)

138 Muscle Dance
LENGTH: 50 and 150 ft.   © No reg.
PRODUCER: [Kinetoscope Exhibiting Company.]
CAMERA: William Heise.
CAST:
PRODUCTION DATE: By September 1895.
LOCATION: Black Maria, West Orange, N.J.
SOURCE:
DESCRIPTION:
SUBJECT: Vaudeville–performances. Dancing. Danse du ventre.
ARCHIVE:
CITATIONS: List of Films Shipped to Atlanta, Sept. 4, 1895, MH-BA.
NOTE: The Muscle dance was also known as the couchee-couchee or Oriental dance. See the photograph of large capacity kinetoscopes in a saloon reproduced in Musser's *The Emergence of Cinema*, 85: one machine features *Muscle Dance*.

In late July Theodore Robert Heise, William Heise's son and camera assistant, was sent to London to take films with a kinetograph for the Continental Commerce Company. (William E. Gilmore to Thomas A. Edison, 15 July 1895, TAEP, 135:0878.) Young Heise was to bring them back to West Orange for development, but his trip was a failure and there are no known subjects that came from this undertaking. (Miller to Gilmore, 28 August 1895, TAEP, 135:0886.)

Annabelle Whitford returned for the third of her four documented appearances before Edison's kinetograph in the spring or summer of 1895.

139 *Annabelle Serpentine Dance / Serpentine Dance / Annabelle Serpentine / [Annabelle Serpentine Dance, no. 3]*
LENGTH: 50 ft.   © No reg.
PRODUCER: William Heise, Continental Commerce Company.
CAMERA: William Heise.
CAST: Annabelle Whitford.
PRODUCTION DATE: April-August 1895.
LOCATION: Black Maria, West Orange, N.J.
SOURCE: *Annabelle Serpentine Dance* (Edison film no. 49, August 1894).
DESCRIPTION: By the famous "Annabelle." These dances are among the finest for the effects of costume, light and shade, and are very popular. (Ohio Phonograph Co., *The Edison Kinetoscope. Price List*, August 1895, 7.)
SUBJECT: Vaudeville–performances. Dancing.
ARCHIVE: DLC-AFI, UkLNFA.

CITATIONS: Maguire & Baucus, *Edison Films*, 20 January 1897, 7; Maguire & Baucus, *Edison and International Photographic Films*, April 1897, 3.
NOTE:

40 ***Annabelle Butterfly Dance / Butterfly Dance / Annabelle Butterfly / [Annabelle Butterfly Dance, no. 3]***
LENGTH: 50 ft.   © No reg.
PRODUCER: William Heise, Continental Commerce Company.
CAMERA: William Heise.
CAST: Annabelle Whitford.
PRODUCTION DATE: April-August 1895.
LOCATION: Black Maria, West Orange, N.J.
SOURCE: *Annabelle Butterfly Dance* (Edison film no. 48, August 1894).
DESCRIPTION: By the famous "Annabelle." These dances are among the finest for the effects of costume, light and shade, and are very popular. (Ohio Phonograph Co., *The Edison Kinetoscope. Price List*, August 1895, 7.)
SUBJECT: Vaudeville–performances. Dancing.
ARCHIVE: NNMoMA.
CITATIONS: Maguire & Baucus, *Edison Films*, 20 January 1897, 6; Maguire & Baucus, *Edison and International Photographic Films*, April 1897, 3; Maguire & Baucus, Fall Catalogue, 1897, 11; *Edison Films,* March 1900, 28.
NOTE:

41 **Annabelle Sun Dance / Sun Dance / Annabelle Sun / [Annabelle Sun Dance, no. 3]**
LENGTH: 50 ft.   © No reg.
PRODUCER: William Heise, Continental Commerce Company.
CAMERA: William Heise.
CAST: Annabelle Whitford.
PRODUCTION DATE: April-August 1895.
LOCATION: Black Maria, West Orange, N.J.
SOURCE: *Annabelle Sun Dance* (Edison film no. 50, August 1894).
DESCRIPTION: By the famous "Annabelle." These dances are among the finest for the effects of costume, light and shade, and are very popular. (Ohio Phonograph Co., *The Edison Kinetoscope. Price List*, August 1895, 7.)
SUBJECT: Vaudeville–performances. Dancing.
ARCHIVE:
CITATIONS: Maguire & Baucus, *Edison Films*, 20 January 1897, 6; Maguire & Baucus, *Edison and International Photographic Films*, April 1897, 3.
NOTE:

42 ***The Execution of Mary, Queen of Scots / Execution***
LENGTH: 50 ft.   © No reg.
PRODUCER: Alfred Clark, Raff & Gammon.
CAMERA: William Heise.
CAST: Robert Thomae (Mary).
PRODUCTION DATE: 28 August 1895.
LOCATION: Edison Laboratory, West Orange, N.J.
SOURCE:
DESCRIPTION: A realistic reproduction of this famous historical scene. Costumes of the period, and shows beheading of the ill-fated Queen. (F.Z. Maguire & Co., *Catalogue,* [March 1898], 29.)
SUBJECT: Historical reenactments. Executions and executioners. Mary, Queen of Scots.

ARCHIVE: NNMoMA, DLC.

CITATIONS: Raff & Gammon to Columbia Phonograph Company, invoice, 23 September 1895, 1:682, MH-BA. Maguire & Baucus, *Edison and International Photographic Films*, April 1897, 7; Maguire & Baucus, *Fall Catalogue*, 1897, 11.

NOTE:

143 *Joan of Arc / Burning of Joan of Arc

LENGTH: 50 ft.   © No reg.

PRODUCER: Alfred Clark, Raff & Gammon.

CAMERA: William Heise.

CAST:

PRODUCTION DATE: 28 August 1895.

LOCATION: Edison Laboratory, West Orange, N.J.

SOURCE:

DESCRIPTION: Representing the burning of the Maid of Orleans. Costumes of the period. A realistic historical subject. (F.Z. Maguire & Co., *Catalogue*, [March 1898], 29.)

SUBJECT: Historical reenactments. Executions and executioners. Joan of Arc, Saint.

ARCHIVE: CaOOANF.

CITATIONS: Raff & Gammon to L.F. Douglas, invoice, 16 October 1895, 1:68[4], MH-BA. Maguire & Baucus, *Edison and International Photographic Films*, April 1897, 10; Maguire & Baucus, *Fall Catalogue*, 1897, 12.

NOTE:

The Leigh Sisters appeared at Keith's Union Square Theatre for the week commencing 29 January 1894 and at the Casino Roof Garden from 10 June into early September 1895, billed as novelty dancers (sharing the stage with the "Passing Show Pickaninnies" formerly known as Lucy Daly's Pickaninnies). They toured the West Coast during much of the 1895-96 theatrical season with The Passing Show.

144 *Umbrella Dance / Umbrella

LENGTH: 50 ft.   © No reg.

PRODUCER: Alfred Clark, Raff & Gammon.

CAMERA: William Heise.

CAST: Edna Leigh, Stella Leigh (Leigh Sisters).

PRODUCTION DATE: [September 1895.]

LOCATION: Black Maria, West Orange, N.J.

SOURCE: *The Passing Show* (revue).

DESCRIPTION: Then two smiling blondes danced under a big umbrella. First they danced with the umbrella over their heads, and their short skirts swayed and their white slippers twinkled. Then the umbrella was whirled in front of them, and only their white feet were seen underneath. They danced out of its shield and their dresses changed colors—not both the same color, but two different colors. ("The Vitascope at Keith's," *Boston Herald*, 19 May 1896.)

A very novel and attractive subject for a projecting machine, by the Leigh Sisters. Has proved very popular. Especially attractive when colored. (*Edison Films*, March 1900, 29.)

SUBJECT: Vaudeville–performances. Dancing. Umbrellas. Motion pictures–colored.

ARCHIVE:

CITATIONS: Raff & Gammon to Columbia Phonograph Co., invoice, 23 September 1895, 1:635, MH-BA; *New York Clipper*, 4 January 1896, 694. Maguire & Baucus, *Edison Films*, 20 January 1897, 6; Maguire & Baucus, *Edison and International Photographic Films*, April 1897, 16; Maguire & Baucus, *Fall Catalogue*, 1897, 13; F.Z. Maguire & Co., *Catalogue*, [March 1898], 27.

NOTE: One of the films shown at Koster & Bial's Music Hall, on opening night of the Vitascope, 23 April 1896. This film was seen recently at John E. Allen, Inc. but was subsequently misplaced.

45 Trilby Dance / Acrobatic Dance

LENGTH: 50 ft.   © No reg.
PRODUCER: Alfred Clark, Raff & Gammon.
CAMERA: William Heise.
CAST: Edna Leigh, Stella Leigh (Leigh Sisters).
PRODUCTION DATE: [September 1895.]
LOCATION: Black Maria, West Orange, N.J.
SOURCE: *The Passing Show* (revue).
DESCRIPTION: The Leigh Sisters Acrobatic Act in which these beautiful young ladies with amazing and startling abandon turn somersault and display their graceful forms is unique and startling. (Raff & Gammon, *List of New Subjects,* in Hendricks notes.)

A graceful acrobatic dance by the famous Leigh Sisters. (Maguire & Baucus, *Edison and International Photographic Films,* April 1897, 15.)
SUBJECT: Vaudeville–performances. Dancing.
ARCHIVE:
CITATIONS: Maguire & Baucus, *Edison Films,* 20 January 1897, 6; Maguire & Baucus, *Fall Catalogue,* 1897, 13; F.Z. Maguire & Co., *Catalogue,* [March 1898], 27.
NOTE:

Casino Roof Garden...One of the novelties to be presented here tomorrow night is a Trilby dance by the Misses Leigh, which they will execute with bare feet. (*New York World*, 16 June 1895.)

Casino Roof Garden...and the Sisters Leigh in their sensational and popular bare-legged Trilby dance. (*New York World*, 18 August 1895.)

EDNA LEIGH

Who as one of the Leigh Sisters has become well known in the realms of farce comedy and vaudeville, was born in Louisville, Ky., and, with her sister, made her professional debut five years ago, in a production of "Babes in the Woods" at Niblo's, this city. Since that time she has appeared in farce comedy productions, and between road seasons has played many of the principal variety houses of the country. Her first road engagement was with Charles A. Loder, in "Oh! What a Night!" and she afterwards appeared with Charles E. Blaney's "A Summer Blizzard;" with Donnelly and Girard, in "The Rainmakers," and last season went to the Pacific coast as a member of "The Passing Show" Co. During this time her dancing has been received with favor, a natural aptitude for that line of work, and a spirit of enterprise in developing new ideas, maintaining the specialty done by herself and sister in popular demand. She possesses an attractive face and figure, is active and graceful, and has gained an enviable position in the profession. (*New York Clipper*, 25 July 1896, 326.)

Lola Yberri, billed as a Spanish dancer and high kicker from the Crystal Palace in London, performed at New York's Eden Musee on 16 October 1893 and remained there until the end of the 1893-94 theatrical season. She appeared at the American Roof Garden that summer and continued to do her Spanish dances in and around New York for the next several seasons.

LOLA YBERRI
AMERICAN
ROOF
GARDEN

46 Cyclone / Cyclone Dance

LENGTH: 50 ft.   © No reg.
PRODUCER: Alfred Clark, Raff & Gammon.
CAMERA: William Heise.
CAST: Lolo or Lola Yberri (Dolores Santa-Maria Yberri).
PRODUCTION DATE: [September 1895.]
LOCATION: Black Maria, West Orange, N.J.
SOURCE:

DESCRIPTION: Spanish dance by Senorita Lola Yberri. (Maguire & Baucus, *Edison and International Photographic Films*, April 1897, 5.)

SUBJECT: Vaudeville–performances. Dancing. Spaniards.

ARCHIVE:

CITATIONS: *New York Herald*, 22 July 1894, 6D (with illustration). Maguire & Baucus, *Fall Catalogue*, 1897, 11; F.Z. Maguire & Co., *Catalogue*, [March 1898], 27.

NOTE:

147 Fan Dance (Spanish dance)

LENGTH: 50 ft.   © No reg.

PRODUCER: Alfred Clark, Raff & Gammon.

CAMERA: William Heise.

CAST: Lolo or Lola Yberri (Dolores Santa-Maria Yberri).

PRODUCTION DATE: [September 1895.]

LOCATION: Black Maria, West Orange, N.J.

SOURCE:

DESCRIPTION: Characterisitc Spanish dance by Senorita Lola Yberri. (Maguire & Baucus, *Edison and International Photographic Films*, April 1897, 8.)

SUBJECT: Vaudeville–performances. Dancing. Spaniards.

ARCHIVE:

CITATIONS: *New York Herald*, 22 July 1894, 6D (with illustration). Maguire & Baucus, *Fall Catalogue*, 1897, 12; F.Z. Maguire, *Catalogue*, [March 1898], 27.

NOTE:

Another dance will be brought out by Lolo Yberri at Eden Musée this week–a typical Spanish one. The step varies from the graceful slow and wavelike movements of the Spanish glide to the rapid, vivacious action in the castanet and tambourine dances. Yberri's mantilla will be of red lined with yellow, the Spanish colors. (*New York Herald*, 20 May 1894, 2E.)

SPANISH DANCERS QUARREL.
Senoritas Tortajada and Yberri Come to Blows Over a Question of Stage Costume.
TWO CLOAKS THE CAUSE OF IT ALL.
Jealousy, However, Is Said by Those Who Know To Have Been at the Bottom of the Difficulty.
LAWSUITS ARE THREATENED.

Senorita Consuelo Tortajada, the première danseuse at the Eden Musée, no longer dances in wild abandon the fandango and the Habanera.

She lies on a bed of pain and tells of the treatment she received on Tuesday night at the hands of at least one of the directors of the Eden Musée, and perhaps more. This trouble is the result of the jealousies of women.

Senorita Tortajada is a Spaniard who dances with all the passion of her race. To her a Spanish cloak, which she whirled and swirled as a skirt depending from the neck, was a natural feature of her dance.

Her cloak was made of red satin lined with blue and trimmed with gold braid. She never failed to reap a harvest of bravos when she placed the cloak into circulation. Her engagement was renewed again and again as much upon the strength and vigor of the cloak as anything else she did. Her cloak became famous. It covered a multitude of pesetas.

THE RIVAL APPEARS.

The cloak begot rivals as well as coin. Senorita Lola Yberri, a secondo at the Eden Musée, who speaks English much better than Spanish and dances like an American, had a cloak made precisely like Senorita Tortajada's. It was also of red satin, but lined with yellow. She whisked it about in her mad American way in imitation of the pretty Barcelonienne. Senorita Lola danced before Senorita Consuelo and her imitation cloak took much of the premiere's prestige.

Senorita Tortajada complained, therefore, on Tuesday afternoon and laid her grievances before the directors of the Eden Musée. She complained that her methods and costume were being hypothecated and declared that she would have no more of it. Like wise men the directors temporized and assured the Spaniard that the obnoxious cloak of Senorita Yberri should be removed.

So night came, and with it the performance. Like Carmencita and a hundred other Spanish heroines, Consuelo lurked in the wings, watching for her rival, Lola. She came out of her dressing room, wearing the same imitation cloak.

With a bound Consuelo had seized the spurious garment and dragged it off her rival. The Americo-Spaniard screamed and fell back. A large negress who attended her and carried her fan smote the Senorita a smart blow across the cheek. Blind with pain and rage Senorita Tortajada fell into the grasp of Director Pomeroy, who, she says, gave her so sharp a twist that the danseuse fell against a box and hurt her side. She immediately retired from the theatre assisted by her family and friends and cancelled her engagement with the Eden Musée.

CONSUELO IN BED.

In order to verify the details of this tragic story I visited Senorita Tortajada yesterday afternoon. I was admitted to the injured senorita's room. There, propped up on pillows and with eyes dancing with rage, lay the broken reed of the Musée ballet.

Her mother, her husband, her sister and two sympathizing friends sat about the bed. The sufferer showed me a scarred ear as a result of the fan blow. The mother took down from a hook on the wall a fur paletot tattered and torn as the result of Director Pomeroy's alleged violence.

Senorita Tortajada described the alleged assault with more vehemence and gesture than one could expect from any but a Spanish invalid. Her relatives and friends interjected many Spanish remarks and proverbs. The Senorita's mother at last produced the ill-fated cloak and placed it about her shoulders.

She assured me that she had already secured a lawyer and proposed to sue Senor Pomeroy to the full extent of the law. She also produced a doctor's certificate relative to her injuries and state of nerves.

THE OTHER SIDE OF THE STORY.

Afterward I heard Senorita Yberri's version of the trouble. She belied her Spanish name somewhat by saying to me frankly:–

"Say! I was never in a 'scrap' before, but I hate to get hit in the back."

She then said that she had been at the Eden Musée for ten months, while Torta Jada had only been there for three months.

"I have been billed as the Spanish dancing wonder," she exclaimed, "and I knew that my Spanish dances killed hers. On Tuesday night I was already to go on with my cloak, which really doesn't resemble hers a bit, when I felt my cloak snatched off and I was hit in the back.

"Managers Crane and Pomeroy then interfered and got between us, for the woman was white with rage. My maid Tillie–or Juanita Myorga, rather–came up with a big umbrella to fight. Pomeroy said, 'Go on, Miss Yberri.' I said, 'How can I?'

"I then went on the stage, went on with my dance and took a curtain."

"Poor Mr. Pomeroy! She says he struck her in the ribs. He didn't do anything of the sort."

The management stated frankly last night that it was all a question of woman's jealousy. Miss Yberri seems to have more friends at court, and therefore the Torta Jada has been discharged.

Miss Yberri's manager says he will have Senorita Torta Jada put under bonds to keep the peace and got a warrant for her, but the court officer found the fair Spaniard in bed and there the matter rests.

Senor Pomeroy declined to be seen or spoken to on the subject, but let it be known through others that he deeply regretted the whole occurrence. (*New York Herald*, 24 May 1894, 6.)

Alfred Clark organized the filming of a second group of historical subjects, most of which featured sensational American situations.

148 Duel between Two Historical Characters

LENGTH: 50 ft. © No reg.
PRODUCER: Alfred Clark, Raff & Gammon.
CAMERA: William Heise.
CAST:
PRODUCTION DATE: [Late September 1895.]
LOCATION: Edison Laboratory, West Orange, N.J.
SOURCE:
DESCRIPTION:
SUBJECT: Historical reenactments. Dueling.
ARCHIVE:
CITATIONS: Raff & Gammon to Smiles & Carter, invoice, 14 October 1895, 1:82, MH-BA.
NOTE:

149 A Frontier Scene / Lynching Scene

LENGTH: 50 ft. © No reg.
PRODUCER: Alfred Clark, Raff & Gammon.
CAMERA: William Heise.
CAST:
PRODUCTION DATE: [Late September 1895.]

LOCATION: Edison Laboratory, West Orange, N.J.

SOURCE:

DESCRIPTION: Lynching of a horse thief by a band of cowboys. A typical frontier scene. (F.Z. Maguire & Co., *Catalogue,* [March 1898], 29.)

SUBJECT: Historical reenactments. Lynchings. Executions and executioners. Criminals. Cowboys.

ARCHIVE:

CITATIONS: Raff & Gammon to L.F. Douglas, invoice, 28 October 1895, 1:695, MH-BA. Maguire & Baucus, *Edison and International Photographic Films*, April 1897, 11; Maguire & Baucus, *Fall Catalogue*, 1897, 12.

NOTE:

150 Indian Scalping Scene / Scalping Scene

LENGTH: 50 ft.   © No reg.

PRODUCER: Alfred Clark, Raff & Gammon.

CAMERA: William Heise.

CAST:

PRODUCTION DATE: [Late September 1895.]

LOCATION: Edison Laboratory, West Orange, N.J.

SOURCE:

DESCRIPTION: A settler pursued, overtaken and scalped by Indians. (Maguire & Baucus, *Fall Catalogue*, 1897, 13.)

SUBJECT: Historical reenactments. Indians of North America. Battles.

ARCHIVE:

CITATIONS: Raff & Gammon to L.F. Douglas, invoice, 28 October 1895, 1:695, MH-BA. Maguire & Baucus, *Edison and International Photographic Films*, April 1897, 15; Maguire & Baucus, *Fall Catalogue*, 1897, 12; F.Z. Maguire & Co., *Catalogue*, [March 1898], 29.

NOTE:

151 Rescue of Capt. John Smith by Pocahontas / Pocahontas / Pocahontas Rescuing Capt. John Smith

LENGTH: 50 ft.   © No reg.

PRODUCER: Alfred Clark, Raff & Gammon.

CAMERA: William Heise.

CAST:

PRODUCTION DATE: [Late September 1895.]

LOCATION: Edison Laboratory, West Orange, N.J.

SOURCE:

DESCRIPTION: A fine representation of the Indian princess saving the life of Captain John Smith. Interesting and historical. (F.Z. Maguire & Co., *Catalogue*, [March 1898], 29.)

SUBJECT: Historical reenactments. Indians of North America. Executions and executioners. English. Pocahontas. John Smith.

ARCHIVE:

CITATIONS: Maguire & Baucus, *Edison and International Photographic Films*, April 1897, 14; Maguire & Baucus, *Fall Catalogue*, 1897, 13.

NOTE:

By the fall of 1895, the fading popularity of Edison's kinetoscope had brought film production to a halt. Filmmaking would not resume until the following year, with the arrival of projection.

As Raff & Gammon prepared to market "Edison's Vitascope"—a motion picture projector invented by C. Francis Jenkins and Thomas Armat, which was then being manufactured in Edison's factories—they recognized the need for an array of new motion picture subjects. Film production resumed in March and in May, the Edison Manufacturing Company had introduced a new, portable camera, freeing production from the limits of the Black Maria and laboratory grounds. By summer they were filming Niagara Falls and Coney Island, as well as scenes of marching street sweepers, the annual Asbury Park baby parade, and Chinese Viceroy Li Hung Chang.

Nonetheless, the first films that the Edison crew made for projection were very much like those made for the peep-hole kinetoscope. Raff & Gammon brought several dancers to the Black Maria on a wintery day in late March. There they cavorted before the kinetograph, with considerable reluctance given the chilly weather.

Amy Muller, novelty dancer, was one of the features of Robert G. Morris' Empire City Stars Co. during the 1894-95 season. She worked more irregularly during 1895-1896, filling a two-week engagement at Carncross' Theatre in Philadelphia during January 1896 and dancing in the New Imperial Theatre in Chicago during part of April 1896.

152 *Amy Muller

LENGTH: 50 and 150 ft.   © No reg.
PRODUCER: Raff & Gammon.
CAMERA: William Heise.
CAST: Amy Muller.
PRODUCTION DATE: [24 March 1896.]
LOCATION: Black Maria, West Orange, N.J.
SOURCE:

DESCRIPTION: The best colored picture yet shown in the Vitascope was the Amy Muller fantastic toe dance, one of those put on yesterday. Almost every movement of the agile and graceful figure displays some new color, till the whole thing begins to assume a kaleidoscopic aspect. (*Boston Herald*, 30 June 1896, 9.)

A beautiful fantastic toe dance. A good subject colored. (F.Z. Maguire & Co., *Catalogue*, [March 1898], 27 and 28.)

SUBJECT: Vaudeville–performances. Dancing. Motion pictures–colored.
ARCHIVE: NR-GE, DLC-Hendricks, CLAc.
CITATIONS: Raff & Gammon to Gilmore, 25 March 1896. Maguire & Baucus, *Edison Films*, 20 January 1897, 6; Maguire & Baucus, *Edison and International Photographic Films*, April 1897, 3 and 17; Maguire & Baucus, *Fall Catalogue*, 1897, 11.
NOTE:

153 Dolorita Passion Dance / Dolorita / Dolarita [sic]

LENGTH: 50 ft.   © No reg.
PRODUCER: Raff & Gammon.
CAMERA: William Heise.
CAST: Dolorita.
PRODUCTION DATE: [24 March 1896.]

LOCATION: Black Maria, West Orange, N.J.
SOURCE:
DESCRIPTION: A characteristic midway dancer. (Maguire & Baucus, *Edison and International Photographic Films*, April 1897, 7.)

Musicians are seated, playing, while the graceful Dolorita dances. It is the Danse-du-Ventre, the famous Oriental muscle dance. (*The Phonoscope*, January 1899, 15.)

SUBJECT: Vaudeville—performances. Dancing. Danse du ventre.
CITATIONS: Raff & Gammon to W.D. Stansifer, 6 May 1896, MH-BA. Maguire & Baucus, *Fall Catalogue*, 1897, 11; *Edison Films,* July 1901, 52.
ARCHIVE:
NOTE: In any case, this film had been shot by the beginning of May 1896.

A press screening of for the vitascope was held at the Edison Laboratory on 3 April 1896. Edison was the master of ceremony, and Thomas Armat, while present, stayed discretely in the background. ("Life-less Skirt Dancers," New York Journal, 4 April 1896, scrapbook, MH-BA.)

The first editorial cartoon for the screen commented on a territorial dispute that erupted between England and Venezuela in the first months of 1896. It involved the boundary between Venezuela and the colony of British Guiana. After Great Britain threatened the South American nation, the United States intervened, encouraging England to agree to a mediated settlement.

154 The Monroe Doctrine / Venezuela Case
LENGTH: 50 ft.   © No reg.
PRODUCER: Raff & Gammon.
CAMERA: William Heise.
CAST: [Charles F. Walton and John Mayon.]
PRODUCTION DATE: By mid-April 1896.
LOCATION: Black Maria, West Orange, N.J.
SOURCE:
DESCRIPTION: Shows John Bull bombarding a South American shore, supposedly to represent Venezuela. John is seemingly getting the better of the argument when the tall lanky figure of Uncle Sam emerges from the back of the picture. He grasps John Bull by the neck, forces him to his knees and makes him take off his hat to Venezuela. (*Boston Herald*, 17 May 1896, 32.)

Burlesque. Uncle Sam teaching John Bull a lesson. (F.Z. Maguire & Co., *Catalogue*, [March 1898], 31.)

SUBJECT: Editorial Cartoons. Monroe Doctrine. United States—Foreign Relations—Latin America.
ARCHIVE:
CITATIONS: "Will Enforce the Monroe Doctrine," *New York Herald*, 14 March 1895, 6; *New York Daily News*, 24 April 1896, scrapbook, MH-BA.
NOTE: Gordon Hendricks tentatively identified the performers in this picture as Walton & Mayon. This is one of the films shown at the premiere of Edison's Vitascope at Koster & Bial's Music Hall, 23 April 1896.

Which Monroe Doctrine?

The Connecticut republicans have made the profound Bunsbyan deliverances that "we believe in maintaining the flag of America" and "we believe in the Monroe doctrine."

These broad utterances are perfectly safe, since it would be difficult to find any American who does not share the sentiments expressed.

But what Monroe doctrine is it in which belief is thus declared? There has come to be a great variety of these doctrines. That proclaimed by Monroe and maintained by our statesmen of former years was that the United States would not look with unconcern upon any foreign monarchical encroachment dangerous to our national peace or safety. But the latter day jingo version would extend the doctrine to every trivial boundary dispute which does not concern us and thus make it a mere pretext for fomenting foreign entanglements.

The Connecticut republicans are discreetly silent as to what particular Monroe doctrine they believe in. (*New York Herald*, 23 April 1896, 10.)

TRIUMPH OF THE MONROE DOCTRINE.
President Cleveland and Secretary Olney Score One of the Signal
Victories of American Diplomacy in the Venezuelan Question.
SUPREME ON THE CONTINENT.
Far Reaching Effort of Great Britain's Concessions as to Disputed Lands in Guiana.
ARBITRATION TO CONTROL ALL.
Fifty years Decided as the Limit of Occupation in the Settled Delta Districts.
THE TERMS OF THE TREATY.
Complete Confirmation of the Herald's Exclusive Report of the Final Arrangements.
...Washington. Nov. 10, 1896.
In the Herald of October 17 last the announcement was exclusively made that a definite understanding had been made between Great Britain and the United States on all the main questions involved in the Venezuelan boundary dispute. It was also stated that the President would be able to announce in his annual message to Congress an amicable settlement of the long pending controversy through the medium of arbitration.

It was then stated in the course of a long despatch that Sir Julian Pauncefote was coming to this country with instructions authorizing him to close up the details of an arbitration treaty, and that the main point to be considered in the late negotiations related to the adjustment of the differences between the countries involved as to the contending governments jurisdiction over their respective settled districts in the disputed territory.

The Herald's News Confirmed.
There is now ample official confirmation of every statement that was made in the Herald at that time....If the Venezuelan dispute has done nothing else it has forced the admission from the foremost nation of Europe that on the American continent the United States is supreme....(*New York Herald,* 11 November 1896, 11.)

Norman Raff and Frank Gammon hired former kinetoscope exhibitor James H. White in mid-April 1896. White quickly became one of their key employees, overseeing the productions of films.

May Irwin and John C. Rice were the two principal actors appearing in the New York stage hit The Widow Jones, *which was performed for the first time on 19 August 1895 at Brockton, Mass. and opened in New York at the Bijou Theatre on 16 September 1895. They staged their kiss for Edison's camera at the behest of the* New York World. *The resulting* May Irwin Kiss *was the most popular film to be shown in Edison's vitascope during 1896.*

155 *May Irwin Kiss / Kiss Scene / Kiss
LENGTH: 50 ft.   © No reg.
PRODUCER: *New York World.*
CAMERA: William Heise.
CAST: May Irwin, John C. Rice (John C. Hilburg).
PRODUCTION DATE: Mid-April 1896.
LOCATION: Black Maria, West Orange, N.J.
SOURCE: *The Widow Jones* (musical comedy).
DESCRIPTION: By May Irwin and John Rice. This subject has met with unequaled success, and is the most popular ever shown on the kinetoscope or projecting machine. (F.Z. Maguire, *Catalogue,* [March 1898], 31.)

By May Irwin and John Rice. They get ready to Kiss, begin to Kiss, and Kiss and Kiss and Kiss in a way that brings down the house every time. (*Edison Films,* March 1900, 36.)
SUBJECT: Musicals–performances. Courtship. Kissing.
ARCHIVE: NNMoMA, DLC, DLC-Hendricks.
CITATIONS: Maguire & Baucus, *Edison Films,* 20 January 1897, 6; Maguire & Baucus, *Edison and International Photographic Films,* April 1897, 11; Maguire & Baucus, *Fall Catalogue,* 1897, 12; *Edison Films,* July 1901, 70.
NOTE:

MAY IRWIN AS THE WIDOW.

BIJOU THEATRE.—The Widow Jones, a farce comedy in three acts, by John J. McNally.

Billy Bilke	John C. Rice
John James Jones	Jacques Kruger
Beatrice Byke	May Irwin
Senor Romero Canovas	George W. Barnum
Felicity Jones	Ada Lewis
Michael McCarthy	Joseph M. Sparks
Cassie Cartee	Sally Cohen
Flossie Cartee	Kathleen Warren
Janet Johnson	Grace Vaughan
Daisey Davis	Agnes Milton
Clifford Prout	Richard J. Jones
Marcela Mendelshoun	Maud M. Chandler
Marle Pose	Mable Power
A.J. Premium	Roland Carter
Mandy Noir	Gertrude Mansfield
Farm hand	George R. Donaldson
Farm hand	John H. Connolly
Baby Flo	Herself

Opinions about women are apt to differ, and so "The Widow Jones" may not be to everybody's taste. But as depicted by May Irwin she is such a jolly, unaffected and engaging person that it was not at all surprising to find that most of the men in the play and more than half in the auditorium were in love with her long before the evening was over.

Younger women, slenderer women, prettier women disported themselves before your eyes, but they were not one-half so sympathetic and attractive as the widow herself. Sincerity, you see, is such a potent quality upon the stage. Fortunately, May Irwin possesses this virtue as few actresses of farce comedy possess it. You believe her always, yes, even when she endeavors to address an audience and breaks down before she has spoken a word. I have seen all sorts of stage tears. Miss Irwin's emotion was genuine and her tears were real. She could not for the life of her have said another word after that little ovation last evening. As for the play itself, it is no better and no worse than a hundred other farce comedies that have held the stage of late years. It is a boisterous and not infrequently, a rather gross affair, in which the characters rush in and off the scene incessantly, though there is not the slightest reason for their doing so. You all know the manner, for you have seen it in every one of Mr. Hoyt's extravaganzas.

The dialogue, too, reminds you not a little of the bard of Twenty-fourth street. Audacious slang for the most part, not wit, it is that distinguishes Mr. MacNally's lines. Many of them were greeted with peals of laughter, simply because they were spoken in such a pointed, and yet in such an insouciant, manner by May Irwin. But it was as a songstress of negro melodies that she again achieved her brightest triumph. In such things she is really beyond compare. "The New Bully," in which she describes the experiences of a colored gentleman going down the alley armed with axe and razor to "wipe out" his rival, is in its way a gem. It is worth a score of "Throw Him Down, McCluskey's" and other popular ditties. An excellent bit of character acting was the Felicity Jones of Miss Ada Lewis. It was the most attractive new woman that has yet been seen here, and there was John Rice, who, as Billy Bilke, was a veritable virtuoso in the art of osculation. George Barnum, as the ardent Portuguese, was really what the programme claimed for him, "erratic and artistic," and John Sparks, as a Maine farmer, did much to enliven the performance. A word for the theatre, too, which is now one of the prettiest and brightest in New York. The Watteau panels are charming and everything now is in really very good taste.

ACT I.—McCarthy's farm at Maranacook, Me. Beatrice Byke, who is pestered by the attention of a couple of lovers, passes herself off as the widow of a Mr. Jones, who, it is claimed, committed suicide near the farm two years ago.

ACT II.—Apartments in Paris, where we meet all our old friends from Maine. What brought them to the gay capital is a mystery and what occurs is equally inexplicable. That song of the razor slashing negro, however, is sung with such finesse by Miss Irwin that you don't bother about the plot.

ACT III.—Home of the Widow Jones, Thousand Islands, where everything comes to an end with the usual choral effects. (*New York Herald*, 17 September 1895, 7.)

The Anatomy of a Kiss
At the Request of The Sunday World May Irwin and John Rice Posed
Before Edison's Kinetoscope—Result: 42 Feet of Kiss in 600 Pictures.
WIDOW JONES'S KISS FORTY-TWO FEET LONG.
It Was of Fifteen Seconds Duration, but the Kinetoscope Caught 600 Views of It.
THE FIRST KISS EVER PUBLISHED IN A NEWSPAPER.

A FORTY-TWO foot kiss! This does not mean a kiss given at forty-two feet range, but a kiss that measures forty-two linear feet. For the first time in the history of the world it is now possible to see what a kiss looks like. Byron and all the other famous poets tried to describe and the men who make dictionaries tried to define a kiss. Novel writers have spoiled thousands of white pages trying to convey in words an adequate idea of a kiss. Scientists have decided that kisses are dangerous, but all the world goes right on in the same old way, content to enjoy without knowing what it all is.

But now the Sunday World publishes the pictures of a kiss taken for it. Such pictures were never before made. In the forty-two feet of kiss recorded by the kinetoscope every phase is shown with startling distinctness. Six hundred different views of the forty-two foot kiss were made. It would require half a dozen pages of The World to print all of this long drawn out osculation.

What the camera did not see in the kiss did not exist.

The Widow Jones and Billie Bilkes have a kiss in the last act of "The Widow Jones" that is the work of art and action. The widow isn't much of a hand at kissing. In fact, the characters about her are not of the kissable kind. So when in the last act the widow and Billie come to the widow's only kiss in the play, it stands out as prominently as a hill on a prairie.

It was the hottest kind of a hot day when May Irwin and John Rice posed at the request of the Sunday World in front of the kinetoscope camera at the Edison works in Orange. It was hot everywhere, but in the [Maria], with the roof open to the sun, and the black walls to gather and hold the heat, it was all but a fiery furnace.

THE KINETOSCOPIST LAUGHED

When the old photographer was told what was wanted he shook with laughter.

"A kiss! That's the funniest thing I ever made. I've done kicks and blows and fights and dances, and all sorts of things but a kiss!" And Heyse [sic] laughed again as he fixed the machine and placed chairs for the demonstrators. "It must last fifteen seconds," said the photographer, "and you'd better rehearse to get it into time. Get ready! Go!"

The Widow Jones: "I don't see much room for argument at such close range."

With a sudden start, "What's the matter with you, Billie? You're dizzy."

Rice—"I'm not, either. I'm not moving. It's you."

May Irwin and Rice were staring at each other in perplexity. A curious wavy sensation prevailed to the camera. The operators were laughing.

"That's enough," called the photographer, and a young man came from without and joined in the laugh.

"Say, we're all on a track, Billie," laughed May Irwin.

"The camera revolves to catch the sun," explained Manager Gilmore.

"Begin again," called the photographer. "If you don't hurry the sun will get into a cloud."

HOW THE KISS WAS PHOTOGRAPHED.

The kiss was practiced, pruned down and hurried up until the photographer was satisfied. The machine was run into a dark room for a last loading of the camera. Taking a kinetoscope photograph is not like ordinary photography. It is a much more delicate operation. Rings had been drawn on the floor about the chair legs, so that they could not be moved an inch without being noticed before the picture was finally taken. The least trifle out of the way and a picture would be spoiled.

At the word "Go" the Widow Jones told Billie Bilkes that the room between their lips admitted no argument. Bilkes thought he was out of practice, but could accomplish something in the osculatory line. Then he twisted his mustache out of the way and the Widow held up a pair of tempting lips.

The photographer stood, watch in hand, counting the seconds as Bilkes caught the Widow's face in his hands and the scene went on. The camera facing the Widow and Bilkes sounded like a coffee mill grinding slowly.

The kiss went on and the camera ground and whirred its way to the end of the film. It seemed to consume ten minutes, but the photographer dropped his watch and called: "Fifteen seconds. There is no need of another. I can assure you that every motion and section of that kiss will be distinct. It was one of the best things I ever did. I'm sure nothing could be better."

DEVELOPING THE OSCULATION.

It was three days before the kiss was developed and transferred to a film. It was just fourteen yards long.

The first section was devoted to what apparently was a kiss, but was really only the preparation for one. These pictures show very distinctly how easily a person watching a couple might think they kissed when they didn't.

The real kiss is a revelation. The idea of a kinetoscopic kiss has unlimited possibilities.

Judges and juries have been called upon to fix a value upon a kiss without heretofore having the slightest idea what sort of a kiss the article was. Hereafter, in such cases where young women place a $10,000 estimate on a kiss or a dozen kisses, the judge or jury will simply have to say to counsel for plaintiff:

"Show us what kind of a kiss your plaintiff's is, and we will tell you whether it is worth that much."

In this way no man will be required to pay for a kiss that is not as good as other kisses.

When a young woman insists on sending her betrothed kisses by mail, she may simply tear one by one yard of them from a kinetoscope strip, and the recipient will know what he gets.

The Widow Jones' kiss is the kind which shows the value of a big mouth where "I can talk to you out of one corner and you can kiss me on the other," as she explains.

Six hundred different phases of a kiss leave little to the imagination. Mrs. McGuirk. (*New York World*, 26 April 1896, 21.)

"Edison's Vitascope" had its commercial debut at Koster & Bial's Music Hall on 23 April 1896.

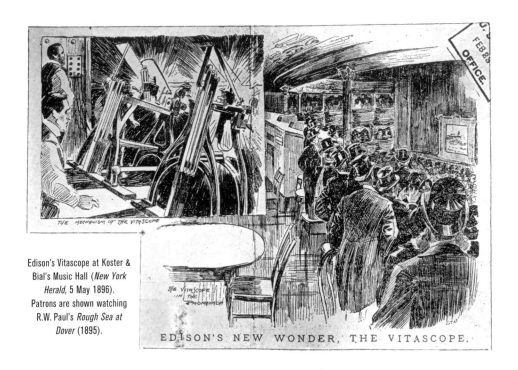

Edison's Vitascope at Koster & Bial's Music Hall (*New York Herald*, 5 May 1896). Patrons are shown watching R.W. Paul's *Rough Sea at Dover* (1895).

EDISON'S NEW WONDER, THE VITASCOPE.

WONDERFUL IS THE VITASCOPE.
Such Was the Verdict of the Audience Which Saw Edison's Invention.
IT BEATS THE KINETOSCOPE.
Pictures, Life Size, Lifelike and Full of Color, Thrown on a Screen.
MAKES A THRILLING SHOW.

The feature of the programme last evening at Koster & Bial's Music Hall was the first public exhibition ever given of Edison's vitascope. This invention has already been described in the HERALD. It has been called an enlarged kinetoscope, because it works somewhat on the principle of that machine, but in the case of the latter one must look into it to see reproductions of pictures about three inches in size, whereas, in the case of the vitascope these same pictures are thrown through a lens and appear on a screen magnified 600 diameters. Moreover, the vitascope reproduces all the colors of a picture. The vitascope was the seventh number on the programme last night, and it was nearly ten o'clock when it was reached. The house was packed, and as picture after picture was thrown on the screen the applause was tremendous.

REALISTIC PICTURES.

The first picture shown was that of two dancers. It seemed as though they were actually on the stage, so natural was the dance, with its many and graceful motions. Next came a picture of a tumbling surf on the Jersey shore. The waves were high and boisterous as they dashed after one another in their rush for the sandy beach, over which they ebbed and flowed. The white crests of the waves and the huge volume of water were true to life. Only the roar of the surf was needed to make the illusion perfect. A boxing bout between a long, thin man and a short, stout one was the next picture. The boxers were photographed in their bout some time ago by the kinetoscope. Every move and step and blow of the boxers was faithfully reproduced on the screen last night. A scene from "The Milk White Flag" was next shown. It was an animated picture, which elicited loud cries of "Bravo!"

JOHN BULL AND UNCLE SAM.

"The Monroe Doctrine" was the title of the next picture. At first John Bull was shown bombarding a South American shore, supposed to represent Venezuela. John was getting the better of the argument when the tall, lank figure of Uncle Sam emerged from the back of the picture. He grasped John Bull by the neck, forced him to his knees and made him take off his hat to Venezuela. This delighted the audience, and applause and cheers rang through the house, while somebody cried, "Hurrah for Edison!"

The "skirt dance" was the last picture shown, and its success equalled that of the others. When the dancer disappeared from view there was a long burst of applause, and everybody agreed that the vitascope was "wonderful." (*New York Herald*, 24 April 1896, 11.)

Cissy Fitzgerald was one of the original "Gaiety Girls" who arrived in New York in September 1894. She was to have danced the serpentine before Edison's camera on 1 November 1894, but became ill. Her visit to the Black Maria in early May 1896 made up for that absence. By then she had become a star, the hit of The Foundling, *a farce comedy which had its New York debut on 25 February 1895. Ads urged potential patrons to "See Cissy Wink" and gave the precise time of her appearance (9:45)—for those interested in coming to enjoy that highpoint, which the Edison staff subsequently recorded on film. She went on to be a top attraction at Koster & Bial's Music Hall, opening the new 1896-97 theatrical season on 7 September 1896, as the headline attraction, then taking the Cissy Fitzgerald Company to Boston and other cities.*

156 Cissy Fitzgerald

LENGTH: 50 ft.   © No reg.

PRODUCER: Raff & Gammon.

CAMERA: William Heise.

CAST: Cissy Fitzgerald.

PRODUCTION DATE: 4-8 May 1896.

LOCATION: Black Maria, West Orange, N.J.

SOURCE: *The Foundling* (farce comedy).

DESCRIPTION: Cissy Fitzgerald, in all her finery of billowy lace, with graceful and agile movements, and kick and wink, danced down to the footlights in that daring fashion with which so many became familiar when she visited Boston a short time ago. This reproduction was very much like the original, and elicited loud applause. (*Boston Herald,* 26 May 1896, 7.)

The Queen of the English variety stage, a leading attraction at Koster & Bial's, in a clever dance. (F.Z. Maguire, *Catalogue,* [March 1898], 28.)

A new dance by this celebrated English artist. Her famous wink adds to the interest of the picture. (*Edison Films*, March 1900, 29.)

SUBJECT: Vaudeville–performances. Dancing.

ARCHIVE:

CITATIONS: "Tribulations of 'The Foudling,'" *New York Herald,* 26 February 1895, 6; "Cissy Fitzgerald on Correct Underwear," *New York Herald,* 24 May 1896, 29; "Tremont Theatre," *New York Clipper,* 31 October 1896, 555. Maguire & Baucus, *Edison Films,* 20 January 1897, 6; Maguire & Baucus, *Edison and International Photographic Films,* April 1897, 5; Maguire & Baucus, *Fall Catalogue,* 1897, 11; *Edison Films,* July 1901, 52.

NOTE: Cissy Fitzgerald would eventually return to moviemaking, appearing in both silent and sound films.

<hr>

"THE FOUNDLING."

It was probably accidental, but I got one. It must have been accidental, although, of course, it would be more satisfactory were it otherwise. Still, I got one, just as I was leaning back in my seat at Hoyt's Theatre last night, prepared to put on a blase expression that, I flatter myself, is very becoming. It reached me in a moment, and–oh! what a difference in the morning. The blase expression wouldn't fit at all, listlessness was impossible; I sat up and waited for another. Guess what it was that proved so useful? But you couldn't guess, of course, so I'll tell you my secret, mommer, dear. Do not hate me for it. Think of me when I am least bad. Oh, mother, mother–Cissy–Cissy Fitzgerald winked at me. I gasped; then I had palpitation of the eyelids; then I realized that it was mine, mine forever, that fat, glad wink. I shall press it in me Shakespeare, and look at it regularly once a week.

Candor compels me to admit that Cissy threw a lot of winks away last night. It must have been a souvenir night, handsome winks being distributed to everybody not a lady. Cissy's eyelids are quite as active as her little toe-lets. She was in a radiant humor, appearing as an incident in the "The Foundling" although I rather think that she was the play, and "The Foundling," the incident. She certainly ruled the roost. Once during the performance she made a little slip, stating an important period as thirty-five years, instead of twenty-five. Was she overwhelmed with confusion? Did she blush, and look awkward? No, mother, dear. She giggled. She enjoyed it. She set the stage a-laughing. So Miller Kent lost his equanimity, and broke up into small pieces. Mr. Humphreys was amused, and the audience enjoyed it. At another time Miss Cissy kept the stage waiting, while E.M. Holland–the only E.M. Holland–was on it. She didn't care a hang. On she came, late, but winking, and the audience forgave her. So much for a wink. Learn to wink, ye actresses. A wink covers a multitude of sins.

Miss Fitzgerald's dance (fancy me calling her "miss" after that wink!) is not nearly as good as the one she did in "The Gaiety Girl." In fact, it is scarcely a dance–merely a gorgeous display of the lace that popular tradition insists shall not be displayed. That is to say, the lace was–well, don't force me to explain, for I'm still young, mother dear. A line on the programme last night declared that "children under seven years of age shall not be admitted." Need I say more? Cissy wore a hideous gown that was most unbecoming. It cost a great deal probably, but it was the sort of dress that a very Western leading-lady would buy when her manager suggested that she look luxurious. I hope that Cissy will resume her pretty English simplicity, discard that frumpish gown and throw away the horrid monumental hat with feathers that replaced the simple Puritan bonnet she wore at Daly's. Do this, for my sake, Cissy, please. I had heard that Cissy gave away h's with her winks, but I found none. In fact, I was surprised to see what a good interpretation she gave of the tricky little Maybird. Her speech was as pleasing as her acting. Cissy's no greenhorn, I'd have you know.

As for "The Foundling," by W. Lestocq and E.M. Robson–well, it makes you laugh. It isn't as good as "Too Much Johnson"–my pet farce–but it is bright, and full of funny situations. A man looking for a mother and finding two, one an acidulated spinster and the other a prosperous married woman, will remove all traces of solemnity from the most austere. The entire episode is most humorous. Silly people say that it is broad, but it's simply laughable. That dreadful accusation of broadness is really too droll. Could anything be broad in New York? That's what I want to know. Why take all the humors of unconventional situations as breaches of decorum? Life is full of them. We see them around us; we hear them; they positively exist; we roar at them in the cafe or the smoking-room. As for all this talk of constructing sweet little poetic affairs for the matinee girl–well, just watch the matinee girls at the theatre. Didn't they flock to see "Sowing the Wind?" Do you think that wild buffaloes could drag them to "Shore Acres," or "Esmeralda?" Let us laugh and enjoy ourselves, for we live but once, and we're a long time dead. If we never get anything naughtier than "The Foundling" we shall not fare badly. Besides, there's a sweet little play called "Lethe" that precedes it. "Lethe" is so sweet that it gives one a sensation of nausea. It will pass into the oblivion that its titles suggests to-morrow night. Its dainty subject hovers around the love of a mommer and daughter for the same person–and what a person! Nobody calls "Lethe" naughty, but to my mind it is worse than all the alleged risque-ness of "The Foundling." There are some clever people engaged in that farce. E.M. Holland is exceedingly good, and S. Miller Kent has the right idea of farce. Then Joseph Humphreys's cockney sketch is a capital piece of work, and Helen Tracy is almost as good as Kate Meek in "Too Much Johnson," and Miss Meek stands alone. Maggie Holloway and Margaret Craven must also be complimented. Go to Hoyt's and get winked at. Perhaps you won't get such a nice wink as I received. I wonder if Cissy saw me and was attracted by the flamboyant beauty of my personality? Joyous thought! I shall go again, for winks are winks, and they are things that money can't buy. ALAN DALE. (*New York Evening World*, 1 March 1895, 4.)

The vitascope people, by the way, are making constant additions to their collection of pictures. Miss Cissy Fitzgerald went down to Menlo Park [sic] one day last week, and she will soon be giving her famous wink on the screen at Koster & Bial's. Mr. Wilson Lackaye, in the Svengali death scene from "Trilby" is also to be "vitascoped," and Chevalier, too, is to be presented. He will sing some of his songs into a phonograph, and while his picture is being shown the audience will hear him sing. (*New York Herald*, 10 May 1896, 6F.)

Due to the bulky nature of the kinetograph, Edison film production had been limited to the Black Maria or its immediate environs. Edison and his staff had recognised the need for a portable camera for some time, and by 6 May 1896 this new kinetograph was ready to be tried out. Five days later a crew took it to New York City to shoot several scenes of metropolitan life.

157 Central Park / Fountain / Fountain in Central Park
LENGTH: 50 ft.   © No reg.
PRODUCER: James White, Raff & Gammon.
CAMERA: William Heise.
CAST:
PRODUCTION DATE: 11 May 1896.
LOCATION: Central Park, New York, N.Y.
SOURCE:

DESCRIPTION: A bit of Central Park, with a fountain playing, and children walking along the curb of the basin, and older people sauntering by, was another view. (*Boston Herald*, 19 May 1896.)

A scene in Central Park, New York City. The water glistening in the sunlight makes fine effects. (Maguire & Co., *Catalogue*, [March 1898], 29.)

SUBJECT: City and town life–New York. Parks. Fountains. Children.

ARCHIVE:

CITATIONS: Maguire & Baucus, *Edison and International Photographic Films*, April 1897, 8; Maguire & Baucus, *Fall Catalogue*, 1897, 12.

NOTE:

158 Herald Square / Herald Square, N.Y.

LENGTH: 50 ft.   © No reg.

PRODUCER: James White, Raff & Gammon.

CAMERA: William Heise.

CAST:

PRODUCTION DATE: 11 May 1896.

LOCATION: New York, N.Y.

SOURCE:

DESCRIPTION: The street cars moved along, the elevated was visible at the extreme left, and men and women walked with various gaits and at different speeds along the street. (*Boston Herald*, 19 May 1896.)

A scene covering Herald Square in New York, showing the noonday activity of Broadway at that point as clearly as if one were spectator of the original seems incredulous, nevertheless is presented life-like. The cable cars seem to move in opposite directions and look real enough to suggest a trip up and down that great thoroughfare, while at the same time the elevated trains are rushing overhead, pedestrians are seen moving along the sidewalks or crossing to opposite sides of the street, everything moving, or as it is seen in real life. (*Buffalo Courier*, 7 June 1896, 10.)

Showing "Herald" Building, Street, and Elevated Railroad. (Maguire & Baucus, *Edison and International Photographic Films*, April 1897, 10.)

Formed by the junction of Broadway, 6th avenue and 35th street. The picturesque low roofed Herald building is plainly shown; also the passing crowds and group of idlers. (*Edison Films*, March 1900, 42.)

SUBJECT: City and town life–New York. Urban transportation.

ARCHIVE:

CITATIONS: "The Blizzard of '95," *New York Herald,* 17 February 1895, 3D (with illustrations); "Herald Square is the Magnet," *New York Herald,* 19 April 1896, 2E. Maguire & Baucus, *Fall Catalogue*, 1897, 12; F.Z. Maguire & Co., *Catalogue*, [March 1898], 34; *Edison Films,* July 1901, 88.

NOTE: *Herald Square* and other outdoor scenes were inspired by open air subjects taken for the Lumière cinématographe and the Lathams' eidoloscope.

HERALD SQUARE "VITASCOPED."

All of the animation, life and movement peculiar to Herald Square on any bright pleasant afternoon was depicted on photographic film by Raff and Gammon, by means of Edison's vitascope, yesterday afternoon, and the result will be shown at Koster & Bial's next week. The photographers settled down to work at two o'clock yesterday afternoon, when the square was crowded with cable cars, carriages and vehicles of all sorts, while now and then an "L" train would thunder by. They chose a window on the lower end of the square, where they were within full view of the Herald Building, and at the same time took in Broadway and Sixth avenue for a radius of several blocks. Copies of the film will be sent to all parts of the world for use wherever a vitascope has been put up. The fountain in Central Park, with thousands of children playing about it, was also photographed yesterday. (*New York Herald*, 12 May 1896, 9.)

159 *Elevated Railway Station, 23rd Street, New York / Elevated Railroad / Elevated Train

LENGTH: 50 ft.   © No reg.

PRODUCER: James White, Raff & Gammon.

CAMERA: William Heise.

CAST:

PRODUCTION DATE: [11 May 1896.]

LOCATION: New York, N.Y.

SOURCE:

DESCRIPTION: Showing the train approaching the 23d St. station, New York. (Maguire & Co., *Catalogue*, [March 1898], 29.)

SUBJECT: City and town life–New York. Urban transportation.

ARCHIVE: NNMoMA.

CITATIONS: "Keith's New Theatre," *Boston Herald*, 24 May 1896, 11. Maguire & Baucus, *Edison and International Photographic Films*, April 1897, 7; Maguire & Baucus, *Fall Catalogue*, 1897, 11.

NOTE:

With a vow to professionalize and dignify street cleaning, Colonel George E. Waring, Jr. drew much attention to the sanitation activities of his New York City department. The parade he staged on 26 May 1896 represented a formal, public display of these efforts. White Wings' Parade was the first parade to be filmed by the Edison Manufacturing Company. Such planned events were well suited for filmmakers, who could carefully set up their cameras in advance. The Edison staff would make increasing elaborate arrangements to film important parades and would soon use multiple crews in appropriate situations.

160 **White Wings' Parade / Waring's White Wings / Parade of New York City Crossing Sweepers / White Wings**

LENGTH: 50 ft.   © No reg.

PRODUCER: James White, Raff & Gammon.

CAMERA: William Heise.

CAST:

PRODUCTION DATE: 26 May 1896.

LOCATION: New York, N.Y.

SOURCE:

DESCRIPTION: Those who have never witnessed the uniquely clad individuals whom Col. Waring has clean the streets of New York should make it a point to see them march, with police escort, as so realistically reproduced in Edison's invention. (*Boston Herald*, 14 July 1896, 6.)

New York Street cleaners on parade. (Maguire & Co., *Catalogue*, [March 1898], 29.)

SUBJECT: Parades. Street Cleaners. George E. Waring, Jr.

ARCHIVE:

CITATIONS: "Colonel Waring's Brand New Broom," *New York Herald*, 6 January 1895, 9D (with illustration); "Denounce Waring," *New York Herald*, 11 March 1895, 9; "Address by Mr. Waring," *New York Herald*, 17 March 1895, 3; "Street Cleaning Plans," *New York Herald*, 30 March 1895, 6; " 'White Wings' Parade," *New York Herald*, 26 May 1896, 4; "White Wings in Array," *New York World*, 27 May 1896, 13 (with illustration); "White Wings Grow Weary. All Work Makes Dull Boys, so They'll Take an Outing," *New York Herald*, 16 June 1896, 12; *Boston Herald*, 12 July 1896, 11; *New York World*, 4 October 1896, 14. Maguire & Baucus, *Edison Films*, 20 January 1897, 7; Maguire & Baucus, *Edison and International Photographic Films*, April 1897, 16; Maguire & Baucus, *Fall Catalogue*, 1897, 13.

NOTE: The Edison Manufacturing Company shot a similar film, *White Wings on Review*, on 29 April 1903. It survives in the Paper Print Collection.

'TWAS WARING'S DAY.

He Surprises New York with a Parade of Unequal Beauty and No Little Novelty.

MAYOR STRONG DELIGHTED.

The Men Marched Well and the Whole Equipment of the Department Shone Brilliantly.

MUSIC, FLOWERS AND CHILDREN.

Realistic Exhibition of the Transformation He Has Wrought in the Street Cleaning Department.

Colonel Waring stood under the frowning, ivy clad battlements of our grandfathers' reservoir, at Forty-second street and Fifth avenue, yesterday and saw his enemies broken under the wheels of the newly painted ash carts, trucks and hose carts of his stable brigade.

He saw the frivolous and envious Aldermen who would not give him a grand stand worthy of his parade torn into pieces with the plaudits of a vast assemblage, which went wild with enthusiasm over the white duck army revealed for the first time to the public eye in its strength, its splendor and its admirable drill.

After yesterday's spectacle Waring must no longer be reckoned a mere Commissioner. He is a poet, a colorist, a showman if you will, but no mere street cleaning commander. He injected into the dreary subject matter of mud, garbage and ashes a new significance. The man who gathers the refuse from the street in front of your window was idealized by Waring and nobody will ever be able to think slightly of him again.

IMAGINATION RAN RIOT.

Waring forgot nothing. His parade made the annual police turnouts look silly by comparison, for the reason that he variegated his line with novel devices, brilliant flowers, music and startling surprises of all kinds.

Lest the general effect should prove monotonous, this Wagner of the street cleaning brigade shot his white battalions through and through with suggestive, not to say striking ideas. Music was so abundant that the ear was ravished, and when the quivering air was suffered for a moment to be still the eye in turn was caught with unexpected symmetries and inimitable contrasts.

Like all necromancers the Colonel did not leave the children out of his calculations, and, as if to emphasize his bigheartedness, there rolled immediately at the heels of his plunging charger two truckloads of little girls of the east side auxiliaries, apparelled in the hues of the flower garden and chanting the good Colonel's praises.

And bringing up the rear of the line were four companies of boys bearing banners, marching like soldiers and cheering in wild shrill trebles. The mayor was so overcome by this spectacle that he dropped his hat.

THE COLONEL'S MUSTACHE.

Everything about this parade was done with military precision. The rendezvous was at Fifth avenue and Fifty-ninth street, and promptly at half-past three o'clock the head of the line was in motion. An immense crowd had gathered at the Plaza to give the white army a send off. Some disappointment was expressed when it was discovered that the Colonel wore no uniform.

But disappointment grew into anguish when it was seen that the Colonel had clipped his mustache to a mere bristle, and had even sacrificed the waxed ends. The band struck up "The Lost Cord" and many eyes were dimmed.

Colonel Waring wore an undress uniform coat of blue without braid, a pair of gray trousers strapped to his boots, and his famous white helmet. His progress was that of an uncrowned king. His horse minced along sidewise and kicked every time the big drum was beaten. Cheers mingled with the blare of trumpets and the crash of carts. The very streets rose up and called him blessed.

AT THE REVIEWING STAND.

The reviewing stand was built behind the reservoir railings. Mayor Strong drew up before it in a hired hack with rubber tires shortly before three o'clock and proceeded to give the "glad hand" to General McCook, James C. Carter, Sheriff Tamsen, Corporation Counsel Scott, President of the Board of Health Wilson, General Emmons Clark, Fire Commissioner La Grange and Charity Commissioner Faure.

When the stand was reached Commissioner Waring and Deputy Gibson dismounted gracefully from their horses and walked to places which had been reserved for them near the Mayor. The line proceeded under the leadership of Grand Marshall H.C. Cushing and fourteen aides. Colonel Waring and Deputy Gibson remained in the stand until the procession had passed, when they remounted and rode to the end of the line to the point of dispersal at Madison avenue and Twenty-sixth street.

The men made a fine appearance in their white duck suits and helmets, and all things considered, put up a doughty and, in some cases, admirable march. There were fourteen hundred sweepers in line, representing eleven districts. They passed the stand in squads of twelve, marching in single rank. Each district was commanded by the district superintendent, either on horseback or in a buggy, while the squads in each instance were commanded by a picked man.

RUMBLE OF THE CARTS.

One of the imposing features of the display were the six hundred ash carts, ash trucks, horse carriages, express wagons and dirt carts, representing the nine stables of the department, and commanded by the stable foreman. All had been newly painted and the hose carts were in many cases, decorated with flags and flowers. The drivers wore dark brown uniforms and drove their springless charges three abreast with commendable grace and precision. At the head of the column were nine prize ash carts, which were judged by G.L. Herbert, while Captain M.J. Whalen passed upon the proficiency of the sweepers.

Upon two two-horse platform trucks practical illustrations were afforded of the processes of street cleaning. One of the trucks was labelled "Bag carriers for street cleaning," and the other "Ash cans for house ashes." Men shovelled dirt into the bags and ashes into the cans in a most realistic manner. When a cartload of little girls passed the reviewing stand the children cried, "Hooray! hooray! hooray! We are the children of the C.A.A.A.A." Mayor Strong said after it was over that the parade had been a surprise to him. He had not expected anything half so fine. He was not the only one who thought so. Citizens in all walks of life were heard to extol the showing of the department, and one man said emphatically:–

"After this he can have all the money he wants." (*New York Herald*, 27 May 1896, 9.)

In late May and early June, under the prodding of Raff & Gammon, William Heise took Edison's newly portable camera on its first long-distance production trip. The crew traveled to Columbus, Ohio; Niagara Falls; and possibly Scranton, Pennsylvania. The trip consumed considerable time, due in part to bad weather conditions (filming could only take place on sunny days), and the results were not very satisfactory. Only one of the films found its way into Edison's catalogs, and then only briefly. If this gamble did not entirely pay off, such trips became frequent and ultimately routine in the months and years ahead.

161 [Knights of Templar Parade]

LENGTH: © No reg.
PRODUCER: James White, Raff & Gammon.
CAMERA: William Heise.
CAST:
PRODUCTION DATE: 26 May 1896.
LOCATION: Scranton, Pa.
SOURCE:
DESCRIPTION:
SUBJECT: Parades. Secret Societies.
ARCHIVE:
CITATIONS: "Two Magnificent Pageants on Scranton Streets Today," and "Knights of Templar Parade," *Scranton Times*, 26 May 1896, 1; *Boston Herald*, 2 June 1896, 7.
NOTE: This film may have been planned, but it seems extremely unlikely that it was taken, given that the Knights of Templar parade was the same day as the parade of Street Cleaners in New York City. If by some chance this film was taken, suggesting two separate production units at this early date, this film was not successful and was never shown commercially.

The Edison filming of a railway collision on Decoration Day is suggestive of fundamental cultural change, along the lines suggested by John Higham, Warren Susman and other historians. The railway locomotive—symbol of speed, technological prowess and productivity—was turned into a momentary spectacle to be consumed by voyeuristic fun seekers. Correspondingly, Decoration Day had been used to commemorate the war dead and the preservation of the Union and was anything but a day of frivolity.

162 Railway Smash-up

LENGTH: © No reg.
PRODUCER: James White, Raff & Gammon.
CAMERA: William Heise.
CAST:
PRODUCTION DATE: 30 May 1896.
LOCATION: Columbus, Ohio.
SOURCE:
DESCRIPTION:
SUBJECT: Railroads–trains. Railroads–accidents. Amusement parks.
ARCHIVE:
CITATIONS:
NOTE: This film was not very successfully realized. Because motion picture cameras at this time did not have a panning mechanism, the smash-up occurred outside the camera frame. The film was shown infrequently and with generally unsatisfactory results. The Edison Manufacturing Company shot a similar subject, *Railroad Smashup*, at Revere Beach, Massachusetts, on 27 August 1904.

It is announced that some great scenes will be shown next week, including a view of that terrible railroad collision at Columbus, Ohio, between two trains and detailed in the Sunday papers. This collision was pre-arranged especially to be photographed for the vitascope, and an immense picture will be the result. A view of the Whirlpool rapids and a march of the Knights of Templar in Scranton, Pa., will also be shown, probably next week. (*Boston Herald*, 2 June 1896, 7.)

Announcement was made that next week the great pre-arranged railroad disaster, and views of Niagara Falls and the Whirlpool rapids, where Capt. Webb lost his life, would be given. (*Boston Herald*, 9 June 1896, 7.)

RAILROAD WRECK MADE TO ORDER.
Unique and Costly Entertainment provided for the Opening of a Park in Ohio.
COLLISION OF ENGINES GOING 50 MILES AN HOUR.
(Special Correspondence of the Sunday World.)

Columbus, O., June 4. A Railroad wreck marked the opening of Buckeye Park, a pleasure ground near this city on Decoration Day. It was made to order and was witnessed by more than 20,000 people. The affair had been widely advertised and proved a great attraction. People came for miles to witness a railroad wreck that was to embrace all the features of those which are accidental except in the matter of killed and maimed.

A special track one mile long was laid near the main line of the C., H.V. and T. Railway, where it passes Buckeye Park. On this special track two locomotives were advertised to meet in collision while running at a high rate of speed. The programme was carried out faithfully. The iron monsters were headed toward each other, the throttles opened wide, the engineers jumped off and the huge machines came together with a deafening crash. It was expected that both engines would be demolished, and the expectation was not amiss. After the collision the locomotives were a heap of iron fit only for the scrap heap.

A TERRIFIC COLLISION.

A.L. Streeter was the manager of the collision. For several years he has had the idea in his head, and he thought the opening of the beautiful Buckeye Park a suitable time. The affair was widely advertised, and the Hocking Valley Railroad, which furnished the engines and cars, secured much more in passenger receipts than the engines and cars were worth. The old engines were selected to end their days of usefulness before a concourse of pleasure seekers. Both had been in the service of the road ever since it was built, twelve years ago. They were repainted and decked in gala attire for their execution, and were rechristened, one the "A.L. Streeter," and the other "W.H. Fisher," the latter after the general passenger agent of the railroad. Behind each engine three loaded coal cars and a caboose were coupled. This made a heavy train and insured sufficient weight to make the collision realistic.

The engines were separated by a distance of about a mile and a half, and at the firing of a bomb they were started towards each other. Gradually they increased their speed until they were going ten miles an hour. Then the engineers opened the throttles wide and jumped from the steps of the cabooses. At every revolution of the driving wheels the engines gained speed, and when they crashed together they were going at least fifty miles an hour.

ONE MAN SERIOUSLY INJURED.

One of the engines had a down grade and it ran faster than the other, so that the collision did not occur exactly where it was expected, but only missed the spot about fifty yards, which was regarded as close figuring. A group of railroad men were standing within 200 feet of the spot where the collision occurred. Two flying pieces of metal came whistling through the air and one struck Thomas C. Peck, chief clerk in the passenger department, breaking both bones of the left leg below the knee.

Ropes had been stretched to keep the crowds at a safe distance. As soon as the engines met the air was filled with escaping steam and smoke. Immediately the crowds broke through the ropes and crowded around the wreck. While the drive wheels were still whirling rapidly in the air the relic-hunters begun removing pieces of the broken machinery as souvenirs and soon the engines were dismantled. Every bit of metal small enough to be portable was carried away by the enthusiastic spectators, who yelled themselves hoarse over the success of the entertainment.

AMATEUR PHOTOGRAPHERS AT WORK.

Several hundred cameras were leveled at the wreck and views were taken of the engines just before they met and after the collision. One of the best is reproduced in the Sunday World. As the two iron monsters struck they rose up in the air like stallions fighting and then crashed together so compactly that it was difficult to tell which engine was which. The coal cars behind the engines telescoped and were almost as badly wrecked as the engines but the cabooses did not suffer greatly.

The engine named "W.H. Fisher" was known as No. 12 during its term of service. It had been driven during all its life by Engineer Pat Clauney, and it was his hand that opened the throttle that started the doomed mass of machinery on its last run. The "A.L. Streeter" was formerly No. 21. J.D. Loomis, one of the oldest engineers on the road, had sat in the cab for a dozen years and he can say that he stayed with the machine to the last, as he started it and then jumped, allowing the machine he had operated for so long to go forward into what he had succeeded in avoiding for so many years.

The collision, which was the most expensive entertainment ever provided for an Ohio audience, was a tremendous success in every way. All day Sunday the spot was crowded by visitors, who looked in awe on the pile of iron which the day before had been two valuable locomotives and seemingly endowed with life. (*New York World*, 7 June 1896, 26.)

DECORATION DAY.

It must be gratifying to every true American that the time has come at last when Decoration Day can be observed without bitterness. It is no longer a day when memories of a bloody struggle are passionately recalled. The flowers which are placed on the graves of the dead are no longer manifestations of animosity to the living. They are rather evidence of a desire to honor courage and fidelity to principle without insisting that those who once held opposing principles must be forever proscribed and anathematized.

The war has at last passed into history. Its animosities are no longer a force in the affairs of the country, as they were even as late as ten years ago. Fifteen years ago the country was still "Federal" or "Confederate." Now those words are anachronistic. The conditions they described have disappeared. It is no longer of practical importance to know whether a man is an "ex-Federal" or an "ex-Confederate." The country has new ideas, new methods, new hopes, and in these all Americans are alike concerned.

It happens thus that Decoration Day has come to be what it ought to be—the celebration of the preservation of the Union, of a true union in citizenship, in patriotism and in the determination to do all that can be done for the welfare and advancement of the country. What better meaning than this could flowers have when they are placed on the graves of the soldier dead? (Editorial, *New York World*, 30 May 1896, 6.)

In taking films of Niagara Falls, the Edison crew was frustrated by bad weather and other difficulties. The films were not apparently of very good quality, despite the hoopla surrounding their exhibition. Some of these pictures, such as those of the Canadian Falls, may never have found their way into distribution. More generally, their commercial life was short and they were quickly replaced by a new set of Niagara Falls films taken in December 1896.

Niagara Falls had long been a favorite subject for still photographers; they had already been filmed by the Lathams for their eidoloscope by early May 1896. Lumière cameraman Alexander Promio would film them in September 1896.

163 Niagara Falls, Gorge / View from Gorge Railroad

LENGTH: 150 ft.   © No reg.

PRODUCER: James White, Raff & Gammon.

CAMERA: William Heise.

CAST:

PRODUCTION DATE: Early June 1896.

LOCATION: Niagara Falls, Canada.

SOURCE:

DESCRIPTION: The most sensational view was that of the gorge and Whirlpool rapids at Niagara, a panoramic picture obtained from the rear end of a swiftly-moving train on the Niagara Gorge railway, and one that has never been equalled for completeness of detail and general effect. In this view the stone bluffs of the gorge, the telegraph poles, rail fences and the waters of the great river go rushing by with incredible swiftness, but yet plain enough for one to note everything in a general way, just as though seated in an observation car. The Whirlpool rapids are in sight one moment and lost to view the next, their whirling eddies and foam-flecked waves sparkling in the sun's rays, forming a very beautiful picture. The imaginary trip ends just beneath the famous suspension bridge, a capital view of which is caught just before the picture ceases to show on the curtain. (*Boston Herald*, 23 June 1896, 9.)

From rear of swiftly moving train. (Maguire & Baucus, *Fall Catalogue*, 1897, 14.)

SUBJECT: Railroads. Waterfalls. Bridges. Tourist trade. Niagara Falls.

ARCHIVE:

CITATIONS: *Buffalo Courier*, 7 June 1896, 7; "Koster & Bial's," *New York Dramatic Mirror*, 20 June 1896, 28; Purdy & Kiefaber to Raff & Gammon, 21 June 1896, MH-BA. F.Z. Maguire & Co., *Catalogue*, [March 1898], 31.

NOTE: The Lumière film of Venice, taken from a moving gondola, had already been shown in the United States (on a vitascope) and doubtlessly inspired the Edison crew to shoot this scene from a moving vehicle, in this instance a train. The making of these Niagara Falls films was mentioned in the press as early as mid-May. (*Boston Herald*, 17 May 1896, 32.)

164   Niagara Falls, Whirlpool
LENGTH: 150 ft.   © No reg.
PRODUCER: James White, Raff & Gammon.
CAMERA: William Heise.
CAST:
PRODUCTION DATE: Early June 1896.
LOCATION: Niagara Falls, [Canada].
SOURCE: *Whirlpool Rapids, Niagara Falls* (Eidoloscope film, May 1896).
DESCRIPTION:
SUBJECT: Waterfalls. Tourist trade. Niagara Falls.
ARCHIVE:
CITATIONS: Purdy & Kiefaber to Raff & Gammon, 21 June 1896, MH-BA.
NOTE: This film may be a shorter version of *Niagara Falls, Gorge.*

165   Niagara Falls (From the West Side of the American Falls)
LENGTH: 150 ft.   © No reg.
PRODUCER: James White, Raff & Gammon.
CAMERA: William Heise.
CAST:
PRODUCTION DATE: Early June 1896.
LOCATION: Niagara Falls, N.Y.
SOURCE:
DESCRIPTION:
SUBJECT: Waterfalls. Tourist trade. Niagara Falls.
ARCHIVE:
CITATIONS: *Boston Herald*, 23 June 1896, 9.
NOTE:

166   Niagara Falls (From the East Side of the American Falls)
LENGTH: 150 ft.   © No reg.
PRODUCER: James White, Raff & Gammon.
CAMERA: William Heise.
CAST:
PRODUCTION DATE: Early June 1896.
LOCATION: Niagara Falls, N.Y.
SOURCE:
DESCRIPTION: The little steamer, the Maid of the Mist, familiar to every visitor of Niagara, as well as those who have seen it in pictures (for it always seems a necessary part of a picture of Niagara), can be discerned making her way across the mighty river, and seemingly almost under the immense mass of water that seems as if it must sweep her to destruction. (*Boston Herald*, 21 June 1896, 11.)
SUBJECT: Waterfalls. Tourist trade. Niagara Falls. Steamships.
ARCHIVE:
CITATIONS: *Boston Herald*, 23 June 1896, 9.
NOTE:

167   [Niagara Falls (Canadian Falls)]
LENGTH: © No reg.
PRODUCER: James White, Raff & Gammon.
CAMERA: William Heise.
CAST:
PRODUCTION DATE: Early June 1896.
LOCATION: Niagara Falls, Canada.
SOURCE:
DESCRIPTION:

SUBJECT: Waterfalls. Tourist trade. Niagara Falls.
ARCHIVE:
CITATIONS: *Boston Herald*, 21 June 1896, 10.
NOTE:

Niagara

Niagara is a corruption of the Seneca word "neagara," meaning "across the neck," an allusion to the strip of land between the lakes. The name has been subjected to many changes since the discovery of the cataract, more than 30 different readings being found in the writings of the various early explorers and geographers. (*Scranton Times*, 26 May 1896, 8.)

After the problematic production trip to Niagara Falls and Columbus, Ohio, Edison's film crew returned to shooting local street scenes in New York City.

168 Bowling Green at a Busy Hour / The Busiest Hour at Bowling Green / Bowling Green, New York / Bowling Green

LENGTH: 50 ft.   © No reg.
PRODUCER: James White, Raff & Gammon.
CAMERA: William Heise.
CAST:
PRODUCTION DATE: By 23 June 1896.
LOCATION: New York, N.Y.
SOURCE:
DESCRIPTION: Bowling Green Park, New York, with its moving horse cars and teams of all descriptions, busy pedestrians, etc. (*Boston Herald*, 21 July 1896, 9.)
A Scene on lower Broadway. (Maguire & Baucus, *Fall Catalogue*, 1897, 11.)
New York City's oldest Park, dating way back to the early Dutch settlers. On this green, during the Revolutionary war, the Patriots pulled down a leaden statue of George III, and melted him into bullets. (*Edison Films*, March 1900, 42.)
SUBJECT: City and town life–New York. Parks. Urban transportation.
ARCHIVE:
CITATIONS: *Boston Herald*, 28 June 1896, 11; *New York World*, 20 September 1896, 14. Maguire & Baucus, *Edison Films*, 20 January 1897, 7; Maguire & Baucus, *Edison and International Photographic Films*, April 1897, 4; F.Z. Maguire & Co., *Catalogue,* [March 1898], 34; *Edison Films*, July 1901, 90.
NOTE:

Bowling Green, at the foot of Broadway, is a little oval park, with a weary fountain in its centre, and surrounded by ocean-steamship offices, foreign consulates, etc., and the great Produce Exchange, Washington Building, and Standard Oil Company's Building. (M.F. Sweetser and Simeon Ford, *How to Know New York City*, 1895, 33.)

169 Battery Park

LENGTH: 50 and 150 ft.   © No reg.
PRODUCER: James White, Raff & Gammon.
CAMERA: William Heise.
CAST:
PRODUCTION DATE: By 23 June 1896.
LOCATION: New York, N.Y.
SOURCE:
DESCRIPTION: Showing ferry boat coming into slip, with tugs, yachts and steamers coming and going. Beautiful water effects. (F.Z. Maguire & Co., *Catalogue*, [March 1898], 32.)
SUBJECT: City and town life–New York. Harbors. Ferries. Parks.
ARCHIVE:
CITATIONS: *Philadelphia Record*, 7 July 1896, 2. Maguire & Baucus, *Fall Catalogue*, 1897, 14; F.Z. Maguire & Co., *Catalogue*, [March 1898], 30.
NOTE:

Battery (the) is the oldest park in the city. It covers 21 acres at the seaward end of the island with trees, lawns, and walks, and a fine promenade around the sea-wall. Here stood the Battery erected by the Dutch founders of the city; and in the latter days, the aristocratic houses of the city fronted on its lawns. Sir Guy Carleton's British army embarked here on Nov. 25, 1783, a day still celebrated as Evacuation Day. On one side is Castle Garden, and on another the United-States Revenue Barge-Office. Here the elevated railways terminate. There are beautiful harbor-views from the sea-wall.... (M.F. Sweetser and Simeon Ford, *How to Know New York City*, 1895, 32.)

170 **Ferryboat Leaving Dock, New York / Ferryboat Starting from Dock, New York**
LENGTH: 50 ft.   © No reg.
PRODUCER: James White, Raff & Gammon.
CAMERA: William Heise.
CAST:
PRODUCTION DATE: By 23 June 1896.
LOCATION: New York, N.Y.
SOURCE:
DESCRIPTION:
SUBJECT: City and town life–New York. Harbors. Ferries.
ARCHIVE:
CITATIONS: *Boston Herald*, 28 June 1896, 10 and 11.
NOTE: It is tempting to see this film as the same film as *Battery Park*. Yet the description indicates the ferry is leaving in this film and arriving in the other. It is quite likely that this film was made on the same occasion (and from the same camera position), but was a different take.

James White and William Heise next took their camera to Coney Island and Brooklyn, filming a variety of summer-time attractions. Most of these subjects were taken at a new amusement resort, Bergen Beach, a section of Coney Island (itself part of Brooklyn). Managed by Percy G. Williams, it opened for the first time on 29 May 1896 and had 20,000 to 75,000 visitors per day when the weather was good. Bergen Beach featured the vitascope among its many concessions.

171 ***Scene on Surf Ave., Coney Island / Surf Ave.**
LENGTH: 50 ft.   © No reg.
PRODUCER: James White, Raff & Gammon.
CAMERA: William Heise.
CAST:
PRODUCTION DATE: 18-23 June 1896.
LOCATION: Coney Island, N.Y.
SOURCE:
DESCRIPTION: A scene from America's most noted seaside resort. (F.Z. Maguire & Co., *Catalogue*, [March 1898], 29.)
SUBJECT: Amusement parks. City and town life–Brooklyn.
ARCHIVE: NR-GE.
CITATIONS: Maguire & Baucus, *Edison and International Photographic Films*, April 1897, 15; Maguire & Baucus, *Fall Catalogue*, 1897, 13.
NOTE:

172 **Pony Race / Pony Race at Coney Island / Coney Island Horse Race**
LENGTH: 50 ft.   © No reg.
PRODUCER: James White, Raff & Gammon.
CAMERA: William Heise.
CAST:
PRODUCTION DATE: 18-23 June 1896.
LOCATION: Coney Island, N.Y.
SOURCE:
DESCRIPTION: Showing five frolicsome boys racing on ponies. A good subject. (F.Z. Maguire & Co., *Catalogue*, [March 1898], 29.)

SUBJECT: Amusement parks. Amusement rides. Horse racing.

ARCHIVE:

CITATIONS: *Boston Herald*, 28 June 1896, 11; Wilson & Ball to Vitascope Company, 2 October 1896, MH-BA. Maguire & Baucus, *Edison and International Photographic Films*, April 1897, 15; Maguire & Baucus, *Fall Catalogue*, 1897, 13.

NOTE:

---

173 *Shooting the Chutes / Shooting the Chutes at Coney Island

LENGTH: 50 and 150 ft.   © No reg.

PRODUCER: James White, Raff & Gammon.

CAMERA: William Heise.

CAST:

PRODUCTION DATE: 18-23 June 1896.

LOCATION: Bergen Beach, Coney Island, N.Y.

SOURCE:

DESCRIPTION: This gives a correct view of the famous Boyton Water Chute, and is full of life and motion. A success. (Maguire & Co., *Catalogue*, [March 1898], 32.)

SUBJECT: Amusement parks. Amusement rides. Paul Boyton.

ARCHIVE: NR-GE, DLC-Hendricks, CLAc.

CITATIONS: Paul Boyton World's Water Show Co., advertisement, *New York Clipper,* 4 April 1896, 77; 18 April 1896, 111; *Boston Herald*, 28 June 1896, 11; 12 July 1896, 11. Maguire & Baucus, *Edison Films*, 20 January 1897, 6; Maguire & Baucus, *Edison and International Photographic Films*, April 1897, 15 and 19; Maguire & Baucus, *Fall Catalogue*, 1897, 13 and 14.

NOTE:

---

174 Camel Parade / Streets of Cairo / [Streets of Cairo, no. 1] / Streets in Cairo

LENGTH: 50 ft.   © No reg.

PRODUCER: James White, Raff & Gammon.

CAMERA: William Heise.

CAST:

PRODUCTION DATE: 18-23 June 1896.

LOCATION: Bergen Beach, Coney Island, N.Y.

SOURCE:

DESCRIPTION: Showing young ladies and children riding on camels. (*The Phonoscope*, November 1896, 16.)

A scene showing happy children taking a ride aboard the "Arks of the Desert." (F.Z. Maguire & Co., *Catalogue,* [March 1898], 30.)

SUBJECT: Amusement parks. Amusement rides. Camels. Egyptians.

ARCHIVE:

CITATIONS: *Boston Herald,* 28 June 1896, 10. Maguire & Baucus, *Edison Films*, 20 January 1897, 6; Maguire & Baucus, *Edison and International Photographic Films*, April 1897, 6; Maguire & Baucus, *Fall Catalogue*, 1897, 11.

NOTE: The title "Streets of Cairo" was quickly dropped so as not to be confused with film no. 241.

---

175 The Ferris Wheel

LENGTH: [50 ft.]   © No reg.

PRODUCER: James White, Raff & Gammon.

CAMERA: William Heise.

CAST:

PRODUCTION DATE: 18-23 June 1896.

LOCATION: Bergen Beach, Coney Island, N.Y.

SOURCE:

DESCRIPTION:

SUBJECT: Amusement parks. Amusement rides. Ferris Wheels.
ARCHIVE:
CITATIONS: *Boston Herald*, 28 June 1896, 11.
NOTE:

Bergen Beach

The attractions which may now be seen at Bergen Beach are sufficiently numerous and diversified to satisfy the taste of everyone. While all the various enterprises are now in ship shape, the proprietors are still on the lookout for meritorious novelties which will be put in as rapidly as found. Negotiations are now pending which will probably result shortly in the addition of several important entertainments to the already long list of attractions. Of those already there the vaudeville performance in the Casino is one of the most potent magnets among visitors, many of whom go to the beach each week, knowing that they will see an entire change of bill, not a single act permitted to hold over. Edison's greatest invention, the vitascope, is now in running order and daily delights hundreds by its almost perfect simulation of moving scenes in real life. This is the first one of these marvelous machines ever exhibited on Long Island. The big Bergen Beach wheel is working at last and many persons have already been carried nearly two hundred feet up into the air, whence a magnificent view of Jamaica bay, with the ocean beyond, may be obtained. Paul Boyton's world's water show has lost none of its popularity and the addition of many new acts has served to make it practically another entertainment. The latest recruit to the long list of attractions is the Egyptian encampment, where a novel entertainment is provided by the natives and their troupes of camels, donkeys, etc. The mystic Morrish maze is novel; the royal automaton theater, where marionettes give an entire vaudeville performance; the big merry go round, the largest and most elaborate in the world, and the bicycle carousel are well patronized. (*Brooklyn Eagle*, 21 June 1896, 23.)

The Edison Manufacturing Company took advantage of its newly mobile camera to shoot the first American film of a horse race. In England, meanwhile, R.W. Paul had already filmed the Derby for a second time.

176 Suburban Handicap

LENGTH: [150 ft.]   © No reg.
PRODUCER: James White, Raff & Gammon.
CAMERA: William Heise.
CAST:
PRODUCTION DATE: 23 June 1896.
LOCATION: Sheepshead Bay Race Track, Coney Island, N.Y.
SOURCE:
DESCRIPTION: The new pictures were great successes, especially the reproduction of the Suburban handicap race, showing the finish between Henry of Navarre, the Commoner, and Clifford, which elicited great applause. The portion of the picture showing the field was somewhat obscured by the dust raised by the racers, but the finish on the stretch, showing the judges' box and grand stand crowded with spectators was extremely realistic. ("Keith's New Theatre," *Boston Herald*, 30 June 1896, 9.)
SUBJECT: Horse racing. The Suburban Handicap.
ARCHIVE:
CITATIONS: "Clifford Beats Henry of Navarre," *New York Herald*, 22 September 1895, 4B; "Navarre's Great Race," *Brooklyn Eagle*, 24 June 1896, 5.
NOTE: Clifford had beaten Henry of Navarre in the Oriental Handicap, 21 September 1895. The Edison Manufacturing Company returned to film the Suburban Handicap in 1897.

HENRY OF NAVARRE 2;07
Mr. Belmont's Great Horse Surprised the Talent by Winning the Thirteenth Suburban Handicap.
THE PUBLIC BACKED HIM.
Clifford Was a Hot Favorite and Fortunes Were Lost When He Ran Third.
A SLEEPER FROM THE WEST.
Hanover's Son, The Commoner, at Long Odds, Led the Field and Finished Second.
IT WAS AN EXCITING RACE.
Society Came by Coach, Boat and Train to Plunge on the Beaten Clifford.
FIFTEEN THOUSAND THERE.

...Henry of Navarre is king of the American turf. He won the thirteenth Suburban at the Sheepshead Bay track yesterday afternoon carrying the top weight on the card, and with a length to spare. W.M. Wallace's The

Commoner ran a surprising second, while the mighty Clifford trailed into third place. The latter was a hot favorite, but at no time during the race did he look dangerous.

Fifteen thousand spectators were present and testified their appreciation of Navarre's victory by giving him a great ovation after the race. Much credit is due to Harry Griffin for the masterly way in which the winner was handled. Both weather and track were perfect.

Perhaps never in the history of the Suburban has so much money been won and lost. Much more than a million dollars was at stake. A great deal of it was lost by the bookmakers throughout the country....(*New York Herald*, 24 June 1896, 3.)

THE SUBURBAN

New York had one day's grateful relief yesterday from the eternal talk of politics. It was Suburban day.

Politics? Who would talk politics on Suburban day? Silver? Who would talk silver and 16 to 1 in preference to Commoner at the same ratio, or Henry of Navarre at enticing odds? Who would bother to argue on Suburban day about the East versus the West on the currency question with such an object lesson in view as an Eastern stable's crack like Navarre and a Western representative like Commoner nose and nose half a furlong from home with the Eastern horse, backed with some money to win, beating the life out of the 16 to 1 animal from the land of the silverites in the final tussle on the homestretch. Politics? Why it beats politics hands down as a good live interesting topic of conversation.

It was a great Suburban day, gloriously successful in all its details, even if it was the proverbially unlucky thirteenth revival of the popular event. The day was perfect overhead. True, few were travelling that way, but it was equally charming under foot. The picturesque grounds never looked prettier, the track was in superb condition, as the time showed; handsome women and elegant costumes were more than ever in evidence: the great attendance proved that despite anti-racing legislation, the public are as much in love with the turf as ever; the race itself was anybody's until the horses were nearly home, and we all picked the winner. At least, if we did not, we are all ready to swear we would have done so had we been there.

What more than all these blessings could we have asked in the way of a perfect Suburban? What else, indeed? Henry of Navarre's victory was sentimentally a popular one. The Blemton stable stands for so much that is sound and square and sportsmanlike on the turf that its victories are rejoiced in by the public. Its horses are run honestly and fairly—for the glory more than for the emoluments of the race course. Indeed, it is said that Navarre won nothing but the honors of the day yesterday, yet was ready to be ridden out to the utmost limit of his strength to win for the public. Therefore, Navarre's success was hailed as a popular triumph. Practically it brought no such pleasure to the main body of the turf spectators, who went to the race course in a Pullman palace car, backed the favorite, Clifford, and walked home on the railway ties—unhappy individuals who went down with anticipation of "a bird and a bottle" on their return but came home to meditate over it with the price of a sandwich and a pint of beer left. But this is descending to petty and unpleasant details.

The Coney Island Jockey Club's spring season of 1896 has opened auspiciously, and while the Suburban, of course, dwarfed all other events on the day's programme, the character of the racing, from the initial scramble to the concluding event of yesterday's list, was of an interesting character and foreshadows in the immediate future many pleasant afternoons at Sheepshead Bay. (Editorial, *New York Herald*, 24 June 1896, 8.)

177 **Bathing Scene at Coney Island / Surf Bathing at Atlantic City**

LENGTH: © No reg.

PRODUCER: James White, Raff & Gammon.

CAMERA: William Heise.

CAST:

PRODUCTION DATE: Late June to early July 1896.

LOCATION: [Coney Island, N.Y.]

SOURCE:

DESCRIPTION:

SUBJECT: Bathing beaches. Seashore.

ARCHIVE:

CITATIONS: *Mail and Express*, 18 July 1896, 7; *Boston Herald*, 21 July 1896, 9; *Philadelphia Record*, 21 July 1896, 2.

NOTE: The negative of this film was not of very high quality since the subject was quickly replaced by "a newer and brighter bathing scene." (See *Bathing Scene at Rockaway*, Edison film no. 191.)

Bicycling had become an immensely popular pastime by the summer of 1896; and its impact on society was being reported in the press on a daily basis. Bicycle parades were ways of demanding—or celebrating—improved roadways. One of the biggest of these gatherings was in Brooklyn.

178 Parade of Bicyclists at Brooklyn, New York / Bicycle Parade

LENGTH: 50 and 150 ft.   © No reg.

PRODUCER: James White, Raff & Gammon.

CAMERA: William Heise.

CAST:

PRODUCTION DATE: 27 June 1896.

LOCATION: Brooklyn, N.Y.

SOURCE:

DESCRIPTION: That immense bicycle parade which took place in Brooklyn was photographed specially for Edison's marvellous invention. (*Boston Herald*, 12 July 1896, 11.)

Bicyclists who are interested in seeing what a Brooklyn parade is like should see that shown in the Vitascope, with its mounted band and all the pomp and

BROOKLYN'S GREAT BICYCLE PARADE PASSING THE REVIEWING STAND.

glory that pertains to such an occasion. (*Boston Herald*, 14 July 1896, 6.)

On the boulevard, New York. (F.Z. Maguire & Co., *Catalogue*, [March 1898], 32.)

SUBJECT: City and town life–Brooklyn. Parades. Bicycles. Marching bands.

ARCHIVE:

CITATIONS: "All New York Was Cycle Mad," *New York Herald*, 7 June 1896, 3-4; "Finest of All Cycle Parades," *Brooklyn Eagle*, 28 June 1896, 5. Maguire & Baucus, *Edison Films*, 20 January 1897, 7; Maguire & Baucus, *Edison and International Photographic Films*, April 1897, 5 and 17; Maguire & Baucus, *Fall Catalogue*, 1897, 11 and 14; F.Z. Maguire & Co., *Catalogue*, [March 1898], 29.

NOTE: The event shown in this film can easily be confused with a large bicycle parade occurring in Manhattan on 6 June 1896, sponsored by the *New York Evening Telegram*. One programme identifies this as a film of the Denver Wheel Club. (*Scrapbook*, Raff & Gammon Collection, vol. 5, MH-BA.)

WHEELS WHIRLED IN FINE ARRAY.
Seven Thousand Bicyclists Open the Return Path from Coney Island with a Parade.
MAYOR WURSTER PRESENT.
He Reviews the Wheelmen from the Grand Stand and Is Greatly Pleased with the Show.
NEW YORK CLUBS IN LINE.
Crack Century Riders Out in Force and Harlem Wheelmen Received an Ovation.

Seven thousand bicyclists were in line in the parade which signalized the opening of the return path along the Ocean Pathway from Brooklyn to Brighton yesterday.

They trooped steadily by the reviewing stand for an hour or more in platoons four abreast, with bands playing, flags flying and silvery wheel bells tinkling salutes to Mayor Wurster and the Park Commissioner, who reviewed them.

It was a fine and inspiring sight, and it gave the politicians and pharisees a deep feeling of respect for the bicycle vote. If ten thousand wheelmen can open such a magnificent bicycle path, surely the half million wheelmen in the State should be well able to convert every road and lane from Brooklyn to Buffalo into a smooth and fascinating bicycle dream.

Incidentally, the demonstration may be called the second annual parade of the Good Roads Association. Every wheelman in Greater New York who has fought in the direction of road reform was in line.

The grand stand was located in the Ocean Parkway, south of avenue C. It was tastefully hung with flags and bunting from end to end. All along the parkway from Prospect Park half way to Brighton Beach the houses and hotels were festooned with flags in honor of the occasion.

On either side of the path, which, by the way, looked like an infinitely long strip of lavender ribbon, the spectators began to gather at noon. The parade was set for two o'clock. Those who did not rally along the path with their wheels rallied in the trolley cars and on foot. They came from all directions and converged upon the grand stand, and along the ropes which were supposed to guard the line of parade from intrusion.

The policemen had their hands full half an hour before the parade began to move. They fussed and fumed among the dense throng of spectators, but in spite of all they could do the crowd insisted on encroaching upon the track. The spectators were four deep along both sides of the path for a mile or more. Half of them could ride wheels themselves, and were sorry they had not brought their bikes along.

Scores of pretty girls darted up and down the path or stood by the wayside holding their wheels and chatting with friends. Many of them had taken part in the great Evening Telegram parade [June 6], and several were there who had drawn prizes on that occasion.

START OF THE PAGEANT.

Mayor Wurster and the Park dignitaries arrived at two o'clock and took the points assigned them on the grand stand. Then the band struck up a bicycle march and away down the path toward the Park the first division fell into line. It was composed of the Brooklyn Wheelmen.

They were preceded by twenty gray coated Park policemen on wheels, who cleared the track. The Brooklyn men made a very fine appearance, with their blue coats and white duck knickerbockers, and the crowd cheered them heartily. Just behind this detachment rolled a squad of duplex wheels. More policemen followed, after which the Kings County Wheelmen, more than a hundred strong, glided down the double hedge of gaping and cheering spectators.

As the leaders of each division passed the reviewing stand they lifted their hats to the Mayor and the Commissioners, who bowed in return. Between the division, in what might be termed the neutral ground, a great many curious things could be seen.

Just behind the Kings County Wheelmen rode a young man with a basket attachment slung in front of his handle bars. In this basket sat a yellow dog of low degree, which appeared to be utterly contented with its lot. Then came two sociable looking family duplexes covered with awnings, under which the wheel people pedalled at their ease.

Behind the fine squadron of Long Island Wheelmen came two bicycles in single file connected by a rope at the end of which was a very small boy in a very small cart. It was a gay looking tandem, but the spectators envied the boy far more than the wheelmen.

NEW WOMAN IN EVIDENCE.

Almost before the tandem had disappeared the new woman came into view. She wore blue golf stockings with red diamonds at the top, tight brown knickerbockers, a man's coat and a rakish jockey cap. "I tell you it's a woman," said a pretty girl on the grand stand in a shrill whisper. "Well, did you ever?" murmured her companion: "It's a woman, as sure as you're born. Well, I don't blame men for making fun of some people! Just look at her! Low handle bars, too!"

Then both girls made that peculiar feminine clucking with their tongues, which means a great deal or nothing, according to circumstances.

And still the wide and noiseless stream poured on. Mayor Wurster was kept busy bowing and scraping and smiling, and the Commissioners hats were in the air constantly. Those who passed in review were composed of all ages, sexes and conditions. There were old men, young men and boys, old women, young women and girls.

There were also all sorts of uniforms. The Bushwick Wheelmen looked very fine in their uniforms of gray. The South Brooklyn Wheelmen were also loudly cheered. Just behind this division in the neutral ground rode a tall young woman in tight fitting green knickerbockers, a frock coat and a red Tam O'Shanter. She went sprinting by at a fifteen mile gait and everybody in the grand stand turned to look after her.

Bloomers were exceedingly numerous, but somehow they did not look half so well as the neat little skirts, shirt waists and sailor hats of some of the women riders. The Kings County Wheelmen turned out a large delegation and formed one of the finest looking detachments of the parade.

CENTURY WHEELMEN SCORCHED.

The Century Wheelmen, the winners of the Telegram prize, were the first of the New York division to appear. A long distance separated them from the riders in advance, and they came scorching past the stand at a great rate, scarcely taking time to bow to the Mayor and Commissioners. They were evidently out of line, for close behind them came the Williamsburg Wheelmen and the Y.M.C.A. Park Wheelmen, the later numbering hundreds.

Preceding the Ocean Parkway Wheelmen next in line were a party of women riders, who jingled their bells in a silvery chorus as they passed the stand. Then came the Gilberts, in dark brown, and the Logans, in light yellow, forming pleasing contrasts in varying colors of the parade. A pretty woman riding a wheel literally covered with flowers glided past the stand, looking neither to the right nor to the left.

A moment later the blare of a band was heard away down the line of march, and the famous Olympic Band, which created such a sensation at the Evening Telegram parade, rolled into view. The players seemed to find no difficulty in holding their machines straight with one hand and playing with the other. The leader even missed a crescendo flourish in order to raise his hat to the grand stand.

By this time the crowd were prepared for almost anything. Consequently, they were not very much surprised when a wheelman riding an old fashioned lofty machine came flying by with one wheel in the air.

OVATION FOR HARLEMITES.

The Harlem Wheelmen were given a regular ovation as they came down the path, four abreast. They were dressed in cream colored uniforms and made a very handsome appearance.

Following the second division came the New Jersey clubs and the Good Roads Associations, behind which hundreds upon hundreds of unattached riders fell into line. Among these unattached riders there were some very pretty sights. Between the saddles of a tandem pedalled by a man and woman was slung a little seat in which sat a very small, white clad child.

Behind this family party there came three little girls dressed in white and wearing red sashes. The next person upon which the crowd showered their attentions was a little four-year-old boy in red knickerbockers. He scorched past the Mayor in a way that made that official open his eyes. (*New York Herald*, 28 June 1896, 5C.)

Some time in the summer of 1896 (the exact date is uncertain), Raff & Gammon opened a make-shift, roof-top studio above their offices at 43 West 28th Street. This facility offered more convenient location for filming theatrical performers than the Black Maria in Orange, New Jersey.

179 Little Jake and the Big Dutch Girl / Clog Dance / Little Jake and Big Dutch Girl

LENGTH: 150 ft.   © No reg.
PRODUCER: James White, Raff & Gammon.
CAMERA: William Heise.
CAST:
PRODUCTION DATE: By late June 1896.
LOCATION: [Raff & Gammon's roof-top studio, New York, N.Y.]
SOURCE:
DESCRIPTION: A burlesque dance, showing a comical little man and a very large Dutch girl in an abbreviated dancing costume. (F.Z. Maguire, *Catalogue*, [March 1898], 28.)
SUBJECT: Vaudeville–performances. Dancing. German Americans.
ARCHIVE:
CITATIONS: *Boston Herald,* 30 June 1896, 9. Maguire & Baucus, *Edison and International Films*, April 1897, 18; Maguire & Baucus, *Fall Catalogue*, 1897, 14.
NOTE:

The Lumière cinématographe had its American premiere at Keith's Union Square Theatre in New York City on 29 June 1896.

Vernona Jarbeau, after purportedly failing to find an appropriate play to show off her talents as a star, joined The Passing Show, *then on tour, in mid-September 1894 (New York Dramatic Mirror, 22 September 1894, 4). Eventually she made a hit with her burlesque imitation of Mme. Emma Calvé in* Carmen *(it was not yet part of her act when* The Passing Show *returned to New York City on 29 October 1894). After she left* The Passing Show, *Jarbeau became a headline attraction in vaudeville and appeared at Keith's Union Square Theatre for two weeks commencing 24 February 1896, still featuring her Calvé burlesque. By the summer she was performing at New York City's roof garden theatres. By February 1897, she was rehearsing for the leading role in* Little Miss Chicago, *at Clifford's Gaiety Theatre in Chicago. She played Koster & Bial's Music Hall and other vaudeville houses during the 1900-1901 season.*

180 Vernona Jarbeau

LENGTH: 50 and 150 ft.   © No reg.
PRODUCER: James White, Raff & Gammon.
CAMERA: William Heise.
CAST: Vernona Jarbeau.
PRODUCTION DATE: 30 June-5 July 1896.
LOCATION: [Raff & Gammon's roof-top studio, New York, N.Y.]
SOURCE: The Passing Show (revue).
DESCRIPTION: "Calve's notable dance in "Carmen." (*Boston Herald*, 26 July 1896, 10.)
SUBJECT: Vaudeville–performances. Opera–performances. Dancing. Emma Calvé.
ARCHIVE:

CITATIONS: *New York Herald*, 23 February 1896, 7C; *New York Clipper,* 16 January 1897, 737; 20 February 1897, 811. Maguire & Baucus, *Edison and International Photographic Films*, April 1897, 16 and 19; Maguire & Baucus, *Fall Catalogue*, 1897, 13; F.Z. Maguire & Co., *Catalogue*, [March 1898], 28.

NOTE: *Munsey's Magazine,* which routinely featured photographs of legitimate theatrical actresses, did not run a picture of Jarbeau as suggested in the *Dramatic Mirror* report.

Triumphant Re-engagement of
Vernona Jarbeau

The Charming Vocaliste and Brilliant Comedienne, Whose Success the Past Week Was Instant and Emphatic, Miss Jarbeau Will Be Heard in Several New Songs, Retaining Her Capital Imitation of Mme. Calvé's Carmen, in Which She Will be Assisted by a Full Chorus. (*New York Herald*, 1 March 1896, 6C.)

Jack Hirsh is busily engaged in booming Vernona Jarbeau. In one of the big Sunday papers of June 29 he had a page with pictures giving the history of her legs. During last week he had the X rays turned on her by Nikola Tesla, the electrician, and had her pose for Edison's Vitascope and the kinetoscope, and for *Munsey's* and *Metropolitan.* (*New York Dramatic Mirror*, 11 July 1896, 18.)

181   Frog Dance
LENGTH: © No reg.
PRODUCER: James White, Raff & Gammon.
CAMERA: William Heise.
CAST:
PRODUCTION DATE: [30 June-5 July 1896.]
LOCATION: [Raff & Gammon's roof-top studio, New York, N.Y.]
SOURCE:
DESCRIPTION:
SUBJECT: Vaudeville–performances. Dancing. French.
ARCHIVE:
CITATIONS: A.F. Rieser to Raff & Gammon, 22 July 1896, MH-BA.
NOTE:

182   Trick Bicycle Riding / Bicycle Riding / Lee Richardson
LENGTH: 150 ft.   © No reg.
PRODUCER: James White, Raff & Gammon.
CAMERA: William Heise.
CAST: Levant Richardson.
PRODUCTION DATE: [30 June-5 July 1896.]
LOCATION: [Raff & Gammon's roof-top studio, New York, N.Y.]
SOURCE:
DESCRIPTION: By Levant Richardson, champion trick bicycle rider of the world. (F.Z. Maguire & Co., *Catalogue*, [March 1898], 31.)
SUBJECT: Vaudeville–performances. Bicycles.
ARCHIVE:
CITATIONS: A.F. Rieser to Raff & Gammon, 22 July 1896, MH-BA. Maguire & Baucus, *Edison and International Photographic Films*, April 1897, 17; Maguire & Baucus, *Fall Catalogue*, 1897, 14.
NOTE:

Trick Riding

The average wheelman sits upon the saddle, grasps the handle bar, and propels his machine by pressing the pedals with his feet. The expert, the "trick rider," scorns this commonplace method of maneuvering a bicycle. He stands upon the saddle and handle bar, or balances himself upon the former alone, standing or kneeling. He rides on the hind wheel alone, rising the front wheel from the ground then he bends forward, detaches the front wheel, and still pedals forward while he takes half of his machine to pieces. He rides backward–Lee Richardson has ridden half a mile backward in two minutes and a half. He turns his machines upside down and makes the wheels revolve, balancing on the pedals. He rides a single wheel–the large wheel of an old fashioned "ordinary"–with neither saddle nor handle, supporting and balancing himself on the pedals. One trick rider plays the banjo while he performs this feat. He carries a man upon his shoulders, and even a second passenger upon the shoulders of the first. The riders shown on page 143 have an "act" in which the entire family of brothers and sisters ride upon a single wheel.

In all, more than a hundred styles of fancy riding are reckoned, and the control that some of its exponents have over their machine seems, to those who watch it on track or stage, nothing less than magical. ("The World Awheel," *Munsey's Magazine*, May 1896, 155.)

183 *Passaic Falls / Paterson Falls

LENGTH: 50 ft.   © No reg.

PRODUCER: James White, Raff & Gammon.

CAMERA: William Heise.

CAST:

PRODUCTION DATE: By early July 1896.

LOCATION: Paterson, N.J.

SOURCE:

DESCRIPTION: A beautiful picture of the Paterson Falls, on the Passaic River. One of the best subjects we offer. (F.Z. Maguire & Co., *Catalogue*, [March 1898], 30.)

SUBJECT: Waterfalls. Paterson Falls. Bridges.

ARCHIVE: NR-GE, DLC-Hendricks, CLAc.

CITATIONS: *Philadelphia Record*, 12 July 1896, 11. Maguire & Baucus, *Edison Films*, 20 January 1897, 6; Maguire & Baucus, *Edison and International Photographic Films*, April 1897, 14; Maguire & Baucus, *Fall Catalogue*, 1897, 13; *Edison Films*, March 1900, 47; *Edison Films*, July 1901, 94.

NOTE: The International Film Company also took a film of this subject and it is possible that the International film rather than the Edison one survives. In the Maguire & Baucus catalog of April 1897, the Edison film is entitled *Paterson Falls*, the International film, *Passaic Falls*.

184 The Haymakers at Work / Hay Makers

LENGTH: 50 ft.   © No reg.

PRODUCER: James White, Raff & Gammon.

CAMERA: William Heise.

CAST:

PRODUCTION DATE: By mid-July 1896.

LOCATION:

SOURCE:

DESCRIPTION: A view of a wheat binder at work in a western field. (*Boston Herald*, 21 July 1896, 9.)

Showing the cutting of grass with a scythe and sickle in a manner true to life. (*The Phonoscope*, November 1896, 16.)

The primitive manner of making hay; with scythe, sickle and hand rake, one of the sharpest subjects we have, and very popular. (F.Z. Maguire & Co., *Catalogue*, [March 1898], 31.)

SUBJECT: Farms. Agriculture. Harvesting.

ARCHIVE:

CITATIONS: *Boston Herald*, 21 July 1896, 9. Maguire & Baucus, *Edison Films*, 20 January 1897, 6; Maguire & Baucus, *Edison and International Photographic Films*, April 1897, 10; Maguire & Baucus, *Fall Catalogue*, 1897, 12.

NOTE:

185 *Love in a Sleigh

LENGTH: 50 ft.   © No reg.

PRODUCER: James White, Raff & Gammon.

CAMERA: William Heise.

CAST:

PRODUCTION DATE: By mid-July 1896.
LOCATION:
SOURCE:
DESCRIPTION:
SUBJECT: Courtship. Kissing.
ARCHIVE: NNMoMA.
CITATIONS: A.F. Rieser to Raff & Gammon, 22 July 1896, MH-BA.
NOTE:

Fatima had become a star at the Midway Plaisance, along with Little Egypt, at the 1893 Columbian Exposition in Chicago. In 1894-1895, she toured with Little Egypt as part of Reilly & Woods Big Show (playing Miner's Bowery Theater for the week of 12 November).

186 ***Fatima's Coochee-Coochee Dance / Fatima's Couchee-Couchee Dance / Couchee Dance**
LENGTH: 150 ft.   © No reg.
PRODUCER: James White, Raff & Gammon.
CAMERA: William Heise.
CAST: Fatima.
PRODUCTION DATE: By late July 1896.
LOCATION: [Raff & Gammon's roof-top studio, New York City or Coney Island, N.Y.]
SOURCE:

DESCRIPTION: This is the lady whose graceful interpretations of the poetry of motion has made this dance so popular of recent years. (*The Phonoscope*, January 1899, 15.)
SUBJECT: Vaudeville–performances. Dancing. Danse du ventre.
ARCHIVE: NNMoMA.
CITATIONS: Purdy & Kiefaber to Raff & Gammon, 7 August 1896, MH-BA; Purdy & Kiefaber to Raff & Gammon, 17 August 1896, MH-BA. *Edison Films*, March 1900, 28; *Edison Films*, July 1901, 52.
NOTE: Charles Webster and Edmund Kuhn of the International Film Company made a film of Fatima and it is possible that the surviving films are theirs. It is also possible that this subject entered the Edison catalog via the acquisition of International Film Company negatives in the late 1890s, once the company was defunct. Peter Williamson at the Museum of Modern Art has identified two different takes of this subject, both of which can be found at NNMoMA.

Fatima, snake charmer, received a serious bite from one of her largest serpents, March 5, at Davis' Museum, Pittsburg, and may not be able to work for a number of weeks. (*New York Clipper*, 17 March 1894, 23.)

THEY SAW FATIMA DANCE.
Two or Three Politicians Blushed and Beat a Retreat.

The Seymour Club, the leading democratic organization of Williamsburg, had its annual outing on Monday at Donnelly's Grove, College Point. Nearly six hundred persons attended. During the day the danse du ventre was given by Fatima, formerly of the Midway Plaisance. The exhibition was in a nearby resort, and the prices of admission were from fifty cents to four dollars. To such lengths did Fatima go in the latter part of her dance that two or three of the witnesses of the display left the place. She did not accompany the excursion on the steamer, but was taken over from this city on the Ninety-second street ferry by her manager, who is known as Professor Sheck. The managers of the excursion disclaim any responsibility for the performance. (*New York Herald*, 24 August 1894, 9.)

HAMMERSTEIN'S OLYMPIA...Fatima, an oriental dancer who has become particularly well-known in this city and vicinity, also danced in the second scene of "Marguerite," and apparently found much favor with the audience. Many of the objectionable features of her performance were omitted, but, nevertheless, her motions throughout the dance strongly suggested the "couchee-couchee." (*New York Clipper*, 4 April 1896, 70.)

FATIMA
THE GREATEST ORIENTAL DANCER,
Just close six weeks successful engagement at Hammerstein's Olympia, N.Y. City. Has a few weeks open. Address 111 W. 33d St., N.Y.C. (Advertisement, *New York Clipper*, 23 May 1896, 191.)

Edison production was being influenced by the Lumières even before the cinématographe had its U.S. premiere. The first Lumière "story film" or "comic vignette" to be remade by the Edison group was, as one might expect, Arroseur et arrosé. *In some respects, this film was not only an imitation but a burlesque of the Lumière subject.*

187 *****Bad Boy and the Gardener / Garden Scene**
LENGTH: 50 and 150 ft.   © No reg.
PRODUCER: James White, Raff & Gammon.
CAMERA: William Heise.
CAST:
PRODUCTION DATE: By 23 July 1896.
LOCATION:
SOURCE: *Arroseur et arrosé* (Lumière film, 1896).

DESCRIPTION: The garden scene was humorous, inasmuch as the bad boy was getting in his work on the gardener by dowsing him with water, though he finally gets caught and receives a licking. (*Boston Herald*, 28 July 1896, 7.)
A lady watering the garden with a hose, a mischievous boy stops the flow of water until she looks for the cause, when he permits the water to flow, resulting in the lady taking an unexpected bath. The father then appears and chastises the youthful culprit. One of the best films ever made. (F.Z. Maguire & Co., *Catalogue*, [March 1898], 30.)
SUBJECT: Gardening. Boys. Practical jokes. Punishment.
ARCHIVE: CaOOANF.
CITATIONS: *New York World*, 20 September 1896, 14. Maguire & Baucus, *Edison Films*, 20 January 1897, 6-7; Maguire & Baucus, *Edison and International Photographic Films*, April 1897, 9 and 18; Maguire & Baucus, *Fall Catalogue*, 1897, 12 and 14; *Edison Films*, March 1900, 36; *Edison Films*, July 1901, 71.
NOTE: Listed as 110-foot subject in 1901. The role of the woman is played by a man in drag. The description which appears in the *Boston Herald* may be explained by this fact. There may also have been two Edison films of this gag or, conceivably, a Lumière film was shown at Keith's vaudeville house in Boston.

188 **Street Sprinkling and Trolley Cars / Edison Laboratory / Street Scene near Edison's Laboratory**
LENGTH: 50 ft.   © No reg.
PRODUCER: James White, Raff & Gammon.
CAMERA: William Heise.
CAST:
PRODUCTION DATE: By 23 July 1896.
LOCATION: West Orange, N.J.
SOURCE:
DESCRIPTION: The street sprinkling scene was such as may be seen on almost any thoroughfare, with a lot of urchins dancing about. (*Boston Herald*, 28 July 1896, 7.) Showing the front of Mr. Edison's laboratory, boys playing, trolley cars passing and porter sprinkling street. Sure to interest the public. (F.Z. Maguire & Co., *Catalogue*, [March 1898], 32.)
SUBJECT: City and town life–Orange. Boys. Streets–maintenance and repair. Urban transportation. Thomas A. Edison.
ARCHIVE:

CITATIONS: *New York World*, 20 September 1896, 14. Maguire & Baucus, *Edison Films*, 20 January 1897, 6; Maguire & Baucus, *Edison and International Photographic Films*, April 1897, 7; Maguire & Baucus, *Fall Catalogue*, 1897, 11.
NOTE:

189 "Grand Republic" / Landing of the "Grand Republic"
LENGTH: 150 ft.　　© No reg.
PRODUCER: Raff & Gammon.
CAMERA: William Heise.
CAST:
PRODUCTION DATE: By 23 July 1896.
LOCATION: Rockaway Beach, N.Y.
SOURCE:
DESCRIPTION: Showing the noted excursion boat unloading her passengers at Rockaway Beach. (F.Z. Maguire & Co., *Catalogue*, [March 1898], 32.)
SUBJECT: Ferries. Seashore.
ARCHIVE:
CITATIONS: Maguire & Baucus, *Edison and International Photographic Films*, April 1897, 18; Maguire & Baucus, *Fall Catalogue*, 1897, 14.
NOTE:

190 Return of the Fishermen
LENGTH:　　　© No reg.
PRODUCER: James White, Raff & Gammon.
CAMERA: William Heise.
CAST:
PRODUCTION DATE: By 23 July 1896.
LOCATION: [Rockaway Beach, N.Y.]
SOURCE:
DESCRIPTION: A splendid subject, full of life and motion, the sea, the boat, the rowers, and the landing of the fish all being clear and distinct. (*Boston Herald*, 28 July 1896, 7.)
SUBJECT: Seashore. Fishing. Boats and boating.
ARCHIVE:
CITATIONS:
NOTE: Given the positive review this film received in the *Boston Herald*, it is puzzling why it did not enter the Edison catalog. Perhaps the negative was damaged during the course of initial printing. Or was it a Lumière film that somehow slipped onto the vitascope?

191 Bathing Scene at Rockaway / Bathing Scene
LENGTH: 50 and 150 ft.　　© No reg.
PRODUCER: James White, Raff & Gammon.
CAMERA: William Heise.
CAST:
PRODUCTION DATE: By 23 July 1896.
LOCATION: Rockaway Beach, N.Y.
SOURCE: *Bathing Scene at Coney Island* (Edison film no. 177, June-July 1896).
DESCRIPTION: "A new and brighter bathing scene." (*Boston Herald*, 26 July 1896, 10.) Shows a beach full of bathers. They sport in and out of the water. Surf breaks and recedes. Bathing suits cling to their figures in a very picturesque fashion. (*Edison Films*, July 1901, 45.)
SUBJECT: Bathing beaches. Seashore.
ARCHIVE:
CITATIONS: *New York World*, 13 September 1896, 14. Maguire & Baucus, *Edison Films*, 20 January 1897, 6-7; Maguire & Baucus, *Edison and International Photographic Films*, April 1897, 3 and 17; Maguire & Baucus, *Fall Catalogue*, 1897, 11 and 14; F.Z. Maguire & Co., *Catalogue*, [March 1898], 29; *Edison Films*, March 1900, 25.
NOTE:

92 **[Boxing Match Between a Man and a Woman]**
LENGTH: © No reg.
PRODUCER: James White, Raff & Gammon.
CAMERA: William Heise.
CAST:
PRODUCTION DATE: By 23 July 1896.
LOCATION:
SOURCE:
DESCRIPTION:
SUBJECT: Sports. Boxing.
ARCHIVE:
CITATIONS: "Keith's New Theatre," *Boston Herald*, 26 July 1896, 10.
NOTE: This film was announced at Keith's New Theatre in Boston for the week of 27 July 1896 but was not reviewed and may have never been shown. It may also have been an advance announcement for *Boxing Contest Between Tommy White and "Solly" Smith* (film no. 193), in which the manager thought "Solly" was a woman.

193 **Boxing Contest Between Tommy White and Solly Smith**
LENGTH: © No reg.
PRODUCER: James White, Raff & Gammon.
CAMERA: William Heise.
CAST: "Tommy" White, "Solly" Smith.
PRODUCTION DATE: By early August 1896.
LOCATION:
SOURCE:
DESCRIPTION:
SUBJECT: Sports. Boxing.
ARCHIVE:
CITATIONS: "Smith-Erne Fight a Draw," *New York Herald*, 3 October 1894, 13; "Solly Smith Loses on a Foul," *New York Herald*, 28 November 1894, 11; *Chicago Tribune*, 9 August 1896, 27.
NOTE: Although White and Smith were both in New York City in the summer of 1896 ("Griffo and Everhardt Draw," *Scranton Times*, 26 May 1896, 5), it is possible that this film was an old subject under a new title. The only reference to its existence, which I have found, is to its presentation at Hopkins Theatre in Chicago. In this case, the film was announced in the theater's advertisement but not mentioned in the *Chicago Tribune*'s short review of that week's bill. (See also note for film no. 192.)

SMITH DEFEATS PATERSON.
A fair sized crowd witnessed the bouts last night held under the auspices of the Eastern Athletic Club at Palace Rink, Brooklyn. The first bout was eight rounds, between "Eddie" Sweeney, of Brooklyn, and "Joe" Hopkins, of this city. The men weighed in at 135 pounds. It was a draw. Frank Paterson, of Brooklyn, and "Solly" Smith, of California, were the principals in the next bout, which was for ten rounds at 122 pounds. Smith was awarded the decision. (*New York Herald*, 23 June 1896, 5.)

Military scenes shown on the Lumière cinématographe were extremely popular and encouraged Raff & Gammon and the Edison Manufacturing Company to produce similar kinds of subjects.

194 **Firing of Cannon at Peekskill By the Battery of Artillery / Artillery, Second Battery / Artillery Practice**
LENGTH: 50 ft. © No reg.
PRODUCER: James White, Raff & Gammon.
CAMERA: William Heise.
CAST:
PRODUCTION DATE: July 1896.
LOCATION: Peekskill, N.Y.
SOURCE:

DESCRIPTION: This film shows very fine smoke effects upon the discharge of the gun. (*The Phonoscope*, November 1896, 16.)

SUBJECT: Armies–United States. Artillery.

ARCHIVE:

CITATIONS: "Dull Day in Camp," *New York Herald*, 29 June 1896, 7; P.W. Kiefaber to Frank Gammon, 31 July 1896, MH-BA; *Boston Herald*, 4 August 1896, 7; *Mail and Express*, 12 September 1896, 10. Maguire & Baucus, *Edison Films*, 20 January 1897, 7; Maguire & Baucus, *Edison and International Photographic Films*, April 1897, 3; Maguire & Baucus, *Fall Catalogue*, 1897, 11; F.Z. Maguire & Co., *Catalogue*, [March 1898], 31.

NOTE:

195 [Artillery Scene at Peekskill]

LENGTH: © No reg.

PRODUCER: James White, Raff & Gammon.

CAMERA: William Heise.

CAST:

PRODUCTION DATE: July 1896.

LOCATION: Peekskill, N.Y.

SOURCE:

DESCRIPTION: The vitascope pictures were novel and interesting, especially the two illustrating the movements and drill of a battery of artillery. (*Boston Herald*, 4 August 1896, 7.)

SUBJECT: Armies–United States. Artillery.

ARCHIVE:

CITATIONS:

NOTE:

196 *Mess Call

LENGTH: 50 ft.   © No reg.

PRODUCER: James White, Raff & Gammon.

CAMERA: William Heise.

CAST:

PRODUCTION DATE: July 1896.

LOCATION: Peekskill, N.Y.

SOURCE:

DESCRIPTION: Showing soldiers at New York State camp going to dinner. (F.Z. Maguire & Co., *Catalogue*, [March 1898], 31.)

SUBJECT: Armies–United States. Military camps.

ARCHIVE: NNMoMA.

CITATIONS: Maguire & Baucus, *Edison and International Photographic Films*, April 1897, 12; Maguire & Baucus, *Fall Catalogue*, 1897, 12.

NOTE: Identification of this film by Ray Phillips is compelling if not absolutely conclusive.

SOLDIER BOYS TAKE PEEKSKILL.
Opening of the State Camp Signalized by the Booming of the National Salute.
TROOP A FIRST ON THE FIELD.
Followed by the Gallant Eighth and the Men of the Separate Companies.
MANY FAMILIAR FACES SEEN.
Initial Drill Was a Great Success but There Are Very Few Visitors Present.
(BY TELEGRAPH TO THE HERALD.)

STATE CAMP, PEEKSKILL, N.Y., June 27, 1896.–It was just twenty minutes to three o'clock this afternoon when the Eighth regiment, preceded by Squadron A and followed by the battalion of separate companies, marched into camp. As the head of the regimental column reached the brow of the hill the first of the twenty-one guns of the national salute rang out, the colors were run up on the flagstaffs and the camp season of 1896 was officially inaugurated.

FIRST IN THE FIELD.
Squadron A was the first to arrive in camp. Orders had been issued to march up from the city, but subsequently

they were changed and the command came to camp by train. They were expected a little after eleven o'clock this morning, but their train was side tracked somewhere along the line, and it was a quarter past one when they arrived, having disembarked at the Peekskill freight depot and trooped over from the village. The State caterers had dinner all ready and it was eaten with a relish as soon as the horses were cared for.

Just before the infantry arrived Mayor Roe and the squadron rode down the hill to escort them into camp. The Seventy-fourth Regiment Band, of Buffalo, under Bandmaster J.G. Miller, was waiting at the top of the hill, and when the cavalry had passed "fell in" at the head of the Infantry. It was then that Sergeant J.G. Janssen and the detail from the West battery fired the salute. The troops marched at once to the East Parade Ground, where they were dismissed to quarters. Shortly after every one was in his own tent, busy getting things to rights.

MANY NEW TENTS ADDED.

The camp is much larger this year than ever before, about 150 new tents having been added to the park, making sixteen company streets....

VERY FAMILIAR FACES.

At State headquarters there are many familiar faces. General E.A. McAlpin occupies his usual quarters and received the troop when they marched in to-day. Colonel J.G. Story has the tent he has occupied many years...Colonel Robert M. Hall, United States infantry, has also been detailed to camp by the government as an inspector of drills and of the National Guard in general.

The evening parade was a very pretty one, but only a few visitors were present. At its conclusion Squadron A had a short drill. Services to-morrow will be conducted by Rev. Charles De Witt Bridgeman, of the regiment.

SCHEDULE OF DUTY.

Go where you will—a cleaner or better disciplined camp cannot be found, or one where harder work is performed, or time utilized to better advantage. From five o'clock in the morning until eleven o'clock at night the men are subject to military duty....The camp is laid out with perfect gravel walks and drives, lighted by electricity, has a perfect drainage and sewerage system, bath houses and kindred conveniences, sentry boxes and a mess pavilion with culinary department sufficient in capacity for feeding about twelve hundred men and their officers in a manner equal to that of a first class hotel. Meals being furnished by contract, the men are saved from all of the labor incidental to camp cooking, including the issuing and distribution of rations, &c., which allows them more time for strictly military instruction. The food is all cooked by machinery and inspected and the meals are never late.

OPPORTUNITY FOR DRILLS.

The programme of instruction, which is carefully prepared before the camp opens, embraces the drill regulations which cannot be successfully practised in the armories, and this year colonels are to drill their regiments, something which they have not done at camp for several years, the drills heretofore being by battalion under the majors. The heavy storms of the past winter and spring made no exception of the State camp ground and surroundings. Many trees were blown down and washouts were numerous, and it took a great deal of work to get it in shape in time for the opening. Additional streets of company tents have been put up and there are now sixteen of them, while the principal street, or Broadway, as the line officers' street is called, has been widened and straightened.

In order to take precaution against a water famine, an additional tank, holding thirty thousand gallons, has been put up alongside the old one. More sinks have been added, and an extension to the mess hall. The shower baths have been improved. The Y.M.C.A. will have a larger tent than usual for the free use of guardsmen, stocked with reading matter, writing paper, &c. The famous "Dunphy's Canteen" is open again on the outskirts of the camp, where the boys can get a cool drink occasionally, and "Luxury Row," where the State officers have their tents, is on the same old bluff. (*New York Herald*, 28 June 1896, 5.)

Keith's...The vitascope will have new views, the most attractive of which will be the evolutions of one of New York's crack regiments, the first pictures of the kind exhibited by Edison's wonderful invention. (*New York Herald*, 2 August 1896, 10.)

197 **Swimming School / Bode & Daly's Swimming School / Bode and Daly's Swimming School**

LENGTH: 50 and 150 ft.   © No reg.

PRODUCER: James White, Raff & Gammon.

CAMERA: William Heise.

CAST:

PRODUCTION DATE: By early August 1896.

LOCATION: Fifth Avenue, New York, N.Y.

SOURCE:

DESCRIPTION: Bathers swimming, diving and turning somersaults in the water.
(Maguire & Baucus, *Fall Catalogue*, 1897, 13.)

A lively bathing scene in a Fifth avenue swimming school. (Maguire & Baucus, *Fall Catalogue*, 1897, 14.)
A bathing scene in a 5th avenue swimming school, showing a number of ladies and gentlemen indulging in their morning dip. (F.Z. Maguire & Co., *Catalogue*, [March 1898], 32.)

SUBJECT: Swimming pools. Aquatic sports. Social elites.

ARCHIVE:

CITATIONS: A. Holland to Raff & Gammon, 3 September 1896, MH-BA and Wm. Rock to Raff & Gammon, 16 November 1896, MH-BA. Maguire & Baucus, *Edison Films*, 20 January 1897, 7; Maguire & Baucus, *Edison and International Photographic Films*, April 1897, 15 and 19.

NOTE:

SWIMMING PARTIES SOCIETY'S NEWEST FAD.

Society has a new fad. Swimming parties are the proper thing for those who, by social law, are now deprived of the pleasures of 5 o'clock teas, dancing, theatre parties and other amusements of the season just closed.

Fashionable folk have literally taken to the water—not to the surfs of the great seaside resorts, not to the mountain lakes, but to an artificial pond of fresh water right in the centre of the swell residence district of this city.

The swimming parties are usually made up of about twenty women and men and are, of course, exclusive, invitation affairs. Not many of these aquatic functions have been held, but there have been enough of them to make the sport an established fad and arrangements have been made for many more, some even so far ahead as next fall.

WHERE THEY SWIM.

The scene of the gayety is at the Fifth Avenue Swimming School Bath and Gymnasium, just off the avenue on Forty-fifth street. This place is, in fact, the only one in the city where such functions could be held, as there is no other swimming institution outside of clubs of sufficient size and exclusiveness open the year round. It is on the site of the well-known swimming school established in 1853 by Prof. Gebhard. It is very complete in its appointments and admirably adapted to the uses to which society is putting it. The swimming pool measures 60 by 35 feet and is from 2 1/2 to 6 feet deep, there being a gradual descent from one end to the other. Its capacity is 80,000 gallons. By clever arrangement of picturesque scenery the water appears to come tumbling down a mountain side, and flows over a huge rustic waterwheel into the pool. As the water is constantly changing it is always inviting. It is kept at a comfortable temperature.

Over the pool is a gymnasium consisting of climbing ropes, rings, "horses," spring-boards, trolleys, trapezes, &c.

The accompanying illustration shows one of the fashionable swimming parties as it appeared a few nights ago. That the participants had a hilarious time can readily be imagined. All drawing-room dignity must be left outside by those joining such a party. It is impossible for any one clad in a bathing suit to look dignified while in swimming. A score of people who are among those supposed to set the pace in proper decorum present an odd appearance paddling and splashing in this tank, diving from spring-boards, vaulting over "horses," swinging in rings and at times yelling like the original inhabitants of Manhattan Island.

The party remains in the water about a half hour. Then the women dry and arrange their hair, while the men enjoy cigars in the cafe. After that all drive to the Waldorf or Delmonico's, where a dinner is served.

"Harry" Beecher, of football fame, was a guest at the last swimming party. He was the central figure in the thrilling incident of the evening. In diving he went too deep and struck the bottom of the tank. A contusion of the scalp and a severe shock were the result, but he soon resumed swimming, and showed his nerve by having the wound dressed and attending the dinner at Delmonico's with the rest of the party.

OUTINGS IN THE CITY.

Strange as it may seem, arrangements are being made by parties at the fashionable seaside resorts, where an ocean of superior bathing water is handy, to come to the city occasionally during the summer to indulge in the new-found fad. "Outings in the city" these bathing parties might be called under such conditions.

Some have planned to go to the swimming school early in the evening, and, after a half-hour swim, eat a light dinner in the restaurant on the premises and then go to a roof garden. Others instead of having a dinner at one of the fashionable restaurants or going to a roof garden, will have an informal dance in Hodgson's Hall, which adjoins the school. It is the intention to organize regular swimming clubs next fall.

ORIGIN OF THE FAD.

Hanging on the wall of the hall leading to the swimming pool is a picture which, in a measure, explains how swimming parties came to be a society fad. It is a photograph taken many years ago at Newport and shows Oliver and August Belmont in swimming when they were tots of ten, with Prof. Gebhard, their tutor.

The Belmonts, as well as nearly all of the millionaire families of New York, were constant patrons of Prof. Gebhard's school on Fifth avenue and continue to be patrons of the institution under its new management. Among these families are the Vanderbilts, the Iselins, the Appletons, the Kipps, the De Jongs, the Emmets, the Sands and many others. They swam there when they were children, their children swim there now, and it was perfectly natural when they felt the need of a new diversion for their minds to revert to the old "swimmin' hole." (*New York World,* 7 June 1896, 21.)

198   Rope Dance

LENGTH: © No reg.
PRODUCER: James White, Raff & Gammon.
CAMERA: William Heise.
CAST:
PRODUCTION DATE: By early August 1896.
LOCATION: [Raff & Gammon's roof-top studio, New York, N.Y.]
SOURCE:
DESCRIPTION:
SUBJECT: Vaudeville–performances. Dancing.
ARCHIVE:
CITATIONS: Purdy & Kiefaber to Raff & Gammon, 17 August 1896, MH-BA.
NOTE:

On August 5th, the New York Evening World *reported that it received a donation of $25 for its Sick Babies' Fund from the Vitascope Company. It was almost certainly connected with the production of several pictures: three films of J. Stuart Blackton executing lightning sketches and one of a harbor outing for infants sponsored by the Sick Babies' Fund. J. Stuart Blackton's appearance before the kinetograph introduced the struggling entertainer (and his partner Albert E. Smith) to movie-making. The film of Blackton executing a sketch of Edison became a hit, boosted the entertainer's career and piqued his interest in motion pictures.*

199   *Blackton Sketches, no. 1 / Inventor Edison Sketched by World Artist / Sketching Mr. Edison / Sketch of Thomas A. Edison

LENGTH: 150 ft.   © No reg.
PRODUCER: James White, Raff & Gammon.
CAMERA: William Heise.
CAST: J. Stuart Blackton.
PRODUCTION DATE: Ca. 5 August 1896.
LOCATION: [Raff & Gammon's roof-top studio, New York, N.Y.]
SOURCE:

DESCRIPTION: Represents him as drawing a large picture of Mr. Thomas A. Edison. (*The Phonoscope,* November 1896, 16.)
A free-hand sketch of the noted "Wizard" by Blackton, the *World* artist. (F.Z. Maguire & Co., *Catalogue,* [March 1898], 32.)
SUBJECT: Vaudeville–performances. Drawing. Thomas A. Edison.
ARCHIVE: NNMoMA.
CITATIONS: Maguire & Baucus, *Edison and International Photographic Films,* April 1897, 19; Maguire & Baucus, *Fall Catalogue,* 1897, 14.
NOTE: The claim that Edison posed for this picture is apochraphal; it is highly unlikely that the film was even shot at the Black Maria.

200   Blackton Sketches, no. 2 / Political Cartoon

LENGTH: 150 ft.   © No reg.
PRODUCER: James White, Raff & Gammon.
CAMERA: William Heise.

CAST: J. Stuart Blackton.
PRODUCTION DATE: Ca. 5 August 1896.
LOCATION: [Raff & Gammon's roof-top studio, New York, N.Y.]
SOURCE:
DESCRIPTION: Showing the artist drawing pictures of McKinley and President Cleveland. (*The Phonoscope*, November 1896, 16.)
SUBJECT: Vaudeville–performances. Drawing. William McKinley. Grover Cleveland.
ARCHIVE:
CITATIONS: Maguire & Baucus, *Edison and International Photographic Films*, April 1897, 18; Maguire & Baucus, *Fall Catalogue*, 1897, 14; F.Z. Maguire & Co., *Catalogue*, [March 1898], 30.
NOTE:

201 **Blackton Sketches, no. 3 / Humorous Cartoon**
LENGTH: 150 ft.   © No reg.
PRODUCER: James White, Raff & Gammon.
CAMERA: William Heise.
CAST: J. Stuart Blackton.
PRODUCTION DATE: Ca. 5 August 1896.
LOCATION: [Raff & Gammon's roof-top studio, New York, N.Y.]
SOURCE:
DESCRIPTION: Is a humorous selection, showing the artist drawing a life-size picture of a female figure, in which the expressions of the countenance are rapidly changing. (*The Phonoscope*, November 1896, 16.)
SUBJECT: Vaudeville–performances. Drawing.
ARCHIVE:
CITATIONS: Maguire & Baucus, *Edison and International Photographic Films*, April 1897, 18; Maguire & Baucus, *Fall Catalogue*, 1897, 14; F.Z. Maguire & Co., *Catalogue*, [March 1898], 32.
NOTE:

ART AND MAGIC AID.
Blackton, the Cartoonist, and A.E. Smith Entertain for the Fund.

The entertainment given for the benefit of the Sick Babies' Fund in the Brunswick Hotel Casino, Asbury Park, by the Royal Entertainment Company, of New York, proved a grand success, $15.85 being realized.

Albert E. Smith opened the programme with a series of skillful experiments in prestidigitation. Using no mechanical appliances and only such articles as he could borrow from the audience, the most wonderful results were produced. He terminated the first number with his humorous shadowgraphs–the swan dressing its plumage, the wolf swallowing a bone and a pigeon in flight were very natural in their motions, while the comical antics of six different characters in grotesque pantomime caused the audience to howl with delight.

J. Stuart Blackton, the well-known cartoonist and humorist certainly has no rival in rapid cartoon and caricature work. He won his audience at the start by a series of humorous sketches of people in the audience, accompanying each drawing with a running fire of good natured talk that kept everyone in a roar. His wonderful pencil fairly flew over the large sheets of paper, and the drawings were as finely finished in appearance as the illustrations in a comic paper.

The political cartoons were a series of striking likenesses, especially Senator Hill's sad expression and McKinley's smile, and his remarks apropos the political situation tickled the audience immensely. There was a rush for Mr. Blackton's signed sketches after the entertainment which netted a good round sum for the poor suffering little tots. Some of the guests of the Hotel Bristol who had been invited but were unable to attend sent in a donation of $3 for the Fund. (*New York Evening World*, 27 July 1896, 5.)

202 **The New York "World" Sick Baby Fund / Outing of the Babies / Outing of Babies**
LENGTH: 50 ft.   © No reg.
PRODUCER: James White, Raff & Gammon.
CAMERA: William Heise.
CAST:
PRODUCTION DATE: Ca. 5 August 1896.
LOCATION: New York, N.Y.
SOURCE:

DESCRIPTION: Showing the children of the poor people enjoying themselves in swings and on hobby horses. (*The Phonoscope*, November 1896, 16.)

Showing babies aboard a harbor excursion boat. Babies swinging, &c., under auspices of New York *World* Sick Baby Fund. (F.Z. Maguire & Co., *Catalogue*, [March 1898], 30.)

SUBJECT: Newspapers. Steamships. Infants. Charities.

ARCHIVE:

CITATIONS: Maguire & Baucus, *Edison and International Photographic Films*, April 1897, 13; Maguire & Baucus, *Fall Catalogue*, 1897, 13.

NOTE:

203 **"Rosedale" / Steamer "Rosedale"**

LENGTH: 50 ft.　© No reg.

PRODUCER: James White, Raff & Gammon.

CAMERA: William Heise.

CAST:

PRODUCTION DATE: [Ca. 5 August 1896.]

LOCATION: New York, N.Y.

SOURCE:

DESCRIPTION: Showing the ill-fated steamer, which, while loaded with passengers, was recently sunk in New York Harbor in collision with the ferry boat Oregon. (*The Phonoscope*, November 1896, 16.)

The ferryboat Rosedale sunk in collision last week. (*New York Mail and Express,* 12 September 1896, 12.)

THE SINKING OF THE ROSEDALE.

SUBJECT: Steamships. Ferries. Harbors. Accidents.

ARCHIVE:

CITATIONS: *Pittsburgh Dispatch*, 6 September 1896. Maguire & Baucus, *Edison and International Photographic Films*, April 1897, 14; Maguire & Baucus, *Fall Catalogue*, 1897, 13; F.Z. Maguire & Co., *Catalogue*, [March 1898], 29; *Edison Films*, March 1900, 42.

NOTE:

STEAMER SUNK; PASSENGERS SAFE.

Ferryboat Oregon Makes a Big Hole in the Rosedale's Hull and She Rapidly Fills.

PANIC ABOARD BOTH BOATS.

Tugs Go to the Rescue of Those on the Rosedale After She Was Aground.

RESPONSIBILITY A QUESTION.

Captain of Each Vessel Says He Was Not to Blame for the Collision.

The Bridgeport day boat Rosedale was sunk yesterday morning in the East River off the foot of Broome street. She was in collision with the ferry boat Oregon, of the New York and Brooklyn Ferry Company, opposite South Fifth street, Brooklyn, and with a hole fifteen feet long in her hull below the water line attempted to run ashore, but settled in sixteen feet of water.

The Rosedale, which is of the sidewheel type, was bound down the river on her trip from Bridgeport to her pier at the foot of Market street. She had made her first landing at the foot of East Thirty-first street, where more than half of the two hundred and fifty passengers who left Bridgeport, according to the purser, were landed.

The Oregon left her pier at the foot of Broadway, Williamsburg, at half-past eleven o'clock, on her way to the East Twenty-third street ferry slip. She had reached mid-stream on her diagonal course when the Bridgeport boat was seen coming directly downstream. A tug with barges in tow was bound up stream two or three hundred feet to the westward of the Oregon.

The gap between the Oregon and the Rosedale was rapidly closing and yet there was no diminution of the headway. Both vessels held their course. When about three hundred feet apart it was evident that a collision was inevitable. The Rosedale's whistle was blown twelve short, sharp blasts, and here engines were reversed. Her course was changed as if to pass to the right and clear the Oregon, whose engines were also reversing. The headway of both vessels, however, together with the tide behind the Oregon, carried them swiftly together.

The port quarter of the ferryboat went ploughing under the Rosedale's upper works and into her hull. The Oregon's passengers, who were mostly standing on the front or up stream end of the boat a moment before, ran through the cabins and narrow passageways toward the stern. Many were jammed in the companion ways when the crash came, which sent many to the floor. The horses on the boat suffered the same fate, and their struggles added to the panic.

Aboard the Rosedale the excitement was greater. As the Oregon backed clear of the Rosedale the water was seen pouring into a huge hole fifteen feet long and extending below her water line. Eight or ten of the Rosedale's crew climbed over the side and jumped aboard the ferryboat. Cries of "You're sinking! Get aboard of us!" reached the ears of Captain William Witherwax of the Rosedale, who was in the pilot house with the pilot, Rawlins, and added to the panic on his steamer. An attempt was made to get a line from the Oregon aboard the sinking steamer, but Captain Witherwax had already signalled ahead at full speed, and the attempt was abandoned.

FILLED RAPIDLY.

The Rosedale had already begun to settle forward and her water line astern was three or four feet above the surface as she was seen from the Oregon making for the shore. William Thompson, first mate, and P.M. Dinkens, purser, of the Rosedale, drove the passengers from the main to the upper deck as the vessel settled lower and lower. Her bow was within fifty feet of the pier at the foot of Broome street when she touched bottom.

Henry Schade, chief engineer, stood waist deep in water in the engine room, when he felt her touch. The fires were out, but the engines were still working. He shut off the steam and waded to the stairs leading to the promenade deck.

A shrieking, fighting mob was running frantically about the deck. Three tugs were coming at full speed to the rescue, and the passengers fought as they came up to be the first to leave the Rosedale. The officers and crew assured them that all would be saved, as the boat was resting easily on the bottom, but only a few believed it.

The tug Olympia, Captain Charles McLaren, was the first to get a line to the Rosedale. Sixty-four passengers jumped aboard of her, and such pieces of their hand baggage as was saved were thrown after them.

In her hurry to reach the side of the Olympia Mrs. Jennings of Bridgeport, plunged down the stairway of the Rosedale, though water was nearly up to the top of it, and disappeared. Joseph Garrigan, fireman of the Olympia, jumped after her and brought her to the surface. He said he found her clinging to a stanchion at the foot of the stairs. The Olympia landed her passengers at the foot of Delancey street.

The tug Katheryn was close behind the Olympia, and took off a load from the star-board side of the Rosedale. The lighter Gipsy Girl and tug Jupiter rescued the remainder.

ABANDONED HER BABY.

As the last of the passengers were about to leave, the first mate, William Thompson, noticed a baby alone and crying lustily on one of the cabin seats. It was put aboard a tug and sent ashore to its mother, who had abandoned it in her fright. There were many claims for baggage at the company's office yesterday at the Market street pier. Most of it was in the hold forward, and many pieces were seen floating out through the hole when the vessel sank. The freight consisted mostly of carriages and machinery, and will be damaged but slightly.

The responsibility for the accident is in dispute. Captain Witherwax said:–

"I saw the Oregon leave her slip and head for the Rosedale, when we were opposite the foot of Thirtieth street. I signalled the Oregon to pass to my right when I was a quarter of a mile away. She paid no attention to the signal, and when about one hundred yards away I signalled her again. I then signalled my engineer to reverse, and also blew my alarm whistle. The Oregon held her course, and only reversed her engines after she had answered my alarm signal."

The statement of Rawlins, the pilot, agreed with that of the captain. He said that at first it was reported to him that there was no leak in the Rosedale, and a moment later that she was sinking.

The captain of the Oregon, E.G. Colloway, says there was no signal from the Rosedale except the alarm whistle, and that he had reversed his engines as soon as he saw the danger. He said the Rosedale should have passed astern of the Oregon, as in any case the tug going up the river would have made it dangerous to cross between her and the Oregon. Captain Colloway said he had been on the ferry for seventeen years, and this was his first accident. Captain Witherwax said the same thing.

The Rosedale was built at Norfolk, Va., in 1877, and has been on the Bridgeport line ever since. She was formerly considered the fastest boat on the Sound. She is 215 feet over all in length, 60 feet beam and is valued at $60,000. She was insured.

The derrick Monarch, of the Chapman Wrecking Company, was placed alongside the Rosedale last night, and the work of raising her, which, it is said, will be comparatively easy, will be begun to-day. At high tide last night the water was washing over the Rosedale's upper deck. (*New York Herald*, 4 September 1896, 5.)

At the insistence of Vitascope states rights owner Peter W. Kiefaber, an Edison crew traveled to Asbury Park to film the resort's seventh annual baby parade. While part of the film was offered for sale as a regular subject, another portion was exhibited primarily at Asbury Park's Electrical Casino. As local views these motion pictures made a big hit.

204 **[Asbury Park Baby Parade, no. 1]**
LENGTH: 200 ft.   © No reg.
PRODUCER: James White, Raff & Gammon, Thomas Henry.
CAMERA: William Heise.
CAST: A.R. Parsons, William Wallace Totten
PRODUCTION DATE: 15 August 1896.
LOCATION: Asbury Park, N.J.
SOURCE:
DESCRIPTION: The pictures are over three hundred feet long, and represent two scenes.
The first shows Mr. A.R. Parsons, of the Brunswick, in the lead, closely followed by
Voss's Band. Then comes the Japanese children carrying a banner, then William
Wallace Totten dressed as a gold bug, and led by his father, doll carriages, etc.
(*Asbury Park Daily Journal*, 24 August 1896, 1.)
SUBJECT: Parades. Infants. Children. Marching bands. Japanese. Voss's Band.
ARCHIVE:
CITATIONS:
NOTE:

205 **Baby Parade at Asbury Park / Baby Parade / [Asbury Park Baby Parade, no. 2]**
LENGTH: 150 ft.   © No reg.
PRODUCER: James White, Raff & Gammon, Thomas Henry.
CAMERA: William Heise.
CAST:
PRODUCTION DATE: 15 August 1896.
LOCATION: Asbury Park, N.J.
SOURCE:
DESCRIPTION: After an intermission of ten
minutes the second picture is produced. Fifty or more gayly decorated
carriages are displayed, among them
the "Birth of the Queen of Hearts,"
which won first prize as the best decorated carriage. The picture caught one
of the mothers just as she was trying
to get out of range of the camera, but
was unsuccessful. Both pictures are
excellent, and will prove the greatest

SOME OF THE BABIES IN THE PARADE AT ASBURY PARK

attraction at the Vitascope. (*Asbury Park Daily Journal*, 24 August 1896, 1.)
Showing hundreds of babies in the annual parade. An interesting view. (F.Z.
Maguire & Co., *Catalogue*, [March 1898], 32.)
SUBJECT: Parades. Infants. Parade floats.
ARCHIVE:
CITATIONS: Maguire & Baucus, *Edison Films*, 20 January 1897, 7; Maguire & Baucus,
Edison and International Photographic Films, April 1897, 18; Maguire & Baucus,
Fall Catalogue, 1897, 14.
NOTE:

Asbury Park–Edison's Vitascope at the Casino under the management of Thomas Henry (last season with Frank
Bush) has become one of the best paying attractions at this resort. (*New York Clipper*, 1 August 1896, 343.)

BABY'S DAY BY THE SEA.
Asbury Park Held an Infant Parade That Fond Mothers Hugely Enjoyed.
PRETTY MAMAS, SWEET BABIES.
Vehicular Parents of the Future Parade Unconscious of Breeches and Bloomers.
PRIZES ARE GIVEN TO THE BEST.
The Exhibition Reflected Credit on Founder Bradley, Mothers, Fathers and Children Too.
The song of the sea breaking up against the famous Board Walk at Asbury Park was subordinated for an hour yes-
terday afternoon to the prattling of infants and to the voices of fond mamas and admiring friends, who had turned
out by tens of thousands to do homage to the babies.

It was "'Babies' Day," one of the many peculiar institutions of Founder Bradley's highly moral resort. Seven years ago the great censor of seaside conduct conceived the idea that New Jersey mothers would take delight in exhibiting their children in gala attire and he made no mistake, for each year the Babies' Day parade has been more popular than before.

So yesterday nearly five hundred mothers entered their "tootsie wootsies" with the judges in order that they might compete for the handsome prizes offered for different types of babies and for vehicles in which they were shown. They came from all over the state.

The babies were first taken to the auditorium at the end of the boardwalk, and when all were there under the one roof the cooing and laughing, the squalling and the prattling made up an infantile symphony calculated to throw a bachelor into a fit. The childless philanthropist, Bradley, went about chucking the babies under their chins and complementing their mothers in a prize-convincing way.

There were at least 40,000 persons on the board walk on either side when a brass band came out of the auditorium at the head of the babies parade, playing the "Doll's Chorus" from "Wang."

From one end of the line to the other during the whole parade could be heard little else than a succession of such impressions as:

"Oh! ain't he sweet?" "Just too lovely for anything." "Oh, I could eat you, you little darling." "My gracious, look at that fat one."

All sorts of babies were in line, some on foot, some in arms, but most of them in gorgeously decorated vehicles. There were Japanese babies, and one little baby that was born near the North Pole, she being little Maria Ahnighte Peary, the child of the Arctic explorer who was born while the Lieutenant and his wife were in Greenland. She was shown off to advantage in a carriage all covered with white cotton that looked like a cradle of snow.

The mothers showed much ingenuity in displaying their darlings to advantage. There were two sets of triplets, all girls, and a half-dozen mothers entered twins. Two little Alabama girls were mounted on a dainty chariot, one dressed all in silver tinsel and the other all in gold. The baby dressed in silver fell off and scratched her nose.

The political issue of the day found other representatives. Willie Brady, the three-year-old son of W.A. Brady, who is Prizefighter Corbett's manager, was dressed up as a farmer sitting on a load of hay driven by two goats. He carried a banner which read "16 to 1." Papa Brady is a silver enthusiast and says he has money to bet on Bryan.

Some of the larger babies carried banners. Some of these read: "Out of the Mouths of Babes He Shall Ordain Praise." "And a Little Child Shall Lead Them." "The Child is the Father of the Man." "What Would the World Be Without Us?"...(*New York World*, 16 August 1896, 42.)

Baby Parade at the Vitascope.

A picture of Asbury Park's seventh annual baby parade is now on exhibition at the vitascope, in the Electrical Casino, corner First and Ocean avenues. The picture was shown for the first time last Saturday. It was taken on the brick walk, just below the turn from the Auditorium, by special representatives of the Edison company. As it was taken it was 350 feet long, but had to be cut in half to be presented here. The first half represents Voss band and the youngsters that follow it up to the coaches. The second section represents the decorated carriages. It is as natural as life. The faces of the participants may readily be recognized by acquaintants. The prize carriage is plainly visible, as are, indeed, almost all that participated. The picture will remain on exhibition indefinitely. To Mr. Henry, the manager of the casino, is due the credit of its production. Only after repeated solicitations were the workmen sent here to take the picture. (*Asbury Park Daily Press*, 24 August 1896, 1.)

206 ***Sea Beach Scene**
LENGTH: 50 ft.   © No reg.
PRODUCER: James White, Raff & Gammon.
CAMERA: William Heise.
CAST:
PRODUCTION DATE: Mid-August 1896.
LOCATION: Asbury Park, N.J. or Atlantic City, N.J.
SOURCE:
DESCRIPTION: Under the big umbrella at Atlantic City. A fine beach scene.
(F.Z. Maguire & Co., *Catalogue*, [March 1898], 31.)
SUBJECT: Bathing beaches. Seashore. Umbrellas.
ARCHIVE: NR-GE, DNA.
CITATIONS:
NOTE:

207 ***Watermelon Eating Contest / Watermelon Contest / Water Melon Contest**
LENGTH: 50 ft.   © No reg.
PRODUCER: James White, Raff & Gammon.
CAMERA: William Heise.
CAST:
PRODUCTION DATE: By early September 1896.
LOCATION: [Raff & Gammon's roof-top studio, New York, N.Y.]
SOURCE:
DESCRIPTION: Shows two of the colored gentry eating melons on a wager. This picture created a furor in New York. Fine effect when colored. (F.Z. Maguire & Co., *Catalogue*, [March 1898], 32.) 
SUBJECT: Afro-Americans. Contests–food. Watermelons. Motion pictures–colored.
ARCHIVE: NNMoMA.
CITATIONS: *Pittsburgh Dispatch*, 6 September 1896. Maguire & Baucus, *Edison Films*, 20 January 1897, 7; Maguire & Baucus, *Edison and International Photographic Films*, April 1897, 16; Maguire & Baucus, *Fall Catalogue*, 1897, 13; *Edison Films*, March 1900, 36.
NOTE:

Li Hung Chang, former Viceroy of China, had watched a Lumière film screening at Kurhans-hotel in Scheveningen (near The Hague) in late May 1896. On a round-the-world tour, he arrived in New York, via Southampton, England, aboard the S.S. "St. Louis" on 28 August 1896. Li was greeted by a tremendous outpouring of good will from the American press and from American citizenry more generally. His brief stay in the American metropolis, during which time he met President Grover Cleveland, was front-page news. Not surprisingly, the Edison staff made considerable effort to film the celebratory events surrounding his visit. Many of these events were also filmed by W.K.L. Dickson and the American Mutoscope Company.

208 **American Line Pier**
LENGTH: 50 ft.   © No reg.
PRODUCER: James White, Raff & Gammon.
CAMERA: William Heise.
CAST:
PRODUCTION DATE: 28 August 1896.
LOCATION: New York, N.Y.
SOURCE:
DESCRIPTION: Showing the crowds at the pier awaiting the arrival of Li Hung Chang. (Maguire & Baucus, *Edison and International Photographic Films,* April 1897, 3.)
SUBJECT: Steamships. Harbors–New York. Piers. China–Foreign Relations–United States. Li Hung Chang. American Line. International Navigation Company.
ARCHIVE:
CITATIONS: "Viceroy Li Disgraced," *New York Herald,* 19 September 1894, 9; "Viceroy Li Hung Chang," *New York Herald,* 21 June 1896, 9. Maguire & Baucus, *Fall Catalogue*, 1897, 11; F.Z. Maguire & Co., *Catalogue,* [March 1898], 34.
NOTE:

209 **Baggage Wagons / Baggage of Li Hung Chang**
LENGTH: 50 ft.   © No reg.
PRODUCER: James White, Raff & Gammon.
CAMERA: William Heise.
CAST:
PRODUCTION DATE: 28 August 1896.
LOCATION: New York, N.Y.
SOURCE:

DESCRIPTION: Li Hung Chang's Baggage wagons leaving the American pier. (Maguire & Baucus, *Edison and International Photographic Films*, April 1897, 4.)

SUBJECT: Harbors–New York. Piers. China–Foreign Relations–United States. Li Hung Chang. American Line. International Navigation Company.

ARCHIVE:

CITATIONS: Maguire & Baucus, *Fall Catalogue*, 1897, 11; F.Z. Maguire & Co., *Catalogue*, [March 1898], 34.

NOTE:

HAIL! PUISSANT LI HUNG CHANG!
Ambassador of the Emperor of China Received at the Gateway
to the United States with Naval and Military Honors.
SALUTED BY THE NEW YORK.
Hundreds of Pleasure Craft Piped a Greeting; Governor's Island's Guns Belched a Welcome.
AN OVATION IN THE CITY.
Escorted by Crack Squadrons of Cavalry and Cheered by Thousands on His Way to the Hotel.
HE TALKS FOR THE HERALD.
An Elaborate Programme Outlined for the Viceroy and Chinatown Will Hold a Jubilee.

Li Hung Chang, who has for thirty years held the destinies of China within the hollow of his hand, yesterday set foot upon a new world, under a new sky, among a new people, with a government for which his language has no equivalent, and he smiled.

It was appreciation and not satire that turned this ancient diplomat's fancy. He was a Westerner among Easterners; he had dreamed of the sun setting while his country but saw it rise. He journeyed forth and went into the land where the sun lived after it was born, and he is satisfied.

No tribute to a great man could have been more frank or more magnificent than that which descended upon the St. Louis as she brought Li within the environments of the Republic. He was not regarded only as the servant of his master, the Emperor of the oldest Empire; it was in acknowledgement of his own greatness. He was as Bismarck, as Gladstone. He was one of the three great men who are now living who have built empires, fought battles that have saved their sovereigns, made laws that have secured them, lived lives which have been given as lessons to their countrymen.

It was a Splendid Welcome.

From the time the American liner with her distinguished passenger passed the bar until she reached her pier she passed through a continuous salute, a splendid welcome. Li Hung Chang was greeted by the representatives of the government. He received the salutes of the army and the navy of this country, which he knows commercially, but which is a terra incognita to him politically. Then in an extraordinary journey from Fulton street to the Hotel Waldorf he received the cheers and the congratulations of the citizens of the freest country on earth–he the representative of the most absolute absolutism.

The estimate of Li Hung Chang among those who saw him and conversed with him yesterday is that he is one of the elect of the earth. A man of seventy-four years, full of power, mental and physical; virile with that authority which knows no questioning, admirable in physical proportions, cautious, courteous and reserved, he is one of those exceptional characters in the world's history that are numbered with the centuries and whose records live with the ages. Li Hung Chang was welcomed by America with unmistakable hospitality. Will he stand as a barrier and erect more lasting barriers between his countrymen's traditions and everlasting progress? (*New York Herald*, 29 August, 1896, 3.)

---

210 The Arrival of Li Hung Chang / Li Hung Chang

LENGTH: 50 ft.   © No reg.

PRODUCER: James White, Raff & Gammon.

CAMERA: William Heise.

CAST: Li Hung Chang.

PRODUCTION DATE: 29 August 1896.

LOCATION: New York, N.Y.

SOURCE:

DESCRIPTION: Shows Li Hung Chang entering his carriage at the door of the Waldorf Hotel, with a file of the Sixth U.S. Cavalry, with drawn sabres, standing near by. (*The Phonoscope*, November 1896, 16.)

Shows the great Celestial Viceroy

leaving the Hotel Waldorf and entering a carriage, attended by native servants. (F.Z. Maguire & Co., *Catalogue*, [March 1898], 30.)

SUBJECT: China–Foreign Relations–United States. Chinese. Cavalry. Hotels. Sixth U.S. Cavalry. Waldorf Hotel.

ARCHIVE:

CITATIONS: "Welcome at Waldorf," *New York Herald*, 29 August 1896, 4. Maguire & Baucus, *Edison and International Photographic Films*, April 1897, 11; Maguire & Baucus, *Fall Catalogue*, 1897, 12.

NOTE:

PRESIDENT GREETS LI.
Mr. Cleveland Extends the Welcome of the Nation to the Chinese Viceroy.
AT WILLIAM C. WHITNEY'S HOUSE.
Formal Reception by the Chief Executive and His Cabinet–Mayor Strong Calls on the Noted Visitor.
A GRAND BANQUET IN THE EVENING.
Tendered to Earl Li by Former United States Ministers to China and Other Distinguished Men–The Guest Pleased, but He Ate Not.

Li Hung Chang, China's great old mandarin, guest of the city and of the nation, had a very pleasant time yesterday. He seemed to enjoy himself. He arose early, and during the day when he was not asking questions he was smoking cigarettes.

President Cleveland came from Buzzard's Bay to officially receive Li Hung and welcome him. Mr. Cleveland came on the yacht Sapphire of Mr. James Stillman, President of the City Bank. Mr. Cleveland landed at 8:30 A.M. and boarded the yacht again at 2:30 P.M., being in New York six hours.

The official reception was held at the residence of William C. Whitney, former Secretary of the Navy, Fifth avenue and Fifty-seventh street. Li was escorted from the Waldorf by the United States cavalrymen who had been ordered here to do him honor. Immense crowds greeted the Viceroy, and made him feel very much at home. He was gratified. Several gentlemen, some who had been United States Ministers to China, others who have met Li Hung Chang in various capacities, invited Li to dinner last night. His excellency seemed to enjoy himself, but ate nothing. Chinatown was crowded with the ex-patrioted compatriots of Li, who duly celebrated the occasion. (*New York Herald*, 30 August 1896, 1.)

The American-built S.S. "St. Louis" not only had brought Viceroy Li Hung Chang to the United States from England, but had broken the speed record for its route during its previous trip. Such achievements were felt to have important implications for the future of American ship building. This steamship was thus noteworthy in its own right, and the Edison camera crew returned to shoot its departure.

211 **Steamer "St. Louis" Leaving Dock / Steamship "St. Louis" / The Sailing of the American Trans-Atlantic Steamship "St. Louis," for Southampton, England / "St. Louis"**

LENGTH: 50 ft.   © No reg.

PRODUCER: James White, Raff & Gammon.

CAMERA: William Heise.

CAST:

PRODUCTION DATE: 2 September 1896.

LOCATION: New York, N.Y.

SOURCE:

DESCRIPTION: Showing one of the fastest transatlantic steamers afloat, sailing down the river, as she starts on her long voyage. (*The Phonoscope*, November 1896, 16.)

THE AMERICAN LINE STEAMER ST. LOUIS.
She Has Beaten the Ocean Record from Southampton to New York.

Shows the American Line record breaker leaving her New York dock. The only picture extant of an ocean greyhound. (F.Z. Maguire & Co., *Catalogue*, [March 1898], 31.)

SUBJECT: Steamships. Harbors–New York. Speed records. American Line. International Navigation Company.

ARCHIVE:

CITATIONS: *New York World*, 11 October 1896, 14. Maguire & Baucus, *Fall Catalogue*, 1897, 13.

NOTE:

QUEEN OF THE SEAS.
The St. Louis, of American Line, Breaks the Record from Southampton to New York.
PACE SET FOR THE ST. PAUL.
Wins the Title of Champion Ocean Greyhound in 6 days 2 Hours and 24 Minutes.
CAMPANIA WAS BAFFLED BY FOG.
Augusta Victoria Eclipses Her Own Record—Prominent Passengers on the Three Ships.

The ocean speed record from Southampton to New York was broken into little bits yesterday. The St. Paul, of the American line, had held it, with a record of 6 days 5 hours and 32 minutes. Now the St. Louis, her narrow waisted sister, has set the pace at 6 days, 2 hours and 24 minutes.

"And they will be fleet ones that beat it," quoth John Walls, the sturdy old engineer, yesterday, as he stood among his engines and listened to their pantings.

Everybody knew that something in the way of a record would have to go when the St. Louis was signalled from Fire Island at such an early hour in the morning. And as she came within the ken of the observer at Sandy Hook, it was seen that she was out for a record. Under the bows of the long backed liner was a hill of foam, smoke was streaming from her twin funnels in a straight line astern, and in her wake rolled a swell like a tidal wave. "Well done," was the signal that waved from the signal tower as the speeding racer brought the finish point abeam. Well done, indeed. The race had been over a course 3,055 miles in length, and it had been traversed at the average speed of nearly 21 knots an hour—20.867 knots to be exact. This, too, with twenty-one hours of fog, during which the engines had to be slowed at times.

At a sober gait the vessel threaded her way through the channel, and arrived off Quarantine at thirty minutes past 12 o'clock. The Health Officer did not detain her long, and one hour later her passengers were being landed.

CONDITIONS WERE FAVORABLE.

In speaking of his rapid voyage, Captain Randle told me that everything had been favorable for the record breaking trip which the St. Louis had made. She was just out of dry dock, where she had been cleaned, and scraped, and her engines given an overhauling. Winds had ceased from troubling and seas were at peace when the voyage was begun, and these conditions of quiet lasted. The daily runs were 477, 519, 530, 510, 499.

The passengers were enthusiastic over the qualities of the ship. When it was made known that the St. Louis had eclipsed all previous speed records on the Southampton route several enthusiastic passengers passed around their hats taking up a collection for the engineers' force, that their might not be an empty triumph.

A purse of $175 was raised and divided among the stokers, firemen and oilers. Then there was a raffle for a bicycle, which the manager of a bicycle concern inaugurated. The wheel was won by Louis Bame, a passenger and the proceeds donated to the Seaman's Friends' Society. The usual concert was held Wednesday evening. A series of resolutions was drafted by a committee chosen from among the passengers, complimenting Captain Randle, the company and the builders of the record breaker....(*New York Herald,* 8 August 1896, 5.)

Ocean Steamers' Speed.

When the International Navigation Company—more commonly called the American Line—began building the St. Louis and St. Paul many friends of foreign shipbuilders assiduously spread the report that these two vessels were intended to make a higher speed than any other ships afloat. Inasmuch as they did not have the size or the horse power of the Lucania and the Campania, this report originated in either ignorance or malice, for no such superiority of speed was contemplated, by their owners or their builders.

Nevertheless, most people familiar with their construction felt confident that they would give a good account of themselves as soon as their machinery had reached it highest efficiency. In spite of the greater distance they have had to cover—from Southampton to New York, compared to the run from Liverpool to New York—the new American line steamers have been landing their passengers here on Friday within an hour or two of the debarkation of the travellers who have come over in the Lucania and the Campania. But the American liners have not tried to make this run of more than three thousand miles at a higher speed than that maintained by the fast Cunarders.

It is true that they have been making new records for the run between Southampton and New York, but their average speed across the Atlantic has been less than that made by the two Cunarders on their record breaking voyages. Yet the trip of the St. Louis, ending at Sandy Hook last Friday, was worthy of special attention, for it indicates the superiority of the hulls and motive power of American built steamers over the best product of the British yards. The distance of 3,055 miles was covered by the St. Louis in 6 days, 2 hours and 24 minutes—the shortest time on record—the average run per day being more than five hundred miles. The average speed was 20.867 knots. The Lucania on her fastest run averaged 22.01 knots across the Atlantic, and when the Campania made her best effort she averaged 21.82 knots.

But although two of the Cunarders, therefore, have a higher speed than the St. Louis or the St. Paul, they secure it by such excess in size and extravagance in coal consumption that relatively the American steamers are evidently far superior to their British built rivals. For the American ships are commercially profitable, while it is generally understood that the Lucania and the Campania are very far short of being so. Being much larger than the St. Louis and her twin they cost more than the sum charged up to the construction account for the American steamers and yet there is not the corresponding increase in the Cunarder's carrying capacity. And when coal consumption is considered the economy of running the American built vessels is wonderful. Naturally the exact figures are not accessible, but experts credit the St. Louis and St. Paul with securing their splendid results on a consumption of not more than eighty per cent of the coal needed to drive the larger ships at their highest speed, and some estimates are as low as sixty per cent. It is understood that the Cunarders burn more than five hundred tons a day.

It is apparent, therefore that had the American line really wished to outspeed the Lucania and the Campania and had ordered vessels of similar size the actual speed records would have long since passed into our hands.

All the indications are in favor of the resumption by the American shipbuilder in steel of the superiority that he formerly possessed in wood. The civil war gave Great Britain her great opportunity to get away from us our prestige as the best naval constructors and shipwrights in the world, and the change from wood to iron and from iron to steel helped her further. But steadily we have gone ahead in the new industry, and the day is not far distant when the standard of comparison, in commercial as well as war vessels, will be the best output of our American yards. (Editorial, *New York Herald,* 13 August 1896, 8.)

Clotilde Antonio, "equilibrist" and "contortionist" appeared for seven weeks at Koster & Bial's Music Hall commencing 9 September 1895. She probably appeared before Edison's kinetograph while performing either at Proctor's 23rd Street Theatre for the week beginning 9 August 1896 or at Keith's Union Square Theatre for the week beginning 31 August 1896.

212   **Lotilde Antonio [sic] / Clotilde Antonio**

LENGTH: 50 and 150 ft.   © No reg.

PRODUCER: James White, Raff & Gammon.

CAMERA: William Heise.

CAST: Clotilde Antonio.

PRODUCTION DATE: [9 August-5 September 1896.]

LOCATION: [Raff & Gammon's roof-top studio, New York, N.Y.]

SOURCE:

DESCRIPTION: The noted Lady Acrobat in Hand Dancing, Head Balancing, Playing Violin, &c. (F.Z. Maguire & Co., *Catalogue,* [March 1898], 33.)

SUBJECT: Vaudeville–performances. Acrobats. Dancing. Violin.

ARCHIVE:

CITATIONS: Maguire & Baucus, *Edison and International Photographic Films,* April 1897, 11 and 18; Maguire & Baucus, *Fall Catalogue,* 1897, 12 and 14.

NOTE: Description is for the 150 ft. version.

213   **New Skirt Dancer / Lucille Sturgis**

LENGTH: 50 ft.   © No reg.

PRODUCER: James White, Raff & Gammon.

CAMERA: William Heise.

CAST: Lucille Sturgis.

PRODUCTION DATE: By early September 1896.

LOCATION: [Raff & Gammon's roof-top studio, New York, N.Y.]

SOURCE:

DESCRIPTION: A pleasing skirt dance, excellent for coloring. (Maguire & Baucus, *Edison and International Photographic Films,* April 1897, 11.)

Shows this clever artist in an entirely new dance. For variety of posture and grace of movement she is second to none. (*Edison Films,* March 1900, 29.)

SUBJECT: Vaudeville–performances. Dancing. Motion pictures–colored.

ARCHIVE:

CITATIONS: *New York World,* 13 Sept. 1896, 14; *Pittsburgh Dispatch,* 20 Sept. 1896, 21. Maguire & Baucus, *Edison Films,* 20 January 1897, 6; Maguire & Baucus, *Fall Catalogue,* 1897, 11; F.Z. Maguire & Co., *Catalogue,* [March 1898], 27.

NOTE:

In late August or early September, the kinetograph crew took a series of motion pictures showing characteristic New York City street scenes—locations that were routinely mentioned in sight-seeing guides to the metropolis.

214 Newsboys Scrambling for Pennies
LENGTH: [50 ft.]   © No reg.
PRODUCER: James White, Raff & Gammon.
CAMERA: William Heise.
CAST:
PRODUCTION DATE: By early September 1896.
LOCATION: Park Row, New York, N.Y.
SOURCE:
DESCRIPTION: A group of street gamins struggling for money on Park Row. (*Mail and Express*, 12 September 1896, 10.)
SUBJECT: City and town life–New York. Boys. Newspaper carriers.
ARCHIVE:
CITATIONS: *New York World*, 13 September 1896, 14.
NOTE:

215 Broadway at P.O. / Broadway at Post Office / Broadway
LENGTH: 50 ft.   © No reg.
PRODUCER: James White, Raff & Gammon.
CAMERA: William Heise.
CAST:
PRODUCTION DATE: [By mid-September 1896.]
LOCATION: Broadway, New York, N.Y.
SOURCE:
DESCRIPTION: Shows the continuous stream of daily traffic on New York City's greatest business artery. The constantly changing crowds are a bewildering spectacle. (*Edison Films*, March 1900, 42.)
SUBJECT: City and town life–New York. Postal service. Urban transportation.
ARCHIVE:
CITATIONS: Maguire & Baucus, *Edison Films*, 20 January 1897, 7; Maguire & Baucus, *Edison and International Photographic Films*, April 1897, 4; Maguire & Baucus, *Fall Catalogue*, 1897, 11.
NOTE:

Post Office, at the junction of Broadway and Park Row, is an immense triangular building of Dix-Island (Maine) granite, which cost nearly $7,000,000, and was finished in 1875. Over 600,000,000 letters, newspapers, etc. are handled annually. The office yields a profit, annually, of nearly $3,000,000, and is the largest in the United States. (M.F. Sweetser and Simeon Ford, *How to Know New York City*, 1895.)

216 Fourteenth and Broadway
LENGTH: 150 ft.   © No reg.
PRODUCER: James White, Raff & Gammon.
CAMERA: William Heise.
CAST:
PRODUCTION DATE: [By mid-September 1896.]
LOCATION: Union Square, New York, N.Y.
SOURCE:
DESCRIPTION: Looking Down Broadway from Union Square. (Maguire & Baucus, *Fall Catalogue*, 1897, 14.)
It was here in the early days of New York that Broadway came to an end. An active scene of daily life. (*Edison Films*, March 1900, 42.)
SUBJECT: City and town life–New York.
ARCHIVE:
CITATIONS: H.R. Kiefaber to Raff & Gammon, 6 October 1896, MH-BA. Maguire & Baucus, *Edison and International Photographic Films*, April 1897, 18.
NOTE:

217 Broadway at 14th Street / Dead Man's Curve / Broadway and Fourteenth Street / 14th Street and Broadway
LENGTH: 50 and 150 ft.   © No reg.

PRODUCER: James White, Raff & Gammon.
CAMERA: William Heise.
CAST:
PRODUCTION DATE: [By mid-September 1896.]
LOCATION: Union Square, New York, N.Y.
SOURCE:
DESCRIPTION: A Scene at "Death Curve." (Maguire & Baucus, *Edison and International Photographic Films*, April 1897, 4.)
SUBJECT: City and town life–New York.
ARCHIVE:
CITATIONS: Maguire & Baucus, *Edison Films*, 20 January 1897, 7; Maguire & Baucus, *Edison and International Photographic Films*, April 1897, 18; Maguire & Baucus, *Fall Catalogue*, 1897, 11 and 14; F.Z. Maguire & Co., *Catalogue*, [March 1898], 34.
NOTE: Dead Man's Curve was so named because streetcar motormen took the curve very fast and often had accidents.

Union Square is a park of 3 1/2 acres, with fountains, trees, statues of Lincoln and Washington, electric lights, and other bravery, between 14th and 17th streets and Broadway and Fourth Avenue. All around are hotels, restaurants, theatres, shops and offices, the centre of an ever busy and picturesque life. It's northern part is an open *plaza* for parades, with a platform for speakers or reviewing-officers. (M.F. Sweetser and Simeon Ford, *How to Know New York City*, 1895, 36.)

218 Sidewalks of New York

LENGTH: 50 and 150 ft.   © No reg.
PRODUCER: James White, Raff & Gammon.
CAMERA: William Heise.
CAST:
PRODUCTION DATE: [By mid-September 1896.]
LOCATION: Bowery, New York, N.Y.
SOURCE:
DESCRIPTION: This view is taken in Mott Street, New York City, and shows a busy throng of people. (*The Phonoscope*, November 1896, 16.)
A street scene from the old Bowery District. The largest number of people ever shown on a film. Full of action. (*Edison Films*, March 1900, 43.)
SUBJECT: City and town life–New York.
ARCHIVE:
CITATIONS: Maguire & Baucus, *Edison and International Photographic Films*, April 1897, 19; Maguire & Baucus, *Fall Catalogue*, 1897, 12 and 14.
NOTE:

Take Your Time–New Yorkers conduct business as though life were fleeting. Go down town and watch the men in the streets. Every one seems in a desperate hurry; and the visitor, without realizing it, is apt to become imbued with the all pervading hurry and scurry, and finds himself rushing and elbowing his way through the crowd. This haste is characteristic of all New-Yorkers, and the traveler who wishes to see the city well must avoid their example. He must go slow, and enjoy what he sees. Nothing is more fatiguing than sight-seeing. (M.F. Sweetser and Simeon Ford, *How to Know New York City*, 1895, 4.)

219 Washington Market

LENGTH: 50 ft.   © No reg.
PRODUCER: James White, Raff & Gammon.
CAMERA: William Heise.
CAST:
PRODUCTION DATE: [By mid-September 1896.]
LOCATION: Washington Market, New York, N.Y.
SOURCE:
DESCRIPTION: The famous old market place. (Maguire & Baucus, *Fall Catalogue*, 1897, 13.)
SUBJECT: City and town life–New York. Markets.
ARCHIVE:

CITATIONS: Maguire & Baucus, *Edison Films*, 20 January 1897, 7; Maguire & Baucus, *Edison and International Photographic Films*, April 1897, 16; F.Z. Maguire & Co., *Catalogue*, [March 1898], 34.
NOTE:

Washington Market, bounded by Washington, West, Vesey and Fulton Streets. This is the largest of the markets and the principal centre for the distribution of meats and vegetables throughout the city and country. (M.F. Sweetser and Simeon Ford, *How to Know New York City*, 1895, 56.)

Because the Edison Manufacturing Company was not yet selling dupe negatives of films by foreign producers in 1897, it appears likely that Charles Webster, who had taken the vitascope to Europe in April 1896, acquired or possibly shot one or more films for the Edison company while on his travels.

220 **Grand Boulevard, Paris / Scenes on the Bois de Boulogne**
LENGTH: 50 ft.   © No reg.
PRODUCER: [Charles Webster.]
CAMERA: [Charles Webster?]
CAST:
PRODUCTION DATE: June 1896 to March 1897.
LOCATION: Paris, France.
SOURCE:
DESCRIPTION: This scene shows the stylish equipages and promenaders on one of the finest avenues of the gay metropolis. (Maguire & Baucus, *Edison and International Photographic Films*, April 1897, 16.)
The passing crowds on this great boulevard are always interesting to watch. Bicyclists, pedestrians, carriages and cabs whirl by in kaleidoscopic profusion. A steam train enters in the distance, marking its route with light puffs of steam. An interesting feature of the picture is the pool of water on the crossing in the foreground which causes temporary embarrassment to some of the ladies who are obliged to take long strides to step over same. (*Edison Films*, March 1900, 39.)
SUBJECT: City and town life–Paris. Urban transportation.
ARCHIVE:
CITATIONS:
NOTE:

In mid-September White and Heise shifted the center of their filmmaking activities from New York City back to the Black Maria studio and the surrounding Orange-Newark area. According to at least one news item, actor Robert Bruce Mantell, then performing at the Bijou Theatre in Pittsburgh, Pa., traveled to Edison's laboratory to be filmed in selected scenes from his shows. Since none of the results appeared either on the screen or in Edison catalogs, this report must be greeted with considerable skepticism. Nonetheless it is dangerous for the historian to disregard completely such information. The following three entries are tentative.

221 **[Select Scenes from *The Corsican Brothers*]**
LENGTH: © No reg.
PRODUCER: James White, Raff & Gammon.
CAMERA: William Heise.
CAST: Robert Mantell.
PRODUCTION DATE: 13-19 September 1896.
LOCATION: Black Maria, West Orange, N.J.
SOURCE: *The Corsican Brothers* (play).
DESCRIPTION:
SUBJECT: Drama–performances.
ARCHIVE:
CITATIONS: "Robert Bruce Mantell," *New York Clipper*, 5 September 1896, 422; advertisement, *New York Clipper*, 25 July 1896, 336.
NOTE:

222 [Select Scenes from *Monbars*]
LENGTH: © No reg.
PRODUCER: James White, Raff & Gammon.
CAMERA: William Heise.
CAST: Robert Mantell.
PRODUCTION DATE: 13-19 September 1896.
LOCATION: Black Maria, West Orange, N.J.
SOURCE: *Monbars* (play).
DESCRIPTION:
SUBJECT: Drama–performances.
ARCHIVE:
CITATIONS:
NOTE:

223 [Select Scenes from *The Face in the Moonlight*]
LENGTH: © No reg.
PRODUCER: James White, Raff & Gammon.
CAMERA: William Heise.
CAST: Robert Mantell.
PRODUCTION DATE: 13-19 September 1896.
LOCATION: Black Maria, West Orange, N.J.
SOURCE: *The Face in the Moonlight* (play).
DESCRIPTION:
SUBJECT: Drama–performances.
ARCHIVE:
CITATIONS:
NOTE:

Robert Mantell, while playing at the Bijou [Pittsburgh] last week, accepted an offer from Mr. Ryan, Thomas A. Edison's representative, and with company, scenery and properties went to Edison's laboratory, at Menlo Park [sic], where photographs of important scenes in "The Corsican Brothers," "Monbars," and "The Face in the Moonlight" were taken for use in Edison's vitascope. The pictures are to be developed and displayed in a week or two at the Bijou. (*New York Clipper*, 26 September 1896, 471.)

224 *The Lone Fisherman
LENGTH: 50 and 150 ft.   © No reg.
PRODUCER: James White, Raff & Gammon.
CAMERA: William Heise.
CAST:
PRODUCTION DATE: By mid-September 1896.
LOCATION: [Fanwood, N.J.]
SOURCE: *Fisherman's Luck* (painting by James Maffit).
DESCRIPTION: Illustrating "Fisherman's Luck." (Maguire & Baucus, *Fall Catalogue*, 1897, 12.) A scene from every-day life in the country, depicting the eager fisherman, sitting on the end of a plank, patiently waiting for a

bite. The practical joker appears and removes the stone from the other end of plank, causing a compulsory immersion. Promotes laughter and is sure to make a hit. (F.Z. Maguire & Co., *Catalogue*, [March 1898], 32.)
SUBJECT: Fishing. Practical jokes. Bridges.
ARCHIVE: CaOOANF, NR-GE, DLC-Hendricks.
CITATIONS: Maguire & Baucus, *Edison Films*, 20 January 1897, 7; Maguire & Baucus, *Edison and International Photographic Films*, April 1897, 11 and 18; Maguire & Baucus, *Fall Catalogue*, 1897, 14; *Edison Films*, March 1900, 36; *Edison Films*, July 1901, 71.
NOTE: NR-GE and DLC have the long version, CaOOANF the short. Although Hendricks has identified the location for this film, he did not provide his source.

225 *Interrupted Lovers / Interrupted Lover

LENGTH: 150 ft.   © No reg.
PRODUCER: James White, Raff & Gammon.
CAMERA: William Heise.
CAST:
PRODUCTION DATE: By mid-September 1896.
LOCATION:
SOURCE:

DESCRIPTION: Another instance where "the course of true love never runs smooth." (Maguire & Baucus, *Edison and International Photographic Films*, April 1897, 10.)
A pair of bucolic lovers discovered by the wrathful father, who teaches the gallant a lesson. Has made a hit. (F.Z. Maguire & Co., *Catalogue*, [March 1898], 30.)

SUBJECT: Courtship. Child rearing.
ARCHIVE: NR-GE, DLC-Hendricks, CLAc.
CITATIONS: Maguire & Baucus, *Edison Films*, 20 January 1897, 6; Maguire & Baucus, *Fall Catalogue*, 1897, 12; *Edison Films*, March 1900, 35; *Edison Films*, July 1901, 69.
NOTE: Listed as a 140-foot subject in 1901.

226 *Tub Race

LENGTH: 50 ft.   © No reg.
PRODUCER: James White, Raff & Gammon.
CAMERA: William Heise.
CAST:
PRODUCTION DATE: By mid-September 1896.
LOCATION:
SOURCE:
DESCRIPTION: Depicting the difficulties of paddling in wash tubs. (Maguire & Baucus, *Fall Catalogue*, 1897, 13.)
This turns out to be as much of a bathing scene as it is a race. Everyone who has participated or witnessed a tub race will enjoy the picture. (*Edison Film*, March 1900, 25.)

SUBJECT: Aquatic sports. Contests. Boys.
ARCHIVE: [Paul Killiam.]
CITATIONS: Maguire & Baucus, *Edison Films*, 20 January 1897, 7; Maguire & Baucus, *Edison and International Photographic Films*, April 1897, 16; F.Z. Maguire & Co., *Catalogue*, [March 1898], 30; *Edison Films,* July 1901, 45.
NOTE: A similar subject was taken by Alfred C. Abadie of the Edison Manufacturing Company in August 1903 (*Tub Race*, © 1 September 1903).

227 Boat Rescue

LENGTH: 50 and 150 ft.   © No reg.
PRODUCER: James White, Raff & Gammon.
CAMERA: William Heise.
CAST:
PRODUCTION DATE: By mid-September 1896.
LOCATION:
SOURCE:
DESCRIPTION: Three small boys chased from a dock, jump into the river and are rescued by a passing row boat. (F.Z. Maguire & Co., *Catalogue*, [March 1898], 32.)
SUBJECT: Boys. Rivers. Boats and boating. Life saving. Piers.
ARCHIVE:
CITATIONS: Maguire & Baucus, *Edison and International Photographic Films*, April 1897, 17; Maguire & Baucus, *Fall Catalogue*, 1897, 14; *Edison Films*, March 1900, 38.
NOTE:

228 *Carpenter Shop

LENGTH: 50 ft.   © No reg.
PRODUCER: James White, Raff & Gammon.
CAMERA: William Heise.
CAST:
PRODUCTION DATE: By mid-September 1896.
LOCATION: Black Maria, West Orange, N.J.
SOURCE:
DESCRIPTION: Showing three carpenters busily engaged at the work bench. (*The Phonoscope*, November 1896, 16.)
    A realistic representation, in which every blow of the hammer, movement of the saw and jack-plane, and falling of the shavings are clearly defined. Sure to prove a success. (F.Z. Maguire & Co., *Catalogue*, [March 1898], 31.)
SUBJECT: Working classes. Carpenters.
ARCHIVE: CaOOANF.
CITATIONS: *New York World*, 27 September 1896, 14. Maguire & Baucus, *Edison Films*, 20 January 1897, 6; Maguire & Baucus, *Edison and International Photographic Films*, April 1897, 6; Maguire & Baucus, *Fall Catalogue*, 1897, 12.
NOTE:

229 **Irish Way of Discussing Politics / Irish Political Discussion / Irish Politics / Political Debate / Discussion**

LENGTH: 50 ft.   © No reg.
PRODUCER: James White, Raff & Gammon.
CAMERA: William Heise.
CAST:
PRODUCTION DATE: By mid-September 1896.
LOCATION: Black Maria, West Orange, N.J.
SOURCE: *Bar Room Scene* (Edison film no. 37, spring 1894).
DESCRIPTION: Showing two Irishmen discussing politics over a glass of whiskey. (Maguire & Baucus, *Fall Catalogue*, 1897, 12.)
    This is a typical Irish argument in which a can of beer, clay pipes and two sons of Erin form the principal parts. (F.Z. Maguire & Co., *Catalogue*, [March 1898], 32.)
SUBJECT: Irish Americans. Taverns, etc. Alcoholic beverages. Politics, practical.
ARCHIVE:
CITATIONS: Jannopoulo & Gumpertz to Vitascope Company, 12 September 1896, MH-BA; *New York World*, 27 September 1896, 14. Maguire & Baucus, *Edison Films*, 20 January 1897, 6; Maguire & Baucus, *Edison and International Photographic Films*, April 1897, 10; Maguire & Baucus, *Fall Catalogue*, 1897, 12; *Edison Films*, March 1900, 36.
NOTE:

230 **Pat and the Populist / Pat vs. Populist**

LENGTH: 50 ft.   © No reg.
PRODUCER: James White, Raff & Gammon.
CAMERA: William Heise.
CAST:
PRODUCTION DATE: By mid-September 1896.
LOCATION:
SOURCE:
DESCRIPTION: Showing the Populist endeavoring to convert Pat to his own political views. (*The Phonoscope*, November 1896, 16.)
    A humorous scene beween an Irish hod-carrier and a politician. (Maguire & Baucus, *Edison and International Photographic Films*, April 1897, 14.)
    Pat ascends a ladder with a hod of bricks. Is approached by a Populist politician. Shows his displeasure by dropping bricks on the politician. (*Edison Films*, March 1900, 36.)
SUBJECT: Politics, practical. Working classes. Irish Americans. Building. Bricks. Violence. Democratic Party.
ARCHIVE:

CITATIONS: Jannopoulo & Gumpertz to Vitascope Company, 12 September 1896, MH-BA; *New York World*, 11 October 1896, 14. Maguire & Baucus, *Fall Catalogue*, 1897, 13; F.Z. Maguire & Co., *Catalogue,* [March 1898], 32; *Edison Films*, July 1901, 71.

NOTE:

231 The Old German Mill / The Old Mill

LENGTH: 50 ft.   © No reg.

PRODUCER: James White, Raff & Gammon.

CAMERA: William Heise.

CAST:

PRODUCTION DATE: By late September 1896.

LOCATION: [Black Maria, West Orange, N.J.]

SOURCE: *Sausage Factory* (Lumière film, 1896).

DESCRIPTION: In which one of the millers thrusts a woman into the hopper of the mill and she soon emerges from beneath it, having apparently been run through the machinery. (*The Phonoscope*, November 1896, 16.)

SUBJECT: German Americans. Practical jokes. Machinery.

ARCHIVE:

CITATIONS: *New York World*, 4 October 1896, 14.

NOTE:

232 German Children's Parade / German Children, Parade / Children's Parade

LENGTH: 50 and 150 ft.   © No reg.

PRODUCER: James White, Raff & Gammon.

CAMERA: William Heise.

CAST:

PRODUCTION DATE: By late September 1896.

LOCATION:

SOURCE:

DESCRIPTION: Showing a procession of children and adults, with a German band. (*The Phonoscope*, November 1896, 14.)

A scene in a German picnic grounds, showing over 200 children in line. (F.Z. Maguire & Co., *Catalogue*, [March 1898], 30.)

SUBJECT: Marching bands. Parades. German Americans. Children.

ARCHIVE:

CITATIONS: *New York World*, 4 October 1896, 14. Maguire & Baucus, *Edison and International Photographic Films*, April 1897, 6 and 17; Maguire & Baucus, *Fall Catalogue*, 1897, 11 and 14.

NOTE:

233 Bryan Train Scene at Orange / Bryan Passing Through Orange / Train Scene at Orange.

LENGTH: 150 ft.   © No reg.

PRODUCER: James White, Raff & Gammon.

CAMERA: William Heise.

CAST: William Jennings Bryan.

PRODUCTION DATE: 23 September 1896.

LOCATION: Orange, N.J.

SOURCE:

DESCRIPTION: Showing Mr. Bryan addressing a crowd of people from the rear platform of a moving train. (*The Phonoscope*, April 1897, 14.)

SUBJECT: Politics, practical. Presidential candidates. Democratic Party. Speeches, addresses, etc. Railroads.

ARCHIVE:

CITATIONS: "Political Notes," *Orange Chronicle*, 26 September 1896, 5; *New York Herald*, 18 October 1896, 7C. Maguire & Baucus, *Edison and International Photographic Films*, April 1897, 19; Maguire & Baucus, *Fall Catalogue*, 1897, 14; F.Z. Maguire & Co., *Catalogue*, [March 1898], 32.

NOTE:

234 *Fast Train

LENGTH: 50 ft.　© No reg.
PRODUCER: James White, Raff & Gammon.
CAMERA: William Heise.
CAST:
PRODUCTION DATE: [Late September to mid-
October 1896?]
LOCATION: Mohawk Valley, N.Y.
SOURCE:
DESCRIPTION: An express train of the Hudson
River and New York Central R.R. passing
around a curve in the picturesque Mohawk
Valley at very fast speed. (Maguire &
Baucus, *Edison and International Photo-
graphic Films*, April 1897, 7.)
SUBJECT: Railroads. New York Central Railroad.
ARCHIVE: NR-GE.
CITATIONS: ["Express Train Approaching Depot"] Kiefaber to Raff & Gammon, 6
November 1896. Maguire & Baucus, *Fall Catalogue*, 1897, 12.
NOTE: It is possible that this film was taken late in 1896 or in early 1897. The identifi-
cation, by Gordon Hendricks, is far from certain.

235 Fast Trains
LENGTH: 150 ft.　© No reg.
PRODUCER: James White, Raff & Gammon.
CAMERA: William Heise.
CAST:
PRODUCTION DATE: [Late September to mid-October 1896?]
LOCATION: [Mohawk Valley], N.Y.
SOURCE:
DESCRIPTION: Express Trains passing on the New York Central R.R. (Maguire &
Baucus, *Edison and International Photographic Films*, April 1897, 18.)
Showing express trains passing north and south on the H.R.R.R. (F.Z. Maguire &
Co., *Catalogue*, [March 1898], 32.)
SUBJECT: Railroads. New York Central Railroad.
ARCHIVE:
CITATIONS: Maguire & Baucus, *Fall Catalogue*, 1897, 14.
NOTE: H.R.R.R. is the Harlem River Railroad, a division of the New York Central. It is
possible that this film was taken late in 1896 or in early 1897.

Although the Edison Manufacturing Company sold Telephone Appointment *and*
Interrupted Supper *separately, its catalogs encouraged exhibitors to show the two
scenes together, making them a very early example of the multi-shot story film.*

236 Telephone Appointment / An Appointment by Telephone
LENGTH: 50 ft.　© No reg.
PRODUCER: James White, Raff & Gammon.
CAMERA: William Heise.
CAST:
PRODUCTION DATE: By early October 1896.
LOCATION: Black Maria, West Orange, N.J.
SOURCE:
DESCRIPTION: First Scene–A gay young man in a Wall Street broker's office, with
wicked intentions makes an engagement with a pretty typewriter. The sequel
brings about his discomforture and the triumph of the typewriter. (F.M. Prescott,
Catalogue of New Films, 1899, 18-19.)
The admirer of the fair sex is first seen making an appointment with a pretty ste-
nographer but is overheard by his wife. (F.Z. Maguire & Co., *Catalogue*, [March
1898], 31.)

SUBJECT: Adultery. Telephone. Businessmen. Secretaries. Brokerage firms.

ARCHIVE:

CITATIONS: *Orange Chronicle*, 30 October 1896, 5. Maguire & Baucus, *Edison and International Photographic Films*, April 1897, 15; Maguire & Baucus, *Fall Catalogue*, 1897, 13; *Edison Films*, March 1900, 36.

NOTE: This subject was subsequently reworked by the Edison Manufacturing Company as the first scene of *Appointment by Telephone* (© 15 May 1902).

237 The Interrupted Supper / Supper Interrupted

LENGTH: 50 ft.   © No reg.

PRODUCER: James White, Raff & Gammon.

CAMERA: William Heise.

CAST:

PRODUCTION DATE: By early October 1896.

LOCATION: Black Maria, West Orange, N.J.

SOURCE:

DESCRIPTION: Second Film–The gay young man with the wicked intentions, from his Wall Street broker's office, hies himself to the place of appointment and meets the pretty typewriter. Just as they are sitting down to supper his irate wife appears upon the scene and there is a denouement. The wicked young man is exposed and disgraced by his wife's explanation. (F.M. Prescott, *Catalogue of New Films*, 1899, 18-19.)

SUBJECT: Adultery. Taverns, etc. Businessmen. Secretaries.

ARCHIVE:

CITATIONS: Maguire & Baucus, *Fall Catalogue*, 1897, 13.

NOTE: This subject was subsequently reworked by the Edison Manufacturing Company as the third and final scene of *Appointment by Telephone* (© 15 May 1902).

CONCERNING THE TYPEWRITER.

Jokes About Her as a Rule are Senseless and Uncalled for.

Probably there is no more maligned woman in the world than the typewriter, unless it is the mother-in-law. Because a typewriter gets most of her patronage from men, she seems to be regarded as a fair mark by the propounder of would-be witticisms which are often in the worst of taste.

In spite of all this there is probably no more sedate class of young women than this self same person who supports herself and oftentimes her family by the agility of her fingers. This is largely due to the fact that the young women realize the unusual nature of their business and are always careful.

But what is the etiquette of typewriters? Books on etiquette tell us not to eat soup with our fork and not to put our feet on the table while dining, and lots of other senseless things, but no mention is made of the typewriter.

For example, a man has been dictating to a woman for months, possibly for years: it has been a matter of business between them always and it is quite certain that they have never been regularly introduced after the conventional fashion. He may admire her for her good sense or her adroitness on the machine, but a suggestion that he might ask her to dine or might send her tickets for the theatre might be misunderstood.

Typewriters in the hotels are in an exceptionally equivocal position. Many hotel proprietors to-day will not employ women as typewriters. It is the male guests who ordinarily want to dictate and they generally want to do so in their rooms, where they can be at their ease.

For that reason, and the fact that most all of the accommodations furnished typewriters in hotels are adjuncts of either the cafe or barroom, the number of women operators in hotels is becoming very considerably lessened. (*New York Herald*, 7 November 1894, 13.)

238 Bag Punching

LENGTH: 50 ft.   © No reg.

PRODUCER: James White, Raff & Gammon.

CAMERA: William Heise.

CAST: Michael Leonard.

PRODUCTION DATE: By early October 1896.

LOCATION: Black Maria, West Orange, N.J.

SOURCE:

DESCRIPTION: An exhibition by Mike Leonard, the famous trainer. (Maguire & Baucus, *Edison and International Photographic Films*, April 1897, 4.)

SUBJECT: Vaudeville–performances. Boxing.
ARCHIVE:
CITATIONS: Maguire & Baucus, *Fall Catalogue*, 1897, 11; F.Z. Maguire & Co., *Catalogue*, [March 1898], 33.
NOTE:

239 *Turkish Harem / Turkish Harem Scene**
LENGTH: 150 ft.   © No reg.
PRODUCER: James White, Raff & Gammon.
CAMERA: William Heise.
CAST:
PRODUCTION DATE: By early October 1896.
LOCATION: Black Maria, West Orange, N.J.
SOURCE:
DESCRIPTION: A characteristic Turkish dance in costume. (Maguire & Baucus, *Fall Catalogue*, 1897, 14.)
SUBJECT: Vaudeville–performances. Turks. Dancing. Danse du ventre.
ARCHIVE: DLC-AFI.
CITATIONS: Maguire & Baucus, *Edison and International Photographic Films*, April 1897, 19; F.Z. Maguire, *Catalogue*, [March 1898], 28.
NOTE:

240 **Cuban Liberty**
LENGTH: 50 ft.   © No reg.
PRODUCER: Raff & Gammon.
CAMERA: William Heise.
CAST:
PRODUCTION DATE: [Mid-October 1896?]
LOCATION: Black Maria, West Orange, N.J.
SOURCE: Political cartoon.
DESCRIPTION: Burlesque. Uncle Sam bringing to a close the row between Cuba and Spain. (F.Z. Maguire & Co., *Catalogue*, [March 1898], 31.)
SUBJECT: Editorial Cartoons. United States–Foreign Relations–Latin America.
ARCHIVE:
CITATIONS:
NOTE: A cartoon appearing in the *New York Herald* (16 October 1896, 3.) conforms to this basic allegory and could have served as inspiration. The reverse (film inspiring cartoon) may also be possible.

The Edison Manufacturing Company hired James Henry White away from Raff & Gammon in October 1896. As head of the Kinetograph Department, he was paid $100 a month plus a 5% commission on film sales. This move recentralized film production within the Edison organization and coincided with the company's decision to copyright its most important negatives in the name of Thomas A. Edison, president and sole owner of this unincorporated business.

241 √Streets of Cairo / [Streets of Cairo, no. 2]**
LENGTH: 50 ft.   © Thomas A. Edison, 23 October 1896.
PRODUCER: James White, Raff & Gammon.
CAMERA: William Heise.
CAST:
PRODUCTION DATE: September-October 1896.
LOCATION: [Coney Island, N.Y.]
SOURCE:
DESCRIPTION: Showing four Egyptian Girls in full native costumes executing the fascinating "Midway dance." (*The Phonoscope*, December 1896, 16.)
SUBJECT: Amusement parks. Dancing. Egyptians. Danse du ventre.

ARCHIVE:
CITATIONS: Maguire & Baucus, *Edison Films*, 20 January 1897, 7; Maguire & Baucus, *Edison and International Photographic Films*, April 1897, 15; Maguire & Baucus, *Fall Catalogue*, 1897, 13; F.Z. Maguire & Co., *Catalogue*, [March 1898], 25.
NOTE: A "Streets of Cairo" show was also at Atlantic City during the summer and early fall of 1896.

COOCHEE-COOCHEE STOPPED AT CONEY.
Police Fail to See How It Can Possibly Rank as a Sacred Concert.
GLOOM IN CAIRO'S STREETS.
Troubled Turks to Appeal to Mayor Wurster for a Sunday Dance Permit.
BIG CROWDS AT THE ISLAND.

The cloudy weather yesterday made things dismal at Coney Island for a while, but in the afternoon an old time crowd began to pour in from the steamboat piers and railroad depots, and by three o'clock more than 70,000 visitors were at that resort. In short order the fakirs were on deck with their little games running in full blast, while the managers of the many amusement places in the Bowery were disturbing the peace with vociferous announcements of the excellence of their respective shows.

The danse du ventre was the great drawing card, however, in the Streets of Cairo, in the Midway Plaisance, and in a dozen or more alleged Turkish theatres. Everything was going along in good order, with the box office man busy raking in the dimes, when Deputy Police Commissioner George Crosbey happened to drop into the Streets of Cairo and saw the "great Adjy" doing the "Coochee" in the lion's den.

NOT AT ALL SACRED.

The Deputy Commissioner could not possibly see how the dance came under the head of a "sacred concert," and immediately ordered it stopped. There were protests by the Turks who own the show, but the dance had to be discontinued, and there was gloom in Cairo's streets during the balance of the day. Later the Deputy Commissioner with a policeman, visited all of the halls where the danse du ventre was being given, and told the managers that it would not be permitted on Sundays.

In the evening Mr. Rodita called upon Justice Finnerty and wanted to know if he would not issue a permit to allow the danse du ventre to go on. The Justice told the Egyptian manager that it was beyond his power to grant such a permit and the only official that could help him out of his trouble was Mayor Wurster.

TO AMUSE THE MAYOR.

Manager Rodita will call upon that official this morning with Adjy and if necessary, give the dance in City Hall....(*New York Herald,* 8 June 1896, 11.)

242 √**Wine Garden Scene / Wein Stube in Harlem**
LENGTH: 150 ft.   © Thomas A. Edison, 23 October 1896.
PRODUCER: James White, Raff & Gammon.
CAMERA: William Heise.
CAST:
PRODUCTION DATE: October 1896.
LOCATION: New York, N.Y.
SOURCE:
DESCRIPTION: This is a scene which may be witnessed by a visitor at a noted German wine garden in Harlem. Shows a number of people seated at tables drinking, etc., two of whom are playing cards; a pretty waitress serves the refreshments and proves very attractive to one of the guests. A sharp, clear film and full of action. (F.Z. Maguire & Co., *Catalogue,* [March 1898], 26.)

SUBJECT: Taverns, etc. Alcoholic beverages. German Americans.
ARCHIVE:

CITATIONS: *The Phonoscope*, December 1896, 16; Maguire & Baucus, *Edison Films*, 20 January 1897, 7; Maguire & Baucus, *Edison and International Photographic Films*, April 1897, 19; Maguire & Baucus, *Fall Catalogue*, 1897, 14; *Edison Films*, March 1900, 38.

NOTE:

243 *Feeding the Doves

LENGTH: 50 ft.   © Thomas A. Edison, 23 October 1896.
PRODUCER: James White, Raff & Gammon.
CAMERA: William Heise.
CAST:
PRODUCTION DATE: Mid-October 1896.
LOCATION:
SOURCE:

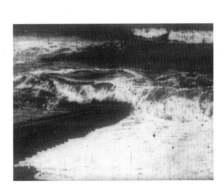

DESCRIPTION: A typical farm scene showing a beautiful girl and her baby sister dealing out the morning meal to the chickens and doves. The doves and chickens form a beautiful spectacle as they flutter and flock around the givers—a beautiful picture, which would appeal to the sentiments of any audience. (*The Phonoscope*, December 1896, 16.)
SUBJECT: Farms. Chickens. Doves. Children.
ARCHIVE: NNMoMA, NR-GE, CLAc, CaOOANF, DLC-Hendricks.
CITATIONS: Maguire & Baucus, *Edison Films*, 20 January 1897, 4; Maguire & Baucus, *Edison and International Photographic Films*, April 1897, 8; Maguire & Baucus, *Fall Catalogue*, 1897, 12; *Edison Films*, March 1900, 39.
NOTE: The Lumière organization and the International Film Company both made films that were very similar to this one. The Edison picture preceded *Farmyard Scene,* made by the International Film Company, but the position of the Lumière film in this sequence is unclear.

244 *Surf at Long Branch / Surf Scene / Surf After the Storm / After the Storm

LENGTH: 50 and 150 ft.   © Thomas A. Edison, 23 October 1896.
PRODUCER: James White.
CAMERA: William Heise.
CAST:
PRODUCTION DATE: October 1896.
LOCATION: Long Branch, N.J.
SOURCE: *Rough Sea at Dover* (R.W. Paul film, 1895).
DESCRIPTION: Photographed at Long Branch just after a severe storm. Shows a heavy surf dashing along a pier and breaking upon the beach close to the camera. An excellent subject for water effects, the glittering spray being distinctly reproduced. (Maguire & Baucus, *Edison Films*, 20 January 1897, 5.)
SUBJECT: Ocean waves. Seashore. Storms. Piers.
ARCHIVE: CaOOANF.
CITATIONS: Maguire & Baucus, *Edison and International Photographic Films*, April 1897, 14 and 19; Maguire & Baucus, *Fall Catalogue*, 1897, 13; F.Z. Maguire & Co., *Catalogue,* [March 1898], 25; *Edison Films*, March 1900, 44.
NOTE: The International Film Company took a very similar film, *Storm on the Sea Coast*, also apparently a Long Branch, at about the same time. The Flaherty collection in which this film survives apparently consists exclusively of Edison films.

The American Mutoscope Company's biograph exhibition service opened in Pittsburgh in mid-September 1896, played in New York City for the week of October 4th, and had its official premiere on October 11th. The company quickly became Edison's principal American competitor. Since the "Biograph Company," worked in a different gauge (68mm or 70mm) and did not sell its films on the open market, the Edison Manufacturing Company often remade its rival's hits.

245 ***A Morning Bath**

LENGTH: 50 ft.   © Thomas A. Edison, 31 October 1896.

PRODUCER: James White.

CAMERA: William Heise.

CAST:

PRODUCTION DATE: October 1896.

LOCATION: Black Maria, West Orange, N.J.

SOURCE: *A Hard Wash* (Biograph film no. 39, summer 1896).

DESCRIPTION: This scene presents a dusky African mother in the act of giving her struggling pickaninny a bath in a tub of suds. This is a clear and distinct picture in which the contrast between the complexion of the bather and the white soapsuds is strongly marked. A very amusing and popular subject. (Maguire & Baucus, *Edison Films*, 20 January 1897, 4.)

SUBJECT: Afro-Americans. Infants. Hygiene. Baths. Child rearing.

ARCHIVE: NNMoMA, NR-GE, DLC-Hendricks, CLAc.

CITATIONS: Maguire & Baucus, *Edison and International Photographic Films*, April 1897, 12; Maguire & Baucus, *Fall Catalogue*, 1897, 12; F.Z. Maguire & Co., *Catalogue*, [March 1898], 26; *Edison Films*, March 1900, 35; *Edison Films*, July 1901, 69.

NOTE:

NEGRO BABIES ON EXHIBITION.

Four Prizes Offered at the Novel Show in Atlantic City.

[By Telegraph to the Herald.]

Atlantic City, N.J., August 20, 1896. What was probably the first and only baby show ever given for infants of the African race only was held on the pier in this city this morning. The dark faced contestants, whose ages ranged from six months to two years, numbered about fifty and attracted a great deal of attention from the thousands of white folks who flocked to the novel exhibition. Four prizes were offered—one for the handsomest, one for the cutest, the third for the fattest, and the fourth for the handsomest pair of twins. As there is no standard comparison of colored beauty, the voting was carried on with no little mirth. (*New York Herald*, 12 August 1896, 9.)

246 ***Clark's Thread Mill / Employees Leaving Factory / Clark's Thread Mills**

LENGTH: 50 and 150 ft.   © Thomas A. Edison, 31 October 1896.

PRODUCER: James White.

CAMERA: William Heise.

CAST:

PRODUCTION DATE: Late October 1896.

LOCATION: East Newark, N.J.

SOURCE: *Employees Leaving the Lumière Factory* (Lumière film, 1895).

DESCRIPTION: Showing about 500 employees (men, women and children) leaving this great factory at the end of their week's toil, their faces lighted up with happiness in anticipation of the day of rest at hand. The facial expression of each of this vast army of toilers is clearly defined. (*The Phonoscope*, December 1896, 16.)

SUBJECT: City and town life–Newark. Working classes. Factories.

ARCHIVE: CaOOANF.

CITATIONS: Maguire & Baucus, *Edison and International Photographic Films*, April 1897, 7 and 18; Maguire & Baucus, *Fall Catalogue*, 1897, 11 and 14.

NOTE: Later sold in lengths of 50 and 100 feet. (F.Z. Maguire & Co., *Catalogue*, [March 1898], 26.)

247 *****The Burning Stable**

LENGTH: 50 and 150 ft.   © Thomas A. Edison, 31 October 1896.

PRODUCER: James White.

CAMERA: William Heise.

CAST:

PRODUCTION DATE: Late October 1896.

LOCATION:

SOURCE: *Stable on Fire* (Biograph film no. 44, 1896).

DESCRIPTION: Shows a barn actually in flames, from which four horses and a burning wagon are rescued by firemen and stable hands. The scene is exciting, full of action from beginning to end, and all its details are clearly and sharply defined. Thick volumes of smoke pouring from the doors and windows of the stable add greatly to the realistic effect. (Maguire & Baucus, *Edison Films*, 20 January 1897, 2.)

SUBJECT: Fire fighters. Horses. Fires. Stables.

ARCHIVE: NNMoMA, NR-GE, CLAc, DLC-Hendricks.

CITATIONS: Maguire & Baucus, *Edison and International Photographic Films*, April 1897, 4 and 17; Maguire & Baucus, *Fall Catalogue*, 1897, 11 and 14; *Edison Films*, March 1900, 28; *Edison Films*, July 1901, 54.

NOTE: 50 and 100 ft. according to F.Z. Maguire & Co., *Catalogue* [March 1898], 25.

In late October an Edison camera crew took the kinetograph to Central Park, where curiosity seekers could spy likely entries for the upcoming New York Horse Show, 9-14 November 1996.

248 **East Side Drive, no. 1 / East Side Drive—Central Park, N.Y. / East Side Drive**

LENGTH: 50 ft.   © Thomas A. Edison, 31 October 1896.

PRODUCER: James White.

CAMERA: William Heise.

CAST:

PRODUCTION DATE: Late October 1896.

LOCATION: Central Park, New York, N.Y.

SOURCE:

DESCRIPTION: Taken at the fashionable driving hour and shows many stylish equipages drawn by spirited and high-bred horses—the sharpest driving scene ever presented. Sharp, clear and full of action. (F.Z. Maguire & Co., *Catalogue*, [March 1898], 26.)

SUBJECT: City and town life–New York. Horses. Carriages and carts. Social elites. Parks.

ARCHIVE:

CITATIONS: *The Phonoscope*, December 1896, 16; Maguire & Baucus, *Edison Films*, 20 January 1897, 7; Maguire & Baucus, *Edison and International Photographic Films*, April 1897, 7; Maguire & Baucus, *Fall Catalogue*, 1897, 12; *Edison Films*, March 1900, 41.

NOTE:

249 **East Side Drive, no. 2**

LENGTH: © Thomas A. Edison, 31 October 1896.

PRODUCER: James White.

CAMERA: William Heise.

CAST:

PRODUCTION DATE: Late October 1896.

LOCATION: Central Park, New York, N.Y.

SOURCE:

DESCRIPTION:

SUBJECT: City and town life–New York. Horses. Carriages and carts. Social elites. Parks.

ARCHIVE:

CITATIONS:

NOTE:

The mounted police were practicing for competition in Class 109, Municipal Police Horses, of the New York Horse Show, 9-14 November 1896.

250 **√Park Police, Dismounting and Mounting / Park Police Drill—Mount and Dismount / Mounted Police Drill, [no. 1]**

LENGTH: 50 ft.   © Thomas A. Edison, 31 October 1896.

PRODUCER: James White.

CAMERA: William Heise.

CAST: Sergeant Eagan.

PRODUCTION DATE: Late October 1896.

LOCATION: Central Park, New York, N.Y.

SOURCE:

DESCRIPTION: These two films [with *Park Police, Left, Wheel and Forward*] show a full battalion of New York's famous mounted police, commanded by Sergeant Eagen, drilling in preparation for the Annual Horse Show, held at Madison Square Garden. (*The Phonoscope*, December 1896, 16.)

SUBJECT: Police. Horses. New York Police Department. New York Horse Show. Parks.

ARCHIVE:

CITATIONS: Maguire & Baucus, *Edison Films*, 20 January 1897, 2; Maguire & Baucus, *Edison and International Photographic Films*, April 1897, 12; Maguire & Baucus, *Fall Catalogue*, 1897, 12; F.Z. Maguire & Co., *Catalogue,* [March 1898], 26; *Edison Films*, March 1900, 43.

NOTE:

251 **Park Police, Left Wheel and Forward / Park Police Drill—Left, Wheel and Forward / Mounted Police Drill, [no. 2]**

LENGTH: 50 ft.   © Thomas A. Edison, 31 October 1896.

PRODUCER: James White.

CAMERA: William Heise.

CAST: Sergeant Eagan.

PRODUCTION DATE: Late October 1896.

LOCATION: Central Park, New York, N.Y.

SOURCE:

DESCRIPTION: These two films [with *Park Police, Dismounting and Mounting*] show a full batallion of New York's famous mounted police, commanded by Sergeant Eagan, drilling in preparation for the Annual Horse Show, held at Madison Square Garden. (*The Phonoscope*, December 1896, 16.)

SUBJECT: Police. Horses. New York Police Department. New York Horse Show. Parks.

ARCHIVE:

CITATIONS: Maguire & Baucus, *Edison Films*, 20 January 1897, 2; Maguire & Baucus, *Edison and International Photographic Films*, April 1897, 11; Maguire & Baucus, *Fall Catalogue*, 1897, 12; F.Z. Maguire & Co., *Catalogue,* [March 1898], 26; *Edison Films*, March 1900, 43.

NOTE:

252 *Mounted Police Charge
LENGTH: 50 ft.   © Thomas A. Edison, 2 November 1896.
PRODUCER: James White.
CAMERA: William Heise.
CAST: Sergeant Eagan.
PRODUCTION DATE: Late October 1896.
LOCATION: Central Park, New York, N.Y.
SOURCE: *Charge of the Seventh French Cuiras-
siers* (Lumière film, 1896).

DESCRIPTION: Shows a battalion of New York's
famous mounted police in full dress uniform. From the distance the mounted officers are seen approaching the audience at a
break-neck gallop and as they halt for
inspection of the reviewing officer, each
horse and rider is brought into life size. (*The Phonoscope*, December 1896, 16.)
SUBJECT: Police. Horses. New York Police Department. Parks.
ARCHIVE: NNMoMA, DLC-Hendricks.
CITATIONS: Maguire & Baucus, *Edison Films*, 20 January 1897, 2; Maguire & Baucus,
Edison and International Photographic Films, April 1897, 11; Maguire & Baucus,
Fall Catalogue, 1897, 12; *Edison Films*, March 1900, 43.
NOTE:

253 √Runaway in the Park / The Runaway in the Park / Runaway
LENGTH: 50 ft.   © Thomas A. Edison, 2 November 1896.
PRODUCER: James White.
CAMERA: William Heise.
CAST:
PRODUCTION DATE: Late October 1896.
LOCATION: Central Park, New York, N.Y.
SOURCE:

DESCRIPTION: Just as we had finished taking
the mounted police a horse and carriage
was observed coming toward us at a furious
rate, closely pursued by two mounted officers. They rode on either side of the
affrighted runaway and thus approached
the camera. The officers could not stop the
running horse until they had passed our
photographer, hence we are unable to show the result. That portion, however,
which we did get forms the most exciting subject ever presented in this or any other
country. Remarkably clear and sharp. (F.Z. Maguire & Co., *Catalogue*, [March
1898], 26.)
SUBJECT: Police. Horses. Rescues. Parks.
ARCHIVE:
CITATIONS: *The Phonoscope*, December 1896, 16; Maguire & Baucus, *Edison and
International Photographic Films*, April 1897, 14; Maguire & Baucus, *Fall
Catalogue*, 1897, 12; *Edison Films*, March 1900, 44; *Edison Films*, July 1901, 90.
NOTE: This subject would be reworked and elaborated almost ten years later as one
scene in *Life of an American Policeman* (Edison film, © 6 December 1905).

And Now the Horse Show.

The entries for New York's annual Horse Show have closed, and in another column of to-day's Herald you can learn
all that you want to know in regard to how the classes filled and what notable animals will be ready to step into
the ring to contest for the blue ribbons. All New York will be there when Horse Show week is inaugurated at
Madison Square Garden, on November 9, and the usual fashionable crush will continue until the last contest is
decided and the last ribbon has been given out. As a display of fine horses, handsome women and pretty toilets
the show is always a sporting and a social success, and the exhibition of 1896 bids fair to be as interesting as any
that has gone before.

The entries are not quite so numerous as in '95, but quality rather than quantity is what is most desirable, and the former is decidedly in evidence. In fact, the list shows a marked advance in that respect, and the lessening in numbers is due to a wise system of weeding out competitors and the elimination of some uninteresting classes. (Editorial, *New York Herald,* 24 October 1896, 8.)

MUNICIPAL POLICE HORSES.

Judged by Mr. George C. Clausen.

Class 109–The best and best trained police horses to be ridden by officers; appointment and uniforms also to be considered.–First prize, $200 (in money or plate) Patrolman James Frawley's Jim b.g. 15.3, eight years, Thirty-first precinct; second prize, $100 (in money or plate), Patrolman Hermann Heemsoth's Jim, b.g. 15.3, six years, Thirty-third precinct; third prize, $50 (in money or plate) Patrolman Michael Voght's Fritz, b.g. 15, twelve years, Thirty-second precinct; highly commended, Roundsman John Popper's Walsh, b.g. 15.3, nine years, Thirty-eight precinct. (*New York Herald*, 13 November 1896, 4.)

The Edison Manufacturing Company took several negatives of the sound money parade, a pro-McKinley demonstration on the eve of the election. The chants offered by this refined group—which featured large contingents of businessmen, Wall Street financiers, lawyers and students from Columbia University—included:

> *Who is Bryan?*
> *Tell me, who?*
> *First in chin, first in cheek*
> *First in the heart of every freak.*

("Marshaling the Host," New York Herald, 1 November 1896, 3.)

254 ***[McKinley Parade, no. 1]**
LENGTH: © No reg.
PRODUCER: James White.
CAMERA: William Heise.
CAST:
PRODUCTION DATE: 31 October 1896.
LOCATION: Fifth Avenue, New York, N.Y.
SOURCE:
DESCRIPTION:
SUBJECT: Parades. Politics, practical. Gold. Republican Party. Flags–United States. William McKinley.
ARCHIVE: NR-GE, DNA.
CITATIONS:
NOTE: In many respects, the assignment of this picture to this particular title is arbitrary, since there is no way to establish the order of filming or the specific title designated for the different films of this event.

255 ***McKinley Parade, no. 2 / McKinley Parade / The Great McKinley Parade**
LENGTH: 50 and 150 ft. © Thomas A. Edison, 7 November 1896.
PRODUCER: James White.
CAMERA: William Heise.
CAST:
PRODUCTION DATE: 31 October 1896.
LOCATION: Fifth Avenue, New York, N.Y.
SOURCE:
DESCRIPTION: We have several negatives of this, the greatest political parade which has ever taken place in New York City. Thousands of men in line, and spectators, with banners flying and flags waving, are clearly and distinctly shown, making a spectacle which cannot fail to arouse the enthusiasm of an audience. (F.Z. Maguire & Co., *Catalogue*, [March 1898], 26.)

SUBJECT: Parades. Politics, practical. Gold. Republican Party. Flags–United States. William McKinley.

ARCHIVE: NR-GE, NNMoMA.

CITATIONS: *The Phonoscope*, December 1896, 16; Maguire & Baucus, *Edison and International Photographic Films*, April 1897, 12 and 18; Maguire & Baucus, *Fall Catalogue*, 1897, 12.

NOTE: The film at NNMoMA may be *Sound Money Parade*, taken by the International Film Company of this same event.

256 **[McKinley Parade, no. 3]**

LENGTH: © No reg.

PRODUCER: James White.

CAMERA: William Heise.

CAST:

PRODUCTION DATE: 31 October 1896.

LOCATION: Fifth Avenue, New York, N.Y.

SOURCE:

DESCRIPTION:

SUBJECT: Parades. Politics, practical. Gold. Republican Party. Flags–United States. William McKinley.

ARCHIVE:

CITATIONS:

NOTE:

PAGEANT OF PATRIOTISM.
Under October's Golden Sun Marched 100,000 Soldiers of the New Grand Army of the Republic.
GREATEST DEMONSTRATION IN THE NATION'S HISTORY.
The City was Swathed in Red, White and Blue, and the Golden Yellow
Chrysanthemum Became the Emblem of National Honor.
AN IMPRESSIVE REVOLT AGAINST REPUDIATION.
Men in line, by actual count–99,195. Head of Parade reached Reviewing Stand, 10h. 55m.
Parade finished at Reviewing Stand, 6 h. 30 m. Actual time in motion. 7h. 35m.

New York yesterday beheld a new Grand Army of the Republic marching through its streets. It was an army of peace, but it was a mighty and overpowering host. It marched bearing aloft the United States flag, shouting aloud the championship of the national honor, keeping step to the martial music of patriotic American sirs.

It paraded, giving an exhibition of the spontaneous outburst of the American spirit against Bryanism, Altgeldism, and Tillmanism. As a demonstration it has no parallel in the history of this country. No such emphatic protest against a political party gone astray, or against political leadership gone daft has ever been recorded.

And yet it was not a partisan demonstration. It was political only in the sense that it was directed against a political creed adopted at Chicago in July. It was essentially patriotic. It sent the blood tingling to the finger tips. It stirred the deeper emotions. It fanned the fires of patriotism as briskly as they blazed during the civil war. The sturdy business citizenship of New York seemed to have arisen as one man to stand up and be counted for honest money. Without regard to party they stood up and were counted, and the count actually made by HERALD reporters shows 99,195 men to have been in line, while it is estimated that at least 15,000 more grew weary of waiting for the order to fall in and went home without going over the route.

Greater Than All Others.

What this means can only be grasped when compared with similar parades in this city which have been regarded as "record breakers." The great political parades were those for Cleveland and Blaine in 1884, the Cleveland business men's parade in 1892, and the Harrison parade in 1881. The great civic demonstrations were the Grant funeral procession, in August 1885, and the Washington Inaugural Centennial parade, May 1, 1889.

Both the Cleveland and Blaine parades in 1884, stretched into one, would not have extended more than half way down the line of yesterday's great array. The Cleveland parade of business men in 1892 was a pigmy. There were less than 30,000 men in line, and it just about equalled the first two divisions of the thirty-nine divisions of yesterday's pageant of the new Grand Army of the Republic.

For instance, the Cleveland parade of 1892 was two hours passing the reviewing stand. Compare that with the line that yesterday swept by in review for seven and one-half consecutive hours. So, too, with the procession that followed Grant to Riverside in 1885. The actual number of men in line was 33,000. Let us continue the comparison to the Centennial pageant, May 1, 1889. Then it was believed that the high water mark was reached for parades in this country. Only 50,000 men participated, according to the highest estimates. Yet this was probably exaggerated.

Perfect Day, Unbounded Enthusiasm.

With this illustration by comparison fixed in the mind one has only to consider the character of the marchers in this new Grand Army of the Republic and the surroundings of the marching to get at what such a demonstration means in this city.

Every branch of business in New York was represented—not by a few in each trade, but by practically all the men engaged in it. The dry goods trade turned out almost enough men to make up a division in the field. The Produce Exchange furnished a brigade. So did the paper trade, and so also did the Cotton and Coffee exchanges. There were enough lawyers to make four regiments. Democrats and republicans were side by side, elbow to elbow, all fully determined "to fire both barrels" at popocracy and Bryanism by voting for McKinley.

The day was perfect, and the welcome that awaited the new Grand Army of the Republic was superb. Bright sunlight flashed from a cloudless sky upon the red, white and blue of the national colors. Brisk breezes kept the colors flying. The outer walls of all the buildings in the streets through which the parade passed were fairly covered with the national emblem. It was Flag Day, and the flag was everywhere. Each parader carried a flag. Each spectator had a flag. The flags were constantly waved, and when the wind caught those in the marchers' hands and sent them all fluttering in the same direction the effect was very pretty.

It was also Chrysanthemum Day. Yellow chrysanthemums were in demand. Yellow meant gold. White chrysanthemums were a drug on the market. White meant nothing in particular. Where all the yellow chrysanthemums came from is one of the mysteries of the campaign. Everybody wore them. Ladies wore them strung together in wreaths and chains. Each spectator had a flower. Each parader had one. It is true that some of the marchers did not have a yellow gold bug, but if a parader did not have a yellow chrysanthemum and a flag he was driven out of the line by his fellows, in disgrace.

Everything Yellow is Gold.

Yellow was the predominating color. There was great applause when a division went by with yellow hats. Yellow medallions of McKinley six inches in diameter were worn. A company captain with yellow hair made a distinct hit. A man with a bad attack of jaundice would have been cheered, and a well developed case of yellow fever would have been regarded as a most excellent thing. Indeed, everybody seemed to have yellow fever.

And so, with tossing flags and flaunting yellow flowers, with "McKinley" the battle cry and gold the sign of victory, this new Grand Army of the Republic went by the reviewing stand where Mr. Hobart, Governor Morton, Mr. Woodruff, Mayor Strong, Mayor Wurster and a party of sound money democrats stood greeting the sturdy patriots.

It went by with a speed which made men familiar with such demonstrations open their eyes. In close ranks, at a brisk pace, without long lapses between divisions, the men went at the rate of nearly 17,000 an hour.

Porter is Proud.

This was the estimate of General Horace Porter, the chief marshal, made last night. No one thought he could do it. Yet without a hitch the line moved, and men who had seen trained soldiers fail to do so well marveled. General Porter was credited with having accomplished something unheard of in parading. When the parade was over General Porter said:–

"The parade passed the reviewing stand at the rate of 17,000 an hour, and there has not been the slightest trouble. It is a greater parade than the review of Sherman's army at Washington after the war, which I witnessed in company with General Grant."

It is estimated that there were 15,000 men left out of the parade by the promptness with which the line moved. The lumber trade organization, 1,000 strong, did not march, because of the lateness of the hour. The whole downtown district was filled with similar organizations shut out. (*New York Herald*, 1 November 1896, 3-5.)

After the American Mutoscope Company produced and exhibited several films of fire runs and fire fighting activities, the Edison Manufacturing Company emulated their success with a number of similar subjects in November 1896.

257 ***Starting for the Fire**

LENGTH: 50 ft.   © Thomas A. Edison, 16 November 1896.

PRODUCER: James White.

CAMERA: William Heise.

CAST:

PRODUCTION DATE: Early November 1896.

LOCATION: Newark, N.J.

SOURCE: *New York Fire Department* (Biograph film no. 87, October 1896).

DESCRIPTION: Newark, N.J., forms the background of this picture, which shows almost the entire Fire Department of that city, led by the Chief, responding to an alarm. The horses present a beautiful spectacle as they dash madly by, reeking with foam, and puffing from the exertion of their long gallop. The first exhibition of this film in New York was cheered to the echo. (F.Z. Maguire & Co., *Catalogue*, [March 1898], 23.)

SUBJECT: Fire fighters. Horses. Fire runs.

ARCHIVE:

CITATIONS: Maguire & Baucus, *Fall Catalogue*, 1897, 13; *Edison Films*, March 1900, 30.

NOTE: A copyright frame or some other kind of identification survives for neither this film nor *Going to the Fire*. This makes it virtually impossible to establish a definitive identification. Both films apparently survive, but this problem has yet to be fully sorted out.

258 **Going to the Fire*

LENGTH: 50 and 150 ft.   © No reg.

PRODUCER: James White.

CAMERA: William Heise.

CAST:

PRODUCTION DATE: 14 November 1896.

LOCATION: Newark, N.J.

SOURCE: *New York Fire Department* (Biograph film no. 87, October 1896); *Starting for the Fire* (Edison film no. 257, November 1896).

DESCRIPTION: This scene shows almost the entire Fire Department led by the Chief, responding to an alarm. The horses, said to be the finest of their kind in the country, present a thrilling spectacle as they dash rapidly by, flecked with foam, and panting from the exertion of their long gallop. (Maguire & Baucus, *Edison Films*, 20 January 1897, 2.)

SUBJECT: Fire fighters. Horses. Fire runs.

ARCHIVE: NR-GE, DLC-Hendricks, CLAc.

CITATIONS: Maguire & Baucus, *Edison and International Photographic Films*, April 1897, 8.

NOTE: Edison-related catalogs used the same descriptions for both *Going to the Fire* and *Starting for the Fire*, although these were undoubtedly two separate films made on different days.

259 **A Morning Alarm / Morning Fire Alarm*

LENGTH: 50 ft.   © Thomas A. Edison, 27 November 1896.

PRODUCER: James White.

CAMERA: William Heise.

CAST:

PRODUCTION DATE: 14 November 1896.

LOCATION: Newark, N.J.

SOURCE:

DESCRIPTION: This shows the Fire Department leaving headquarters for an early morning fire. The scene is remarkable for its natural effect. The opening of the engine house doors, the prancing of the horses, and even the startled expression upon the faces of the spectators are all clearly depicted. (Maguire & Baucus, *Edison Films*, 20 January 1897, 2.)

SUBJECT: Fire fighters. Horses. Fire runs.

ARCHIVE: DLC-Hendricks.

CITATIONS: Maguire & Baucus, *Edison and International Photographic Films*, April

1897, 12 and 18; Maguire & Baucus, *Fall Catalogue*, 1897, 12; F.Z. Maguire & Co., *Catalogue*, [March 1898], 23; *Edison Films*, March 1900, 29; *Edison Films,* July 1901, 54-55.

NOTE:

260 *Fighting the Fire

LENGTH: 50 ft.   © Thomas A. Edison, 27 November 1896.
PRODUCER: James White.
CAMERA: William Heise.
CAST:
PRODUCTION DATE: 14 November 1896.
LOCATION: Newark, N.J.
SOURCE: *Fire Engine at Work* (Biograph film no. 23, July 1896).
DESCRIPTION: Representing a fire engine in action. The black smoke rising from the engine stack and the firemen placing ladders and directing streams of water against a burning building serve to make a very interesting scene. (Maguire & Baucus, *Edison Films*, 20 January 1897, 2.)

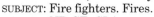

SUBJECT: Fire fighters. Fires.
ARCHIVE: NR-GE, CLAc.
CITATIONS: Maguire & Baucus, *Edison and International Photographic Films*, April 1897, 8; Maguire & Baucus, *Fall Catalogue*, 1897, 12; F.Z. Maguire & Co., *Catalogue*, [March 1898], 23; *Edison Films*, March 1900, 30.
NOTE:

Run of Firemen With Carriage and Engine Past An Edison Kinetograph.
THE DEPARTMENT IN ACTION.

Nearly Three Thousand Pictures in Less Than a Minute of the Dash to a Fire and the Hosemen at Work.

Newarkers had a fine chance to view the efficiency of their fire department to-day, and the remarks of the hundreds of people who lined Broad street, from Market to William street, were very complimentary.

It didn't take long to noise around the news that the Edison Vitascope Company were going to take a series of pictures of a portion of the Fire Department passing at full speed to an imaginary fire.

At 11 o'clock there were barely a score of interested persons grouped about Engine House No. 1, 819 Broad street, but an hour later when the company of firemen and steeds were running at full tilt down Broad street, there were fully 2,000 persons straining their eyes to watch the test.

Photographer J.H. White, with two assistants, had the kinetograph, stationed on a wagon a few feet above the City Hall. Everybody regarded the big walnut box with a great deal of interest, but the two operators kept the black cloth snugly wrapped around it, and the only view they got of it was when the lens was exposed.

A LIVELY MACHINE.

The kinetograph contains a reel of fine film, one inch high, in small strips, one and one-half inches wide. When the instrument is in action this strip of film, 150 feet long, is run off onto another reel in 50 seconds.

During this time 2,760 pictures are taken, all representing the subject in motion, and taking in the minutest detail.

After the pictures are developed they are placed in that wonderful instrument of Edison's, the vitascope. They are then thrown on a large screen, the small pictures passing so rapidly before the eye as to give the impression of a large picture, showing the subject in constant motion.

When the pictures taken to-day of the fire department running to a fire are thrown on the screen, the spectator will see the Chief, Assistant Chief, hook and ladder, engine, hose cart and chemical engine all speeding towards a fire. Every action and motion of horses and men will be shown with minute details, and the spectator will not think of the 2,760 pictures on the 150 feet of film that go towards composing the one, big living picture.

RUNNING FOR A PICTURE.

It took some time before everything was ready. The crowd kept surging in front of the lens, and the two policemen had their hands full. The irrepressible small boy was out in full force, and was in evidence everywhere. Commissioner Rommell hurried hither and thither, directing things, occasionally grabbing a small boy and hustling him out of the way. Finally everything was in readiness.

Photographer White stationed himself in front of the Central Railroad depot, took off his tall hat and waved it in the air. One of his assistants grasped a crank in the rear of the kinetograph while the other exposed the lens.

With the clang of bells, the clatter of hoofs and rumble of wheels, the procession of firemen and horses sped down Broad street. Chief Kiersted, with Driver Cleveland, was in the lead.

The chief handled the reins skillfully, and the small black horse, Ned, responded nobly. It was a hot pace and the gray head of Assistant Chief Astley's horse, George, almost touched the rubber tired wheels. With Astley was driver Wallace, but the assistant chief did the guiding.

Swerving from side to side, with the two powerful grays and the big black, known as 51, 52 and 53, tugging and straining every nerve, ploughed the big hook and ladder. Captain Exall, with Driver White, were in the front seat, while W.H. Robotham manned the wheel. The other firemen were W.J. Vesey, E.A. Crossman, C.B. Vandegrift, W.J. Nevitt, C.F. Clark, J. McCree and A.E. Newton.

A short space intervened between the long hook and ladder and Engine No. 1. Harry and Doc pulled at the big engine as though they were drawing a toy express. James Vreeland was the driver and with him on the box were ex-Captain Holtenbach and Engineer Stiff.

Then came Hose Cart No. 1, with Pete between the thills. W.E. Moore was the driver and Captain Hamberger, Firemen Bercaugh, Hank, Van Ness, O'Connor, Storch and Carr were in the cart. Last of all was Chemical Engine No. 1, with Pete, a black horse and Harry, a sorrel, at the pole. Captain Van Volkenberg, Driver Davis, and Fireman Wallroff were on the engine.

FIFTY SNAPS A SECOND.

The long procession swung down the street over the Belgian blocks at a rattling pace, each horse on a gallop, and each driver urging his horses to their utmost. It was a fine sight and when they were in focus the man at the crank began turning it. The pictures were recorded on the sensitive film at the rate of fifty to a second and the procession had passed the kinetograph in less than a minute.

After a short rest a view was taken of them coming out of Engine House and Hook and Ladder House No. 1. Every man was putting on his coat, the firemen were stoking and the drivers were being strapped to their seats.

The next view was taken in front of Engine House No. 4, on High street, below Orange street, showing that fire company putting out a fire. The tall building was scaled by ladders, long lines of hose were run up and the water was turned on. It was a realistic scene and completed the series. (*Newark Daily Advertiser*, 14 November 1896, 2.)

261 **Charge of West Point Cadets / Cadets' Charge / Charge of the West Point Cadets**
LENGTH: 50 ft.   © Thomas A. Edison, 27 November 1896.
PRODUCER: James White.
CAMERA: William Heise.
CAST:
PRODUCTION DATE: November 1896.
LOCATION: West Point, N.Y.
SOURCE: *Charge of the Seventh French Cuirassiers* (Lumière film, 1896), *West Point Cadet Cavalry* (Biograph film no. 56, September 1896).
DESCRIPTION: Showing a Squadron of cavalry (at the U.S. Military Academy, West Point, N.Y.), charging towards the camera at headlong speed. The flashing of their sabres in the sunlight as they are brandished aloft adds vim to the picture. (Maguire & Baucus, *Edison Films*, 20 January 1897, 2.)
SUBJECT: Armies–United States. Cavalry. Military cadets. U.S. Military Academy (West Point, N.Y.).
ARCHIVE:
CITATIONS: Maguire & Baucus, *Edison and International Photographic Films*, April 1897, 5; Maguire & Baucus, *Fall Catalogue*, 1897, 11; F.Z. Maguire & Co., *Catalogue*, [March 1898], 23.
NOTE:

At the end of November James H. White and William Heise traveled along the Lehigh Valley Railroad, taking pictures with that railroad company's sponsorship and support. The trip, which took them to Buffalo and Niagara Falls, lasted approximately two weeks.

262 **Black Diamond Express / [Black Diamond Express, no. 1]**
LENGTH: 50 ft.   © Thomas A. Edison, 12 December 1896.
PRODUCER: James White.
CAMERA: William Heise.
CAST:
PRODUCTION DATE: 1 December 1896.

LOCATION: Lake Cayuga, N.Y.

SOURCE: *Empire State Express* (Biograph film no. 77, September 1896).

DESCRIPTION: This scene presents the famous Lehigh Valley "flyer" emerging from a wood in the distance and approaching the camera under full head of steam. A section gang in the foreground, engaged in repairing track, wave their hats to the engineer, who is leaning out of the cab window. The snowy linen which the porters wave from the platform of the dining car adds to the effect produced. The "Black Diamond" is undoubtedly the handsomest and one of the fastest trains in America, and the subject is the only one in existence showing an express train making seventy miles an hour. (Maguire & Baucus, *Edison Films*, 20 January 1897, 3.)

SUBJECT: Railroads. Lehigh Valley Railroad.

ARCHIVE:

CITATIONS: Maguire & Baucus, *Edison and International Photographic Films*, April 1897, 4; Maguire & Baucus, *Fall Catalogue*, 1897, 11.

NOTE: The Lehigh Valley Railroad and the New York Central Railroad were locked in a serious commercial rivalry, in part built around competition for traffic between New York and Buffalo. The Black Diamond Express and the Empire State Express, which provided the premier service for each of the railways, were potent symbols in this competition. Significantly this rivalry was extended into the world of cinema as the Edison Manufacturing Company came to be associated with the Lehigh Valley Railroad and the American Mutoscope Company with the New York Central Railroad.

VALLEY'S BLACK DIAMOND.
The Fastest Flyer to be Put on the Lehigh Today.

New York, May 18.–The Black Diamond express, the new and magnificent train which the Lehigh Valley Railroad company will put into commission Monday, inaugurating a fast limited service over their road between this city and Buffalo, was on exhibition yesterday at the company's terminal in Jersey City and was inspected by large crowds. The train consists of four cars, each built especially for the new service and the company claims they are the most perfectly appointed and handsome in the world. There are two Pullman coaches, built after the latest approved models, a mammoth combination baggage, dining and cafe car, and a Pullman observation car. An exact duplicate of the train exhibited in Jersey City was on exhibition in Buffalo, and both trains will be put in operation simultaneously from New York and Buffalo Monday.

They will be run daily, Sunday excepted, leaving their terminal at noon, arriving at destination at 10 p.m. Connection with these trains will be made to and from Philadelphia, at Bethlehem. The new flyer will go against time on its first trip through the state Monday, and the officials of the company declare that the "Black Diamond express" will prove to be the "queen of the fast trains of the world." (*Scranton Times*, 23 May 1896, 3.)

Photographed the Black Diamond.

General Passenger Agent Chas. S. Lee, of the Lehigh Valley, Superintendent O.O. Esser and Private Secretary Edgar R. Reets, all of the same company, stopped over in town last night and saw De Wolf Hopper. They, with Mr. White, one of Thomas Edison's cleverest men, have been along the road taking vitascope views of various things interesting. For example, they took yesterday a vitascope picture of the Black Diamond Express up near Lake Cayuga, and when it was coming on at the rate of a mile a minute. They caught the flyer a mile down the track and took sixty-six pictures a second until it was out of sight. To-day they went to Mauch Chunk to catch the famous Lehigh Valley flyer as it enters the Switzerland of America. (*Wilkes-Barre Leader*, 2 December 1896, 8.)

SOME MARVELS OF PHOTOGRAPHY
Edison's Men Take Pictures of the Black Diamond as it Rushes Through Space Sixty Miles an Hour.

The science of photography has become so all conquering nowadays that the average layman has ceased to be surprised at the steps of progress and can only stand agape and wonder like the Simple Simon at the art gallery. Wizard Edison has been at work of late on the vitascope idea and many of the earlier difficulties have been overcome so that it is now possible to see pictures of moving life and action, so natural to make one wonder if they are really a counterfeit presentation or the real thing. This week a company of Lehigh Valley railroad people and three of Edison's men in charge of J.H. White rode over the road to get some samples of fast moving trains. Up in the Lake Cayuga region they pointed the camera at the Black Diamond and though the Express was cutting through space at the rate of sixty miles an hour it could not escape the eye of the sensitive film. General Passenger Agent Chas. S. Lee, Edgar Reets, private secretary to the general superintendent, and Supt. O.O. Esser accompanied the Edison people and took a warm interest in all that transpired. The party occupied a private car and the trip both as a means of enjoyment and as an aid to science was a great success. The Black Diamond photograph was taken on one of the coldest but one of the clearest and brightest days of this week.

A vantage point was taken at a place where a view of the track could be had for three quarters of a mile. The express was due in ten minutes and there was not more than time enough to adjust the apparatus. The railroad people watched the details carefully and the scientists worked, silently and with a keen intelligence of the situation. Nothing went wrong and no time was wasted. The photographing apparatus is nothing wonderful to the eye. It looks like a well made camera about eighteen inches square and having an outside covering of hard wood. On the open side there is a covering of chamois skin, very thick and in the middle of this are two holes which are filled in with two short sleeves, these sleeves ending in the narrow confinement of rubber bands. The point is you see that the inside of this wonderful apparatus is secret and if the operator has anything to adjust while a crowd is standing around he simply works his hands into these rubber banded sleeve holes and fusses around as long as he wishes without anybody getting as much as a peep. The lens, so Mr. White explains, is very sharp and powerful and specially ground. The camera box is set up on a strong tripod and the operators under Mr. White's watchful eye put the black cloth over their heads, adjust and focus the lens and do such other bits of preliminary work as will familiarly strike one who has had his picture taken. Then the sensitive film is slipped inside. This is rolled up closely .... hand is led within a tin box, the diameter of which is about three inches. This size box is large enough to hold a film that will take 2200 impressions. The operator pushes his hands inside the camera and adjusts the film to the gearing, just how of course the layman is not permitted to see. A crank about ten inches long hitches to a little projection at the back of the camera box. He touches it gently and gives it a cautious quarter turn just to see that it is caught and that the gearing is going to work all right.

"No, something is wrong. How much time have we?"

"Just three minutes and she is due around the bend. Be quick," says Mr. White.

The bystanders look on anxiously. The operator pushes his hands inside the sleeves again and fusses in a mysterious way. One minute–two minutes.

Will he get it fixed? is the anxious inquiry. Half a minute remains and he withdraws his hands nodding his head that everything is all right.

Hand on the crank! Ha! A streak of steam! There she is. The man slowly turns the crank, the shutter has been opened and as the train sweeps into view three-quarters of a mile away the whirring sound inside the box indicates that every wave of steam every detail of motion of that train goes into the eye of the lens and is recorded on the retina. Whirr, whirr, goes the machine. The train grows into your vision as if by magic. You have been holding your watch just forty seconds when the Black Diamond, with a roar and a hiss of steam, sweeps past right before your eyes. Before you have time to think of anything but admiration of the whole thing the machine has ceased to whirr and the train is disappearing a mile away. But the story of the train's passage along that distance has been recorded at the rate of forty-eight impressions a second. In other words, there has been nearly three thousand distinct and separate pictures taken in less than a minute. That's all there is to it. The operators gather up the camera and re-enter the private car. A few minutes with the developer and they come forth to announce that the thing had been entirely successful and that the picture will be all right. That means that in three weeks or less the people in London will sit in their cosy theatres and see before them on the screen just what has been seen there around that curve and the Black Diamond will sweep across their vision at the rate of sixty miles an hour. And if you are in New York in about three weeks time the chances are that you will have a chance to see the same thing there. After the experiments alluded to the party returned as far as Wilkes-Barre, spent the night there and the next morning attached their private car to the 8 o'clock train and at Mauch Chunk the apparatus was taken on the bridge and pointed at the river as the water tumbles over the dam there. In the right of this picture a train is seen coming round the curve. It had been the intention to get at this point another picture of the Black Diamond, but the day was thought to be a little too dark for such delicate work and the attempt was put off until another time. The railroad officials went on to Bethlehem and Philadelphia and Mr. White and his assistants returned to get a picture of Niagara Falls a thing which ought to be one of the most interesting achievements of the vitascope process. (*Wilkes-Barre Leader*, 6 December 1896, 4.)

263 Chicago and Buffalo Express

LENGTH: 50 ft.   © Thomas A. Edison, 12 December 1896.
PRODUCER: James White.
CAMERA: William Heise.
CAST:
PRODUCTION DATE: Early December 1896.
LOCATION: Geneva, N.Y.
SOURCE:
DESCRIPTION: This scene shows the arrival at a station, and passengers alighting from

and boarding the train, together with the usual bustling activity of the baggage men, etc. It is an interesting and impressive subject of its kind. (Maguire & Baucus, *Edison Films*, 20 January 1897, 3.)

SUBJECT: Railroads. Railroad stations. Lehigh Valley Railroad.
ARCHIVE:
CITATIONS: Maguire & Baucus, *Edison and International Photographic Films*, April 1897, 5; Maguire & Baucus, *Fall Catalogue*, 1897, 11; F.Z. Maguire & Co., *Catalogue*, [March 1898], 23.
NOTE:

264 Special Photographing Train
LENGTH: [50 ft.]   © Thomas A. Edison, 12 December 1896.
PRODUCER: James White.
CAMERA: William Heise.
CAST:
PRODUCTION DATE: Early December 1896.
LOCATION: N.Y.
SOURCE:
DESCRIPTION:
SUBJECT: Railroads. Motion pictures. Photography. Lehigh Valley Railroad.
ARCHIVE:
CITATIONS:
NOTE:

Although F.Z. Maguire's catalog for March 1898 contends that Edison personnel shot the new Niagara Falls films between 11 and 13 December 1896, this would not have been possible for the first two films in this series which were copyrighted on December 12th, indicating a somewhat earlier shooting date. These films were meant to replace those taken in June 1896 (nos. 163-167).

New Niagara Falls Series
The following subjects were all taken on the latest and most improved clear stock during December, 1896, and should not be confounded with former negatives, which were not entirely satisfactory. (Maguire & Baucus, *Edison Films*, 20 January 1897, 5.)

265 *American Falls from Above, American Side / American Falls from Top of American Shore
LENGTH: 50 ft.   © Thomas A. Edison, 12 December 1896.
PRODUCER: James White.
CAMERA: William Heise.
CAST:
PRODUCTION DATE: Early December 1896.
LOCATION: Niagara Falls, N.Y.
SOURCE: Niagara Falls films (Edison, June 1896).
DESCRIPTION: Shows glittering ice background and a group of photographers preparing to take pictures. (Maguire & Baucus, *Edison Films*, 20 January 1897, 5.)
SUBJECT: Waterfalls. Niagara Falls. Lehigh Valley Railroad.
ARCHIVE: DLC-Hendricks.

CITATIONS: Maguire & Baucus, *Edison and International Photographic Films*, April 1897, 4; Maguire & Baucus, *Fall Catalogue*, 1897, 11; F.Z. Maguire & Co., *Catalogue*, [March 1898], 25; *Edison Films*, March 1900, 47; *Edison Films*, July 1901, 95.
NOTE:

266 Rapids Above American Falls / Rapids at "Cave of the Winds"
LENGTH: 50 ft.   © Thomas A. Edison, 12 December 1896.

PRODUCER: James White.
CAMERA: William Heise.
CAST:
PRODUCTION DATE: Early December 1896.
LOCATION: Niagara Falls, N.Y.
SOURCE: Niagara Falls films (Edison, June 1896).
DESCRIPTION: A scene taken from the American Shore below the Falls, showing swirling water and ice background. (Maguire & Baucus, *Edison Films*, 20 January 1897, 5.)
SUBJECT: Waterfalls. Niagara Falls. Lehigh Valley Railroad.
ARCHIVE:
CITATIONS: Maguire & Baucus, *Edison and International Photographic Films*, April 1897, 14; Maguire & Baucus, *Fall Catalogue*, 1897, 13; F.Z. Maguire & Co., *Catalogue*, [March 1898], 25; *Edison Films*, March 1900, 47; *Edison Films*, July 1901, 95.
NOTE:

267 √**American Falls—From Incline R.R. / American Falls from Incline Railroad**
LENGTH: 50 ft.   © Thomas A. Edison, 24 December 1896.
PRODUCER: James White.
CAMERA: William Heise.
CAST:
PRODUCTION DATE: 11-13 December 1896.
LOCATION: Niagara Falls, N.Y.
SOURCE: Niagara Falls films (Edison, June 1896).
DESCRIPTION:
SUBJECT: Waterfalls. Niagara Falls. Lehigh Valley Railroad.
ARCHIVE:
CITATIONS: Maguire & Baucus, *Edison Films,* 20 January 1897, 5; Maguire & Baucus, *Edison and International Photographic Films*, April 1897, 3; Maguire & Baucus, *Fall Catalogue*, 1897, 11; F.Z. Maguire & Co., *Catalogue*, [March 1898], 25; *Edison Films*, March 1900, 47.
NOTE:

268 **Horseshoe Falls—From Luna Isle / Horse Shoe Falls (from Luna Island)**
LENGTH: 50 ft.   © Thomas A. Edison, 24 December 1896.
PRODUCER: James White.
CAMERA: William Heise.
CAST:
PRODUCTION DATE: 11-13 December 1896.
LOCATION: Niagara Falls, N.Y.
SOURCE: Niagara Falls films (Edison, June 1896).
DESCRIPTION: Showing top of Falls, a portion of the rapids above them and the Catholic Convent (on Canadian side) in background. (Maguire & Baucus, *Edison Films,* 20 January 1897, 5.)
SUBJECT: Waterfalls. Convents. Niagara Falls. Lehigh Valley Railroad.
ARCHIVE:
CITATIONS: Maguire & Baucus, *Edison and International Photographic Films*, April 1897, 10; Maguire & Baucus, *Fall Catalogue*, 1897, 12; F.Z. Maguire & Co., *Catalogue*, [March 1898], 25; *Edison Films*, March 1900, 48; *Edison Films*, July 1901, 95.
NOTE:

269 √**American Falls From Bottom, Canadian Shore / American Falls from Bottom of Canadian Shore / American Falls (from Canada Shore, below)**
LENGTH: 50 ft.   © Thomas A. Edison, 24 December 1896.
PRODUCER: James White.

CAMERA: William Heise.

CAST:

PRODUCTION DATE: 11-13 December 1896.

LOCATION: Niagara Falls, Canada.

SOURCE: Niagara Falls films (Edison, June 1896).

DESCRIPTION: This give the best general view of Niagara, and is so clear that the mist is shown arising and gradually settling over the falls. Sea gulls flying over the great cataract are plainly distinguishable. (F.Z. Maguire & Co., *Catalogue*, [March 1898], 25.)

SUBJECT: Waterfalls. Niagara Falls. Seagulls. Lehigh Valley Railroad.

ARCHIVE:

CITATIONS: Maguire & Baucus, *Edison Films*, 20 January 1897, 5; Maguire & Baucus, *Edison and International Photographic Films*, April 1897, 3; Maguire & Baucus, *Fall Catalogue*, 1897, 11; *Edison Films*, March 1900, 48.

NOTE:

270 √**Horseshoe Falls—From Table Rock (Canadian Side) / Horse Shoe Falls (from Table Rock) / Horseshoe Falls from Table Rock, Canadian Side**

LENGTH: 50 ft.   © Thomas A. Edison, 24 December 1896.

PRODUCER: James White.

CAMERA: William Heise.

CAST:

PRODUCTION DATE: 11-13 December 1896.

LOCATION: Niagara Falls, Canada.

SOURCE: Niagara Falls films (Edison, June 1896).

DESCRIPTION: This is the best general view of the Horse Shoe Falls and shows nearly a mile of the seething rapids above this point. The picture is sharp and clear. (Maguire & Baucus, *Edison Films*, 20 January 1897, 5.)

SUBJECT: Waterfalls. Niagara Falls. Lehigh Valley Railroad.

ARCHIVE:

CITATIONS: Maguire & Baucus, *Edison and International Photographic Films*, April 1897, 10; Maguire & Baucus, *Fall Catalogue*, 1897, 12; F.Z. Maguire & Co., *Catalogue*, [March 1898], 25; *Edison Films*, March 1900, 48; *Edison Films*, July 1901, 95.

NOTE:

271 **Whirlpool Rapids—From Canadian Shore / Whirlpool Rapids from Bottom of Canadian Shore / Whirlpool Rapids**

LENGTH: 50 ft.   © Thomas A. Edison, 24 December 1896.

PRODUCER: James White.

CAMERA: William Heise.

CAST:

PRODUCTION DATE: 11-13 December 1896.

LOCATION: Niagara Falls, Canada.

SOURCE: *Niagara Falls, Whirlpool* (Edison film no. 164, June 1896).

DESCRIPTION: Showing the place where Captain Webb met his tragic death; the most turbulent and dangerous spot in the entire gorge. (Maguire & Baucus, *Edison Films*, 20 January 1897, 5.)

SUBJECT: Waterfalls. Niagara Falls. Matthew Webb. Lehigh Valley Railroad.

ARCHIVE:

CITATIONS: "Captain Webb Missing Yet," *New York Times*, 26 July 1883, 1; "Capt. Webb's Body Found," *New York Times*, 29 July 1883, 1; "Captain Webb's Fate," *New York Times*, 30 July 1883, 1. Maguire & Baucus, *Edison and International*

Photographic Films, April 1897, 16; Maguire & Baucus, *Fall Catalogue*, 1897, 13; F.Z. Maguire & Co., *Catalogue*, [March 1898], 25; *Edison Films*, March 1900, 48; *Edison Films*, July 1901, 95.

NOTE:

CAPT. WEBB DROWNED
LOST IN THE NIAGARA WHIRL-POOL RAPIDS.
HE GOES SAFELY THROUGH THE BIG RAPIDS, BUT IS OVERCOME
IN THE WHIRLPOOL, THROWS UP HIS ARMS AND DISAPPEARS.

Buffalo. July 24–Capt. Webb, the champion swimmer, who successfully swam the British Channel, was drowned in the Whirlpool Rapids, in the Niagara River to-day. He came to the city last evening and spent the night in the Genesee House. At noon to-day he went to Niagara Falls with the avowed intention of swimming the Whirlpool Rapids. The announcement that he would undertake so perilous a feat was not credited, and very few persons paid any attention to it. There were no more visitors at the Falls than on ordinary days. Residents of the place scoffed at the idea that any man would throw his life away in such a manner. The appearance of Capt. Webb at the Falls, however, finally aroused some local curiosity, and when it was given out that he would make the plunge at 4 o'clock people began to follow his movements. He paid no heed to warnings of danger, and very coolly and in a few words declared his perfect ability to swim the rapids in safety. Shortly before 4 o'clock he descended to the ferry below the falls and engaged the ferryman to row him as far down the stream as he dared to go, then started toward the railroad suspension bridge, which is about two miles from the Falls, and proceeded something more than half the distance when the ferryman said he could go no further, the current was becoming too powerful and the situation too dangerous. Capt. Webb then stripped off his clothing retaining nothing but a breech-cloth, and dived into the river, but appeared promptly on the surface. This was at 4:02 o'clock, and it is estimated that about 500 persons saw the start. People who have visited the falls and the rapids below will remember that the river becomes narrow as well as terribly swift. At the bridge it is about 350 feet wide.

Below it is still narrower. In the middle the stream is terribly swift. At the edge the current is checked by friction with the banks, and the effect is to force the stream up, making it highest in the middle. No one can look at it and not shudder at the thought of a human being struggling in it. It is frightening to look upon. A stick thrown into the stream is borne along almost with the swiftness of a cannon-shot, but when the rapids are reached it disappears.

Capt. Webb started nearly in the middle of the stream, and kept near the middle. He had looked the situation over beforehand, and had evidently regarded that as his only safety. He was carried along apparently with perfect ease, but no one could tell what difficulties he encountered. Occasionally he would disappear, going under the water, and a few seconds later be seen on the surface again, a long distance below where he went under so swiftly did the current carry him on. When the first rapids were reached he was watched by the spectators with the most intense anxiety. He went under, but seemed to be out of sight but a single instant and reappeared again and passed on as before. It is impossible to follow the bank below the bridge, and the spectators may only visit it at different points where stairways and descending cars have been constructed for their accommodation. When the Captain was started therefore, many people hastened to the first Whirlpool Rapids and were on the river bank to see him pass. These rapids are at the very neck of the Whirlpool itself, and nearly a mile below the bridge. The river is but 220 feet wide, and rushes violently on. Those waiting near the point saw the swimmer approach, in what condition it was impossible to say. If alive, however, he must have been completely exhausted. On reaching the rapids the water necessarily swept over him as at the rapids above, but he did not appear at the surface again. The excited spectators watched in breathless suspense. They looked below, to the sides, and all about, but could see no sign of him. They rushed down the river bank as far as they could go, but saw nothing of the strong swimmer. They looked at each other, and said, "The man is lost." Capt. Webb was drowned. The hour was 4:19, just 17 minutes had elapsed after his dive from the boat. The spectators went to the Whirlpool and strained their eyes in looking for the body of the swimmer. Some of them thought they saw it, but no one was sure of it. Captain Webb's manager and a party of friends, after looking in vain for signs of the body in the Whirlpool, took carriages and drove to Queenstown, the place on the Canada side where the river empties into Lake Ontario. There they took a boat and went as far up the river as possible, searching for the body. They returned to Niagara Falls, knowing nothing beyond the fact that Capt. Webb had disappeared in the first Whirlpool Rapids, and had not been certainly seen again. That he is dead, no one doubts, as bodies which go over the Falls often float for days in the Whirlpool. It is quite possible that Capt. Webb's body is now there and that within a day or two it may be discovered....(*New York Times*, 25 July 1883, 1.)

"DOING" NIAGARA FALLS
Members of the President's Cabinet Spend a Day Seeing the Sights.
[BY TELEGRAPH TO THE HERALD]

NIAGARA FALLS, N.Y., Oct. 14, 1894. The Cabinet party, consisting of Secretaries Greeham, Carlisle, Smith and

Herbert, and First Assistant Postmaster Jones, Fourth Assistant Postmaster General Maxwell, Mrs. Carlisle, Mrs. Greeham, Mrs. Smith, Mrs. Thurber, and Mrs. Micon, spent to-day in visiting the various attractive spots about the falls under the escort of Superintendent T.V. Welch, of the State Reservation.

The visitors were taken around the islands crossing to the Three Sister Islands, and Luna Island, going out to Terrapin Rock. They descended the incline railway in Prospect Park, and all received a thorough drenching from the spray below the American Falls.

They drove across the suspension bridge to Canada, where two private cars were in waiting on the Niagara Falls Park and River Railroad. A trip on the electric road running along the gorge from Chippewa to Queenstown was made.

Secretary Daniel Lamont and Mrs. Lamont arrived from Buffalo this morning and joined the party on the electric road trip.

Returning to this city, the visitors were the guests of George Porter in the old Porter homestead, overlooking the American Rapids. After luncheon in the Cataract House a brief reception was held in the hotel parlors.

Secretary Lamont left soon after two o'clock for the East, intending to visit his mother before returning to Washington. Mrs. Lamont remained with the party, all of whom left early this evening. Secretary and Mrs. Gresham going to Chicago and the rest to Washington. (*New York Herald*, 15 October 1894, 7.)

272 ***Buffalo Horse Market / Horse Market, Buffalo, N.Y.**
LENGTH: 50 ft.   © Thomas A. Edison, 24 December 1896.
PRODUCER: James White.
CAMERA: William Heise.
CAST:
PRODUCTION DATE: Mid-December 1896.
LOCATION: Buffalo, N.Y.
SOURCE:

DESCRIPTION: Photographed at the most famous stock yards in America, from which as many as 5,000 horses are frequently shipped in one day. The spirited animals are seen being led to the cars and the passing of a pair of high-stepping coachers hitched to a light runabout lends additional activity to an already lively scene. (Maguire & Baucus, *Edison Films*, 20 January 1897, 3.)
SUBJECT: Markets. Horses. Lehigh Valley Railroad.
ARCHIVE: CaOOANF.
CITATIONS: Maguire & Baucus, *Edison and International Photographic Films*, April 1897, 9; Maguire & Baucus, *Fall Catalogue*, 1897, 12; F.Z. Maguire & Co., *Catalogue*, [March 1898], 24; *Edison Films,* July 1901, 50.
NOTE:

High Class Horses
...New York, Philadelphia and Boston obtain all their supplies of high class horses from the Buffalo market. (*Buffalo Courier,* 5 December 1896, 6.)

273 ***Hurdle Race—High Jumpers / Hurdle Race / Hurdle Race and High Jumping**
LENGTH: 50 ft.   © Thomas A. Edison, 24 December 1896.
PRODUCER: James White.
CAMERA: William Heise.
CAST:
PRODUCTION DATE: Mid-December 1896.
LOCATION: Buffalo Country Club, Buffalo, N.Y.
SOURCE:

DESCRIPTION: This scene, photographed at the Buffalo "Country Club," shows a number of thoroughbred horses (prize winners at the recent Horse Show in New York) taking an extremely high hurdle, which was so placed that the racers are seen coming straight at the audience. A subject full of

action and very interesting. (Maguire & Baucus, *Edison Films*, 20 January 1897, 3.)
SUBJECT: Horsemanship. Horse racing. Country clubs. Lehigh Valley Railroad. New York Horse Show. Buffalo Country Club.
ARCHIVE: CLAc.
CITATIONS: Maguire & Baucus, *Edison and International Photographic Films*, April 1897, 10; Maguire & Baucus, *Fall Catalogue*, 1897, 12; F.Z. Maguire & Co., *Catalogue*, [March 1898], 23; *Edison Films*, March 1900, 26; *Edison Films,* July 1901, 50.
NOTE:

274 *Tally-Ho—Arrival / Tally-Ho, the Arrival**
LENGTH: 50 ft.   © Thomas A. Edison, 24 December 1896.
PRODUCER: James White.
CAMERA: William Heise.
CAST:
PRODUCTION DATE: Mid-December 1896.
LOCATION: Buffalo Country Club, Buffalo, N.Y.
SOURCE:
DESCRIPTION: Another scene taken at the Buffalo Country Club, in which are seen many of the elite of Buffalo driving up and alighting from their four-horse drag at the door of the clubhouse. Introductions, handshakings and greetings make a lively and attractive subject. (F.Z. Maguire & Co., *Catalogue* [March 1898], 24.)
SUBJECT: Social elites. Carriages and carts. Country clubs. Lehigh Valley Railroad. Buffalo Country Club.
ARCHIVE: CaOOANF.
CITATIONS: Maguire & Baucus, *Edison Films*, 20 January 1897, 3; Maguire & Baucus, *Edison and International Photographic Films*, April 1897, 15; *The Phonoscope*, April 1897, 13; Maguire & Baucus, *Fall Catalogue*, 1897, 13; *Edison Films*, March 1900, 26; *Edison Films,* July 1901, 50.
NOTE:

275 Tally-Ho—Departure / Tally-Ho, the Departure**
LENGTH: 50 ft.   © Thomas A. Edison, 24 December 1896.
PRODUCER: James White.
CAMERA: William Heise.
CAST:
PRODUCTION DATE: Mid-December 1896.
LOCATION: Buffalo Country Club, Buffalo, N.Y.
SOURCE:
DESCRIPTION: The same group is shown leaving the club, waving adieux to friends in the background. (F.Z. Maguire & Co., *Catalogue*, [March 1898], 24.)
Shows a four-horse drag leaving the club house of the Buffalo Country Club. The passengers wave farewells to their friends in the background. (*Edison Films,* July 1901, 50.)
SUBJECT: Social elites. Carriages and carts. Country clubs. Lehigh Valley Railroad. Buffalo Country Club.
ARCHIVE:
CITATIONS: Maguire & Baucus, *Edison Films*, 20 January 1897, 3; Maguire & Baucus, *Edison and International Photographic Films*, April 1897, 15; *The Phonoscope*, April 1897, 14; Maguire & Baucus, *Fall Catalogue*, 1897, 13; *Edison Films*, March 1900, 27.
NOTE:

Vitascopic Pictures.

A party of the officials of the Lehigh Valley Railroad paid a visit on Wednesday [December 23rd] to the Edison Phonograph Works, by invitation, to see the vitascopic results of a number of pictures taken of the fast train[s] on the road. There were first thrown on the screen some pictures taken at the Country Club, of Buffalo, of four-in-hand coaching parties, which were well defined. Then came a number of pictures of different trains on the Lehigh Valley road, including one of the celebrated Black Diamond Express, coming almost directly towards the spectators, at the speed of sixty miles an hour. This also was excellent. The exhibition closed with a number of views of Niagara Falls, and rapids above and below the falls, including the celebrated rapids where Captain Webb lost his life. The officials in the party were: C.S. Lee, General Passenger Agent; W.H. Gummere, General Baggage Agent; A.W. Nonnemaker, Assistant General Passenger Agent; H.H. Kingston, General Traffic Agent, and E.R. Reets, Assistant General Superintendent. (*Orange Chronicle*, 26 December 1896, 7.)

276 √Cock Fight / [Cock Fight, no. 3]
LENGTH: 50 ft.   © Thomas A. Edison, 24 December 1896.
PRODUCER: James White.
CAMERA: William Heise.
CAST:
PRODUCTION DATE: 21 December 1896.
LOCATION: Black Maria, West Orange, N.J.
SOURCE: *Cock Fight, no. 2* (Edison film no. 53, summer 1894).

DESCRIPTION: A lively and exciting encounter between two genuine game birds, in which their respective owners are seen in the background exchanging bets on the probable finish. When projected upon canvas the birds appear much larger than in life and every feather (including those which are shed in the fray) is distinctly shown. (Maguire & Baucus, *Edison Films*, 20 January 1897, 4.)
SUBJECT: Cockfighting. Gambling.
ARCHIVE:
CITATIONS: Maguire & Baucus, *Edison and International Photographic Films*, April 1897, 6; Maguire & Baucus, *Fall Catalogue*, 1897, 11; F.Z. Maguire & Co., *Catalogue*, [March 1898], 24; *Edison Films*, March 1900, 27; *Edison Films*, July 1901, 51.
NOTE:

No sooner were the films of Buffalo, the Black Diamond Express and Niagara Falls completed and shown to Lehigh Valley Railroad executives on December 23rd than James White and William Heise left on another trip, travelling to Harrisburg, Pennsylvania. There they shot a group of films intended to be shown on Edison's newly designed motion picture projector, the projectoscope, which was having its debut at a local theatre.

277 [Rockville Bridge and Train Crossing]
LENGTH: © No reg.
PRODUCER: James White.
CAMERA: William Heise.
CAST:
PRODUCTION DATE: 24 December 1896.
LOCATION: Harrisburg, Pa.
SOURCE:
DESCRIPTION:
SUBJECT: Railroads. Bridges.
ARCHIVE:
CITATIONS:
NOTE: This film was apparently never distributed or shown.

278 √Police Patrol Wagon / Police Patrol
LENGTH: 50 ft.   © Thomas A. Edison, 8 January 1897.
PRODUCER: James White.
CAMERA: William Heise.
CAST: Sergeant McCann.
PRODUCTION DATE: 24 December 1896.
LOCATION: Harrisburg, Pa.
SOURCE:

DESCRIPTION: A scene in which a number of men engage in a rough-and-tumble street fight. The police appear, the patrol wagon dashes up and the combatants are arrested and driven off to the police station. A realistic picture: sharp, clear and sure to excite interest wherever exhibited. (Maguire & Baucus, *Edison Films*, 20 January 1897, 4.)

SUBJECT: Police. City and town life–Harrisburg. Violence.

ARCHIVE:

CITATIONS: Maguire & Baucus, *Edison and International Photographic Films*, 14; Maguire & Baucus, *Fall Catalogue*, 1897, 13; F.Z. Maguire & Co., *Catalogue*, [March 1898], 24; *Edison Films*, July 1901, 90.

NOTE:

279 √The Farmer's Troubles / Farmer's Trouble

LENGTH: 50 ft.   © Thomas A. Edison, 8 January 1897.

PRODUCER: James White.

CAMERA: William Heise.

CAST:

PRODUCTION DATE: 24 December 1896.

LOCATION: Harrisburg, Pa.

SOURCE:

DESCRIPTION: A rather dilapidated farm wagon loaded with cabbages is being driven along the market place, where a dark miscreant trundling a wheelbarrow succeeds in colliding with one of the rear wheels. The wheel parts company with the vehicle, and wrecking it, scatters the contents in all directions. The farmer, convinced that the darkey was responsible for the breakdown,

jumps from his wagon and a pugilistic encounter takes place, in which the bystanders interfere. A clear picture of a ludicrous subject. (Maguire & Baucus, *Edison Films*, 20 January 1897, 4.)

SUBJECT: City and town life–Harrisburg. Farmers. Afro-Americans.

ARCHIVE:

CITATIONS: Maguire & Baucus, *Edison and International Photographic Films*, April 1897, 8; Maguire & Baucus, *Fall Catalogue*, 1897, 12; F.Z. Maguire & Co., *Catalogue*, [March 1898], 24; *Edison Films*, March 1900, 34; *Edison Films*, July 1901, 69.

NOTE: Listed as a 45-foot subject in 1901.

Local Projectoscope Views

This afternoon a large crowd assembled on Market street, near Third to watch two projectoscope people take a picture of two drunken men engaged in a fight and their arrest by Sergeant McCann and a couple of officers. The police patrol wagon dashed up and hustled the men off to the county jail. Of course, it was all play. Tomorrow the City Grays will be taken and other local views will be secured.

Pictures of the Rockville bridge and a train crossing were also obtained to-day. (*Harrisburgh Daily Telegraph*, 24 December 1896, 1.)

280 *The First Sleigh-Ride

LENGTH: 50 ft.   © Thomas A. Edison, 8 January 1897.

PRODUCER: James White.

CAMERA: William Heise.

CAST:

PRODUCTION DATE: 24 December 1896.

LOCATION: Harrisburg, Pa.

SOURCE:

DESCRIPTION: This subject taken just after the recent first fall of snow, shows two enthusiastic horsemen indulging in a "brush" with their respective horses and cutters. (Maguire & Baucus, *Edison Films*, 20 January 1897, 4.)

SUBJECT: City and town life–Harrisburg. Sleighs and sledges. Horse racing.

ARCHIVE: NR-GE, DLC-Hendricks, CLAc.

CITATIONS: Maguire & Baucus, *Edison and International Photographic Films*, April 1897, 8; Maguire & Baucus, *Fall Catalogue*, 1897, 12; F.Z. Maguire & Co., *Catalogue* [March 1898], 24.

NOTE: Taken on River Road.

281 *Market Square, Harrisburg, Pa.

LENGTH: 50 ft.   © Thomas A. Edison, 8 January 1897.

PRODUCER: James White.

CAMERA: William Heise.

CAST:

PRODUCTION DATE: 24 December 1896.

LOCATION: Harrisburg, Pa.

SOURCE:

DESCRIPTION: A Typical Holiday Season Street Scene, showing many shoppers lugging home their Holiday purchases. Trolley cars and vehicles are passing back and forth, and the well-known Commonwealth Hotel looms up in the background. (Maguire & Baucus, *Edison Films*, 20 January 1897, 4.)

SUBJECT: City and town life–Harrisburg. Urban transportation. Christmas.

ARCHIVE: CaOOANF.

CITATIONS: Maguire & Baucus, *Edison and International Photographic Films*, April 1897, 12; Maguire & Baucus, *Fall Catalogue*, 1897, 12; F.Z. Maguire & Co., *Catalogue*, [March 1898], 24.

NOTE:

282 Pennsylvania State Militia, Single Time / Governor's Guard / The Governor's Troop / Pennsylvania State Militia, [no. 1]

LENGTH: 50 ft.   © Thomas A. Edison, 8 January 1897.

PRODUCER: James White.

CAMERA: William Heise.

CAST: Captain Hutchinson.

PRODUCTION DATE: 25 December 1896.

LOCATION: Harrisburg, Pa.

SOURCE:

DESCRIPTION: This subject, taken at Harrisburg, Pa. shows the Governor's Guard en route for the Capitol Grounds. Various manœuvres were executed while the pictures were being taken, all of which are distinctly shown. The scene is interesting, clear and sharp. (Maguire & Baucus, *Edison Films*, 20 January 1897, 3.)

SUBJECT: National Guard–Pennsylvania. Armories. Parades.

ARCHIVE:

CITATIONS: Maguire & Baucus, *Edison and International Photographic Films*, April 1897, 9; Maguire & Baucus, *Fall Catalogue*, 1897, 13; F.Z. Maguire & Co., *Catalogue*, [March 1898], 24.

NOTE:

283 √**Pennsylvania State Militia, Double Time / Infantry Manœuvres / Infantry Manœuvres, The City Grays / Pennsylvania State Militia, [no. 2]**

LENGTH: 50 ft.   © Thomas A. Edison, 8 January 1897.

PRODUCER: James White.

CAMERA: William Heise.

CAST: Captain Hutchinson.

PRODUCTION DATE: 25 December 1896.

LOCATION: Harrisburg, Pa.

SOURCE:

DESCRIPTION: This scene was also taken at Harrisburg, and shows the State Militia executing orders on "double-quick" time. The best subject of its kind yet produced. (Maguire & Baucus, *Edison Films*, 20 January 1897, 3.)

SUBJECT: National Guard–Pennsylvania. Armories. Parades.

ARCHIVE:

CITATIONS: "At the Bijou," *Harrisburg Daily Telegraph*, 19 January 1897, 4. Maguire & Baucus, *Edison and International Photographic Films*, April 1897, 10; Maguire & Baucus, *Fall Catalogue*, 1897, 13; F.Z. Maguire & Co., *Catalogue*, [March 1898], 24.

NOTE:

284 *****The Morning Alarm / [Harrisburg Fire Run]**

LENGTH: 150 ft.   © No reg.

PRODUCER: James White.

CAMERA: William Heise.

CAST:

PRODUCTION DATE: 25 December 1896.

LOCATION: Harrisburg, Pa.

SOURCE:

DESCRIPTION: Our artists, while in a very large city, were able to secure an exceedingly interesting picture of almost the entire fire department on the way to a large fire. Shows the Chief in his buggy, followed by a smoking fire engine, hose wagon, hook and ladder truck, insurance patrol wagon, another engine and a chemical engine, all coming down the street straight into the foreground of the picture, the horses snorting and galloping at full speed. A very realistic and stirring scene, magnificent horse effects, with the invariable accompaniment of barking dog, policemen and impatient crowd.

Note: This film must not be confused with the 50-foot strip previously listed as it is entirely new, being by far the best of the several fire alarm pictures. 150 feet only. (F.Z. Maguire & Co., *Catalogue*, [March 1898], 23.)

SUBJECT: Fire fighters. Fire runs. Horses. Police.

ARCHIVE: DLC-Hendricks.

CITATIONS: "The New Machine," *Harrisburg Daily Telegraph*, 16 January 1897, 4. Maguire & Baucus, *Edison Films*, 20 January 1897, 7; Maguire & Baucus, *Fall Catalogue*, 1897, 14; *Edison Films*, July 1901, 54.

NOTE:

AN EXHIBITION RUN
Portion of the Fire Department Photographed for the Projectoscope

An exhibition of several companies of the Harrisburg fire department was given for photographing for projectoscope use in Market square yesterday under direction of Fire Chief Holstein.

The apparatus of the Friendship, Citizen, Paxton, Reily, and Mt. Vernon companies was brought together on Market street near Third and at one tap from 112 at the Ruse building, was run to the square. The machines were not run straight across the square but made a turn into Second street, and owing to the great speed two of them nearly upset in crossing the trolley car curves. One of the poles in the Mt. Vernon truck's three horse team was broken, but no one was hurt. The photographs were taken with the horses at full gallop and were very successful.

In the morning the City Grays in state uniform were photographed at company drill in front of the armory on North Second street. (*Harrisburg Patriot*, 26 December 1896, 2.)

Interior of the Black Maria (circa 1894-1897).

Edison's portable camera equipment worked with increasing ease and reliability dur-ing 1896. After their second and more successful trip to Niagara Falls in December 1896, Edison camera crews displayed much greater mobility. In the first months of 1897, Edison personnel traveled twice to the Washington, D.C., area to take films relat-ed to the Inauguration of President William McKinley. In the spring, they returned to Buffalo and then traveled to Cleveland and Chicago. By mid-1897 James Henry White, the head of the Kinetograph Department, had begun a world tour that took him to Yellowstone National Park, the West Coast, Colorado and eventually into Mexico. The trip continued in the first months of 1898 as he traveled to China, Japan, and the Hawaiian Islands.

The Edison Manufacturing Company's reliance on a peripatetic camera unit reflected White's romantic and self-interested outlook toward life. But it also responded to the diversity of views being offered by French producers such as the Lumières and British firms such as R.W. Paul and the Warwick Trading Company. The American Mutoscope Company had also sent a camera to Europe in the first months of 1897 and was soon sending back views from England and the continent. Edison's two-man Edison crew, consisting of White and Frederick W. Blechendyn, set out in the opposite direction. All of their travels were subsidized by various railroad and transportation companies.

To compensate for White's protracted absence, William Heise headed a second produc-tion unit that was based in West Orange. He made a selection of comedies and staged films in the Black Maria and otherwise confined his filmmaking to the New York-New Jersey area.

285 √**Parisian Dance**

LENGTH: 50 ft.　© Thomas A. Edison, 15 January 1897.

PRODUCER: James White.

CAMERA: William Heise.

CAST: [Barrison Sisters.]

PRODUCTION DATE: Early January 1897.

LOCATION: Black Maria, West Orange, N.J.

SOURCE:

DESCRIPTION: A dance in street costume by two pretty young ladies. An excellent subject for coloring. (Maguire & Baucus, *Edison and International Photographic Films*, April 1897, 14.)

A typical dance by two well-known vaude-ville artists, reproduced exactly as per-formed by them at Hammerstein's "Olympia," New York City. This is a full-size pic-ture, and shows clearly the combination of black and white colors, making a very striking and beautiful effect. The dance performed is the famous can-can. (F.Z. Maguire & Co., *Catalogue*, [March 1898], 22.)

SUBJECT: Vaudeville–performances. Dancing. French. Motion picture–colored.

ARCHIVE:

CITATIONS: Misc. programme, ca. 1897, Raff & Gammon Scrapbook, MH-BA. Maguire & Baucus, *Fall Catalogue*, 1897, 14; *Edison Films*, March 1900, 28; *Edison Films*, July 1901, 52.

NOTE: A programme in the Raff & Gammon Collection identifies the Barrison Sisters as appearing in this film. It is also possible that the Earl Sisters (Hazel and Maud), who were performing an identical act at the time that this film was made, were the actual subjects for this picture.

286 √**The Milker's Mishap**

LENGTH: 50 ft.   © Thomas A. Edison, 11 February 1897.

PRODUCER: James White.

CAMERA: William Heise.

CAST:

PRODUCTION DATE: January 1897.

LOCATION:

SOURCE:

DESCRIPTION: A comic subject. Farmer milking a Holstein, which becomes irritated from the work of the farmhands in the barnyard, kicks over the milker and milk pail, and the hands quarrel over the spilt milk. Figures are clear and large. (F.Z. Maguire & Co., *Catalogue*, [March 1898], 23.)

SUBJECT: Farms. Cows. Milk. Accidents.

ARCHIVE:

CITATIONS: Maguire & Baucus, *Edison and International Photographic Films*, April 1897, 12; Maguire & Baucus, *Fall Catalogue*, 1897, 12; *Edison Films*, March 1900, 34; *Edison Films*, July 1901, 69.

NOTE: Listed as a 45-foot subject in 1901.

An Edison camera crew traveled to Washington, D.C., and environs early in 1897. Doubtlessly this was linked to preparations for the filming of William McKinley's Inauguration—the selection of locations and so forth—but the group also took this occasion to make a number of films.

287 √**Guard Mount, Fort Myer (Va) / Guard Mount**

LENGTH: 50 ft.   © 11 February 1897.

PRODUCER: James White.

CAMERA: William Heise.

CAST:

PRODUCTION DATE: January 1897.

LOCATION: Fort Myer, Va.

SOURCE:

DESCRIPTION: This shows a detachment of the U.S. Army starting out to relieve guard, preceded by the Fort Band. The sun shining on the musical instruments and arms produces a bright and interesting effect. Sharp, clear, life-size figures. (F.Z. Maguire & Co., *Catalogue* [March 1898], 22.)

SUBJECT: Armies–United States. Marching bands. Sixth U.S. Cavalry.

ARCHIVE:

CITATIONS: Maguire & Baucus, *Edison and International Photographic Films*, April 1897, 9; Maguire & Baucus, *Fall Catalogue*, 1897, 12.

NOTE:

288 √**Pennsylvania Avenue, Washington, D.C. / Pennsylvania Avenue**

LENGTH: 50 ft.   © Thomas A. Edison, 11 February 1897.

PRODUCER: James White.

CAMERA: William Heise.

CAST:

PRODUCTION DATE: January 1897.

LOCATION: Washington, D.C.

SOURCE:

DESCRIPTION: This is a veritable street scene taken on the principal avenue of the national Capital, looking east, with the Capitol building showing sharply and clearly in the background. Cable cars are seen passing, also vehicles, pedestrians, etc.

Very clear and distinct. (F.Z. Maguire & Co., *Catalogue*, [March 1898], 22.)

SUBJECT: City and town life–Washington. Urban transportation.

ARCHIVE:

CITATIONS: Maguire & Baucus, *Edison and International Photographic Films*, April 1897, 13; Maguire & Baucus, *Fall Catalogue*, 1897, 13.

NOTE:

289 √Pile Driving, Washington Navy Yard / Steam Pile-Driver / Pile Driver in Washington Navy Yard

LENGTH: 50 ft.   © Thomas A. Edison, 11 February 1897.

PRODUCER: James White.

CAMERA: William Heise.

CAST:

PRODUCTION DATE: January 1897.

LOCATION: Washington, D.C.

SOURCE:

DESCRIPTION: Showing a pile-driver at work in the Washington Navy Yard. This subject is sharp and clear and depicts the actual operation as the pony engine slowly lifts the two ton iron weight to the top of derrick and allows the same to descend with great rapidity on the piles. A good subject for effects. (Maguire & Baucus, *Edison and International Photographic Films*, April 1897, 15.)

This picture depicts a large steam pile driver at work, showing the workmen attending to their respective duties, engine in full operation, steam issuing from the exhaust, etc. Realistic, with picturesque steam effects, sharp and clear. (F.Z. Maguire & Co., *Catalogue*, [March 1898], 22.)

SUBJECT: Navies–United States. Construction equipment. Steam. Machinery. Working classes. Motion pictures–sound effects.

ARCHIVE:

CITATIONS: Maguire & Baucus, *Fall Catalogue*, 1897, 13.

NOTE:

290 American and Cuban Flag / Old Glory and Cuban Flag / [Old Glory and Cuban Flag, no. 1]

LENGTH: 50 ft.   © Thomas A. Edison, 5 March 1897.

PRODUCER: James White.

CAMERA: William Heise.

CAST:

PRODUCTION DATE: February 1897.

LOCATION:

SOURCE:

DESCRIPTION: Showing the Stars and Stripes and the flag of Cuba Libre fluttering in the breeze. The flags appear in the foreground, one after the other, and the effect is very dramatic. Appeals to the prevailing popular sentiment. (F.Z. Maguire & Co., *Catalogue*, [March 1898], 22.)

SUBJECT: Flags–United States. Flags–Cuba. Patriotism.

ARCHIVE:

CITATIONS: Maguire & Baucus, *Edison and International Photographic Films*, April 1897, 13; Maguire & Baucus, *Fall Catalogue*, 1897, 12.

NOTE: This film was subsequently remade as *[Old Glory and the Cuban Flag, no. 2]*.

291 ***Fifth Avenue, New York**
LENGTH: 50 ft.   © Thomas A. Edison, 5 March 1897.
PRODUCER: James White.
CAMERA: William Heise.
CAST:
PRODUCTION DATE: Late February 1897.
LOCATION: Fifth Avenue, New York, N.Y.
SOURCE:
DESCRIPTION: A spirited picture, showing the
   famous parade of fashion on the avenue.
   Figures very large and distinct, and the
   action brisk. A flower fakir in the fore-
   ground makes a pleasing foil to the parade
   of fashion that the picture portrays. We
   consider it one of the best films Mr. Edison
   has made. (F.Z. Maguire & Co., *Catalogue*, [March 1898], 22.)
SUBJECT: City and town life–New York. Social elites. Flowers.
ARCHIVE: NNMoMA.
CITATIONS: Maguire & Baucus, *Edison and International Photographic Films*, April
   1897, 8; Maguire & Baucus, *Fall Catalogue*, 1897, 12; *Edison Films*, March 1900,
   42; *Edison Films,* July 1901, 88.
NOTE:

292 **Sleigh Riding, Central Park / Sleighing in Central Park**
LENGTH: 50 ft.   © Thomas A. Edison, 5 March 1897.
PRODUCER: James White.
CAMERA: William Heise.
CAST:
PRODUCTION DATE: Late February 1897.
LOCATION: Central Park, New York, N.Y.
SOURCE:
DESCRIPTION: An effective picture of the fashionable amusement in New York City,
   depicting one of the rare occasions when its fashionable turnouts are seen to most
   picturesque advantage. Horses and equipages going and coming directly in front of
   the camera in life-size. A success. Rapid picture, spirited and full of action. (F.Z.
   Maguire & Co., *Catalogue,* [March 1898], 23.)
SUBJECT: Sleighs and sledges. Sleighing. City and town life–New York. Social elites. Parks.
ARCHIVE:
CITATIONS: Maguire & Baucus, *Edison and International Photographic Films*, April
   1897, 15; Maguire & Baucus, *Fall Catalogue*, 1897, 13; *Edison Films*, March 1900, 48.
NOTE:

*The leading filmmaking companies in the United States—Edison, International,
Biograph and Lumière—all sent camera crews to Washington, D.C., in order to shoot
the ceremonies surrounding William McKinley's inauguration as President of the
United States. The Edison Manufacturing Company managed to achieve a diversity of
camera positions with the eleven Inauguration films that it copyrighted, suggesting
that it sent more than one camera to cover the quadrennial ritual. This occasion, therefore, was the first time that the Edison organization engaged in multi-camera coverage
of an important news event. Variety of shots was also achieved by employing two lenses
of different focal lengths.*

293 √**McKinley and Cleveland Going to the Capitol / McKinley and Cleveland**
LENGTH: 100 ft.   © Thomas A. Edison, 15 March 1897.
PRODUCER: James White.
CAMERA: [William Heise.]
CAST: William McKinley, Grover Cleveland.
PRODUCTION DATE: 4 March 1897.
LOCATION: Washington, D.C.

SOURCE:

DESCRIPTION: Going to the Capitol. This film is one of much interest as it shows the accident of the day. The picture opens with Troop A, of the Black Horse Cavalry of Cleveland, Ohio, the personal guard of the president-elect. The troopers are mounted on prancing horses and make an extraordinary fine appearance. Following this body guard comes the four-horse barouche occupied by President Cleveland and Major McKinley. At this point in the scene, one of the rear horses, attached to the President's  carriage, slipped and fell on the pavement, the accident happening immediately in front of the camera. The carriage stops, mounted police galop to the rescue and thus enabled the operator to get the only effective photograph of the retiring and incoming Presidents that the great parade afforded. Extremely clear, with strong light effects and life-size throughout. (*The Phonoscope*, March 1897, 14.)

SUBJECT: Inauguration Day. Presidents–United States–Inauguration. National Guard–Ohio. Police. Cavalry. Parades. Accidents.

ARCHIVE:

CITATIONS: Maguire & Baucus, *Edison and International Photographic Films*, April 1897, 17; Maguire & Baucus, *Fall Catalogue*, 1897, 14; F.Z. Maguire & Co., *Catalogue*, [March 1898], 21; *Edison Films*, March 1900, 23.

NOTE: NNMoMA has several film fragments of this event. Two shots seem to conform to the above title, but the camera position is different, suggesting that these subjects were taken by a different production company, probably the International Film Company.

294 √**McKinley Taking the Oath**

LENGTH: 50 ft.   © Thomas A. Edison, 15 March 1897.

PRODUCER: James White.

CAMERA: [William Heise.]

CAST: William McKinley, Melville Weston Fuller.

PRODUCTION DATE: 4 March 1897.

LOCATION: Washington, D.C.

SOURCE:

DESCRIPTION: An interesting picture of an historical scene. Showing the multitude of people waving handkerchiefs, hats and flags to the new Executive, who, with Chief Justice Fuller and other officials of the Government, appear on the inauguration stand in front of  the National Capitol. A remarkable view of an enormous crowd on a rare occasion. Very clear and sharp. (F.Z. Maguire & Co., *Catalogue*, [March 1898], 21.)

SUBJECT: Inauguration Day. Presidents–United States–Inauguration.

ARCHIVE:

CITATIONS: Maguire & Baucus, *Edison and International Photographic Films*, April 1897, 12; Maguire & Baucus, *Fall Catalogue*, 1897, 12.

NOTE:

PAGEANTRY OF THE INAUGURAL.
Nearly Four Hundred Thousand People Cheer the New President.
NO FLAW IN THE PROGRAMME
Clear Skies, Gorgeous Parades, a Great and Enthusiastic Throng.
INAUGURAL ADDRESS & SURPRISE
The New President Announces Himself in Favor of the Peace Treaty.
FRANKLY OUTLINES HIS POLICY.

...WASHINGTON, March 4.–Under a brilliant sun that shone from a cloudless sky William McKinley, of Ohio, was made the twenty-fifth President of the United States at 1:35 P.M. to-day. Never has the city known a fairer day. From sunrise to sunset there was not a trace of white in the blue of heaven.

A cool breeze tempered the hot rays and kept flags and bunting aquiver. There were perhaps 150,000 strangers in the city. Four years ago, when former President Cleveland was inaugurated, the visitors numbered nearly 300,000. It was a fine and gorgeous spectacle to-day, and cost a deal of money. All the departments of the Government joined in contributing to its splendor.

The foremost men of the land were gathered to see a plain and simple citizen of a little city in Ohio receive the greatest honor that a people can bestow. It gave tens of thousands of other plain citizens opportunity to realize the pomp and ceremony and the forms of law which surround the installation of a Chief Magistrate of the republic. It gave opportunity for half a dozen Governors and their staffs to show themselves and be admired, and it also demonstrated how abominably Washington can treat a big crowd.

It is a remarkable fact that the inauguration of the President who received the largest popular vote ever given a candidate should have been attended with less enthusiasm than has ever been known in modern times.

The greeting to President McKinley was warm, earnest and sincere, but there was no outburst of feeling. Those who came to Washington expecting to see a great throng carried away by emotion were disappointed.

There were gatherings everywhere–at the White House, at the Capitol, along the line of march. About 22,000 men were in the parade. It was three hours in passing. There were probably 25,000 people gathered at the Capitol to see the inauguration ceremonies. Every available place for seeing the procession was occupied. Yet nowhere was there any memorable demonstration.

Yet it was perhaps one of the most notable occasions in the history of this country, because an incoming President had the courage to stand before 25,000 people and commend in the most emphatic terms the crowning act of his predecessor's official career.

When President McKinley lifted his voice in favor of the arbitration treaty and urged the early action of the Senate thereon, "not merely as a matter of policy, but as a duty to mankind," there was a moment of silence that was followed by applause that was warmer, more spontaneous than was aroused by anything else that he had said.

It is significant that this utterance and that relative to the protection of American citizens travelling abroad were received with as much favor as what he said about the tariff question.

His announcement that he would appoint a monetary commission and call a special session for March 15 made those familiar with inaugurals of Presidents open their eyes with surprise. His address is causing more talk in Washington to-night than anything else connected with his installation as President.

Amid the gorgeousness of the demonstration one body of men shone out with peculiar splendor. Even the decorations paled when the radiant staff of Gov. Black passed up the avenue. Gov. Black himself achieved conspicuousness. He was the only Governor who did not appear on horseback. From the time that President McKinley appeared on his way to the White House he received the warmest of greetings. There were cheers on the way to the Capitol, and Mr. Cleveland came in for a share. Ohio was chock full of enthusiasm, but her people could not arouse the great crowd. It was the New York representatives who received the warmest greeting when they passed the President's stand.

The parade was fine and brilliant, but it was very like other parades. The United States troops interested people more than did the National Guards. The buildings were decorated with a lavishness that has never been surpassed. Mrs. McKinley was overcome when walking to her place on the inaugural stand, but she soon revived and was able to appear on the reviewing stand for an hour during the afternoon.

The inauguration ball was a brilliant function. The Pension Office was transformed into a fairyland, and hundreds upon hundreds of people were glad to pay $5 to be a part of the crush. (*New York World*, 5 March 1897, 2.)

The parade which followed the inauguration of President William McKinley consisted of a small escort which accompanied the parade's Grand Marshall, General Horace Porter, and the new President. Next in the order of march was a Military Grand Division consisting of U.S. military forces (Division One), national guards and state militia (Division Two), and veterans organizations (Division Three). The Civic Grand Division was then made up of a series of Republican organizations.

295   ***Return of McKinley from the Capitol**
LENGTH: 150 ft.   © Thomas A. Edison, 15 March 1897.
PRODUCER: James White.
CAMERA: [William Heise.]
CAST: William McKinley, Grover Cleveland.
PRODUCTION DATE: 4 March 1897.
LOCATION: Washington, D.C.
SOURCE:

DESCRIPTION: Shows the famous Black Horse Cavalry, Troop A, of Cleveland, Ohio, escorting President McKinley, who is seen seated on the right-hand side of ex-President Cleveland. This scene depicts President McKinley raising his hat and bowing to the populace, who are waving handkerchiefs, hats and flags as he passes by. The carriage is followed by a detachment of veterans of the Twenty-third Ohio Volunteers, who march 32 abreast. This is a very demonstrative and stirring scene, and the only kinetograph picture taken of

the President on his way to the White House. Exceedingly fine and clear. (F.Z. Maguire & Co., *Catalogue*, [March 1898], 22.)

SUBJECT: Inauguration Day. Presidents–United States–Inauguration. National Guard–Ohio. Veterans. Cavalry. Parades.

ARCHIVE: NNMoMA.

CITATIONS: "Order of the Parade," *New York Herald*, 3 March 1897, 6. Maguire & Baucus, *Edison and International Photographic Films*, April 1897, 18; Maguire & Baucus, *Fall Catalogue*, 1897, 14; *Edison Films*, March 1900, 24.

NOTE:

296 √**Marines from U.S. Cruiser "New York"**
LENGTH: 150 ft.   © Thomas A. Edison, 15 March 1897.

PRODUCER: James White.

CAMERA: [William Heise.]

CAST:

PRODUCTION DATE: 4 March 1897.

LOCATION: Washington, D.C.

SOURCE:

DESCRIPTION: Leading their section of the parade, and stepping to the lively airs of the band, the Jack Tars, accompanied by their famous Goat, which is the mascot of the Cruiser, certainly made a fine and pleasing spectacle. Followed by other Marine troops, and showing the usual

Inauguration crowds. Excellent definition. (Maguire & Baucus, *Edison and International Photographic Films*, April 1897, 18.)

SUBJECT: Inauguration Day. Presidents–United States–Inauguration. Marines–United States. Marching bands. Parades. Mascots. William McKinley.

ARCHIVE:

CITATIONS: "Order of the Parade," *New York Herald*, 3 March 1897, 6; "The Marine Corps," *Washington Evening Star*, 4 March 1897, 4. Maguire & Baucus, *Fall Catalogue*, 1897, 14; F.Z. Maguire & Co., *Catalogue*, [March 1898], 21; *Edison Films*, March 1900, 23.

NOTE: Sold as a 50 or 150-foot film in 1900.

297 √**Battery A, Light Artillery, U.S. Army**
LENGTH: 50 ft.   © Thomas A. Edison, 15 March 1897.

PRODUCER: James White.

CAMERA: [William Heise.]

CAST:

PRODUCTION DATE: 4 March 1897.

LOCATION: Washington, D.C.

SOURCE:

DESCRIPTION: Shows a battalion of light artillery in rapid movement. Figures well in the background, and the pictures filled with men, horses, cannon and ammunition carriages. Effective perspective and stirring subject; full of action and martial spirit. Scene on Pennsylvania Ave., with mounted police restraining crowds in foreground. (Maguire & Baucus, *Edison and International Photographic Films*, April 1897, 4.)

Artillery scene. A clear film full of action and martial spirit. Shows a battalion of light artillery in rapid movement. Figures well in the foreground, and the picture thick with men, horses, cannon and ammunition carriages, all large size and prominent. Effective perspective and stirring subject. Scene on Pennsylvania avenue, with crowd in background and mounted police restraining crowd in foreground. (F.Z. Maguire & Co., *Catalogue*, [March 1898], 21.)

SUBJECT: Inauguration Day. Presidents–United States–Inauguration. Armies–United States. Artillery. Parades. Police. William McKinley.

ARCHIVE:

CITATIONS: "Order of the Parade," *New York Herald*, 3 March 1897, 6. Maguire & Baucus, *Fall Catalogue*, 1897, 11.

NOTE:

298 √**Vice-President Hobart's Escort**

LENGTH: 150 ft.   © Thomas A. Edison, 15 March 1897.

PRODUCER: James White.

CAMERA: [William Heise.]

CAST:

PRODUCTION DATE: 4 March 1897.

LOCATION: Washington, D.C.

SOURCE:

DESCRIPTION: The Essex troop of Newark, N.J., mounted on coal black chargers, a fine body of men and horses, as they appeared while acting as escort to the new Vice-President. Film of good quality with clear figures and good action. (*The Phonoscope*, March 1897, 14.)

SUBJECT: Inauguration Day. Presidents–United States–Inauguration. National Guard–New Jersey. Parades. William McKinley. Garret Augustus Hobart.

ARCHIVE:

CITATIONS: "Order of the Parade," *New York Herald*, 3 March 1897, 6. Maguire & Baucus, *Edison and International Photographic Films*, April 1897, 19; Maguire & Baucus, *Fall Catalogue*, 1897, 14; F.Z. Maguire & Co., *Catalogue*, [March 1898], 21; *Edison Films*, March 1900, 23.

NOTE: Sold as a 50 or 150-foot film in 1900.

THE ESSEX TROOP.
It Excited General Comment on Account of Its Fine Appearance.

The Essex troop, First Troop N.G. New Jersey, was organized at Newark, N.J., June 1890, by Captain Fleming, formerly of the volunteer service in the war of the rebellion in the Pennsylvania cavalry. The troop consists of seventy members, and carries on its rolls the name of some of the most respected families in Newark and vicinity. Lawyers, doctors, bankers and merchants compose its membership. It is officered by Captain Frelinghuysen, Lieutenant Parker and Heath, and Surgeons Ward and Dougherty.

The troop as organized by Captain Fleming equipped itself, and for three years was independent of the National Guard of the state; for three years, however, it has been in the guard. It is a thoroughgoing military organization performing at all times all the duties of cavalrymen. Though the men are engaged in professional and commercial life, as troopers they do their own stable work, horse cleaning, guard duty, and all the hard work pertaining to a trooper in service. In the Columbian parade in New York the troop evoked the most favorable comments. The comment passed on the company at that time was "for precision and style in cavalry evolutions there was nothing to surpass it in the entire parade." The First Troop has grown steadily to an average of seventy active members. In rifle practice the troop has led the state for the last three years in organization figure of merit.

In October, 1893, the troop paraded in Trenton at the unveiling of the battle monument; in October 1894, in Philadelphia at the dedication of the McClellan monument. An armory building has been started, while the riding hall was completed in December 1896, at a cost of $45,000, without any aid from the state.

In June 1895, the enlistment of twenty-five charter members ran out, and all but two or three re-enlisted. Captain Fleming, the founder of the troop, retired at that time amid general regret, and First Lieutenant Frederick Frelinghuysen was unanimously elected in his place. Second Lieutenant Parker was promoted to be first lieutenant, and First Sergeant Charles Heath to be second lieutenant.

The troop excited general comment in the parade today on account of its fine appearance, the beautiful horses ridden and the splendid accoutrements of the men, military precision and discipline seemed to be almost perfected. (*Washington Evening Star*, 4 March 1897, 13.)

299 √**71st Regiment, New York / Seventy-First Regiment, New York**

LENGTH: 150 ft.   © Thomas A. Edison, 15 March 1897.

PRODUCER: James White.

CAMERA: [William Heise.]

CAST: Francis V. Greene.

PRODUCTION DATE: 4 March 1897.

LOCATION: Washington, D.C.

SOURCE:

DESCRIPTION: The opening of the film shows the famous Seventh Regiment Band starting to play, with Fife and Drum Corps accompanying. The Seventy-first Regiment follows, in formation 32 abreast, commanded by Col. F.V. Greene, of New York, and mounted aides. As the troop approaches, completely filling the great avenue from curb to curb, the company executes interesting military manoeuvres directly in line of the camera, completing the evolution while within focus. The picture abounds in detail and movement, and is pleasantly varied by the change which occasional mounted officers make in the panorama. Very sharp and clear. (F.Z. Maguire & Co., *Catalogue*, [March 1898], 22.)

SUBJECT: Inauguration Day. Presidents–United States–Inauguration. National Guard–New York. Marching bands. Parades. William McKinley. 71st Regiment.

ARCHIVE:

CITATIONS: "Order of the Parade," *New York Herald*, 3 March 1897, 6. Maguire & Baucus, *Edison and International Photographic Films*, April 1897, 18; Maguire & Baucus, *Fall Catalogue*, 1897, 14; *Edison Films*, March 1900, 23 and 24.

NOTE: Sold as a 50 or 150-foot film in 1900.

THE SEVENTY FIRST.
It Has a Splendid Record for Service During the War.

The 71st Regiment, National Guard of the state of New York, which took such a prominent part in the great parade today, is one of the best known military organizations in the country. Its history, running back for almost a half century, is a most creditable one, and the 71st has always been famous for the qualities that go to make up a model regiment. Its armory at the corner of 34th street and Park avenue is one of the handsomest in New York city, and its roster includes many men prominent in New York business and social life.

A complete history of the regiment would contain a number of references to Washington. Its present commanding officer, Col. Francis V. Greene, is well known in this city, for he was formerly in the regular army and was stationed here as assistant to the Engineer Commissioner. When on April 17, 1861, President Lincoln issued a call for 75,000 troops, the 71st was one of the first to respond and to reach the capital. Four days later it embarked from New York to Annapolis whence it made a forced march to Washington. It was temporarily quartered in the inaugural ball room, but was afterward stationed for some time at the navy yard. The regiment saw a great deal of hard service during the war and has taken the field on a number of occasions since when emergencies have arisen.

The regiment was organized in August 1852. The American Rifles, a battalion of four companies formed the nucleus of the regiment. September 21, 1870, the 37th Regiment was consolidated with the 71st Regiment, Companies E, D, H, A, G, K, and B of the 37th Regiment being consolidated with Companies A, C, D, E, F, G, and K of the 71st Regiment respectively. In 1861 it entered the United States service for three months, from April 21 to July 30: in

1862 it re-entered the same service May 29 for three months, at the expiration of which it volunteered to remain, and remained until September 1; in 1863 it was mustered in the United States service for thirty days, and served from June 17 to July 22. It participated in engagements at Aguia creek, June 20, 1861; Bull Run, Va., July 21 1861; Kingston, Pa., June 26, 1863; Port Washington, Pa., June 29, 1863; draft riots in New York city, July 1863; Orange riots in 1871; railroad riots in 1877; switchmen's strike at Buffalo, August 1892, and motormen's strike at Brooklyn, January 1895....(*Washington Evening Star*, 4 March 1897, 12.)

300 √Drum Corps and Militia

LENGTH: 50 ft. © Thomas A. Edison, 15 March 1897.

PRODUCER: James White.

CAMERA: [William Heise.]

CAST:

PRODUCTION DATE: 4 March 1897.

LOCATION: Washington, D.C.

SOURCE:

DESCRIPTION: Fife and Drum Corps, with marching troops and mounted officers. A pleasing subject, showing a detachment of the Minnesota National Guard. Very clear film. (Maguire & Baucus, *Edison and International Photographic Films*, April 1897, 6.)

SUBJECT: Inauguration Day. Presidents–United States–Inauguration. National Guard–Minnesota. Parades. Marching bands. William McKinley.

ARCHIVE:

CITATIONS: "Order of the Parade," *New York Herald*, 3 March 1897, 6. Maguire & Baucus, *Fall Catalogue*, 1897, 11; F.Z. Maguire & Co., *Catalogue*, [March 1898], 21.

NOTE:

301 √Washington Continental Guards

LENGTH: 50 ft. © Thomas A. Edison, 15 March 1897.

PRODUCER: James White.

CAMERA: [William Heise.]

CAST:

PRODUCTION DATE: 4 March 1897.

LOCATION: Washington, D.C.

SOURCE:

DESCRIPTION: This scene opens with the Marine Fife and Drum Corps seen approaching, followed by the Continental Guards in their picturesque and showy uniforms. The reflection of the sun on the gun barrels and buckles adds greatly to the effect of the picture. (Maguire & Baucus, *Edison and International Photographic Films*, 16.)

SUBJECT: Inauguration Day. Presidents–United States–Inauguration. National Guard–Washington, D.C. Parades. Marching bands. Marines–United States. William McKinley.

ARCHIVE:

CITATIONS: "Order of the Parade," *New York Herald*, 3 March 1897, 6. Maguire & Baucus, *Fall Catalogue*, 1897, 13.

NOTE: No organization in the order of march was identified by the name under which this film was copyrighted. There were several Washington, D.C.-based groups that could have been filmed for this subject.

302 *Umbrella Brigade

LENGTH: 50 ft. © Thomas A. Edison, 15 March 1897.

PRODUCER: James White.

CAMERA: [William Heise.]

CAST:

PRODUCTION DATE: 4 March 1897.

LOCATION: Washington, D.C.

SOURCE:

DESCRIPTION: Incidents of the great parade on Pennsylvania Avenue, showing a marching Club carrying red, white and blue umbrellas, which they revolve while marching, giving fine pin-wheel effects. This feature of the parade discloses a large American flag which, unfurling in the breeze, adds to the spirit of the occasion. (*The Phonoscope*, March 1897, 14.)

SUBJECT: Inauguration Day. Presidents–United States–Inauguration. Flags–United States. Patriotism. Parades. Republican Party. Umbrellas. Cook County Republican Marching Club. William McKinley.

ARCHIVE: CaOOANF.

CITATIONS: "Order of the Parade," *New York Herald*, 3 March 1897, 6. Maguire & Baucus, *Edison and International Photographic Films*, April 1897, 16; Maguire & Baucus, *Fall Catalogue*, 1897, 11; F.Z. Maguire & Co., *Catalogue*, [March 1898], 21.

NOTE:

In the civic division of the parade many political clubs that did effective work in the campaign appeared. A great many states were represented. The handsome uniforms worn and the fine marching of many of the bodies showed to what perfection campaigning by means of clubs has been brought in many parts of the Union. Below will be found descriptions of notable organizations in line:

COOK COUNTY CLUB.
The Big Marching Republican Organization of Chicago.

For the first time in her history Chicago was represented at a republican inauguration today. This representative was the Cook County Republican Marching Club, which occupied a place in the third division of the civic portion of the parade at the head of the five organizations from the sate of Illinois. There were 300 men in line, headed by a band of forty pieces, and the club made an exceptionally fine showing. The regular marshal of the club, Capt. William F. Knoch, was in command. The uniform worn consisted of black box overcoats, black cutaway coats and silk hats, and each member in line carried an umbrella. The club marched with military precision and ably represented the great city of the west, receiving a large share of applause all the way along the line.

The Cook County Republican Marching Club was organized at the Great Northern Hotel, Chicago, January 19, 1894. The objects of the club were, and are, to maintain a well-drilled body of men to march at the request of the central republican organization and to act as an escort to conventions and to prominent republicans who visit the city of Chicago. Any republican, if he is a resident of Cook county, may become a member and no candidates are indorsed by the club until they have been nominated in regular convention. (*Washington Evening Star*, 4 March 1897, 14.)

303 √**Young Men's Blaine Club of Cincinnati**

LENGTH: 50 ft.   © Thomas A. Edison, 15 March 1897.

PRODUCER: James White.

CAMERA: [William Heise.]

CAST:

PRODUCTION DATE: 4 March 1897.

LOCATION: Washington, D.C.

SOURCE:

DESCRIPTION: This is a spirited picture of Pennsylvania avenue, with the National Capitol shown in the background one mile and a half away. The members of the Blaine Club march by in white high hats and light-colored spring overcoats, with badges. There is a large crowd of people in the foreground, and the usual inauguration crowd fills the sidewalk on either side of

the street. (F.Z. Maguire & Co., *Catalogue*, [March 1898], 21.)
SUBJECT: Inauguration Day. Presidents–United States–Inauguration. Republican Party. Parades. Young Men's Blaine Club of Cincinnati. William McKinley.
ARCHIVE:
CITATIONS: "Order of the Parade," *New York Herald*, 3 March 1897, 6. Maguire & Baucus, *Edison and International Photographic Films*, April 1897, 16; Maguire & Baucus, *Fall Catalogue*, 1897, 13.
NOTE:

NAMED FOR BLAINE.
A Big Cincinnati Club That Attracted Much Notice.
Preceded by the 1st Ohio Regiment Band of fifty pieces and attired in fawn-colored overcoats of the latest cut, dark trousers, white plug hats and kid gloves, jauntily swinging canes: the famous Young Men's Blaine Club of Cincinnati, Ohio, 300 strong, commanded by Capt. Frank S. Krug, made a handsome appearance. This organization was one of the popular ones in the procession, and their appearance was the signal always for an outburst of cheers. They marched well and made an excellent appearance in every way. The club was organized the evening of June 6, 1884, the day James G. Blaine was nominated for the presidency and is composed of the most prominent men in Cincinnati, men of means and standing in that city. A fine club house is owned by the organization, and its members, when not engaged in political warfare, repair there to enjoy themselves. The club took an active part in the last campaign, and also attended the St. Louis convention. The members traveled to Washington in a special car, magnificently fitted up with every convenience, and for more than a month they have been drilling constantly. Hence their fine bearing in the parade today. Among the selections rendered by their fine band was the "Vim, Vigor and Victory March," composed by Miss Beiser, the sixteen-year-old daughter of Mr. Julius Beiser, a member of the club.…(*Washington Evening Star*, 4 March 1897, 14.)

Thomas A. Edison has offered to the National Museum at Washington a set of photographic films for the kinetoscope taken during President McKinley's inauguration. They show the president taking the oath of office, Cleveland and McKinley driving to the capitol, and views of the parade. It is intended to have these films sealed hermetically and marked: To be opened by the Curator of the National Museum thirty years after President McKinley's inauguration. (*Milwaukee Journal*, 26 March 1897, TAEP, 146:1097.)

One Edison crew remained in the Washington, D.C., area after the inauguration; the group filmed the new President attending church, and several military scenes at Fort Myer, Va.

304 √**McKinley Leaving Church / President McKinley Coming from Church**
LENGTH: 50 ft.   © Thomas A. Edison, 21 April 1897.
PRODUCER: James White.
CAMERA: [William Heise.]
CAST: William McKinley, Mrs. William McKinley (mother of the President).
PRODUCTION DATE: 7 March 1898.
LOCATION: Metropolitan Church, Washington, D.C.
SOURCE:
DESCRIPTION: This picture was recently taken in Washington, and shows the President leaving Metropolitan Methodist Church, Washington, D.C. As he descends the steps, his mother, who accompanies him, can be seen leaning heavily on his arm, thus making a very effective and attractive scene, with multitudes of people lifting their hats as a token of respect to the new leader. A very clear picture. (F.Z. Maguire & Co., *Catalogue*, [March 1898], 16.)
SUBJECT: Presidents–United States. Church buildings. Worship.
ARCHIVE:
CITATIONS: "President at Church," *Washington Post*, 8 March 1897, 1. Maguire & Baucus, *Fall Catalogue*, 1897, 10; F.M. Prescott, *Catalogue of New Films*, 1899, 11.
NOTE: The F.M. Prescott catalog fictitiously locates this scene at the Continental Baptist Church in Washington, D.C.

THE PRESIDENT'S MOTHER.
The Venerable Woman Who Saw Her Son's Inauguration.

Mrs. William McKinley, mother of the President, has reached her eighty-fourth year, and has at that venerable age good health and undimmed faculties. She has grown old gracefully, her simple and retired life having passed along quietly and serenely. Sharing all the ambitions of her children, and especially of her distinguished son, the honors which have come to him seem to her the most natural thing in the world. The President's devotion to his wife is only equaled by his affectionate solicitude for his mother. Every spare minute he has had away from one has been passed with the other.

Mrs. McKinley has a modern home near that of the now famous wooden house in Canton, and to which she will probably return after paying a visit to the White house. The honors paid her son made no difference in the simple regularity of her household direction. She is a good housekeeper, fond of household duties and could be seen all last summer and fall almost any morning sweeping off her front porch and ready to chat with any neighbor who passed along. Mrs. McKinley has a very sweet voice and a very pleasant way of saying nice things. No member of her family has taken a deeper interest nor displayed a more accurate knowledge of the scenes she has witnessed since she came to Washington.

Miss Helen McKinley, the President's unmarried sister, lives with her mother, and with the two also live the orphan wards of the President, the son and daughter of his brother James, who died in San Francisco a few years ago. (*Washington Evening Star*, 4 March 1897, 15.)

THE PRESIDENT'S SUNDAY.
He Attended the Metropolitan M.E. Church and Heard Bishop Newman.

President McKinley, accompanied by his mother, Gen. Osborne and Private Secretary and Mrs. Porter, attended divine service at the Metropolitan M.E. Church yesterday morning and listened to an able and impressive sermon by Bishop John P. Newman, formerly pastor of the church. The President will be a regular attendant at the Foundry Church during his term of office, but he was anxious to hear Bishop Newman yesterday, and his first appearance at church as President was at the Metropolitan.

It was known in advance what his plans were, and the result was that a crowd that far exceeded the seating capacity of the church gathered long before the regular hour for service, and when the President's party entered the church was crowded to its utmost limit and hundreds were turned away unable to obtain admission. The distinguished party was shown directly to the pew that was used by President Grant when he was in the White House. Rev. Dr. Hugh Johnston, the regular pastor, assisted the bishop, and with them on the platform was Rev. Dr. Manchester of Canton, Mr. McKinley's former pastor.

During the afternoon the President, accompanied by Mr. McWilliams of Chicago, took a short walk through the northwest section of the city. Many pedestrians were enjoying the beautiful afternoon, and Mr. McKinley was generally recognized. Passersby bowed and he was noticeably careful in returning every salutation. Late Saturday afternoon, after his day's work was over, Mr. McKinley left the White House and took a quiet stroll through the streets. The fact that he has begun in this way has been most favorably commented upon on all sides by people, who hope for a return to the days when the President of the United States will not seek to hold himself aloof, but will think it not beneath his dignity to mingle with the crowds in public places.

Vice President and Mrs. Hobart, accompanied by their son, Garret A. Hobart, Jr., attended service in the morning at the Church of the Covenant, occupying the pastor's pew.

Secretary and Mrs. Alger and Miss Frances Alger attended service at the New York Avenue Presbyterian Church, Secretary and Miss Long at All Souls' Church, and the Attorney General at St. Matthew's. (*Washington Evening Star*, 8 March 1897, 12.)

305 √**Pennsylvania Avenue, Washington**

LENGTH: 50 ft.   © Thomas A. Edison, 21 April 1897.

PRODUCER: James White.

CAMERA: William Heise.

CAST:

PRODUCTION DATE: March 1897.

LOCATION: Washington, D.C.

SOURCE:

DESCRIPTION:

SUBJECT: City and town life–Washington, D.C.

ARCHIVE:

CITATIONS:

NOTE:

306 √**Bareback Hurdle Jumping**
LENGTH: 50 ft.   © Thomas A. Edison, 21 April 1897.
PRODUCER: James White
CAMERA: William Heise.
CAST:
PRODUCTION DATE: March 1897.
LOCATION: Fort Myer, Va.
SOURCE:

DESCRIPTION: A subject taken at Fort Myer,
Va., showing a troop of United States
Cavalry, in command of Col. Sumner. Each
man is seen standing astride of three spirited horses, and approaching the hurdle, the
rider stands erect, and the jump is made in
this extremely difficult manner, the men
having great difficulty in keeping their footing as the horses leap over the hurdle. A
very exciting scene. (F.Z. Maguire & Co., *Catalogue*, [March 1898], 16.)
SUBJECT: Horsemanship. Horses. Armies–United States. Cavalry. Sixth U.S. Cavalry.
ARCHIVE:
CITATIONS: "The Sixth Cavalry," *Washington Evening Star,* 4 March 1897, 4. Maguire
& Baucus, *Fall Catalogue*, 1897, 10; *Edison Films*, March 1900, 45; *Edison Films,*
July 1901, 92.
NOTE:

307 √**Hurdle Jumping and Saddle Vaulting / Vaulting in Saddle and Jumping Hurdle**
LENGTH: 50 ft.   © Thomas A. Edison, 21 April 1897.
PRODUCER: James White.
CAMERA: William Heise.
CAST:
PRODUCTION DATE: March 1897.
LOCATION: Fort Myer, Va.
SOURCE:

DESCRIPTION: Another interesting subject
taken at Fort Myer, Va. The rider in this
picture is handling two spirited and energetic cavalry horses, seated in the saddle of
one and leading the other. As he nears the
hurdle, he jumps to the ground, running
beside his own mount until both horses rise
to make the hurdle jump, when he vaults over the back of the horse he had formerly ridden, gracefully alighting in the saddle of the horse he had been leading. This
is regarded by military men as an extremely difficult feat, and in the picture we
secured it is performed by over thirty cavalrymen, who jumped the hurdles with
double mounts in rapid succession. This picture cannot help but arouse the enthusiasm of an audience. (F.M. Prescott, *Catalogue of New Films*, 1899, 11.)
SUBJECT: Horsemanship. Horses. Armies–United States. Cavalry. Sixth U.S. Cavalry.
ARCHIVE:
CITATIONS: Maguire & Baucus, *Fall Catalogue*, 1897, 9; F.Z. Maguire & Co., *Catalogue*,
[March 1898], 16; *Edison Films*, March 1900, 45; *Edison Films,* July 1901, 92.
NOTE:

308 √**Cavalry Passing in Review**
LENGTH: 50 and 150 ft.   © Thomas A. Edison, 21 April 1897.
PRODUCER: James White.
CAMERA: William Heise.
CAST:
PRODUCTION DATE: March 1897.
LOCATION: Fort Myer, Va.
SOURCE:

DESCRIPTION: Troop A, U.S. Cavalry, Fort Myer, Va., is first seen at a distance of more than half a mile, rounding the bend of a beautiful Southern road, and coming toward the camera in columns of four. As they approach the audience they seem to be riding harder and harder, growing into life-size as they pass out of view. Even the dust and turf is distinguished as it is thrown up by the horses' hoofs. When this picture was taken the troopers were in full-dress uniform, and they make a striking and effective picture as  their armor and uniform decorations flash in the bright sunlight. A fine, clear picture, sure to create applause. (F.Z. Maguire & Co., *Catalogue*, [March 1898], 17.)

SUBJECT: Armies–United States. Cavalry. Sixth U.S. Cavalry.

ARCHIVE:

CITATIONS: Maguire & Baucus, *Fall Catalogue*, 1897, 10 and 15; *Edison Films*, March 1900, 45.

NOTE:

MAKING OF A WAR HORSE.
How Steeds are Trained for the Cavalry Service of Uncle Sam.
THE SCHOOL AT FORT MYER.
Taken From the Plains, Broken and Taught to Do Many Strange Things.

PHILADELPHIA, Pa., April 11–One of the most interesting feature of the busy war preparations which have been going on during the past six weeks is the training of a large number of cavalry horses at Fort Myer, Va. Although most important and significant, the work has been carried on without the knowledge of the general public. And to-day finds Uncle Sam well equipped with horses for the cavalry service, says the Times. Its importance cannot be over-estimated, for the cavalry is one of the most effective adjuncts of a military force and the horse the essential factor in its efficiency....

Horses are too expensive to maintain in numbers exceeding actual requirement. In war times the requisite number is, of course, greatly increased. The augmentation of the number could not be left to the last minute, however, for the training of a horse requires considerable time.

What He Must Do.

He must learn to stand steady under fire and in the midst of flashing sabres; he must learn to obey the slightest pressure upon his flanks when running with loose rein; he must learn to lie down and form a barricade for his rider, in short, there are a hundred minor details which must be taught him before he becomes sufficiently skilled for field use. To teach a horse these tactics requires time and the greatest patience. Every one is not capable of doing it and in consequence the great time is consumed in training a large number. In fact the work is left almost entirely to one man, Lieut. Short, who, at Fort Myer, furnishes trained horses for the entire Eastern division of the army.

The horses are brought raw from the West and have never felt the weight of a saddle. They have little intelligence, but are simply creatures of habit. All that is required to teach them cavalry tactics is to make them understand what is expected of them and let them know they must do it. What is once learned they never forget.

Upon his arrival at Fort Myer the new recruit is tabled with the other horses. He is probably travel sick from the effect of his long ride on the car. The first thing to do is to get him in good physical shape and make him feel at home amid his new surroundings. He is just like a new boy at school; he is shy and everything is strange to him.

After he has been thoroughly rested he is taken out into the paddock some morning and given his first lesson in cavalry tactics. The initial instruction is in kneeling and lying down. In order to make him understand what is required of him a simple arrangement of harness is used.

First Lesson.

A surcingle is placed around his belly, to which are attached two iron rings, one underneath and one at the horse's back. Straps containing rings are also placed about each foreleg just above the hoof and another strap is placed about the head just above the nose. The officer in charge is supplied with two long ropes, by mean of which the horse is rendered quite at the mercy of his instructor.

One rope is fastened to the rings on the right leg, extends up through the ring on the surcingle under the horse's belly down to the ring on the left leg and back again through the surcingle ring. The other end of the rope is held by the officer. The minute the horse begins to show a fractious spirit, a strong pull on the rope brings him down on his knees.

The other rope passes on the right side of the horse from the ring just above the nose to that in the surcingle at the horse's back. A pull on this brings the animal's head around close to the right shoulder, and he is powerless. A pull on both ropes at once will cause him to lose his equilibrium, and down he comes on his left side.

A few repetitions of this administered in such a way as to demonstrate to the horse that he is entirely at the mercy of the trainer and the first lesson is over. The horse is taken back to his stable, often without a stroke of a whip, in some instances, however, it is found necessary to apply the lash with discretion.

The next step is to mount him. A light snaffle bridal is adjusted, and while the horse is on the ground the officer hands the rope holding the animal in check to one of his men. Then they are slackened and as the horse attempts to struggle to his feet the officer leaps on his back. With a snort of surprise the equine recruit jumps and rears. Another pull on the ropes and down he comes again to the turf, with the trainer leaping from him as he falls. He lies there trembling; a few softly spoken words, a gentle caress and it is tried all over again. Finally the pupil, who has previously learned to realize that he is powerless, gets used to the weight on his back and doesn't mind it....

The greatest shock to his nerves is yet in store for his horseship. This is getting accustomed to firearms. While the animal is down on the ground, the trainer takes a pistol and fires it close to his ear. Then in rapid order he fires the weapon over his back, under his neck, between his legs, anywhere that an opening presents itself during the horses futile struggles. Not until he sinks back exhausted, all a-tremble, and showing the whites of his eyes does the pistol practice cease.

After two or three lessons of this kind it is considered safe to mount him with a bridle furnished with a curb bit. Up to this time the horse has never felt a curb. The light snaffle is still retained and the curb bridle is only given a gentle pressure at first—just enough to let him know that it is there. Gradually the strength of the pull is increased, and with this safeguard the horse is taught to stand fire from his rider's pistol or carbine. In carbine practice the horse must be thoroughly broken, as both hands are required in using the weapon, whereas with the pistol the rider may retain the bridle with one hand. Then comes sabre practice, and that is another trial to the horse. Again is he thrown to the ground and he probably can't understand why he should have to suffer this indignity all over again, for he has learned that lesson very well. But when the bright blade of the sabre, with quick thrusts flashing before his eyes and cutting the air in close proximity to his ears, appears to him, he is again terror-stricken.

But the lesson he has earned from the smell of gun powder stands him in good stead, and he soon gets over his fear. And even with a man on his back and another mounted upon a seasoned horse coming at him with sabre raised in the air or slashing left and right he knows that it is all a part of his education and something to be expected. So he stands his ground or cavorts about the other horse, while the two troopers indulge in their sabre practice.

Jumping.

With his instructions in jumping the new recruit's education is nearly completed. He is drilled in what is known as large jumping that is to say he is placed in a shoot, with two high fences converging toward a gate. He is still kept in check by a long rope, held by a man outside the fence.

Two other men run at his flanks with whips, and in order to escape the lash he is bound to jump. If he doesn't go over clear, the rails are tied up and at the next attempt he comes a cropper on the tanbark, landing in a heap. The next time with the whips and the fear of another fall, he clears the bars like a bird.

After a little practice of this sort the horse knows just what he has to do, and then a man mounts him. With the extra weight the jump is made lower, and he eventually takes his final degree as a full-fledged cavalry horse.

As to the time required by the process a great deal depends upon the horse. Some can be thoroughly broken to this service in three weeks and be perfectly trustworthy. With others it may take as long as six months. There is a small class, a very small class, which seem never able to learn, and their education is finally abandoned. These cases, however, are few and far between. (*New York World*, 14 April 1898, 8.)

309 ***Grace Church, New York / View of Grace Church, New York***

LENGTH: 50 and 150 ft.   © Thomas A. Edison, 21 April 1897.

PRODUCER: James White.

CAMERA: William Heise.

CAST:

PRODUCTION DATE: 4 April 1897.

LOCATION: Broadway, New York, N.Y.

SOURCE:

DESCRIPTION: A very sharp, clear picture, taken on Easter Sunday, 1897, showing the fashionable congregation of that historical church on Broadway, New York, leaving the edifice at the close of morning service. The picture is full of action from start to finish, and will be found interesting by

thousands of people throughout the country, who have heard of Grace Church, but have never had the opportunity of seeing it. (F.M. Prescott, *Catalogue of New Films*, 1899, 11.)

SUBJECT: Church buildings. Easter. Worship.
ARCHIVE: CaOOANF.
CITATIONS: Maguire & Baucus, *Fall Catalogue*, 1897, 15; F.Z. Maguire & Co., *Catalogue*, [1898], 18.
NOTE:

Grace Church looks down Broadway from 10th Street, and is a very sumptuous and ornate edifice of marble, with a lofty marble spire. The interior is rich in delicate carvings, lines of stone columns, forty stained-glass windows, etc. Renwick built the church in 1845. Dr. Huntington is rector. You should visit the beautiful little chantry, opening off the south aisle, and erected by Christine Wolf's bounty. (M.F. Sweetser and Simeon Ford, *How to Know New York City*, 1895, 71.)

310 Now I Lay Me Down to Sleep / Children Saying Their Prayer

LENGTH: 50 ft.   © Thomas A. Edison, 21 April 1897.
PRODUCER: James White.
CAMERA: William Heise.
CAST:
PRODUCTION DATE: Mid-March to mid-April 1897.
LOCATION: Black Maria, West Orange, N.J.
SOURCE:
DESCRIPTION: A very pretty scene of home life, showing an indulgent mother performing her last duties of the day in putting her two little children to bed, one of whom refuses to say its prayers, and is crying. The other is kneeling by the mother's knee, with his head bowed in prayer. They are finally kissed by the loving parent, and as they are snugly wrapped in the bed cover the scene ends, making a very touching and pleasing picture. (F.Z. Maguire & Co., *Catalogue*, [March 1898], 17.)
SUBJECT: Children. Worship. Family. Beds.
ARCHIVE:
CITATIONS: Maguire & Baucus, *Fall Catalogue*, 1897, 10; F.M. Prescott, *Catalogue of New Films*, 11.
NOTE:

311 *Seminary Girls / Scene in a Seminary

LENGTH: 50 and 150 ft.   © Thomas A. Edison, 21 April 1897.
PRODUCER: James White.
CAMERA: William Heise.
CAST:
PRODUCTION DATE: Mid-March to mid-April 1897.
LOCATION: Black Maria, West Orange, N.J.
SOURCE: *A Pillow Fight* (Biograph film, March 1897).
DESCRIPTION: A most amusing and life-like scene, in which a number of young ladies clad in their night robes, are seen engaged in a midnight frolic; starting in smoking cigarettes, drinking tonic and ending in a pillow fight. They are suddenly interrupted by the Principal appearing on the scene (with candle in hand) when a general stampede occurs, one girl being very conspicuous in her frantic efforts to get under the bed, and thus escape the wrath of the school marm, but the scene ends in the young lady being caught, pulled from under the bed and punished. A very ludicrous picture. (F.M. Prescott, *Catalogue of New Films*, 1899, 11.)
SUBJECT: Schools. Girls. Cigarettes. Punishment. Pillows. Beds.
ARCHIVE: CLAc, DLC.
CITATIONS: Maguire & Baucus, *Fall Catalogue*, 1897, 10 and 15; F.Z. Maguire & Co., *Catalogue*, [March 1898], 17; *Edison Films*, March 1900, 34; *Edison Films*, July 1901, 69.
NOTE: The Lumières also made a pillow fight film that may have preceded the Edison subject in terms of production date. See also Edison film no. 343, *Pillow Fight*.

312 ***The Washerwoman's Troubles / Trouble with the Washerwoman**
LENGTH: 50 and 150 ft. © Thomas A. Edison, 21 April 1897.
PRODUCER: James White.
CAMERA: William Heise.
CAST:
PRODUCTION DATE: Mid-March to mid-April 1897.
LOCATION: Black Maria, West Orange, N.J.
SOURCE:

DESCRIPTION: A woman is first seen at the tub, washing, when the typical iceman enters, drops a large cake of the frozen moisture into the chest, breaking many of the dishes and upsetting the eatables, whereupon he is scolded by the washerwoman. He then seeks to amuse himself by dropping a piece of ice down the woman's back which she resents with a blow from a bunch of wet linen. He then thrusts his arm around her neck and attempts to kiss her. In the scuffle which ensues the tub is overthrown and the water and suds flood the floor, running toward the audience. In the meantime the iceman is driven from the kitchen in disgrace. This picture cannot fail to amuse an audience, as it is very realistic and life-like. (F.M. Prescott, *Catalogue of New Films*, 1899, 11.)
SUBJECT: Working classes. Kitchens. Sexual harassment. Ice.
ARCHIVE: CaOOANF.
CITATIONS: Maguire & Baucus, *Fall Catalogue*, 1897, 10 and 15; F.Z. Maguire & Co., *Catalogue*, [March 1898], 17-18; *Edison Films*, March 1900, 34; *Edison Films*, July 1901, 69.
NOTE:

313 **√The Elopement**
LENGTH: 50 ft. © Thomas A. Edison, 21 April 1897.
PRODUCER: James White.
CAMERA: William Heise.
CAST:
PRODUCTION DATE: Mid-March to mid-April 1897.
LOCATION:
SOURCE:

DESCRIPTION: A pretty New England farmhouse forms the background of this picture. A young girl suddenly appears at the door; her lover rides to meet her, mounted on a fine black horse, and leading a mount for his intended bride. The mutual friend then appears and assists the young lady to her saddle, and as they ride away her father comes from the house, but too late to check their departure. He can then be seen to remonstrate with the friend for aiding the couple in running away. This picture will not only be found amusing, but the surroundings are both natural and beautiful. (F.Z. Maguire & Co., *Catalogue*, [March 1898], 17.)
SUBJECT: Elopement. Farms. Courtship. Horses.
ARCHIVE:
CITATIONS: Maguire & Baucus, *Fall Catalogue*, 1897, 10.
NOTE:

The Black Diamond Express had proved so popular that the negative soon became worn and a new one was needed. An Edison crew returned to north-eastern Pennsylvania and took new negatives of this subject as well as two new and related views (one shot from the rear of the train, and a "rear view" of the Black Diamond Express that could function, in some respects, as a reverse angle of the popular film subject). Exhibitors could then sequence these films and show the train hurtling down the tracks from several perspectives.

Filming the Black Diamond Express near Towanda, Pa. (April 1897).
James White rests his elbow on the kinetograph. William Heise stands next to him, his hand touching the camera.

314 √Panoramic Scene, Susquehanna River / Panoramic View of the Susquehanna River

LENGTH: 50 ft.   © Thomas A. Edison, 21 April 1897.

PRODUCER: James White.

CAMERA: William Heise.

CAST:

PRODUCTION DATE: April 1897.

LOCATION: Near Towanda, Pa.

SOURCE:

DESCRIPTION: In this picture we introduce a very novel effect. Our camera was placed on the rear of a moving train and as it steamed along at a high rate of speed we were able to get a good view of the passing scenery. Near the end of the film the train passes a small station, where a number of ladies and gentlemen stand waving adieux

to some of their friends who are on the disappearing train. This picture will be found interesting, both for its novel effect and beautiful scenery. (F.Z. Maguire & Co., *Catalogue*, [March 1898], 18.)

SUBJECT: Railroads. Rivers. Railroad stations. Lehigh Valley Railroad. Susquehanna River.

ARCHIVE:

CITATIONS: Maguire & Baucus, *Fall Catalogue*, 1897, 10.

NOTE:

315 √Receding View, Black Diamond Express / Receding View of the Black Diamond Express / Rear View of the Black Diamond Express / [Receding View, Black Diamond Express, no. 1]

LENGTH: 50 ft.   © Thomas A. Edison, 21 April 1897.

PRODUCER: James White.

CAMERA: William Heise.

CAST:

PRODUCTION DATE: April 1897.

LOCATION: Near Towanda, Pa.

SOURCE:

DESCRIPTION: Quite unlike the approaching scene of this most popular train, the audience first sees the tracks and mountain scenery in the background, when the train suddenly dashes into view, going at the rate of about seventy miles an hour. This is the first picture ever taken of a receding train, and the effect is most pleasing, as the passengers are seen in the windows and on the rear end of the train, waving their handkerchiefs, hats, etc. In this manner the train speeds down the track for more than half a mile, when it rounds a curve in the road, disappearing from view. A very clear, sharp picture which will be found pleasing and interesting, particularly if shown immediately after the approaching view of the same train. (F.M. Prescott, *Catalogue of New Films*, 1899, 12.)

SUBJECT: Railroads. Rivers. Mountains. Lehigh Valley Railroad.

ARCHIVE:

CITATIONS: Maguire & Baucus, *Fall Catalogue*, 1897, 10; F.Z. Maguire & Co., *Catalogue,* [March 1898], 18.

NOTE:

316 **Black Diamond Express, no. 1 / Lehigh Valley Express "Black Diamond" / Black Diamond Express (New Negative) / [Black Diamond Express, no. 2]*

LENGTH: 50 and 150 ft.   © Thomas A. Edison, 27 April 1897.

PRODUCER: James White.

CAMERA: William Heise.

CAST:

PRODUCTION DATE: April 1897.

LOCATION: Near Towanda, Pa.

SOURCE: *Black Diamond Express* (Edison film no. 262, December 1896).

DESCRIPTION: This picture was taken near Towanda, Pa., on the shore of the Susquehanna River, and is truly one of the most picturesque spots on the line of the Lehigh Valley Railroad, a gigantic mountain forming the background. The train is first observed rounding a curve at a distance of nearly a mile, and as she bowls along at a speed exceeding 70 miles an hour, the engineer blows a whistle, warning a gang of road men engaged in repairing the roadway. As the train approaches, the passengers and others are seen waving their handkerchiefs, hats, etc., from windows and platforms, the pictures being so sharp that the numbers can be clearly discerned, and the engineer is plainly seen, looking from the cab window, with his hand upon the starting lever. (F.M. Prescott, *Catalogue of New Films*, 1899, 12.)

SUBJECT: Railroads. Rivers. Mountains. Lehigh Valley Railroad. Susquehanna River.

ARCHIVE: NNMoMA, UkLNFA.

CITATIONS: Maguire & Baucus, *Fall Catalogue*, 1897, 15; F.Z. Maguire & Co., *Catalogue,* [March 1898], 18; *Edison Films*, March 1900, 46.

NOTE: In this film a hand truck appears on the left, behind several men waving at the passing train. Passengers also wave with handkerchiefs, and there is a narrow white sign on the right of the tracks—clearly placed by the filmmakers—identifying the film.

317 **Black Diamond Express, no. 2 / Black Diamond Express / [Black Diamond Express, no. 3]*

LENGTH: 50 ft.   © Thomas A. Edison, 27 April 1897.

PRODUCER: James White.
CAMERA: William Heise.
CAST:
PRODUCTION DATE: April 1897.
LOCATION: Near Towanda, Pa.
SOURCE: *Black Diamond Express* (Edison film no. 262, December 1896).
ARCHIVE: CaOOANF.
DESCRIPTION:
SUBJECT: Railroads. Rivers. Mountains. Lehigh Valley Railroad. Susquehanna River.
ARCHIVE:
CITATIONS: *Edison Films*, March 1900, 46.
NOTE: A reserve negative for this popular subject. It is also possible that this second negative was used for making all 50-foot prints of this subject.

318 √**Receding View, Black Diamond Express / [Receding View, Black Diamond Express, no. 2]**
LENGTH: [150 ft.]   © Thomas A. Edison, 27 April 1897.
PRODUCER: James White.
CAMERA: William Heise.
CAST:
PRODUCTION DATE: April 1897.
LOCATION: Near Towanda, Pa.
SOURCE:
DESCRIPTION:
SUBJECT: Railroads. Rivers. Mountains. Lehigh Valley Railroad.
ARCHIVE:
CITATIONS:
NOTE: A reserve negative for this popular subject. See film no. 315.

If Barnum and Bailey's Circus had come to the kinetograph in 1895, two years later the kinetograph came to Barnum and Bailey's Circus. Now the Edison crew could film twelve trained elephants or seventy disciplined horses performing in the ring. Only one scene, of a performing acrobat, was of a type familiar from the 1894-1895 era.

319 √**Chas. Wertz, Acrobat [sic] / Acrobat Charles Werts / Charles Werts**
LENGTH: 50 ft.   © Thomas A. Edison, 27 April 1897.
PRODUCER: James White.
CAMERA: William Heise.
CAST: Charles Werts.
PRODUCTION DATE: 5-24 April 1897.
LOCATION: New York, N.Y.
SOURCE:

DESCRIPTION: A picture made at the Barnum & Bailey Circus, showing this famous acrobat, known in the profession as "Chad Werts," performing a number of difficult acrobatic feats, such as double back handsprings, etc. A particularly clear film, and full of action from start to finish. (F.Z. Maguire & Co., *Catalogue*, [March 1898], 20.)
SUBJECT: Circus performers. Acrobats. Tumbling. Barnum & Bailey's Circus.
ARCHIVE:
CITATIONS: Maguire & Baucus, *Fall Catalogue*, 1897, 10; F.M. Prescott, *Catalogue of New Films*, 1899, 13.
NOTE:

320 Horse Dancing Couchee Couchee

LENGTH: 50 ft.   © Thomas A. Edison, 8 May 1897.

PRODUCER: James White.

CAMERA: William Heise.

CAST: Mr. O'Brien.

PRODUCTION DATE: 5-24 April 1897.

LOCATION: New York, N.Y.

SOURCE:

DESCRIPTION: This undoubtedly is the most novel performance ever photographed by our apparatus, being a perfect rendition of the famous Midway Plaisance dance by a horse trained by Mr. O'Brien, of the Barnum & Bailey circus. The horse goes through all the steps of this much-talked-of dance, keeping perfect time to the music, with his trainer mounted on his back. It is, without doubt, the most wonderful exhibition of animal intelligence now before the public. Sure to create laughter wherever shown. (F.Z. Maguire & Co., *Catalogue*, [March 1898], 20.)

SUBJECT: Circus animals. Horses. Dancing. Danse du ventre. Barnum & Bailey's Circus.

ARCHIVE:

CITATIONS: Maguire & Baucus, *Fall Catalogue*, 1897, 9; *Edison Films,* July 1901, 49.

NOTE:

321 O'Brien's Trained Horses

LENGTH: 50 ft.   © Thomas A. Edison, 8 May 1897.

PRODUCER: James White.

CAMERA: William Heise.

CAST: Mr. O'Brien.

PRODUCTION DATE: 5-24 April 1897.

LOCATION: New York, N.Y.

SOURCE:

DESCRIPTION: The opening of this film shows seventy trained horses performing at one time in a forty-foot ring. They are commanded by Mr. O'Brien, of Barnum & Bailey's circus, and go through many interesting and amusing tricks, finishing by forming a pyramid, with their trainer mounted on a beautiful white horse at the top of the pedestal, fifteen feet in height, in the center of the ring. A clear picture and sure to please. (F.Z. Maguire & Co., *Catalogue*, [March 1898], 20.)

SUBJECT: Circus animals. Horses. Animal trainers. Barnum & Bailey's Circus.

ARCHIVE:

CITATIONS: Maguire & Baucus, *Fall Catalogue*, 1897, 10.

NOTE:

322 Tandem Hurdle Jumping

LENGTH: 50 ft.   © Thomas A. Edison, 8 May 1897.

PRODUCER: James White.

CAMERA: William Heise.

CAST:

PRODUCTION DATE: 5-24 April 1897.

LOCATION: New York, N.Y.

SOURCE:

DESCRIPTION: This shows two of Barnum and Bailey's expert horsewomen, each mounted on a spirited horse and driving three other horses tandem. They are first observed racing on a turn of the circus track, and as they approach, jump some extremely high hurdles, the entire eight horses making the jump at one time. A very exciting scene, which will arouse the enthusiasm of all who witness it. (F.Z. Maguire & Co., *Catalogue*, [March 1898], 20.)

SUBJECT: Circus animals. Horses. Horsemanship. Barnum & Bailey's Circus.

ARCHIVE:

CITATIONS: Maguire & Baucus, *Fall Catalogue*, 1897, 10; *Edison Films,* July 1901, 49.

NOTE:

323 √Trick Elephants, no. 1
LENGTH: 50 ft. © Thomas A. Edison, 8 May 1897.
PRODUCER: James White.
CAMERA: William Heise.
CAST:
PRODUCTION DATE: 5-24 April 1897.
LOCATION: New York, N.Y.
SOURCE:

DESCRIPTION: A very funny picture, indeed. Twelve of Barnum and Bailey's famous trick elephants are seen performing at one time in a ring. One elephant rolls a barrel, another stands on his head on a pedestal, and others go through equally interesting and ludicrous manoeuvres. (F.Z. Maguire & Co., *Catalogue*, [March 1898], 20.)
SUBJECT: Circus animals. Elephants. Barnum & Bailey's Circus.
ARCHIVE:
CITATIONS: Maguire & Baucus, *Fall Catalogue*, 1897, 10; *Edison Films*, March 1900, 25; *Edison Films,* July 1901, 49.
NOTE:

324 √Trick Elephants, no. 2
LENGTH: 50 ft. © Thomas A. Edison, 8 May 1897.
PRODUCER: James White.
CAMERA: William Heise.
CAST:
PRODUCTION DATE: 5-24 April 1897.
LOCATION: New York, N.Y.
SOURCE:

DESCRIPTION: Showing a number of elephants forming a pyramid, while others march around the ring at the same time, performing many comical and amusing tricks. (F.Z. Maguire & Co., *Catalogue*, [March 1898], 20.)
SUBJECT: Circus animals. Elephants. Barnum & Bailey's Circus.
ARCHIVE:
CITATIONS: Maguire & Baucus, *Fall Catalogue*, 1897, 10; *Edison Films*, March 1900, 25; *Edison Films,* July 1901, 49.
NOTE:

In the 1890s, the deceased Ulysses S. Grant—former U.S. President and Civil War General—was still considered one of the foremost heroes in United States history. On April 27th, Grant's Day, Grant's Tomb on Riverside Drive at 122nd Street, New York City, was dedicated and turned over to the municipal government. Hundreds of thousands of spectators were expected to watch the pageantry surrounding these ceremonies, but inclement weather spoiled the festivities. The day's events had three principal elements: speeches, a land parade and a naval parade. Edison's camera(s) shot the first two while ignoring the last, taking sixteen copyrighted films of the day's events.

325 √McKinley's Address / President McKinley's Address / Address of President McKinley
LENGTH: 50 ft. © Thomas A. Edison, 8 May 1897.
PRODUCER: James White.
CAMERA: William Heise.
CAST: William McKinley, Horace Porter, William L. Strong.
PRODUCTION DATE: 27 April 1897.

LOCATION: Grant's Tomb, New York, N.Y.

SOURCE:

DESCRIPTION: We were within thirty feet of the President when he was addressing the multitude of people gathered at Grant's Tomb on April 27th, 1897, and were thus enabled to obtain a clear, life-size picture of the new Executive, with the great crowd waving their handkerchiefs and hats in the foreground. This is a remarkable view of a very historical occasion, showing a perfect reproduction of the President's gestures when delivering his speech. (F.Z. Maguire & Co., *Catalogue*, [March 1898], 19.)

SUBJECT: Speeches, addresses, etc. Presidents–United States. Ulysses S. Grant.

ARCHIVE:

CITATIONS: Maguire & Baucus, *Fall Catalogue*, 1897, 10; F.M. Prescott, *Catalogue of New Films*, 1899, 12; *Edison Films*, March 1900, 24.

NOTE: Taken on the 75th anniversary of Ulysses S. Grant's birth. Grant Day Series.

326 √General Porter's Oration

LENGTH: 50 ft.   © Thomas A. Edison, 8 May 1897.

PRODUCER: James White.

CAMERA: William Heise.

CAST: Horace Porter, William L. Strong, William McKinley.

PRODUCTION DATE: 27 April 1897.

LOCATION: Grant's Tomb, New York, N.Y.

SOURCE:

DESCRIPTION: Introducing the same foreground as in President McKinley's address, with an excellent picture of our new Ambassador of France, who was the President of the Grant Tomb Association, as he delivers his oration. Hon. Wm. L. Strong, Mayor of New York, can be seen sitting on General Porter's right, and President McKinley on his left, as also many other noted men. (F.Z. Maguire & Co., *Catalogue*, [March 1898], 19.)

SUBJECT: Speeches, addresses, etc. Presidents–United States. Ulysses S. Grant.

ARCHIVE:

CITATIONS: Maguire & Baucus, *Fall Catalogue*, 1897, 10.

NOTE: Grant Day Series. Gen. Horace Porter was the new ambassador to France.

327 √Buffalo Bill and Escort

LENGTH: 50 ft.   © Thomas A. Edison, 8 May 1897.

PRODUCER: James White.

CAMERA: William Heise.

CAST: William Frederick Cody.

PRODUCTION DATE: 27 April 1897.

LOCATION: Grant's Tomb, New York, N.Y.

SOURCE:

DESCRIPTION: An excellent picture of Hon. W.F. Cody, former chief of U.S. Army Scouts, mounted on a spirited chestnut stallion, riding at the head of a company of cavalry. (F.Z. Maguire & Co., *Catalogue*, [March 1898], 19.)

SUBJECT: Parades. Cavalry. Veterans–United States. Ulysses S. Grant.

ARCHIVE:

CITATIONS: "Marching of the Mighty Army," *New York Herald*, 27 April 1897, 7. Maguire & Baucus, *Fall Catalogue*, 1897, 10; F.M. Prescott, *Catalogue of New Films*, 1899, 12.

NOTE: Grant Day Series.

328 √**Sixth U.S. Cavalry / Sixth U.S. Cavalry, Fort Myer, Va. / Sixth U.S. Cavalry, Fort Meyer, Va. [sic]**

LENGTH: 50 and 150 ft.   © Thomas A. Edison, 8 May 1897.

PRODUCER: James White.

CAMERA: William Heise.

CAST:

PRODUCTION DATE: 27 April 1897.

LOCATION: Grant's Tomb, New York, N.Y.

SOURCE:

DESCRIPTION: This picture shows the entire regi-ment passing very close to our camera, mak-ing a splendid military appearance, each man finely mounted and every movement showing perfection of military discipline. Full of action, showing over 500 horses. (F.Z. Maguire & Co., *Catalogue*, [March 1898], 19.)

SUBJECT: Parades. Armies–United States. Cavalry. Ulysses S. Grant. Sixth U.S. Cavalry.

ARCHIVE:

CITATIONS: "The Sixth Cavalry," *Washington Evening Star,* 4 March 1897, 4; "Marching of the Mighty Army," *New York Herald*, 27 April 1897, 7. Maguire & Baucus, *Fall Catalogue*, 1897, 10 and 15; *Edison Films*, March 1900, 45.

NOTE: Edison's cameras filmed the Sixth U.S. Cavalry on numerous occasions in the 1890s. Grant Day Series.

329 √**7th and 71st Regiment, New York / Seventh and 71st Regiments of New York / New York's 7th and 71st Regiments**

LENGTH: 150 ft.   © Thomas A. Edison, 8 May 1897.

PRODUCER: James White.

CAMERA: William Heise.

CAST: Francis V. Greene.

PRODUCTION DATE: 27 April 1897.

LOCATION: Grant's Tomb, New York, N.Y.

SOURCE:

DESCRIPTION: The start of this film shows the famous 7th Regiment Band beginning to play. The 71st Regiment follows in columns thirty-two abreast, commanded by Col. F.V. Green[e], of New York. After they have passed, the 7th Regiment of New York comes into view and marches by, forming a very striking spectacle with their showy uniforms and equipments. Thus we were able to record a moving view of two of New York's crack regiments. (F.M. Prescott, *Catalogue of New Films*, 1899, 13.)

SUBJECT: Parades. Marching bands. Armies–United States. Ulysses S. Grant. Seventh Regiment. 71st Regiment.

ARCHIVE:

CITATIONS: "Marching of the Mighty Army," *New York Herald*, 27 April 1897, 7. Maguire & Baucus, *Fall Catalogue*, 1897, 10 and 15; F.Z. Maguire & Co., *Catalogue*, [March 1898], 19-20; *Edison Films*, March 1900, 24.

NOTE: Sold as a 50 or 150-foot film in 1900. Grant Day Series.

330 √**Old Guard, New York City / Old Guard of New York City**

LENGTH: 50 ft.   © Thomas A. Edison, 8 May 1897.

PRODUCER: James White.

CAMERA: William Heise.

CAST:

PRODUCTION DATE: 27 April 1897.

LOCATION: Grant's Tomb, New York, N.Y.

SOURCE:

DESCRIPTION: An excellent picture of this celebrated Company, as they march under the Triumphal Arch at the east corner of Grant monument. Their uniforms being white, the picture comes out sharp and clear, and they are thus seen to good advantage. (F.Z. Maguire & Co., *Catalogue*, [March 1898], 19.)

SUBJECT: Parades. Armies–United States. Ulysses S. Grant.

ARCHIVE:

CITATIONS: "Marching of the Mighty Army," *New York Herald*, 27 April 1897, 7. Maguire & Baucus, *Fall Catalogue*, 1897, 10.

NOTE: Last group in the second brigade, Col. Thomas E. Sloan commanding. Grant Day Series.

331 √**Battery B, Governor's Troop, Penna. / Battery B, Governor's Troop, State of Pennsylvania / State of Pennsylvania, Battery "B" Government Troop**

LENGTH: 50 ft.   © Thomas A. Edison, 8 May 1897.

PRODUCER: James White.

CAMERA: William Heise.

CAST:

PRODUCTION DATE: 27 April 1897.

LOCATION: Grant's Tomb, New York, N.Y.

SOURCE:

DESCRIPTION: An artillery scene, wonderfully clear and full of action, showing a company of artillery marching under the Triumphal Arch at the east corner of Grant's tomb, with many hundreds of the National Guard of Pennsylvania forming the background. A remarkably fine and interesting picture. (F.Z. Maguire & Co., *Catalogue*, [March 1898], 19.)

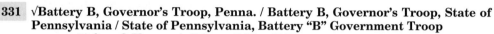

SUBJECT: Parades. Artillery. National Guard–Pennsylvania. Ulysses S. Grant.

ARCHIVE:

CITATIONS: "Marching of the Mighty Army," *New York Herald*, 27 April 1897, 7. Maguire & Baucus, *Fall Catalogue*, 1897, 10; F.M. Prescott, *Catalogue of New Films*, 1899, 12.

NOTE: Grant Day Series.

332 √**Governor Cook and Staff, Connecticut [sic] / Governor Cook's Escort, Hartford, Conn. [sic] / [Governor Cooke and Staff, Connecticut]**

LENGTH: 150 ft.   © Thomas A. Edison, 8 May 1897.

PRODUCER: James White.

CAMERA: William Heise.

CAST: Lorrin A. Cooke, Henry E. Hyde, Jr.

PRODUCTION DATE: 27 April 1897.

LOCATION: Grant's Tomb, New York, N.Y.

SOURCE:

DESCRIPTION: A fine, clear picture, showing the Governor of Connecticut and staff, followed by the Governor's Foot Guard, commanded by Major Henry E. Hyde, Jr., with the entire Connecticut National Guard in the background. A very clear and attractive picture. (F.Z. Maguire & Co., *Catalogue*, [March 1898], 20.)

SUBJECT: Parades. National Guard–Connecticut. Governors–United States. Ulysses S. Grant.

ARCHIVE:

CITATIONS: "Marching of the Mighty Army," *New York Herald*, 27 April 1897, 7. Maguire & Baucus, *Fall Catalogue*, 1897, 10.

NOTE: Grant Day Series.

---

333 √**National Lancers, Boston / National Lanciers of Boston**

LENGTH: 50 ft.   © Thomas A. Edison, 8 May 1897.

PRODUCER: James White.

CAMERA: William Heise.

CAST: O.A. Jones.

PRODUCTION DATE: 27 April 1897.

LOCATION: Grant's Tomb, New York, N.Y.

SOURCE:

DESCRIPTION: A fine, clear picture of this cele-brated troop, as they appear at the head of the National Guard of Massachusetts, com-manded by Captain O.A. Jones. They march by very close to the camera, and con-sequently show full life-size. The picture is full of action and martial spirit, the horses being very lively. (F.Z. Maguire & Co., *Catalogue*, [March 1898], 18.)

SUBJECT: Parades. National Guard–Massachusetts. Cavalry. Ulysses S. Grant.

ARCHIVE:

CITATIONS: "Marching of the Mighty Army," *New York Herald*, 27 April 1897, 7. Maguire & Baucus, *Fall Catalogue*, 1897, 10; *Edison Films*, March 1900, 24.

NOTE: Grant Day Series.

---

334 √**Amoskeag Veterans, New Hampshire / Amoskeag Veterans of New Hampshire**

LENGTH: 50 ft.   © Thomas A. Edison, 8 May 1897.

PRODUCER: James White.

CAMERA: William Heise.

CAST: Frank P. Kimball.

PRODUCTION DATE: 27 April 1897.

LOCATION: Grant's Tomb, New York, N.Y.

SOURCE:

DESCRIPTION: Commanded by Major Frank P. Kimball. A very clear and attractive picture of these celebrated veterans, as they march by the tomb. Their uniform is a perfect copy of the old Continental uniform of buff and blue, of Revolutionary times. (F.Z. Maguire & Co., *Catalogue*, [March 1898], 19.)

SUBJECT: Parades. Veterans–United States. Ulysses S. Grant.

ARCHIVE:

CITATIONS: "Marching of the Mighty Army," *New York Herald*, 27 April 1897, 7. Maguire & Baucus, *Fall Catalogue*, 1897, 10.

NOTE: Grant Day Series.

---

335 √**Governor of Ohio and Staff**

LENGTH: 50 ft.   © Thomas A. Edison, 8 May 1897.

PRODUCER: James White.

CAMERA: William Heise.

CAST: A.S. Bushnell, H.A. Axline.

PRODUCTION DATE: 27 April 1897.

LOCATION: Grant's Tomb, New York, N.Y.

SOURCE:

DESCRIPTION: Showing Governor Bushnell, of Ohio, followed by Gen. H.A. Axline and staff, mounted on spirited horses, with a long line of Cavalry Guards of Ohio forming the background. Very clear, sharp picture. (F.Z. Maguire & Co., *Catalogue*, [March 1898], 19.)

SUBJECT: Parades. National Guard–Ohio. Cavalry. Governors–United States. Ulysses S. Grant.

ARCHIVE:

CITATIONS: "Marching of the Mighty Army," *New York Herald*, 27 April 1897, 7. Maguire & Baucus, *Fall Catalogue*, 1897, 10.

NOTE: Grant Day Series.

---

336 √**Corcoran Cadets, Washington / Corcoran Cadets, Washington, D.C.**
LENGTH: 50 ft.   © Thomas A. Edison, 8 May 1897.
PRODUCER: James White.
CAMERA: William Heise.
CAST:

PRODUCTION DATE: 27 April 1897.
LOCATION: Grant's Tomb, New York, N.Y.
SOURCE:

DESCRIPTION: This body of men presents a fine military appearance as they pass under the Triumphal Arch at Grant's tomb, and march by our camera, where we show them to good advantage. (F.Z. Maguire & Co., *Catalogue*, [March 1898], 18.)

SUBJECT: Parades. Armies–United States. Military cadets. Ulysses S. Grant.

ARCHIVE:

CITATIONS: "Marching of the Mighty Army," *New York Herald*, 27 April 1897, 7. Maguire & Baucus, *Fall Catalogue*, 1897, 10.

NOTE: Grant Day Series.

---

337 √**Grant Veterans—G.A.R. / Grant Post, G.A.R.**
LENGTH: 50 ft.   © Thomas A. Edison, 8 May 1897.
PRODUCER: James White.
CAMERA: William Heise.
CAST:

PRODUCTION DATE: 27 April 1897.
LOCATION: Grant's Tomb, New York, N.Y.
SOURCE:

DESCRIPTION: Showing U.S. Grant Post No. 237, Department of New York. An excellent picture of this famous company of veterans, as they pass the tomb of their former leader, making a very impressive scene, and one which always proves interesting to G.A.R. posts throughout the country. (F.Z. Maguire & Co., *Catalogue*, [March 1898], 19.)

SUBJECT: Parades. Veterans–United States. Ulysses S. Grant.

ARCHIVE:

CITATIONS: "Marching of the Mighty Army," *New York Herald*, 27 April 1897, 7. Maguire & Baucus, *Fall Catalogue*, 1897, 10; F.M. Prescott, *Catalogue of New Films*, 1899, 12.

NOTE: Grant Day Series.

WHERE ALL PICTURES FAIL

Of course, no picture, or series of pictures, can give more than a meagre conception of the spectacle as it will be seen by the thousands of people along the line of parade. All the brilliance and color, all the spirit and rhythmic cadence of the march–no picture, not even the marvellous work of the kinetoscope, can reproduce these. (*New York World*, 25 April 1897, 33.)

SEATS $1 AND UPWARD
MONUMENT CIRCLE STAND
RIVERSIDE DRIVE, NEAR 122D ST.,

opposite Monument adjoining President McKinley's reviewing stand. Finest view both Land and Naval Parade. Perfect sanitary and toilet accommodations. Excellent Restaurant and Cafe. Seats and boxes 1201 Broadway, near 29th st. Open all day Sunday and Monday 8 A.M. to 11 P.M. Also at stand.

Grant Parade.

Choice $2, $3, $4, and $5 Seats and Boxes on highest elevation on Riverside Drive, southeast corner 105th st. Stand accepted by Department; near 104th st. L station. Ladies' retiring room, with attendant. Tickets on sale at Radner's Hotel, 42d st and Lexington ave. or telephone 463 Harlem, F.S. Baker. 228 West 116th Street or Tyson's, Ruilman's, Bretano's and at stand. (*New York World*, 25 April 1897, 15.)

TRIBUTE OF MILLIONS TO THE NATION'S HERO.
Dedication of the People's Monument to the Memory of Gen. Grant.
The Most Magnificent Pageant Ever Seen in This Country.
AN ICY NORTHWEST GALE COULD NOT SPOIL IT.
Soldiers from Far and Near, the Battle-Ships of Many Nations, the Men
Who Fought Grant and Who Fought Under Him, United to Do Him Honor.
THE PRESIDENT ADDRESSED A GIGANTIC GATHERING.

It should have been the nation's first great fete day, for the tribute to Gen. Grant was not a set and formal thing. It was an outpouring of the pride and patriotism of a free people glorying in the memory of a man who preserved the nation's heritage.

A fierce and vicious wind made it a day of suffering. It so marred the occasion that no one can tell what it might have been. Clouds obscured the sun. Yet it was the greatest pageant that the country has ever known. For the first time in its history the people dedicated a noble and splendid mausoleum which they themselves had builded.

No acknowledgement that the living could pay was lacking. President McKinley looked upon a million of his fellow-citizens. Perhaps twice that number saw the parade. Fifty-four thousand men marched through the gale in the gay trappings of war that may come and the war that has passed. They marched through a multitude that was slashed and shrivelled by the wind.

Men were there who fought with Grant. Men were there who fought against him. Gathered about the tomb were the diplomats of the foreign nations, the executives and lawmakers of the United States; men from the plains, Indian and white. There was a great chorus, whose great volume of song was carried away from the tomb. There were bands a-plenty, and speechmaking which the wind conquered.

Not 300 people heard the great address made by President McKinley, Gen Horace Porter cut his speech almost in half. Thousands of people were literally driven from the stand in front of the tomb by the cold. The stands erected along the line of march, which were built to hold 360,000 people, were not more than half filled, because people could not stand the exposure.

The arrangements were admirable. The vast crowd was handled with marvellous success and consideration. The parade moved promptly and arrived at the tomb ahead of time. There were many small accidents and two that will likely prove fatal. (*New York World*, 28 April 1897, 1.)

GRANT'S TOMB NOW–OUR SACRED TRUST
The Hero's Last Resting Place Transferred to the City by the Men Who Built it,
in the Presence of Representatives of the Nations of the Earth.
FIFTY-THREE THOUSAND IN LINE: 561,135 VISITORS.

The tomb of General Ulysses S. Grant yesterday became the sacred charge of the city of New York. Father Knickerbocker took his post as sentinel on the windiest knoll of windy Riverside a few minutes after noon, when the beautiful and massive memorial pile was formally turned over to the municipality by General Horace Porter, president of the Grant Monument Association, and the trust on behalf of Greater New York was accepted by Mayor Strong.

This transfer was made the occasion for a patriotic demonstration unequalled in the history of the country, unapproached in the history of the world. It was divided into three great spectacles–the impressive ceremonial at the tomb, the parade of the army, the National Guard and civic bodies, and the review of the navy and the merchant marine on the Hudson. It was more than national: it was international and worldwide–a tribute paid to a great modern soldier and statesman nearly twelve years after his death.

SURRENDER OF THE MEMORIAL.

Many thousand persons gathered at the tomb to witness the ceremonies and the review. The day was clear, but a strong wind blew across the Hudson, whirling the sand and dust and making participation in the affair a positive hardship. Mayor Strong presided at the tomb. The President and Vice President of the United States, the members of the Cabinet, the Speaker of the House of Representatives, former President Cleveland, the representatives at Washington of all the foreign countries, the family of General Grant and distinguished Union and Confederate generals were conspicuous on the main stand. There was music by a carefully selected chorus led by Frank Damroach, and Bishop J.P. Newman, one of Grant's closest friends, offered a prayer. The address of President McKinley was in reality an oration, and his eloquent periods struck responsive chords in the hearts of the multitude. General Porter's oration concluded with the surrender of the memorial, which his energy had completed, to the city, and Mayor Strong's acceptance was full of dignity.

PAGEANT ON LAND.

Then came the military and civic parade, led by General Grenville M. Dodge, the Chief Marshal. By the time the head of the line went swinging up the Riverside Drive the fury of the wind had doubled, and the marchers seemed like men hurrying through the smoke of battle. Men seldom marched under greater disadvantages in time of war.

By actual count made for the HERALD 53,516 men passed the reviewing stand. Many of the old veterans, on account of the long wait and the discomforts of the day, had to fall out of line. The display of the United States regulars was the finest seen in this country for many years. The entire National Guard of this State turned out 18,000 strong. Pennsylvania, New Jersey, Connecticut, Massachusetts, Maryland, New Hampshire, Virginia, Rhode Island, Vermont, Ohio, Illinois, and the District of Columbia were finely represented. Many of the Governors rode ahead of their troops. New York's did not.

THE NAVAL REVIEW.

While the veteran organizations were still flowing past, the President left the reviewing stand to Vice President Hobart and Mayor Strong and boarded the Dolphin for the naval review. The North Atlantic squadron, under Rear Admiral Bunce, the revenue marine and the foreign men-of-war were anchored in double column in the river in front of Riverside. The Dolphin ran up the President's flag, and the whole fleet saluted.

Then, the President's boat steamed down the lines, while the war ships saluted once again and the merchant marine blew their whistles; and thus the day closed with a stirring maritime spectacle just as the sun sank below the Palisades.

At night there was a reception to the President at the Union League and a dinner to Mrs. McKinley at the Windsor. The HERALD had an accurate count kept of all the visitors in the city by the various ferries and railroad lines. This shows that there were 561,135 visitors here attracted by "Grant Day." (*New York Herald*, 28 April, 1897, 3.)

The practice of showing a film within a play had been introduced in the fall of 1896, when the eidoloscope film of a bullfight was shown during a stage version of Carmen. *The short, one-shot film entitled* The Little Reb *was likewise intended to be shown within the play* Winchester. *Although the play was written by the spring of 1897, it was not produced for another four years, having its debut on 22 April 1901 at the American Theatre in New York. By that time, the idea of showing a filmed insert was no longer novel and the motion picture was replaced by an actual rendering of the dramatic high point using a real horse and Mr. Neil Burgess's racing machine.*

338 √**The Little Reb**

LENGTH: 50 ft.   © Margaret M. Fish, 8 May 1897.

PRODUCER: James White.

CAMERA: William Heise.

CAST: Margaret May (stage name for Margaret M. Fish?).

PRODUCTION DATE: Late April to early May 1897.

LOCATION:

SOURCE: *Winchester* (play).

DESCRIPTION: The scene opens with a girl on horseback riding at a break-neck speed. The girl has a pardon for her lover, who is about to be shot and she is followed by an enemy of her lover, who tries to take the pardon away from her, when she shoots him and he falls from his horse. Taken from Guy Fish's drama "Winchester." (*New Orleans Picayune*, 29 August 1897, 2.)

A scene taken from the war play "Winchester," about to be placed upon the stage, in which the heroine is carrying a pardon to her lover, who is condemned to be shot. As she comes into view, mounted on a fleet horse, a soldier suddenly appears at a bend in the road and starts in pursuit of the girl. He overtakes her after they have galloped about half a mile, and as he endeavors to lift her from her horse she thrusts a revolver in his face and fires, when he falls heavily to the ground from his running horse, and the heroine, accompanied by the riderless horse of the spy, passes out of the foreground of the picture. Both life-size. Very realistic, and sure to become very popular. (Maguire & Baucus, *Catalogue*, [March 1898], 17.)

SUBJECT: Drama. United States–History–Civil War. Guy Fish. Violence.

ARCHIVE:

CITATIONS: Maguire & Baucus, *Fall Catalogue*, 1897, 10; *Edison Films*, March 1900, 45.

NOTE: Margaret M. Fish was almost certainly the married name for the actress Margaret May, who played the heroine when the drama finally premiered.

The Spanish war has yielded little in the way of dramatic material. Dramatists who want to write successful war plays still hark back to the civil war. A new play of this period will be produced at the American Theatre tomorrow night. It is called "Winchester," has been written by Mr. Edwin McWade, and in the preliminary announcements much is made of the circumstances that it will introduce a new actress and a new horse. In fact, the horse, named Mazeppa, is to be presented in what is said to be a "sensational" and "thrilling" episode for which Mr. Neil Burgess' racing machine, similar to those used in "The Country Fair" and in "Ben-Hur," has been secured.

The heroine of "Winchester"–scene laid in the Shenendoah Valley, 1863–is Miss Virginia Randolph, a Southern girl who falls in love with a Federal officer. Learning telegraphy from him, she keeps the Southern army informed of the plans of the Northern commander. When Major Kearney, the officer she loves, is in consequence suspected of being a spy, is court martialled and sentenced to death, she secures a reprieve, mounts her horse, shoots the villain and, jumping a fence on horseback, lands right in front of the shooting party in time to save Major Kearney from death. The actress who is to do all this, as Virginia Randolph, is Miss Margaret May, who comes from the West. She is known as a fine horsewoman, has won prizes at the horse shows and has trained Mazeppa herself. So what more can be asked to make Winchester quite an event on the West Side this week. (*New York Herald*, 21 April 1901, 7F.)

NEW WAR PLAY AT THE AMERICAN.
"Winchester" Has Many Stirring Scenes That Pleased the Audience Last Night.
HEROINE ON HORSEBACK.

AMERICAN THEATRE–WINCHESTER, a play in five acts, by Mr. Edward McWade.

General Thorton	Logan Paul
Colonel Dayton	Menifee Johnstone
Major Frank Kearney	Ralph Stuart
Phillip Allen	Harde Kirkland
Colonel Tom Eustis	Hermann Sheldon
Henry Clay Randolph	Thomas J. Keogh
Benny Clancy	Horace Vintoh
Uncle Rasmus	Frank Linden
Julius	Miss Anna Buckley
Baker	Emilé Cohlas
Sentry	Frank Peele
Officer of firing squad	A.E. Dexter
Virginia Randolph	Miss Margaret May
Madge Childress	Miss Georgia Welles
Mrs. Randolph	Miss Julia Blanc

"Winchester," a new war play by Mr. Robert McWade, was produced for the first time at the American Theatre last night. Although it threshes over the old civil war situation so dear to the dramatist, it pleased the large audience and at times aroused enthusiasm.

In plays of this sort it is just as essential to have a Northern officer fall in love with the loyal Southern girl as in comic opera it is imperative to start in with an innkeeper dusting the table. The chief trouble–and fortunately one that can be remedied–is that the five acts are far too talky. The hyper-critical might take exception to an officer–he was the villain–who rushes in from the battlefield with beautifully creased trousers and to a spy who is clean shaven in the first act but two hours later, in the second act, has grown a black mustache.

The cast was a competent one. Miss Margaret May did well as the heroine; Miss Georgia Welles was a charming

Madge Childress; Mr. Ralph Stuart was a manly hero, and Mr. Johnstone a highly polished villain, who earned the immediate dislike of the gallery gods. "Winchester," with the stirring scene at the end where the heroine rides in on horseback, just in time to save her lover, is likely to be heard from again next season. (*New York Herald*, 23 April 1901, 11.)

Annabelle Whitford gave her last performance before Edison's rapid firing kinetograph in late April or early May 1897.

339 *****Serpentine Dance—Annabelle / Serpentine Dance / [Annabelle Serpentine Dance, no. 4]**

LENGTH: 50 ft.   © Thomas A. Edison, 8 May 1897.

PRODUCER: James White.

CAMERA: William Heise.

CAST: Annabelle Whitford.

PRODUCTION DATE: Late April to early May 1897.

LOCATION: Black Maria, West Orange, N.J.

SOURCE: *Annabelle Serpentine Dance* (Edison film no. 49, summer 1894)

DESCRIPTION: We are pleased to announce that we have recently made new negatives of the famous dancer, Annabelle, in her "Sun" and "Serpentine" dances. (F.Z. Maguire & Co., *Catalogue*, [March 1898], 27.)

SUBJECT: Vaudeville–performances. Dancing.

ARCHIVE: CaOOANF.

CITATIONS: Maguire & Baucus, *Fall Catalogue*, 1897, 11; *Edison Films*, March 1900, 28.

NOTE: The film at the Canadian National Film Archives appears to be this version of the film.

340 *****Sun Dance—Annabelle / Sun Dance / [Annabelle Sun Dance, no. 4]**

LENGTH: 50 ft.   © Thomas A. Edison, 8 May 1897.

PRODUCER: James White.

CAMERA: William Heise.

CAST: Annabelle Whitford.

PRODUCTION DATE: Late April to early May 1897.

LOCATION: Black Maria, West Orange, N.J.

SOURCE: *Annabelle Sun Dance* (Edison film no. 50, summer 1894).

DESCRIPTION: We are pleased to announce that we have recently made new negatives of the famous dancer, Annabelle, in her "Sun" and "Serpentine" dances. (F.Z. Maguire & Co., *Catalogue*, [March 1898], 27.)

SUBJECT: Vaudeville–performances. Dancing.

ARCHIVE: DLC.

CITATIONS: Maguire & Baucus, *Fall Catalogue*, 1897, 11; *Edison Films*, March 1900, 28.

NOTE: Ray Phillips kindly brought this film, which matches the frames submitted for copyright, to my attention.

341 *****Husking Bee**

LENGTH: 50 ft.   © Thomas A. Edison, 24 May 1897.

PRODUCER: James White.

CAMERA: William Heise.

CAST:

PRODUCTION DATE: May 1897.

LOCATION:

SOURCE:

DESCRIPTION: Shows a party of young people in front of a barn door searching for the red ear, which is discovered, and the penalty exacted from one of the group who resists payment of the forfeit, creating thereby confusion and merriment. The group is animated, and is made up of real farmer boys and girls. During the progress of husking the farmer arrives, wheeling his little daughter to the sport on a barrow. (F.Z. Maguire & Co., *Catalogue,* [March 1898], 15.)

SUBJECT: Farms. Courtship. Kissing. Corn-husking.

ARCHIVE: NR-GE, CLAc.

CITATIONS: Maguire & Baucus, *Fall Catalogue,* 1897, 9; *Edison Films,* March 1900, 35.

NOTE:

---

342 √**Making Soap Bubbles / Soap Bubbles**

LENGTH: 50 ft. © Thomas A. Edison, 24 May 1897.

PRODUCER: James White.

CAMERA: William Heise.

CAST:

PRODUCTION DATE: May 1897.

LOCATION:

SOURCE:

DESCRIPTION: A group of seven children gathered about a tub of soap suds, pushing and jostling for preferences. This is an exterior scene, full of animation and free from artificiality. The figures are clearly defined, well in the foreground and the group well composed. The familiar scenes of children blowing soap bubbles from clay pipes is here shown under natural conditions. (F.Z. Maguire & Co., *Catalogue,* [March 1898], 16.)

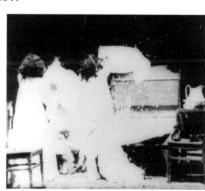

SUBJECT: Children. Soap bubbles.

ARCHIVE:

CITATIONS: Maguire & Baucus, *Fall Catalogue,* 1897, 10.

NOTE:

---

343 *****Pillow Fight**

LENGTH: 50 ft. © Thomas A. Edison, 24 May 1897.

PRODUCER: James White.

CAMERA: William Heise.

CAST:

PRODUCTION DATE: May 1897.

LOCATION: Black Maria, West Orange, N.J.

SOURCE: *A Pillow Fight* (Biograph film no. 158, March 1897).

DESCRIPTION: A comic subject, clear, bright, and characteristic, shows four girls in their night dresses, engaged in an animated pillow fight. During the action the pillows become torn and the feathers fly over their heads and about the room in great numbers, producing with the white dresses and black background, a novel effect. Sharp, full of action, and popular in character. (F.Z. Maguire & Co., *Catalogue,* [March 1898], 15.)

SUBJECT: Girls. Pillows. Beds.

ARCHIVE: NR-GE, DNA, CLAc.

CITATIONS: Maguire & Baucus, *Fall Catalogue*, 1897, 10; *Edison Films*, March 1900, 35; *Edison Films*, July 1901, 69.

NOTE: Listed as a 45-foot film in 1901. The Lumières also made a pillow fight that may have preceded the Edison subject in terms of production date.

---

344 *** Mr. Edison at Work in His Chemical Laboratory**

LENGTH: 50 ft.   © Thomas A. Edison, 24 May 1897.

PRODUCER: James White.

CAMERA: William Heise.

CAST: Thomas A. Edison.

PRODUCTION DATE: May 1897.

LOCATION: Black Maria, West Orange, N.J.

SOURCE: Photograph of Edison at work in his chemical laboratory.

DESCRIPTION: This film is remarkable in several respects. In the first place it is full life size. Secondly, it is the only accurate recent portrait of the great inventor. The scene is an actual one, showing Mr. Edison, in working dress, engaged in an interesting chemical experiment in his great laboratory. There is sufficient movement to lead the spectator through the several processes of mixing, pouring, testing, etc., as if he were side by side with the principal. The lights and shadows are vivid, and the apparatus and other accessories complete a startling picture that will appeal to every beholder. (F.Z. Maguire & Co., *Catalogue*, [March 1898], 15.)

SUBJECT: Inventors. Publicity. Chemical laboratories.

ARCHIVE: NNMoMA, DNA, CLAc, NR-GE.

CITATIONS: Maguire & Baucus, *Fall Catalogue*, 1897, 10; *Edison Films*, March 1900, 38.

NOTE:

---

345 √**Boating on the Lake**

LENGTH: 50 ft.   © Thomas A. Edison, 5 June 1897.

PRODUCER: James White.

CAMERA: William Heise.

CAST:

PRODUCTION DATE: May 1897.

LOCATION:

SOURCE:

DESCRIPTION: Depicts a boating scene on an inland lake at a popular summer resort. Two boat loads of pleasure seekers start from the wharf and come to the front of the picture. One of the oarsmen, losing his oar, jumps headlong into the water, while his boat and its female occupants float out of reach. The figures are large and well defined, and the effect of the sunlight on the rippling water adds brightness to the scene. (F.Z. Maguire & Co., *Catalogue*, [March 1898], 16.)

SUBJECT: Boats and boating. Lakes. Swimming. Accidents. Piers.

ARCHIVE:

CITATIONS: Maguire & Baucus, *Fall Catalogue*, 1897, 10; *Edison Films*, March 1900, 38.

NOTE:

---

346 *** Chicken Thieves**

LENGTH: 50 ft.   © Thomas A. Edison, 5 June 1897.

PRODUCER: James White.

CAMERA: William Heise.

CAST:

PRODUCTION DATE: May 1897.

LOCATION:

SOURCE:

DESCRIPTION: A capital picture, depicting an occupation commonly attributed to and sometimes proven against the colored race. The hen house occupies the entire left foreground of the picture, running back to the nearby road. The main foreground is filled with tall grass, swept by the wind, the naturalness of which effect is remarkable. A darky thief appears around the corner, car-

rying a tattered sack. He suspiciously approaches the window from which two fowls are handed to him by a black confederate, who himself suddenly appears at the window, falling out head first, but clinging tenaciously to a fluttering white bird. Both darkies start to run, when the farmer and his hand appear in the foreground, one with a scythe and the other with a gun. Just as the marauders disappear around the corner, the farmer, back to, but still shown at life size in the picture, aims and fires twice. The smoke effect from the gun at this close range is startling and beautiful, and the entire picture is one of the best composed and most ingenious we have made. (F.Z. Maguire & Co., *Catalogue*, [March 1898], 15-16.)

SUBJECT: Afro-Americans. Farms. Chickens. Criminals. Violence. Vigilantes.

ARCHIVE: NR-GE, CaOOANF, CLAc.

CITATIONS: Maguire & Baucus, *Fall Catalogue*, 1897, 10; *Edison Films*, March 1900, 43.

NOTE:

847 √**Children's Toilet**

LENGTH: 50 ft.   © Thomas A. Edison, 5 June 1897.

PRODUCER: James White.

CAMERA: William Heise.

CAST:

PRODUCTION DATE: May 1897.

LOCATION: Black Maria, West Orange, N.J.

SOURCE:

DESCRIPTION: Three children at the wash bowl. The picture opens with one of the little ones taking the others out of bed, followed by the washing, in which one splashes water over the other. The picture is interesting, and its domestic color pleasing. (F.Z. Maguire & Co., *Catalogue*, [March 1898], 17.)

SUBJECT: Children. Hygiene. Baths. Family. Beds.

ARCHIVE:

CITATIONS: Maguire & Baucus, *Fall Catalogue*, 1897, 10.

NOTE:

In July 1897, the Edison Manufacturing Company began to copyright its motion pictures (still in the name of its owner and president Thomas A. Edison) by submitting complete paper prints of each subject (rather than a few frames on nitrate film). These have subsequently been transferred back onto film. As a result, a large percentage of Edison motion picture subjects survive for the remaining period covered by this filmography.

The first motion pictures submitted as paper prints were taken on a tour subsidized if not sponsored by the Erie Railroad. The Edison crew traveled to the Catskill Mountains, Buffalo, Cleveland and finally Chicago. Such filmmaking expeditions were becoming common.

848 *****Waterfall in the Catskills**

LENGTH: 50 ft.   © Thomas A. Edison, 31 July 1897.

PRODUCER: James White.

CAMERA: [William Heise.]
CAST:
PRODUCTION DATE: June 1897.
LOCATION: Haines' Falls, N.Y.
SOURCE:

DESCRIPTION: Haines Falls is a picturesque and almost inaccessible mountain cataract in the Catskills. This view of it shows the water effects against a dark background. The falls have a drop of 160 feet, only a part of which is shown. The rugged surroundings of the falls are impressive. (F.Z. Maguire & Co., *Catalogue*, [March 1898], 44.)

SUBJECT: Waterfalls. Catskill Mountains (N.Y.). Erie Railroad.

ARCHIVE: DLC-pp.

CITATIONS: *Catskill Mountains* (Roundout, N.Y.: Passenger Department, Ulster & Delaware R.R., 1892), 63-64. *The Phonoscope*, August-September 1897, 15; Maguire & Baucus, *Fall Catalogue*, 1897, 9; *Edison Films*, March 1900, 47; *Edison Films*, July 1901, 94.

NOTE: It is possible, if unlikely, that James White was working with cameraman Frederick W. Blechynden on this filming expedition.

349 ***Falls of Minnehaha**

LENGTH: 50 ft.   © Thomas A. Edison, 31 July 1897.

PRODUCER: James White.

CAMERA: [William Heise.]

CAST:

PRODUCTION DATE: June 1897.

LOCATION: Haines' Falls, N.Y.

SOURCE:

DESCRIPTION: A capital picture of the universally known waterfall celebrated in Longfellow's "Hiawatha." The picture was taken on a clear day, and is a good view of the "Laughing Waters." (F.Z. Maguire & Co., *Catalogue*, [March 1898], 45.)

SUBJECT: Waterfalls. Catskill Mountains (N.Y.). Erie Railroad.

ARCHIVE: DLC-pp.

CITATIONS: *Catskill Mountains* (Roundout, N.Y.: Passenger Department, Ulster & Delaware R.R., 1892), 63-64. Maguire & Baucus, *Fall Catalogue*, 1897, 9; *Edison Films*, March 1900, 47; *Edison Films*, July 1901, 95.

NOTE: The "Falls of Minnehaha" are mythical and do not correspond to Haines' Falls or any others.

HAINES' FALLS HOUSE.

This very popular resort has been enlarged, and has one hundred and sixty feet of piazza fronting the Kaaterskill Grove, and the splendid view through it. Over the plains and the Hudson may be seen the Berkshires of Massachusetts and the Mount Riga in Connecticut.

Mr. C.W. Haines, the proprietor, has a Western Union Telegraph Office, with direct wire to New York, for the convenience of his guests. Parties visiting the falls make a payment of twenty-five cents, once for the whole season. At the entrance of the grove take the shady path leading to the right and to the top of the falls. Looking from the projecting rocks the scene is wild and grand, the water leaps and dashes through the gorge 475 feet in less than one-fourth of a mile.

Half-way down the stairs is Crystal Spring, an appropriate name on account of the purity and coolness of the water. From the foot of the stairway a fine view of the falls is had, even when the ordinary stream is running, but while there, a large body of water is allowed to plunge over the rocks above, and the scene then is wild and exciting. The dashing waters encircle the many irregular bowlders in the stream, and rush wildly to the cascades below.

THE FIVE CASCADES.

Walk down the stream a few yards, and cross it at the top of the first cascade where a steep but safe set of stairs leads to its base.

Cross the stream and descend the second cascade, following the distinct path on below the fifth cascade to Shelving Rock, overhanging the Naidad's Bath.

The view here is grand beyond description. Looking up the gorge are the five cascades, from 30 to 90 feet each in height, and you see the top of Spray Falls above them 400 feet from your position.

A visitor, having spent five years in Europe and California, declares this view from Shelving Rock to be the most beautiful scene of the kind he has ever witnessed.

This charming spot was visited years ago by Cole, Durand, Kensett, Cassilear, and others, when ropes and ladders had to be used in descending and ascending the ledges at the cascades.

The paths are now good, and none should fail to visit this favorite resort of the artists. (*Van Loan's Catskill Mountain Guide with Bird's-Eye View, Maps and Choice Illustrations*, 1890, 22-24.)

350 ***Buffalo Stockyards / Buffalo Stock Yards**

LENGTH: 150 ft.   © Thomas A. Edison, 31 July 1897.

PRODUCER: James White.

CAMERA: [William Heise.]

CAST:

PRODUCTION DATE: Early June 1897.

LOCATION: Buffalo, N.Y.

SOURCE: *Buffalo Horse Market* (Edison film no. 272, December 1896).

DESCRIPTION: An interesting subject full of moving horses, ponies, mules, etc., taken at the Buffalo yards of the Erie Railroad. A long line of horses being led, driven and ridden in the yards where they are sold and distributed. Has much animation and freedom of action, and the figures are large. Equal to or better than our successful "Buffalo Horse Market" film. (*The Phonoscope*, October 1897, 13.)

SUBJECT: Markets. Horses. Stockyards. Erie Railroad.

ARCHIVE: DLC-pp.

CITATIONS: Maguire & Baucus, *Fall Catalogue*, 1897, 9; F.Z. Maguire & Co., *Catalogue*, [March 1898], 44; *Edison Films*, March 1900, 43; *Edison Films*, July 1901, 50.

NOTE: Listed as part of the Erie Railroad Series.

351 ***Buffalo Police on Parade**

LENGTH: 50 ft.   © Thomas A. Edison, 31 July 1897.

PRODUCER: James White.

CAMERA: [William Heise.]

CAST:

PRODUCTION DATE: 10 June 1897.

LOCATION: Buffalo, N.Y.

SOURCE:

DESCRIPTION: A street scene showing parade of the entire Buffalo Police Department, sixteen men abreast, preceded by a military band. The marching is excellent and precise, and this is as good an example of a marching subject as we have ever taken. The clear background presents a long view down the crowded street. (F.Z. Maguire & Co., *Catalogue*, [March 1898], 45.)

SUBJECT: Police. Parades. Marching bands. Erie Railroad.

ARCHIVE: DLC-pp, CaOOANF.

CITATIONS: Maguire & Baucus, *Fall Catalogue*, 1897, 9; *The Phonoscope*, November 1897, 13.

NOTE:

THOUSANDS SAW POLICE PARADE.
Highly Creditable Turnout of Buffalo Bluecoats.
REVIEW AT THE FRONT.
Mayor Jewett and Other City Officials Greatly Pleased with the Men.
DRILLED LIKE VETERANS.
Evolutions of the Mounted Squad Attracted Especial Attention–Presentation of Badges.

It would be a hard thing to tell just how many people witnessed the annual parade of the local Police Department yesterday, but a statistican would say that everybody in the city who was able to get out was somewhere along the line of march, or at the Front for the drill and review.

And they didn't miss anything, for the new uniforms of the men were as neat and natty as possible, the batons shone, the horses were well groomed and well trained and the music was so catchy that the men could not have marched poorly had they tried.

Gus Schneider twirled the baton in front of the band. That alone was worth a journey to the front.

Review at the Front.

It was shortly after 1:30 o'clock that the officers and spectators began to assemble at the Front. Men and women on foot, on wheels and in carriages came from all directions. To the east of the parade ground a spacious review-ing stand had been constructed and from this splendid vantage point Mayor Jewett, Commissioners Curtiss and Rupp and Detective Heidelburg of New York, the city officials and many invited guests watched the evolutions of the 500 bluecoats.... (*Buffalo Courier-Record*, 11 June 1897, 7.)

352 ***Buffalo Fire Department in Action**
LENGTH: 50 ft.   © Thomas A. Edison, 31 July 1897.
PRODUCER: James White.
CAMERA: [William Heise.]
CAST:
PRODUCTION DATE: Early June 1897.
LOCATION: Buffalo, N.Y.
SOURCE:

DESCRIPTION: Another of those stirring fire scenes which have proved so popular. There are ten pieces of apparatus in the picture. Every piece fully manned is under full headway, and is shown almost head-on to the beholder. Several of the engines and wagons are drawn by three horses abreast. Firemen appear putting on their coats, etc., while the engines and trucks rush by. Many of the engine horses in the picture are white and the speed at which they break into the scene and pass full size under the very eye of the observer is star-tling. The engines are fired up and there are dust, steam and smoke effects all through the film. This picture is very full and complete. (F.Z. Maguire & Co., *Catalogue*, [March 1898], 44.)
SUBJECT: Fire fighters. Fire runs. Erie Railroad.
ARCHIVE: DLC-pp.
CITATIONS: Maguire & Baucus, *Fall Catalogue*, 1897, 9.
NOTE:

353 ***Giant Coal Dumper**
LENGTH: 50 ft.   © Thomas A. Edison, 31 July 1897.
PRODUCER: James White.
CAMERA: [William Heise.]
CAST:
PRODUCTION DATE: June 1897.
LOCATION: Cleveland, Ohio.
SOURCE: June 1897.
DESCRIPTION: This picture illustrates vividly one of the modern labor saving means of landing enormous loads without effort. It shows how a full car load of coal is loaded into a vessel every thirty seconds, at the great Erie Railroad Docks, Cleveland, Ohio. The view discloses first the backing of the loaded train into an enormous iron cylinder. One of the cars is detached, and the huge cylinder with its contents is

rolled mechanically up an inclined track. Thus, turning completely over, it discharges the contents instantly, and the giant dumping cylinder comes back into place for the next car, which pushes out the empty one on an extension of the track. The Erie Railroad claims this to be the only device of the kind in existence, and it is being constantly visited by engineers from all parts of the United States. The rising coal dust in clearly seen, and adds to the naturalness of the view. (F.Z Maguire & Co., *Catalogue,* [March 1898], 41-42.)

SUBJECT: Railroads–Fuel. Railroads, industrial. Coal. Labor productivity. Erie Railroad.

ARCHIVE: DLC-pp.

CITATIONS: Maguire & Baucus, *Fall Catalogue,* 1897, 9; *Edison Films,* March 1900, 23.

NOTE:

354 ***Corner Madison and State Streets, Chicago**

LENGTH: 50 ft.   © Thomas A. Edison, 31 July 1897.

PRODUCER: James White.

CAMERA: [William Heise.]

CAST:

PRODUCTION DATE: June-July 1897.

LOCATION: Chicago, Ill.

SOURCE:

DESCRIPTION: An animated picture of the busiest corner in Chicago. Crowded with pedestrians and the movement of street traffic. A cable car makes the turn into State Street in the midst of the crowd. Shows hundreds of shoppers crossing Madison Street, with a correct view of State Street looking north toward the Masonic Temple. This picture gives a good idea of the care displayed in handling the street traffic of a busy corner in a big city. (F.Z. Maguire & Co., *Catalogue,* [March 1898], 44.)

SUBJECT: City and town life–Chicago. Urban transportation. Erie Railroad.

ARCHIVE: DLC-pp.

CITATIONS: Maguire & Baucus, *Fall Catalogue,* 1897, 9; *Edison Films,* March 1900, 23.

NOTE: Taken on a Sunday, probably either June 13th or 20th. Placards passing through the scene promote Electric Park.

ELECTRIC PARK–Chicago's Playground
OPEN FROM 10 A.M. to 12 P.M.
Free Day for Chicago's Wage Earners
Bring a line from your employers and you will be admitted FREE today.
Balloon ascensions. High diving. Dancing in Mammoth Music Temple.
Elston, Clybourn, Belmont ave cars to entrance.
(Advertisement, *Chicago Inter-Ocean,* 20 June 1897, 30.)

355 ***Armour's Electric Trolley**

LENGTH: 50 ft.   © Thomas A. Edison, 31 July 1897.

PRODUCER: James White.

CAMERA: [William Heise.]

CAST:

PRODUCTION DATE: June-July 1897.

LOCATION: Chicago, Ill.

SOURCE:

DESCRIPTION: Shows the private electric railway of Messers Armour & Co. in their great Chicago yards. The motor is drawing a loaded train of their products, and passes near to the audience at the left of the picture. (*The Phonoscope*, October 1897, 13.)

SUBJECT: Stockyards. Railroads, industrial. Armour & Co. Erie Railroad.

ARCHIVE: DLC-pp.

CITATIONS: Maguire & Baucus, *Fall Catalogue*, 1897, 9; F.Z. Maguire & Co., *Catalogue*, [March 1898], 44.

NOTE:

356 *Sheep Run, Chicago Stockyards

LENGTH: 50 ft.   © Thomas A. Edison, 31 July 1897.

PRODUCER: James White.

CAMERA: [William Heise.]

CAST:

PRODUCTION DATE: June-July 1897.

LOCATION: Chicago, Ill.

SOURCE:

DESCRIPTION: A large flock of sheep being driven over the runs from the cars to the slaughter beds. The sheep pressed by the driver and frightened by the surroundings and the confusion, move very fast. Several of the animals in their fright jump over an obstruction in the runway. Strong effects of light and shade, showing the white coated animals in agreeable contrast, add to the merit of an excellent negative. The picture has good action, and will be interesting. (*The Phonoscope*, October 1897, 13.)

SUBJECT: Stockyards. Sheep. Erie Railroad.

ARCHIVE: DLC-pp.

CITATIONS: Maguire & Baucus, *Fall Catalogue*, 1897, 9; F.Z. Maguire & Co., *Catalogue*, [March 1898], 43; *Edison Films*, March 1900, 23.

NOTE:

357 *Cattle Driven to Slaughter

LENGTH: 50 ft.   © Thomas A. Edison, 31 July 1897.

PRODUCER: James White.

CAMERA: [William Heise.]

CAST:

PRODUCTION DATE: June-July 1897.

LOCATION: Chicago, Ill.

SOURCE:

DESCRIPTION: A life-like photograph of a herd of long horn cattle being driven through the Chicago stock yard gates to the slaughter house, where 280 of the animals are killed every hour of the day. The drove comes pell-mell into the foreground of the picture before passing out of view, and the figures are large and interesting. The atmospheric effects correspond with those invariably seen where large bunches of animals are driven at close quarters. (F.Z. Maguire & Co., *Catalogue*, [March 1898], 43.)

SUBJECT: Stockyards. Cattle. Erie Railroad.

ARCHIVE: DLC-pp.

CITATIONS: Maguire & Baucus, *Fall Catalogue*, 1897, 9; *The Phonoscope*, November 1897, 13.

NOTE:

James White and the Edison crew filmed several horses races in late June and over the July 4th weekend. They returned to Sheepshead Bay to shoot the Suburban Handicap for the second time.

358 ***Racing at Sheepshead Bay**
LENGTH: 50 ft.   © Thomas A. Edison, 31 July 1897.
PRODUCER: James White.
CAMERA: William Heise.
CAST:
PRODUCTION DATE: 22 June 1897.
LOCATION: Sheepshead Bay Race Track, Coney Island, N.Y.
SOURCE:
DESCRIPTION: The finish and weighing out of a running race with nine starters. Won by the famous Clifford, with Sloane up. Shows a good view of the track and the race. (*The Phonoscope*, October 1897, 13.)
SUBJECT: Horse racing.
ARCHIVE: DLC-pp.
CITATIONS: "Summaries of the Races," *New York Tribune*, 23 June 1897, 3. Maguire & Baucus, *Fall Catalogue*, 1897, 9; F.Z. Maguire & Co., *Catalogue*, [March 1898], 45; *Edison Films*, March 1900, 31; *Edison Films*, July 1901, 56.
NOTE: This was the first race of the new season at Sheepshead Bay.

359 ***Suburban Handicap, 1897**
LENGTH: 50 and 150 ft.   © Thomas A. Edison, 31 July 1897.
PRODUCER: James White.
CAMERA: William Heise.
CAST: Willie Simms.
PRODUCTION DATE: 22 June 1897.
LOCATION: Sheepshead Bay Race Track, Coney Island, N.Y.
SOURCE: *Suburban Handicap* (Edison film no. 176, 1896).
DESCRIPTION: This race was photographed on a 150-foot strip. The event, which is one of the notable races of the American turf, takes place annually at the Sheepshead Bay track of the Coney Island Jockey Club. The purse

yields $6,000 to the winner. The race this year was won by Ben Brush, ridden by Simms. As this is such an important event, several views were taken of the race as follows: First showing the parade past the stand to the starting post. Then, as the runners pass the stand just after the start, all in a bunch. The finish, with Ben Brush winning. The Winner second and Havoc third, with others strung out, all coming down in the dust under whip and spur. Finally, the weighing-out, well in the foreground, showing jockeys on their mounts saluting in front of the judges' stand, followed by the dismount and unsaddling. Ben Brush, the winner, can be distinguished by the plain white colors of his jockey, and is the first horse that returns to the judges' stand.
We can also supply a 50 foot strip, showing start and finish and weighing-out as above. (F.Z. Maguire & Co., *Catalogue*, [March 1898], 45.)
SUBJECT: Horse racing. Suburban Handicap.
ARCHIVE: DLC-pp.
CITATIONS: "Ben Brush's Suburban," *New York Tribune*, 23 June 1897, 3. Maguire & Baucus, *Fall Catalogue*, 1897, 9 and 15; *The Phonoscope*, November 1897, 13; *Edison Films*, March 1900, 30; *Edison Films*, July 1901, 56.
NOTE: The Suburban Handicap was the fourth race of the day at Sheepshead Bay. The favorite, Ben Brush, had already won the Kentucky Derby. This film is noteworthy for its four-shot structure.

360 *****Free-For-All Race at Charter Oak Park / $6,000 Free For All Race at Charter Oak Park**

LENGTH: 50 ft.   © Thomas A. Edison, 31 July 1897.

PRODUCER: James White.

CAMERA: William Heise.

CAST:

PRODUCTION DATE: 5 July 1897.

LOCATION: Charter Oak Park, Hartford, Conn.

SOURCE:

DESCRIPTION: In this photograph we have taken the principal events of the Independence Day Meeting at the famous Hartford track. Shows a part of the enormous crowd on that occasion, and the start and finish of the free-for-all pacing race, in which the fastest harness horse in the world, John R. Gentry (2:00 1/2), the coming Star Pointer and Frank Egan competed for a purse of $6,000. The heat we photographed was won by Star Pointer in the fast time of 2:04 3/4. The start and finish are shown closely following each other, so there is no wait. On the same strip is also shown Gentry's attempt (start and finish) to beat the old-fashioned high-wheel sulky record of 2.061/4. In this exhibition the champion was accompanied by a running mate hitched to a bicycle sulky. (F.Z. Maguire & Co., *Catalogue*, [March 1898], 45.)

SUBJECT: Horse racing.

ARCHIVE: DLC-pp, CaOOANF.

CITATIONS: Maguire & Baucus, *Fall Catalogue*, 1897, 9; *Edison Films*, March 1900, 30.

NOTE:

RACING AT CHARTER OAK PARK AGAIN.
Star Pointer Defeats John R. Gentry and Frank Egan.

Hartford, Conn., July 5.–The largest crowd that ever assembled at Charter Oak Park was present to-day at the reopening of this famous track. Though there was some disappointment at the time made by the acknowledged fastest side-wheelers in the world in the free-for-all pace, and also at John R. Gentry's failure to lower Johnson's high sulky record of 2:06 1/2 at Chicago thirteen years ago, still the card arranged by the management was so attractive that there was no dissatisfaction. A conservative estimate places the attendance at twenty-five thousand, Greater New York was represented by a special train of eight cars....(*New York Tribune*, 6 July 1897, 2.)

Some of the Edison people were on hand to make pictures for the vitascope, if Gentry had beaten the high wheel sulky pacing record or if one of the pacers hit the 2-minute mark. (*Hartford Courant*, 6 July 1897, 6.)

361 *****Philadelphia Express, Jersey Central Railway**

LENGTH: 50 ft.   © Thomas A. Edison, 31 July 1897.

PRODUCER: [James White.]

CAMERA: [William Heise.]

CAST:

PRODUCTION DATE: June-July 1897.

LOCATION: Elizabeth, N.J.

SOURCE:

DESCRIPTION: The scene of this picture is itself interesting being the overhead crossing of the Pennsylvania and Jersey Central Railroads at Elizabeth, N.J. While a Pennsylvania train is passing over the arch, moving to the right, the Philadelphia Express on the Central Railroad comes dashing underneath at full speed, head-on to the audience. It passes off the canvas apparently straight into the audience with thrilling effect. At this point in the picture, the camera is within a few inches of the fast moving train. (F.Z. Maguire & Co., *Catalogue*, [March 1898], 44.)

SUBJECT: Railroad bridges. Railroads. Pennsylvania Railroad. Jersey Central Railroad.
ARCHIVE: DLC-pp, CaOOANF.
CITATIONS: Maguire & Baucus, *Fall Catalogue*, 1897, 9.
NOTE: The print at CaOOANF is much more complete than the currently available paper print copy.

Several New York producers were making advertising films by 1897, including the Edison Manufacturing Company, the International Film Company, and the American Mutoscope Company. Admiral Cigarette *was one of the Edison organization's first efforts of this kind, at least if films made in association with railroad companies are excluded. James White had probably left on his world tour, leaving William Heise in charge of the Black Maria studio, when this was made.*

362 ***Admiral Cigarette***

LENGTH: [50 ft.]   © Thomas A. Edison, 5 August 1897.
PRODUCER: [William Heise.]
CAMERA: William Heise.
CAST:
PRODUCTION DATE: July 1897.
LOCATION: [Black Maria, West Orange, N.J.]
SOURCE:
DESCRIPTION:
SUBJECT: Advertising. Cigarettes.
ARCHIVE: DLC-pp.
CITATIONS:
NOTE:

62.1 ***Crawford Shoe Store***

LENGTH: [50 ft.]   © No reg.
PRODUCER: [William Heise?]
CAMERA: [William Heise?]
CAST:
PRODUCTION DATE: [1897.]
LOCATION: [New York, N.Y.?]
SOURCE:
DESCRIPTION:
SUBJECT: Advertising. Shoes. Stores. City and town life.
ARCHIVE: NR–GE.
CITATIONS:
NOTE: Despite Edison's claim to copyright which appears on this film, there is no known registration. The Edison Manufacturing Company made other advertising films, which generally were not copyrighted. See also *Lickmann's Cigar and Photo Store* (Edison film no. 549).

The tracing of William Heise filmmaking activities continue with film no. 380.

Members of the Young People's Society of Christian Endeavor, which was affiliated with the Presbyterian Church, left Orange, New Jersey, as part of a state-wide contingent of 175 and traveled to their national conference in San Francisco in early July. They may have been escorted by James H. White and Frederick W. Blechynden who were beginning their ten-month world tour. In any case, they were joined by White and Blechynden who accompanied them to Yellowstone National Park on their return trip.

The New Jersey Endeavorers started from San Francisco on their return on Tuesday [July 13th]. Spokane should be reached this morning and Helena to-night, where Sunday will be spent. Monday will be devoted to seeing the wonders of the Yellowstone park. The train will also stop at St. Paul and Chicago, New Jersey being reached on July 23rd. ("Young People's Society of Christian Endeavor," *Orange Journal*, 17 July 1897, 2.)

On July 16th the Endeavorers were in Tacoma and then Seattle, Washington, where they had a brief sail on Lake Washington (Seattle Times, 17 July 1897). They reached Helena, Montana on Saturday, July 18th, where they attended services.

363 ***Overland Express Arriving at Helena, Mont.**

LENGTH: 50 ft.   © Thomas A. Edison, 4 April 1900.

PRODUCER: [James White.]

CAMERA: [Frederick Blechynden.]

CAST:

PRODUCTION DATE: [Ca. 19 July 1897.]

LOCATION: Helena, Mont.

SOURCE:

DESCRIPTION: It is train time. We look down the long platform, crowded with people, and see the famous N.P. Railway Overland Express approaching rapidly. In a moment the engine passes by, slowing down. Then comes one, two, three, four express cars, and behind them seven coaches and Pullmans. Passengers alight, baggage is unloaded, friends greet each other, station men rush here and there, the whole scene being one of great interest and activity. (*Edison Films*, July 1901, 9.)

SUBJECT: Tourist trade. Railroads. Young People's Society of Christian Endeavor. Northern Pacific Railroad.

ARCHIVE: DLC-pp.

CITATIONS: "A Memorable Day," *Helena Daily Herald*, 19 July 1897, 4. *New York Clipper*, 21 April 1900, 184.

NOTE: This film may have been taken by Thomas Crahan and Robert K. Bonine on a subsequent filming expedition in September or October 1899.

364 **Tourist Train Leaving Livingston, Mont.**

LENGTH: 50 ft.   © No reg.

PRODUCER: James White.

CAMERA: Frederick Blechynden.

CAST:

PRODUCTION DATE: Ca. 19 July 1897.

LOCATION: Helena, Mont.

SOURCE:

DESCRIPTION: Here we have a party of Christian Endeavorers en route for Yellowstone Park. Engine 627 puffs and starts slowly. The train gathers headway rapidly and car after car passes the camera. Every window shows a head and a waving handkerchief and the platforms are crowded with tourists waving goodbye. They are off for a good time and they will have it, too, if train service and N.P. management are up to standard. (*Edison Films*, July 1901, 9-10.)

SUBJECT: Tourist trade. Railroads. National parks and reserves. Young People's Society of Christian Endeavor. Northern Pacific Railroad. Yellowstone National Park.

ARCHIVE:

CITATIONS: *New York Clipper*, 21 April 1900, 184.

NOTE:

LIVINGSTON TO MAMMOTH HOT SPRINGS.

The Park tour may really be said to begin at Livingston. The fifty-one mile ride on the cars up the Yellowstone Valley to Cinnabar is a glorious prelude to what follows and can hardly be disassociated from it. Soon after leaving Livingston the train passes through the Gate of the Mountains into Paradise Valley.

Large fields of grain extend from the river far up the slopes to the very mountains. The peaks rise to great lengths. The grandest of them is Emigrant Peak, 10,629 feet above the sea. It is a massive one, and if seen when its upper regions are covered with snow, will not soon be forgotten.

At Yankee Jim's Cañon the railroad is carried along the face of a rocky bluff, with the river far below.

No finer trout-fishing is to be found than in the rapids of the Yellowstone between the Gate of the mountains and

Cinnabar. Those who have once experienced the thrill of angling thereabouts, are never content until they again haunt the pools and whip the rapids for the eager, gamey beauties found there.

At Cinnabar the train is exchanged for the stagecoach, and the traveler enters upon a new experience. Three miles beyond Cinnabar a small collection of log huts and stores is passed. This is Gardiner City. Here the road swings to the right and follows the Gardiner River, a rapid stream beset with immense boulders, almost to Mammoth Hot Springs. Among the crags that overhang the river an eagle's nest or two can be descried. (Olin D. Wheeler, *Wonderland '96: Picturing the Country, the Cities, the Resorts, the Game Found Along the Northern Pacific Railroad*, 1896, 58.)

365 *Coaches Arriving at Mammoth Hot Springs / Arrival of Yellowstone Park Coaching Party

LENGTH: 50 ft. © Thomas A. Edison, 4 January 1899.
PRODUCER: James White.
CAMERA: Frederick Blechynden.
CAST:
PRODUCTION DATE: 19-25 July 1897.
LOCATION: Yellowstone National Park, Wyo.
SOURCE:

DESCRIPTION: The scene is the broad piazza of the Mammoth Hot Springs Hotel, and shows the arrival of the tourists. Up dashes a spanking team of six, seemingly as fresh and spirited as when they started. Friends who are waiting on the piazza rush to greet the new arrivals and help them alight. (*Edison Films*, July 1901, 12.)

SUBJECT: National parks and reserves. Tourist trade. Carriages and carts. Hot springs. Young People's Society of Christian Endeavor. Yellowstone National Park.
ARCHIVE: DLC-pp.
CITATIONS:
NOTE:

REACH THE PARK.
Fourth Cavalry Band Greeted the C.E. Visitors at Mommoth.

Mammoth Hot Springs, July 20—Two special trains brought 500 more Christian Endeavorers to the park yesterday. The first train contained the New York contingent besides a few from Pennsylvania. The other was laden with the remainder of the New Jersey delegation the first section of which arrived Saturday.

They were being successfully handled by the Park Transportation company, without accident and on schedule time. When the coaches drove up to the Mammoth Hot Springs hotel, the musicians of the Fourth Cavalry, Fort Yellowstone, were stationed to the left of the main entrance of the hotel and welcomed them with inspiring music. The keystone delegation was headed by J. Wilbur Chapman, the evangelist of John Wannamaker's Presbyterian church in Philadelphia. (*Helena Evening Herald*, 20 July 1897, 1.)

366 *Tourists Going Round Yellowstone / Coaching Party, Yellowstone Park

LENGTH: 50 ft. © Thomas A. Edison, 4 January 1899.
PRODUCER: James White.
CAMERA: Frederick Blechynden.
CAST:
PRODUCTION DATE: 19-25 July 1897.
LOCATION: Yellowstone National Park, Wyo.
SOURCE:

DESCRIPTION: Rapidly one after the other coach after coach passes before the camera. First comes a big one, six horses, crowded top and inside with tourists. They wave their hats and handkerchiefs as they pass. Then comes another; then follows four more, each drawn by a four-horse team, while ten or a dozen more are strung out far into the distance. This is the Christian Endeavor excursion touring through the Yellowstone Park under the able management of the Northern Pacific Railway Company. (*Edison Films*, July 1901, 12.)

SUBJECT: National parks and reserves. Tourist trade. Carriages and carts. Young People's Society of Christian Endeavor. Northern Pacific Railroad. Yellowstone National Park.

ARCHIVE:

CITATIONS:

NOTE:

A Talk to Tourists

The Park tour is planned so as to enable ordinary persons, those of moderate means, to see the most at a minimum expense and in *a reasonable time*. Those who can afford the time and money can prolong their stay to weeks if desired, and thus see far more, and as leisurely, as inclination prompts. The ordinary tourist does not and can not in the time allowed, see thoroughly even the most important objects. As a matter of fact, a week could be spent at both the Upper Geyser Basin and the Grand Cañon. The five and one-half days' tour *does* give the tourist the opportunity, if the time be utilized aright, to see fairly well the choice morsels to be found there, and to carry away an intelligent idea of them and render him thankful for what he has seen. Even then it is necessary that much walking and some climbing be done. The stages can not and do not go everywhere. At Mammoth Hot Springs the terraces must be climbed more or less; at the Geyser Basins the geysers, and at the Grand Cañon, the falls and cañon, must be, to an extent, visited on foot. The coaches convey the tourists from hotel to hotel, etc., and this is sufficient work for horses and drivers as every reasonable person will allow.

From the hotels some of the objects of interest can be partially visited if the tourist prefers to pay the extra price. At the Lower Geyser and the Upper Geyser Basins and also at the Grand Cañon, tourist wagons make the rounds of such places as can be thus visited, for a reasonable fare. Many of the most interesting spots to be seen at all must be visited wholly or partially afoot. (Olin D. Wheeler, *Wonderland '96: Picturing the Country, The Cities, The Resorts, The Game Found Along the Northern Pacific Railroad*, 1896, 56.)

367 Wild Bear in Yellowstone Park

LENGTH: 50 ft.   © No reg.

PRODUCER: [James White.]

CAMERA: [Frederick Blechynden.]

CAST:

PRODUCTION DATE: 19-25 July 1897.

LOCATION: Yellowstone National Park, Wyo.

SOURCE:

DESCRIPTION: Here he is, fresh from his forest lair, devouring the carcass of his prey. At first he looks in dumb astonishment at the machine that is taking his picture, then growling fiercely he seizes a large bone, rises to his hind feet, pivots around and trots off to the woods in the background. (*Edison Films*, July 1901, 12.)

SUBJECT: Bears. National parks and reserves. Tourist trade. Yellowstone National Park.

ARCHIVE:

CITATIONS:

NOTE: See note for film no. 368.

368 *Old Faithful Geyser

LENGTH: 100 ft.   © Thomas A. Edison, 6 May 1901.

PRODUCER: [James White?]

CAMERA: [Frederick Blechynden?]

CAST:

PRODUCTION DATE: [19-25 July 1897.]

LOCATION: Yellowstone National Park, Wyo.

SOURCE:

DESCRIPTION: This geyser is one of the celebrated and popular curiosities of the great National Park. It takes its name from the fact of its never failing to give an exhibition of its wonderful action every seventy minutes. As we see it here in the height of its action, sending immense volumes of steam and hot water hundreds of feet in the air, there to take on fanciful forms indescribable in words, it forms one of the most beautiful subjects ever presented to a motion picture camera. (*Edison Films*, July 1901, 12.)

SUBJECT: Geysers. National parks and reserves. Tourist trade. Yellowstone National Park.

ARCHIVE: DLC-pp.

CITATIONS:

NOTE: It is possible that this film, and some of the other films of Yellowstone National Park, were taken at a later date by Thomas Crahan and Robert K. Bonine. Crahan was selling almost two dozen "New Films of the Northwest" in late 1900, many of Yellowstone. (*New York Clipper*, 1 December 1900, 895.)

Whether the films copyrighted by Thomas Edison were taken in 1897 or on some later occasion, for instance on Bonine's and Crahan's filmming expedition in the summer and fall of 1899, is unclear. If there was a second expedition to Yellowstone, films copyrighted in 1901 would very likely date from this later period.

369 *****Riverside Geyser, Yellowstone Park / Riverside Geyser, Yellowstone National Park**

LENGTH: 65 ft.   © Thomas A. Edison, 24 May 1901.

PRODUCER: [James White?]

CAMERA: [Frederick Blechynden?]

CAST:

PRODUCTION DATE: [19-25 July 1897.]

LOCATION: Yellowstone National Park, Wyo.

SOURCE:

DESCRIPTION: On the side of the Fire Hole River just below the Upper geyser basin, Yellowstone Park, is situated this remarkable feature of the National Park. Spouting at an angle, alternately jets of hot water and steam, this natural fountain presents an ever changing and interesting sight. Our artist was fortunate in securing a picture of one of its most vigorous and diversified eruptions. (*Edison Films*, July 1901, 11-12.)

SUBJECT: Geysers. National parks and reserves. Tourist trade. Yellowstone National Park.

ARCHIVE: DLC-pp.

CITATIONS:

NOTE: See note for film no. 368.

370 *****Upper Falls of the Yellowstone / Upper Falls of the Yellowstone, Yellowstone National Park**

LENGTH: 65 ft.   © Thomas A. Edison, 6 May 1901.

PRODUCER: [James White?]

CAMERA: [Frederick Blechynden?]

CAST:

PRODUCTION DATE: [19-25 July 1897.]

LOCATION: Yellowstone National Park, Wyo.

SOURCE:

DESCRIPTION: This picture shows this celebrated spectacle of nature in the highest state of its grandeur. As this immense volume of angry water falls from its dizzy height, clearly defined against its rocky background and striking with such force on the bed of the river below, you imagine you can almost hear the roar of the cataract and feel the spray you see rising in the clouds settling on your faces. (*Edison Films*, July 1901, 12.)

SUBJECT: Waterfalls. National parks and reserves. Tourist trade. Yellowstone National Park.
ARCHIVE: DLC-pp.
CITATIONS:
NOTE: See note for film no. 368.

---

371 ***Lower Falls, Grand Canyon, Yellowstone***

LENGTH: [50 ft.]   © Thomas A. Edison, 4 January 1899.
PRODUCER: James White.
CAMERA: Frederick Blechynden.
CAST:
PRODUCTION DATE: 19-25 July 1897.
LOCATION: Yellowstone National Park, Wyo.
SOURCE:
DESCRIPTION:
SUBJECT: Waterfalls. Canyons. National parks and reserves. Tourist trade. Yellowstone National Park.
ARCHIVE: DLC-pp.
CITATIONS:
NOTE:

THE LOWER FALLS.

In a good many years of sight-seeing in the West, I have found it quite unsatisfactory to make comparisons. There is usually some important factor in connection with one of the members of the equation absent from the other, that renders the comparison valueless. There are in the United States several large and now well-known falls. Four that constitute, perhaps, the greatest quartet are Niagara, Shoshone in Idaho, the Yosemite, and the Great, or Lower, Falls of the Yellowstone. Of these the only two that it seems possible to couple, comparatively, are Niagara and Shoshone. And these are so entirely different in important characteristics as to render it senseless to attempt it. None of them can honestly be compared with the Yellowstone for the same reason. Nor is there any need of it. They are all great, beautiful, grand, powerful, each in its own way. The heights of the Lower Falls is given in the old guide-books as 360 feet. Careful measurements by the United States Geological Survey proved that 308 feet was their correct height. In the same way the Upper Falls have been estimated at 140 and 150 feet, when they are really 109 feet. The depth of the cañon is wildly stated at from 1,500 to 2,500 feet when the truth is that 1,200 feet is the maximum height of the walls. Neither the falls nor the cañon need exaggeration in any respect, and we may as well be truthful about it. At the very edge of the Lower Falls there is a platform, well railed, from which the falls may be seen in all their glory from this position—looking down upon them. As the water, green and clear, plunges over the brink it becomes a mass of spray and foam, white as the driven snow. At times I have seen on the left side of it–the side upon which the platform is built–a green ribbon, gradually growing fainter and fainter, stretching down, seemingly one-fourth the height of the falls. There is a fascination in simply standing and watching the falls. Now one feature presents itself strongly, then another....(Olin D. Wheeler, *Wonderland '96: Picturing the Country, the Cities, the Resorts, the Game Found Along the Northern Pacific Railroad*, 1896, 75.)

---

372 ***Coaches Going to Cinnabar from Yellowstone***

LENGTH: © Thomas A. Edison, 4 January 1899.
PRODUCER: James White.
CAMERA: Frederick Blechynden.
CAST:
PRODUCTION DATE: 19-25 July 1897.
LOCATION: Yellowstone National Park, Wyo.
SOURCE:
DESCRIPTION:
SUBJECT: National parks and reserves. Tourist trade. Carriages and carts. Young People's Society of Christian Endeavor. Yellowstone National Park.
ARCHIVE: DLC-pp.
CITATIONS: "Cowboy Chris in Cinnabar," *Beadle's Popular Library* 1 July 1891.
NOTE:

After their tour of Yellowstone National Park, James H. White and Frederick W. Blechynden quickly traveled to Seattle. The Alaskan Gold Rush had begun there in earnest on the very day that the Christian Endeavorers had passed through Seattle, on 17 July 1897, as the S.S. "Portland" docked in Seattle with gold and successful prospectors on board. White and Blechynden were staying at the Hotel Stevens by 6 August 1897. From this base they filmed a number of local scenes that recorded the frantic efforts of men to reach the Klondike before winter had set in. Few actually succeeded.

373 ***S.S. "Queen" Loading**
LENGTH: 50 ft.   © Thomas A. Edison, 25 October 1897.
PRODUCER: James White.
CAMERA: Frederick Blechynden.
CAST:
PRODUCTION DATE: 6 August 1897.
LOCATION: Seattle, Wash.
SOURCE:

DESCRIPTION: Shows the S.S. "Queen" at Seattle with an immense crowd of miners crowding the decks of the boat and the docks, carrying aboard baggage, implements, etc. Taken at the height of the excitement and gives a good idea of the vast numbers that started for the gold fields. (F.Z. Maguire & Co., *Catalogue*, [March 1898], 34.)
SUBJECT: Gold mines and mining. Steamships. Harbors–Seattle. Piers. Klondike River Valley (Yukon)–Gold discoveries. Northern Pacific Railroad.
ARCHIVE: DLC-pp.
CITATIONS: *Seattle Intelligencer*, 7 August 1897, 8.
NOTE:

374 ***Loading Baggage for Klondike, no. 6 / Loading Baggage, S.S. "Queen"**
LENGTH: 50 ft.   © Thomas A. Edison, 25 October 1897.
PRODUCER: James White.
CAMERA: Frederick Blechynden.
CAST:
PRODUCTION DATE: 6 August 1897.
LOCATION: Seattle, Wash.
SOURCE:

DESCRIPTION: Shows the baggage of the miners, enroute to the new found Eldorado, being loaded aboard the S.S. "Queen" at Seattle, Wash. This picture was taken when the excitement was at its highest pitch and the crowd of anxious gold seekers, with their implements, provisions, clothing, etc., are shown life size. The huge derrick hoisting load after load, is shown to good advantage, while the hotel busses, driving up with passengers, add to the action. The picture is sharp and clear. (*The Phonoscope*, January 1898, 12.)
SUBJECT: Gold mines and mining. Steamships. Harbors–Seattle. Piers. Klondike River Valley (Yukon)–Gold discoveries. Northern Pacific Railroad.
ARCHIVE: DLC-pp.
CITATIONS: *Seattle Intelligencer*, 7 August 1897, 8. *New York Clipper*, 18 December 1897, 699; F.Z. Maguire & Co., *Catalogue*, [March 1898], 33.
NOTE:

375 ***S.S. "Queen" Leaving Dock**
LENGTH: 50 ft.   © Thomas A. Edison, 25 October 1897.
PRODUCER: James White.
CAMERA: Frederick Blechynden.

CAST:

PRODUCTION DATE: 7 August 1897.

LOCATION: Seattle, Wash.

SOURCE:

DESCRIPTION: Shows S.S. "Queen" backing out from the dock of Northern Pacific R.R., Seattle, Wash., the decks covered with a mass of passengers, leaving for the new gold field. (*The Phonoscope*, January 1898, 12.)

SUBJECT: Gold mines and mining. Steamships. Harbors–Seattle. Piers. Klondike River Valley (Yukon)–Gold discoveries. Northern Pacific Railroad.

ARCHIVE: DLC-pp.

CITATIONS: *Seattle Intelligencer*, 7 August 1897, 8. *New York Clipper*, 18 December 1897, 699; F.Z. Maguire & Co., *Catalogue*, [March 1898], 33.

NOTE:

376 ***Horses Loading for Klondike, no. 9 / Horses Loading for the Klondike**

LENGTH: 50 ft.   © Thomas A. Edison, 25 October 1897.

PRODUCER: James White.

CAMERA: Frederick Blechynden.

CAST:

PRODUCTION DATE: 7 August 1897.

LOCATION: Seattle, Wash.

SOURCE:

DESCRIPTION: Taken at the wharf of the Northern Pacific R.R., in Seattle, and shows a number of horses being loaded aboard the S.S. "Williamette" for transportation to the "Klondike" country. The horses are placed in large boxes or slings, hoisted with derricks to the deck and then lowered into the hold of the ship. The usual crowd of curious onlookers, in addition to the owners, stevedores, longshoremen and ship hands are shown life size. The waiting horses are seen in the foreground. As the sling is hoisted the head and neck of the affrighted horse are shown tossing about. The men hurrying around the decks and wharf add to the action, making an interesting subject, sharp and clear. (F.Z. Maguire & Co., *Catalogue*, [March 1898], 35.)

SUBJECT: Gold mines and mining. Steamships. Horses. Harbors–Seattle. Piers. Klondike River Valley (Yukon)–Gold discoveries. Northern Pacific Railroad.

ARCHIVE: DLC-pp.

CITATIONS: "Pack Horses for Trail," *Seattle Intelligencer*, 8 August 1897, 2. *New York Clipper*, 18 December 1897, 699; *Edison Films*, July 1901, 10.

NOTE: Virtually all of these horses died en route to the gold fields.

376.1 **Loading Baggage for Klondike**

LENGTH: 50 ft.   © No reg.

PRODUCER: James White.

CAMERA: Frederick Blechynden.

CAST:

PRODUCTION DATE: 7 August 1897.

LOCATION: Seattle, Wash.

SOURCE:

DESCRIPTION: This was the first [sic] ship sailing for the Klondike from Seattle during the gold rush of 1897. The picture shows the excitement and enthusiasm that attended the great Klondike exodus. Crowds of anxious gold seekers watch the loading of their outfits, clothing, kits and provisions into the hole of the "Williamette." (*Edison Films*, July 1901, 10.)

SUBJECT: Gold mines and mining. Steamships. Harbors–Seattle. Piers. Klondike River Valley (Yukon)–Gold discoveries. Northern Pacific Railroad.

ARCHIVE:

CITATIONS: *Seattle Intelligencer*, 7 August 1897, 8.

NOTE: This may have been an uncopyrighted subject that was placed into distribution as other negatives wore out. Or, this may have been an inaccurate description for *Loading Baggage for Klondike, no. 6,* which shows the S.S. "Queen."

377   ***S.S. "Williamette," Leaving for Klondike**

LENGTH: 50 ft.   © Thomas A. Edison, 25 October 1897.

PRODUCER: James White.

CAMERA: Frederick Blechynden.

CAST:

PRODUCTION DATE: 9 August 1897.

LOCATION: Seattle, Wash.

SOURCE:

DESCRIPTION: Shows the steamer backing out from the docks of the Northern Pacific R.R. Co., at Seattle Wash., with its immense load of passengers waving adieux to relatives and friends. In the foreground can be seen a large crowd of men and women, life size, all filled with the prevailing excitement and enthusiasm. (F.Z. Maguire & Co., *Catalogue,* [March 1898], 35.)

SUBJECT: Gold mines and mining. Steamships. Harbors–Seattle. Piers. Klondike River Valley (Yukon)–Gold discoveries. Northern Pacific Railroad.

ARCHIVE: DLC-pp.

CITATIONS: *Seattle Intelligencer*, 10 August 1897, 1. *New York Clipper*, 18 December 1897, 699.

NOTE:

378   ***First Avenue, Seattle, Washington / Fifth Avenue, Seattle, Wash.**

LENGTH: 50 ft.   © Thomas A. Edison, 25 October 1897.

PRODUCER: James White.

CAMERA: Frederick Blechynden.

CAST:

PRODUCTION DATE: 6-9 August 1897.

LOCATION: Seattle, Wash.

SOURCE:

DESCRIPTION: A street scene taken during the "Klondike" excitement. The most notable feature lies in the fact that the buildings, trolley cars and vehicles are covered with large banners and signs with "Klondike" in large letters showing prominently. (*The Phonoscope*, January 1898, 12.)

SUBJECT: City and town life–Seattle. Gold mines and mining. Urban transportation. Klondike River Valley (Yukon)–Gold discoveries.

ARCHIVE: DLC-pp.

CITATIONS: *New York Clipper*, 18 December 1897, 699; F.Z. Maguire & Co., *Catalogue,* [March 1898], 35; *Edison Films*, March 1900, 38; *Edison Films*, July 1901, 9.

NOTE: Tim Muir indicates that this film was almost certainly taken on First Avenue.

T.A. EDISON'S PROJECTOSCOPE.
Animated Pictures of Seattle to Be Re-produced.

One of the latest enterprises of Thomas A. Edison, the electrical inventor, is that of sending a representative around the world to obtain animated pictures to be reproduced on the Edison Projectoscope and other instruments employed for that purpose. The person selected for that important work is Mr. James H. White of Orange, New Jersey. Mr. White is now at the Hotel Stevens, on his trip around the world, and a reporter of The Times was accorded the privilege of an interview with him this morning.

"My object," said Mr. White, "is to obtain animated pictures of Seattle and other places for the purpose of illustrating life in the West, including its industries, mode of travel, transactions and life in general. The pictures I take are distributed throughout the world and will be reproduced on the Edison Projectoscope and other instruments for the reproduction of animated pictures.

"Our apparatus is able to record fifty or sixty pictures per second of any moving object. The instrument was invented by Mr. Edison in 1892. In making a subject 150 feet of negative is used, and about 3,300 distinctive pictures are taken on this length."

This is Mr. White's first trip so far west, and the reporter had the curiosity to ask how Seattle compared with Eastern cities of the same size.

"Why," he said, "there is simply no comparison. I have stopped in every city of any account and I find Seattle the smartest and most pushing city I have visited. There is a push and enterprise here far beyond the comprehension of people in the East. When Eastern men and women want to get away from the rustlers for a brief vacation they mustn't come to Seattle."

While in the city it is Mr. White's purpose to take a series of pictures of the Ocean dock when the Williamette is preparing to sail for Dyea and other living moving scenes that will represent our every day life in Seattle. (*Seattle Times*, 7 August 1897.)

'TIS NOW A STAMPEDE.
Six Steamers to Sail for Alaska by End of the Week.
THEY WILL CARRY 2800 MINERS.
The Williamette Sailed at Noon Yesterday, With Nearly 900 Passengers and All the Freight She
Could Carry–Her Departure the Most Notable Event in the History of the Water Front–
Thousands Crowd Every Foot of the Pacific Coast Steamship Company's Dock–Picturesque
Incidents at the Departure–Ellen Anderson to Get Away for St. Michael's Today–Steamer Bristol
to Sail With 1,100 From Victoria Tomorrow–Utopia Next With 150–The Mexico Due From Dyea.

The stampede of gold hunters to the Klondike reaches flood tide this week. No less than 2,800 persons will be sailing the billowy for the various Alaskan ports at the end of the week. Besides six steamers, carrying from 150 to 1,200 passengers, there are several scows loaded with provisions and fuel, and two barges carrying 300 horses to be used in transporting miners and freight over the White pass and Chicat [i.e. Chilkoot] pass, above Dyea. The stampede now exceeds in picturesque incidents even the rush of the Argonauts to California in '49.... (*Seattle Intelligencer*, 10 August 1897, 1.)

379 ***Fast Mail, Northern Pacific Railroad / Fast Mail, N.P.R.R.**
LENGTH: 50 ft.   © Thomas A. Edison, 6 December 1897.
PRODUCER: James H. White.
CAMERA: Frederick Blechynden.
CAST:
PRODUCTION DATE: [July-August 1897.]
LOCATION: Portland, Oreg.
SOURCE:

DESCRIPTION: Taken on the line of the N.P.R.R., between Portland and Beatty on its journey of 2,000 miles to St. Paul. This train was made up of two baggage cars, one mail car and nine passenger coaches, a total of twelve cars. It is the fastest and best train crossing the continent and the view we have is most striking. The picture was taken in a valley and the hills formed a sharp background. The high waving grass alongside the train stands out sharp and clear, while a number of people, including some ladies standing on the side of the track add to its realism. The train moves at a high rate of speed and the dust and smoke effects are vivid. The picture is sharp and clear, all tending to make one of the best train scenes ever photographed. (F.Z. Maguire & Co., *Catalogue*, [March 1898], 34.)

SUBJECT: Railroads. Northern Pacific Railroad.
ARCHIVE: DLC-pp.
CITATIONS: *New York Clipper*, 18 December 1897, 699; *Edison Films*, March 1900, 47; *Edison Films*, July 1901, 9.
NOTE:

The tracking of White's and Blechynden's filmmaking activities resume with film no. 389.

While James White was globe trotting, William Heise stayed behind in Orange, New Jersey, and assumed charge of local production. Horses—racing, jumping, performing in circuses, on fire runs or in the cavalry—were popular film subjects during the first year of projected motion pictures (as popular as railroads). Even as White was filming travel scenes with the assistance of West Coast railroad companies, William Heise took films of the Monmouth County Horse Show in Long Branch, New Jersey, where he had previously filmed the surf after a storm.

380 ***Teams of Horses / Team of Horses**

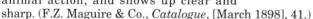

LENGTH: 50 ft.   © Thomas A. Edison, 25 October 1897.
PRODUCER: William Heise.
CAMERA: William Heise.
CAST:
PRODUCTION DATE: 13 August 1897.
LOCATION: Long Branch, N.J.
SOURCE:
DESCRIPTION: Shows six teams of high stepping harness horses, hitched to fashionable park traps of several styles, passing by full life size at a fast trot. The grand stand, with crowds of fashionable occupants, forms an attractive background. The picture is full of animal action, and shows up clear and sharp. (F.Z. Maguire & Co., *Catalogue*, [March 1898], 41.)
SUBJECT: Horse shows. Social elites. Carriages and carts. Monmouth County Horse Show.
ARCHIVE: DLC-pp.
CITATIONS: *New York Clipper*, 25 December 1897, 722; *Edison Films*, March 1900, 26; *Edison Films*, July 1901, 50.
NOTE: The two-month delay in copyrighting these Monmouth County Horse Show subjects has several possible explanations. Certainly one is that the films became more topical and commercial as the New York Horse Show (early November) approached.

381 ***Judging Tandems**
LENGTH: 50 ft.   © Thomas A. Edison, 25 October 1897.
PRODUCER: William Heise.
CAMERA: William Heise.
CAST:
PRODUCTION DATE: 13 August 1897.
LOCATION: Long Branch, N.J.
SOURCE:

DESCRIPTION: Taken at the Monmouth County Horse Show, Long Branch, N.J., and shows five tandem teams hitched to their carts in their exhibition for prizes. The teams come full head-on to the audience, the horses going at a fast trot, and show up full life-size. The film is full of action from start to finish, and makes a subject full of animation. A team of ponies, hitched tandem and driven by a small boy, accompanied by a boy groom, adds to the interest of a good subject. (F.Z. Maguire & Co., *Catalogue*, [March 1898], 41.)
SUBJECT: Horse shows. Social elites. Carriages and carts. Boys. Monmouth County Horse Show.
ARCHIVE: DLC-pp.
CITATIONS: *New York Clipper*, 25 December 1897, 722; *Edison Films*, March 1900, 26; *Edison Films*, July 1901, 50.
NOTE:

382 ***Single Harness Horses**

LENGTH: 50 ft.   © Thomas A. Edison, 25 October 1897.

PRODUCER: William Heise.

CAMERA: William Heise.

CAST: Charles "Fatty" Bates.

PRODUCTION DATE: 13 August 1897.

LOCATION: Long Branch, N.J.

SOURCE:

DESCRIPTION: Shows ten horses hitched to fashionable carts driven past the judges and grandstand to show their style, action and high-stepping movements. Among the drivers, Charles F. (Fatty) Bates, the noted whip, shows up very prominently. The horses are all of very high class, and the action is of the very best. The film is clear, sharp and catchy. (F.Z. Maguire & Co., *Catalogue*, [March 1898], 41.)

SUBJECT: Horse shows. Social elites. Carriages and carts. Monmouth County Horse Show.

ARCHIVE: DLC-pp.

CITATIONS: *New York Clipper*, 25 December 1897, 722; *Edison Films*, March 1900, 26; *Edison Films,* July 1901, 50.

NOTE: When Charles F. Bates died of an illness on 2 March 1900, the *New York Times* gave the horseman a front-page obituary and described him as one of the best known figures in the city (see document below).

383 ***Ladies' Saddle Horses**

LENGTH: 50 ft.   © Thomas A. Edison, 25 October 1897.

PRODUCER: William Heise.

CAMERA: William Heise.

CAST:

PRODUCTION DATE: 13 August 1897.

LOCATION: Long Branch, N.J.

SOURCE:

DESCRIPTION: This picture represents a number of lady riders on handsome horses, with full and complete mountings, galloping around the course, the judges being seen passing to the stand. An immense crowd of people are shown waving handkerchiefs, etc., at their favorites. The picture is very animated, clear and sharp, and the effect is very starting. (F.Z. Maguire & Co., *Catalogue*, [March 1898], 41.)

SUBJECT: Horse shows. Social elites. Monmouth County Horse Show.

ARCHIVE: DLC-pp.

CITATIONS: *New York Clipper*, 25 December 1897, 722. *Edison Films*, March 1900, 26; *Edison Films,* July 1901, 50.

NOTE:

384 ***Exhibition of Prize Winners**

LENGTH: 50 ft.   © Thomas A. Edison, 25 October 1897.

PRODUCER: William Heise.

CAMERA: William Heise.

CAST: Charles "Fatty" Bates.

PRODUCTION DATE: 14 August 1897.

LOCATION: Long Branch, N.J.

SOURCE:

DESCRIPTION: This shows a characteristic view of the winning horses at the recent horse show at Long Branch, N.J., taken on Ocean avenue, with the great West End

Hotel forming the background. The procession was led by the well-known and popular whip, Mr. Charles F. Bates, known to his friends generally as "Fatty" Bates, driving a handsome park coach, filled both inside and outside with well-known society people, and drawn by four energetic and spirited horses, with a mounted "cock" horse in the lead, followed by the well-known and beautiful prize winning horse, "Coxey," hitched to a high cart, followed in turn by tandems, spike teams, carts, etc., all driven

exactly the same as in the ring, but at a much higher rate of speed. The picture shows the high-knee action of the horses, and the effect, as a whole, is both interesting and attractive. (F.Z. Maguire & Co., *Catalogue*, [March 1898], 41.)

SUBJECT: Horse shows. Social elites. Carriages and carts. Hotels. Monmouth County Horse Show.

ARCHIVE: DLC-pp.

CITATIONS: "Long Branch Show Ended," *Brooklyn Eagle*, 15 August 1897, 3. *New York Clipper*, 25 December 1897, 722; *Edison Films*, March 1900, 26; *Edison Films,* July 1901, 50.

NOTE: Coxey was Bates's top prize winning horse (see obituary below).

385 *****Dancing Darkey Boy**

LENGTH: 50 ft.   © Thomas A. Edison, 25 October 1897.

PRODUCER: William Heise.

CAMERA: William Heise.

CAST:

PRODUCTION DATE: 12-14 August 1897.

LOCATION: Long Branch, N.J.

SOURCE:

DESCRIPTION: Shows a small colored boy, about ten years old, amusing the stable hands with a characteristic negro dance. He is placed on a table and is surrounded by a crowd of stablemen, jockeys, etc., all of

whom pat time and unconsciously follow the movements of the performer. The dance is a combination of jig, clog and negro cake walk steps. The audience is composed of about fifteen, all of whom, including the principal, show up full life size and are all action. The film is sure to please, being clear and sharp. (F.Z. Maguire & Co., *Catalogue*, [March 1898], 41.)

SUBJECT: Afro-Americans. Dancing. Horse shows. Boys. Monmouth County Horse Show.

ARCHIVE: DLC-pp.

CITATIONS: *New York Clipper*, 25 December 1897, 722; *Edison Films*, March 1900, 27; *Edison Films*, July 1901, 52.

NOTE:

HORSE SHOW LIONS.
Governor Griggs Will Be Added To-Day to the List of Distinguished Visitors.
FACES SEEN IN THE BOXES.
Carl Otto Peters Entertained the Russian Consul General and Other Diplomats.
SUMMARIES OF THE AWARDS.
C.F. Bates, as Usual, Carried Off the Brewster Prize for the Best Pair of Park Horses.

There were former Governors, United States and State Senators and millionaires to be seen at the second day of the Monmouth County Horse Show, in Long Branch, N.J., yesterday, but to-day there is to be an up-to-date Governor there—Governor Griggs sent word last night that he would be attended by two of his military staff, Colonel Barbour and Kuser....

SUMMARY OF THE AWARDS.
Louis W. Wormser's Don Wilkes and His Excellency Defeated.

Brewster & Co. for several seasons have given a special prize at all the horse shows near New York for the best pair of park horses shown before a demi-mail or spider or Stanhope phaeton, and almost as regularly C.F. Bates has won it. This was the first class called yesterday. Under the conditions of the competition carriage and appointments count for fifty per cent. In a matter of this sort Mr. Bates is invariably perfect: liveries, harness, turnout, everything is just right. The famous Bates horse show smile was largely in evidence when the blue ribbon came his way again.

There was a keen contest between pairs over 15 and not exceeding 15.3 hands in class 10, and here the Bates entry had again, as the day before, to play second fiddle to L.W. Wormser's great steppers Superior and Surprise. The latter is a swaybacked horse, but he fully compensates for this by his dashing style of action, knees and hocks moving like machinery. Amusement and Amazement are a closely matched pair of deep cherry bays, with black joints, and move as one horse, but they are inexperienced in show ring manners. At the National Horse show in November this pair should be about ripe....

ONE MORE FOR MR. BATES

Class 7–For best single harness horse, that has not taken a first prize in single harness in the year 1895, 1896 or 1897, or the National, Philadelphia, Boston, or Long Branch horse shows; stallion, mare or gelding, over 14.1 hands and not exceeding 15 hands.–First prize won by C.F. Bates's bay gelding The Whirl of the Town; Strauss & Hexter's chestnut gelding Amadon second, L.W. Wormser's chestnut gelding His Excellency third, G.S. Gagnon's bay gelding Gold Pointer fourth.

Class 24–For best lady's hack, not under 14.1 hands and not exceeding 15.3, special prize donated by W. Rice Hochester. –Won by W.A. McGibben's bay gelding Jubilee, ridden by Miss Adelaide Doremus; J.A. Scrimser's bay mare Lady O (Mrs. Squire), second; Mrs. J.A. Logan's chestnut mare Killarney (Miss Beach) third; G.S. Gagnon's chestnut mare Brier Rose (Mrs. Beech), fourth. (*New York Herald,* 14 August 1897, 6.)

CHARLES F. BATES IS DEAD
Well-Known Horseman Passes Away After Two Weeks' Illness.
Was One of the Best Whips in the Country and a Familiar figure at the Annual Horse Show.

Charles F. Bates, more familiarly known as "Fatty" Bates, died last night at 8:30 o'clock at his apartments in the Dakota Flats, 1 West Seventy-second Street. Mr. Bates was thirty-five years of age. His death was due to bronchial pneumonia. He was stricken two weeks ago with grip, which developed into pneumonia. He lived with his father, C. Francis Bates, his mother having died some years ago.

Mr. Bates was in his way one of the best known figures in the city and it was to his interest in and association with horses that he had in his peculiar line more than a local fame. He was one of the best whips in the country, and in the horse world gained an enviable record as a breeder and dealer in fine stock.

Every one for ten years back who has visited the annual Horse Show knew Mr. Bates, at least by sight, and indeed, that yearly gathering would have been considered incomplete without his presence. He not only entered his own horses at the New York Horse Show, but he was equally well known at the shows in Philadelphia, Atlantic City, Long Branch, and Newport, where for several years he had shown his skill as a driver.

Many New Yorkers will recall him in one of his whimsical poses in Madison Square Garden during Horse Show week, tooling a coach and four around the tanbark dressed not unlike Samuel Weller, his coach followed by a boy in odd costume, on a cock horse trailing behind. But it was really with a more serious view that Mr. Bates made his annual entries at this institution. He carried away many prizes, and what was more to the point, sold many a fine prize animal at a fancy price.

It was he who introduced the fashion of docking trotting horses tails, then training the animals to the knee and hock action, and succeeded in beating, according to the dictum of horsemen, the English hackneys "at their own game."

Something over ten years ago Mr. Bates began the breeding of line horses. He established a farm at Hubbard, Ohio, where he kept at all times from 150 to 200 animals, principally of the high-stepping, coach and heavy harness type. At his two stables up town in this city he had on hand almost constantly at least 100 horses.

During his career Mr. Bates won as prizes over 500 ribbons at the various shows where he made entries, his most famous prize winner being the American trotter Coxey. In the intervals between his professional appearances Mr. Bates naturally was much seen on the road, and along the fine driveways of New York his equipages in matter of appointment were not, infrequently the envy of many a wealthier patron of the turf.

It was often his boast that he held the world's record in making quick changes of horses to a road coach, his time being forty-two seconds. His nearest competitor in this feat, so dear to the professional whip, was James Selby, who it was his delight to say ran behind him by five seconds.

Some two or three years ago Mr. Bates figured in a breach of promise suit. His last public appearance in the courts was in a suit against Assistant Secretary Hyde of the National Horse Show Association for the care of a horse. In the course of the suit the Grand Jury was asked to indict Mr. Hyde, but refused to do so. Thereupon Mr. Bates brought this refusal to the attention of the Mazet Committee toward the close of its session. Nothing ever came of it, as the committee adjourned sine die a few days later. Mr. Bates's breezy mannerisms in the committee room, it was recalled yesterday furnished much amusement to the spectators.

Mr. Bates was President of the New York Coach Horse and Cob Company, and a member of the Colonial Club. He was the last member of his father's family, his birthplace being at Newport, R.I. One of his sisters, Mrs. Daniel Saxton, died some time ago, and the other, who was the wife of Captain F.W. Dickens of the United States Navy, died in Washington last July as the result of a naphtha explosion at her home. As showing the fatality which seemed to pursue the family, it was said last night that two sisters of his father were killed some time ago by a subway explosion in Boston.

Mr. Bates will be buried in Mount Auburn Cemetery in Cambridge, Mass. (*New York Times*, 3 March 1900, 1.)

William Heise also produced a number of acted films, both outdoors and in the Black Maria.

386 *Fisherman's Luck

LENGTH: 50 ft.   © Thomas A. Edison, 20 September 1897.
PRODUCER: William Heise.
CAMERA: William Heise.
CAST:
PRODUCTION DATE: August-September 1897.
LOCATION:
SOURCE: *Fisherman's Luck* (painting by James Maffit).

DESCRIPTION: Shows two German anglers, who are plainly novices, engaged in fishing from a narrow dock. No fish have been caught, but one of them, who is sitting down, finally gets his hook fast. He has, apparently, a fish of unusual size on the line, requiring a great effort to land it. When brought to the surface a piece of stove pipe instead of the expected fish is brought to view. The look of astonishment on both the disappointed faces is most amusing. The companion who is standing in the rear is so surprised that he loses his balance and falls backward into the water. His efforts to regain the dock prove unsuccessful, until he is assisted by his friend. Their combined efforts are attended with many interesting and laughable movements. A boat load of young people rowing past lend a pleasing addition. The film is clear and sharp and the figures are life size. (F.Z. Maguire & Co., *Catalogue*, [March 1898], 43.)

SUBJECT: Fishing. German Americans. Boats and Boating. Accidents.
ARCHIVE: DLC-pp.
CITATIONS: *New York Clipper*, 25 December 1897, 722; *Edison Films*, March 1900, 34; *Edison Films*, July 1901, 69.
NOTE:

387 *Bowery Waltz

LENGTH: 50 ft.   © Thomas A. Edison, 24 September 1897.
PRODUCER: William Heise.
CAMERA: William Heise.
CAST: James T. Kelly, Dorothy Kent.
PRODUCTION DATE: September 1897.
LOCATION: Black Maria, West Orange, N.J.
SOURCE:

DESCRIPTION: Shows James T. Kelly and Dorothy Kent, of Waite's Comedy Company, in the famous "Bowery Dance." The dancers are dressed in costumes characteristic to the surroundings, and the dance as shown is an exact reproduction.

The subject shows many humorous situations, is clear, sharp, and the figures show full life size. Suitable for coloring. (F.Z. Maguire & Co., *Catalogue*, [March 1898], 42.)

SUBJECT: Dancing. Working classes. Motion pictures–colored. Waite's Comedy Company. James R. Waite.

ARCHIVE: DLC-pp.

CITATIONS: *New York Clipper*, 25 December 1897, 722.

NOTE:

388 ***Charity Ball**

LENGTH: 50 ft.   © Thomas A. Edison, 24 September 1897.

PRODUCER: William Heise.

CAMERA: William Heise.

CAST: James T. Kelly, Dorothy Kent.

PRODUCTION DATE: September 1897.

LOCATION: Black Maria, West Orange, N.J.

SOURCE:

DESCRIPTION: Shows James T. Kelly and Dorothy Kent, of Waite's Comedy Company, in their popular dance known as the "Charity Ball." The dance is a reproduction of one of the figures of the german, as danced at the famous Charity Ball, which is given each year by the "400" of New

York. The performers are in full dress, Miss Kent's costume being white, thus making it suitable for coloring. The picture is clear, sharp, the figures full life size and the subject pleasing. (F.Z. Maguire & Co., *Catalogue*, [March 1898], 42.)

SUBJECT: Dancing. Motion pictures–colored. Social elites. Waite's Comedy Company. James R. Waite.

ARCHIVE: DLC-pp.

CITATIONS: *New York Clipper*, 25 December 1897, 722.

NOTE:

EDISON EMPLOYEE IS ARRESTED.
Is Charged With Stealing a Series of Kinetoscope Films.
Manager of an Exhibition in Newark Accused of Receiving Stolen Property–Denies Felonious Intent.

Julius Manger, of 249 Bergen street, this city, was arrested by Detective Fallon yesterday afternoon in Edison's works in West Orange on a charge of stealing from the Edison Company half a dozen kinetoscope pictures representing six rounds of the Corbett-Courtney contest, valued at $172, and of disposing of them in Newark for $25. When taken before S.W. Schwab, the superintendent of the works, the accused electrician confessed. He would not, however, disclose who his accomplice was. The Edison people say they have suffered from several similar thefts of late. George E. Mansfield, 52 years old, of 507 West Twenty-third street, New York, who is giving an exhibition at 663 Broad street, this city, was arraigned in the First Precinct Police Court this morning charged with fraud and larceny by Mr. Schwab, representing the Edison Manufacturing Company. It was alleged that Mansfield bough films from Manger at a nominal sum and with the knowledge that the goods were stolen. Mansfield said Manger misrepresented himself to him. He supposed the goods which he bought were second-hand. Schwab said he was willing to drop the complaint against Mansfield. The defendant was paroled for the Grand Jury. (*Newark Daily Advertiser*, 15 September 1898, 5.)

The documenting of Heise's filmmaking activities from his base at Edison headquarters in Orange, N.J., is resumed with film no. 426. The next section continues to trace White and Blechynden's filmmaking from film no. 379.

James White and Frederick W. Blechynden found their ten-month tour of the United States, Mexico, Hawaii and the Far East heavily subsidized, in fact made possible by, transportation companies—particularly railroads. The passenger departments of these railroads were interested in bolstering tourism in the Far West as a way to increase ticket sales. Virtually all these companies published tourist guides, many describing and illustrating the very sites (spots of scenic beauty, hotels, tourist attractions, etc.) that these two men filmed.

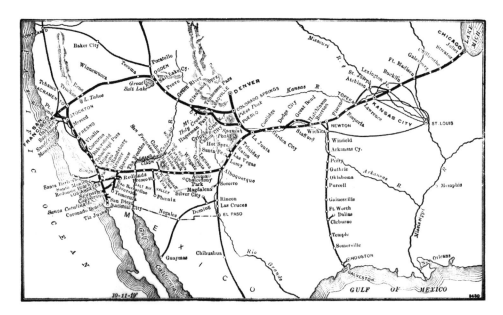

Map showing the railroad lines of the Southern Pacific Railroad (1897).

389 ***Southern Pacific Overland Mail / Overland Mail at Tunnel No. 9**

LENGTH: 100 ft.   © Thomas A. Edison, 25 October 1897.

PRODUCER: James White.

CAMERA: Frederick Blechynden.

CAST:

PRODUCTION DATE: July-August 1897.

LOCATION: Leland Station, Oreg.

SOURCE:

DESCRIPTION: Taken on the line of the Southern Pacific Railroad at tunnel No. 9, near Leland Station, Ore. The scene opens showing a group of women and children standing along the tracks at the mouth of the tunnel. The train, composed of two engines, one baggage car, one mail car and nine coaches, comes rushing out of the tunnel and passes before the audience full size, going at a high rate of speed. After the train has passed the smoke follows out of the mouth of the tunnel in immense volumes, producing a most attractive and realistic effect. The background is formed by rugged hills which show clear and sharp. The picture is one of the best train scenes we have photographed and will prove a very attractive subject. (F.Z. Maguire & Co., *Catalogue*, [March 1898], 37.)

SUBJECT: Railroads. Tunnels. Southern Pacific Railroad.

CITATIONS: *New York Clipper*, 18 December 1897, 699. *Edison Films*, March 1900, 21; *Edison Films*, July 1901, 43.

ARCHIVE: DLC-pp.

NOTE: This film could have been taken at a slightly earlier or later stage of White and Blechynden's filming trip.

By mid-August 1897, White and Blechynden had arrived in San Francisco and were shooting local touristic scenes. They subsequently used the city as a base for their filming expeditions, passing through it almost a half-dozen times during their world tour.

390 ***Leander Sisters / Leander Sisters, Yellow Kid Dance**

LENGTH: 50 ft.   © Thomas A. Edison, 25 October 1897.

PRODUCER: James White.
CAMERA: Frederick Blechynden.
CAST: Leander Sisters.
PRODUCTION DATE: 22 August 1897.
LOCATION: San Francisco, Calif.
SOURCE:

DESCRIPTION: Shows the Leander Sisters in a novel character dance, which they call the "Yellow Kid," performed at Sutro Baths, San Francisco, Cal. One is dressed in an up-to-date long frock coat, to represent the "Yellow Kid." The costumes show a combination of pearl, gray and white, with excellent color effects. The dance is unique, full of action and graceful movements. The figures are life size, with features clearly defined. A large crowd of bathers in costume add to the merit of an excellent subject. (F.Z. Maguire & Co., *Catalogue*, [March 1898], 40.)

SUBJECT: Vaudeville–performances. Dancing. Sutro Baths. Southern Pacific Railroad.
ARCHIVE: DLC-pp.
CITATIONS: *New York Clipper*, 18 December 1897, 699; *Edison Films*, March 1900, 27; *Edison Films,* July 1901, 51.
NOTE:

391 *****Cupid and Psyche / Cupid and Psyche Dance**
LENGTH: 50 ft.   © Thomas A. Edison, 25 October 1897.
PRODUCER: James White.
CAMERA: Frederick Blechynden.
CAST: Leander Sisters.
PRODUCTION DATE: 22 August 1897.
LOCATION: San Francisco, Calif.
SOURCE:

DESCRIPTION: An original dance by the Leander Sisters, performed at the Suthro Baths, San Francisco, Cal. One is dressed as Cupid, with the accompanying wings, bow and arrow; the other represents Psyche. The dance is full of grace and action, and the figures show life size and very clear. The costumes are white, and show up in beautiful contrast to the dark background, which is composed of bathers in bathing costume and two tiers of spectators. The film is in every way an attractive subject. (F.Z. Maguire & Co., *Catalogue*, [March 1898], 40.)

SUBJECT: Vaudeville–performances. Dancing. Sutro Baths. Southern Pacific Railroad.
ARCHIVE: DLC-pp, DLC-AFI.
CITATIONS: *New York Clipper*, 18 December 1897, 699; *Edison Films*, March 1900, 27; *Edison Films,* July 1901, 54.
NOTE:

At the Sutro Baths this afternoon, a fine bill of specialties will be presented, in addition to aquatic features…the Leander sisters will present their novelty dances. (*San Francisco Chronicle*, 22 August 1897, 27.)

392 *****Sutro Baths, no. 1**
LENGTH: 50 ft.   © Thomas A. Edison, 20 September 1897.
PRODUCER: James White.
CAMERA: Frederick Blechynden.
CAST:
PRODUCTION DATE: 22 August 1897.
LOCATION: San Francisco, Calif.
SOURCE:

DESCRIPTION: Taken at the Sutro Baths, San Francisco, Cal., and shows a large crowd of bathers in a small area. The picture is full of action from beginning to end, caused by numerous and varied feats of diving, somersaults, etc. A toboggan slide 50 feet long, at an angle of 45 degrees, furnishes sport for the bathers. Instead of coming down in a car, they slide rapidly down the incline in all manner of postures. On striking the pool, the water is splashed to a height of 10 to 12 feet. One following another in rapid succes-

sion keeps the water churned to a milky foam, which is also the case in all parts of the pool, as bathers are continually jumping, diving, etc., from floats, rafts and the lower floor. The film is replete with ludicrous and humorous scenes. The bathers are clad in black trunks, which show in striking contrast to their exposed flesh and the foam. The background shows the ground floor and two balconies filled with spectators. The picture is exceedingly sharp and clear, and is without doubt one of the best film subjects we have made. (F.Z. Maguire & Co., *Catalogue*, [March 1898], 39.)

SUBJECT: Aquatic sports. Swimming pools. Diving. Sutro Baths. Southern Pacific Railroad.

ARCHIVE: DLC-pp, NR-GE.

CITATIONS: *New York Clipper*, 18 December 1897, 699; *The Phonoscope*, January 1898, 12; *Edison Films*, March 1900, 24; *Edison Films*, July 1901, 45.

NOTE: The Sutro Baths opened in February 1896, a gift of Adolph Heinrich Joseph Sutro, who was mayor of San Francisco from 7 January 1895 to 3 January 1897. The baths cost more than $1,000,000.

393 ***Sutro Baths / Sutro Baths, no. 2**

LENGTH: 50 ft.   © Thomas A. Edison, 25 October 1897.

PRODUCER: James White.

CAMERA: Frederick Blechynden.

CAST:

PRODUCTION DATE: 22 August 1897.

LOCATION: San Francisco, Calif.

SOURCE:

DESCRIPTION: A different view of the same baths, in which less area is taken in, and as a consequence the figures show larger with less background. This film, if possible, contains more action than No. 1, a particular feature being a spring board, from which some remarkable diving feats are per-

formed. It also contains the toboggan slide, and is also exceedingly sharp and clear, and just as interesting as No. 1. (F.Z. Maguire & Co., *Catalogue*, [March 1898], 39.)

SUBJECT: Aquatic sports. Swimming pools. Sutro Baths. Diving. Southern Pacific Railroad.

ARCHIVE: DLC-pp.

CITATIONS: *New York Clipper*, 18 December 1897, 699; *Edison Films*, March 1900, 25; *Edison Films*, July 1901, 45.

NOTE: *Sutro Baths* (copyright title) quickly became *Sutro Baths, no. 2* in Edison catalogs.

394 ***Lurline Baths / Lurline Baths, San Francisco**

LENGTH: 50 ft.   © Thomas A. Edison, 25 October 1897.

PRODUCER: James White.

CAMERA: Frederick Blechynden.

CAST:

PRODUCTION DATE: August 1897.

LOCATION: San Francisco, Calif.

SOURCE:

DESCRIPTION: Taken at the Lurline Baths, San Francisco, Cal., and is a picture full of action and very clear and sharp. The principal feature is a toboggan, down which the bathers slide, some sitting up, others lying down feet first, others head first. There is a continuous stream of people gliding down the slide, and, as they strike the water, it is thrown up in large volumes and churned into milky foam, producing a most pleasing effect. At the same time, other bathers are jumping and diving in the pool, making a

picture full of action and very realistic. In the background can be seen a large crowd going up the stairs to the top of the toboggan. The figures are life size and show clear and distinct. (F.Z. Maguire & Co., *Catalogue*, [March 1898], 40.)

SUBJECT: Aquatic sports. Swimming pools. Lurline Baths. Diving. Southern Pacific Railroad.

ARCHIVE: DLC-pp.

CITATIONS: *New York Clipper,* 18 December 1897, 699; *Edison Films*, March 1900, 25; *Edison Films*, July 1901, 45.

NOTE:

395 *Fisherman's Wharf

LENGTH: 50 ft.   © Thomas A. Edison, 25 October 1897.

PRODUCER: James White.

CAMERA: Frederick Blechynden.

CAST:

PRODUCTION DATE: August 1897.

LOCATION: San Francisco, Calif.

SOURCE:

DESCRIPTION: Shows the wharf at San Francisco, Cal., with a large fleet of fishing boats at anchor. The crews are engaged in mending nets, arranging lines, etc., all of which lend action to the view. The figures are clear and life size, and the scene is truthfully reproduced. (F.Z. Maguire & Co., *Catalogue*, [March 1898], 39.)

SUBJECT: Fishing boats. Harbors–San Francisco. Piers. Southern Pacific Railroad.

ARCHIVE: DLC-pp.

CITATIONS:

NOTE:

396 *Fishing Smacks / Fishing Smacks, San Francisco

LENGTH: 50 ft.   © Thomas A. Edison, 25 October 1897.

PRODUCER: James White.

CAMERA: Frederick Blechynden.

CAST:

PRODUCTION DATE: August 1897.

LOCATION: San Francisco, Calif.

SOURCE:

DESCRIPTION: Taken at Fisherman's Wharf, San Francisco, Cal., with a large fleet of fishing boats at anchor. The crews are engaged in mending nets, arranging lines, etc., all of which lend action to the view. The figures are clear and life size, and the scene is truthfully reproduced. (F.Z. Maguire & Co., *Catalogue*, [March 1898], 39.)

SUBJECT: Fishing boats. Harbors–San Francisco. Piers. Southern Pacific Railroad.
ARCHIVE: DLC-pp.
CITATIONS: *New York Clipper*, 18 December 1897, 699.
NOTE:

397 ***Arrest in Chinatown, San Francisco, Cal.**
LENGTH: 50 ft.   © Thomas A. Edison, 25 October 1897.
PRODUCER: James White.
CAMERA: Frederick Blechynden.
CAST:
PRODUCTION DATE: August 1897.
LOCATION: San Francisco, Calif.
SOURCE:

DESCRIPTION: Taken in San Francisco, Cal., in the famous Chinatown district, where more Chinamen are quartered than any other place of equal size in the United States. The scene is an actual one and shows the arrest of two Chinamen, one a high-binder and the other a hatchet-man, terms applied to two of the worst classes of Chinese crimi-nals. The scene opens showing one of the criminals being forced by a policeman up the street toward the audience. The prisoner's look of anger and hatred is very clearly portrayed. The street is full of pedestrians, all more or less excited, among them being one woman, who clearly shows her fright and hastens across the street to get away from the crowd. In order to get a picture of the patrol wagon it was nec-essary to move the camera, which caused a change in background. The last portion shows the arrival and leaving of the patrol wagon, with prisoners, officers, detec-tives, etc. The whole films is full of action and is a clear and sharp subject. (F.Z. Maguire & Co., *Catalogue*, [March 1898], 97.)
SUBJECT: City and town life–San Francisco. Chinese Americans. Police. Criminals. Southern Pacific Railroad.
ARCHIVE: DLC-pp.
CITATIONS: *New York Clipper*, 18 December 1897, 699.
NOTE:

398 ***S.S. "Coptic" at Dock / Steamer "Coptic" at Dock, San Francisco / Steamship "Coptic" at Dock**
LENGTH: 50 ft.   © Thomas A. Edison, 25 October 1897.
PRODUCER: James White.
CAMERA: Frederick Blechynden.
CAST:
PRODUCTION DATE: 2 September 1897.
LOCATION: San Francisco, Calif.
SOURCE:

DESCRIPTION: Taken at the docks of the Pacific Steamship Co., San Francisco, Cal., which is operated in connection with the Southern Pacific Railroad Co. The "Coptic" is one of the best appointed, largest and fastest ves-sels that traverse the Pacific Ocean, and this view was taken as she was leaving for a voyage to Sandwich Islands, Japan and China. The multitude of people crowding the decks and dock, waving hands, hats, &c, to each other, makes a stirring and life like scene. The picture is clear and sharp and the figures show life size. (F.Z. Maguire & Co., *Catalogue*, [March 1898], 37.)
SUBJECT: Harbors–San Francisco. Steamships. Chinese Americans. Southern Pacific Railroad. Occidental and Oriental Steamship Company.
ARCHIVE: DLC-pp.

CITATIONS: "Departure of China Steamer," *San Francisco Chronicle*, 3 September 1897, 10. *New York Clipper*, 18 December 1897, 699.
NOTE: The next departure of the "Coptic" was 18 November 1897.

399 ***S.S. "Coptic" in the Harbor / Steamer "Coptic" in the Harbor / Steamship "Coptic" in the Harbor***
LENGTH: 50 ft.   © Thomas A. Edison, 25 October 1897.
PRODUCER: James White.
CAMERA: Frederick Blechynden.
CAST:
PRODUCTION DATE: 2 September 1897.
LOCATION: San Francisco, Calif.
SOURCE:
DESCRIPTION: Shows the vessel away from the dock and slowly turning. The vessel is seen to good advantage, the four masts, smokestack and hull being faithfully reproduced. Clouds of smoke pour out of the funnel, and volumes of steam out of the exhaust pipe. In the foreground is a dense crowd, among which are numerous Chinamen. Clear and sharp with figures life-size. (F.Z. Maguire & Co., *Catalogue*, [March 1898], 37.)
SUBJECT: Harbors–San Francisco. Steamships. Chinese Americans. Southern Pacific Railroad. Occidental and Oriental Steamship Company.
ARCHIVE: DLC-pp.
CITATIONS: *San Francisco Chronicle*, 3 September 1897, 10. *New York Clipper*, 18 December 1897, 699.
NOTE: The paper print of this film was mistakenly copyrighted as *S.S. "Coptic" Sailing Away*. The labels for these two subjects were apparently switched by an Edison employee while preparing the materials for copyright.

400 ***S.S. "Coptic" Sailing Away / Steamer "Coptic" Sailing Away / Steamship "Coptic" Sailing Away***
LENGTH: 50 ft.   © Thomas A. Edison, 25 October 1897.
PRODUCER: James White.
CAMERA: Frederick Blechynden.
CAST:
PRODUCTION DATE: 2 September 1897.
LOCATION: San Francisco, Calif.
SOURCE:
DESCRIPTION: Shows the vessel after she has been fully turned and on her way across the Pacific. The boat shows large and clear with smoke coming from the stack. In the foreground is a constantly changing crowd of people composed of men, women and children. Action is added by some late comers who rush to the dock to wave their last farewell. Life-size, sharp and clear. (F.Z. Maguire & Co., *Catalogue*, [March 1898], 38.)
SUBJECT: Harbors–San Francisco. Steamships. Southern Pacific Railroad. Occidental and Oriental Steamship Company.
ARCHIVE: DLC-pp.
CITATIONS: *San Francisco Chronicle*, 3 September 1897, 10. *New York Clipper*, 18 December 1897, 699.
NOTE: The paper print of this film was mistakenly copyrighted as *S.S. "Coptic" in the Harbor*. The labels for these two subjects were apparently switched by an Edison employee while preparing the materials for copyright.

401 ***Stanford University, California***
LENGTH: 50 ft.   © Thomas A. Edison, 25 October 1897.

PRODUCER: James White.
CAMERA: Frederick Blechynden.
CAST:
PRODUCTION DATE: Ca. 3 September 1897.
LOCATION: Palo Alto, Calif.
SOURCE:
DESCRIPTION: Taken at the above University, noted the world over, being the personal gift of the late Senator Leland Stanford. The view shows an immense arch in the background through which are seen coming groups of students, some walking, others on

bicycles. The figures show life size, clear and distinct. The ivy covered walls of the building form the background to a pleasing picture. (F.Z. Maguire & Co., *Catalogue*, [March 1898], 38.)
SUBJECT: Universities. Bicycles. Stanford University. Southern Pacific Railroad. Leland Stanford.
ARCHIVE: DLC-pp.
CITATIONS: *New York Clipper*, 18 December 1897, 699.
NOTE:

Leland Stanford Jr. University

Among the broadest educators the idea is gaining ground that it is better for Eastern young men and women to attend a Western college and *vice versa.* While California, in the past, has sent many students to Eastern colleges and universities, it is only since the opening of the Leland Stanford Jr. University, at Palo Alto, California, that an Eastern tide of students has set toward this State. When this magnificent institution opened its doors, October 1, 1891, almost every State east of the Rocky Mountains, beside other sections more remote, was represented in the hundreds of students that thronged its hall and corridors. In fact, the majority of the students were from the East. It would, perhaps, be an interesting study to ascertain the reasons for this westward-taking of such a large student course. While California's superior climate, so favorable to out-of-door life and exercise, is certainly an element of attraction, it cannot be a very great one, or it would have been operative in the past to a greater degree than it has been. The fact that the Leland Stanford Jr. University is one of the most nobly endowed universities in the world; that it numbers among its professors many of the most advanced educators of the day; that every appointment is designed to be as nearly perfect as an intelligent expenditure of almost unlimited means can make it–these are perhaps some of the reasons why Stanford University has become the Eastern student's Mecca of the West.

The founding of the University as a magnificent monument to an only son; the princely endowment of lands and money; the rapid launching upon the sea of active and practical work–these facts are familiar to almost every one, east or west, who has read the newspapers during the past few years. An institution of learning located thirty miles from San Francisco, in the midst of an estate of more than eight thousand acres, matchless in grace of outline and fertility of soil, is certainly an object to be widely talked about. Beside the Palo Alto estate there are properties in other parts of the State, aggregating some 28,000 acres, making a total of 36,000 acres, this being the land endowment of the great University. From the day of its opening it has taken honorable rank among the prominent universities of the world, its management having been such as to establish it firmly in the confidence of the people. The buildings of the University are one story in height, of gray sandstone. Those thus far completed–extensive as they are, they are but the beginning of a system of structures–are arranged around a quadrangle 586 feet in length by 246 feet in width, inclosing three and one-fourth acres. Extending around the entire quadrangle is a continuous length of wide corridors into which every room opens. Within this sheltered [i]nclosure are gardens in which are grown the rarest trees and plants. Many other buildings have been erected on the domain for dormitory, residence and other purposes, including a beautiful structure for a museum. Students from abroad reside at the University, or at any of the adjacent towns, and many come daily from their own homes along the line of the railroad from San Francisco to San Jose. Tuition and all lectures are free, and visitors to the lecture-rooms are always cordially received. There are at present about eight hundred students enrolled, and some seventy resident professors. (*California for Health, Pleasure and Profit: Why You Should Go There*, 189?, 66.)

White and Blechynden arrived at the Hotel Vendome in San Jose on Friday, 3 September 1897. (San Jose Daily Mercury, *4 September 1897, 6.) They apparently traveled from there to the Lick Observatory on Saturday so they could be present for "visitor's night."*

402 ***Hotel Vendome, San Jose, Cal.**
LENGTH: 50 ft.   © Thomas A. Edison, 25 October 1897.
PRODUCER: James White.
CAMERA: Frederick Blechynden.
CAST: Mr. Ross.
PRODUCTION DATE: Ca. 4 September 1897.
LOCATION: San Jose, Calif.
SOURCE:

DESCRIPTION: The world famous hotel, with
   crowded piazzas, which forms the background, is one of the best in the State of
   California, and is the principal stop for
   tourists en route to the famous Lick
   Observatory. The picture shows two four-
   horse coaches, two teams and two single
horse carriages, loaded with tourists under the guidance of Mr. Ross, proprietor of
the Mt. Hamilton Transportation Co., starting for the Observatory. The picture is
full of action, the figures life size and clear, and the background of hotel, trees and
foliage very true to life. (F.Z. Maguire & Co., *Catalogue*, [March 1898], 38.)
SUBJECT: Hotels. Tourist trade. Carriages and carts. Lick Observatory. Mt. Hamilton
   Transportation Co. Southern Pacific Railroad.
ARCHIVE: DLC-pp.
CITATIONS: *New York Clipper*, 18 December 1897, 699; *Edison Films*, March 1900, 21.
NOTE:

403 ***Lick Observatory, Mt. Hamilton, Cal.**
LENGTH: 50 ft.   © Thomas A. Edison, 25 October 1897.
PRODUCER: James White.
CAMERA: Frederick Blechynden.
CAST:
PRODUCTION DATE: 4 September 1897.
LOCATION: Mt. Hamilton, Calif.
SOURCE:

DESCRIPTION: The background of this picture is
   the Lick Observatory, Mount Hamilton,
   Cal. This observatory, the gift of James
   Lick, of Pennsylvania, was constructed at a
   cost of $700,000, being equipped with one of
   the most powerful telescopes that has ever
   been produced, and is famous the world
over. The view of the Observatory is very complete, showing the style of architecture, including the glass covered dome in which are placed the various astronomical
instruments. Every Saturday night throughout the year is set apart for visitors to
inspect the Observatory and look through the great glass. This view shows a coach
load driving up and alighting. (F.Z. Maguire & Co., *Catalogue*, [March 1898], 38.)
SUBJECT: Tourist trade. Carriages and carts. Observatories. Lick Observatory. Mt.
   Hamilton Transportation Co. Southern Pacific Railroad. James Lick.
ARCHIVE: DLC-pp.
CITATIONS: *New York Clipper*, 18 December 1897, 699.
NOTE:

LICK OBSERVATORY.

Although Lick Observatory—on the summit of Mount Hamilton, Santa Clara county (4,209 feet above sea-level)—is
only thirteen miles from San Jose in an air line, yet, to preserve a comfortable and easy grade, the magnificent
driveway leading to it is some twenty-six miles in length. A more delightful outing trip cannot be imagined than a
visit to this site of the largest telescope in the world, especially if one goes in the spring or early summer, or
immediately after the first autumn rains. The journey is a continuous series of new and fascinating surprises in the
way of wildly romantic views, and an ever-changing combination of nearly all the varieties of tree and shrub and
wild-flower peculiar to California mountain sections.

The tourist usually leaves San Jose in the early morning, either by one of the regular stages or as one of a party going by private carriage. An exception to this hour of starting is generally made on Saturday, when the stages leave later as Saturday night is "visitors' night" at the Observatory. On this night the entire force of astronomers and professors is resolved into a reception committee to introduce the crowds of visitors to the wonders of the heavens through the great telescope and other lesser glasses. During the season, that is from early spring to late autumn, from 150 to 200 visitors are entertained every Saturday night.

The last few miles of the road before reaching the summit of the mountain are exceedingly circuitous in order to keep the grade within the limit of six feet to one hundred, the road being very wide and well kept. As one rounds turn after turn of the last peak, until the ascent seems like threading the spirals of an immense screw, a vision of magnificent distance is opened before him, unexcelled in the world. Over the summit of the Coast Range is seen at various points the Pacific Ocean. Far to the north is the snow-capped peak of Lassen's Butte, 175 miles distant is the Sierra Nevada; while the great range of the Sierra Nevada comes out clear and sharp at sunrise. At no other observatory in the world is the air so uniformly clear, or are there so many nights favorable for astronomical observation. The visitor is received at the main entrance of the Observatory, and, after registering his name in the "Visitors' Book," and looking around awhile at interesting objects without number, passes up a stairway into the great dome seventy-five feet in diameter, where is placed the great thirty-six inch telescope. Seating himself in the gallery which encircles the dome, he awaits his turn at the glass, where one of the astronomers is stationed explaining and answering questions. After he has gazed his allotted time he reluctantly gives place to some one else, and goes over to the twenty-five-foot dome at the end of the "long hall" and joins another crowd at the twelve inch telescope.

James Lick, the founder of the observatory which bears his name, and whose body lies buried under the pier upon which rests the great telescope, was an eccentric Pennsylvanian, who came to California in 1847, leaving home, it has been asserted, on account of an unhappy love affair. He never married. By wise and careful investments in lands and other properties in San Francisco and Santa Clara County he was, at his death, many times a millionaire. Nearly all his property was deeded for different benevolent purposes. The gift which will do the most good and immortalize his name was the $700,000 donation for his monument—the Lick Observatory, with its mammoth telescope, on the summit of Mount Hamilton. (*California for Health, Pleasure and Profit: Why You Should Go There*, 189?, 60-61.)

404 ***Surf at Monterey**
LENGTH: 50 ft.   © Thomas A. Edison, 25 October 1897.
PRODUCER: James White.
CAMERA: Frederick Blechynden.
CAST:
PRODUCTION DATE: Ca. 5 September 1897.
LOCATION: Monterey, Calif.
SOURCE: *Rough Sea at Dover* (R.W. Paul film, 1895).

DESCRIPTION: This is one of the ever popular surf scenes and was taken at Monterey, Cal. In the foreground are two large rocks over which the surf breaks in volumes, at times completely covering them. The water breaking over the rocks, is dashed in silvery like spray and thrown many feet high. The film is very clear and sharp, with exceptionally fine water effects, and will prove a subject interesting to any audience. (F.Z. Maguire & Co., *Catalogue*, [March 1898], 38.)
SUBJECT: Ocean waves. Seashore. Southern Pacific Railroad.
ARCHIVE: DLC-pp.
CITATIONS: *New York Clipper*, 18 December 1897, 699; *Edison Films*, March 1900, 21; *Edison Films*, July 1901, 43.
NOTE:

405 ***Hotel Del Monte / Hotel Del Monte, Monterey, Cal.**
LENGTH: 50 ft.   © Thomas A. Edison, 25 October 1897.
PRODUCER: James White.
CAMERA: Frederick Blechynden.
CAST:
PRODUCTION DATE: Ca. 5 September 1897.

LOCATION: Monterey, Calif.

SOURCE:

DESCRIPTION: This magnificent and well-known hotel, located at Monterey, Cal., on the line of the Southern Pacific Railroad, forms the background. It is one of the largest and best appointed hotels in the country. It is surrounded by a luxuriant growth of Palms, Oleander, Cypress, Pampas Grass and other tropical plants, many of which are shown in the picture. The view shows a party starting on what is known as the sev-

enteen mile drive, being conveyed in a six-horse coach, two four-horse wagons and one two-horse vehicle, all of which lend action to an artistic subject. (F.Z. Maguire & Co., *Catalogue*, [March 1898], 38)

SUBJECT: Hotels. Tourist trade. Carriages and carts. Southern Pacific Railroad.

ARCHIVE: DLC-pp.

CITATIONS: *New York Clipper*, 18 December 1897, 699; *Edison Films*, March 1900, 21.

NOTE:

Del Monte.

Said an enthusiastic lady recently, after visiting this beautiful resort: "If I had the choice between Del Monte and Elysium I am much afraid that I should take Del Monte." This is perhaps an emphasized expression of the feelings of all who have visited the place. It would be difficult to find another spot where nature and art have been so fortunately united in the realization of such truly artistic ideals.

Situated on the beautiful Bay of Monterey, whose natural loveliness is enhanced by the many historic and romantic memories which attach to it, with a climate remarkable for its genial and unchanging mildness, three hours by rail from San Francisco, and easily accessible from all parts of the State, Del Monte unquestionably deserves the admiration it receives.

The hotel, a magnificent structure capable of comfortably accommodating four or five hundred guests, is set in the midst of a beautiful park of one hundred acres. In the grounds immediately adjoining the buildings the skill of the landscape gardener and florist has been taxed to the utmost, and the wilderness of rare and beautiful blossoms, the year round, is a constant marvel to the visitor.

A few yards from the hotel is the bay, whose slow rolling breakers mingle their never-ceasing sound with the sighing of the stately pines which surround the place, until the charmed listener is puzzled to distinguish the dominant note of this "married music." The commingling of sea air with the odor of the pines produces an atmosphere peculiarly rich in ozone, and is probably one secret of the remarkable healthfulness of the place.

Every facility for salt-water bathing in all varieties is found at Del Monte, warm swimming-baths and luxurious tub-bathing happily supplementing the regular ocean "dip." In the wooded hills and ravines surrounding the bay, hunting and angling can be enjoyed at pleasure, as well as the fishing in the waters of the bay.

Within a few minutes' walk of Del Monte, and connected with it by street car, is the old historic town of Monterey, the first territorial capital of California, and also the seat of the second of the California Missions, as well as the home of the first missionary president, Father Junipero Serra. Many old adobe buildings and other quaint remembrances yet remain to tell of bygone days; and the relic-hunter and one interested in the reminiscences of a romantic past can find ample opportunity for the gratification of his taste in Monterey and surroundings.

Some two or three miles beyond Monterey is Pacific Grove, which began existence as a seaside camping-place, but has developed into a lovely little city of homes, and one of the pleasantest seaside resorts on the Coast.

A magnificent drive, known as the seventeen-mile drive, girdles the peninsula upon which the two towns are located, and gives one a glorious view of the old Pacific unsubdued by island, or land modifier of any sort. No one who visits Del Monte should miss the seventeen-mile drive. Neither should he forget to see the ruins of Carmel Mission, some seven miles from Monterey, the site chosen by Father Serra for the relocation of the Mission of San Carlos at Monterey. (*California for Health, Pleasure and Profit: Why You Should Go There*, 189?, 62-63.)

406 *Boxing for Points

LENGTH: 50 ft.   © Thomas A. Edison, 25 October 1897.

PRODUCER: James White.

CAMERA: Frederick Blechynden.

CAST: Private Darrin, Corporal Healy.

PRODUCTION DATE: 9 September 1897.

LOCATION: Presidio, San Francisco, Calif.

SOURCE:

DESCRIPTION: This subject was taken at the Grand Military Athletic Tournament, Presidio Military Reservation, San Francisco, Cal., Sept. 9, 1897, held under the auspices of the Lincoln Monument League. It shows Private Darrin, Battery G., Third Artillery, and Corporal Healy, Troop B, Fourth Cavalry, in a lively fistic encounter, seconded by their respective officers. This is one of the regular features, the points counting in the final score. As a

consequence, a fast, hard hitting, scientific battle ensues, during which one of the contestants scores a knock-down. An immense crowd of spectators is shown in the background. A sharp, clear picture with action from start to finish. (F.Z. Maguire, *Catalogue*, 1898, 40.)

SUBJECT: Sports. Boxing. Armies–United States. Southern Pacific Railroad.

ARCHIVE: DLC-pp.

CITATIONS: *New York Clipper*, 18 December 1897, 699.

NOTE:

407 ***Wall Scaling**

LENGTH: 50 ft.   © Thomas A. Edison, 25 October 1897.

PRODUCER: James White.

CAMERA: Frederick Blechynden.

CAST:

PRODUCTION DATE: 9 September 1897.

LOCATION: Presidio, San Francisco, Calif.

SOURCE:

DESCRIPTION: Taken at the Grand Military Athletic Tournament, Presidio Military Reservation, San Francisco, Cal., Sept. 9, 1897, held under the auspices of the Lincoln Monument League, shows a team from Company G, First Infantry, and a team from Company D, First Infantry, in

full equipment, scaling a sixteen foot wall. The pictures show the men running to the fence, climbing on each other's shoulders, thus reaching the top, and then leaping to the ground on the opposite side. A true reproduction of a difficult and exciting military manoeuvre, full of action, with figures life-size. (F.Z. Maguire & Co., *Catalogue,* [March 1898], 40.)

SUBJECT: Sports. Armies–United States. Southern Pacific Railroad.

ARCHIVE: DLC-pp.

CITATIONS:

NOTE:

PRESIDIO ATHLETICS ATTRACT THOUSANDS.
REVEL IN A PERFECT DAY.
BENEFIT OF LINCOLN MONUMENT FUND.
There Was a Brave Military Showing That Gave Spirit to the Occasion.

A perfect day brought several thousand people out to the Presidio yesterday to witness the military and athletic games by the United States troops stationed at San Francisco and vicinity. The tournament was under the auspices of the Lincoln Monument League, and the proceeds will go to the monument fund.

The games and events were under the control and management of a board of officials selected from among the United States Army officers, and as usual under such management were brought off promptly, and the field arrangements were excellent. The manager was Lieutenant Leon S. Roudiez, Quartermaster First Infantry; assistant manager, Second Lieutenant Dennis E. Nolan, First Infantry; general referee, First Lieutenant J.M. Neall, Fourth Cavalry; special referee for light artillery events, Captain Charles W. Hobbs, Third Artillery; special referee for boxing, First Lieutenant R.C. Croxton, First Infantry; judges, Captain James S. Pettit, First Infantry; Captain James Lockett, Fourth Cavalry; Captain Charles G. Starr, First Infantry; timekeepers, Captain Louis P. Brant, First Infantry; First Lieutenant Hiram McL. Powell, First Infantry; Second Lieutenant James N. Pickering, First Infantry; starter, First Lieutenant J.P. Hains, Third Artillery; clerk of course, Second Lieutenant D.W. Kilburn, First Infantry; assistant clerk of course, Sergeant John Salter, Company E, First Infantry; scorer, Private Brook, Troop B, Fourth Cavalry.

Among the athletic events, those of a military character were probably the most interesting to the general body of the spectators, and of these, the cavalry and artillery events brought out the most applause.

In the afternoon there was a grand display drill of a battalion of light artillery, consisting of Light Batteries C and F, Third Artillery, under command of Lieutenant Colonel E.B. Williston. The dash and spirit of the drill evoked round after round of applause from the great throngs which saw it.

The results of the athletic and military events were as follows:...

Boxing for Points, lightweights–Springfield first, Healy second, Petees third; heavyweights, Smith first, Hendrie second, Weatherly third....

Wall scaling, ten feet, two runs–First run team of Company D, First Infantry, first; team of Battery H, Third Artillery, second. Time, 0:36 4-5; second run, team of Company A, First Infantry, first; team of Battery G, Third artillery, second. Time: 0:37 3-5....(*San Francisco Chronicle*, 10 September 1897, 7.)

---

408 ***Beach Apparatus-Practice**
LENGTH: 50 ft.   © Thomas A. Edison, 25 October 1897.
PRODUCER: James White.
CAMERA: Frederick Blechynden.
CAST:
PRODUCTION DATE: September 1897.
LOCATION: Presidio, San Francisco, Calif.
SOURCE:

DESCRIPTION: Taken during drill hours at Pacific Coast Life Saving Service, Fort Point Station, Presidio, San Francisco, Cal., Capt. Joseph Hodgson commanding, and illustrates how a crew is rescued from the mast of a sunken vessel. In the foreground the crew is seen engaged in arranging the apparatus; the dynamite mortar is taken from its carriage, set in place, loaded, sighted and fired, projecting the life line over the mast. The shore end of the life line is then made fast to a large hawser, which is hauled out and made fast to the topmast. By means of this hawser a buoy is subsequently sent to the imperiled mariners, which they fasten around their bodies and then slide down the inclined rope to the shore. The film is very clear, the smoke effects are fine and the subject full of action. (F.Z. Maguire & Co., *Catalogue*, [March 1898], 36.)
SUBJECT: Life saving apparatus. Seashore. U.S. Life Saving Service. Capt. Joseph Hodgson.
ARCHIVE: DLC-pp.
CITATIONS: *New York Clipper*, 18 December 1897, 699.
NOTE:

---

409 ***Rescue-Resuscitation**
LENGTH: 50 ft.   © Thomas A. Edison, 25 October 1897.
PRODUCER: James White.
CAMERA: Frederick Blechynden.
CAST:
PRODUCTION DATE: September 1897.
LOCATION: Presidio, San Francisco, Calif.
SOURCE:
DESCRIPTION: Taken at the Pacific Coast Life-Saving Service, Fort Point Station, Presidio, San Francisco, Cal., Capt. Joseph Hodgson commanding, and shows the actual process of rescuing and resuscitating drowning people. The film opens showing a man on an overturned boat waving his hat for help, two of the life-saving corps then shoot a life line to him, which he catches and fastens around his body.

The shipwrecked man is then hauled through the water to the shore by the full corps of five men, who pick him up, lay him across a log and go through the resuscitating operations. The picture is full of action, the figures showing up full life-size, sharp and clear. (F.Z. Maguire & Co., *Catalogue*, [March 1898], 36.)

SUBJECT: Life saving apparatus. Seashore. Ocean waves. U.S. Life Saving Service. Capt. Joseph Hodgson.

ARCHIVE: DLC-pp.

CITATIONS: *New York Clipper*, 18 December 1897, 699; *Edison Films*, March 1900, 20; *Edison Films*, July 1901, 42.

NOTE:

410 ***Launch of Life Boat / Launch of a Lifeboat, Fort Point Sta., Cal.**

LENGTH: 50 ft.   © Thomas A. Edison, 25 October 1897.

PRODUCER: James White.

CAMERA: Frederick Blechynden.

CAST:

PRODUCTION DATE: September 1897.

LOCATION: Presidio, San Francisco, Calif.

SOURCE:

DESCRIPTION: Taken at the Pacific Coast Life Saving Service, Fort Point Station, Presidio, San Francisco, Cal., commanded by Capt. Joseph Hodgson, and shows the crew in the act of starting for a wreck. The scene opens with the opening of the boat-house door, followed by the boat speeding down a runway into the water. The sailors, with oars pointing upward, and the splashing waters, are clearly reproduced, making an interesting scene. (F.Z. Maguire & Co., *Catalogue*, [March 1898], 35.)

SUBJECT: Life saving apparatus. Seashore. U.S. Life Saving Service. Capt. Joseph Hodgson.

ARCHIVE: DLC-pp.

CITATIONS: *New York Clipper*, 18 December 1897, 699.

NOTE:

411 ***Capsize of Lifeboat.**

LENGTH: 50 ft.   © Thomas A. Edison, 25 October 1897.

PRODUCER: James White.

CAMERA: Frederick Blechynden.

CAST:

PRODUCTION DATE: September 1897.

LOCATION: Presidio, San Francisco, Calif.

SOURCE:

DESCRIPTION: Taken at Pacific Coast Life Saving Service, Fort Point Station, Presidio, San Francisco, Cal., Capt. Joseph Hodgson commanding, and shows the crew capsizing a life boat. These boats are self-righting and self-bailing, and this act is rehearsed daily, so that they are prepared for any such accident. The scene opens with the boat on its beam ends, the crew standing on the lower gunwale holding fast to the upper one. They succeed in turning the boat completely over, remaining beneath it. The boat subsequently rights itself, carrying the sailors with it. The subject is very novel, and is faithfully reproduced. (F.Z. Maguire & Co., *Catalogue*, [March 1898], 36.)

SUBJECT: Life saving apparatus. Seashore. U.S. Living Saving Service. Capt. Joseph Hodgson.

ARCHIVE: DLC-pp.

CITATIONS: *New York Clipper*, 18 December 1897, 699; *Edison Films*, March 1900, 20; *Edison Films*, July 1901, 42.

NOTE:

---

412   *Boat Wagon and Beach Cart / Boat, Wagon and Beach Cart

LENGTH: 50 ft.   © Thomas A. Edison, 25 October 1897.

PRODUCER: James White.

CAMERA: Frederick Blechynden.

CAST:

PRODUCTION DATE: September 1897.

LOCATION: Golden Gate Park, San Francisco, Calif.

SOURCE:

DESCRIPTION: Taken at Pacific Coast Life Saving Service, Golden Gate Park, Ocean Beach, San Francisco, Cal., Capt. George H. Varney commanding, and shows the lifeboat crew rushing out of the boat-house drawing the lifeboat on a four-wheel wagon, followed by the beach cart. A pet bulldog running at full speed after the apparatus makes a pleasing addition to a subject full of action. The figures are full life size, sharp and clear. (F.Z. Maguire & Co., *Catalogue*, [March 1898], 36.)

SUBJECT: Life saving apparatus. Seashore. Dogs. U.S. Life Saving Service. Capt. George H. Varney.

ARCHIVE: DLC-pp.

CITATIONS: *New York Clipper*, 18 December 1897, 699.

NOTE:

---

413   *Launch of Surf Boat / Launching of Surf Boat / Launching the Surf Boat

LENGTH: 50 ft.   © Thomas A. Edison, 25 October 1897.

PRODUCER: James White.

CAMERA: Frederick Blechynden.

CAST:

PRODUCTION DATE: September 1897.

LOCATION: Golden Gate Park, San Francisco, Calif.

SOURCE:

DESCRIPTION: Taken at Pacific Coast Life Saving Service, Golden Gate Park Station, Ocean Beach, San Francisco, Cal., Capt. George H. Varney commanding. The beginning shows the crew of seven men, dressed in cork jackets, wading through the surf and pushing the boat into deep water. When deep water is reached they climb into the boat and row out over the rough surf. The point at which this was taken is the most dangerous on the Pacific Coast, and the most difficult place to launch a boat. The surf is very high, and the boat riding the waves produces a fine effect. The white-capped waves and water breaking on the shore make a beautiful and realistic surf scene. A sharp and clear subject. (F.Z. Maguire & Co., *Catalogue*, [March 1898], 36.)

SUBJECT: Life saving apparatus. Seashore. Ocean waves. U.S. Life Saving Service. Capt. George H. Varney.

ARCHIVE: DLC-pp.

CITATIONS: *New York Clipper*, 18 December 1897, 699; *Edison Films*, March 1900, 20; *Edison Films*, July 1901, 42.
NOTE:

414 *Return of Lifeboat / Return of the Life Boat

LENGTH: 50 ft.   © Thomas A. Edison, 25 October 1897.
PRODUCER: James White.
CAMERA: Frederick Blechynden.
CAST:
PRODUCTION DATE: September 1897.
LOCATION: Golden Gate Park, San Francisco, Calif.
SOURCE:
DESCRIPTION: Taken at Pacific Coast Life Saving Service, Golden Gate Park Station, Ocean Beach, San Francisco, Cal., Capt. Geo. H. Varney commanding. Shows a life boat attempting to reach the shore through the breakers. The surf is so very wild that the boat tosses about like a cork, showing the extreme difficulty and danger attending the landing. The waves are high and the water effects beautiful. An interesting subject, with the figures showing large and clear. (F.Z. Maguire & Co., *Catalogue*, [March 1898], 37.)
SUBJECT: Life saving apparatus. Seashore. Ocean waves. U.S. Life Saving Service. Capt. George H. Varney.
ARCHIVE: DLC-pp.
CITATIONS: *New York Clipper*, 18 December 1897, 699; *Edison Films*, March 1900, 20.
NOTE: The filmmkers used crude camera movements to keep the boat in frame.

PACIFIC LIFE SAVING SERVICE SERIES

These subjects are illustrative of the work performed by the Life Saving Corps of the United States Government, and show the methods in vogue at one of the most important stations on either side of our Continent. The exact routine pursued in actual practice is clearly illustrated. We are particularly indebted to Major T.J. Blackeney, Superintendent of the U.S. Life Saving Service, 12th District, San Francisco, Cal., and Captain W.C. Coulson, of the U.S. Revenue Cutter, San Francisco, for their kind cooperation. We are thus enabled to bring before the public generally absolutely true and accurate pictures of one of our most worthy as well as interesting institutions, the crews of which are constantly risking their own lives for the preservation of others. (*Edison Films*, March 1900, 20.)

415 *The Sea Lions' Home

LENGTH: 50 ft.   © Thomas A. Edison, 25 October 1897.
PRODUCER: James White.
CAMERA: Frederick Blechynden.
CAST:
PRODUCTION DATE: September 1897.
LOCATION: San Francisco, Calif.
SOURCE:

DESCRIPTION: A scene taken near the Golden Gate Beach and shows the sea lions in their wild state. The water surrounding the rocks is considered to be the roughest on the Pacific Coast, and none but the stoutest boats can live therein sufficiently close to the rocks to secure a picture. Through the kindness of Maj. T.J. Blackeney, Sup't U.S. Life Saving Service, our photographers were furnished specially with a life boat commanded by Capt. Geo. H. Varney, Golden Gate Station, from which this picture was obtained. The sea lions are clearly shown, some lying on the rocks, others swimming about in the water and others diving off the rocks into the water. The rugged rocks in the background and the water breaking against the rocks combine

to make an attractive subject. (F.Z. Maguire & Co., *Catalogue*, [March 1898], 37.)
The famous Seal Rocks at Golden Gate Park are here shown. Sea lions in their wild
state are lying on the rocks and swimming and diving in the water. (*Edison Films*,
March 1900, 20.)

SUBJECT: Ocean waves. Seashore. Sea lions. U.S. Life Saving Service. Capt. George H.
Varney. Maj. T.J. Blackeney.

ARCHIVE: DLC-pp.

CITATIONS: *New York Clipper*, 18 December 1897, 699.

NOTE:

*In late September or early October, James White and Frederick Blechynden left the San
Francisco bay area for Colorado, where they arranged to shoot the Festival of Mountain
and Plain.*

416 ***Masked Procession**

LENGTH: 50 ft.   © Thomas A. Edison, 24 February 1898.

PRODUCER: James White.

CAMERA: Frederick Blechynden.

CAST:

PRODUCTION DATE: 5 October 1897.

LOCATION: Denver, Colo.

SOURCE:

DESCRIPTION: Taken during the Festival of
Mountain and Plain at Denver, Col., with
the grand-stand and its immense throng of
people forming the background. This film is
remarkable for the number of people
shown, all of whom are dressed in most gro-
tesque costumes. The masqueraders are seen marching on the right, while a procession of bicyclists in fantastic costumes pass to the left in the opposite direction. (*The
Phonoscope*, March 1898, 14.)

SUBJECT: Parades. Masqueraders. Bicycles. Festival of Mountain and Plain. Denver &
Rio Grande Railroad.

ARCHIVE: DLC-pp.

CITATIONS: *Edison Films*, 15 March 1898, 7; F.Z. Maguire & Co., *Catalogue*, [March
1898], 13; *Edison Films*, March 1900, 18.

NOTE:

417 ***Cripple Creek Floats**

LENGTH: 50 ft.   © Thomas A. Edison, 24 February 1898.

PRODUCER: James White.

CAMERA: Frederick Blechynden.

CAST:

PRODUCTION DATE: 5 October 1897.

LOCATION: Denver, Colo.

SOURCE:

DESCRIPTION: Taken at Denver, Col., at the
Festival of Mountain and Plain, at the same
point as the above mentioned films, with
the same background. The film opens disclosing a large float, representing an
immense rock, across the center of which
has been painted a representation of run-
ning water. The front of the float shows the opening of a mine, in front of which are
standing several miners. The first float is followed by another, drawn by four black
horses, each horse being led by a groom in a long flowing gown. This float represents
the shaft or entrance to a mine. It is beautifully decorated with flowers, and on
either corner is a pedestal, each surrounded by a young girl, while high up on the
centre of the float another young girl sits in state. The conception is most unique,

and the effects produced are remarkably fine. The film is sharp, and the objects come well in the foreground, showing life size. (*Edison Films*, 15 March 1898, 7.)

SUBJECT: Parades. Parade floats. Gold mines and mining. Children. Festival of Mountain and Plain. Denver & Rio Grande Railroad.

ARCHIVE: DLC-pp.

CITATIONS: F.Z. Maguire & Co., *Catalogue*, [March 1898], 13; *Edison Films*, March 1900, 18.

NOTE: Same camera position as above.

GOLDEN CRIPPLE

Cripple Creek was represented by a severely plain float, yet it told a story that is scarcely credited by anyone outside the state. On the float were arranged seven pyramids ranging from a very small one to one almost mountain high. The pyramids were labeled as follows: 1891, $126,000; 1892, $1,200,000; 1893, 2,600,000; 1894: 4,260,000; 1895, eleven tons of pure gold; 1896, sixteen tons of pure gold; 1897, two tons of gold per month. The Eastern people who noted this display could not comprehend the magnitude of measuring gold by the ton.

The Victor float was the richest county display in the parade. It was a picture of a mountain of solid gold pierced by the famous Ulniah tunnel–and on either side was built of silver a stamp mill and tramway. On the corners of the float rode the four fairest daughters of Victor, representing the Portland, Independence, Gold Coin and Granite mines. The brilliancy of this float defies description. (*Denver Post*, 5 October 1897, 8.)

418 ***Procession of Mounted Indians and Cowboys***

LENGTH: 150 ft.   © Thomas A. Edison, 24 February 1898.

PRODUCER: James White.

CAMERA: Frederick Blechynden.

CAST:

PRODUCTION DATE: 5 October 1897.

LOCATION: Denver, Colo.

SOURCE:

DESCRIPTION: Taken at Denver, Col., at the junction of Broadway and Colfax avenues, at the annual festival of Mountain and Plain. The official grand-stand with its throngs of people, forms the background. This is another section of the same parade, in which are shown mounted indian braves and squaws of the Pueblos, Apaches and Utes, in full Indian costume and war paint. Several floats characteristic of the country, including a float which carries an old miner and his donkey, pass. The procession ends with a group of rough cowboy riders on their half-tamed broncos. (*Edison Films*, 15 March 1898, 6.)

SUBJECT: Parades. Gold mines and mining. Indians of North America. Cowboys. Ute Indians. Pueblo Indians. Apache Indians. Festival of Mountain and Plain. Denver & Rio Grande Railroad.

ARCHIVE: DLC-pp.

CITATIONS: F.Z. Maguire & Co., *Catalogue*, [March 1898], 13; *Edison Films*, March 1900, 18.

NOTE: Same camera position as above.

419 ***Horticultural Floats, no. 9***

LENGTH: 50 ft.   © Thomas A. Edison, 24 February 1898.

PRODUCER: James White.

CAMERA: Frederick Blechynden.

CAST:

PRODUCTION DATE: 5 October 1897.

LOCATION: Denver, Colo.

SOURCE:

DESCRIPTION: Taken at the junction of Broadway and Colfax Avenues, Denver, Col., at the annual fete known as the "Festival of Mountain and Plain." The official grand-stand, crowded with citizens of Denver and visitors, forms the background. A continuous line of vehicles, going in either direction, pass the reviewing stand. The floats are mammouth in size and heavily massed with flowers, each wheel of the vehicles being a large rosette of flowers. The horses drawing the floats are beautiful and spirited animals. (*Edison Films,* 15 March 1898, 6.)

SUBJECT: Parades. Parade floats. Horticulture. Festival of Mountain and Plain. Denver & Rio Grande Railroad.

ARCHIVE: DLC-pp.

CITATIONS: *The Phonoscope*, March 1898, 14; F.Z. Maguire & Co., *Catalogue*, [March 1898], 12.

NOTE: Same camera position as above.

420 ***Decorated Carriages, no. 11**

LENGTH: 50 ft.   © Thomas A. Edison, 24 February 1898.

PRODUCER: James White.

CAMERA: Frederick Blechynden.

CAST:

PRODUCTION DATE: 5 October 1897.

LOCATION: Denver, Colo.

SOURCE:

DESCRIPTION: Taken at the same point as the above mentioned films, with the same background. In this scene are shown the most fashionable equipages of the Denverites, all of which are beautifully decorated with flowers. The occupants, consisting of ladies and gentlemen, are also specially costumed for the occasion. There are also horse-back riders, and one [of] the equestrians is having considerable trouble to manage his unruly mount. (*Edison Films*, 15 March 1898, 7.)

SUBJECT: Parades. Social elites. Carriages and carts. Festival of Mountain and Plain. Denver & Rio Grande Railroad.

ARCHIVE: DLC-pp.

CITATIONS: F.Z. Maguire & Co., *Catalogue*, [March 1898], 13; *Edison Films*, March 1900, 19.

NOTE: Same camera position as above.

421 ***Chinese Procession, no. 12**

LENGTH: 50 ft.   © Thomas A. Edison, 24 February 1898.

PRODUCER: James White.

CAMERA: Frederick Blechynden.

CAST:

PRODUCTION DATE: 5 October 1897.

LOCATION: Denver, Colo.

SOURCE:

DESCRIPTION: Taken at the Festival of Mountain and Plain, and shows the Celestials who take part in the procession, dressed in their native costumes, playing their crude barbaric musical instruments and carrying their national flag, embellished with dragon and serpents. The woman riding the pony is said to be a native princess, descended from royal blood. Sharp and clear. (*Edison Films*, 15 March 1898, 7.)

SUBJECT: Parades. Chinese Americans. Flags–China. Festival of Mountain and Plain. Denver & Rio Grande Railroad

ARCHIVE: DLC-pp.

CITATIONS: *The Phonoscope*, March 1898, 14; F.Z. Maguire & Co., *Catalogue*, [March 1898], 13.

NOTE: Same camera position as above.

PHOTOGRAPHS
The Parades Will Be "Taken" by All the New Moving Picture Processes.

All the latest inventions for obtaining life-like pictures of the week's parade will be in use. The viviascope, which is the very latest creation of this character, the product of C.S. Jackson, son of Denver's famous photographer, W.H. Jackson, will be given its first practical work. It was tested on Saturday and proved that it is capable of accomplishing the designs of its inventor. The viviascope not only takes pictures at the rate of 30 per second but displays them on canvas. Mr. Jackson will take pictures of the scenes from a vantage point in the grand stand.

A great many views will be obtained by members of the Colorado Camera club which has a stand erected at Colfax and Broadway expressly for this work. The views are to be utilized by members of the club for instruction and enlargement.

The local representatives of the New York Biograph company will obtain many views for use in theaters and the Edison vitascope will also catch all that can be secured of the parades, balls and other moving panoramas, all guaranteed that millions of amusement-seeking people throughout the union will be reminded of the Festival of Mountain and Plain during the next year as a result of scientific discoveries. (*Denver Post*, 4 October 1897, 3.)

Although James White and Frederick Blechynden may have shot the following two films at the Santa Clara Indian Reservation as indicated by the respective catalog descriptions, it seems much more likely that these dances were conveniently filmed at the local city park during the Festival of Mountain and Plain.

422 *Wand Dance, Pueblo Indians

LENGTH: 50 ft.   © Thomas A. Edison, 24 February 1898.

PRODUCER: James White.

CAMERA: Frederick Blechynden.

CAST:

PRODUCTION DATE: [3-8 October 1897.]

LOCATION: [City Park, Denver, Colo.]

SOURCE:

DESCRIPTION: Taken at Santa Clara. The foreground of this picture is formed by five small Indian papooses, who face the audience, full life size. The dancers are dressed in their native costumes, including war paint and feathers. The dance, while not particularly rapid, is weird in the extreme, and is a faithful reproduction of this peculiar custom. They go through the ceremony with the usual stolidity and lack of expression characteristic of the race. The music for the dance is furnished by a lone tom-tom player, who stands at the centre of the group. Sharp and clear. (*Edison Films,* 15 March 1898, 8.)

SUBJECT: Indians of North America. Dancing. Drums. Santa Clara Pueblo Indians from Espanola, N. Mex. Festival of Mountain and Plain. Denver & Rio Grande Railroad.

ARCHIVE: DLC-pp.

CITATIONS: "Indians," *Denver Post*, 4 October 1897, 3. *The Phonoscope*, March 1898, 14; F.Z. Maguire & Co., *Catalogue*, [March 1898], 13; *Edison Films*, March 1900, 19; *Edison Films*, July 1901, 41.

NOTE:

423 *Eagle Dance, Pueblo Indians

LENGTH: 50 ft.   © Thomas A. Edison, 24 February 1898.

PRODUCER: James White.

CAMERA: Frederick Blechynden.

CAST:

PRODUCTION DATE: [3-8 October 1897.]

LOCATION: [City Park, Denver, Colo.]

SOURCE:

DESCRIPTION: Taken at Santa Clara. The background is formed by a group of Indians, with tom-tom player in the foreground. Two of the braves, dressed in full war costume, decorated with feathers, go through the steps of this very eccentric dance. Sharp and clear. (*Edison Films*, 15 March 1898, 8.)

SUBJECT: Indians of North America. Dancing. Drums. Santa Clara Pueblo Indians from Espanola, N.Mex. Festival of Mountain and Plain. Denver & Rio Grande Railroad.

ARCHIVE: DLC-pp.

CITATIONS: F.Z. Maguire & Co., *Catalogue*, [March 1898], 13-14; *Edison Films*, March 1900, 19; *Edison Films*, July 1901, 41.

NOTE: Same camera position as above.

THE INDIANS
Aborigines With Sportive Hearts but Dignified Mien Own City Park.

The sound of the tom-tom echoed from lake to lake; tepee fires curled lazily in the morning air, and with a subdued monotonous murmur the morning chant of the Apaches swelled indistinctly through the City park....

To the right of the large lake and in front of the pavilion is the teepees of the Santa Clara Pueblos. There are forty clean-looking, straight-limbed Southerners in the eight tepees. To the left of the smaller lake is the mess tent and the villages of the Jicarilla Apaches and the Utes from the Ute reservation, numbering in all 86. The two tribes occupy separate tepees placed several yards from each other. The Indians arrived yesterday afternoon. They were taken directly in street cars to City park, where before evening the tepees were up, the fires were lighted and the strange visitors were perfectly at home and in peace with the world.

Clerk L.A. Knackstedt of the Southern Ute reservation, in charge of the Utes, remarked as the Indian train pulled into the depot: "If the Utes had been on the wrecked Rio Grande train they would have scattered to the four corners of the surrounding country and no power on earth would have stopped them." As it was each Indian enjoyed to the utmost the novel experience of riding on a railroad.

...The band of Utes are the largest at City park. Old chief Buckskin is in charge, with Julian Buck, his son, and old Severo, also a chief, who dresses in a blue infantry uniform with brass buttons because of his position as an Indian policeman. For seeing that order is maintained among the Utes on the reservation he draws a salary of $15 a month from the government. At the park the Utes will go through the dog dance for the feast. The cauldron simmers over a briskly burning fire when the dance begins. During its process the dog is secured, killed and thrown into the pot. When it is ready for serving the frenzied swaying of the tom-toms ceases and the feast begins.

Other dances are the bear dance, typical of spring, the first appearance of the bear after winter's sleep, his capture and consumption, and the harvest dance. (*Denver Evening Post*, 4 October 1897, 3.)

424 ***Denver Fire Brigade**

LENGTH: 150 ft.   © Thomas A. Edison, 24 February 1898.

PRODUCER: James White.

CAMERA: Frederick Blechynden.

CAST:

PRODUCTION DATE: Early October 1897.

LOCATION: Denver, Colo.

SOURCE:

DESCRIPTION: Taken in the city of Denver, with fine prospective of a long, wide street. The brigade consists of twelve pieces, which rush by the camera in the following order: Chief in single carriage; chemical engine, drawn by two horses; hook and ladder, drawn by four horses; hose carriage, drawn by two horses; engine by two horses; chief in single carriage; steamer drawn by two horses; steamer by two horses; steamer drawn by two horses; truck by two horses; steamer by two horses and water tower drawn by three horses. The scene is exceptionally animated and the interest is kept up from beginning to end. The usual crowd of bystanders lines the street. An excellent picture of a good subject. (*Edison Films*, 15 March 1898, 9.)

SUBJECT: Fire fighters. Fire runs. Denver & Rio Grande Railroad.
ARCHIVE: DLC-pp.
CITATIONS: F.Z. Maguire & Co., *Catalogue*, [March 1898], 14-15.
NOTE:

The chronicling of White's and Blechynden's trip resumes with film no. 431. The follow-ing continues the documentation of Heise's filmmaking activities from film no. 388.

During the fall of 1897, William Heise produced a significant number of subjects at the behest of local groups, such as the Record Ambulance Fund. These films were often intended to be used, at least initially, for benefit performances.

425 *Ambulance Call

LENGTH: 50 ft.   © Thomas A. Edison, 25 October 1897.
PRODUCER: William Heise.
CAMERA: William Heise.
CAST:
PRODUCTION DATE: 8 October 1897.
LOCATION: Orange, N.J.
SOURCE:

DESCRIPTION: Shows the Record Ambulance of Orange, N.J., leaving the stable in answer to a call. The scene opens with the barn door being opened, the ambulance comes out, turns up the street toward the audi-ence and rushes by with horse at full speed. The Chief of the Fire Department, in his gig, follows. A large furniture van, which has been held back by a policeman, comes out of an alley, adding to the action and realism of the subject. The figures are life size, the films clear and sharp and the subject true to life and full of action. (F.Z. Maguire & Co., *Catalogue*, [March 1898], 42.)

SUBJECT: Ambulances. City and town life–Orange. Stables. Firefighters. Police.
ARCHIVE: DLC-pp.
CITATIONS: "First Ambulance Performance," *Orange Chronicle*, 19 February 1898, 8; "The Lyceum Stock Company and Ambulance Pictures," *Orange Chronicle,* 21 May 1898, 6. *New York Clipper*, 25 December 1897, 722; *Edison Films*, March 1900, 38.
NOTE:

426 *Ambulance at the Accident

LENGTH: 50 ft.   © Thomas A. Edison, 25 October 1897.
PRODUCER: William Heise.
CAMERA: William Heise.
CAST: John Tierney (the victim).
PRODUCTION DATE: 8 October 1897.
LOCATION: Orange, N.J.
SOURCE:

DESCRIPTION: Shows the injured man lying in the fender of a trolley car, with the usual curious crowd held in check by two police-men. The ambulance drives up, the stretch-er is taken out and put in position. The injured man is placed upon it, then lifted into the ambulance and driven to the hospi-tal. A realistic scene, and is sharp, clear and life size. (F.Z. Maguire & Co., *Catalogue*, [March 1898], 42.)

SUBJECT: Ambulances. Accidents. City and town life–Orange. Urban transportation. Police.
ARCHIVE: DLC-pp.
CITATIONS: *New York Clipper*, 25 December 1897, 722; *Edison Films*, March 1900, 38.
NOTE:

Making Vitascopic Pictures of the Ambulance

Some interesting kinetoscopic films were made yesterday morning on the Main street of the Record Ambulance and its work. William Heise, of the Edison Laboratory, who has charge of this department, brought the apparatus down and set it up at first on William and Day streets. Here two films were made of the ambulance coming out of the station at full speed. Then the instrument was moved to the front of the Orange National Bank and directed towards the corner of Day street. Three films were made here. The first of them was of a man supposedly struck by a trolley car and lying on the fender. The victim was "Jack" Tierney, of Music Hall. The ambulance came up at full speed and he was picked up and carried off to the hospital.

The next film showed him lying on the ground after being run over by a trolley car. Then the ambulance came up and he was again picked up and carried off. The third scene was a repetition of the first, a number of people passing to and fro and the action in the three Main street scenes was excellent. The films were taken at the request of the Ambulance Trustees to be used at the theatrical series to show the ambulance service. They will be shown in the usual way wherever the vitascopic exhibitions are made. (*Orange Chronicle*, 9 October 1897, 7.)

Crissie Sheridan performed with the New City Sports Company during the 1893-94 season. By the 1895-96 season she was the star of this burlesque company, which she now headed with Flynn. During the 1896-97 season, Flynn and Sheridan's Big Sensation Double Show was also touring the theatrical circuit. Sometime in the first months of 1897 Sheridan & Flynn added motion pictures (on the cinematascope). to at least one of their shows. This film could have been made for exhibition in the companies' projectors as a way for Sheridan to retain a presence without actually appearing in the show.

427 ***Crissie Sheridan / Serpentine Dance in National Colors [?]***

LENGTH: 50 ft.   © Thomas A. Edison, 25 October 1897.

PRODUCER: William Heise.

CAMERA: William Heise.

CAST: Crissie Sheridan.

PRODUCTION DATE: September-October 1897.

LOCATION: Black Maria, West Orange, N.J.

SOURCE:

DESCRIPTION: A picture of the popular serpentine dance as performed by this well-known artist. A dance full of grace and action. The costume being white makes it a fine subject for coloring. Sharp, clear and life size. (F.Z. Maguire & Co., *Catalogue*, [March 1898], 42.)

SUBJECT: Burlesque–performances. Dancing. Motion pictures–colored.

ARCHIVE: DLC-pp.

CITATIONS: "Westminister Theater," *Providence Journal*, 6 April 1897, 10. *New York Clipper*, 25 December 1897, 722; *The Phonoscope*, May 1898, 6.

NOTE:

Westminister Theatre.

The new City Sports Big Show, described as the Barnum of its class, began a week's engagement yesterday at the Westminister Theatre. Flynn and Sheridan have made a number of changes in the company since it appeared here last season, and two new burlesques–"The Cadet's Reception" and "A Night with Pity-Us"–were procured for the City Sports. The leaders in these were Crissie Sheridan, Fanny Lewis, George Synder, David Foster, Harry Buckley, Phil Sheridan, and Joe. J. Mackie. The usual number of songs, dances, and marches was introduced, and the comedians in outlandish costume had all the desired opportunities for making themselves ridiculous. The costumes were good, the dialogues were notable for political hits and and the audience appeared to be satisfied with the City Sports and their show.

Charles E. Johnson, who was here with a creole company a year or two since, and Dora Dean had the best comedy act on the programme. Mr. Johnson's gyrations were remarkable; his dancing was decidedly novel, and Miss Dean also excelled as a dancer and vocalist. They were complimented with several recalls. Mlle. Meza, the Spanish girl, had a contortion act different from anything in this line previously exhibited at the Westminister. Some of her feats were astonishing. Mlle. Delmore and Lillian Jerome had a grotesque dance; Dave Foster and Fanny Lewis exchanged smart remarks; Miss Lewis, the best singer in the company, sang the latest songs, and Kitty Howard and Ida Earl had character songs....(*Providence Journal*, 25 October 1897, 8.)

The People's

Coming to the popular People's this afternoon is Flynn and Sheridan's Big Sensation Double Show, the attraction that created such a favorable impression on the patrons of this amusement resort last season. The show is in every way a double one, being composed of two separate and distinct companies, one of twenty white artists and one of fifteen Creole performers. The following are a few of the many artists who will appear: Mlle Zittella, the fair burlesquer; Lancaster and Collins, the grotesque dancers; Cunningham and Grant, the "Brutal Brothers;" the Sisters Howe, in choice selections; May Lafting, the charming soubrette; a grand clog tournament by ten young ladies, led by Sophie Thorne, champion clog dancer; a gavotte, by ten Creole maidens; Billy Farrell, champion cake walker; Smart and Williams, Afro-American comedians–and dancers and a host of others.

A special feature has been engaged for the People's in the Moorish Troupe of Oriental Dancers, seven women and two men. These foreigners have been creating quite a furor in this country with their unique dances, feats of strength, etc. This will be their initial appearance. (*Cincinnati Commercial Tribune*, 3 January 1897, 11.)

---

428 *****Pie Eating Contest**

LENGTH: 50 ft.   © Thomas A. Edison, 25 October 1897.
PRODUCER: William Heise.
CAMERA: William Heise.
CAST:
PRODUCTION DATE: October 1897.
LOCATION:
SOURCE:

DESCRIPTION: Shows two well-known contestants engaged in a spirited pie eating contest. The participants have their hands tied behind their backs, eating pies direct from the plates. The picture opens with clean faces and shirts. The pies are made of huckleberries, and as they are consumed the faces and clothes are thoroughly smeared, producing a most laughable effect. The motions are rapid, full of animation, and the faces contorted in many mirth producing expressions, making an extremely ludicrous subject. The figures are life size and are perfect photographs. An excellent subject for coloring. (F.Z. Maguire & Co., *Catalogue*, [March 1898], 42-43.)
SUBJECT: Contests–food. Pies. Motion pictures–colored.
ARCHIVE: DLC-pp.
CITATIONS: *New York Clipper*, 25 December 1897, 722; *Edison Films*, March 1900, 34.
NOTE:

---

429 *****Rainmakers**

LENGTH: 50 ft.   © Thomas A. Edison, 25 October 1897.
PRODUCER: William Heise.
CAMERA: William Heise.
CAST:
PRODUCTION DATE: October 1897.
LOCATION:
SOURCE:

DESCRIPTION: A humorous subject in which the small boy and the farmer play the leading parts. The small boy has placed a sign on the fence reading "Drop a nickel in the slot and see it rain." In order to give the curious their money's worth, the boy is stationed behind the fence with a large hose. The countryman walks up, notices the sign, is interested and proceeds to gratify his curiosity. Immediately as he drops the coin he raises his umbrella with a look of puzzled expectancy. This is changed to wondering surprise when the water begins falling. A ludicrous and humorous subject, with figures life size and clear. (F.Z. Maguire & Co., *Catalogue*, [March 1898], 43.)
SUBJECT: Boys. Farmers. Practical jokes. Umbrellas.

ARCHIVE: DLC-pp.
CITATIONS: *New York Clipper*, 25 December 1897, 722.
NOTE:

430 ***The Jealous Monkey***

LENGTH: 50 ft.   © Thomas A. Edison, 25 October 1897.
PRODUCER: William Heise.
CAMERA: William Heise.
CAST:
PRODUCTION DATE: October 1897.
LOCATION:
SOURCE: 
DESCRIPTION: A monkey and a dog in friendly
  scrap. Full of action. (*New York Clipper*, 25
  December 1897, 722.)
  Shows a party of three men sitting at a
  table on which is a monkey and a dog. The
  owner is attentive to the dog, which arous-
  es the jealousy of the monkey and starts
  him fighting. The monkey jumps at the dog, strikes him, grabs him around the neck
  and bites him. The dog fights back, and the monkey, to avoid being caught, leaps off
  and on the table, making a picture full of action from beginning to end. The figures
  are life size, sharp and clear. (F.Z. Maguire & Co., *Catalogue*, [March 1898], 42.)
SUBJECT: Animal fighting. Monkeys. Dogs.
ARCHIVE: DLC-pp.
CITATIONS:
NOTE:

*The documentation of Heise's filmmaking activities continues with film no. 440. The fol-
lowing entries resume the chronicling of White's and Blechynden's trip from film no. 424.*

*After the Festival of Mountain and Plain in early October, James H. White and
Frederick W. Blechynden left Denver and toured substantial sections of the Denver and
Rio Grande Railroad's "Trip Around the Circle," a journey, designed for tourists, which
normally took four days. The railroad company, which had already published a popular guidebook to the many sites of natural beauty included in this tour of Colorado,
provided the filmmakers with the necessary assistance for taking motion pictures of the
high points along its tracks.*

431 ***Circle Dance / Circle Dance. Ute Indians***

LENGTH: 50 ft.   © Thomas A. Edison, 24 February 1898.
PRODUCER: James White.
CAMERA: Frederick Blechynden.
CAST:
PRODUCTION DATE: October 1897.
LOCATION: Ignacio, Colo.
SOURCE: 
DESCRIPTION: Taken at the Ute Indian
  Reservation, Ignacio, Col. In the immediate
  background can be seen two native teepees,
  while in the distant background can be
  seen the low foothills rising from the prai-
  rie. The Indians perform their dance in the
  immediate foreground, formed in a compact
  circle, with arms across each other's shoul-
  ders, and moving round and round. (*Edison Films*, 15 March 1898, 9.)
SUBJECT: Indians of North America. Dancing. Ute Indians. Denver & Rio Grande
  Railroad.
ARCHIVE: DLC-pp.

CITATIONS: F.Z. Maguire & Co., *Catalogue*, [March 1898], 14; *Edison Films*, March 1900, 19; *Edison Films*, July 1901, 41.
NOTE:

432 ***Buck Dance / Buck Dance. Ute Indians**
LENGTH: 50 ft.   © Thomas A. Edison, 24 February 1898.
PRODUCER: James White.
CAMERA: Frederick Blechynden.
CAST:
PRODUCTION DATE: October 1897.
LOCATION: Ignacio, Colo.
SOURCE:

DESCRIPTION: Taken at the Ute Indian Reservation, Ignacio, Col., and shows a number of Buck Indians of this noted tribe indulging in their favorite amusement, which is dancing to the tune of a single base drum. Their movements are grotesque in the extreme. In the foreground are shown a group of Bucks and Squaws sitting on the ground, while in the background can be seen the tepees. The figures are sharp and clear and the subject novel. (*Edison Films*, 15 March 1898, 8-9.)
SUBJECT: Indians of North America. Dancing. Ute Indians. Denver & Rio Grande Railroad.
ARCHIVE: DLC-pp.
CITATIONS: F.Z. Maguire & Co., *Catalogue*, [March 1898], 14; *Edison Films*, March 1900, 19; *Edison Films*, July 1901, 41.
NOTE: Same camera position as above.

433 ***Serving Rations to the Indians, no. 1**
LENGTH: 50 ft.   © Thomas A. Edison, 24 February 1898.
PRODUCER: James White.
CAMERA: Frederick Blechynden.
CAST:
PRODUCTION DATE: October 1897.
LOCATION: Ignacio, Colo.
SOURCE:

DESCRIPTION: Taken at the Indian Reservation, Ignacio, Colorado, and shows a number of Ute Indian squaws leaving the reservation issue house, after having been served with their semi-monthly allowance of rations. The superstition with which these people regarded the camera is remarkable and this is plainly perceptible in their frantic attempts to escape from the vision of the lens. The only buck in the scene rides away, followed by a very small papoose on another horse. A large number of lean, lanky looking dogs, which are always a part of an Indian encampment, are seen moving about. The picture is taken at short range and the figures show life size, the features of the Indians being particularly clear. (*Edison Films,* 15 March 1898, 14.)
SUBJECT: Indians of North America. Ute Indians. Dogs. Denver & Rio Grande Railroad.
ARCHIVE: DLC-pp.
CITATIONS: F.Z. Maguire & Co., *Catalogue* [March 1898], 14; *Edison Films*, March 1900, 19; *Edison Films*, July 1901, 41.
NOTE:

434 ***Serving Rations to the Indians, no. 2 / Serving Rations, no. 2**
LENGTH: 50 ft.   © Thomas A. Edison, 24 February 1898.
PRODUCER: James White.
CAMERA: Frederick Blechynden.

CAST:
PRODUCTION DATE: October 1897.
LOCATION: Ignacio, Colo.
SOURCE:
DESCRIPTION: A large number of lean, lanky looking dogs are prowling around, looking for a share of the rations that are distributed to the squaws. (*Edison Films*, March 1900, 19.)

Taken at the same point [as *Serving Rations to Indians, no. 1*], and is another view of this interesting procedure. The film is equally sharp and clear. (*Edison Films*, 15 March 1898, 8.)

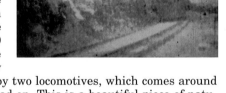

SUBJECT: Indians of North America. Ute Indians. Dogs. Denver & Rio Grande Railroad.
ARCHIVE: DLC-pp.
CITATIONS: F.Z. Maguire & Co., *Catalogue*, [March 1898], 14; *Edison Films*, July 1901, 41.
NOTE:

Indian Reservations.–The reservations of the Jicarilla Apaches and Southern Utes are traversed by the line of the Denver & Rio Grande Railroad. The agencies are located respectively at Dulce, 372 miles from Denver, and Ignacio, 424 miles from Denver. (Passenger Department of the Denver and Rio Grande R.R., *Around the Circle: One Thousand Miles Through the Rocky Mountains, Being a Description of a Trip Over the Passes and Through the Canons of Colorado*, 1903, 45.)

435 ***Cañon of the Rio Grande / [Canyon of the Rio Grande]**
LENGTH: 50 ft. © Thomas A. Edison, 24 February 1898.
PRODUCER: James White.
CAMERA: Frederick Blechynden.
CAST:
PRODUCTION DATE: October 1897.
LOCATION: Black Canyon, Colo.
SOURCE:
DESCRIPTION: Taken along the line of the Denver and Rio Grande R.R. in the above Canon of the Rocky Mountains. The Canon is 16 miles long and the two sides rise abruptly to a height of from 2,000 to 2,500 ft. The background is formed by these rugged rocks. Action is lent to the scene by the approach of a passenger train, drawn by two locomotives, which comes around a sharp curve and passes the audience, head-on. This is a beautiful piece of natural scenery, and is one of the points of interest to which the attention of passengers is particularly drawn. (*Edison Films*, 15 March 1898, 6.)
SUBJECT: Rocky Mountains. Tourist trade. Canyons. Railroads. Denver & Rio Grande Railroad.
ARCHIVE: DLC-pp.
CITATIONS: *The Phonoscope*, March 1898, 14; F.Z. Maguire & Co., *Catalogue*, [March 1898], 12; *Edison Films*, July 1901, 41.
NOTE:

Black Cañon.–Twenty-five miles west from Gunnison. Along many miles of this grand gorge the railroad lies upon a shelf hewn from the living rock, which rises frequently to an altitude of over two thousand feet. The canon is sixteen miles in length and abounds in many striking features. (Passenger Department of the Denver and Rio Grande R.R., *Around the Circle: One Thousand Miles Through the Rocky Mountains, Being a Description of a Trip Over the Passes and Through the Canons of Colorado*, 1903, 49.)

436 ***Royal Gorge**
LENGTH: 50 ft. © Thomas A. Edison, 24 February 1898.
PRODUCER: James White.

CAMERA: Frederick Blechynden.

CAST:

PRODUCTION DATE: October 1897.

LOCATION: Royal Gorge, Colo.

SOURCE:

DESCRIPTION: Taken along the line of the Denver and Rio Grande R.R., and is a photograph of the famous "Royal Gorge," known also as the "Cañon of the Arkansas." It is a panoramic view taken from the rear end of a moving train, and is a good photograph of this noted rocky and picturesque American scenery. (*Edison Films*, 15 March 1898, 6.)

SUBJECT: Rocky Mountains. Canyons. Railroads. Tourist trade. Denver & Rio Grande Railroad.

ARCHIVE: DLC-pp.

CITATIONS: *The Phonoscope*, March 1898, 14; F.Z. Maguire & Co., *Catalogue*, [March 1898], 12; *Edison Films*, July 1901, 41.

NOTE:

The Royal Gorge

The crowning wonder of this wonderful Denver & Rio Grande Railroad is the Royal Gorge. Situated between Canon City and Salida, it is easy of access either from Denver or Pueblo. After the entrance to the canon has been made, surprise and almost terror comes. The train rolls round a long curve close under a wall of black and banded granite, beside which the ponderous locomotive sinks to a mere dot, as if swinging on some pivot in the heart of the mountain, or captured by a centripetal force that would never resign its grasp. Almost a whole circle is accomplished, and the grand amphitheatrical sweep of the wall shows no break in its zenith-cutting facade. Will the journey end here? Is it a mistake that this crevice goes through the range? Does not all this mad water gush from some powerful spring, or boil out of a subterranean channel impenetrable to us? No, it opens. Resisting centripetal, centrifugal force claims the train, and it breaks away at a tangent past the edge or around the corner of the great black wall which compelled its detour and that of the river before it. Now what glories of rock piling confront the wide-distended eye! How those sharp-edged cliffs, standing with upright heads that play at handball with the clouds, alternate with one another, so that first the right, then the left, then the right one below strike our view, each one half obscured by its fellow in front, each showing itself level browed with its comrades as we come even with it, each a score of hundreds of dizzy feet in height, rising perpendicularly from the water and the track, splintered atop into airy pinnacles, braced behind against the almost continental mass through which the chasm has been cleft. This is the Royal Gorge. (Passenger Department of the Denver and Rio Grande R.R., *Around the Circle: One Thousand Miles Through the Rocky Mountains, Being a Description of a Trip Over the Passes and Through the Canons of Colorado*, 1903, 40-41.)

37 *Cattle Fording Stream*

LENGTH: 150 ft. © Thomas A. Edison, 24 February 1898.

PRODUCER: James White.

CAMERA: Frederick Blechynden.

CAST:

PRODUCTION DATE: October 1897.

LOCATION: [El Paso County, Colo.]

SOURCE:

DESCRIPTION: Shows a herd of 300 head of cattle being driven across the River Platte. Five cowboys mounted on horses are forcing them across the stream. The fording place is narrow and the current of the stream very swift at this point, so that it is with great difficulty the wild cattle are kept to the crossing. They rush back and forth through the water, throwing up immense quantities of spray. They finally emerge on the bank nearest the audience and then pass directly in front of the camera. The scene is full of action and the photograph was made at close quarters, showing animals life size. This is an exceptionally good subject and should prove very attractive. (*Edison Films*, 15 March 1898, 9.)

SUBJECT: Cattle drives. Ranches. Cowboys. Rivers. Denver & Rio Grande Railroad.

ARCHIVE: DLC-pp.

CITATIONS: *The Phonoscope*, March 1898, 14.

NOTE:

---

438   *Calf Branding

LENGTH: 50 and 150 ft.   © Thomas A. Edison, 24 February 1898.

PRODUCER: James White.

CAMERA: Frederick Blechynden.

CAST:

PRODUCTION DATE: October 1897.

LOCATION: El Paso County, Colo.

SOURCE:

DESCRIPTION: This picture was secured during the annual "round-up" on the ranch of the Alfalfa Land and Cattle Co., El Paso County, Colorado, which is one of the largest and best known ranches in the state. It shows a mounted cowboy leaving the vast herd of cattle and dragging a calf at the end of his lariat. The calf struggles frantically to escape and is repeatedly thrown to the ground, until it is finally overcome, when red-hot brands are burned into his hide, the smoke from the brand being plainly seen. This operation is repeated on both sides of the calf. The fire in which the irons are heated is in the centre of the picture. A large herd of restless cattle make up the background of the picture. (*Edison Films*, 15 March 1898, 11.)

SUBJECT: Cattle–marking. Ranches. Cowboys. Alfalfa Land and Cattle Co. Atchison, Topeka & Santa Fe Railroad.

ARCHIVE: DLC-pp.

CITATIONS: F.Z. Maguire & Co., *Catalogue*, [March 1898], 10.

NOTE:

---

439   *Indian Day School

LENGTH: 50 ft.   © Thomas A. Edison, 24 February 1898.

PRODUCER: James White.

CAMERA: Frederick Blechynden.

CAST:

PRODUCTION DATE: October-November 1897.

LOCATION: Isleta, N.Mex.

SOURCE:

DESCRIPTION: Taken at the Pueblo Indian village of Isleta, along the line of the Atchison, Topeka & Santa Fe R.R. It was taken at very short focus, showing the Indian children running in and out of the doorway. The coarse, black, straight hair of the children shows in striking contrast with their white garments. The figures are life size, and the high cheek bones of the little Indian children are very noticeable. Particular attention is drawn to the very simple costumes and the looks of wonderment on their little faces. The school house which forms the background is of adobe, a structure common to the country. Sharp and clear. (*Edison Films*, 15 March 1898, 11.)

SUBJECT: Indians of North America. Santa Clara Pueblo Indians from Espanola, N.Mex. Schools. Atchison, Topeka & Santa Fe Railroad.

ARCHIVE: DLC-pp.

CITATIONS: F.Z. Maguire & Co., *Catalogue*, [March 1898], 10.

NOTE:

Isleta

This is by far the largest of the Tañoan pueblos, numbering over [one] thousand inhabitants. It is also the most westerly of the Tañoan pueblos except the little village of Hano, which occupies one of the Hopi means. The village is pleasantly located on the west bank of the Rio Grande River, about thirteen miles south of Albuquerque, and within a stone's throw of the main line of the Santa Fe Railway.

There is a station at the village, and hence the pueblo may be easily visited by leaving the railroad at the station or by a drive of about two hours from the city of Albuquerque. The drive from Albuquerque to the village is strongly recommended.

Although of unusual size for an Indian pueblo, Isleta has lost many of the characteristics of a true Indian town, this being due probably to the presence of a large Roman Catholic church and the constant attendance of a priest. The country about the pueblo is fertile in the extreme and is crossed and recrossed by irrigating ditches, which make possible prosperous crops of alfalfa and wheat.

Not withstanding the presence of a well preserved church, together with the well kept quarters of the padre, Isleta still possesses an estufa or native temple, in which certain ancient religious observances are retained, and from which the priests appear at the time of their annual festival on August 28th. The visitor probably will be struck at once with the fact that, modern as the pueblo seems in many ways, he will probably be unable to obtain admission to this kiva, or half-sunken, circuclar underground temple, which may be entered only from the hole in the roof.

The houses and streets of the pueblo are well kept and clean, and inasmuch as the dwellings of the village are, like the Mexican quarters generally of this region, of a single story, the pueblo covers a large area. Within the houses are many evidences of the white man's civilization, such as beds, chairs and domestic utensils; but the primitive method of grinding corn into meal is still retained and in the majority of the houses one may see in the corner a bin with a stone metate for this purpose.

Isleta was for many years the home of that interesting writer, Mr. Charles F. Lummis, who has written impressions of his visit here in his delightful books "Strange Corners of Our Country," and "A Tramp Across the Continent." (George A. Dorsey, *Indians of the Southwest*, 1903, 76-77.)

To continue with White's and Blechynden's trip, go to film no. 444. The following section resumes the chronology of Heise's production from film no. 432.

While White and Blechynden were touring the western United States, Heise continued to make films from company headquarters in Orange, N.J. The Edison Manufacturing Company took three films of the Orange-based and locally fashionable National Guard unit, Gatling Gun Company A. The films were subsequently shown as part of a benefit for the group's Athletic Committee, held at the local Armory on 17 December 1897.

440 *Mount and Dismount, Gatling Gun / Mount & Dismount, Gatling Gun**
LENGTH: [50 ft.]   © Thomas A. Edison, 18 December 1897.
PRODUCER: William Heise.
CAMERA: William Heise.
CAST:
PRODUCTION DATE: 25 November 1897.
LOCATION: East Orange, N.J.
SOURCE:
DESCRIPTION:
SUBJECT: National Guard–New Jersey. Gatling guns. Gatling Gun Company A, N.G.N.J. Richard J. Gatling.
ARCHIVE: DLC-pp.
CITATIONS: "Gatling Gun Company A," *Orange Chronicle*, 11 December 1897, 5.

NOTE: Shot near the Armory (North Clinton and Carleton streets).

441 *Gatling Gun Crew in Action**
LENGTH: [50 ft.]   © Thomas A. Edison, 18 December 1897.
PRODUCER: William Heise.
CAMERA: William Heise.
CAST:

PRODUCTION DATE: 25 November 1897.
LOCATION: East Orange, N.J.
SOURCE:
DESCRIPTION:
SUBJECT: National Guard–New Jersey. Gatling guns. Gatling Gun Company A, N.G.N.J. Richard J. Gatling.
ARCHIVE: DLC-pp.
CITATIONS:
NOTE:

442 ***Firing by Squad, Gatling Gun**
LENGTH: [50 ft.]   © Thomas A. Edison, 20 December 1897.
PRODUCER: William Heise.
CAMERA: William Heise.
CAST:
PRODUCTION DATE: 25 November 1897.
LOCATION: East Orange, N.J.
SOURCE:
DESCRIPTION:
SUBJECT: National Guard–New Jersey. Gatling guns. Gatling Gun Company A, N.G.N.J. Richard J. Gatling.
ARCHIVE: DLC-pp.
CITATIONS:
NOTE:

Gatling Gun Company A

A large number of members and friends attended the performance of "The Old Homestead" at the Newark Theatre on Monday night, which was given for the benefit of the company. The share of the receipts which the company receives will place a very handsome sum to the credit side of its ledger.

Plans were discussed last Saturday night for improving the Armory, so that the active and associate members may have additional facilities for their enjoyment. The room over the assembly room, on the second floor, which is vacant, will be converted into a gymnasium, and will be connected with the Quartermaster's room by a hallway leading to the back stairway, and, which will lead to a bath-room on the first floor, now occupied as a wardrobe room by the commissioned officers. Among the projects are a card room and other forms of amusement. Dancing classes will also be formed. The idea is to make the Armory a pleasant and delightful place for those connected with the company. The rules of the Armory positively forbid in any form whatever, the use of intoxicating liquors.

Several new names were handed in to the Recruiting Committee last Saturday night. The company will no doubt have its full membership by the opening of the new year. It is expected that at least five new members will come up for election at the monthly meeting to be held next Saturday night.

After several postponements some very good vitascope pictures were taken of the gun crews on Thanksgiving morning, in the field near the Armory, by an attache of the Edison laboratory. Firing in different directions, dismounting and mounting, etc., were executed. Fifty blank cartridges were used. (*Orange Chronicle*, 27 November 1897, 5.)

Richard Gatling Has Invented a New Gun.
It Is an Eight-Inch Rifle Forged of Solid Steel and Drilled—Will be Rifled at Washington.

CLEVELAND, O., March 11.–The inventor of the Gatling gun, Dr. Richard J. Gatling, will soon ship to Washington a new eight-inch gun which he has been making by a new process, of which he expects great things....

Dr. Gatling is a native of North Carolina. He has lived here many years. He is a medical man, but for years has devoted his attention to mechanics and gun making. In manners he is mild, and in disposition kind. He says the terrible scenes of the Civil War led him to devise the Gatling gun in the interest of humanity, and he believes it has done much to prevent bloodshed.

"Only recently," said Dr. Gatling, "General Miles told me of an experience on the frontier–in Utah, I believe it was. A certain chief threatened to create a disturbance, and he had braves enough on the warpath to do a great deal of damage. Under a flag of truce General Miles got him to come to his camp and see his power. One of the battery of Gatlings was charged and turned on a distant tree. After about 800 shots had been fired the chief, whose name was Crow Day, threw up his hands and left. He reported that the white man had a 'devil gun,' and straightway he and his braves picked up their blankets and walked. The chief never stopped to see whether the tree had been hit or not."

Speaking further of that invention he said that his idea was that if a gun could be made with which one man might do the work of a hundred, then ninety-nine would be spared the horror of camp hospital and battle-field.

"My early difficulties were many," he said. "I made my plans easily enough and finally had a battery of six guns built. When these guns were nearly completed and all paid for, some one–doubt not a scoundrel of a rebel spy–set fire to the factory and they were destroyed. I went to work again, and battery of thirteen guns was made in Cincinnati and sent to Washington as soon as completed. Here there were more troubles. Gen. Ripley, the chief of ordinance, would have none of my gun. Finally my agent started back on his way to the James River, and exhibited the battery to him. He was most enthusiastic and purchased twelve guns and carriages and a thousand rounds of ammunition for each for $12,000." (*New York World*, 12 March 1898.)

Making *What Demoralized the Barbershop* (1897). Heise sits in the barber's chair.

Despite the copyright date of 16 December 1898 for What Demoralized the Barbershop, *information on the film reads "Copyrighted 1897." Photographic documentation at NjWOE shows Heise making this film, though he had retired from film production by late 1898. It was almost certainly made while White was on his far-flung tour. Interestingly, the film never entered the Edison catalog.*

443   ***What Demoralized the Barbershop**

LENGTH: 50 ft.   © Thomas A. Edison, 16 December 1898.

PRODUCER: William Heise.

CAMERA: William Heise.

CAST:

PRODUCTION DATE: [November-December 1897?]

LOCATION: Black Maria, West Orange, N.J.

SOURCE: *The Barbershop* (Edison film no. 18, 1893).

DESCRIPTION:

SUBJECT: Barbershops. Prostitutes.

ARCHIVE: DLC-pp, NNMoMA, NR-GE.

CITATIONS:

NOTE:

The documentation of Heise's production continues with film no. 492. White's and Blechynden's trip is resumed from film no. 439.

James White and Frederick Blechynden followed the rails south and into Mexico, where two of that nation's largest railroad companies, like their American counterparts, were eager to encourage—and subsidize—North Americans who wished to take motion pictures that might bolster tourism.

444 ***Branding Cattle**

LENGTH: 50 and 150 ft.   © Thomas A. Edison, 24 February 1898.

PRODUCER: James White.

CAMERA: Frederick Blechynden.

CAST:

PRODUCTION DATE: November 1897.

LOCATION: Sabinas, Mexico.

SOURCE:

DESCRIPTION: Taken at Hacienda de Soledad, Sabinas, Mexico, and shows a number of Mexican cowboys, clad in their typical costumes, going through the semi-yearly routine of branding stock. A large refractory steer is lassoed, dragged from the herd to the fire and forcibly thrown to the ground. The red-hot irons are then applied, deeply burning the brand letters into his hide, the smoke from the burning hair and hide showing distinctly. After the branding is completed the steer is permitted to rise and is drawn around by the cowboys until the branded side is towards the audience, when the newly made letters are plainly distinguished. This is a sharp, clear film, is a true reproduction, and will prove a subject of unusual interest. (*Edison Films*, 15 March 1898, 2.)

SUBJECT: Cowboys. Mexicans. Cattle–marking. Ranches. Mexican International Railroad.

ARCHIVE: DLC-pp.

CITATIONS: F.Z. Maguire & Co., *Catalogue*, [March 1898], 11.

NOTE:

445 ***Lassoing Steer / Lassoing a Steer**

LENGTH: 50 ft.   © Thomas A. Edison, 24 February 1898.

PRODUCER: James White.

CAMERA: Frederick Blechynden.

CAST:

PRODUCTION DATE: November 1897.

LOCATION: [Sabinas, Mexico.]

SOURCE:

DESCRIPTION: Shows eight mounted cowboys in pursuit of a lone steer. As they ride at full speed, swinging their lassoes, one of them deftly throws his and lands it over the head of the steer; his horse is suddenly stopped and the mad career of the steer is brought to an abrupt halt; he seems to leap completely off the ground, is turned fully half way round and thrown violently to the ground. The steer rises and again starts running, the one cowboy being unable to control him. Another cowboy then lassoes him around both hind feet. The two riders separate until their lines are taut, and the steer is brought violently to the ground a second time. This photograph is mechanically perfect, is full of action, with the figures full size and well defined. It is an excellent subject and is sure to please. (*Edison Films*, 15 March 1898, 3.)

SUBJECT: Cowboys. Mexicans. Cattle. Ranches. Mexican International Railroad.

ARCHIVE: DLC-pp, NR-GE.

CITATIONS: F.Z. Maguire & Co., *Catalogue,* [March 1898], 12; *Edison Films*, March 1900, 23.

NOTE:

446 ***Cattle Leaving the Corral**
LENGTH: 50 ft.   © Thomas A. Edison, 24 February 1898.
PRODUCER: James White.
CAMERA: Frederick Blechynden.
CAST:
PRODUCTION DATE: November 1897.
LOCATION: Sabinas, Mexico.
SOURCE:

DESCRIPTION: Taken at Hacienda de Soledad, Sabinas, Mexico, and shows a herd of 900 cattle being driven out of the corral, after having been branded. This immense herd, driven by Mexican cowboys, comes through the gates head-on to the audience. The cattle with their large horns, as they crowd together and push rapidly out through the gates, make an interesting picture. (*Edison Films*, 15 March 1898, 2.)
SUBJECT: Cowboys. Mexicans. Cattle. Ranches. Mexican International Railroad.
ARCHIVE: DLC-pp.
CITATIONS: *The Phonoscope*, March 1898, 14; F.Z. Maguire & Co., *Catalogue*, [March 1898], 11.
NOTE:

447 ***Bull Fight, no. 1**
LENGTH: 50 ft.   © Thomas A. Edison, 10 March 1898.
PRODUCER: James White.
CAMERA: Frederick Blechynden.
CAST:
PRODUCTION DATE: November-December 1897.
LOCATION: Durango, Mexico.
SOURCE:

DESCRIPTION: Taken at Durango, Mexico, on the Mexican International R.R. The arena in which this bull-fight took place is considered the finest bull-ring in the Republic of Mexico, and the bull-fighters who participate in the contest compose the best troupe in the Mexican country. The background is formed by the sides of the arena, surmounted by tiers of seats, which are densely filled with spectators. The opening discloses a mounted picador coming in focus, the bull well in the foreground, and several foot picadors in the background. The bull, enraged by numerous bandilleros, which protrude him from his sides and back, makes a furious charge after the picadors, but is cleverly avoided. One of the picadors then runs across the arena and implants a bandillero in the bull, which is resented by another mad but futile rush. He is next tantalized by one of the picadors, who waves his mantilla in the face of the bull, which provokes another charge. The action is aggressive, lively and exciting throughout, figures life size and very sharp. (*Edison Films*, 15 March 1898, 1.)
SUBJECT: Bullfights. Mexicans. Mexican International Railroad.
ARCHIVE: DLC-pp.
CITATIONS: F.Z. Maguire & Co., *Catalogue*, [March 1898], 11; *Edison Films*, March 1900, 17; *Edison Films*, July 1901, 39.
NOTE:

448 ***Bull Fight, no. 2**
LENGTH: 50 ft.   © Thomas A. Edison, 10 March 1898.
PRODUCER: James White.
CAMERA: Frederick Blechynden.
CAST:

PRODUCTION DATE: November-December 1897.
LOCATION: Durango, Mexico.
SOURCE:
DESCRIPTION: Taken at the same place, on the same day, and shows a portion of a different fight. The scene opens with the matador, sword in hand, and the bull in the right foreground. The bull at first slowly approaches the matador; this is suddenly changed into a fierce charge. The bull is again the aggressor, with the matador facing him but slowly retreating; suddenly the

matador leaps forward and thrusts his sword between the shoulder blades of the bull, inflicting the death-wound. The action is maintained throughout the film, the figures life size and very sharp. (*Edison Films*, 15 March 1898, 1.)
SUBJECT: Bullfights. Mexicans. Mexican International Railroad.
ARCHIVE: DLC-pp.
CITATIONS: F.Z. Maguire & Co., *Catalogue*, [March 1898], 11; *Edison Films*, July 1901, 40.
NOTE:

449 ***Bull Fight, no. 3**
LENGTH: 50 ft.   © Thomas A. Edison, 10 March 1898.
PRODUCER: James White.
CAMERA: Frederick Blechynden.
CAST:
PRODUCTION DATE: November-December 1897.
LOCATION: Durango, Mexico.
SOURCE:
DESCRIPTION: The opening shows the bull making a mad rush for the picadors, head-on to the audience; the first rush is followed by another. The picadors jump in every direction, with remarkable cleverness and agility. The scene then changes; the bull has received the matador's thrust and stands in

the centre of the arena, surrounded by five of the picadors. He backs around, his strength perceptibly ebbing away, then sinks to the ground. The picadors, still unsatisfied, continue to torture the bull, and with a last effort he staggers to his feet. The action in this film is well maintained, and the figures are large and exceptionally sharp. (*Edison Films*, 15 March 1898, 2.)
SUBJECT: Bullfights. Mexicans. Mexican International Railroad.
ARCHIVE: DLC-pp.
CITATIONS: *Edison Films*, March 1900, 17; *Edison Films*, July 1901, 40.
NOTE:

450 ***Wash Day in Mexico / Washday in Mexico.**
LENGTH: 50 ft.   © Thomas A. Edison, 24 February 1898.
PRODUCER: James White.
CAMERA: Frederick Blechynden.
CAST:
PRODUCTION DATE: November-December 1897.
LOCATION: Durango, Mexico.
SOURCE:
DESCRIPTION: Taken at Durango, Mexico, and is a scene that may be witnessed on any Monday throughout the Republic. It shows a large number of the native women, bareheaded and on their knees on the bank of a rapidly running stream of water. In front of

each woman is a large flat rock, which they use as a scrubbing board. They dip the clothes into the stream, and after soaping them, rub them vigorously over the flat stones. At the right of the picture, in the foreground, is seen a little naked Mexican child. (*Edison Films*, 15 March 1898, 3.)

SUBJECT: City and town life–Mexico. Laundries. Children. Mexicans. Mexican International Railroad.

ARCHIVE: DLC-pp.

CITATIONS: *The Phonoscope*, March 1898, 14; F.Z. Maguire & Co., *Catalogue*, [March 1898], 11; *Edison Films*, March 1900, 17; *Edison Films*, July 1901, 40.

NOTE:

451 ***Train Hour in Durango, Mexico**

LENGTH: 50 ft.   © Thomas A. Edison, 24 February 1898.

PRODUCER: James White.

CAMERA: Frederick Blechynden.

CAST:

PRODUCTION DATE: November-December 1897.

LOCATION: Durango, Mexico.

SOURCE:

DESCRIPTION: This view was taken at the station of the Mexican International R.R., Durango, Mexico, and demonstrates the unusual commotion caused in this Mexican town by the so common occurrence as a train arrival. The inhabitants, arrayed in native costumes, the men with sombreros and serapes, the women with bare heads and mantillas on their shoulders, are anxiously scanning the alighting passengers for recognition of friends. As Durango is the least Americanized of any of the interior cities in the Republic of Mexico, the types of the people shown in the picture are truly typical. (*Edison Films*, 15 March 1898, 2-3.)

SUBJECT: City and town life–Mexico. Mexicans. Railroad stations. Mexican International Railroad.

ARCHIVE: DLC-pp.

CITATIONS: F.Z. Maguire & Co., *Catalogue*, [March 1898], 11; *Edison Films*, March 1900, 17; *Edison Films*, July 1901, 40.

NOTE:

452 ***Repairing Streets in Mexico**

LENGTH: 50 ft.   © Thomas A. Edison, 24 February 1898.

PRODUCER: James White.

CAMERA: Frederick Blechynden.

CAST:

PRODUCTION DATE: November-December 1897.

LOCATION: Durango, Mexico.

SOURCE:

DESCRIPTION: Taken at Durango, Mexico, and illustrates the method employed by the Mexican government in repairing and paving streets and doing all manner of public work. The convicts, under a strong guard of national troops, are marched from the prison through the public streets and compelled to perform the arduous task of carrying and laying the heavy stones used throughout Mexico in street paving. The slow and painful movements of the barefooted convicts walking over the sharp stones, lend a pathetic but humorous aspect to the scene. The figures are well in the foreground and show life size. (*Edison Films,* 15 March 1898, 3.)

SUBJECT: City and town life–Mexico. Streets–maintenance and repair. Criminals. Convict labor. Mexicans. Mexican International Railroad.

ARCHIVE: DLC-pp.
CITATIONS: F.Z. Maguire & Co., *Catalogue*, [March 1898], 12.
NOTE:

453 *Surface Transit, Mexico / Surface Transit in Mexico

LENGTH: 50 ft.   © Thomas A. Edison, 24 February 1898.
PRODUCER: James White.
CAMERA: Frederick Blechynden.
CAST:
PRODUCTION DATE: December 1897.
LOCATION: Mexico City, Mexico.
SOURCE:

DESCRIPTION: The scene opens with a street car, drawn by two mules, standing in the left foreground. It is an open car, the sides being protected by huge curtains to keep the hot rays of the sun from beating on the passengers. A number of passengers alight from the car and go their various ways. In the meantime the mules have turned about, so as to face the car. Their deliberation, combined with the efforts of the driver to start the mules in the right direction, is highly amusing. In order to succeed he is forced to use his whip very freely. (*Edison Films*, 15 March 1898, 5.)

Mule power is all right when time is no object, as is shown in the picture. Mules balk, and passengers all leave the open air car. (*Edison Films*, March 1900, 18.)

SUBJECT: City and town life–Mexico. Mexicans. Mules. Urban transportation. Mexican Central Railroad.
ARCHIVE: DLC-pp.
CITATIONS: F.Z. Maguire & Co., *Catalogue*, [March 1898], 8; *Edison Films*, March 1900, 18; *Edison Films*, July 1901, 40.
NOTE:

454 *Spanish Ball Game

LENGTH: 50 ft.   © Thomas A. Edison, 24 February 1898.
PRODUCER: James White.
CAMERA: Frederick Blechynden.
CAST:
PRODUCTION DATE: December 1897.
LOCATION: Mexico City, Mexico.
SOURCE:

DESCRIPTION: Taken in the City of Mexico, and represents the Spanish game of La Pelota, or ball game. It is somewhat similar to the American game of hand-ball, except that the players use scoops, instead of their bare hands. Exciting and full of activity. (*Edison Films*, 15 March 1898, 5.)

SUBJECT: Sports. Jai alai. Mexicans. Mexican Central Railroad.
ARCHIVE: DLC-pp.
CITATIONS: F.Z. Maguire & Co., *Catalogue*, [March 1898], 8.
NOTE:

455 *Mexican Rurales Charge / Mexican Rurales Charging

LENGTH: 50 ft.   © 24 February 1898.
PRODUCER: James White.
CAMERA: Frederick Blechynden.
CAST: Francisco de P. Benavides.
PRODUCTION DATE: December 1897.
LOCATION: Mexico City, Mexico.

SOURCE: *Charge of the Seventh French Cuirassiers* (Lumière film, 1896).

DESCRIPTION: This picture was taken at Guadalupe Hidalgo, on a fine level plain, with Mexican hills rising abruptly in the background. It shows the 4th Company Rurales de la Federacion, led by the famous warrior, Col. Francisco de la Benavides, making the charge. They are clad in their picturesque full-dress regulation uniform. The picture opens with the cavalry, with drawn sabres, charging at full speed, head

on to the audience. They pass the audience close to the camera, wheel about and make as vivid a charge in the other direction. As they sweep by the audience they leave a dense cloud of dust, from which they emerge in the distance. These men are famed for their horsemanship and skill with the sword. Full of action, charp and clear. (*Edison Films*, 15 March 1898, 4.)

SUBJECT: Mexicans. Cavalry. Armies–Mexico. Mexican Central Railroad.

ARCHIVE: DLC-pp.

CITATIONS: F.Z. Maguire & Co., *Catalogue*, [March 1898], 7; *Edison Films*, March 1900, 17; *Edison Films*, July 1901, 40.

NOTE:

456 ***Sunday Morning in Mexico**

LENGTH: 50 ft.   © 24 February 1898.

PRODUCER: James White.

CAMERA: Frederick Blechynden.

CAST:

PRODUCTION DATE: December 1897.

LOCATION: Mexico City, Mexico.

SOURCE:

DESCRIPTION: Taken in the fashionable park in Mexico City on Sunday morning and shows the fashionable set in their usual after-church promenade. These promenaders comprise the best people in Mexico, who appear quite Americanized. It will be

noticed in this picture that no typical Mexican costumes are in evidence, which is due to the fact that the Peons, or lower classes, are not allowed to mingle with the "Four Hundred." The concourse is made up of people of all nationalities, including several groups of pretty Senoritas. This is an interesting subject, with the figures showing life size. Clear and distinct. (*Edison Films*, 15 March 1898, 4-5.)

SUBJECT: City and town life–Mexico. Mexicans. Social elites. Mexican Central Railroad.

ARCHIVE: DLC-pp.

CITATIONS: F.Z. Maguire & Co., *Catalogue*, [March 1898], 7; *Edison Films*, March 1900, 18; *Edison Films*, July 1901, 40.

NOTE:

457 ***Market Scene, City of Mexico**

LENGTH: 50 ft.   © 24 February 1898.

PRODUCER: James White.

CAMERA: Frederick Blechynden.

CAST:

PRODUCTION DATE: December 1897.

LOCATION: Mexico City, Mexico.

SOURCE:

DESCRIPTION: Taken at the famous market place in the City of Mexico, where native Mexicans and Indians dispose of their produce of chillies, sweet-potatoes, sugar-cane, sweet-meats, pottery, etc. It is a motley crowd of all sizes and types. The

Mexicans and Indians are going to and departing from the market, with various articles of merchandise in their hands. Their features are sharply defined, and their different expressions are plainly seen. This is considered one of the "sights" of Mexico, and is witnessed by all tourists who visit this very interesting capital. (*Edison Films*, 15 March 1898, 4.)

SUBJECT: City and town life–Mexico. Markets. Mexicans. Tourist trade. Mexican Central Railroad

ARCHIVE: DLC-pp.

CITATIONS: F.Z. Maguire & Co., *Catalogue*, [March 1898], 7; *Edison Films*, March 1900, 17; *Edison Films*, July 1901, 40.

NOTE:

---

458   *Mexico Street Scene / Mexico City Street Scene

LENGTH: 50 ft.   © Thomas A. Edison, 24 February 1898.

PRODUCER: James White.

CAMERA: Frederick Blechynden.

CAST:

PRODUCTION DATE: December 1897.

LOCATION: Mexico City, Mexico.

SOURCE:

DESCRIPTION: Taken in the City of Mexico, on the Plaza de la Constitucion, or the Plaza Mayor. The Zocola Gardens of the Cathedral (Church of the Asuncion de Maria Santissima) form the background, while a number of pack-mules, street cars, vehicles and pedestrians pass in the foreground, all typical view of this wonderful city. (*Edison Films*, 15 March 1898, 5.)

SUBJECT: City and town life–Mexico. Urban transportation. Mules. Church buildings. Mexicans. Mexican Central Railroad

ARCHIVE: DLC-pp.

CITATIONS: F.Z. Maguire & Co., *Catalogue*, [March 1898], 8; *Edison Films*, March 1900, 18; *Edison Films*, July 1901, 40.

NOTE:

---

459   *Las Vigas Canal, Mexico City / Las Vigas Canal, City of Mexico

LENGTH: 50 ft.   © Thomas A. Edison, 24 February 1898.

PRODUCER: James White.

CAMERA: Frederick Blechynden.

CAST:

PRODUCTION DATE: December 1897.

LOCATION: Las Vigas Canal, Mexico City, Mexico.

SOURCE:

DESCRIPTION: Taken at the small suburban village of Santa Anita, on the outskirts of the City of Mexico, and shows the native men and women, bare-footed and in their grotesque native costumes, propelling their flat-bottomed boats and unloading therefrom cargoes of vegetables. Unlike the method in this country, the canal boats are propelled by poling. The boats rapidly pass each other on the canal, while a large crowd of natives, mostly women, are seen on the bank unloading the garden truck. A sharp, clear film, and the light and shadow effects falling on the water produce a striking effect. The figures are full life size. (*Edison Films*, 15 March 1898, 4.)

SUBJECT: City and town life–Mexico. Canals. Boats and boating. Markets. Mexicans. Mexican Central Railroad.

ARCHIVE: DLC-pp.

CITATIONS: F.Z. Maguire & Co., *Catalogue*, [March 1898], 7; *Edison Films*, March 1900, 17.

NOTE:

460 ***Mexican Fishing Scene**

LENGTH: 50 ft.   © Thomas A. Edison, 24 February 1898.

PRODUCER: James White.

CAMERA: Frederick Blechynden.

CAST:

PRODUCTION DATE: December 1897.

LOCATION: Las Vigas Canal, Mexico City, Mexico.

SOURCE:

DESCRIPTION: Taken on the Las Vigas Canal, City of Mexico. This is a humorous subject, and shows two Mexican Muchachos, clad in their scant costumes, consisting of a pair of trunks, engaged in their favorite occupation of fishing for eels. A flat-bottomed vegetable boat, suddenly appearing from the background, collides with the boys' craft, and they are unceremoniously precipitated into the water. The boys scramble hastily into their boat to resume their fishing. The background is formed by a luxuriant field of sugar-cane. A sharp, clear film with fine water effects and full of action. (*Edison Films*, 15 March 1898, 5.)

SUBJECT: City and town life–Mexico. Canals. Fishing. Boys. Boats and boating. Mexicans. Mexican Central Railroad.

ARCHIVE: DLC-pp.

CITATIONS: F.Z. Maguire & Co., *Catalogue*, [March 1898], 8.

NOTE:

White and Blechynden's itinerary continues with film no 464.

The Passion play, performed each year in Horitz, Bohemia (part of Austria-Hungary), had become a tourist attraction—a modest rival to the Passion play produced in Oberammergau. After seeing one such event, Frenchman Charles Hurd approached the theater group about making a film of their performance and negotiated a contract which called for the actors to be paid 1,500 Austrian Florins and the company to receive 2,000 florins per year for five years. Exhibitions were also to be limited to non-German speaking countries. The American theatrical producers Klaw & Erlanger acquired these motion picture rights from Hurd and sent W.W. Freeman to supervise the production. The films were shot using "the Lumière process." The resulting evening-length program opened on 22 November 1897 at Philadelphia's Academy of Music. After Thomas A. Edison sued Klaw & Erlanger for infringing on his patents, his company assumed control of the negatives in the settlement (7 April 1898) and made prints for resale, from which Klaw and Erlanger received a royalty.

461 **The Horitz Passion Play / Passion Play of Horitz**

LENGTH: 2,400 ft.   © No reg.

PRODUCER: Walter W. Freeman, Klaw & Erlanger.

CAMERA: Charles Webster.

CAST: Jordan Willochko (Christ), Anna Wenzieger (Mary), Joseph Frephies (Caiaphas).

PRODUCTION DATE: Summer 1897.

LOCATION: Horitz (Horice), Bohemia, Austro-Hungarian Empire.

SOURCE: *The Passion Play* (religious drama).

DESCRIPTION:

SUBJECT: Passion plays. Catholicism. Miracles. Jesus Christ. Religious ceremonies. City and town life–Austria-Hungary. Austrians.

ARCHIVE:

CITATIONS: *The Phonoscope*, November-December 1897, 9; *Philadelphia Record*, 21 November 1897, 16; "Passion Play Tableaux," *Philadelphia Record*, 23 November 1897, 6; "The Passion Play," *Philadelphia Inquirer*, 23 November 1897, 5; "The Passion Play at Horticultural Hall," *Philadelphia Record*, 28 November 1897, 16; "The Passion Play at Daly's," *New York Herald*, 15 March 1898, 13; Thomas A Edison, Marc Klaw, Abraham L. Erlanger,

THE FLIGHT INTO EGYPT.

Walter W. Freeman, and William Harris, contract, 7 April 1898, NjWOE; Zdenek Stabla, *Queries Concerning the Horice Passion Film* (Prague: Film Institute, 1971); Charles Musser, "Passions and the Passion Play: Theater, Film and Religion, 1880-1900," *Film History* 5, no. 4 (1993), 419-456. *New York Clipper*, 9 April 1898, 99.

NOTE: Here, as is the case with several other large-scale film projects, it is more appropriate to think of each scene as an individual film. However, for purposes of filmographic efficiency, they are grouped as a single entry. Fifty films totaling 5,000 ft. were said to be shot. Forty-two were exhibited at the premiere, while 30 films totaling 2,400 ft. were offered for sale through the Edison Manufacturing Company.

THE "PASSION PLAY" GIVEN HERE IN BOSTON.
SPLENDID REPRODUCTION OF THE IMPRESSIVE SPECTACLE.
Oberammergau [sic] and its Peasant Actors Vividly Shown at the Museum with the Aid of the Cinematograph–Not a Single Suggestion of Irreverence in the Whole Representation.

Prof. Ernest Lacy's famous reproduction of the Oberammergau [sic] "Passion Play" entered last night at the Boston Museum upon what promises to be one of the most successful fortnights ever devoted in this city to a popular theatrical entertainment. The augury of the occasion was a splendid audience, including in its numbers not only regular theatregoers, but a considerable contingent of people who are much oftener to be found at church than attending a play.

But beyond and above this attitude of the public was the complete rendering, without even the appearance of a hitch, given by performers who neither by love nor by money could have been induced to quit the Bohemian forests in the midst of which they annually represent the chief incidents in the life of Christ. The whole spectacle was a surprise to people unacquainted with the thaumaturgy of the cinematograph, and the interest grew more and more absorbing as the climax was approached. The audience was enthusiastic, and its applause unstinted.

The pictures thrown on the screen last night at the Museum had their origin some months ago in the thoughts of Dr. W.W. Freeman, after witnessing a performance of the "Passion Play" in Horitz Bohemia, that possibly the peasants taking part might be induced to give a representation for use in the cinematograph. His scheme proved successful, and all last summer, as well as part of the previous winter, he spent at Horitz "taking" the various scenes in the play, as well as other pictures suited to reproduction.

The result is the fine exhibition given last night at the Museum, consisting of a complete set of moving pictures of the "Passion Play," with an explanatory lecture by Prof. Lacy and some excellent singing and instrumental music.

The representation, as could be seen at a glance, faithfully reproduced the scenes enacted annually by the peasants at Horitz. In one very remarkable way the cinematographic method showed its advantage for a sacred play over both living figures and mere pictures in panorama. A machine like that used last night disposes forever of the objection of irreverence.

It is a fact that, through all the ages of the Christian era, men have loved to imagine the Godlike in the human; have ever sought to discover their conception of the divine beneath the earthly form of Jesus of Nazareth. Yet from any attempt to thus personate deity by means of an ordinary man, the sensitive religious conscience of modern times has always shrunk. It did this several times in Europe, and still more recently in the United States.

But, in the representation at the Museum, all ground of protest on this score is entirely removed. The great world-drama is not acted in any true sense of the word nor does anybody, from one end of the lecture to the other, take upon himself the responsibility of suggesting in flesh and blood what Christ might have looked like when he was on earth. The startling incongruities by which Bible scenes have been so often degraded to the level of "living tableaux"; the rude touch of the stage realist from which the tender ideals of a delicate imagination come forth hopelessly ruined—these have no part or place in the representation at the Museum. And if the disadvantages insepara-ble from the acting of the "Passion Play" have been avoided, the boldness, the inactivity, the "dead calm" of the picture are equally absent. What is given to the spectator is a union of the best features of the acted play, with its real personages in living relief, and of the lifelike reproduction which only the smooth surfaces of a photograph can ever be expected to yield.

The figures are always in motion, yet their "tone" is such as to obtrude the personal element as little as possible. There is, moreover, an element of mystery inseparable from the manner in which they change on the screen, and though each figure represents an actual person, all seem idealized to an extent which harmonizes well with the character of the piece.

At first the spectator thinks of the pictures only as a representation of a representation—regards them in the light of an effort to show how the peasants at Horitz acted their "Passion Play." It therefore seems in order to attend to the way in which the effects are being produced to calculate the probable speed of the machine, and watch for the right focussing of the images. This one can do at one's ease while Prof. Lacy is sketching, in the style of a lit-erary artist, the environs of Horitz, as such pictures as "The Village Street," "The Stone Cutters," "Peasants Working in the Fields" and "The Passions-Spielhaus" fall upon the screen.

But when the play begins there is a new mental attitude toward the representation. The thought that one is gazing at a mere pictorial representation seems to pass away, and in its place comes, somehow or other, the notion that the people seen are real people, and that on the screen there are moving the very men and women who acted the "Passion Play" last summer in the Bohemian forest to the delight of thousands of foreigners.

So it goes on for a while, as the spectators follow with increasing interest the various introductory pictures which present Old Testament incidents, such as "Adam and Eve in the Garden," "The Flood," "Moses in the Bulrushes" and "The Angels Appearing to Mary."

Then the players begin to depict the birth and life of Christ, and with this change of the subject there comes a new change of the mental attitude. So absorbing becomes the interest of the pictures that the onlooker, from merely regarding the figures as the figures of the real, live people who acted the play in Bohemia, begins to forget all about what was done in Bohemia and henceforth is lost in the thought that the faces and forms before him are the real people who lived in Palestine 2000 years ago, and with their own eyes witnessed the crucifixion of Christ.

This triumph of the representation is greatly aided by the splendid face and excellent acting of Jordan Willschko, the Christus of the play, and hardly less so by the vivid manner in which Prof. Lacy re-enforces the effect by his descriptions. (*Boston Herald*, 4 January 1898, 6.)

The Edison Manufacturing Company and its affiliates, notably F.Z. Maguire & Co. (headed by one of the partners of Maguire & Baucus), distributed this sensational film of a hanging, in which someone demonstrably dead looked amazingly life-like.

462 **The Hanging of Wm. Carr / The Hanging of William Carr**

LENGTH: 50 ft.   © No reg.

PRODUCER: Frederick Guth.

CAMERA: Frederick Guth.

CAST: William Carr, Sheriff J.H. Hymer.

PRODUCTION DATE: 17 December 1897.

LOCATION: Liberty, Mo.

SOURCE:

DESCRIPTION: Taken at Liberty, Missouri, December 17, 1897. This Photographic Film shows just as plainly as if you were there, every act and every motion of the pro-ceedings on the gallows, the adjusting of the rope and black cap, and the springing of the trap door by Sheriff Hymer, and being a cold morning, you can see the little clouds of breath from the mouths of the participants. (F.Z. Maguire & Co., *Catalogue*, [March 1898], 48.)

SUBJECT: Executions and executioners. Hanging.

ARCHIVE:

CITATIONS: "No Longer a Mystery," *Kansas City Star*, 25 October 1897, 1; "Are Sure He Killed Her," *Kansas City Star*, 26 October 1897, 1; "Carr's Trial Very Short," *Kansas City Star*, 13 November 1897, 2; "Carr to Die, December 17th. The Child Murderer Sentenced by Judge Broaddus," *Kansas City Star*, 16 November 1897, 1; "Last Visits Paid to Carr," *Kansas City Star*, 16 December 1897, 1.

NOTE: William Carr was a farm laborer who killed his three-year-old daughter on October 10th by throwing her into the river with a rope around her neck and attached to a rock. The case broke open two weeks later after her body was found.

His wife, the girl's step mother, was also a suspect though never tried. At the time Frank Guth made this film, he was locked in a commercial rivalry with the Vitascope. The individual who supplied Frank Guth with the equipment was almost certainly Edward Amet (not Arnet as indicated in the following documentation). The Kansas Phonograph Company had been buying films from the Edison company since the kinetoscope era.

THE ONLY GENUINE
LUMIERE CINEMATOGRAPHE
AT LIBERTY AFTER NOV. 27.
SIXTY (60) Foreign and American views, including
QUEEN JUBILEE and BULL FIGHT Pictures.
Vaudeville managers write. Repertoire managers wishing to strengthen
their show with the biggest novelty act before the public, address
F. GUTH
This week and next at Auditorium Theatre, Kansas City, Mo.
(Advertisement, *New York Clipper*, 27 November 1897, 651.)

KANSAS CITY, Mo.–While a deputy sheriff was rubbing soap into the rope which was to strangle to death William Carr, child murderer, at Liberty yesterday, while the sheriff was placing the forbidding black cap over the condemned man's head, and when the awful drop came and in the silence a dying man swung, barely touching the trodden snow with his throng-bound feet, a merry clicking punctuated the silence. It was the soundings of a little machine that was taking pictures of the scene at the rate of forty-six a second.

Before the execution there was erected just outside the stockade and back of the gallows a little house. Through the big fence was cut a hole–so small that not one of the morbid crowd in the inclosure noticed it. In the little house was the photographic machine, known as the American cinematograph. It was operated by Frank Guth, manager of the Kansas City agency of the American Phonographic Company. Storage batteries furnished the motive power of the machine. Before leaving Kansas City there was placed in the camera a strip of films [sic] 1,000 feet long and $1^{1/2}$ inches wide. Percy N. Arnet of Waukegan, Ill., came West for the express purpose of taking the pictures, being an experienced man with the cinematograph. But after reaching Liberty he weakened, saying that he wouldn't see the hanging if he was paid at the rate of $100 for every picture he should take.

"Rather than abandon my p'ans," said Mr. Guth, "I decided to take the pictures myself. I'm not an expert with the machine, but I didn't want to come back to Kansas City without making a trial, so I left Arnet at the hotel and did the work myself. As soon as the preparations began I started the machine and it ran right through until Carr was dropped. Then the mob tried to break down the stockade and shake it so I stopped the cinematograph and left. I'd like to have had a picture of that mob, though, but I was afraid they would smash my camera if they saw it, so I slid out."

"In the afternoon we tried a piece of the strip in a gallery at Liberty and the picture was perfect. About 500 feet in all were used."

The strips can be run in a kinetoscope or any one of the many projecting machines. The pictures will be placed on exhibition in Kansas City and St. Louis. This is the first time pictures of this kind were taken of an execution. (*The Phonoscope*, December 18987, 11.)

NOW SHOWING TO STANDING ROOM ONLY AT KANSAS CITY, MO.
THE
HANGING OF WILLIAM CARR
THE SELF CONFESSED CHILD MURDERER.
This film was taken by me at the jail enclosure on the day of the Hanging, Dec. 17, 1897–is controlled exclusively by us, and is the only film ever taken of a real hanging. These films, for all machines, can be had of us only. Will not be sold, but can be had on royalty. See K.C. papers for the comment the showing of this picture has caused. The film alone is as strong a feature as any attraction can get. Full information from F. Guth, Mgr. Cinematographe Co. 425 Delaware Street, Kansas City, Mo. (Advertisement, *New York Clipper*, 29 January 1898, 799.)

WE BUY AND SELL
FILMS,
Projecting Machines, Calcium Tanks and all other scientific devices of merit. As we purchase only goods which can be sold with a STRONG GUARANTEE, we have no use for inferior quality. We are the only house in existence supplying its customers with PLANS how to SUCCEED FINANCIALLY with a small investment. Our NOVELTIES are the best money makers the market has ever been able to furnish; what we don't handle is not worth handling. All

Instructions furnished by our Manager, who is the oldest and only practical successful exhibitor in the field. References: Dunn, Bradstreets and the First National Bank, Kansas City. Write for a catalog. THE EDISON AMERICAN PHONOGRAPH CO., F. GUTH, Manager, 811 Main Street, Kansas City, Mo. (Advertisement, *New York Clipper,* 26 August 1899, 527.)

Under its president, Richard Hollaman, the Eden Musee moved into production late in 1897. It realized two ambitious projects, both instances of filmed theater, before being sued by Thomas A. Edison for patent infringement. The first undertaking was designed to upstage the Klaw & Erlanger production of The Horitz Passion Play. *As part of his settlement with Edison, Hollaman turned over his Passion play negatives to the Edison Manufacturing Company, which licensed and then marketed them. Edison subsequently purchased the negatives and rights in 1899.*

463 *The Passion Play of Oberammergau (Salmi Morse Version)**

LENGTH: 2,200 ft.   © No reg.

PRODUCER: Richard Hollaman.

CAMERA: William Paley.

CAST: Frank Russell (Christ).

PRODUCTION DATE: December 1897 to January 1898.

LOCATION: New York, N.Y.

SOURCE: *The Passion* (play by Salmi Morse).

DESCRIPTION: About 2,200 feet in 23 subjects, averaging 100 feet in length.

1. Shepherds Watching their Flocks in the Night.
2. First Scene in the Temple.
3. Attempted Assassination.
4. The Flight to Egypt.
5. Massacre of the Innocents.
6. Herodius Pleads for John the Baptist's Head.
7. Salome's Dance Before Herod.
8. Death of John the Baptist.
9. The Brook of Cedron.
10. The Messiah's Entry into Jerusalem.
11. Suffer Little Children to Come Unto Me.
12. Raising of Lazarus.
13. The Last Supper.
14. Second Scene-Judas' Betrayal.
15. Third Scene-The Messiah's Arrest.
16. The Jews and Pilate in the Temple.
17. Christ Before Pilate.
18. Condemnation.
19. Carrying the Cross.
20. The Crucifixion.
21. Taking Down from the Cross.
22. The Resurrection.
23. The Ascension.

Photographed by William Paley under license of Thomas A. Edison. (F.Z. Maguire & Co., *Catalogue,* [March 1898], 4-5.)

SUBJECT: Passion plays. Catholicism. Miracles. Jesus Christ.

ARCHIVE: NR-GE.

CITATIONS: "The Passion Play. The Eden Musee Views Were Made in New York, Not Oberammergau," *New York Herald,* 1 February 1898, 7; "Passion Play at the Eden Musee," *New York Mail and Express,* 1 February 1898, 3; "Passion Play at the Eden Musee," *New York World,* 1 February 1898, 8; Terry Ramsaye, *A Million and One Nights* (New York: Simon & Schuster, 1926), 367-376; Charles Musser, "Passions and the Passion Play: Theater, Film and Religion, 1880-1900," *Film History* 5, no. 4 (1993), 419-456.

NOTE: See also film no. 491, *Opera of Martha—Second Act.*

SCENES OF BIBLE SUBJECTS.
AN EXHIBITION OF PASSION PLAY PICTURES AT THE EDEN MUSEE.

A series of Passion Play pictures was presented at the Eden Musée yesterday by the cinematograph. It was intended as a press view, though such visitors as happened to be in the Musée at the time also saw it. The pictures will be regularly presented to the public for the first time on Monday. Twenty-three scenes are shown, beginning with the shepherds watching their flocks and ending with the ascension. It would thus be more accurate to describe the series simply as a Scriptural play, since it is not confined to the scenes of the Passion.

Allowance being made for the lack of preparation, which will be remedied before the pictures are publicly shown, they were presented, for the most part, with good effect. A mistake was made in announcing them as representing the Passion Play of Oberammergau. Pictures of the celebrated play of that place cannot have been taken for use in the cinematograph, for the obvious reason that marvellous machine had not been invented at the time when the play was last given, in 1890. Nor do these pictures even approach a close imitation of the Oberammergau play. Of the twenty-three scenes shown yesterday, eleven do not occur at all in the play of Oberammergau, which begins with the entry of Christ into Jerusalem.

These pictures have their own excellencies, and they are quite capable of standing on their own bottom, and should be allowed to do so. The best of them were the flight into Egypt, the raising of Lazarus, the crucifixion and the descent from the cross. While the first two of these are not given in the Oberammergau play, the other two more nearly resemble that representation than anything else that was shown. That which takes half an hour or so on the stage had to be compressed into a few minutes on the screen, but the action had the appearance of being modelled after the famous Bavarian play. Perhaps these scenes were done better than the others for the very reason that they were harder to do. The exhibition seemed to make a favorable impression on those who saw it, and it is likely to interest the frequenters of the Musée. (*New York Tribune*, 29 January 1898, 9.)

James H. White and Frederick W. Blechynden arrived in San Diego on 20 December 1897 (San Diego Union, 21 December 1897, 3), remaining in the area between three and ten days. The duo quickly resumed their shooting of touristic scenes that were often mentioned in the travel books published by the Atchison, Topeka & Santa Fe Railroad. According to one San Diego newspaper,

James H. White and Fred. W. Blechynden are here today representing the Edison laboratory. They have taken kinetograph pictures of the rabbit chase at Coronado, spaniel[s] in the surf, ostriches and a moving double decker car of Fifth street, passing Marston's store. The views will be developed and exhibited over the world. (*San Diego Sun*, 23 December 1897, 8.)

464 ***Street Scene, San Diego / Street Scene in San Diego, Cal.**
LENGTH: 50 ft. © Thomas A. Edison, 17 February 1898.
PRODUCER: James White.
CAMERA: Frederick Blechynden.
CAST:
PRODUCTION DATE: 21-23 December 1897.
LOCATION: San Diego, Calif.
SOURCE:

DESCRIPTION: There is a long perspective, with a large double-decked trolley car in the distance, which approaches and passes the audience. Both decks are crowded with passengers, on their way to a football game, which is advertised on the side of the car. When close to the camera they rise to their feet and wave their handkerchiefs and hats. A large number of bicycle riders, pedestrians, bystanders and carriages add to the action. Sharp and clear. (*Edison Films*, 15 March 1898, 11.)

SUBJECT: City and town life–San Diego. Urban transportation. Atchison, Topeka & Santa Fe Railroad.

ARCHIVE: DLC-pp.

CITATIONS: F.Z. Maguire & Co., *Catalogue*, [March 1898], 10; *Edison Films*, March 1900, 20; *Edison Films*, July 1901, 42.

NOTE:

465 [Ostriches in San Diego]
LENGTH: 50 ft.   © No reg.
PRODUCER: James White.
CAMERA: Frederick Blechynden.
CAST:
PRODUCTION DATE: 21-23 December 1897.
LOCATION: San Diego, Calif.
SOURCE:
DESCRIPTION:
SUBJECT: Ostriches. Farms. Tourist trade.
ARCHIVE:
CITATIONS:
NOTE:

The City of San Diego.

San Diego has grown to a population of upward of 20,000 and is a city showing life and modern improvements. Briefly enumerated, its public conveniences are a comprehensive water system, costing over a million and a half dollars, a well-equipped electric street car system, whose twenty-five miles of track extend to all portions of the city; two public parks (one consisting of 1400 acres overlooking the bay); large and commodious operahouses, numerous public and private schools, and a State normal school now in course of construction; church buildings of all denominations and a public library circulating over eight thousand volumes per month. There are many fraternal and secret societies as well as literary and musical associations of a high order, showing wealth and refinement on all sides. The city has four daily newspapers, besides a number of weeklies, six banks, well-stocked whole sale and retail stores, and all told more than three score manufacturing plants, employing over one thousand men. The city is provided with fine hotels and good restaurants and lodging-houses, thus making it easy for the large number of tourists who come here each year to find suitable accommodations. (*Los Angeles Times,* "Annual Midwinter Number," 1 January 1898, 40.)

San Diego and Vicinity

Fringing the bay that for a dozen miles glows like a golden mirror below its purple rim, San Diego stands up a slope that rises from the water to the summit of a broad mesa....One may be happy in San Diego and do nothing. Its soft sensuous beauty and caressing air create in the breast a new sense of joy of mere existence. But there is besides, abundant material for the sight-seer. (C.A. Higgins, *To California and Back,* February 1900, 74-75.)

466 *Off for the Rabbit Chase / Off to the Rabbit Chase
LENGTH: 50 ft.   © Thomas A. Edison, 17 February 1898.
PRODUCER: James White.
CAMERA: Frederick Blechynden.
CAST:
PRODUCTION DATE: 21-23 December 1897.
LOCATION: Hotel del Coronado, San Diego, Calif.
SOURCE:

DESCRIPTION: Shows the world-renowned Hotel del Coronado, San Diego, Cal., on the right background, while the left background is taken up by a beautiful park which fronts the hotel. The film opens with a group of horseback riders coming head-on to the audience at full gallop, accompanied by a large pack of hounds. A second group follows, also accompanied by hounds. The figures show clear and distinct and the scene is full of action. (*Edison Films,* 15 March 1898, 10.)
SUBJECT: Hotels. Tourist trade. Hunting. Horses. Dogs. Atchison, Topeka & Santa Fe Railroad.
ARCHIVE: DLC-pp.
CITATIONS: F.Z. Maguire & Co., *Catalogue,* [March 1898], 10; *Edison Films,* March 1900, 20.
NOTE:

467 *Dogs Playing in the Surf
LENGTH: 50 ft.   © Thomas A. Edison, 17 February 1898.

PRODUCER: James White.
CAMERA: Frederick Blechynden.
CAST:
PRODUCTION DATE: 21-23 December 1897.
LOCATION: Hotel del Coronado, San Diego, Calif.
SOURCE:
DESCRIPTION: Taken at the Coronado, San Diego, Cal. Shows a variety of dogs, including Water Spaniels, Fox Terrier, Pug and St. Bernard plunging into the water and retrieving sticks thrown by their master. The breakers dash over the dogs, completely submerging them at times. It will be noticed that the pug dog conspicuously avoids getting wet. The dogs are well in the foreground and show life size. Sharp and clear. (*Edison Films*, 15 March 1898, 10.)
SUBJECT: Hotels. Dogs. Seashore. Ocean waves. Tourist trade. Atchison, Topeka & Santa Fe Railroad.
ARCHIVE: DLC-pp.
CITATIONS: F.Z. Maguire & Co., *Catalogue*, [March 1898], 10; *Edison Films*, March 1900, 20.
NOTE:

Connected by ferry and by railroad with the mainland, Coronado bears the same relation to San Diego that fashionable suburbs bear to many Eastern cities, and at the same time affords recreative pleasures which the inhabitants of those suburbs must go far to seek. Here the business-man dwells in Elysian bowers by the sea, screened from every reminder of business cares, yet barely a mile from office or shop....On the ocean side, just beyond reach of the waves, stands the hotel whose magnificence has given it leading rank among the famous hostelries of the world. It is built around a quadrangular court, or *patio*–a dense garden of rare shrubs and flowering plants more than an acre in extent. Upon this patio many sleeping rooms open by way of the circumjacent balcony, besides fronting upon ocean and bay, and a glass covered veranda, extending nearly the entire length of the western frontage, looks over the sea toward the peaks of the distant Coronado islands. (C.A. Higgins, *To California and BacK*, February 1900, 80-81.)

468 ***California Orange Groves, Panoramic View***
LENGTH: 50 ft.   © Thomas A. Edison, 24 February 1898.
PRODUCER: James White.
CAMERA: Frederick Blechynden.
CAST:

PRODUCTION DATE: 30 December 1897.
LOCATION: Riverside, Calif.
SOURCE:
DESCRIPTION: This panoramic view was taken on the Southern Pacific R.R., branch motor line. The train ran through grove after grove of heavily laden orange trees, which show in striking contrast to the almost snow-white road-bed. An immense mountain, well-defined, looms up in the approaching background. A typical California scene. Sharp and clear. (*Edison Films*, 15 March 1898, 12-13.)
SUBJECT: Orchards. Oranges. Mountains. Railroads, industrial. Southern Pacific Railroad.
ARCHIVE: DLC-pp.
CITATIONS: F.Z. Maguire & Co., *Catalogue*, [March 1898], 9; *Edison Films*, March 1900, 22.
NOTE:

469 ***Picking Oranges***
LENGTH: 50 ft.   © Thomas A. Edison, 24 February 1898.

PRODUCER: James White.
CAMERA: Frederick Blechynden.
CAST:
PRODUCTION DATE: 30 December 1897.
LOCATION: Riverside, Calif.
SOURCE:
DESCRIPTION: Taken in Mr. Newcomb's orchard with a large, heavily laden orange tree taking up the entire background. Two long ladders are placed against the tree and eight persons are busily engaged picking the fruit, some on the ladders and others on the ground. One of the pickers in descending the ladder accidentally misses his footing and falls to the ground, adding a humorous incident. This picture is a remarkable piece of photography. (*Edison Films*, 15 March 1898, 12-13.)
SUBJECT: Orchards. Harvesting. Oranges. Accidents. Southern Pacific Railroad. Mr. Newcomb.
ARCHIVE: DLC-pp.
CITATIONS: F.Z. Maguire & Co., *Catalogue*, [March 1898], 9.
NOTE:

RIVERSIDE AND VICINITY.

A locality renowned for oranges, and oranges, and still more oranges, white and odorous with the bloom of them, yellow with the sheen of them, and rich with the gains of them; culminating in a busy little city overhung by the accustomed mountain battlements and the pendant to a glorious avenue many miles in length, lined with tall eucalyptus, drooping pepper and sprightly magnolia trees in straight lines far as eye can see, and broken only by short lateral driveways through palm, orange and cypress to mansion homes. The almost continuous citrus groves and vineyards of Riverside are the result of twenty years of co-operative effort, supplemented by some pre-ponderating advantages of location. (C.A. Higgins, *To California and Back*, February 1900, 98-100.)

Riverside, December 31.

Two representatives of the Edison Kinetoscope Company yesterday visited one of the packing houses and secured a number of pictures of the orange packers to show in the Eastern States. (*Los Angeles Evening Express*, 31 December 1897, 3.)

White and Blechynden arrived at the Hollenback Hotel in Los Angeles on 30 December 1897. ("Hotel Arrivals," Los Angeles Times, 1 January 1898, 15.)

470 *****South Spring Street, Los Angeles / South Spring Street, Los Angeles, Cal.**
LENGTH: 50 ft.   © Thomas A. Edison, 24 February 1898.
PRODUCER: James White.
CAMERA: Frederick Blechynden.
CAST:

PRODUCTION DATE: Ca. 31 December 1897.
LOCATION: Los Angeles, Calif.
SOURCE:
DESCRIPTION: Street scene, showing various equipages, including a tally-ho drawn by six white horses. As each party passes the camera they salute the artists with the bugle. When the carriages are close to the camera a rut is encountered, which jolts the passengers and causes them to bounce from their seats. A trolley car local to California and of a type not familiar in the East, comes down the street. It is open at each end and closed in the centre. Various persons are seen *riding* their bicycles, while other vehicles and pedestrians are passing both ways. Sharp and clear. (*Edison Films*, 15 March 1898, 12.)

SUBJECT: City and town life–Los Angeles. Urban transportation. Carriages and carts. Bicycles. Southern Pacific Railroad.

ARCHIVE: DLC-pp.

CITATIONS: "Business Blocks," *Los Angeles Times,* "Annual Midwinter Number," 1 January 1898, 69. F.Z. Maguire & Co., *Catalogue,* [March 1898], 8-9; *Edison Films,* March 1900, 22; *Edison Films,* July 1901, 43.

NOTE: A sign for Tally's Phonograph Parlor, 311 South Spring Street, can be seen on the left side of the screen.

HOLLYWOOD

Nestling near the foot of the Cahuenga Pass is Hollywood, a small but growing settlement with a picturesque setting among the hills. The advent of a perfect irrigation system has provided the district with much needed water, within the past year, and promises a marked advance within the immediate future. Laurel Cañon, reached by a suburban line, one of the most beautiful mountain resorts of Southern California, is near by, to the west, while within two miles to the north is the splendid tract of 6000 acres, known as Griffith Park, which was recently presented to the city of Los Angeles by Mr. Griffith J. Griffith. The settlement of Hollywood has schools, churches and stores; a population of about one hundred, and is six miles from Los Angeles. (*Los Angeles Times,* "Annual Midwinter Number," 1 January 1898, 34.)

The United States acquired an overseas empire in the year 1898, as it quickly defeated Spain in a war and took over its colonies in the Caribbean and the Pacific: Cuba, Puerto Rico, and the Philippines. Films of U.S. battleships, including the sunken "Maine" in Havana Harbor, served the colonialist agenda and did much to inflame the jingoistic passions of Americans, which made war possible. Edison-licensed cameraman William Paley filmed American troops gathering in Tampa, Florida, and then accompanied them on their invasion of Cuba. James White and Frederick Blechynden embarked on a tour of Asia which matter-of-factly documented Western supremacy. European economic penetration was everywhere in evidence while the port cities of Canton, Shanghai and Yokohama were depicted as exotic sites for tourists. (Such easy self-confidence would be shattered two years later by the Boxer Rebellion.) The pair also filmed the Hawaiian Islands, as they were in the process of being annexed by the United States, and then returned to San Francisco in time to film U.S. troops departing for the Philippines. By August they were shooting one of the first events to celebrate these imperialist victories.

Thomas Edison also launched a legal offensive, suing his competitors for infringing on his motion picture patents. Because only a few motion picture producers were ready to do battle with the famed inventor in the U.S. courts, many of his rivals went out of business, while others became licensees. Despite these commercial triumphs, the Edison Manufacturing Company was being squeezed on the high end of the film market by the American Mutoscope & Biograph Company with its large format (68/70mm) film and exclusive contracts with first-class vaudeville houses. On the low end Sigmund Lubin, the Philadelphia producer, competed effectively by consistently selling his films for a lower price than Edison.

James White and Fred Blechynden filmed the Ninth Annual Tournament of Roses in Pasadena on New Years' Day, 1898. The Rose Bowl had not yet been built.

471 ***Marching Scene**

LENGTH: 50 ft.   © Thomas A. Edison, 24 February 1898.

PRODUCER: James White.

CAMERA: Frederick Blechynden.

CAST:

PRODUCTION DATE: 1 January 1898.

LOCATION: Pasadena, Calif.

SOURCE:

DESCRIPTION: Taken at the Tournament of Roses, at Pasadena, Cal. Shows a large company of young men, marching nine abreast. They are dressed in white uniforms, each carrying a flag and wearing a sash of roses. As they march along they skillfully perform various evolutions in wheeling and counter-wheeling, which readily wins applause from an audience. Sharp and clear. (*Edison Films*, 15 March 1898, 12.)

SUBJECT: Parades. Flowers. Tournament of Roses. Southern Pacific Railroad. Americus Drum Corps.

ARCHIVE: DLC-pp.

CITATIONS: F.Z. Maguire & Co., *Catalogue*, [March 1898], 8; *Edison Films*, March 1900, 22; *Edison Films*, July 1901, 43.

NOTE:

472 *Parade of Coaches**

LENGTH: 50 ft.   © Thomas A. Edison, 24 February 1898.
PRODUCER: James White.
CAMERA: Frederick Blechynden.
CAST:
PRODUCTION DATE: 1 January 1898.
LOCATION: Pasadena, Calif.
SOURCE:

DESCRIPTION: Taken at Pasadena, Cal., during the annual fete of the "Tournament of Roses." Shows three large coaches, each drawn by six horses. The wheels are festooned with roses, and the coaches otherwise decorated with this flower. On the top of each coach are seated from a dozen to fifteen young ladies, dressed in white; the drivers of the coaches are also in appropriate costume. The marshalls pass on horseback, their horses having large garlands of roses about their necks. Sharp and clear. (*Edison Films*, 15 March 1898, 12.)

SUBJECT: Parades. Carriages and carts. Parade floats. Flowers. Tournament of Roses. Southern Pacific Railroad.
ARCHIVE: DLC-pp.
CITATIONS: F.Z. Maguire & Co., *Catalogue*, [March 1898], 8; *Edison Films*, March 1900, 22; *Edison Films*, July 1901, 43.
NOTE: Same camera position as above.

The Tournament of Roses

Blue and Gold, the sunshiny colors of Pasadena, and the bright signals of our Southern California skies—how jubilantly they fluttered and glittered and bloomed in Pasadena yesterday!

Everywhere blue and gold. The streets were festooned and pennoned with them, windows beamed with them, they flaunted from poles, wires and gables, men disported them, fair women set them off, violets and honey suckle wore them, and a mile of brilliant procession did them honor.

It was the day of Pasadena's ninth annual Tournament of roses, and a day of happy achievement. There is only one Pasadena, and only one Rose Tournament on New Year's day, this ninth of the festivals was in all respects worthy of the applause that greeted it from the throngs which came to see. There were crowds on every street, they packed the electric and steam cars, they drove to town on tally-hos with bugles blowing, and behind old Dobbin with old dog Tray under the wagon, they came from city and plain, and it is estimated that there were 20,000 strangers in Pasadena....

Ideal weather, a picturesque pageant, a spectacle of floral luxuriance, maidenly beauty, childhood's charm and manhood's pride, heightened by all that art could devise with the spectrum's tints and skill could execute, with music, games, and good cheer, these made up the day which is now such a delightful memory.

Whence came all the flowers? There were more than anybody imagined there would be, after the inroads of the recent frost, and the exhibit was a new vindication of Pasadena's claims as a winter garden. Perhaps the scarlet glory of the geranium dominated, but there were roses, wreaths, and bouquets and banks of them together with pinks, acacias, orange blossoms, marigolds, poppies, stock, honeysuckles, pointsettas—most voluptuous blooms of them all—red peppers, yellow daisies and all the flowers of this exuberant valley, intertwined with smilax and supported with ferns. Even a few callas had been spared by the destroyer of this eventful anniversary.

From the bugler of Robin Hood's band, in his green doublet, who heralded the approach of the column, to the historic mules from Wilson's Peak, and the fire engines that closed the rear, the procession stretched out more than a mile. It formed on Walnut street, and the avenues intersecting it, and all the morning the town was gay with marching companies and decorated carriages, making their way to the quarters of the different divisions, while bands were pouring in. It had been just a year since Pasadena saw such an inspiring forenoon.

"Forward!" was heard soon after 11 o'clock, and it was just noon when the right of the line reached the palm decorated reviewing stands on Orange Grove avenue. The parade was half an hour in passing, and there was not an uninteresting moment....

A MILE OF FLOWERS
Detailed Description of the Parade, Beautiful Costumes.

The procession itself was about a mile in length. It was headed by a platoon of police mounted on bay horses, with collars of smilax, roses and geraniums on each horse....

Immediately following the vanguard of police came the officers of Pasadena Tournament of Roses Association, M.H.

Weight, president....Next in the order of march was the Seventh Regiment Band of Los Angeles, D.M. Parker, manager; twenty pieces; followed by Troop D., N.G.C. of Los Angeles, mounted in full heavy marching costume, forty in number....

Next came the Americus Club Drum Corps, A.C. Jones, leader; followed by the Americus Club, officered by Maj. N.S. Bangham....The staff and major rode elegant mounts, and wore wreaths of smilax and yellow marguerites across their shoulders, and in their epaulets were entwined the same flower. The horses wore white saddle blankets, trimmed with yellow, well covered with smilax and marguerites, and collars of smilax. Each of the men wore a sash of smilax and yellow marguerites. The club never made a finer appearance, and its drilling, especially the fancy movements, was applauded the entire length of the line.

...Next came the equestrian division....

The six-in-hand of Troop Polytechnic Institute came next. Preceding the coach was Elliott Howe in a beautiful silk costume, officiating as bugler....The coach was trimmed with marigolds and smilax and was drawn by six bay horses. The saddle blankets were yellow and the floral decorations were marigolds and smilax. The young ladies occupying the coach wore white, accordion-plaited capes, black poke bonnets, with black ostrich plumes and long black gloves; each of them also carried a yellow silk bag....

The Hotel Green coach was drawn by six large bay horses, with harness wrapped in green and scarlet–the hotel colors–and this effect was carried out in the decorations of the coach. The flowers were principally red geraniums, many thousands being employed in the decorations. The only other color used was green, composed of immense quantities of smilax. The ladies occupying the coach were costumed in white capes with scarlet ruchings, scarlet hats, white lace parasols, trimmed with scarlet ribbons and geraniums....

The Pasadena High School coach followed. Six white horses with harness trimmed with white satin, drew a white tally-ho laden with beautiful young ladies, wearing white gowns, capes, and hats trimmed with red and carrying parasols of red. (*Los Angeles Sunday Times,* 2 January 1898, 10.)

473 *Ostriches Feeding

LENGTH: 50 ft.   © Thomas A. Edison, 24 February 1898.

PRODUCER: James White.

CAMERA: Frederick Blechynden.

CAST:

PRODUCTION DATE: Early January 1898.

LOCATION: South Pasadena, Calif.

SOURCE:

DESCRIPTION: Taken at a South Pasadena Ostrich Farm, on the Atchison, Topeka & Santa Fe R.R., and shows these giant birds in the act of feeding. Nothing seems to come amiss to them from a grain of corn to a piece of rock. The picture is taken at short range, the birds being immediately in front of the camera and life size. Their plumage shows up sharp and clear. In the background is shown a thrifty California orchard. An exceedingly sharp and clear picture. (*Edison Films,* 15 March 1898, 10.)

SUBJECT: Ostriches. Farms. Tourist trade. Atchison, Topeka & Santa Fe Railroad.

ARCHIVE: DLC-pp.

CITATIONS: F.Z. Maguire & Co., *Catalogue,* [March 1898], 9; *Edison Films,* March 1900, 19; *Edison Films,* July 1901, 42.

NOTE:

474 *Ostriches Running, no. 1

LENGTH: 50 ft.   © Thomas A. Edison, 24 February 1898.

PRODUCER: James White.

CAMERA: Frederick Blechynden.

CAST:

PRODUCTION DATE: Early January 1898.

LOCATION: South Pasadena, Calif.

SOURCE:

DESCRIPTION: A comical picture, showing these gigantic birds striding awkwardly about as the keeper, whip in hand, chases them around their enclosure. He finally rounds them up, and they are seen feeding at their seemingly indigestible repast. Sure to produce shouts of laughter. (*Edison Films,* 15 March 1898, 10.)

SUBJECT: Ostriches. Farms. Tourist trade. Atchison, Topeka & Santa Fe Railroad.

ARCHIVE: DLC-pp.

CITATIONS: F.Z. Maguire & Co., *Catalogue,* [March 1898], 9; *Edison Films,* July 1901, 42.

NOTE: It is impossible to establish if *Ostriches Running, no. 1* or *Ostriches Running, no. 2* was listed as *Ostriches Running* in *Edison Films,* March 1900, 19.

475 *Ostriches Running, no. 2

LENGTH: 50 ft.   © Thomas A. Edison, 24 February 1898.

PRODUCER: James White.

CAMERA: Frederick Blechynden.

CAST:

PRODUCTION DATE: Early January 1898.

LOCATION: South Pasadena, Calif.

SOURCE:

DESCRIPTION: Taken at the same Ostrich Farm, and shows a large flock of the birds running around the enclosure in which they are kept, just as if they were on a track. They are running at a terrific speed, with wings outstretched. A sharp, clear film. (*Edison Films,* 15 March 1898, 10.)

SUBJECT: Ostriches. Farms. Tourist trade. Atchison, Topeka & Santa Fe Railroad.

ARCHIVE: DLC-pp.

CITATIONS: F.Z. Maguire & Co., *Catalogue,* [March 1898], 9.

NOTE:

476 *California Limited, A.T. & S.F.R.R. / California Ltd., A.T. & S.F.R.R.

LENGTH: 50 ft.   © Thomas A. Edison, 24 February 1898.

PRODUCER: James White.

CAMERA: Frederick Blechynden.

CAST:

PRODUCTION DATE: Early January 1898.

LOCATION: Arcadia, Calif. [Santa Anita, Calif.]

SOURCE:

DESCRIPTION: Shows an engine and five cars approaching from quite a distance. Taken at Santa Anita, Cal., at the well-known ranch of "Lucky" Baldwin, on the Atchison, Topeka & Santa Fe R.R. Shows an engine with one combination and four passenger cars approaching at a high rate of speed.

The train is seen for a long distance, and finally passes very close to the camera. A good scene of an ever popular train subject. A sharp, clear film. (*Edison Films,* 15 March 1898, 11.)

SUBJECT: Railroads. Ranches. Atchison, Topeka & Santa Fe Railroad. E.J. "Lucky" Baldwin.

ARCHIVE: DLC-pp, NR-GE.

CITATIONS: "The Woman Suffers; The Man Goes Free," *San Francisco Chronicle,* 21 January 1897, 14 (paternity suit—Lillian A. Ashley vs. E.J. "Lucky" Bladwin). F.Z. Maguire & Co., *Catalogue,* [March 1898], 10; *Edison Films,* March 1900, 20; *Edison Films,* July 1901, 42.

NOTE:

"LUCKY" BALDWIN LOST A DOLLAR.

...SAN FRANCISCO, June 25, 1894.–E.J. Baldwin first heard of the victory of Rey El Santa Anita through a friend at the Midwinter Fair grounds. The friend remarked to Mr. Baldwin that Rey El Santa Anita had won the Derby.

"No, he did not," replied Mr. Baldwin, who thought his friend was joking.

"I'll bet you a hundred against one," was the quick response.

"I will have to take that bet," retorted the owner of Rey El Santa Anita. So it cost Mr. Baldwin a big American dollar to find out about the triumph of his colt, but as he won $50,000 in stakes and bets he has no regrets, for Mr. Baldwin had put up $500 against $20,000 in the winner books.

"Fifty thousand dollars would not buy Rey El Santa Anita," said Mr. Baldwin on Saturday night. "Of course I was a little bit surprised to win, as I had read so much about Domino and Senator Grady. I knew I had a slashing good colt and thought I had a chance, otherwise I would not have bet $500." (*New York Herald*, 26 June 1894, 11.)

Turfman "Lucky" Baldwin
Something about the Millionaire Californian Who Owns Rey El Santa Anita and Other Flyers.

One of the wealthiest, if not the very wealthiest, turfmen in the United States is Mr. E.J. Baldwin, or "Lucky" Baldwin, as he is more familiarly known. He races for pastime, just as a small boy would play marbles or fly a kite. Several times he has attempted to retire from the turf, but it inevitably lures him back for another "farewell" appearance.

Mr. Baldwin is a lean, straight, thin-faced old man, with silky white hair standing out from under a broad-brimmed hat, and the keenest of hazel eyes looking out from under bushy, gray eyebrows. His florid face is always smooth shaven except for a silvery mustache. He is a multi-millionaire, but he does not look the part. He resembles more an unsuccessful business man whose best days have gone by. But behind his plain face and brow there is one of the brightest business brains in the country. His small, bright eyes can see further into the merits or demerits of a race horse than most of the men who follow the turf for a livelihood.

Like that other sterling supporter of the turf, Marcus Daly, Mr. Baldwin went to California forty years ago, a young man without a dollar. He began his Western life in San Francisco as the keeper of a livery stable. Then he went to selling groceries, and got a lot of stock in different mines in settlement of his bills. This apparently worthless stock he put carefully away and then went over to Japan to bring over a Japanese troupe as a sort of theatrical enterprise. He was gone several months, and when he returned he found that the Comstock lode had been discovered and that the mining stock he had put away was worth considerably over a million dollars. This was where he earned his sobriquet of "Lucky."

HIS VAST WEALTH

Not withstanding his sudden accession to wealth, Mr. Baldwin went about over the country with his Japanese troupe until his contract was filled. Then he went back to San Francisco and reinvested his money, and he is now said to be worth fully $20,000.000. He owns vast ranches in Southern California, a hotel at Lake Tahoe, the Baldwin Theatre and hotel in San Francisco, and several valuable gold mines.

It is at his Santa Anita ranch that Mr. Baldwin's celebrated racing stables are located. It is there that the king of the Santa Anita ranch, the celebrated Emperor of Norfolk, is located. In one year, his great stallion cleared $79,000 for Mr. Baldwin. Santa Anita ranch is in the San Gabriel Valley, about 20 miles from Los Angeles, and consists of 50,000 acres. Mr. Baldwin breeds, raises, and trains every horse that carries the Maltese cross. The stables are plain and simple and utterly without the usual filigree told about in connection with the quarters of Maud 8 and other flyers. Mr. Baldwin is not a believer in such things. There are no gilt edge stalls. The horses, some of which are valued at from $25,000 to $50,000 each, live in plain wooden stalls, fifteen feet square, which are kept in utmost neatness and order by attentive stable attendants. Near the stables is a beautiful mile track, on which the horses are exercised.

LIKES EVERYTHING SPANISH

Mr. Baldwin is a great lover of everything Spanish, and most of his horses are given Spanish names. The best known are Chiquita, Floriana, Santa Cruz, Rey Del Caredes and Rey El Santa Anita. Four times Mr. Baldwin has won the Derby. On the last occasion it was Rey El Santa Anita that carried the Maltese cross to victory. Mr. Baldwin manages the stable as a business enterprise, and he makes it pay, although it is doubtful if he would worry much if it should prove a losing venture. He pays little attention to horses himself and drives but seldom.

In addition to his racing stock Mr. Baldwin keeps on his ranch a large stock of Devens and Durhams, and his dairy turns out 2,000 pounds of butter a week. He has 1,000 hogs and 25,000 sheep on his ranch, and the amount of good old wine in his cellars is stupendous. On the ranch alone he has 300,000 gallons of wine and 50,000 gallons of brandy, from three to twenty years old.

Mr. Baldwin is a hard worker and a man of not many amusements. One of these, however, is a quiet and moderate game of poker. His career on the turf covers over twenty years. Last fall he made up his mind to retire from racing on account of a pressure of business and, although he sold some of his horses, he could not part with all. At present he devotes more of his time to breeding fine horses than racing them.

Outside of Mr. Baldwin's turf history his career has been a checkered one. He has been married three times, and although over seventy years of age, is hale and hearty, and promises to live a great many years longer. (*New York Herald*, 13 August 1894, 9.)

477 *****Going Through the Tunnel**
LENGTH: 100 ft.   © Thomas A. Edison, 24 February 1898.
PRODUCER: James White.
CAMERA: Frederick Blechynden.
CAST:
PRODUCTION DATE: Early January 1898.
LOCATION: Santa Monica, Calif.
SOURCE:

DESCRIPTION: Taken on the Southern Pacific R.R., on the way to Santa Monica, Cal. This picture was taken from the front end of a train while it approached, ran through and emerged from a tunnel. During the action of the picture a train running in the opposite direction is passed. A number of track men giving signals to the train lends action to the scene. A very novel subjects and one that should please. (*The Phonoscope*, March 1898, 14.)
SUBJECT: Railroads. Tunnels. Southern Pacific Railroad.
ARCHIVE: DLC-pp.
CITATIONS: *Edison Films*, 15 March 1898, 12; F.Z. Maguire & Co., *Catalogue*, [March 1898], 9; *Edison Films*, March 1900, 21; *Edison Films*, July 1901, 43.
NOTE: The railroad bed in this film appears to have become the present day West Coast Highway.

478 *****Sunset Limited, Southern Pacific Railway / Sunset Ltd., Southern Pacific Railroad**
LENGTH: 150 ft.   © Thomas A. Edison, 24 February 1898.
PRODUCER: James White.
CAMERA: Frederick Blechynden.
CAST:
PRODUCTION DATE: Mid-January 1897.
LOCATION: Fingal, Calif.
SOURCE:
DESCRIPTION: Taken at the small station of Fingal, Cal., where the world renowned "Sunset Limited" trains pass each other. One of the trains is run on a side track and the crews and passengers alight to salute the train which is approaching, and which passes at a high rate of speed. Immediately the approaching train has passed a switchman turns the switch and the train on the siding passes on to the main track and receding out of view. (*Edison Films*, 15 March 1898, 13.)
SUBJECT: Railroads. Southern Pacific Railroad.
ARCHIVE: DLC-pp.
CITATIONS: F.Z. Maguire & Co., *Catalogue*, [March 1898], 9; *Edison Films*, March 1900, 21; *Edison Films*, July 1901, 43.
NOTE:

479 *****Freight Train**
LENGTH: 100 ft.   © Thomas A. Edison, 10 March 1898.
PRODUCER: James White.
CAMERA: Frederick Blechynden.
CAST:
PRODUCTION DATE: Early to mid-January 1898.
LOCATION: Calif.

SOURCE:

DESCRIPTION: Taken on the line of the Southern Pacific R.R. Shows a freight train with two engines in front, followed by nineteen freight cars, another engine and caboose. The background is formed by very high mountains, which rise abruptly to immense heights. The scene opens showing the train part way out of a tunnel, creeping slowly around a curve and up a heavy grade to the audience. As the front end comes in the foreground the worst of the

grade has been passed and the speed increases. In the centre of the train a brakeman is standing on top of one of the cars. When the rear engine passes the whistle is blown, the escaping steam producing a fine effect. As the train passes out of view the mouth of the tunnel is fully exposed, from which immense volumes of smoke issue forth and rise along the sides of the mountains. A good photograph, the background being especially fine. (*Edison Films*, 15 March 1898, 15.)

SUBJECT: Railroads. Tunnels. Mountains. Motion pictures–sound effects. Southern Pacific Railroad.

ARCHIVE: DLC-pp.

CITATIONS: *Edison Films*, March 1900, 21; *Edison Films*, July 1901, 43.

NOTE:

White and Blechynden kinetographed a group of scenes centered on the launching of the Japanese battleship "Chitose." For many, Japan's choice of an American shipyard signaled U.S. technological superiority, particularly in the construction of warships.

480 ***Launch of Japanese Man-of-War "Chitosa" [sic] / Launching Japanese Man-of-War "Chitose" / Launching of Japanese Man-of-War "Chitose"**

LENGTH: 50 ft.   © Thomas A. Edison, 10 March 1898.

PRODUCER: James White.

CAMERA: Frederick Blechynden.

CAST:

PRODUCTION DATE: 22 January 1898.

LOCATION: San Francisco, Calif.

SOURCE:

DESCRIPTION: Taken at the docks of the Union Iron Works, San Francisco, Cal., and shows the launching of this mammoth modern war vessel. The scene opens with a group of three people in the immediate foreground and another group of three just behind them in small row-boats. The large ship slides slowly

down the ways, stern first, and the water line showing high up, even exposing the keel under the bow. As the boat floats out of sight another row-boat comes slowly into focus in the left foreground. The small boats rise and fall over the swells created by the launching. Immediately the ship has passed out of sight two of the occupants of the row-boat in the right background are seen to plunge into the water, while more boats come into focus. This is a scene which very few people have an opportunity to witness, and as the picture is very true to life it should prove a subject of great interest to the public. This film is very sharp, with the figures well defined. (*Edison Films*, 15 March 1898, 14.)

SUBJECT: Ships–launching. Navies–Japan. Japanese. Boats and boating. Piers. Boys. Union Iron Works. Southern Pacific Railroad.

ARCHIVE: DLC-pp, CLAc.

CITATIONS: "Two Cruisers for Japan," *Washington Post*, 1 January 1897, 2; "Chitose in Old Ocean's Arms," *San Francisco Chronicle*, 23 January 1898, 40. *Edison Films*, March 1900, 22.

NOTE:

481 *Launching, no. 2

LENGTH: 50 ft.   © Thomas A. Edison, 10 March 1898.
PRODUCER: James White.
CAMERA: Frederick Blechynden.
CAST:
PRODUCTION DATE: 22 January 1898.
LOCATION: San Francisco, Calif.
SOURCE:

DESCRIPTION: The camera was changed after the former subject had been photographed and the ship is seen nearly head-on, bow first, still floating backward into the harbor, while in the foreground are seen numerous row-boats with their occupants. As the boat passes out of view the row-boats constantly move around and increase in numbers, thereby lending action to the scene. This film is also exceedingly sharp, and being shown in connection with the launching proper would prove interesting. (*Edison Films,* 15 March 1898, 15.)
SUBJECT: Ships–launching. Navies–Japan. Japanese. Boats and boating. Union Iron Works. Southern Pacific Railroad.
ARCHIVE: DLC-pp.
CITATIONS:
NOTE:

482 *After Launching

LENGTH: 50 ft.   © Thomas A. Edison, 10 March 1898.
PRODUCER: James White.
CAMERA: Frederick Blechynden.
CAST:
PRODUCTION DATE: 22 January 1898.
LOCATION: San Francisco, Calif.
SOURCE:

DESCRIPTION: Taken near the Union Works, San Francisco, Cal., immediately after the launching of the Japanese Man-of-war "Chitose." The scene opens with the pleasure yacht "Unadilla" passing in the immediate foreground, her decks loaded with passengers. The boat slowly passes, until the stern is directly to the audience. The water in the wake of the yacht is churned by her screw propeller into a milky stream. As the yacht recedes and the perspective widens, a fishing smack shows on the left, while in the right foreground is a small row-boat. Sharp and clear. (*Edison Films,* 15 March 1898, 15.)
SUBJECT: Ships–launching. Navies–Japan. Japanese. Boats and boating. Union Iron Works. Southern Pacific Railroad.
ARCHIVE: DLC-pp.
CITATIONS:
NOTE:

483 *Union Iron Works

LENGTH: 50 ft.   © Thomas A. Edison, 10 March 1898.
PRODUCER: James White.
CAMERA: Frederick Blechynden.
CAST:
PRODUCTION DATE: 22 January 1898.
LOCATION: San Francisco, Calif.
SOURCE: *Employees Leaving a Factory* (Lumière film, 1895), *Clark's Thread Mill* (Edison film no. 246, October 1896).
DESCRIPTION: Taken at these well known ship yards at San Francisco, Cal., and shows

the employees leaving the factory for their mid-day lunch. This film shows the immense throng of employees life size. The figures are well defined, the features showing up very distinctly. The action is lively for a scene of this nature, the people being full of animal spirits. This film compares very favorably with any of its nature that has ever been made. (*Edison Films*, 15 March 1898, 15.)

Here was built the peerless battleship "Oregon." The scene is taken at lunch hour, and shows a great throng of employees leaving the shop. (*Edison Films*, March 1900, 22.)

SUBJECT: Shipyards. Navies–Japan. Working classes. Union Iron Works. Southern Pacific Railroad.

ARCHIVE: DLC-pp.

CITATIONS:

NOTE: A reminder that the export of armaments meant jobs.

Japan's New Battle Ships.

In reading the HERALD'S description of the two Japanese battle ships recently launched in England, navy officers cannot fail to be impressed with the inferiority of these vessels compared with the United States armored craft of the Indiana type. Except in speed, the Fuji is a far less efficient ship than the Indiana, although the former has about twenty per cent more displacement than the latter.

The Indiana's battery power enormously exceeds that of the Japanese vessels, and the Indiana's protection for her guns is so much superior to the Fuji's that the latter's fire would be silenced by an impact of shot and shell that would not affect the service of the Indiana's guns.

While the Fuji is designed for a speed about two knots greater than that of the Indiana, this quality would be of little value in ordinary circumstances. It is very improbable that any battle ship will steam into action at a higher speed than fifteen knots.

In general the new Japanese vessels are far inferior to our first class war ships. Japan is about to make a large addition to her navy, and the English are making heroic efforts to secure the contracts for the new vessels; but if she really wants the best she must come to American naval constructors for designs and to American shipyards for workmanship. (*New York Herald*, 22 April 1896, 10.)

JAPAN ORDERS FAST CRUISERS.
Description of the Vessels That Will Be Built by American Shipbuilders.

The Imperial Japanese government has concluded negotiations with the William Cramp and Sons' Ship and Engine Building Iron Works of Philadelphia and the Union Iron Works, of San Francisco, for the building of two protected cruisers, which promise to surpass anything of their class. With the experiences of actual naval combat fresh in their minds, the Japanese have a thorough appreciation of what a war ship should be, and the contracts for their new cruisers were awarded only after mature deliberation and an exhaustive consideration of plans submitted by builders in England, France, Germany, and the United States. The Japanese Commissioners, moreover, visited the establishments of all the contesting builders and made themselves thoroughly conversant with their respective facilities for turning out good work.

COMMERCE DESTROYERS

The new Japanese ships will be commerce destroyers and the contracts will call for a speed of 22 1/2 knots. Since the vessel, once in Japanese waters, will be brought into close and critical comparison with the cruisers of all the navies of the world, the builders will undoubtedly try to build ships that credit themselves and their flag.... (*New York Herald*, 9 November 1896, 9.)

JAPAN'S BIG NEW CRUISER.
THE CHITOSE, RECENTLY LAUNCHED AT SAN FRANCISCO, ONE OF THE FINEST MODERN TYPE.

San Francisco, Feb. 5.–The new Japanese cruiser Chitose, launched Saturday, January 22 at the Union Iron works in this city, and built to the order of the Imperial Japanese Government, is one of the finest types of the modern cruiser. The final delivery to her Government will be made in next September. The Chitose will cost, when completed, $1,500,000. She is 374 feet long, 48 feet 9 inches in middle width, and 17 feet 9 inches in draught, with a displacement of about 4,750 tons. She is to have longitudinal and transverse bulks divided into compartments, with an armored conning, tower and engine and boilers protected underneath with a double bottom.

The main battery will consist of two eight-inch guns, one on the forecastle and the other on the poop, and a secondary battery, which is to have ten four and seven inch guns, twelve of twelve centimetres, and six two-and-a-half pounders. Five torpedo tubes will complete the armament. The guns are now being manufactured in England by Armstrong, and are to be installed on the cruiser on her arrival at the Navy Yard Station of Northern Japan. Three thousand five hundred tons of the best American steel and five hundred tons of other materials have been used in the construction of the vessel. Her engines are to be of the triple-expansion type, with cylindrical boilers. The quarters of the crew and galleys have been built to conform to the Japanese idea of comfort and utility. The Chitose will have a speed of twenty-two and one-half knots under forced draught, and will be able to outstrip any vessel of the American Navy, with the exception of the Minneapolis. In structure and speed the Chitose is to be a sister ship of the famous cruiser Yoshino of the Japanese Imperial Navy, which won honors at the naval battle of the Yaloo and Wei-Hai-Wei. (*New York Tribune*, Illustrated Supplement, 6 February 1898, 1.)

CHITOSE IN OLD OCEAN'S ARMS.
New Japanese Cruiser Leaves Her Ways. Doves of Peace Hover Over the Ship of War.
The Successful Ceremony is Witnessed by About 200 Distinguished Guests.

San Francisco gave to old ocean yesterday another bride, when the Japanese cruiser Chitose was launched at 10:25 o'clock A.M. As the first tremor of her frame told of the vessel's surrender to the waters the wine of California dashed against her bows and a moment later mingled with the tide. Her parting from the ways released four snow-white doves which rose in the air half a hundred feet in joy at their freedom and with joyous circlings watched the baptism of the war ship.

The fierce whistling of steamers, the softer music of the band and the hurrahs of thousands of spectators echoed the greeting splash of the mighty cruiser as she dipped into her future element, and as she gently moved across the bosom of the bay, builder and captain, Japanese and American, grasped hands in delight at their success. There was not a hint of hitch or other delay to mar the beauty of the ceremony, and during the following half hour there was loud booming of firework bombs, mingled with martial airs of musicians and the praises of the immense concourse of visitors.

Miss May Budd, niece of California's Governor and a fair daughter of the State, christened the vessel with a generous bottle of native champagne, and the little niece of Mayor Phelan, Gladys Sullivan, with her tiny finger on the electric button, gave the signal that struck away the last bond that held the Chitose to shore. Around these two were gathered many of the most distinguished men of the city, a sprinkling of charming women, officers of Army and Navy, resplendent in brilliant uniforms, members of the Governor's staff, officials of the State and the city and representatives of foreign governments. The party of invited guests took their stand on a platform high up by the prow of the ship, on which was a table holding the mimic guillotine which severed the cord restraining the last shoe under the cradle. The pressure of the button made the electric connection that cut the tie and sent the cruiser into the waves....

Many Japanese of all grades of life were present and their patriotic cries and handclapping was a pleasing feature of the launching. Among the most distinguished of the invited guests was Captain Sakurai of the Imperial navy and constructor of the Chitose for the Japanese government, who wore a striking uniform. His assistants were Chief Engineer Wadagaki and Engineers Otsuka and Nakayama. Consular Secretary Amano was accompanied by his wife and infant child, and in the party of Consul Segawa were Dr. I. Katsuki, Messers K. Yamada, G.Y. Okada, C. Tourntain, U. Snyekawa, T. Asahina, S. Hagihara, A. Segawa, M. Maila and Messers Saite, Ichihashi, Mikami, Miyatani, Fujisawa, Tamai, Sakanouye and Uyeda.

Captain Sakurai was overwhelmed with congratulations, as was Irving Scott of the Union Iron Works, who was indefatigable in looking after the comfort of his guests. The gold lace of the military men with the bunting, streamers and gayly colored ribbons decorating the stand and the beauty of the ladies made a fine show which the camera fiends made the most of. An Edison animatoscope caught the fleeting cruiser in a series of moving pictures which are to be sent to Japan for the edification of the public there, the Home Government favoring the project....(*San Francisco Chronicle*, 23 January 1898, 40.)

484 *Feeding Sea Gulls

LENGTH: 50 ft.   © Thomas A. Edison, 10 March 1898.

PRODUCER: James White.

CAMERA: Frederick Blechynden.

CAST:

PRODUCTION DATE: Ca. 22 January 1898.

LOCATION: San Francisco, Calif.

SOURCE:

DESCRIPTION: Taken from the rear end of a ferry boat which runs between San Francisco and Oakland, Cal. In the background are seen the hills and mountains which surround the bay. The opening of the film shows a small tug going across the bay towing a large barge or scow, while in the immediate foreground can be seen numerous sea gulls flying through the air and fluttering in the rear of the boat. In the wake of the boat the water seethes and surges. The effect is novel, the film is very sharp and clear and will prove an attractive subject. (*Edison Films,* 15 March 1898, 14.)

SUBJECT: Sea gulls. Ferries. Harbors–San Francisco. Southern Pacific Railroad.

ARCHIVE: DLC-pp.

CITATIONS: *Edison Films,* March 1900, 22; *Edison Films,* July 1901, 44.

NOTE:

On 24 January 1898, James White and Fred Blechynden filmed a parade in San Francisco, which celebrated the 50th anniversary of the discovery of gold in California.

485 *Procession of Floats

LENGTH: 50 ft.   © Thomas A. Edison, 10 March 1898.

PRODUCER: James White.

CAMERA: Frederick Blechynden.

CAST:

PRODUCTION DATE: 24 January 1898.

LOCATION: San Francisco, Calif.

SOURCE:

DESCRIPTION: Taken at San Francisco, Cal., at the Golden Jubilee. In the foreground are seen crowds of people, all being very close to the camera. The first float is drawn by four white horses and is at least twenty feet long. It carries a full load of little school girls, who sit along its full length facing the sides of the street. This is followed by a corps of firemen, and they in turn by a unique float drawn by six mules. Particular attention is drawn to the actions of a small boy who stands very close to the camera and who partially obstructs the view. He was requested by the photographer to leave his position, and the startled look and hasty disappearance lends a humorous incident. Sharp and clear. (*Edison Films,* 15 March 1898, 14.)

SUBJECT: Parades. Parade floats. Anniversaries–California–Gold discoveries.

ARCHIVE: DLC-pp.

CITATIONS:

NOTE:

486 *Native Daughters

LENGTH: 50 ft.   © Thomas A. Edison, 10 March 1898.

PRODUCER: James White.

CAMERA: Frederick Blechynden.

CAST:

PRODUCTION DATE: 24 January 1898.

LOCATION: San Francisco, Calif.

SOURCE:

DESCRIPTION: Taken at San Francisco, Cal., at the Golden Jubilee. In the foreground is shown an immense concourse of people, including ladies and children, while the background is formed by very high buildings, from the windows of which numerous flags are waving. The film opens showing the native daughters mounted on horses, passing through the immense throngs of on-lookers. They are dressed in white costumes, wear white Alpine hats, and are followed by a beautifully decorated float, drawn by white horses. (*Edison Films,* 15 March 1898, 13.)

SUBJECT: Parades. Parade floats. Children. Anniversaries–California–Gold discoveries.
ARCHIVE: DLC-pp.
CITATIONS: "Jubilee Begins," *San Francisco Chronicle*, 25 January 1898, 1.
NOTE: Taken from same camera position as above.

487 *Parade of Chinese
LENGTH: 50 ft.   © Thomas A. Edison, 10 March 1898.
PRODUCER: James White.
CAMERA: Frederick Blechynden.
CAST:
PRODUCTION DATE: 24 January 1898.
LOCATION: San Francisco, Calif.
SOURCE:

DESCRIPTION: Taken at San Francisco, Cal., at the Golden Jubilee. This picture shows a procession of the resident Chinese of San Francisco, carrying banners, flags, etc. They are followed by an immense float drawn by four white horses. In the background is seen a beautiful arch, while across the street are hung numerous flags, which wave in the wind. (*Edison Films,* 15 March 1898, 13.)
SUBJECT: Parades. Chinese Americans. Parade floats. Anniversaries–California–Gold discoveries.
ARCHIVE: DLC-pp.
CITATIONS:
NOTE: Taken from same camera position as above.

SKIES SMILE AS THE GREAT PARADE PASSES
The Procession, Its Mass and Detail. A Brilliant Spectacle in the City's Streets.
Vast Crowds View and Cheer the Marching Host. Scenes and Incidents of a Day That Sons and Daughters of California Will Not Soon Forget.

It was a right royal jubilee parade, through and through, backed by every accessory of color and music that could be gathered to prove how heartily California celebrated the passage of fifty years of the reign of gold. The yellow metal has its sins to answer for, no doubt, but the manifold blessings that it also brings to humanity were probably never more strikingly exemplified anywhere in the world than on the streets of San Francisco yesterday. The well-dressed thousands, the happy, contented faces; the magnificence and solid appearance of the business structures through which the procession passed and the general air of joyous prosperity all served to emphasize the immensity of the debt that the Golden State owes to the discovery made by "Jimmy" Marshall on that January morning half a century ago....

Young California in Line

The fourth division represented distinctively Young California. It was made up almost exclusively of Native Son and Native Daughter organizations, but much originality was shown in the design and arrangements of floats and in the introduction of features representative or symbolical of California life or California history.
The Native Daughters of the Golden West formed a part of this section, some riding in carriages, while about thirty in white riding habits trimmed in gold were mounted on horses. They were all excellent riders and they made one of the most pleasing features of the parade, attracting much attention and receiving many complimentary remarks along the entire route....

Woes of the Celestials

Division 12 was allotted to the Chinese and they made of it the most picturesque section of the Jubilee pageant. Although they were subjected to all sorts of annoyance, they brought their display through in safety, and received their reward in the words of praise that came from spectators all along the streets. To begin with the Chinese division was compelled to wait for two hours on the inhospitable cobbles of Battery Street before it was given the order to march. It was hardly started up Market street before its line was rudely broken by a big traction engine which was sent out of Second street by the National Association of Stationary Engineers, which had been assigned to a place further down the line. While the Chinese were marching down Montgomery street, near Montgomery avenue, they were set upon by a crowd of toughs, who sought to destroy their banners and to clamber on their floats. The Chinese gave the hoodlums battle, and with the aid of the police managed to preserve their costly fabrics entire.
Among the unique features of this division were two floats, each representative of a Chinese historical event. On each float were mounted several Chinese, disguised as celebrated personages of some long-forgotten dynasty in

the empire beyond the seas. To this mute play there was an accompaniment of weird music from kettledrums and cymbals. Then there were seven Chinese boys arrayed as warriors bold of the land of their ancestors. And leading these were Chinese men bearing aloft gorgeous lanterns. About it all the rich, vari-colored banners waved an air of mystery, and the people, as the pageant passed, marveled anew at the unfathomable nature of these who believe the brightest stars of the firmament to be but the spirits of those who on earth were good and great. In command of the Chinese was Robert L. Park, who had for his assistants Leonard Leon, James Ah Chung, Leon Poon and Lee Chin. In carriages were many prominent Chinese Native Sons. One carriage was occupied by Chin Toy and Leung Dew, pioneer miners. Chin Toy came to the California diggings in 1852 and located at Oroville, Butte county, where he remained for many years. (*San Francisco Chronicle*, 25 January 1898, 1-2.)

488 ***Mount Tamalpais R.R., no. 1 / Mount Tamaltais R.R., no. 1 [sic]**
LENGTH: 50 ft.   © Thomas A. Edison, 10 March 1898
PRODUCER: James White.
CAMERA: Frederick Blechynden.
CAST:
PRODUCTION DATE: January 1898.
LOCATION: Mount Tamalpais, Marin County, Calif.
SOURCE:

DESCRIPTION: Taken on the line of the Mount Tamaltais [sic] Scenic R.R., Marin County, Cal. This scene was taken from the rear end of a train. The train on which the camera is placed moves forward and is followed by another train, engine first, with two men standing on the cow-catcher. From this a receding effect is produced, but the engine with the men on the cow-catcher are constantly in the immediate foreground. The depot gradually recedes from view, while immense mountains loom up in the background. The effect is extremely novel. Sharp and clear. (*Edison Films*, 15 March 1898, 16.)
SUBJECT: Mountains. Railroads. Tourist trade. Southern Pacific Railroad. Mount Tamalpais Scenic R.R.
ARCHIVE: DLC-pp.
CITATIONS: *Edison Films*, March 1900, 22; *Edison Films*, July 1901, 44.
NOTE:

489 ***Mount Tamalpais R.R., no. 2 / Mount Tamaltais R.R., no. 2 [sic]**
LENGTH: 50 ft.   © Thomas A. Edison, 10 March 1898.
PRODUCER: James White.
CAMERA: Frederick Blechynden.
CAST:
PRODUCTION DATE: January 1898.
LOCATION: Mount Tamalpais, Marin County, Calif.
SOURCE:

DESCRIPTION: Taken on the line of the Mount Tamaltais [sic] Scenic R.R., Marin County, Cal. This was taken from a flat car immediately following the engine. On the front end of the flat car is seen a lady, whose feathers and ribbons flutter in the wind, also a brakeman, who from time to time sets up or loosens the brake as the grades demand. The background is a panoramic view of the hills and valleys as the train ascends the mountain and winds around the curves. In different points of the film the engine takes up all the foreground and the working of the piston rods and revolving of the wheels are distinctly seen. The effect is very pleasing. Sharp and clear. (*Edison Films,* 15 March 1898, 16.)
SUBJECT: Mountains. Railroads. Tourist trade. Southern Pacific Railroad. Mount Tamalpais Scenic R.R.

ARCHIVE: DLC-pp.
CITATIONS: *Edison Films,* March 1900, 22; *Edison Films,* July 1901, 44.
NOTE:

490 ***Mount Taw R.R., no. 3 / Mount Tamaltais R.R., no. 3 [sic] / Mount Tamalpais R.R., no. 3**
LENGTH: 50 and 150 ft.   © Thomas A. Edison, 15 March 1898.
PRODUCER: James White.
CAMERA: Frederick Blechynden.
CAST:
PRODUCTION DATE: January 1898.
LOCATION: Mount Tamalpais, Marin County, Calif.
SOURCE:

DESCRIPTION: Taken on the line of the Mount Tamaltais [sic] Scenic R.R., Marin County, Cal. Whereas the foregoing views were ascending, this is a descending view, the camera being placed on the front end of a train, which follows another, consisting of two passenger coaches and an engine, down the steep grades and around numerous curves. The background constantly changes, in some instances being formed by mountains looming up in the distance and in still other cases over valleys with clouds in the extreme background. The background in this picture is particularly beautiful, in some instances immense rocks showing, in others dark jagged rocks and in other instances trees and underbrush. The film is exceptionally good from a photographic standpoint, and the constantly changing view makes it a subject of unusual interest. The light and shadow effects are exceptionally fine, and the foliage of the trees stands out clear and distinct. (*Edison Films,* 15 March 1898, 16.)
SUBJECT: Mountains. Railroads. Tourist trade. Southern Pacific Railroad. Mount Tamalpais Scenic R.R.
ARCHIVE: DLC-pp.
CITATIONS: *Edison Films,* March 1900, 22; *Edison Films,* July 1901, 44.
NOTE:

Documentation of White and Blechynden's world tour continues with film no. 496.

After the success of The Passion Play of Oberammergau, *the Eden Musee quickly produced a second ambitious example of filmed theater,* Opera of Martha, *which was not shown publicly until January 1899.*

491 **Opera of Martha—Second Act**
LENGTH: 1,350 ft.   © No reg.
PRODUCER: Richard Hollaman.
CAMERA: William Paley.
CAST: Grace Golden (Lady Harriet), Lizzie Macnichol (Nancy), H.N. Knight (Lord Tristan).
PRODUCTION DATE: February 1898.
LOCATION: New York, N.Y.
SOURCE: *Martha* (opera).
DESCRIPTION: The second Act of this beautiful opera. Consists of five scenes, about 1,300 feet in length. 1. Duet outside the Inn. 2. Quartette inside the Inn. 3. Spinning Wheel Chorus. 4. Martha singing "Last Rose of Summer." 5. Good Night Quartette. This film shows a quartette of well-known opera singers acting and singing their parts in this ever popular opera. The subjects are taken with the greatest care and the films manufactured by the Edison Manufacturing Company.
Managers can arrange to produce this exhibition throughout the country and can obtain a quartette of church singers to remain behind the scenes and sing the parts and produce a remarkably fine entertainment, besides giving a local interest to the

same by utilizing local talent. If it is desired to do so, however, the quartette can be engaged to travel with the exhibition.

Other operas and plays in preparation.

Complete Set, 5 scenes, about 1,300 feet, $320. (*Edison Films*, March 1900, 2.)

SUBJECT: Opera. Castle Square Opera Company.

ARCHIVE:

CITATIONS: "Police Guarded Souvenirs," *New York Herald*, 8 February 1898, 7.

NOTE: The Edison Manufacturing Company ended up acquiring these films as part of a settlement for Edison's patent infringement suit against Richard Hollaman at the Eden Musee.

"MARTHA" AT THE AMERICAN.

The versatile Castle Square Opera Company again changed its bill at the American Theatre last night and sang "Martha." You can look at "Martha" and listen to it and renew your youth just as well as you can by staring into a sea-coal fire. It is an opera that will stand an infinite amount of killing. It has seldom, if ever, been attempted by a company that was bad enough to take the melody out of it. Certainly the Castle Square company is not bad enough for that. The old tunes that the opera troupes of all sizes have sung for so many years sounded fresh and bright, and so did the applause that greeted them. The opera-goer of experience might have found it convenient to forget more pretentious performances, but he had only to send his memory further back to a time when he was less exacting and when "Martha" was "Martha," and then—well then "Martha" was "Martha" again. Miss Grace Golden again gratified her hearers with her singing of the little part, and Miss Lizzie Macnichol did a particularly clever piece of acting as Nancy. The chorus had its usual spirit and vigor, and the setting of the piece was bright and pretty. The company quite regained what it lost last week by its rather cheap performance of the rather cheap "Paul Jones." The performance of last night was celebrated as the fiftieth of the company in this theatre. The announcement that something would be given for nothing, namely souvenirs, brought such crowds to the theatre that the guard rails at the entrance were nearly wrecked and the police captain in charge had to send to his station for reserves, who arrived to the number of about twenty in time to save the audience from perishing under its own feet in its efforts to get into the house. (*New York Tribune,* 8 February 1898, 7.)

The following section continues Heise's filmmaking activities from film no. 443.

492 ***Coasting***

LENGTH: 50 ft. © Thomas A. Edison, 17 February 1898.

PRODUCER: William Heise.

CAMERA: William Heise.

CAST:

PRODUCTION DATE: 1-3 February 1898.

LOCATION: Newark, N.J.

SOURCE:

DESCRIPTION: Taken on Court Street, Newark, N.J., in mid-winter, showing a large number of school children coasting down a steep hill, on bobs and sleds of all descriptions. As the coasters come down the hill they are snowballed by a crowd of school boys who stand on the sidewalks. Kruger's magnifi-

cent residence shows up prominently in the background. The scene is full of boyish animation, which lends action and makes it an interesting film. This is a novel subject, of which an animated picture has never been made, and will be appreciated where these scenes are unknown. The continuity of this film is not interrupted, it can be run as long as wished. (F.Z. Maguire & Co., *Catalogue* [March 1898], 6.)

SUBJECT: Sleds. Coasting. Winter sports. Boys. Mr. Kruger.

ARCHIVE: DLC-pp, [NNMoMA].

CITATIONS: *Edison Films*, 15 March 1898, 17; *Edison Films*, March 1900, 48; *Edison Films*, July 1901, 95.

NOTE:

493 ***Snowballing the Coasters***

LENGTH: 50 ft. © Thomas A. Edison, 17 February 1898.

PRODUCER: William Heise.
CAMERA: William Heise.
CAST:
PRODUCTION DATE: 1-3 February 1898.
LOCATION: Newark, N.J.
SOURCE:

DESCRIPTION: This scene was taken at short focus, showing a large number of school boys in the foreground on either side of the street, busily engaged making snowballs, with which they are bombarding the coasters as they come rapidly down the hill on their bobs and sleds. Although they try to dodge the shots, many are hit by the missiles, thus making a picture full of excitement. This was also taken in Newark on Court street, and shows a large church in the background. The figures are life size, and the scene is full of action from beginning to end. (F.Z. Maguire & Co., *Catalogue* [March 1898], 6.)
SUBJECT: Sleds. Coasting. Winter sports. Boys. Snowballing. Church buildings.
ARCHIVE: DLC-pp, NR-GE, CLAc.
CITATIONS: *Edison Films*, March 1900, 48; *Edison Films*, July 1901, 95.
NOTE:

494 *A Mid-Winter Brush
LENGTH: 50 ft.   © Thomas A. Edison, 24 February 1898.
PRODUCER: William Heise.
CAMERA: William Heise.
CAST:
PRODUCTION DATE: 1-3 February 1898.
LOCATION: East Orange, N.J.
SOURCE:

DESCRIPTION: Taken on Central avenue, East Orange, N.J., when the sleighing season was at its height. Shows a sharp brush between at least twenty different cutters. The day was cold and clear, and the steam from the horses' nostrils, as well as the snow thrown by their flying hoofs, is plainly shown. The camera was focused so that there was a very long perspective, and the horses come head-on to the audience at high speed. A couple of very exciting races occur, and the horses appear to enter into the spirit of the contest with as much interest as the drivers. This is the best film of its class that we have listed. (F.Z. Maguire & Co., *Catalogue*, [March 1898], 7.)
SUBJECT: Sleighs and sledges. Winter sports. City and town life-Orange.
ARCHIVE: DLC-pp.
CITATIONS: *Edison Films*, 15 March 1898, 17.
NOTE:

Sleighing at its Height
Conditions of City Streets and Country Roads Better Than for Years—Trolley Car Gong Out-sounded.
The clang of the trolley car gong was out-sounded to-day by the merry jingle of sleigh bells. There were bells of all tones to be heard, as there were sleighs of all kinds to be seen, from the big lumbering delivery vans of the department stores to the neat and jaunty cutters, drawn by high steppers in shining harnesses. Indeed of all the vehicles to be seen on the streets, those on runners are much more in evidence just now than those on wheels. The majority of the milkmen driving into town on their early morning routes have for the time being substituted sleighs for their usual wagons, and not a few of them because the conditions of many of suburban roads have rendered the wheel vehicles almost useless. These were the sleighs that were the earliest seen on the streets this morning. Market sledges from the country were also noticeable in the early hours.

As the morning wore on the sledges of the business houses appeared and later the pleasure sleighs were out in force. Despite the brilliant sunlight the snow has remained in excellent condition, thanks to the crisp, frosty air, and on many of the streets where there are no car tracks the sound of sleigh bells has been almost incessant. Despite the non-arrival of the extra snowstorm that was predicted for last night and this morning, the streets of the city and the roads of the surrounding country were in better condition for sleighing than at any time during last winter. The longest continuous period of sleighing then was three days and today marks the third day of the present season....

The tariff of prices for sleighs that prevails in Newark livery stables is virtually uniform. For a two-seat, one-horse cutter, $4 is charged for an afternoon, with the right to stay out from 1 o'clock until 6, and for the night, say from 7:30 until 12 or 1 o'clock, the rate for a single cutter is $5. A two-horse sleigh costs $8 for an afternoon and $10 for a night ride. For a four-horse sleigh the price is $10 for the afternoon and $15 at night. All these sleighs are furnished with heavy fur robes for the comfort of the passengers. The Russian plumes, that are to be noticed on thoroughly equipped private sleighs, are not hired out by the livery stables.

"If we got such prices as they do in New York," said a local liveryman, "we could afford to put on plumes and such like gewgaws, too, but where they get $20 for a rig over there, we can't possibly charge more than $10."

A popular route is out the River road to Passaic. Through the Oranges and to many of the suburban places out of Newark many parties go. (*Newark Evening News*, 3 February 1898, 2.)

---

495 **Hockey Match on the Ice*

LENGTH: 150 ft.   © Thomas A. Edison, 24 February 1898.

PRODUCER: William Heise.

CAMERA: William Heise.

CAST:

PRODUCTION DATE: February 1898.

LOCATION: Crystal Lake, Newark, N.J.

SOURCE:

DESCRIPTION: Taken in mid-winter on Crystal Lake. This film shows the opposing team batting the disk to and fro in their endeavors to land it in their respective goals. The contestants skating back and forth and swinging their hockeys make a scene of full animation. The figures show full Life size. (F.Z. Maguire & Co., *Catalogue*, [March 1898], 6.)

SUBJECT: Ice hockey. Winter sports.

ARCHIVE: DLC-pp.

CITATIONS: *Edison Films*, 15 March 1898, 17; *Edison Films*, March 1900, 48.

NOTE:

To follow Heise's filming activities go to film no. 526. The next section continues White's and Blechynden's journey from film no. 491.

On 3 February 1898, James H. White and photographer Frederick W. Blechynden left San Francisco for Hong Kong via Yokohama on the S.S. "Coptic," operated by the Occidental and Oriental Steamship Company. ("Departure of the China Steamer," San Francisco Chronicle, 4 February 1898, 10.)

---

496 **S.S. "Coptic" Lying To / [S.S. "Coptic," no. 1]*

LENGTH: 50 ft.   © Thomas A. Edison, 21 April 1898.

PRODUCER: James White.

CAMERA: Frederick Blechynden.

CAST:

PRODUCTION DATE: Ca. 13 February 1898.

LOCATION: Pacific Ocean.

SOURCE:

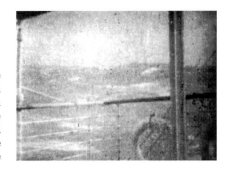

DESCRIPTION: This view was taken aboard the S.S. "Coptic" while making a trip from San Francisco to Japan. The scene was taken from one side of the upper deck, after one of the most severe hurricanes that this vessel had ever passed through, as soon as it was possible to set up the machine. The entire perspective

is formed by the angry waters. At one moment it appears as though the vessel were climbing up a mountain of water, and again the waves sink so that they are almost out of sight, as the vessel rides the crest of the waves. The effect produced is of a grandeur that must be seen to be appreciated. The picture is photographically perfect and it is certainly one of the finest subjects that we have ever taken. (*War Extra: Edison Films*, 20 May 1898, 11.)
SUBJECT: Steamships. Storms. Ocean waves. Occidental and Oriental Steamship Company.
ARCHIVE: DLC-pp.
CITATIONS: *Edison Films*, March 1900, 14; *Edison Films,* July 1901, 37.
NOTE:

497　***S.S. "Coptic" / S.S. "Coptic," no. 2**
LENGTH: 50 ft.　© Thomas A. Edison, 21 April 1898.
PRODUCER: James White.
CAMERA: Frederick Blechynden.
CAST:
PRODUCTION DATE: Ca. 13 February 1898.
LOCATION: Pacific Ocean.
SOURCE:

DESCRIPTION: Taken on the same trip as the one before described, from the forward deck, near the bridge. The former picture [no. 496] was made when there was no sunlight, but in this one the sun has just broken through the clouds. As the waters surge and roll, the tops of the waves are covered with a milk-white foam, making a striking contrast to the inky blackness of the billows. If there is any discrimination, this film is even better than No. 1, and it would prove a most attractive addition to any list of subjects. (*War Extra: Edison Films*, 20 May 1898, 12.)
SUBJECT: Steamships. Storms. Ocean waves. Occidental and Oriental Steamship Company.
ARCHIVE: DLC-pp.
CITATIONS: *Edison Films*, March 1900, 14; *Edison Films,* July 1901, 37.
NOTE:

498　***S.S. "Coptic" Running Against the Storm**
LENGTH: 50 ft.　© Thomas A. Edison, 21 April 1898.
PRODUCER: James White.
CAMERA: Frederick Blechynden.
CAST:
PRODUCTION DATE: Ca. 13 February 1898.
LOCATION: Pacific Ocean.
SOURCE:

DESCRIPTION: The view point of this picture is midships, straight ahead and shows the vessel running head-on through the heavy sea that still prevails. The bow of the vessel is plainly shown, with one of the crew stationed at his post as lookout. As the vessel runs into the heavy billows, the water breaks in huge volumes over the prow and is dashed into clouds of spray. A monster wave comes along and the lookout disappears, but bobs up the next moment; and the water may be seen running in streams from the deck. This is a very sharp and clear photograph. (*War Extra: Edison Films*, 20 May 1898, 12.)
SUBJECT: Steamships. Storms. Ocean waves. Occidental and Oriental Steamship Company.
ARCHIVE: DLC-pp, DLC, NNMoMA.
CITATIONS: *Edison Films*, March 1900, 14; *Edison Films,* July 1901, 37.
NOTE: Possibly also sold as *S.S. "Coptic" in a Storm on the Pacific Ocean* with the fol-

lowing description: "In some miraculous manner with the ship pitching and heaving at a tremendous rate, the operator was able to lash his camera to the deck of the vessel, and to get a thrilling picture of the ocean rising and falling in the great fury of a storm. A portion of the ship is shown very plainly, and the effect of the waves has never been equalled in any film so far produced." (*New York Clipper*, 30 April 1898, 153.)

499 *Heaving the Log / Heaving the Log, S.S. "Coptic" in a Storm on the Pacific Ocean

LENGTH: 50 ft.   © Thomas A. Edison, 21 April 1898.
PRODUCER: James White.
CAMERA: Frederick Blechynden.
CAST:
PRODUCTION DATE: Ca. 13 February 1898.
LOCATION: Pacific Ocean.
SOURCE:

DESCRIPTION: Taken abroad the S.S. "Coptic" just after the hurricane. The vessel has been driven out of her bearings, and the sailors in their oilskins are heaving the log. Another sailor is raising and lowering a flag, evidently signalling some other vessel. The billows are heaving and the effect of the whitecaps is fine. A long wake of foam stretches into the distance. Immense volumes of smoke pour from the funnels and recede in the background. The effect produced by the combined action of the water and the flying smoke is awe inspiring. A sharp clear picture of an excellent subject. (*War Extra: Edison Films*, 20 May 1898, 12.)

SUBJECT: Steamships. Storms. Ocean waves. Occidental and Oriental Steamship Company.
ARCHIVE: DLC-pp.
CITATIONS: *Edison Films*, March 1900, 14; *Edison Films,* July 1901, 37.
NOTE:

500 *S.S. "Coptic" Running Before a Gale

LENGTH: 50 ft.   © Thomas A. Edison, 24 December 1898.
PRODUCER: James White.
CAMERA: Frederick Blechynden.
CAST:
PRODUCTION DATE: Ca. 13 February 1898.
LOCATION: Pacific Ocean.
SOURCE:

DESCRIPTION: Taken from a point well up in the bow of the "Coptic" and shows the waves and spray breaking again and again high into the air, as the vessel pitches and tosses in the heavy sea. (*Edison Films,* July 1901, 37.)

SUBJECT: Steamships. Storms. Ocean waves. Occidental and Oriental Steamship Company.
ARCHIVE: DLC-pp.
CITATIONS: *Edison Films*, March 1900, 14.
NOTE:

THE "COPTIC" ARRIVES AT LAST
TERRIBLE EXPERIENCES IN THE PACIFIC

The Coptic, which arrived in Yokohama Harbor about 11:30 on Thursday morning, four days overdue, encountered terrible weather during her passage. The steamer, which is one of the best in the Occident and Oriental Company's service, left San Francisco on the 3rd inst. and made a good passage up to the 11th. About 1 a.m. on that day a terrific gale sprung up from the west, and the wind blew with fearful violence for two days. Great waves swept the steamer from stem to stern, and the passengers had a terrible time of it. One huge billow descended with tremendous force on the "whaleback" of the steamer's bow, and smashed and bent it in all directions, injuring the anchor gear, and completely washing out the forecastle. The forty or fifty men who were there narrowly escaped with their lives, having to fight their way aft through eight feet of water and through the wreck of the broken bulkheads. Fortunately, however, no one was washed overboard. The Coptic's ill-luck did not cease here, for some days after she ran into a succession of westerly gales. In her damaged condition it was not possible to force her against the sea and the captain had to go considerably out of his course. It will be some time before the damage done can be properly repaired. (*Japan Weekly Mail*, 26 February 1898, 216.)

James H. White and Frederick W. Blechynden reached Yokohama, Japan, on the S.S. "Coptic," 24 February 1898.

501   *S.S. "Coptic" Coaling

LENGTH: 50 ft.   © Thomas A. Edison, 22 June 1898.
PRODUCER: James White.
CAMERA: Frederick Blechynden.
CAST:
PRODUCTION DATE: 24-25 February 1898.
LOCATION: Yokohama, Japan.
SOURCE:

DESCRIPTION: Shows the "human elevator" process of coaling in Japan. A gang of fifty coolies will empty a coal lighter in an incredibly short time. (*Edison Films*, March 1900, 16.)
SUBJECT: Steamships. Harbors–Japan. Coal. Stevedores. Working classes. Japanese. Occidental and Oriental Steamship Company.
ARCHIVE: DLC-pp.
CITATIONS:
NOTE:

After a brief fueling stop White, Blechynden and the S.S. "Coptic" continued on to Hong Kong, arriving on 6 March 1898.

502   *Street Scene in Hong Kong

LENGTH: 50 ft.   © Thomas A. Edison, 22 June 1898.
PRODUCER: James White.
CAMERA: Frederick Blechynden.
CAST:
PRODUCTION DATE: 7-31 March 1898.
LOCATION: Hong Kong, China.
SOURCE:
DESCRIPTION: Here is an excellent view of one of the main business streets in the Chinese quarter of Hong Kong. Prosperous looking stores line both sides of the wide street, with their strange business signs reading up and down. (*The Phonoscope*, August 1898, 15.)
SUBJECT: Great Britain–Colonies. City and town life–China. Tourist trade. Stores. Occidental and Oriental Steamship Company.
ARCHIVE: DLC-pp.
CITATIONS: *Edison Films*, March 1900, 15; *Edison Films*, July 1901, 38.
NOTE:

503   *Government House at Hong Kong

LENGTH: 50 ft.   © Thomas A. Edison, 22 June 1898.
PRODUCER: James White.

CAMERA: Frederick Blechynden.
CAST:
PRODUCTION DATE: 14 March 1898.
LOCATION: Hong Kong, China.
SOURCE:

DESCRIPTION: Our artist seized the opportune moment to catch this picture when the distinguished guests were gathering to do honor to Prince Henri, of Prussia at the official residence of the governor; the occasion being a garden party. The guests arrive at the pillared gates in chairs carried on the shoulders of Chinamen, who make their living at this occupation. (*The Phonoscope*, August 1898, 15.)

SUBJECT: Great Britain–Colonies. Diplomatic and consular service. City and town life–China. Occidental and Oriental Steamship Company. Prince Henry of Prussia.

ARCHIVE: DLC-pp.

CITATIONS: "Hong Kong," *Hong Kong Weekly Press and China Overland Mail*, 19 March 1898, 220. *Edison Films*, March 1900, 15; *Edison Films*, July 1901, 38.

NOTE:

504 ***Hong Kong Regiment, no. 1**
LENGTH: 50 ft.   © Thomas A. Edison, 22 June 1898.
PRODUCER: James White.
CAMERA: Frederick Blechynden.
CAST:
PRODUCTION DATE: 7-31 March 1898.
LOCATION: Hong Kong, China.
SOURCE:

DESCRIPTION: A splendid infantry regiment raised in India, composed of Punjabis, Paithans, and Hindoostanis, 1,023 strong, commanded by Major J.M.A. Retallick. They march forward and wheel by the companies during the Adjutant's parade under Lieut. Berger. (*The Phonoscope*, August 1898, 15.)

SUBJECT: Great Britain–Colonies. Armies–Great Britain. East Indians. Occidental and Oriental Steamship Company. J.M.A. Retallick. Lieut. Berger.

ARCHIVE: DLC-pp.

CITATIONS: *Edison Films*, March 1900, 15.

NOTE:

505 ***Hong Kong Regiment, no. 2**
LENGTH: 50 ft.   © Thomas A. Edison, 22 June 1898.
PRODUCER: James White.
CAMERA: Frederick Blechynden.
CAST:
PRODUCTION DATE: 7-31 March 1898.
LOCATION: Hong Kong, China.
SOURCE:

DESCRIPTION: Shows same regiment at bayonet drill, keeping time with full regimental band. The uniform is the British scarlet coat and black trousers, bound tightly below the knee with their peculiar cloth leggings. The "puggri" or turban, is of dark blue and red. (*The Phonoscope*, August 1898, 15.)

SUBJECT: Great Britain–Colonies. Armies–

Great Britain. Bands (music). East Indians. Occidental and Oriental Steamship Company. J.M.A. Retallick. Lieut. Berger.
ARCHIVE: DLC-pp.
CITATIONS:
NOTE:

506 *Sheik Artillery, Hong Kong / [Sikh Artillery, Hong Kong]
LENGTH: 50 ft.   © Thomas A. Edison, 22 June 1898.
PRODUCER: James White.
CAMERA: Frederick Blechynden.
CAST:
PRODUCTION DATE: 7-31 March 1898.
LOCATION: North Point Fort, Hong Kong, China.
SOURCE:

DESCRIPTION: This picture shows a squad of men forming part of this fine regiment of Sheiks [sic], from East India, under command of their Subadar, or native commissioned officer. They may be seen working the 12 ton cannon in North Point Fort. (*The Phonoscope*, August 1898, 15.)
SUBJECT: Great Britain–Colonies. Armies–Great Britain. Artillery. East Indians. Occidental and Oriental Steamship Company.
ARCHIVE: DLC-pp.
CITATIONS:
NOTE:

507 *River Scene at Macao, China
LENGTH: 50 ft.   © Thomas A. Edison, 22 June 1898.
PRODUCER: James White.
CAMERA: Frederick Blechynden.
CAST:
PRODUCTION DATE: 7-31 March 1898.
LOCATION: Macao, China.
SOURCE:

DESCRIPTION: Here are the great warehouses and a forest of masts, indicating the enterprise of this Portuguese settlement. At anchor in the foreground lies a Chinese Junk with its high poop. (*Edison Films*, March 1900, 16.)
SUBJECT: Ships. Warehouses. Rivers–China. Harbors–China. Portugal–Colonies. Occidental and Oriental Steamship Company.
ARCHIVE: DLC-pp.
CITATIONS:
NOTE:

508 *Hong Kong Wharf Scene
LENGTH: 50 ft.   © Thomas A. Edison, 22 June 1898.
PRODUCER: James White.
CAMERA: Frederick Blechynden.
CAST:
PRODUCTION DATE: 7-31 March 1898.
LOCATION: Hong Kong, China.
SOURCE:

DESCRIPTION: A Macao steamer has just arrived, and the coolies are seen passing through the small gate on the left, jostling each other in their hurry to reach the steamer to unload both freight and passenger luggage. (*The Phonoscope*, August 1898, 15.)

SUBJECT: Great Britain–Colonies. Steam-ships. City and town life–China. Harbors–China. Stevedores. Working classes. Piers. Chinese. Occidental and Oriental Steamship Company.

ARCHIVE: DLC-pp.

CITATIONS: *Edison Films*, March 1900, 15; *Edison Films,* July 1901, 38.

NOTE:

509 *Tourists Starting for Canton

LENGTH: 50 ft.   © Thomas A. Edison, 22 June 1898.

PRODUCER: James White.

CAMERA: Frederick Blechynden.

CAST:

PRODUCTION DATE: 7-31 March 1898.

LOCATION: Hong Kong, China.

SOURCE:

DESCRIPTION: Shows a party of English people in their chairs. This is the only safe way of getting about in Canton, as the streets are indescribably filthy. (*Edison Films*, March 1900, 15.)

SUBJECT: Great Britain–Colonies. City and town life–China. Tourist trade. English. Oc-cidental and Oriental Steamship Company.

ARCHIVE: DLC-pp.

CITATIONS: *Edison Films,* July 1901, 38.

NOTE:

510 *Canton River Scene

LENGTH: 50 ft.   © Thomas A. Edison, 22 June 1898.

PRODUCER: James White.

CAMERA: Frederick Blechynden.

CAST:

PRODUCTION DATE: 7-31 March 1898.

LOCATION: Canton, China.

SOURCE:

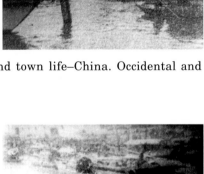

DESCRIPTION: The large boats are used as freight carriers. The smaller boats carry passengers. They are the Sampans; the rickshaws of the water traffic. Women row them, as well as men. (*Edison Films*, March 1900, 16.)

SUBJECT: Boats and boating. Rivers–China. Harbors–China. Chinese. Sampans. City and town life–China. Occidental and Oriental Steamship Company.

ARCHIVE: DLC-pp.

CITATIONS:

NOTE:

511 *Landing Wharf at Canton

LENGTH: 50 ft.   © Thomas A. Edison, 22 June 1898.

PRODUCER: James White.

CAMERA: Frederick Blechynden.

CAST:

PRODUCTION DATE: 7-31 March 1898.

LOCATION: Canton, China.

SOURCE:

DESCRIPTION: An immense number of strange shaped river and canal boats are seen. One-half the population of Canton lives on the water in these floating houses. (*Edison Films*, March 1900, 15.)

SUBJECT: Riverboats. Harbors–China. City and town life–China. Occidental and Oriental Steamship Company.

ARCHIVE: DLC-pp.

CITATIONS: *Edison Films*, July 1901, 38.

NOTE:

512 ***Canton Steamboat Landing Chinese Passengers**

LENGTH: 50 ft.   © Thomas A. Edison, 22 June 1898.

PRODUCER: James White.

CAMERA: Frederick Blechynden.

CAST:

PRODUCTION DATE: 7-31 March 1898.

LOCATION: Canton, China.

SOURCE:

DESCRIPTION:

SUBJECT: Steamships. Harbors–China. Occidental and Oriental Steamship Company.

ARCHIVE: DLC-pp.

CITATIONS:

NOTE:

*The S.S. "Gaelic" left Hong Kong, with White and Blechynden aboard, on 1 April 1898. It arrived at Shanghai about April 7th. (*China Overland Report and Hong Kong Weekly Press, 9 April 1898, 292; North China Herald, 11 April 1898.)

513 ***Shanghai Street Scene, no. 1**

LENGTH: 50 ft.   © Thomas A. Edison, 22 June 1898.

PRODUCER: James White.

CAMERA: Frederick Blechynden.

CAST:

PRODUCTION DATE: 6-10 April 1898.

LOCATION: Shanghai, China.

SOURCE:

DESCRIPTION: The street in this picture is the Bund, or the road nearest the river Yangtse Kiang; really the principal business street; containing as it does nearly all the banks and offices. It is also the fashionable drive where at sundown the European residents turn out in full array. (*The Phonoscope*, August 1898, 15.)

SUBJECT: City and town life–China. Tourist trade. Rickshaw men. Urban transportation. Occidental and Oriental Steamship Company.

ARCHIVE: DLC-pp.

CITATIONS: *Edison Films*, March 1900, 16; *Edison Films,* July 1901, 39.

NOTE:

514 ***Shanghai Street Scene, no. 2**

LENGTH: 50 ft.   © Thomas A. Edison, 22 June 1898.

PRODUCER: James White.

CAMERA: Frederick Blechynden.

CAST:

PRODUCTION DATE: 6-10 April 1898.

LOCATION: Shanghai, China.

SOURCE:

DESCRIPTION: Here is another view on the Bund, with The Garden on the left, with its high arched conservatory. As in the former scene, the peculiar wheelbarrows prove to be the central attraction. Evidently some tourists are enjoying the novel vehicle, as shown by the hilarity of the party that passes by in front of our artists. A barrow is often loaded with three or four passengers, although but one man propels it. (*The Phonoscope*, August 1898, 15.)

SUBJECT: City and town life–China. Tourist trade. Rickshaw men. Urban transportation. Occidental and Oriental Steamship Company.

ARCHIVE: DLC-pp.

CITATIONS: *Edison Films*, March 1900, 16.

NOTE:

515 *Shanghai Police

LENGTH: 50 ft.   © Thomas A. Edison, 22 June 1898.

PRODUCER: James White.

CAMERA: Frederick Blechynden.

CAST:

PRODUCTION DATE: 6-10 April 1898.

LOCATION: Shanghai, China.

SOURCE:

DESCRIPTION: Passing out of the gates at the government offices, the Shanghai police pass in full view on their way to their respective stations. (*The Phonoscope*, August 1898, 15.)

Just coming from inspection at the government office. Europeans, Punjabis, and Chinamen, both mounted and afoot. Crowds of open-mouthed spectators watch the parade. (*Edison Films*, March 1900, 16.)

SUBJECT: Police. Parades. Municipal buildings–China. Rickshaw men. Occidental and Oriental Steamship Company.

ARCHIVE: DLC-pp.

CITATIONS: *Edison Films*, March 1900, 14; *Edison Films*, July 1901, 37.

NOTE:

S.S. "Gaelic" left Shanghai, China, for Nagasaki, Japan, about 8 April 1898, with White and Blechynden aboard.
Lumière cameraman Constant Girel had already taken films of Japan, in September and October 1897. Pioneering Japanese cameraman Tsunekichi Shibata was also taking some scenes of Tokyo, using Lumière technology, in April 1898, about the time that White and Blechynden were filming in Japan. (Futoshi Koga, ed., Lumière, 1995.)

516 *S.S. "Gaelic"

LENGTH: 50 ft.   © Thomas A. Edison, 22 June 1898.

PRODUCER: James White.

CAMERA: Frederick Blechynden.

CAST:

PRODUCTION DATE: Early April 1898.

LOCATION: Pacific Ocean.

SOURCE:

DESCRIPTION:

SUBJECT: Steamships. Occidental and Oriental Steamship Company.

ARCHIVE: DLC-pp.

CITATIONS:

NOTE:

517 ***S.S. "Gaelic" at Nagasaki / S.S. "Gaelic" Coaling at Nagasaki**
LENGTH: 50 ft.   © Thomas A. Edison, 22 June 1898.
PRODUCER: James White.
CAMERA: Frederick Blechynden.
CAST:
PRODUCTION DATE: 10-12 April 1898.
LOCATION: Nagasaki, Japan.
SOURCE:

DESCRIPTION: Here is a group of Japanese engaged in the arduous task of coaling the great steamer anchored out in the harbor. The scaffolding on which they stand is built up from the deck of the lighter which brings out the coal. It is constructed with bamboo cross pieces on wooden uprights; and the coolies stand in tiers, one above the other, passing the small straw coal-filled baskets from hand to hand with great rapidity. (*The Phonoscope*, July 1898, 14.)

SUBJECT: Steamships. Coal. Harbors–Japan. Stevedores. Japanese. Working classes. Occidental and Oriental Steamship Company.
ARCHIVE: DLC-pp.
CITATIONS: *Edison Films*, March 1900, 16; *Edison Films,* July 1901, 39.
NOTE:

S.S. "Gaelic," with White and Blechynden aboard, arrived in Yokohama, Japan, on about April 14th. The filmmakers remained in Japan while the "Gaelic" continued on its eastward journey.

518 ***Street Scene in Yokohama, no. 1**
LENGTH: 50 ft.   © Thomas A. Edison, 22 June 1898.
PRODUCER: James White.
CAMERA: Frederick Blechynden.
CAST:
PRODUCTION DATE: 14-30 April 1898.
LOCATION: Yokohama, Japan.
SOURCE:

DESCRIPTION: Gives a capital view of Japan's main seaport, the street being the principal thoroughfare in the English section. The feature of the picture is the Jinrikisha, or, as it is popularly abbreviated, Rickshaw. This conveyance constitutes the popular cab service of Japan. It is a small two-wheeled affair, and is drawn by man power. (*The Phonoscope*, July 1898, 14.)

SUBJECT: City and town life–Japan. Urban transportation. Rickshaw men. Japanese. Occidental and Oriental Steamship Company.
ARCHIVE: DLC-pp.
CITATIONS: *Edison Films*, March 1900, 15; *Edison Films,* July 1901, 38.
NOTE:

519 ***Street Scene in Yokohama, no. 2**
LENGTH: 50 ft.   © Thomas A. Edison, 22 June 1898.
PRODUCER: James White.
CAMERA: Frederick Blechynden.
CAST:
PRODUCTION DATE: 14-30 April 1898.
LOCATION: Yokohama, Japan.
SOURCE:
DESCRIPTION: Shows the native quarter of Yokohama, the camera being stationed

directly opposite one of the native clothing stores or shops. These are low, pagoda-like structures, with curious tiling, and lanterns hanging in front. A typical group of jap men, women and toddling children are gathered on the roadside, watching the native band, which at that moment passes by. (*The Phonoscope*, July 1898, 14.)

SUBJECT: City and town life–Japan. Stores. Japanese. Bands (music). Children. Occidental and Oriental Steamship Company.

ARCHIVE: DLC-pp.

CITATIONS: *Edison Films*, March 1900, 15; *Edison Films,* July 1901, 38.

NOTE:

---

520 *Theatre Road, Yokohama

LENGTH: 50 ft.   © Thomas A. Edison, 22 June 1898.

PRODUCER: James White.

CAMERA: Frederick Blechynden.

CAST:

PRODUCTION DATE: 14-30 April 1898.

LOCATION: Yokohama, Japan.

SOURCE:

DESCRIPTION: An excellent view of the busy thoroughfare in the native quarter of Yokohama. Most of the Japanese theatres are on this street, and crowds are always to be seen gazing at the old theatre posters. In the immediate foreground is a group of curious Japanese children, attracted by our artists. (*The Phonoscope*, July 1898, 14.)

SUBJECT: City and town life–Japan. Theaters. Japanese. Children. Occidental and Oriental Steamship Company.

ARCHIVE: DLC-pp.

CITATIONS: *Edison Films*, March 1900, 15; *Edison Films,* July 1901, 38.

NOTE:

---

521 *Railway Station at Yokohama / Railroad Station at Yokohama

LENGTH: 50 ft.   © Thomas A. Edison, 22 June 1898.

PRODUCER: James White.

CAMERA: Frederick Blechynden.

CAST:

PRODUCTION DATE: 14-30 April 1898.

LOCATION: Yokohama, Japan.

SOURCE:

DESCRIPTION: The scene presented is just outside the depot, and gives a capital view of passengers just arrived from Tokyo as they pass out into the street. To the left is seen a row of rickshaws, with their barelegged runners wearing the peculiar white mushroom-shaped hats, eagerly soliciting faces. (*The Phonoscope*, July 1898, 14.)

SUBJECT: City and town life–Japan. Railroad stations. Rickshaw men. Japanese. Occidental and Oriental Steamship Company.

ARCHIVE: DLC-pp.

CITATIONS: *Edison Films*, March 1900, 15; *Edison Films,* July 1901, 38.

NOTE:

522 *Arrival of Tokyo Train
LENGTH: 50 ft.   © Thomas A. Edison, 22 June 1898.
PRODUCER: James White.
CAMERA: Frederick Blechynden.
CAST:
PRODUCTION DATE: 14-30 April 1898.
LOCATION: Yokohama, Japan.
SOURCE:
DESCRIPTION: Here is a Japanese railway depot, something quite different from the bustle and hustle of our American railroad stations. A train is just arriving at Yokohama. The engine is of a modified American type, while the passenger coaches are

similar in construction to the accepted English idea. The first and second-class coaches are quite modern looking and have glass windows, in distinction from the third class. (*The Phonoscope*, July 1898, 14.)
SUBJECT: City and town life–Japan. Railroad stations. Occidental and Oriental Steamship Company.
ARCHIVE: DLC-pp.
CITATIONS: *Edison Films*, March 1900, 15; *Edison Films,* July 1901, 38.
NOTE:

523 *Going to the Yokohama Races
LENGTH: 50 ft.   © Thomas A. Edison, 22 June 1898.
PRODUCER: James White.
CAMERA: Frederick Blechynden.
CAST:
PRODUCTION DATE: 14-30 April 1898.
LOCATION: Yokohama, Japan.
SOURCE:
DESCRIPTION: This picture was taken on the occasion of the annual Yokohama races, and shows one of the roads over the bluffs. This is the favorite suburb where Europeans have their residences. The pretty detached houses, standing within neatly

walled compounds with flowering shrubs and creepers, make an attractive setting for this scene of active traffic. (*The Phonoscope*, July 1898, 14.)
SUBJECT: Horse racing. Occidental and Oriental Steamship Company.
ARCHIVE: DLC-pp.
CITATIONS: *Edison Films*, March 1900, 15; *Edison Films,* July 1901, 38.
NOTE:

524 *Returning from the Races
LENGTH: 50 ft.   © Thomas A. Edison, 22 June 1898.
PRODUCER: James White.
CAMERA: Frederick Blechynden.
CAST:
PRODUCTION DATE: 14-30 April 1898.
LOCATION: Yokohama, Japan.
SOURCE:
DESCRIPTION: In this picture one gets an excellent idea of the Jap pleasure seekers who have been out to "play" the annual Yokohama races. At the roadside is seen a Japanese mother with her toddling child, who carries a miniature national flag on a slender bamboo stick. An old blind beggar

is being led along holding one end of a bamboo stick, the other end of which is guided by his son. (*The Phonoscope*, July 1898, 14.)

SUBJECT: City and town life–Japan. Horse racing. Japanese. Infants. Flags–Japan. Beggars. Blindeness. Occidental and Oriental Steamship Company.

ARCHIVE: DLC-pp.

CITATIONS: *Edison Films*, March 1900, 16; *Edison Films*, July 1901, 39.

NOTE:

---

525 *Japanese Sampans

LENGTH: 50 ft.   © Thomas A. Edison, 22 June 1898.

PRODUCER: James White.

CAMERA: Frederick Blechynden.

CAST:

PRODUCTION DATE: 14-30 April 1898.

LOCATION: Yokohama, Japan.

SOURCE:

DESCRIPTION: A view taken in Yokohama harbor from the landing stage, or British Hatoba, and presents a lively head-on race between these peculiar crafts, the Sampans. They have just carried out passengers to one of the steamships lying in the offing, and are seen racing like "night hawk cabbies" for the remaining passengers standing on the jetty. (*The Phonoscope*, August 1898, 14.)

SUBJECT: Boats and boating. Sampans. Harbors–Japan. Japanese. Occidental and Oriental Steamship Company.

ARCHIVE: DLC-pp.

CITATIONS:

NOTE:

To follow the continuation of White's and Blechynden's journey, go to film no. 566. The next section resumes the documentation of Heise's filmmaking from film no. 495.

Heise remained based in West Orange, continuing to shoot actualities and make fiction vignettes. His response to the war fever growing out of the sinking of the "Maine" (15 February 1898) was limited to a few films of the American and Cuban flags.

526 *Sea Waves

LENGTH: 50 ft.   © Thomas A. Edison, 10 March 1898.

PRODUCER: William Heise.

CAMERA: William Heise.

CAST:

PRODUCTION DATE: March 1898.

LOCATION: Long Branch, N.J.

SOURCE: *Surf at Long Branch* (Edison film no. 244, October 1896).

DESCRIPTION: Taken near Long Branch, N.J., immediately after a very severe storm. In the immediate foreground are seen two rows of spiles, which formerly supported the board-walk that has been washed away by the fierce storm. Over these spiles the exceedingly high waves break, churning the water into a milky foam and throwing spray many feet in the air. The picture is very sharp and the water effects are exceedingly fine. (*Edison Films*, 15 March 1898, 18.)

SUBJECT: Ocean waves. Seashore. Storms. Piers.

ARCHIVE: DLC-pp.

CITATIONS: *Edison Films*, March 1900, 43; *Edison Films*, July 1901, 91.

NOTE:

527 ***An Unwelcome Visitor**
LENGTH: 50 ft. © Thomas A. Edison, 10 March 1898.
PRODUCER: William Heise.
CAMERA: William Heise.
CAST:
PRODUCTION DATE: February to early March 1898.

LOCATION: Black Maria, West Orange, N.J.
SOURCE:
DESCRIPTION: The scene is laid in a bedroom. The film opens showing a man in bed and a monkey dragging the clothes off the sleeper, which partially awakens him. The monkey then crawls under the bed and lifts it from the floor, causing further concern to the occupant. He sits up and looks around for the cause of the trouble, but is unable to discover anything; then leans over the edge of the bed and looks underneath it, but in the meantime the monkey has come from under the bed and belabors him from the rear. This thoroughly arouses the would-be sleeper, he jumps out of bed, discovers the cause of his annoyance and proceeds to wreak his vengeance. He makes a grab for his tormentor, but unfortunately catches his tail, which parts company with its owner. The surprise that comes over the face of the man is ludicrous in the extreme. In the scuffle which ensues the night-shirt of the man is torn and his clothes, as well as his temper, are considerably ruffled. The situations in this view are sure to provoke mirth, the subject as a whole being extremely laughable. The figures are full life size, sharp and clear, with features well defined. (*Edison Films*, 15 March 1898, 17-18.)
SUBJECT: Monkeys. Nightmares. Dreams. Beds.
ARCHIVE: DLC-pp, NR-GE.
CITATIONS:
NOTE:

528 ***Acrobatic Monkey**
LENGTH: 50 ft. © Thomas A. Edison, 15 March 1898.
PRODUCER: William Heise.
CAMERA: William Heise.
CAST:
PRODUCTION DATE: February to early March 1898.

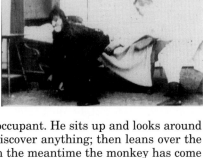

LOCATION: Black Maria, West Orange, N.J.
SOURCE:
DESCRIPTION: This film shows a man, disguised as a monkey, performing various acrobatic feats on two perpendicular ropes. The disguise is perfect and the representation very clever. The feats performed are more or less difficult and there is action from beginning to end. The acrobat is well in the foreground and as a consequence shows up life size. The background is white, which tends to make the pseudo monkey stand out more sharply. (*Edison Films*, 15 March 1898, 18.)
SUBJECT: Monkeys. Acrobats.
ARCHIVE: DLC-pp.
CITATIONS:
NOTE:

529 ***Old Glory and the Cuban Flag / [Old Glory and the Cuban Flag, no. 2] / Old Glory and the Cuban Flag, in Colors**
LENGTH: 50 ft. © Thomas A. Edison, 15 March 1898.
PRODUCER: William Heise.
CAMERA: William Heise.

CAST:

PRODUCTION DATE: February to early March 1898.

LOCATION: Black Maria, West Orange, N.J.

SOURCE: *American and Cuban Flag* (Edison film no. 290, winter 1897).

DESCRIPTION: Our special artists produce a beautiful effect in the coloring. The regular price is $10, and the cost of coloring $5 extra. (*New York Clipper*, 30 April 1898, 153.) The stars and stripes and the flag of Cuba Libre flutter in the breeze, one after the other. Very dramatic. Appeals to the popular sentiment. Excellent when colored. (*Edison Films*, March 1900, 38.)

SUBJECT: Flags–United States. Flags–Cuba. Patriotism. Spanish-American War. Motion pictures–colored.

ARCHIVE: DLC-pp.

CITATIONS: *The Phonoscope*, May 1898, 6.

NOTE: This film was taken against a black background and was probably used when requests for hand-colored films were made.

530 *American Flag / [American Flag, no. 1]

LENGTH: 50 ft. © Thomas A. Edison, 15 March 1898.

PRODUCER: William Heise.

CAMERA: William Heise.

CAST:

PRODUCTION DATE: February to early March 1898.

LOCATION: Black Maria, West Orange, N.J.

SOURCE:

DESCRIPTION: This picture shows our National flag waving in the breeze. Coloring adds greatly to the effectiveness of this film. (*Edison Films*, March 1900, 38.)

SUBJECT: Flags–United States. Patriotism. Spanish-American War. Motion pictures –colored.

ARCHIVE: DLC-pp.

CITATIONS:

NOTE: This film was taken against a black background and was probably used when requests for hand-colored films were made.

531 *Old Glory and the Cuban Flag / [Old Glory and the Cuban Flag, no. 3]

LENGTH: 50 ft. © Thomas A. Edison, 17 March 1898.

PRODUCER: William Heise.

CAMERA: William Heise.

CAST:

PRODUCTION DATE: February to early March 1898.

LOCATION: Orange, N.J.

SOURCE:

DESCRIPTION:

SUBJECT: Flags–United States. Flags–Cuba. Patriotism. Spanish-American War.

ARCHIVE: DLC-pp.

CITATIONS:

NOTE:

532 *American Flag / [American Flag, no. 2]

LENGTH: 50 ft. © Thomas A. Edison, 17 March 1898.

PRODUCER: William Heise.

CAMERA: William Heise.

CAST:

PRODUCTION DATE: February to early March 1898.

LOCATION: Orange, N.J.

SOURCE:

DESCRIPTION: This picture shows our National flag waving in the breeze. (*Edison Films*, March 15 1898, 18.)

SUBJECT: Flags–United States. Patriotism. Spanish-American War.

ARCHIVE: DLC-pp.

CITATIONS:

NOTE:

THE BRAVE AND THE FAIR MAKE THE FLAG OF THE FREE.
How Pretty Maids and Salty Old Sea Dogs Work Upon the
Most Glorious Emblem in the World at the Brooklyn Navy-Yard.

It is an excellent time to talk about flags, particularly the American flag–the finest of them all. It takes an incredible number of them to supply the annual demands of the nation.

Nobody knows how many are made. There is one firm in Elizabeth street that manufactures more than 150,000,000 each year, and there are scores of other makers in this country. From which it may be inferred that there are half a dozen flags made annually for each man, woman and child in the United States.

Of course the majority of these flags are little affairs three inches long and two inches wide, which sell for 27 cents a gross. They are printed on muslin and are turned out by the million. Cheap muslin flags are made 6 feet long and 40 inches wide.

The good flags, those made of bunting, sewed together, and with carefully arranged stars, are manufactured by flag-making firms and by every sail and awning maker in the country.

The most interesting place where flags are made is in Building No. 7 in the Brooklyn Navy-Yard. There every flag used in the United States navy is made. There are the various United States flags, signal flags, pennants, ensigns, flags of high officials, from the President of the United States down, and the flags of forty three foreign nations. Wherefore it will be seen that the flag outfit of a United States warship is pretty extensive.

Just now the workers under James Crimmins, master flagmaker, are very busy. The preparations for war have affected him. Nowhere are flags so carefully made. Every star, stripe, bar and device is measured to geometrical accuracy, and each flag must stand a strength test. They are being turned out at the rate of 100 a week.

The bunting is made in Massachusetts. It is entirely of wool and of the best quality. It must have so many threads and a fixed-tensile strength. The colors must be fast.

The stripes are cut out just as clothing is cut, in many layers at a time, by means of a circular knife that is kept as sharp as a razor. Then they are sent to the sewing-room, where skillful young women sew the stripes together and place the blue field in place.

The stars are cut out thirty at a time by means of a cold chisel and a big iron-bound mallet. Folds of goods, smoothly woven, of a standard grade, are laid in yard lengths, thirty thicknesses together, on a large square block made of cubes of oak, put together with the grain running in different directions. A metal star, used as a model, is placed on the muslin and carefully marked around with a lead pencil. Then the workman places his chisel on a pencil line and drives it through. Four blows and a constellation of thirty showy stars are released.

The sewing of the stars upon the blue field is very exacting work. There are ninety stars on each flag, forty-five on either side, and they are put on so evenly and carefully that when the flag is held up to the light there appears to be but one star. The stitching is wonderfully even and dainty.

The flagmakers are the most picturesque workers. They are two old sailors and expert sailmakers. It is their business to put on the finishing touches–the tings, the tape that adds strength, and many other things. They wear a white canvas uniform, use the queer sailmakers' thimble and talk in a fascinating sea jargon.

Directly the flags are finished they must be measured. Triangles, squares and stars of polished brass mark off the floor. If a flag is an inch or two out of the way it is rejected. The width of an American ensign must be 10-19 of its length. The largest flag made at the Navy-Yard is 36 feet long and 19 feet wide.

The foreign flags give the greatest trouble. Some of the designs are extremely intricate and the colors are as Joseph's coat. At one time these designs were painted, but they didn't last. Now the color is cut out by itself and sewed in place. It requires expert needlewomen to do this work.

One of the most difficult flags to make is that of China. It is triangular in shape, a brilliant yellow, with a black, open-mouthed dragon crawling about. One of the most beautiful flags is that of the President of the United States.

It has the coat-of-arms of the nation on a blue field, surrounded with stars. The eagle is white, and the shield he holds is properly colored.

There has been a deal of dispute over the evolution of the American flag. When the Revolutionary War broke out the flags used by the colonists were English ensigns, bearing the Union Jack, upon which were written "Liberty and Union" or other similar expressions. Then were developed the Pine-Tree flag, the Rattlesnake flag and many others.

The American ensign was adopted in 1777 by the Continental Congress. There is a dispute as to the significance of the flag. The explanation accepted as most probable is that the blue field is intended to represent the night of affliction that in 1777 surrounded the thirteen States, which were typified by the white stars arranged in a circle, signifying the endless duration of the new nation, while the stripes were chosen out of compliment to New York and the Dutch Republic and were a compliment to Republican principles.

The number of stripes symbolized the thirteen States, the first and thirteenth, both red, representing New Hampshire and Georgia respectively. Gen. Washington was a member of the committee appointed to design the flag. Mrs. John Ross, of Philadelphia, made the first flag. She designed the five pointed star.

John Paul Jones put the new flag to the first public use. He ran it up on the masthead of the Ranger. The flag, strangely enough, had but twelve stars, probably due to a blunder. Jones had the same flag on the Bon Homme Richard.

Of course everybody knows that each star in the flag represents a state, and that for the [   ] ensign had fifteen stripes, the additional ones representing Vermont and Kentucky. The flag has not changed save for the adding of stars, since then. (*New York World*, 13 March 1898, 9.)

William Daly Paley was given a contract as a licensed Edison cameraman on 7 March 1898. (William E. Gilmore to William Paley, 7 March 1898, NjWOE.) He left New York City for Key West, Florida, circa 15 March 1898. (William Paley to Edison Manufacturing Company, 12 March 1898, NjWOE.) His assignment was to take films of Cuba and U.S. military activities in that area. This was done in cooperation with William Randolph Hearst's New York Journal, *specifically with one of its correspodents—Karl C. Decker.*

533 *Burial of the "Maine" Victims / The Funeral of Nine of the Victims of the "Maine" Disaster / Burial of "Maine" Victims**

LENGTH: 150 ft.   © Thomas A. Edison, 21 April 1898.

PRODUCER: William Paley, Karl C. Decker.

CAMERA: William Paley.

CAST:

PRODUCTION DATE: 27 March 1898.

LOCATION: Key West, Fla.

SOURCE:

DESCRIPTION: Taken at Key West, Fla., March
27, 1898. First comes a detachment of sail-
ors and marines in the left foreground,
while at the right is seen a crowd of small
colored boys, which precedes any public
procession in the South. Then follow nine
hearses, each coffin draped with the flag.
At the side of each wagon walk the pall bearers, surviving comrades, their heads bowed in attitudes of grief. Next comes naval officers and marines, and lastly a procession of carriages, followed by a large crowd on foot. The scene is reproduced as it actually occurred. The figures are life size and well in the foreground. (*War Extra: Edison Films*, 20 May 1898, 4.)

SUBJECT: Spanish-American War. Funerals. Navies–United States. Afro-Americans. Boys. Disasters.

ARCHIVE: DLC-pp.

CITATIONS: *New York Clipper*, 30 April 1898, 153.

NOTE:

534 *War Correspondents**

LENGTH: 50 ft.   © Thomas A. Edison, 21 April 1898.

PRODUCER: William Paley, Karl C. Decker.

CAMERA: William Paley.

CAST: Karl Decker (in carriage).
PRODUCTION DATE: Late March to early April 1898.
LOCATION: Key West, Fla.
SOURCE:
DESCRIPTION: Shows a phase of the war excitement as it affects newspaper men at Key
West, Florida. About a dozen war correspondents of the different New York newspapers
are running up the street in a bunch to the
cable office to get copy of cablegrams to be
in turn transmitted to their different

papers. They rush directly toward the audience, turn a corner in the immediate foreground and disappear down a side street. A good-natured struggle occurs here, to see
who will make the turn first. Curious natives watch the unusual scene. A horse and
carriage follow at a seemingly slow pace, showing by comparison what a rapid head-
on foot race has been witnessed. (*War Extra: Edison Films*, 20 May 1898, 5.)
SUBJECT: Spanish-American War. Journalists. Telegraph. Carriages and carts.
ARCHIVE: DLC-pp.
CITATIONS:
NOTE:

535 *****N.Y. Journal Despatch Yacht "Buccaneer" / N.Y. Journal Despatch Yacht
"Buccaneer," War Correspondents on Board**
LENGTH: 50 ft.   © Thomas A. Edison, 21 April 1898.
PRODUCER: William Paley, Karl C. Decker.
CAMERA: William Paley.
CAST: Karl Decker (on the bridge).
PRODUCTION DATE: 17 March-8 April 1898.
LOCATION: Off Key West, Fla.
SOURCE:
DESCRIPTION: The "Buccaneer" is shown pro-
ceeding under full steam, Carl Decker on
the bridge. A most interesting picture of
well-known "Journal" yacht. (*New York
Clipper*, 30 April 1898, 153.)

Shows the despatch boat of the "New York
Journal" steaming through the water, hav-
ing aboard the war correspondents. This is one of the fastest yachts engaged in the
business. She approaches rapidly and as she cuts through the sea her prow throws
the water in a white spray on either side. This is an excellent picture of a good sub-
ject. The bow waves are especially fine. (*War Extra: Edison Films*, 20 May 1898, 7.)
SUBJECT: Spanish-American War. Journalists. Yachts and yachting.
ARCHIVE: DLC-pp.
CITATIONS: *Edison Films*, March 1900, 13.
NOTE:

KARL DECKER DIES, CORRESPONDENT, 73
Hearst Reporter Many Years Rescued Evangelina Cisneros From a Cuban Prison
FEAT WIDELY ACCLAIMED
Long With Universal Service–Began Career in Capital–Retired Few Years Ago

Karl Decker, who was one of William Randolph Hearst's outstanding correspondents during the Spanish-American
War, died Wednesday afternoon, after a two-weeks' illness, at Roosevelt Hospital. He was 73 years old.

Before America declared war on Spain, Mr. Decker was sent to Cuba. He wrote a series of articles exposing the
alleged grave brutalities inflicted upon the natives of that island by their Spanish rulers. These stories aided mea-
surably in stirring up indignation in this country and prepared the way for the war with Spain.

When the war came American newspapers, notably those controlled by Mr. Hearst and Joseph Pulitzer, rushed correspondents to the island. Many of them, particularly Richard Harding Davis, made journalistic reputations. Few,
however, had the astounding adventures of Mr. Decker.

Rescued Cuban From Jail

He was assigned to rescue Evangelina Cosio y Cisneros, the daughter of a Cuban revolutionary, who had insisted upon going to jail with her father when he was arrested by the Spanish authorities. Because she was young and beautiful her voluntary imprisonment naturally made good copy for the newspapers. Many American women, stirred by the stories of the beautiful Cuban languishing in jail, signed petitions urging her release.

Mr. Decker arrived in Cuba, learned where she was incarcerated, and laid his plans to rescue her. He climbed to the roof of a building next door to the jail. Then he lowered himself to a window from which he twisted a rusted iron bar. He got her out of jail, smuggled her upon a vessel chartered by the Hearst newspapers and sent his story of the rescue to New York.

When the ship arrived great throngs were on hand to greet the beautiful Evangelina, for whom a great celebration was staged at the old Madison Square Garden.

Once on Morning Telegraph

After the war Mr. Decker continued to work as reporter and correspondent for the Hearst organization. In 1924 he was on the staff of The Morning Telegraph, but later returned to the Universal Service, a Hearst news service. For Universal he returned to Cuba in 1933 and wrote a series of several articles on the political situation in the island.

Mr. Decker was a newspaper man since his early manhood. He was born at Stauton, Va. He grew up in Georgetown in the District of Columbia, and after graduating from the Washington High School found work as a cub reporter on Washington newspapers. He later became Washington correspondent of The Baltimore Sun and then joined Mr. Hearst, publisher of The New York American and The New York Journal.

Ill health forced his retirement from active newspaper work several years ago. He resided at 48 West 75th Street with his wife, Mrs. Maud Decker. (*New York Times*, 5 December 1941, 24.)

536 **Wreck of the Battleship "Maine" / The Wreck of the "Maine" in Havana Harbor*

LENGTH: 50 ft.   © Thomas A. Edison, 21 April 1898.

PRODUCER: William Paley, Karl C. Decker.

CAMERA: William Paley.

CAST:

PRODUCTION DATE: 17 March-1 April 1898.

LOCATION: Havana Harbor, Cuba.

SOURCE:

DESCRIPTION: Taken in Havana Harbor from a moving launch, and shows the wreck of the "Maine" surrounded by wrecking boats and other vessels. The warped and twisted remains show how thoroughly the immense mass of iron and steel was blown out of all semblance of a vessel. The background of this picture is formed by the shores of Havana Harbor, and as the yacht moves around, a panoramic view of the shores adds an interesting feature. (*War Extra: Edison Films*, 20 May 1898, 7.)

SUBJECT: Harbors–Cuba. Spanish-American War. Navies–United States. Spain–Colonies.

ARCHIVE: DLC-pp.

CITATIONS: "The Maine's Fine Run," *New York Herald*, 26 September 1894, 9; "The Maine's Good Speed," *New York Herald,* 18 October 1894, 11. *New York Clipper*, 30 April 1898, 153; *The Phonoscope*, May 1898, 6.

NOTE:

TUG RIGHT ARM RETURNS FROM THE MAINE WRECK.
Capt. McGee Says the Warship Was Undoubtedly Blown Up from Outside.

The tug Right Arm, which returned Saturday night from working on the wreck of the Maine in Havana Harbor, was tied up at the Weehawken coal docks yesterday morning. Capt. McGee said that the Right Arm lay alongside the Maine twenty-three days.

"During that time," said Capt. McGee, "the divers were constantly bothered by Spaniards who made insulting remarks and tried to interfere with their work."

Capt. McGee declared that the Maine was undoubtedly blown up by a mine under the ship.

In one of the compartments forward, where the Maine sailors slept, Capt. McGee said the divers counted fifty-three bodies, but were unable to reach them on account of a mass of twisted steel beams and plates that barred the way. (*New York World*, 22 March 1898, 2.)

537 *Morro Castle, Havana Harbor / Panoramic View, Showing Entrance to Havana Harbor and Morro Castle

LENGTH: 50 ft.   © Thomas A. Edison, 21 April 1898.
PRODUCER: William Paley, Karl C. Decker.
CAMERA: William Paley.
CAST:
PRODUCTION DATE: 17 March-1 April 1898.
LOCATION: Havana Harbor, Cuba.
SOURCE:

DESCRIPTION: The Journal tug "Buccaneer," which was placed at the disposal of Mr. Paley and Carl Decker, ran close in, taking a panoramic view of the harbor and the fortifications. (F.Z. Maguire, advertisement, *New York Clipper,* 30 April 1898, 153.) A most excellent picture of the grim old fortress which stands at the entrance of Havana Harbor. The high ramparts and lofty battlements look very formidable. Parts of the stronghold date back to the seventeenth century. While the yacht from which the picture is taken sails around the promontory, an excellent view is afforded of the entire fortress. Waves are seen dashing up against the rocks at the foot of the abutments. The lighthouse and sentry-box are so near that the guard is plainly seen pacing up and down. The photograph is excellent; and in view of a probable bombardment, when the old-fashioned masonry will melt away like butter under the fire of 13-inch guns, the view is of historic value. (*War Extra: Edison Films,* 20 May 1898, 5.)
SUBJECT: Spanish-American War. Spain–Colonies. Fortresses. Harbors–Cuba. Lighthouses.
ARCHIVE: DLC-pp.
CITATIONS: *New York Clipper*, 30 April 1898, 153; *The Phonoscope*, May 1898, 6.
NOTE:

CORRESPONDENTS QUIT HAVANA.
One Deported to Cadiz Without His Baggage, Despite the Protest of the British Consul.
HAVANA, March 30.–Few correspondents are left here now, and most of them will go north before to-morrow evening because of the quarantine going into effect April 1. It is probable that only seven American correspondents will remain in Havana. George C. Musgrave, the correspondent of a New York newspaper, was deported to-day. He was charged with having come direct from the camp of Gen. Gomez. Mr. Musgrave claims to be a British subject, and British Consul Gollannos tried to prevent the deportation. The young man was sent on board the mail steamer Buenos Ayres, without his baggage. She is bound for Cadiz, making her first stop at Porto Rico. The trip usually takes about thirteen days. (*New York World,* 31 March 1898, 4.)

Three attempts were made by our representatives to get pictures in the vicinity of Havana. They were run out of the city by Spanish officers, insulted, and spat upon by the people. (Advertisement, F.Z. Maguire & Co., *New York Clipper*, 30 April 1898, 153.)

538 *U.S.S. "Castine" / Panoramic View of U.S.S. "Castine"

LENGTH: 50 ft.   © Thomas A. Edison, 21 April 1898.
PRODUCER: William Paley, Karl C. Decker.
CAMERA: William Paley.
CAST:
PRODUCTION DATE: 17 March-8 April 1898.
LOCATION: Off Key West, Fla.
SOURCE:

DESCRIPTION: Shows the gunboat "Castine," assembled with the fleet in the Dry Tortugas. The view is taken from the steam launch, which approaches and passes the vessel. The decks are filled with sailors and marines, while the gunners are shown leaning over their guns from the various port-holes. The flag which is trailing from the stern is very large, and as it waves in the breezes produces a fine effect. In the background is seen the side wheeler "Whitney." The picture is sharp and clear. (*War Extra: Edison Films,* 20 May 1898, 7.)

SUBJECT: Spanish-American War. Navies–United States. Flags–United States.

ARCHIVE: DLC-pp.

CITATIONS: *New York Clipper,* 30 April 1898, 153; *The Phonoscope,* May 1898, 6; *Edison Films,* March 1900, 13.

NOTE: The U.S. fleet was assembled in the Dry Tortugas at the time that the Edison catalog was published in mid-May 1898, but was located off Key West when Paley actually took the films.

---

539 ***U.S. Battleship "Iowa" / U.S.S. "Iowa"**

LENGTH: 50 ft.   © Thomas A. Edison, 21 April 1898.

PRODUCER: William Paley, Karl C. Decker.

CAMERA: William Paley.

CAST:

PRODUCTION DATE: 28 March-1 April 1898.

LOCATION: Off Key West, Fla.

SOURCE:

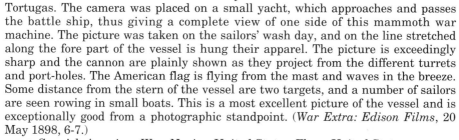

DESCRIPTION: A panoramic view of this majestic ship in the harbor, showing sailors passing to and fro, and other action which makes a remarkably interesting film. (*New York Clipper,* 30 April 1898, 153.)

Shows the U.S. Battle Ship "Iowa" at anchor at the rendez-vous near the Dry Tortugas. The camera was placed on a small yacht, which approaches and passes the battle ship, thus giving a complete view of one side of this mammoth war machine. The picture was taken on the sailors' wash day, and on the line stretched along the fore part of the vessel is hung their apparel. The picture is exceedingly sharp and the cannon are plainly shown as they project from the different turrets and port-holes. The American flag is flying from the mast and waves in the breeze. Some distance from the stern of the vessel are two targets, and a number of sailors are seen rowing in small boats. This is a most excellent picture of the vessel and is exceptionally good from a photographic standpoint. (*War Extra: Edison Films,* 20 May 1898, 6-7.)

SUBJECT: Spanish-American War. Navies–United States. Flags–United States.

ARCHIVE: DLC-pp.

CITATIONS: *New York Clipper,* 30 April 1898, 153; *Edison Films,* March 1900, 13.

NOTE:

---

540 ***U.S. Battleship "Indiana" / U.S.S. "Indiana" Coaling at Sea**

LENGTH: 50 ft.   © Thomas A. Edison, 21 April 1898.

PRODUCER: William Paley, Karl C. Decker.

CAMERA: William Paley.

CAST:

PRODUCTION DATE: 28 March-1 April 1898.

LOCATION: Off Key West, Fla.

SOURCE:

DESCRIPTION: Taken at the Dry Tortugas, and shows the most powerful fighting machine in the world to-day as she lies at anchor taking on coal. The decks are covered with marines and sailors. An immense barge lies along side from which a large gang of negroes are hustling "King coal" into the battleship, on whose decks the coal passers run to and fro. The view is taken from a moving yacht and gives the effect of the vessel itself passing through the water. As the yacht passed the starboard quarter, the powerful 13-inch, 8-inch and 6-inch guns bristle from their turrets. She looks every inch of her great length, 348 feet. The photograph is excellent. (*War Extra: Edison Films*, 20 May 1898, 9.)

SUBJECT: Spanish-American War. Navies–United States. Coal. Afro-Americans.

ARCHIVE: DLC-pp.

CITATIONS: *New York Clipper*, 30 April 1898, 153; *Edison Films*, March 1900, 13.

NOTE:

---

541 ***Cruiser "Cincinnati" / Panoramic View of U.S.S. "Cincinnati"**

LENGTH: 50 ft.   © Thomas A. Edison, 21 April 1898.

PRODUCER: William Paley, Karl C. Decker.

CAMERA: William Paley.

CAST:

PRODUCTION DATE: 28 March-1 April 1898.

LOCATION: Off Key West, Fla.

SOURCE:

DESCRIPTION: An excellent picture of the protected cruiser type. The "Cincinnati" is about 300 feet in length, and as she swings at anchor at the Dry Tortugas, she presents a magnificent spectacle. From the main mast floats the American flag, and from the forward tops are swung the signal lanterns. Her death-dealing guns seem to point directly at our camera. The massive barbettes, turrets and armored belt look invulnerable. A sailor at the stern is signaling to the "Indiana" close by. He frantically waves a blue flag, white square in the center (P in the International Code). Several small boats moving in the foreground lend action to the scene. A very interesting subject. (*War Extra: Edison Films*, 20 May 1898, 8-9.)

SUBJECT: Spanish-American War. Navies–United States. Flags.

ARCHIVE: DLC-pp.

CITATIONS: *New York Clipper*, 30 April 1898, 153; *The Phonoscope*, May 1898, 6; *Edison Films*, March 1900, 13.

NOTE:

---

542 ***U.S. Cruiser "Nashville" / Panoramic View of U.S.S. "Nashville"**

LENGTH: 50 ft.   © Thomas A. Edison, 21 April 1898.

PRODUCER: William Paley, Karl C. Decker.

CAMERA: William Paley.

CAST:

PRODUCTION DATE: 17 March-8 April 1898.

LOCATION: Off Key West, Fla.

SOURCE:

DESCRIPTION: Taken at the Dry Tortugas where the "Nashville" is awaiting orders to sail. She is a gunboat, built in 1893, of about 1400 tons displacement. She differs in design from the rest of our navy, having very tall unprotected smoke-stacks. As she goes out of view, smoke is seen rising from the rear funnel. The honor of capturing the first prize of the war, the Buena Ventura (literally "Good Luck"), belongs to this speedy gunboat. A very strong picture, outlines well defined. The water is wonderfully calm and the reflection effects are marvelous for an ocean view. (*War Extra: Edison Films*, 20 May 1898, 9.)

SUBJECT: Spanish-American War. Navies–United States.

ARCHIVE: DLC-pp.

CITATIONS: *New York Clipper*, 30 April 1898, 153; *The Phonoscope*, May 1898, 6; *Edison Films*, March 1900, 13.

NOTE:

43 *Cruiser "Detroit" / Panoramic View of U.S.S. "Detroit"**

LENGTH: 50 ft.   © Thomas A. Edison, 21 April 1898.
PRODUCER: William Paley, Karl C. Decker.
CAMERA: William Paley.
CAST:
PRODUCTION DATE: 17 March-8 April 1898.
LOCATION: Off Key West, Fla.
SOURCE:

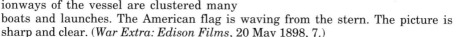

DESCRIPTION: This picture shows the cruiser "Detroit" lying at anchor in the Dry Tortugas. The effect produced is as though the vessel were approaching and passing the audience. The decks are filled with marines and sailors, while at the companionways of the vessel are clustered many boats and launches. The American flag is waving from the stern. The picture is sharp and clear. (*War Extra: Edison Films*, 20 May 1898, 7.)
SUBJECT: Spanish-American War. Navies–United States. Flags–United States.
ARCHIVE: DLC-pp.
CITATIONS: *New York Clipper*, 30 April 1898, 153; *The Phonoscope*, May 1898, 6; *Edison Films*, March 1900, 13.
NOTE:

44 *Flagship "New York" / Flagship "New York," Panoramic View / U.S. Flagship "New York" / The "New York"**

LENGTH: 50 ft.   © Thomas A. Edison, 26 April 1898.
PRODUCER: William Paley, Karl C. Decker.
CAMERA: William Paley.
CAST:
PRODUCTION DATE: 17 March-8 April 1898.
LOCATION: Off Key West, Fla.
SOURCE:

DESCRIPTION: Here is a capital view of the most popular and widely known boat in the U.S. Navy, the armored cruiser "New York." She has three funnels, same as her sister ship, the "Brooklyn." It is wash day, as evidenced by the display on her forward deck, drying in the bright sunshine and gentle breeze. She has just coaled, and with steam up and smoke pouring out of rear funnel, is waiting orders. Her maximum coaling capacity is 1200 tons, fitting her for long and swift cruising. The active part taken by Admiral Sampson and the "New York" at the bombardment of San Juan, makes this picture of great interest to any audience. (*War Extra: Edison Films*, 20 May 1898, 8.)
SUBJECT: Spanish-American War. Navies–United States. William Thomas Sampson.
ARCHIVE: DLC-pp.
CITATIONS: *New York Clipper*, 30 April 1898, 153; *The Phonoscope*, May 1898, 6; *Edison Films*, March 1900, 13.
NOTE:

45 *Cruiser "Marblehead" / U.S.S. Gunboat "Marblehead" / U.S. Cruiser "Marblehead"**

LENGTH: 50 ft.   © Thomas A. Edison, 22 April 1898.
PRODUCER: William Paley, Karl C. Decker.
CAMERA: William Paley.
CAST:
PRODUCTION DATE: 2-6 April 1898.
LOCATION: Key West, Fla.
SOURCE:

DESCRIPTION: This view of another vessel of Sampson's squadron is taken as she lies coaling at her wharf in Key West. It is a busy scene; coal passers, stevedores, sailors and officers all seem imbued with a spirit of hustle. All except the coons on the wharf, watching the work. One of them slowly gets up, stretches, yawns and walks off to the right scratching his head. The "Marblehead" distinguished herself at the bombardment of San Juan, Porto Rico; which makes the view a valuable momento of the occasion. Outlines of vessel are clear, and the wharf-loungers in the foreground are full life-size. (*War Extra: Edison Films*, 20 May 1898, 7.)

SUBJECT: Spanish-American War. Navies–United States. Coal. Harbors–Key West. Afro-Americans. Piers. Stevedores.

ARCHIVE: DLC-pp.

CITATIONS: *New York Clipper*, 30 April 1898, 153; *The Phonoscope*, May 1898, 6; *Edison Films*, March 1900, 13.

NOTE:

546 ***Monitor "Terror" / U.S.S. Monitor "Terror" Taking on Ammunition and Coaling at Dock / U.S. Monitor "Terror"**

LENGTH: 50 ft.   © Thomas A. Edison, 22 April 1898.

PRODUCER: William Paley, Karl C. Decker.

CAMERA: William Paley.

CAST:

PRODUCTION DATE: 2-6 April 1898.

LOCATION: Key West, Fla.

SOURCE:

DESCRIPTION: Coaling at dock in Key West. Monitors belong to a class of war ships that is the connecting link between the modern leviathan like the "Indiana," and the first type evolved by the genius of Ericsson, and consequently, this picture is an interesting

study. Low main deck, heavy armor belt, and revolving turrets. Military tops filled with rapid fire machine guns. A terror in deed as well as in name. Lots of action in picture. Coal car arrives and dumps into chute; another dumps, and away she goes. A bunch of coal passers are seen working further down the wharf. The "Marblehead" is coaling just beyond. Three sailors watch the work in the foreground and discuss the situation briskly. No collection of pictures complete without this one. (*War Extra: Edison Films*, 20 May 1898, 7.)

SUBJECT: Spanish-American War. Navies–United States. Stevedores. Coal. Harbors–Key West. Piers.

ARCHIVE: DLC-pp.

CITATIONS: "Terror Goes to Key West This Morning," *New York World,* 24 March 1898, 4; "Terror Fires Shot into Fleeing Spanish Steamship," *New York World*, 29 April 1898, 5. *New York Clipper*, 30 April 1898, 153; *The Phonoscope*, May 1898, 6; *Edison Films*, March 1900, 13.

NOTE:

KEY WEST FLEET CLEARED FOR ACTION.
Two Battle-Ships, Five Cruisers, Three Gunboats and Six Torpedo Boats
to Engage an Enemy's Warships or Shell Havana on Fifteen Minutes' Notice.
SLATE-COLORED PAINT ON DECK ENCUMBRANCES ASHORE AND GUNS SHOTTED.
Naval Officers Believe the Squadron Can Whip Any Fleet Spain Can Send
and Every Sailor Aboard Is Ready to Shed Blood for the Honor of the Country.

...KEY WEST, Fla., April 1.–Within twenty minutes after getting orders Capt. William T. Sampson, commanding officer of the North Atlantic Squadron, can sail for Havana or on any duty designated. The last of the slate-colored paint was put on the Cincinnati this morning, which completed the work of preparing the fleet for service. The Marblehead is taking on coal to-night. The other ships have a full supply. The flagship New York, with Capt. Sampson on board, lies off the bar six miles away, with the battle-ship Iowa a cable's length away to the westward, and the battle-ship Indiana the same distance to the eastward, all with steam up ready to get away.

Careful discipline is maintained and but little shore leave is allowed to officers or men. The launches come off each day for supplies, but are not allowed to stay long. No one is allowed to approach at night. Merchant vessels have been warned not to take chances.

It is an inspiring sight to witness the crews at work. Every man aboard each ship seems to feel that nation's honor depends on him. When nightfall comes buglers and drummers appear on the quarter-decks and sound the reveille. Every man on deck faces aft, and as the flag is hauled down salutes the colors he is bound to defend to the last drop of his blood.

Not a thing has been left undone to prepare the fleet for instant action. Inside the harbor are the torpedo boats and the other ships of the fleet. Each one is in the same condition as those lying in the roadstead. All now are looking anxiously for the monitors Puritan and Terror. They will probably arrive Monday. If the time for action arrives before they reach here there will be no delay. Still with these big brutes at [his] command Capt. Sampson will have a formidable fleet.

The naval officers here feel that the monitors can destroy any battle-ship afloat. While they have no secondary battery the crew is so well protected that it would probably not suffer much unless the vessel sunk.

Omitting the monitors Captain Sampson has under him now the battle-ships Indiana and Iowa, the cruisers New York, Detroit, Marblehead, Montgomery and Cincinnati, the gunboats Nashville, Wilmington and Castine, and the torpedo boats Dupont, Cushing, Porter, Winslow, Ericsson and Foote.

But little has been taken off the ships to prepare them for action. From the flagship a few things that would encumber the deck have been sent to shore. These would naturally go overboard if the ship cleared for action. The American Navy hold the record for clearing ship. After the signal was given it has been accomplished in fifteen minutes.

A few of the officers have sent important private papers ashore. These were things that could not be duplicated. This has not been done generally. The rooms of most of the officers look exactly as they usually do.

It is not yet understood here why the Texas and Massachusetts were sent north. Apparently there is much mystery in the movement. But their absence is counter-balanced by the coming of the monitors.

The plan of campaign is much discussed. It is thought that Captain Sampson may proceed directly to Havana with most of the fleet. Others may go to Matanzas. If there is simply a blockade Havana cannot last long, as already pointed out in The World, as the food supply is short.

If action is to be had Spain has near Cuba the armored cruisers, Oquendo and Vizcaya. The Alphonse XII is of no use, as she cannot get away from her moorings. If either of the first-named ships get out of Havana harbor she will be sunk in fifteen minutes by our battle-ships. The batteries on shore are not of much use. The twelve-inch rifles can not be handled well and the supply of ammunition is short. The mortars cannot range more than three miles. By keeping outside the ranges of the mortars, the American ships can batter the shore fortifications to pieces in a short time. So the opportunities for distinguishing themselves are not many for American officers and men. Spain has no fleet to ravage the coast of the United States, so naval officers here feel that if war comes she will stake all on one decisive naval engagement. They feel anxious, too, as to what the Government is to do about intercepting the fleet of torpedo destroyers now on the way to Port Rico. The Flying squadron, they say, ought to be able to intercept them at sea and if it does not capture them, at least it can destroy them before they have an opportunity to harass the fleet here. They also think that half of the campaign is to worry Spain with two or three cruisers by making night attacks on cities. This plan has long been under consideration at Washington.

The Nashville has about completed the laying of the cable to Tortugas. The line is complete from Tortugas to reef Northwest Key West. There is trouble in getting the cable over the reef. The Nashville got aground there yesterday for a moment, but backed right off.

The Government is to send telegraph operators to Tortugas Saturday. (*New York World*, 2 April 1898, 2.)

547 ***Secretary Long and Captain Sigsbee / Secretary of the Navy Long and Captain Sigsbee, the Hero of the "Maine," Coming From the Navy Department**
LENGTH: 50 ft. © Thomas A. Edison, 21 April 1898.
PRODUCER: William Paley, Karl C. Decker.
CAMERA: William Paley.
CAST: John Davis Long, Charles Dwight Sigsbee.
PRODUCTION DATE: Ca. 13 April 1898.
LOCATION: Washington, D.C.
SOURCE:

DESCRIPTION: This scene was taken in Washington and represents Captain Sigsbee and Secretary Long descending the steps of the Navy Department and stopping to receive the first news of reading of the President's message in Congress. (*New York Clipper*, 30 April 1898, 153.)

Taken at Washington, in front of the Navy Department, and shows Secretary of the Navy Long and Captain Sigsbee of the ill-fated "Maine" coming down the steps. As they reach the bottom a waiting attaché approaches the Secretary and hands him a letter. In the meantime Capt. Sigsbee and his friend walk toward the immediate foreground, in earnest conversation. They are quickly joined by the Secretary and the attaché. Here they halt and apparently debate some important question. Additional action is lent to the scene by ladies and gentlemen descending the steps. The background is formed by the handsome building of the Navy Department. The figures are full life size, and are excellent portraits of the famous Captain and the Secretary. This picture excites the keenest interest whenever it is shown. (*War Extra: Edison Films*, 20 May 1898, 4-5.)

SUBJECT: Spanish-American War. Navies–United States.

ARCHIVE: DLC-pp.

CITATIONS: "Sigsbee Leaves Havana on the Olivette," *New York World*, 28 March 1898, 16; "Captain Sigsbee Lionized at the National Capitol," *New York World*, 31 March 1898, 4. *New York Clipper*, 30 April 1898, 153.

NOTE:

Capt. Sigsbee returned to his home in Washington to-day and was warmly welcomed. He spent much of the day with Secretary Long who took him to the White House. (*New York World*, 30 March 1898, 3.)

Paley returned to New York City circa 14 April 1898. (New York Journal and Advertiser, *16 April 1898, 11.)*

THE JOURNAL'S VIVID MOVING WAR PICTURES
Squadron at Key West in Evolution and Havana Scenes Depicted with Life and Action.

The Journal is arranging that the public may see the fleet of battleships about Key West and the scenes in Havana Harbor, with all the vivid impression that an eye witness gets in viewing an unusual or striking situation.

William Paley has just returned from Cuba after spending several weeks. He took with him elaborate apparatus for securing a series of moving pictures. These animated reproductions show many interesting scenes which have occurred in the neighborhood of Havana and Key West.

Karl Decker accompanied Mr. Paley in his selection of many subjects and the results are remarkably interesting. The Buccaneer was placed at their disposal so they could go where they pleased.

One of the most striking series of pictures shows the burial of the Maine victims. First comes the crowd of small colored boys, which precedes any public procession of the South; then follow the nine hearses covered with flowers. At each side walk surviving comrades, with their heads bowed in attitudes of grief. Next come naval officers and marines in imposing array, and lastly a procession of carriages. The whole scene passes before the spectator just as it occurred, and its effect is particularly realistic.

In lighter vein is a scene of the various newspaper correspondents rushing to file "war copy" at the little telegraph office in Key West. They run down the street at full speed and just at the door there is a good-natured scuffle between those in the lead, which lets in one of those who had been a bit behind in the race. Karl Decker took a carriage for this race and arrived with the Journal copy before the leaders in the foot race.

There are a number of animated pictures of the big battle ships performing their various evolutions in the vicinity of Key West. That of the Iowa getting ready for target practice shows the big ship slowly moving through the water. As she turns, one gets a splendid view of the great guns and the battle ship appears so near that one might almost touch the armor-plated sides. The crew are seen hurrying about the decks getting ready for the target practice.

A pretty scene shows the Buccaneer under full speed, carrying dispatches from Havana to Key West.

The Indiana taking coal shows the big, grimy coal barge at one side and the negroes passing the coal on deck. The Detroit, Cincinnati and other gunboats are shown moving about as if ready to repel Spanish invaders.

The scenes in Havana harbor show the wrecking companies' tugs at work on the Maine and take the spectator through the narrow passage by Morro Castle, under the very walls of the grim Cabanas and up to the side of the Viscaya and Alfonso XII.

Mr. Paley was warned that if he took his photographic apparatus to Havana the Spanish officials would make him pay dearly for such a reckless proceeding, for they do not desire the Maine and its surroundings reproduced.

When he entered the harbor at Havana the pilot attempted to throw the photographic apparatus overboard. This caused a personal encounter, in which Mr. Paley was victorious. Spanish officers also boarded the yacht and attempted to arrest the photographer. He managed to evade them sufficiently to get all the important scenes that are worth reproducing in the harbor.

This series of moving pictures give the first adequate idea of what will probably be a scene of battle in the near future. The moving battle ships shown by this method give a better notion of their great size and power than could be obtained by really seeing them unless one had exceptional facilities for getting very close to them. (*New York Journal*, 16 April 1898, 11.)

With war fever at its height, reporters were eager to print Edison's views on the looming conflict, and also to report on his latest technological invention, deemed certain to transform modern warfare.

EASY TO WHIP SPAIN, SAYS EDISON.

Spain? What's fighting with Spain? There isn't enough of a fight to make an American inventor enthusiastic. It's mere child's play, because the Spaniards can't fight. They can't shoot. If they had a lot of English gunners on their warships we might have something to look after.

Spain? Why, when the shooting began they'd all go crazy. They wouldn't know what they were doing. I'll bet ten cents they'd shoot each other and think they were killing Americans all the time.

We ought to wallop Spain without an effort. I don't know what we are waiting for, except that the Spaniards are not fit to fight with. Nobody wants to play chess with a fool. Spain? Easy. Easy.

The Great Wizard of Electricity Devises Cheap, Practical "Light Bombs"
Which, Thrown from Our Battle-ships at Night, Will Illuminate the Sea for Miles,
Revealing the Movements of the Enemy's Torpedo Boats and Making Them Harmless.

THOMAS A. EDISON has made a discovery, or rather applied a principle that will revolutionize modern naval warfare. At present night and fog are the greatest enemy a war fleet at sea can know. It is under cover of the darkness that the torpedo boats sneak up to within hailing distance of the great ships and aim deadly blows at them.

By day nothing is so feeble as a torpedo boat. It must get within half a mile of its mark ere it can spit its venom, and this it cannot do. It is as swift in flight and as harmless in offense as a rabbit. Its decks are so thin, that it bends under the feet, its sides so frail that the smallest rapid-fire gun will riddle it.

Built for speed rather than strength the torpedo boat is inept in the daylight. It is only in storm or fog that it can, even then at peril of its own life, approach close enough to deal the blow that may send a great warship sluicing down into the cool sea depths.

Now even the night is to lose its terrors, if the United States Navy will act upon Mr. Edison's suggestion, and the officers and men of the American Navy may laugh at the Spaniards and their war fleet.

Not only does Mr. Edison's invention render the strongest element of the Spanish Navy–its torpedo boat flotilla–absolutely harmless, but it makes naval battle at night a deadly possibility....(*New York World*, 10 April 1898, 25.)

See also: "Wizard Edison's New Sea Light," New York World, 24 April 1898, 18.

William Paley's filmmaking continues to be traced with film no. 552.
The following section resumes the documentation of Heise's production activities from film no. 532.

548 ***Snow Storm**
LENGTH: 50 ft.   © Thomas A. Edison, 21 April 1898.
PRODUCER: William Heise.
CAMERA: William Heise.
CAST:
PRODUCTION DATE: 5 April 1898.
LOCATION: Llewellyn Park, Orange, N.J.
SOURCE:
DESCRIPTION: We present this picture as being one of the most novel that has ever been shown to the public. It was taken during an actual snow storm, not a ray of sunshine visible. The background is formed by the entrance to Llewellyn Park, Orange, N.J., the

lodge house with its roof covered with snow being to the right. The limbs of the trees are heavily loaded down, and even the falling flakes are distinctly shown. Several carriages and pedestrians with uplifted umbrellas approach and lend action to the scene. One of the walkers is a high stepper, and every lift of his foot throws a ball of snow forward. Just as the picture ends his foot sends a snowball apparently right into the audience. This picture is very clear, and the subject entirely out of the ordinary line of animated pictures. (*War Extra: Edison Films,* 20 May 1898, 10.)

SUBJECT: Snow storms. City and town life–Orange.
ARCHIVE: DLC-pp.
CITATIONS: *Orange Chronicle,* 9 April 1898, 7.
NOTE: Three inches of snow fell in Orange, New Jersey, on Tuesday, 5 April 1898.

J. Stuart Blackton and Albert E. Smith commissioned two films used for advertising purposes by their short-lived company, the Commerical Advertising Bureau. It is possible that they were made by William Heise and the Edison Manufacturing Company.

549 Lickmann's Cigar and Photo Store
LENGTH: [50 ft.]   © No reg.
PRODUCER: [William Heise], J. Stuart Blackton, Albert E. Smith.
CAMERA: [William Heise.]
CAST:
PRODUCTION DATE: April 1898.
LOCATION: New York, N.Y.
SOURCE:
DESCRIPTION:
SUBJECT: City and town life–New York. Advertising. Stores. Photography.
ARCHIVE:
CITATIONS: Commercial Advertising Bureau, accounts, Albert Smith Collection, CL-UC.
NOTE: For a similar type of advertising film, see *Crawford Shoe Store* (film no. 362.1).

550 North Side Dental Rooms
LENGTH: [50 ft.]   © No reg.
PRODUCER: [William Heise], J. Stuart Blackton, Albert E. Smith.
CAMERA: [William Heise.]
CAST:
PRODUCTION DATE: April 1898.
LOCATION: [New York, N.Y.]
SOURCE:
DESCRIPTION:
SUBJECT: City and town life–New York. Advertising. Dentistry.
ARCHIVE:
CITATIONS: Commercial Advertising Bureau, accounts, Albert Smith Collection, CL-UC.
NOTE:

If William Heise did take the preceding advertising films, he probably took the following film on the same trip.

551 *A Street Arab
LENGTH: 50 ft.   © Thomas A. Edison, 21 April 1898.
PRODUCER: William Heise.
CAMERA: William Heise.
CAST:
PRODUCTION DATE: April 1898.

LOCATION: [New York, N.Y.]

SOURCE:

DESCRIPTION: Shows one of New York's street gamins going through various acrobatic evolutions; he turns handsprings backward and forward, walks the crab, does cart wheels and other kindred feats. An exceptionally unique part of the performance is his standing on his head and twisting around like a top. It is safe to say he will be bald-headed at an early age. (*War Extra: Edison Films*, 20 May 1898, 10.)

SUBJECT: Acrobats. Afro-Americans. Boys.

ARCHIVE: DLC-pp.

CITATIONS: *Edison Films*, March 1900, 24; *Edison Films*, July 1901, 45.

NOTE:

William Heise's filmmaking activities continue with film no. 578. The following section traces William Paley's motion picture production from film no. 547.

William Paley traveled to Florida a second time, leaving New York City about 21 April 1898 in anticipation of a declaration of the war. (F.Z. Maguire to William E. Gilmore, 20 April 1898, NjWOE.) He traveled to Tampa, which quickly became the jumping off point for the invasion of Cuba. On April 27th, newspapers reported that "camping grounds are being laid out for 35,000 men, which is the number of volunteers expected here next week." ("Getting Ready at Tampa for an Army of 35,000," New York World, 27 April 1898, 7.) From this site, Paley began to send films back to the Edison factory in West Orange.

552 ***10th U.S. Infantry, 2nd Battalion, Leaving Cars**

LENGTH: 100 ft.   © Thomas A. Edison, 20 May 1898.

PRODUCER: William Paley.

CAMERA: William Paley.

CAST:

PRODUCTION DATE: 1 May 1898.

LOCATION: Ybor City, Fla.

SOURCE:

DESCRIPTION: Hurrah-here they come! Hot, dusty, grim and determined! Real soldiers, every inch of them! No gold lace and chalk belts and shoulder straps, but fully equipped in full marching order: blankets, guns, knapsacks and canteens. Train in the

background. Crowds of curious bystanders; comical looking "nigger dude" with a sun-umbrella strolls languidly in the foreground, and you almost hear that "yaller dog" bark. Small boys in abundance. The column marches in fours and passes through the front of the picture. More small boys—all colors. The picture is excellent in outline and full of vigorous life. (*War Extra: Edison Films*, 20 May 1898, 3-4.)

SUBJECT: Spanish-American War. Armies–United States. Railroads. Afro-Americans. Umbrellas. 10th U.S. Infantry.

ARCHIVE: DLC-pp.

CITATIONS: "Ordered to Tampa," *New York World*, 30 April 1898, 3; "Army of Invasion About to Move," *New York World*, 2 May 1898, 10. *Edison Films*, March 1900, 13; *Edison Films*, July 1901, 36.

NOTE: The 10th regiment left Mobile, Alabama, on April 30th—arriving in Tampa on May 1st.

553 ***10th U.S. Infantry Disembarking from Cars**

LENGTH: 100 ft.   © Thomas A. Edison, 20 May 1898.

PRODUCER: William Paley.
CAMERA: William Paley.
CAST:
PRODUCTION DATE: 1 May 1898.
LOCATION: Ybor City, Fla.
SOURCE:
DESCRIPTION: A stirring scene; full of martial energy. No ordinary dress parade this, but a picture of soldiers—men with a high purpose. They march up the platform in fours, and left wheel just in front of the camera, passing out of sight in a cloud of dust. The customary small boy is in evidence in great numbers. While the rear guard passes, the train pulls out of the station. Literally "out of sight." (*War Extra: Edison Films*, 20 May 1898, 3.)

Disembarking from cars at Ybor City and marching to Camp at Tampa, Fla. (*New York Clipper*, 28 May 1898, 220.)
SUBJECT: Spanish-American War. Armies–United States. Boys. Railroad stations. 10th U.S. Infantry.
ARCHIVE: DLC-pp.
CITATIONS: *Edison Films*, March 1900, 12; *Edison Films*, July 1901, 36.
NOTE:

554 ***U.S. Cavalry Supplies Unloading at Tampa, Florida / U.S. Cavalry Unloading Ambulance Supplies / Cavalry Supplies Unloading at Tampa**
LENGTH: 100 ft.   © Thomas A. Edison, 20 May 1898.
PRODUCER: William Paley.
CAMERA: William Paley.
CAST:
PRODUCTION DATE: 1 May 1898.
LOCATION: Tampa, Fla.
SOURCE:
DESCRIPTION: Here is a freight train of thirty cars loaded with baggage and ambulance supplies for the 9th U.S. Cavalry. In the foreground a score of troopers are pulling, lifting and hauling an ambulance from a flat car. It slides down the inclined planks with a sudden rush that makes the men

"hustle" to keep it from falling off. Drill engine on the next track darts past with sharp quick puffs of smoke. A very brisk scene. (*War Extra: Edison Films*, 20 May 1898, 2.)
SUBJECT: Spanish-American War. Armies–United States. Cavalry. Railroads. Ninth U.S. Cavalry.
ARCHIVE: DLC-pp.
CITATIONS: "Army of Invasion Moving to Cuba," *New York World*, 1 May 1898, 1; *New York Clipper*, 28 May 1898, 220.
NOTE: The 9th U.S. Cavalry arrived in Chickamauga Park on April 23rd and left for Tampa on April 29th.

555 ***9th U.S. Cavalry Watering Horses / Ninth U.S. Cavalry Watering Horses**
LENGTH: 100 ft.   © Thomas A. Edison, 20 May 1898.
PRODUCER: William Paley.
CAMERA: William Paley.
CAST:
PRODUCTION DATE: 1-13 May 1898.
LOCATION: Tampa, Fla.
SOURCE: *The Horse Fair* (Rosa Boneur painting, 1848).
DESCRIPTION: Taken at Tampa, Fla. Up the road from the camp comes a double file of

cavalrymen, a hundred or more, each man leading another horse beside his own. The leader rides a magnificent dapple gray. They approach at a fast walk, with an occasional frisky animal prancing and pirouetting. As they pass by, the spirited action reminds one forcibly of Rosa Bonheur's celebrated 100,000 dollar painting, "The Horse Fair." The figures of both men and horses stand out in bold relief. (*War Extra: Edison Films*, 20 May 1898, 3.)

SUBJECT: Spanish-American War. Armies–United States. Cavalry. Horses. Military camps. Ninth U.S. Cavalry.

ARCHIVE: DLC-pp.

CITATIONS: "Boys in Blue Throng Chickamauga Park," *New York World*, 24 April 1898, 2; "Troops Move on to Tampa," *New York World*, 29 April 1898, 8. *New York Clipper*, 28 May 1898, 220 and 221.

NOTE: Rosa Boneur's painting, *The Horse Fair*, was popular and much evoked. A critic compared the Lumière film *The Horse Trough* (1896) to this painting, which was at the Metropolitan Museum of Art in New York.

556 *Battery B Arriving at Camp / Battery B, Fourth U.S. Artillery / [Battery B, Fourth U.S. Artillery, no. 1] / Battery B Arriving in Camp

LENGTH: 50 ft.   © Thomas A. Edison, 20 May 1898.

PRODUCER: William Paley.

CAMERA: William Paley.

CAST:

PRODUCTION DATE: 29 April-2 May 1898.

LOCATION: Tampa, Fla.

SOURCE:

DESCRIPTION: When Battery B of the 4th U.S. Artillery came to Tampa, Fla, it meant business, and the picture shows it. One by one the big artillerymen pass by in front and reappear in the background, dismounting, unloosing saddle girths and bridles and leading away their mounts. Limbers, gun

carriages and caissons in the distance. The sweating horses and the vigorous switching of their tails tell a mute story of hot weather and fly-time. A picture full of reality. (*War Extra: Edison Films*, 20 May 1898, 2.)

SUBJECT: Spanish-American War. Armies–United States. Military camps. Artillery. Horses. Fourth U.S. Artillery.

ARCHIVE: DLC-pp.

CITATIONS: "Troops Move on to Tampa," *New York World*, 29 April 1898, 8. *New York Clipper*, 28 May 1898, 220 and 221.

NOTE: The Fourth Artillery was in Chickamauga Park by 21 April 1898. Two batteries of artillery left Chicakamauga Park for Tampa on April 28th. The remainder were to follow shortly.

557 *Battery B Pitching Camp / Battery B, Fourth U.S. Artillery / [Battery B, Fourth U.S. Artillery, no. 2]

LENGTH: 50 ft.   © Thomas A. Edison, 20 May 1898.

PRODUCER: William Paley.

CAMERA: William Paley.

CAST:

PRODUCTION DATE: 29 April-2 May 1898.

LOCATION: Tampa, Fla.

SOURCE:

DESCRIPTION:

SUBJECT: Spanish-American War. Armies–United States. Military camps. Artillery. Fourth U.S. Artillery.
ARCHIVE: DLC-pp.
CITATIONS: "Troop Gather in Camps of War," *New York World,* 22 April 1898, 8; "Troops Move on to Tampa," *New York World*, 29 April 1898, 8; "Army of Invasion About to Move," *New York World,* 2 May 1898, 10. *New York Clipper*, 28 May 1898, 220, 221.
NOTE:

558 *Steamer "Mascotte" Arriving at Tampa

LENGTH: 50 ft.   © Thomas A. Edison, 20 May 1898.
PRODUCER: William Paley.
CAMERA: William Paley.
CAST:
PRODUCTION DATE: [1-3 May 1898.]
LOCATION: Tampa, Fla.
SOURCE:

DESCRIPTION: Here is the staunch little transport "Mascotte" arriving at Tampa with the 2nd Battalion of 24th Colored Infantry on board. Her speed is shown by the high bow spray she throws. Clouds of exhaust steam rise from the port-hole at the water line. A stiff breeze is blowing, and her three flags stand out as straight as boards. Decks literally covered with transports—a very attractive picture, owing to bright sunshine, sharp shadow contrasts and brilliant wave effects. (*War Extra: Edison Films*, 20 May 1898, 6.)
SUBJECT: Spanish-American War. Armies–United States. Navies–United States. Afro-Americans. Transports. Harbors–Tampa. 24th U.S. Infantry.
ARCHIVE: DLC-pp.
CITATIONS: "The Mascotte Arrives at Key West with 96 Americans," *New York World*, 7 April 1898, 2. *New York Clipper*, 28 May 1898, 220.
NOTE: The 24th Infantry left Camp Thomas, Chickamauga Park on April 30th. Soldiers from this camp generally traveled by rail.

559 *Colored Troops Disembarking / Colored Troops Disembarking (24th U.S. Infantry)

LENGTH: 50 ft.   © Thomas A. Edison, 20 May 1898.
PRODUCER: William Paley.
CAMERA: William Paley.
CAST:
PRODUCTION DATE: [1-3 May 1898.]
LOCATION: Tampa, Fla.
SOURCE:

DESCRIPTION: The steamer "Mascotte" has reached her dock at Port Tampa, and the 2nd Battalion of Colored Infantry is going ashore. Tide is very high, and the gang plank is extra steep; and it is laughable to see the extreme caution displayed by the soldiers clambering down. The commanding officer struts on the wharf, urging them to hurry. Two boat stewards in glistening white duck coats, are interested watchers—looking for "tips" perhaps. The picture is full of fine light and shadow effects. (*War Extra: Edison Films*, 20 May 1898, 6.)
SUBJECT: Spanish-American War. Armies–United States. Navies–United States. Afro-Americans. Transports. Harbors–Tampa. Piers.

ARCHIVE: DLC-pp.
CITATIONS: *New York Clipper*, 28 May 1898, 220.
NOTE:

560 *9th Infantry Boys' Morning Wash / Ninth U.S. Infantry Boys at Their Morning Wash / Ninth Infantry "Boys'" Morning Wash**
LENGTH: 50 ft.   © Thomas A. Edison, 20 May 1898.
PRODUCER: William Paley.
CAMERA: William Paley.
CAST:
PRODUCTION DATE: 27 April-13 May 1898.
LOCATION: Tampa, Fla.
SOURCE:

DESCRIPTION: Imagine forty or fifty soldier boys each with a pail of water on the ground before him, sousing and spattering and scrubbing away for dear life. Soap and towels too. Every man jack of them looks as if he were enjoying the wash immensely, and also the novelty of having his picture taken. The big fellow in the center of the picture is laughing heartily. All the figures are clearly outlined, and the whole group is true to life. (*War Extra: Edison Films*, 20 May 1898, 3.)
SUBJECT: Spanish-American War. Armies–United States. Military camps. Ninth U.S. Infantry.
ARCHIVE: DLC-pp.
CITATIONS: "Army of Invasion Moving to Cuba," *New York World*, 1 May 1898, 1; "9th Regiment Infantry," *New York World,* 8 May 1898, 22; "Ninth Infantry Took Broadway," *New York World*, 25 May 1898, 4. *New York Clipper*, 28 May 1898, 220 and 221.
NOTE: The Ninth U.S. Infantry left Camp Thomas, Chickamauga April 30th.

561 *Military Camp at Tampa, Taken from Train / Military Camp, Tampa, Panoramic View**
LENGTH: 50 ft.   © Thomas A. Edison, 20 May 1898.
PRODUCER: William Paley.
CAMERA: William Paley.
CAST:
PRODUCTION DATE: 1-13 May 1898.
LOCATION: Tampa, Fla.
SOURCE:

DESCRIPTION: A wide plain, dotted with tents, gleaming white in the bright sunshine. Soldiers moving about everywhere, at all sorts of duties. In the background looms up a big cigar factory; giving the prosaic touch to the picture needful to bring out in sharp contrast the patriotism with which the scene inspires us. The camera was on a rapidly moving train, so the panoramic view is a wide one and remarkably brilliant. (*War Extra: Edison Films*, 20 May 1898, 3.)
SUBJECT: Spanish-American War. Armies–United States. Military camps. Factories. Railroads.
ARCHIVE: DLC-pp.
CITATIONS: "Army of Invasion About to Move," *New York World,* 2 May 1898, 10. *New York Clipper*, 28 May 1898, 220 and 221.
NOTE:

ALL ARE EAGER FOR THE ADVANCE ON CUBA

TAMPA, Fla., May 2....Around the port are arranged the camps of cavalry and infantry, while the five companies of light artillery–the First, Second, Third, Fourth, and Fifth Batteries–are all there and ready for work. Their 3.2-10 rifles, breechloaders, have an effective range of three to four miles, and can be fired to good advantage four times a minute taking good aim, and six times a minute without aim. It would be a brave and foolhardy column to try to stand before such a rain of shot and shell. The men are of the best material, are in spick-span condition, full of mettle and anxious to try their guns on the plains. Under Lieut. Treat they have been drilled at firing at moving targets. One, seven by sixteen, was struck ten times by ten shots, and riddled at a distance of three miles. (*New York World*, 3 May 1898, 4.)

LACK OF SYSTEM DOWN AT TAMPA.
Arriving Troops Subjected to Great Privations on Account of the Inadequacy of the Preparations.
SOME WERE WITHOUT WATER FOR FIFTEEN HOURS.
One Regiment Was Dumped Out of the Cars and Left Without Supplies for Three Days—Seventy-First in Camp.
(Special to The World.)

TAMPA, Fla., May 16.–The preparations here for the reception of troops has been so inadequate as to elicit something like a rebuke from the War Department.

One regiment had no water for fifteen hours after its arrival and another was dumped beside a railroad track and given no supplies for three days. The Seventh arrived two days ago and hasn't been able to secure supplies yet.

"It's lucky that we brought thirty days' rations with us or we might have starved for all the aid we got from the commissary department here," said an officer of that command to-day.

It is well known that the commissaries are way behind on orders for blankets, leggings and many other supplies. One regiment got no coffee for three days. Some of the officers blame the railroads for not delivering goods quickly, claiming that whole carloads of goods and supplies have been lost or sidetracked somewhere. This the railroads deny. The officers of the regiments say that the commissaries are to blame. The War Department is putting the blame on the commanding officers.

Gen. Shafter's plans have been fully carried out, and in his department everything moves like clockwork.

The Plant system people think of building some forty miles of side tracks between here and Port Tampa to accommodate the cars loaded with supplies that are expected in soon. Lakeland, where the First and Tenth Cavalry and the Seventy-first New York volunteers are camped, will be made another big camp according to present plans. It has a first-rate water supply and is an excellent camping ground. Miami and Jacksonville are being investigated with a view to having camps there. (*New York World*, 17 May 1898, 3.)

71ST REGIMENT HAPPY IN CAMP.
Change from Hempstead Storms to Florida Breezes Thoroughly Appreciated.
NEW CAMP IS AN IDEAL ONE.
(Special to The World.)

TAMPA, May 19.–"The World can say to our friends in New York," said Col. Francis V. Greene, of the Seventy-first New York Volunteers, this afternoon, "that we are enjoying life under the moss-covered oak trees of Florida. The men are in fine spirits, and are all well and enjoying the change from the cold rains at Camp Black to the delightful breezes here.

"It's a little warm, perhaps, but the boys will soon get used to that. We had two cases of men being overcome by heat, but they soon recovered, and to-day all the men are in A1 condition and ready for marching orders."

The camp of the Seventy-first is an ideal one, located one mile east of the railroad in an oak and pine grove on the banks of Lake Morton. The company streets run to the water's edge. The boys greatly enjoy the afternoons under the swaying trees, while the cool breezes from off the water lull them into slumber.

The regiment had a hard experience coming down. To begin with, they were kept twenty-four hours on the boat, and when they finally started were famished. All the way down they made forays upon the restaurants at the stopping-points and managed to keep their appetites appeased.

The boys of Company K were bound to get food before reaching camp, and the hustlers, led by Jack McDonald, had landed three pigs, six chickens, four geese, two dogs and a lot of bacon before Savannah was reached.

First Lieut. Rafferty, of Company F, managed to get his boys through in great shape. At Trilby, where they arrived Tuesday morning, he managed to get a gallon coffee-pot. Fires were built along the line while the train waited and from various sources enough food was got to make a good meal.

The men arrived here tired, hot and dusty. Their supply train was delayed and for the first twenty-four hours hard tack and beans comprised the entire menu. The F boys were the only ones to get their tents up so as to sleep under cover last night.

"We have had a tough time," said Lieut., now Acting Capt., Rafferty, "but are in ship-shape again. It's a little hard for the boys, the transition from cold storms at Camp Black to the heat of Florida, but the boys are getting used to it."

The boys are anxious for a dash into the cool lake, but until the wells are driven they have to go to another lake half a mile away....

Private Cooper, of Company E, enjoys the reputation of being able to drink more ice-cold sodas in a given time than any other man. This being a strictly Prohibition town, soda and lemonade are the strongest drinks sold. Lieut. W.E. Gallagher, of Mount Vernon, had a hard time getting into a sheltered spot last night during the rain and finally found refuge under his cot. Young Julian Hawthorne is making a model soldier. The boys say that the people here imagine the Seventy-first is made up of millionaires and fix prices accordingly.

Col. Greene is something of a martinet and believes in teaching the boys war is not a picnic. Drills are had from 6:30 till 7:30 and 9:30 till 10:30. Few men are allowed to leave the camp, only twenty passes being given to each company.

"That would be all right," said the first sergeant, "if we could only get enough to eat. Hard tack, bad coffee and corn beef is rather a tough menu. New York State gives us 48 cents daily for rations, while the Government only allows 21 cents. But as soon as our commissary gets into shape we hope to be in better trim, and the boys will not be so discontented."...

The glee clubs of Companies K, F and L entertained the regiment last night. A country band of four pieces was brought up from Lakeland by Carson, of Company K, and serenaded Col. Greene and his staff. It created much fun....

L.W. Iseman is after a Spanish flag. His father, a brewer, has promised that in case he captures a Spanish flag he will give him a half interest in the business. He also allows him $50 monthly for pocket money, or four times the amount Uncle Sam pays, while he is hunting the flag.

The Massachusetts boys have named their quarters Camp Little Eat. It is appropriate. (*New York World*, 20 May 1898, 3.)

"KIND-HEARTED" WAR.
A Pen Picture of the Results of the War Policy of Lumber-Dealer Alger.
(Poultney Bigelow, in *Harper's Weekly*.)

With the Troops Under Canvas, May 22, 1898. Down here (Tampa) we are sweltering in day and night with the thermometer ninety-eight in the shade. Nobody complains, for fear of appearing unpatriotic. Still it will do us no harm to hear a little of the truth, for this affair is turning out just as officers of the regular army have foreseen.

Here we are thirty days after the declaration of war, and not a regiment is yet equipped with uniforms suitable for hot weather. The United States troops sweat night and day in their cowhide boots, thick flannel shirts and winter trousers. In addition to this, they wear a tunic at inspection—a piece of torture.

Who is responsible for this? No one knows.

The poor men have to sleep on the ground in the heavy, dirty sand. Their sweaty clothing picks it up, and their food is full of it. Every whiff of hot air blows fine dust about, and every horse cart or even passing person adds discomfort to men already miserable. How little it would cost to have the camp sprinkled once or twice a day! Or at least the Government might have provided rough boards from which the men could have sawed themselves a few feet of flooring.

We are in the habit of pitying the soldier of Europe as hardly treated. For downright neglect I have seen nothing to beat the way the American is treated by Uncle Sam.

The troops are supplied with only that which is most unseasonable—greasy pork, and beans of that brown quality that makes one ready to spend the rest of the day in a watermelon patch. It is a wonder that the men develop an abnormal thirst, and rush off to satisfy this craving as best they can—some with plain water, some with milk-shakes, some with beer, some with compounds? The result is that already the camp doctors are busy every morning with men and officers suffering from varying degrees of dysentery. We hush this up as well as we can, but to do so altogether is impossible. Who is responsible? No one can tell.

The war is thirty days in swing. It took less time than that for Germany to put half a million well-trained men on the French frontier in 1870. To-day we look in vain for a single regiment fit to take the field. Every day raw recruits are dumped down here out of an incoming train, and they are taken out into the deep sand and made to move their legs up and down until exhausted nature cries out for rest. The ordinary man asks why were not these recruits licked into shape up in the cool North, and sent down properly clothed and armed. Who is responsible?

The army is lumbered up with civilian staff officers whose duty it is to see that our men are properly located and taken care of. The colonels and captains of the individual regiments are powerless in this matter; they can but obey the orders of their superiors on the staff.

In no army of Europe, not even in Spain, have I seen troops so badly treated through the incompetence of staff officers, who are to-day strutting about in new uniforms when they ought to be whistled out of camp as frauds.

While the nation has been patriotically voting men and money for this campaign of alleged philanthropy, promotions have not been spent in active military work, but from the ranks of politicians who may have had a smattering of militia drill, or may have worn a uniform forty years ago.

To-day, thirty days after the declaration of war, there has not been held at Tampa a single military field exercise likely to be of service to generals of brigade or division, let alone an army corps. The main reason is, no doubt, that there are no brigadiers or major-generals in Tampa who would know how to go to work in the matter.

If people up North could see what I have been seeing, there would be a cry of indignant protest throughout the country. Nothing, I am sure, is so well calculated to encourage Spain in her obstinate resistance as the knowledge that our military resources are being squandered as recklessly as were those of France in 1870.

Finally, let us insist that for the successful conduct of a war there must be one man, and one man only, responsible for the command.

To-day no one is in command. There are half a dozen people in Washington pretending to be directing operations. Gen. Miles sits at the War Department with no more influence than his doorkeeper.

There is no head to the army. The railway, express, telegraph, steamship and other corporations are getting fat out of this war; so are all contractors who deal with politics. The more inefficient the army, the better it suits them. If this war should be dragged out for a year or so they would be more than delighted. Meanwhile brave boys in blue will be dying in the heat of Tampa, to say nothing of the Cuban swamps.

We can thrash Spain any time we choose. But just now it would do us all much more good to discover why, thirty days after war is declared, our troops are losing their vitality in Florida, with not a single regiment fit to take the field. (*New York World,* 6 June 1898, 6.)

562 *Transport "Whitney" Leaving Dock

LENGTH: 50 ft.   © Thomas A. Edison, 20 May 1898.
PRODUCER: William Paley.
CAMERA: William Paley.
CAST:
PRODUCTION DATE: 7 May 1898.
LOCATION: Tampa, Fla.
SOURCE:

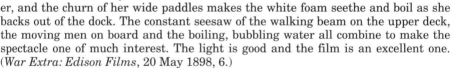

DESCRIPTION: (The first to leave with troops for the front), with a battalion of the 5th Infantry on board leaving dock for Dry Tortugas. (*New York Clipper,* 28 May 1898, 221.) This boat was the first to leave for the South with troops. On board is a battalion of the 5th U.S. Infantry. She is a sidewheeler, and the churn of her wide paddles makes the white foam seethe and boil as she backs out of the dock. The constant seesaw of the walking beam on the upper deck, the moving men on board and the boiling, bubbling water all combine to make the spectacle one of much interest. The light is good and the film is an excellent one. (*War Extra: Edison Films,* 20 May 1898, 6.)
SUBJECT: Spanish-American War. Armies–United States. Navies–United States. Harbors–Tampa. Transports. Fifth U.S. Infantry.
ARCHIVE: DLC-pp.
CITATIONS: *New York Clipper,* 28 May 1898, 220; *Edison Films,* March 1900, 13.
NOTE: This is one of the films that was duped illegally by J. Stuart Blackton and Albert E. Smith of the American Vitagraph Company and served as evidence in the subsequent copyright case brought against them by Thomas A. Edison. The "Whitney" also appears in the background of film no. 538.

Tampa–The Whitney, the sister ship of the Gussie, which sailed for Dry Tortugas Saturday, with two companies of the 5th Infantry. (*New York World,* 10 May 1898, 1.)

563 *Cuban Refugees Waiting for Rations

LENGTH: 50 ft.   © Thomas A. Edison, 20 May 1898.
PRODUCER: William Paley.
CAMERA: William Paley.
CAST:
PRODUCTION DATE: 4-13 May 1898.
LOCATION: Tampa, Fla.
SOURCE:
DESCRIPTION: A group of escaped reconcentrados, saved from the fate of starvation imposed by the Butcher, Weyler. They stand in line waiting, each man with his tin dish and cup. One expects to see just such men as these, after the centuries of Spanish oppression and tyranny. As they come forward, their walk, even, is listless

and lifeless. The picture affords an exceedingly interesting racial character study. At one side stands a group of officers from the camp near by, accompanying several ladies who are seeing the sights. (*War Extra: Edison Films*, 20 May 1898, 4.)

SUBJECT: Spanish-American War. Cubans. Armies–Officers. Refugees. Tourist trade.

ARCHIVE: DLC-pp, NR-GE.

CITATIONS: *New York Clipper*, 28 May 1898, 220 and 221.

NOTE:

564 The Cuban Refugees Going to Breakfast

LENGTH: [50 ft.]   © No reg.

PRODUCER: William Paley.

CAMERA: William Paley.

CAST:

PRODUCTION DATE: 4-13 May 1898.

LOCATION: Tampa, Fla.

SOURCE:

DESCRIPTION:

SUBJECT: Spanish-American War. Cubans. Refugees.

ARCHIVE:

CITATIONS: *New York Clipper*, 28 May 1898, 220.

NOTE:

565 *Cuban Volunteers Marching for Rations

LENGTH: 50 ft.   © Thomas A. Edison, 20 May 1898.

PRODUCER: William Paley.

CAMERA: William Paley.

CAST:

PRODUCTION DATE: 4-13 May 1898.

LOCATION: West Tampa, Fla.

SOURCE:

DESCRIPTION: Taken at the Cuban Volunteer Camp at West Tampa, Fla. Men are falling into line, two abreast, every man with his tin cup and dish. Command is given "forward march," and the column approaches the audience. A fine looking body of men, worthy of a people battling for freedom.

Figures are life size and life like. Prominently displayed upon their military hats is the emblem Cuba Libre, a single star in a red tri-cornered field. An accurate and interesting subject. (*War Extra: Edison Films*, 20 May 1898, 4.)

SUBJECT: Spanish-American War. Cubans. Armies–Cuba. Military Camps.

ARCHIVE: DLC-pp.

CITATIONS: *New York Clipper*, 28 May 1898, 220 and 221.

NOTE:

CUBANS ENLIST TO GET REVENGE.

Hundreds Volunteer at Tampa, Anxious to Avenge Murder of Loved Ones.

GOMEZ NEARING THE COAST.

Notifies the Junta He is Pushing On to Matanzas to Connect with Our Forces.

TROOPS NOT TO LEAVE TO-DAY.

Transports Will Not Arrive at Tampa Until Friday and No Immediate Invasion of Cuba is Expected.

(Special to The World.)

TAMPA, May 3.–The Cubans are coming here with a rush and enlisting for active service. Nine out of ten of them have personal wrongs to avenge. The faces of murdered relatives and friends will nerve them in battle, and now, with the certainty of arms and ammunition, they are only too anxious to return to help drive the Spaniards from Cuba. Late last night the Cuban volunteers began arriving from New York, and to-day those from Philadelphia, Jacksonville, New Orleans and other points came, and 200 or more arrived from Key West to-night. The young men hurried at once to Cespides Hall and enlisted.

Dr. Echeverria was in charge. He told the recruits the Cuban army was to fight; that it had no money and little food and there is no chance for soft places. Enlistment meant war and hard work. The volunteers cheerfully accepted the chances and signed.

A tall youth from Georgia, James Futch, came in and asked to enlist. "We have no money, the army has no tents; it will be fighting under difficulties and hard work," said the doctor. "That's all right," replied Futch. "That's what I want: the Spaniards killed my brother in cold blood. Fighting is all I want."

Scores of the Cubans gave such replies. One had a mother to avenge, another a son and daughter; while one stalwart fellow, with tears in his eyes, told of the butchery of his wife, two daughters and a young boy by the Spanish troops two months ago.

A letter was received here to-day from Gen. Gomez. He is pushing toward Matanzas, and will be ready to co-operate with the United States forces.

The officer sent by the United States authorities reached him safely, and delivered his despatches. Gen. Gomez expressed his joy that deliverance is near at hand.

He also reported that the country people were wild with joy over the prospects of having arms to fight with. Hundreds are flocking to him daily, and as soon as he can secure arms he will have from ten to twenty thousand extra troops within a week or so. He reports that the Spanish forces in the interior of Cuba are demoralized and discouraged. The blockade had greatly vexed and worried the army. The appearance of the fleet and the American captures reported has caused them to recognize their helplessness.

The Cubans here fear the defeat of the Spanish fleet at Manila will lead to the murder of reconcentrados about Havana, unless the fleet takes possession of the city soon.

The troops will not leave here for several days at least. The transports are not expected until Friday and some will not be here next week, therefore no immediate invasion of Cuba is possible....(*New York World*, 4 May 1898, 7.)

To follow Paley's ongoing filmmaking expedition go to film no. 585.
The following section continues James H. White's and Frederick W. Blechynden's journey from film no. 525.

White and Blechynden left Yokohama, Japan, about 30 April 1898 on S.S. "Doric."

566 ***S.S. "Doric."***
LENGTH: 50 ft.   © Thomas A. Edison, 22 June 1898.
PRODUCER: James White.
CAMERA: Frederick Blechynden.
CAST:
PRODUCTION DATE: Ca. 30 April 1898.
LOCATION: Off Yokohama, Japan.
SOURCE:

DESCRIPTION: Passing the lightship two miles out from Yokohama. The black smoke pours from her funnels and the British flag waves at her stern. (*Edison Films*, March 1900, 16.)
SUBJECT: Steamships. Flags–Great Britain. Occidental and Oriental Steamship Company.
ARCHIVE: DLC-pp.
CITATIONS: *Edison Films*, July 1901, 38.
NOTE: Compare this film to *S.S. "Gaelic"* (film no. 516).

567 ***Afternoon Tea on Board S.S. "Doric" / Afternoon Tea on S.S. "Doric"***
LENGTH: 50 ft.   © Thomas A. Edison, 22 June 1898.
PRODUCER: James White.
CAMERA: Frederick Blechynden.
CAST:
PRODUCTION DATE: May 1898.
LOCATION: Pacific Ocean.

SOURCE:

DESCRIPTION: Shows a jolly little tea party on the saloon deck. One young man is suddenly seized with a pang, and dashes to the rail. (*Edison Films*, March 1900, 16.)

SUBJECT: Steamships. Tourist trade. Tea parties. Occidental and Oriental Steamship Company.

ARCHIVE: DLC-pp.

CITATIONS:

NOTE: Films taken aboard the "Doric" in mid-ocean could also have been taken after the ship's stopover in Honolulu.

568 *S.S. "Doric" in Mid-Ocean

LENGTH: 50 ft.　© Thomas A. Edison, 22 June 1898.

PRODUCER: James White.

CAMERA: Frederick Blechynden.

CAST:

PRODUCTION DATE: May 1898.

LOCATION: Pacific Ocean.

SOURCE:

DESCRIPTION: Shows passengers enjoying a bath on deck in a huge canvas tank filled with sea water. A very novel subject. (*Edison Films*, March 1900, 16.)

SUBJECT: Steamships. Tourist trade. Baths. Swimming pools. Occidental and Oriental Steamship Company.

ARCHIVE: DLC-pp.

CITATIONS: *Edison Films,* July 1901, 38.

NOTE:

569 *Game of Shovel Board on Board S.S. "Doric" / Game of Shovel Board on S.S. "Doric" / S.S. "Doric": Game of Shovel Board

LENGTH: 50 ft.　© Thomas A. Edison, 22 June 1898.

PRODUCER: James White.

CAMERA: Frederick Blechynden.

CAST:

PRODUCTION DATE: May 1898.

LOCATION: Pacific Ocean.

SOURCE:

DESCRIPTION: Both ladies and gentlemen are participating in this pleasant pastime. One of the members just made a very close shot and is greatly excited. (*Edison Films*, March 1900, 16.)

SUBJECT: Steamships. Games. Tourist trade. Occidental and Oriental Steamship Company.

ARCHIVE: DLC-pp.

CITATIONS:

NOTE:

The S.S. "Doric" arrived in Honolulu on 9 May 1898 with James H. White and Frederick W. Blechynden aboard. (Hawaiian Gazette, 13 May 1898, 3.)

570 *Kanakas Diving for Money, no. 1 / Kanakas Diving for Money

LENGTH: 50 ft.　© Thomas A. Edison, 22 June 1898.

PRODUCER: James White.

CAMERA: Frederick Blechynden.

CAST:
PRODUCTION DATE: 10 May 1898.
LOCATION: Honolulu, Hawaii.
SOURCE:
DESCRIPTION: The diving boys at Honolulu are always on the lookout for the tourist's spare change. The picture shows them splashing in the water at the end of the wharf. (*Edison Films*, March 1900, 16.)
SUBJECT: Harbors–Honolulu. Hawaiians. Tourist trade. Steamships. Boys. Piers. Occidental and Oriental Steamship Company.
ARCHIVE: DLC-pp.
CITATIONS: "Hawaii is Now American," *New York Times*, 8 July 1898, 7. *Edison Films*, July 1901, 39.
NOTE:

571 *Kanakas Diving for Money, no. 2
LENGTH: 50 ft.   © Thomas A. Edison, 22 June 1898.
PRODUCER: James White.
CAMERA: Frederick Blechynden.
CAST:
PRODUCTION DATE: 10 May 1898.
LOCATION: Honolulu, Hawaii.
SOURCE:
DESCRIPTION: The boys are diving, treading water and turning somersaults. The white foam and spray is thrown high into the air. (*Edison Films*, March 1900, 16.)
SUBJECT: Harbors–Honolulu. Hawaiians. Tourist trade. Steamships. Boys. Piers. Occidental and Oriental Steamship Company.
ARCHIVE: DLC-pp.
CITATIONS: *Edison Films*, July 1901, 39.
NOTE:

572 *Honolulu Street Scene
LENGTH: 50 ft.   © Thomas A. Edison, 22 June 1898.
PRODUCER: James White.
CAMERA: Frederick Blechynden.
CAST:
PRODUCTION DATE: 10 May 1898.
LOCATION: Honolulu, Hawaii.
SOURCE:
DESCRIPTION: An interesting picture in the chief city of the Sandwich Islands now a part of the United States of America. (*Edison Films*, March 1900, 17.)
SUBJECT: City and town life–Honolulu. Urban transportation. Occidental and Oriental Steamship Company.
ARCHIVE: DLC-pp.
CITATIONS: *Edison Films*, July 1901, 39.
NOTE:

573 *Wharf Scene, Honolulu
LENGTH: 50 ft.   © Thomas A. Edison, 22 June 1898.
PRODUCER: James White.
CAMERA: Frederick Blechynden.

CAST:
PRODUCTION DATE: 10 May 1898.
LOCATION: Honolulu, Hawaii.
SOURCE:
DESCRIPTION: The "Doric" is just leaving, home-
ward bound. Crowds stand on the pier,
waving their good-byes. The steamer's pro-
pellor makes fine water effects. (*The
Phonoscope*, November 1898, 15.)
SUBJECT: Steamships. Harbors–Honolulu. Piers.
Occidental and Oriental Steamship Company.
ARCHIVE: DLC-pp.
CITATIONS:
NOTE:

Honolulu in Kinetoscope

The two kinetoscope men aboard the S.S. Doric secured several thousand yards of Honolulu film for use in the States. The travelers have been getting material in China and Japan, but were especially anxious to have some Honolulu views. With their special camera they made a number of exposures in the bay, getting steamers, laborers, boat crews and the Bennington. Views were taken on King, Nuuanu and Fort street. These pictures will prove of much advertising value to Honolulu, as they will be shown throughout the United States. (*Hawaiian Gazette*, 13 May 1898, 3.)

The S.S. "Doric" set sail from Honolulu on 10 May 1898 and arrived in San Francisco on May 16th. ("Doric Arrives from Hong Kong," San Francisco Chronicle, 17 May 1898, 10.) Before heading East, White and Blechynden took a series of films related to the American occupation of the Philippines.

574 ***14th U.S. Infantry Drilling at the Presidio**
LENGTH: 50 ft.   © Thomas A. Edison, 22 June 1898.
PRODUCER: James White.
CAMERA: Frederick Blechynden.
CAST:
PRODUCTION DATE: 17-23 May 1898.
LOCATION: Presidio, San Francisco, Calif.
SOURCE:
DESCRIPTION:
SUBJECT: Spanish-American War. Armies
–United States. Military camps.
ARCHIVE: DLC-pp.
CITATIONS:
NOTE:

575 ***California Volunteers Marching to Embark / California Troops Marching to Embark**
LENGTH: 50 ft.   © Thomas A. Edison, 22 June 1898.
PRODUCER: James White.
CAMERA: Frederick Blechynden.
CAST:
PRODUCTION DATE: 23 May 1898.
LOCATION: San Francisco, Calif.
SOURCE:
DESCRIPTION:
SUBJECT: Spanish-American War. Armies–
United States. Harbors–San Francisco.
Ships. Parades.
ARCHIVE: DLC-pp.
CITATIONS: "California Sons are on Their Way
to War," *San Francisco Chronicle*, 24 May 1898, 3.
NOTE:

576 ***Troops Embarking at San Francisco**
LENGTH: 50 ft.   © 22 June 1898.
PRODUCER: James White.
CAMERA: Frederick Blechynden.
CAST:
PRODUCTION DATE: 23 May 1898.
LOCATION: San Francisco, Calif.
SOURCE:
DESCRIPTION:
SUBJECT: Spanish-American War. Transports. Armies–United States. Harbors–San Francisco. Ships.
ARCHIVE: DLC-pp.
CITATIONS: "California Sons are on Their Way to War," *San Francisco Chronicle*, 24 May 1898, 3.
NOTE:

OFF TO THE PHILIPPINES TO FIGHT THE SPANIARDS.
First California Regiment Marched Aboard the Transport City of Peking to Sail for Manila To-day.
SAN FRANCISCO WILD OVER ITS DEPARTURE TO WAR.
Shouting Men and Weeping Women Followed to the Docks–a Pandemonium of Noise–
Other Troops to Embark To-day.

SAN FRANCISCO, Cal., May 23–California said good-by to her First Regiment of Volunteers to-day. The men left camp on the Presidio at 8 A.M. and marched to the Pacific Mail dock, where the big steamer City of Peking lay ready for them. By noon the soldiers were all on board. Before night everything was in readiness for their departure to Manila. They probably will sail to-morrow.

The farewell demonstration by the people of San Francisco will long be remembered by the soldiers of the First Regiment. Every street leading from the Presidio to the Pacific Mail dock, a distance of about five miles, was lined with people, who after the soldiers passed, followed in their wake and marched with them to the dock....

As the marching men neared the water front bombs were fired, steam whistles blown, and every device imaginable for making a noise was put into operation. The jam at the dock was terrific. In vain the police and the mounted signal corps attempted to keep the crowd back. They would not be denied and rushed the dock in the wake of the soldiers.

Arrived at the dock, the volunteers were marched on board the transport without delay. It took considerable time for each man to be assigned to his quarters, but this task was accomplished with but very little confusion. After the soldiers were once on board, the police cleared the dock and the gates were shut. All day a big crowd hung about the dock in the hope of getting one more glimpse of the men who are going to sail 6,000 miles to fight for their country.

The First Regiment of California Volunteers is commanded by James F. [   ] and consists of 1,086 officers and men. To-morrow the Second Regiment of Oregon Volunteers, one battalion of the Fourteenth infantry, United States Regulars, and a detachment of California heavy artillery will board the steamer City of Sydney. It is probable that the Peking and the Sydney will depart in company when supplies are taken on board. (*New York World*, 24 May 1898, 3.)

577 ***Troop Ships for the Philippines / Troop Ships for Philippine Islands**
LENGTH: 150 ft.   © Thomas A. Edison, 22 June 1898.
PRODUCER: James White.
CAMERA: Frederick Blechynden.
CAST:
PRODUCTION DATE: 25 May 1898.
LOCATION: San Francisco, Calif.
SOURCE:
DESCRIPTION:
SUBJECT: Spanish-American War. Armies–United States. Harbors–San Francisco. Ships.
ARCHIVE: DLC-pp, NNMoMA.
CITATIONS: "Local Transports at Anchor in Bay. Fleet Will Probably Sail this Afternoon," *San Francisco Chronicle*, 25 May 1898, 3. *The Phonoscope*, June 1898, 4.
NOTE: Troop ships were S.S. "Australia" and S.S. "City of Peking."

THREE SHIPS FULL OF MEN AND AMMUNITION START TO DEWEY'S AID.
Peking, Sydney and Australia Leave San Francisco
Under Gen. Anderson with 2,500 Troops and a Year's Supplies.

SAN FRANCISCO, May 25.–The start was made for Manila late this afternoon. At 4 o'clock this afternoon Brig. Gen. Anderson signalled from the Australia for the City of Peking and the City of Sydney to get under way. The signal was seen from the shore and the waiting crowds began to cheer. In a short time the anchors were up and the vessels were under way. Then the 2,500 soldiers who had been impatiently awaiting the signal to start let themselves loose. They climbed to the rigging and swarmed all over the big ships, shouting and cheering. The big transports steamed slowly along the water front and the crowd on shore moved along to keep them in sight. The noise made by patriotic citizens on sea and shore was something terrific. As the Australia passed Alcatraz Island, in the lead of the other ships, the battery of United States artillery stationed there fired a salute to Gen. Anderson.

After the pilots were dropped, the vessels went ahead at full speed, and in six days they will enter Honolulu Harbor and join the Charleston. The transports carried close on to 2,500 men. The expedition, which is under command of Brig. Gen. Anderson, consists of four companies of regulars under command of Major Robe, the First Regiment California volunteers, Col. Smith; the First Regiment Oregon volunteers, Col. Summers; a battalion of fifty heavy artillery, Major Gary; about 180 sailors and 11 naval officers.

The fleet is loaded with supplies to last a year and carries a big cargo of ammunition and naval stores for Admiral Dewey's fleet. It is thought here that the fleet that left to-day will not keep company with the Charleston after leaving Honolulu. They all carry enough coal to steam at full speed from Honolulu to Manila, while the Charleston, in order to economize coal, will not steam faster than ten knots an hour. If the transports do not wait for the cruiser, they may be expected to arrive at Manila about June 20. The first battalion of the Tenth Regiment, Pennsylvania Volunteers, numbering 602 men and 18 officers, arrived in this city to-day. (*New York World*, 26 May 1898, 2.)

White's and Blechynden's filmmaking expedition ended in San Francisco. To continue tracing White's producing activities, go to film no. 601. The following section traces William Heise's motion picture productions, picking up from film no. 551.

Given the large number of news and actuality films flowing into the Edison Manufacturing Company, William Heise sought to provide some diversity in subject matter by producing a series of short comics.
Belle Gordon teamed with Billie Curtis as a comedy boxing duo from about 1896 to 1900. After this partnership dissolved, Belle Gordon started another all-girl boxing duo, the Gordon Sisters.

578 ***Comedy Set-to**

LENGTH: 50 ft.   © Thomas A. Edison, 20 May 1898.
PRODUCER: William Heise.
CAMERA: William Heise.
CAST: Billie Curtis, Belle Gordon.
PRODUCTION DATE: April to mid-May 1898.
LOCATION: Black Maria, West Orange, N.J.
SOURCE:

DESCRIPTION: Shows Curtis and Gordon in one
of their cleverest acts. Miss Belle Gordon
holds the Police Gazette medal as Champion
Lady Bag Puncher of the World. The bout is
a combination of popular leads and blows
used by all pugilists, and the grace and ease
with which Miss Gordon does a cross-under or throws an upper-cut or an under-cut
at Billy Curtis, is so quick and clever that one wishes the round was three times
longer. From the handshake to the finish it is refined, scientific and a genuine comedy. Belle is as frisky a little lady as ever donned a boxing outfit, and her abbreviated
skirts, short sleeves and low necked waist make a very jaunty costume. Plenty of
action and sure to be a great favorite. (*War Extra: Edison Films*, 20 May 1898, 9.)
SUBJECT: Vaudeville–performances. Boxing. Women.
ARCHIVE: DLC-pp.
CITATIONS: Advertisement, *New York Clipper*, 20 June 1896, 257.
NOTE: Belle Gordon may have also appeared in the Edison film *Gordon Sisters Boxing*
    (© 6 May 1901).

THE ORIGINATORS
Billie CURTIS and GORDON Belle

The hit of the show at the Westminister Theatre, Providence, week of May 11; big hit at Lyceum Theatre, Boston, last week; engaged to strengthen the Rentz-Stanley Show, Brooklyn, this week. N.B.–MISS GORDON is the FIRST LADY who ever introduced Bag Punching on the American stage, and is always open for contest. Have a few weeks open for roof gardens or Summer resorts. Address Care of UNIQUE THEATRE, Brooklyn, N.Y. (Advertisement, *New York Clipper*, 30 May 1896, 206.)

Tony Pastor's...Curtis and Gordon did well with their bag punching and boxing act. (*New York Clipper*, 20 June 1896, 248.)

I, BELLE GORDON,
OF CURTIS AND GORDON,
Do hereby challenge ANY LADY BAG PUNCHER IN THE WORLD for $300 a side.
Money now in THE POLICE GAZETTE OFFICE, New York City.
I have had $100 deposited in said office since July 2, which has NEVER BEEN COVERED.

To the Profession in General: We do not travel on our ability as Fighters, but as Performers, and wish this distinctly understood; we are closing the olio with the Rentz-Stanley Co; one of the features and the hit of the Show. Please note the following: "MISS GORDON: I have witnessed your performance and am very favorably impressed by same, and if there is any chance to get on a bona fide match, I will bet $250 on you against any Female Bag Puncher in the world. This is a bona fide offer, and you can use it any way you see fit. Very truly yours, Sam C. Austin, Sporting Editor Police Gazette." Well, we are with a good Show, getting our salary and are happy, and, together with the ELINORE SISTERS, are growing fat. Our kindest regards to O'BRIEN, JENNINGS AND O'BRIEN. (Advertisement, *New York Clipper*, 10 October 1896, 515.)

Dissolved Partnership Curtis & Gordon
I wish to say to Managers at home that I have something new in preparation,
which I shall be pleased to negotiate for later.
Regards to all, friend or no friend, just so long as you are an American.
Miss Belle Gordon

(Advertisement, *New York Clipper,* 3 March 1900, 22.)

At the Casino [Paris, France]...Curtis and Gordon are doing fine. (*New York Clipper*, 10 March 1900, 27.)

The Only Lady Boxing Act
GORDON SISTERS

THIS WEEK–Grand Central Theatre, Montreal.
(Advertisement, *New York Clipper*, 3 November 1900, 803.)

A GOOD ACT! WHO WANTS IT?
Bessie GORDON SISTERS Minnie
IN THEIR BAG PUNCHING AND SCIENTIFIC ACT.

Have some open time. Open for next season. Would like to hear from Park Managers. Address: 226 2d Ave., New York, or our agent TED MARKS, Broadway and 57th Street, N.Y.C. (Advertisement, *New York Clipper*, 16 February 1901, 1140.)

BILLY CURTIS

Billy Curtis, 60, former vaude performer and in recent years a night club revue producer, died at the Southern Methodist hospital in Tuscon, Ariz., Dec. 9. He was troubled with a complication of diseases. As a boy he went on the vaudeville stage with a partner, and after many years in that field drifted into booking acts. He was acknowledged one of the best in the nite club business before retiring on account of his health. (*Variety*, 11 December 1934, 62.)

Edison filmmakers continued to rely on the stage to generate film material that audiences would recognize and enjoy. The Burglar *appropriated a scene from* A Parlor Match *a popular farce comedy that had long featured Charles E. Evans and William Hoey. These performers first appeared together during 1882 in* The Book Agent, *a farce comedy that was subsequently elaborated by playwright Charles H. Hoyt and then retitled* A Parlor Match. *The new piece was first performed at Asbury Park, New Jersey, on 5 September 1884 and had its New York City premiere on 22 September 1884 at Tony*

Pastor's Theatre. Evans and Hoey gave 2,551 performances of this farce, kept fresh by the infusion of specialty acts and new gags, until April 1894 when the Evans-Hoey partnership was dissolved. Evans promptly became manager of the Herald Square Theatre, while Hoey performed on his own. The duo was reunited on 21 September 1896 as their old farce was successfully dusted off and reopened at the Herald Square Theatre with French chanteuse Anna Held performing one of the show's many specialties. The play continued to tour into the twentieth century, although by 1899 other actors had replaced Evans and Hoey.

579 *The Burglar / [The Burglar, no. 1]**
LENGTH: 50 ft.   © Thomas A. Edison, 20 May 1898.
PRODUCER: William Heise.
CAMERA: William Heise.
CAST:
PRODUCTION DATE: April to mid-May 1898.
LOCATION: Black Maria, West Orange, N.J.
SOURCE: *A Parlor Match* (farce comedy).

DESCRIPTION: Here's one of those bold daylight robbers you read about. In steals the villain, mask, dark lantern, jimmy, hand-drill and full outfit. Sees the solid looking safe, starts to drill out the combination. Hears some one coming and hides. Office boy comes in briskly with a coal scuttle, opens safe and discloses coal bin inside. Fills his scuttle, shuts safe door with a slam and goes out. This is the well known scene in "The Parlor Match," made famous by Evans and Hoey. The burglar during this episode is a sight to behold. Curiosity, surprise, rage, mortification and disgust seize him, and he slinks away, a crestfallen man. The whole affair is very laughable, the disclosure of coal in a safe being sure to make a great outburst of genuine merriment. (*War Extra: Edison Films*, 20 May 1898, 10.)
SUBJECT: Burglars. Coal. Boys.
ARCHIVE: DLC-pp.
CITATIONS: "Tony Pastor's Theatre—'A Parlor Match,'" *New York Herald*, 23 September 1884, 10; "A Parlor Match at Tony Pastor's" *New York Sun*, 23 September 1884, 3; "Now It Is the Herald Square," *New York Herald*, 1 May 1894, 6; "The Bijou Theatre," *Pittsburg Post*, 11 April 1899, 4.
NOTE: The above film was remade two months later with more elaborate sets and a variation on the above gag; see *[The Burglar, no. 2]*, film no. 601.

MORE SNAP STILL TO "A PARLOR MATCH."
Mlle. Anna Held Makes a Successful Debut at the Herald Square Theatre.
IS VERY CHIC AND DAINTY.
...HERALD SQUARE THEATRE.–A PARLOR MATCH, a farce comedy in three acts.

Role	Actor
L. McCorker	Charles E. Evans.
Old Hoss	William Hoey.
Captain William Kidd	James T. Galloway.
Ephraim Bellomont	M.J. Sullivan.
Ralph Bellomont	William M. Armstrong.
McKee, of Allon, M.P.	Hugh Mack.
Asa High	William Keough.
Abel Leever	Stuart Connover.
St. Claire Todd	Peter Randall.
Euphonia Allen	Harriet Sheldon.
Lucille Kidd	Aliene Crater.
Aline Kidd	Aimee Van Dane.
Vesta Bule	Beatrice Tait.
Gladys Riche	Millie Tait.
Marie Quick	Grayee Scott.
Lady Little	Estelle Henriques.

Nora Marks . . . . Lillian Claiborne.
Innocent Kidd . . . . Minnie French.

There is never a fizzle to the "Parlor Match." It was struck on Broadway last night in the pretty Herald Square Theatre and flared up as brilliant as ever. "Old Hoss" and McCorker renewed their youth and mirth provoking abilities in their new box. Miss Minnie French was as irresistible as ever as Innocent Kidd, and as these old time favorites came one by one on the scene, by ladder, on foot and in a goat cart, they were received with the heartiest of greetings. Every one knows the absurdities of "A Parlor Match," and every one appreciates the clever work of the people who enter into the spirit of the piece with song and dance.

There are many old faces in the cast and some new ones. The voices are generally good, and the woman sufficiently fresh and pretty in various costumes, with a latitude between tights and ball room gowns. The very crowded house would doubtless have dwelt more on all these points, as of yore, had there not been a general sense of expectancy in the air. All the audience had seen Evans and Hoey many a time before, but very few had ever seen Mlle. Anna Held. What would she be like—as clever as Gilbert, as suggestive as Fougere? Would she be as chic and pretty as her pictures or fade into insignificance beside the highly colored posters?

It was during the spiritualist seance in the second act that the public was given an opportunity to decide. The lights were lowered, then turned up to a full blaze to display Miss Held pausing for a moment in the door of the mysterious cabinet, from which all the "specialties" of the "Parlor Match" are produced. As she sprang forward to the footlights the women in the stalls exclaimed: "How dainty!"—the men kept their eyes glued to their opera glasses, a greater compliment still.

They saw a pretty young woman with a mass of soft brown hair clinging about her brow, big, gray eyes, and exceedingly svelte and pretty figure, and a very expressive mouth. The costume consisted of a very decollete bodice, held up by the merest slips of shoulder bands, and a single white satin skirt, which disclosed in almost every movement a pair of pink pantalettes, ruffled with blue—all worn with the aplomb and grace which is denied to other women than the French.

Without any ado Miss Held began the strains of "La Marcheuse." Like all French music hall singers her voice is well placed and flexible, with less shrillness, than is usually born of the café chantant. Her enunciation is pretty and distinct, her airs and graces, of course, perfect. She was evidently a bit alarmed, and glowed visibly under the storm of applause that greeted her first song.

This she followed with a funny bit of French wit, "Mlle. Colignon," and afterwards gave "La Contre-Basse," finishing up with an English song, "Come and Play with Me," which quite brought down the house, for "Old Hoss," who was sitting on the stage at the time, "played up" to her, as they say on the stage, in quite an unpremeditated way, which her quick Gallic wit used to the best purpose. Of course then she had to make a little speech in very nice English, thanking every one so much for their kindness and begging them either to come again to hear all her repertoire, which was so long, indicated by a gesture of arms and legs which only a Parisienne could accomplish.

"Oh! yes; she'll be the rage," said every one as she disappeared at last with a last flurry of the pantalettes. And not only on but off the stage, for Mlle. Held has already received invitations to sing in private houses, notably at an entertainment to be given in Newport by Senator Brice to Lord Chief Justice Russell. As for the luncheons and suppers to which she has been bidden it makes her manager weary to keep tab on them. Her engagement at the Herald Square is for four weeks only. (*New York Herald*, 22 September 1896, 12.)

Heise made two variations on the same basic telephone gag (the second was copyrighted in July). The first one plays off the relationship, and potential confusion, between presence and absence.

580 ***The Telephone / [The Telephone, no. 1]**
LENGTH: 50 ft.   © Thomas A. Edison, 20 May 1898.
PRODUCER: William Heise.
CAMERA: William Heise.
CAST:
PRODUCTION DATE: April to mid-May 1898.
LOCATION: Black Maria, West Orange, N.J.
SOURCE:
DESCRIPTION: A practical illustration of the value of this modern invention. Posted up on the wall is the startling sign. *Don't travel. Use the telephone. You can get anything you want.* Man comes in, rings up, takes telephone, talks, then waits a moment; opens little door at the bottom of receiver, and takes out—a

glass of beer! Blows off the foam, takes a deep draught, and telephones for a cigar. Waits a moment; gets impatient and calls again, when out comes a blast of flour, plastering his face and clothes so that he looks like a miller. Sure to create barrels of fun. The man's face is a study. From satisfied contentment over his beer to utter disgust about the flour, the contrast and changes are most accurately shown. (*War Extra: Edison Films*, 20 May 1898, 10-11.)

SUBJECT: Telephones. Practical jokes. Alcoholic beverages. Cigars.

ARCHIVE: DLC-pp.

CITATIONS:

NOTE: *The Telephone* was remade in July 1898; see *[The Telephone, no. 2]*, film no. 602.

581 ***See-Saw Scene***

LENGTH: 50 ft.   © Thomas A. Edison, 20 May 1898.

PRODUCER: William Heise.

CAMERA: William Heise.

CAST:

PRODUCTION DATE: April to mid-May 1898.

LOCATION: Edison Laboratory, West Orange, N.J.

SOURCE:

DESCRIPTION: Two factory boys get a huge barrel during their noon hour, and with a couple of planks they make an old-fashioned seesaw. Sitting on either end, they go up and down like a pair of kids. 'Long comes a third party with a brim full water pail, and a practical joke. He pushes off the boy nearest him, and substitutes the pail, which being lighter—away she goes, with comical results. The dripping boy wipes the water out of his eyes and off his clothes with a good-natured grin, while the other two laugh till their sides ache. Audience joins in every time this picture is shown. A very acceptable subject as a mirth provoker. Figures true to life and distinct. (*War Extra: Edison Films*, 20 May 1898, 11.)

SUBJECT: Practical jokes. Boys. Games. Seesaws.

ARCHIVE: DLC-pp.

CITATIONS: *Edison Films*, March 1900, 36.

NOTE: The Edison Laboratory is in the background.

582 ***The Ball Game***

LENGTH: 50 ft.   © Thomas A. Edison, 20 May 1898.

PRODUCER: William Heise.

CAMERA: William Heise.

CAST:

PRODUCTION DATE: [16-18 May 1898.]

LOCATION: Newark, N.J.

SOURCE:

DESCRIPTION: The Reading pitcher has just let a Newark batsman walk to first. Our cameraman is stationed about twenty feet from the bag, and the satisfied grin of the runner is great as he touches first and gets up on his toes for second. Next man up cracks first ball pitched for a two bagger, and races for the base with a wonderful burst of speed. First baseman just misses a put out. Very exciting. Man on the coaching line yells, and umpire runs up and makes decision. Small boy runs past back of the catcher close to the grand stand, where there is great commotion. A most excellent subject, treated brilliantly. (*War Extra: Edison Films*, 20 May 1898, 11.)

SUBJECT: Baseball. Sports.

ARCHIVE: DLC-pp.

CITATIONS:

NOTE:

583 ***Parade of Buffalo Bill's Wild West Show, no. 1 / Buffalo Bill's Wild West Show, no. 1**
LENGTH: 50 ft.   © Thomas A. Edison, 22 June 1898.
PRODUCER: William Heise.
CAMERA: William Heise.
CAST: William Frederick Cody.
PRODUCTION DATE: 20 May 1898.
LOCATION: Newark, N.J.
SOURCE:

DESCRIPTION: First comes the gilt coach, drawn by eight horses. Then Buffalo Bill and his famous Rough Riders of the World. Crowds of people watch. (*The Phonoscope*, November 1898, 14.)
SUBJECT: Wild west shows. Parades. Cavalry. Buffalo Bill's Wild West.
ARCHIVE: DLC-pp.
CITATIONS: "Buffalo Bill's Street Parade," *Newark Evening News*, 20 May 1898, 7.
NOTE: Despite the titles for this film, William W. Cody's show was known as Buffalo Bill's Wild West and not as Buffalo Bill's Wild West Show.

584 ***Parade of Buffalo Bill's Wild West Show, no. 2 / Buffalo Bill's Wild West Show, no. 2**
LENGTH: 150 ft.   © Thomas A. Edison, 22 June 1898.
PRODUCER: William Heise.
CAMERA: William Heise.
CAST:
PRODUCTION DATE: 20 May 1898.
LOCATION: Newark, N.J.
SOURCE:

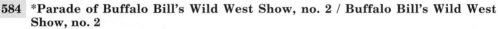

DESCRIPTION: Same parade, but shows the whole procession. Mounted cavalry, Indians, Arabs, Cossacks, Turks, Abyssinians and hosts of strange riders. Full of spirited interest and action. (*The Phonoscope*, November 1898, 14.)
SUBJECT: Wild west shows. Parades. Cavalry. Arabs. Cossacks. Indians of North America. Turks. Abyssinians. Buffalo Bill's Wild West.
ARCHIVE: DLC-pp.
CITATIONS: "Buffalo Bill's Street Parade," *Newark Evening News*, 20 May 1898, 7.
NOTE:

To continue with Heise's filmmaking activities go to film no. 601.
The following section continues the documentation of Paley's production of war films from film no. 565.

585 ***Blanket-Tossing a New Recruit**
LENGTH: 50 ft.   © Thomas A. Edison, 22 June 1898.
PRODUCER: William Paley.
CAMERA: William Paley.
CAST:
PRODUCTION DATE: Mid-May to early June 1898.
LOCATION: Tampa, Fla.
SOURCE:

DESCRIPTION: Company F, 1st Ohio Volunteers, initiating a new man. Nineteen times he bounces in the blanket, and each toss is funnier than the last one. (*Edison Films*, March 1900, 13.)

SUBJECT: Armies–United States. Spanish-American War. Initiation rites. Blankets. First Ohio Volunteer Infantry.

ARCHIVE: DLC-pp, CLAc.

CITATIONS: *Edison Films*, July 1901, 36.

NOTE:

586 *Soldiers Washing Dishes

LENGTH: [50 ft.]   © Thomas A. Edison, 22 June 1898.

PRODUCER: William Paley.

CAMERA: William Paley.

CAST:

PRODUCTION DATE: Mid-May to early June 1898.

LOCATION: Tampa, Fla.

SOURCE:

DESCRIPTION:

SUBJECT: Armies–United States. Spanish-American War.

ARCHIVE: DLC-pp.

CITATIONS:

NOTE:

587 *Wagon Supply Train En Route

LENGTH: 50 ft.   © Thomas A. Edison, 22 June 1898.

PRODUCER: William Paley.

CAMERA: William Paley.

CAST:

PRODUCTION DATE: Mid-May to early June 1898.

LOCATION: Tampa, Fla.

SOURCE:

DESCRIPTION: Each heavily loaded wagon is drawn by six army mules. On top of each load are the armed guards and the driver. (*Edison Films*, March 1900, 13.)

SUBJECT: Armies–United States. Spanish-American War. Transportation, military. Mules.

ARCHIVE: DLC-pp.

CITATIONS:

NOTE:

588 *9th and 13th U.S. Infantry at Battalion Drill

LENGTH: [100 ft.]   © Thomas A. Edison, 22 June 1898.

PRODUCER: William Paley.

CAMERA: William Paley.

CAST:

PRODUCTION DATE: Mid-May to early June 1898.

LOCATION: Tampa, Fla.

SOURCE:

DESCRIPTION:

SUBJECT: Armies–United States. Spanish-American War.

ARCHIVE: DLC-pp.

CITATIONS: "Cheers and Tears as Soldiers Start," *New York World,* 20 April 1898, 3; "General Wade Takes Command of the Army Camps at Tampa," *New York World,* 22 April 1898, 8; "13th Regiment in Camp Tampa," *New York World.*

NOTE: Elements of the 13th Infantry left Governor's Island, New York, N.Y., on 19 April 1898 and arrived in Tampa, Fla., on April 21st.

589 *Trained Cavalry Horses

LENGTH: 50 ft.   © Thomas A. Edison, 22 June 1898.
PRODUCER: William Paley.
CAMERA: William Paley.
CAST:
PRODUCTION DATE: Mid-May to early June 1898.
LOCATION: Tampa, Fla.
SOURCE:

DESCRIPTION: Shows the wonderful intelligence of these Troop F, 6th U.S. Cavalry, horses. At a command they lie down promptly and at another order scramble to their feet. (*Edison Films*, March 1900, 13.)
SUBJECT: Armies–United States. Spanish-American War. Cavalry. Horses–training. Sixth U.S. Cavalry.
ARCHIVE: DLC-pp.
CITATIONS: "Troops Gather in Camps of War," *New York World*, 22 April 1898, 8; "Troops Arrive at Tramp," *New York World*, 14 May 1898, 3. *Edison Films*, July 1901, 36.
NOTE: The Sixth Cavalry was normally based at Fort Myer (see film nos. 287, 306-308). The Sixth Cavalry was encamped at Chickamauga Park by 21 April 1898 and arrived in Tampa on May 13th.

The army boarded the transport ships at Tampa on June 8th. Paley filmed the embarkation and then sent his negatives to West Orange, New Jersey, for development by the Edison Manufacturing Company.

590 *Roosevelt's Rough Riders Embarking for Santiago

LENGTH: [50 ft.]   © Thomas A. Edison, 22 June 1898.
PRODUCER: William Paley.
CAMERA: William Paley.
CAST:
PRODUCTION DATE: 8 June 1898.
LOCATION: Tampa, Fla.
SOURCE:
DESCRIPTION:

SUBJECT: Harbors–Tampa. Piers. Transports. Armies–United States. Spanish-American War. Cavalry. First U.S. Cavalry (Volunteer).
ARCHIVE: DLC-pp.
CITATIONS: "Lieut.-Col. Roosevelt at the Head of Cowboy Cavalry," *New York World*, 26 April 1898, 1; "Roosevelt Sworn in as Lieutenant Colonel," *New York World*, 7 May 1898, 4; "Eastern Rough Riders in Earnest," *New York World*, 9 May 1898, 2; "Rough Riders Gather," *New York World*, 9 May 1898, 16; "Roosevelt's Men at Work," *New York World*, 19 May 1898, 5; "Rough Riders Watchful," *New York World*, 22 May 1898, 4; "New York Dudes Schooled by Cowboys," *New York World*, 22 May 1898, 33; "Teddy's Terrors Objects of Wonder," *New York World*, 23 May 1898, 4; "Profanity for Rough Riders," *New York World*, 26 May 1898, 4; "Rough Drill Language Horrifies Fifth Ave. Contingent of Rough Riders," *New York World*, 29 May 1898, 4; "Rough Riders Off to Tampa," *New York World*, 30 May 1898, 3; "Embarkation of Army at Port Tampa," *New York Times*, 12 June 1898, 3.
NOTE: Troops embarked onto "Yucatan" or "Leona."

591 *Cuban Volunteers Embarking

LENGTH: [50 ft.]   © Thomas A. Edison, 22 June 1898.
PRODUCER: William Paley.
CAMERA: William Paley.
CAST:

PRODUCTION DATE: 8 June 1898.
LOCATION: Tampa, Fla.
SOURCE:
DESCRIPTION:
SUBJECT: Harbors–Tampa. Piers. Armies–
Cuba. Transports. Spanish-American War.
ARCHIVE: DLC-pp.
CITATIONS: "Embarkation of Army at Port
Tampa," *New York Times*, 12 June 1898, 3.
NOTE:

592 ***71st New York Volunteers Embarking for Santiago***
LENGTH: [100 ft.]   © Thomas A. Edison, 22 June 1898.
PRODUCER: William Paley.
CAMERA: William Paley.
CAST:
PRODUCTION DATE: 8 June 1898.
LOCATION: Tampa, Fla.
SOURCE:
DESCRIPTION:
SUBJECT: Harbors–Tampa. Piers. Armies–
United States. Transports. Spanish-Amer-
ican War. 71st Regiment.
ARCHIVE: DLC-pp.
CITATIONS: "Seventy-First is Off for the Front,"
New York World, 13 May 1898, 8; "Seventy-
First Regiment Mustered Into Service,"
New York World, 11 May 1898, 7; "71st on Its Way to Tampa," *New York World*, 15
May 1898, 11; "71st Regiment Happy in Camp," *New York World*, 20 May 1898, 3.
NOTE: The 71st Regiment left the New York area for Tampa on May 14th.

593 ***Loading Horses on Transport***
LENGTH: [50 ft.]   © Thomas A. Edison, 22 June 1898.
PRODUCER: William Paley.
CAMERA: William Paley.
CAST:
PRODUCTION DATE: 8 June 1898.
LOCATION: Tampa, Fla.
SOURCE:
DESCRIPTION:
SUBJECT: Harbors–Tampa. Piers. Armies–
United States. Spanish-American War.
Cavalry. Horses. Transports.
ARCHIVE: DLC-pp.
CITATIONS:
NOTE:

594 ***Transport Ships at Port Tampa***
LENGTH: [50 ft.]   © Thomas A. Edison,
22 June 1898.
PRODUCER: William Paley.
CAMERA: William Paley.
CAST:
PRODUCTION DATE: 8 June 1898.
LOCATION: Tampa, Fla.
SOURCE:
DESCRIPTION:
SUBJECT: Harbors–Tampa. Piers. Navies–

United States. Armies–United States. Spanish-American War. Transports.
ARCHIVE: DLC-pp.
CITATIONS:
NOTE:

EMBARKATION OF THE ARMY AT PORT TAMPA.
The Regulars and Volunteers Board Transports in High Spirits.
STIRRING SCENE OF THE WAR.
Generals, Majors, Colonels, Rough Riders and Infantrymen, All in Order.
MILES AND SHAFTER CHEERED.
Five Hours Consumed in Transporting the Troops from the Docks to the Ships.

(Written at Port Tampa on Wednesday and sent from Tampa Saturday, with the permission of Gen. Miles.)

PORT TAMPA BAY, June 8–(Delayed in transmission).–The first American army to be embarked by the United States in a war with a foreign country is afloat. The army, whose proportions, of course, cannot be given, marched to-day on board transports, and under convoy of the United States Navy prepared to execute the orders of the President delivered through Major Gen. Miles, the acting commander-in-chief of the United States Army.

The embarkation of Uncle Sam's trained fighters, of whom more than two-thirds were regulars, was one of the most spirited and fascinating combinations of marine and military spectacles ever presented. The men, admirably equipped for the rigorous service demanded of them, acted with the most splendid courage and enthusiasm.

The orders of the Secretary of War, particularly announced in Washington on Tuesday, that the troops were to be placed on board the transports under convoy of the gunboats awaiting them and convoyed to some place where actual land hostilities intended to carry out the mandate of commanders and to drive the Spaniards out of the island are soon to begin.

Invokes General Admiration.

But the extraordinary achievement of to-day in preparing so vast a body of troops for a hostile expedition into a foreign country invoked the admiration of representatives of nine European and Asiatic Governments who were stationed here to witness them.

Within ten hours from the time of the actual embarkation of the troops–their artillery, ammunition and supplies–was inaugurated, they were ready. As a matter of fact, several of the transports bearing the pick of the regular and volunteer regiments now at Tampa, sturdy of limb, bronzed in face and as enthusiastic as they are brave, had already begun to move out of Tampa Bay toward the Gulf of Mexico.

Three hundred miles only separated them from the country they were ordered to invade. When Gen. Miles and Gen. Shafter reported to the President and Secretary of War at midday of Wednesday this fleet was still waiting.

From each of the troopships were wafted sounds of joyous songs. The men were in excellent spirits and impatient for the word expected every minute. The destination of the troopships and their transports cannot of course be learned.

Good-Natured but Fighters.

Trains from various camps arrived and were rushed and jerked down the narrow mile of docks that juts out from the mainland into the bay, depositing a miscellaneous collection of good-natured and boisterous troopers, mammoth pyramids of boxes and a collection of every conceivable convenience that fighting men require, from a case of court plaster to a war balloon.

The word to embark was not generally known to the officers of the army until late on Tuesday night, but from the time they received them until their men and camp accoutrements were huddled and jammed among the railway tracks and stringpieces of the docks lying between the double line of great transports, black of hull and with brass trimmings resplendent as gold under the tropical sun, there was enacted such a scene of systematized and orderly activity as has not been witnessed in this country for a great many years.

The camps of the various regiments which were to embark in the transports covered a range of territory twenty miles in area. The headquarters of the army at the Tampa Bay Hotel, where Gen. Miles, the commander-in-chief of the land forces, and Major Gen. Shafter, who was to lead the expedition ordered to sail away, were up all night, and their aides and orderlies were flying about on horseback issuing commands to the various regiments to move at once to Port Tampa.

All Done in Quick Time.

The camp tents were struck and packed on mule trains, and within three hours from the receipt of the orders the railway traversing the nine miles from Tampa to the shore had a continuous procession of trains loaded with troops.

In the wagon roads, fetlock-deep with sand that arose in clouds under the shoes of the mules and horses, long wagon trains of commissary supplies, all under convoy of armed guards, made the sight lively with noises and oaths peculiar to the handling of a mule train.

Two hundred porters and orderlies were packing bundles and the equipage of field service in the officers' rooms in the hotel. A full train of four cars was required to carry the luggage of the generals, colonels and majors. One of the cars was filled with the warlike paraphernalia of reporters who are going with the army to report its operations. There were fifty-five of these reporters. Some of them came from St. Petersburg, Berlin sent two, Paris three. London writers and reporters were common. New York was represented by a full quota, Chicago and San Francisco two or three each.

They were a keen, picturesque lot of chaps, a few with records of daring exploits under the suns of India and in the icefields of the frozen zone.

Men Who Have Spurs to Win.

The majority, however, were new at the game. These carried a ferocious assortment of belt artillery and bowie knives, and their backs were strained under the weight of immense Haversacks, bags, boxes, tent poles, collapsing folding-beds, bundles of tin cups and plates that dangled about their legs from strings. They were garbed in all sorts of uniforms supposed to be suitable for the event. One or two correspondents were freighted with stuff enough to start a bride and groom off housekeeping in a Harlem flat in a very respectable style.

Most of the officers who were to go were organized in suits of khaki, a dusty brown material used by the English army in India. Major Gen. Shafter, who was to lead the expedition, was in blue fatigue uniform, with two gold stars on his shoulder-straps and a stout walking-stick in his hand.

Lieut.-Col. John Jacob Astor, in a snug-fitting suit of khaki, and carrying his sword in his right hand, jostled Hallet Alsops Borrowe, of the Rough Riders, who has charge of the gelatine high explosive guns. Lieut.-Col. Roosevelt, in the picturesque uniform of his unique command, was lamenting the fact that his men couldn't take all their horses because the War Department had ordered the cavalry to leave them behind.

Rough Riders Taking Leave.

Creighton Webb, who is an inspector-general, Woodbury Kane and Willie Tiffany, Rough Riders, were taking leave of their families and friends and carrying packages. The streets about the hotel were filled with marching soldiers and noisy with the call of orders from officers, and at daylight the special train that was to bear the officers to the port pulled out from the hotel yard on the way to Port Tampa, where the transports were.

Nowhere in the world was ever a more busy scene witnessed than at Port Tampa. Way down the road as far as the eye could reach was a seemingly interminable line of railway tracks, losing themselves in the distance.

Thousands of enthusiastic boys in blue and brown were impatiently waiting for their turn to come to march aboard the waiting transports, which were opened ready for them to embark. Now that the hour to strike hard had arrived they were eager to be on their way toward Cuba.

Applause for Hardy Regulars.

One by one the trains slowly advanced along the road and debarked, the freight on the platform, the train drawing out again to make room for the next. Cheer rolled up after cheer as the hardy regulars fell into line and marched without confusion into the steamers.

Little time was lost after leaving the trains. Baggage was quickly gathered and sorted and stowed in the capacious holds. A line of eight steamers lay at the dock, probably the largest pier in the country.

Its value as a port of departure and a base of supplies is enhanced by the facilities for loading and unloading. The trains run all the way to the end of the wharf, and it is but a step from car to steamer. These terminal facilities cost an immense sum of money and time.

No place South is so admirably situated for the rendezvous of a transport fleet. Twenty miles or more from the Gulf the narrow, tortuous and shallow channel practically prohibits the entrance of a hostile fleet. At night a search light is necessary to pick out the channel.

If the Spaniards should enter, the chances are they would run aground and stay there. So the transports had little to fear as they took aboard their complement of troops. As soon as one was filled it slowly drew out, took its position in the bay and anchored while another quietly took its place.

There was no confusion, no disorder, everything went off smoothly, and except for a few minor details the movement reflected great credit on those who managed and planned it. As the ropes were let go from the mooring posts and the ships quietly swung away from the last hold of their native shores, the troops, swarming upon the upper decks, and perched up in the rigging, gave way to prolonged cheers, the bands struck up patriotic airs, and throngs of civilians on the wharf shouted words of encouragement.

Cheers for Popular Generals.

The cheers were taken up by the soldiers still on the trains and in the neighboring camps, and long after they had ceased on the docks far away hurrahs came echoing down the line. The coming of Gens. Miles and Shafter with their staffs was a signal for another outbreak of enthusiasm.

Gen. Miles was attired in a civilian's suit of blue serge and mingled freely with the boys on the wharf. He seemed deeply interested in the embarkation, and was evidently pleased and satisfied with the showing made by the army. The scene that unfolded itself was imposing. The regulars, in their rough costume of blue flannel shirt, regulation trousers, felt hat, brown canvas leggings and formidable-looking cartridge belts, swarmed along the board walk. Staff officers in their brand-new uniforms were everywhere. It is a noticeable fact that few of the regular line officers outside of the staff have provided themselves with the new uniform. Hundreds of gayly-attired sightseers from

Tampa and neighboring towns were down to view the movement. The large number of the gentler sex, many of them wives, sisters or sweethearts of departing officers, lent color to the scene.

The day was unusually warm, and a run was made on the only bar in the place. Its stock was quickly exhausted. The troops had just been paid and were longing to spend their money. There is but one restaurant on the long pier, and it will ordinarily accommodate from eight to ten persons.

Uniforms of All Nations.

All sorts and conditions of men in all sorts of uniforms were jammed and jostled along the track, where cars were being shunted and shifted or unloaded. A Russian lieutenant of infantry, with bloomer-like trousers tucked into loose glazed boots and a square yachting-shaped cap, walked arm in arm with Capt. Pope, of the British Army, very cool and fresh-looking in duck and gold lace.

A Swedish surgeon general, a German count in the uniform of his regiment, yellow-ribbed and picturesque; a Norwegian artillerist in tight-fitting uniform, and a dapper little Japanese rider, looking very much like a cavalry cadet in his first uniform, represented the foreign contingent, and became hopelessly entangled among the brawny-looking buffalo soldiers of the Ninth Regular Cavalry Regiment, which is composed of colored men, and rough-riders from Fifth avenue and the Indian Territory.

A brilliant and uncomfortable tropical sun reflected from the smooth, glassy bosom of the bay sapphire and green in spots. Far away to the south the waters of the Gulf could be seen through a strong glass, and a score of white-masted [schooners] and black transports and tramp steamers, with long trails of smoke in their wakes, hung against the horizon.

The con[   ] of the sun through the gray mists witnessed the start of the embarkation. The reporters with their war trousseaus went first in a little tender to the transport Olivette, which is to be their home until they are land-ed to write up the doings of the army.

They tugged their belongings through the lines of colored troopers, and Cuban guides almost as dark hued of com-plexion, who regarded them curiously and held aside their guns and ugly-looking machetes to let them pass. The half-hundred mascot dogs and the mascot goat of the Seventy-first New York Volunteer Regiment barked and pulled at the regulars, but they did not mind.

Five Hours to Get All Aboard.

The Olivette was the first of the transports to get under way. She steamed to a point 100 feet off the starboard quarter of a gunboat. The regular infantry came next. Immediately, the transports prepared for them, and they speedily steamed out to join the gunboats.

Five hours were actually consumed in transporting the troops from the docks to the cluster of troops ships and gunboats half a mile off shore. The air was black with the smoke of the transports.

The Massachusetts volunteers were on a transport that was easy to distinguish. From it came distinct cries of "What's the matter with Boston?" and this couplet:

> We want to go back, we want to go back,
> We want to go back to Boston.

The Ohio men were in a boat near a gunboat and were the first to see the blue, yellow and red flag run up the sig-nal halyards. They did not know what it meant until a deckhand read it for them. Then they lifted up their lusty voices and informed the rest of the transport about it.

"Remember the Maine!" "Remember the Maine!"

The Men in the rigging sent the battle cry to the men on the decks below. It was a most inspiring spectacle, and the weary troopers and civilians on shore cheered and cheered again as the cry reached them.

The highest pitch of enthusiasm and the supreme moment of the embarkation however, was when the Fourth Infantry Band started up the "Star-Spangled Banner." A gunboat had just started down the bay to go ahead of the fleet. This was at 2 o'clock. The last transport she passed played the national air.

Ten thousand voices on the transports and from the decks took up the refrain and the Spaniards could have heard it ten miles away. Hats went off as the first strains of the grand old air rang out and they remained off until the last word died away.

"In all Europe," said Gen. Miles, by whose side I stood, "there is no such soldiers as these. I have never seen such a scene of enthusiastic patriotism. I am proud of my soldiers."

The singing of patriotic songs continued until the gunboat was out of sight. "My Country 'Tis of Thee," by the men on some of the transports, the "Red, White and Blue" by others. The last transport to steam away carried colored troop-ers. Their band played "There'll Be a Hot Time in the Old Town To-night," and the dusky troopers sang it merrily.

All the boats were soon clustered within the space of a mile, the nearest half a mile off shore. Ten thousand troop-ers and civilians watched them from the decks. There was a wait of half an hour, then a gun sounded from the lit-tle three-pounder of the flagship Annapolis, the salute to the commanding officer, Gen. Shafter, as he went aboard his transport.

It was construed as the signal to start and a mighty cheer went up. But there was another long wait and finally a steam launch put off from the dock and hung under the gray outline of the Annapolis.

An officer in the launch delivered some despatches. There was instantly an exciting scene on the Annapolis. A signal officer, with a bunch of flags under his arm, mounted the bridge and wagged them. Officers from the transports and other gunboats answered them in a similar manner.

Stopped at the Last Moment.

They finally got the message "Wait; draw near the docks." In half an hour the order was obeyed, and at first there was just disappointment.

Then word came that the delay was only temporary; that orders to sail against the Spaniards would come before many hours, and the men settled down to the routine of their duties and waited for word to come. The soldiers ashore went back to their camp. LOUIS SEIBOLD. (*New York World*, 12 June 1898, 2.)

DEPARTURE FROM TAMPA
A STIRRING SPECTACLE.
(Special to The World.)

TAMPA, Fla., June 12–The first division of the army of invasion started from Tampa to-day for Key West, which will be reached to-morrow. There the fleet of thirty-two transport boats will be met by the convoy of twelve naval vessels and will, it is believed, make a speedy start for Cuba.

It was a mighty procession that swept out of Tampa Bay to-day and started gallantly across the waters; a stately procession, too, moving along in column as well aligned and as steadily as a regiment of soldiers on land. There are no stragglers in this magnificent march, no weaklings.

The embarkation had been a rapid one and these boats steamed out into the sea awaiting the order "On to Cuba." The big fleet filled the harbor, anchoring, however, as far out as possible, so that no time might be lost when the order came to move. Major-General Shafter, in command of the army, spent much time in port and then the wires to Washington began to work. There were questions and answers, suggestions and orders, commands and counter-commands, and the hours passed away while still the "tick, tick" of the telegraph-sounder spelled out the words that might mean great glory for our nation or death to thousands.

The people of Tampa and the soldiers left behind had flocked to the water front to share a farewell. From the transports came cheer after cheer, shouts were taken up from one vessel to another, and then songs that rolled along the long line like an almost ceaseless echo.

At last the signal, "Up anchor," was floated from the mast of the flagship.

Gen. Shafter had sent his last message to Washington, received his last command.

"Eight knots an hour," said the signals, and "eight knots an hour" were the orders to engineers.

The boats were ranged in a double column as close as safety would permit, but with allowance for plenty of steerage-way.

On the sides and on the smokestacks of each of the transports was painted a large white number, and by these numbers the boats were officially known, their original names being discarded. This was for the purpose of facilitating signalling between the flagship and the other boats of the fleet.

Here is the list, with names of officers and number of soldiers:

1–Miami, McDonald, 1,200 men.
2–Santiago, Leighton, 950 men.
3–Gussie, Birney, 400 men.
4–Cherokee, Carvin, 1,000 men.
5–Seneca, Decker, 900 men.
6–Alamo, Hix, 900 men.
7–Comal, Evans, 950 men, 176 horses.
8–Xucatan, Robertson, 950 men.
9–Berkshire, Diser, 474 men, 174 horses.
10–Whitney, Staples, 100 men.
11–Olivette, Stevenson, 400 men, 15 horses.
12–Seguranca (flag), Hansen, 600 men.
13–[   ], [   ], [   ].
14–Concho, Rick, 1,300 men.
15–Florida, Miner, 600 men.
16–City of Washington, Stevens, 900 men.
17–Allegheny, Nickerson, 450 men, 190 horses.
18–San Marcos, Itzen, 1,100 men, 20 horses.
19–Decatur H. Miller, Peterson, 350 men, 300 miles.
20–Saratoga, Johnson, 900 men.
21–Leone, Wilder, 1,250 men.
22–Rio Grande, Staples, 1,100 men.

23–Vigilancia, McIntosh, 1,200 men.
24–Orizaba, Downs, 1,200 men.
25–Iroquois, Kimble, 950 men.
26–Matteawan, Lewis, 800 men, 400 horses.
27–Morgan, Staples, [   ].
28–Stillwater, Gault, [   ].
29–Breakwater, Rivero, [   ].
30–Cumberland, [   ], [   ].
31–Knickerbocker, [   ], 900 men.
32–Clinton, [   ], [   ].
State of Texas (hospital), Young, [   ].
Barges–Bessie, Martha.
Tug–Captain Sam.
At Key West the fleet will be met by the convoy of at least twelve warships, and when the start for Cuba is made the stately Indiana will be in the lead.
Along the flanks of the double column of transports will range the naval vessels–the bodyguard. Just behind the Indiana will steam the Puritan and the Wilmington. On the flanks will be the Helena, the Manning, Terror, Rodgers, Wasp, Bancroft, Newport, and Mayflower. In the rear the St. Louis will keep guard. On board the transports the men will be permitted a certain amount of liberty, but on the naval vessels the discipline will be very much more rigid. The men will sleep at their guns–those who sleep at all–and not the slightest relaxation will be permitted. The prize they are guarding is a rich one–17,000 brave soldiers, the flower of our army–and this prize must be guarded well.
Before leaving Tampa Gen. Shafter communicated with Washington in regard to the news that three Spanish gun-boats had sallied forth from Havana only recently and had been driven back by Commodore Watson's cruisers. It was believed that the Spanish gunboats had been sent out to create an impression that the Spaniards were pre-pared to attack transports, but their speedy flight on the approach of our cruisers showed that this action was only a "bluff." Even if the gunboats had escaped the vigilance of Commodore Watson they could have made but a ridiculous stand against the invading American fleet, for not one of the Spanish boats was equal in power to the smallest of our cruisers. (*New York World*, 13 June 1898, 1.)

The U.S. troop ships left Port Tampa on 12 June 1898. Reporters and physicians were on the "Olivette," which returned to port on June 15th but quickly rejoined the convoy. Troops began to land at Daiquiri on June 22nd and the forces were fully landed by June 26th.

595 ***U.S. Troops Landing at Daiquiri, Cuba / U.S. Troops Landing at Baiquiri, Cuba**
LENGTH: 50 ft.   © Thomas A. Edison, 5 August 1898.
PRODUCER: William Paley.
CAMERA: William Paley.
CAST:
PRODUCTION DATE: 22-26 June 1898.
LOCATION: Daiquiri, Cuba.
SOURCE:

DESCRIPTION: These are the first U.S. troops to land on Cuban soil, June 22, 1898. The pic-ture shows a long perspective view of the pier at Baiquiri, the point chosen so strate-gically for the landing of General Shafter's army. At the end of the wharf are the coal dumps and ore elevators used by the min-ing company operating the famous iron mines at Juragua, five miles away. On the right of the picture is seen the stern of a huge transport as she rides at anchor, and in the distance, stretching far out to the horizon, are other vessels of the fleet. (*The Phonoscope*, October 1898, 15.)
SUBJECT: Armies–United States. Navies–United States. Spanish-American War. Transports. Landing operations. Piers.
ARCHIVE: DLC-pp, NR-GE, CLAc.
CITATIONS: *Edison Films*, March 1900, 10; *Edison Films*, July 1901, 33.
NOTE:

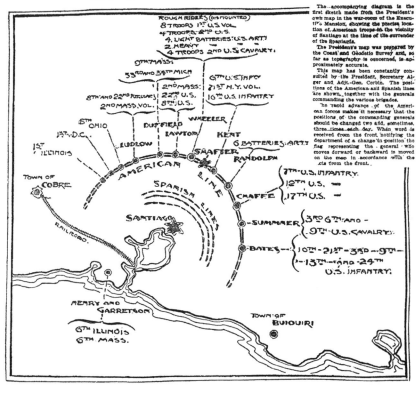

THE WORLD: FRIDAY, JULY 15, 1898.

PRESIDENT'S MAP SHOWING LOCATION OF OUR TROOPS.

Map showing location of American troops around Santiago, Cuba (July 1898).

596 *Mules Swimming Ashore at Daiquiri, Cuba / Army Mules Swimming Ashore at Baiquiri, Cuba

LENGTH: 50 ft.   © Thomas A. Edison, 5 August 1898.

PRODUCER: William Paley.

CAMERA: William Paley.

CAST:

PRODUCTION DATE: 22-26 June 1898.

LOCATION: Daiquiri, Cuba.

SOURCE:

DESCRIPTION: They just tossed the mules overboard and let 'em swim for it. Transport No. 10 [the "Whitney"] lies in the near distance, and is discharging her four-footed in this novel manner. Other transports lie at anchor further out, with tenders and rowboats in attendance. In the foreground two mules are swimming toward the beach. One of them seems to be exhausted, and the men in the row boat are urging it along. (*The Phonoscope*, October 1898, 15.)

SUBJECT: Armies–United States. Spanish-American War. Mules. Transports. Landing operations.

ARCHIVE: DLC-pp.
CITATIONS: *Edison Films*, March 1900, 10; *Edison Films*, July 1901, 33.
NOTE:

597 *Packing Ammunition on Mules, Cuba**
LENGTH: [50 ft.]   © Thomas A. Edison, 5 August 1898.
PRODUCER: William Paley.
CAMERA: William Paley.
CAST:
PRODUCTION DATE: 22-26 June 1898.
LOCATION: Daiquiri, Cuba.
SOURCE:

DESCRIPTION: Dotting the horizon on the right of the picture is the great fleet of transports, while scattered all along the beach and piled high to the left are hundreds upon hundreds of ammunition cases. Soldier boys in the foreground are packing the boxes on the patient army mules. An officer stands by bossing the job. Two boxes are tied on each mule. (*The Phonoscope*, October 1898, 15.)
SUBJECT: Armies–United States. Armies–Officers. Spanish-American War. Mules. Transports.
ARCHIVE: DLC-pp.
CITATIONS:
NOTE:

598 *Major General Shafter**
LENGTH: 50 ft.   © Thomas A. Edison, 5 August 1898.
PRODUCER: William Paley.
CAMERA: William Paley.
CAST: William Rufus Shafter.
PRODUCTION DATE: Late June 1898.
LOCATION: Daiquiri, Cuba.
SOURCE:
DESCRIPTION: This view is taken at the camp at Baiquiri. In the distance under the trees are tents and a camp fire, beyond which stretches the broad expanse of the Caribbean Sea. An officer gallops toward the front, reins in his horse, and wheeling rapidly, stands at attention. Other officers are seen galloping across the camp. A party of officers is seen rapidly approaching. He with the white helmet and broad expanse of shirt bosom is Major General Shafter, commanding the 5th Army Corps. His avoirdupois distinguishes him from his subordinates. They gallop forward, taking the trail leading to Santiago. An excellent picture of this capable and brave General. (*The Phonoscope*, October 1898, 15.)
SUBJECT: Armies–Officers. Armies–United States. Spanish-American War.
ARCHIVE: DLC-pp.
CITATIONS: *Edison Films*, March 1900, 10; *Edison Films*, July 1901, 34.
NOTE: Gen. Shafter commanded U.S. military operations in Cuba culminating with the capitulation of the Spanish Army and the surrender of Santiago.

TWO ROADS FROM BAIQUIRI LEAD TO THE REAR OF SANTIAGO.

Baiquiri or Daiquiri, as it is more commonly called, is situated about little more than one-third distance from Morro Castle, Santiago, to the entrance of Guantanamo Bay.
Baiquiri is an important collection of huts. There is a small river which flows into the sea. There is a small bay. Two miles northwest is a village of a dozen huts, called Demayayabo. There are iron mines near Baiquiri of manganese ore. The mineral railway from Santiago skirts the coast to within a distance of perhaps five miles of Baiquiri. Then it turns inland when it reaches to Juragua River. Playa del Este is on the eastern side of the bay that makes

up near Baiquiri. Playa means beach, and Este east–East Beach. The country in the rear of Playa del Este is high and rolling. There is a hill called the Pillar, which is a sort of landmark. The land bordering the sea is low. Looking inland west of north six miles is a hill known as a landmark on the coast, called Del Indio.

The general aspect of the country about the landing place is low near the sea with irregular hills inland, and a very sparse population.

There are two roads to Santiago. One follows near the coast, the other goes inland by way of Santa Barbara. The coast road is the most direct. Any one here would call it a pretty tough highway. Like nearly all the roads of Santiago Province, it is almost impassable except for ox-carts.

The location of Playa del Este is about half-way from Morro Castle to Guantanamo Bay.

There is a good landing at Baiquiri. It used to be an iron pier. The distance by highway from Santiago is from fifteen to eighteen miles.

There are no poisonous reptiles in Cuba. It is a peculiarity of the island. There are snakes, but inoffensive ones. There are scorpions and tarantulas spiders and centipedes.

These together with cactus-spikes and as lively mosquitoes as there are in the world, will not conduce to the comfort of the troops. (*New York World*, 23 June 1898, 1.)

Army Disembarked at Three Points, Meeting Little Resistance.
CUBANS AND THE TEXAS ATTACK IN THE WEST.
One Man Killed in the Fleet–To March on Santiago Without Delay.
(Copyright, 1898, by the Press Publishing Company, New York World.)
(Special Cable Despatch to The World.)

OFF SANTIAGO, June 22 (via Port Antonio, Jamaica).–Gen. Shafter is a man of action. He began to disembark a large portion of his army at noon to-day at Baiquiri, Jurugua Bay and the Bay of Baconao, twelve and fifteen miles east of Santiago.

While the troops were being landed Admiral Sampson's ships bombarded several points simultaneously to confuse the Spaniards. The Cuban forces and the battle-ship Texas made a joint land and water attack on Nimanima, a few miles westward of Santiago, at the same time to create a diversion in that direction.

The landing is being made with great success.

Long before this despatch is read in New York the American troops will be driving the Spanish outposts into Santiago. The landing has been successfully made, and Cuba is invaded by the United States army's beautiful co-operation with the navy.

Shafter's plan of invasion involved, first, an attack on Manterola, west of Santiago, by the Cuban soldiers under Tabi; second, the shelling of Mazzamorra blockhouse by the warships; third, the shelling of hills overing every cove where a landing might be affected east of harbor; fourth, the grouping of coal transports to the west to make the Spaniards believe the landing would take place there. As soon as Mazzamorra was taken.

Daybreak saw the counterfeit transports steaming to the west and the real troop transports in the east, the latter gathering off Baconoo.

One battle-ship, one cruiser, also the gunboats Helena, Louise, Suwanee and several auxiliary yachts were assigned to cover the landing. Fires soon began to blaze in the town up the bay, showing that the Spaniards were destroying it.

It was a beautiful day and the water was smooth. Boats were towed beside the transports whose troops were to go first. On the decks of the transports, which had now been forty hours off Santiago, the crowded troops huddled, impatient to land. Spanish riflemen dotted the hills, but there was no sign of fortifications.

Fifteen miles west of this point the strategic game opened at 8 o'clock, when Rabi's two thousand Cubans attacked the Spanish forces at Mazzamorra. The battleship Texas at the same time ran close inshore and opened on a blockhouse back of Cabanas Bay. The Estrella battery opened on the Texas, the shots coming near, for the range was short. The Texas silenced the battery in forty minutes. Then a Spanish field battery ran down to the beach and opened on the Texas, but was quickly driven off by the rapid-fire guns. The battery opened again, but was again driven off.

Meantime the Spanish and Cubans became hotly engaged. The fierce fire was heard on Cervera's ships in the harbor and they opened fire on the Cubans on the plateau at Little Bay Julici, where is the hut that Tweed lived in when he landed in Cuba. A yacht believed to be the Scorpion opened fire on the hills.

Another diversion was made on the slopes in the harbor of Juruaguay by the Helena, Newport, Bancroft and yacht Vixen. Shrapnel burst all over the hillside and the Spanish riflemen fled.

Still another diversion was made when the battle-ship left the convoy and returned to the fleet.

Admiral Sampson, leaving Schley in command with orders to smash Cervera if he came out of the harbor, steamed down to Baconas to superintend the naval part of the operations there. The gunboats continued their raking fire. The Iowa took a hand and engaged the water batteries beneath Morro, silencing them. The gunboats continued raking Juragua with shells, the Texas still firing, as was the Scorpion.

The line of battle was twenty miles long. The New York at Baconos, opened with her big guns, clearing the beach. A bugle call rang over the water, the troops clattered into boats and the real landing of the army began.

The events which led up to the only great American operation of American soldiers since the war of the rebellion were picturesque. When The World's despatch boat left Santiago this noon final arrangements had been made for landing a portion of the army of invasion at Signa, Bay of Baconao and at Juraqua.

Plans for the landing had been completed at a conference held at Gen. Shafter's headquarters on board the flag-ship Sequranca Tuesday night.

Gen. Shafter concluded to strike quickly, get his troops ashore rapidly and move on Santiago at once, when nothing would interfere with his movement on Porto Rico.

The transports, which had been riding far out at sea, came stealing into the bay early Wednesday morning. They were convoyed by the battle-ship Indiana, the gunboats Helena and Bancroft and the auxiliary cruisers.

The troops eagerly crowded the decks, scanning the shores of Baracao Bay. Here are iron mines. Beyond the huge iron dock fires blazed. There had been fighting here earlier with the insurgents. The Spaniards fled, but before their hurried retreat had fired the town.

The troops on the twenty-six warships asked many questions as they waited for the troops to clear the way. The prospect ashore was pleasant to the eye, with wooded hills, frowning mountains and little hamlets, with here and there a Spanish block house.

Powerful glasses showed the Spanish infantry on the hills.

Indications of firing were made out some fifteen miles the other side of Santiago harbor, and it was apparent that Mazamorro had been attacked by land and sea, and that Spanish soldiers were hurrying from Santiago harbor to repel an expected landing at a point east of the harbor, an easy landing-place for infantry.

One of the torpedo boats reported that Spanish soldiers were collected on the hillsides as though they expected an attack at that point.

The challenge was accepted and soon one of the auxiliary yachts was b[lasting] away at the Spaniards and sending them helter skelter to the plateau near the point where the ships still menaced Sigus with its blazing houses.

Four warships ran into the bay of Juragua, in front of Baiquiri, and began to plow up the hillsides and scatter the Spanish soldiers there.

One of the attacking ships was the Bancroft. It was the first time she had been in action and she did beautiful shooting.

The shore batteries beneath Morro opened on a scouting torpedo boat.

One of the armorclads waiting for Cervera, the Texas, it is believed, steamed in and silenced the batteries. The coast fronting Santiago was menaced at all points. At one time it was seemingly more serious on the west than on the east, and the beleaguered city could not tell where the blow would come. (*New York World*, 23 June 1898, 1.)

599 *Pack Mules with Ammunition on the Santiago Trail, Cuba / Pack Mules with Ammunition, Santiago**

LENGTH: 50 ft.   © Thomas A. Edison, 5 August 1898.
PRODUCER: William Paley.
CAMERA: William Paley.
CAST:
PRODUCTION DATE: Late June to early July 1898.
LOCATION: Daiquiri, Cuba.
SOURCE:
DESCRIPTION: The narrow trail shown in this picture leads from Baiquiri westward to Sibony, thence northward to Santiago. It will be seen it is hardly more than a wood-path. At first it was overgrown with brush and shut in close by chaparral, but the passage of thousands of soldiers has broadened it considerably. A great bunch of pack  mules swings into vision. The advance scout or guide is evidently a Cuban, and he approaches rapidly followed by the train. It is a fine sight. (*The Phonoscope*, October 1898, 15.)

SUBJECT: Armies–United States. Spanish-American War. Mules. Transportation, military. Cubans.
ARCHIVE: DLC-pp, DLC-Roosevelt, CLAc, NR-GE.
CITATIONS: *Edison Films*, March 1900, 10; *Edison Films*, July 1901, 33.
NOTE:

THE ARMY MULE.

Washington, D.C., June 4, The mule–the American mule, the long-eared, short-tailed animal whose sweet song and sturdy virtues have endeared it for so many years–is making trouble for the American Government just now.

He and his mate, the "Jinny," tangled up the War Department in a discussion of the project to invade Cuba to-day and is responsible for considerable feeling between two members of the President's official family.

It has only been within the last two weeks that the American mule has become so important a feature in the proposed operations of our army in Cuba. His value was discovered when Gen. Miles, the commander of the land forces, made an estimate that the services of 18,000 mules would be required to transport supplies along with the invading army.

A majority of the members of the Cabinet disagreed with the General. They thought 2,000 mules would be as many as could be managed to carry the food of the troops to be landed: at any rate they thought the army would be sufficiently busy fighting the Spaniards without taming more than 2,000 of the obstinate beasts. But Miles knew better.

MILES AND MULES WIN.

There was a long controversy over the subject, the end of which was that the distinguished statesmen in the Cabinet recanted and the General was instructed to go ahead and get the mules–if he could.

The Quartermaster-General made a canvass of the country and discovered that the value of mules had appreciated from 50 to 200 per cent. A mule that could have been bought for $30 three months ago, for instance, is now considered by his owner to be worth at least $100, and even at the top figures not more than 6,000 "Jacks" and "Jinnies" are to be obtained.

The Quartermaster made known the result of his investigations into the mule supply to-day and there was a lot of things said on the subject in official circles that would not do to print. The Quartermaster reported that the owners of mules did not want to part with them; they love them too dearly: their eyes fill with tears at the bare thought of selling their dear mules–companions of their waking hours, sharers of their toil and soothers of their slumber by touching lullabies in the night's still watches–that is, not for less than $75 to $100 per.

Apparently, this official reported, there were enough mules in the country in 1890 to carry the supplies of an army of a million strong, but there were not enough at present to equip one army corps. He recommended that as soon as possible the owners of mules be required to register every month the number and quality of their stock, so that the Government may be informed as to the number available in case of an emergency.

LIGHT TALK; GRAVE TOPIC.

When the subject of mules was first made known to the Cabinet by Secretary of War Alger, Secretary of the Treasury Gage made light of the request for 18,000 mules.

Secretary Alger retorted that the request did not call for humorous discussion, but was very serious indeed, and there was an entertaining exchange of opinions on the subject between the two gentlemen, which was not entirely in the nature of a joke.

The discussion was terminated by Mr. Gage saying: "Well, if the conduct of the war depends on mules, why don't you send your troops to Cuba and take what the Spaniards have? I understand they have so many mules down there that they are eating them."

Such is the love which the mule has inspired and the unwillingness of the average owner to part with him that it is probable that the army of invasion of Cuba will be equipped with 6,000 or 7,000 "Jacks" and "Jinnies" instead of the larger number.

THE MULE YARD IN WASHINGTON.

Even at this, the mule yard in Washington presents a busy, stirring, interesting scene. Some 1,500 mules are scattered over 100 acres of ground. When they plaintively sing for their dinner in chorus the effect is surprising. They are generally fed promptly from wagons which move over the whole yard, fodder being thrown off by the teamster men. Even corn and oats are thrown upon the ground in little heaps; but there is surprisingly little waste for the mule is an enterprising feeder and saves the crumbs.

There is on the ground a hastily constructed blacksmith shop, with ten smiths to shoe the mules. Some of the animals squeal and lash out with their heels when shoeing is attempted. For these a number of racks have been provided, similar to the "frames" used in shoeing oxen in New England.

There will be dire alarm in the Spanish breast when this formidable array of mules move on Cuba. As for the brave conscripts, neither yellow fever nor short rations have any terrors for them. (*New York World*, 5 June 1898, 27.)

600 **Troops Making Military Road in Front of Santiago*
LENGTH: 50 ft.   © Thomas A. Edison, 3 September 1898.
PRODUCER: William Paley.
CAMERA: William Paley.
CAST:
PRODUCTION DATE: Late June to early July 1898.
LOCATION: Santiago, Cuba.

SOURCE:

DESCRIPTION: Here is a detail of the 34th Michigan Regiment engaged in road making. Under command of Captain Dodd of Troop E, 3rd Regular Cavalry, they are road making, that the siege guns may go to the front. The chaparral and thick underbrush has been cleared away, and the soldiers are working with picks and shovels, to make the way passable. (*The Phonoscope*, October 1898, 15.)

SUBJECT: Armies–United States. Spanish-American War. Roads, construction. 34th Michigan Infantry. Captain Dodd.

ARCHIVE: DLC-pp, NR-GE.

CITATIONS: *Edison Films*, March 1900, 10; *Edison Films*, July 1901, 34.

NOTE:

"Bill Paley, the Kinetoscope Man"

Half a dozen New York theatres and dozens of others throughout the country are displaying moving pictures of stirring scenes around the coast of Cuba with the American fleet, and of the Cuban and American soldiers before Santiago. They are wargraphs or cinematographs, or go by some similar name. "Kinetoscope pictures" is what most persons call them, and the man who took the original photographs was known among the naval officers at Key West and the army officers around Santiago and the war correspondents everywhere as "Bill Paley, the Kinetoscope Man."

William Paley, whose work is delighting the amusement-loving public just now, came home from Siboney, Cuba, on the transport Seneca a sick man. He was so ill and his particular form of fever was so suspicious that Health Officer Doty kept him in Quarantine after the other passengers from that much-abused ship had got their liberty. Paley didn't have yellow fever, and it is expected that he will be able soon to be out again. In Twenty-fourth street, from Broadway to Sixth avenue, Paley's is a familiar figure. He has lived and done photographic work in and around that block for several years.

Paley went to Oberammergau and obtained pictures of the Passion Play in his camera, and he has done many other conspicuous things in the photographic line. He is a large man, corpulent and slow-moving, and his work with the navy and the army during the present war has been more difficult than a younger and more wiry man would have found it. He has had to climb in and out of small boats that tipped dangerously under his weight, and the personal discomforts he endured while following the troops in Cuba would have discouraged a less plucky man. With it all he was good-natured that the war correspondents, in whose company he found himself often, liked him immensely and assisted him in his work whenever the opportunity offered.

It is told to me that somewhere in this town there is a vivid and moving wargraph, portraying the Key West correspondents in a mad race for the cable office, after the arrival of a naval dispatch boat with news from the fleet. The men posed for Paley out of good nature, although for some of them that hundred yards dash meant much loss of breath and much perspiration for an hour afterward.

Paley's final experience in his efforts to furnish to the New York public the latest views from life of the scene around Santiago nearly finished him. It was related by Charles E. Hands, the war correspondent of the London Daily Mail, who came back from Cuba with Paley on the Seneca.

"Paley got an army teamster finally to carry his machine and himself from Siboney to Shafter's headquarters," said Mr. Hands. "Then he got another wagon and started for El Caney, where the refugees from Santiago had gathered. It had rained and the road was bad. Half way to El Caney the wagon broke down, and as it was close to nightfall and he had no tent, Paley remained where he was for the night. With darkness came rain, but he stuck to the wagon seat, and in the morning they managed to fix the vehicle up and get into El Caney.

"When he started in to take pictures Paley found that his machine wouldn't work. Whether it was water-soaked or whether it had got broken by the jolting in the rough wagon I don't know, but anyway, it refused to take pictures. Paley got back to Shafter's headquarters that night and crawled under somebody's dog tent. He was pretty well broken up.

"All that night it rained, and he got soaked to the skin again. He had a bad case of fever in the morning. He was helpless, of course, owing to his great bulk. I hustled around and got a wagon that would take us down to Siboney. Bill and his machine gun got on and I rode with them as far as La Guisima, where the trail over the mountains joins. I took the mountain trail on foot, and Bill and the wagon went along the valley road. It rained hard for about six hours, and the wagon got stuck and couldn't go any further. So Paley spent that night, his third, in the rain. When he got into Siboney in the morning he was a wreck. The Seneca was going out in the afternoon, and we

were both lucky enough to get aboard. Paley was wretched all during the trip. He lay out on the deck all day on a cot that somebody got for him, and never changed his position at night. I'm glad he's getting better now."
Mr. Hands is one of the many war correspondents who bought horses in Tampa and then were unable to take them to Cuba, owing to the lack of transportation. A friend asked him where his horse was.
"I don't know, and I don't dare send to Tampa to inquire," he said. "The blooming beast probably has eaten his head off long ago, and his hind heels as well. The livery man will have to keep him for the oats he's been feeding him. But there are others, as you Americans say." Monte Cutler. (*The Phonoscope*, August 1898, 7.)

Paley concluded his efforts to film the Spanish-American War with film no. 600. The following section traces James White's and William Heise's production activities, picking up from entry nos. 577 and 584.

White returned from his Far Eastern tour a sick man, but presumably had begun to recover sometime in June. The mise-en-scène for studio films made after his return were more elaborate.
Heise reworked the gags in two of his previous films, The Telephone *and* The Burglar, *using a set with distinctive wallpaper that would appear in other Edison films. The camera is a greater distance from the mise-en-scène. Was the Black Maria renovated, or did the Kinetograph Department develop new production facilities on its West Orange properties?*

601 *The Burglar / [The Burglar, no. 2]

LENGTH: 50 ft.   © Thomas A. Edison, 18 July 1898.
PRODUCER: William Heise, [James White].
CAMERA: William Heise.
CAST:
PRODUCTION DATE: June to mid-July 1898.
LOCATION: [Black Maria], West Orange, N.J.
SOURCE: *The Burglar* (Edison film no. 579, May 1898); *A Parlor Match* (farce comedy).
DESCRIPTION:
SUBJECT: Burglars. Coal.
ARCHIVE: DLC-pp.
CITATIONS:
NOTE: See relevant documents and commentary under film no. 579, *[The Burglar, no. 1].*

602 *The Telephone / [The Telephone, no. 2]

LENGTH: 50 ft.   © Thomas A. Edison, 18 July 1898.
PRODUCER: William Heise, [James White].
CAMERA: William Heise.
CAST:
PRODUCTION DATE: June to mid-July 1898.
LOCATION: [Black Maria], West Orange, N.J.
SOURCE: *The Telephone* (Edison film no. 580, May 1898).
DESCRIPTION:
SUBJECT: Telephones. Practical jokes.
ARCHIVE: DLC-pp.
CITATIONS:
NOTE:

603 *Fake Beggar

LENGTH: 50 ft.   © Thomas A. Edison, 5 August 1898.
PRODUCER: [James White.]
CAMERA: [William Heise.]
CAST:
PRODUCTION DATE: [July 1898.]
LOCATION: [New York, N.Y.]

SOURCE:

DESCRIPTION: This picture is taken on a crowded street of a great city, and affords a fine perspective view of a long broad avenue. Crowds of people are passing, and in the thick of the throng is seen an apparently legless beggar, propelling himself across the sidewalk with his small hand-crutches. His companion is a genuine cripple, a poor little street arab whose legs are very short indeed. The fake cripple has a sign around his neck "Help the Blind," and his eyes

stare forth a mute, glassy appeal. Kindly passers-by drop an occasional coin in his hat. One coin drops on the sidewalk, and the blind man calmly looks around and reaches for it. At this moment a cop who has been watching him closely, steps up and lays hold of his arm. The fakir sees he is found out and jumps to his feet, disclosing the fact that he has good sound legs deceitfully doubled up under him. After a lively foot race down the street, the policeman catches him and the crowd follows to see the finish. (*The Phonoscope*, November 1898, 14.)

SUBJECT: City and town life–New York. Impersonations. Beggars. Police. Blindness. Fakirs.

ARCHIVE: DLC-pp, NR-GE, CLAc.

CITATIONS: *Edison Films*, March 1900, 36; *Edison Films*, July 1901, 71.

NOTE:

604   *Shooting Captured Insurgents

LENGTH: 50 ft.   © Thomas A. Edison, 5 August 1898.

PRODUCER: [James White.]

CAMERA: [William Heise.]

CAST:

PRODUCTION DATE: [July 1898.]

LOCATION:

SOURCE:

DESCRIPTION: A file of Spanish soldiers approaches guarding some Cuban prisoners, hatless and shoeless. Officer commands "Halt." They place their miserable victims face toward a blank wall and step back four or five paces. The Spanish officer, resplen-

dent in gold lace and buttons, raises his sword. One can imagine his commands by his gestures. "Aim!" "Fire!" and four poor fellows have joined the ranks of martyrs for the cause of Cuba Libre. Their death struggles are painful to witness. One of them dies hard, so the officer helps him into the next world with his sword. (*The Phonoscope*, November 1898, 14.)

SUBJECT: Spanish-American War. Armies–Cuba. Armies–Spain. Spaniards. Cubans. Executions and executioners. Historical re-enactments.

ARCHIVE: DLC-pp.

CITATIONS: *Edison Films*, March 1900, 10; *Edison Films*, July 1901, 34.

NOTE: A staged "re-enactment." Conceivably made by William Paley.

605   *Cuban Ambush

LENGTH: 50 ft.   © Thomas A. Edison, 5 August 1898.

PRODUCER: [James White.]

CAMERA: [William Heise.]

CAST:

PRODUCTION DATE: [July 1898.]

LOCATION:

SOURCE:

DESCRIPTION: Concealed in the upper story of a ruined building on a sugar plantation is a party of Cubans, lying in wait for their hated enemy. A scouting party of Spaniards appears through the thick underbrush, led by an officer. They suspect the presence of an enemy, but evidently not concealed above their heads: for not until the Cubans pour forth a sudden volley are the Spaniards conscious that they are ambushed. One falls, the others drop on knee and fire at random at the upper windows. It is noticeable that the brave Spanish lieutenant moves rapidly close in to the wall, out of range. There is no further shooting, however, as the lifeless forms of the Cubans are still, excepting one, who in his terror jumps from the window, a sheer twenty-foot drop, right into danger instead of out of it. He is quickly dispatched by a shot from one of the Spaniards, aided by a sword thrust by the brave officer. (*The Phonoscope*, November 1898, 14.)

SUBJECT: Spanish-American War. Armies–Cuba. Armies–Spain. Spaniards. Cubans. Battles. Historical re-enactments.

ARCHIVE: DLC-pp.

CITATIONS: *Edison Films*, March 1900, 10; *Edison Films*, July 1901, 34.

NOTE: A staged "re-enactment." Conceivably made by William Paley.

Filmmakers J. Stuart Blackton and Albert E. Smith, whom Thomas A. Edison had sued for patent and copyright infringement on 12 July 1898, signed an agreement with the renowned inventor on August 2nd. This document recognized Edison's motion picture patents and paved the way for the partners to continuing working as licensees affiliated with the Edison Manufacturing Company.

On August 20th, Edison's Kinetograph Department "equipped three parties to secure views" of "The Great Naval Parade in the North River" (i.e. the Hudson River), which celebrated the victory of Admiral Sampson's North Atlantic Squadron over the Spanish fleet. These filmmaking efforts were co-ordinated by James H. White, though his supervisory role was almost certainly very limited. One or two of these "parties" were headed by Blackton and Smith of American Vitagraph. At least one crew consisted of Edison employees, including William Heise. This early example of multi-camera coverage yielded fourteen copyrighted subjects.

606 ***Excursion Boats, Naval Parade**

LENGTH: [50 ft.]   © Thomas A. Edison, 3 September 1898.

PRODUCER: James White.

CAMERA:

CAST:

PRODUCTION DATE: 20 August 1898.

LOCATION: New York Harbor, New York, N.Y.

SOURCE:

DESCRIPTION: At many points along the line of the parade, all the rules of river traffic were practically suspended, and the services of the Police boats were very necessary. This picture shows a tug and a ferryboat backing out of the way of the warships. (*The Phonoscope*, October 1898, 15.)

SUBJECT: Harbors–New York. Parades. Navies–United States. Spanish-American War. Police boats. Boats and boating.

ARCHIVE: DLC-pp.

CITATIONS: "Hours of Triumph for Naval Heros," *New York Herald*, 21 August 1898, 3; "Miles of People Saw the Parade," *New York Herald*, 21 August 1898, 5; "Countless Craft with Gay Crowds," *New York Herald*, 21 August 1898, 6; "Splendid Fleet's

Mighty Triumph" and "Proud March of the Ships of War," *New York World*, 21 August 1898, 1.

NOTE:

607 ***Police Boats Escorting Naval Parade / Policeboats Escorting Naval Parade**

LENGTH: [50 ft.]   © Thomas A. Edison, 3 September 1898.

PRODUCER: James White.

CAMERA:

CAST:

PRODUCTION DATE: 20 August 1898.

LOCATION: New York Harbor, New York, N.Y.

SOURCE:

DESCRIPTION: Shows the two police boats, "Robert A Van Wyck" and "Patrol" heading the great naval parade. They are steaming along at full speed, their propellers churning the water into white swirling eddies as they pass. The picture is taken at quarter of eleven as the procession is approaching the Battery, from the anchorage off Staten Island. (*The Phonoscope*, September 1898, 14.)

SUBJECT: Harbors–New York. Parades. Navies–United States. Police boats. Spanish-American War.

ARCHIVE: DLC-pp.

CITATIONS:

NOTE:

608 ***The Fleet Steaming up the North River / The Fleet Steaming up North River**

LENGTH: 150 ft.   © Thomas A. Edison, 3 September 1898.

PRODUCER: J. Stuart Blackton, Albert E. Smith, James White.

CAMERA: J. Stuart Blackton and/or Albert E. Smith.

CAST:

PRODUCTION DATE: 20 August 1898.

LOCATION: Hudson River, New York, N.Y.

SOURCE:

DESCRIPTION: Affords a magnificent nearby view of the port side of the "Brooklyn," as she slowly forges ahead of the yacht on which our artists were stationed. Every detail is brought out with wonderful clearness. The bright sunshine plays on her grim armor plated side, showing every porthole, 1-pounder, 6-pounder, 5-inch and 8-inch guns. The jackies are lined up along the rails, spotless in holiday white. (*The Phonoscope*, September 1898, 14.)

Shows the "Brooklyn," flying Schley's twin-stared blue flag. Every detail brought out with wonderful clearness. Excursion craft in the distance. Bow of the "Indiana" appears toward end of film. (*Edison Films*, July 1901, 35.)

SUBJECT: Harbors–New York. Parades. Navies–United States. Spanish-American War. Winfield Scott Schley.

ARCHIVE: DLC-pp.

CITATIONS: *Edison Films*, March 1900, 11.

NOTE: The authorship of this film and several others of the Naval Parade can be identified because the pictures were listed on vaudeville programs featuring the Vitagraph, before the films had been copyrighted and offered for sale. And Vitagraph billed these pictures as presented "for the First Time on any stage Graphic Motion Pictures of the Grand Naval Parade."

609 ***Victorious Squadron Firing Salute**

LENGTH: 50 and 150 ft.   © Thomas A. Edison, 3 September 1898.

PRODUCER: James White.
CAMERA:
CAST:
PRODUCTION DATE: 20 August 1898.
LOCATION: Hudson River, New York, N.Y.
SOURCE:

DESCRIPTION: The Flagship "New York" reached Grant's tomb at precisely 11:30, and four seconds after the picture begins, fired the first shot of the national salute of 21 guns. The "Massachusetts" follows example, close behind. As she approaches, the smoke thickens. The "Oregon" now comes into sight. By this time the firing has become general; and as she looms up through the thickening smoke her outlines grow more and more distinct until she finally emerges into full view. The effect is magnificent. One can only wonder how the "men behind the guns" could have aimed so accurately and with such deadly effect in their victorious fight with the Spanish ships. This entire view is without doubt the finest moving picture film that has ever been taken. Not only are the smoke effects superb, but the detail and definition of the picture leave absolutely nothing to be desired. (*The Phonoscope*, September 1898, 14.)

A grand view of the National salute at Grant's tomb. The Flagship "New York" is followed by the "Massachusetts" and "Oregon." The smoke thickens as the firing becomes general. The film is one of the finest ever taken. 150 ft. $22.50.

Flagship "New York," 50 foot strip. "Massachusetts," 50 foot strip. "Oregon," 50 foot strip. (*Edison Films,* March 1900, 12.)

SUBJECT: Harbors–New York. Parades. Navies–United States. Spanish-American War.
ARCHIVE: DLC-pp, NR-GE.
CITATIONS:
NOTE:

610 *Reviewing the "Texas" at Grant's Tomb

LENGTH: 50 ft.   © Thomas A. Edison, 3 September 1898.
PRODUCER: J. Stuart Blackton, Albert E. Smith, James White.
CAMERA: J. Stuart Blackton and/or Albert E. Smith.
CAST:
PRODUCTION DATE: 20 August 1898.
LOCATION: Hudson River, New York, N.Y.
SOURCE:

DESCRIPTION: The background is formed by the commanding heights of Riverside park, on the crest of which Grant's Tomb rears its snow white dome against the sky. The bow of the "Texas" swings into view; and Old Glory seems to wave right through the screen, so close were our artists. (*The Phonoscope*, September 1898, 14.)

SUBJECT: Harbors–New York. Parades. Navies–United States. Spanish-American War. Flags-United States.
ARCHIVE: DLC-pp.
CITATIONS: *Edison Films*, March 1900, 12.
NOTE:

611 *U.S. Cruiser "Brooklyn," Naval Parade

LENGTH: 50 ft.   © Thomas A. Edison, 3 September 1898.
PRODUCER: James White.
CAMERA:
CAST:
PRODUCTION DATE: 20 August 1898.
LOCATION: Hudson River, New York, N.Y.

SOURCE:

DESCRIPTION: Taken after the salute was fired, as she swung around to port to take position for the trip down the Hudson. Several tugs and small yachts are in the foreground, gaily decked with flags and bunting. Excursion crafts of every description are seen in the background, toward the Jersey shore. Admiral Schley's twin-starred flag of blue flies from the main mast together with other small flags, evidently a signal of some kind. (*The Phonoscope,* September 1898, 14.)

SUBJECT: Harbors–New York. Parades. Navies–United States. Spanish-American War. Winfield Scott Schley.

ARCHIVE: DLC-pp.

CITATIONS: *Edison Films,* March 1900, 12.

NOTE:

612 **U.S. Battleship "Oregon"*

LENGTH: 50 and 150 ft.　© Thomas A. Edison, 3 September 1898.

PRODUCER: J. Stuart Blackton, Albert E. Smith, James White.

CAMERA: J. Stuart Blackton and/or Albert E. Smith.

CAST:

PRODUCTION DATE: 20 August 1898.

LOCATION: Hudson River, New York, N.Y.

SOURCE:

DESCRIPTION: Here is a wonderful war vessel that does so much credit to her Pacific coast builders. A 10,000 mile journey without a mishap; and then, without repairs or overhauling of any kind, active and glorious service at Santiago. She dashes by at full speed, preceded and followed by hosts of yachts, tugs, river steamboats and excursion crafts of all kinds. Her commander, the

brave Captain Barker, stands on the bridge with his navigating officer. Strung along on her decks are the crew, in picturesque fashion. (*The Phonoscope,* September 1898, 14.)

SUBJECT: Harbors–New York. Parades. Navies–United States. Spanish-American War. Albert Smith Barker.

ARCHIVE: DLC-pp.

CITATIONS: *Edison Films,* March 1900, 12.

NOTE:

613 **Observation Train Following Parade*

LENGTH: [50 ft.]　© Thomas A. Edison, 3 September 1898.

PRODUCER: James White.

CAMERA:

CAST:

PRODUCTION DATE: 20 August 1898.

LOCATION: Hudson River, New York, N.Y.

SOURCE:

DESCRIPTION: There were two freight trains standing on the tracks between the river and the Riverside Park, and they furnished a perfect impromptu observation train service to the men and boys who clambered up on the cars to get a view of

the parade. They saw the vessels go up and then waited for their return. As the ships came back the engineer of one of the trains started it for the freight yards at Thirty-third Street, and a crowd of about 2,000 was carried along, perched up on the roof of the cars. (*The Phonoscope*, October 1898, 15.)

SUBJECT: Harbors–New York. Parades. Navies–United States. Spanish-American War. Railroads.
ARCHIVE: DLC-pp.
CITATIONS:
NOTE:

---

614 *The "Massachusetts," Naval Parade*

LENGTH: 50 ft.   © Thomas A. Edison, 3 September 1898.
PRODUCER: J. Stuart Blackton, Albert E. Smith, James White.
CAMERA: J. Stuart Blackton and/or Albert E. Smith.
CAST:
PRODUCTION DATE: 20 August 1898.
LOCATION: Hudson River, New York, N.Y.
SOURCE:

DESCRIPTION: This is the only battleship of the seven that looks as if she had been fighting, and even so, the damages probably are very slight. She has a dull, faded, dirty appearance—a "respectably" dirty appearance, as some one said. Along her hull, near the water line, are rusty looking patches. A good clear view is afforded, as the yacht with the operator on board was quite near. (*The Phonoscope*, October 1898, 15.)
SUBJECT: Harbors–New York. Parades. Navies–United States. Spanish-American War.
ARCHIVE: DLC-pp.
CITATIONS: *Edison Films*, March 1900, 12; *Edison Films*, July 1901, 36.
NOTE:

---

615 *Close View of the "Brooklyn," Naval Parade*

LENGTH: 50 ft.   © Thomas A. Edison, 3 September 1898.
PRODUCER: J. Stuart Blackton, Albert E. Smith, James White.
CAMERA: J. Stuart Blackton and/or Albert E. Smith.
CAST:
PRODUCTION DATE: 20 August 1898.
LOCATION: Hudson River, New York, N.Y.
SOURCE:

DESCRIPTION: Here is a picture that presents Schley's flagship at close range, as she steams past on her way back to the anchorage. It is the starboard side of the cruiser. By looking sharply one can see a shot hole on her middle funnel, about a third way up from the deck. (*The Phonoscope*, October 1898, 15.)
SUBJECT: Harbors–New York. Parades. Navies–United States. Spanish-American War. Winfield Scott Schley.
ARCHIVE: DLC-pp.
CITATIONS: *Edison Films*, March 1900, 12; *Edison Films*, July 1901, 36.
NOTE:

---

616 *The "Texas," Naval Parade*

LENGTH: 50 ft.   © Thomas A. Edison, 3 September 1898.
PRODUCER: J. Stuart Blackton, Albert E. Smith, James White.
CAMERA: J. Stuart Blackton and/or Albert E. Smith.

CAST:
PRODUCTION DATE: 20 August 1898.
LOCATION: Hudson River, New York, N.Y.
SOURCE:
DESCRIPTION: An excellent view of the trim lit-
tle "Texas" taken on her way down the
Hudson, after the salute. The background
is the Riverside Park, at about 98th Street.
Church steeple in the distance. (*The Phono-
scope*, October 1898, 15.)
As she dashes by she looks as trim as a
yacht in her fresh coat of paint. Philip's
new Commodore's flag flies aloft. (*Edison
Films*, July 1901, 36.)
SUBJECT: Harbors–New York. Parades. Navies–United States. Spanish-American War.
John W. Phillip.
ARCHIVE: DLC-pp.
CITATIONS: *Edison Films*, July 1901, 36.
NOTE:

617 *The "Glen Island" Accompanying Parade

LENGTH: [50 ft.]   © Thomas A. Edison, 3 September 1898.
PRODUCER: J. Stuart Blackton, Albert E. Smith, James White.
CAMERA: J. Stuart Blackton and/or Albert E. Smith.
CAST:
PRODUCTION DATE: 20 August 1898.
LOCATION: Hudson River, New York, N.Y.
SOURCE:
DESCRIPTION: The Mayor of New York City is
on this boat with the city officials and their
friends, together with the special commit-
tees in charge of the local end of the cele-
bration of welcome. She is decked from
stem to stern with flags and streamers.
(*The Phonoscope*, October 1898, 15.)
SUBJECT: Harbors–New York. Parades.
Navies–United States. Spanish-American
War. Steamships. Robert Anderson Van Wyck.
ARCHIVE: DLC-pp.
CITATIONS:
NOTE:

618 *Admiral Sampson on Board the Flagship

LENGTH: [50 ft.]   © Thomas A. Edison, 3 September 1898.
PRODUCER: J. Stuart Blackton, Albert E. Smith, James White.
CAMERA: J. Stuart Blackton and/or Albert E. Smith.
CAST: William Thomas Sampson.
PRODUCTION DATE: 20 August 1898.
LOCATION: New York Harbor, New York, N.Y.
SOURCE:
DESCRIPTION: After the run down the Hudson
the "New York" lay off Bedloe's Island for a
short time, while the Admiral held a recep-
tion, before proceeding to the anchorage
ground at Staten Island. (*The Phonoscope*,
October 1898, 15.)
SUBJECT: Harbors–New York. Parades.
Navies–United States. Spanish-American
War.

ARCHIVE: DLC-pp.
CITATIONS:
NOTE:

619 ***Statue of Liberty**
LENGTH: [50 ft.]   © Thomas A. Edison, 3 September 1898.
PRODUCER: J. Stuart Blackton, Albert E. Smith, James White.
CAMERA: J. Stuart Blackton and/or Albert E. Smith.
CAST:
PRODUCTION DATE: 20 August 1898.
LOCATION: New York Harbor, New York, N.Y.
SOURCE:

DESCRIPTION: Turning homeward from the fare-well to Sampson, one sees the Statue of Liberty, standing on Bedloe's Island in New York harbor. The statue was a gift to the people of the United States by the people of France. (*The Phonoscope*, October 1898, 15.)
SUBJECT: Harbors–New York. Parades. Navies–United States. Spanish-American War. Monuments. France. William Thomas Sampson.
ARCHIVE: DLC-pp.
CITATIONS:
NOTE:

Aug. 20–5:40 A.M.–Rear Admiral Sampson's fleet sighted off Sandy Hook.
Aug. 20–8 A.M.–The fleet arrived at Tompkinsville.
Aug. 20–10 A.M.–Mayor Van Wyck and committee of Citizens received by Rear Admiral Sampson.
Aug. 20–10:15 A.M.–The fleet started from Tompkinsville in naval review.
Aug. 20–11:30 A.M.–The fleet arrived in the Hudson opposite Grant's Tomb.
Aug. 20–1 P.M.–The return of the fleet to the anchorage ground began.
Aug. 20–3 P.M.–The fleet arrived at Tompkinsville. (*New York World*, 21 August 1898, 1.)

NEW YORK'S WELCOME TO OUR VICTORIOUS NAVY

Sampson and Schley and their hard fighting, straight shooting men came home in six steel ships yesterday morning, and to them was accorded a welcome so magnificent, so patriotic, so inspiring, that naval history finds few spectacles to equal it since men began to fight by sea. The voice of the American people greeting the conquerors of Cervera was as the voice of all England hailing Nelson and the old Victory. The President sent his Cabinet officers to meet them. The Mayor of New York and a committee of distinguished citizens told them of their country's pride and gratitude, and gave them the keys of the city at its gate.

Ship and Shore Cheered Conquering Fleet's Return.

It was a glorious morning when, clothed in their simple suits of battle drab, stripped as for action, scarred by Spanish shells, the embodiment of terrible power, the victorious fleet steamed up the harbor in majestic single column, saluted and saluting, and accompanied by a flotilla of steamboats, yachts, tugs and launches two miles long, densely packed and extending from shore to shore. New York had seen no such spectacle before. Full throated from a million or more of their proud countrymen and countrywomen on two shores rose the chorus of welcome to the returning heroes. The heart of a thankful nation was in the cry. Steadily through the crowded waters ploughed the cruisers and battle ship–seven in all when the Texas joined them–keeping the signaled distance apart, moving at the signalled speed of eight knots, guided by the same sure hands which had made them irresistible.

Saluted at Grant's Tomb.

Thus they moved until they reached the tomb of him who said "Let us have peace," set on a hill, the verdure of which was hidden by a cheering flag waving multitude. Then for the first time the fleet saluted as a whole. The New York set a string of signal flags and steamed on, firing from starboard and port until she moved in a cloud of her own creation.

The mighty Iowa took up the note, then the Indiana, the Brooklyn, the Massachusetts, the Oregon, the Texas–until there was a line of smoke and flame reminding one of the scene off Santiago on the morning of July 3, when Cervera dashed himself against the same impregnable line and lost his ships and all but honor. Heedless of the jostling, shrieking launches, yachts and steamboats which seemed to make evolutions without accident an impossibility the New York turned gracefully about and headed south again, her consorts swinging easily round the circle marked by her wake.

Seven Reasons for Peace.

It was a triumph of seamanship in itself. But seen under these circumstances, with the thunder of batteries ashore, the cheers of a might host, the numberless harbor craft laden with sightseers, it stirred the heart rarely and piled wonder on wonder. Many who saw the war ships as they swept on with flashing guns could not but see in them seven potent reasons why we have peace to-day. Down the course again, with the observation fleet packed closer than ever about them, cheered more widely, still thundered at by field batteries, still making the signalled speed and holding their position as if they were in the open sea, the fighting ships swept back to Governor's Island.... (*New York Herald*, 21 August 1898, 3.)

On Saturday morning August 20, 1898, six grim black battleships of Admiral Sampson's North Atlantic Squadron sailed into New York Harbor; and joined by their sister ship, the "Texas," which had preceded them, sailed in proud and formidable procession up the Hudson, with a characteristic promptness astonishing to New York sightseers, accustomed to hours of delays in parades. Sailed up the Hudson to receive a welcome from the people and to fire a salute of victory in sight of the tomb of the great soldier hero of another war.

We equipped three parties to secure views from all points: The results have been exceedingly gratifying; and we present the following films to the public as our share in the celebration; by means of which we can not only satisfy the curiosity of people living too far distant to be present, but can also stimulate their patriotism, and perpetuate forever the glory of the occasion. (*Edison Films*, March 1900, 11.)

620 ***Merry-Go-Round**

LENGTH: [50 ft.]   © Thomas A. Edison, 3 September 1898.

PRODUCER:

CAMERA:

CAST:

PRODUCTION DATE: [August 1898.]

LOCATION: [New York, N.Y.]

SOURCE:

DESCRIPTION: This picture was taken at a German picnic ground; and is so lifelike that one almost hears the organ that goes with every merry-go-round, grinding out its ear splitting tunes. Flags and lanterns decorate the structure. The children ride around gaily, astride of lions, zebras, camels, elephants, horses, elks and other strange and wonderful animals. (*The Phonoscope*, November 1898, 14.)

SUBJECT: Merry-go-round. Amusement rides. German Americans. Children.

ARCHIVE: DLC-pp.

CITATIONS:

NOTE:

621 ***Farmer Kissing the Lean Girl / Farmer Kissing "The Lean Gal"**

LENGTH: [50 ft.]   © Thomas A. Edison, 3 September 1898.

PRODUCER: James White.

CAMERA: [William Heise.]

CAST: Mr. and Mrs. Byron Spaun.

PRODUCTION DATE: August 1898.

LOCATION: [Black Maria], West Orange, N.J.

SOURCE:

DESCRIPTION: Mr. and Mrs. Byron Spaun excel in their "Farmer and Lean Gal" specialty. He looks every bit of an old hayseed, and she certainly lives up to her name. The old chap is in a museum, and has taken a fancy to the thin "freak." In a secluded corner he proposes to kiss her. She objects—a little— but finally consents. The kiss is of the gimlet order. It is as if his lips were an augur,

and he boring for maple sugar sap in spring time. It's such a rotary brac-and-bit sort of a kiss that it brings down the house every time. (*The Phonoscope*, November 1898, 14.)
SUBJECT: Vaudeville–performances. Farmers. Courtship. Kissing.
ARCHIVE: DLC-pp, CLAc.
CITATIONS:
NOTE:

Mr. and Mrs. Byron Spaun
"The Farmer and the Lean Gal"
Home address: 401 MICHIGAN AVE., Detroit, Mich.
(Advertisement, *New York Clipper*, 28 May 1898, 220.)

As the popularity of war films faded in September 1898, J. Stuart Blackton and Albert E. Smith made a series of short comedies and magic films which appeared as exclusives on their Vitagraph programs. Several months later, the filmmakers turned these negatives over to Edison's Kinetograph Department for distribution, as part of their licensing arrangement.

622 *****The Vanishing Lady**
LENGTH: 50 ft.   © Thomas A. Edison, 16 December 1898.
PRODUCER: J. Stuart Blackton, Albert E. Smith.
CAMERA: J. Stuart Blackton.
CAST: Albert E. Smith (magician).
PRODUCTION DATE: Late August to early September 1898.
LOCATION: Vitagraph's roof-top studio, New York, N.Y.
SOURCE: "The Vanishing Lady" (vaudeville trick), *The Vanishing Lady* (Méliès film, 1896), *The Vanishing Lady* (Biograph film no. 271, July 1897).
DESCRIPTION:
SUBJECT: Magic tricks. Magicians. Women.
ARCHIVE: DLC-pp.

CITATIONS: Proctor's Pleasure Palace, programmes, 12 and 19 September 1898; Proctor's 23rd Street Theatre, programme, 19 September 1898, Harvard Theatre Collection.
NOTE:

623 *****The Burglar on the Roof**
LENGTH: 50 ft.   © Thomas A. Edison, 12 December 1898.
PRODUCER: J. Stuart Blackton, Albert E. Smith.
CAMERA: Albert E. Smith.
CAST: J. Stuart Blackton (burglar), Charles Urban.
PRODUCTION DATE: September 1898.
LOCATION: Vitagraph building's roof top, New York, N.Y.
SOURCE:
DESCRIPTION: He finds a loose skylight, pries it up, and crawls in to investigate. Two women appear upon the scene. One grabs him by the foot and the other belabors him with a broom. (*Edison Films*, March 1900, 37.)
SUBJECT: Tramps. Burglars. Violence.
ARCHIVE: DLC-pp.
CITATIONS: Proctor's Pleasure Palace, programme, 3 October 1898, Harvard Theatre Collection. *Edison Films*, July 1901, 77.
NOTE:

624 *Elopement on Horseback

LENGTH: 50 ft. © Thomas A. Edison, 26 November 1898.

PRODUCER: [J. Stuart Blackton, Albert E. Smith.]

CAMERA:

CAST:

PRODUCTION DATE: [August-October 1898.]

LOCATION:

SOURCE:

DESCRIPTION: The fair one appears at a window, rather scantily clothed. She climbs out, gets upon a horse behind her lover, who kisses her rapturously, and off they go. (*Edison Films*, March 1900, 37.)

SUBJECT: Courtship. Horses. Elopement.

ARCHIVE: DLC-pp.

CITATIONS: *Edison Films*, July 1901, 77.

NOTE:

625 *The Cavalier's Dream

LENGTH: 75 ft. © Thomas A. Edison, 16 December 1898.

PRODUCER: [J. Stuart Blackton, Albert E. Smith.]

CAMERA: [J. Stuart Blackton and/or Albert E. Smith.]

CAST:

PRODUCTION DATE: [September-October 1898.]

LOCATION: [Vitagraph's roof-top studio, New York, N.Y.]

SOURCE:

DESCRIPTION: He sits asleep at a bare table; old witch enters, raps three times, then disappears; cavalier sees table spread for a sumptuous repast. Mephistopheles appears; then the old witch, who suddenly changes to a beautiful young girl. The changes and magical appearances are startling and instantaneous. (*Edison Films*, March 1900, 40.)

SUBJECT: Dreams. Magic. Devil. Witches. French.

ARCHIVE: DLC-pp.

CITATIONS: *New York Clipper*, 11 February 1899, 854.

NOTE:

626 *Little Mischief

LENGTH: 50 ft. © No reg.

PRODUCER: J. Stuart Blackton, Albert E. Smith.

CAMERA: [J. Stuart Blackton and/or Albert E. Smith.]

CAST:

PRODUCTION DATE: [September 1898 to February 1899.]

LOCATION: [Vitagraph's roof-top studio, New York, N.Y.]

SOURCE:

DESCRIPTION: Papa is reading his newspaper and his little girl tickles his neck with a long straw. Thinking it is a fly papa "shoos" away the supposed fly with his hand. The tickling continues now on his ear, and papa waves his newspaper round his head. Not yet content, the little mischief maker continues her fun, and the man loses all patience, and makes such a wild commotion that he loses his balance, and falls over backwards, chair and all.

Sure to make fun for the children, both great and small. (*Edison Films*, March 1900, 37.)

SUBJECT: Child rearing. Accidents. Girls. Newspapers. Practical jokes.

ARCHIVE: DLC.

CITATIONS: *Edison Films*, July 1901, 71-72; *Edison Films,* September 1902, 80.

NOTE: This identification from the Library of Congress seems tentative.

627 Family Troubles

LENGTH: 25 ft.   © No reg.

PRODUCER: [J. Stuart Blackton, Albert E. Smith.]

CAMERA: [Albert E. Smith.]

CAST: [J. Stuart Blackton.]

PRODUCTION DATE: [September 1898 to February 1899.]

LOCATION: [Vitagraph's roof-top studio, New York, N.Y.]

SOURCE:

DESCRIPTION: Mrs. Smith can't make stove burn. Bad draught. Crooked stovepipe. Little Lucy toasts her fingers, shivering and unhappy. Papa Smith comes in. Of course he can fix it! Tries. Tries again. It don't burn. Gets mad and kicks it over. Tableau. (*Edison Films*, March 1900, 37.)

SUBJECT: Children. Family. Accidents.

ARCHIVE:

CITATIONS:

NOTE:

628 Up-to-Date Cakewalk

LENGTH: 75 ft.   © No reg.

PRODUCER: [J. Stuart Blackton, Albert E. Smith.]

CAMERA: [J. Stuart Blackton and/or Albert E. Smith.]

CAST:

PRODUCTION DATE: [September 1898 to February 1899.]

LOCATION: [Vitagraph's roof-top studio, New York, N.Y.]

SOURCE:

DESCRIPTION: On a raised platform sit the Music Committee, with banjo and guitar, furnishing reels and jigs and breakdowns for the coon cake-walkers. The fancy steps and grotesque evolutions of the dancers are novel and amusing. (*Edison Films*, March 1900, 36.)

SUBJECT: Afro-Americans. Dancing. Bands (music).

ARCHIVE:

CITATIONS: *Edison Films*, July 1901, 71; *Edison Films,* September 1902, 80.

NOTE:

629 Race Track Scene

LENGTH: 50 ft.   © No reg.

PRODUCER: [J. Stuart Blackton, Albert E. Smith.]

CAMERA: [J. Stuart Blackton and/or Albert E. Smith.]

CAST:

PRODUCTION DATE: [May-November 1898.]

LOCATION:

SOURCE:

DESCRIPTION: A bunch of twenty horses is shown in a close finish. The bright sunshine makes every detail clear and distinct. Shows also the weighing out. (*Edison Films*, March 1900, 31.)

SUBJECT: Horse racing.

ARCHIVE:

CITATIONS: *Edison Films*, July 1901, 57.

NOTE: These two horse racing films (nos. 629 and 630) entered the Edison catalog in December 1898, well-after the racing season was over and, given the titles and descriptions, well after this specific race had been run. Vitagraph's Blackton and Smith are the likely producers.

630 **Betting Field**
LENGTH: 100 ft.   © No reg.
PRODUCER: [J. Stuart Blackton, Albert E. Smith.]
CAMERA: [J. Stuart Blackton and/or Albert E. Smith.]
CAST:
PRODUCTION DATE: [May-November 1898.]
LOCATION:
SOURCE:
DESCRIPTION: Horses are seen in the distance, coming around the turn. The finish is made in a great cloud of dust. The crowd pours back across the betting field to interview the bookies. (*Edison Films*, March 1900, 31.)
SUBJECT: Horse racing. Gambling.
ARCHIVE:
CITATIONS: *Edison Films*, July 1901, 57.
NOTE:

James White and William Heise continued to use the Black Maria to make films of vaudeville performers, placing them against a simple, typically black background.

631 ***Ella Lola, a la Trilby**
LENGTH: [50 ft.]   © Thomas A. Edison, 7 October 1898.
PRODUCER: James White.
CAMERA: William Heise.
CAST: Ella Lola.
PRODUCTION DATE: September 1898.
LOCATION: Black Maria, West Orange, N.J.
SOURCE:
DESCRIPTION:
SUBJECT: Vaudeville–performances. Dancing.
ARCHIVE: DLC-pp.
CITATIONS:
NOTE: Dancing "a la Trilby" meant dancing barefoot.

632 ***Turkish Dance, Ella Lola**
LENGTH: [50 ft.]   © Thomas A. Edison, 7 October 1898.
PRODUCER: James White.
CAMERA: William Heise.
CAST: Ella Lola.
PRODUCTION DATE: September 1898.
LOCATION: Black Maria, West Orange, N.J.
SOURCE:
DESCRIPTION:
SUBJECT: Vaudeville–performances. Dancing.
ARCHIVE: DLC-pp.
CITATIONS:
NOTE:

633 *Balloon Ascension, Marionettes

LENGTH: [50 ft.]   © Thomas A. Edison, 7 October 1898.
PRODUCER: James White.
CAMERA: William Heise.
CAST:
PRODUCTION DATE: Mid to late September 1898.
LOCATION: Black Maria, West Orange, N.J.
SOURCE:
DESCRIPTION:
SUBJECT: Marionettes. Gray's Royal Marionettes. Waite's Comedy Company. James R. Waite.
ARCHIVE: DLC-pp.
CITATIONS: "Waite's Comedy Co.," *Orange Chronicle*, 17 September 1898, 5.
NOTE:

634 *Dancing Chinaman, Marionettes

LENGTH: [50 ft.]   © Thomas A. Edison, 7 October 1898.
PRODUCER: James White.
CAMERA: William Heise.
CAST:
PRODUCTION DATE: Mid to late September 1898.
LOCATION: Black Maria, West Orange, N.J.
SOURCE:
DESCRIPTION:
SUBJECT: Marionettes. Gray's Royal Marionettes. Waite's Comedy Company. James R. Waite.
ARCHIVE: DLC-pp.
CITATIONS: "Waite's Comedy Co.," *Orange Chronicle*, 17 September 1898, 5.
NOTE:

635 *Skeleton Dance, Marionettes

LENGTH: [50 ft.]   © Thomas A. Edison, 7 October 1898.
PRODUCER: James White.
CAMERA: William Heise.
CAST:
PRODUCTION DATE: Mid to late September 1898.
LOCATION: Black Maria, West Orange, N.J.
SOURCE:
DESCRIPTION:
SUBJECT: Marionettes. Gray's Royal Marionettes. Waite's Comedy Company. James R. Waite.
ARCHIVE: DLC-pp.
CITATIONS: "Waite's Comedy Co.," *Orange Chronicle*, 17 September 1898, 5.
NOTE:

JAMES R. WAITE

Whose claim to the credit of being the pioneer of popular priced travelling entertainment is generally acknowledged, has been before the public for many years as actor and manager. After a varied experience in legitimate roles, and engagements with a number of the leading companies of the day, he left the profession for a time, and when he returned to the fold it was at the helm of his own company. At that time the several organizations touring in the vicinity of Colorado, where he was then living, were, with but few exceptions, meeting with indifferent success, and he decided that the scale of prices then prevailing was mainly responsible for this. Resolving that the company he contemplated organizing should be conducted upon a policy that would obviate this difficulty, he caused the scale of prices to be fixed at an extremely low rate, and afterward made a still further reduction, playing at ten, twenty and thirty cents. These prices have since been maintained and the first Waite Comedy Company, which began its career in 1880, met with phenomenal success, and played entirely in the West up to 1883. Finding that popular prices and capable productions were generously recognized by the public, he widened his field of operations, and an Eastern comedy company and an opera organization eventually bore his name. Fortune treated him most kindly, and all three companies have prospered. Mr. Waite spends much of his leisure time at his residence in Poughkeepsie, N.Y., where ample grounds and a roomy residence, afford him every opportunity to entertain his friends in generous fashion. (*New York Clipper*, 13 January 1900, 954.)

From late August through October 1898, victorious American troops returning from the Spanish-American War paraded through the nation's streets. These celebrations were tempered by reports of numerous deaths and serious illnesses in the American army, even among those soldiers who had never gone to Cuba but remained in U.S. military camps. Poor sanitation and food as well as the hazards of living and fighting in a tropical climate during the summer months had been more effective than the Spanish Army. Perhaps because scenes of the Naval Parade had met the demand, the Edison Manufacturing Company and its licensed cameramen did not shoot any films of returning troops until late September.

636 *Advance Guard, Return of New Jersey Troops**
LENGTH: [50 ft.]   © Thomas A. Edison, 7 October 1898.
PRODUCER: James White.
CAMERA: William Heise.
CAST:
PRODUCTION DATE: 20-30 September 1898.
LOCATION:
SOURCE:
DESCRIPTION:
SUBJECT: Armies–United States. National Guard–
   New Jersey. Parades. Spanish-American War.
ARCHIVE: DLC-pp.
CITATIONS:
NOTE:

637 *Return of 2nd Regiment of New Jersey**
LENGTH: [150 ft.]   © Thomas A. Edison, 7 October 1898.
PRODUCER: James White.
CAMERA: William Heise.
CAST:
PRODUCTION DATE: 20-30 September 1898.
LOCATION:
SOURCE:
DESCRIPTION:
SUBJECT: Armies–United States. National Guard–
   New Jersey. Parades. Spanish-American
   War. Second New Jersey Volunteers.
ARCHIVE: DLC-pp.
CITATIONS:
NOTE:

HALF A REGIMENT ILL.
At Pablo Beach a Second New Jersey Man Describes the Sufferings.
THESE MEN HALF STARVED.
Men Receive Only a Portion of the Governmental Ration–Gives Figures to Prove It.
When the men of the Second New Jersey Volunteers reach home and are mustered out an exhibition of scandalous official neglect and cruelty will be unveiled to their friends. One of the most popular men in the regiment is an athlete known all over the country and up to the outbreak of the war the occupant of a Government position in Hoboken. This man has written a letter to one of his Hoboken friends from Pablo Beach, Fla., dated Sept. 12. After describing the moving of the regiment from Jacksonville to Pablo Beach the letter continues:

"Such a lot of sick, weak, broken-down and dejected-looking men as those of the Second New Jersey Regiment were never seen before. You will not believe it when I tell you the cause is starvation.

Rutherford Company's Fate.

"There is not a company in the regiment with less than twenty sick men on the list, and one company, Company L, of Rutherford, has fifty-eight sick and ten of their men have died.

"When Col. Morse came down here as a representative of the Government he found no less than 325 on the sick list and as many more sick in their tents. Does that look like 2 or 3 per cent? No, but 50 per cent. Why, you can hardly find a man that is well.

"What is at the bottom of all this? Nothing but the insufficient food given the men. Take the bread question, for instance. The Government allows us flour enough for 160 loaves and we get but from 20 to 50 loaves a day. This cannot be due to oversight, but to bold and outrageous robbery. Coffee, meat and potatoes are short in the same proportion.

Hopes to Use His Testimony.

"I have a detailed account before me of what we are allowed by the Government and exactly what we have received since July 1, and hope some day to be able to use it as evidence against those who are responsible for our rations."

The writer describes the number of vain protests lodged by the men with their superior officers on the food question, also of a vote taken in the regiment on the question of home or Cuba, with the result that 95 per cent voted for home. (*New York World*, 19 September 1898, 2.)

---

638 *Return of Troop C, Brooklyn

LENGTH: 50 ft.   © Thomas A. Edison, 12 October 1898.

PRODUCER: [James White.]

CAMERA: [William Heise.]

CAST:

PRODUCTION DATE: 1 October 1898.

LOCATION: Prospect Park Plaza, Brooklyn, N.Y.

SOURCE:

DESCRIPTION: The finest cavalry picture we have. They present a grand appearance as they approach 16 abreast, with drawn sabers. The background shows the Plaza Circle, Prospect Park. (*Edison Films*, March 1900, 11.)

SUBJECT: Armies–United States. Cavalry. Parades. Spanish-American War.

ARCHIVE: DLC-pp.

CITATIONS: "Troop C Outdoors," *New York Herald*, 1 June 1896, 3; "Troop C Ready. To Fight Now," *New York World*, 24 April 1898, Brooklyn Supplement; "Troops A and C Break Camp To-day," *New York World*, 22 May 1898, 8; "Ovation for the Gallant Troopers Bound for War," *New York World*, 23 May 1898, 4; "N.Y. Troops in Camp Alger," *New York World*, 24 May 1898, 4; "Brave Fighting Men Parade and Are Reviewed by Thousands of Proud People of Brooklyn," *New York World,* 2 October 1898, 14. *Edison Films,* July 1901, 35.

NOTE:

---

639 *Parade of Marines, U.S. Cruiser "Brooklyn"

LENGTH: 150 ft.   © Thomas A. Edison, 12 October 1898.

PRODUCER: [James White.]

CAMERA: [William Heise.]

CAST:

PRODUCTION DATE: 1 October 1898.

LOCATION: Prospect Park Plaza, Brooklyn, N.Y.

SOURCE:

DESCRIPTION: First comes the famous Marine Band of the "Brooklyn," with the mascot goat alongside of the brass drum. The 300 marines follow in rapid marching order, a sixteen file front in each company. Fine looking men and excellent marching. (*Edison Films*, March 1900, 11.)

SUBJECT: Parades. Marines–United States Spanish-American War. Mascots.
ARCHIVE: DLC-pp.
CITATIONS: "Brave Fighting Men Parade and Are Reviewed by Thousands of Proud People of Brooklyn," *New York World,* 2 October 1898, 14. *Edison Films,* July 1901, 35.
NOTE:

Great Martial Day.
Parade of Brooklyn Troops a Magnificent Spectacle.
REVIEW AT THE PLAZA.
The Home Coming Soldiers, Escorted by the Local Commands That Were Kept at Home, Get a Fine Reception From the Citizens of the Borough, Who Turn Out by Thousands Along the Line of March and Mass in Hordes About the Reviewing Stand—How the Various Regiments Appeared as They Marched in Line—Scenes and Incidents of a Big Military Pageant. The Starting of the Parade and Its Progress Along the Route.

Yesterday's parade of the returning soldiers of Brooklyn borough, escorted by the commands left at home, and the scene attending it, will always be remembered by those who were lucky enough to get a place to stand overlooking the Plaza. The greeting the soldiers received was a warm one, but it was not of the soul stirring, blood tingling character that [compares to] the reception of the soldiers when they arrived from the front or Southern camps. There were cheers, but not of the hysterical order, and women did not weep as they waved their flags, nor did men hug each other in the wild excitement of a month ago when the war craze was at its height.

Yet from a picturesque standpoint nothing more beautiful could have been imagined than the marching, the countermarching, the massing and the maneuvers of those brave soldiers in the plaza. From a patriotic view nothing could have been more inspiring than the old war flags in tatters and shreds, endeared with a new significance, or rather a renewed significance, by the events of the recent past; the heavy campaign uniforms and accoutrements of the young soldiers and the splendid appearance all the troops and sailors made.

The men were not dirty, bewhiskered and weary. They were bright, light-footed and light-hearted and marched with quick steps and admirable precision and the crowds applauded them with hand clapping and now and then with a real, good, old fashioned cheer. Except for the momentary outbursts for Troop C, for the Fourteenth, the remnant of the Thirteenth, "Russell's Tigers," and a rousing cheer for the Brooklyn boys of the Seventy-first Regiment, as well as a burst of enthusiasm over the Second Naval Battalion, the brave boys of the Sylvia, the applause was rather for excellent marching than for the fact that a war has just been concluded and that many of those men have still a chance to see duty, because of that war, in foreign lands. Yet, with all that, the soldier boys have no reason to complain, for what it lacked in enthusiasm the crowd made up in numbers and the committee has every reason to be proud of one of the most magnificent processions and receptions that has ever been arranged in this community or will ever be seen again, probably, in this generation.

Vast Crowd at the Plaza.
While all Brooklyn was decorated in honor of the event and every street had its picturesque point of interest and each citizen seemed to be striving to add to the general effect, the great place of interest was, of course, the plaza; and it was there the greater portion of the crowd gathered. The people began to arrive hours before the parade was formed miles away at the fountain on Bedford avenue. They started in to worry the police at a little after 11 o'clock, and by 12 o'clock they threatened to take possession of the whole plaza and monopolize the seats set out for the German singing societies. Finally the squads from the different police precincts arrived in force and drove the multitudes back to behind the ropes that surrounded the plaza. Then the crowd took to the little parks and climbed the trees, sat on fences, spread out over the hills, covered every grass plot and simply transformed the entire surrounding scenery into one vast, good natured, hustling mass of humanity. Every tree that had a decent sized limb or two swayed with animated bunches of them that were occasionally plucked by the police, but only grew in greater numbers the next moment.

The crowd was irrepressible. It broke through the lines and encroached on forbidden territory every time the police left any spot unprotected. Then it would good naturedly be swept back again, only to jam itself into a smaller compass and a merrier one. It grew and grew until the new arrivals were forced to be content with positions on the side streets and only half a chance to see what was going on and still it grew. Deputy Chief Mackellar walked up and down the long lines of police and encouraged them with compliments and suggestions and smiled at their efforts to keep the crowds back without being too harsh. In fact, the excellent management of the police was one of the features of a great show....

Warm Reception for Troop C.
And now the crowd leaped to its feet, flags began to wave excitedly in the air, while cheer after cheer rolled along from one end of the plaza to the other. With these cheers came the cry, "Troop C." "Here come the Porto Rico boys." Men jumped on their seats and women clung to them, while every one yelled just as loud as he or she could.

Captain Clayton smiled wearily and tried to look unconcerned. He was pale and showed the effects of his illness.

But this only added to the effect and stirred the crowds to greater efforts. As for the gallant troopers themselves, they were fitted up for just that ovation and wore broad grins and dirty shirts with sleeves rolled up to the elbow, everything about their costumes looking businesslike and almost gory. They had no reason to complain of the apathy of the crowd....

Marines in Fine Form.

Prior to this, while the scene was pleasing from a spectacular standpoint, there was nothing in the parade but what the ordinary citizen has seen and is in the habit of seeing from time to time. But when the next section of the procession came up it proved something new in the way of military display. The marching of the United States Marine Corps at this point surpassed anything that had been seen in the previous part of the procession. They were about 400 strong and the manner in which they kept step and alignment evoked no end of applause. (*Brooklyn Eagle*, 2 October 1898, 1 and 5.)

William Heise left Edison's employ in October 1898. His replacements as cameraman are unclear, but possible candidates include Robert K. Bonine, Alfred C. Abadie, Charles Kayser, Heise's son Theodore, and Charles Webster (hired in 1899).

640 *The Burglar in the Bed Chamber
LENGTH: 50 ft.   © Thomas A. Edison, 16 December 1898.
PRODUCER: James White.
CAMERA:
CAST:
PRODUCTION DATE: Mid-October to early December 1898.
LOCATION: [Black Maria], West Orange, N.Y.
SOURCE:
DESCRIPTION:
SUBJECT: Tramps. Burglars. Police.
ARCHIVE: DLC-pp.
CITATIONS:
NOTE:

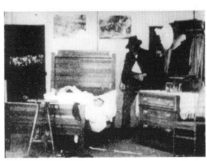

641 *The Tramp in the Kitchen
LENGTH: [50 ft.]   © Thomas A. Edison, 26 November 1898.
PRODUCER: James White.
CAMERA:
CAST:
PRODUCTION DATE: November 1898.
LOCATION: [Black Maria], West Orange, N.J.
SOURCE:
DESCRIPTION: He gathers all the movable articles on the table as he eats. He also tries to kiss the cook. She grabs a double handful of dough from a pan, and plasters it all over his face. (*Edison Films*, March 1900, 37.)
SUBJECT: Tramps. Kitchens. Food. Sexual harassment. Punishment. Kissing.
ARCHIVE: DLC-pp.
CITATIONS:
NOTE: Same wallpaper as *The Burglar [no. 2]* (film no. 601), *The Telephone, [no. 2]* (film no. 602), and *Farmer Kissing the Lean Girl* (film no. 621).

642 *The Cop and the Nurse Girl
LENGTH: 50 ft.   © Thomas A. Edison, 12 December 1898.
PRODUCER:
CAMERA:
CAST:
PRODUCTION DATE: [October-November 1898.]
LOCATION:
SOURCE:

DESCRIPTION: They have a little flirtation, finally kissing each other. While this is going on a jealous rival creeps up and pushes the baby carriage down the hill right into the water. (*Edison Films*, March 1900, 37.)

SUBJECT: Police. Nannies. Courtship. Kissing. Jealousy.

ARCHIVE: DLC-pp.

CITATIONS:

NOTE: Possibly made by Vitagraph's Blackton and Smith.

643 *Sleighing Scene / Sleigh Scene

LENGTH: 50 ft.   © Thomas A. Edison, 16 December 1898.

PRODUCER: [James White?]

CAMERA:

CAST:

PRODUCTION DATE: 28-29 November 1898.

LOCATION: Central Park, New York, N.Y.

SOURCE:

DESCRIPTION: A view taken on the West Side drive in Central Park. Shows a continuous stream of handsome rigs and turnabouts passing in both directions. Pedestrians watch the gay carnival. (*Edison Films*, March 1900, 48.)

SUBJECT: Sleighs and sledges. City and town life–New York.

ARCHIVE: DLC-pp.

CITATIONS:

NOTE: Possibly made by Vitagraph's Blackton and Smith.

By the beginning of 1899 Thomas A. Edison had come to rely heavily on licensed came-ramen and their exhibition services for his motion picture business—a group that was to include William Paley, J. Stuart Blackton and Albert E. Smith, and Thomas Crahan. During this year these affiliates also achieved a new level of prosperity and stability. In the second half of 1899, Blackton and Smith's American Vitagraph Company and William Paley's Kalatechnoscope exhibition service were hired on a regu-lar, open-ended basis by first-class vaudeville houses—by Tony Pastor's and the Proctor circuit respectively. The newly formed, Edison-affiliated Kinetograph Company, which was headed by Percival Waters, established a similar relationship—exhibiting at Huber's 14th Street Museum.

These venues required a steady output of new films, which bolstered and regularized production, at least to some degree. Many of these pictures were eventually offered for sale by the Edison Manufacturing Company, which also copyrighted them in the inventor's name. Yet licensees typically made films for purposes of vaudeville exhibition rather than for sale through the Edison organization. Because sales were often an after-thought, many films were of marginal commercial value by the time Edison's Kinetograph Department could have advertised them in the trades. Licensees were able to retain considerable latitude in their operations, even as they benefited indirectly by being under the umbrella of Edison's sponsorship.

By 1899—even as Vitagraph and other concerns had open-air, roof-top studios with considerable room for actors and sets—the Black Maria studio had become a largely outmoded facility. James White, head of the Kinetograph Department, and other Edison personnel shot at least some of their films, such as Love and War *(no. 724) and* The Astor Tramp *(no. 725), outdoors and on make-shift stages.*

Because the relationship between licensee and licensor offered benefits which were often intangible, neither side was very happy with the arrangement and each tried to improve its situation in relation to the other. Conflict was perhaps inevitable. Like the local populations in the United States' new colonies, the licensed filmmakers worked for the dominant power—Edison—but remained restless, testing the will of the domi-nant force and waiting for an opportunity to rebel.

The new year began with an Edison cameraman filming the transfer of governmental authority in Havana, Cuba, from Spanish to American forces.

644 Spaniards Evacuating / Spanish Evacuating a Fort

LENGTH: 50 ft.   © No reg.

PRODUCER: [James White?]

CAMERA:

CAST:

PRODUCTION DATE: 1 January 1899.

LOCATION: Havana, Cuba.

SOURCE:

DESCRIPTION: In the background of this picture are the grim walls of Morro. Down the steep hill come the Spaniards, horsemen, soldiers and mules. As the procession zig-zags in and out on the narrow trail, it presents a very picturesque scene. The men look dogged and dejected. The mules carry all kinds of supplies; personal baggage, camp utensils, cannon, ammunition, cannon wheels, and all the paraphernalia of an army. (*The Phonoscope*, January 1899, 15.)

SUBJECT: Spanish-American War. Fortresses. Armies–Spain. Military occupation. Mules. Transportation, military.

ARCHIVE:

CITATIONS: *New York Clipper*, 11 February 1899, 854; *Edison Films*, March 1900, 9.
NOTE:

645 ***General Lee's Procession, Havana**
LENGTH: 100 ft.   © Thomas A. Edison, 20 January 1899.
PRODUCER: [James White?]
CAMERA:
CAST: Fitzhugh Lee.
PRODUCTION DATE: 1 January 1899.
LOCATION: Havana, Cuba.
SOURCE:

DESCRIPTION: A magnificent view of the Prado, from the balcony of the United States Club. The procession is headed by a troop of horsemen. Prominent among them is General Lee. Then come the soldiers, file after file and company after company; filling the broad avenue from curb to curb and as far as the eye can reach with marching men. It is the Seventh Army Corps. Great crowds of people fill the sidewalks: and through the trees that line the promenade in the middle of the Prado, are seen carriages and vehicles following the parade. The crowning event of the Spanish-American war! The great procession on Evacuation Day. (*The Phonoscope*, January 1899, 15.)
SUBJECT: Spanish-American War. Armies–United States. Military occupation.
ARCHIVE: DLC-pp.
CITATIONS: *New York Clipper*, 11 February 1899, 854; *Edison Films*, March 1900, 9.
NOTE:

646 ***Troops at Evacuation of Havana / U.S. Troops at Evacuation of Havana**
LENGTH: 150 ft.   © Thomas A. Edison, 20 January 1899.
PRODUCER: [James White?]
CAMERA:
CAST:
PRODUCTION DATE: 1 January 1899.
LOCATION: Havana, Cuba.
SOURCE:

DESCRIPTION: The picture is taken at the end of the Prado, Havana's famous boulevard. The troops are turning in from a side street, where stands a triumphal arch erected by the Cubans, but which Gen. Brooke, the Military Governor of Cuba, would not permit to be finished, as he allowed no demonstrations of any kind. The soldiers are the First Texas troops. The streets are crowded with people. Many typical Cubans are seen lounging in the foreground, with here and there a Spaniard, if one may judge by sour looks and solemn demeanor. The buildings are all low stone structures, with heavy barred windows, from which are displayed small Cuban flags. An excellent picture of life in Havana, New Year Day, 1899. (*The Phonoscope*, January 1899, 15.)
SUBJECT: Spanish-American War. Armies–United States. Military occupation. Cubans. Flags–Cuba. First Texas Infantry. John Rutter Brooke.
ARCHIVE: DLC-pp.
CITATIONS: *New York Clipper*, 11 February 1899, 854; *Edison Films*, March 1900, 9.
NOTE:

IMPRESSIVE CEREMONIES OF SURRENDER
Great Historic Act of the Transfer of the Sovereignty of Cuba Takes Place in the Palace at Havana.
SPAIN'S FLAG TAKEN DOWN AHEAD OF TIME.
Spaniards Attempt to Avoid Humiliation by Secretly Removing It from Its Place.
HAVANA'S CHEERS FOR LEE.
Great Ovation for the General During the Parade of the Seventh Army Corp.
BIG FLAG OVER THE MAINE.
Cuban Generals Witnessed the Surrender, but Cuban Citizens are Still Surly.

[FROM THE HERALD'S SPECIAL CORRESPONDENT.]

HAVANA, Cuba, Sunday—Spain's flag did not fall from above the Captain General's palace at noon to-day, for the very good reason that there was no flag there to fall. Up to the final moment of the surrender of sovereignty the representatives of the Spanish government pursued the same petty policy that caused the loss of the island to them. Indeed, in conduct and attitude to-day they appeared as small in comparison with the American officials as did the Spanish troops when compared physically with the army of occupation.

It is hardly too much to say they ran away from final humiliation. Captain General Castellanos failing to make good his word that he would meet the moment with fortitude—more, would add honor to Spanish glory.

After the general programme of surrender had been agreed to the Spaniards in effect at least, broke all their promises. At ten o'clock a Spanish officer lowered the crimson and gold flag that floated over the palace and dis- appeared with it. As noon approached it was learned that no other flag had been provided, and when Major Butler protested, he was met with shrugs that meant everything or nothing.

Then as the Spanish and American officers gathered in the reception room of the palace for the final ceremonies it was seen that while the Americans were in full dress uniforms the Spanish wore fatigue uniforms without side arms. However, they suffered in comparison for this lack of courtesy. The Americans, physical giants anyway, led by Brooke, who towered over Castellanos as an oak over a weeping willow, had their stature increased by their toggery. Had it not been for their discourteous conduct the Spaniards would have had general sympathy instead of what approached contempt.

After the ceremony General Castellanos, instead of bidding his friends goodby, led an immediate and tearful pro- cession to the water front, where he took a launch for the steamer Ribot, vowing he would never again set foot on Cuban soil.

An Impressive Ceremony.

In spite of all these incidents the ceremony was impressive and one never to be forgotten by those who saw it. A cordon of United States troops of the Tenth Infantry kept all without passes two blocks from the palace, in front of which six companies were massed. Drawn along directly in front of the palace and facing the American soldiers were two companies of the Leon battalion, with Colonel Raffael Salamanca in command. Just at half-past eleven o'clock Major Generals Wade and Butler, with their staffs, rode down Obispo street, and as they wheeled into the palace plaza the Eighth infantry band, with Jacob Haest, who is six feet and six inches tall, as drum major, struck up the Royal March of Cadiz, in which the Spanish bugle corps joined. Next to arrive were Major Generals Brooke and Ludlow and staffs in carriages. As they stepped to the street the "Stars and Stripes Forever" was played. Next to arrive were Generals Chaffee, Humphrey, Davis and Keifer, who were honored with a fanfare from the Spanish trumpeters.

Perhaps the most dramatic incident of the morning and of more moment was the arrival of the Cuban Generals Rodriguez, Menocal, Vidal, Lacret, Cardenas, Agramonte, Modarso, Valiente and José Gomez. The Americans had been saluted by the Spanish officers as they arrived and greeted by Spanish trumpets. The Cubans received no salute. No blare of trumpets announced their appearance. From the Americans, however, they received every cour- tesy, and the Second Illinois regiment band played in their honor a medley which sounded much like the Cuban national hymn.

Last to arrive was Major General Fitzhugh Lee, with his staff and guard, making a most imposing appearance as they encircled the palace.

By this time it was approaching the hour of noon. General Brooke had sent word to Major Butler not to insist upon having the Spanish flag raised. Generals Brooke and Wade led the procession up the wide but broken marble steps running from the central court of the palace to the reception room on the second floor. Following them were Generals Butler, Lee, Ludlow, Humphrey, Chaffee, Davis and Keifer and then the staff officers and the invited guests.

Castellanos Not Cordial.

General Castellanos advanced and shook hands coldly with Generals Brooke and Wade. The Spaniards were gath- ered in small groups at the south end of the room. General Castellanos being supported by his two sons and aids, and Colonels Girauta, Benitez and Galvez, with a few others of lesser rank. The Americans made an imposing group at the north of the room.

After their positions had been taken General Lacret marched into the room with his associates of the insurgent army. They were given a position of advantage at right angles to the others and half facing them.

Behind the American generals stood Acting British Consul Jerome, who has represented the United States in Havana. With the Spaniards stood French Consul Martin. He was the only one in the group not in full dress uniform. It was noted as places were taken that the Marquis de Montero, a member of the Spanish Evacuation Commission, was absent.

Promptly as the big clock in the palace struck the first note of the twelfth hour came the thunder of cannon from Cabana across the harbor. Three distinct echoes followed, so that the second gun sounded before the first had ceased to reverberate. A Spanish bugle sounded a note in the courtway below, and Captain General Castellanos, pale to sallowness, advanced, meeting General Wade in the centre of the room.

The Formal Surrender.

There was a moment of hushed expectancy as all listened for the strangest words ever pronounced within those grim wall that had known Spanish power and glory and were now to know Spanish humiliation. While his conduct had been petty for a man in his position, there is no doubt that General Castellanos felt deeply. For a moment he was absolutely unable to proceed. Tears tolled down his stern old face, and when he spoke his voice was broken with emotion. He spoke in Spanish, and beautifully.

At the conclusion of his speech, Captain Hart, attached to the American Commission, advanced and, taking from General Castellanos a roll of manuscript, translated that which the Spanish Captain General had just said. Captain Hart is almost as large a man as General Brooke, and he presented a heroic figure acting as the instrument through which the transfer of sovereignty was made. He was pale, too, but his voice was unbroken, and as he read every one within the room heard his words.

At the conclusion of Captain Hart's reading, General Wade turned to General Brooke and in a dignified manner announced as briefly as possible that the command of the American forces in Cuba henceforward rested with him. General Brooke spoke feelingly, Captain Hart translating, accepting the responsibility and expressing the goodwill of the American government and the people for Spain.

Raising of the Flag.

In the meantime a signal had been given and Major Butler raised Old Glory over the Palace, which ceased at that moment to represent Spanish power and oppression. As the Stars and Stripes floated in the breeze two bands stationed in the plaza played the "Star Spangled Banner," while the troops presented arms in salute. From thousands of throats a song of welcome came, and whether it was heartfelt, or not, which the future only can tell, it was certainly long and loud.

Thunders of salutes from the harbor still continued to roll over the city, and from every available staff the American flag was unfolded to receive the plaudits of the people who during the morning had remained within doors, but who were now pouring into the streets literally in thousands.

General Castellanos had informed the Americans that he would be happy to receive any one who might come to pay his respects, but at the last moment his heart failed him. As the simple ceremonies closed the officers fell to the right and left, opening a passage to the throne room, along which Castellanos and his aids passed. Immediately strapping on their side arms, they filed solemnly down the stairs to the plaza, which they crossed accompanied by General Clous and Captain Hart, to the harbor front, where they took launches for the steamship Ribot, which later took General Castellanos to Matanzas.

As they departed the American troops all stood at attention. No voice was raised in exultation, the grief of the conquered being respected. As the party approached the water front a woman appeared upon the balcony of a building, shook out the Spanish flag, and in shrill tones cried "Viva España."

Tearful Farewell to Havana.

General Castellanos and his aides halted, saluted their flag and with tear broken voices gave three feeble "Vivas." As they reached their launch they were all sobbing as though broken hearted. General Castellanos last words after bidding goodby to General Clous were that he would never set foot on Cuban soil but should live while at Matanzas and Clenguegos on board the Ribot.

At the harbor front marines from the cruiser Brooklyn formed a guard of honor for the Castellanos party, escorting them through thousands who had gathered to bid them goodbye. The marines also accompanied the Spaniards in a second launch to the Ribot.

After the withdrawal of the Spanish officials General Lacret made a brief speech, in which he pledged the loyalty of the Cuban troops and people in giving every assistance to the American forces in establishing in Cuba a free and independent government. General Brooke responded, evading the delicate reference to Cuban independence.

"I have been sent by my government," he said, "to establish in Cuba that order which has been unknown in the island for years. To do this it is necessary that I should have your support. In you I place the greatest trust. From you I expect extraordinary assistance. From the people I expect co-operation."

As the Cuban generals withdrew representatives of the Ayuntamiento were presented to General Brooke, who signified the desire that they should act in full accord with the American plans as made public by him. The faculty of the university appeared in full gowns, and pledged their heartfelt support to the new order of affairs. General

Brooke thanked them and expressed a desire that their work should proceed without interruption. The most spectacular incident within the palace was when the bombaras, Havana's firemen, dressed in full uniform, crowded into the reception room unexpectedly and gave three rousing cheers for "Los Americanos." They captured General Brooke's heart, and the genial old General shook hands all around with them.

A hurried inspection of the palace was made, showing that the Spaniards before their departure had stripped the rooms of everything save a broken lot of furniture. The pictures had been stripped from the walls with the exception of a portrait of Spain's boy King, which still graces the wall of the throne room. Early in the afternoon Captain Mott placed a guard about the palace, closing it to the public. The old building will be completely renovated before it is again occupied.

The people of Havana were up early on this last day of Spanish control. The air was charged with suspense. The detailed programme of the day's ceremonies was known to every inhabitant, but everywhere was the nervous fear that something unexpected and discreditable might occur. There is no denying Cuban disaffection. Where five days ago the city was one flash of colors, with flags and bunting everywhere, to-day to display a Cuban flag is to announce one's self opposed to Cuban independence.

In all quarters where Cuban sentiment is strong flags have disappeared. In the business portion decorations are maintained, but that is because a majority of the businessmen of Havana are Spaniards, which means they are annexationists. Had a permit been given for an insurgent parade Havana would have been filled with rejoicing people proclaiming the greatness of the United States. (*New York Herald*, 2 January 1899, 3-4.)

OVATION TO GENERAL LEE.
Tremendous Cheers for Him and His Troops During a Parade in Havana.
[FROM THE HERALD'S SPECIAL CORRESPONDENT.]

HAVANA, Cuba, Sunday–General Fitzhugh Lee reaped the honors of the American army during the re-view to-day. He was received as he rode at the head of the Seventh Army Corps with an enthusiasm which may have reminded him of his reception when he rode down Pennsylvania avenue, in Washington, as grand marshal of Grover Cleveland's inauguration parade in 1885.

The review of American troops proved a good idea. The people did not take it as a menace. They were pleased with the soldiers, though curiosity had something to do with their pleasure. Havana within the last three years has seen 300,000 Spanish soldiers march through the streets. It was never impressed with them as it was this afternoon with a few thousand troops of the United States marching up the Prado and out through Cerro to their camp.

Immediately after the conclusion of the ceremonies at the palace General Lee rode with his staff, to the Punta, where the regiments were massed. The parade was at once taken up. General Lee was mounted on a splendid iron grey charger. All the members of his staff were well mounted. Their appearance at the head of the troops caused great enthusiasm. All along the route the people cried "Long live Lee!" and "Long live the American troops." They also showered the commanding general with flowers, which were thrown from balconies by fair hands. General J. Warren Kiefer and his staff and Colonel Wheaton and his staff rode at the head of their divisions.

Opposite Central Park and in front of the Hotel Inglaterra General Lee halted while his troops passed in review before Generals Brooke, Wade, Ludlow and Chaffee. This was the order of the parade:–

> Second Louisiana Regiment
> First Texas Regiment
> Fourth Virginia Regiment
> Forty Ninth Iowa Regiment
> Sixth Missouri Regiment
> First North Carolina Regiment
> Second Illinois Regiment
> 161st Indiana Regiment

Captain Sigsbee and other naval commanders stood beside the generals of the army. National airs, which were played by the regimental bands, seemed to please the people greatly. Some laxness of discipline was apparent. Ambulances and water wagons were profusely decorated with both American and Cuban flags. Some of them had more Cuban banners than American ensigns. The last company of the 161st Indiana regiment was carrying small Cuban flags. This pleased the people greatly. Their enthusiasm was dampened when the Indiana company was reprimanded for the violation of army regulations and compelled to remove the flags.

The review as a whole had a good effect in giving people an opportunity to see the troops and receive them as friends. It was an incident and not a feature of the day, and was meant for nothing more. After the parade was ended a dozen or more insurgent officers rode through the city. They were in uniform, but did not have their side arms. They were everywhere received with enthusiasm. (*New York Herald*, 2 January 1899, 4.)

American Vitagraph submitted a group of film negatives to Edison's Kinetograph Department, which copyrighted and distributed them.

647 *****Raising Old Glory Over Morro Castle**
LENGTH: [50 ft.]   © Thomas A. Edison, 4 February 1899.
PRODUCER: J. Stuart Blackton, Albert E. Smith.
CAMERA: J. Stuart Blackton and/or Albert E. Smith.
CAST:
PRODUCTION DATE: Ca. 2 January 1899.
LOCATION: Vitagraph's roof top studio, New York, N.Y.
SOURCE:
DESCRIPTION: Down goes the Spanish flag, and up floats the Stars and Stripes. Down falls the symbol of tyranny and oppression that has ruled in the new world for four hundred years, and up goes the Banner of Freedom. In the distance are the turrets and battlements of Morro, the last foothold of Spain in America. (*The Phonoscope*, January 1899, 15.)
SUBJECT: Spanish-American War. Flags— United States. Military occupation.
ARCHIVE: DLC-pp.
CITATIONS:
NOTE:

648 *****Willie's First Smoke**
LENGTH: [50 ft.]   © Thomas A. Edison, 4 February 1899.
PRODUCER: J. Stuart Blackton, Albert E. Smith.
CAMERA: J. Stuart Blackton and/or Albert E. Smith.
CAST:
PRODUCTION DATE: [January 1899?]
LOCATION: Vitagraph building's roof top, New York, N.Y.
SOURCE:
DESCRIPTION:
SUBJECT: Boys. Cigarettes.
ARCHIVE: DLC-pp.
CITATIONS:
NOTE:

649 *****Panoramic View of Brooklyn Bridge / Brooklyn to New York via the Bridge / From Brooklyn to New York over the Bridge**
LENGTH: 150 and 300 ft.   © Thomas A. Edison, 4 February 1899.
PRODUCER: [J. Stuart Blackton, Albert E. Smith.]
CAMERA: [J. Stuart Blackton and/or Albert E. Smith.]
CAST:
PRODUCTION DATE: [January 1899?]
LOCATION: Brooklyn Bridge, New York, N.Y.
SOURCE:
DESCRIPTION: Taken from moving cable car leaving Brooklyn train yard, crossing entire span and arriving at New York terminus in City Hall station. (Advertisement, American Vitagraph Company, *New York Clipper,* 13 May 1899, 217.)
SUBJECT: Bridges. Railroads.
ARCHIVE: DLC-pp.
CITATIONS:
NOTE: Given that the two other films copyrighted by Thomas Edison on 4 February

1899 were made by Blackton and Smith and that films by licensees were often copyrighted in batches, it seems very likely that this film was also made by the Vitagraph producers.

650 *Astor Battery on Parade*

LENGTH: [50 ft.]   © Thomas A. Edison, 27 January 1899.
PRODUCER: J. Stuart Blackton, Albert E. Smith.
CAMERA: J. Stuart Blackton and/or Albert E. Smith.
CAST:
PRODUCTION DATE: 23 January 1899.
LOCATION: Union Square, New York, N.Y.
SOURCE:
DESCRIPTION: As they appeared in New York on Saturday, January 21 [sic], 1899, on their return from active service in the Philippines. The picture is taken as they cross Broadway, Union Square, north. First come the mounted police, proud and prancing, then the band, then the famous Astor Battery, marching twenty-four abreast. As the second file approaches, the order is given to "change arms" and the rifles shift from right to left shoulder. The men march well, with rapid gait, and present a fine spectacle, dressed in their long dark overcoats. A group of ladies on a balcony wave their handkerchiefs, and the crowds that line the sidewalks show their enthusiasm.  As the Battery passes out of sight, men and boys run across the street, and a hansom cab brings up the rear. The picture was taken late in the afternoon, and the exposures were slow; consequently the film must be reproduced slowly to give the best results. (*The Phonoscope*, January 1899, 15.)
SUBJECT: Parades. Armies–United States. John Jacob Astor.
ARCHIVE: DLC-pp.
CITATIONS: "Collegians and Athletes Rush to Join Crack Astor Battery," *New York World,* 28 May 1898, 3; "Great Rush to Join Astor Battery," *New York World,* 29 May 1898, 4; "Ovation Awaits Astor Battery," *New York Herald,* 22 January 1899, 5; "Astor Battery is Home from Manila," *New York Herald,* 23 January 1899, 4.
NOTE: The Astor Battery was financed and raised privately—John Jacob Astor's gift to the United States for use in its war with Spain. The military unit, which enjoyed extensive press coverage, was sent to fight in the Philippines. The date of filming provided in Edison catalogs is inaccurate; the picture had to be shot on the 23 of January 1899.

THRONGS CHEER ASTOR BATTERY
Great Demonstration During the Parade and Line of March Is Gay with Colors.
REVIEW BY MAYOR VAN WYCK
After Their Return to the Armory the Soldiers and Fair Visitors Had an Impromptu Dance.
WORK OF MUSTERING OUT.
By the End of the Week It Is Expected the Men Will Have Been Discharged.

New York turned out yesterday afternoon to greet the members of the Astor battery as they paraded from the Seventy-first Regiment Armory, at Park avenue and Thirty-fourth street, to Union square and back.

The Astor battery, under the escort of Battery I, one hundred men, of the Fifth United States artillery, left the Seventy-first Regiment Armory shortly after three o'clock, marched up Park avenue to Fortieth street, thence down Fifth avenue to Union square and Seventeenth street, where it was reviewed by Mayor Van Wyck. The battery then marched up Fourth avenue to Twenty-third street, and back to the armory, where the men and their escort, and their relatives and friends were treated to a luncheon provided by Mr. E.B. Ely, the representative of Colonel John Jacob Astor. For hours before the time set for the start of the parade, great crowds had gathered in front of the armory, around Union square and all along the line of march.

BUNTING ON THE BUILDINGS.

In honor of the returned soldiers flags and bunting were displayed on nearly all the buildings which the battery passed. As the men reported at the armory they presented a fine appearance. They wore the regular army uniforms, with long coats and leggings. The majority of them had spent Sunday night with relatives or friends, while others had gone to hotels. Very few of them slept in the armory. In place of the usual army rations the men were treated to a hearty breakfast, ordered by Mr. Ely.

ARRIVAL OF THE ESCORT.

Finally the throng that was gathered in Thirty-fourth street about two o'clock heard the inspiring strains of martial music to the west of them, and presently Battery I of the Fifth United States artillery from Fort Hamilton, preceded by the regimental band and under the command of Lieutenant Marcellus G. Spinks, marched up the street.

When Battery I reached the armory Captain March lined his men up on the floor of the big drill room and called the roll. All responded to their names, including the two who had missed the connection in Colorado, but who had taken the next train for the East. The men were dressed in heavy marching order and carried their knapsacks and other accoutrements. They wore blue trousers and brown leggings, blue overcoats without capes and regulation hats with crossed cannons.

Bugler Barrett sounded the call shortly after three o'clock, and then Captain March and his men filed out of the armory, only to be greeted by the wild cheers of the assembled thousands.

The battery took up its position after the Fort Hamilton regulars, and the parade was started in the following order:– Squad of mounted police; regimental band, under the direction of Frederick Franke; Battery I, Fifth United States artillery, under the command of Lieutenant Spinks, and the Astor battery, under the command of Captain March.

In a hansom after his comrades rode Corporal Van Horne. He was unable to march with them, for he had left half of his right leg on the field of Manila in the fighting of August 13, when the Astor boys charged the Spanish lines with pistols only.

The battery marched down Fifth avenue, to the accompaniment of enthusiastic cheering and the waving of flags, Astor battery ribbons and handkerchiefs on the part of the assembled multitudes, while the band played patriotic airs and the "Astor Battery March."

While the battery was parading down Fifth avenue at Fortieth street the horse of Mounted Policeman George Neil, of the Highbridge station, became frightened and fell, breaking the rider's leg.

REVIEWED BY THE MAYOR.

At seventeenth street the parade turned toward Union square, where Mayor Van Wyck reviewed the soldiers from the balcony of the cottage on the plaza. On the balcony besides the Mayor were the members of the Reception Committee, composed of relatives and friends of the battery, who had planned the reception and parade. Among those were Colonel C.H. Blair and Mrs. Blair, Mr. and Mrs. James Taylor, Mr. and Mrs. William P. Baker, Mr. Joseph W. Beacham, Major and Mrs. L.L. Robbins, Mr. V.L. Hardenbrush and Mrs. Guibert, the mother of Corporal Van Horne. On the balcony also were committees from the Board of Aldermen and the Municipal Assembly, city officials and representatives of Grand Army posts, including Corporation Counsel Whalen, Tax Commissioner Feitner, Commissioner Keating, Controller Coler, Charities Commissioner Keller, Commissioner of Corrections Lantry, Register Fromme, Captain Stewart M. Brice, Mr. Hermann Oelrichs, Police Commissioners York and Hess, Superintendent of Buildings Brady, and Commissioner Clausen.

As the battery filed past the reviewing stand the band played the "Astor Battery March," the great crowd cheered and applauded, and Boojum was very much in evidence, for he ran between the lines of the soldiers and barked all the time.

When the regulars and the battery marched in to the big armory it was just a quarter past four. The rest of the day was given over to enjoyment. The luncheon provided by Mr. Ely was soon disposed of. Then the band played some dance music, and the Astor boys, with their sweethearts or their sisters, whirled about the spacious drill room and proved that they could dance as well as they could fight. The college boys in the battery sang glees between the dances.

The formal mustering out of the Astor battery began yesterday morning, when General Randolph, who has superintended the mustering of many volunteer companies since his own return from Santiago, where he commanded the artillery brigade, reached the armory and took charge of matters. Captain E.R. Hills, of the Fifth artillery, will attend to the details of the mustering out, and will have the aid of half a dozen clerks. It is believed the mustering out will be finished before the end of the week. (*New York Herald*, 24 January 1899, 8.)

Mr. Smith broke all records in photography and caused considerable newspaper talk by taking an animated picture of the parade on Union Square at 4:00 PM and developing, printing, and exhibiting it by 9 PM the same evening at several New York theatres. (*Mahatma*, February 1899, 81.)

James White hired members of the New Jersey National Guard to "reenact" a number of stirring scenes from the Spanish-American war, a practice that the Edison Manu-

facturing Company continued to pursue in the years ahead—with the Philippine Insurrection (1899), the Boer War (1901), and the Russo-Japanese War (1904). Although the Second Regiment of New Jersey had been mobilized (see film no. 637), it never left American soil. Some of its members finally had at least the vicarious satisfaction of re-enacting the war's most heroic moments.

651 Sailors Landing Under Fire / Sailors Landing on Cuban Soil Under Fire
LENGTH: 50 ft.   © No reg.
PRODUCER: James White.
CAMERA:
CAST:
PRODUCTION DATE: [January to early February 1899.]
LOCATION:
SOURCE:
DESCRIPTION: A long boat dashes up to the shore, oars up. Out jump the men, a score or more, knee deep into the water. They line up and fire volley after volley, advancing meanwhile up the beach. (*The Phonoscope*, January 1899, 15.)
SUBJECT: Navies–United States. Spanish-American War. Battles.
ARCHIVE:
CITATIONS: *New York Clipper*, 11 February 1899, 854; *Edison Films*, March 1900, 10; *Edison Films*, July 1901, 33.
NOTE: *The Phonoscope* was published a month late in this period, and fell further behind during the course of 1900.

652 Battle of San Juan Hill
LENGTH: 100 ft.   © No reg.
PRODUCER: James White.
CAMERA:
CAST:
PRODUCTION DATE: [January to early February 1899.]
LOCATION: Orange Mountains, West Orange, N.J.
SOURCE:
DESCRIPTION: This is one of the greatest war films ever placed on the market. The enemy is seen scouting in the underbrush at the foot of a steep hill. Suddenly our own soldier boys appear under the order of "Forward by rushes," and gallantly charge up the hill. A struggle takes place, but our boys are victorious and they plant our flag there to stay. The most realistic part of this scene is the explosion of the bombs thrown by the enemy in close proximity to a soldier who has fallen, and who is being cared for by the Red Cross staff, who finally carry him away on a stretcher. A most exciting picture. (*The Phonoscope*, April 1899, 17.)
SUBJECT: Historical Reenactments. Armies–United States. Spanish-American War. National Guard–New Jersey. First U.S. Cavalry (Volunteer). Second New Jersey Volunteers. Red Cross.
ARCHIVE:
CITATIONS: *New York Clipper*, 11 February 1899, 854; *Edison Films*, March 1900, 10; *Edison Films*, July 1901, 34.
NOTE:

"Spaniards" Would Not Fight
Vitascope Man Badly Treated by Men He Hired to Mimic the Battle of San Juan.

A photographer for a moving picture machine had hard luck at Orange, N.J., recently in his attempt to depict an engagement on San Juan Hill. He engaged eighteen negroes to represent the Spaniards and an equal number of volunteers from the Second Regiment, N.G.N.J., for the American army and costumed them appropriately, taking the two commands upon Orange Mountain, where they were to engage in a bloody conflict.

He paid the negroes 75 cents each in advance, gave them some beer, in order that they might be in fighting trim, and then adjusted his photographing apparatus. When ready the Vitascope man found that the "Spaniards" had disappeared, taking with them 200 rounds of blank cartridges.

The police found a number of the pseudo Spaniards later engaged in a game of craps, but as they fled no arrests were made. (*The Phonoscope*, April 1899, 15.)

HAMILTON FISH, JR., AND TWELVE ROUGH RIDERS AND CAVALRYMEN KILLED IN BATTLE BY SPANIARDS.
Fifty Americans, Including Six of the Officers, Were Wounded–Ten Will Probably Die.
SPANIARDS LEFT TWELVE DEAD ON FIELD OF BATTLE.
Gen. Young and Col. Wood Were Reinforced and Now Hold the Position,
Which Overlooks the City of Santiago De Cuba.
FIGHT LASTED OVER AN HOUR AND WAS SHARPLY CONTESTED.
The Men Were Making a Reconoissance in Advance of the Army, Which Was Closing in on the City.

PLAYA DEL ESTE, June 24.–Roosevelt's Rough Riders and the United States regular cavalrymen proved their mettle this morning in a fierce and sanguinary fight with the Spaniards five miles from Santiago.

Less than a thousand Americans, fighting as dismounted cavalrymen, charged two thousand Spaniards in the thickets. Although the enemy had the great advantage in numbers and position, they were routed from the dense brush.

They rallied around a blockhouse, but the Rough Riders and troopers were not to be denied and drove them into the city.

The fight lasted an hour. Thirteen Americans were killed and at least fifty wounded, of whom ten will die. Among the killed were Capt. Allyn K. Capron, of the Rough Riders, and two non-commissioned officers. Six officers were wounded.

Twelve dead Spaniards were left behind by their flying comrades. Undoubtedly their loss was much greater.

The engagement took place in the course of the general advance against Santiago.

Gen. Young commanded the regulars. Col. Leonard Wood was at the head of the Rough Riders, who had pleaded to be hurried forward and who advanced west of the regulars.

Both commands came upon the Spaniards together. The enemy was hidden in the underbrush, where they had thrown up rude intrenchments of tree trunks.

The Spaniards, lying in the grass, opened fire. The cavalrymen charged.

The difficulty of the way, their falling comrades, did not stay them.

As they charged the enemy retreated, but fighting stubbornly. There were many hand-to-hand encounters.

Falling back on a block-house, their officers rallied the Spaniards. Rough Riders and troopers charged them again, they broke and ran, scattering over the mountains.

After fight ended the dismounted cavalrymen were reinforced by the Seventh, Twelfth and Seventeenth Infantry, part of the Ninth Cavalry, the Second Massachusetts and the Seventy-first New York.

Our troops, of course, hold the position at the threshold of Santiago. More troops are constantly moving forward and assault on the city is imminent. (*New York World*, 25 June 1898, 1.)

ROOSEVELT TELLS OF BATTLE IN WHICH THE ROUGH RIDERS LOST SO MANY.
Spanish Firing Surprisingly Accurate, Fearfully Heavy.
"Every One of Our Men Did His Duty Up to the Handle–Not a Man Flinched."

"There must have been nearly 1,500 Spaniards in front and to the sides of us." They held the ridges with rifle pits and machine guns, and hid a body of men in ambush in the thick jungle at the side of the road over which we were advancing. Our advance guard struck the men in ambush and drove them out, but they lost Capt. Capron, Lieut. Thomas and about fifteen men killed or wounded.

"The Spanish firing was accurate, so accurate, indeed, that it surprised me; and their firing was fearfully heavy.

"I want to say a word for our own men. Every officer and man did his duty up to the handle. Not a man flinched."

Lieut.-Col. Roosevelt's description of the battle in which Hamilton Fish, jr, and fifteen others were killed. (*New York World*, 27 June, 1898, 1.)

653 Defending the Colors
LENGTH: 50 ft.   © No reg.
PRODUCER: James White.
CAMERA:
CAST:
PRODUCTION DATE: [January to early February 1899.]
LOCATION: Orange Mountains, West Orange, N.J.
SOURCE:
DESCRIPTION: The enemy has taken the fort. In one corner, with their last cannon, stand a handful of soldiers, guarding the flag to the last. They fire their cannon. An answering volley kills several; the last are overcome in a hand to hand conflict. (*The Phonoscope*, January 1899, 15.)
SUBJECT: Armies–United States. Spanish-American War. Battles. Second New Jersey Volunteers.
ARCHIVE:

CITATIONS: *New York Clipper*, 29 April 1899, 178.
NOTE:

654 Red Cross at the Front

LENGTH: 100 ft.   © No reg.
PRODUCER: James White.
CAMERA:
CAST:
PRODUCTION DATE: [January to early February 1899.]
LOCATION: Orange Mountains, West Orange, N.J.
SOURCE:
DESCRIPTION: Wounded soldiers are lying around, watching the arrival of a poor fellow on a stretcher from the front. The nurses and attendants all wear the red cross on their arms. (*Edison Films*, March 1900, 10.)
SUBJECT: Armies–United States. Red Cross. Spanish-American War. Battles. Second New Jersey Volunteers.
ARCHIVE:
CITATIONS: *Edison Films*, July 1901, 34.
NOTE: Dating of this production is based primarily on the "code word" designation in Edison catalogs.

655 Surrender of General Toral

LENGTH: 50 ft.   © No reg.
PRODUCER: James White.
CAMERA:
CAST:
PRODUCTION DATE: [January to early February 1899.]
LOCATION: [Orange Mountains, West Orange, N.J.]
SOURCE:
DESCRIPTION: The white flag of truce is prominent in the center of the picture. Shafter and Wheeler are on the left, conferring with staff officers. Toral hands his sword to General Shafter, who returns it with a courteous bow. (*Edison Films,* March 1900, 10.)
SUBJECT: Historical Reenactments. Armies–United States. Armies–Spain. Spanish-American War. Second New Jersey Volunteers. William Rufus Shafter. Joseph Wheeler. General Toral.
ARCHIVE:
CITATIONS: "General Toral Says He Will Not Surrender," *New York World*, 15 July 1898, 1; "Toral's Appeal to a Generous Foe," *New York World*, 18 July 1898, 2. *Edison Films*, July 1901, 34.
NOTE: Dating of this production is based primarily on the "code word" designation in Edison catalogs.

NINTH INFANTRY FIRST TO ENTER.
Triumphant Entry of Gen. Shafter–Crowds Welcome Him.
SPAIN'S GENERALS DO HIM HONOR.
Spain's Troops Lay Down Their Arms and Camp Outside the City Limits.

SANTIAGO, July 17.–At noon to-day the American flag was hoisted over the city of Santiago, while in the streets of the ancient town our bands played "The Star-Spangled Banner."

Officers and men reverently saluted the colors as they went sailing up the tall staff which a few hours before had supported the yellow and red emblem of Spain.

The hoisting of our flag meant the actual occupation of the city by our troops. At 11 A.M. the official entrance to the town began. As soon as possession had been taken Gen. Chambers McKibbin was appointed Military Governor of Santiago.

NINTH INFANTRY FIRST.

The first troops to enter were the men of the Ninth Infantry. The position of honor was given them as a reward for their heroic assault on San Juan hill during the first days of the fighting against Santiago.

Gen. Shafter and his staff as they rode into the town were escorted by the Second Cavalry....Gens. Shafter, Wheeler, Kent, Lawton, Ames, Sumner and McKibbin rode straight to the Captain-General's palace, where they were met by the municipal authorities, the Archbishop of Santiago and the generals of the defeated Spanish army.

GEN. LINARES'S REGRETS.

Gen. Toral apologized for the non-appearance of Lieut.-Gen Linares, who was prevented from being present by a serious wound. He will call and pay his respects to Gen. Shafter as soon as he is able to leave his cot.

An elaborate dinner was prepared at the Captain-General's palace for fifteen generals, and at this banquet many of the details of the surrender which have not been settled were discussed.

For the present the Spanish municipal authorities will remain in control of the city.

While our troops were marching into the city the vanguard of the defeated army began to march out, the Spanish soldiers depositing their arms at the edge of the city. All of the Spanish troops are going into camp on open ground between the former firing lines, where it will be comparatively easy to keep them under control until the arrival of the transports to carry them back to Spain....(*New York World*, 18 July 1898, 1.)

---

656 *Answering the Alarm

LENGTH: 50 ft.   © No reg.

PRODUCER:

CAMERA:

CAST:

PRODUCTION DATE: [January to early February 1899.]

LOCATION: New York, N.Y.

SOURCE:

DESCRIPTION: Shows the fire department of Greater New York going about its business. A great picture. Engine drawn by three horses, hook and ladder truck, hose cart and patrol wagon, all come dashing up the street at furious speed. Men and boys follow, running in the middle of the roadway. An excellent film in every respect, clear, distinct and full of exciting action. (*Edison Films*, March 1900, 30.)

SUBJECT: Fire fighters.

ARCHIVE: NR-GE.

CITATIONS: *Edison Films*, July 1901, 54.

NOTE: Listed as a 40-foot subject in 1901.

---

657 *Mr. and Mrs. Calif at Dinner

LENGTH: 50 ft.   © No reg.

PRODUCER:

CAMERA:

CAST:

PRODUCTION DATE: [January to early February 1899.]

LOCATION: Central Park, New York, N.Y.

SOURCE:

DESCRIPTION: Shows a tank in the Zoo at Central Park, New York. Two hippopotamuses are being fed by their keeper, who drops loaves of bread into their wide open jaws. (*Edison Films*, March 1900, 26.)

SUBJECT: Hippopotamuses. Zoos. Food.

ARCHIVE:

CITATIONS:

NOTE: This film survives and has been screened, but before it was recognized to be an Edison subject. The archive where the film is located needs to be established.

---

658 *Rapids Below Suspension Bridge

LENGTH: 50 ft.   © 17 February 1899.

PRODUCER: James White.

CAMERA:

CAST:

PRODUCTION DATE: [January to early February 1899.]

LOCATION: Niagara Falls, Canada.

SOURCE: *Niagara Falls, Gorge* (Edison film no. 163, June 1896)

DESCRIPTION: A panoramic view of nature's greatest waterfall, taken from the narrow railway that skirts the gorge, at the foot of

Niagara Falls. (*Edison Films*, March 1900, 47.)
SUBJECT: Waterfalls. Bridges. Niagara Falls. Railroads.
ARCHIVE: DLC-pp.
CITATIONS:
NOTE:

659 ***Larks Behind the Scene / Larks Behind the Scenes**
LENGTH: 50 ft.   © Thomas A. Edison, 17 February 1899.
PRODUCER: James White.
CAMERA:
CAST:
PRODUCTION DATE: January to early February 1899.
LOCATION: [Black Maria], West Orange, N.J.
SOURCE:

DESCRIPTION: Clever high kicking in the dressing room of a theatre. The ladies are in excellent spirits, judging by their actions; and excellent spirits are in the ladies, judging by the empty bottles. (*Edison Films*, March 1900, 29.)
SUBJECT: Dancing. Alcoholic beverages. Actresses.
ARCHIVE: DLC-pp.
CITATIONS: *Edison Films*, July 1901, 52.
NOTE: See *Jones Gives a Private Supper* (film no. 669) for a very similar subject.

660 ***Poker at Dawson City**
LENGTH: 50 ft.   © Thomas A. Edison, 17 February 1899.
PRODUCER: James White.
CAMERA:
CAST:
PRODUCTION DATE: January to early February 1899.
LOCATION: Black Maria, West Orange, N.J.
SOURCE: *A Bar Room Scene* (Edison film no. 37, spring 1894).
DESCRIPTION: A decided shady game. Shows a novel way of filling a bobtail flush. Game breaks up in a general scrimmage. The barkeeper cools off the fighters by the judicious use of a siphon of vichy. (*Edison Films*, March 1900, 36.)
SUBJECT: Taverns, etc. Alcoholic beverages. Gold mines and mining. Gambling. Poker. Violence. Klondike River Valley (Yukon)-Gold discoveries.
ARCHIVE: DLC-pp.
CITATIONS: *New York Clipper*, 11 February 1899, 854.
NOTE:

In March 1899, the Edison Manufacturing Company announced the availability of "Four New Humorous Subjects," under the rubric "What Happened to Jones." (New York Clipper, 11 March 1899, 40.) The "What Happened to Jones" series listed in Edison's catalogs soon consisted of more than a half dozen short comedies focusing on the travails of an alcoholic clubman.

661 ***Jones' Return from the Club / [Jones' Return from the Club, no. 1] / Jones Returns from the Club**
LENGTH: 50 ft.   © Thomas A. Edison, 20 February 1899.
PRODUCER: James White.
CAMERA:
CAST: [James White?]

PRODUCTION DATE: January to early February 1899.

LOCATION: [Llewellyn Park, West Orange, N.J.]

SOURCE:

DESCRIPTION: The scene is laid in a prominent private park and opens by depicting the belated Jones returning from his club, clad in a dress suit, smoking a cigar, and armed with the inexhaustible whiskey bottle. Jones' house is shown in the background, but Jones himself, after travelling waist deep through the snow in the opposite direction from his home finally becomes bewildered and leans against a tree, the expression on his face alternating between happiness and disgust. A friendly policeman appears on the scene and endeavors to start Jones off in the right direction; an argument follows, which ends by Jones knocking off the policeman's hat and pitching him head first in a neighboring snow drift. Jones now dons the policeman's helmet and appropriates his club, then makes an attempt to arrest the worthy officer of the law. The picture finally ends by the unfortunate Jones being rolled heavily in the snow. (*The Phonoscope*, February 1899, 14.)

SUBJECT: Alcoholism. Police. Violence. Practical jokes.

ARCHIVE: DLC-pp.

CITATIONS: *Edison Films*, March 1900, 31; *Edison Films*, July 1901, 61.

NOTE: Three similar yet distinct films were submitted for copyright under this one title.

---

662 *Jones' Return from the Club / [Jones' Return from the Club, no. 2]

LENGTH: 50 ft. © Thomas A. Edison, 20 or 25 February 1899.

PRODUCER: James White.

CAMERA:

CAST: [James White?]

PRODUCTION DATE: January to early February 1899.

LOCATION: [Llewellyn Park, West Orange, N.J.]

SOURCE:

DESCRIPTION:

SUBJECT: Alcoholism. Police. Violence. Practical jokes.

ARCHIVE: DLC-pp.

CITATIONS: *Edison Films*, March 1900, 31.

NOTE: Three similar yet distinct films were submitted for copyright under this one title.

---

663 *Jones' Return from the Club / [Jones' Return from the Club, no. 3]

LENGTH: 50 ft. © Thomas A. Edison, 25 February 1899.

PRODUCER: James White.

CAMERA:

CAST: [James White?]

PRODUCTION DATE: January to early February 1899.

LOCATION: [Llewellyn Park, West Orange, N.J.]

SOURCE:

DESCRIPTION:

SUBJECT: Alcoholism. Police. Violence. Practical jokes.

ARCHIVE: DLC-pp.

CITATIONS: *Edison Films*, March 1900, 31.

NOTE: Three similar yet distinct films were submitted for copyright under this one title.

664 *****Jones and His Pal in Trouble**
LENGTH: 50 ft.   © Thomas A. Edison, 25 February 1899.
PRODUCER: James White.
CAMERA:
CAST: [James White?]
PRODUCTION DATE: January to early February 1899.
LOCATION: [West Orange, N.J.]
SOURCE:

DESCRIPTION: Jones feels that he needs assistance to get home, and finds a friend to help him. They are two of a kind. They come down the snow covered pathway, stopping frequently to sample a large flask. They finally stick their canes into a snow bank, and between them they finish up the whiskey. Just then the policeman appears, with blood in his eye. The two happy ones are too much for the officer, and after a short wrestle he is thrown down into the deep snow. Jones staggers away, leaving his friend to fight it out. He and the officer have a very exciting rough and tumble fight in the snow. Jones comes back to the rescue and the policeman gives up the job. (*The Phonoscope*, February 1899, 18.)
SUBJECT: Alcoholism. Police. Violence.
ARCHIVE: DLC-pp.
CITATIONS: *Edison Films*, March 1900, 31; *Edison Films*, July 1901, 61.
NOTE:

665 *****Jones' Interrupted Sleighride**
LENGTH: 50 ft.   © Thomas A. Edison, 25 February 1899.
PRODUCER: James White.
CAMERA:
CAST: [James White?]
PRODUCTION DATE: January to early February 1899.
LOCATION: [West Orange, N.J.]
SOURCE:

DESCRIPTION: Jones and his friend go out for a ride still in a happy condition. They meet a policeman, who remonstrates about their manner of driving. Jones stands upon the seat and tells the officer to mind his own business, whereupon the officer jumps into the sleigh, and, grappling with Jones, they fall out into a snow drift. The friend drives off as fast as he can, tacking from one side of the road to the other. The cop pursues the sleigh, and Jones escapes. As the sleigh disappears among the trees the cop gives up the chase and comes back for his helmet. Jones comes back also to argue the question and the cop promptly arrests him. (*The Phonoscope*, February 1899, 18.)
SUBJECT: Alcoholism. Police. Violence. Sleighs and sledges. Punishment.
ARCHIVE: DLC-pp.
CITATIONS: *Edison Films*, March 1900, 31-32; *Edison Films*, July 1901, 61.
NOTE:

666 **Jones Interviews His Wife**
LENGTH: 50 ft.   © No reg.
PRODUCER: James White.
CAMERA:
CAST:
PRODUCTION DATE: February 1899.
LOCATION: [Black Maria], West Orange, N.J.
SOURCE:

DESCRIPTION: He finally reaches home, pretty late, and finds his wife sitting up for him. He begins to disrobe, throwing his hat and cane on the floor, and scattering his clothes all round the room. His wife at first is very much ashamed of him, then indignant and finally angry. She picks up a basin full of water and empties it over his head, drenching him from head to foot. The water pours off in streams as he stands with fingers outstretched, shocked almost into soberness. Very comical. (*The Phonoscope*, February 1899, 18.)

SUBJECT: Alcoholism. Married people. Punishment.

ARCHIVE:

CITATIONS: *Edison Films*, March 1900, 32; *Edison Films*, July 1901, 61.

NOTE:

667 *Jones Makes a Discovery

LENGTH: 50 ft.   © Thomas A. Edison, 8 March 1899.

PRODUCER: James White.

CAMERA:

CAST:

PRODUCTION DATE: February 1899.

LOCATION: [Black Maria], West Orange, N.J.

SOURCE:

DESCRIPTION: Jones' wife has been telling her troubles to his friend, who becomes very loving and affectionate. He abuses Jones' confidence in him and consoles the lady with most touching sympathy. Just at this point the door opens and Jones appears in his nightgown. He is still in a happy state, but not too much so to appreciate the position. Grasping the false one by the collar, he throws him bodily out of the window; his hat, stick and valise follow. Taking his wife by the arm, he pushes her from the room. Overcome by the excitement and the exertion, he collapses in the middle of the room. (*Edison Films*, March 1900, 32.)

SUBJECT: Alcoholism. Adultery. Punishment.

ARCHIVE: DLC-pp.

CITATIONS: *Edison Films*, July 1901, 62.

NOTE:

668 Jones' Return from a Masquerade

LENGTH: 50 ft.   © No reg.

PRODUCER: James White.

CAMERA:

CAST:

PRODUCTION DATE: February to early March 1899.

LOCATION: [Black Maria], West Orange, N.J.

SOURCE:

DESCRIPTION: Jones comes home from a masquerade ball, clad in a Scotch costume and his usual confused condition. He gets into his neighbor's apartments instead of his own. He hears his neighbor and wife coming into their rooms, and being now thoroughly frightened, crawls under the bed to hide. His neighbor discovers him, hauls him out, and, by way of punishment, throws him through the window. (*Edison Films*, July 1901, 62.)

SUBJECT: Alcoholism. Violence. Beds. Punishment.

ARCHIVE:

CITATIONS: *Edison Films*, March 1900, 32.

NOTE:

669 Jones Gives a Private Supper

LENGTH: 50 ft.   © No reg.

PRODUCER: James White.

CAMERA:

CAST:

PRODUCTION DATE: February to early March 1899.
LOCATION: [Black Maria], West Orange, N.J.
SOURCE:
DESCRIPTION: This picture shows Jones entertaining three young ladies after the theatre. They have a private room, and are evidently enjoying themselves very much. Jones sets up wine freely, and the party becomes hilarious. The girls dance in turn for Jones, each vieing with the other in executing novel, and startling terpsichorean effects. (*The Phonoscope*, February 1899, 14.)
SUBJECT: Taverns, etc. Alcoholism. Dancing.
ARCHIVE:
CITATIONS: *Edison Films*, March 1900, 32; *Edison Films*, July 1901, 62.
NOTE: See film no. 659, *Larks Behind the Scene*.

Mr. Edison's Latest Discovery.

We have made a complete revolution in our printing and developing departments, employing an entirely new process for making animated film subjects. The results surpass anything hitherto produced. The pictures when projected show great improvements both in clearness and definition, and have that soft mellow tone which has been so long sought for, but not until now attained. (Edison Manufacturing Company, advertisement, *New York Clipper*, 11 March 1899, 40.)

The following four films were all taken against the same backdrop at the same studio, almost certainly the Black Maria. By this point, the spring of 1899, Edison films rarely showed performers against plain backgrounds—a marked departure from previous practice.

670 **[Bicycle Trick Riding, no. 1]**
LENGTH: 50 ft.   © No reg.
PRODUCER: James White.
CAMERA:
CAST: Neidert.
PRODUCTION DATE: March 1899.
LOCATION: [Black Maria], West Orange, N.J.
SOURCE:
DESCRIPTION:
SUBJECT: Vaudeville–performances. Bicycles.
ARCHIVE:
CITATIONS:
NOTE:

671 ***Bicycle Trick Riding, no. 2**
LENGTH: 50 ft.   © Thomas A. Edison, 20 March 1899.
PRODUCER: James White.
CAMERA:
CAST: Neidert.
PRODUCTION DATE: March 1899.
LOCATION: [Black Maria], West Orange, N.J.
SOURCE:
DESCRIPTION: "Neidert," of national fame, does stunts on his wheel that are simply wonderful. Makes his bicycle rear up, and rides around the stage on his back wheel; besides a lot of other easy things, such as riding on one pedal and riding backward, seated on the handlebars. (*The Phonoscope*, July 1899, 14.)

SUBJECT: Vaudeville–performances. Bicycles.
ARCHIVE: DLC-pp.
CITATIONS: *Edison Films*, March 1900, 25; *Edison Films,* July 1901, 49.
NOTE:

672 ***Arabian Gun Twirler**
LENGTH: 50 ft.　© Thomas A. Edison, 20 March 1899.
PRODUCER: James White.
CAMERA:
CAST: Hadji L. Cheriff.
PRODUCTION DATE: March 1899.
LOCATION: [Black Maria], West Orange, N.J.
SOURCE:

DESCRIPTION: An interesting exhibit by Hadji
Cheriff, of the original Midway Plaisance.
Twirls his rifle over shoulder, behind back,
under leg, both hands and one hand. (*The
Phonoscope*, July 1899, 14.)
SUBJECT: Jugglers. Arabs. Rifles and rifle prac-
tice. Wild west shows.
ARCHIVE: DLC-pp.
CITATIONS: *Edison Films*, March 1900, 25; *Edison Films,* July 1901, 49.
NOTE: Cheriff had previously appeared before Edison's cameras, in film no. 75, *Hadji
Cheriff*. See that entry for relevant documentation on Cheriff.

SHIEK HADJI TAHAR writes THE CLIPPER as follows: "The excitement at the Erie Ferry, foot of West Twenty-third
Street, Saturday afternoon, June 9, was caused by Sheik Hajah Takar's [sic] Oriental contingent of forty people,
dressed in parade costume, leaving for the Pan-Continental Amusement Carnival at Olean, N.Y. Among the number
who left were Hadji Cheriff, dervish and gun spinner, with his troupe of Arabian acrobats; Seignor El Francol, and
his Filipino company of singers and dancers, and Negib Farras' troupe of Oriental musicians, sword fighters and
dancers." (*New York Clipper*, 23 June 1900, 371.)

673 ***Three Acrobats**
LENGTH: 50 ft.　© Thomas A. Edison, 20 March 1899.
PRODUCER: James White.
CAMERA:
CAST: The Bouffons.
PRODUCTION DATE: March 1899.
LOCATION: [Black Maria], West Orange, N.J.
SOURCE:
DESCRIPTION: The Bouffons are artists in their
line. They rumble in and out of trick doors,
disappear and reappear in unexpected plac-
es in most unexpected ways. Sure to amuse
children. (*The Phonoscope*, July 1899, 14.)
SUBJECT: Vaudeville–performances. Aerialists.
Acrobats.
ARCHIVE: DLC-pp.
CITATIONS: *Edison Films*, March 1900, 25;
Edison Films, July 1901, 49.
NOTE: The backdrop behind the facade of trick doors is the same as for *Arabian Gun
Twirler* and *Bicycle Trick Riding, no. 2*.

*A devastating fire swept through the Windsor Hotel on Fifth Avenue, Manhattan, on
17 March 1899, St. Patrick's Day. Dozens of people died and many more were injured.
The disaster quickly yielded several films, which were listed a month later in Edison
advertisements.*

674 **Panorama of Windsor Hotel Ruins**
LENGTH: 50 and 100 ft.　© No reg.
PRODUCER: [J. Stuart Blackton, Albert E. Smith.]
CAMERA: [J. Stuart Blackton and/or Albert E. Smith.]
CAST:
PRODUCTION DATE: Ca. 18 March 1899.

LOCATION: Fifth Avenue, New York, N.Y.
SOURCE:
DESCRIPTION:
SUBJECT: Fire ruins.
ARCHIVE:
CITATIONS: *New York Clipper*, 15 April 1899, 136.
NOTE:

675 Reproduction of Windsor Hotel Fire
LENGTH: 100 ft.   © No reg.
PRODUCER: J. Stuart Blackton, Albert E. Smith.
CAMERA: J. Stuart Blackton and/or Albert E. Smith.
CAST:
PRODUCTION DATE: 18-25 March 1899.
LOCATION: New York, N.Y.
SOURCE:
DESCRIPTION:
SUBJECT: Fires. Fire fighters.
ARCHIVE:
CITATIONS: *New York Clipper*, 15 April 1899, 136.
NOTE: This film was made using a miniature.

676 *Firemen Rescuing Men and Women / Rescuing Men and Women by Firemen
LENGTH: 75 ft.   © No reg.
PRODUCER: [J. Stuart Blackton, Albert E. Smith?]
CAMERA: [J. Stuart Blackton and/or Albert E. Smith?]
CAST:
PRODUCTION DATE: 18-25 March 1899.
LOCATION:
SOURCE:
DESCRIPTION: The efficiency of the modern life-saving methods and apparatus now in use by the fire department is illustrated by this picture. The view is the front of a burning building where two ladders have been raised. Through a thick cloud of smoke and sparks we see the members of the fire companies ascending. Entering the windows they pass unfortunate occupants, whose only means of exit has been cut off by the flames, to their comrades, who in turn take them down to safety. (*Edison Films*, September 1902, 66.)
SUBJECT: Fires. Fire fighters.
ARCHIVE: NNMoMA.
CITATIONS: *New York Clipper*, 15 April 1899, 136; *Edison Films*, July 1901, 55.
NOTE:

RUIN IN BIG FIRE THAT RAZED THE WINDSOR HOTEL.
Great Fifth Avenue Structure Suddenly a Mass of Flames and
Terror Stricken Guests Leap to Death and Injury.
TWO SCORE OF SUFFERERS IN THE HOSPITAL.
Match Cast Among Lace Curtains Started Conflagration Which Caused
Property Loss of More Than a Million Dollars and Made Scene of Awful Suffering.
WARREN F. LELAND INSANE, HIS WIFE AND CHILD DEAD.

The historic Windsor Hotel Fifth Avenue and Forty-sixth street was entirely destroyed by fire yesterday.

Eight persons who perished in the fire had been identified at midnight. Five more dead await identification, but this does not, it is believed represent the full number of persons who lost their lives. There were two hundred and seventy-five patrons registered at the hotel when the fire was discovered in one of the bedroom windows. It spread with marvellous rapidity. In less that forty minutes the great building was almost entirely in flames.

Nobody knows how many persons—patrons and servants—will be found under those ruins. A man who works in the engine room said that he stopped on the lower floor of the burning Hotel as long as he could, but when he left he saw many trying to escape. Twenty-two persons are missing. If they are not in the ruins they have not been otherwise accounted for. Fifty three are injured, most of them by jumping from the windows and the roof before there was any necessity for their doing so.

The panic in the hotel was something fearful. Men and women rushed about the corridors and the rear courtyard of the hotel crazy from fright. Some jumped when they were warned not to, for rescue was at hand. Others declined to be taken to a place of rescue when they had the chance.

Warren Leland Crazed by Grief.

The thickly thronged streets around the burning building added to the confusion. It was St. Patrick's Day, and the procession was due to pass the hotel just about the time the fire was discovered. There were throngs out to see it. The whole machinery of the Fire and Police Department was put into operation, but the crowd was too powerful for them to battle with. Hysterical women ran about with frightened children clinging to their skirts. Many of them were injured before they could be removed from the vicinity of the hotel.

The Windsor was last leased by Warren Leland, who lost his wife and daughter in the flames. The former died at nine o'clock last night from burns in the Flower Hospital. Fifteen minutes later the body of a young woman who had been hitherto unidentified at the Fifty-first street station house was discovered to be that of Miss Leland. The calamity has utterly unbalanced Mr. Leland's mind. Last night it was necessary to put him under restraint.

There was no escape by the courtyards save through the burning building. (*New York Herald*, 18 March 1899, 3.)

---

677 *Casey at the Bat / Casey at the Bat, or the Fate of a "Rotten" Umpire

LENGTH: 50 ft.   © Thomas A. Edison, 22 April 1899.

PRODUCER: James White.

CAMERA:

CAST:

PRODUCTION DATE: Early to mid-April 1899.

LOCATION: [New Jersey.]

SOURCE:

DESCRIPTION: The umpire makes a decision that Casey don't like, and an argument follows, during which Casey deftly trips him up, and continues the argument on the ground. The other players run from the bench and join in the rumpus. The fielders come running in and the pile on the home plate looks like a foot ball scrimmage. A solemn warning to all rotten umpires. (*The Phonoscope*, July 1899, 14.)

SUBJECT: Baseball. Violence.

ARCHIVE: DLC-pp.

CITATIONS: *New York Clipper*, 15 April 1899, 136; 29 April 1899, 178; *Edison Films*, March 1900, 35; *Edison Films*, July 1901, 70.

NOTE:

---

678 *Tommy Atkins, Bobby and Cook / Tommy Atkins, Bobby and the Cook

LENGTH: 75 ft.   © 22 April 1899.

PRODUCER: James White.

CAMERA:

CAST:

PRODUCTION DATE: [March to mid-April 1899.]

LOCATION: [Black Maria], West Orange, N.J.

SOURCE:

DESCRIPTION: Here is a soldier enjoying the hospitality of the kitchen maid, and having a real good time. There comes a knock on the door, and he hides behind a screen, while cook hurriedly clears the table. In comes a bobby, who kisses the maid, and sits down to the table and eats. He hears a noise behind the screen and gets up to investigate. Discovers the soldier, and a rough and tumble fight follows. (*Edison Films*, March 1900, 37.)

SUBJECT: Soldiers. Police. Violence. Courtship. Kitchens.

ARCHIVE: DLC-pp.

CITATIONS: *Edison Films*, July 1901, 77.

NOTE: Same wallpaper as in entry nos. 601, 602, 621, 641.

---

679 *A Wringing Good Joke

LENGTH: 50 ft.   © Thomas A. Edison, 22 April 1899.

PRODUCER: James White.
CAMERA:
CAST:
PRODUCTION DATE: [March to mid-April 1899.]
LOCATION: Black Maria, West Orange, N.J.
SOURCE: *A (W)ringing Good Joke* (Biograph film no. 884, March 1899).

DESCRIPTION: Grandpa sits nodding in his arm chair in the kitchen where a woman is at work over a wash tub. Small boy plans mischief. She is called away from her work, and while she is talking at the door, small boy ties a string from the tub handle to grandpa's chair, which suddenly tips over backward, upsetting the tub, soap suds and clothes all over him. The small boy dances in wicked glee; especially when the woman, in trying to help the old man up, slips on a piece of soap, and herself falls into the mess. (*Edison Films*, March 1900, 35.)
SUBJECT: Boys. Practical jokes. Kitchens.
ARCHIVE: DLC-pp.
CITATIONS: *New York Clipper*, 1 July 1899, 360.
NOTE:

680 ***Cripple Creek Bar-Room Scene***
LENGTH: 50 ft.   © Thomas A. Edison, 22 April 1899.
PRODUCER: James White.
CAMERA:
CAST:
PRODUCTION DATE: March to mid-April 1899.
LOCATION: Black Maria, West Orange, N.J.
SOURCE: *A Bar Room Scene* (Edison film no. 37, 1894), *Poker at Dawson City* (Edison film no. 660, 1899).

DESCRIPTION: Shows tap room of the "Miner's Arms," stout lady at bar, and three men playing stud horse. Old toper with a silk hat asleep by the stove. Rough miner enters, bar maid serves him with Red Eye Whisky and he proceeds to clean out the place. Barmaid takes a hand with a siphon of vichy, and bounces the intruder; with the help of the card players, who line up before the bar and take copious drinks on the house. (*Edison Films*, March 1900, 35.)
SUBJECT: Taverns, etc. Alcoholic beverages. Gold mines and mining. Poker. Violence. Gambling.
ARCHIVE: DLC-pp.
CITATIONS: *New York Clipper*, 23 September 1899, 619; *Edison Films*, July 1901, 70-71.
NOTE:

681 ***104th Street Curve, New York Elevated Railway / Panoramic View, Elevated R.R., N.Y., 104th St. Curve / 104th St. Curve, New York Elevated Railway***
LENGTH: 75 and 150 ft.   © Thomas A. Edison, 22 April 1899.
PRODUCER: James White.
CAMERA:
CAST:
PRODUCTION DATE: Late March to mid-April 1899.
LOCATION: New York, N.Y.
SOURCE:
DESCRIPTION: Taken from the front platform of a special train run backward over this celebrated S curve. Not only are the passing trains and crowded platforms of great interest, but the view of uptown New York is an excellent one, showing acre upon

acre of roofs, towers, steeples and towering apartment houses. As the "special" slows up at 92nd street, a Harlem express dashes by, the engineer leaning out of his cab, and waving a good-bye. (*The Phonoscope*, June 1899, 17.)

SUBJECT: Railroads. Urban transportation.

ARCHIVE: DLC-pp.

CITATIONS: *New York Clipper*, 29 April 1899, 178; *Edison Films*, March 1900, 42; *Edison Films*, July 1901, 89.

NOTE:

New Yorkers had looked forward to greeting the U.S. "Raleigh" with large scale celebrations. However, the cruiser, the first of Admiral George Dewey's warships to return to the United States, arrived in New York harbor hours late—well after all the excursion boats that were waiting to greet it had given up and gone home. The following day was cold and wet, dampening moods and precluding effective filming of the celebration. The Edison crew had to be satisfied with shooting the warship one day after the disappointing reception.

682 *****Morning Colors on U.S. Cruiser "Raleigh"**

LENGTH: 75 ft.   © Thomas A. Edison, 28 April 1899.

PRODUCER: James White.

CAMERA:

CAST:

PRODUCTION DATE: 17 April 1899.

LOCATION: Hudson River, New York, N.Y.

SOURCE:

DESCRIPTION: Shows a group of sailors and an officer at the stern. The flag runs out in a ball to the end of the staff, and, at the signal, is broken. Proudly the stars and stripes wave in the morning breeze, while the officer salutes. A very pretty picture of man-o-war life. (*The Phonoscope*, June 1899, 17.)

SUBJECT: Harbors–New York. Navies–United States. Spanish-American War. Flags–United States.

ARCHIVE: DLC-pp.

CITATIONS:

NOTE:

683 *****U.S. Cruiser "Raleigh" / U.S. Cruiser "Raleigh," New York Harbor**

LENGTH: 50 ft.   © Thomas A. Edison, 22 April 1899.

PRODUCER: James White.

CAMERA:

CAST: Joseph B. Coughlan.

PRODUCTION DATE: 17 April 1899.

LOCATION: Hudson River, New York, N.Y.

SOURCE:

DESCRIPTION: A panoramic view of the "Raleigh," as she lies at anchor off 27th street, North River, April 17, 1899. Captain Coghlan stands among a group of officers near the bridge. The "Raleigh" fired the first gun at Manila, and is the first boat of the Pacific Squadron visiting New York. All the details of the famous battleship are clearly shown as the launch from which the picture was taken moves rapidly around her. (*The Phonoscope*, June 1899, 17.)

SUBJECT: Harbors–New York. Navies–United States. Navies–officers. Spanish-American War.

ARCHIVE: DLC-pp.

CITATIONS: "Returning Raleigh Fired First Shot at Manila," *New York Herald*, 2 April 1899, 3E; "Crowds Ashore Cheered Cruiser," *New York Herald,* 17 April 1899, 4. *New York Clipper*, 29 April 1899, 178; *Edison Films*, March 1900, 5.

NOTE:

84 *Pilot Boats in New York Harbor

LENGTH: 75 ft.   © Thomas A. Edison, 22 April 1899.

PRODUCER: James White.

CAMERA:

CAST:

PRODUCTION DATE: 17 April 1899.

LOCATION: New York Harbor, New York, N.Y.

SOURCE:

DESCRIPTION: A close view of an eighty-footer, schooner rigged, trim as a private yacht, skimming over the waters of the harbor, near Robin's Reef, which picturesque little light house is seen in the near background. A steamer decked with bunting also passes by at close range. (*The Phonoscope*, June 1899, 17.)

SUBJECT: Harbors–New York. Yachts and yachting. Steamships. Pilot boats. Lighthouses.

ARCHIVE: DLC-pp.

CITATIONS: "Pilot Boats Sigh," *New York Herald,* 7 June 1896, 10D. *Edison Films*, March 1900, 42.

NOTE:

THE RALEIGH REACHES QUARANTINE AT MIDNIGHT.
THOUSANDS WAITED FOR THE RALEIGH
Disappointed Multitudes Thronged Water Front and Steamers Eager to Welcome the Homecoming Cruiser.
CITY GAY WITH BUNTING FROM BATTERY TO BRONX
Expectant Fleet Cruised at the Harbor Gates in the Wake of the Glen Island, with the Mayor Aboard.
CITY OFFICIALS IN THE PARTY.
Riverside Drive Packed with Crowds Who Longed for a Sight of the Famous Fighting Ship.

The United States cruiser Raleigh made an unobtrusive entrance into the harbor last night and came to anchor off Tompkinsville at midnight. There was none to welcome her except the Herald's tug, which had been on the look out throughout the day. Upon hailing the vessel immediately after her anchor had been let go, I learned from the officer of the deck that the trip from Bermuda had been without incident of any sort except for a bit of rough weather encountered on Thursday. The vessel came into port wet with new paint and trying to look her best for the reception which awaits her today. The Raleigh was delayed in Bermuda by difficulty in getting the coal delivered alongside. Everybody was anxious to get away on Wednesday night, but the trouble with the coaling, combined with the threatening weather, made that impossible. She sailed at daylight on Thursday, hoping to make up lost time, but as soon as she was clear of the island she encountered a strong northwest wind, with a heavy sea. This necessitated a slowing down. About midnight Friday, just as the vessel had opened out to a fourteen knot gale, a gauge glass in one of the boilers blew out, filling the fire room with steam and driving the firemen from it. This delayed the ship thirty minutes. Thousands by land and sea waited for the Raleigh all day yesterday, and went home at night disappointed....(*New York Herald,* 16 April 1899, 2G.)

VICTOR'S TRIUMPH FOR THE RALEIGH
Flying the Flags She Flew at Cavite, the First of Admiral Dewey's Renowned Fleet to Return
Steams Up the North River While Watching Thousands Applaud.
MAYOR BESTOWS THE CITY'S FREEDOM ON HER OFFICERS.
Though Rain Decreased the Throng of Spectators, Their Ardor Was Not Dampened,
and in the Cruiser's Wardroom Happy Officers Toasted the Raleigh's Achievement.
CLAIM THE HONOR OF THE FIRST SHOT IN THE PHILIPPINES.

The fine cruiser Raleigh, looking grim in her coat of fighting gray, achieved another triumph yesterday when, greeted by the cheers and shouts of thousands, she steamed up the river under escort of the fleet which had been sent to do her honor.

It was to praising mortals and weeping skies that this last act of the Raleigh's dramatic cruise was played to the end. Skies leaden as her own garb of "Dewey gray," an ill east wind which drove the sloping drizzle into the faces of the patient crowd and a generally cheerless aspect of the weather all tended to make her home coming devoid of the enthusiasm that goes with the excursion gayety of fairer days.

But the greeting that awaited her no rain could dampen, and the moral of that mighty welcome lies in the sincerity of it. The excursion fleet was not as large as some that have paraded up the North River, but then excursions cannot be inaugurated offhand, and the Raleigh was expected the day before she got in. Had she arrived on time her passage up the river would have been marked by the size of the flotilla that was waiting to do her honor. She did not arrive in time for that, but in the long stretch of water front, with pier heads everywhere black with people to become white with fluttering handkerchiefs and reverberant with cheers the moment she drew near, the gallant crew of the Raleigh had a more convincing testimonial than any excursion fleet could have given. (*New York Herald*, 17 April 1899, 3.)

In late May, the Edison Manufacturing Company produced a series of films "illustrating movements of our troops in the Philippine Islands" against the insurgent forces of Emilo Aguinaldo in late March 1899. (New York Clipper, 10 June 1899, 297.) Once again they employed members of the local National Guard.

685　***Advance of Kansas Volunteers at Caloocan / Advance of 20th Kansas Volunteers**
LENGTH: 75 ft.　© Thomas A. Edison, 5 June 1899.
PRODUCER: James White.
CAMERA:
CAST:
PRODUCTION DATE: May 1899.
LOCATION: [Orange Mountains, West Orange, N.J.]
SOURCE:

DESCRIPTION: From the thick underbrush where the Filipinos are massed comes volley after volley. They are making one of those determined stands that marks Caloocan as the bloodiest battle of the Filipino rebellion. Suddenly, with impetuous rush, Funston's men appear. They pause but a moment, to fire, reload and fire. The bearer falls, but the standard is caught up by the brave Sergeant Squires and waves undaunted in the smoke and dine of the receding battle. This is one of the best battle pictures ever made. The first firing is done directly toward the front of the picture, and the advance of the U.S. troops apparently through the screen is very exciting; the gradual disappearance of the fighters sustaining the interest to the end. (*Edison Films*, March 1900, 4.)
SUBJECT: Historical Reenactments. Armies–United States. Philippines–History–Insurrection (1899-1901). Frederick Funston. Sergeant Squires.
ARCHIVE: DLC-pp.
CITATIONS: "Through the Bush and Swamp Our Brave Men Dash," *New York Herald*, 2 April 1899, 1D. *The Phonoscope*, May 1899, 14; *New York Clipper*, 10 June 1899, 297; 23 September 1899, 619; *Edison Films*, July 1901, 30.
NOTE: See also film no. 721, *Colonel Funston Swimming the Bagbag River.*

686　***Rout of the Filipinos / Rout of Filipinos**
LENGTH: 75 ft.　© Thomas A. Edison, 10 June 1899.
PRODUCER: James White.
CAMERA:
CAST:
PRODUCTION DATE: May 1899.
LOCATION: [Orange Mountains, West Orange, N.J.]
SOURCE:
DESCRIPTION: A dense thicket at Caloocan showing the tropical foliage and large trees.

First one straggler, then another, then a whole body of flying Filipinos, retreating in disorder, firing occasionally, falling in the brush, and finally disappearing. A smokey haze hangs over the scene like a pall. Then comes the U.S. Infantry, crouching in the underbrush, firing and advancing steadily around the waving flag. Just as the advance is in full swing, the officer in command is shot. Down drops his upraised sword and he falls forward. The scene is well chosen, and from a photographic standpoint, as well as dramatically, the picture is an excellent one. (*Edison Films*, March 1900, 4.)

SUBJECT: Historical Reenactments. Armies–United States. Philippines–History–Insurrection (1899-1901).

ARCHIVE: DLC-pp.

CITATIONS: *The Phonoscope*, May 1899, 14; *New York Clipper*, 10 June 1899, 297; 23 September 1899, 619; *Edison Films*, July 1901, 30.

NOTE:

687 ***U.S. Troops and Red Cross in the Trenches Before Caloocan / Red Cross and U.S. Troops in the Trenches Before Caloocan / Red Cross in the Trenches**

LENGTH: 75 ft.   © Thomas A. Edison, 5 June 1899.

PRODUCER: James White.

CAMERA:

CAST:

PRODUCTION DATE: May 1899.

LOCATION: [Orange Mountains, West Orange, N.J.]

SOURCE:

DESCRIPTION: Our troops have driven the Filipinos out of the trenches, and, after firing one or two volleys, press on in pursuit. The enemy returns the fire and the forward rush is marked by a trail of dead and wounded. Following close behind is the hospital corps. Stretchers are quickly brought out and the nurses tenderly care for the fallen and carry them to the rear. (*Edison Films*, March 1900, 4.)

SUBJECT: Historical Reenactments. Armies–United States. Philippines–History–Insurrection (1899-1901). Red Cross.

ARCHIVE: DLC-pp.

CITATIONS: *The Phonoscope*, May 1899, 14; *New York Clipper*, 10 June 1899, 297; 23 September 1899, 619; *Edison Films*, July 1901, 33-31.

NOTE:

According to Filipino accounts a thousand Americans have been killed, the fatalities being especially heavy at Caloocan, where the United States troops "rushed like madmen against a storm of bullets." (*New York World*, 25 March 1899, 1-2.)

VALIANT CHARGE OF AMERICAN TROOPS

The American troops charged fiercely through the brush and heavy growth in the bamboo groves. They never faltered in the onward rush.

Strategists of the enemy had prepared many obstacles and ingeniously concealed trenches to frustrate the advance of the American troops. They were futile.

The loss of the Americans is much less than that of the Filipinos. The enemy lost heavily from the effective fire of the American artillery. The Filipinos were driven out of the trenches....

GENERAL OTIS REPORTED HEAVY FIGHTING.

Weaton's brigade at Caloocan drove enemy one and a half miles north, across the river. Hall on extreme right encountered considerable force and routed it. Fighting heavy near Caloocan. Movement continues in morning....Otis. (*New York World*, 26 March 1899, 1.)

The insurgents stopped firing when our doctors went forward to get the Filipino wounded. (*New York Herald*, 26 March 1899, 1.)

688 ***Filipinos Retreat from Trenches / Filipinos Retreat from the Trenches**
LENGTH: 75 ft. and 50 ft.   © Thomas A. Edison, 5 June 1899.
PRODUCER: James White.
CAMERA:
CAST:
PRODUCTION DATE: May 1899.
LOCATION: [Orange Mountains, West Orange, N.J.]
SOURCE:
DESCRIPTION: An incident of the Battle of the Trenches at Candabar. The enemy threw up a high earth embankment during the night, and are defending it with great stubbornness. The pits are crowded with Filipinos, who fire volley after volley. The artillery of the Americans plays havoc with their ranks and

they fall back, leaving many dead. Their retreat is hotly covered by a company of U.S. Infantry, with mounted officer. They rumble over the embankment into the trench, fire volley and advance. The officer carefully examines the earthworks, his horse picking his way cautiously over the bodies of the fallen foe. (*Edison Films*, March 1900, 4.)
SUBJECT: Historical Reenactments. Armies–United States. Philippines–History–Insurrection (1899-1901).
ARCHIVE: DLC-pp.
CITATIONS: *The Phonoscope*, May 1899, 14; *New York Clipper*, 10 June 1899, 297; 23 September 1899, 61; *Edison Films,* July 1901, 31.
NOTE:

689 ***Capture of Trenches at Candaba / Capture of Trenches at Candabar / Capture of the Trenches at Candabar**
LENGTH: 75 ft.   © Thomas A. Edison, 10 June 1899.
PRODUCER: James White.
CAMERA:
CAST:
PRODUCTION DATE: May 1899.
LOCATION: [Orange Mountains, West Orange, N.J.]
SOURCE:
DESCRIPTION: The Filipinos execute a flank movement and re-occupy the trenches, cutting off the advance guard of Americans. The rebel flag waves over the ditch and they defend their position bravely. A fierce charge by our soldiers makes them give way and

they scatter in all directions. The officer in command pays dearly for his desperate sortie. Just as his horse clears the embankment the officer throws up his hands and falls backward with a crash; while the riderless horse dashes off toward the American lines. A picture full of exciting action and excellent detail. (*Edison Films*, March 1900, 4-5.)
SUBJECT: Historical Reenactments. Armies–United States. Philippines–History–Insurrection (1899-1901).
ARCHIVE: DLC-pp.
CITATIONS: *The Phonoscope*, May 1899, 14; *New York Clipper*, 10 June 1899, 297; 23 September 1899, 619; *Edison Films,* July 1901, 31.
NOTE:

690 ***U.S. Infantry Supported by Rough Riders at El Caney / U.S. Infantry Supported by Rough Riders before El Caney / U.S. Troops at El Caney**
LENGTH: 100 ft.   © Thomas A. Edison, 5 June 1899.
PRODUCER: James White.
CAMERA:
CAST:
PRODUCTION DATE: May 1899.
LOCATION: [Orange Mountains, West Orange, N.J.]

SOURCE:
DESCRIPTION: Up the road comes a detachment of infantry, firing, advancing, kneeling and firing again and again. The advance of the foot soldiers is followed by a troop of Rough Riders, riding like demons, yelling and firing revolvers as they pass out of sight. Other troops follow in quick succession, pressing on to front. (*The Phonoscope*, June 1899, 17.)
SUBJECT: Historical Reenactments. Armies–United States. Spanish-American War. First U.S. Cavalry (Volunteer).
ARCHIVE: DLC-pp.
CITATIONS: *The Phonoscope*, June 1899, 14; *New York Clipper*, 10 June 1899, 297; 1 July 1899, 360; *Edison Films*, March 1900, 11.
NOTE: "Re-enacts" a scene from the American invasion of Cuba.

691 ***Skirmish of Rough Riders**
LENGTH: 75 ft.   © Thomas A. Edison, 10 June 1899.
PRODUCER: James White.
CAMERA:
CAST:
PRODUCTION DATE: May 1899.
LOCATION: [Orange Mountains, West Orange, N.J.]

SOURCE:
DESCRIPTION: Shielded by a thick bit of timber at a turn of the road stands a company of mounted men, awaiting the order to advance. In the foreground, left by the flotsam of battle, is a dead horse from the shelter of which two marksmen are picking off the enemy. Suddenly the command, "Forward," and the riders dash up the road, out of sight, leaving behind them a great cloud of dust and smoke. A detachment of infantry covers the advance and volley repeatedly as they press forward. (*Edison Films*, March 1900, 10-11.)
SUBJECT: Historical Reenactments. Armies–United States. Spanish-American War. First U.S. Cavalry (Volunteer).
ARCHIVE: DLC-pp.
CITATIONS: *The Phonoscope*, June 1899, 14; *Edison Films*, July 1901, 34.
NOTE:

692 ***New York Police Parade, June 1st, 1899**
LENGTH: 150 ft.   © Thomas A. Edison, 10 June 1899.
PRODUCER:
CAMERA:
CAST: William S. Devery.
PRODUCTION DATE: 1 June 1899.
LOCATION: Union Square, New York, N.Y.
SOURCE:
DESCRIPTION: An excellent view of "The Finest," on their annual parade and inspection June 1, 1899. The head of the column is just turning into 14th street from

Broadway, the Morton House forming part of the background. Crowds line both sides of the cable car tracks, falling back as the band heading the first division swings around Dead Man's Curve, and passes the camera. Chief Devery makes a fine showing; as also do his men, with their white gloves and helmets, shining buttons and spick and span appearances in general. (*The Phonoscope*, June 1899, 17.)

SUBJECT: Parades. Police.

ARCHIVE: DLC-pp.

CITATIONS: *Edison Films*, March 1900, 43; *Edison Films*, July 1901, 91.

NOTE:

POLICE ON PARADE: THE CROWDS CHEER.
Brave Bluecoats March Over a Long Route and Receive a Warm Greeting.
MEN REVIEWED BY NOTABLES.
Gen. Joseph Wheeler on the Stand Along with the Mayor and Commissioners.
RHINELANDER MEDAL FOR SCHLEPP.
At the Crowd's Behest the Brooklyn Patrolman Is Made Roundsman on the Spot.

New York saw the biggest police parade in its history yesterday. There were 5,000 bluecoats in line. Applause greeted them all along the line from the Battery up Broadway and Madison avenue to Fifty-ninth street and back again down Fifth avenue to Madison Square.

The parade got away promptly on schedule time–1 P.M. At the head marched the Twelfth Regiment band, and right behind it came Chief Devery, riding a prancing charger.

Meanwhile the two grand stands at Twenty-sixth street began blossoming like flower gardens. All the friends of the force were there, and many notables, including Mayor Van Wyck, Magistrate Simms, Comptroller Coler, Gen. Wheeler, Health Commissioner Jenkins, Corporation Counsel Whalen, James J. Coogan and Dr. John T. Nagie.

Chief Devery and his full staff, all mounted, reached the stand at 3:45.

That was the signal for the Mayor and President York to get in their carriage, and the other Commissioners in theirs, while Chief Devery escorted them up Fifth avenue, from one end of the line to the other.

The reviewing party returned, and Patrolman John E. Schlepp of Brooklyn, stepped forward to receive the Rhinelander medal, annually awarded to the bluecoat who shows the most bravery. He rescued a woman and five children at a fire on April 14 last.

Mayor Van Wyck pinned the medal on Schlepp's breast.

"Make him a 'roundsman'!" yelled the crowd.

"I nominate him for the post of roundsman," said Chief Devery.

"Then the Police Board unanimously approves the nomination," said President York.

There were rousing cheers, and then the parade. All the well-known captains got ovations, particularly Capt. Chapman and Capt. Stephenson.

When Capt. Price swung along there was a roar–half cheers and some hisses. Just opposite the reviewing stand Capt. Price turned his ankle and he dropped his baton.

In the rear came the mounted police and the bicycle squad. They didn't get a hand though the mounted men looked superbly. The Seventh Regiment Band got a rousing reception all along the route and another at the stand.

The Maset Committee saw the parade at the corner of Franklin street and Broadway, having lunched at a cafe nearby.

There were two notable absentees, Capt. Creedon and Capt. Schmittberger.

"I used my judgement in leaving Schmittberger out," said Chief Devery. "I do not consider him a proper person to have any one under him in the Police Department."

At the conclusion of the parade nearly one hundred members of the Broadway Squad went to Schuetsen Hall, No. 12 St. Mark's place and had a dinner.

It was decided that hereafter a dinner shall be held annually on the day of the parade. (*The World*, 2 June 1899, 5.)

The boxing match between heavy-weight world champion Robert Fitzsimmons and challenger James Jeffries led to a series of films made before, during, and after the actual bout. Blackton and Smith's American Vitagraph Company filmed the challenger in training before the match. The filmmakers had also arranged to film the fight itself—indoors at night, under a bank of arc lamps. Unfortunately for those involved, the electrical system failed almost at the outset. If successful, films of this eleven-round fight, which made Jeffries the new champion, would have been extremely lucrative. In all likelihood, Vitagraph sought to recover from this embarrassing setback by filming a reenactment of the fistic encounter.

693 Jeffries Throwing Medicine Ball

LENGTH: 50 ft.   © No reg.
PRODUCER: J. Stuart Blackton, Albert E. Smith.
CAMERA: J. Stuart Blackton and/or Albert E. Smith.
CAST: James J. Jeffries, Jack Jeffries, Jim Daly, Tom Ryan.
PRODUCTION DATE: 7 June 1899.
LOCATION: Asbury Park, N.J.
SOURCE:
DESCRIPTION: An absolutely perfect picture of the champion heavyweight of the world, James J. Jeffries, throwing the medicine ball. (*Edison Films,* September 1902, 28.)
SUBJECT: Boxing. Training. Althetics.
ARCHIVE:
CITATIONS: American Vitagraph Company, advertisement, *New York Clipper,* 21 April 1900, 192.
NOTE: The Edison staff took films of James J. Jeffries in his training camp before his fight with Gus Ruhlin on 15 November 1901 in Los Angeles. It seems very likely, however, that in addition to those films, two of the three negatives taken by Blackton and Smith were dusted off for use. *Fun in Training Camp* or *Fun in the Training Quarters* (75 ft.) was apparently not used.

694 Jeffries Skipping Rope / Jeffries Skipping the Rope

LENGTH: 85 ft.   © No reg.
PRODUCER: J. Stuart Blackton, Albert E. Smith.
CAMERA: J. Stuart Blackton and/or Albert E. Smith.
CAST: James J. Jeffries, Jack Jeffries.
PRODUCTION DATE: 7 June 1899.
LOCATION: Asbury Park, N.J.
SOURCE:
DESCRIPTION: A splendid subject showing the champion heavyweight of the world exercising in his training quarters. After showing his skill in side stepping and fancy steps, while skipping the rope at a phenomenal speed, the champion's trainers peel off his sweater and administer a rub-down, during which application the mighty muscles on the champion's chest and back are seen to perfection. (*Edison Films,* September 1902, 29.)
SUBJECT: Boxing. Training. Althetics.
ARCHIVE:
CITATIONS: American Vitagraph Company, advertisement, *New York Clipper,* 21 April 1900, 192.
NOTE: Vitagraph offered this film for sale in April 1900 as a 100 ft. subject.

FITZSIMMONS AND JEFFRIES LET UP IN THEIR WORK, INTENSE HEAT CAUSED CAUTION IN BOTH CAMPS.
Jeffries Has a Day of Pleasure, Takes Another Ocean Bath Before a Moving Camera and Has Fun with Jim Daly in a Public Three Round Bout–Boiler-Maker Surprises Daly and the Crowd by His Cleverness.
ASBURY PARK, N.J., June 7. Jeffries boxed Jim Daly three short rounds at the theatre here to-night. They came on between acts of "The Widow From the West," and Jeffries was introduced by Ross O'Neill as the coming champion of the world.
Jeffries danced around Daly, tapping him on the head and body and avoiding the vicious swings that were launched in his direction. The round was about a minute and a half. The second round was stopped at the end of one minute by an upper cut on the chin that rattled the teeth in Daly's head.
It was somewhat harder than Jeff intended it to be and the audience was as much surprised as Daly. He came back after the minute's rest and roughed it for thirty seconds. It was no sparring match for points on Daly's part. That uppercut had hurt him and he was trying to pay it back.
He failed to land a good one and Jeffries put on more steam. Daly was knocked and tossed about the stage in the

last half-minute of the round as if he had been a child. His 190 pounds counted for nothing in the hands of the young giant and at any moment Jeffries could have put him out. Jeffries will probably not don the gloves again until he enters the ring.

Ocean Bath Before the Camera.
(Special to The World.)

ASBURY PARK, N.J., June 7.–Quiet and restful was the order of things at Loch Arbor training quarters this morning. Billy Delaney prohibited the long morning run and during the sultry hours, from 8 o'clock to 11, Jeffries lolled in a hammock on the veranda or was sprawled on the grass in the shade.

The one thing done that was like work was posing before a vitagraph for moving pictures. This occupied the entire afternoon. The series began with the medicine ball. Daly, Jack Jeffries and Tommy Ryan each took their turn with Jim before the camera and were successively bowled over like sticks. The big ball left his hands as if sent from a machine, and the three trainers were willing enough to pose in lighter work.

A comic scene in which Jeffries and Ryan engaged in a water fight with the hose, which ended up in a wrestling match in which Ryan was worsted, was followed by rope skipping and a rub down. The entire party, including about a dozen visitors, then repaired to the beach in front of the life-saving station and ground out pictures by the hundred. Jeffries, Jim Daly, Bill Delaney, Marty McCue, Jack Jeffries and Dick Toner sported in the high surf for twenty minutes. After returning to the house a few minutes of bag punching ended the day's work.

No one connected with the training quarters had anything to say about Chief Devery's announced intention to stop the fight if there was any slugging.

Tommy Ryan, who had worked hard and faithfully to prepare himself for his bout with Mysterious Billy Smith on June 13, was greatly disappointed to hear that Smith had been overcome by heat and would be unable to meet him. (*New York World,* 8 June 1899, 8.)

695 [The Jeffries-Fitzsimmons Fight]
LENGTH: © No reg.
PRODUCER: J. Stuart Blackton, Albert E. Smith.
CAMERA: J. Stuart Blackton and/or Albert E. Smith.
CAST: Robert Fitzsimmons, James J. Jeffries.
PRODUCTION DATE: 9 June 1899.
LOCATION: Coney Island, N.Y.
SOURCE:
DESCRIPTION:
SUBJECT: Sports. Boxing.
ARCHIVE:
CITATIONS:
NOTE: This filmmaking effort was unsuccessful due to the failure of the electrical lighting system designed to illuminate the arena where the boxing match was being shot.

JEFFRIES WINS IN ELEVEN ROUNDS.
The Big Californian Wrests the World's Championship
from "Bob" Fitzsimmons in a Fast and Hard-Fought Contest.
GETS LEAD EARLY AND HOLDS IT.
With Odds Against Him, the Boiler-Maker Upsets the Gamblers' Expectations
and Has the Battle in His Favor Throughout–Immense Crowd Sees the Bout.
DEVERY THERE, BUT DOES NOT INTERFERE.
Betting at the Ringside Heavy, with the Odds at 2 to 1 on Fitzsimmons Until the Fight Is Half Over,
When They Change to 7 to 5 on the Ex-Champion–Mrs. Fitzsimmons Sees the Fight.
Jeffries, the New Champion, to The World After the Fight.
(Special to The World.)

Coney Island Sporting Club, June 9.

The result of this battle, for which I have trained as few men ever trained for a fight, did not surprise me. I expected to win, as I have stated before to The World, and my surprise would have been almost as great as my disappointment if the battle had gone against me.

There is no depreciation of my feelings in the matter, either, for to be victorious in this fight meant a great deal more to me than to some others who have held the title of champion.

I had an idea when I went into the ring what blow would win for me, as I expected to stagger him with the left and put him out with the right. I had given little consideration to the round in which I would win, as I knew I was thoroughly capable of going the entire twenty-five.

I had been well drilled in the fact that Fitz was a wonderful fighter and a hard man to beat, but from that very fact I gained courage, as I knew the greater glory would be mine for defeating him.

When I knocked him down the first time I thought I had him out. His vitality was too great and he fought as hard afterward as he did before. One cut on the eye was all I got, but he opened that several times.

As the fight went on I became more and more convinced that I would get him directly. There was not much time to think, but it did occur to me to be thankful for the hard work I had done and the good training I had.

One thing that makes me specially proud and happy for this victory is the fact that I am not only the undisputed champion of the world but the undefeated champion as well, and the title has been won without a single slur ever being cast upon my motives, without a single boast and without my ever having struck a foul blow or taken an undue advantage of any antagonist.

Fitzsimmons was and still is my friend, so is Julian. I have the kindest feelings toward them both, and give Fitz great credit for his splendid fighting ability.

I am an American born and bred, and as an American will defend my present title against all comers. In a short time I will go with my brother to my home in Los Angeles, Cal., and spend some time with my father and mother.

I have no other plans at present and have no idea whom I shall fight next.

I think I had many friends in the audience judging from the demonstration.

From the demonstrations when I won and as I was leaving the ring I think I made many more–at least I hope I did.

I expect to hold this title many years, defending it as occasions arise, and as a young man in perfect health I believe my chance for doing so is bright. Very truly, JAMES JEFFRIES. (*New York World*, 10 June 1899, 1.)

The Films That Failed
Emergency Experiences in Trying to Electrically Illuminate a Prize Fight

On Friday, June 9, at the building of the Coney Island Athletic Club, there was attempted a solution of an electrical and photographic problem, which, had it succeeded, would have resulted in successful kinetoscope films of the big prize-fight, in which Robert Fitzsimmons and James Jeffries were the principals.

The light conditions to be obtained were the illumination of a platform about 24 feet square, to such an intensity as to permit successful instantaneous photography of any objects or persons standing upon it.

It was essentially a hurry up job. A great deal of money was spent in making haste, and if so much haste had not been necessary there might have been more light. The lamps were 24 in number, and were supposed to consume from 50 to 80 amperes each at 80 volts. This current load it was found impossible to obtain either from the local lighting or railway circuits, and the immediate erection of a temporary plant, rheostats and systems of wiring was necessary; whereby hangs a tale.

The boiler of this installation was an upright tubular affair standing, with its short stack, some 30 feet high, and which, in its gaunt uncovered condition, looked as if it might have been resurrected from some saw-mill. Indeed, the local boiler inspector seemed to think so, for rumor has it that he objected to certain features of its construction, and declined to permit it to be used, and it is also said that this difficulty was gotten over by the simple device of passing both the inspector and the boiler. Certain it is that about 12 o'clock on the day of the contest steam was up in the boiler and hissing ominously out of the safety valve.

The engine which this boiler supplied was a bulky, single cylinder, Corliss type, and was mounted on a not too secure foundation of a few railway ties imbedded in the sand. The exhaust was piped off to a sufficient distance so as not to annoy the engineer, that being the only requisite which the occasion demanded.

When the engine was revolving at full speed there was a decided sense of insecurity, as it rocked and swayed, and there was every prospect of the fly-wheel suddenly finding the bottom of the pit which had been excavated for it, in which case engine and boiler would have undoubtedly constituted a very energetic and destructive merry-go-round, surpassing anything that has been seen, even on Coney Island. A long belt connected the engine with a generator which apparently was capable of developing as much as 150 kilowatts and rated at a pressure of 220 volts. A few beams driven into the ground, with two or three cross-beams, supported an ammeter and voltmeter and a telephone connected with the lamp platform, and a canvas roof, stretched upon posts stuck in the sand, housed the installation.

One of the leads of the dynamo was sent directly to the arc lamps and became a common positive for them all. The negative wire was split up into 24 sections, each passing through a rheostat on its way to the individual lamp that it supplied. The rheostats were of the liquid type, and here local conveniences were utilized, for each rheostat consisted of a substantial beer barrel in which were immersed two metal plates, the barrel being filled with water to which a suitable modicum of salt was added. The arc lamps themselves were supported on a square platform surrounding the ring side and some 30 feet above its level. Each lamp was mounted on the floor of this platform and its beams were directed on the floor of the ring. The lamps consisted of a sheet-iron reflector on the back of which were mounted stout oak bars. The whole was pivoted at its lower end on a universal joint. Short projections from either end of the wooden bar accommodated a brass carbon holder adapted to carry an inch carbon. The upper carbon holder was provided with a rack attachment enabling the carbon to be fed down as occasion required or to be manipulated for the purpose of striking the arc, which occasion [was] required much more frequently. Poised on thin supports the lamps looked over the edge of the platform like 24 interested and animated coal hods mounted on nodding stems. A switch and fuse-block completed the equipment of each lamp. Some of the switches of these lamps were capable of carrying fully 300 amperes and others were closely allied to the "baby"-knife class. Altogether it was as heterogeneous a collection as might be imagined. There were quick breaks, slow breaks and those that didn't break at all. The lamp circuits themselves were connected in many cases with wire equivalent to perhaps No. 12, and the fuse-blocks protecting them were found to contain short and very healthy looking pieces of No. 10 copper wire. As far as can be learned none of these fuses ever blew; they would doubtless have been a very permanent part of the installation had it not been that the management decided that it was better to remove them and replace them with fuse wire.

Some hours before the fight the plant was started up and each arc lamp was adjusted singly, telephone communication being had between the arc-lamp platform and the dynamo. The operator adjusted the carbons and called for more salt in the rheostats until the light was "about right," and the lamp was then extinguished and the next one adjusted in the same way. Each lamp operated alone gave a magnificent illumination and seemed to flood the ring with light, and it was fondly hoped that if each light proved thus satisfactory they would operate simultaneously with equal effectiveness. They were mostly adjusted for 60 amperes. Now, 60 times 24 is 1,440, and if the machine had this ampere capacity its total necessary watt output at 220 volts would be 317 kilowatts, a very fair over-load for a machine of apparently 150-kilowatt capacity at the very most. It seemed quite safe to predict its early decline and fall when the total lamp-load was called for.

And so indeed it proved. When the principals in the contest appeared and took their chairs in the respective corners, everyone was ordered to light up, but the success was by no means as general as the order. Perhaps 12 of the 24 lights lighted. The rest gave interesting little flashes and would not hold a permanent arc in spite of the utmost ingenuity in manipulating the adjustment screws.

While the operators were endeavoring to get their lamps started, the engine outside was laboring heavily; the piston was leaky and it could not develop anything like its full horse-power, and at any suggestion of a demand for current in the dynamo the entire plant slowed down. Finally, the likeliest looking lamps which had the saltiest rheostats were picked out to operate, and the others were turned out. The light was perhaps equal to about four of the lamps burning as they should have burned, and the kinetoscope films developed out innocent of any marks that would suggest a negative.

Subsequent manipulation of the circuits after the big fight was over, showed that the device of placing two of the lamps in series had a very beneficial result, and transferred some of the energy which was being consumed in the barrels on the outside of the building to the arcs within the reflectors, and subsequent unimportant bouts occurring on succeeding evenings were very efficiently lighted. The entire essay seemed to demonstrate that even in a hastily constructed plant where economy is no consideration it is well to make a few little engineering calculations as, for instance, those which compare the capacity of the machinery with the load that is to carry, and it also demonstrates the advisability of preliminary trial before risking an installation on an important venture. The actual money lost in this attempt could not have been far short of $5,000, and it is easily possible that the kinetoscope films had they been successful might have realized $100,000.

Ample excuse for the projectors of the enterprise may be found in the lack of time, which, when it is taken into consideration, makes it surprising that any plant at all was erected; its subsequent successful performance when it was not needed is only a sad reminder of what might have been, although it demonstrates that, had there been time to properly install and connect the equipment, unqualified success was certain. (*The Phonoscope,* May 1899, 14.)

696 **Reproduction of the Jeffries-Fitzsimmons Fight**

LENGTH: 1,350 and 750 ft.   © No reg.

PRODUCER: [J. Stuart Blackton, Albert E. Smith.]

CAMERA: [J. Stuart Blackton and/or Albert E. Smith.]

CAST: [Robert Fitzsimmons, James J. Jeffries.]

PRODUCTION DATE: June-July 1899.

LOCATION:

SOURCE:

DESCRIPTION: We are prepared to furnish the six important rounds, including the knockout, Jeffries-Fitzsimmons Fight, Faithfully reproduced, just as it took place at Coney Island on the night of June 9, 1899.

The six rounds are 750 feet long . . . . Price $150
Entire Fight, Eleven Rounds, 1,350 feet . . . Price $270
(*New York Clipper,* 12 August 1899, 474.)

SUBJECT: Sports. Boxing.

ARCHIVE:

CITATIONS:

NOTE: Relatively little definitive information is available on this film, which was sometimes said to have featured the actual contestants. Sigmund Lubin also filmed a reenactment of the fight but used stand-ins.

697 ***Mesmerist and Country Couple**
LENGTH: 100 ft.   © Thomas A. Edison, 17 June 1899.
PRODUCER: [J. Stuart Blackton, Albert E. Smith.]
CAMERA: [Albert E. Smith.]
CAST: [J. Stuart Blackton (professor).]
PRODUCTION DATE: [May to mid-June 1899.]
LOCATION: [Vitagraph's roof-top studio, New
   York, N.Y.]
SOURCE:

DESCRIPTION: Mr. and Mrs. Hayseed have
   heard of the wonderful Professor, and come
   to his office. They waken him from a trance,
   give him a fee and he hypnotizes them. The
   stunts they do while under his influence
   would make the Sphinx laugh for joy.
   Hayseed stands on his head, balances him-
self on a chair and takes off his clothes. Mrs. Hayseed also begins to disrobe, but she
goes behind a screen. Her bare arm appears over the top, and she drops her clothes
on the floor. It is a hair raising moment to guess what she's going to do next. The
mystical appearances and lightning changes are managed with wonderful cleverness. (*Edison Films*, March 1900, 40.)
SUBJECT: Hypnotism. Farmers.
ARCHIVE: DLC-pp.
CITATIONS: *New York Clipper*, 23 September 1899, 619; *Edison Films,* July 1900, 84-85.
NOTE:

698 ***Strange Adventure of a New York Drummer / Adventures of a New York**
Drummer / Strange Adventures of a New York Drummer
LENGTH: 75 ft.   © Thomas A. Edison, 17 June 1899.
PRODUCER: [James White.]
CAMERA:
CAST:
PRODUCTION DATE: May to mid-June 1899.
LOCATION:
SOURCE:

DESCRIPTION: This commercial traveler has evidently had a wet day judging from the
   strange things he sees at his hotel. The hall
   boy shown him to his room, puts down his
   grips, and then calmly disappears—through
   the ceiling. Drummer pushes button five
   times for a drink and waiter appears—
   through the floor. Drummer is overcome
with surprise and turns to sit down on the bed—it promptly disappears. He fights
with the waiter, is overcome and waiter locks him in a trunk, and sits on it. After a
while opens trunk; behold! its empty. Drummer appears mysteriously, picks up a big
book, hits waiter on head, and drives him through the floor. Drummer dances in
delirious glee. (*Edison Films*, March 1900, 40.)
SUBJECT: Alcoholism. Hallucinations.
ARCHIVE: DLC-pp.
CITATIONS: *New York Clipper*, 23 September 1899, 619; 10 February 1900, 1064; *Edison
   Films,* July 1901, 84.
NOTE: Filmed on an outdoor stage (not the Black Maria), perhaps the same one used
   for *Love and War* and *The Astor Tramp*. "Drummer" was a slang expression for
   traveling salesman.

699 *The Bibulous Clothier

LENGTH: 75 ft.   © Thomas A. Edison, 23 June 1899.

PRODUCER: James White.

CAMERA:

CAST:

PRODUCTION DATE: May to mid-June 1899.

LOCATION: [Black Maria], West Orange, N.J.

SOURCE:

DESCRIPTION:

SUBJECT: Alcoholism.

ARCHIVE: DLC-pp.

CITATIONS: *New York Clipper*, 23 September 1899, 619.

NOTE:

700 *A Fair Exchange Is No Robbery

LENGTH: 50 ft.   © Thomas A. Edison, 28 June 1899.

PRODUCER: James White.

CAMERA:

CAST:

PRODUCTION DATE: June 1899.

LOCATION:

SOURCE:

DESCRIPTION: The coachman sleepeth. The broad piazzas look cool and nap provoking. Even the horse droopeth his ears and shutteth one eye contemplatively. All at once, the small boy! and with him the butler, whom he hath impressed as prime minister in the joke. Horse awakeneth and unhitcheth and leadeth away. Boy bringeth billy goat, and fasteneth to the runabout. Coachman still sleepth, boy doubleth in joy and butler shaketh. Dude comes with lady, who entereth the wagon. Dude graspeth the situation but not the joke. Awakeneth Jehu sasseth the dude, who scrappeth and bruiseth Jehu and his hat. Small boy weepth for very joy. (*The Phonoscope*, July 1899, 14.)

SUBJECT: Practical jokes. Carriages and carts. Boys. Horses. Goats.

ARCHIVE: DLC-pp.

CITATIONS: *New York Clipper*, 23 September 1899, 619.

NOTE:

In June 1899, White and the Edison staff again returned to northeastern Pennsylvania to film along the Lehigh Valley Railroad. This time they placed the camera on the front end of a locomotive (or on an observation car coupled ahead of the engine) and filmed a series of "phantom rides" from the moving train. These were designed to display the region's scenic beauty. Edison cameraman Robert Kates Bonine was originally from Altoona, Pa., and could have shot these films shortly before leaving for the Klondike on 8 June 1899.

701 *Panoramic View, Horseshoe Curve from Penna. Ltd. / Panorama of Susquehanna River Taken from the Black Diamond Express / [Panoramic View, Horseshoe Curve, Pa. Ltd., no. 1]

LENGTH: 100 ft.   © Thomas A. Edison, 22 June 1899

PRODUCER: James White.

CAMERA: [Robert K. Bonine.]

CAST:

PRODUCTION DATE: June 1899.

LOCATION: Near Altoona, Pa.

SOURCE:

DESCRIPTION: There is hardly a lovelier spot along the whole Lehigh Valley railroad than this stretch of road. We are on a gently curving bit of track, mountains on both sides. We glide beneath a slender bridge, pass a crossing and a wayside station and run out on a steep embankment. Suddenly the road dips into the hills, then out again, round a point, and the valley of the Susquehanna bursts upon our view. Far away in the blue distance the river glistens like a silver thread. There are bridges and houses and barns and steeples. There are checker board farms, and broad patches of virgin forest, all calm and serene in the glory of God's sunshine. (*Edison Films*, March 1900, 46.)

SUBJECT: Railroads. Mountains. Bridges. Rivers. Susquehanna River. Lehigh Valley Railroad. Tourist trade.
ARCHIVE: DLC-pp.
CITATIONS:
NOTE:

702 *Panoramic View, Horseshoe Curve, Pa. Ltd., no. 2

LENGTH: 150 ft.   © Thomas A. Edison, 7 July 1899.
PRODUCER: James White.
CAMERA: [Robert K. Bonine.]
CAST:
PRODUCTION DATE: June 1899.
LOCATION: Near Altoona, Pa.
SOURCE:
DESCRIPTION: On the right is the river, lost to view as the track curves toward the hills. Then a straightway thousand yards, as the train approaches a cleft in the hills. On the left a giant excavator and scores of little gravel cars. Then into a rock cut; and out again with a slight curve. For a short moment the rails glisten like a shining ribbons as the sun catches their polished surfaces. Past a puffing freight engine, a huge mogul pulling seemingly endless box cars. Another slight curve, and a broad valley greets us. Kittaning Point on the right and far away up in the hills the Altoona reservoir. Under the bridge, past a signal power, and a broad expanse of meadow and forest, bathed in sunshine. (*Edison Films*, March 1900, 46.)

SUBJECT: Railroads. Bridges. Rivers. Lehigh Valley Railroad.
ARCHIVE: DLC-pp.
CITATIONS:
NOTE:

703 *A Ride Through Pack Saddle Mountains, Penna. R.R.

LENGTH: 150 ft.   © Thomas A. Edison, 7 July 1899.
PRODUCER: James White.
CAMERA: [Robert K. Bonine.]
CAST:
PRODUCTION DATE: June 1899.
LOCATION: Near Altoona, Pa.
SOURCE:
DESCRIPTION: The picture shows a beautiful panoramic view of ever changing interest. First a straight bit of track, fine roadbed, long vista of telegraph poles. Suddenly the road curves in toward the mountain side. On one hand a study in foliage; on the other a deep ravine, with a fringe of far off blue mountains in the background. A

block signal tower comes into momentary sight, as the train whizzes along, past track walkers and a gang of section hands. Taken from the front platform of a "special" furnished through the courtesy of the Pennsylvania R.R. Co. (*Edison Films*, March 1900, 47.)

SUBJECT: Railroads. Mountains. Pennsylvania Railroad.

ARCHIVE: DLC-pp.

CITATIONS: *Edison Films*, July 1901, 94.

NOTE:

---

704 *Running Through Gallitzen Tunnel, Penna., R.R.

LENGTH: 150 ft.   © Thomas A. Edison, 7 July 1899.

PRODUCER: James White.

CAMERA: [Robert K. Bonine.]

CAST:

PRODUCTION DATE: June 1899.

LOCATION: Near Altoona, Pa.

SOURCE:

DESCRIPTION: We overtake a freight train as we approach the tunnel. First we catch the caboose, then overhaul, car by car, the entire train, then pass the puffing, blustering camel-back. The track curves, and we see a cavern in the hillside; exhaling great breaths of smoke as if a lair of some fabled monster. An eye-wink and we're in the tunnel. The blackness is dense and cooling. As we become accustomed to the gloom, we see an EYE far ahead; a half-closed eye, growing larger and larger as we approach. It glistens on the converging rails; it grows larger; it grows brighter. We see a delicate picture outlined in that tiny space; a picture of a station, a tower, bright trees, shining meadows; and suddenly we're right in the midst of it all. The semaphore beckons us on; and on we go, on and through the heart of the mountains; those tree-clad slopes that make famous the scenery along the Pennsylvania railroad. (*Edison Films*, March 1900, 46.)

SUBJECT: Railroads. Tunnels. Pennsylvania Railroad.

ARCHIVE: DLC-pp.

CITATIONS: *Edison Films*, July 1901, 93.

NOTE:

Blackton and Smith are the cameramen who most probably took these films of the "Columbia" and "Defender" as they prepared for the America's Cup races. The race off of Larchmont was the first head to head competition between these two boats.

705 Trial Race, "Columbia" and "Defender," [no. 1]

LENGTH: 150 ft.   © No reg.

PRODUCER: [J. Stuart Blackton, Albert E. Smith?]

CAMERA: [J. Stuart Blackton and/or Albert E. Smith?]

CAST:

PRODUCTION DATE: 8 July 1899.

LOCATION: Long Island Sound, Larchmont, N.Y.

SOURCE:

DESCRIPTION: Taken off Larchmont, July 8. Boats are shown one after the other, rounding the south-east stake boat, the Columbia leading. As they approach the Judge's boat the wonderful spread of canvas is shown, three jibs, sheet, topsail and spinnaker set. The Defender's boom dips into the water every now and then, throwing the spray high into the air. Close views of both yachts are also shown, giving details of crews and rigging. The nearby view of the Defender shows her swinging off on another tack. (*Edison Films*, March 1900, 5.)

SUBJECT: Yacht racing. America's Cup races.

ARCHIVE:

CITATIONS: *Edison Films*, July 1901, 31-32.

NOTE: This attribution is based on the fact that Vitagraph was then the only 35mm exhibition service with a regular venue in vaudeville, where such timely subjects were in great demand. Moreover, Vitagraph took a particularly active role in the filming of the America's Cup films that October and this was probably a practice run for them as well as the boats. On the other hand, the very brief remarks and advertisements in newspapers and trade journals of this period fail to link Vitagraph to these films.

706   Trial Race, "Columbia" and "Defender," no. 2

LENGTH: 150 ft.   © No reg.

PRODUCER: [J. Stuart Blackton, Albert E. Smith?]

CAMERA: [J. Stuart Blackton and/or Albert E. Smith?]

CAST:

PRODUCTION DATE: 8 July 1899.

LOCATION: Long Island Sound, Larchmont, N.Y.

SOURCE:

DESCRIPTION: The Columbia leads the Defender the second time over the course. Both yachts are shown in different positions and on different tacks. The picture also shows the Columbia crossing the line at the finish, with the judges taking time and making notes. (*Edison Films*, March 1900, 5.)

SUBJECT: Yacht racing. America's Cup races.

ARCHIVE:

CITATIONS: *The Phonoscope*, July 1899, 14.

NOTE:

DEFENDER TO BE TRIAL HORSE FOR THE SYNDICATE'S NEW YACHT.
$25,000 Will Be Spent to Tune the Conqueror of the Valkyrie Up to
Racing Trim—Will Be Moved to the Herreshoff Yards Shortly.

That good speedy craft, the Defender, will be the trial horse of the Morgan-Iselin syndicate yacht, which is to safeguard the America's Cup against the Shamrock, Sir Thomas Lipton's challenger.

It has been decided to spend $25,000 on the Defender to tune her up to racing trim and make her as swift as she was in her victorious races against the Valkyrie.

Capt. Nat Herreshoff made a trip recently to New Rochelle, where the Defender has been laid up in Echo Bay since the memorable cup races. He made a thorough examination of the yacht and decided it would cost about $25,000 to put her in first-class shape.

Within a couple of weeks the Defender will be towed to Bristol, R.I., where she was built and where the tuning up will be done.

The placing of the Defender in commission merely as a trial horse shows that no money is to be spared to keep the America's Cup safe on these shores. The cost of refitting her ($25,000) is only one item of placing her in commission. A racing crew for her numbers more than thirty men, and the incidental expenses besides the crew's pay are many and great.

The estimated cost of the new yacht which will meet the Shamrock is $150,000, and this, with the expenses of racing her, and of the Defender, will bring the total cost to the syndicate up to the $300,000 mark. (*New York World*, 16 September 1898, 8.)

CLOSE WORK BY THE BIG RACING YACHTS.
The Columbia and Defender Sail Over a Triangular Course of Thirty Miles on
Long Island Sound Under Larchmont Auspices, and the New Boat Wins by 3m. 13s.
RACE WAS MEANT TO HAVE BEEN THIRTY-EIGHT MILES.
Going to Her Moorings off New Rochelle the Columbia Fouled the
Defender and Snapped Her Steel Boom Off Two-Thirds from the Last.
GREAT SKILL IS SHOWN IN HANDLING THE OLDER CRAFT.

Most satisfactory to all concerned was the race between those wonderful sloop yachts the Columbia and Defender, which was held on Long Island Sound yesterday. In a strong steady breeze and over a smooth sea the new cup defender beat the old by three minutes and thirteen seconds, actual time, over a course that would measure short of thirty miles. Experts, basing their calculations upon yesterday's test, predict a five minute margin for the Columbia when she has her formal trial with the Defender over a full thirty mile course in September.

The Columbia and Defender met yesterday under the auspices of the Larchmont Yacht Club for a cup offered by Commodore Clarence A. Portley, known to all yachtsmen as the owner of the racing schooner Colonia.

The Larchmont committee having the important meeting in hand made the necessary provisions for the occasion, such as the laying out of a special course and the chartering of the required number of boats to follow the racers. The business was attended to with the proverbial enthusiasm of the committee, and had the racing skippers given attention to the descriptions and charts of the course left in their hands the contest would go on record as particularly interesting and showing, to some additional extent, the relative merits of the new and old vessels.

Cut the Course Short.

The Larchmont committee laid out a course of nineteen miles, two legs of which were of eight nautical miles each and the third of three nautical miles. This twice over makes thirty-eight nautical miles, the distance intended to be sailed.

The racers cut the course about eight miles, sailing as near as can be guessed, about thirty nautical miles. On the first leg they turned a false mark said to have been one of the Riverside Yacht Club's, whose annual regatta was fixed for yesterday, and repeated the error the second time around, although the committee endeavored to set them right when they reached the home mark the first time. So, take eight miles from the course laid out, and some thirty nautical miles as the distance sailed, will be somewhat near correct.

The committee in charge felt so disappointed over the error made by the racing yachts that they omitted to take time for a while, agreeing that no official figures should go on record, but they changed their minds, and finally did take time when the boats finished the first time around.... (*New York Herald*, 9 July 1899, 3.)

707 A Quiet Little Smoke

LENGTH: 50 ft.   © No reg.

PRODUCER: J. Stuart Blackton, Albert E. Smith.

CAMERA: [Albert E. Smith.]

CAST: [J. Stuart Blackton.]

PRODUCTION DATE: By July 1899.

LOCATION: Vitagraph's roof top studio, New York, N.Y.

SOURCE:

DESCRIPTION: Baby sits in his high chair and papa is playing with him. Papa is smoking his evening pipe. Baby claps his hands, points to pipe and wants it. So papa puts on baby's hood, and baby smokes papa's pipe. The child's face is full of expression, and is as pretty a picture of baby life as was ever made for a moving picture machine. Sure to delight the children. (*The Phonoscope*, July 1899, 14.)

SUBJECT: Tobacco. Infants. Child rearing.

ARCHIVE:

CITATIONS: *New York Clipper*, 23 September 1899, 619; *Edison Films*, March 1900, 35; *Edison Films*, July 1901, 69-70.

NOTE:

708 *The Prentis Trio [sic] / [The Prentice Trio]

LENGTH: [50 ft.]   © Thomas A. Edison, 4 August 1899.

PRODUCER: [James White.]

CAMERA:

CAST: Harry C. Prentice, Anna B. Prentice, Nellie M. Prentice.

PRODUCTION DATE: [July 1899.]

LOCATION:

SOURCE:

DESCRIPTION: Performing at a lawn fete. This is a decided novelty in acrobatics. Surrounded by a background of trees, with the soft grass of a carpet, this man, woman and child go through their various acts with great dexterity. The child stands on his father's shoulders, jumps, turns a somersault and alights on the woman's shoulder with an accuracy, the envy of many an

amateur. The man does some great tumbling; and the woman some backward som-
ersaults that are very interesting indeed. (*The Phonoscope,* July 1899, 14.)
SUBJECT: Vaudeville–performances. Acrobatics. Children.
ARCHIVE: DLC-pp.
CITATIONS: Advertisements, *New York Clipper,* 20 January 1900, 993; 12 May 1900,
253; 16 June 1900, 365.
NOTE: There is no presently-available evidence that the Prentice Trio performed for the
American Mutoscope Company's biograph camera as the following advertisement
suggests. There are several possible explanations for this discrepancy, including the
possibility that *The Prentice Trio* was shot in the late summer of 1898.

What the N.Y. World, Jan. 29, 1899 Says About the
PRENTICE TRIO
HARRY C.   ANNA B.   NELLIE M.

Little Nellie Prentice, the remarkable athlete; her repertoire includes all the acrobatic tricks to be seen on the
stage. She stands on her father's shoulders and turns a complete somersault to her mother's shoulders. One of the
turns the trio goes through is a somersault from the floor to shoulder.–N.Y. WORLD, Jan. 29, 1899. The best
Singing, Dancing, Acrobatic Comedy in the country, BAR NONE, and the only act of the kind ever put in the
American biograph. AT LIBERTY FOR BALANCE OF SEASON. Ad. H.C. Prentice, 89 Vanderpool St., Newark, N.J. or
N.Y. Agts. 25 minutes all laughs. P.S.–I have a riding habit that cost me $10,000, but I have another habit that
cost me twice as much. P.S. But it does not interfere with my business. (Advertisement, *New York Clipper*, 4
February 1899, 832.)

The Prentice Trio gave a good exhibition of dancing and acrobatic comedy. The work of Nellie, a child six years
old, was splendid. (*Washington Post*, 25 April 1899, 7.)

GRAND OPERA HOUSE, WASHINGTON, D.C., THIS WEEK.
THE HARRY **PRENTICE** ANNA **TRIO** LITTLE NELLIE

Just closed with WOLFORD SHERIDAN STOCK CO. Read what Manager says about us: AMERICAN EXCHANGE, April
20, 1899–THE PRENTICE TRIO has just closed an engagement with my co. They were engaged as a SPECIAL
FEATURE and proved to be a GREAT DRAWING CARD. I consider THE PRENTICE TRIO the best singing and
Dancing Acrobatic Comedy Act before the public today.–ARNOLD WOLFORD, Wolford Sheridan Stock Co. WE ARE
AT LIBERTY FOR SUMMER SEASON. Just the act for Parks; cannot fail to make good with any audience.
THE PRENTICE TRIO, 89 Vanderpool Street, Newark, N.J. (Advertisement, *New York Clipper,* 29 April 1899, 177.)

The only Singing and Dancing Acrobats doing 3 Highs and Somersaults across from shoulder to
shoulder, and the only Soubrette Comedy Kid doing Spotting Somersaults on shoulders.
HARRY C.   ANNA B.   NELLIE M.
The   PRENTICE   TRIO

July 3 and 10, Rocky, Point, R.I.; A FEW WEEKS OPEN AFTER THAT. Read what managers says about us:
Mr. Prentice–Though unsolicited I wish to convey to you my sincere appreciation of the act of the Prentice Trio. I
unqualifiedly pronounce it the strongest act of its kind ever presented in this city, and one which will add brilliancy
to any bill. The marvelous talent of little Nellie places her in a class all by herself, and the manner in which she has
nightly captured the large audiences drawn to the Park by the act should be a matter of great pride to you. In conclusion, I beg to say there will at all times be a place on our bill for the Prentice Trio. It is useless to wish you success–your more than clever work assures you of that, and wise managers should "fall over each other" to book you.
Yours, very truly, J.A. Prizzini,
Manager Athletic Park,
Regards to Montgomery and Stone
Richmond, Va. (Advertisement, *New York Clipper,* 1 July 1899, 367.)

*The Kinetograph Department arranged with Thomas Crahan of Montana to shoot
films of the Klondike Gold Rush in the summer of 1899, sending along cameraman
Robert K. Bonine as Edison's representative. For this expedition, Edison's technical
staff built two new cameras that used a large-format film comparable in size to the film
stock then being used by the American Mutoscope & Biograph Company. This equipment, however, failed to work properly. Bonine also shot standard 35mm films as well
as photographs for lantern slides. The expedition left West Orange on June 8th, passed
through Seattle on June 16th* (Seattle Intelligencer, *16 June 1899) and arrived in*

Map showing the route from Dyea and Skagway to the Klondike gold fields (1898).

Dawson City, Yukon Territory, by July 21st. ("Local Brevities," Klondike Nugget, 22 July 1899.) Crahan and Bonine headed home on September 5th, departing Skagway on September 19th on the S.S. "Humboldt" and arriving in Seattle early Friday morning, September 22nd. What had been a grueling and dangerous journey just the previous summer had become comparatively easy.

There were two popular points of entry to the gold fields in 1897-1899, both towns on the Alaskan coast that had not existed two years earlier. From Skagway (or "Skaguay") gold seekers traveled the Skagway trail over White Pass to Lake Bennett. Others left Dyea on the Dyea Trail over the Chilkoot (more often "Chilcoot") Pass to Lake Lindemann. Travelers who crossed either lake then had to survive the ordeal of Miles Canyon.

On leaving the mountain lakes, each boat had to run the gantlet of Miles Canyon and the rapids beyond it before the river proper could be reached. All heard of this canyon, but few knew exactly where it was until, at a turn in the river, they saw a piece of red calico and then a board upon whose rough surface the single word CANNON had been scrawled. Suddenly, dinning into their ears, came the roar of tumbling waters beyond.

And there before them lay the gorge, a narrow cleft in a wall of black basalt with an unholy whirlpool at its center. Beyond this dark fissure lurked two sets of rapids: the Squaw Rapids, where the river raced over a series of jutting rocks; and the White Horse Rapids, so called because the foam upon them resembled white steeds leaping and dancing in the sunlight. (Pierre Berton, *The Klondike Fever: The Life and Death of the Last Great Gold Rush,* 1958, 279.)

709 *****Panoramic View of the White Pass Railroad / Panoramic View from the White Pass Railroad**

LENGTH: 75 ft.   © Thomas A. Edison, 6 May 1901.

PRODUCER: Thomas Crahan.

CAMERA: Robert K. Bonine.

CAST:

PRODUCTION DATE: Early July to 18 September 1899.

LOCATION: Yukon Territory, Canada.

SOURCE:

DESCRIPTION: This scene was taken shortly after the completion of this railroad in 1899. The impression received by the audience is that of riding on the pilot of an engine. Shortly after starting, you plunge into the darkness of the tunnel, afterwards to emerge, and crossing a high trestle skirting the edge of a deep chasm, you continue to wind about among the mountains and gorges. The ice-covered peaks of the distant mountains form an every changing background. (*Edison Films,* July 1901, 49.)

SUBJECT: Gold mines and mining. Railroads. Tunnels. Mountains. Klondike River Valley (Yukon)–Gold discoveries. White Pass and Yukon Railway Company.

ARCHIVE: DLC-pp.

CITATIONS:

NOTE: The White Pass was named after Sir Thomas White, Canadian Minister of the Interior. (Berton, *Klondike Fever,* 147.)

710 *****White Horse Rapids / White Horse Rapids (Klondike)**

LENGTH: 50 ft.   © Thomas A. Edison, 4 April 1900.

PRODUCER: Thomas Crahan.

CAMERA: Robert K. Bonine.

CAST:

PRODUCTION DATE: Early July to 18 September 1899.

LOCATION: Yukon Territory, Canada.

SOURCE:

DESCRIPTION: This picture was taken at the historical point signified by the above title, where so many daring and venturesome miners have lost their lives in attempting to shoot these mad and turbulent rapids in their flat bottom boats, constructed for the purpose of navigating the treacherous Yukon River, which flows through the rich gold fields of Alaska. This picture was secured at the time a party of miners in a boat were making their way over one of the very rough spots. As they are tossed about by the mad current, the waves and spray are seen to dash high into the air and at times entirely envelop the eager gold seekers. This is a very realistic and exciting picture. (*Edison Films*, July 1901, 10.)

SUBJECT: Gold mines and mining. Boats and boating. Rivers. Klondike River Valley (Yukon)–Gold discoveries.

ARCHIVE: DLC-pp.

CITATIONS: *New York Clipper*, 21 April 1900, 184.

NOTE:

711 *****Miles Canyon Tramway / Miles Cañon Tramway**

LENGTH: 75 ft.   © Thomas A. Edison, 6 May 1901.

PRODUCER: Thomas Crahan.

CAMERA: Robert K. Bonine.

CAST:

PRODUCTION DATE: Early July to 18 September 1899.

LOCATION: Yukon Territory, Canada.

SOURCE:

DESCRIPTION: This primitive railway made of rough logs shows one of the means adopted by the miners in conveying supplies in a new country. Each car, as it approaches, can be seen as it passes to be loaded with all sorts of supplies, which are being transferred by this method from the steamer seen in the distance to another at a point above the rapids. The activity shown in handling these supplies at this point shows that time is an important item in the Klondyke. (*Edison Films,* July 1901, 11.)

SUBJECT: Gold mines and mining. Canyons. Steamships. Railroads, industrial. Klondike River Valley (Yukon)–Gold discoveries.

ARCHIVE: DLC-pp.

CITATIONS:

NOTE: Miles Canyon had ruined many prospectors racing to the Klondike in the spring of 1898. In the first days of the stampede, 150 boats were wrecked and ten men drowned. According to Pierre Berton, "Meanwhile an enterprising young man named Norman Macaulay was building a tramway with wooden rails and horse-drawn cars around the rapids. When it was completed, he made a small fortune charging twenty-five dollars to take a boat and outfit beyond the fast water." (*Klondike Fever*, 281.)

712 *****Pack Train on Chilcoot Pass / Burro Pack Train on the Chilcoot Pass**

LENGTH: 50 ft.   © Thomas A. Edison, 6 May 1901.

PRODUCER: Thomas Crahan.

CAMERA: Robert K. Bonine.

CAST:

PRODUCTION DATE: Early July to 18 September 1899.

LOCATION: Yukon Territory, Canada.

SOURCE:

DESCRIPTION: The burro, or pack mule, is an almost indispensable adjunct to the miners in a new country. A long line of these sure-footed animals is seen in this view, loaded with supplies, wending their way toward the spectator. The expansive view of the snow-capped peaks of the distant mountains shows some of the difficulties these persistent animals encountered before reaching the present part of the trail.

(*Edison Films,* July 1901, 11.)

SUBJECT: Gold mines and mining. Mules. Mountains. Klondike River Valley (Yukon)– Gold discoveries.

ARCHIVE: DLC-pp.

CITATIONS:

NOTE: The title of this film is suspect since Chilkoot Pass itself was too steep for all pack animals. If a man was too poor to hire packers, he had to climb Chilkoot Pass forty times to bring his outfit across. By the spring of 1898, a tramway had been opened to transport goods to the summit of Chilkoot Pass. (Berton, *Kondike Fever,* 252 and 254.)

713 ***Packers on the Trail**

LENGTH: 75 ft.   © Thomas A. Edison, 24 May 1901.

PRODUCER: Thomas Crahan.

CAMERA: Robert K. Bonine.

CAST:

PRODUCTION DATE: Early July to 18 September 1899.

LOCATION: Yukon Territory, Canada.

SOURCE:

DESCRIPTION: A snow covered slope with narrow trail is seen in the foreground of this picture. In the distance, some figures are seen approaching. As they draw nearer we recognize a dog team and sledge loaded with supplies, and followed by miners loaded with tools and materials, trudging their way over the well run trail into the heart of the Klondike. This picture gives the observer some idea of the hardships of the miners in the Alaskan Gold Field. (*Edison Films,* July 1901, 49.)

SUBJECT: Gold mines and mining. Sleighs and sledges. Dogs. Klondike River Valley (Yukon)–Gold discoveries.

ARCHIVE: DLC-pp.

CITATIONS:

NOTE:

714 **Burro Pack Train on Main Street, Dawson City/ Burro Pack Train on Main St., Dawson City**

LENGTH: 50 ft.   © No reg.

PRODUCER: Thomas Crahan.

CAMERA: Robert K. Bonine.

CAST:

PRODUCTION DATE: 21 July-5 September 1899.

LOCATION: Dawson City, Yukon Territory, Canada.

SOURCE:

DESCRIPTION: The fascination for gold which leads men into the hardship of a rough, unsettled country, is clearly shown by this picture. Here you see all kinds of material lashed on the backs of burros, the only means of transportation in the Klondike country. This train is about leaving Dawson City for the workings on the hills. (*Edison Films,* July 1901, 10.)

SUBJECT: Gold mines and mining. City and town life–Dawson City, Canada. Mules. Klondike River Valley (Yukon)–Gold discoveriess.

ARCHIVE:

CITATIONS: *New York Clipper,* 21 April 1900, 184.

NOTE:

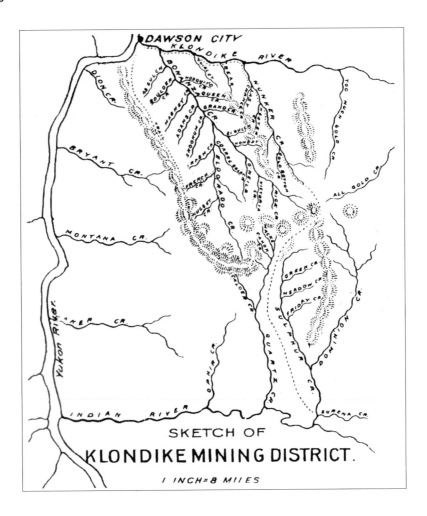

715 ***Rocking Gold in the Klondike / Rocking Gold in the Klondyke**
LENGTH: 65 ft.   © Thomas A. Edison, 6 May 1901.
PRODUCER: Thomas Crahan.
CAMERA: Robert K. Bonine.
CAST:
PRODUCTION DATE: 21 July-22 August 1899.
LOCATION: Yukon Territory, Canada.
SOURCE:
DESCRIPTION: Here we see one of the methods
employed in the search for gold, where
water is scarce. We see the workmen using
the water over and over again in the rocker
until it becomes too thick with earth for
further use. The scene is one of action, as
the valuable character of the ground

enables many to work profitably in close quarters. An interesting and instructive
subject. (*Edison Films,* July 1901, 11.)
SUBJECT: Gold mines and mining. Working classes. Klondike River Valley (Yukon)–
Gold discoveries.
ARCHIVE: DLC-pp.
CITATIONS:
NOTE:

716 *Washing Gold on 20 Above Hunker, Klondike / Washing Gold on 20 Above Hunker in the Klondyke

LENGTH: 65 ft.   © Thomas A. Edison, 6 May 1901.

PRODUCER: Thomas Crahan.

CAMERA: Robert K. Bonine.

CAST:

PRODUCTION DATE: 21 July-22 August 1899.

LOCATION: Yukon Territory, Canada.

SOURCE:

DESCRIPTION: This picture shows the miners washing out gold by what is known as the sluice box method. Here we see the miners shovelling from both sides the soil containing the gold into the sluice boxes, where the water, rushing at a rapid rate, carries away the dirt and stones, leaving the precious metal, which settles to the bottom of the box, to be recovered in the clean up at the end of the day's work. This is a very good subject, full of action and detail. (*Edison Films,* July 1901, 11.)

SUBJECT: Gold mines and mining. Working classes. Klondike River Valley (Yukon)– Gold discoveries.

ARCHIVE: DLC-pp.

CITATIONS:

NOTE:

Klondike Exhibit.

Col. Miles, who has taken the lead in the matter of preparing a Klondike exhibit for the Paris exposition, feels certain that the undertaking can be carried to a successful close. Mr. [William] Ogilvie has given assurances of all the assistance in his power, and will furnish the colonel with letters to officers of the government at Ottawa. Col. Miles also has promises of help from the White Pass and Yukon Railway Company and other transportation companies.

The following outline has been drawn up as to what shall constitute the exhibit:

Samples of gold dust from each creek, bench and hillside to the amount of $1,000.

A general exhibit of gold dust, coarse and fine, with nuggets large and small, not limited in amount or value.

Samples of bedrock containing gold, also gold and copper ores, platinum and all other minerals to be found here.

One cubic foot of pay dirt from each creek, viz., Bonanza, Eldorado, Dominion, Sulphur, Hunker and Bear, to be exhibited in glass cases, showing at least two inches of bedrock. It is also proposed to have one cubic foot adjoining this intact sample washed out and exhibited with its proceeds in dust, together with the affidavit of the man from whose claim it was taken.

It is also proposed to have an exhibit of the formation of different layers of muck, gravel, etc., from the surface to bedrock, in a glass tube in sections of five feet each.

Specimens of agricultural products, native grasses, wild flowers, fruits, etc.

Specimens of game birds, animals and fish, furs and fur-bearing animals.

Samples of all kinds of timber found here.

Photographs of scenes and scenery from Skaguay to St. Michaels. Also pamphlets containing reliable information for tourists as well as investors of capital; large photographs showing general topography of mining districts, correct maps of mining districts, showing locations and reservations.

An exhibit of fossil remains, in the interest of science.

Any person having samples of ores, nuggets of gold in quartz or rare samples of minerals of any kind from the district that they wish to have exhibited in Paris can leave the same with Governor Ogilvie, who will receive and receipt for the same.

All fossil remains, viz., ivory tusks, bones, skulls with horns attached, etc., found in the mines, should be carefully preserved.

Specimens of Indian work and relics. (*The Klondike Nugget,* 14 June 1899.)

KLONDIKE AT THE PARIS EXPOSITION.
A Display of Everything Pertaining to the Gold Fields Will Be Made.

A NUGGET representative called at the office of the Klondike Exposition Company last evening and found Manager Thomas Crahan and R.K. Bonine, Mr. Edison's representative, busy by getting ready for several weeks of hard work, which will begin next Monday, in Dawson and on the creeks. The work will consist of the taking of moving and stationary pictures by the large new Edison kinetoscope [sic], by which the methods of mining, transportation and living in the Klondike will be shown at the Paris Exposition next year, and throughout the United States and Canada the coming winter and in foreign countries after the Exposition.

Mr. Crahan has visited many of the large cities of the United States and Canada since last January, and has been to Paris to arrange for space for the Klondike exhibit, and says that in every section visited by him a deep interest has been taken in the Klondike Exhibition Company and in this country.

"The people of France," said Mr. Crahan, "know very little of this country as yet, only a few of their countrymen having visited this section, and among the ones who have been here a number were unreliable. At the beginning of the rush to this section an order was sent broadcast throughout France by the president warning the people to stay away from the Klondike and that order stands to this day, the masses of the people of France being of the opinion that getting into this country is next to impossible and that sure death awaits the stampeder on the passes and trails.

"While in Paris I met many men of capital who had invested and lost large amounts in South African stocks, and who are now at a standstill and awaiting a new field in which to speculate. France has not been worked by the mining promoter, and for that reason is a good field from which to draw capital for Klondike investments, and much capital will be put into the mines here if a creditable exhibit of the products and resources of this country are made at Paris next year. In the first place, a large amount of gold ingots, nuggets and gold dust should be shown, accompanied by letters from bankers and business men of Dawson stating that it was [a] product of this country.

"We are now preparing a collection of moving and stationary views such as the world has never seen, and will show to the outside world in this unique way the incontrovertible truth concerning the peculiarities and resources of this wonderful country. We will show the old way of transportation and travel into this country by pack trains and scows, and the new way, by railroad trains and palatial steamers.

"By our new large moving pictures, which can be projected 50x100 feet in size, we will show exactly how mining is carried on here—the thawing of the ground, the hoisting of the dirt, the washing of the same, and the transportation of the gold dust to Dawson by pack trains.

"We will show steamers plying on the Yukon, landing at the various stations, discharging freight and passengers, etc. Street scene in Dawson will be taken, showing things as they are in the metropolis of the Yukon Territory.

"Think of what an interesting picture the 'Miner at Work' will be! We will first show him by moving picture preparing his wood for a fire by thawing; next the miner is seen lighting his fire, the smoke can be seen curling up, and the flames leaping out here and there. He will be shown next at the windlass hoisting his dirt, and later washing the same in his sluice boxes. We will show him sharpening his pick at his portable forge, his working of the bellows, and the blows struck on the pick point while at white heat; he can be seen dipping the pick in a tub o[r] bucket of water for the purpose of tempering it, and the white steam can be seen arising.

"We will show the loading and unloading of pack trains, dog teams, etc., and in this way will make our exhibit one of interest and education and of great good to this country.

"We desire the co-operation of the miners and business men of this district in getting up a fine exhibit for Paris next year, and claim owners wishing to have the products of their properties exhibited at the World's Exposition next year may call at our office and arrange for same.

"We will be pleased to have parties call on us who have curios and relics, so that we may arrange for securing the same and for their shipment to Paris."

Mr. Crahan is an affable and energetic gentleman, and a few moments' conversation is sufficient to convince the listener that the work of representing the Klondike at the Paris Exposition is in the very best hands. (*Klondike Nugget*, 22 July 1899.)

Mr. R.K. Bonine, who is preparing the kinetoscope views of the Klondike for the Klondike Exposition Co., has completed his labors on the creeks. The claims shown will be Nos. 20 and 22 above the Hunker, Judge Dugas' claim on Dominion, Dr. Falkner's claim on Gold Hill and No. 2 above on Bonanza, owned by Alex McDonald. He was shown every facility by the owners and men in charge and will be able to portray the several features of Klondike mining in a most complete way. (*Klondike Nugget*, 23 August 1899.)

Messers. C[r]ahan and Bonine who have been preparing kinetoscope pictures of the Klondike for exhibition at world's fair left on the Bonanza King Tuesday having completed their labors here. They will stop at the Yellowstone Park on their way east and take a few shots at the glaciers there. (*Klondike Nugget*, 6 September 1899.)

RUSHING TO SEATTLE
Alaska People Seek Warmer Climes.
The Humboldt Brings Down a Large Number of Passengers.
Glacier Ice Broken Off by the Recent Earthquake Encountered.

It is no longer a one way business with the Alaska steamship companies, taking people and freight north and coming down empty. Business is exceptionally brisk both ways and every boat arriving brings down a full list of return-ing prospectors and Alaska business people. In four steamer arrivals this week so far fully 700 paid passengers have returned. The "Alaska Flyer," the Humboldt, Capt. Bonifield, got in this morning at 3 o'clock full of a happy, contented crowd of people. There were 177, among them several rich prospectors. Billy Chappell, a Klondike king, and his wife, and "Skiff" Mitchell, little less famous in his way, were among the Humboldt's passengers.

Purser Charley Carroll had $40,000 in his strong box for safe keeping for several passengers and there was consid-erable dust retained by the passengers themselves on the way down. One man in the party had $18,000.

The Humboldt left Skagway about 4 p.m. of the 19th and made her usually quick run to the home port. The weath-er was pleasant and the only incident of the voyage up and back was the big field of ice encountered off Taku gla-cier, which was knocked to pieces by the recent earthquake. The steamer "fouled" none of the bergs, but she had to slow down for over an hour while threading her way through them. No further details of the "quake" were brought down by the Humboldt's officers.

The Humboldt's passengers are:...Thomas Crahan,...R.K. Bonine. (*Seattle Daily Times*, 22 September 1899.)

On their way back East, Thomas Crahan and Robert K. Bonine may well have stopped off in Yellowstone National Park to take a series of motion pictures of the geysers and other tourist attractions. If so, a number of Edison films copyrighted in May 1901 were probably taken at this time (see entry nos. 368, 369, 370). By the later part of October they were in Boston.

Moving Pictures of the Klondike.

R.K. Bonine and Thomas Crahan, who were sent out by Thomas A. Edison last spring to take a series of moving pictures in the Klondike, returned home last week after a most successful trip. The party left on June 8, this year, and made the trip from Skaguay on the Alaskan coast to Dawson in the Yukon territory and from thence south into the gold fields. They took pictures of the most notable scenic subjects illustrating the old and new methods of reaching the gold fields, among them the tram road around the famous White Horse Rapids, and also secured a number of fine stationary pictures of the Canadian police patrol, and the different stations in the gold territory. Numerous pictures were also taken to illustrate the methods of securing the gold by thawing out the ground.

The pictures were taken in the interest of the "Klondike Exposition Company," in which Mr. Edison is largely inter-ested, and which intends to put these pictures on view at the Paris Exposition next spring. Previous to this the company will give a series of entertainments in the larger cities of this country this fall. Messrs. Bonine and Crahan brought back with them a team of the famous "huskies" or Alaskan dogs, which are a cross between the wolf and the Spitz dog. They are now in Boston at the home of Mr. Crahan, but will be brought to this city in a short time. (*Orange Chronicle*, 28 October 1899, 6.)

717 ***Boston Horseless Fire Department**

LENGTH: 200 ft.   © Thomas A. Edison, 15 September 1899.

PRODUCER: [James White.]

CAMERA:

CAST:

PRODUCTION DATE: August to early September 1899.

LOCATION: Boston, Mass.

SOURCE:

DESCRIPTION: Positively the most realistic and exciting fire run ever offered to exhibitors. It shows the entire horseless fire depart-ment of Boston accompanied by the old style apparatus which is drawn by the horses running at a terrific pace down Batterymarch Street, Boston, on its way to a fire. There are four horseless engines and the black smoke rolls from the smokestacks in great volumes, adding unequalled excitement to the picture. Another view on this same film shows a por-tion of the Boston fire department making a quick hitch in the engine-house and running out with the horses on a gallop. (*Edison Films*, March 1900, 29.)

SUBJECT: Fire fighters. Fire runs.

ARCHIVE: DLC-pp.

CITATIONS: *New York Clipper*, 23 September 1899, 619; *Edison Films*, July 1901, 54.

NOTE:

718 *New Brooklyn to New York via Brooklyn Bridge, no. 1

LENGTH: [100 ft.]   © Thomas A. Edison, 22 September 1899.
PRODUCER: [James White?]
CAMERA:
CAST:
PRODUCTION DATE: September 1899.
LOCATION: Brooklyn Bridge, New York, N.Y.
SOURCE: *Panoramic View of Brooklyn Bridge* (Edison film no. 649, January 1899).
DESCRIPTION:
SUBJECT: Bridges. Railroads.
ARCHIVE: DLC-pp.
CITATIONS:

NOTE: Why *Panoramic View of Brooklyn Bridge* (no. 649) was remade so quickly is unclear. Was the negative damaged or was the subject so popular that it wore out? And had the Edison staff remade a subject that was initially produced by a licensee as a way to avoid paying royalties? Or did Blackton and Smith also shoot this subject?

719 *New Brooklyn to New York via Brooklyn Bridge, no. 2 / New, Brooklyn to New York via Brooklyn Bridge

LENGTH: 150 ft.   © Thomas A. Edison, 22 September 1899.
PRODUCER: [James White?]
CAMERA:
CAST:
PRODUCTION DATE: September 1899.
LOCATION: Brooklyn Bridge, New York, N.Y.
SOURCE: *Panoramic View of Brooklyn Bridge* (Edison film no. 649, January 1899).
DESCRIPTION: This is a new negative showing the entire trip from Brooklyn to New York, in which the immense towers stand out clear and distinct against the sky. Positively the best picture of the Brooklyn Bridge yet secured. (*Edison Films*, March 1900, 42.)
SUBJECT: Bridges. Railroads.
ARCHIVE: DLC-pp.
CITATIONS: *Edison Films*, July 1901, 90.
NOTE: The film's designation as a second negative was dropped in Edison's July 1901 catalog.

720 *The Early Morning Attack

LENGTH: 75 and 100 ft.   © Thomas A. Edison, 22 September 1899.
PRODUCER: James White.
CAMERA:
CAST:
PRODUCTION DATE: June to mid-September 1899.
LOCATION:
SOURCE:
DESCRIPTION: This shows a body of U.S. Infantrymen attacking a force of Filipino Insurgents, who are strongly intrenched on a high hill. The U.S. soldiers make a gallant charge up the hill, headed by an officer mounted on a white horse, and after fierce fighting, capture the Filipino stronghold. (*Edison Films*, March 1900, 5.)
SUBJECT: Armies–United States. Philippines–History–Insurrection (1899-1901).
ARCHIVE: DLC-pp.
CITATIONS: *Edison Films,* July 1901, 31.
NOTE:

721 ***Colonel Funstan Swimming the Baglag River [sic] / Colonel Funston Swimming the Bagbag River**

LENGTH: 100 ft.   © Thomas A. Edison, 23 September 1899.

PRODUCER: James White.

CAMERA:

CAST:

PRODUCTION DATE: June to mid-September 1899.

LOCATION:

SOURCE:

DESCRIPTION: He throws off his coat, takes the rope in his mouth, dives from the raft into the river, and under a hot fire swims to the opposite shore, which is lined with Filipinos, hauling the raft after him and safely landing his men, who put the Filipinos to flight. Highly exciting and true to history. (*Edison Films*, March 1900, 5.)

SUBJECT: Armies–United States. Armies–officers. Philippines–History–Insurrection (1899-1901). Frederick Funston.

ARCHIVE: DLC-pp.

CITATIONS: "Praise for Col. Funston," *New York Times,* 1 April 1899, 2.

NOTE:

MACARTHUR'S MEN WHIP AGUINALDO AND GO FORWARD.
...
MARILAO IS CAPTURED AFTER A SHARP ENGAGEMENT.
Six American Killed and Forty Wounded in Practically the Only Fighting of the Day.

Manila, Monday.–MacArthur's division pushed its way to Marilao to-day, and is encamped in and about that town to-night....As the column neared Marilao white roofs and steeples were seen among the green trees beyond the river, looking not unlike a Massachusetts village. The rebels had the advantage of an unfordable river in front of them, and they poured in a fire so effective that it showed they were veterans, probably members of the native militia which the Spaniards organized.

Artillerymen Put an End to Battle.

The American artillery put a dramatic end to the battle. Approaching under cover of the bushes to about sixty yards from the trenches, the artillerymen emerged upon an open space commanding the town. When the Americans appeared they gave a great yell, and the Filipinos were panic stricken, about a hundred seeking safety in flight, while a white flag was raised by those who were in the trenches, who also shouted "Amigos!" ("Friends").

Colonel Funston, with twenty men of the Kansas regiment, swam across the river to the left of the railroad bridge and captured eighty prisoners, with all their arms....(*New York Herald*, 28 March 1899, 1.)

PRAISE FOR COL. FUNSTON.

KANSAS CITY, Mo., March 31. Col. Frederick Funston of the Twentieth Kansas Infantry, who was the first man to enter Malolos to-day, and whose brilliant record since the Philippine campaign opened has attracted much atten-tion, is a son of ex-Congressman E.H. Funston of the Second Kansas District. He was born in Ohio thirty-three years ago, and is a graduate of the Kansas State University.

In his younger days Funston was a reporter on The Fort Smith Tribune. During President Harrison's Administration he was sent to Alaska by the Government in search of specimens and had many thrilling experiences. He made a canoe trip alone 900 miles up the Yukon. In the Fall of 1894 Funston went to Cuba and enlisted in the Cuban Army. For two years he fought for the cause of the insurgents. At one time he was commissioned a Colonel and commanded the entire artillery forces of the Cubans under Gen. Garcia. He fired the first dynamite gun used by the Cubans in their war against the Spanish, and was in many severe battles. In one charge, he received a bullet just below the heart.

He returned to Kansas and had barely recovered from his wound when Gov. Leedy appointed him Colonel of the Kansas regiment. Last Fall, Col. Funston was called to Florida and gave Gen. Miles much information of value regard-ing Cuba. Funston's friends have urged him for appointment as Brigadier General. (*New York Times,* 1 April 1899, 2.)

722 ***Fun in Camp**

LENGTH: 50 ft.   © Thomas A. Edison, 27 November 1899.

PRODUCER: James White.
CAMERA:
CAST:
PRODUCTION DATE: June-September 1899.
LOCATION: [Orange, N.J.]
SOURCE:
DESCRIPTION: Showing a group of soldiers and Red Cross nurses being amused by a number of small children who are riding upon the backs of trick bears. A remarkably fine picture, with U.S. Infantry camp in the background. (*Edison Films,* March 1900, 34.)

SUBJECT: Armies–United States. Nurses. Children. Bears. Red Cross. Circus animals.
ARCHIVE: DLC-pp.
CITATIONS: *Edison Films,* July 1901, 68.
NOTE: Although copyrighted in late November, the scenery indicates a summer shooting date. Copyrighted at the same time as *Love and War,* the first shot of this film could have been incorporated into that picture as the second scene.

723 **Trick Bears*
LENGTH: [100 ft.]   © Thomas A. Edison, 27 November 1899.
PRODUCER: James White.
CAMERA:
CAST:
PRODUCTION DATE: June-September 1899.
LOCATION: [Orange, N.J.]
SOURCE: *[Trained Bears]* (Edison film no. 36, spring 1894).
DESCRIPTION:
SUBJECT: Armies–United States. Bears. Circus animals. Trainers.
ARCHIVE: DLC-pp.
CITATIONS:
NOTE:

The Edison Manufacturing Company made several "Picture Songs," probably in association with the Eaves Shadowgraph Company which was promoting them by mid-October 1899:

SONGS, ORIGINAL
WITH MOVING PICTURES,

Dancing News Girl and Organ Grinder, Impecunious Composer with German Band, Tenderloin After Two in the Morning, Astor Unwelcome Tramp Visitor, Love and War. Six scenes. Will illustrate any song. Action in accord with music. Terms reasonable. Professional copies. EAVES SHADOWGRAPH CO., 63 East 12th St., New York. (Advertisement, *New York Clipper,* 14 October 1899, 688.)

The Edison Manufacturing Company later advertised two of these multi-shot films, designed for accompaniment by specially written songs as Love and War *and* The Astor Tramp. *A third picture song,* Tenderloin at Night, *was perhaps considered too bawdy to sell publicly.*

724 **Love and War*
LENGTH: 200 ft.   © James H. White, 28 November 1899.
PRODUCER: James White.
CAMERA:
CAST:
PRODUCTION DATE: June-September 1899.
LOCATION: [Orange, N.J.]
SOURCE:

DESCRIPTION: An illustrated song telling the story of a hero who leaves for the war as a private, is promoted to the rank of captain for bravery in service, meets the girl of his choice, who is a Red Cross nurse on the field, and finally returns home triumphantly as an officer to the father and mother to whom he bade good-by as a private. The film presents this beautiful song picture in six scenes, each of which has a separate song, making the entire series a complete and effective novelty.

PARTING.—"Our hero boy to the war has gone." Words and music.

CAMPING.—"What! A letter from home." Words and music.

FIGHTING.—The battle-prayer. "Father, on Thee I Call." Words and music.

CONVALESCING—"Weeping, Sad and Lonely." Words and music.

SORROWING.—The mother's lament. "Come back, my dear boy, to me." Words and music.

RETURNING.—When our hero boy comes back again. Hurrah! Hurrah! "Star Spangled Banner." Words and music.

The above scene can be illustrated either by a soloist, quartette or with an orchestra, and with or without stereopticon slides. This series of animated pictures, when properly illustrated or announced by stereopticon reading matter, should make a great success. Length 200 feet, complete with words of song and music. (*Edison Films*, July 1901, 13.)

SUBJECT: Armies–United States. Soldiers. Courtship. Battles. Red Cross. Armies–Officers. Motion pictures–sound.

ARCHIVE: DLC-pp.

CITATIONS: Eaves Shadowgraph Co., advertisement, *New York Clipper,* 14 October 1899, 688; 18 November 1899, 801; *Edison Films*, March 1900, 3.

NOTE: Scenes were filmed during the summer or early fall. Completion and copyright may have been delayed by numerous high-priority projects of a timely nature—the Dewey celebrations, the Sharkey-Jeffries Fight, etc. It is also possible that James White, a talented singer in his own right, was performing with the films before putting them on the market. The full image indicates that interior scenes were shot on an open-air stage, obviously not the Black Maria. Not all the scenes described in this film were copyrighted and are in the surviving paper print. The full subject appears to have included at least two additional scenes—shorter films which were made, sold, and probably copyrighted separately.

The Astor Tramp *was based on a well-known incident that occurred five years earlier and was quickly incorporated into New York City lore. Tramp John Garvey (aka John Garvin) slept in a millionaire's house and became an instant celebrity, courtesy of the New York Herald. The situation was most ironic in that the Astors owned and operated the Waldorf Hotel just around the corner from their home, with a companion accommodation (the Astoria) in the planning stages. The following articles suggest the genealogy of "the Astor tramp"—a motion picture forerunner of Charlie Chaplin's tramp persona. The transformation was furthered by Tony Pastor's comic song "The Tramp Who Slept at P_Astor's," which he sang in his theater in early December 1894.*

25 ***The Astor Tramp / Astor Unwelcome Tramp Visitor**

LENGTH: 100 ft.   © Thomas A. Edison, 27 November 1899.

PRODUCER: James White.

CAMERA:

CAST:

PRODUCTION DATE: June-September 1899.

LOCATION: [Orange, N.J.]

SOURCE:

DESCRIPTION: A side splitting subject, showing the mistaken tramp's arrival at the Wm. Waldorf Astor mansion and being discovered comfortably asleep in bed, by the lady of the house. (*Edison Films*, March 1900, 3.) A side splitting subject, showing the mistaken tramp's arrival at the famous New York hotel, the Waldorf-Astoria. The tramp inquires as to changing his nationality and asks also as to the results of this prospective change. The music and words accompanying are explanatory and can be either sung or spoken. The tramp calls to ask Waldorf's opinion as to whether he should become an English citizen, and finding no flunky at the door, he climbs upstairs. He sees an inviting bed and says he will lie down and wait for Waldorf. A lady discovers the tramp asleep. He was arrested, but discharged. He is extremely humorous, as he uses a puff powder, standing very vainly before a mirror as he makes himself up. Length 100 feet, complete with words of song and music. (*Edison Films*, July 1901, 3.)

SUBJECT: Tramps. Newspapers. Beds. Hotels. Social elites. Motion pictures–sound. William Waldorf Astor. Waldorf-Astoria Hotel.

ARCHIVE: DLC-pp.

CITATIONS: "How a Bowery Tramp Got Into Society," *New York World*, 25 November 1894, 25. Eaves Shadowgraph Co., advertisement, *New York Clipper,* 14 October 1899, 688.

NOTE: The catalog description does not refer to the second scene of this film in which the Astor Tramp reads about his escapades in the newspaper. The film was shot on an outdoor stage, probably the one used for *Love and War*. William Waldorf Astor was the son of William Blackhouse Astor, who was estimated to be worth $200 million at the time of his death in 1875. Mrs. Wm. Astor, who occupied the house that was entered by tramp John Garvey (aka as "the Astor tramp") was the widow of William Blackhouse.

YET ANOTHER ASTOR HOTEL.
John Jacob Is Contemplating Building One to Adjoin and Connect with the Waldorf.
ON MRS. WILLIAM ASTOR'S PROPERTY
It Has Not been Decided Yet, However, and No Plans Have Been Drawn.
TO BE LARGE AND COSTLY.

Real estate men were talking yesterday of a gigantic new hotel which, it was said, John Jacob Astor contemplated building at the corner of Fifth avenue and Thirty-fourth street, adjoining the Waldorf.

It was stated that Architect Henry J. Hardenbergh, of No. 10 West Twenty-third street, was drawing plans for the structure, which was to be eighteen stories high and finished in the most sumptuous and costly manner.

DISCUSSED IN THE EXCHANGES.

The gossip of the exchanges had it that the new hotel was to be built and run as a rival to the Waldorf, which is the property of William Waldorf Astor, John Jacob's first cousin.

The story proved on investigation to be only partly true. Little could be learned in detail, because all information was refused at Mr. Astor's office in East Twenty-sixth street, except that the subject of a new hotel on the site in question has been spoken of. Mr. Astor himself was in the city, but declined to be seen in regard to the matter.

Mr. Hardenbergh, the architect, said, when asked if he had been commissioned to draw plans for such a hotel, that he was not at liberty to say anything about the matter whatever.

From wholly unofficial sources, however, it was learned that John Jacob Astor conceived the idea of building a hotel adjoining the Waldorf some time during the summer and made no secret of it among his personal friends.

NOT TO BE A RIVAL.

It is a mistake though, that his purpose was in any way to rival his cousin's hotel, but rather to build a hotel to be run, if possible, in connection with the Waldorf. No decision, however, has been reached as to the desirability of the scheme.

At the time the Waldorf was built it was extensively published that Mrs. William Astor, who owns the adjoining property on Thirty-fourth street, was opposed to the project. She lived, and still lives, in the house on the corner of Fifth avenue and Thirty-fourth street, separated from the hotel only by a vacant lot, which is also her property.

Since her new house is nearly completed, it is presumable that she has abandoned her opposition. If the new hotel is erected, there is plenty of property on which to build it, as the tax map show that Mrs. Astor owns not only the corner property where her house stands, but nearly half the block west on the south side of Thirty-fourth street. (*New York Herald*, 2 November 1894, 11.)

THIEVES AIM FOR BIG PRIZES
One Caught in Bed in a Servant's Room on an Upper Floor of
Mrs. William Astor's Mansion in Fifth Avenue.
LOCKED IN THE ROOM.
But a Servant Heard Him and a Policeman Made Him Dress and Took Him to a Cell.
LIVELY CHASE IN A HOTEL.
A Son of Ex-Secretary Endicott Found a Man Rifling His Valise in the Fifth Avenue Hotel.
HE FINALLY CAUGHT HIM
An Unusual Number of Burglaries and Robberies Reported at One Police Station.

A roughly dressed man, thirty-two years old, gained an entrance in some unknown manner to the residence of Mrs. William Astor, at No. 350 Fifth avenue, last evening and was discovered hidden in a servant's room on the fourth floor of the mansion shortly before midnight.

The policeman broke in the door and found the man in bed. He was taken to the West Thirtieth street station where he said he was John Garvin, of No. 96 Bowery. He would tender no explanation as to how he gained entrance to the house or what his purpose was.

The family had retired, and the house was wrapped in darkness, when at eleven o'clock a laundress employed by Mrs. Astor went to her room on the fourth floor to retire. She placed her hand on the knob of the door and tried to open it, but it resisted all her efforts.

She heard at the same time the sound of somebody moving about the room, and, thoroughly alarmed, she ran down stairs to the basement and notified one of the man servants that her room was occupied by somebody, who had locked himself in.

FOUND IN BED.

While the chef ran up to the room and stood on guard in the hall in front of the door a servant ran up Fifth avenue looking for a policeman. He returned accompanied by Policeman Harty of the West Thirtieth street station, who was admitted and went at once to the fourth floor.

He seized the door knob and shook it, loudly demanding at the same time that he be admitted without delay. There was not response, but the policeman could hear some person moving about. "Open this door," he shouted, "or I shall break it in!"

When no answer was made the policeman placed his should against the door and pushed it in.

The gas was lighted but turned down. On the floor beside the bed was a complete suit of clothes and stretched out full length under the covers was a man's figure. The man was apparently asleep.

With his night stick the policeman made the stranger jump from under the bed clothing and stand before him. He was a rough looking man, about thirty years old, with a dark mustache and scrubby beard of several days' growth.

He was taken to the West Thirtieth street police station, followed by a curious crowd which had been attracted by the unusual sight of a policeman entering the Astor mansion.

When arraigned before Sergeant Sheehan in the station house the prisoner was inclined to be morose and uncommunicative, but finally, in reply to the sergeant's persistent questioning, said he was John Garvin, thirty-one years old, of No. 96 Bowery, which he said was a lodging house. Although accused of entering the house for the purpose of robbery, he refused to answer any questions or even to tell how he had gained an entrance to the house. He was finally locked up, when the sergeant decided that further questioning was useless.

At the house, No. 350 Fifth avenue, a careful examination of all the doors and windows was made, but everything was found tightly closed and locked, and those there were unable to suggest any reasonable explanation of the man's presence in the house. That his object in hiding in the house was for the purpose of robbery the police are almost positive, and it was suggested that perhaps believing that he was in an unoccupied room, he intended to wait until everybody had retired and then to admit others, who would help him in looting the house.

When I called at the house at midnight my ring at the bell was answered by the chef, who appeared at a basement window and told me that nobody in the house could explain the appearance of the man in the house.

"He was found in the servant's room on the top floor," he said. "But how he got there nobody knows but himself. He has been taken to the station house and locked up as a suspicious person. He frightened the servants, but did not steal anything, and it was fortunate that he was discovered." (*New York Herald,* 18 November 1894, 5.)

ASTOR SEES TRAMP GARVIN.
Believes He Entered Mrs. Astor's House to Steal and Wants Him More Severely Punished.

John Jacob Astor, accompanied by his brother-in-law, Orne Wilson, paid a visit to the Jefferson Market Police Court yesterday morning to make inquiries about John Garvin, who walked into the home of Mrs. William Astor, at

Thirty-fourth street and Fifth avenue, on Saturday night, as told in the Herald, and went to bed in the room of the laundress. Garvin was brought before Justice Voorhis on Sunday and fined $5 for disorderly conduct. He did not have the money, and went to jail. He was still in a cell at Jefferson Market Court yesterday morning.

As soon as Mr. Astor came into court, he was invited to take a seat on the bench with Justice Hogan. Mr. Astor explained to him that he was very much worried concerning the presence of the man in his mother's house.

"I was out of town on Sunday," he said, "and didn't known anything about it until I read it in the newspapers. I came down to court this morning expecting to appear against this fellow and I find that he has been before a justice and sentenced. I do not understated such doings, and it does not seem right to me that a man can enter a house of any citizen and only be fined $5. Why if he had happened to have the money, he could have got away at once, and then we never could have gotten hold of him. My mother is frightfully alarmed over the matter, and something must be done to punish this man, so that he will not repeat his offence. If he goes free in this way there will be hundreds of others doing the same thing, and I cannot have that."

Garvin was sent for. He came slouching into the little room. His eyes had the same sullen, hard look that has been their chief characteristic since his arrest.

Mr. Astor asked Garvin how he had gotten into the house.

"I just walked in," said Garvin. "The door was open and I went in. I didn't want to steal anything, but I had no place to go, and some people on the sidewalk told me to go in there and go to bed. I did, and then they arrested me."

"Were you really asleep?" asked Mr. Astor.

"Why 'cert,' " said the tramp.

"How was it, then that you didn't wake up when they broke open the door?"

"Did they break open the door?" asked Garvin. "I didn't know that."

Then Garvin went back into his cell.

Mr. Astor had another conference with Justice Hogan and left the court room. Before leaving he said that he was firmly convinced that the man had not been asleep; that he had entered the place to steal, and had hidden himself as best he knew how.

"I am not going to let this thing rest here," he said. "My mother is very much upset, and I am going to take steps to have this fellow rearrested and punished as soon as his time is up. I shall consult with my lawyers and see what can be done."

After Justice Hogan had announced that he expected to have additional charges preferred against Garvin in the morning, and had gone home, a representative of the firm of Burnett, Stayton & Hogan called at the prison, paid Garvin's fine, which amounted to $3, and took him away with him. The lawyer positively declined to tell for whom they were acting. (*New York Herald*, 20 November 1894, 5.)

ASTOR'S TRAMP AGAIN IN CUSTODY
Tired John Garvin Rearrested in the Bowery on Charges of Attempted Burglary.
HE LAUGHED AT HIS FATE.
Thought His Captor Was the Liberal Proprietor of a Dime Museum.
ENVY OF BROTHER HOBOES.

Like Lord Byron, tired John Garvin, tramp and Bowery flotsam, woke up and found himself famous.

'Tis true, he woke up in a bed that was not his, but to-day he is the scorn and envy of trampdom, from Maine to California and from the Great Lakes to the Gulf. His dime museum value causes the great army that is forever marching on its uppers to curse fate in one grand, hoarse chorus.

John Garvin's nap in the Fifth avenue residence of Mrs. William Astor was rudely interrupted by a policeman Saturday midnight. John spent the remainder of the hours of darkness in West Thirtieth street station. Sunday morning found him sentenced to five days in prison in default of $5 fine imposed by Justice Voorhis. Monday evening saw him a free man through the liberality of an enterprising newspaper reporter, who paid the city $4 for relinquishing the pleasure of John's society for the remaining days of his sentence. Happy but weary John fled immediately to his beloved Bowery.

John was rearrested yesterday afternoon in the lodging house at No. 89, on a warrant sworn out before Justice Hogan by Thomas Hayes, Mr. Astor's butler, who charges the tramp with attempted burglary. Garvin was locked up temporarily in the Macdougal street police station and will be arraigned in Jefferson Market Police Court this morning.

MR. ASTOR'S PERSISTENCE.

It has already been told in the Herald how angry John Jacob Astor was when he learned that Garvin had escaped with so light a sentence. He went down to court post haste and demanded that the tramp be rearrested. This Justice Hogan was unwilling to permit, unless sufficient evidence could be adduced upon which to base a charge. Mr. Astor was in court yesterday morning to renew his application, and a warrant was finally issued on evidence given by Johanna Best, the laundress, in whose bedroom Garvin was caught, supplemented by the testimony of Hayes and John Brennan, the Astor Butler and footman.

The warrant, however, was sworn out by Butler Hayes, who is a servant of imposing mien, assertive disposition and the majesty of a Russian Grand Duke. Hayes has never forgiven Garvin for being able to elude his vigilance. As soon as their business in the court was done the butler, the footman and the slightly agitated laundress drove away in one carriage, while Mr. Astor and his brother-in-law, Orme Wilson, were swept away in another.

Mr. Astor said while waiting in Justice Hogan's private room:

"My mother is really very worried over this matter, and I do not wish to have it rest where it is. I am utterly at a loss to understand why any one should want to pay the fellow's fine and let him get away. I think it was a most outrageous act. The idea of a man's being able to enter a house at night and escape with the punishment of a few days in prison. Such a thing is not to be tolerated, and I for one do not propose that it shall."

THE BOWERY MAN HUNT.

The warrant was given to Court Policeman Bernard J. Connolly for service.

Connolly is a big, powerful fellow, with lots of good nature in him. He knows his Bowery as a good boy does his multiplication table.

"I'll find him in an hour," said Connolly, as he started out. First he asked for tired John at No. 6 Bowery. Here you can get a bed and bath for twenty-five cents, or a bed for fifteen cents. There is a large sitting room, with a big stove in the centre, where the unfortunate who have the price may thaw themselves out in cold weather. Connolly asked for Garvin.

"He ain't in," said the clerk, suspiciously. "He wuz in 'bout ten o'clock, but I guess he's out receivin' the congratulations of his frens."

Connolly received this information incredulously. "Say," he remarked, "guess you don't know who I am. I am no spotter. I'm a dime museum proprietor, I am, and I want's to make the boy an offer."

"How much?" inquired the clerk, his eyes sparkling.

"Oh, about $300 a week."

"By gum!" exclaimed the clerk. "I tole him this mornin' he oughter make his mark." With that he walked to the foot of the stairs and shouted.

"Hey, Johnnie! Here's a mug down here what wants you for a freak."

AND GARVIN LAUGHED.

The tramp did not recognize Connolly and went away with him gladly. But he did not talk much. All he said was:–

"De boys is sore of me. Dey says 'Ully gee, Johnnie, we wishes we'd a slep' in dat roost. Yer made, Johnnie, yer made.' "

After a block had been traversed Connolly said:–"Look here, Garvin, I ain't no freak chiseller. I'm a policeman and I've got a warrant for your arrest."

Garvin laughed. "The first time," said Connolly, "I ever saw him laugh, and then he became as solemn as a judge and kept that way until I locked him up."

But Connolly has a tender heart. The poor tramp, scantily clad, shivered in the cold November wind. So the policeman took him into a neighboring restaurant and told him to order what he wanted. Garvin devoured a steak, a stack of buckwheats, two of "draw one" and half a dozen "sinkers."

Mr. Astor was very much pleased when he learned from Connolly that the tramp was in custody and announced his intention of being in court this morning to press the charge against him. (*New York Herald*, 21 November 1894, 7.)

GARVEY TO STAND TRIAL.
The Tramp Invader of Mrs. William Astor's Residence Must Answer to the Burglary Charge.

When John Garvey re-enters the realms of trampdom he will have acquired such a smattering of law, and all on account of his having sought slumber in the residence of Mrs. William Astor, as will enable him to hold large audiences of fellow vagrants on the park benches in nightly sessions for many months while he tells of legal twists.

Garvey was arraigned before Judge Fitzgerald again yesterday, when Lawyer William H. Stayton intended to talk his client out of court and from beneath the pending indictment for burglary in the second degree. The lawyer did talk, but, notwithstanding that, Garvey will be placed on trial next Monday.

When Garvey changed his lodgings for one night from his fifteen cent Bowery couch to those of one of Mrs. Astor's housemaids he did not possess that well nourished body that he had yesterday. There were two causes for this.

In the first place, Garvey does not have to "hustle" for food. It is brought to him, and the only trouble he has is that of masticating it. Secondly, some warm hearted woman who has been carried away with Garvey's social aspirations and desire to better his surroundings has given Warden Fallon carte blanche to feed Garvey twice a day at her expense. Notwithstanding this, Garvey's lawyer holds that the prisoner is not quite right mentally.

A warm cell and nutritious food have made Garvey's beard grow like unto a hot house plant. It is stubbly now, but ere the spring sets in Garvey will wear it a la Van Dyke.

Garvey sat listlessly by the side of his lawyer while the latter pleaded with Judge Fitzgerald that Garvey had been convicted in the Jefferson Market Police Court of disorderly conduct.

The jury agreed with Judge Fitzgerald that Garvey's offence could not be construed as disorderly conduct, as the house of Mrs. Caroline W. Astor was not a public place or a public thoroughfare. To break into that residence was burglary.

With these legal formalities concluded Assistant District Attorney Macdona announced that the trial would have to be postponed, as he had permitted his witnesses to go for the day. Mr. Stayton wanted the trial to proceed, as he had six witnesses present and one of whom was from New Jersey.

The New Jersey witness was Isaac Taylor, a tea merchant, of No. 35 Grove street, Jersey City, for whom Garvey worked as clerk for several months. Taylor said Garvey was a good clerk, but a little queer at time. He would not call the man insane. Mr. Taylor's statement will be used during the trial on Monday.

Having achieved the proud distinction of reclining on the couch of an Astor, Garvey's high social and literary ambition will probably inspire him with a consuming desire to possess a copy of the marvellous Christmas number of the HERALD, which appears to-morrow. (*New York Herald*, December 8, 1894, 3.)

TRAMP GARVEY CONVICTED.
The Invader of Mrs. William Astor's house Found Guilty of "Unlawful Entry."

Sleepy John Garvey, the tramp who sought seclusion and repose in the residence of Mrs. William Astor, No. 350 Fifth avenue, on the night of November 17, was tried yesterday before Judge Fitzgerald and convicted of "unlawful entry." He was remanded until Thursday for sentence.

Garvey seemed to be the least interested of any in the courtroom. He leaned back in his chair and buried the lobes of his ears behind an upturned coat collar. Now and then he smiled at the criticisms of Assistant District Attorney Macdona, upon whom devolved the duty of prosecuting him. In his opening Mr. Macdona told the jurors that a grave injustice had been done Garvey by reportorial artists, who had pictured Garvey as having slept under swansdown coverlets, beneath an Oriental canopy and in a mahogany bed chased with gold. Mr. Macdona said that, as a matter of fact, Garvey had slumbered, perchance to dream, in a very ordinary bedstead, over which there was no canopy. Mr. Macdona explained how Garvey entered the Astor residence from the rear, and called Jane Dougherty as the first witness.

Mrs. Dougherty is the laundress for Mrs. Astor, and testified that she went to her room at ten o'clock on the night of November 17. She found her room door locked. Her efforts to open it were fruitless, and then Laundress Dougherty called Johanna Best, who has been in Mrs. Astor's employ twenty-five years. The two women rattled the door. The key was discovered to be on the inside. John Brennan, footman, was summoned, and the door was opened. Garvey was discovered in bed. His clothing was neatly folded and laid on a chair.

To Mrs. Best's question, "What are you doing here?" Garvey made no response, and made no reply when Mrs. Best told him to get up and dress himself. Mrs. Best testified that she saw Garvey ten days before that, when Mrs. Astor's ten servants were dining. He came to the kitchen and got something to eat.

Butler John Hade testified to having ordered Garvey out. Mrs. Dougherty went for Policeman Harty, who went to the room and asked Garvey, "What are you doing?" to which Garvey replied, "Takin' a sleep." When asked what right he had to come there and sleep Garvey replied, "Persons outside told me to come in and take a sleep."

Assistant District Attorney Macdona concluded his case and elected to take away the charge of burglary from the jury. Lawyer William H. Stayton, for the defence, declared that he thought Garvey's mind was affected.

An affidavit of Isaac Taylor, of No. 381 Grove street, Jersey City, was read, and John Coffey testified that he believed Garvey was weak minded. Michael Donnelly testified that he had known Garvey for several years. Garvey, he said, was a member of a highly respectable family, and was himself respectable until recently.

Garvey was then called. Lawyer Stayton asked:–"How did you get into Mrs. Astor's house?"

"The door was open and I walked in." Garvey replied. He repeated the story about persons on the outside telling him to go there and sleep. Garvey said he was a porter for Park & Tilford for two years and a half. One time he kept a grocery at No. 753 Ninth avenue. Joseph McQuade, keeper in the Tombs, testified that Garvey when he wasn't eating was asleep. (*New York Herald*, 11 December 1894, 7.)

TRAMP GARVEY NOT SENTENCED.
Judgement Postponed on the Ground That the Verdict Was Improperly Recorded.

John Garvey, who was convicted last Monday of unlawfully entering the residence of Mrs. William Astor, No. 350 Fifth avenue, was arraigned before Judge Fitzgerald yesterday for sentence, when Lawyer William H. Stayton secured a postponement by moving to set the verdict aside.

Lawyer Stayton asked that the verdict be amended, as it now appeared that the record had been changed and was not the verdict as rendered by the jury. The lawyer said that Garvey was convicted of "unlawfully entering a building," while the record read, "Guilty of unlawfully entering a building with the intention of committing a crime."

The lawyer said that the addition of the last few words made a serious difference to the defendant, as no sentence could be imposed on the verdict as originally handed in. The verdict of the jury, he said, showed no intention on Garvey's part to commit a crime.

Mr. Stayton contended that the jurymen who tried Garvey had assured him (the lawyer) that they could not find, in their discussions, that Garvey had tried to commit any crime. Garvey was remanded until to-day, when Lawyer Stayton will again appear with affidavits of jurors in support of his assertions. (*New York Herald*, 14 December 1894, 9.)

ONE YEAR FOR TRAMP GARVEY.
Won't Find Lodging as Pleasant as in the Astor Residence.

John Garvey, tramp, convicted of "unlawful entry" into Mrs. William Astor's house, was sentenced to one year's imprisonment yesterday by Judge Fitzgerald.

He said Garvey was either an insane man, who went to the residence without a motive, or a sane man who went there with a motive. The Judge considered the tramp a fairly intelligent man. The necessity of protecting lives and property would not permit him being sentenced for less than one year. (*New York Herald*, 15 December 1894, 5.)

726 *****Tenderloin at Night / Tenderloin After Two in the Morning**
LENGTH: [100 ft.]   © Thomas A. Edison, 27 November 1899.
PRODUCER: James White.
CAMERA:
CAST:
PRODUCTION DATE: [June-September 1899.]
LOCATION: [West Orange, N.J.]
SOURCE:
DESCRIPTION:
SUBJECT: Prostitutes. Criminals. Police. Alcoholism. Motion pictures–sound.
ARCHIVE: DLC-pp.
CITATIONS: Eaves Shadowgraph Co., advertisement, *New York Clipper,* 14 October 1899, 688.
NOTE:

727 *****The Diving Horse**
LENGTH: 100 ft.   © Thomas A. Edison, 23 September 1899.
PRODUCER: James White.
CAMERA:
CAST: King or Queen (diving horse).
PRODUCTION DATE: Late August to early September 1899.
LOCATION: Coney Island, N.Y.
SOURCE:
DESCRIPTION: The only picture extant showing this wonderful performance of a horse diving from a staging 40 feet in height into the water. Scenes secured at the Shoot the Chutes pond at Coney Island, and depicts a truly wonderful feat. (*Edison Films*, March 1900, 44.)
SUBJECT: Horses. Circus Animals. Diving. Amusement parks. Paul Boyton.
ARCHIVE: DLC-pp.
CITATIONS: Advertisements, *New York Clipper,* 16 September 1899, 589; 7 July 1900, 425. *Edison Films,* July 1901, 91.
NOTE:

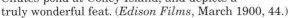

THE WHITE WONDERS!
The Most Powerful Outdoor Attraction Ever Presented to the Public,
PROF. G.F. HOLLOWAY'S HIGH DIVING ARABIAN HORSES,
KING AND QUEEN
GENUINE, NATURAL DIVERS.

No traps or devise to assist or force them. They drew more than 100,000 people at Woodside Park, Phila. The vast Chute Grounds, at Coney Island, are packed to the gates daily by the crowds that come to see them. They are the talk of all New York. Come and see the act and the enormous crowds it attracts. A FEW DATES OPEN. Managers of parks and resorts who want the strongest drawing card in existence, write or telegraph to PAUL BOYTON, Manager [of] the Diving Horses, Coney Island, N.Y. (Advertisement, *New York Clipper*, 9 September 1899, 566.)

728 ***Shoot the Chutes Series***

LENGTH: 100, 200 and 275 ft.   © Thomas A. Edison, 23 September 1899.

PRODUCER: James White.

CAMERA:

CAST:

PRODUCTION DATE: Late August to early September 1899.

LOCATION: Coney Island, N.Y.

SOURCE:

DESCRIPTION: This is positively the most wonderful series of pictures ever secured by an animated pictures camera. The first scene is taken from the pond of the chutes, and shows a number of boats laden with gay Coney Island pleasure-seekers coming down into the water in rapid succession. The next scene is taken from the top of the incline, showing the boats being loaded, starting away, running down the chutes and dashing into the water. The next and most wonderful picture was secured by placing the camera in the boat, making a panoramic view of the chutes while running down and dashing into the water. (*Edison Films*, March 1900, 44.)

SUBJECT: Amusement parks. Amusement rides. Paul Boyton.

ARCHIVE: DLC-pp.

CITATIONS: *Edison Films*, July 1901, 90.

NOTE:

Coney Island.–Captain Paul Boyton's Shooting the Chutes Park has been converted into a fairy land by his constantly adding new features, all of which are of that dare-devil, risky, hazardness nature that has marked the career of the man who heads the concern. One of the most curious as well as interesting things to be enjoyed there is "The River," which runs through a wild and romantic glen, winding in and out through the high peaks and long rocky ranges that rise abruptly in towers and pinnacles, splintered and riven in all manner of fantastic shapes and is about an eighth of a mile in length. It is picturesque, and scenically is one of the most remarkable things ever invented to please the public. Another novelty, that will be seen here for the first time this week, is Prof. G.F. Holloway's white wonders, plunging and high diving horses. These are as fine a pair of Arabian horses as can be found in this country. Mr. Holloway raised them, and he has pedigrees as long as his arm for each horse. Undoubtedly these diving horses are the greatest feature ever seen at this place of wonders. Thousands of people are attracted to the performances, and the act is as daring as it is really surprising and awe inspiring. The other specialties are Prof. Ben Woodger, the aquatic comedian, as Ally Sloper, in his famous water pantomime, "The Walrus Hunt" and "Sloper's Picnic;" Richard Vrooman, in his thrilling ride down the chute on a bicycle at a speed of 100 miles an hour; Martie Sprague, female high diver, who makes a descent each afternoon, and a sensational fire dive at night; Hall McFall, expert water log performer; Andre and Golden, high divers; Joseph Columbia in his terrific slide of 700 feet, while suspended from his teeth; H.H. Robins, Monte Cristo sack dive and under water long distance swimmer; [and] Wild Burt's remarkable feats in marksmanship. A pleasing display of stereopticon pictures and the grand naval battle wind up the programme. Other attractions are Robinson Crusoe and his island home, sea lions, turtles and several species of wild and tame fowls. (*New York Clipper*, 26 August 1899, 514.)

Coney Island.–Capt. Paul Boyton's Shooting the Chute Park is the chief attraction at this famous seaside resort. The captain adds something new with each week, beside the other regular features seen there. The whole performance, with a ride down the chute, can be enjoyed for ten cents. (*New York Clipper*, 9 September 1899, 560.)

Admiral George Dewey stopped off at Gibraltar on his way to the United States and an almost endless series of victory celebrations, of which the first was to be in New York.

729 ***Admiral Dewey Landing at Gibraltar***

LENGTH: [150 ft.]   © Thomas A. Edison, 27 September 1899.

PRODUCER: [James White?]

CAMERA:

CAST: George Dewey.

PRODUCTION DATE: [5 September 1899.]

LOCATION: [Gibraltar.]
SOURCE:
DESCRIPTION:
SUBJECT: Navies–United States. Navies–officers. Spanish-American War. Great Britain–Colonies.
ARCHIVE: DLC-pp.
CITATIONS:
NOTE: That an Edison cameraman went all the way to Gibraltar to take a single film of Dewey is puzzling and somewhat difficult to accept. Was this film acquired from a free-

lance cameraman, perhaps even someone on board the admiral's flagship? Was it faked? Or did James White use this opportunity to return to his peripatetic ways? The lack of advertising for this film only adds to the mystery.

ADMIRAL DEWEY SPEAKS OF THE WAR IN THE PHILIPPINES.
Expresses a Favorable Opinion as to the Outcome of the Conflict and Hopes that the Next Dry Season Will See the Insurrection Quelled.
EXPECTS TO RETIRE WHEN HIS TIME IS UP.
Now Housed in a Wretched Hotel in Gibraltar, but It Is the Best in the Place–Pleased with Programme Arranged for His Welcome in New York City.
PRAISES HIGHLY THE WORLD'S PHOTOGRAPH OF HIM.
Looks Proudly on Officers and Men of Olympia and Asks "What More Can I Want than to Be a Full Admiral in the United States Navy?"

...GIBRALTAR, Sept. 5.–Nothing could be in more striking contrast than Admiral Dewey's surrounding at the hotel here and what awaits him in New York.

He came ashore at 8 o'clock this morning, his Chinese servants bringing his small steamer trunk. The hotels here are poorer than those in small country towns in the United States. The officers of the garrison either have houses or live at mess.

The hotel where the Admiral is stopping is no exception. He and Lieut. Brumby have two rooms adjoining as large as the hotel affords, such as rent for $4 a week furnished in New York. But the rooms are quiet, and the Admiral has made himself quite comfortable.

In the morning he visited the garrison library, and at the Mediterranean Club he took luncheon with Consul Sprague.

In the afternoon Major-Gen. Slade, commanding the artillery forces, and Major-Gen. Sir Henry Colville, commanding the infantry forces garrisoned at Gibraltar, as well as other officers, called.

Among these was Col. Dundas, assistant adjutant-general, who was commanding the troops on the British transport from India which gave passage to the then Capt. Dewey, who was just recovering from a surgical operation.

The Admiral never forgot Dundas's kindness, and the Colonel has always remembered the good stories Capt. Dewey told. They met here to-day for the first time in thirteen years.

The hospitality of the club and of the messes was extended to the officers of the wardroom of the Olympia.

Coaling began early this morning, and the Olympia will depart Sept. 10. (*New York World*, 6 September 1899, 1.)

James White mobilized the Edison Manufacturing Company's staff as well as its licensees to cover the Dewey celebrations in New York City. According to Edison advertisements and catalogs:

Eight parties were equipped on the occasion of Admiral Dewey's arrival in New York, Wednesday, September 27, 1899, and secured the following excellent moving pictures of the Admiral and his great ship, together with the stirring events of Dewey Day, September 29, the day of the Naval Parade and Dewey Day, September 30, the day of the Land Parade. This was the only photographic apparatus on board the U.S. Cruiser Olympia on this memorial occasion. The Admiral posed especially for this camera. (*The Phonoscope*, September 1899, 14.)

The make-up of these camera crews remains uncertain, although American Vitagraph supplied two if not three units. Paley fielded at least one, possibly two. James White and the Edison staff would have probably put two crews in the field, including cameramen Alfred C. Abadie and Charles Webster. Might have Edwin Porter, then an exhibitor at the Eden Musee, been enlisted for this occasion? The degree to which James White co-ordinated this filming is unclear. It would have made sense for these crews to pool their films, but competition in the local theaters may have limited such sharing. In any case, this undertaking doubtlessly represented the largest single co-ordinated effort to film a pre-planned event in nineteenth-century America.

730 Admiral Dewey's First Step on American Shore / Arrival of Admiral Dewey
LENGTH: 50 ft.   © No reg.
PRODUCER: James White.
CAMERA:
CAST: George Dewey.
PRODUCTION DATE: 27 September 1899.
LOCATION: Brooklyn Navy Yard, Brooklyn, N.Y.
SOURCE:
DESCRIPTION:
SUBJECT: Navies–United States. Navies–officers. Spanish-American War.
ARCHIVE:
CITATIONS: *New York Clipper*, 14 October 1899, 685; *Edison Films*, March 1900, 8.
NOTE: Shot approximately 3:00 pm.

> **DEWEY SETS FOOT ON AMERICAN SOIL.**
> **Makes His First Landing in His Native Country Since He Won Fame.**
> **VISITS BROOKLYN NAVY-YARD.**
> **Attired in New Admiral's Uniform, He Makes Official Call on Rear-Admiral Philip.**
> **STRANGERS AT THE YARD DELIGHTED.**
> **Press Forward to Shake the Brave Man's Hand, but Only Three Women Succeed.**
> For the first time since he won fame Admiral Dewey set foot on his native soil yesterday, when he visited the Brooklyn Navy-Yard to officially return the call of Rear-Admiral Philip, the commandant. He arrived at 3 o'clock in Admiral Philip's barge, the Undine. There were perhaps 250 visitors in the yard who had no expectation of seeing the great man, and they were simply overcome with delight. There were no warning whistles or guns to tell of his arrival. The little blue flag with four white stars apparently attracted no attention. But when the Undine drew up to the landing at the foot of Main street in the Navy-Yard the workmen all about dropped their tools and ran with all their might. The admiral was in full dress. His coat sleeves were covered with gold lace as far as the elbows. The four gold stars on the collar told of his rank. His fore-and-aft chapeau was new and shiny. His trousers had most amazing creases and his white gloves fitted perfectly....(*New York World*, 28 September 1899, 1.)

731 Police Boats and Pleasure Craft on Way to "Olympia"
LENGTH: 50 and 100 ft.   © No reg.
PRODUCER: James White.
CAMERA:
CAST:
PRODUCTION DATE: 27-29 September 1899.
LOCATION: New York Harbor, New York, N.Y.
SOURCE:
DESCRIPTION: Showing Hospital Boat Missouri and Gun Boat Dupont, the Latter Under Full Speed. (*New York Clipper*, 7 October 1899, 664.)
SUBJECT: Harbors–New York. Police boats. Yachts and yachting. Steamships. Navies–United States. Spanish-American War. George Dewey.
ARCHIVE:
CITATIONS: *New York Clipper*, 14 October 1899, 685 and 688; *Edison Films*, March 1900, 7; *Edison Films*, July 1901, 32.
NOTE:

732 *Admiral Dewey Receiving the Washington and New York Committees / Reception Committee on Board the "Olympia" / Committee of Arrangements' Visit to Admiral Dewey
LENGTH: 100 ft.   © Thomas A. Edison, 2 October 1899.
PRODUCER: James White.
CAMERA:
CAST: George Dewey, Nelson Appleton Miles, William Thomas Sampson, Octavius L. Pruden.

PRODUCTION DATE: 28 September 1899.
LOCATION: New York Harbor, New York, N.Y.
SOURCE:
DESCRIPTION: Showing Committee of Arrange-
ments visit to the Admiral on board the
U.S. Cruiser Olympia. (*Edison Films*,
March 1900, 7.)
SUBJECT: Harbors–New York. Parades.
Navies–United States. Navies–officers.
Spanish-American War.
ARCHIVE: DLC-pp.
CITATIONS: *New York Clipper*, 7 October 1899,
664; 14 October 1899, 688; 4 November
1899, 760.
NOTE:

733 *****Admiral Dewey Taking Leave of the Washington Committee on the U.S.
Cruiser "Olympia" / Admiral Dewey Taking Leave of the Committee of
Arrangements / Admiral Dewey Taking Leave of Committee**
LENGTH: 75 and 100 ft.   © Thomas A. Edison, 2 October 1899.
PRODUCER: James White.
CAMERA:
CAST: George Dewey, Nelson Appleton Miles,
William Thomas Sampson, Octavius L.
Pruden.
PRODUCTION DATE: 28 September 1899.
LOCATION: New York Harbor, New York, N.Y.
SOURCE:
DESCRIPTION: Showing the gallant Admiral
standing directly in front of the camera, life
size, his head bare, graciously bidding his
guests adieu. This was exhibited at the Eden
Musee and Koster and Bial's, New York, to
18,000 people the next day after the picture was taken. (*Edison Films*, March 1900, 7.)
SUBJECT: Harbors–New York. Navies–United States. Parades. Navies–officers.
Spanish-American War.
ARCHIVE: DLC-pp.
CITATIONS: *New York Clipper*, 7 October 1899, 664; 14 October 1899, 688; 4 November
1899, 760; *Edison Films*, July 1901, 32.
NOTE:

Brought McKinley's Greeting.

Hardly was the last medal pinned on the breast of the last man when the guns began to boom. Alongside were the
committeemen from Washington. They got thirteen guns because in the entourage were Gen. Miles and Rear-
Admiral Sampson. Along were a company of gold-laced aides and several citizens. With them was Major Pruden,
who came to bear the President's good wishes–he being Mr. McKinley's executive clerk. "Come in, come in,"
exclaimed the Admiral, meeting them at the gangway. They were invited to the cabin and there they discussed the
details of the celebration. Meanwhile all visitors of the celebration were barred from coming aboard....

Dewey Always Calm

Everybody was excited but Dewey. "I am glad to see you, General," he said to General Miles, head of the
Washington committee. (*New York World*, 29 September 1899, 2.)

734 **Panoramic View of "Olympia" in New York Harbor**
LENGTH: 150 ft.   © No reg.
PRODUCER: James White.
CAMERA:
CAST:
PRODUCTION DATE: 28-29 September 1899.
LOCATION: New York Harbor, New York, N.Y.

FORMATION AND ROUTE OF THE NAVAL PARADE.

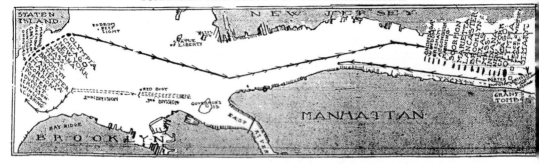

Map showing the progress of the Dewey Naval Parade (29 September 1899).

SOURCE:
DESCRIPTION: With Entire White Squadron in the Back Ground. (*New York Clipper*, 7 October 1899, 664.)
SUBJECT: Harbors–New York. Navies–United States. Parades. Spanish-American War. George Dewey.
ARCHIVE:
CITATIONS: *New York Clipper*, 14 October 1899, 688; 4 November 1899, 760; *Edison Films*, March 1900, 7.
NOTE: May also have been sold under the title *Panoramic View of Squadron, "Olympia" in the Lead*. (*New York Clipper*, 14 October 1899, 685.)

734.1 Panoramic View of Cruiser "Olympia"
LENGTH: 150 ft.   © No reg.
PRODUCER: James White.
CAMERA:
CAST:
PRODUCTION DATE: 28-29 September 1899.
LOCATION: New York Harbor, New York, N.Y.
SOURCE:
DESCRIPTION: With Entire White Squadron in the backround. (*Edison Films*, March 1900, 8.)
SUBJECT: Harbors–New York. Navies–United States. Parades. Spanish-American War. George Dewey.
ARCHIVE:
CITATIONS: *New York Clipper*, 4 November 1899, 760.
NOTE:

735 *U.S. Cruiser "Olympia" Leading Naval Parade / U.S. Cruiser "Olympia" Firing Salute
LENGTH: 200 ft.   © Thomas A. Edison, 7 November 1899.
PRODUCER: James White.
CAMERA:
CAST:
PRODUCTION DATE: 29 September 1899.
LOCATION: Hudson River, New York, N.Y.
SOURCE:
DESCRIPTION:
SUBJECT: Harbors–New York. Navies–United States. Parades. Spanish-American War. George Dewey.
ARCHIVE: DLC-pp.
CITATIONS: *New York Clipper,* 4 November 1899, 760; *Edison Films*, March 1900, 7.
NOTE:

736 Flagship "Olympia" and Cruiser "New York" in Naval Parade
LENGTH: 150 ft.   © No reg.
PRODUCER: James White.
CAMERA:
CAST:
PRODUCTION DATE: 29 September 1899.
LOCATION: Hudson River, New York, N.Y.
SOURCE:
DESCRIPTION:
SUBJECT: Harbors–New York. Navies–United States. Parades. Spanish-American War.
    George Dewey.
ARCHIVE:
CITATIONS: *Edison Films*, March 1900, 7; *Edison Films*, July 1901, 33.
NOTE:

737 *Panoramic View of Floral Float "Olympia" / Panoramic View of Naval Float "Olympia"*
LENGTH: 50 ft.   © Thomas A. Edison, 5 October 1899.
PRODUCER: James White.
CAMERA:
CAST:
PRODUCTION DATE: 29 September 1899.
LOCATION: Hudson River, New York, N.Y.
SOURCE:
DESCRIPTION:
SUBJECT: Harbors–New York. Parade floats.
    Parades. Spanish-American War. George
    Dewey.
ARCHIVE: DLC-pp.
CITATIONS: *New York Clipper*, 7 October 1899,
    664; and 4 November 1899, 760.
NOTE:

738 *Panorama at Grant's Tomb, Dewey Naval Procession / Panoramic View, Grant's Tomb / Panoramic View of Grant's Tomb*
LENGTH: 150 and 200 ft.   © Thomas A. Edison, 4 October 1899.
PRODUCER: James White.
CAMERA:
CAST:
PRODUCTION DATE: 29 September 1899.
LOCATION: Riverside Drive, New York, N.Y.
SOURCE:
DESCRIPTION: Showing throngs on the river
    banks watching parade. (*Edison Films*,
    March 1900, 7.)
SUBJECT: Parades. Navies–United States.
    Spanish-American War. George Dewey.
ARCHIVE: DLC-pp.
CITATIONS: *New York Clipper*, 14 October 1899, 685 and 688; 4 November 1899, 760.
NOTE:

GREATEST MARINE PAGEANT IN AMERICAN HISTORY.
DEWEY COMMANDS A FLEET GATHERED TO DO HIM HONOR.
Imposing Array of Warships, Followed by Countless Yachts,
Excursion Steamers and Other Craft, Moves from Tompkinsville to Grant's Tomb and Return.
NEVER HAD ANY HERO WARMER WELCOME.

...The whole North River [i.e., Hudson River], the piers and the houses, the open spaces like Castle Point and the
Palisades of New Jersey and the parks and squares of New York formed one magnificent amphitheatre–an amphi-
theatre such as the world never saw before–and there five million people were gathered.
Between these millions steamed the Olympia with her squadron trailing out behind. Every ferry-boat, every steam-

ship and every factory along the route had steam up to where the safety valve lifted and every whistle was thrown wide open as the Admiral passed. There was no distinct blast–it was an unceasing roar that, though coming from afar, was deafening and yet thrilling beyond description. And where whistles were lacking bells rung furiously and fireworks bombs were hurled aloft and exploded so lavishly that the sounds were in a way like those of the battle of Manila itself.

Squadron of Locomotives.

But even the continuous roar of the lower city was to be outdone by the noise at the railroad piers about Thirtieth street, for there a squadron of locomotives (so to speak) had been massed on the piers and these made such weird shriekings as might have awakened the dead....

And though it had seemed as if every sort of harbor craft that the port and all neighboring ports had afforded had been afloat in the lower bay, a fleet of sailing yachts that numbered scores was found at anchor opposite the park, each one with its spectators and each one rejoicing in a yacht cannon that belched smoke and noise in the most exhuberant fashion as the Olympia passed.

At last the float that bore the statue of Peace was under the bows of the Olympia–and a beautiful statue it was–and when that was passed came the float that bore old Neptune and his steeds as its most conspicuous feature. It had been partly wrecked but was still striking in its design and execution.

The Turn at Grant's Tomb.

And then the turn was reached just above the tomb of General Grant. Very slowly the Olympia rounded the old schoolship, while the police boats went snorting and screaming about to clear the way....(*New York World*, 30 September 1899, 2-3.)

MULTITUDE AT GRANT'S TOMB WILD WITH ENTHUSIASM.
It Was as Inspiring a Spectacle in Its Way as the Procession of Olympia Led Ships Up the Great River.
NONE LIKE IT EVER SEEN THERE BEFORE.

Riverside Park and Drive began to fill up with spectators at 9 o'clock in the morning, although it was not expected that the Olympia would appear off Grant's Tomb until 3 o'clock in the afternoon. The Admiral did, however, according to his wont, appear ahead of time, as it was only 2:30 when he turned the stake-boat St. Mary's, and he had then been in sight of the cheering half million people half an hour.

After 9 o'clock the crowds poured in many great streams from the elevated stations and the cable and electric roads, until by 1 o'clock those who came–and there were thousands more–had only the crowds to watch, for the last foothold affording even a half view of the river was then overcrowded.

But even they, the late comers, were repaid for their trip, for a view of that crowd was an inspiring sight.

There was a thrill of delight and surprise when at 2 o'clock the distant but unmistakable din heralding the hero's progress came floating up between the high banks of the river.

There was something awe-inspiring in that first faint sound, made up of the shriek of whistles, clanging of bells, booming of guns and roar of voices. For many minutes all these sounds were blended into one echoing rumble that seemed the effect of some force of nature, and it quieted the waiting thousands strangely.

At 2:15 the Olympia came in sight even to those on the upper part of the parkway, and then sounds became distinguishable. New Jersey was doing herself proud. Land batteries and little craft under the shadow of the Jersey heights began thundering away, each its appointed seventeen guns, in a brave manner, and then, as the Olympia slowly, with stately movement, moved up toward the stake-boat off One Hundred and Twenty-fifth street, New York took up the booming, the ringing, the shrieking: but yet that vast concourse on the park slope was silent.

It was waiting for something. Dewey could not be seen.

The smoke of the saluting guns along the shore drifted across the water between the park and the Olympia so that individual figures on the ship could not be made out.

But at 2:30, when the Olympia had cautiously swung around the stake-boat, and after she had fired a General's salute of twenty-one guns and her own powder smoke had drifted away, the crowds, by some inspiration which, like a panic almost, seizes a vast number at the same instant, made out on the bridge below the first fighting top of the Olympia's foremast the figure of a man. It was little more than a dark line, seemingly no longer than a woman's finger, but it was known in that instant that the Admiral was at last in sight.

Then such a shout! High-pitched and tumultuous at first, then a deep, sonorous, grand volume of sound, which was heard out on the flagship over all the dim of gun and whistle; for the little figure, seen as through the reducing lens of an opera-glass, slowly lifted a hat in acknowledgement.

Then the tone and character of the shout changed. It became a frantic uproar. Men shrieked and danced and women wept as they cheered.

"What is it?" a little girl in a carriage asked, frightened to see her mother in such hysterics.

The mother grasped the child and held it aloft.

"Look, baby! Look!" she cried. "On the bridge there in the front of that first big boat! See! It's Dewey!"

That was a scene typical of the two-mile-long crowd.

J. Stuart Blackton in top hat preparing to film Admiral Dewey receiving the Loving Cup (30 September 1899).

The Olympia steamed slowly down to about One Hundred and Tenth street and there dropped anchor. She was immediately surrounded by scores of steam craft which miserably obstructed the view of the thousands on the slopes, and in spite of what seemed to be some sort of an effort made by some of the torpedo-boats to keep them off, they remained there during all the time the Admiral was endeavoring to review the returning fleets.

The warships anchored in turn below Olympia, each being cheered for various special reasons as she came to a halt in her appointed place.

Then the formation of the several divisions was abandoned and boats turned at will, some without going to the stake-boat, and made quick way down the river.

The only unfortunate incident of that part of the day's happenings was the partial wreck of the float bearing a heroic figure of Victory. The plaster-covered wooden structure of the figure, weakened by a collision the day previous, fell into the river in pieces when the wind freshened in the morning and the outstretched wings of Victory caught the full force of the breeze. (*New York World*, 30 September 1899, 4.)

739   Presentation of Loving Cup at City Hall, New York

LENGTH: 150 and 200 ft.   © No reg.

PRODUCER: J. Stuart Blackton, Albert E. Smith, James White.

CAMERA: J. Stuart Blackton.

CAST: George Dewey, Robert Anderson Van Wyck, Richard Croker.

PRODUCTION DATE: 30 September 1899.

LOCATION: New York, N.Y.

SOURCE:

DESCRIPTION: This shows the Admiral, life size. (*Edison Films*, March 1900, 7.)

SUBJECT: Spanish-American War. Ceremonies.

ARCHIVE:

CITATIONS: *New York Clipper*, 7 October 1899, 664; 14 October 1899, 688; 4 November 1899, 760.

NOTE:

ADMIRAL DEWEY RECEIVES THE CITY'S LOVING CUP.
CITY PRESENTS A LOVING CUP OF GOLD TO ADMIRAL DEWEY.
Simple Ceremonies at the City Hall Hurried Through So Quickly, however, that
2,000 School Children Meet a Sad Disappointment.
SCHEDULED TO SING TO THE HERO.
When They Arrived the Admiral Had Gone, The Reception to Him
in the Office of Mayor Van Wyck Having Been Omitted.

"I haven't got my eyes open yet," said Admiral Dewey to the members of the Reception Committee when they landed on the Olympia from the police boat Patrol yesterday morning. St. Clair McKelway was at the head of the escort. With him were Senator Depew, Richard Croker and Assistant Secretary McAdoo.

The admiral boarded the launch at 7:30 A.M. On the way down the river he chatted with the committeemen. Turning suddenly to St. Clair McKelway he said: "Mr. McKelway, what are your politics?"

"I belong to the same political faith as Mr. Croker," replied Mr. McKelway, "but we never vote the same ticket."

There were no honors given by the fleet at anchor. The breakfast flag was flying and "colors" had not yet been raised.

The Admiral wore full dress uniform. He was pale, as from fatigue. He said he felt very tired. He did not know what he would have to face.

At Pier A, which he reached at 8:20 A.M., he was met by members of the Reception Committee, headed by William Berri. The Admiral walked down the long pier with a quick, brisk step. There was a delay of about five minutes at the Battery while the Admiral was introduced to the other members of the committee.

Troop A His Escort.

Troop A, with an escort of police, were at the pier to meet the Admiral. He took a seat in a brougham with St. Clair McKelway.

While waiting for the procession to start he said to the reporters:

"I haven't really awakened yet. I'm in the hands of my friends. The display last night was magnificent. What pleases me the most is that this display is by the people. It is spontaneous. It is the outpouring of the great American people."

There were about 1,500 persons in Battery Park. The Admiral responded cordially to their greetings, and with every raising of his chapeau to the cheers he would say "Good morning."

His carriage moved across Battery Park to Broadway. A trooper from Squadron A rode beside the carriage. At Beaver street his horse became unmanageable and plunged backward into the front wheel of the carriage, kicking viciously. The Admiral paid no attention to the antics of the horse.

The horses moved up Broadway on a trot. There were not many persons in the streets, but lack of numbers was made up in enthusiasm. To all the cheers, the waving of handkerchiefs and hats Admiral Dewey responded with salutes.

He was greatly amused by the reception given Senator Depew. The crowd recognized the Senator more quickly than any person in the party. His journey from the Battery to City Hall was marked by a wave of cheers. One man, who looked as if he hailed from the Bowery, greeted him with the remark:

"Hello, Chauncey, old sport, how are you this fine morning!"

From Broadway the Admiral's carriage swung into Park Row, and he descended in City Hall Park to receive the gold loving-cup.

A Disappointment.

Here was a disappointment for Dewey and his friends alike. Two thousand child singers who came to City Hall Park to sing "My Country 'Tis of Thee" to Admiral Dewey were disappointed.

They sang, but not to Dewey. He had gone. Sore was the disappointment of these children, whose fine voices had won them the honor of representing New York's 300,000 school children in singing patriotic songs to the hero of Manila.

Admiral Dewey was on time. He came behind the clattering cavalrymen acting as an escort shortly after half-past 8. It was then planned to have a reception of half an hour or so in the Mayor's office. Instead the ceremony of presenting the $5,000 gold loving-cup to the Admiral was pushed right along.

Why Admiral Dewey was hurried off before the hour set for his departure was not explained. There was no hand-shaking or introduction of officials in Mayor Van Wyck's office, as scheduled. There was no rest. The hero was simply hurried on the platform, hurried off and into a carriage and driven away.

An hour before the time set City Hall Park and Park Row in front of The World Building were crowded with people. They had taken points of vantage to see and hear Admiral Dewey. Thousands were streaming from surface cars.

Three troops of Squadron A were drawn up in line in front of City Hall at 7:30. A crowd of school children bound uptown in charge of teachers marched across to Broadway, singing "The Star-Spangled Banner." The cavalrymen presented swords as the little procession passed, and the national colors were dipped.

Gov. Roosevelt, accompanied by Adt. Gen. Avery A. Andrews, was among the first arrivals. They were ushered into

Mayor Van Wyck's office. Then came Rear Admiral Jack Philip. Rear-Admiral Schley received an ovation. He was received by Gen. Howard Carroll, and as he walked across the platform to the City Hall the crowd gave him cheer after cheer.

Before Admiral Dewey's arrival Admiral Schley was the hero of the hour. He was kept busy shaking hands and listening to eulogistic comments in Mayor Van Wyck's office. Chauncey M. Depew greeted Capt. Coghlan as he entered with "Hoch der Kaiser."

There was a laugh. Capt. Coghlan bowed, smiled, shook Depew's hand and seemed to appreciate the joke.

Soon the tramp of cavalry was heard on Park Row. The people massed around the carriage of Admiral Dewey and the police had all they could do to keep the crowd back.

The guests in Mayor Van Wyck's office were hurriedly arranged in line. They walked out on the platform, led by Mayor Van Wyck and Secretary Downes.

The gold loving-cup was placed on a pedestal. Admiral Dewey hurriedly walked toward Mayor Van Wyck and, shaking him by the hand, said:

"Good morning, Mr. Mayor, I hope you had a good night's rest. What a lovely day. The air is a little chilly to me. I feel it more because I was so long in a warm climate."

Mayor Van Wyck was nervous, and evidently disappointed because the stands in front of the City Hall were not crowded with people.

Schley and Dewey Meet.

Admiral Dewey saw Rear-Admiral Schley. He rushed toward him with hands outstretched:

"Schley, my dear old boy," he said, "I'm delighted. God bless you, old fellow, and how are you?"

These two heroes had not met since they had achieved fame, one at Manila, the other at Santiago.

"Fine as silk, Admiral," answered Schley.

"Here, here, Schley, drop that Admiral business. I'm plain, old George Dewey to you, my boy."

The meeting between these two men was strongly affectionate, and none interrupted their little talk. Then Admiral Dewey was formally presented to a number of guests.

"Shall we proceed or wait a few minutes?" said Mayor Van Wyck.

The remark was overheard by Admiral Dewey, and he said, with a smile: "I am quite ready now, Mr. Mayor."

He stood at attention, facing Mayor Van Wyck with Richard Croker at his back.

Presenting the Cup.

Mayor Van Wyck took from his pocket a manuscript and read a speech of presentation. He said in part:

"Your countrymen are interested in and know every detail of your life. They have traced your ancestry and your character and deeds from the cradle, rocked by a fond mother, to the Olympia, rocked by the rolling waves of the mighty deep.

"They listen with delight to the story of your pointing out, when a mere child, to your father the pictures in the clouds of a [   ]ing his country's flag from the disabled ship; of your service under Admiral Farragut in the Gulf Squadron as the executive officer of the Mississippi, when you plunged iron shot and shell through the armor of the Confederate ram Manassas; of the sturdy and fearless manner in which you defended your ship against the guns of Port Hudson, and the quiet and orderly manner in which you abandoned her when she sunk.

"The world stood enthralled and then broke out in loud huzzahs, which can never be silenced, when the electric spark flashed the news over the globe that on the 1st of May, 1898, your fleet had destroyed in Manila Bay the Spanish Navy, silencing the forts and taking the Philippine Islands, thus stripping the East of every vestige of Spanish domination.

His Crowning Achievement.

"This all was accomplished in a naval battle of less than seven hours, including the cooly ordered intermission for breakfast. Not an American killed, but 200 Spaniards laid low, 700 wounded, the Spanish Navy destroyed and an empire lost to her forever. History records no achievement of such superb completeness as the battle in Manila Bay.

"This demonstration is no mere tribute to a personal friend, a fellow citizen. It is a simple and deserved recognition of the debt due the public servant who has proved himself grandly and efficiently faithful to his country's welfare and honor.

"You are called a man of destiny. You are—but it is the destiny of merit and worth—the conscientious obedience to duty of one skilled in art and judgement.

"Our Republic has no reason to fear a comparison of her sea fighters with those of other nations. The birth of the Republic gave her Paul Jones; the war of freedom of ocean highways gave her Perry, and the war for her moral and physical integrity gave her Farragut. She points with pride to any one of this trinity and says to all nations, Match him if you can.

"The war against Spain, waged for common humanity's sake in behalf of her island neighbors, gave her Dewey, who can safely be proclaimed chief among the naval heroes of the world.

"To the Mayor has been assigned the personally pleasant duty of presenting to you in the name of the city of New York, the metropolis of our country, this loving-cup, a keepsake to remind you from time to time of her love for you and her special pride in your deeds of valor, which she believes will for ages to come insure full respect of all nations and people for our starry flag, whether flung to the breeze over the man-of-war or the ship of commerce." Admiral Dewey heaved two big sighs while the Mayor was reading his speech. He nodded at the mention of the brave deeds of Paul Jones, but praise of himself was received with impassive face. Admiral Dewey only glanced at the gold loving-cup once. Then he said:

"Mr. Mayor, it would be quite impossible to express in words how deeply I am moved by this—by all these honors, one after the other—this beautiful cup, the freedom of the city, this great, magnificent reception.

"I cannot find words to say what I want to, but speaking for myself and the gallant squadron I had the honor to command at Manila, I thank you from the bottom of my heart."

Then in his quick, impetuous way Admiral Dewey said:

"These are the men who did it. Without them I could not have won the victory. Mr. Mayor, I want you to meet my captains, and they want to meet you."

Capts. Lamberton, Wildes, Dyer, Wood and Coghlan were presented.

The ceremonies lasted less than twenty minutes....

Off for the Parade.

When he re-entered his carriage Mayor Van Wyck was his companion. The police and the troops fell quickly into line and the march to the East River line pier, where the Sandy Hook lay, began. The street was crowded. As the pier was crowded with freight there was some delay with the carriages. Admiral Dewey walked from his carriage to the rear cabin of the Sandy Hook. His route was through two lines of policemen with batons at present.

Gen. Miles was one of the first persons the Admiral met on the boat.

"Miles," he said, "it's regular soldier weather, isn't it?"

"Not exactly," replied Miles. "I'd call it Dewey weather."

The Admiral went to breakfast as soon as he boarded the boat. Mayor Van Wyck sat down with him. He partook only of a cup of boullion, and declined a cigar.

When the Governor of Vermont was introduced Dewey said: "Glad to meet you. Glad to see you back."

The Admiral turned and introduced the blushing Governor from the Green Mountain State to every man in sight. The Governor was visibly embarrassed, and Dewey is so simple in his ways that he never even noticed it.

Something was said about the old people of Vermont.

His Remark on Old Age.

"Now, here is the best example," he said. "Here's Gov. Morton. He is seventy-six. Think of it! Children die in Vermont, but when we get past that period we live to an old age."

A young man was introduced as a relative of Ensign Worth Bagley.

"I remember him," said the Admiral. "I saw him play football. He saved the game for Annapolis. He was a brave boy—a brave boy. We need all like him we can get."

When asked if he had read the newspapers, he said:

"Not yet, but I'm saving them. When you have a Mayor who wakes you up at 7 A.M. you haven't any time for papers." Speaking of the parade, he said:

"It's a great thing when a grand city like New York gives up two days to do honor to one man."

The Governors of North and South Carolina, New Jersey and Tennessee were grouped before the Admiral.

"Gentlemen, it's a long time between drinks."

"Let's make it a quadruple," said Gov. McMillan. (*New York World*, 1 October 1899, 4.)

740 **Admiral Dewey and Mayor Van Wyck Going Down Riverside Drive / Admiral Dewey and Mayor Van Wyck**

LENGTH: 150 ft.   © No reg.

PRODUCER: James White.

CAMERA:

CAST: George Dewey, Robert Anderson Van Wyck.

PRODUCTION DATE: 30 September 1899.

LOCATION: New York, N.Y.

SOURCE:

DESCRIPTION: Showing battleship saluting at Hudson River. (*Edison Films*, March 1900, 8.)

SUBJECT: Navies–United States. Parades. Spanish-American War.

ARCHIVE:

CITATIONS: *New York Clipper*, 7 October 1899, 685; 4 November 1899, 760.

NOTE:

741 ***Admiral Dewey Leading Land Parade, [no. 1]**

LENGTH: 100 and 200 ft.   © Thomas A. Edison, 5 October 1899.

PRODUCER: James White.

CAMERA:

CAST: George Dewey, Robert Anderson Van Wyck, Nelson Miles, William Thomas Sampson, Winfield Scott Schley.

PRODUCTION DATE: 30 September 1899.

LOCATION: New York, N.Y.

SOURCE:

DESCRIPTION: On Riverside Drive; showing Naval Brigade of North Atlantic Fleet, followed by Schley, Sampson, Miles and other celebrities. The Admiral is in the carriage with Mayor Van Wyck. (*Edison Films*, March 1900, 7.)

SUBJECT: Spanish-American War. Navies–officers. Navies–United States. Armies–Officers. Parades.

ARCHIVE: DLC-pp.

CITATIONS: *New York Clipper*, 7 October 1899, 685; *Edison Films*, July 1901, 32-33.

NOTE:

---

742 *Admiral Dewey Leading Land Parade, no. 2 / Admiral Dewey Leading Land Parade, (Eighth Ave.)

LENGTH: 100 and 200 ft.   © Thomas A. Edison, 7 October 1899.

PRODUCER: James White.

CAMERA:

CAST: George Dewey, Robert Anderson Van Wyck, Nelson Miles, William Thomas Sampson, Winfield Scott Schley.

PRODUCTION DATE: 30 September 1899.

LOCATION: New York, N.Y.

SOURCE:

DESCRIPTION: Showing Central Park in the back-ground. (*Edison Films*, March 1900, 8.)

SUBJECT: Spanish-American War. Parades. Navies–officers. Armies–officers.

ARCHIVE: DLC-pp.

CITATIONS:

NOTE:

---

743 Mounted Police, Sousa's Band and Sailors of "Olympia"

LENGTH: 150 ft.   © No reg.

PRODUCER: James White.

CAMERA:

CAST:

PRODUCTION DATE: 30 September 1899.

LOCATION: New York, N.Y.

SOURCE:

DESCRIPTION:

SUBJECT: Police. Parades. Navies–United States. Marching bands. Spanish-American War. George Dewey. John Philip Sousa.

ARCHIVE:

CITATIONS: *New York Clipper*, 14 October 1899, 685.

NOTE: This film may be an alternate title or excerpt of *Admiral Dewey Leading Land Parade* (nos. 1 or 2).

---

744 *Admiral Dewey Passing Catholic Club Stand

LENGTH: 75 ft.   © Thomas A. Edison, 5 October 1899.

PRODUCER: James White.

CAMERA:

CAST: George Dewey.

PRODUCTION DATE: 30 September 1899.
LOCATION: New York, N.Y.
SOURCE:
DESCRIPTION:
SUBJECT: Spanish-American War. Parades.
Navies–officers. Catholicism.
ARCHIVE: DLC-pp.
CITATIONS: *New York Clipper*, 7 October 1899,
685.
NOTE:

ADMIRAL'S TRIUMPHAL PROGRESS TO THE REVIEWING STAND.
His Carriage Passes Between Living Walls for the Entire Distance and No Token of Popular Affection and Respect Is Omitted.
CHILDREN GREATLY PLEASE THE ADMIRAL.

Admiral Dewey did not leave his chair on the Sandy Hook during the trip up to One Hundred and Twenty-ninth street following the loving-cup ceremonies. When any one was introduced he begged pardon for not rising. He said he was tired already and had five hours of standing before him.

Dewey was the last to leave the boat with Mayor Van Wyck and an orderly. He sat on the right side of an open carriage drawn by four horses. An orderly occupied the seat with him. It was 11:10 A.M. when the Admiral left the boat.

No time was lost when Admiral Dewey and the Mayor arrived. One hundred mounted police had galloped ahead to form a wedge. Gen. Roe and staff had taken their places next. Sousa's Band had hastened forward and took its stand in front of the battalion of sailors from the Olympia, who were commanded by Lieut.-Commander Colvocoresses.

The Line Is Formed.

Meanwhile Major Green, of Gen. Roe's staff, had gone back to the rear and placed the carriages in their proper place. Gen. Roe looked back, saw that everything was taking shape and gave the word "Forward," Sousa's Band struck up with the inspiring march "El Captain," and while thousands on either side shouted and waved myriads of handkerchiefs and flags the greatest parade in the history of American demonstrations moved forward.

Salutes from the warships of the North Atlantic squadron thundered from the river to the north, bands chimed in on every side where the soldiers were in waiting to "fall in," and as far as the eye could see down Riverside Drive a waving mass of people lined the way, overflowing the gayly bedecked stands and crowding the neighboring house tops.

Bowed to the Children.

At One Hundred and Second street hundreds of children from the Hebrew Orphan Asylum had banked themselves on a huge platform. Two juvenile cornet bands played patriotic airs in front of the throng of orphans. Admiral Dewey turned and looked at the children a long time in passing, apparently lost to all others. He smiled and bowed and waved his plumed chapeau at them.

After the carriages came the naval brigade of the North Atlantic fleet, made up of United States marines, sailors of the warships New York, Texas, Indiana, Massachusetts, Brooklyn, Lancaster and the Dolphin. The marines and sailors were heartily cheered all down the line.

The Seventh, Sixty-ninth and Seventy-first Regiments and Troops A and C received the most applause, but the Seventh was also hissed at several points on the line. Gov. Roosevelt, who rode a magnificent black horse, was very warmly received. The children [on the] enormous stand at Seventy-second street and Central Park West sang "My Country 'Tis of Thee" and the Governor [was] kept busy raising his hat in response to the many calls of "Roosevelt! Roosevelt! What's the matter with Roosevelt?"

A large stand at Ninety-ninth street and Riverside Drive was occupied by five thousand children from the New York Juvenile Asylum, the Hebrew Sheltering Guardian Asylum and other [like] institutions. The children were plainly delighted with everything they saw, all cheered and yelled themselves hoarse.

Bothered by Paper Tape.

At Seventy-sixth street a string of paper tape fell across the Admiral's carriage. It got entangled in his hat. He put it aside at first and then tore it as it became more annoying.

In Seventy-second street the crowd became more dense. The people got closer to his carriage. His greetings became more cordial. In front of one house flowers were strewn in the road way.

In another house he recognised someone. He removed his chapeau and bowed. More flowers were thrown, and a boy handed him a bouquet.

In the same street one of the gold epaulets fell from his shoulder. Mayor Van Wyck had a hard time fastening it. The spectators lost a good view of his face.

The parade halted at Seventy-second and Central Park West, while the children sang. When they had finished Dewey rose in his carriage for the first time and bowed. Then he wrapped himself in his cloak and resumed the usual salutes.

It was just 5 o'clock when the last division of the parade–that division in which marched the veterans of the civil war, reached 42nd street and Fifth avenue.

The dust filled eyes of the spectators were alredy tired from watching.

Behind the band, which reportedly played "Onward Christian Soldiers," rode Gen. O.O. Howard, U.S.A, retired, and behind him were fourteen organizations of veterans of the civil war–G. A.R. men from all parts of the country. The General had a large staff.

They marched down the hill from Thirty-ninth street behind the men from the District of Columbia and soon the white pillars of the arch appeared, and then the officers of Gen. Howard's staff and veterans knew they would soon see Dewey.... (*New York World*, 1 October 1899, 2.)

745 Dewey's Arrival at Triumphal Arch

LENGTH: 100 ft.   © No reg.

PRODUCER: James White.

CAMERA:

CAST: George Dewey, William Thomas Sampson, Winfield Scott Schley.

PRODUCTION DATE: 30 September 1899.

LOCATION: New York, N.Y.

SOURCE:

DESCRIPTION: Greeted by Admirals Schley and Sampson. (*New York Clipper*, 7 October 1899, 664.)

SUBJECT: Spanish-American War. Parades. Navies–officers.

ARCHIVE:

CITATIONS: *New York Clipper*, 14 October 1899, 688.

NOTE:

THE ADMIRAL AMAZED.

When the carriage stopped, almost under the shadow of the big white arch, Admiral Dewey gazed up at the towering structure in amazement. He saw the magnificent colonnades of the approaches. He saw far up in the sky a hundred or more American flags and flags bearing his name which were apparently suspended in mid-air, but which were in fact attached to the strings of strong kites. He seemed to be lost in amazement until Mayor Van Wyck, who sat with him, touched him on his glove.

Casting his eyes then around the great amphitheatre of stands Admiral Dewey seemed for the first time to realise the overwhelming enthusiasm which his appearance had created among the ten thousand persons about him.

He stood up in the carriage, doffed his hat and bowed profoundly at least a dozen times. Then he stepped out of the carriage, ran nimbly up the steps of the reviewing stand, and there turned to again acknowledge the greetings of the people.

He stood there a few moments, still bowing and smiling, the flush of gratification showing on his bronzed cheeks. Then Mayor Van Wyck led him to a corner where were many sandwiches and almost as many bottles. Dewey ate a sandwich and sipped a goblet of champagne, while from the carriages following his alighted Rear-Admirals Sampson, Schley, Philip and a glittering crowd of lesser naval officers, most of them Dewey's own, of the Olympia, and their escorts of the city's committee.

The reviewing stand was just to the north of the great arch and on the west side of Fifth avenue. A canopy of blue and white was supported by eight slender iron columns, each surmounted by a gilt eagle. From the tops of the corner columns hung great wreaths of laurel and evergreen. The front edge of the stand was adorned with figures of dolphins and big baskets of pink roses, over which a butterfly, far wandering from the fields, occasionally hovered.

Two handsome armchairs of oak, carved, upholstered in blue velvet, stood at the front of the stand, one for the Admiral, the other for the Mayor. It may interest some people to know the chairs cost $40 apiece.

Back of these were arranged fifty comfortable armchairs, in which other prominent persons sat.

Far above the stand, suspended on kite strings, waved a streamer with "Welcome" in big letters, a number of Admirals' pennants and a big American flag. (*New York World*, 1 October 1899, 2.)

746 U.S. Marines in Dewey Land Parade

LENGTH: 100 ft.   © No reg.

PRODUCER: James White.

CAMERA:
CAST:
PRODUCTION DATE: 30 September 1899.
LOCATION: New York, N.Y.
SOURCE:
DESCRIPTION:
SUBJECT: Parades. Marines–United States. Spanish-American War. George Dewey.
ARCHIVE:
CITATIONS: *Edison Films*, July 1901, 33.
NOTE:

NOW THE BLUE JACKETS.

Right back of Gen. Roe and his staff came a battalion of blue jackets and marines, sturdy as young oaks, and with skins browned by tropical suns. They were the crew of Admiral Dewey's flagship, the Olympia. They were marching with that easy rolling swing which is characteristic of sailors ashore. Their arms were at port. They carried no equipment except canteens. They were nearly all young fellows and nearly every one had a broad grin on his face.

A good right they had to smile, for they knew that they were being honored quite as much as Dewey was; that the cheers were as much for the men behind the guns as for the master mind that directed them....

There was a complete brigade of sailors and marines from the North Atlantic fleet, made up of the crews of the New York, the Texas, Indiana, Massachusetts, Brooklyn and Lancaster.

As the jack tars swung by the reviewing stand, each battalion headed by its own ships band, the boys could not resist the temptation to turn their heads so as to get a good look at Admiral Dewey. It was against regulations, but the Admiral did not seem to mind that, and when he saw how the eyes of the jackies lighted up at the sight of him he smiled responsively. As each ship's flag was dropped before him he raised his chapeau and bowed reverently. (*New York World*, 1 October 1899, 2.)

---

747 ***West Point Cadets***
LENGTH: 75 ft.   © Thomas A. Edison, 7 October 1899.
PRODUCER: James White.
CAMERA:
CAST:
PRODUCTION DATE: 30 September 1899.
LOCATION: New York, N.Y.
SOURCE:
DESCRIPTION: In Dewey land parade. (*Edison Films*, March 1900, 8.)
SUBJECT: Armies–United States. Parades. Military cadets. Spanish-American War. George Dewey. U.S. Military Academy (West Point, N.Y.)
ARCHIVE: DLC-pp.
CITATIONS: *Edison Films*, July 1901, 33.
NOTE:

THE REGULARS

Following the sailors came the United States troops, a full brigade, commanded by Col. John I. Rogers, Fifth United States Artillery. They were headed by 350 of the West Point cadets, and it did not take long to demonstrate the fact that the future generals of the army hold a warm place in the people's hearts. The cheering for them was deafening, and they deserved it. In their gray coats, white duck trousers and black shakos, they presented a particularly trim appearance, and they marched with that precision for which the cadets have always been famous.

They were probably the only organization in the whole line that resisted the temptation to turn their heads toward the reviewing stand and get a good look at the Admiral.... (*New York World*, 1 October 1899, 2.)

---

748 ***Battery K Siege Guns***
LENGTH: 50 or 75 ft.   © Thomas A. Edison, 5 October 1899.
PRODUCER: James White.
CAMERA:
CAST:

PRODUCTION DATE: 30 September 1899.
LOCATION: New York, N.Y.
SOURCE:
DESCRIPTION: In Dewey land parade. (*Edison Films*, March 1900, 8.)
SUBJECT: Parades. Armies–United States. Artillery. Spanish-American War. George Dewey.
ARCHIVE: DLC-pp.
CITATIONS: *Edison Films*, July 1901, 33.
NOTE:

749 *****Governor Roosevelt and Staff / Governor Roosevelt and Staff in Dewey Land Parade**
LENGTH: 50 ft.   © Thomas A. Edison, 7 October 1899.
PRODUCER: James White.
CAMERA:
CAST: Theodore Roosevelt.
PRODUCTION DATE: 30 September 1899.
LOCATION: New York, N.Y.
SOURCE:
DESCRIPTION: In Dewey land parade. (*Edison Films*, March 1900, 8.)
SUBJECT: Spanish-American War. Parades. National Guard–New York. Governors–United States. George Dewey.
ARCHIVE: DLC-pp.
CITATIONS: *Edison Films*, July 1901, 33.
NOTE:

ROOSEVELT'S SALUTE.

Roosevelt rode his horse, not in the wild Western cowboy style which he delights to ride a polo pony or bronco, but he sat up stiff and straight. As he approached Admiral Dewey he turned his head toward him, took off his high hat with a flourish and swung it around with his right hand until it rested on his left breast.

Admiral Dewey responded to the salute by taking off his own elegant chapeau and bowing and smiling but Gov. Roosevelt did not bow in return. He sat stiff as a ramrod, trying to look unconcerned. Squadron A rode as an escort to the Governor. (*New York World*, 1 October 1898, 2.)

750 *****Dewey Parade, 10th Pennsylvania Volunteers**
LENGTH: 50 ft.   © Thomas A. Edison, 7 October 1899.
PRODUCER: James White.
CAMERA:
CAST:
PRODUCTION DATE: 30 September 1899.
LOCATION: New York, N.Y.
SOURCE:
DESCRIPTION: In Dewey land parade. (*Edison Films*, March 1900, 8.)
SUBJECT: Armies–United States. Parades. National Guard–Pennsylvania. Spanish-American War. Philippines–History–Insurrection (1899-1901). George Dewey.
ARCHIVE: DLC-pp.
CITATIONS: *Edison Films*, July 1901, 33.
NOTE:

Quick Moving Parade.

The parade was moving along at a lively pace....New York's State troops had all passed and the militia of other states were to come. Pennsylvania was first in the line. Gov. Stone and his staff rode at the head of five of the best regiments of the State. The Governor was given a splendid reception by the crowd and made a fine figure on horseback. The Pennsylvania regiments in the line were the First, 450 men; the Second, 450 men; the Ninth, 350 men; the Third, 200 men; and the Tenth, 600 men. The Pennsylvanians were commented on for their excellent marching and for their business-like appearance. But it was the Tenth Regiment, of Pennsylvania, commanded by Col. Barnett, which the people were especially looking for, and when it came along the men of that command received the greatest welcome that was given to any organization in the entire parade. The Tenth Regiment of Pennsylvania only returned from the Philippine Islands a few weeks ago, after a long campaign in which they had fought many hard engagements and covered themselves with glory. Naturally, then, the crowd became wildly enthusiastic as they came along. (*New York World,* 1 October 1899, 2.)

751 *The Dewey Arch—Troops Passing Under

LENGTH: [100 ft.]   © Thomas A. Edison, 5 October 1899.
PRODUCER: James White.
CAMERA:
CAST:
PRODUCTION DATE: 30 September 1899.
LOCATION: New York, N.Y.
SOURCE:
DESCRIPTION:
SUBJECT: Armies–United States. Parades.
    Spanish-American War. George Dewey.
ARCHIVE: DLC-pp.
CITATIONS:
NOTE:

Gen. Merritt, as commander of the Department of the East, stood up beside Admiral Dewey to review the troops of the regular army as they passed. There was a battalion of engineers, four battalions of artillery and one battalion of mounted artillery. Some of the men wore their old campaign hats, and they caught the fancy of the crowd. They looked warlike. The battalion of mounted artillery, with half a dozen wicked looking four inch guns, each mounted upon the new high gun carriages, and with a score of smaller field pieces and ammunition wagons, won the plaudits of the people. The men rode their horses as though they were part of them. There was a full brigade of these United States troops, making the best display of regular army soldiers that has ever been seen in a street parade in this city....(*New York World,* 1 October 1899, 2.)

After his triumphant reception in New York City and amid considerable speculation about the admiral becoming a presidential candidate, Dewey headed South to another celebration, this time in the nation's capital.

752 Presentation of Nation's Sword to Admiral Dewey

LENGTH: 100 and 175 or 200 ft.   © No reg.
PRODUCER: J. Stuart Blackton, Albert E. Smith.
CAMERA: J. Stuart Blackton and/or Albert E. Smith.
CAST: George Dewey, John Davis Long, William McKinley.
PRODUCTION DATE: 3 October 1899.
LOCATION: Washington, D.C.
SOURCE:
DESCRIPTION: By Secretary Long at Washington, showing President McKinley, the Admiral and many other celebrities. Clear, sharp and lifelike. (*Edison Films,* July 1901, 33.)
SUBJECT: Spanish-American War. Ceremonies.
ARCHIVE:
CITATIONS: "Gift of a Nation," *Washington Evening Star,* 3 October 1899, 3-13. *New York Clipper,* 14 October 1899, 685; 4 November 1899, 760; *Edison Films,* March 1900, 7.
NOTE:

DEWEY RECEIVES FROM THE PRESIDENT THE SWORD VOTED HIM BY CONGRESS.
Mr. McKinley, in Presenting the Beautiful Weapon, Said the Fruits of the
Victory of Manila Would be Stoutly Defended by the United States.
TEARS IN ADMIRAL'S EYES AS HE TOOK THE GIFT.
Herald Bureau Corner of Fifteenth and G Streets, N.W., Washington, D.C., Tuesday. Admiral Dewey was made the

hero of the nation to-day by a ceremony which in impressiveness has not been equalled since the foundation of the republic.

The entire national government assembled to do him honor. By his side, on the spot where Presidents are inaugurated, stood President McKinley to bestow upon him the magnificent sword which Congress had voted should be given to him upon his return from Manila. Behind him were grouped the members of the Cabinet and the Justices of the Supreme Court of the United States. The Senate and House of Representatives were present in the persons of their more distinguished members.

The navy, of which he himself is the head, was represented by the rear admirals and the captains of the ships which destroyed the fleets of Spain. Major General Miles and his staff headed the parade, which represented every branch of the service, and which passed in review before him.

Governors of many States, with their staffs, were on the platform, and, finally on every hand, as far as the eye could reach, stretched a mass of wildly enthusiastic spectators.

ADMIRAL SHOWS EMOTION.

It was a perfect day, Dewey weather. When the Admiral stood up in his glittering uniform, to receive the nation's gift, the hearts of the multitude warmed toward him as they saw him raise his white gloved hand to brush back the emotion from his eyes, it was a scene which none who saw it will forget.

John D. Long, Secretary of the Navy, delivered the formal oration in which he recounted the events in Manila Bay and told Admiral Dewey why it was that the representatives of the nation assembled to do him honor. While Secretary Long was speaking, Dewey's eyes filled with tears, and it was evident to all that he was struggling to restrain his emotion.

President McKinley applauded every mention of Dewey's bravery and the Admiral repaid the compliment when the Secretary spoke of the part played by his chief in the war with Spain.

At the conclusion of his speech Secretary Long aided by Admiral Dewey, unfastened the lid of the white oak box in which the sword lay. As he lifted it and the crowd saw the sun flash on the diamond studded hilt they cheered frantically.

PRESIDENT PRESENTED THE SWORD.

President McKinley, who had kept himself in the background, rose from his chair as Secretary Long concluded and stepped forward until he and Admiral Dewey faced each other. Both men are almost of the same height and figure, but Admiral Dewey looked ruddy above his gold embroidered collar, while McKinley's, in his dark overcoat, seemed pale.

"Admiral Dewey," said the President, "from your entrance in the harbor of New York with your gallant crew and valiant ships the demonstrations which everywhere have greeted you reveal the public esteem of your heroic action and the fullness of love in which you are held by your country...."

Admiral Dewey replied simply and sincerely. His voice was firm and his bearing easy and natural as he took the splendid sword from the President's hand....

Again and again the crowd cheered as the Admiral referred to the sword and to the allusion to Washington as his home. The band struck up "My Country 'Tis of Thee," and all who were on the platform rose and stood hatless until the last note.

Cardinal Gibbons mounted the steps of the reviewing stand as the anthem ended. Standing between the Admiral and the President who bowed their heads, he delivered a benediction.

Mounted policemen with difficulty cleared a broad lane through the crowd in order to release General Miles and his staff, who had been hemmed in and to make way for the parade. While this was being done there were cries from the crowd of "Hold up the sword," and Admiral Dewey obligingly lifted it so that all might see. A woman on the inner edge of the crowd lifted her little girl who threw a kiss toward the reviewing stand. The Admiral saw it and returned it by lifting his hat with a smile. He also bowed to several of his friends in the crowd, among them Senator Depew....(*New York Herald*, 4 October 1899, 12.)

Following the enthusiastic celebrations that greeted him in New York and Washington, Dewey began to tour many other large American cities, beginning with Boston. Despite its citizens' general lack of enthusiasm for the recent war against Spain, Boston greeted Dewey with impressive energy.

753 ***Admiral Dewey at State House, Boston, Mass. / Dewey at the State House, Boston**

LENGTH: 100 and 150 ft.   © Thomas A. Edison, 25 October 1899.
PRODUCER: James White.
CAMERA:
CAST: George Dewey, Roger Wolcott.
PRODUCTION DATE: 14 October 1899.

LOCATION: Boston, Mass.

SOURCE:

DESCRIPTION: This picture shows Dewey coming down the State House steps, leaning on the arm of Governor Walcott [sic]; also reviewing the parade, leaving the stand and going away in a carriage. (*Edison Films*, March 1900, 8.)

SUBJECT: Parades. Spanish-American War.

ARCHIVE: DLC-pp.

CITATIONS: *New York Clipper*, 21 October 1899, 707.

NOTE: An Edison advertisement for this film in the *New York Clipper* (2 October 1899) indicates that the company was selling additional films of "The Boston Dewey Celebration," but does not provide titles.

HONOR TO THE HERO.
Dewey Rides Through Boston to Music of Cheers.
ALL NEW ENGLAND APPLAUDS HIM.
Solid Ranks of Soldiers Follow the Brave Admiral, Who Reviews Them.

ADMIRAL George Dewey received yesterday, from early morning until late at night, the greatest ovation ever extended by Boston to any man.

The Boston that cheered itself hoarse and struggled for a sight of the hero of Manila bay, was not the Boston of every day. It was a Boston filled full to overflowing with its own people and the people of all surrounding New England, gathered to pay special tribute to Admiral Dewey, the man who is always on time or ahead of time.

The admiral's day began early. He arose at 6 o'clock, after 10 hours of restful sleep at the Hotel Touraine, and at 6:30 breakfasted with his son, George G. Dewey, Lieut. Brumby and General Manager McKeever of the Rutland railroad. About 9 there arrived the special committee from the school committee, deputized to conduct the admiral to the children's exercises on the Common....

Then there was a presentation of a sword on the part of a Boston newspaper, the mayor acting as spokesman.

Promptly at 9:50 o'clock the admiral left the hotel for the exercises by the children, on the Common. He was escorted by Mayor Quincy.

At exactly 9:58–two minutes before programme time–Admiral Dewey's carriage entered the Common by the Park square entrance, and 25,000 school children greeted him and sang patriotic airs as told in detail on page 13 of today's Sunday Herald.

From the Common the admiral and his party went to City Hall where he arrived at 10:38, and where he was presented with the city's gift–a watch.

What Mayor Quincy said in presenting the watch and how the exercises were carried out, may be found today on page 21 of today's Sunday Herald.

The exercises at City Hall over, Admiral Dewey re-entered his carriage, and was driven to the home of Mr. J. Montgomery Sears, where luncheon was served.

At 11:50 Admiral Dewey, a little ahead of time, as ever, accompanied by Lieut.-Gov. Crane, Mayor Quincy and Lieut. Brumby, left the Sears residence and entered the four-horse barouche which was in waiting. It was two minutes and a half before 12 o'clock when the bugles at the head of the line gave notice the parade has started, and a few seconds later the admiral's carriage began to roll over the smooth macadam of Arlington street.

When the party came from Mrs. Sears' house there were hearty cheers, and most of the men within view uncovered, but the enthusiasm was nothing to that which marked the line of march after the parade got fairly started.

The route traversed was a long one, but the wisdom which prompted the extension of the original programme was early made manifest. If an attempt had been made to confine yesterday's parade to the business streets of Boston there would have been disappointment, instead of general satisfaction and serious disaster would almost inevitably had attended the confining of the throngs to the streets originally set apart for the march.

After the admiral's carriage turned from Arlington into Beacon street the first sign of the great enthusiasm which was to follow was seen....

The mounted police, the Olympia battalion and its band proceeded directly up Beacon street, in front of the State House. Gov. Wolcott, who headed the parade, turned up Mt. Vernon street, accompanied by his staff officers. They were soon joined by Admiral Dewey and the other guests and members of the committee who rode in carriages.

The party entered the State House from the arch, and then, passing through, came out the front steps from the main corridor. Sergeant-at-Arms Adams led the way, and then came Gov. Wolcott and Admiral Dewey, followed by the staff officers and invited guests.

A stand for review had been constructed directly in front of the State House grounds, and here the reviewing party took their places. Gov. Wolcott and Admiral Dewey stood in the centre, while grouped about them were Gov. Dyer of Rhode Island, Gov. Rolling of New Hampshire, and Lieut. Gov. Crane, with other dignitaries closely ranged around them. It was scarcely five minutes after 2 o'clock when the column began to pass by the reviewing officers.

As the columns marched by the reviewing officers, Admiral Dewey expressed himself as very favorably impressed on several occasions. He showed a keen interest in finding out about the various organizations, what section each one came from, how long it had been in service, what service it saw during the Spanish-American war, and who the officers were....

It was just 3 o'clock when the last soldier passed the reviewing stand, and the great spectacle was over....

As soon as the review was over Admiral Dewey was taken in charge again by Lieut.-Gov. Crane, and was escorted to his carriage. He took his side, and Mayor Quincy and Lieut. Brumby on the opposite seat. The marines and blue-jackets from the Olympia, under the command of Lieutenant-Commander Colvocresses, who had been massed along the front of the reviewing stand, swung to the right and marched off down Beacon Street toward the Common. Behind them came Admiral Dewey and the carriages containing Gov. Rollins of New Hampshire, Gov. Dyer of Rhode Island, and other staff officers and members of the committee. In the rear was the fine appearing battalion of marines from the navy yard, under the command of Lieut.-Col. Crane.

While this little procession was forming, Gov. Wolcott and the members of his staff mounted their horses again and took position at the head of the line.

This little procession then moved down Beacon street toward the Common....(*Boston Herald*, 15 October 1899, 1-2.)

The yacht races for the America's Cup were consistent front-page news during most of October 1899. The contest between the "Columbia" and Sir Thomas Lipton's challenger, the "Shamrock," began on October 3rd. This race was canceled due to insufficient wind. The next three attempts to race were also unsuccessful. One of the notable features of the races in this period was the reporting of the boats' progress by Marconi wireless. The first official race was on 16 October 1899, the second on 17 October 1899 and the third and final race on 20 October 1899. The American boat won all three races and retained the cup.

This event may have been covered by more than one Edison-affiliated camera crew, but Blackton and Smith's American Vitagraph Company was at least responsible for most of the pictures. Then the only 35mm exhibition service with an established venue in New York vaudeville, Vitagraph showed films of each race on the evening of the day it occurred—a strong indication that Blackton and/or Smith took these films. A selection of these subjects was then offered for sale through the Edison Manufacturing Company, with the following announcement:

International Yacht Race Films. The following have created a great sensation in New York City where they were thrown on the screen by our apparatus the same night of the happening of each event. We secured many moving pictures of these races, but we only list below those which are perfect in every detail and which show the yachts clear and distinct. (*New York Clipper*, 4 November 1899, 760.)

754 *Pictures Incidental to Yacht Race / Pictures Incidental to International Yacht Races

LENGTH: 150 ft.   © Thomas A. Edison, 7 November 1899.
PRODUCER: J. Stuart Blackton, Albert E. Smith.
CAMERA: J. Stuart Blackton and/or Albert E. Smith.
CAST:
PRODUCTION DATE: 3-20 October 1899.
LOCATION: New York Harbor, New York, N.Y.
SOURCE:
DESCRIPTION: Showing a full rigged ship under sail passing out of New York Harbor, pleasure boats, tugs, etc., and the Official Timekeeper of the races signalling Commodore Kane's Committee boat by means of the army wigwag signals. (*Edison Films*, March 1900, 6.)
SUBJECT: Yachts and yachting. Yacht racing. America's Cup races. S. Nicholson Kane.

ARCHIVE: DLC-pp.
CITATIONS: "Tony Pastor's," *New York Dramatic Mirror*, 14 October 1899, 18. *New York Clipper*, 4 November 1899, 760.
NOTE:

755 *After the Race—Yachts Returning to Anchorage

LENGTH: 100 ft.   © Thomas A. Edison, 20 October 1899.
PRODUCER: J. Stuart Blackton, Albert E. Smith.
CAMERA: J. Stuart Blackton and/or Albert E. Smith.
CAST:
PRODUCTION DATE: 3-16 October 1899.
LOCATION: Off Sandy Hook, N.J.
SOURCE:
DESCRIPTION: Shows the yachts returning to anchorage. (*New York Clipper*, 4 November 1899, 760.)
SUBJECT: Yacht racing. America's Cup races.
ARCHIVE: DLC-pp.
CITATIONS: *Edison Films*, March 1900, 6.
NOTE:

756 *"Shamrock" and "Columbia" Yacht Race, First Race, [no. 1]

LENGTH: 100 ft.   © Thomas A. Edison, 20 October 1899.
PRODUCER: J. Stuart Blackton, Albert E. Smith.
CAMERA: J. Stuart Blackton and/or Albert E. Smith.
CAST:
PRODUCTION DATE: 16 October 1899.
LOCATION: Off Sandy Hook, N.J.
SOURCE:
DESCRIPTION: This picture shows the two yachts rounding the stakeboats and jockeying for a start. (*Edison Films*, March 1900, 6.)
SUBJECT: Yacht racing. America's Cup races.
ARCHIVE: DLC-pp.
CITATIONS: *New York Clipper*, 4 November 1899, 760.
NOTE:

757 *"Shamrock" and "Columbia" Yacht Race, First Race, no. 2 / "Columbia" and "Shamrock" Tacking [?]

LENGTH: 100 ft.   © Thomas A. Edison, 7 November 1899.
PRODUCER: J. Stuart Blackton, Albert E. Smith.
CAMERA: J. Stuart Blackton and/or Albert E. Smith.
CAST:
PRODUCTION DATE: 16 October 1899.
LOCATION: Off Sandy Hook, N.J.
SOURCE:
DESCRIPTION:
SUBJECT: Yacht racing. America's Cup races.
ARCHIVE: DLC-pp.
CITATIONS: *New York Clipper*, 4 November 1899, 760.
NOTE: It is not certain that the second title refers to this film. *"Columbia" and "Shamrock" Tacking* might possibly be the name for another film that was not copyrighted.

COLUMBIA WINS FIRST RACE; SHAMROCK A MILE BEHIND.
Big Sloops Start in Thick Fog on a Thrash to Windward,
with Wind Varying from Eight to Twelve Miles an Hour.
AMERICAN BOAT'S SUPERIORITY OVER HER RIVAL WAS EVIDENT.
Columbia Draws Away from Shamrock in the Beat to the Outer Mark
and Starts on the Homeward Run with a Lead of Nearly Ten Minutes.
SHAMROCK AT HER BEST BEFORE THE WIND ON HER WAY HOME.
As a Result of This Race Public Opinion Has Entirely Changed.
Betting Is All in Favor of the Columbia, and Belief Is General that It Will Be Three Straight.

COLUMBIA wins! After two long weeks of fruitless waiting and depressing efforts, a breeze was found at the famous old yacht-racing ground yesterday that was fit to drive both the cup challenger Shamrock and the cup defender Columbia over the prescribed course. It was not a strong breeze; it was a light one only, for it required more than five hours for the sluggard to cover the course, but in spite of the fears and faint-heartedness of the weaklings, Columbia won by a most pleasing margin of time.

The day was foggy, and at one time a drizzling mist filled the air. The wind came from the east, and it varied in speed, as estimated, at from eight to ten knots per hour. It may have been somewhat better than that during the last hour or so, but it was never much better. The course was fifteen miles to windward and back.

The sea was as smooth as it ever will be under a working easterly breeze, and the excursion boats were kept so well clear that the racers had every opportunity to do their best.

In short, it was the cleanest, fairest test of yachts in a breeze varying from light to moderate ever seen in the history of the cup, and Columbia won by 10 minutes and 8 seconds of time, and by a space of a little less than a mile and a quarter.

STEADFAST BETTORS PROFITED.

The World begs to congratulate those sporting men with red blood in their veins who upon its reports bet their money on Columbia and did not hedge when The World's esteemed contemporaries without exception were scared by what they thought they saw in the days of flukes. (John R. Spears, *New York World*, 17 October 1899, 1.)

758 *"Shamrock" and "Columbia" Jockeying for a Start

LENGTH: 100 ft.   © Thomas A. Edison, 7 November 1899.
PRODUCER: J. Stuart Blackton, Albert E. Smith.
CAMERA: J. Stuart Blackton and/or Albert E. Smith.
CAST:
PRODUCTION DATE: [17 October 1899.]
LOCATION: Off Sandy Hook, N.J.
SOURCE:
DESCRIPTION:
SUBJECT: Yacht racing. America's Cup races.
ARCHIVE: DLC-pp.
CITATIONS: *Edison Films*, March 1900, 6.
NOTE: This film could have been taken on any one of several different occasions.

COLUMBIA WINS AGAIN. SHAMROCK CRIPPLED.
Challenger's Skipper Carries Mr. Fife's Enormous Club Topsail
in a Freshening Breeze Until the Oregon Pine Topmast Snaps Short.
HAD RACED ONLY TWENTY-FOUR MINUTES.
Cup Defender Was Gaining and Capt. Hogarth Knew That
to Set a Smaller Sail Would Mean Defeat—He Preferred to Risk His Spars.
COLUMBIA WENT OVER THE COURSE ALONE.
She Showed Herself Better Than the Challenger In Exactly the Sort of
Weather the British Yachtsmen Have Said Was Needed to Show Their Boat at Her Best....

Columbia wins the second race of the series. On Monday we had a light-to-fresh breeze test of the speed of the two models, with Columbia winning by a margin of ten minutes and eight seconds. Yesterday we had a fresh-breeze-moderate-sea test of the construction of the two racers, and Columbia won by a topmast.

Hoping that Mr. Fife's judgment in planning the spars and sails of his boat was good, and driven to desperation by the defeat the white wonder of Bristol had given him on the previous day, the captain of the Shamrock set a club topsail that was all the yacht could stagger under in the breeze that prevailed just before the start, and then held on to it when the breeze freshened after crossing the line.

BREEZE NOT A STRONG ONE.

It was not a strong breeze. It was at most not so strong as what Sir Thomas has often expresses a wish for. It was less than fifteen knots an hour. Nor was the sea at all bad. There were a few lumps and an occasional mound to be crossed, but it was a sea often faced by Columbia in her summer's work. Nevertheless Shamrock had been across the line but twenty-four minutes when her topmast snapped short off at the cap, fell over to leeward and there slatted to and fro to the roll of the hulk. Necessarily Capt. Hogarth at once gave up the race and headed for home.

HAD THE BEST OF THE START.

At the start of the race Shamrock had the best of it by getting the weather berth and holding Columbia fairly blanketed for two minutes after crossing the line–an advantage equal to about one minute, it is guessed.

But Shamrock found the hills too steep on the starboard tack, on which she had crossed, and went about, leaving the wind open for Columbia, and so while Shamrock's mast held good there was a fair test of the two boats in a fresh breeze, with the result, as it appeared from The World's despatch boat, that Columbia had a least made up all she lost through Hogarth's good seamanship at the start.

MEANT A LEAD AT THE TURN.

And that is to say that Columbia would have rounded the first turn from three to four minutes ahead of her rival. After that, as the two remaining legs were reaches in a wind that moderated at least to six or eight knots, it is fair to suppose that she would have steadily increased her lead. Columbia covered the course in three hours and thirty-seven minutes, a length of time that showed to those who saw her during the summer's work that she is in still better form for fresh-breeze work that she was then. It should be noted that the mutual agreement whereby any yacht that breaks down in a race shall suffer the loss of the race if its rival can cover the course in the time limit was made at the request of Mr. Fife. He had been deeply impressed by the fact that Columbia had broken a mainmast and a club topsail sprit during her trials. (John R. Spears, *New York World*, 18 October 1899, 1.)

759 *"Shamrock" and "Columbia" Rounding the Outer Stake Boat, [no. 1] / "Shamrock" and "Columbia" Rounding the Outer Stakeboat, [no. 1]

LENGTH: 100 ft.   © Thomas A. Edison, 24 October 1899.
PRODUCER: J. Stuart Blackton, Albert E. Smith.
CAMERA: J. Stuart Blackton and/or Albert E. Smith.
CAST:
PRODUCTION DATE: 20 October 1899.
LOCATION: Off Sandy Hook, N.J.
SOURCE:
DESCRIPTION: This picture shows the two yachts racing at 20 miles an hour, the crew manipulating the sails as they round the outer mark. Columbia leading the Shamrock by thirteen seconds. (*Edison Films*, March 1900, 6.)
SUBJECT: Yacht racing. America's Cup races.
ARCHIVE: DLC-pp.
CITATIONS: *New York Clipper*, 4 November 1899, 760.
NOTE:

760 *"Shamrock" and "Columbia" Rounding the Outer Stake Boat, no. 2 / "Shamrock" and "Columbia" Rounding the Outer Stakeboat, no. 2

LENGTH: 100 ft.   © Thomas A. Edison, 25 October 1899.
PRODUCER: J. Stuart Blackton, Albert E. Smith.
CAMERA: J. Stuart Blackton and/or Albert E. Smith.
CAST:
PRODUCTION DATE: 20 October 1899.
LOCATION: Off Sandy Hook, N.J.
SOURCE:
DESCRIPTION: This picture shows the two yachts racing at 20 miles an hour, the crew manipulating the sails as they round the outer mark, Columbia leading the Shamrock by thirteen seconds. (*Edison Films*, July 1901, 32.)

SUBJECT: Yacht racing. America's Cup races.
ARCHIVE: DLC-pp.
CITATIONS: *Edison Films*, March 1900, 6.
NOTE:

761 *"Columbia" Winning the Cup**
LENGTH: 100 ft.   © Thomas A. Edison, 24 October 1899.
PRODUCER: J. Stuart Blackton, Albert E. Smith.
CAMERA: J. Stuart Blackton and/or Albert E. Smith.
CAST:
PRODUCTION DATE: 20 October 1899.
LOCATION: Off Sandy Hook, N.J.
SOURCE:

DESCRIPTION: This picture shows the Columbia
crossing the line, leading the Shamrock by
about 1/2 mile. The Shamrock is plainly
seen in the distance and she later comes up
and crosses the line in the same picture.
(*Edison Films*, March 1900, 6.)
The decisive moment in the great
International Yacht Races is shown in this
picture. Against a background of well
defined clouds, the Light Boat is seen
marking the finishing line in this great aquatic struggle. As the Columbia crosses
the line, followed closely by the Shamrock, we see the steam from the whistle of the
Light Ship announcing the well earned victory of the American yacht. (*Edison
Films*, July 1901, 32.)
SUBJECT: Yacht racing. America's Cup races.
ARCHIVE: DLC-pp.
CITATIONS: *New York Clipper*, 4 November 1899, 760.
NOTE:

GRAND TRIUMPH FOR COLUMBIA AND YANKEE BUILDERS.

COLUMBIA wins again! It is the third race of the series. She has had an uninterrupted succession of victories, and
that of yesterday was not only decisive, but it was the most glorious victory in the history of the cup.
In fact, all three victories, whether taken together or considered singly, are without parallel.
The first, that of last Monday, was especially notable. The designer of the challenger had lightened his ship by
removing ballast in order to make her travel at a breath, and had succeeded in this scheme so far as to scare every
thin-blooded American that ever saw a yacht, while even men who really knew better got white around the gills.
All this because in light and unsteady breezes when no yacht could cover the course Shamrock had had the better luck.
But when a light breeze that would hold true and heavy enough to allow the yachts to cover the course in the time
limit did come, the white wonder was wafted home the victor by 10 minutes and 8 seconds.
That shut tight and forever the mouths of those who had said Shamrock would win as soon as a little more wind
came.

THE SECOND RACE.

As it happened, there was a little more wind next day, and with it came enough of a sea to give a new test of the
racers, and a test for which special provision had been made at the especial request of the challenger.
The sea gave "a test of the strength of construction" of the two yachts.
Goaded by his loss of the previous race Capt. Hogarth crowded sail on his untried yacht beyond her limit of endu-
rance and Columbia won by a topmast.
In spite of the queer sentiment displayed in some of the New York newspapers next day, Columbia's victory on
Tuesday was entirely creditable to her builder and to Mr. Iselin. Few more creditable victories have been recorded.
Well, the challenger then gave up hope of success in moderate breezes, and while getting a new topmast up and
shrouded to stay she took in more ballast–3,383 pounds more. She was now fit at last, her backers said, and they
added rather gratuitously that there had been as yet no real test of the yachts!
They said that for a real test wind and a plenty of it was needed. If only they could get a whole sail breeze–
something from fifteen to eighteen knots or better–the pride of Erin would show what the dour Scotch designer
could do in the way of building racers.

The sun came up yesterday in a murk so thick that only such rays as could permeate a Hatteras fog were found to tell the tale.

But out of the north was coming a wind that was like the breath of inspiration, for it filled and satisfied the hearts of the faithful.

It was a magnificent, a most glorious breeze–the half gale for which the Shamrocks had wished, and it was to hold its force throughout the race and shift only for the benefit of the green challenger from over the sea.

With sails driving them at a speed that made them laugh at tugs the giant racers reached out to the old red light-ship, and there made ready for the starting gun.

Was it a good breeze–all that any one wanted?

Even the "powerful" Shamrock sent up a working topsail only, although the course was laid dead before the wind, and now, if ever, was the time to use every thread she could carry.

But if small topsails only could be spread they could both carry spinnakers, and when at last they were off, with the honors of the start resting on Columbia's quarterdeck, the spectators saw such a picture as has rarely been seen before.

Nor was it only the picturesque that held the spectators for a time spellbound. Columbia was not only Yankee-built, she was Herreshoff-modelled, and she was driving through the water at a speed that drove the Shamrocks desperate.

Columbia had started astern and was steadily overhauling the pride of Erin.

Needless to tell it is that she had a struggle before her. The brave captain of the Shamrock would not yield till he must. Columbia had started to windward as well as astern–that is, out on the spinnaker side of Shamrock–but Hogarth tuned the green racer out until Iselin was content to head through his lee.

So for a time it looked to the spectators who were poorly placed as if Shamrock had suddenly begun to gain–a nightmare of a delusion that lasted half an hour, and then–well, Shamrock had seemed to begin to gain a half hour after starting, but when still another half hour had gone the nightmare fled, for Columbia was seen to be ahead of Shamrock–she had gained the minute that was between them at the start.

A little later down came her spinnaker and around the turn she went, seventeen seconds in the lead, while every whistle screamed and every patriot in that crowd of excursionists went wild.

The race was already decided though but half done.

Still the friends of the green racer were hopeful that in windward work she could redeem herself. Hadn't she been designed to go to windward in a gale, and hadn't she had 3,383 pounds of lead stowed on board?

Stand by, said they, and see what happens.

ALL WATCHED THE FINAL TEST.

So all stood by and with bulging eyes they saw–yes, they saw Shamrock reach through Columbia's lee just as she did on a fluke day–PRECISELY as she did then.

She did this by reaching away off the wind and so losing lengths while fools thought she was gaining.

From the moment she came to the wind Columbia opened the sweet light between her and Shamrock, and she continued to pen it until Hogarth was driven to splitting tacks, after the fashion he had followed in previous trials.

But he continued to drop astern until well up to Navesink Highlands, when kindly fortune, to save him from utter despondency, came with a favoring breath.

Influenced by the green Jersey hills, perhaps–at any rate, for some reason–the wind suddenly shifted from north-northeast to north by west.

And the shift came when Shamrock was well inshore, well to westward of Columbia, and it left Shamrock on the weather quarter of the fleet Columbia.

HOGARTH TOOK EVERY CHANCE.

At that Capt. Hogarth took a desperate chance. The wind was freshening and neither yacht had had a topsail of any kind up for a long time, but Hogarth luffed up and set a club-topsail.

Then he filled away, and the way the green racer heeled to it made the oldest of the old sharps gasp.

And at that Columbia footed away from him faster than ever, winning at the last by a mile in space and 6 minutes and 34 seconds in time.

Sir Thomas proved to be a good loser, and her received as much attention as if he had been a winner. After the race he hoisted the American flag over the Shamrock's flag. He went aboard the Corsair, where J. Pierpont Morgan and C. Oliver Iselin embraced him. He held a reception aboard his own boat.

A joint testimonial to Sir Thomas and Mr. Iselin has been proposed, and a cup presentation to the Shamrock's owner is also on the programme. (John R. Spears, *New York World*, 21 October 1899, 1.)

762 *"Shamrock" and "Erin" Sailing

LENGTH: 100 ft.   © Thomas A. Edison, 25 October 1899

PRODUCER: J. Stuart Blackton, Albert E. Smith.

CAMERA: J. Stuart Blackton and/or Albert E. Smith.

CAST:
PRODUCTION DATE: [20 October 1899.]
LOCATION:
SOURCE:
DESCRIPTION:
SUBJECT: Yachts and yachting. America's Cup races.
ARCHIVE: DLC-pp.
CITATIONS: *New York Clipper*, 4 November 1899, 760; *Edison Films*, March 1900, 6.
NOTE:

Ten days after the America's Cup races concluded and two weeks after Dewey's reception in Boston, an Edison or Edison-affiliated cameraman traveled to Quebec to film Canadian troops leaving for South Africa and the Boer War.

763 ***2nd Special Service Battalion, Canadian Infantry, Parade / Second Special Service Battalion, Canadian Infantry, Embarking for South Africa (part) / Canadian Troops Departing from Quebec for the Transvaal (part)**
LENGTH: 100, 200, 300 and 525 ft.   © Thomas A. Edison, 7 November 1899.
PRODUCER: [James White.]
CAMERA:
CAST:
PRODUCTION DATE: 30 October 1899.
LOCATION: Quebec, Canada.
SOURCE:

DESCRIPTION: This picture shows the Canadian troops departing from Quebec for the war in Transvaal. The scene opens with the soldiers clad in campaign uniform, marching under the triumphal arch, cheered by thousands of spectators who are waving English flags. The troops next appear marching upon the wharf and finally embarking upon the transport Sardinia[n], which is to carry them to far away South Africa. (*Edison Films*, March 1900, 3.)
SUBJECT: South African War, 1899-1902. Armies–Canada. Parades. Transports.
ARCHIVE: DLC-pp.
CITATIONS: "Le départ du contingent," *L'Événement*, 30 October 1899, 4.
NOTE: *2nd Special Service Battalion, Canadian Infantry, Parade* provided the first section of *Canadian Troops Departing from Quebec for the Transvaal*, also titled *Second Special Service Battalion, Canadian Infantry, Embarking for South Africa.*

764 ***2nd Special Service Battalion, Canadian Infantry, Embarking for So. Africa / Second Special Service Battalion, Canadian Infantry, Embarking for South Africa (part) / Canadian Troops Departing from Quebec for the Transvaal (part)**
LENGTH: 100, 200, 300 and 525 ft.   © Thomas A. Edison, 7 November 1899.
PRODUCER: [James White.]
CAMERA:
CAST:
PRODUCTION DATE: 30 October 1899.
LOCATION: Quebec, Canada.
SOURCE:
DESCRIPTION: This picture shows the Canadian troops departing from Quebec for the war in Transvaal. The scene opens with the soldiers clad in campaign uniform, marching under the triumphal arch, cheered by thousands of spectators who are waving English flags. The troops next appear marching upon the wharf and finally

embarking upon the transport Sardinia[n], which is to carry them to far away South Africa. (*Edison Films*, March 1900, 3.)

SUBJECT: South African War, 1899-1902. Armies—Canada. Parades. Transports. Piers.

ARCHIVE: DLC-pp.

CITATIONS: "Le départ du contingent," *L'Évé-nement*, 30 October 1899, 4.

NOTE: *2nd Special Service Battalion, Canadian Infantry, Embarking for So. Africa.* provided the second section of Canadian *Troops Departing from Quebec for the Transvaal*, also titled *Second Special Service Battalion, Canadian Infantry, Embarking for South Africa.*

OFF FOR THE WAR
Cannons Thunder When Contingent Leaves Quebec.
EARL MINTO SPEAKS
Governor-General Bids Boys Godspeed in Africa.
THOUSANDS ON ESPLANADE
Farewell to the Soldiers Are Enthusiastic as the Good Ship Sardinian Leaves Her Mooring.

Quebec, October 30–(Special).–His Excellency the Governor-General received the following telegram this afternoon from the Secretary of State for the colonies:–

"London, October 30.–Referring to your telegram of October 29, Her Majesty's Government offer hearty congratulations to the Canadian Government and military authorities for the rapid organization and embarkation of the contingent. Enthusiasm displayed by the people of the Dominion is a source of much gratification here. CHAMBERLAIN."

Quebec, October 30.–(Special)–Every possible point of vantage around the Esplanade was seized this morning by tens of thousands to see the grand review of the special service contingent of the Royal Canadian Regiment, which marched down from the Citadel, accompanied by detachments from the local military organizations and from outside the city. The Montreal detachment was preceded by a detachment of the 5th Royal Scots, with their pipes and by the officers of other Montreal corps. As each detachment came down Citadel hill, they were loudly cheered by the immense throng present. The various detachments of the contingent marched like veterans, and their appearance was highly creditable alike to the corps from which they were drawn and to the country which was sending them forth.

A stand had been erected by the citizens' reception committee on the Esplanade and early in the day places were at a premium. Before the arrival of General Hutton, Mayor Parent and the whole City Council took their place on the stand. Mayor Prefontaine, of Montreal, was also present, as were Hon. Sir Mackenzie Powell, Hon. C. Fitzpatrick, Ald. Graham, representing the mayor of Toronto; the Lord Bishop of Quebec, Hon. F.G. Dechene, and Hon. Jules Tessier. Lieutenant-Governor Jette arrived later and took his place on the platform.

The local visiting militia formed a cordon to keep the field free. The bands were massed in rear of the troops and greeted the arrival of General Hutton with appropriate music. Col. Otter put his regiment through the manual, after which General Hutton, with a staff, inspected the regiment, company by company. During the inspection the R.C.A. band, the Royal Scots pipe band and local corps' bands rendered appropriate music.

EARL OF MINTO SPEAKS.

The Governor-General was greeted on his arrival by the strains of the National Anthem. His Excellency was accompanied by Hon. Sir Wilfrid Laurier, Hon. A.G. Blair, Hon. W.S. Fielding, and Hon. James Sutherland, a military staff consisting of Lieut.-Col. Irwin, Lieut.-Col. Evanturei, Lieut.-Col. Sherwood, hon. A.D.C.'s, and Captain Graham, A.D.C., being in waiting. His Excellency also inspected the regiment, which had been formed to imitate three sides of a square.

His Excellency then addressed the men, congratulating them on their zest and soldierly appearance. They came from all sections of the country, from the Rockies to the Maritime Provinces, and he was sure they all felt pride in being chosen to represent this country in the Imperial army. He closed with words of wise advice, and wished the officers and men God-speed.

Sir Wilfrid Laurier also addressed the men, saying in conclusion in French:–"I will only say two or three words to my French-speaking compatriots. You will be called upon to fight troops which are among the most celebrated in the world. I will only ask you to so conduct yourselves as to prove yourself worthy of your origin."...

MARCH TO THE SHIP.

Major-General Hutton also said a few words, and after rousing cheers for the Queen, the regiment started on its march for the place of embarkation, at the Allan's wharf, taking in the principal streets of the city en route. Crowds were stationed at every point of vantage and the streets were crowded with citizens and visitors who cheered and applauded their citizen soldiers most heartily.

Arrived at the Allan's wharf, the regiment was drawn up in companies while arrangements were completed for embarking them on the Sardinian. The neighboring streets, wharves and the cliffs above were crowded, while Dufferin Terrace and the Glacis were black with enormous crowds. The police and military guards at the wharf had a great difficulty in keeping a space clear for the troops, the crowd pressing so vigorously that the police were frequently carried bodily within the lines. There were demonstrations as well known military and political men appeared, but the heartiest plaudits were given to the four lady nurses as they made their way to the steamer. When the embarkation of the men commenced it did not take long to put the whole regiment aboard, everything being well managed by the officers in charge. The men were in the best of spirits and appreciated the hearty good wishes of the people who shook them by the hand and wished them good luck wherever they could reach them. There were about twenty-five badly disappointed men who were left behind, there being that number enrolled over the actual number authorized and for whom accommodation had been furnished.

CASTS OFF HER MOORINGS.

Shortly after 4 o'clock, the Sardinian cast off her moorings, the men covered her deck and swarmed in the rigging, singing patriotic songs, "Rule Britannia," and "Soldiers of the Queen." As the ship moved slowly away from the wharf the big guns of the Citadel boomed out a salute, the crowds cheered wildly and were answered by the gallant Royal Canadians, handkerchiefs and flags were waved, and amid the plaudits of thirty thousand spectators, the contingent began its voyage to South Africa. As the Sardinian steamed slowly down the river, it was cheered by the crowds lining every projecting wharf, the steamers along the river side, and a fleet which accompanied the Sardinian blowing their whistles and firing rockets, etc. It was not until the good ship had steamed out of sight that the crowds began slowly to disperse and the farewell was over.

The splendid behavior of the men while in Quebec is greatly admired, it would be difficult to bring together a finer body of men, physically and morally, they are a credit to the Dominion. The character of the men was shown at the service in the cathedral on Sunday when one-third of the regiment partook of the communion, up to that time the authorities had refused to listen to any application for the appointment of a Church of England clergyman, but the silent appeal of this service was too strong for the military authorities, and at the last moment Rev. Mr. Alwood, a well-known Church of England clergyman was allowed to go with the regiment as one of their chaplains.

There were probably 10,000 strangers in the city today to assist in the good-bye, and on every side was heard self-congratulatory remarks on their good fortune in having assisted at an occasion which will be historical.

The Sardinian was reported outwards at Grosse Isle and L'Islet and as the night is fine it will probably pass Father Point at a very early hour to-morrow. (*Montreal Gazette*, 31 October 1899, 7.)

The American Mutoscope & Biograph Company made elaborate arrangements to film the Jeffries-Sharkey Fight, working closely with the boxers and promoters. Nevertheless, two Edison-affiliated camera crews sneaked into the stadium and filmed sections of the bout surreptitiously. This surreptitious filming became the basis for many colorful stories about "the pioneering" days of cinema.

765   The Battle of Jeffries and Sharkey for Championship of the World
LENGTH: © James H. White, 4 November 1899.
PRODUCER: James White, Joe Howard, Ida Emerson.
CAMERA: Albert E. Smith, James B. French, Joe Howard.
CAST: James J. Jeffries, Thomas Joseph "Sailor Tom" Sharkey.
PRODUCTION DATE: 3 November 1899.
LOCATION: Coney Island, N.Y.
SOURCE:
DESCRIPTION:
SUBJECT: Boxing. Sports.
ARCHIVE:
CITATIONS:
NOTE: One of two titles related to the fight between James J. Jeffries and Thomas Sharkey that the head of Edison's Kinetograph Department submitted for copyright purposes, perhaps as a way to distance Edison from this dubious venture.

766   *The Jeffries-Sharkey Contest
LENGTH: © James H. White, 4 November 1899.

PRODUCER: James White, Joe Howard, Ida Emerson.

CAMERA: Albert E. Smith, James B. French, Joe Howard.

CAST: James J. Jeffries, Thomas Joseph "Sailor Tom" Sharkey.

PRODUCTION DATE: 3 November 1899.

LOCATION: Coney Island, N.Y.

SOURCE:

DESCRIPTION:

SUBJECT: Boxing. Sports.

ARCHIVE: DLC-AFI.

CITATIONS:

NOTE: One of two titles related to the fight between James J. Jeffries and Thomas Sharkey that the head of Edison's Kinetograph Department submitted for copyright purposes, perhaps as a way to distance Edison from this dubious venture.

JEFFRIES DEFEATS SHARKEY AND IS STILL CHAMPION
Could Not Knock the Sailor Out, but Was Declared the Winner
on Points After the Most Remarkable Fistic Battle in Recent Years.
STRUGGLE CONTINUED FOR TWENTY-FIVE ROUNDS.
Ring Generalship Was Well Displayed During the Early Part of the Encounter,
but Then Came a Gradual Collapse of Both Men, and Brutality Supplanted Cleverness.
LOSER VERY BITTER IN DEFEAT, DENOUNCES THE REFEREE.
Winner, James Jeffries. Decision given on points. Number of rounds fought, twenty-five.

James Jeffries and Thomas Sharkey, giant gladiators of the modern arena, met in the greatest championship contest of their time before a multitude of ring followers at Coney island last night. A struggle that brought to the surface all the determination, pluck, endurance and knowledge of the tactics possessed by either man resulted in a decision for Jeffries after the full limit of twenty-five rounds had been fought.

That struggle did more than prove the superiority of the one. After the winner had taken a decisive lead, it developed the remarkable brute courage, the willingness to take punishment by the loser. Toward the last he had only the forlorn hope of landing a chance blow, but gamely he stood up to the punishment, intent upon staying until nerves could no longer force flesh and muscle to withstand the terrible onslaught....

To some it may have seemed that a draw would have been more in keeping with the work done by the two men, but the decision given by Mr. Siler was undoubtedly the one that should have been given....(*New York Herald*, 4 November 1899, 3.)

JEFFRIES CRIES "FOUL."
Champion Says That the Sailor Butted Him and He Declared "No More Picture Machines for Me."

"Sharkey was lucky. My left hand went back on me in the seventh round, or I would have knocked him out. No more picture machines for me. The intense heat from the electric lights bothered me considerably and made me very weak at times...." (*New York Herald*, 4 November 1899, 4.)

CLANDESTINELY TOOK PICTURES OF THE FIGHT.
"Enterprise" of Seven Men Which Affects the Biograph Company.

(SPECIAL BY LEASED WIRE, THE LONGEST IN THE WORLD.)

NEW YORK, November 5.—The Biograph Company which made such elaborate preparations for taking moving pictures of the Sharkey-Jeffries fight, may find that all its expensive work will amount to naught.

Another moving-picture concern, by clandestine plans scarcely paralleled, says that it also took moving pictures of the fight. These latter pictures, according to a report in circulation to-night, have been copyrighted, and to-morrow, the same authority says, a lawyer will ask for an injunction prohibiting the Biograph Company from exhibiting its pictures.

Maurice Kraus, manager of the Dewey Theatre, said that he had been approached by Joe Howard, of the Howard & Emerson vaudeville troupe, as agent for the non-Biograph pictures, with a proposal to show them at that theatre. Kraus saw the fight and has looked at several feet of film of these pictures. "They are genuine pictures," he said to-night. "They show Jeffries, Sharkey and Siler all in the ring, just as plain as can be. They are no sham pictures; that much is certain."

The Edison moving picture machines are said to have been used for making the films. The Examiner's informant says that Howard and six confreres did the work. The machines were strapped around their waists. Over the machines they wore mackintoshes with big capes. As it was a rainy night, the wearing of mackintoshes excited no suspicion.

It is said there were 150 men in various parts of the house guarding against cameras being brought in. These safe-guards, however, did not prevent the men in question from entering the building with their instruments and taking places on both sides of the arena, in what was known as the mezzanine seats. Four of the men sat on one side of the house and three on the other, and in this way they secured the pictures. (*San Francisco Examiner*, 6 November 1899, 7.)

DON'T BE FOOLED BY FAKE PICTURES OF THE
SHARKEY-JEFFRIES BATTLE
WHEN YOU CAN GET THE REAL THING AT A REASONABLE FIGURE.
Our Special Photographers

were at the Coney Island Club on the night of November 3, and photographed the great fight between Sharkey and Jeffries, under the special direction of MESSERS. HOWARD AND EMERSON. Our pictures are copyrighted and fully protected at the Library of Congress at Washington, D.C.

WE WILL PROTECT OUR RIGHTS AGAINST ALL FAKE EXHIBITION OF THESE FILMS.

The copyrighted laws of the United States make it a felony to exhibit illegitimate copies of a copyrighted article. We will vigorously prosecute infringements of these films. Don't discourage the public by shoddy exhibitions when you can give them something good for the same money.

FOR TERMS FOR EXHIBITION OF THE SHARKEY-JEFFRIES FILMS APPLY TO

EDISON MANUFACTURING COMPANY, ORANGE, N.J. AND 135 FIFTH AVENUE, NEW YORK.

(Advertisement, *New York Clipper*, 11 November 1899, 776.)

JEFFRIES and SHARKEY
10 Mins.; One and Full Stage (Spe)
Boxing
Loew's State (V-P)

James J. Jeffries, former world's heavyweight champion, conqueror of Bob Fitzsimmons, James J. Corbett and other leading heavies of his day, is touring the Loew Circuit in a three-minute boxing exhibition, coupled with Tom Sharkey, old foeman of Jeff's and a heavy-weight who fought Jeff a 25-round bout and a 20-round bout in the long ago.

Both are bald but Jeffries seems in remarkable physical condition, due, no doubt, to his outdoor life at Burbank, Cal. Sharkey has been connected with the race track at Tia Juana, working for "Sunny" Jim Coffroth.

Their vaudeville turn consists of three one-minute rounds in which the old boys endeavor to give the present generation an idea of what they looked like in their pugilistic primes. Jeff still shows a clever left hand. Sailor Tom's chest is just as prowlike as ever but his wind has given its tribute to the old boy with the scythe.

Introduced by Tom O'Brien, coast fight promoter and picture man, the pair were given an unusual ovation. It's 16 years since Jeffries made an unsuccessful attempt to come back to the ring and started the White Hope era by losing to Jack Johnson. His record proves him a real champion.

Imagine a present day title-holder defending it nine times in a year against challengers like Sharkey, Fitz, Ruhlin, Corbett, etc.–and for donuts. *Con.* (*Variety*, 14 July 1926, 20.)

William Paley placed his Kalatechnoscope exhibition service into Proctor's vaudeville houses as a permanent attraction, commencing 9 October 1899. Each week he tried to film one or more newsworthy subjects, presenting them to patrons as kalatechnoscope exclusives. Paley retained his status as an Edison licensee, and many of his films eventually ended up in Edison catalogs. Some were copyrighted in the inventor's name. One of the first showed an automobile parade sponsored by the newly formed Automobile Association of America, which was seeking to influence public opinion at a time when opposition to this novel form of transportation was strong and being translated into laws sharply restricting its use.

767 *Automobile Parade / Parade of Automobiles

LENGTH: 50 and 100 ft.   © Thomas A. Edison, 6 February 1900.

PRODUCER: William Paley.

CAMERA: William Paley.

CAST:

PRODUCTION DATE: 4 November 1899.

LOCATION: Madison Square, New York, N.Y.

SOURCE:

DESCRIPTION: The famous Madison Square Garden forms the background of this excellent picture. A number of very fine automobiles pass in this strip, coming close to the camera and show clear and life size. A very strange coincidence in the closing of the picture is two old ladies who drive by in a dilapidated looking buggy drawn by a long eared mule. This is a remarkable picture showing up-to-date means of transportation in New York City, and the incident of the mule and the two old ladies adds a sufficient amount of humor. (*The Phonoscope,* December 1899, 10.)

SUBJECT: Parades. Automobiles. Mules. Social elites. Automobile Club of America.

ARCHIVE: DLC-pp.

CITATIONS: *New York Clipper,* 10 February 1900, 1064; *Edison Films,* March 1900, 38; *Edison Films,* July 1901, 78.

NOTE:

AUTOMOBILES NOW BARRED FROM PARK
President Clausen Has an Ordinance to That Effect Hurriedly Passed by the Commission.
WILL GIVE PUBLIC HEARING.
He Makes Explanation of His Course, in Which He Speaks of a "Questionable" Offer.
REFERS TO "TRICKY" ACTS.
Messrs. Lyon and Buzby Emphatically Resent the Insinuation Made Against Them and the Club.

Owing to the efforts being made by members of the Automobile Club of America, to obtain entrance for horseless carriages to Central Park, the Park Commissioners, at a meeting yesterday, resolved to give a public hearing in the matter, on Thursday, November 9. President Clausen, at the same time, hurried through an ordinance to the effect that no horseless carriages or motor wagons shall enter the Park except by permission of the department....

MR. CLAUSEN'S EXPLANATION

"My object in offering this resolution," said Mr. Clausen, "is for the purpose of having adopted a second resolution, which I will offer after having made a verbal statement. As this hearing is set for next Thursday, and as we have had an intrusion in Central Park by automobilists, or, as I consider it, a violation of the rules on the part of several individuals, I wish to prevent a repetition by having a second resolution passed."

Mr. Clausen referred to Winslow E. Buzby, who, accompanied by Whitney Lyon, entered Central Park last Friday on his automobile. Mr. Buzby was arrested, but was afterward discharged by Magistrate Olmsted, who refused to entertain the complaint against him.

"I wish to state," said Mr. Clausen, with some heat, "that these men who were arrested first wanted me to become a member of the Automobile Club, and for obvious reasons offered to waive the initiation fee. They asked for a permit to enter the Park, and I was obliged to refuse. I thought that it was extremely discourteous on their part to make an attempt to enter twenty-four hours later without one."...(*New York Herald,* 3 November 1899, 9.)

AUTOMOBILE CLUB HAS FIRST PARADE
Brave Display Made in the Initial Run Is Applauded by Crowds Along the Route.
GENERAL ANDREWS LEADS.
Forty Self-Propelled Vehicles, with Club Members and Their Guests in Line.
TO CLAREMONT AND RETURN.
Frightened No 1 Run Was Voted a Success.

Automobiles had the right of way in Fifth avenue yesterday. Led by Adjunct General Avery D. Andrews in an electric victoria, forty self-propelled carriages belonging to members of the Automobile Club of America, moved in parade from the Waldorf-Astoria to Claremont and return. It was a brave and varied show. Thousands of spectators assembled along the route and applauded the vehicles and their occupants. From start to finish the initial run of the newly organized Automobile Club of America was a success. Not an accident marred its pleasure, and not a horse took fright at the long line of self-propelled carriages.

There were amusing incidents when grades were encountered, which retarded the speed of some motors and enabled others to push ahead, and in brushes for supremacy between steam, gasoline and electric vehicles.

'TWAS AN OBJECT LESSON.

Although the automobilists who arranged the run sought primarily their own pleasure, they afforded the general public an object lesson in progress yesterday, which, they said, should not fail to have it effect upon Park Commissioners and any other persons who have opposed the introduction of horseless carriages in the streets and drives of this city.

Before the start there was a gathering at the Waldorf-Astoria that in itself was instructive. Automobile after automobile rolled up to the entrance, and after discharging its human freight was tooled around to Astor Court, where it immediately was surrounded by a crowd of enthusiasts, who studied its mechanism.

Owners of motors of different types compared notes of their own experiences and asked innumerable questions about vehicles of other makes. French carriages undoubtedly were more showy and had more of their machinery exposed, and the steam motors came next.

While a crowd surged around the horseless vehicles in Astor court and Thirty-third street, members of the club and their guests assembled for luncheon at one o'clock in the ballroom on the Waldorf side of the hotel....(*New York Herald*, 5 November 1899, 6.)

768 **An Exchange of Good Stories / Two Old Pals / Two Old Cronies**
LENGTH: 50 ft.   © No reg.
PRODUCER: William Paley.
CAMERA: William Paley.
CAST: [Chauncey Depew], [Marshall Wilder.]
PRODUCTION DATE: [11 November 1899?]
LOCATION: New York, N.Y.
SOURCE:
DESCRIPTION: The World's Greatest Raconteurs, Hon. Chauncey M. Depew and Marshall P. Wilder in "An Exchange of Good Stories." (Taken yesterday at Mr. Depew's Club.) (*New York Herald*, 12 November 1899, 15.)
  The interest manifested by these two gentlemen (who are evidently of similar taste, and the best of friends) in the illustrations they are examining, is made so very apparent by their facial expressions and gestures, that it requires no words to convey its meaning to the audience. The hearty laughter resulting from their evident buoyant remarks and illusions are alike indulged in by actors and audiences. (*Edison Films*, July 1901, 77.)
SUBJECT: Facial expressions. Storytelling.
ARCHIVE:
CITATIONS: *New York Clipper*, 21 April 1900, 184.
NOTE: It is possible that *An Exchange of Good Stories* and *Two Old Pals/Two Old Cronies* are not the same picture. It is also possible that the well-known personalities mentioned in the initial announcement were impersonated by actors for the film (which would help to explain the lack of subsequent references). This subject was remade by American Mutoscope and Biograph Company on 20 November 1899 as *Two Old Cronies*. The Biograph film was subsequently copyrighted on 24 February 1903.

769 ***Dick Croker Leaving Tammany Hall**
LENGTH: 50 ft.   © Thomas A. Edison, 9 February 1900.
PRODUCER: William Paley.
CAMERA: William Paley.
CAST: Richard Croker.
PRODUCTION DATE: [18 November 1899?]
LOCATION: New York, N.Y.
SOURCE:

DESCRIPTION: A splendid life-motion picture taken at the Democratic Club yesterday. (*New York Herald*, 19 November 1899, 13A.)
  A very lifelike picture of the famous New York politician and Tammany Hall boss. This picture was taken on Sunday morning [sic] as he was leaving the 14th Street Wigwam, accompanied by a number of prominent New York politicians. (*The Phonoscope*, December 1899, 10.)
SUBJECT: Politics, practical. Democratic Party.
ARCHIVE: DLC-pp.

CITATIONS: *New York Clipper*, 10 February 1900, 1064; *Edison Films,* March 1900, 41; *Edison Films*, July 1901, 88.

NOTE: It is possible that the Proctor announcement quoted from the *New York Herald* was a rhetorical flourish signifying "up-to-dateness" and that indeed the film had been taken on the previous Sunday (November 12th).

An Edison camera crew filmed a football game between the local Orange and Newark athletic clubs, in part to prepare for the shooting of a much bigger sporting event—the Army-Navy football game in Philadelphia, which occurred the following week.

770 Football Game Between Orange Athletic and Newark Athletic Clubs / Football Game

LENGTH: 50, 100, 200, 550 ft.   © No reg.

PRODUCER: James White.

CAMERA:

CAST:

PRODUCTION DATE: 30 November 1899.

LOCATION: Orange, N.J.

SOURCE:

DESCRIPTION: Between the Orange Athletic Club and the Newark Athletic Club, at the Orange Oval, on Thanksgiving Day, 1899. This is the greatest foot-ball picture ever attempted and shows many exciting plays, kick-offs, touch-downs, rushes, etc. (*Edison Films*, March 1900, 30.)

SUBJECT: Football. Sports.

ARCHIVE:

CITATIONS: *New York Clipper*, 9 December 1899, 865; 10 February 1900, 1064.

NOTE:

O.A.C. 6; Newark A.C. 0

The Orange Athletic Club established its superiority over the Newark Athletic Club on the oval Thursday morning, when these two clubs met for the first time in the contest for the amateur championship of the East, the prize being a silver cup offered by Albert Rothschild. Each had a fine record behind it, the Newarks having been defeated but twice, while the Orange team had only one score against it. There was a fine turnout at the Oval, fully five thousand spectators being present and of these one third were Orange residents and the remainder from Newark. The Orange players appeared to be much larger and heavier than the Newark men but this was only apparent. The official weight of the eleven men on the Newark team and the twelve that played on Orange side show that the average weight of the entire team was precisely the same. Newark had its team work down to a finer point than Orange, but the latter excelled in the agility of its backs and effective bucking the center. The general effect was the that the Newark team was clearly outplayed, the ball being in their territory most of the time and the Orange goal never being seriously threatened. The game was clean and notably free from slugging and unnecessary roughness. There were only two penalizations, one on each side for off side play.

Newark won the toss and took the north goal, giving Orange the kick off. Mohor kicked off sending the leather well into Newark territory. Miller tried for a gain but was downed with a net loss of three yards. Backus punted out to the Orange 40 yard line and then began a fine pushing of the pigskin by successive bucking of the center and mass plays through the tackles or around the ends by Torrey, Tucker, Gibson, Reinhart, Joralemon, and Estey, one of which was a pretty end run of 15 yards by Gibson, and these carried the ball steadily despite all efforts of Newark to her 15 yard line. Here Newark braced up and held Orange steady, getting the ball at last on a fumble. Then the Newarks began offensive play. Dodd and Wiedenmayer made good gains through the tackles. Newark was given 5 yards for Orange holding, and Miller made a pretty end run of 20 yards to the 45 yard line. Fierce plays by Dodd, Connery and Carr pushed the pigskin to the Orange 30 yard line, where Orange braced up and took the ball on downs. Reinhart then punted to the Newark 25 yard line, Torrey breaking through and capturing the ball for Orange. Joralemon made a good gain but in the next play Orange lost the ball on a fumble on the Newark 20 yard line. Dodd punted out to center field, Lee catching the leather and gaining 15 yards to the Newark 40 yard line. Then Orange settled down once more to steady bucking of the center and tackles. Laneon, Kyle, Reimer, Tucker, Gibson and Reinhart pushed the leather to within two yards of the Newark goal. Reimer plunged through, having the pigskin within six inches of the line, and on the next play Tucker was sent through for a touchdown. Time 23 1/2 minutes. Lee kicked the goal. Score: Orange 6, Newark 0. Before any further gains were made time was called.

In the second half no scores were made. Twice during the half Orange forced the ball dangerously near the

Newark goal, once to within 15 yards and once to within 5 yards, the first time losing the ball on downs and the second on a fumble and each time the ball being punted out and the score saved. Another feature was the attempt of Reinhart to kick a place goal from the field which barely failed of success. The half was open and punts were frequent on each side. In the last play of the game just as time was called Gibson hurt his head and had to be carried from the field in a dazed condition. He recovered soon after. When time was called the leather was on the Orange 35 yard line....(*Orange Chronicle,* 2 December 1899, 8.)

771 The Great Football Game Between Annapolis and West Point / Great Football Game
LENGTH: 100 and 200 ft.   © No reg.
PRODUCER: James White.
CAMERA:
CAST:
PRODUCTION DATE: 2 December 1899.
LOCATION: Philadelphia, Pa.
SOURCE:
DESCRIPTION: Between West Point and Annapolis at Philadelphia, on Saturday, December 2, 1899. This picture includes incidental scenes, a panoramic view of the grand stand and all the important plays in the game. (*Edison Films,* March 1900, 30.)
SUBJECT: Football. Sports. Navies–United States. Armies–United States. Naval cadets. Military cadets. U.S. Military Academy (West Point, N.Y.).
ARCHIVE:
CITATIONS: *New York Clipper,* 9 December 1899, 865; 10 February 1900, 1064.
NOTE:

Twenty-five Thousand Persons Cheered and Wept Over Victory or Defeat.
ARMY OFFICERS DANCED JIGS.
Secretary Long and Secretary Root Grew Enthusiastic as the Great Game Progressed.
GEN. MILES HUGGED MRS. MILES.
Young Cassad, Who Made the First Touchdown, Was for the Time the Greatest of Heroes.
(Special to The World.)

PHILADELPHIA, Pa., Dec. 2.–It's the army, 17 to 5. West Point has scored an upset on Annapolis. Here on Franklin Field to-day before a cheering host of 25,000 patriots the youngsters who are soon to be lieutenants triumphed nobly over the other youngsters who are soon to be ensigns. The middies were the cards to win; the cadets wiped them off the gridiron with consummate ease.

It was a great game. It was likewise the first football game between army and navy for six years. Before that the boys had not met on the gridiron but four times, and the Severn-bred lads had wrested the palm three times out of four from the youngsters up Hudson River way. Only pleading and praying with the powers that be at Washington got the game this year.

And so, again let it be said that it was a great game. Both academies got a day's furlough. The embryo army officers left West Point early this morning in full regimentals, dress coats, caps and gray overcoats, on a special train. The embryo naval heroes left Annapolis about the same time on another special train clad in their trim blue blouses and blue fatigue caps. They wore no overcoats–it was a cold day in more ways than one for them.

And what a difference between other football games and this. Money wouldn't buy a seat to-day. It was "the army and navy together; three cheers for the Red, White and Blue!"

If you weren't asked you couldn't get in.

The University of Pennsylvania was the host; all the army and navy its guests. More than 25,000 invitations were issued. Every one was accepted. Not a cent was taken in at the gates–this game was for blood and glory, and not to wax fat the treasuries of any college athletic associations.

Each academy had 6,000 seats; the rest went to the Pennsylvania boys, and every seat was filled. Never did a more notable company assemble on the gridiron's sides. Washington must have been deserted to-day; certainly every army post and every ship within a thousand miles were.

Secretary Long and Gen. Miles There.

They came by special train and in carriages. There were heroes of three wars and fledglings still unaccustomed to their bright new shoulder straps. There were the Secretary of the Navy, Mr. Long, and the Commander-in Chief of the Army, Gen. Miles. It was a fight for blood, as you may guess by this.

The strangers found that Philadelphia was ready for them. All trolleys led to Franklin Field. All the hotels were jammed with army and navy officers eager to bet. It was 10 to 9 on the middies but few takers. Hadn't Annapolis held the great Princeton team down to one touchdown while West Point was run off the earth, 24 to 0.

So the navy folk were jubilant. They and the north stand. They had gold and blue–their colors–galore. They had the marine band. They also had their secretary present that was no better than the army, for Mr. Root was on hand, too. There on the army side were Assistant Secretary Melkle John; Adjt. Gen. Corbin, Assistant Adjts. Gen. Simpson and Carter, Gen. Merritt, Gen. Miles, Col. Hein and Gen. Charles F. Roe, head of New York's National Guard....

How the Men Lined Up.

But the game–out tumbled the army boys in gray blankets; the navy had blue sweaters. A preliminary pass or two and the first game in four years, between Uncle Sam's fighters to be was on. This was the line up:

West Point	Positions	Annapolis
Smith (Capt.)	Left End	Long
Farnsworth	Left Tackle	Wortham (Capt.)
Hopkins	Left Guard	Halligan
Boyers	Right Guard	Belknap
Bunker	Right Tackle	Nichols
Burnett	Right End	Berrien
Cassad	Left Half-Back	Fowler
Wesson	Quarter-Back	Osterhaus
Clark	Right Half-Back	Gannon
Jackson	Full-Back	Wade
Bettison	Centre	Adams

Umpire–Robert D. Wrenn. Referee–Edgar Wrightington. Timekeeper–"Bert" Waters, all of Harvard.

Tier upon tier. The rooters cheered. The two bands brayed again. The air was full of yellow and blue, and of black and gray and yellow. A coin flipped. West Point won. Silence, the cry "Play!" and the mighty struggle was on. And off went Clark after the kick-off with a wondrous 30 yards for the army. Generals danced madly, captains rolled on the ground. Who cared for dignity or discipline now? Hadn't the army started off to win? In vain the navy sang:

> Hello, Hello, Hello,
> Hello, the quarter-back,
> Hello, the half-back,
> Hello, the full-back, too.
> Our tackles and ends are fine
> So in all our time
> Fowler will make a gain,
> Gannon will do the same;
> Across the line we'll roll,
> Navy wake up!
> Wortham will kick the goal.

Back came the army with more songs to the "Hello, My Baby" tune too. And then more cheers: "Ray, ray, ray! Bah, rah, rah, rah, rah, rah, rah, rah, rah! West Point!" The navy yelled in turn, "Highty, tighty! Highty, tighty, um-ti-ighty, navee!"

Urged on in this way, the Annapolis backs pushed holes through West Point for fifteen yards, but then the navy lost the ball. And now–West Point!

Every time they tried the army gained. Clark was showing himself a wonder. The vaunted navy rush line was as a broken reed before his onslaught, and never once in fifteen minutes did West Point have to kick. Each time the army boys kept on making the necessary five yards before they lost the ball on downs.

Army Makes a Touch-Down.

Clark jumped clean over the navy line for five yards, and Gen. Miles hugged Mrs. Miles. The ball was on the navy's ten-yard line.

"Right, low, parry, heave!" yelled the West Pointers, thinking of their drill, and the ball went three yards nearer. A whirling wedge, a mass play–"Four yards for a touch-down!" was the cry, and the army shrieked its glee. The navy tried to cheer back, but it was a feeble try.

Smash, mash, bang! A West Pointer lay over the goal line half dead, but he was still holding that elusive pigskin–a touch-down for the army!

And now picture the sight! Pales Gettysburg, Bunker Hill, Santiago, Manila, at the sight. The army had scored on the navy, and little Cassad, who did it, was a bigger hero than if he had led an army corps into successful battle. A goal was easy for the limber-toed Bettison. It was West Point, 6, Annapolis, 0! Revenge at last, after years of defeat with only a single victory!

"This is the army's year!" sang the West Pointers to the tune of "She is My Rag-Time Gal!"

"A navy yell!" shrieked the youngster who led the Annapolis cheering, but he got a feeble reply.

Annapolis kicked off, and back and forth went the ball on punts and rushes till Osterhaus got it for the navy. He smashed 15 yards into the army's centre before they downed him.

"85–10!"–a mystic signal–and Wade plunged twenty-five yards through the army's thin line. Yard by yard the navy did what the army had done before. It looked like a score for Annapolis, but a fumble in the line spoiled it all. "There'll be a hot time in the army ....

Secretary Long Enthusiastic.

"Touchdown! Root, boys!" yelled Secretary Long, flinging his high hat in the air, forgetting dignity; but it never came. West Point's gallant line held the navy with only a yard to spare. The army band went crazy, and the big brass drummer hopped around on one leg, beating time madly to the West Point cheers. And so the navy lost the ball on downs. Then the army kicked out of danger. Sang West Point then:

"They will go under,
"Navy to thunder,
"This is the army's game."

Gannon got the ball and tried to run. He went down in his tracks with three future lieutenants on top of him. Fowler, tried it–no use. Wade had a hack at the line; he failed to gain. The navy punted in desperation; the army punted back cheerfully to the navy's 25-yard line.

"Time!" cried the referee and the first half was over.

"Well, it might have been worse!" remarked Admiral Sampson to Admiral McNair.

But West Point was ahead by six points, and the red-striped band blared gloriously, while a white mule in the army colors and trousers was trotted down the line. The navy band tooted, too, but it had not the inspiration of six points to nothing. The army went around hugging itself, for victory was already in the air. Discipline went to the winds.

The sun was in the middies' eyes in the second half, when they defended the western end of the field, but they went in with another plan of attack. The articles of war had been discussed thoroughly in dressing-rooms, and both teams had their plan of attack and defense mapped out to decide the struggle. Gen. Miles and Secretary Long diverted attention from the game for several minutes as they walked across the field after play had been started.

Navy Plan Changed in Vain.

Wade found his ranges early in the half, and on the kick-off landed the projectile within a few feet of the sea dogs' goal. Gannon was cruising about that portion of the field and took the missile aboard. He sounded the gongs for the engines to get up speed. The response was quick, but a well-directed shot in the shape of Bunker stopped the run and sank the middies on the twenty-yard line.

Berrien and Long were sent out on scouting duty, when Wade fell back for a punt. Burnett and Smith were on the same tack for the soldiers, and stopped them for an interesting argument in the centre of the field.

Berrien sat on Smith's head for a few seconds, and Long insisted that Burnett show cause why he should not be put off the play. The West Pointers' end started to do this, and the ball went far over their heads. Clark was ready to receive it, and Halligan was anxious to embrace them both. On straight-line plays, varied with but one attempt to skirt the end, West Point plunged eighty yards up the field for a second touchdown. Rockwell going over the line and Bettison kicking an easy goal. It was now 12 to 0 for the army. The band tooted hoarsely.

Belknap is Injured.

Belknap was hurt in this scrimmage, and Gen. Fremont's grandson, Fremont, took his place. The kick off not returned, Freyer replaced Fowler, and the navy took a brace. Stimulated by heartfelt yells, they plunged at the soldiers and disputed their every attempt to gain. Another kick off and the same story. Inch by inch the army gained and scored again. It was 17 to 0 for West Point, because Bettison missed the goal.

At last the navy got a chance.

"Tear 'em up!" screamed the undaunted Annapolis rooters.

They did. They came back with revolving wedges, mass plays, V's end plays, runs–a touchdown by Wade! How the Marine Band blared now! But it was of no use. The navy failed to kick the goal, and when time was called a minute later the ball was in the middle of the field and the army had won a glorious victory–the first in years–to the tune of 17 to 5.

Special trains took the dignitaries back to Washington and the cadets back to their two academies. It was a great game, though, and a great victory. (*New York World*, 3 December, 1899, 8.)

A number of motion picture subjects entered Edison's catalog in early December 1899. Never copyrighted, these were made by licensees William Paley and American Vitagraph's Blackton and Smith.

772 **Panoramic View of the Dewey Arch / Panoramic View of the Dewey Arch, New York City**

LENGTH: 50 and 75 ft.   © No reg.

PRODUCER: [William Paley?]

CAMERA: [William Paley?]

CAST:

PRODUCTION DATE: September-November 1899.

LOCATION: New York, N.Y.

SOURCE:

DESCRIPTION: The scene starts at 19th street and Fifth avenue. The picture was taken from an automobile and shows the arch full to life size. During the approach of the camera the spectators imagine themselves passing under the arch and proceeding up Fifth avenue. The automobile then turns suddenly into 26th street, toward Broadway. The graceful arch and wonderful historical columns form a very attractive background. This picture also gives the spectator a glimpse of two of New York's greatest thoroughfares, as the arch is located at the junction of Broadway and Fifth avenue, better known as Madison Square. (*Edison Films*, March 1900, 43.)

SUBJECT: Monuments. Spanish-American War. City and town life–New York. Automobiles. Urban transportation. George Dewey.

ARCHIVE:

CITATIONS: "Shall Dewey Arch Remain Permanent? Proposed Site at 110th Street, 7th Avenue," *New York Herald*, 28 September 1899, 5. *New York Clipper*, 9 December 1899, 865; 10 February 1900, 1064; *Edison Films*, July 1901, 90.

NOTE: This film may have been shot by J. Stuart Blackton and Albert E. Smith.

773   **Panoramic View of the Ghetto / Panoramic View of the Ghetto, New York City**

LENGTH: 100 or 150 ft.   © No reg.

PRODUCER: [William Paley?]

CAMERA: [William Paley?]

CAST:

PRODUCTION DATE: September-November 1899.

LOCATION: New York, N.Y.

SOURCE:

DESCRIPTION: This picture shows the Hebrew quarter of New York which is so graphically described in the Zangwill play. (*Edison Films*, March 1900, 43.)

SUBJECT: City and town life–New York. Jews. Israel Zangwill.

ARCHIVE:

CITATIONS: "Within New York's Little Russia," *New York Herald*, 28 October 1894, 7F. *New York Clipper*, 9 December 1899, 865; 10 February 1900, 1064; *Edison Films*, July 1901, 90.

NOTE: This film may have been shot by J. Stuart Blackton and Albert E. Smith. First offered as a 150-foot subject, then sold at 100 feet.

774   ***A Visit to the Spiritualist**

LENGTH: 100 ft.   © No reg.

PRODUCER: J. Stuart Blackton, Albert E. Smith.

CAMERA: J. Stuart Blackton and/or Albert E. Smith.

CAST:

PRODUCTION DATE: September to early December 1899.

LOCATION: Vitagraph's roof-top studio, New York, N.Y.

SOURCE:

DESCRIPTION: This is acknowledged by exhibitors to be the funniest of all moving magical films. A countryman is seen entering the office of the spiritualist and paying his fee. He is then mesmerized and sees funny things. He drops his handkerchief on the floor and as he reaches for it, it gradually grows larger and larger, dancing up and down, and going through funny antics until before the eye of the spectator it turns into a ghost of enormous proportions. It then vanishes and as the countryman is in the act of sitting in the chair, the ghost suddenly appears and the countryman receives a great fright. He then jumps up and throws off his hat and coat, and they immediately fly back on his body. He repeatedly throws them off and they as often return. This scene finally closes by numerous ghosts and hobgoblins appearing and disappearing before the eyes of the frightened countryman, who finally leaves the room in great haste. (*Edison Films*, March 1900, 40-41.)

SUBJECT: Hallucinations and illusions. Ghosts.
ARCHIVE: CL-UC.
CITATIONS: *New York Clipper*, 9 December 1899, 865; 10 February 1900, 1064; *Edison Films,* July 1900, 85.
NOTE:

775 Flags of All Nations

LENGTH: 75 ft.   © No reg.
PRODUCER: J. Stuart Blackton, Albert E. Smith.
CAMERA: J. Stuart Blackton and/or Albert E. Smith.
CAST:
PRODUCTION DATE: September to early December 1899.
LOCATION: Vitagraph's roof-top studio, New York, N.Y.
SOURCE:
DESCRIPTION: Illustrating Flags of every Nation. (*New York Clipper*, 9 December 1899, 865.)
SUBJECT: Flags.
ARCHIVE:
CITATIONS:
NOTE:

776 *Why Jones Discharged His Clerks

LENGTH: 100 ft.   © Thomas A. Edison, 9 January 1900.
PRODUCER: James White.
CAMERA:
CAST:
PRODUCTION DATE: [December 1899 to early January 1900.]
LOCATION: [Black Maria], West Orange, N.J.
SOURCE:
DESCRIPTION: Great Hit. Two delinquent clerks are seated in a broker's office engaged in a game of cards. The boss suddenly appears walking through the corridor. The cards are thrown down in great haste and when the employer enters the office the clerks are apparently busily engaged in their work. The boss looks over the mail and then sits down behind an adjacent screen to enjoy the morning paper. A lady suddenly enters the office and upon inquiring for the broker, is shown behind the screen by

one of the clerks. He immediately calls the attention of the stenographer and they post themselves upon chairs and engage in looking over the top of the screen. One of the chairs is suddenly tipped over by the office boy and the clerks and screen fall upon the unsuspecting broker. He immediately becomes wrathful, throws off his coat and proceeds to clear out of the office. One of the clerks becomes frightened and jumps through the window into the corridor; the other is unceremoniously fired through the door. This is an extremely humorous picture. (*Edison Films*, March 1900, 32-33.)

SUBJECT: Clerks. Stenographers. Adultery. Brokerage firms. Businessmen. Voyeurism. Punishment.
ARCHIVE: DLC-pp.
CITATIONS: *New York Clipper*, 10 February 1900, 1064; *Edison Films*, July 1901, 62-63.
NOTE:

777 ***Why Mrs. Jones Got a Divorce**

LENGTH: 75 ft. © Thomas A. Edison, 9 January 1900.
PRODUCER: James White.
CAMERA:
CAST:
PRODUCTION DATE: [December 1899 to early January 1900.]
LOCATION: [Black Maria], West Orange, N.J.
SOURCE:
DESCRIPTION: This scene opens by showing a pretty cook mixing bread in the kitchen. Jones comes in unexpectedly from a trip and carries a dress suitcase. He inquires for his wife and is told by the cook that she is absent. Jones is hungry and asks for something to eat. The cook is very obliging

and Jones becomes unruly, chuckles the cook under the chin. The cook puts her arms around Jones' neck and leaves finger imprints of flour on his back. This is where the trouble commences. Jones' wife suddenly appears and accuses Jones of making love to the cook. Jones denies it. She scornfully points to the finger marks on Jones back. Jones still denies it. The wife becomes angry and seizes the pan of flour and turns it upside down on Jones' head, spoiling his best Sunday clothes. Jones escapes and the cook is discharged. This is a very funny picture. (*Edison Films*, March 1900, 33.)
SUBJECT: Kitchens. Food. Adultery. Married people. Servants. Punishment.
ARCHIVE: DLC-pp.
CITATIONS: *New York Clipper*, 10 February 1900, 1064; *Edison Films*, July 1901, 63.
NOTE:

The Black Maria stood between the Edison Laboratory and the Phonograph Works (illustration ca. 1900).

The business year of 1899-1900 showed a marked falling off in Edison's profits from film sales, despite the industry's new level of stability based on regular exhibition outlets in vaudeville. The licensing arrangements with Blackton, Smith, Paley and others were apparently not working to the inventor's benefit. His motion picture business was in a state of crisis. At one point during this final year of the nineteenth century, the American Mutoscope & Biograph Company acquired an option to buy Edison's entire motion picture business. When this arrangement fell through, the situation required bold, new business initiatives. By the fall of 1900, Edison executives had decided to close the Black Maria studio in West Orange and open a glass-enclosed roof-top facility in Manhattan, close to the theater district.

Early in 1900, Thomas Edison also took a more aggressive stance toward his motion picture licensees. On January 29th, shortly after the Vitagraph partners demanded an accounting of the royalties due them from the Edison Manufacturing Company, Edison terminated Blackton and Smith's license. In a desperate effort to rescue their business, the duo sold their company to relatives, who were not bound by previous court injunctions, and continued working as "employees." In a short-term tactical move, Edison restored Blackton and Smith's license in August or September 1900, and many Vitagraph films that were made in this interim period eventually appeared in Edison's catalogs. Vitagraph supplied Edison with many films during 1900, but with the opening of the inventor's new roof-top studio early in 1901, Blackton and Smith's output was deemed unnecessary and their license was again cancelled. With the exception of William Paley, other licensees suffered similar if less dramatic fates.

Although Eberhard Schneider was restricted to showing Edison films by a court injunction, commercial necessity forced him to screen films by other producers. Edison's lawyers served a writ on his exhibition service at a Manhattan theater on 23 January 1900, forcing him to forfeit several infringing films.

MOVING PICTURES SEIZED.

Two deputies of United States Marshal Henkel visited the Dewey Theatre last Tuesday [Jan 23] and seized several films on a writ of attachment issued by Judge Lacombe. It was alleged that the films were being used in defiance of an injunction obtained by Thomas A. Edison, in a suit in equity against Ebherhardt [sic] Schneider for infringement of a patent. A lot of new films was procurred, and the exhibition was given as usual. (*New York Dramatic Mirror*, 3 February 1900, 20.)

---

778 **The Tramp and the Crap Game**

LENGTH: 85 ft.   © No reg.

PRODUCER: [James White.]

CAMERA:

CAST:

PRODUCTION DATE: [January to early February 1900.]

LOCATION:

SOURCE:

DESCRIPTION: A number of darky boys and street arabs are engaged in a crap game just outside of the back entrance of a theatre. The darkies suddenly give up the game of craps for the purpose of indulging in a Southern break down. A grewsome looking Weary Willy who is seated near-by suddenly seizes the opportunity and rushes in to grab the stakes which have been left lying on the ground. The entire crowd of arabs pile on poor Weary Willy and proceed to teach him a lesson in etiquette. A policeman suddenly appears in the scene and attempts to arrest the tramp, who makes a very ludicrous escape. (*Edison Films*, July 1901, 62.)

SUBJECT: Tramps. Afro-Americans. Police. Gambling. Dancing.

ARCHIVE:

CITATIONS: *New York Clipper*, 10 February 1900, 1064; *Edison Films*, March 1900, 33.

NOTE: The film's production date is based on its assigned code word (Uncloaked). The picture could be a dupe of another company's film.

---

779 **Pluto and the Imp**

LENGTH: 200 ft.   © No reg.

PRODUCER:

CAMERA:

CAST:

PRODUCTION DATE: By early February 1900.

LOCATION:

SOURCE:

DESCRIPTION: Pluto appears before the gates of the Infernal Palace, and, sending for his Imp, commands him to bring the Book of Fates. A Mortal then appears upon the scene and Pluto demands him to sign the Book of Fates. The Mortal takes the pen and as he writes upon the book, smoke is seen to arise from the pages (a fine mystery effect). The Imp then commands the Mortal to enter the gates of the Infernal Palace, the Mortal refuses and a duel with swords ensues. The Imp succeeds in killing the Mortal, then proceeds to dismember the body. First a leg, then an arm, then the head and finally the whole body of the Mortal is thrown through the body of Pluto within the gates. The Imp steps to the foreground of the picture and running toward his Master, Pluto, dives through his body and disappears within the gates. A remarkably fine mysterious picture, creating much amusement to an audience. (*Edison Films*, March 1900, 41.)

SUBJECT:

ARCHIVE:

CITATIONS: *The Phonoscope*, December 1899, 10.

NOTE: The film's production date is based on its assigned code word (Uncloak). The picture could be a dupe of another company's film.

---

780 ***Roeber Wrestling Match / The Great Wrestling Match Between Ernest Roeber and August Faust**

LENGTH: 355 ft.   © Thomas A. Edison, 16 December 1901.

PRODUCER: J. Stuart Blackton, Albert E. Smith.

CAMERA: J. Stuart Blackton and/or Albert E. Smith.

CAST: Ernest Roeber, August Faust.

PRODUCTION DATE: [January–March 1900.]

LOCATION: Vitagraph's roof-top studio, New York, N.Y.

SOURCE:

DESCRIPTION: This films shows a most exciting Graeco-Roman Wrestling match between two of the most skillful "Knights of the Mat" and is full of action from start to finish; every muscle stands out in relief as

the Gladiators battle for supremacy. The fall is finally won by Roeber after a hard fought contest which keeps the spectators in a fever of excitement. The match took place in a large Amphitheatre and the referee, timekeeper, judges and seconds who are all well known sporting men, form an animated background to the scene. Photography and action throughout are perfect. (*Edison Films*, September 1902, 64.)

SUBJECT: Wrestling. Germans.

ARCHIVE: DLC-pp.

CITATIONS: "Ernest Roeber, American Champion, Who is to Wrestle Yosouf, the Turk," *New York World*, 16 March 1898, 10; "Roeber Wins on a Foul," *New York World*, 28 March 1898, 8; "Roeber Will Wrestle," *New York World*, 24 April 1898, 20; "The Turk and Roeber," *New York World*, 26 April 1898, 10; "Police Stop Wrestling Match," *New York World*, 1 May 1898, 15. American Vitagraph Company advertisement, *New York Clipper*, 24 March 1900, 96.

NOTE: One of a group of twenty films, made by Blackton and Smith and listed in a preliminary agreement with the Edison Manufacturing Company, dated 10 September 1900. These were turned over to Edison's Kinetograph Department for sales purposes; four were eventually copyrighted while many others were simply added to the Edison catalogs. About the time that this film was made, Sigmund Lubin produced *Reproduction of the Wrestling Match Between Ernest Roeber and Bech Olsen*. Lubin's 250-foot subject used actors. (*New York Clipper*, 31 March 1900, 120.)

LOOK THIS OVER!

The ROEBER-CRANE ATHLETIC COMEDY CO.

HEADED BY THE CHAMPION WRESTLER OF THE WORLD

ERNEST ROEBER,

IN CONJUNCTION WITH THE FAMOUS MUDTOWN RUBES

CRANE BROS.,

And NINE PICKED Vaudeville Acts, NINE. Now Booking Season 98-99.

Address: JAMES H. CURTIN, Olympic Theatre, 129th Street, New York.

(Advertisement, *New York Clipper*, 28 May 1898, 220.)

ROEBER FAVORED BY REFEREE.

Jack Quinn Awarded Him the Decision Over Muller–Match Ended in a Slugging Match.

Ernest Roeber, the German champion, and Caspar Muller, of South Africa, met in a wrestling match at the Theatre Unique, Williamsburg, last evening, and the affair developed into a slugging match.

The principals had agreed on George Considine for referee, but he failed to put in an appearance. Thereupon Jack Quinn, who knew nothing of the science of wrestling, was selected. He watched Muller give Roeber all and more than the German was looking for, and awarded the decision to Roeber after nineteen minutes of scuffling.

The crowd was greatly incensed, and the South African's breath was almost taken away by the action of the referee. The curtain was rung down and the two principals came to blows. They were soon parted, and agreed to meet again to-morrow night. If Roeber fails to throw his man in thirty seconds he is to forfeit the entire box-office receipts. (*New York World*, 27 September 1898, 8.)

781 **The Cragg Family / [The Craggs]**

LENGTH: 50, 100, 150, 200, and 250 ft.   © No reg.

PRODUCER: [J. Stuart Blackton, Albert E. Smith.]

CAMERA: [J. Stuart Blackton and/or Albert E. Smith.]
CAST: Cragg Family.
PRODUCTION DATE: [January-March 1900?]
LOCATION: Koster & Bial's Roof Garden, New York, N.Y.
SOURCE:
DESCRIPTION: A spirited film, showing the entire act performed by this most famous troupe of English acrobats, father and five sons. The Cragg family are famous throughout the world for their sensational acrobatic work and command the highest salary of any acrobatic family in the world, having received $3,000 per week on their last visit to America. The startling feats of head to head and foot to foot balancing, triple somersaults and marvelous hand and foot work accomplished by these premier gymnasts make one of the most wonderful motion pictures ever produced. (*Edison Films,* July 1901, 44.)
SUBJECT: Vaudeville–performances. Acrobats. Family.
ARCHIVE:
CITATIONS: *New York Clipper*, 24 November 1900, 876.
NOTE: An American Vitagraph advertisement indicates that the exhibition service was offering a film of "The Famous Crazy Family, in sensational acrobatic work" (*New York Clipper*, 24 March 1900, 96). This may well be of a film of the Cragg family (gg somehow becoming zy).

The Craggs, owing to previous engagements, will leave "Squatters' Daughter" for a few weeks and fulfill London engagements. Their place in the company will be filled with a cinematograph film 300 feet long, taken at Koster & Bial's Roof Garden, New York, showing the entire acrobatic performance of these well-known artists. (*The Entr'acte*, 14 April 1900.)

Four-times married, father of twenty-four children, the eldest 58 and the youngest 3, thirteen of whom are still alive, and great grand-father of eighteen children, is, according to the *London Evening News*, the record of John Williams Cragg, aged 76, the famous British acrobat. Forty years ago the "Marvelous Craggs" used to top the bills of London music halls, in the days when all the halls were associated with fully licensed drinking saloons, and the chairman who announced the turns, always had a glass of something stimulating at his table.
Cragg began his public career in 1862, and in 1868 he and his partner took an engagement as trapeze performers at Cremorne Gardens. They were both so hungry that Cragg fell, through weakness, forty feet, but disregarded his bruises and finished his performance. When the doctor at the hospital saw him, instead of giving him a bottle of embrocation, he gave him something to nourish him.
He, however, got to the top, and managed to enroll a troupe of six performers. These were often hungry, and when at work their combined salaries totaled $30 a week. From that small beginning, however, the "marvelous Craggs," rose to $2,500 a week, paid them in the United States.
Mr. Cragg runs a public gymnasium in the Kensington Road, London, still keeps in active training, and looks like a man "in the forties," rather than one of 76 years.... (*New York Times*, 25 September 1921, 10G.)

Edison lawyer Richard Dyer seems to have had significant family connections with the United States Navy. This provided James White with entry to Newport naval facilities, where he was able to film naval maneuvers several times over the next few years.

782 Drill of Naval Cadets at Newport
LENGTH: 75 ft.   © No reg.
PRODUCER: James White.
CAMERA:
CAST:
PRODUCTION DATE: January to early February 1900.
LOCATION: Naval Training Station, Newport, R.I.
SOURCE:
DESCRIPTION: This picture shows the Cadets marching, countermarching and a great many interesting maneuvres. (*Edison Films*, March 1900, 45.)
SUBJECT: Navies–United States. Naval cadets. Parades.
ARCHIVE:
CITATIONS: *New York Clipper*, 10 February 1900, 1064; *Edison Films,* July 1901, 26.
NOTE:

783 Military Scenes at Newport, R.I.
LENGTH: 50 ft.   © No reg.
PRODUCER: James White.
CAMERA:
CAST:
PRODUCTION DATE: January to early February 1900.
LOCATION: Naval Training Station, Newport, R.I.
SOURCE:
DESCRIPTION: These pictures were taken at the Newport Naval Training Station and show the Cadets in the act of training and discharging pieces of heavy artillery. (*Edison Films*, March 1900, 45.)
SUBJECT: Navies–United States. Artillery. Naval cadets.
ARCHIVE:
CITATIONS: *New York Clipper*, 10 February 1900, 1064; *Edison Films*, July 1901, 26.
NOTE:

Thomas Edison copyrighted five films on 28 February 1900 which, based on internal evidence, were all made by the same producer, whose identity has yet to be established. Blackton and Smith, the chief generators of Edison trick films in the past, are unlikely candidates since their relationship with the inventor was at this moment adversarial. Paley produced principally actualities, while the mise-en-scène differs noticeably from other films made at the Black Maria under James White.

784 *A Dull Razor / The Dull Razor
LENGTH: 45 ft.   © Thomas A. Edison, 28 February 1900.
PRODUCER:
CAMERA:
CAST:
PRODUCTION DATE: [February 1900.]
LOCATION:
SOURCE:

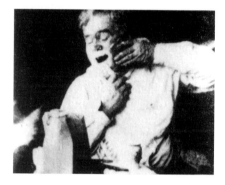

DESCRIPTION: This picture shows an old gentleman seated at his shaving table. The razor is evidently giving him a great deal of trouble, as he catches hold of the brush and with a great show of impatience he hurriedly coats his face with the foaming soap and makes a second attempt at removing his beard. He scrapes and scrapes, and judging from the painful facial expressions, the razor grows duller with every stroke. The old man makes a new and ludicrous twitch of the mouth every time he draws the razor across his face. This is a 50 foot film of an ordinary scene of every day life, and its mirth provoking merits have never been surpassed. (*Edison Films*, July 1901, 70.)
SUBJECT: Facial expressions. Shaving.
ARCHIVE: DLC-pp.
CITATIONS: *New York Clipper*, 24 March 1900, 96.
NOTE:

785 *An Animated Luncheon / The Animated Luncheon
LENGTH: 60 and 75 ft.   © Thomas A. Edison, 28 February 1900.
PRODUCER:
CAMERA:
CAST:
PRODUCTION DATE: [February 1900.]
LOCATION:
SOURCE:
DESCRIPTION: The scene takes place in a fashionable café. A well dressed couple enter and after a careful perusal of the menu, conclude on an order of boiled eggs and

Welsh rarebit. The obliging waiter delivers the order. The guests break open the eggs, and two beautiful white chickens fly across the room. The diners then perform a similar trick with the Welsh rarebit just served, and two beautiful snow white rabbits hop from the dish and are seen kicking and squirming as they are lifted to the floor. It was all a joke but the waiter was not on. Your audience will catch on, for it is a good lively subject, full of action. (*Edison Films*, July 1901, 85.)

SUBJECT: Taverns, etc. Magic tricks. Chickens. Rabbits.

ARCHIVE: DLC-pp.

CITATIONS: *New York Clipper*, 24 March 1900, 96.

NOTE:

786 *Faust and Marguerite

LENGTH: 60 ft.   © Thomas A. Edison, 28 February 1900.

PRODUCER:

CAMERA:

CAST:

PRODUCTION DATE: [February 1900.]

LOCATION:

SOURCE: *Faust and Marguerite* (folk tale).

DESCRIPTION: Marguerite is seated before the fireplace, Faust standing by her side. Mephistopheles enters and offers his sword to Faust, commanding him to behead the fair Marguerite. Faust refuses, whereupon Mephistopheles draws the sword across the throat of the lady and she suddenly disappears and Faust is seated in her place. (*Edison Films*, July 1901, 84.)

SUBJECT: Devil. Magic.

ARCHIVE: DLC-pp.

CITATIONS: *New York Clipper*, 24 March 1900, 96.

NOTE:

787 *The Magician

LENGTH: 60 ft.   © Thomas A. Edison, 28 February 1900.

PRODUCER:

CAMERA:

CAST:

PRODUCTION DATE: [February 1900.]

LOCATION:

SOURCE:

DESCRIPTION: The scene opens on a theatrical stage. The magician enters from the wings, and making a bow to the audience, removes his coat and hat and they disappear mysteriously in the air. He then takes a white handkerchief from his pocket, holds it over his knees, and his long trousers disappear, and behold! he is clad in knickerbockers. He next makes a pass with a magic wand and a table suddenly appears before the audience, on which is a large pile of tissue paper. The magician takes up the paper and shakes it a few times and three live geese fly out upon the floor. This is a highly pleasing and mystifying subject. (*Edison Films*, July 1901, 83.)

SUBJECT: Magic tricks. Magicians. Geese.
ARCHIVE: DLC-pp.
CITATIONS: *New York Clipper*, 24 March 1900, 96.
NOTE:

788 ***Ching Ling Foo Outdone**
LENGTH: 50 and 75 ft.   © Thomas A. Edison, 28 February 1900.
PRODUCER:
CAMERA:
CAST:
PRODUCTION DATE: [February 1900.]
LOCATION:
SOURCE:

DESCRIPTION: The magician enters upon the stage, and removing a covering from a small table, shakes it before the audience to show that there is nothing whatever concealed inside, places the cloth upon the floor, and when he removes it five large geese are found to be swimming in the water. The magician takes the geese out of the tub, and places them on the stage, and they walk away. He again places the cloth over the tub, and when he removes it the tub disappears and a small boy stands in its place. The boy walks off the stage to the astonishment and amazement of the audience. (*Edison Films*, July 1901, 84.)
SUBJECT: Magic tricks. Boys. Magicians. Geese. Ching Ling Foo.
ARCHIVE: DLC-pp.
CITATIONS: *New York Clipper*, 24 March 1900, 96.
NOTE: There were many magicians appearing on the stage who claimed to exceed Ching Ling Foo in one way or another. In this instance, it was the motion picture producer.

THE WONDER,

CHING LING FOO,

FAMOUS CHINESE CONJUROR,

AND HIS

COMPANY OF ORIENTAL ENTERTAINERS

THE UNDISPUTED SENSATION OF THE AGE,

THE LONGEST VAUDEVILLE ENGAGEMENT ON RECORD. 40 CONSECUTIVE WEEKS ON

B.F. KEITH'S CIRCUIT OF THEATRES—NEW YORK, BOSTON, PHILADELPHIA AND PROVIDENCE.

UNQUESTIONABLY THE MOST PROFITABLE ATTRACTION EVER IN VAUDEVILLE.

UNDER SPECIAL CONTRACT FOR A TERM OF YEARS WITH MR. B.F. KEITH AND COL. JOHN D. HOPKINS.

Propositions for a Limited Number of Engagements, Commencing Jan 15, will be Entertained. Address

E.F. ALBEE, General Manager. B.F. KEITH'S ENTERPRISES, UNION SQUARE THEATRE, NEW YORK.

(Advertisement, *New York Clipper*, 16 December 1899, 885.)

CHING LING FOO'S NEW CONTRACT.

The minor differences which have existed between B.F. Keith and John D. Hopkins and Ching Ling Foo, the Chinese conjurer, were all amicably settled during Ching's engagement in Washington two weeks ago, through the kindness of the Chinese Minister, who listened patiently to both sides of the story. E.F. Albee spent two days in Washington and was in consultation with the Chinese Minister six hours of each day. The result of the conferences was that the Minister prepared an entirely new contract, covering a term of years, which was signed by Mr. Albee and Ching in presence of the Minister, who affixed his signature, thus making the affair binding. Ching also made a new contract with his comedian-assistant, who is a great feature of the act, and when the conference was concluded every one concerned was entirely satisfied. Ching will remain absolutely under the control of Keith and Hopkins and cannot play in the United States, Europe or Canada without their consent. Now that everything has been settled, Mr. Albee has been overwhelmed with applications for the services of the Chinaman, who has proven the greatest drawing card ever known in the history of vaudeville. Within a few months Ching will revisit his home in China to settle up his affairs, and will then return to America, to begin the work of amassing the fortune that awaits him. (*New York Dramatic Mirror*, 3 February 1900, 18.)

789 ***The Kiss / The New Kiss**

LENGTH: 50 ft.   © Thomas A. Edison, 9 March 1900.

PRODUCER:

CAMERA:

CAST:

PRODUCTION DATE: [February to early March 1900.]

LOCATION:

SOURCE: *May Irwin Kiss* (Edison film no. 155, April 1896).

DESCRIPTION: Nothing new, but an old thing done over again and done well. Some one has attempted to describe a kiss as "something made of nothing," but this is not one of that kind, but one of those old fashioned "home made" kind that sets the whole audience into merriment and motion, and has always proven a popular subject. It is very fine photographically and an exhibit is not complete without it. (*Edison Films*, July 1901, 70.)

SUBJECT: Kissing.

ARCHIVE: DLC-pp.

CITATIONS: *New York Clipper*, 24 March 1900, 96; 12 May 1900, 260.

NOTE: The screen behind the lovers is the same one appearing in *A Dull Razor* (no. 783) and other films copyrighted 28 February 1900.

An Edison-affiliated cameraman traveled to Halifax, Nova Scotia, to take a series of films of Canadian troops departing for South Africa. Parts of the second contingent left on earlier dates. But the third and final portion was the largest of these groups.

790 **Second Canadian Contingent Leaving Halifax**

LENGTH: 100 ft.   © No reg.

PRODUCER: [William Paley?]

CAMERA: [William Paley?]

CAST:

PRODUCTION DATE: [21 February 1900.]

LOCATION: Halifax, Nova Scotia, Canada.

SOURCE:

DESCRIPTION:

SUBJECT: South African War, 1899-1902. Armies–Canada. Parades.

ARCHIVE:

CITATIONS: *New York Clipper*, 19 May 1900, 284.

NOTE: The delay between this film's production and its entry into Edison's catalog was large enough to suggest that the picture was made by a licensee (William Paley being the most likely candidate), who enjoyed the customary period of exclusivity prior to Edison distribution.

THE EMBARKATION.
OUR CANADIAN BOYS OFF TO THE WAR.
Scenes at the Dockyard, etc.–Names of the Haligonians and Nova Scotians who sailed yesterday.

The Third and largest portion of the Second Canadian Contingent sailed majestically down the harbor yesterday afternoon, and by now are well out on the ocean. They have gone, and with them goes the best wishes of every Canadian. While in Halifax the men all conducted themselves well and made many friends.

At the inspection yesterday afternoon the Armories were packed. At sharp 2 o'clock General Lord Seymour arrived, and accompanied by Sir M.B. Daly, Hon. Dr. Borden, Col. Irving, Col. Biscoe, Capt. Ferguson, and the commanding officers of the Contingent, he inspected the troops. The General was evidently pleased at the splendid appearance of the men. Lord William Seymour then addressed the troops. He told the men they were going to encounter a foe of no common kind in South Africa, situated in a mountainous country, an enemy with rifles and guns of the greatest precision, cunning in warfare against man and beast, but he believed on looking over the Canadians, that the enemy may be encountered on his own terms. He asked the men to endeavor to do their best under all circumstances.

In conclusion the speaker said the late despatches had shown to the world that the first Canadian contingent was not behindhand in its sacrifice of life for the Empire.

"Col. Evans, on behalf of the Imperial forces in Canada, I wish you and your command a prosperous voyage across the ocean, a glorious and decisive campaign when you arrive, and a happy return to the Dominion of Canada."

Governor Daly in his address said that not only Halifax, Nova Scotia, and Canada, but the British Empire applauded the Canadians devotion and self-sacrifice. Her Majesty herself has said from her throne that the brilliant courage and soldier-like qualities of the colonial forces engaged in South Africa have already earned high admiration. In conclusion his honor wished them a speedy and prosperous voyage, a brilliant and successful campaign and a happy return to their homes and families. He said: "My words are but a feeble echo of the sincere and heartfelt sympathy of all your fellow countrymen for your success and welfare. God speed you."...

THE PARADE.

After the addresses the soldiers, headed by the Leinster band playing the United Empire march, left the Drill Hall and were greeted with a roar of cheering, waving of flags, etc., by the solid mass of people who had gathered there. The soldiers were fairly hemmed in, and there was difficulty in keeping the centre of the street open for the boys. From the Drill Hall to Cogswell street the street was so densely thronged that a squad of police had to clear the centre of the street to allow the soldiers to pass along.

A continuous murmur of applause travelled with the huge moving mass of civilians and soldiers and made a cheerful accompaniment to the music of the bands, which, on this occasion, were scattered through the detachment. Never has a more demonstrative gathering assembled in Halifax.

All along the route the men were loyally greeted, and often men and women would break through the crowd and in some instances even stepped into the ranks to bid adieu to their friends and relatives.

The decorations on the route of parade was profuse. Harrington street was lined thickly with people, and a spectator from an upper window stated that every inch of ground was covered.

The Leinster band headed the procession, the detachment being divided into three bodies. The second body was headed by the 65th band and 66th band. The third body was headed by the 1st C.A. and 63rd bands. By this arrangement all the men had the benefit of marching music. (*Arcadian Recorder*, 22 February 1900, 3.)

791 **Snowballing Scene / Snowballing Scene at Halifax, N.S. / Snowballing Scene in Halifax**
LENGTH: 50 ft.   © No reg.
PRODUCER: [William Paley?]
CAMERA: [William Paley?]
CAST:
PRODUCTION DATE: [21 February 1900.]
LOCATION: Halifax, Nova Scotia, Canada.
SOURCE:
DESCRIPTION: An interesting picture secured in Halifax, N.S., on the day of the embarkation of the Canadian contingent for South Africa. The picture shows about 300 small boys in front of the armory engaged in a lively snowballing contest, which finally develops into a fight. The two sides rush each other, and as the contest grow interesting a venturesome teamster passes down the road in a wagon drawn by a white horse. The boys immediately turn their attention to the daring driver and pelt him with snowballs, knock off his hat and disable him generally. This is a very humorous picture. (*Edison Films*, July 1901, 96.)
SUBJECT: Boys. Snowballing. Winter Sports. Armories.
ARCHIVE:
CITATIONS: *New York Clipper*, 24 March 1900, 96; 12 May 1900, 260; *Edison Films*, September 1902, 111.
NOTE:

792 **Panoramic View of the Bay of Fundy**
LENGTH: 50 ft.   © No reg.
PRODUCER: [William Paley?]
CAMERA: [William Paley?]
CAST:
PRODUCTION DATE: [February 1900.]
LOCATION: Bay of Fundy, Nova Scotia, Canada.
SOURCE:
DESCRIPTION: This pictures was taken from the bow of a tug boat running by the light-

house on the Isle of Man in the Bay of Fundy. It shows the waves during a fierce storm dashing against the rock-bound coast and rolling over the breakers in front of the lighthouse. (*Edison Films*, July 1901, 48.)

SUBJECT: Storms. Ocean waves. Tugboats. Lighthouses.

ARCHIVE:

CITATIONS: *New York Clipper*, 24 March 1900, 96; 12 May 1900, 260.

NOTE:

793 Great Newark Fire

LENGTH: 50, 85 and 100 ft.   © No reg.

PRODUCER: [James White.]

CAMERA:

CAST:

PRODUCTION DATE: 28 February 1900.

LOCATION: Newark, N.J.

SOURCE:

DESCRIPTION: This scene was secured at Newark, N.J., February 28th, at the burning of the great dry goods district on Broad Street. The picture was secured the morning of February 28th, while the firemen were at work coping with the flames and smoke. The effect is most graphic. Huge volumes of smoke roll away over the burning building, while the firemen are playing the hose. In one part of the picture part of the walls of one of the buildings is seen to fall to the ground with a crash. (*Edison Films*, July 1901, 55.)

SUBJECT: Fire fighters. Fires. Fire ruins.

ARCHIVE:

CITATIONS: *New York Clipper*, 24 March 1900, 96.

NOTE: The fire fighters shown in such films as *Starting for a Fire* (no. 257), *Going to a Fire* (no. 258) and *A Morning Alarm* (no. 259) were the firemen fighting this destructive blaze.

MILLION DOLLAR FIRE IN NEWARK
Blaze Starts in the Centre of the Broad Street Dry Goods District and Sweeps Through the W.O. Snyder and Other Establishments Before Its Progress is Stopped.
THRILLING RESCUE OF A MAN WITH HIS CLOTHES AFIRE.
O.O. Shackelton, Superintendent of the Snyder Dry Goods House, Hemmed In by Flames, Carried Down a Ladder as Firemen Beat Out the Blaze.
FIREMEN BURIED UNDER A WALL, BUT WERE FINALLY RESCUED.

In the centre of the big Broad street dry goods district of Newark, N.J., fire last night destroyed property valued at $1,000,000.

The flames started about half-past six o'clock in the basement of the five story dry goods house of W.V. Snyder & Co., on the northwest corner of Broad and Cedar streets, and in less than five minutes had run up through the elevator shaft, spreading through every floor, and developed into the biggest fire in the history of the city in its business district.

Just how the fire started no one could tell. Snyder's stores had been closed for business only half an hour before. There were two employees remaining on the ground floor, and one superintendent, O.O. Shackelton, on the third floor. A puff of smoke was seen near the first floor elevator opening, and a message was sent for a chemical engine. Before it arrived the flames burst through the entire structure, and the two men on the first floor fled for their lives. One of them, Watson Snyder, cashier, left his coat behind him.

The man on the third floor could not escape. He ran frantically from one end of the building to the other until the flames hemmed him into a small space near a window on the Cedar street side.

RESCUED WITH CLOTHING AFIRE.

He opened the window, shouted for help and was about to jump, when Policeman Welsh and several others called to him to wait, as a ladder truck was then dashing to the spot only a block away. He waited, though the flames scorched his back and caused him to scream from fright and pain. The crew of the hook and ladder truck No. 1 quickly raised a ladder, and even before it was steadied men were climbing to the rescue.

When they reached Shackelton his clothing was ablaze from head to foot, and he was scarcely able to help himself. He was gotten out through the window and then with firemen above and below him and another keeping pace with him by climbing down the under side of the ladder he was taken safely to the street.

During the climb down the ladder, the firemen were working to put out the flames which were consuming his clothing and burning into his flesh. He was without clothing when the ground was reached and his body was badly burned. He was sent to McMichael's hospital and at midnight it was said he would live. It was rumored that a colored janitor and his wife were in the building and had been burned to death, but up to midnight this could not be verified.

From the first it was seen to be impossible to save the Snyder buildings, and in less than half an hour they were simply a mass of hot bricks and smouldering timbers. Two adjoining buildings in Broad street—Bernstein Brothers shoe store and John M. Mentz, dealer in dry goods and laces—were also totally destroyed within half an hour, and the entire fire force of the city turned its attention to saving surround[ing] property, but seven or eight businesses suffered badly.

FLAMES CROSSED STREET.

The flames leaped across Cedar street, a narrow thoroughfare, and set fire to the building on the southwest corner of Broad and Cedar streets....

During the blaze several firemen were slightly injured, the most seriously being Newton of Truck No. 1, who was hurt by falling debris. As the roofs of the several floors and the side walls of the Snyder, Bernstein and Mentz buildings fell with a succession of crashes, the flames and sparks mounted high into the air, producing a fiery spectacle which attracted more than fifty thousand persons on the scene from all parts of Newark and the surrounding cities and towns.

A force of more than one hundred policemen, under Chief Hopper, Captains Corbitt and Daly and several sergeants and roundsmen, had difficulty in maintaining a fire line; and there were scores of narrow escapes from falling electrical light, trolley, telephone and telegraph wires. To minimize the danger from that source, the lighting companies shut off the power from the wires soon after the fire began.

Late at night it was declared that the fire was started in Snyder's building by a defective electric light wire on the third floor, and that the flames travelled along the wires and through the elevator shafts to the other floors in a few minutes.

FIREMEN UNDER A WALL.

Just before midnight a section of the side wall of the Snyder Building fell with a crash while four firemen and a citizen were just inside of it. It was two stories high, about twenty feet long and two feet thick, and the five men were buried under tons of hot bricks. Half a hundred men at once sprang to the rescue, and in a few minutes four of them were gotten out. They are firemen Elmer Gardner, of No. 4 engine; Andrew Bessinger and Thomas Brown of No. 6 engine, and Joseph Huber, a nephew of Bessinger, who is not a member of the department.

All were badly cut about the head and shoulders and injured about the legs and arms, while Brown and Gardner are believed to be seriously hurt internally. Walter Harrison, lieutenant of Engine No. 4. was completely buried under three feet of bricks and beams, and it took half an hour to dig him out though his head was uncovered after the first few minutes, and he was able to direct the work of his rescuers. He was weak when gotten out and suffered from internal injuries which will cause his death. He and the others were taken to the City Hospital. After the accident all parts of the standing walls were pulled down. Streams were kept on the ruins all night....(*New York Herald*, 28 February 1900, 9.)

794   **Clown Dining at the Infernal Palace**
LENGTH: 175 ft.   © No reg.
PRODUCER:
CAMERA:
CAST:
PRODUCTION DATE: [February to mid-March 1900?]
LOCATION:
SOURCE:
DESCRIPTION:
SUBJECT: Clowns. Hell. Devil.
ARCHIVE:
CITATIONS: *New York Clipper*, 24 March 1900, 96; 21 April 1900, 184; 19 May 1900, 284.
NOTE: May be a dupe of another company's picture.

795   ***An Artist's Dream / The Artist's Dream**
LENGTH: 75 ft.   © Thomas A. Edison, 21 March 1900.
PRODUCER:
CAMERA:
CAST:
PRODUCTION DATE: [February to mid-March 1900.]

LOCATION:

SOURCE: "The Artist's Dream" (magic show by Prof. Hermann); *The Artist's Dream* (Biograph film no. 924, April 1899).

DESCRIPTION: The scene opens in the interior of an artist's studio. Mephisto appears mysteriously and signals the pictures to come to life. They step down from the frames and walk forward, admiring their costumes. Mephisto then touches the artist on the shoulder, awaking him, and disappears. The artist, after rubbing his eyes, sees the

picture on his right hand side and jumps up to embrace her. After embracing her once, he makes a second attempt and she disappears. The artist now wakes up, jumps to his feet and runs to see if the pictures are still in the frames. He examines them and finding that they are still fast on the wall, realizes that he has been dreaming and seeks consolation in the bottle. (*Edison Films*, July 1901, 83.)

SUBJECT: Dreams. Alcoholism. Artists. Devil.

ARCHIVE: DLC-pp.

CITATIONS: *New York Clipper*, 24 March 1900, 96.

NOTE: Apparently made by the same production company as *The Magician* and other films copyrighted on 28 February 1900.

MAGIC AND DRAMA.
Professor Hermann's Two Latest Illusions and the Revolution of Which They May Be the Forerunners.

The two new illusions, "The Artist's Dream" and "Noah's Ark," which Professor Hermann exhibited for the first time in this city at the Columbus Theatre last week are probably the forerunners of a revolution in magical performances. "The public wants novelty and change," said the magician the other day. "The old fashioned entertainment was little more than a string of tricks, which had little or no connection one with the other. It is my idea that what is demanded now is a combination of drama and magic, and that is what I have tried to give in these two new illusions."

"The Artist's Dream," which probably exemplifies this new idea the better of the two, is a pathetic little sketch telling the story of an old French artist who has painted the portrait of his little daughter, who has died. His work has become a part of his life, and every night as he falls to sleep before the easel the child seems to come to life again and to sing and dance around him as she used to do. Of course, when he awakes he finds it has only been a dream. The stage is set to represent the old artist's studio. There are one or two easels, with empty frames, and at one side stands the young girl's portrait. An Irish lackey enters, and in his dusting manages to show the painting to the audience from every side. Then the artist comes in and, after adding a few touches to the picture with his brush, sits down in front of it. He gazes at it awhile, and then apparently drops off to sleep. In a twinkling a fairy appears in one of the empty frames, and as she waves her wand the portrait of the child literally comes to life before the eyes of the spectators. She steps down from the frame and dances and sings around her father's chair. Suddenly he awakes, and presto! the child is back in the frame, a picture once more.

"Noah's Ark" is not quite so good from a dramatic standpoint, although it is a very clever illusion. The stage represents the top of Mount Ararat, with the ark resting on the centre. The magician and his assistant take the vessel all to pieces, put it together again and then apparently fill it with water. Then out are drawn the animals—a flock of pigeons, a half dozen rabbits, a pug dog, a lot of chickens, a turkey, a peacock and a pig. Last of all there bursts apparently from the top of the ark a young girl, carrying a dove in her hand.

In view of the present interest in everything related to Napoleon, Professor Hermann is now at work on a magical sketch in which an incident of the Emperor's life is the central feature. He has numerous other illusions of this same kind in preparation and it is possible that before very long he will have ready a complete play combining a number of these. (*New York Herald*, 18 November 1894, 3D.)

796 ***The Mystic Swing**

LENGTH: 60 ft.   © Thomas A. Edison, 21 March 1900.

PRODUCER:

CAMERA:

CAST:

PRODUCTION DATE: [March 1900?]

LOCATION:

SOURCE:

DESCRIPTION: The professor shows his power to Mephisto by mysteriously placing a young lady in a swing. Mephisto then shows his power by making the young lady disappear from the swing, to the surprise of the professor. The professor makes another mystic pass and produces a second young lady then in the swing, and also a skeleton. (*Edison Films*, July 1901, 85.)

SUBJECT: Magicians. Devil. Rivalries.

ARCHIVE: DLC-pp.

CITATIONS: *New York Clipper*, 24 March 1900, 96.

NOTE: Made by the same production company as *The Magician* and other films copyrighted on 28 February 1900.

'97   *Uncle Josh in a Spooky Hotel / Uncle Josh in a Spook Hotel

LENGTH: 80 or 100 ft.   © Thomas A. Edison, 21 March 1900.

PRODUCER:

CAMERA:

CAST:

PRODUCTION DATE: [March 1900?]

LOCATION:

SOURCE:

DESCRIPTION: The landlord enters with his rural guest. After examining the bed and other things in the room, Josh takes a seat beside the landlord, who tells him that there is a rumor that a ghost appears in that room every night at 12 o'clock. The ghost then appears mysteriously and hits

Josh a slap on the check. Thinking it was the landlord who hit him Josh gets up and knocks the landlord off the chair. After a little row, Josh and the landlord again sit down and the ghost again appears and hits the landlord on the cheek. The landlord, thinking it was Josh, gets up and knocks him off the chair. Each one accuses the other of striking him. Josh discovers that his companion is really the ghost, and in great fright he grabs his things and rushes out of the room, followed by the ghost. (*Edison Films*, July 1901, 87.)

SUBJECT: Farmers. Ghosts. Hallucinations and illusions. Hotels.

ARCHIVE: DLC-pp.

CITATIONS: *New York Clipper*, 24 March 1900, 96; and 12 May 1900, 260.

NOTE: Made by the same production company as *The Magician* and other films copyrighted on 28 February 1900.

---

98   *Uncle Josh's Nightmare

LENGTH: 150 ft.   © Thomas A. Edison, 21 March 1900.

PRODUCER:

CAMERA:

CAST:

PRODUCTION DATE: [March 1900?]

LOCATION:

SOURCE:

DESCRIPTION:

SUBJECT: Dreams. Farmers. Hotels.

ARCHIVE: DLC-pp.

CITATIONS: *New York Clipper*, 24 March 1900, 96.

NOTE: Made by the same production company as *The Magician* and other films copyrighted on 28 February 1900.

799 **Off for the Fox Hunt / The Fox Hunt**

LENGTH: 125 ft.   © No reg.

PRODUCER: [James White.]

CAMERA:

CAST:

PRODUCTION DATE: March-April 1900.

LOCATION: [Bartell's Animal Farm, Orange, N.J.?]

SOURCE:

DESCRIPTION: The anticipation of a great day's sport is very evident by the interest taken alike by horses and hounds in the early part of this picture. As they start forth from the kennels, expectation is apparent in every motion. The vaulting of the steeds over bars and the loping of hounds as they start tend at once to interest all in the exciting chase for the brush that must occur later on. Next comes the triumphal return, where the horses leisurely trot along and the hunters discuss the mishaps and incidents of the day's sport, while the brush at the saddle bow is the trophy in evidence of the enjoyment that they have experienced. (*Edison Films*, September 1902, 89.)

SUBJECT: Fox hunting. Hunting. Horses. Dogs. Social elites.

ARCHIVE:

CITATIONS: *New York Clipper*, 21 April 1900, 184; 23 June 1900, 388; *Edison Films*, July 1901, 79.

NOTE: In 1906 the Biograph Company shot a film entitled *The Fox Hunt* at Bartell's Animal Farm in Orange, N.J, in cooperation with the Union County Hounds of Orange, N.J. It is possible that this locale and organization were used for this earlier Edison film as well. The picture might also have been shot on the Vincent farm where James White staged and filmed a number of Boer War films.

With the Anglo-Boer War dominating the front page of the nation's newspapers, it also became a popular screen subject. The rival Biograph organization had sent cameraman W.K.L. Dickson on location in South Africa. Other films came from or through England and provided a British perspective. James White once again began to produce "re-enactments" of recent battles. Like the Belgians, Dutch, French, and Germans, many Americans were sympathetic to the Boer cause (or were at least anti-British); and so it is not surprising that most of these films treated the Boers with considerable respect. (Stephen Bottomore reports that the Belgians and Dutch also staged battle scenes that were sympathetic to the Boers.) Shortly before these films were made, the following appeared in the New York Clipper:

At the Olympia (Paris, France) they have war scenes displayed by moving picture machines and when the English soldiers appear the whistling and hissing by the audience sounds like escaping steam from a large engine. When the Boer pictures are shown they forget themselves enough to applaud and yell with delight. Our American Rough Riders who took part in our war with Spain are used and passed off as Boers, and their appearance is a signal for cheers. If you are foolish enough to applaud English soldiers it would be made so uncomfortable for you that you would gladly leave the theatre. (*New York Clipper*, 10 March 1900, 27.)

800 ***Boers Bringing in British Prisoners**

LENGTH: 75 ft.   © Thomas A. Edison, 14 April 1900.

PRODUCER: James White.

CAMERA:

CAST:

PRODUCTION DATE: 11 April 1900.

LOCATION: Orange Mountains, West Orange, N.J.

SOURCE:

DESCRIPTION: Here we have a mixed company of Gordon Highlanders, Irish Fusilliers and English Lancers, as a group of prisoners taken to the rear by a troop of Boer Cavalry. The expression of their faces show who is the victor, and who the vanquished.

You can read in the dust and smoke-begrimed countenances of the prisoners, the story of their stubborn resistance to superior numbers before the surrender: while the Boers give expression to their feelings, by cheering and waving their hats in triumph as they pass. (*Edison Films*, July 1901, 29.)
SUBJECT: South African War, 1899-1902. National Guard–New Jersey. Cavalry.
ARCHIVE: DLC-pp.
CITATIONS: *New York Clipper*, 21 April 1900, 184; 28 April 1900, 216.
NOTE:

801 ***Capture of Boer Battery by British / Capture of Boer Battery by the British**
LENGTH: 100 ft.   © Thomas A. Edison, 14 April 1900.
PRODUCER: James White.
CAMERA:
CAST:
PRODUCTION DATE: 11 April 1900.
LOCATION: Orange Mountains, West Orange, N.J.
SOURCE:

DESCRIPTION: Nothing can exceed the stubborn resistance shown by the Gordon Highlanders, as we see them steadily advancing in the face of a murderous fire of the Boers, who are making their guns speak with rapid volleys. One by one the gunners fall beside their guns, and as the smoke clears for an instant the Highlanders are seen gaining nearer and nearer the disputed ground. Finally a grand charge is made, the siege is carried, and amid cheers they plant the colors on the spot they have so dearly earned. (*Edison Films*, July 1901, 28-29.)
SUBJECT: South African War, 1899-1902. National Guard–New Jersey. Battles. Artillery.
ARCHIVE: DLC-pp.
CITATIONS:
NOTE:

802 ***Capture of Boer Battery**
LENGTH: 100 ft.   © Thomas A. Edison, 16 April 1900.
PRODUCER: James White.
CAMERA:
CAST:
PRODUCTION DATE: 11 April 1900.
LOCATION: Orange Mountains, West Orange, N.J.
SOURCE:

DESCRIPTION: By the Gordon Highlanders. In the foreground are two Creusot guns, manned by the Dutch burghers. Smoke effects are due. The Highlanders are seen in the distance, approaching rapidly, easily distinguished by their kilts and bare legs. They sweep all before them, leaving the guns smoking and deserted as they pursue the flying Boers. (*New York Clipper*, 28 April 1900, 216.)
SUBJECT: South African War, 1899-1902. National Guard–New Jersey. Battles. Artillery.
ARCHIVE: DLC-pp.
CITATIONS: *New York Clipper*, 21 April 1900, 184; 28 April 1900, 216; 12 May 1900, 260.
NOTE:

803 ***Charge of Boer Cavalry / [Charge of Boer Cavalry, no. 1]**
LENGTH: 50 ft.   © Thomas A. Edison, 14 April 1900.
PRODUCER: James White.
CAMERA:

CAST:
PRODUCTION DATE: 11 April 1900.
LOCATION: Orange Mountains, West Orange, N.J.
SOURCE: *Charge of the Seventh French Cuirassiers* (Lumière film, 1896).
DESCRIPTION: Shows a wild charge of Mounted Boer up a steep hill. The action of the picture is spirited and photographically it is an excellent film. The opening scene shows a bleak hillside with the Boer cavalry in the distance, galloping rapidly to the front.

They cross the ridge just as the film ends. (*New York Clipper*, 28 April 1900, 216.)
SUBJECT: South African War, 1899-1902. National Guard–New Jersey. Cavalry.
ARCHIVE: DLC-pp.
CITATIONS: *New York Clipper*, 21 April 1900, 184; 12 May 1900, 260.
NOTE:

804 ***Charge of Boer Cavalry / [Charge of Boer Cavalry, no. 2]**
LENGTH: 50 ft.   © Thomas A. Edison, 16 April 1900.
PRODUCER: James White.
CAMERA:
CAST:
PRODUCTION DATE: 11 April 1900.
LOCATION: Orange Mountains, West Orange, N.J.
SOURCE: *Charge of the Seventh French Cuirassiers* (Lumière film, 1896).
DESCRIPTION: In the distance is seen a number of grey objects rapidly approaching, which, upon drawing closer, are recognized as a company of Boer cavalry. As they draw nearer, you can see that they are straining every nerve and urging their horses to the utmost speed. Waving their sabres aloft on they come, so that the audience involuntarily makes an effort to move from their seats in order to avoid being trampled under the horses. (*Edison Films*, July 1901, 28.)
SUBJECT: South African War, 1899-1902. Cavalry. National Guard–New Jersey.
ARCHIVE: DLC-pp.
CITATIONS: *New York Clipper*, 21 April 1900, 184.
NOTE:

INJURED IN SHAM BATTLE
Two Men Wounded in a Reproduction of the Engagement at Spion Kop, in South Africa

Brick Church, N.J., April 11–Two men were injured this afternoon in West Orange at a sham battle in reproduction of the famous engagement at Spion Kop, in South Africa. James H. White, General Manager of the Edison projecting kinetoscope business, had arranged it. The scene was on the rocky side of the eastern slope of the second Orange Mountain, near the Livingstone line. About 200 men had been engaged, half of them in Boer costume posted on the top of the crest, while the remainder attired as British stormed the heights. A good sized cannon was used to heighten the effect and the kinetoscope was placed in a position to take the moving pictures. Through some blunder the cannon was discharged prematurely and Mr. White and one of the men, William McCarthy of 33 South street, Orange, were struck by the wad and burned by the powder. McCarthy's injuries were trivial, but Mr. White was badly lacerated as well as burned, and his condition tonight is reported as serious. (*Philadelphia Ledger*, 12 April 1900, clipping, NjWOE.)

805 ***Battle of Mafeking**
LENGTH: 75 ft.   © Thomas A. Edison, 28 April 1900.
PRODUCER: James White, Mason Mitchell.
CAMERA:
CAST:

PRODUCTION DATE: 15-24 April 1900.

LOCATION: Orange Mountains, West Orange, N.J.

SOURCE:

DESCRIPTION: This scene shows the Boers attacking the British; and after surrounding and killing the greatest part of them, they capture the remainder. (*New York Clipper*, 12 May 1900, 260.)

In the opening of this picture we see in the foreground a company of Highlanders preparing for a charge on the Boer entrenchments seen in the distance. Just in advance of the Highlanders, two pieces of artillery have just been placed in position, and these immediately open fire upon the enemy. After several volleys from the battery, the Highlanders charge. They only reach a point just in advance of the battery, when they are attacked on the flank by a troop of Boer Cavalry, who come on the scene riding like madmen. All the Artillerymen fall about their guns except one, who runs to join the Highlanders but is brought to earth by a shot from one of the Cavalrymen. The Boers close with the Highlanders and a hand to hand fight is waged, in which the smoke becomes so thick that it is difficult to distinguish Boer from Briton. A Cavalryman is seen to fall mortally wounded from his horse, who walks off the field with an empty saddle. This is a very exciting picture. (*Edison Films*, July 1901, 29-30.)

SUBJECT: South African War, 1899-1902. National Guard–New Jersey. Historical reenactments. Battles. Artillery. Cavalry.

ARCHIVE: DLC-pp.

CITATIONS:

NOTE:

806 ***English Lancers Charging / English Lancers Charging at Modder River***

LENGTH: 75 ft. © Thomas A. Edison, 28 April 1900.

PRODUCER: James White, Mason Mitchell.

CAMERA:

CAST:

PRODUCTION DATE: 15-24 April 1900.

LOCATION: Orange Mountains, West Orange, N.J.

SOURCE:

DESCRIPTION: This scene shows the British Infantry and Cavalry attacking the Boers and being repulsed. Very stirring. (*New York Clipper*, 12 May 1900, 260.)

The stubborn resistance of the Boers is shown by the activity and persistency with which they fire the two large field pieces immediately in the foreground. It seems, indeed, a hopeless matter to attempt to capture and overthrown such an invulnerable position. The British lancers are seen advancing, urged on by their officers, with the Royal colors flying in the air. They press the battery of Boers with such vigor that before the position is surrendered, there is scarcely a handful left to retreat, the remainder lying dead and wounded on the battle field. This picture is full of action and very exciting. (*Edison Films*, July 1901, 29.)

SUBJECT: South African War, 1899-1902. National Guard–New Jersey. Historical reenactments. Battles. Cavalry. Artillery.

ARCHIVE: DLC-pp.

CITATIONS:

NOTE:

807 ***Red Cross Ambulance on the Battlefield**
LENGTH: 100 ft.   © Thomas A. Edison, 28 April 1900.
PRODUCER: James White, Mason Mitchell.
CAMERA:
CAST:
PRODUCTION DATE: 15-24 April 1900.
LOCATION: Orange Mountains, West Orange,
   N.J.
SOURCE:
DESCRIPTION: Near the center of this scene we
   see the regimental surgeon directing the
   movements of the Ambulance Corps.
   Tenderly they pick up the unfortunates and
   place them in the ambulance. The numbers
   disabled show that the battle has been a

hot one, and many a poor fellow, if he survives his injuries, will carry to his grave
the scars honorably acquired in his country's cause. (*Edison Films*, July 1901, 29.)
SUBJECT: South African War, 1899-1902. National Guard–New Jersey. Red Cross. Battles.
ARCHIVE: DLC-pp.
CITATIONS:
NOTE:

808 ***Boer Commissary Train Treking**
LENGTH: 25 ft.   © Thomas A. Edison, 28 April 1900.
PRODUCER: James White, Mason Mitchell.
CAMERA:
CAST:
PRODUCTION DATE: 15-24 April 1900.
LOCATION: Orange Mountains, West Orange,
   N.J.
SOURCE:
DESCRIPTION: Shows a Boer supply wagon train
   escorted by cavalry marching down a
   mountain road. (*New York Clipper*, 12 May
   1900, 260.)
   In this picture we see one very important
   adjunct to any well conducted siege. The
   teams are straining at their traces, in order
to move the heavily loaded wagons over the rough roads through the country. It is a
successful General who always manages to keep his commissary department close
to his men, as he may as well give up the struggle as to attempt to fight on short
rations or without ammunition. (*Edison Films*, July 1901, 29.)
SUBJECT: South African War, 1899-1902. National Guard–New Jersey. Cavalry. Transportation, military.
ARCHIVE: DLC-pp.
CITATIONS:
NOTE:

Fake Pictures
False Bearded Boers Meet Buller's Troops—Armies Struck
for $2—Kinetoscope Men Yielded—There'll Be Some Truly Moving Pictures

"Boys," yelled "Jimmy" Burns, who, as Gen. Botha, led the Boer Commando at the battle of Colenso; "boys, are
you dollar and a quarter soldiers?"
"Not by a darned sight!" chorused the braves who were fighting for liberty.
"My force won't move a step under $2," shouted Gen. Butler, waving his sword.
Whereupon the Boer and English armies fraternized and the kinetoscope men, completely routed, agreed to pay
each of the 200 fighters $2 for his day's realistic work.
The kinetoscope men have been making truly moving pictures of the Boer war in Jersey. The battle of Colenso had
been again set when the soldiers, 100 on a side, struck for a raise of 75 cents and got it. This was the second

attempt at the now historic struggle. At the first, a few days ago, a real cannon exploded, wounded two men and scared so many others that the battle was necessarily postponed.

The armies are drawn up on the veldt, Tom Vincent's farm, and for three hours there was murderous slaughter on the kops, two of the Orange Mountains that shadow the farm. Whenever the kinetoscope machine stopped, the dead men, whose pictures will draw tears from New York audiences, got up and went at it again.

A costumer had uniformed the British soldiers as Highlanders and Fusiliers. Some dragoons and lancers were mounted on Vincent's horses. The Boers wore khaki, and a wigmaker provided them with what he called the "real Boer beards." When the fighting got hot some of the Boers took off their beards.

Mason Mitchell, the actor, who fought with Roosevelt's Rough Riders, had rehearsed the armies. The Boers did not drop dead fast enough to please Mr. Mitchell.

"Here, you, drop dead, d'ye hear," Mr. Mitchell shouted at an (Orange) Free State man, who ambushed behind a kraal which looked much like a pig sty.

"Thought you wanted to make it look like the real scrap," retorted the Free Stater, who is an Irishman.

After two hours Englishmen and Boers got tired and the mortality was frightful. Mr. Mitchell got them on their feet and shouted the command:

"Charge Boers, charge! Put on your beards and keep them on!"

The only real casualty was to Gen. Buller's horse. A too-enthusiastic Boer thrust his bayonet into the horse's flank, which promptly threw Buller over its head. (*The Phonoscope*, April 1900, 9.)

Mason Mitchell.

This well known and highly esteemed actor, manager and soldier is at present a star of the first magnitude upon the vaudeville stage. He enlisted in the late war with Col. Roosevelt's Rough Riders, and while gallantly fighting was among the wounded. He is now giving illustrated recitals of personal experiences in the battles of Las Guisamas and Santiago, and his eloquence never fails to arouse among his audiences the utmost enthusiasm. (*New York Clipper*, 1 October 1898, 521.)

809 **Panoramic View of Newport / Panoramic View of Newport, R.I.*
LENGTH: 75 ft.   © Thomas A. Edison, 12 May 1900.
PRODUCER: James White.
CAMERA:
CAST:
PRODUCTION DATE: Late April to early May 1900.
LOCATION: Newport, R.I.
SOURCE:
DESCRIPTION: Possibly the sensation of the flight of a bird can be nearest realized by being on deck of one of the U.S. Government's fleet torpedo boats racing at its highest speed through the water. This picture was taken under these conditions and shows the beautiful scenery comprising the

harbor of Newport, R.I. In the foreground, the spray of the vessel and the form of the water gives a fair idea of the rapidity at which this boat is moving. In the distance can be seen the wharves and shipping, including the large steamers that ply between New York and Boston. Various other objects can be seen passing the rear, and the busy motion of the men on the deck and the immense volumes of smoke escaping from the funnels all add life and energy to this picture. (*Edison Films*, July 1901, 26.)
SUBJECT: Navies–United States. Harbors–Newport.
ARCHIVE: DLC-pp.
CITATIONS: *New York Clipper*, 19 May 1900, 284.
NOTE:

810 **Discharging a Whitehead Torpedo/ Discharging Whitehead Torpedoes / Discharging a Torpedo*
LENGTH: 75 and 100 ft.   © Thomas A. Edison, 12 May 1900.
PRODUCER: James White.
CAMERA:

CAST:
PRODUCTION DATE: Late April to early May 1900.
LOCATION: Newport, R.I.
SOURCE:
DESCRIPTION: This picture was taken on board
the U.S. torpedo boat "Morris," and it
shows the crew placing a Whitehead torpedo into the tube, discharging the torpedo,
which falls into the water with a big splash,
runs out like an enormous whale for a distance of over half a mile and explodes in fifteen fathoms of water, throwing up a volume of water, mud and rocks, for a distance

of over 500 feet in the air. It is a most realistic picture, full of exciting action.
We can supply a 75 Foot Print of this scene, but it does not show the torpedo
exploding. (*New York Clipper*, 19 May 1900, 284.)
SUBJECT: Navies–United States. Torpedo boats. Torpedoes.
ARCHIVE: DLC-pp.
CITATIONS: *Edison Films,* July 1901, 27.
NOTE:

811 *Exploding a Whitehead Torpedo
LENGTH: 25 ft.   © Thomas A. Edison, 12 May 1900.
PRODUCER: James White.
CAMERA:
CAST:
PRODUCTION DATE: Late April to early May 1900.
LOCATION: Newport, R.I.
SOURCE:
DESCRIPTION: The torpedo was exploded in fif-
teen fathoms of water. The picture shows
the water, mud and rocks being thrown
high up in the air, and will give an idea of
the destructiveness of one of these missiles.
We furnish this with the above picture as a
100 foot strip (Uncritical) at the net price of
$15.00. (*Edison Films,* July 1901, 27.)
SUBJECT: Navies–United States. Torpedoes.
ARCHIVE: DLC-pp.
CITATIONS: *New York Clipper*, 19 May 1900, 284.
NOTE:

**812 *Torpedo Boat "Morris" Running / Torpedo Boat "Morris" Running under
Full Speed / U.S. Torpedo Boat "Morris" Running at Full Speed**
LENGTH: 75 ft.   © Thomas A. Edison, 12 May 1900.
PRODUCER: James White.
CAMERA:
CAST:
PRODUCTION DATE: Late April to early May 1900.
LOCATION: Newport, R.I.
SOURCE:
DESCRIPTION: This scene was taken at
Newport, R.I., and shows this wonderful
torpedo boat running at the rate of thirty
miles an hour. When the boat came in front
of the camera it discharged a gigantic
Whitehead torpedo, which is seen to dive
into the water like an enormous fish.
(*Edison Films,* July 1901, 27.)

SUBJECT: Navies–United States. Torpedo boats. Torpedoes.
ARCHIVE: DLC-pp.
CITATIONS: *New York Clipper*, 19 May 1900, 284.
NOTE:

The Road Drivers Association organized a demonstration of horse owners as a display of strength, and as a visual refutation of the notion that automobiles were the wave of the future. Certainly the horse-drawn vehicles far outnumbered the cars assembled by the Automobile Club of America for its parade on November 4th of the previous year, also filmed by William Paley (Automobile Parade, no. 767). Nevertheless, this marshalling of supporters did nothing to slow the emergence of the automobile as the favored form of private transportation.

813 **Roaddrivers' Association Parade / Parade on N.Y. Speedway May 5, 1900 / Parade on the Speedway**
LENGTH: 50, 100, 150, 200, 275 or 300 ft.   © No reg.
PRODUCER: William Paley.
CAMERA: William Paley.
CAST:
PRODUCTION DATE: 5 May 1900.
LOCATION: Speedway, New York, N.Y.
SOURCE:
DESCRIPTION: Taken on New York's famous speedway on Saturday May 5, showing all the famous fast horses of New York City and vicinity walking and trotting by our cameras. The horses and drivers show up full life size and present a remarkably fine spectacle. (*New York Clipper*, 19 May 1900, 284.)
SUBJECT: Parades. Carriages and carts. Horses. Social elites. Road Drivers' Association of New York.
ARCHIVE:
CITATIONS: *New York Clipper*, 12 May 1900, 260; *Edison Films*, July 1901, 56.
NOTE: Two days after this parade, Paley was showing this film in Proctor's theaters with his kalatechnoscope service (*New York World*, 6 May 1900). The following week the Kinetograph Company was exhibiting the film at Huber's Museum.

814 **Racing on N.Y. Speedway May 5, 1900**
LENGTH: 150 ft.   © No reg.
PRODUCER: William Paley.
CAMERA: William Paley.
CAST:
PRODUCTION DATE: 5 May 1900.
LOCATION: Speedway, New York, N.Y.
SOURCE:
DESCRIPTION:
SUBJECT: Parades. Carriages and carts. Horses. Road Drivers' Association of New York.
ARCHIVE:
CITATIONS: *New York Clipper*, 12 May 1900, 260.
NOTE:

FIRST SPEEDWAY PARADE VIEWED BY THRONGS
MILLION AND A HALF IN HORSES ON PARADE
Famous Racers in Procession Six Miles Long Gayly Pass in
Review Up the Speedway Amid the Plaudits of Thousands of Spectators.
EIGHT HUNDRED VEHICLES DRAWN BY SLEEK ROADSTERS.
Steeds of Proud Pedigree and Wondrous Records Restrained by Skilful
Drivers Without a Serious Runaway or Accident to Mar the Day's Success.
GENERAL MILES, INCOGNITO, ALMOST ESCAPES DISCOVERY.

It was a great day for the horse—as distinctly his day as is that of the Derby or the Suburban Handicap, or the opening of the Horse Show. The first annual parade of road horses under the auspices of the Road Drivers' Association of New York, when it ended yesterday at five o'clock was pronounced the most brilliant spectacle in high bred, high priced horseflesh ever witnessed in America. It marked the apotheosis of the Harlem Speedway–that superb stretch three miles long and a hundred feet wide, the beauties of which are not yet known to thousands of New Yorkers.

It registered a living, moving protest–a protest six miles long and $1,500,000 strong–against the utilitarian cynic who professes to see in the whirring automobile the doom of the sleek roadster.

Thousands View the Procession.

When it was all over but the feasting, and Dr. H.H. Kane, president of the association, was being congratulated on the perfect success of the first parade, he announced that there had been eight hundred vehicles in line and that the total value of the horses alone was nearly a million and a half. Nothing approximating such an array has ever before been seen in this country. The procession took nearly an hour to pass a given point.

If evidence was needed to disprove the notion that the advent of electric, steam and gasoline motors has caused popular interest in the smooth limbed trotter or pacer to wane, the presence of eager thousands who lined Riverside Drive and the Speedway from start to finish, and stood in the cool wind until the last equine beauty had passed, was enough to dissipate that idea....(*New York Herald*, 6 May 1900, 5.)

---

815 ***Panorama of Gorge Railway / Panoramic View of the Gorge Railroad**

LENGTH: 100 ft.   © Thomas A. Edison, 26 May 1900.

PRODUCER: James White.

CAMERA:

CAST:

PRODUCTION DATE: May 1900.

LOCATION: Niagara Falls, N.Y.

SOURCE: *Niagara Falls, Gorge* (Edison film no. 163, June 1896).

DESCRIPTION: One of the most interesting places in the vicinity of Niagara Falls is the Whirlpool Rapids, where the immense volume of water which passes from the Falls, speeds along through its rocky and tortuous passage towards the ocean. The camera in securing this picture was placed at the front end of a train ascending the grade at a very rapid rate of speed. The combined motion of the train in one direction and the water in the opposite direction, the latter impeded and interrupted in its course by the rocky path through which it flows, sending beautiful masses of spray and foam many feet in the air, makes an impression on the audience long to be remembered. (*Edison Films*, July 1901, 95.)

SUBJECT: Rivers. Waterfalls. Railroads. Niagara Falls.

ARCHIVE: DLC-pp.

CITATIONS: *New York Clipper*, 19 May 1900, 284.

NOTE:

---

816 **Niagara Falls from the Brink of the Horseshoe**

LENGTH: 75 ft.   © No reg.

PRODUCER: James White.

CAMERA:

CAST:

PRODUCTION DATE: May 1900.

LOCATION: Niagara Falls, N.Y.

SOURCE:

DESCRIPTION:

SUBJECT: Waterfalls. Niagara Falls.

CITATIONS: *New York Clipper*, 7 July 1900, 428.

ARCHIVE:

NOTE:

---

817 ***New Black Diamond Express / [Black Diamond Express, no. 4]**

LENGTH: 50 or 60 ft.   © Thomas A. Edison, 26 May 1900.

PRODUCER: James White.
CAMERA:
CAST:
PRODUCTION DATE: May 1900.
LOCATION: Near Towanda, Pa.
SOURCE: *Black Diamond Express* (Edison film no. 262, December 1896).
DESCRIPTION: This picture was taken at one of the curves on the Lehigh Valley Railroad, along the beautiful Susquehanna River. The train is seen rapidly approaching in the distance, clearly outlined against the grey mountains. Smoke can be seen pour-

ing in volumes from the stack of the locomotive, and as the train approaches closely, she sounds a whistle, warning some section men, who are working on the tracks in the foreground. As she rushes by the camera, the swing motion of the train gives a vivid idea of the lightning speed at which she is traveling. (*Edison Films,* July 1901, 94.)
SUBJECT: Railroads. Rivers. Mountains. Lehigh Valley Railroad. Susquehanna River.
ARCHIVE: DLC-pp.
CITATIONS: *New York Clipper*, 19 May 1900, 284.
NOTE:

James White worked with the New York City Board of Education to take films of school-day activities for the Paris Exposition of 1900. Production involved the careful synchronization of recorded sound and pictures—students performing for the camera while the pre-recorded sound was being played. This was one of at least four attempts to present synchronous sound at the Exposition.

818   A Ride Through the Gheto [sic] / [A Ride Through the Ghetto]
LENGTH: © No reg.
PRODUCER: James White, Alfred T. Schauffler.
CAMERA:
CAST:
PRODUCTION DATE: [May 1900.]
LOCATION: New York, N.Y.
SOURCE:
DESCRIPTION:
SUBJECT: City and town life–New York. Immigrants. Urban transportation. Motion pictures–sound. Board of Education of the City of New York.
ARCHIVE:
CITATIONS:
NOTE:

819   School Assembly, Foreign Children
LENGTH: © No reg.
PRODUCER: James White, Alfred T. Schauffler.
CAMERA:
CAST:
PRODUCTION DATE: [May 1900.]
LOCATION: New York, N.Y.
SOURCE:
DESCRIPTION:
SUBJECT: Schools–Exercises and recreations. Children. Immigrants. Motion pictures–sound. Board of Education of the City of New York.
ARCHIVE:
CITATIONS:
NOTE:

820 Dismissal to the Class Rooms
LENGTH: © No reg.
PRODUCER: James White, Alfred T. Schauffler.
CAMERA:
CAST:
PRODUCTION DATE: [May 1900.]
LOCATION: New York, N.Y.
SOURCE:
DESCRIPTION:
SUBJECT: Schools–Exercises and recreations. Children. Motion pictures–sound. Board of Education of the City of New York.
ARCHIVE:
CITATIONS:
NOTE:

821 Kindergarten games
LENGTH: © No reg.
PRODUCER: James White, Alfred T. Schauffler.
CAMERA:
CAST:
PRODUCTION DATE: [May 1900.]
LOCATION: New York, N.Y.
SOURCE:
DESCRIPTION:
SUBJECT: Schools–Exercises and recreations. Children. Games. Motion pictures–sound. Board of Education of the City of New York.
ARCHIVE:
CITATIONS:
NOTE:

822 Recess Games, Boys
LENGTH: © No reg.
PRODUCER: James White, Alfred T. Schauffler.
CAMERA:
CAST:
PRODUCTION DATE: [May 1900.]
LOCATION: New York, N.Y.
SOURCE:
DESCRIPTION:
SUBJECT: Schools–Exercises and recreations. Children. Boys. Games. Motion pictures–sound. Board of Education of the City of New York.
ARCHIVE:
CITATIONS:
NOTE:

823 Recess Games, Girls
LENGTH: © No reg.
PRODUCER: James White, Alfred T. Schauffler.
CAMERA:
CAST:
PRODUCTION DATE: [May 1900.]
LOCATION: New York, N.Y.
SOURCE:
DESCRIPTION:
SUBJECT: Schools–Exercises and recreations. Children. Girls. Games. Motion pictures–sound. Board of Education of the City of New York.
ARCHIVE:
CITATIONS:
NOTE:

824 A Workshop in Full Operation
LENGTH: © No reg.
PRODUCER: James White, Alfred T. Schauffler.
CAMERA:
CAST:
PRODUCTION DATE: [May 1900.]
LOCATION: New York, N.Y.
SOURCE:
DESCRIPTION:
SUBJECT: Schools. Motion pictures–sound. Board of Education of the City of New
    York.
ARCHIVE:
CITATIONS:
NOTE:

825 Classroom Gymnastics
LENGTH: © No reg.
PRODUCER: James White, Alfred T. Schauffler.
CAMERA:
CAST:
PRODUCTION DATE: [May 1900.]
LOCATION: New York, N.Y.
SOURCE:
DESCRIPTION:
SUBJECT: Schools–Exercises and recreations. Gymnastics. Motion pictures–sound.
    Board of Education of the City of New York.
ARCHIVE:
CITATIONS:
NOTE:

826 Grace Hoop Gymnastic Drill
LENGTH: © No reg.
PRODUCER: James White, Alfred T. Schauffler.
CAMERA:
CAST:
PRODUCTION DATE: [May 1900.]
LOCATION: New York, N.Y.
SOURCE:
DESCRIPTION:
SUBJECT: Schools–Exercises and recreations. Gymnastics. Motion pictures–sound.
    Board of Education of the City of New York.
ARCHIVE:
CITATIONS:
NOTE:

827 Rapid Dismissal to the Street
LENGTH: © No reg.
PRODUCER: James White, Alfred T. Schauffler.
CAMERA:
CAST:
PRODUCTION DATE: [May 1900.]
LOCATION: New York, N.Y.
SOURCE:
DESCRIPTION:
SUBJECT: Schools–Exercises and recreations. Motion pictures–sound. Board of
    Education of the City of New York.
ARCHIVE:
CITATIONS:
NOTE:

828   Ball Games. Football, etc.
LENGTH: © No reg.
PRODUCER: James White, Alfred T. Schauffler.
CAMERA:
CAST:
PRODUCTION DATE: [May 1900.]
LOCATION: New York, N.Y.
SOURCE:
DESCRIPTION:
SUBJECT: Schools–Exercises and recreations. Football. Sports. Motion pictures–sound. Board of Education of the City of New York.
ARCHIVE:
CITATIONS:
NOTE:

829   Assembly in an Uptown School
LENGTH: © No reg.
PRODUCER: James White, Alfred T. Schauffler.
CAMERA:
CAST:
PRODUCTION DATE: [May 1900.]
LOCATION: New York, N.Y.
SOURCE:
DESCRIPTION:
SUBJECT: Schools–Exercises and recreations. Motion pictures–sound. Board of Education of the City of New York.
ARCHIVE:
CITATIONS:
NOTE:

830   Rhythmic Ball Drill to Music
LENGTH: © No reg.
PRODUCER: James White, Alfred T. Schauffler.
CAMERA:
CAST:
PRODUCTION DATE: [May 1900.]
LOCATION: New York, N.Y.
SOURCE:
DESCRIPTION:
SUBJECT: Schools–Exercises and recreations. Motion pictures–sound. Board of Education of the City of New York.
ARCHIVE:
CITATIONS:
NOTE:

831   Cooking Class in Operation
LENGTH: © No reg.
PRODUCER: James White, Alfred T. Schauffler.
CAMERA:
CAST:
PRODUCTION DATE: [May 1900.]
LOCATION: New York, N.Y.
SOURCE:
DESCRIPTION:
SUBJECT: Schools–Exercises and recreations. Food. Kitchens. Motion pictures–sound. Board of Education of the City of New York.
ARCHIVE:
CITATIONS:
NOTE:

832 **Marching Salute to the Flag**
LENGTH: © No reg.
PRODUCER: James White, Alfred T. Schauffler.
CAMERA:
CAST:
PRODUCTION DATE: [May 1900.]
LOCATION: New York, N.Y.
SOURCE:
DESCRIPTION:
SUBJECT: Schools–Exercises and recreations. Flags–United States. Motion pictures–sound. Board of Education of the City of New York.
ARCHIVE:
CITATIONS:
NOTE:

833 **Indian Club Swinging, High School Girls**
LENGTH: © No reg.
PRODUCER: James White, Alfred T. Schauffler.
CAMERA:
CAST:
PRODUCTION DATE: [May 1900.]
LOCATION: New York, N.Y.
SOURCE:
DESCRIPTION:
SUBJECT: Schools–Exercises and recreations. Girls. Sports. Gymnastics. Motion pictures–sound. Board of Education of the City of New York.
ARCHIVE:
CITATIONS:
NOTE:

Our Foreign Correspondence

Paris Exposition, June 29th, 1900.
Editor of The Phonoscope:
A new, novel and instructive entertainment was shown for the first time to-day in Hall C of the Social Economy Palace. Over 500 invitations were sent out to the complete jury; the representation lasted fully an hour and comprised the following scenes:

      1.–A ride through the Gheto.
      2.–School assembly, foreign children.
      3.–Dismissal to the class rooms.
      4.–Kindergarten games.
      5.–Recess games, boys.
      6.– " " girls.
      7.–A workshop in full operation.
      8.–Classroom gymnastics.
      9.–Grace hoop gymnastic drill.
      10.–Rapid dismissal to the street.
      11.–Ball games. Foot ball, etc.
      12.–Assembly in an uptown school.
      13.–Rhythmic ball drill to music.
      14.–Cooking class in operation.
      15.–Marching salute to the flag.
      16.–Indian club swinging, High School girls.

Such activity as could be shown–New York schools by moving pictures. The pictures were made by the Edison Manufacturing Company under the supervision of Mr. James H. White, Manager of the Film Department. The scenes were prepared under the direction of the Associate Superintendent, Mr. A.T. Schauffler of New York City. The Board of Education of the City of New York has spared no expense in making this exhibit, which is the only exhibit of its kind on this elaborate scale at the Paris Exposition. The most novel and original feature of the exhibit is the combination of the Phonograph with the Projectoscope. This makes possible the reproduction not only of the movements of the children, but of their voices in recitation and songs, as well as of the music to which they perform their evolutions and gymnastic exercises. The Board of Education has sent over Mr. A.T. Schauffler, who shortly will be relieved by Supt. J.H. Haaren of Brooklyn, N.Y., and they are assisted by Mr. G.D. Adams as operator, of San Francisco, Cal. The Phonograph was kindly loaned by Mr. Kaiser, who is in charge of the Edison exhibit. Mr. White of the Edison works was present yesterday at the first rehearsal and pronounced same a grand success. G.L. (*The Phonoscope*, April 1900, 9.)

James White was one of several men interested in filming the eclipse. His efforts were probably not successful. If he did exhibit the results, accounts of such an event have yet to be located.

834 [Eclipse]
LENGTH: © No reg.
PRODUCER: James White.
CAMERA:
CAST:
PRODUCTION DATE: 28 May 1900.
LOCATION: Virginia Beach, Va.
SOURCE:
DESCRIPTION:
SUBJECT: Solar eclipses. Sun
ARCHIVE:
CITATIONS: "Natives in a Frenzy Over Queer Darkness," *New York World*, 28 May 1900, 1; "President Saw Eclipse Through Smoked Glass and Smudged His Nose," *New York World*, 29 May 1900, 2.
NOTE:

Took Views of the Eclipse
James H. White, general manager of the kinetoscope department of the Edison laboratory, went to Virginia Beach, near Norfolk, on Sunday and took a series of pictures of Monday's solar eclipse. He had a specially prepared apparatus consisting of a telephoto lens of thirty inches focal length, that produced an image 3-16 of an inch in diameter on the lens of a short focus objective. The latter threw up the image on the sensitized film to 5/8 of inch in diameter. Mr. White made a number of exposures of a minute duration each, showing the first and last contacts, the totality and other phases of the eclipse. The pictures of the totality were remarkably fine and showed the corona and chromosphere with the different phenomena that have so puzzled scientists. The pictures were taken at the rate of about 25 a second, and the actual exposure was 1 100th of a second. (*Orange Chronicle*, 2 June 1900, 7.)

The Total Eclipse of the Sun TOMORROW.
The eclipse at New York enters its first phase at 7.53 A.M. and ends at 10:28 A.M., local mean time. There will be only a partial—or nine-tenths eclipse at this point.
The shadow will be about seventy miles wide and will move at varying speed, but always many miles per minute.
The entire duration of the eclipse throughout its course—from the Pacific Ocean to Upper Egypt—will be five hours and twenty-three minutes.
BY W.B. NORTHROP.
TO-MORROW, for the first time in many years a total eclipse of the sun will take place which will be visible over a considerable part of the United States. There will not be another eclipse of the same character in the same region for eighteen years and twelve days. (*New York World*, Sunday Magazine, 27 May 1900, 1.)

SUN'S TOTAL ECLIPSE, MOST REMARKABLE ON RECORD,
Observed by Astronomers with Instruments of Unprecedented Power,
CASTS SIX GREAT STATES INTO SOMBRE DARKNESS.
ASTRONOMERS DESCRIBE PHENOMENON FOR THE WORLD.
...NORFOLK, Va., May 28.–The observations of the eclipse were made by members of the Hartford Scientific Society's expedition under ideal conditions. About one minute before totality the sky became a purple hue. At the instant of totality the corona appeared and remained almost absolutely uniform in intensity throughout the entire totality. It was of the shape predicted by Prof. Bigelow of Washington. The greatest extension of the corona was toward the west and its length was about two degrees. The brush of light extending farthest from the sun was on the upper side of the corona and stopped about one quarter of a degree short of Mercury. The polar filaments were short, not more than a quarter of a degree in length, but were visible to the naked eye. The extension of the corona

below the sun was less than that above, being not more than three-fifths as great. Mercury was a very conspicuous object just west of the sun. Venus was distinctly visible. No stars of lower magnitude than the first were observed by our party. LEWIS W. RIPLEY Secretary, Hartford Scientific Society. (*New York World,* 29 May 1900, 1-2.)

835 ***High Diving by A.C. Holden / High Diving Scene by Arthur C. Holden, Champion High Diver and Water Exhibitor of the World**
LENGTH: 90 or 100 ft.   © Thomas A. Edison, 20 June 1900.
PRODUCER: [James White.]
CAMERA:
CAST: Arthur C. Holden.
PRODUCTION DATE: Late May to mid-June 1900.
LOCATION: Vailsburg, N.J.
SOURCE:

DESCRIPTION: This picture was secured at the popular bicycle race track at Vailsburg, N.J., where Mr. Holden gave an exhibition of his wonderful skill and judgement before several thousand spectators. In the beginning of the scene Mr. Holden is discovered poised on his lofty perch over the water, preparing to make his first plunge, in which he describes a symmetrical curve, descending like a shot and entering the water as straight as an arrow, throwing the spray high in the air. Mr. Holden included four distinct dives in this picture, including a backward double somersault. The tank is surrounded by some of Mr. Holden's athletic comrades, who cheer when he accomplishes this extremely hazardous and successful feat. (*Edison Films,* July 1901, 45.)
SUBJECT: Aquatic sports. Diving. Swimming pools.
ARCHIVE: DLC-pp.
CITATIONS: *New York Clipper,* 7 July 1900, 428.
NOTE:

JUMPED FROM A FERRYBOAT.
Young Man Anxious for Notoriety Was Fished Out and Locked Up in Jersey City.

As the Pennsylvania ferryboat St. Louis was nearing its slip at Twenty-third Street yesterday afternoon, on its 4:25 o'clock trip from Jersey City, a man, clad only in his undergarments and shoes, dashed from behind a wagon in the carriageway, clambered over the rear guard rail, and plunged into the river. He was picked up by the tugboat Municipal of the New York Dock Department and carried to Jersey City.

In the pockets of the clothing the man had left in the carriageway of the ferryboat papers were found showing that he was A.C. Holden of 116 West Sixty-first Street, this city. An ambulance surgeon's badge and hatband from Roosevelt Hospital were also found. Holden said that he was at one time employed as a diamond cutter at Wanamaker's, but left after the holiday trade was over. Regarding the ambulance surgeon's badge and hatband he explained that he hurt his wrist on New Year's Day, and was sent to the Roosevelt Hospital. While there he found the things, and put them in his pocket. He had forgotten all about them. He denied that he had attempted to commit suicide, and asserted that his only motive was to prove that he could stay in the water longer than Donovan. He added that though he boarded at 116 West Sixty-first Street, New York, his home was at 43 Monmouth Street. He was locked up for the night in a cell at Gregory Street Police Station.

Mrs. Bonner, who occupies the fifth floor of 116 West Sixty-first Street, where Holden had a room, stated last night that the young man was steady in his habits, and there was nothing to indicate that he was not well balanced mentally. He left there about four weeks ago, but had appeared in the house about a week ago with his arm in a sling.

NEWARK, N.J., Jan. 11.–Arthur C. Holden, who jumped from the ferryboat St. Louis, appears to be anxious to attain notoriety of some kind. A few months ago he leaped from the Midland Bridge near Belleville into the Passaic River. He also wanted to leap from the Brooklyn Bridge. At another time he telegraphed to his parents here from New York that while performing in Pastor's Theatre in New York, he had fallen and broken an arm. Two or three times the ambulances and patrol wagons of this city have been called to pick up suicides in the parks and streets of this city only to find it was Holden and that he was faking. (*New York Times,* 12 January 1898, 4.)

836 ***Watermelon Contest / New Watermelon Contest**
LENGTH: 50, 100, and 150 ft.   © Thomas A. Edison, 28 June 1900.

PRODUCER: James White.
CAMERA:
CAST:
PRODUCTION DATE: June 1900.
LOCATION:
SOURCE:
DESCRIPTION: This subject shows four colored chaps eating watermelon on a wager. The interest becomes very intense as the test proceeds, and the finish is a very close one. Fine effect when colored. (*Edison Films*, July 1901, 71.)

SUBJECT: Watermelons. Afro-Americans. Contests–food. Motion pictures–colored.
ARCHIVE: DLC-pp.
CITATIONS: *New York Clipper*, 7 July 1900, 428.
NOTE: Maximum length of 140 ft. was given in *Edison Films*, July 1901, 71.

837 *****Bombardment of Taku Forts / Bombardment of Taku Forts by the Allied Fleets**
LENGTH: 100 ft.   © Thomas A. Edison, 16 August 1900.
PRODUCER:
CAMERA:
CAST:
PRODUCTION DATE: Ca. 19 June 1900.
LOCATION:
SOURCE:
DESCRIPTION: A wonderful and realistic naval battle. (*New York Clipper,* 1 September 1900, 604.)

The scene opens by showing the battleships maneuvering for a position. They finally draw up in line of battle and commence firing on the shore batteries. Immense volume

of smoke arise from the fleet and from the distant shore. Shots are seen to fall thickly among the vessels and immense bodies of water are thrown up by the explosion of mines. A very exciting naval battle. (*Edison Films*, July 1901, 16.)
SUBJECT: Naval battles. Navies. China–History–Boxer Rebellion.
ARCHIVE: DLC-pp.
CITATIONS: "Warships Punish Chinese Defiance," *New York World*, 19 June 1900, 3. *New York Clipper*, 18 August 1900, 564.
NOTE: The bombardment of the forts occurred on 17 June 1900 and was a prominent but brief incident in the Boxer Rebellion. It seems probable that an Edison licensee made the film very shortly after the event, exploited the picture as an exclusive on its exhibition circuit and then turned over the negative to the Edison company.

CHINESE FORTS TAKEN BY THE ALLIED FLEETS.
The World's Hongkong Correspondent Cables That Taku Guns
Fired on Warships of Powers Without Warning.
TIENTSIN NATIVES SHELL THE FOREIGN QUARTERS.
Peking Legations Reported Captured and General Massacre of Ministers and Missionaries is Feared.
(Copyright 1900, by the Press Publishing Company, New York World.)
(Special Cable Despatch to The World.)

Hongkong, British China, June 18.
The Chinese forts at Taku, commanding the entrance to the Peiho River, opened fire upon the allied foreign fleets yesterday (Sunday) morning without warning.
The warships replied, silenced the Chinese guns, sent out landing parties and took possession of the forts.
The casualties of the allied forces in men were: Killed–1 Briton, 1 Frenchman, 3 Germans and 16 Russians. Total, 21.
Wounded–4 Britons, 1 Frenchman, 7 Germans and 45 Russians. Total, 57.
The British gunboat Algerine was damaged.
No news has been received from Admiral Seymour.

OREGON SHORT OF MEN.

The departure from Hongkong of the United States battle-ship Oregon has been delayed owing to a want of men, this ship's complement having been largely reduced by the drafts to make up crews for the new gunboats when they were put in commission.

The British warship Daphne, Commander Winnington-Ingram, left this afternoon for North China.

Two British East Indian regiments are coming to Hongkong to reinforce the garrison here.

LI HUNG CHANG BUYING MAUSERS.

Li Hung Chang, now the Viceroy of Canton, has purchased 700 stands of Mauser rifles at Macao.

400 CHINESE KILLED, 32 WARSHIPS ENGAGED.

LONDON, June 19–3:30 A.M.–China declared war against the world when the Taku forts opened fire upon the international fleet.

One despatch says that the Yorktown participated in the bombardment.

Another asserts that American marines formed part of the storming force of two thousand.

The substance of the special despatches is as follows.

The forts began firing in obedience to orders from Peking, conveyed in a personal edict of the Empress Dowager, by advice of Kang-Yi (President of the Ministry of War).

Several warships were struck by shells from the twelve-inch guns of the forts.

The heavy Russian losses were due to the blowing up of the magazine at Mandshur.

Four hundred Chinese are reported to have been killed.

The Chinese, when retreating, fell into the hands of the Russian land forces.

Two of the forts were blown up.

The thirty-two warships at Taku aggregated two hundred thousand tons and carried more than three hundred guns. The powers are taking prompt action. Four thousand German troops have been ordered to China; 10,000 French troops are waiting to embark at Saigon, capital of French Cochin-China, and from 3,000 to 5,000 more Russians have been ordered from Port Arthur to Taku. (*New York World*, 19 June 1900, 5.)

James White and an unidentified Edison cameraman associate (possibly Alfred C. Abadie) left New York, on the "Kaiserin Maria Theresia," 19 June 1900, bound for Europe and the Paris Exposition.

838 ***A Storm at Sea**

LENGTH: 100 ft.   © Thomas A. Edison, 9 August 1900

PRODUCER: James White.

CAMERA: [Alfred C. Abadie?]

CAST:

PRODUCTION DATE: 19-27 June 1900.

LOCATION: Atlantic Ocean.

SOURCE:

DESCRIPTION: While our photographers were crossing the Atlantic Ocean a most wonderful and sensational picture was secured, showing a storm at sea. The picture was secured by lashing the camera to the after bridge of the Kaiserine Maria Theresa [sic], of the North German Lloyd Line, during one of its roughest voyages. The most wonderful storm picture ever photographed. Taken at great risk. (*Edison Films*, July 1901, 16.)

SUBJECT: Oceans waves. Steamships. Storms. North German Lloyd Line.

ARCHIVE: DLC, DLC-pp.

CITATIONS: *New York Clipper*, 18 August 1900, 564.

NOTE:

839 ***Burning of the Standard Oil Tanks, Bayonne, N.J. / Destruction of Standard Oil Company's Plant at Bayonne, N.J., by Fire on July 5th, 1900**

LENGTH: 50, 100 and 150 ft.   © Thomas A. Edison, 12 July 1900.

PRODUCER

CAMERA:

CAST:
PRODUCTION DATE: 5 July 1900.
LOCATION: Bayonne, N.J.
SOURCE:
DESCRIPTION: This picture shows a street scene at Constable Hook, Bayonne, N.J. In the background rise immense volumes of dense black smoke from the burning oil, reaching high in the heavens. Outlined against this dense oil smoke is seen some of a lighter color. This is from the fire engines and from the houses of the unfortunate residents, whom we see fleeing before the destructive

march of this element of fire. Some of them are bringing out what remains of their homes, and they have pressed into service all manner of vehicles, men in some cases taking the place of horses. Some have saved so little that they can readily carry all that remains of their goods. (*Edison Films*, July 1901, 53.)

SUBJECT: Fire fighters. Fires. Oil. Standard Oil Company.
ARCHIVE: DLC-pp.
CITATIONS:
NOTE:

MILLIONS VANISH IN BLAZING OIL
Lightning Bolt Sets Aflame Twenty Standard Tanks at Constable Hook, N.J.
BAYONNE PANIC STRICKEN
Inhabitants Gather Up Their Belongings and, Urged by Fear, Flee to the Meadows.
A WEIRD SCENE PRESENTED
Three Million Dollars' Worth of Property Destroyed, Seven Men Injured and Four Missing.

Rising inky black to a height of three miles above the surface of New York Bay, a column of smoke yesterday drew all eyes to Constable Hook, Bayonne, N.J., where tanks of petroleum and valuable buildings owned by the Standard Oil Company were being rapidly consumed. The destruction of twenty tanks of inflammable fluids, together with various apparatus and machinery, represented a loss of nearly three million of dollars. Seven men were injured and four are reported as missing. The city of Bayonne was thrown several times into a panic by the fear that the flames would spread to the dwellings. This apprehension was increased by two more conflagrations in different parts of the city, which required a division of the feeble strength of the local fire department. On the waste of sterile meadows were piled the household goods of scores of families, who had been warned by the police to flee for their lives.

Constable Hook is a point of land which juts into the bay to the eastward from the New Jersey shore, and with New Brighton guards the entrance of the Kill van Kull. Passengers who made the daily trip to and from St. George, S.I., will identify the place as one from which inky clouds and banks of the white vapor of chemicals are constantly rising. The Hook points, finger like, across the upper bay, in the direction of South Brooklyn. On this arid waste the Standard Oil Company years ago built oil tanks. There are piers where the lumbering tank steamers receive their cargoes of crude and refined oil for all the world. The tank yards gradually extended their limits, and along the shores of the Hook were built establishments for the manufacture of chemicals.

Most of the factories are purveyors to the great petroleum company. At the tip of the Hook are the crude oil docks. Along the Kill van Kull shore, going from the point to the west, are the works of the Columbia Oil Company, the Orford Copper Company, the Kalbfleisch Chemical Company, the French Oil Works, an abandoned factory, once owned by the C.T. Raynolds & Devoe Company; the Bergen Point Chemical Company and the Thomas White Sulphur Works. Fronting on the bay are the so-called "old yard" of the Standard Oil Company and the "new yard." Back of these are the rows of green tanks owned by the Tidewater Oil Company, an organisation closely affiliated with the Standard.

This region of fume and vapor is connected with the main part of the city of Bayonne, N.J., by East Twenty-second street. The area of the fire may be considered as bounded by East Twenty-second street and a spur of the New Jersey Central Railroad on one side and avenues I and J on the other.

Here was a place which a match or a cigar stump might have easily converted into a Tophet. The torch was applied by the lightning at half past twelve o'clock yesterday morning. The bolt struck tank No. 4, in the new yard, and travelled along the iron pipe connections to tanks 6 and 16. The three great sheet iron receptacles, ninety-five feet in diameter and thirty feet in height, became cauldrons, each seething a 35,000 barrel brew.

EXPLOSION OF THE TANKS.

They boiled and bubbled, while the watchmen fled from the premises. The burning tanks were so close to the great engine house and pumping station that it was impossible to transfer the contents of any of the contiguous tanks. Sheets of flame five hundred feet high shot into the air with deafening explosions as one by one the tanks blew up.

The flames ran along the ground and heated the sides of the neighboring tanks until they bubbled and seethed with the inflammable gases generated in their interiors. The fire ran down to the shores of the bay and caught the scum of oil which rested on the surface. The Standard Oil tugs dragged the ungainly steamers out of harm's way. The red glow brought Staten Islanders from their beds.

Livingston, New Brighton and Sailors' Snug Harbor passed a sleepless night. Bayonne arose and viewed the flames from its housetops. The rattle of engines and the shrieking of whistles were heard in the streets. The roof of tank No. 16 was lifted off by a terrific explosion, and landed on the top of a freight car fifty yards away. The waters of New York Bay caught the red flow, and there was etched against the leaden sky of the summer night the outlines of a black wreath, which widened and expanded like that evil genius in the Arabian tale which was inadvertently released from a bottle.

PANIC IN BAYONNE.

Bayonne had seen oil fires before, and it was not until seven o'clock yesterday morning that the New Jersey municipality awoke to the full danger of the conflagration. There came at seven o'clock a series of explosions. The fire increased in intensity. The Hungarians and Slavs, whose wooden dwellings, dry as tinder, line Twenty-second street near the yards, hastily packed up their goods and, incited by their own fear and the orders of the police, took to the meadows. There they piled their possessions and watched the progress of the fire.

As far as the Bayonne Fire Department was concerned, it did all that could be expected of five engine companies and one hook and ladder company. Its work was supplemented by the hose systems of the various oil and chemical companies. There were a hundred ineffectual streams playing upon the fire. Two more small fires made it necessary for two engines to be sent away. Hurry calls were sent out for the employees of all the companies to assemble.

The Tide Water Company dug trenches to stay the flood of burning oil in case the outer row of tanks should burst. Much of the attention of the fire fighters was bestowed upon a thirty thousand barrel tank of naphtha which bore the number 13. There were two more tanks of the volatile fluid further down the line.

By daylight there appeared above Constable Hook a great column. Its base was dull red flame, its shaft was smoke of inky blackness, and its capital was leaden hued vapor. William A. Eddy, who has for years been studying the atmosphere, found by a careful calculation, by triangulation, that the column was three miles high. The wind along the surface of the earth was northeast. Five hundred feet above the sea level the column drifted with an easterly current, and for two miles further up the expert noticed that the wind was northwest.

KING MAY BE ALIVE.

There were several narrow escapes. Mrs. Cummings kept a boarding house for workmen, known as the Bayview House. This building caught fire and the one hundred laborers fled in terror. Mrs. Cummings and her child narrowly escaped death in the flames. It was reported that Charles King, an electrician, had been killed by the bolt of lightning which struck the tanks. It is believed that he is alive. Those who were injured were John White, a fireman; John Crolles, fireman of an engine company; Owen Sullivan, a watchman; Frank Vetter, a laborer; John Divan, a laborer; John Washko, a watchman; and Frederick Mauer, a workman. None of them is seriously injured. Charles Ross, Charles King and the watchman, whose name the officials could not give yesterday, are on the roll of missing. Estimates given last night place the loss at less than $3,000,000. There were twenty tanks, which cost $12,000 apiece. They were each supposed to contain thirty-five thousand barrels of oil, valued at $2.10 a barrel. The contents of each tank would be worth $73,500. The loss of other property represents $1,000,000 more. This last item includes the engine house, paraffine works, compounding works and numerous pipe connections.

It is expected that the fire will burn for several days. The officials believed last night that they had it under control. There was no insurance, except that which the company carries itself in a special fund.

Three more tanks exploded last evening between the hours of seven and ten o'clock, and three employes of the Standard Oil Company's fire brigade were injured. They were taken to the Bayonnne Hospital. Their names could not be learned. (*New York Herald*, 6 July 1900, 1.)

Early in his European tour, James H. White and his fellow cameraman picked up a panning mechanism for their camera tripod, which allowed them to film scenes with sweeping camera movements. Also putting the kinetograph on moving platforms of various kinds, the Edison crew turned landscape into spectacle.

840 ***Champs Elysees / Driving Scene on the Champs Elysees**
LENGTH: 75 ft.   © Thomas A. Edison, 9 August 1900.
PRODUCER: James White.
CAMERA:
CAST:

PRODUCTION DATE: July 1900.
LOCATION: Champs Elysées, Paris, France.
SOURCE:
DESCRIPTION: Near the main entrance. Hundreds of carriages and characteristic Parisian busses are passing. (*Edison Films,* July 1901, 18.)
SUBJECT: City and town life–Paris. Urban transportation. Carriages and carts. Exhibitions. Paris Exposition of 1900.
ARCHIVE: DLC-pp.
CITATIONS: *New York Clipper*, 11 August 1900, 536; 18 August 1900, 564.
NOTE:

841 *Palace of Electricity / Circular Panoramic View of the Champs de Mars, [no. 1]
LENGTH: 50 ft.   © Thomas A. Edison, 9 August 1900.
PRODUCER: James White.
CAMERA:
CAST:
PRODUCTION DATE: July 1900.
LOCATION: Paris, France.
SOURCE:
DESCRIPTION: In the Exposition grounds with a close view of the Palace of Electricity. (*Edison Films, July 1901, 18.*)
SUBJECT: City and town life–Paris. Exhibitions. Paris Exposition of 1900.
ARCHIVE: DLC-pp.
CITATIONS: *New York Clipper*, 11 August 1900, 536; 18 August 1900, 564.
NOTE:

842 *Panorama of Eiffel Tower / Eiffel Tower, no. 1 / Panoramic View of the Eiffel Tower Taken from the Outside
LENGTH: 90 or 150 ft.   © Thomas A. Edison, 9 August 1900.
PRODUCER: James White.
CAMERA:
CAST: Lyman Howe.
PRODUCTION DATE: July 1900.
LOCATION: Paris, France.
SOURCE:
DESCRIPTION: The camera is slowly raised, thus showing all parts of this immense structure. The height is 980 ft. Then the camera is slowly lowered, showing the wide spreading base, measuring 380 ft. wide. The arch over the street has a span of 230 ft. This wonderful feat of engineering was completed in 1889. (*New York Clipper*, 11 August 1900, 536.)

Showing the entire height of this wonderful structure from the base of the dome and return, with the great Paris Exposition in the background, looking down Champs de Mars. A most realistic picture. (*Edison Films*, July 1901, 17.)
SUBJECT: Monuments. Exhibitions. Tour Eiffel (Paris, France). Paris Exposition of 1900.
ARCHIVE: DLC-pp.
CITATIONS:
NOTE: The earliest camera tilt (a vertical up-down movement) found in surviving Edison productions.

843 ***Panorama of Place de L'Opera / Place de L'Opera / Circular Panoramic View of the Place de L'Opera**
LENGTH: 75 ft.   © Thomas A. Edison, 9 August 1900.
PRODUCER: James White.
CAMERA:
CAST:
PRODUCTION DATE: July 1900.
LOCATION: Place de L'Opera, Paris, France.
SOURCE:

DESCRIPTION: The busiest square in all Paris. (*Edison Films*, July 1901, 18.)
SUBJECT: City and town life–Paris. Urban transportation.
ARCHIVE: DLC-pp.
CITATIONS: *New York Clipper*, 11 August 1900, 536; 18 August 1900, 564.
NOTE:

844 ***Scene from the Elevator Ascending Eiffel Tower / Scene from the Eiffel Tower, Ascending and Descending / Panoramic View from the Eiffel Tower, Ascending and Descending**
LENGTH: 125 and 200 ft.   © Thomas A. Edison, 9 August 1900.
PRODUCER: James White.
CAMERA:
CAST:
PRODUCTION DATE: July 1900.
LOCATION: Paris, France.
SOURCE:

DESCRIPTION: A marvelously clear picture from the top of the elevator of the Eiffel Tower during going up and coming down of the car. This wonderful tower is 1,000 feet in height, and the picture produces a most sensational effect. As the camera leaves the ground and rises to the top of the tower, the enormous white city opens out to the view of the astonished spectator. Arriving at the top of the tower, a bird's eye view of the Exposition looking toward the Trocadero, and also toward the Palace of Electricity, is made, and the camera begins its descent. The entire trip is shown on a 200-foot film. We furnish the ascent...in 125 foot film. (*Edison Films*, July 1901, 18.)

SUBJECT: City and town life–Paris. Monuments. Exhibitions. Paris Exposition of 1900. Tour Eiffel (Paris, France).
ARCHIVE: DLC-pp.
CITATIONS: *New York Clipper*, 11 August 1900, 536; 18 August 1900, 564.
NOTE: *Eiffel Tower, no. 2* and *Eiffel Tower, no. 3* (advertised in *New York Clipper*, 11 August 1900, 536) appear to be sections of this larger film.

845 ***Champs de Mars / Circular Panoramic View of the Champs de Mars, no. 2**
LENGTH: 135 ft.   © Thomas A. Edison, 9 August 1900.
PRODUCER: James White.
CAMERA:
CAST:
PRODUCTION DATE: July 1900.
LOCATION: Paris, France.
SOURCE:

DESCRIPTION: Shows all the prominent buildings on this thoroughfare, ending with a
close view of the base of the Eiffel Tower,
with the Trocadero Palace in the background. (*Edison Films*, July 1901, 18.)

SUBJECT: City and town life–Paris. Monuments. Exhibitions. Paris Exposition of
1900. Tour Eiffel (Paris, France).

ARCHIVE: DLC-pp.

CITATIONS:

NOTE:

846 Paris Exposition from the Trocadero Palace

LENGTH: 50 and 70 ft.   © No reg.

PRODUCER: James White.

CAMERA:

CAST:

PRODUCTION DATE: July 1900.

LOCATION: Paris, France.

SOURCE:

DESCRIPTION: Showing the immense crowds going up the Champs de Mars, with the
Eiffel Tower in the background. (*Edison Films*, July 1901, 17.)

SUBJECT: City and town life–Paris. Monuments. Exhibitions. Paris Exposition of 1900.
Tour Eiffel (Paris, France).

ARCHIVE:

CITATIONS: *New York Clipper*, 18 August 1900, 564.

NOTE: Possible alternate title for *Eiffel Tower from Trocadero Palace* (film no. 847).

847 *Eiffel Tower from Trocadero Palace / Eiffel Tower from Trocadero

LENGTH: 75 ft.   © Thomas A. Edison, 9 August 1900.

PRODUCER: James White.

CAMERA:

CAST:

PRODUCTION DATE: July 1900.

LOCATION: Paris, France.

SOURCE:

DESCRIPTION:

SUBJECT: Monuments. Exhibitions. Paris Exposition of 1900. Tour Eiffel (Paris, France).

ARCHIVE: DLC-pp.

CITATIONS: *New York Clipper*, 11 August 1900,
536.

NOTE:

**848 *Esplanade des Invalides / Circular Panoramic View of the Esplanade des
Invalides**

LENGTH: 100 ft.   © Thomas A. Edison,
9 August 1900.

PRODUCER: James White.

CAMERA:

CAST:

PRODUCTION DATE: July 1900.

LOCATION: Paris, France.

SOURCE:

DESCRIPTION: Beginning with the camera
pointing toward the Invalides entrance,
with the tomb of Napoleon in the background. The camera is slowly revolved until

it rests upon the new and beautiful bridge of Alexander III, showing the immense crowds entering the Exposition. (*Edison Films*, July 1901, 17.)
SUBJECT: City and town life–Paris. Monuments. Exhibitions. Bridges. Paris Exposition of 1900.
ARCHIVE: DLC-pp.
CITATIONS: *New York Clipper*, 11 August 1900, 536; 18 August 1900, 564.
NOTE:

849 *****Panorama of the Paris Exposition from the Seine / Paris Exhibition Viewed from the Seine / Paris Exposition Viewed from the Seine**
LENGTH: 75 and 375 ft.   © Thomas A. Edison, 9 August 1900.
PRODUCER: James White.
CAMERA:
CAST:
PRODUCTION DATE: July 1900.
LOCATION: Paris, France.
SOURCE:
DESCRIPTION: This panoramic scene is taken from a Seine steamboat and gives a rapid view of the banks of the river. The launch steams under six bridges and past the Street of Nations. The United States building is a prominent white domed structure, gay with national flags. The picture ends at the famous three million dollar bridge, the Point [sic] Alexander III.

We supply an excellent strip of the above film, showing the Street of Nations. (*Edison Films*, July 1901, 18-19.)
SUBJECT: City and town life–Paris. Bridges. Rivers. Riverboats. Exhibitions. Paris Exposition of 1900.
ARCHIVE: DLC-pp.
CITATIONS: *New York Clipper*, 11 August 1900, 536.
NOTE: The 75-foot selection from this film was entitled *Street of the Nations*.

850 *****Panorama of the Moving Boardwalk / Moving Sidewalk, no. 1 / Panorama of the Moving Sidewalk at the Paris Exposition / Panoramic View of the Moving Sidewalk at the Paris Exposition**
LENGTH: 100 ft.   © Thomas A. Edison, 9 August 1900.
PRODUCER: James White.
CAMERA:
CAST: Lyman Howe.
PRODUCTION DATE: July 1900.
LOCATION: Paris, France.
SOURCE:
DESCRIPTION: This picture was taken from the stationary platform, showing the rapidly moving board walk on the outer edge, which has a speed of five miles per hour; also shows the middle platform moving two and a-half miles per hour, the third being stationary. At interval there are upright posts to steady passengers passing from one platform to the other. By watching these uprights passing by the camera and passing each other, a good idea of the speed is obtained. The structure is crowded with passengers, some gliding by, standing still, other walking and running and stepping from one platform to the other. (*Edison Films*, July 1901, 17.)

SUBJECT: Exhibitions. Passenger conveyors. Paris Exposition of 1900.
ARCHIVE: DLC-pp.
CITATIONS: *New York Clipper*, 11 August 1900, 536; 18 August 1900, 564.
NOTE:

851 ***Panorama from the Moving Boardwalk / Moving Sidewalk, no. 2 / Panoramic View from the Moving Sidewalk at the Paris Exposition / Panorama from the Moving Sidewalk**
LENGTH: 100 ft.   © Thomas A. Edison, 9 August 1900.
PRODUCER: James White.
CAMERA:
CAST:
PRODUCTION DATE: July 1900.
LOCATION: Paris, France.
SOURCE:

DESCRIPTION: The camera is stationed on the middle walk of the Platform Mobile, as the French call it, and give further views and incidents of this Paris Exposition novelty. (*Edison Films*, July 1901, 17.)
SUBJECT: City and town life–Paris. Exhibitions. Passenger conveyors. Paris Exposition of 1900.
ARCHIVE: DLC-pp.
CITATIONS: *New York Clipper*, 11 August 1900, 536; 18 August 1900, 564.
NOTE:

852 ***Scene in the Swiss Village / Scene in the Swiss Village at the Paris Exposition / [Swiss Village, no. 1]**
LENGTH: 75 ft.   © Thomas A. Edison, 29 August 1900.
PRODUCER: James White.
CAMERA:
CAST:
PRODUCTION DATE: July 1900.
LOCATION: Paris, France.
SOURCE:

DESCRIPTION: The picture opens with a crowd of Swiss boys and girls dressed in native costumes, marching down the street in this very unique and picturesque village. Each happy and smiling face is clearly shown as they pass the camera. The scene ends by the boys and girls congregating in the square and dancing to the strains of an accordion played by one of the happy villagers. (*Edison Films*, July 1901, 19.)
SUBJECT: Swiss. Dancing. Exhibitions. Boys. Girls. Paris Exposition of 1900.
ARCHIVE: DLC-pp.
CITATIONS:
NOTE: According to Roland Casandey, this is the same Swiss village that was filmed by the Lumière camera at the Geneva Exposition of 1896.

853 ***Swiss Village, no. 2**
LENGTH: 100 and 50 ft.   © Thomas A. Edison, 29 August 1900.
PRODUCER: James White.
CAMERA:
CAST:
PRODUCTION DATE: July 1900.
LOCATION: Paris, France.
SOURCE:

DESCRIPTION: The scene opens by showing the village girls driving home a herd of cows, and shows the native peasantry of Switzerland returning from their daily occupation—watching the herds. After driving the cattle to their shelter, the boys and girls congregate in front of the old barn and go through a native dance, to the amusement of the spectators. These pictures are marvelously clear and distinct, showing every feature of the participants.
We can also furnish a strip fifty feet in length...showing the dance, or 50 feet, showing the girls driving the cattle. (*Edison Films*, July 1901, 19.)

SUBJECT: Swiss. Exhibitions. Boys. Girls. Cows. Paris Exposition of 1900.
ARCHIVE: DLC-pp.
CITATIONS:
NOTE:

854 *Panoramic View of the Champs Elysees

LENGTH: 75 ft.   © Thomas A. Edison, 29 August 1900.
PRODUCER: James White.
CAMERA:
CAST:
PRODUCTION DATE: July 1900.
LOCATION: Champs Elysées, Paris, France.
SOURCE:
DESCRIPTION:
SUBJECT: City and town life–Paris.
ARCHIVE: DLC-pp.
CITATIONS:
NOTE:

855 *Panoramic View of the Place de l'Concord [sic] / Panoramic View of Place de la Concorde

LENGTH: 100 ft.   © Thomas A. Edison, 29 August 1900.
PRODUCER: James White.
CAMERA:
CAST:
PRODUCTION DATE: July 1900.
LOCATION: Place de la Concorde, Paris, France.
SOURCE:
DESCRIPTION: Taken from an automobile. This picture was taken during the fashionable driving hour, making a complete circle of the Place de la Concorde, passing hundreds of carriages and busses. The beginning of the picture shows the historical church of the Madeleine in the background, the picture ending by approaching and running under the main entrance to the Paris Exposition. (*Edison Films*, July 1901, 18.)
SUBJECT: City and town life–Paris. Urban transportation. Automobiles. Church buildings. Paris Exposition of 1900.
ARCHIVE: DLC-pp.
CITATIONS:
NOTE:

856 Annual French Military Carousal
LENGTH: 50, 100 and 150 ft.   © No reg.
PRODUCER: James White.
CAMERA:
CAST:
PRODUCTION DATE: July 1900.
LOCATION: Paris, France.
SOURCE:
DESCRIPTION: This is made up of the army officers of France, mounted upon the best picked horses of the French Army. It shows them executing cavalry charges, hurdle jumping, wheeling, high kicking by picked horses, and cutting at heads with swords. (*Edison Films*, July 1901, 19.)
SUBJECT: Armies–France. Armies–officers. Cavalry.
ARCHIVE:
CITATIONS:
NOTE:

857 *Breaking of the Crowd at Military Review at Longchamps [sic] / Breaking up of the Crowd at Military Review at Long Champs
LENGTH: 50 ft.   © Thomas A. Edison, 29 August 1900.
PRODUCER: James White.
CAMERA:
CAST:
PRODUCTION DATE: July 1900.
LOCATION: Long Champs, Paris, France.
SOURCE:
DESCRIPTION: This picture shows thousands of people leaving their seats in the grand stand and going across the parade grounds toward Paris. A very sharp and clear picture. (*Edison Films*, July 1901, 19.)
SUBJECT: Armies–France. City and town life–Paris.
ARCHIVE: DLC-pp.
CITATIONS:
NOTE:

858 Scene on the Boulevard DeCapucines [sic] / Scene on the Boulevard des Capucines
LENGTH: 50 ft.   © No reg.
PRODUCER: James White.
CAMERA:
CAST:
PRODUCTION DATE: July 1900.
LOCATION: Paris, France.
SOURCE:
DESCRIPTION:
SUBJECT: City and town life–Paris.
ARCHIVE:
CITATIONS: *Edison Films*, July 1901, 19.
NOTE:

859 Street Scene at Place de la Concorde, Paris, France
LENGTH: 75 ft.   © No reg.
PRODUCER: James White.
CAMERA:
CAST:
PRODUCTION DATE: July 1900.
LOCATION: Paris, France.
SOURCE:

DESCRIPTION: Shows a troop of French Infantry marching down the street, followed by numbers of carriages and busses, with Tuilleries in the background. (*Edison Films*, July 1901, 19.)

SUBJECT: City and town life–Paris. Armies–France. Parades. Urban transportation.

ARCHIVE:

CITATIONS:

NOTE:

860 Arrival of Train at Paris Exposition

LENGTH: 50 ft.   © No reg.

PRODUCER: James White.

CAMERA:

CAST:

PRODUCTION DATE: July 1900.

LOCATION: Paris, France.

SOURCE:

DESCRIPTION: The scene opens at the Gare de Parre at the Paris Exposition grounds, and shows a long stream of cars drawn by a typical French engine steaming into the station. The train comes to a stop and hundreds of doors of the European compartment cars are opened. The multitudes of people of all nationalities pour out and start with a rush for the main gate of the Exposition. This picture was secured on one of the big days at the great Paris show and an immense crowd is clearly depicted leaving the cars, some of which are double deckers and very unique in construction. This is a typical European train scene, and was secured under most advantageous circumstances. (*Edison Films*, July 1901, 20.)

SUBJECT: City and town life–Paris. Railroad stations. Paris Exposition of 1900.

ARCHIVE:

CITATIONS:

NOTE:

GAYETY REIGNS IN EXPOSITION CITY.
"A Synthesis of the Philosophy and Civilization of the Nineteenth Century."
PARISIANS' HARVEST YEAR.
An Easy and Fascinating Daily Programme for the Fortunate Ones Who Can Afford It.
(Copyright, 1900, by the Press Publishing Company, New York World.)
(Special Cable Despatch to The World.)

PARIS, June 16.–The Parisians are apparently always happy; it is certain that they are always orderly and well-mannered. In the crushes at the Exposition there is only laughter and jokes among the French visitors, and nothing offensive. As M. Loubet says, "Paris just now is a seductive and immense school of mutual instruction."

To many–those who have wealth and leisure–the daily programme is easy and fascinating. Rise at noon, dejeuner; then, if no races are on, sit with the smart bachelordom of Paris behind a sherry cobbler and a cigar in the Cafe de la Paix and watch the ladies pass; then a round through the Exposition for an hour on the "trottoir roulant" (an American moving sidewalk), and then dinner at the Grand Cafe (at famine prices). Coffee and cognac on the boulevards before the theatre at about 8 or the Opera Comique, the Folies Bergere. At midnight the theatres are over, and then half an hour with the youth and beauty of the Cafe Anglais, or at Maxim's; then supper, and then, perhaps, to bed. So it is easily seen how the Exposition is, indeed, as the French say, "a synthesis of the philosophy and civilization of the nineteenth century."

But the tradition that the Parisian is a pleasure-seeker pure and simple is a mistake, for Paris is first and foremost a manufacturing centre of factories and shops and frugal-minded people, with only its superficial upper crust of frivolity. While it is true that the Exposition will bring together examples of the national progress of every civilized country in the world, everything representative of peculiar national ideas and customs and everything typical of the world's advance in science and art during the last century, yet to the Parisians it is a serious, money-making enterprise, and to-day they are saying that foreign pilgrims will bring $300,000,000 to Paris in the next six months. Even though these gigantic figures are not reached, the Exposition will fill the money chests of Paris to overflowing.

Mrs. Agnes Moody, a colored woman from Chicago, is making herself famous in Paris. She is the scientific and artistic cook who presides over the American Corn Kitchen, which has become one of the features of the big fair. It is said that "Aunty" Moody knows how to prepare more delicious corn concoctions than any other living person, and it is expected here that her work in making corn soup, corn cakes, corn muffins and corn dodgers, will prove a campaign of cookers' education for the whole world, besides giving American corn a great boom in Europe.

"Aunty" Moody was born in slavery, and in 1852, at the age of ten, escaped into Canada by the underground railway. She managed to acquire a good education, and in 1866 went to Chicago, where she has lived ever since, and where Commissioner-General Peck discovered her.

The American National Institute of Paris has opened its doors for the benefit of the American girl students, and Miss Smedley, who has been working for the past seven years for the organization of this praiseworthy scheme, has seen her work crowned with success. The importance of the American National Institute cannot be doubted in view of the list of names which are on the working committee for both America and France. The desire which has been achieved—has been to institute for Americans a "Prix de Paris," the competitions for which take place in the United States and it is thus hoped to give an artistic training to those who are worthy of encouragement by having in Paris an institute where these pupils can be taken care of.

The hotels are full of Americans, and New Yorkers are met everywhere, on the avenues and boulevards, in the cafes and theatres and at the Exposition. Col. John Jacob Astor and wife are seen almost nightly dining with distinguished guests at the Hotel Ritz, which is the swell cafe of Paris. Dr. Edmund Charles Wendt, of New York, recently gave a soiree in honor of the United States Commissioners to the Exposition at the Hotel Cap. Among the guests was the Prince of Monaco, attended by his chamberlain, Comte de Yamottee d'Allogny.

The King of Sweden and Norway visited the United States pavilion at the Exposition to-day and was received by the American officials and National Commissioners. Being told that a million of his subjects were in the United States the King replied: "I know that, but you have too many of them."

He inspected the building, and, noticing the American flag, said: "We all respect that." (*New York World*, 17 June 1900, Editorial Section, 1.)

James White and his cameraman apparently left the Paris Exposition in mid July and traveled to Oberammergau where they filmed several scenes of local color that exhibitors could then show in conjunction with the misnamed Passion Play of Oberammergau *(film no. 463), giving a new but more bogus context for the images of the Passion. Although evidence points toward White as the producer of these films, Eberhard Schneider was in Germany at this time and could also have shot them.*

861 ***Train Loaded with Tourists Arriving at Oberammergau**

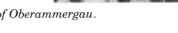

LENGTH: 100 ft.   © No reg.
PRODUCER: [James White.]
CAMERA:
CAST:
PRODUCTION DATE: 23 July 1900.
LOCATION: Oberammergau, Germany.
SOURCE:
DESCRIPTION:
SUBJECT: City and town life—Germany. Passion plays. Tourist trade.
ARCHIVE: NR-GE.
CITATIONS: *New York Clipper*, 25 August 1900, 604; *Edison Films*, July 1901, 2.
NOTE: Sold as part of *The Passion Play of Oberammergau*.

862 ***Opening of the Great Amphitheatre Door for the Intermission**
LENGTH: 50 ft.   © No reg.
PRODUCER: [James White.]
CAMERA:
CAST:
PRODUCTION DATE: 23 July 1900.
LOCATION: Oberammergau, Germany.
SOURCE:
DESCRIPTION:
SUBJECT: City and town life—Germany. Passion plays. Tourist trade.
ARCHIVE: NR-GE.
CITATIONS: *New York Clipper*, 25 August 1900, 604; *Edison Films*, July 1901, 2.
NOTE: Sold as part of *The Passion Play of Oberammergau*.

863 ***Street Scene in Oberammergau**
LENGTH: 50 ft.   © No reg.
PRODUCER: [James White.]
CAMERA:
CAST:
PRODUCTION DATE: 23 July 1900.
LOCATION: Oberammergau, Germany.
SOURCE:
DESCRIPTION:
SUBJECT: City and town life–Germany. Passion
  plays. Tourist trade.
ARCHIVE: NR-GE.
CITATIONS: *New York Clipper*, 25 August 1900,
  604; *Edison Films*, July 1901, 2.
NOTE: Sold as part of *The Passion Play of Oberammergau*.

864 ***Anton Lang's House**
LENGTH: 50 ft.   © No reg.
PRODUCER: [James White.]
CAMERA:
CAST:
PRODUCTION DATE: 23 July 1900.
LOCATION: Oberammergau, Germany.
SOURCE:
DESCRIPTION: This is the man who plays the
  part of Christ in the Passion Play. (*Edison
  Films*, July 1901, 2.)
SUBJECT: City and town life–Germany. Passion
  plays. Tourist trade. Anton Lang.
ARCHIVE: NR-GE.
CITATIONS: *New York Clipper*, 25 August 1900, 604.
NOTE: Sold as part of *The Passion Play of Oberammergau*.

From Oberammergau, White and his cinematographer traveled quickly to London and then back to New York.

865 **Piccadilly Circus, London, England**
LENGTH: 60 ft.   © No reg.
PRODUCER: James White.
CAMERA:
CAST:
PRODUCTION DATE: [25-27 July 1900.]
LOCATION: Piccadilly Circus, London, England.
SOURCE:
DESCRIPTION: A typical London street scene full of action from start to finish, showing
  the famous Piccadilly Circus at one of its busiest hours crowded with carriages,
  omnibuses and pedestrians. A most interesting view. (*Edison Films,* July 1901, 20.)
SUBJECT: City and town life–London. Urban transportation.
ARCHIVE:
CITATIONS: "Piccadilly Crowded in the Afternoon," *New York Herald*, 23 September
  1900, 2C.
NOTE:

866 **Royal Exchange, London, England**
LENGTH: 60 ft.   © No reg.
PRODUCER: James White.
CAMERA:
CAST:
PRODUCTION DATE: [25-27 July 1900.]

LOCATION: London, England.
SOURCE:
DESCRIPTION: With statue of Wellington in the background, looking toward old Broad Street. This is positively the busiest crosswalk in the world. (*Edison Films,* July 1901, 20.)
SUBJECT: City and town life–London. Monuments.
ARCHIVE:
CITATIONS:
NOTE:

867   Tug-o-War on Board an Ocean Steamer
LENGTH: 75 ft.   © No reg.
PRODUCER: James White.
CAMERA:
CAST:
PRODUCTION DATE: 28 July 1900.
LOCATION: Atlantic Ocean.
SOURCE:
DESCRIPTION: This picture shows a tug-o-war between the male and female passengers of the S.S. New York of the American Line. It was taken during the trip from Southampton to New York on July 28th, 1900. After hard tugging for a while, the female passengers are seen to pull the male passengers half the length of the ship. A very exciting picture. (*Edison Films*, July 1901, 19.)
SUBJECT: Steamships. Games. Tourist trade. American Line.
ARCHIVE:
CITATIONS:
NOTE:

In the summer of 1900 Eberhard Schneider went to Germany, where he took a large number of negatives. Schneider made arrangements to license and sell his films through the Edison organization. A group of negatives were turned over to the Edison Manufacturing Company and developed. According to Schneider, these were ruined by bad hypo; and of his six films advertised in September 1900, only one was in the July 1901 catalog—a fact supporting this claim. Another eight films from Schneider's trip entered the catalog at a subsequent date.

868   Johannisfest Marchen Gruppen of the Legends and Fairy Tales of the Past Centuries
LENGTH: © No reg.
PRODUCER: Eberhard Schneider.
CAMERA: [Eberhard Schneider.]
CAST:
PRODUCTION DATE: [July-August 1900.]
LOCATION:
SOURCE:
DESCRIPTION:
SUBJECT: Fairy tales. Germans.
ARCHIVE:
CITATIONS: *New York Clipper*, 1 September 1900, 604.
NOTE:

869   Great Fire Engine Scene in Breslau, Germany
LENGTH: © No reg.
PRODUCER: Eberhard Schneider.
CAMERA: [Eberhard Schneider.]
CAST:
PRODUCTION DATE: [July-August 1900.]
LOCATION: Breslau, Germany.
SOURCE:

DESCRIPTION:
SUBJECT: Fire fighters. Germans.
ARCHIVE:
CITATIONS: *New York Clipper*, 1 September 1900, 604.
NOTE:

870   Fire Drills at Breslau, Germany
LENGTH: 200 ft.   © No reg.
PRODUCER: Eberhard Schneider.
CAMERA: [Eberhard Schneider.]
CAST:
PRODUCTION DATE: [July-August 1900.]
LOCATION: Breslau, Germany.
SOURCE:
DESCRIPTION: Shows the arrival of the engines and apparatus at the fire, with steam blowing off, positions being obtained, etc. In the building, at the upper windows, are seen people trying to get out, whose escape has been cut off by the fire. The firemen immediately spread a large canvas below, and the people are seen jumping down two and three stories into the canvas. A wonderfully realistic scene and one that will cause great astonishment and surprise in an audience. This picture also shows people being rescued and let down by ropes from the third and fourth stories. All the various appliances for rescuing and saving life from a burning building are shown in this picture. In connection with this scene, the shooting out of the carbonic acid gas ladders, the latest acquisition to Germany's fire apparatus, is shown. This is a wonderful ladder, and inasmuch as there is considerable danger in handling it, it is only used in cases of extreme necessity. (*Edison Films,* July 1901, 24.)
SUBJECT: Fire fighters. Germans
ARCHIVE:
CITATIONS:
NOTE:

871   Breslau Fire Department in Action
LENGTH: 200 ft.   © No reg.
PRODUCER: Eberhard Schneider.
CAMERA: [Eberhard Schneider.]
CAST:
PRODUCTION DATE: [July-August 1900.]
LOCATION: Breslau, Germany.
SOURCE:
DESCRIPTION: Here is seen the entire Fire Department of Breslau in action. First is seen a wonderful bicycle motor apparatus dashing down one of the principal streets of the city. It is closely followed by a number of engines, hook and ladder and hose trucks. All sweep by the camera in rapid succession. The scene now changes to the front of an engine house. A general alarm is sounded. The horses rush out to their places in the apparatus, the large doors are swung open and out they dash in a wild rush for the scene of disaster. Next is the scene of the fire. The engines take their positions and the life saving crew hurry with their nets to the rescue of the unfortunate inmates of the burning building, who are seen at the top windows. The nets are spread by the firemen and the people are seen to jump into them and to safety. This is a very exciting fire scene and is sure to make a hit. (*Edison Films,* July 1901, 24.)
SUBJECT: Fire fighters. Fire runs. Germans.
ARCHIVE:
CITATIONS:
NOTE:

872   Market Day in Breslau, Germany
LENGTH: 50 ft.   © No reg.
PRODUCER: Eberhard Schneider.

CAMERA: [Eberhard Schneider.]
CAST:
PRODUCTION DATE: [July-August 1900.]
LOCATION: Breslau, Germany.
SOURCE:
DESCRIPTION: This picture shows the women from the farms around Breslau, coming in all kinds of wagons with their wares to sell them to the storekeepers and others throughout the city. This business is carried on entirely by the women in Germany, and it is wonderful to see them hustling around looking for the best and cheapest they can find. A very exciting an interesting market scene. (*Edison Films*, July 1901, 23.)
SUBJECT: City and town life–Germany. Carriages and carts. Markets.
ARCHIVE:
CITATIONS:
NOTE:

873 The Great Corpus Christi Procession in Breslau
LENGTH: 75 ft.   © No reg.
PRODUCER: Eberhard Schneider.
CAMERA: [Eberhard Schneider.]
CAST: Cardinal Kopp.
PRODUCTION DATE: [July-August 1900.]
LOCATION: Breslau, Germany.
SOURCE:
DESCRIPTION: A large number of Bishops, Priests and laymen are seen in this procession which is headed by his Eminence, Cardinal Kopp, of Germany. The Cardinal, who is the highest Catholic official throughout the German Empire, is seen walking under a great canopy which is mounted with gold and supported by two dozen men. Along the line of march, which is around a small park, are erected small alters at which the Cardinal stops to pray. A very pretty scene, and the only one of its kind extant. (*Edison Films*, July 1901, 23.)
SUBJECT: City and town life–Germany. Religious ceremonies. Catholicism.
ARCHIVE:
CITATIONS:
NOTE:

874 Military Maneuvers of the German Army
LENGTH: © No reg.
PRODUCER: Eberhard Schneider.
CAMERA: [Eberhard Schneider.]
CAST:
PRODUCTION DATE: [July-August 1900.]
LOCATION: Germany.
SOURCE:
DESCRIPTION:
SUBJECT: Armies–Germany.
ARCHIVE:
CITATIONS: *New York Clipper*, 1 September 1900, 604.
NOTE:

875 A German Cuirassier Regiment
LENGTH: 100 ft.   © No reg.
PRODUCER: Eberhard Schneider.
CAMERA: [Eberhard Schneider.]
CAST:
PRODUCTION DATE: [July-August 1900.]
LOCATION: Germany.
SOURCE:
DESCRIPTION: No part of an army has as much daring work to do, or more dangerous,

than the cavalry, hence it is generally the case that only large, stalwart, brawny men are selected for this branch of the service. This picture shows, without any exception whatever, one of the finest bodies of men in all Europe ever collected together in one regiment. Their striking uniform and helmets, the steel-tipped lances they carry, the magnificent horses they ride, their elegant trappings, the majestic manner in which they ride, make this picture one of the most desirable and valuable of our military series. The column is led by a military band on horseback. Horses and men both catch the inspiration of the picture that no exhibitor can afford to be without. It is one of the best drilled and most famous regiments in the German Empire. Be sure to get this picture. (*Edison Films*, July 1901, 25.)

SUBJECT: Armies–Germany. Cavalry. Marching bands.
ARCHIVE:
CITATIONS:
NOTE:

876 Ammunition Wagons Arriving on the Battlefield
LENGTH: 100 ft.   © No reg.
PRODUCER: Eberhard Schneider.
CAMERA: [Eberhard Schneider.]
CAST:
PRODUCTION DATE: [July-August 1900.]
LOCATION: Germany.
SOURCE:
DESCRIPTION: This picture shows the arrival on the battlefield of a host of ammunition wagons, each drawn by four horses, with a soldier to guide and direct the first pair of horses, and another soldier for the rear pair of horses, similar to the way in which horses are handled when hitched to cannon. The men who have charge of the ammunition chests are seen sitting on them while the wagons are in motion. The picture shows a very long line of these wagons coming, which follow each other closely. The ammunition wagons being the most necessary thing on a battlefield, this picture will attract a great deal of attention and cause considerable comment, because of its exact representation, full size, etc. We do not know of any moving pictures ever having been made that show what these pictures do. (*Edison Films*, July 1901, 24.)
SUBJECT: Armies–Germany. Battles. Transportation, military.
ARCHIVE:
CITATIONS:
NOTE:

877 Red Cross of the German Army on the Battlefield
LENGTH: 100 ft.   © No reg.
PRODUCER: Eberhard Schneider.
CAMERA: [Eberhard Schneider.]
CAST:
PRODUCTION DATE: [July-August 1900.]
LOCATION:
SOURCE:
DESCRIPTION: This is an exact reproduction of the work of the Red Cross Society during an engagement. Here we see these brave men rushing around on the field of battle with stretchers, picking up the wounded and hurrying them off to a place of safety where their wounds may be treated. Officers on horseback are seen to be giving instructions as to the handling of the unfortunates who have fallen in the fight. A very pathetic scene in this picture is where an officer falls from his horse with a bullet wound and is picked up, placed on a stretcher and carried off, the horse following behind with bowed head. (*Edison Films*, July 1901, 23.)
SUBJECT: Armies–Germany. Red Cross. Battles.
ARCHIVE:
CITATIONS:
NOTE:

878 Opening of Bismarck's Mausoleum

LENGTH: 75 ft.   © No reg.
PRODUCER: Eberhard Schneider.
CAMERA: [Eberhard Schneider.]
CAST: Herbert Bismarck.
PRODUCTION DATE: [July-August 1900.]
LOCATION: Friedrichsruhe, Germany.
SOURCE:
DESCRIPTION: This picture shows the mausoleum of the Great Bismarck, at Friedrichsruhe, Germany. Special permission to open same was granted to the Krieger Bund Society by General Bismarck's son. Bismarck's son is here shown at the head of the procession of the American Delegation as they march into the mausoleum. The U.S. Flag is carried at the head of the column and a handsome laurel is deposited at the foot of the tomb of the great General. This picture cannot be duplicated. Millions of people have heard and read of this wonderful man, one of the greatest of the nineteenth Century, and will be glad to have an opportunity of seeing his last resting place. (*Edison Films*, July 1901, 23.)
SUBJECT: Monuments. Flags–United States. Parades. Otto von Bismarck.
ARCHIVE:
CITATIONS:
NOTE:

879 Great Waterfall of the Rhein at Shaffhausen, Germany [sic] / Great Waterfall of the Rhein at Shaffhausen, Switzerland [sic]

LENGTH: 75 ft.   © No reg.
PRODUCER: Eberhard Schneider.
CAMERA: [Eberhard Schneider.]
CAST:
PRODUCTION DATE: [July-August 1900.]
LOCATION: Schaffhausen, Switzerland.
SOURCE:
DESCRIPTION: This picture is a perfect representation of the great waterfall of the Rhein, the greatest waterfall in all Europe. A small row boat is seen to pass with the utmost difficulty through the rapids approaching the falls. It is very dangerous and perilous undertaking to pass through these rapids, as the rocks are very large and numerous. One large rock divides the river, and the water rushing on each side of it makes the falls as large as they are. A little way up the rapids is a railroad bridge which crosses the river Rhein, and to add interest to the picture a train is seen crossing the bridge at full speed. A very interesting subject taken in a beautiful country.

We can also furnish a 50-foot strip from this negative. (*Edison Films*, July 1901, 25.)
SUBJECT: Waterfalls. Bridges. Railroads. Boats and boating.
ARCHIVE:
CITATIONS: *New York Clipper*, 1 September 1900, 604.
NOTE:

880 View of the Rhein Falls from the Centre of the Rapids

LENGTH: © No reg.
PRODUCER: Eberhard Schneider.
CAMERA: [Eberhard Schneider.]
CAST:
PRODUCTION DATE: [July-August 1900.]
LOCATION: Schaffhausen, Switzerland.
SOURCE:
DESCRIPTION:
SUBJECT: Waterfalls.
ARCHIVE:
CITATIONS: *New York Clipper*, 1 September 1900, 604.
NOTE:

881   Climbing Snowclad Mountains in Switzerland
LENGTH: © No reg.
PRODUCER: Eberhard Schneider.
CAMERA: [Eberhard Schneider.]
CAST:
PRODUCTION DATE: [July-August 1900.]
LOCATION: Switzerland.
SOURCE:
DESCRIPTION:
SUBJECT: Mountain climbing. Swiss Alps.
ARCHIVE:
CITATIONS: *New York Clipper*, 1 September 1900, 604.
NOTE:

During the summer of 1900, J. Stuart Blackton and Albert E. Smith made numerous films, many of which eventually ended up in the Edison catalog. Some were copyrighted. Most were not. The following motion pictures were shot by the Vitagraph duo, as best as can be determined within this time frame (and most of these subjects were definitely taken in these months).

882   *Leaping Dogs at Gentry's Circus / Leaping Dogs
LENGTH: 100 ft.   © Thomas A. Edison, 16 December 1901.
PRODUCER: J. Stuart Blackton, Albert E. Smith.
CAMERA: J. Stuart Blackton and/or Albert E. Smith.
CAST:
PRODUCTION DATE: [July-August 1900.]
LOCATION:
SOURCE:
DESCRIPTION: In the center of the ring the
   trainer forms a pile of baskets many feet
   in height and over this Gentry's famous
   greyhounds leap in rapid succession, forming a graceful arch and landing on the
   ground as lightly as so many feathers. The
   position of our camera was a most happy
   one, as the dogs appear to leap directly
   toward the audience and the film is both
   beautiful and exciting. (*Edison Films*,
   September 1902, 63.)

SUBJECT: Circus animals. Animal trainers. Dogs. Gentry's Dog and Pony Show.
ARCHIVE: DLC-pp.
CITATIONS:
NOTE: One of a group of twenty films, made by Blackton and Smith and listed in a preliminary agreement with the Edison Manufacturing Company, dated 10 September
   1900. These were turned over to the Edison organization; four were eventually
   copyrighted while many of the others were simply added to Edison catalogs. This
   subject was probably filmed while Gentry's Dog and Pony Circus was performing in
   either Brooklyn or Harlem during the summer of 1900.

The Gentry's
Famous Tented Amusement Enterprises.
Four of the Largest and Richest Trained Animal Exhibitions in the World,
Consisting of Educated Dogs, Ponies, Monkeys and Elephants.

Unlimited capital and conducted on sound business principles. H.B. Gentry has just purchased AMERICA'S GREAT-
EST DOG AND PONY SHOW, formerly owned by Sipe, Dolman & Blake. Has also purchased the WORLD'S GREATEST
DOG AND PONY SHOW, formerly owned by Ogden, Main & Company. These four shows are in Winter quarters at the
following places: Show No. 1 at Houston, Texas, WALLACE W. GENTRY, Manager; SHOW No. 2 at Jacksonville, Fla.,
J. WILLIAM GENTRY, Manager; SHOW No. 3 at Montgomery, Ala., TAYLOR P. COONS, Manager; SHOW No. 4 at
Bloomington, Ind., FRANK H. GENTRY, Manager. (Advertisement, *New York Clipper*, 4 February 1899, 833.)

Brooklyn. Halsey Street and Broadway.–The Gentry Dog and Pony Show opened here 2, with an afternoon and evening performance, before two large crowds. It promises to do as well here as it did last season, when thousands of people enjoyed the antics of the trained animals. Last week it showed to large crowds at Flatbush Avenue and Pacific Street. (*New York Clipper*, 7 July 1900, 416.)

GENTRY'S FAMOUS
DOG AND PONY SHOW.
LIMITED ENGAGEMENT.
Cor. 135th ST. and LENOX AVE.
THIRD WEEK
THE HIT OF THE SEASON.
THE TALK OF THE TOWN.
The Oldest, Largest and Richest Exhibition of its kind in the world. Over 150 All Star DOGS, PONIES, MONKEYS and LILLIPUTIAN ELEPHANTS in a powerful exhibition of animal sagacity. A novelty at last, in which dumb brutes are educated and tutored to that of human intelligence, the power of speech being the only thing lacking.
Capacity of Mammoth Tents Tested at Every Performance.
Two Performances Daily, rain or shine.
MATINEES, 2:30 P.M. NIGHT, 8 P.M.
Seating cool and comfortable.
(Advertisement, *New York Clipper*, 28 July 1900, 483.)

John W. Gentry
John W[illiam] Gentry, 65, one of the three brothers who owned the Gentry dog and pony circuses, died in Miami Dec. 3 following a long illness.
Back in the 1890s, James [sic] Gentry, with his two brothers, Henry B. and Frank Gentry, put out his first dog and pony circus, having served his apprenticeship with the Morris animal show. Since then the Gentry show has played practically every show spot between the two coasts and the Gentrys occupied the same position in the dog and pony show business that Ringling occupied in the larger field. Often they had half a dozen or more outfits on the road, each scaled to the route it was to play, ranging from 20 to 30 cars, according to equipment.
The setup was profitable, with most of the entertainment supplied by the animals, and the Gentry name became as standard in the hinterland as was the Barnum tag in the larger cities. The latter were also played, chiefly neighborhood dates, and the shows have several times played New York City for several weeks at a time, changing lots, but not leaving the city limits. The Gentry outfit was practically the pioneer, in spite of the fact the dog and pony show was not a new idea, and its success was largely responsible for a flock of imitators, none of whom approached the Gentry outfits in size or receipts. (*Variety*, 9 December 1936, 54.)

883 ## How the Professor Fooled the Burglars
LENGTH: 75 ft.   © No reg.
PRODUCER: [J. Stuart Blackton, Albert E. Smith?]
CAMERA: [J. Stuart Blackton and/or Albert E. Smith?]
CAST:
PRODUCTION DATE: [June-September 1900.]
LOCATION: [Vitagraph's roof-top studio, New York, N.Y.]
SOURCE:
DESCRIPTION: The professor, who is a renowned magician, hears some one approaching and instantly changes himself into a cloaked figure with a skull head. Two burglars enter and deal him a terrible blow on the head. One of the burglars now fills his sack. Suddenly the bag changes into the Professor, who springs to the floor, and as he alights changes again into a bag before their astonished eyes. The Professor makes another lightning change and then vanishes himself. Very startling and laughable. (*Edison Films*, July 1901, 83.)
SUBJECT: Burglars. Magicians. Magic.
ARCHIVE:
CITATIONS: "Professor Fights Fleeing Burglars," *New York Herald*, 4 September 1900, 14. *New York Clipper*, 8 December 1900, 920.
NOTE:

884 ## Baby's Meal
LENGTH: 75 ft.   © No reg.

PRODUCER: [J. Stuart Blackton, Albert E. Smith?]
CAMERA: [Albert E. Smith?]
CAST: [J. Stuart Blackton.]
PRODUCTION DATE: [June 1899 to September 1900.]
LOCATION: [Vitagraph's roof-top studio, New York, N.Y.]
SOURCE:
DESCRIPTION: Baby is seated on his high chair, and at a table close by father is enjoying
   a little light lunch. Baby and father both have their bottles, the baby's is milk and
   the father's is Piper Heidsieck. Baby is in a good temper when the meal starts, but
   not being satisfied with his own bottle and being refused the champagne, he pro-
   ceeds to dig his knuckles into his little eyes and bawl as only babies can. Mother
   finally rescues baby and brings the meal to a finish. A pretty picture of home life,
   sure to be a great favorite with ladies and children. (*Edison Films*, July 1901, 79.)
SUBJECT: Child rearing. Infants. Milk. Alcoholic beverages. Alcoholism.
ARCHIVE:
CITATIONS: *Edison Films*, September 1902, 89.
NOTE:

885 ***Harry Thompson's Immitations of Sousa [sic] / Harry Thompson's Imitation
of Sousa / Sousa Leading the Band. Thomson**
LENGTH: 50 ft.   © Thomas A. Edison, 16 December 1901.
PRODUCER: J. Stuart Blackton, Albert E. Smith.
CAMERA: J. Stuart Blackton and/or Albert E. Smith.
CAST: Harry Thom[p]son.
PRODUCTION DATE: June 1899 to September 1900.
LOCATION: Vitagraph's roof-top studio, New York, N.Y.
SOURCE:
DESCRIPTION: The well-known Band Master is
   here imitated "To the life" by the above clev-
   er impersonator who goes through all the
   well known poses familiar to Sousa when
   the latter is in full blast leading his band
   while playing one of his favorite composi-
   tions. (*Edison Films*, September 1902, 87.)
SUBJECT: Vaudeville–performances. Imper-
   sonations. John Philip Sousa.
ARCHIVE: DLC-pp.
CITATIONS:
NOTE: One of a group of twenty films, made by
   Blackton and Smith and listed in a preliminary agreement with the Edison
   Manufacturing Company, dated 10 September 1900. These were turned over to the
   Edison organization; four were eventually copyrighted while many of the others
   were simply added to Edison catalogs. Despite the way Thom[p]son chose to spell
   his name in the *Clipper* advertisement reprinted below, Keith's Boston announce-
   ments included a *p* in his last name.

THE PEOPLE'S CHOICE, HIS HONOR THE MAYOR OF THE BOWERY,
HARRY THOMSON,
On the Keith Circuit, big hit at Philadelphia, March 27; big hit Providence, April 3; and expect the same at Keith's
Boston, this week. P.S.–AND ONLY A WASHLINER. (Advertisement, *New York Clipper*, 15 April 1899, 137.)

886 **Such a Headache**
LENGTH: 125 ft.   © No reg.
PRODUCER: J. Stuart Blackton, Albert E. Smith.
CAMERA: J. Stuart Blackton and/or Albert E. Smith.
CAST:
PRODUCTION DATE: June 1899 to September 1900.
LOCATION: Vitagraph's roof-top studio, New York, N.Y.
SOURCE:

DESCRIPTION: Into a dollar-a-day room in a Bowery hotel enters a New York drummer who has evidently been having a "good time." As soon as he is left alone he begins to "see things." His valise flies around the room in a startling manner, upon opening it a huge demon's head arises therefrom and floats through the air. A bottle on the table changes into a little black dog, which springs to the floor as he reaches to take a drink he rings for the chambermaid, but immediately kicks her out. She returns reinforced with the landlord and the bell-boy. All four now engage in a most furious fight, in which bedclothes, chairs, water pitcher, etc., take an active part. The drummer wraps a towel around his head, and pouring the contents of the ice water pitcher upon it, wearily lies down again. After seeing the picture it is easy to see why we give it the title "Such a Headache." (*Edison Films,* September 1902, 101.)

SUBJECT: Alcoholism. Hotels. Hallucinations and illusions.

ARCHIVE:

CITATIONS: *New York Clipper,* 8 December 1900, 920; *Edison Films,* July 1901, 83.

NOTE: One of a group of twenty films, made by Blackton and Smith and listed in a preliminary agreement with the Edison Manufacturing Company, dated 10 September 1900. These were turned over to the Edison organization; four were eventually copyrighted while many of the others were simply added to Edison catalogs.

887   *****The Mysterious Cafe / The Mysterious Café, or Mr. and Mrs. Spoopendyke Have Troubles with a Waiter**

LENGTH: 100 ft.   © Thomas A. Edison, 16 December 1901.

PRODUCER: J. Stuart Blackton, Albert E. Smith.

CAMERA: J. Stuart Blackton and/or Albert E. Smith.

CAST:

PRODUCTION DATE: June 1899 to September 1900.

LOCATION: Vitagraph's roof-top studio, New York, N.Y.

SOURCE:

DESCRIPTION: As the above title indicates, the scene does not take place in an ordinary restaurant, but one in which all natural rules of order and gravitation are reversed.

The couple above mentioned have a most trying experience while endeavoring to partake of a square meal. They find themselves flying about the room from chairs to table, and vice versa, until they are both completely bewildered, ending in a general mix-up, which is sure to provoke much merriment. (*Edison Films,* September 1902, 95.)

SUBJECT: Taverns, etc. Magic.

ARCHIVE: DLC-pp.

CITATIONS:

NOTE: One of a group of twenty films, made by Blackton and Smith and listed in a preliminary agreement with the Edison Manufacturing Company, dated 10 September 1900. These were turned over to the Edison organization; four were eventually copyrighted while many of the others were simply added to Edison catalogs.

888   **The Mischievous Clerks; or, How the Office Was Wrecked**

LENGTH: 100 ft.   © No reg.

PRODUCER: [J. Stuart Blackton, Albert E. Smith.]

CAMERA: [J. Stuart Blackton and/or Albert E. Smith.]

CAST:

PRODUCTION DATE: [June 1899 to September 1900.]

LOCATION: [Vitagraph's roof-top studio, New York, N.Y.]

SOURCE:

DESCRIPTION: An animated scene during the busy hours in a lawyer's office. As the scene opens an elderly countryman is ushered into the office and requested to take a seat, as the lawyer is busy with another client. He takes a seat on the waiting bench, where another elderly gentleman is waiting, and indulging in a little snooze. The countryman is evidently a little sleepy himself, and while awaiting his interview, also begins to nod. The two mischievous clerks, being for the moment removed from the watchful eye of their employer, note the possibilities of the situation, and hastily procuring a long piece of cord, tie it around the necks of the two old men, who are sitting back to back. After accomplishing this piece of mischief, they tickle the noses of the two dozing victims, who, after making ineffectual efforts to chase away the "flies," suddenly awake and see their tormentors in front of them. Their natural impulse is to spring up and seize the culprits, but as they are securely tied together by the rope around their necks, the result can be imagined; and the vicious fight that ensues completely wrecks the entire office, and makes the participants, including the lawyer and his lady client, the mischievous clerks, and the two old men, the janitor, and the policeman who is called, all fit subjects for the hospital. A highly amusing film with an exceedingly strong climax. (*Edison Films,* July 1901, 66.)

SUBJECT: Practical jokes. Clerks. Law offices. Violence. Police.
ARCHIVE:
CITATIONS:
NOTE: Vitagraph made a film that was listed as *Inquisitive Clerks* in a preliminary agreement with the Edison Manufacturing Company, dated 10 September 1900. It was probably this film.

889 Miniature Railway
LENGTH: 70 ft.   © No reg.
PRODUCER: J. Stuart Blackton, Albert E. Smith.
CAMERA: J. Stuart Blackton and/or Albert E. Smith.
CAST:
PRODUCTION DATE: June 1899 to September 1900.
LOCATION:
SOURCE:
DESCRIPTION: One of the greatest attractions in parks and summer resorts during the past summer has been the miniature railway. The film shows three different views of this novel attraction, first the little engine and line of cars ready to start, passengers, including many children, scramble aboard, the engineer blows the tiny whistle, and they are off. The train is then seen rounding a long curve and coming head on at full speed. It passes with all the dash of a limited express. The camera is then turned and shows a receding view of the same train. (*Edison Films,* July 1901, 91-92.)

SUBJECT: Railroads (miniatures). Children. Amusement parks. Amusement rides.
ARCHIVE:
CITATIONS:
NOTE: One of a group of twenty films, made by Blackton and Smith and listed in a preliminary agreement with the Edison Manufacturing Company, dated 10 September 1900. These were turned over to the Edison organization; four were eventually copyrighted while many of the others were simply added to Edison catalogs.

890 *Children Bathing / The Kiddies Go Bathing
LENGTH: 50 ft.   © Thomas A. Edison, 16 December 1901.
PRODUCER: J. Stuart Blackton, Albert E. Smith.
CAMERA: J. Stuart Blackton and/or Albert E. Smith.
CAST:
PRODUCTION DATE: [Late July to early August 1900.]
LOCATION: [Martha's Vineyard, Mass.]
SOURCE:
DESCRIPTION: A pretty and natural picture in which the principal actors are two tiny tots who are evidently not a bit afraid of the briny deep as they splash around in the waves in very evident delight and enjoyment. The water effects are splendid and this is a beautiful subject of "Child-life." We

recommend this to make a hit with any audience. (*Edison Films*, September 1902, 92.)
SUBJECT: Children. Seashore. Bathing beaches.
ARCHIVE: DLC-pp.
CITATIONS:
NOTE:

Blackton and Smith made a series of short comedies around the tramp character they had developed in earlier films such as Burglar on the Roof *(no. 623). This figure was now called "Happy Hooligan," after the cartoon character drawn by Frederick Burr Opper (1857-1937). The "Happy Hooligan" comic strip began to appear in William Randolph Heart's newspapers in 1900 and quickly became a hit, running into the 1930s. Despite this appropriation of the cartoon strip's name, the tramp character appearing in these Edison films bears no physical resemblance to Opper's tramp. The Edison Manufacturing Company advertised the Happy Hooligan subjects as a series that later included productions by Edwin S. Porter, George Fleming and other Edison employees.*

The Adventures of Happy Hooligan.

A new series of comic pictures in which the principle character, Happy Hooligan Esq., a most disreputable looking tramp, has a number of wonderful and side-splitting adventures, from which, however, he always emerges triumphant, only to get into trouble again by a new prank. Undoubtedly the greatest set of comedy pictures ever invented. An added charm is lent to these pictures by the fact that the surroundings of each film consist of the most beautiful and picturesque scenery. (*Edison Films*, July 1901, 57.)

891 Hooligan and the Summer Boarders / Hooligan and the Summer Girls

LENGTH: 75 ft.   © No reg.
PRODUCER: J. Stuart Blackton, Albert E. Smith.
CAMERA: Albert E. Smith.
CAST: J. Stuart Blackton (Happy Hooligan).
PRODUCTION DATE: Late July to early August 1900.
LOCATION: Martha's Vineyard, Mass.
SOURCE: "Happy Hooligan" (comic strip—name only).
DESCRIPTION: A pretty scene in the woods. Between two trees swings a hammock, and in the hammock sit two charming summer girls eating caramels and reading the inevitable novel. In the distance a farmer is seen mowing the grass, and everything is serene. Suddenly a prowling figure appears, which as it advances, resolves itself into the tattered figure of Happy Hooligan. He executes a wild war dance on seeing the two summer girls alone and unprotected, and then stealing up behind them, he places an arm affectionately around each tender waist. The girls beat a hasty retreat, and Hooligan immediately possesses himself of the hammock, blowing clouds of smoke from his little butt with every appearance of contentment. However, there is trouble in store for Mr. Hooligan. The farmer has seen the whole occurrence, and he is now coming with rapid strides, brandishing his murderous looking scythe. Reaching the hammock, he quickly draws the sharp tool across the ropes which support it, and Hooligan hits the ground with a bump that completely jars him. (*Edison Films*, July 1901, 57-58.)
SUBJECT: Tramps. Sexual harassment. Cigars. Farmers. Harvesting. Hammocks. Punishment.
ARCHIVE:
CITATIONS: *New York Clipper*, 13 October 1900, 740; 8 December 1900, 920.
NOTE: Marketed as part of "The Adventures of Happy Hooligan Series."

892 Hooligan in Central Park / Hooligan Visits Central Park

LENGTH: 75 ft.   © No reg.
PRODUCER: J. Stuart Blackton, Albert E. Smith.
CAMERA: Albert E. Smith.
CAST: J. Stuart Blackton (Happy Hooligan).
PRODUCTION DATE: [Late July to early August 1900.]
LOCATION: [Martha's Vineyard, Mass.]
SOURCE: "Happy Hooligan" (comic strip—name only).

DESCRIPTION: On a shady lawn several young ladies are seated on a bench, also a colored nurse, with two little tots, who are playing on the grass. Happy Hooligan looms into view and sees a chance for a little flirtation. After brushing his rags with his feather duster he seats himself on the bench. The nurse girl immediately seizes the children and flies for protection to a policeman, who is seen in the background. Hooligan slides along the bench to the next young lady. She, and in turn, her companion, both beat a hasty retreat, and as Hooligan is now in full possession of the bench, he stretches himself at full length, his feet curled gracefully over the back, and prepares to enjoy a refreshing sleep. His dreams are rudely dispelled by the policeman's club, which descends with a terrible wack on the soles of his feet. A lively chase then ensues around the bench, with Hooligan in the lead, ending in his ignominious capture. (*Edison Films*, July 1901, 59.)

SUBJECT: Tramps. Police. Children. Afro-Americans. Sexual harassment. Punishment.

ARCHIVE:

CITATIONS: *New York Clipper*, 13 October 1900, 740.

NOTE: Marketed as part of "The Adventures of Happy Hooligan Series."

893 **Hooligan at the Seashore**

LENGTH: 100 ft.   © No reg.

PRODUCER: J. Stuart Blackton, Albert E. Smith.

CAMERA: Albert E. Smith.

CAST: J. Stuart Blackton (Happy Hooligan).

PRODUCTION DATE: Late July to early August 1900.

LOCATION: Martha's Vineyard, Mass.

SOURCE: "Happy Hooligan" (comic strip—name only).

DESCRIPTION: Behind a large rock, upon a beautiful beach, Hooligan sits at ease devouring his mid-day meal. Along the beach comes a natty young dude dressed in the very latest style, white flannels, straw hat, high collar and fancy cane. He pauses on the far side of the rock, and seeing no one in sight, proceeds to undress and go in for a swim. By this time Hooligan is "on," and has been watching the disrobing with interest. As soon as the unfortunate dude enters the water Hooligan immediately commences to annex the dude's clothes, leaving in their place his own horrible rags. He then saunters along the beach, blowing kisses to the frantic young man, who has just discovered his loss. The dude, having nothing else to wear, is obliged to put on Hooligan's cast off rags, and he had just done this when he is chased away by a colored girl from one of the neighboring cottages, who mistakes him for a tramp. The film ends with an exciting fight in the water between Hooligan, the dude, and the servant girl, in which the latter gets very much the best of it. A screaming laugh from start to finish. (*Edison Films*, July 1901, 59-60.)

SUBJECT: Seashore. Bathing beaches. Tramps. Afro-Americans. Mistaken identities. Food.

ARCHIVE:

CITATIONS: *New York Clipper*, 13 October 1900, 740.

NOTE: Marketed as part of "The Adventures of Happy Hooligan Series." This gag was expanded and reworked in the Edison film *Poor Algy!* (1905).

894 **Hooligan Has Troubles with the Cook**

LENGTH: 60 ft.   © No reg.

PRODUCER: J. Stuart Blackton, Albert E. Smith.

CAMERA: Albert E. Smith.

CAST: J. Stuart Blackton (Happy Hooligan).

PRODUCTION DATE: Late July to early August 1900.

LOCATION: Martha's Vineyard, Mass.

SOURCE: "Happy Hooligan" (comic strip—name only).

DESCRIPTION: In this picture Mr. Hooligan introduces himself to the audience and also to a large, juicy apple pie which rests temptingly on the window sill, where the cook has left it to cool. Happy Hooligan slouches around the corner of the house, and, spying the pie, immediately proceeds to get outside of it. Having finished the pie in great style, he next turns his attention to a large pan on the window sill, which unfortunately for him, is full of ready mixed batter and flour. This he succeeds in pulling over his head, and is immediately enveloped in a cloud of white flour dust just as the cook appears in the window and discovers him. She promptly douses poor Hooligan with a large pail of cold water, and he flees in dismay. (*Edison Films*, July 1901, 57.)

SUBJECT: Tramps. Food. Pies. Kitchens. Punishment.

ARCHIVE:

CITATIONS: *New York Clipper*, 13 October 1900, 740.

NOTE: Marketed as part of "The Adventures of Happy Hooligan Series."

895 Hooligan Takes His Annual Bath

LENGTH: 65 or 75 ft.   © No reg.

PRODUCER: J. Stuart Blackton, Albert E. Smith.

CAMERA: Albert E. Smith.

CAST: J. Stuart Blackton (Happy Hooligan).

PRODUCTION DATE: Late July to early August 1900.

LOCATION: Martha's Vineyard, Mass.

SOURCE: "Happy Hooligan" (comic strip—name only).

DESCRIPTION: A very spirited water scene, showing a float and a number of ladies seated thereon and disporting themselves in the water. They are horrified at the sudden appearance of Hooligan, who, in the excitement of taking his annual bath, has even forgotten to remove his clothes. As he splashes toward the raft the ladies all retreat in haste, and a great crowd of men and boys dash into the water and administer a severe and thorough washing to the unfortunate Hooligan. Beautiful photography and very fine water effects. (*Edison Films*, July 1901, 58.)

SUBJECT: Baths. Bathing beaches. Tramps. Lakes. Punishment.

ARCHIVE:

CITATIONS: *New York Clipper*, 13 October 1900, 740.

NOTE: Marketed as part of "The Adventures of Happy Hooligan Series."

896 *Hooligan Causes a Sensation

LENGTH: 100 ft.   © No reg.

PRODUCER: J. Stuart Blackton, Albert E. Smith.

CAMERA: Albert E. Smith.

CAST: J. Stuart Blackton (Happy Hooligan).

PRODUCTION DATE: Late July to early August 1900.

LOCATION: Martha's Vineyard, Mass.

SOURCE: "Happy Hooligan" (comic strip—name only).

DESCRIPTION: In this we see Hooligan, for once in his life, hard at work. He is sawing wood for the proprietress of a laundry. A sign on the shutter reads as follows: "No. 71, Mrs. Marshall, Laundress. Samples in this window. Closed Sunday after 11 A.M." Hooligan evidently feels the heat, as he quits sawing to knock on the shutter and ask for a drink of water. One-half of the shutter opens with a startling result. The wording of the sign has been cleverly arranged, so that when one-half is taken away by the opening of the shutter, the other half which remains in view reads as follows. "I shall undress in this window Sunday A.M." Hooligan immediately sees the point and frantically calls to the passersby, who congregate in large numbers to watch the result. As usual Happy Hooligan gets the worst of it, a policeman coming up at this juncture and hustling him off. (*Edison Films*, July 1901, 58.)

SUBJECT: Tramps. Laundries. Signs. Police. Practical jokes.

ARCHIVE: NNMoMA.

CITATIONS: *New York Clipper*, 13 October 1900, 740.

NOTE: Marketed as part of "The Adventures of Happy Hooligan Series."

897 **Hooligan's Narrow Escape**
LENGTH: 70 or 75 ft.   © No reg.
PRODUCER: J. Stuart Blackton, Albert E. Smith.
CAMERA: Albert E. Smith.
CAST: J. Stuart Blackton (Happy Hooligan).
PRODUCTION DATE: Late July to early August 1900.
LOCATION:
SOURCE: "Happy Hooligan" (comic strip—name only).
DESCRIPTION: Our friend, Happy Hooligan, is here seen traveling from New York to
   Boston, not in a parlor car, but by the time-honored custom of walking the ties.
   From the distance is seen approaching an express train. As it draws near and final-
   ly passes by, Hooligan stops in his tramp long enough to wave his hat at the pass-
   ing train. He is then seen to suddenly look around and make a wild spring down the
   embarkment, and just as his coat-tails disappear a train thunders by in the opposite direction on the very track upon which he was standing an instant before. As it
   passes by and recedes in a cloud of dust, Hooligan limps painfully up the embarkment again and shakes his fist after the train from which he had such a narrow
   escape. (*Edison Films*, July 1901, 59.)
SUBJECT: Tramps. Railroads. Accidents.
ARCHIVE:
CITATIONS: *New York Clipper*, 13 October 1900, 740.
NOTE: Marketed as part of "The Adventures of Happy Hooligan Series."

Cottage City, Mass.
on Martha's Vineyard
August 11th, 1900
[S.O. Edmonds:]
Smith and myself will return from our vacation in a few days. Before leaving New York we attempted to reach you
by phone many times but were never successful. We conversed with White the day before his departure and he
stated that you would close the contract at any time. As we are now ready to get down to business and have on
hand a large number of negatives of comedy subjects, etc., taken during the summer, we should like you to make
an appointment as soon as possible in order that, after arrangements are satisfactory concluded we may ship the
said subjects to Orange, as we understood from White that comic pictures were greatly needed in that quarter.
Please address all communications to my residence 966 E 166th Street, NYC.

Yours truly,
J. Stuart Blackton (signed)

898 **Trial Run of the New Battleship "Alabama" / Trial Run of the Battleship
"Alabama"**
LENGTH: 45 or 50 ft.   © No reg.
PRODUCER: [James White?]
CAMERA:
CAST:
PRODUCTION DATE: 28 August 1900.
LOCATION: Atlantic Ocean (off Cape Ann, Mass.).
SOURCE:
DESCRIPTION: Showing the new $6,000,000.00 battleship recently constructed by the
   Cramp Ship Building Co. making 18 knots an hour on her official trial run off Cape
   Ann, Mass. A most picturesque naval view taken from the deck of the U.S.
   Battleship, "Texas." (*Edison Films*, July 1901, 27.)
SUBJECT: Navies–United States.
ARCHIVE:
CITATIONS: "The Alabama Launched," *New York World*, 19 May 1898, 5. *New York
   Clipper*, 22 September 1900, 666.
NOTE: The "Alabama" was launched 18 May 1898 from Cramps Ship Yard, Phila-
   delphia, "in time for the next war." Edison had the Navy connection but Blackton
   and/or Smith may still have been in Martha's Vineyard (or could easily have
   returned). The delay between production and distribution suggests this film was
   taken by a licensee.

THE ALABAMA MAKES SEVENTEEN KNOTS
New Battle Ship Exceeds Her Contract Speed by Full Knot.
MAY BE NAVY'S QUEEN
Record of the Iowa, Though Apparently a Trifle Better, May Be Eclipsed.

Boston, Mass., Tuesday:–In her speed trial to-day the new battle ship Alabama made an average of seventeen knots an hour for four hours over the thirty-three knot measured course off Cape Ann. This was a knot better than the contract speed but was a trifle less than the battle ship Iowa made on her official trial trip, in April, 1897. The Iowa's record was 17.067 knots an hour.

It is believed that trial corrections will favor the Alabama, and that she may be the fastest battle ship in the United States navy. The official statement of the trial will not be made until the data shall have been submitted to the Secretary of the Navy.

The most remarkable performance of the Alabama was the speed which she attained over the third lap of the course going north. The time for this spurt of 6.6 knots showed that she was moving at the rate of more than eighteen knots an hour probably the highest speed that a first class battle ship ever made at any time.

It may be that the two stakes between which this run was made were closer together than the others, for buoys cannot be anchored out at sea with mathematical precision. The records of official speed trials take no account of spurts, although it was certain that the vessel was going through the water at record pace.

Made a Knot Extra.

The one prime fact developed by the trial is that the ship made a full knot in excess of her contract speed. This in the days of premiums for speed above contract would have netted about $200,000 for the builders, but the Alabama was built for $2,650,000, exclusive of armor, and with no bonus whatever for excess of speed. The additional speed meant merely another achievement for the Cramps.

The Alabama took on the Trial Board and her guests shortly after seven o'clock this morning. There were 240 in the party. The number was larger than usual and as many as desired for such a trip. By eight o'clock the big anchor came up out of President's Roads and the ship passed down the harbor.

She gathered speed as she went toward Cape Ann. The passage up was made in good time, but was remarkably free from incident. She jogged along without making any fuss and without any salutes or noise. The revolutions of the big bronze propellers were steadily increasing and little vibration was noticeable. The battle ship Texas, which served as the landmark for the first buoy of the course, was discerned soon after ten o'clock.

Battle Ships as Stakeboats.

The use of battle ships for stakeboats proved a wise step although not as necessary as would have been the case on a thick or misty day. The weather conditions were absolutely ideal for the run, in fact, could not have been better. There was no swell. The Alabama rode like a Nantasket steamship in harbor. There was little wind.

But for all this, the battle ships made the steering of the Alabama an easier matter, for they could be seen clearly. The six stakeboats were anchored at a distance of 6.6 knots apart.

The Alabama made straight for the course, having warmed up to her work during the run to the cape, and swung over the start with a rush, though her speed seemed to be made without much effort. An onlooker scarcely realized that she was moving as fast as was really the case.

Her screws were making 113 1/2 turns a minute as she settled on her run. They turned 115 at twenty minutes of eleven o'clock, and kept for a long time between 114 and 115, a high rate as it was estimated that 106 revolutions would give the sixteen knots required. The boilers were making steam in a steady manner. There seemed to be no sudden jumps of steam pressure.

It was announced that the ship was already making sixteen and three-quarters knots, and the crowd on board became more excited. The Osceola was passed at seven minutes of eleven o'clock, and figures taken at this time showed that the pace for the first section of the course was about seventeen knots. At this juncture a staid old merchant schooner crossed the battle ship's bow, close on, and nearly met disaster.

Cheers from the Kearsarge.

The magnificent Kearsarge loomed up ahead, and then occurred the most interesting episode of the day. The Kearsarge fairly swarmed with men. They filled the military tops. When the Alabama swept by, as if to efface the last trace of feeling over the fearful fight of nearly forty years ago, the men of the Kearsarge gave three thundering cheers.

The Kentucky, Indiana and Massachusetts were all passed in rapid succession. The great spurt of the day was between the Kearsarge and the Kentucky.

The figures of Captain Redwood D. Sargent, commanding for the builders, and of the Trial Board, were based on Greenwich time. Neither of the speed estimates was official. The two offer a basis of comparison. The total average given by the Board for the run up and back is about a hundredth of a knot less than the seventeen knots really made by the ship, because the averages for each leg of the course were given only to the second decimal point. The third decimal would have resulted in showing a speed more than seventeen knots.

It was one of the most spectacular trials ever held, due to the presence of all the battle ships of the North Atlantic squadron and the splendor of the day at sea. Residents of Rockport, who were in a fine position to see the start and finish, viewed her passage with interest. Soon after two o'clock in the afternoon a black column of smoke indicated her approach on the way back, and she came down the line, passing the many yachts and excursion boats as though they were anchored.

A tremendous white "bone" was rolling up, almost smothering the bow. She received three long blasts in salute from the Texas as she completed the run. After making an experimental turn or two, at the same high speed and in an amazingly short radius, she hurried on back to Boston. She anchored off Boston Light shortly after five o'clock.

The guests and naval men on board enjoyed the experience, for there was no shadow of a drawback to the trip. A stand-up luncheon was served shortly after noon.

Edwin S. Cramp said that not a drop of water was used upon any journal and live steam was not used in any of the receivers. The run was really a fair, every day possibility, he said. The tactical diameter of the turn made by the ship was 700 to 800 feet, a remarkable curve for a ship nearly 400 feet long. He said that the boilers maintained a steam pressure of 180 pounds to the square inch, even blowing off for an extended period during the run. An approximate horse power of 11,500 pounds was developed.

The screw revolutions averages for the port engine were 115.8 to the minute on the run north, and 114.8 on the return trip, while the starboard engine averaged respectively 114.8 and 113.2.

The entire average of the port engine was 115.3 and the starboard engine 114. Together they averaged 114.6 over the entire course.

Mr. Cramp said that the Alabama will start for Philadelphia to-morrow, and that he expects to deliver the vessel to the government within six weeks. The Alabama is more nearly completed than any other ship, which has been tried out over the Cape Ann course. All of her boats and all except some of the small guns are on board. (*New York Herald*, 29 August 1900, 6.)

899 **Girls Frolic at the Seashore / Girl's Frolic at the Lake**
LENGTH: 100 ft.   © No reg.
PRODUCER:
CAMERA:
CAST:
PRODUCTION DATE: [July-September 1900.]
LOCATION:
SOURCE:
DESCRIPTION: A number of girls are seated on the bank of the lake apparently waiting for chums they expect to appear in a boat. The boat appears and a young man and his sweetheart are the only occupants. They are apparently so engaged with their own pleasure and conversation that they will not notice the girls upon the bank, who are calling out to be taken aboard. The girls finally become exasperated and, springing into the water, swim to the boat and proceed to upset it, precipitating the happy couple into the water. (*Edison Films*, July 1901, 67.)
SUBJECT: Bathing beaches. Courtship. Girls. Lakes. Boats and boating. Punishment.
ARCHIVE:
CITATIONS: *New York Clipper*, 22 September 1900, 666.
NOTE:

900 **The Fisherman and the Bathers**
LENGTH: 50 ft.   © No reg.
PRODUCER:
CAMERA:
CAST:
PRODUCTION DATE: [July-September 1900.]
LOCATION:
SOURCE:
DESCRIPTION: On a pile of rocks jutting out into the ocean sits a venturesome fisherman patiently waiting for a bite. A group of mischievous boys and girls in bathing costume are seen creeping up behind the unsuspecting victim. The leader of the band having climbed to a rock just behind the fisherman, gives a sudden spring, and fisherman and bather both roll into water. As they emerge the other bathers reach the scene, and a free fight ensues in which everybody gets ducked. A very lively seaside scene. (*Edison Films*, July 1901, 68-69.)

SUBJECT: Bathing beaches. Seashore. Boys. Girls. Fishing.

ARCHIVE:

CITATIONS:

NOTE: This film bears significant resemblance to *The Lone Fisherman* (Edison film no. 224).

Having returned from Europe with the new panning mechanism he had used to shoot the Paris Exposition, James White promptly employed it to film a variety of landscapes in the United States.

901 **Circular Panoramic View of Niagara Falls / Circular Panorama of Niagara Falls**

LENGTH: 100 ft.   © No reg.

PRODUCER: James White.

CAMERA:

CAST:

PRODUCTION DATE: [August to early September 1900.]

LOCATION: Niagara Falls, N.Y.

SOURCE:

DESCRIPTION: This picture was taken from Goat Island, beginning with the camera placed looking up the rapids above the Horseshoe Falls. The camera is slowly and even turned until the Horseshoe Falls are brought into view, showing the immense volume of water rushing over the precipice. The camera revolves, making a complete circle until the American Falls come into view. (*New York Clipper*, 22 September 1900, 666.)

Taken from Goat Island, beginning with the camera pointed up the Rapids above the Horseshoe Falls, and slowly revolved from left to right until the entire Horseshoe is shown, with the Canadian shore in the background. The camera then turns, looking down the Whirlpool below the Horseshoe Falls, showing the Suspension Bridge in the background; passes the American Falls and ends by looking up the Rapids above the American Falls. This picture affords a complete view of Niagara Falls and the surrounding territory. (*Edison Films*, July 1901, 47.)

SUBJECT: Waterfalls. Bridges. Niagara Falls.

ARCHIVE:

CITATIONS:

NOTE:

902 **Circular Panorama of the American Falls**

LENGTH: 50 ft.   © No reg.

PRODUCER: James White.

CAMERA:

CAST:

PRODUCTION DATE: [August to early September 1900.]

LOCATION: Niagara Falls, N.Y.

SOURCE:

DESCRIPTION: Beginning with the camera pointed toward the Canadian shore, and slowly turning from left to right until a close view of the Suspension Bridge and the whirlpool below the Falls are shown. The camera then rested for a period of about twenty seconds, giving a close view of Luna Island and the American Falls. The picture ends with a close view of the Rapids below Horseshoe Falls. (*Edison Films*, July 1901, 47.)

SUBJECT: Waterfalls. Bridges. Niagara Falls.

ARCHIVE:

CITATIONS:

NOTE:

903 **Circular Panorama of Mauch Chunk, Penna.**

LENGTH: 80 ft.   © No reg.

PRODUCER: James White.

CAMERA:

CAST:
PRODUCTION DATE: [August to early September 1900.]
LOCATION: Jim Thorpe [Mauch Chunk], Pa.
SOURCE:
DESCRIPTION: On the Lehigh Valley Railroad. This place is described in books of travels as "THE SWITZERLAND OF AMERICA." The scene begins with the camera looking down the hill toward the Mansion Hotel. The camera is slowly revolved from right to left, making an entire sweep of this most picturesque city nestled in the hills of the Pohohoka Mountains, with the Susquehanna River winding through their midst. The camera being on the side of the mountains, at an elevation of about 200 feet, furnishes a most excellent view of Mauch Chunk and all the surrounding hills. This picture is absolutely perfect photographically and a most interesting subject. (*Edison Films*, July 1901, 46-47.)
SUBJECT: City and town life–Mauch Chunk. Tourist trade. Mountains. Rivers. Lehigh Valley Railroad.
ARCHIVE:
CITATIONS:
NOTE:

904 Circular Panorama of Atlantic City, N.J.
LENGTH: 100 ft. © No reg.
PRODUCER: James White.
CAMERA:
CAST:
PRODUCTION DATE: [August to early September 1900.]
LOCATION: Atlantic City, N.J.
SOURCE:
DESCRIPTION: The camera was placed with the lens pointed toward the famous board walk in Atlantic City. During the exposure of the film the camera is slowly revolved from left to right, taking in the immense crowds of surf bathers during the revolution of the camera and ending by looking out over the ocean, taking in Young's pier and showing a number of sail boats cruising about close to shore. (*Edison Films*, July 1901, 46.)
SUBJECT: Oceans. Seashore. Bathing beaches. Yachts and yachting. Piers.
ARCHIVE:
CITATIONS:
NOTE:

905 Panoramic View of the Capitol, Washington, D.C.
LENGTH: 40 ft. © No reg.
PRODUCER: James White.
CAMERA:
CAST:
PRODUCTION DATE: [August to early September 1900.]
LOCATION: Capitol Building, Washington, D.C.
SOURCE:
DESCRIPTION: Those who have never been fortunate enough to visit our country's Capital City will now be enabled to view the splendid and massive pile of architecture which constitutes the seat of government at Washington. This film shows a magnificent view of the Capitol beginning at the north end, and, as the camera revolves, bringing into full view the entire building from the dome to the ground. (*Edison Films*, July 1901, 47.)
SUBJECT: Public buildings–United States. City and town life–Washington, D.C.
ARCHIVE:
CITATIONS:
NOTE:

906 Panoramic View of the White House, Washington, D.C.
LENGTH: 125 ft. © No reg.

PRODUCER: James White.
CAMERA:
CAST:
PRODUCTION DATE: [September 1900.]
LOCATION: White House, Washington, D.C.
SOURCE:
DESCRIPTION: By permission our photographers were enabled to obtain a splendid moving panorama of the Executive Mansion taken from the private grounds in the rear. The film shows in perfect detail the beautiful flowers and shrubbery in the President's garden, the fountain and fish pond and as the camera slowly revolves the Washington Monument in the distance comes into full view. Then the beautiful glass conservatories in the grounds, and finally the White House itself, is shown in perfect detail, making a comprehensive and interesting view of the President's home. (*Edison Films*, July 1901, 47.)
SUBJECT: Public buildings–United States. City and town life–Washington, D.C. Presidents–United States. Monuments.
ARCHIVE:
CITATIONS:
NOTE:

907 A Composite Picture of the Principal Buildings in Washington, D.C.
LENGTH: 65 ft.   © No reg.
PRODUCER: James White.
CAMERA:
CAST:
PRODUCTION DATE: [September 1900.]
LOCATION: Washington, D.C.
SOURCE:
DESCRIPTION: A very interesting film, giving views of the Treasury Department, the Corcoran Art Gallery, the War and Navy Building, the White House and other prominent points in the Nation's Capital. These views were taken by using the new circular panoramic attachment which has lately been added to our cameras, and we are thus enabled to present views taken from different points all in one film without breaking the continuity of the view, as the buildings appear to pass slowly before the eye of the spectator. (*Edison Films*, July 1901, 47-48.)
SUBJECT: Public buildings–United States. City and town life–Washington, D.C. Presidents–United States.
ARCHIVE:
CITATIONS:
NOTE:

The Edison Manufacturing Company re-instated J. Stuart Blackton's and Albert E. Smith's license in time for Smith to travel to Galveston, Texas, and film the devastated area shortly after the hurricane and flood of 8 September 1900. Smith brought one of the new panning mechanisms with him for his camera.

908 *Searching Ruins on Broadway, Galveston, for Dead Bodies / Searching the Ruins of Galveston for Dead Bodies / Searching Ruins for Dead Bodies on Broadway
LENGTH: 50 ft.   © Thomas A. Edison, 24 September 1900.
PRODUCER: Albert E. Smith.
CAMERA: Albert E. Smith.
CAST:
PRODUCTION DATE: 11-19 September 1900.
LOCATION: Galveston, Tex.
SOURCE:
DESCRIPTION: This shows the heart of the tremendous drifts in the east end of Galveston. Hundreds of bodies are concealed in these immense masses, and at the time the picture was taken the odor given out could be detected for miles. The

subject shows a gang of laborers clearing away the debris in the search for corpses, one of which was discovered while the picture was being taken. (*Edison Films*, July 1901, 15.)

SUBJECT: Natural disasters. Ruins. Floods.

ARCHIVE: DLC-pp.

CITATIONS: *New York Clipper,* 22 September 1900, 666; 29 September 1900, 676.

NOTE:

909 ***Bird's Eye View of Dock Front, Galveston / Galveston Dock Yard Wreck / Birds-Eye Panorama of the Dock Front, Galveston**

LENGTH: 75 ft.   © Thomas A. Edison, 24 September 1900.

PRODUCER: Albert E. Smith.

CAMERA: Albert E. Smith.

CAST:

PRODUCTION DATE: 11-19 September 1900.

LOCATION: Galveston, Tex.

SOURCE:

DESCRIPTION: Showing dismantled cars, wrecked warehouses, schooners and tugs that had been stranded on the dock; also the tents that had been rigged for the poor people who had been left entirely homeless. (*Edison Films*, July 1901, 16.)

SUBJECT: Natural disasters. Ruins. Floods. Tug boats. Ships.

ARCHIVE: DLC-pp.

CITATIONS: *New York Clipper,* 22 September 1900, 666; 29 September 1900, 676.

NOTE:

910 ***Launching of a Stranded Schooner / Launching a Stranded Schooner from the Docks at Galveston / Launching a Stranded Schooner from the Docks**

LENGTH: 60 or 75 ft.   © Thomas A. Edison, 24 September 1900.

PRODUCER: Albert E. Smith.

CAMERA: Albert E. Smith.

CAST:

PRODUCTION DATE: 11-19 September 1900.

LOCATION: Galveston, Tex.

SOURCE:

DESCRIPTION: During the terrific storm all of the light craft along the dock front was lifted out of water and washed up into the streets, many of them being carried for miles inland. This subject shows a number of boatmen who have banded together to get their craft back into the water, a panoramic view being taken of the schooner as she glided sideways down the improvised ways, forming a very interesting subject. (*Edison Films*, July 1901, 15-16.)

SUBJECT: Natural disasters. Ruins. Floods. Ships–launching.

ARCHIVE: DLC-pp.

CITATIONS: *New York Clipper,* 29 September 1900, 676.

NOTE:

911 ***Panorama of East Galveston / Bird's Eye View of East Galveston / Bird's-Eye Panorama of East Galveston / Panorama of East Galveston, Texas**
LENGTH: 100 ft.   © Thomas A. Edison, 24 September 1900.
PRODUCER: Albert E. Smith.
CAMERA: Albert E. Smith.
CAST:
PRODUCTION DATE: 11-19 September 1900.
LOCATION: Galveston, Tex.
SOURCE:

DESCRIPTION: The cyclone struck the city from this end, which was the most densely populated portion. The houses for blocks around are completely wiped out, while the lumber, furnishings, etc, are piled up in an immense mass to the west and south of the picture. The foreground is strewn with sewing machines, hundred of which were scattered all over the city. (*Edison Films,* July 1901, 15.)
SUBJECT: Natural disasters. Ruins. Floods.
ARCHIVE: DLC-pp.
CITATIONS: *New York Clipper,* 22 September 1900, 666; 29 September 1900, 676.
NOTE:

912 ***Panorama of Galveston Power House / Ruins of the Galveston Power House / Panorama of the Galveston Power House***
LENGTH: 50 ft.   © Thomas A. Edison, 24 September 1900.
PRODUCER: Albert E. Smith.
CAMERA: Albert E. Smith.
CAST:
PRODUCTION DATE: 11-19 September 1900.
LOCATION: Galveston, Tex.
SOURCE:

DESCRIPTION: This building and machinery supplied the electric power and electric light of the entire city of Galveston, including the car system. The building, which is of solid masonry, is a complete wreck, and together with the twisted iron work of the machinery, shows the tremendous power of the cyclone. (*Edison Films,* July 1901, 15.)
SUBJECT: Natural disasters. Ruins. Floods.
ARCHIVE: DLC-pp.
CITATIONS: *New York Clipper,* 22 September 1900, 666; 29 September 1900, 676.
NOTE:

913 ***Panorama of Orphans' Home, Galveston / Galveston Orphans' Home in Ruins / Panorama of the Orphans' Home, Galveston***
LENGTH: 50 ft.   © Thomas A. Edison, 24 September 1900.
PRODUCER: Albert E. Smith.
CAMERA: Albert E. Smith.
CAST:
PRODUCTION DATE: 11-19 September 1900.
LOCATION: Galveston, Tex.
SOURCE:
DESCRIPTION: This is the building in which so many of the poor orphans met their death. The place is completely dismantled. In addition to the orphanage is shown one of the principal streets in Galveston blocked

with overturned houses and other materials. (*Edison Films*, July 1901, 15.)
SUBJECT: Natural disasters. Ruins. Floods. Orphanages.
ARCHIVE: DLC-pp.
CITATIONS: *New York Clipper,* 22 September 1900, 666; 29 September 1900, 676.
NOTE:

914 ***Panorama of Wreckage of Water Front, Galveston / Stranded Schooners on Galveston Beach / Panorama of Wreckage on Water Front, Galveston / Panorama of Wreckage on Water Front**
LENGTH: 40 or 50 ft.   © Thomas A. Edison, 24 September 1900.
PRODUCER: Albert E. Smith.
CAMERA: Albert E. Smith.
CAST:
PRODUCTION DATE: 11-19 September 1900.
LOCATION: Galveston, Tex.
SOURCE:

DESCRIPTION: This picture shows the remains of one of the docks, several freight cars being piled one upon the other, while the most interesting part of the picture shows two schooners literally smashed one into the other, forming a most picturesque mass of wreckage. (*Edison Films*, July 1901, 15.)
SUBJECT: Natural disasters. Ruins. Floods. Piers.
ARCHIVE: DLC-pp.
CITATIONS: *New York Clipper,* 22 September 1900, 666; 29 September 1900, 676.
NOTE:

915 ***Panoramic View of Tremont Hotel, Galveston / Wreck of Tremont Hotel, Galveston / Panoramic View of Galveston from Tremont Hotel / Panoramic View of Galveston / Panorama of Tremont Hotel, Galveston**
LENGTH: 50 ft.   © Thomas A. Edison, 24 September 1900.
PRODUCER: Albert E. Smith.
CAMERA: Albert E. Smith.
CAST:
PRODUCTION DATE: 11-19 September 1900.
LOCATION: Galveston, Tex.
SOURCE:
DESCRIPTION: This picture shows several of the buildings which were wrecked and also shows a rear view of this hotel, which is on the highest point of land in Galveston, and in which several thousand people were saved. (*Edison Films*, July 1901, 15.)
SUBJECT: Natural disasters. Ruins. Floods. Hotels.
ARCHIVE: DLC-pp.
CITATIONS: *New York Clipper,* 22 September 1900, 666; 29 September 1900, 676; 13 October 1900, 740.
NOTE:

HALF OF GALVESTON, DESTROYED BY HURRICANE—INLAND TOWNS IN RUINS. 3,000 DEAD
Destruction Extends Up and Down the Coast a Hundred Miles Either Way
from Galveston—4,000 Houses Destroyed—City Mass of Debris—Ship Lifted Two Miles Inland.
Galveston, Tex., was submerged by the great West Indian hurricane, which struck the city Saturday afternoon and raged until 11 P.M., when the storm somewhat abated. Of the city's population of 39,000 it is estimated that from 1,000 to 3,000 were killed. Gov. Sayers telegraphed The World that according to the advices he had received 3,000 lives had been lost. Four thousand buildings, representing millions of dollars, are in ruins.
The bridges which connect the island on which Galveston is built with the mainland have been damaged and ren-

dered useless. Even telegraph communication with the city is cut off. The latest advices by boat are that the leading hotel is six feet under water. Those who have survived the flood are huddled on high ground.

Virginia Point is the nearest place on the main land to Galveston. A Santa Fe relief train was obliged to turn back six miles from Virginia Point. Those on the train counted 200 bodies of the dead.

Advices received at the Weather Bureau in Washington from unofficial sources at Houston are that Galveston is as if it "Had been bombarded by artillery." Private advices from San Antonio say relief trains going to Galveston found water over the tracks eight miles from the coast.

Port Arthur, Tex., is covered by four feet of water. Many smaller places have been destroyed.

Much of the cotton crop has been ruined and the remainder greatly damaged.

Help is needed. (*New York World*, 10 September 1900, 1.)

At the first news of the disaster by cyclone and tidal wave that devastated Galveston on Saturday, September 8, we equipped a party of photographers and sent them by special train to the scene of the ruin. Arriving at the scene of desolation early last week, our party succeeded at the risk of life and limb in taking about 1,000 feet of moving pictures. In spite of the fact that Galveston was under martial law and that photographers were shot down at sight by the excited police guards, a very wide range of subjects has been secured.

The series, taken as a whole, will give the entire world a definite idea of the terrible disaster unequalled since the Johnstown Flood of 1889. (*New York Clipper*, 22 September 1900, 666.)

Boston Music Hall....The vitagraph shows views taken on the spot at Galveston, Tex., immediately after the great disaster by flood, and the pictures are graphic enough to help swell the relief fund. (*Boston Herald*, 25 September 1900, 9.)

Six weeks after the Galveston Flood, an Edison crew filmed a smaller disaster, closer to home: the Tarrant & Co. explosion and fire in Lower Manhattan.

916   Firemen Fighting the Tarrant Fire

LENGTH: 50 or 125 ft.   © No reg.

PRODUCER: [J. Stuart Blackton, Albert E. Smith.]

CAMERA: [J. Stuart Blackton and/or Albert E. Smith.]

CAST:

PRODUCTION DATE: 29 October 1900.

LOCATION: New York, N.Y.

SOURCE:

DESCRIPTION: Great volumes of smoke and flames are pouring from the ruins. In the background can be seen the ruins of the elevated station, which was blown almost to atoms by the terrific explosion. Another interesting part of the picture is the very fine water effect from the dozen different lines of hose which are continually playing on the ruins. (*Edison Films*, July 1901, 14.)

SUBJECT: Fire ruins. Fire fighters. Fires.

ARCHIVE:

CITATIONS: "Three Explosions in Quick Succession Wreck Entire City Block," *New York Herald*, 30 October 1900, 3. *New York Clipper*, 10 November 1900, 828.

NOTE: Edison advertisements claimed that the films of the Tarrant fire were protected by copyright, though no such entries are in available records at the Library of Congress.

917   The Falling Walls at the Tarrant Explosion

LENGTH: 100 ft.   © No reg.

PRODUCER: [J. Stuart Blackton, Albert E. Smith.]

CAMERA: [J. Stuart Blackton and/or Albert E. Smith.]

CAST:

PRODUCTION DATE: 29 October 1900.

LOCATION: New York, N.Y.

SOURCE:

DESCRIPTION: One of the most interesting pictures ever produced. The picture opens showing the ten stories of walls bulging out, ready to topple over into the street at any moment, and immediately after they are seen to sway and fall. Great clouds of dust rise from the ruins and make this a most interesting subject. (*Edison Films*, July 1901, 14.)

SUBJECT: Fire ruins. Fire fighters.
ARCHIVE:
CITATIONS: *New York Clipper*, 10 November 1900, 828.
NOTE:

918 Searching the Ruins of the Tarrant Fire
LENGTH: 75 ft.   © No reg.
PRODUCER: [J. Stuart Blackton, Albert E. Smith.]
CAMERA: [J. Stuart Blackton and/or Albert E. Smith.]
CAST:
PRODUCTION DATE: 29 October 1900.
LOCATION: New York, N.Y.
SOURCE:
DESCRIPTION: Showing the crowds of workmen searching the ruins for victims. Great
    volumes of steam arise from the debris. This is caused by the many lines of hose
    which are playing on it. This makes a very sensational subject and every detail is
    brought out clearly and distinctly. (*Edison Films*, July 1901, 14.)
SUBJECT: Fire ruins. Fire fighters.
ARCHIVE:
CITATIONS: *New York Clipper*, 10 November 1900, 828.
NOTE:

GREAT LOSS OF LIFE MAY HAVE OCCURRED IN DRUG HOUSE FIRE
Intensity of the Heat in Ruins Prevents Firemen from Ascertaining How Many Persons Have Perished.
FIREMEN AND POLICE DISPLAY GREAT HEROISM
Loss to Property and to Stocks of Mercantile Establishments Not Computed,
but Will Aggregate Millions of Dollars.

Buildings reaching for half a block backed on each side of Warren street, from Greenwich to Washington streets, were utterly destroyed by fire and explosions just after noon yesterday. Not fewer than two hundred persons were injured, many of them supposed to be fatally. The loss of life, although still problematical, is feared to be great. The property loss will reach into the millions.

Chief Croker said at two o'clock this morning that no estimate could be made of the loss of life. He had no doubt there were many bodies in the ruins, but he would not say how many he thought were there.

Of the origin of the fire no exact information is yet to be had. The flames were first seen on the third and fourth floor of the building at the northwest corner of Warren and Greenwich streets, occupied by Tarrant & Co., whole-sale and retail dealers in drugs, and manufacturers of medicinal specialties.

It is possible that the fire resulted from imperfect insulation of electric light wires, but it is the opinion of Fire Chief Croker and Fire Commissioner Scannell that carelessness among chemicals was the cause of the blaze.

Although the city regulations against the storing of chemicals are of the strictest kind, Commissioner Scannell, to a reporter for the Herald, made the specific charge that Tarrant & Co. had paid no heed to the law and had placed in storage chemicals and explosives far exceeding the legal limit. Had it not been for these explosives the blaze would have been easily conquered, but the work of the firemen was rendered extremely hazardous by the explo-sions, which occurred with alarming frequency. Three of these wrought appalling disaster.

Alarm concerning the fire was turned in at the house of Engine Company No. 29, in Chambers street, near Greenwich, about a quarter-past twelve o'clock. This company was quick to respond, and its members did not hes-itate to risk their lives in an effort to rescue those who had been caught in the burning structure.

Deputy Chief Ahearn arrived in time to see the walls of all the buildings in the block facing on Warren street fall out, and caused to be sent to headquarters the emergency alarm, and what is known as the "disaster signal," call-ing for all ambulances that are available.

Panic Follows the Explosion.

The explosions, which occurred as soon as the flames touched the more dangerous chemicals and oils, were of sufficient force to drive the spectators back panic stricken. Every window for a block in all directions was destroyed, the glass being blown into the streets in showers. As the debris poured down upon the heads of those who were fleeing from the flames their terror increased to such an extent that they were unable to use ordinary discretion. Many fell to be trampled under the feet of those who came behind. (*New York Herald*, 30 October 1900, 3.)

THE GREAT NEW YORK EXPLOSION

On Monday, Oct. 29, at a few minutes after noon, down-town New York was shaken by a tremendous explosion, followed at intervals of a few minutes by two other terrific crashes that were more like earthquake shocks than anything New York ever experienced.

These explosions occurred in a large Manufacturing Drug House on the corner of Warren and Greenwich Streets. The tremendous force leveled the entire block on Warren Street and the flames which immediately followed, spread with lightning like rapidity all over the ruins, and also to the buildings lining Greenwich, Warren, Murray, and Washington Streets. The area of ruin was almost an acre in extent.

Within one hour after the first explosion we had a photographer on the spot, and in spite of the strict police and fire lines and the surging crowds of sightseers, we obtained three excellent moving pictures of the ruins, the falling walls and the search for dead bodies and other exciting events that followed the catastrophe.

There have been other fires in the history of the large cities in our country, but no explosion with consequent loss of life has ever equaled this Tarrant explosion. (*New York Clipper,* 3 November 1900, 803.)

In the fall of 1900, Blackton and Smith made a series of trick films, which they soon turned over to the Edison Manufacturing Company for sale and distribution.

919 **The Congress of Nations**

LENGTH: 100 ft.   © Thomas A. Edison, 16 November 1900.

PRODUCER: J. Stuart Blackton, Albert E. Smith.

CAMERA: J. Stuart Blackton.

CAST: Albert E. Smith.

PRODUCTION DATE: September to early November 1900.

LOCATION: Vitagraph's roof-top studio, New York, N.Y.

SOURCE:

DESCRIPTION: A stirring and sentimental picture, treating upon the complicated Chinese question, ending with a marvelous tableau that will evoke applause from every audience. (*New York Clipper*, 17 November 1900, 852.)

A new and sensational film, which deals in a highly up to-date manner with the international situation. A magician steps upon the stage carrying a hoop covered with white paper. Then in quick succession the flags of Germany, Russia, Ireland, England and China are brought forth and from each a soldier is produced corresponding with the flag of each nation. The magician adds a bit of comedy to the scene by producing a decidedly Hiberian policeman from the flag of Erin's Isle. The magician then slowly waves his arms in front of the American flag, and as he dissolves into thin air a striking and patriotic tableau appears. The dissolve effect from the magician to the tableau is a new and unique effect never hitherto achieved in motion photography. (*Edison Films*, July 1901, 81.)

SUBJECT: Magicians. China–History–Boxer Rebellion. Patriotism. Irish. Chinese. Germans. English. Russians. Flags. Flags–United States.

ARCHIVE: DLC-pp.

CITATIONS: *New York Clipper*, 17 November 1900, 852.

NOTE: The dissolve mentioned in the above description is the earliest in any available American film but the technique was used the year before by Georges Méliès in *Cinderella*.

920 **Hooligan Assists the Magician**

LENGTH: 100 ft.   © Thomas A. Edison, 16 November 1900.

PRODUCER: J. Stuart Blackton, Albert E. Smith.

CAMERA: Albert E. Smith.

CAST: J. Stuart Blackton.

PRODUCTION DATE: September to early November 1900.

LOCATION: Vitagraph's roof-top studio, New York, N.Y.

SOURCE:

DESCRIPTION: This is a new adventure in which our friend, Mr. Hooligan, appears in an entirely new capacity. On a stage a professor of magic is performing some wonder-

ful experiments, and when he requests some assistance Happy Hooligan immediately volunteers his services and climbs upon the platform. As he does so, the professor vanishes through the floor and the amateur assistant is left alone with nothing but a couple of barrels, which, however, immediately begin to cut up some remarkable capers. They absolutely refuse to be tampered with, and as fast as Mr. Hooligan knocks them over they regain their balance, and during their evolutions, clowns, ghosts, demons, and goblin appear and disappear in an alarming manner, not, however; without each of them having a crack at the unfortunate Hooligan. Finally he captures two of them, only to find when he yanks them out of the barrels they have changed into immense masses of white muslin, which the professor, who now appears again, divides into two potions, one of which he causes to change into thousands of fluttering bits of paper, while the other at his magic touch forms into a huge and grotesque looking goblin; the whole forming a series of most startling and laughable effects entirely new to animated photography. (*Edison Films*, July 1901, 60.)

SUBJECT: Magicians. Tramps. Magic tricks. Ghosts.
ARCHIVE: DLC-pp.
CITATIONS: *New York Clipper*, 17 November 1900, 852.
NOTE:

921 *The Enchanted Drawing
LENGTH: 100 ft.   © Thomas A. Edison, 16 November 1900.
PRODUCER: J. Stuart Blackton, Albert E. Smith.
CAMERA: Albert E. Smith.
CAST: J. Stuart Blackton.
PRODUCTION DATE: September to early November 1900.
LOCATION: Vitagraph's roof-top studio, New York, N.Y.
SOURCE:

DESCRIPTION: Upon a large sheet of white paper a cartoonist is seen at work rapidly sketching the portrait of an elderly gentleman of most comic feature and expression. After completing the likeness the artist rapidly draws on the paper a clever sketch of a bottle of wine and a goblet, and then, to the surprise of all, actually removes them from the paper on which they were drawn and pours actual wine out of the bottle into a real glass. Surprising effects quickly follow after this; and the numerous changes of expression which flit over the face in the sketch cause a vast amount of amusement and at the same time give a splendid illustration of the caricaturist's art. (*Edison Films*, July 1901, 81.)

SUBJECT: Vaudeville–performances. Drawing. Alcoholic beverages. Facial expressions.
ARCHIVE: DLC-pp.
CITATIONS: *New York Clipper*, 17 November 1900, 852.
NOTE:

922 *Maude's Naughty Little Brother / Maud's Naughty Little Brother, or Wouldn't It Jar You? / Maude's Naughty Little Brother, or Wouldn't It Jar You?
LENGTH: 100 ft.   © Thomas A. Edison, 16 November 1900.
PRODUCER: J. Stuart Blackton, Albert E. Smith.
CAMERA: J. Stuart Blackton and/or Albert E. Smith.
CAST:

PRODUCTION DATE: September to early November 1900.

LOCATION: Vitagraph's roof-top studio, New York, N.Y.

SOURCE:

DESCRIPTION: In a charming dining room a very attractive young lady is seen seated at the table, evidently waiting for the caller who is to share a quiet little dinner for two. A moment later a dude of the regular chappy type enters and seats himself at the table. As soon as the meal commences the inevitable wicked small boy sneaks in unobserved, and producing a piece of rope ties one end securely to the dude's coat tails and fastens the other to the table-cloth. He then crawls under the table and in great glee awaits the result of his operations. At this moment an unexpected interruption occurs. The door is flung rudely open and papa enters the peaceful scene, at sight of whom the dude rises from the table and makes a dash for the door. Unfortunately for him his coat-tails are securely tied to the table cloth, and as he makes his exit he drags off the crockery and table-cloth and overturns the table with a tremendous crash, being forcibly assisted out of the door by the irate parent's shoe-toe, who then rushes back into the room and administers a sound spanking to Maude's naughty little brother. (*Edison Films*, July 1901, 66.)

SUBJECT: Boys. Courtship. Child rearing. Fathers. Family. Punishment. Practical jokes.

ARCHIVE: DLC-pp.

CITATIONS: *New York Clipper*, 17 November 1900, 852.

NOTE:

923 *The Clown and the Alchemist

LENGTH: 80 ft.   © Thomas A. Edison, 16 November 1900.

PRODUCER: J. Stuart Blackton, Albert E. Smith.

CAMERA: [Albert E. Smith.]

CAST: [J. Stuart Blackton?]

PRODUCTION DATE: September to early November 1900.

LOCATION: Vitagraph's roof-top studio, New York, N.Y.

SOURCE:

DESCRIPTION: Although we are led to believe that the ancient alchemists were all powerful, this picture somewhat reverses the order of things. The clown plays some wonderful pranks on the old professor. He appears and disappears in numerous startling positions, using his club with great effect and always escaping punishment. At last the alchemist brings his magic power into use, and calling two hooded assistants, orders a large cauldron brought in. The climax, by which the clown finally disposes of the alchemist, is startling in the extreme. (*Edison Films*, July 1901, 81.)

SUBJECT: Clowns. Magicians. Magic.

ARCHIVE: DLC-pp.

CITATIONS: *New York Clipper*, 17 November 1900, 852.

NOTE:

James White returned to the Newport Naval Training Center for a third time in the fall of 1900 (also see entry nos. 782, 783, 809-812). In producing several of these pictures, he either filmed scenes of a large-scale war game, which took place in September 1900, or shot related types of scenes shortly thereafter.

924 ***Naval Apprentices at Sail Drill on Historic Ship "Constellation"**
LENGTH: 125 ft. © Thomas A. Edison, 22 November 1900.
PRODUCER: James White.
CAMERA:
CAST:
PRODUCTION DATE: September–November 1900.
LOCATION: Newport, R.I.
SOURCE:

DESCRIPTION: This picture opens with the young cadets climbing the rigging and going through the sail drill on board the famous historic ship "Constellation." Loosing sail to buntline, making sail, shortening sail and furling; also loose sail to bowline. This picture is absolutely perfect photographically; also very thrilling, and makes a most interesting subject. (*Edison Films,* July 1901, 25-26.)
SUBJECT: Navies–United States. Naval cadets. Schools–Exercises and recreations. Ships.
ARCHIVE: DLC-pp.
CITATIONS: *New York Clipper*, 1 December 1900, 896.
NOTE:

925 ***Gun Drill by Naval Cadets at Newport Training School**
LENGTH: 50 ft. © Thomas A. Edison, 22 November 1900.
PRODUCER: James White.
CAMERA:
CAST:
PRODUCTION DATE: September–November 1900.
LOCATION: Naval Training Station, Newport, R.I.
SOURCE:

DESCRIPTION: Shows the cadets going through the gun drill, also loading, firing and charging. This is also a very stirring picture and is full of animation. (*Edison Films,* July 1901, 26.)
SUBJECT: Navies–United States. Naval cadets. Schools–Exercises and recreations.
ARCHIVE: DLC-pp.
CITATIONS: *New York Clipper*, 1 December 1900, 896.
NOTE:

926 ***Gymnasium Exercises and Drill at Newport Training School / Gymnasium Exercises and Drill at Newport Naval Training School**
LENGTH: 75 ft. © Thomas A. Edison, 22 November 1900.
PRODUCER: James White.
CAMERA:
CAST:
PRODUCTION DATE: September–November 1900.
LOCATION: Naval Training Station, Newport, R.I.
SOURCE:

DESCRIPTION: This picture shows the young cadets going through their daily exercises and drill, and is full of life, and photographically perfect. (*Edison Films,* July 1901, 26.)
SUBJECT: Navies–United States. Schools– Exercises and recreations. Naval cadets.
ARCHIVE: DLC-pp.

CITATIONS: *New York Clipper*, 1 December 1900, 896.
NOTE:

927 ***Naval Sham Battle at Newport / Naval Sham Battle at Newport Naval Training School**
LENGTH: 100 ft.   © Thomas A. Edison, 22 November 1900.
PRODUCER: James White.
CAMERA:
CAST:
PRODUCTION DATE: September-November 1900.
LOCATION: Naval Training Station, Newport, R.I.
SOURCE:
DESCRIPTION: Showing the attacking forces drawn up in line of battle. They immediately commence firing on the shore batteries. The batteries return the fire with telling effect, but are at last silenced by the overwhelming forces of the enemy. In the distance can be seen the ruins of a bridge destroyed by the invading forces. The smoke thickens as the firing becomes general, and the effect is superb. This picture is full of action, also thrilling and very exciting, and every detail is brought out clearly and distinctly. (*Edison Films,* July 1901, 26.)

SUBJECT: Navies–United States. Sham battles. Artillery. Bridges. Schools–Exercises and recreations. Harbors–Newport.
ARCHIVE: DLC-pp.
CITATIONS: "Hostile Fleet Beaten in Fierce Battle at Newport," *New York Herald*, 25 September 1900, 7; "Lessons Taught by Monday's Sham Battle," *New York Herald*, 26 September 1900, 9. *New York Clipper*, 1 December 1900, 896.
NOTE:

928 **Sham Battle on Land by Cadets at Newport Naval Training School**
LENGTH: 75 ft.   © No reg.
PRODUCER: James White.
CAMERA:
CAST:
PRODUCTION DATE: September-November 1900.
LOCATION: Naval Training Station, Newport, R.I.
SOURCE:
DESCRIPTION: Showing the attacking forces in the distance, led by Commander Hacker. They immediately advance on the enemy and take their position by storm. This is one of the best battle pictures yet produced. The cannon fire is executed directly in front of the camera, and the smoke effects make this one of the most realistic pictures ever taken. Photographically perfect. (*Edison Films,* July 1901, 25.)
SUBJECT: Navies–United States. Sham battles. Artillery. Schools–Exercises and recreations. Naval cadets. Commander Hacker.
ARCHIVE:
CITATIONS: *New York Clipper*, 1 December 1900, 896.
NOTE:

The Naval Drills at Newport.
Despite an advanced intention of the War College, the naval drills at Newport must count for little this year. These exercises it is idle to dignify. Manœuvres have been limited to a period of three days, and one of these days has expired. Reduced to the simplest terms, they mean that a small division of ships, assisted by minor torpedo craft, has been given seventy-two hours in which to attack a smaller division of vessels reinforced by shore batteries and one submarine boat.
These shore batteries are not using their own guns, and the submarine boat is working under favorable circum-

stances that could not be realized in any real conditions. What is more, the whole value of these vaunted drills must amount to little when the limitations of time, place, offence and defence are considered. They are not magnificent, neither are they anything like war. It is evident, for example, that if the element of surprise is to be considered the attack must be delivered on the first or second day, because on the third day this could no longer be a surprise.

Some slight good may result, but nothing that will be convincing. The North Atlantic squadron needs more fleet work at sea. It is suffering from a plethora of flower show demonstrations. Under commanders in chief with sand and sense, like Meade, Bunce, and Sicard, it reached in peace a high degree of efficiency. And this was because the ships were kept together and hard at work clear of harbors and fortifications. When this meaning is attained it will be quite time enough to begin combined operations. (*New York Herald*, 25 September 1900, 10.)

929 Sound Money Parade, New York, Nov. 3, 1900

LENGTH: 50 and 100 ft.   © No reg.
PRODUCER: James White.
CAMERA:
CAST: Theodore Roosevelt.
PRODUCTION DATE: 3 November 1900.
LOCATION: New York, N.Y.
SOURCE: *The Great McKinley Parade* (Edison film no. 255, October 1896).
DESCRIPTION: These films include an excellent picture of Governor Roosevelt. (*New York Clipper*, 17 November 1900, 852.)
SUBJECT: Parades. Politics, practical. Gold. Republican Party. William McKinley. Governors–United States.
ARCHIVE:
CITATIONS: *New York Clipper*, 17 November 1900, 852.
NOTE: Election day was November 6th, so it did not make sense to copyright this film. The picture was doubtlessly shown in New York theaters on the evening immediately following the event.

ROOSEVELT TO McKINLEY–"GREATER THAN 1896!"

At the close of the sound money parade Governor Roosevelt sent the following telegram to President McKinley–
NEW YORK, November 3, 1900.
President WILLIAM McKINLEY, Canton, Ohio.
In spite of the unfavorable weather the sound money parade was an even more magnificent demonstration than four years ago. The aroused civic honesty and business intelligence of the nation are behind you.
THEODORE ROOSEVELT. (*New York World*, 4 November 1900, 3.)

HONEST MONEY'S PARADE, DESPITE RAIN AND CROKER, A GREAT TRIUMPH
Marching Throngs Disregard the Downpour, and Unite in Making the Pageant One of the Most Remarkable Political Demonstrations in History of Country.
REPUBLICAN MANAGERS ELATED OVER AFFAIR
Tammany Chieftain's Efforts to Discredit the Demonstration and His Insults to Marchers Call Forth Condemnation Even from Members of Democratic Organization.

With a cheer which lasted for seven hours almost without a break the republicans and sound money democrats of New York city yesterday voiced their resolve to maintain the gold standard. It came from the throats of more than ninety thousand men who endured discomfort and braved serious danger to their health in their determination to carry out the plans for the great demonstration which marked the close of the anti-Bryan campaign in New York State.

Despite the soaking rain, which fell nearly all day, thousands of the leading business men of Greater New York turned out to walk three miles over wet streets in order to demonstrate the strength of their conviction. Nearly every important trade and industry in the city was represented by men who have long stood in the front rank of success. Behind them marched their subordinates and employees, wildly enthusiastic for the cause of honest finance and sound business policy. Indeed, the discouraging weather seemed rather to add fuel to the enthusiasm than to depress it. Though the number of men in line fell about seven thousand short of the number who marched under clear skies in the great sound money parade four years ago, their enthusiasm was far more intense and their cheers much louder than those of the gold men of 1896.

In many respects the parade of yesterday was one of the most remarkable political demonstrations ever seen in this country. In point of earnestness and significance it has not been surpassed. At times it resembled a triumphal progress rather than a mere political march.

Croker's Effort a Failure.

Richard Croker's attempt to detract from the impressiveness of the parade by causing Bryan banners to be hung out above the heads of the marchers was not only a flat failure, but it had the effect of increasing, rather than of diminishing, the impressiveness of the occasion. It is safe to say that not one of the thousands of paraders and not one in ten of the hundreds of thousands of spectators but carried away from the parade a feeling of the warmest resentment against Mr. Croker's device.

Not only republicans and independents, but even Tammany Hall democrats were disgusted by the puerile short-sightedness of Mr. Croker's attempt to interfere with the parade. They declared that he had added another blunder to the long list of mistakes which cost the democracy the State two years ago, and which have so heavily handicapped him in the present campaign.

To persons who watched the sound money march the ridiculousness of Mr. Croker's repeated assertion that many of the paraders had been coerced into parading was apparent. Never was there a more enthusiastic body of men than those who tramped up Broadway and Fifth avenue yesterday. It was evident to all who saw them that they were marching because they desired to do so and because they believed it to be their duty and not because they were in fear of consequences if they remained away.

Bryan's name was cheered three times by men in the ranks. There was every indication that these cheers were given by men who had been paid to do what they did. As it was, the trick was played in such a shamefaced and hangdog manner that it had no effect.

In the face of many obstacles the management of the parade was a success. The several divisions started promptly, and there were even fewer gaps than in the parade of four years ago. Rank after rank they swept by the reviewing stand, to the number of 91,711, as counted exactly by mechanical means for the Herald. The managers of the parade had expected to have 140,000 men in line, and it is probable that had the weather conditions been favorable, their expectation would have been fulfilled. When the day dawned with rain they would have been satisfied to be assured that 75,000 men would march. The result therefore, left them nothing to desire.

Chief Devery added another credit to the right side of his ledger by the excellence of the police arrangements. There was neither disorder nor disturbance, and the crowds were handled without adding unnecessarily to their discomfort.

Roosevelt Scores a Personal Triumph.

Governor Roosevelt was the popular hero of the day. He stood for seven hours on the reviewing stand with bared head in the rain and listened to shouts of "Hurrah for Teddy!" Both the crowd and the marchers seemed to feel a sort of ownership in the Governor, and his smiling reception of their familiarity indicated that the honors showered upon him had repaid him for his labors during the campaign. (*New York Herald*, 4 November 1900, page 3A.)

When the Boston Music Hall opened on 3 September 1900, American Vitagraph was on the bill and remained to become a permanent attraction. To service this venue, Blackton and Smith took a number of local views in Boston in December 1900 and into the new year. Some of these found their way into Edison catalogs.

930 **The Boston Fire Boat in Action**

LENGTH: 65 ft. © No reg.

PRODUCER: [J. Stuart Blackton, Albert E. Smith.]

CAMERA: [J. Stuart Blackton and/or Albert E. Smith.]

CAST:

PRODUCTION DATE: 28 August-December 1900.

LOCATION: Boston Harbor, Boston, Mass.

SOURCE:

DESCRIPTION: This beautiful picture is one of the most novel that has ever been presented in motion photography. The film shows the fire boat coming head on to the camera. All of the nozzles are in full play, and the effect of the columns of water rising from the bow of the boat is grand. The action of the wind causes the columns to spray out until they look like huge bunches of ostrich feathers blowing in the wind. The subject has a double interest, for, outside of the novel effect of the fire hose, the boat performs some beautiful evolutions in the water, going through the most intricate and marvelous manoeuvres, and with the new panoramic effect on our cameras, we were enabled to follow the boat all over the river, and she is always in the center of the picture. As the craft circles around, the spectators can watch the action of the water from every direction, and the smoke from the funnel, with the steam, the spray, and the beautiful ripple of the waves makes this one of the most interesting subjects that has ever been exhibited on a moving picture machine. It is

sure to give satisfaction. We were enabled to take this picture through the kind courtesy of Mr. L. Webber, Chief of the Boston Fire Department, who extended to us all the assistance in his power. (*Edison Films*, July 1901, 54.)
SUBJECT: Fire fighters. Fireboats. Tugboats. L. Webber.
ARCHIVE:
CITATIONS:
NOTE: Production date somewhat uncertain; conceivably film could have been taken at about the same time as *Trial Run of the New Battleship "Alabama."*

---

931 ***Panoramic View of Boston Subway from an Electric Car / Boston Subway from an Electric Car**
LENGTH: 100 ft.   © Thomas A. Edison, 16 December 1901.
PRODUCER: J. Stuart Blackton, Albert E. Smith.
CAMERA: J. Stuart Blackton and/or Albert E. Smith.
CAST:
PRODUCTION DATE: December 1900.
LOCATION: Boston, Mass.
SOURCE:

DESCRIPTION: Persons who have visited the "Hub," no doubt carried away very vivid recollections of Boston's famous system of Underground Transportation and this film takes the audience from the bright sunshine into the dim obscurity of the subway. The Underground stations and rows of Electric Arc lamps are plainly shown and, after traversing the tunnel for a considerable distance, the car finally emerges opposite the railroad depot. (*Edison Films,* September 1902, 92.)
SUBJECT: Urban transportation. Subways. Tunnels. Railroad stations.
ARCHIVE: DLC-pp.
CITATIONS: *Boston Herald*, 6 January 1901, 14-15.
NOTE: This film opened at the Boston Music Hall on 7 January 1901.

J. Stuart Blackton and Albert E. Smith made a number of comedies and trick films late in 1900, prior to Edison's withdrawal of their license for the second time in January 1901. At least one was copyrighted by Thomas A. Edison late in 1901 and subsequently distributed by the Edison Manufacturing Company.

---

932 ***The Artist's Dilemma / The Artist's Dilemma, or What He Saw in a Nightmare**
LENGTH: 125 ft.   © Thomas A. Edison, 14 December 1901.
PRODUCER: J. Stuart Blackton, Albert E. Smith.
CAMERA: J. Stuart Blackton and/or Albert E. Smith.
CAST:
PRODUCTION DATE: November-December 1900.
LOCATION: Vitagraph's roof-top studio, New York, N.Y.
SOURCE: *An Artist's Dream* (Edison film no. 795, 1900).
DESCRIPTION: The scene opens in an artist's studio, the artist asleep in his chair. A large old-fashioned clock opens and a young lady comes out and awaking the artist, requests him to paint her picture. While the artist is executing the work a clown comes from the clock, takes in the situation and begins to make love to the lady. The artist detects him and compels him to desist his love making. He continues to paint. The clown become interested and asks the artist to allow him to paint the picture, and begins smearing a

whitewash brush over the canvas, when lo, a most perfect image of the young lady appears. The image then steps down from the frame joins the young lady in the studio, and the figures, each a perfect counterpart of the other begin to dance to the great astonishment of the artist. The clown then by waving his hand causes the figures of the two girls to merge into one. The artist then assumes his seat and awakens from his dream with a great shock. (*Edison Films*, September 1902, 96.)

SUBJECT: Dreams. Artists. Magic. Clowns.

ARCHIVE: DLC-pp.

CITATIONS:

NOTE:

933 ***Grandma and the Bad Boys / Grandma and the Bad Boys; or, the Tables Turned**
LENGTH: 60 ft. © Thomas A. Edison, 21 December 1900.
PRODUCER: James White.
CAMERA:
CAST:
PRODUCTION DATE: December 1900.
LOCATION: [Black Maria, West Orange, N.J.]
SOURCE:

DESCRIPTION: The scene opens in the kitchen which is strewn with cooking utensils, indicating that grandma is busy preparing the Christmas pastry. Two bad boys of the red headed, freckled face type, enter. The mischievous expressions on their faces indicate that they have already planned a huge joke on grandma. One of the boys climbs to the kitchen table and takes down the old kitchen bracket lamp, which is equipped with a very large chimney, the other goes to the flour barrel and scoops out a quantity of flour, pouring it into the chimney of the lamp until it is filled to the top and packed down solidly. The lamp is then placed in the bracket. Grandma, who is very near sighted enters, scratches a match, removes the lamp chimney for the purpose of lighting up for the evening, when a large quantity of flour falls upon her head, instantly changing her old gingham wrapper into a snow white frock and giving her a general ghost-like appearance. The flour sticks in her hair and fills her eyes, but this is where she turns the tables. Suspecting the bad boys, she immediately looks for them under the old kitchen table where she finds them, as they thought, safely hidden away and enjoying the joke. She grabs them by the heels, and throws them one after the other, head first into the flour barrel. She then sits them down upon the floor very forcibly with their faces toward the audience and they present a very ludicrous appearance in the mad scramble to remove the flour from their eyes and hair. This is a picture which cannot fail to provoke mirth. (*Edison Films*, July 1901, 65-66.)

SUBJECT: Family. Boys. Practical jokes. Kitchens. Punishment.

ARCHIVE: DLC-pp.

CITATIONS:

NOTE:

934 ***A Wringing Good Joke / New "Wringing Good Joke"**
LENGTH: 60 ft. © Thomas A. Edison, 28 December 1900.
PRODUCER: James White.
CAMERA:
CAST:
PRODUCTION DATE: December 1900.
LOCATION: [Black Maria, West Orange, N.J.]
SOURCE: *A Wringing Good Joke* (Edison film no. 679, March-April 1899).

DESCRIPTION: A remarkably pleasing picture that will appeal to both young and old, for it is the sort of trick that every boy might play on a grandparent. Grandpa sits nodding in his armchair in the kitchen, where a stout jolly wash-woman from the

Emerald Isle is engaged over the tub with the family wash. The woman is called away from the tub by the appearance of the ubiquitous book agent who enters the kitchen door. While she is engaged in conversation with the book agent, the small boy enters, secures a string, ties one end of it to grandpa's chair and the other end he ties to a towel which is hanging over the tub. The washerwoman finally ejects the book agent, who becomes a nuisance, and going back to the tub in a wrathful frame of mind begins vigorously wringing the clothes. The towel

to which the string is secured is suddenly drawn into the wringer, and as grandpa is sitting with his feet on the stove and the chair tilted back a collision is brought about by the string, pulling grandpa and the tub together. Grandpa is thoroughly immersed in the foaming suds to the great amusement of both the boy and the book agent. The scene ends in a very ludicrous manner, as the woman is trying to help the old man up, slips on a piece of soap and herself falls into the mess. This is a crowning success as a comic picture.

Note: The above is a new negative and a great improvement over the Wringing Good Joke from our old negative. (*Edison Films*, July 1901, 65.)

SUBJECT: Boys. Practical jokes. Kitchens. Family. Irish Americans. Washing.

ARCHIVE: DLC-pp.

CITATIONS:

NOTE:

935 ***Love in a Hammock / Love in a Hammok [sic]**

LENGTH: 50 ft.   © Thomas A. Edison, 12 January 1901.

PRODUCER: James White.

CAMERA:

CAST:

PRODUCTION DATE: December 1900 to early January 1901.

LOCATION:

SOURCE: *Love in a Hammock* (Biograph film no. 1137, July 1899).

DESCRIPTION: A happy young couple are seated in a hammock under an old oak tree, ardently making love and evidently totally oblivious to all that is taking place about them. Two bad boys suddenly appear upon the scene, and one of them climbs into the tree while the other keeps watch. The urchin into the tree scrambles out on an overhanging branch, lying flat on his face, so as to be directly over the happy pair to hear what goes on. When the love making reaches a climax the branch on which the boy is lying breaks. The boy falls into the

hammock between the pair of lovers; the hammock breaks with the fall of the boy, and both the boy and the lovers are mixed up in a confused mass upon the ground. The ending is exceedingly ludicrous and we predict that this subject will be highly amusing. (*Edison Films*, July 1901, 67.)

SUBJECT: Courtship. Boys. Practical jokes. Hammocks.

ARCHIVE: DLC-pp.

CITATIONS:

NOTE:

936 **Love's Ardor Suddenly Cooled**

LENGTH: 35 ft.   © No reg.

PRODUCER: [James White.]

CAMERA:

CAST:

PRODUCTION DATE: By early January 1901.

LOCATION:

SOURCE:

DESCRIPTION: The scene opens with a picturesque wood as a background. An old fashioned settee is in the foreground of the picture, and in front of it runs a pretty stream of water, what is known in the country as a brook. A laddie and lass enter the scene and take a seat upon the settee and are busily engaged in telling each other their troubles and incidentally making a little love, when a farm boy enters, and, all unnoticed by the preoccupied lovers, seizes the back of the settee and precipitates the lovers and their seat into the water. The scene is entirely novel and humorous and the action is remarkably natural and true to life. (*Edison Films*, July 1901, 67.)

SUBJECT: Courtship. Boys. Practical jokes.

ARCHIVE:

CITATIONS:

NOTE:

This filmography is part of an ongoing project. There are unresolved enigmas and loose ends. One of the most obvious involves Annabelle Whitford, who may have appeared before Edison's cameras more often than this filmography currently indicates. The following stills remain to be adequately identified:

1.
Woman and child on the grounds of the Edison Laboratory, [1893-1894?]. Frame in Copyright Collection, DLC.

2.
Serpentine dance by three men in drag, [1894-1897]. Possibly *French Dancers* (Edison film no. 53.1). FrBaADF.

3.
*Annabelle
Serpentine Dance,*
[1894?].
The R written in the
corner suggests that
this film might have
been made for Raff
& Gammon some-
times in the fall of
1894.
Still courtesy of Ray
Phillips.

4.
Annabelle perform-
ing the Serpentine
Dance à la Trilby
(i.e. barefoot), [1895-
1897].
CLAc.

5.
Film of New York
City streets.
It has been tempt-
ing to identify this
subject as *Herald
Square* (Edison film
no. 158), but the
match is unsatisfac-
tory. *Broadway at
P.O.* (Edison film
no. 215) is another
possibility.
DLC-Hendricks.

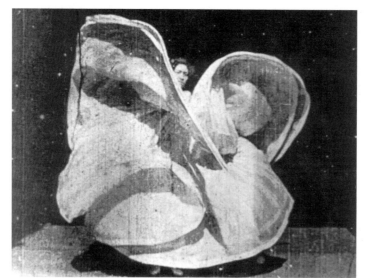

6.
[Serpentine Dance].
A statement appearing on the surviving print(s) claims that the film was copyrighted in 1897, but no copyright record matches with this production.
NNMoMA and CLAc.

7.
[Aunt Dinah's Sleigh Ride] is the name assigned to this film, at NR-GE. It may not be an Edison film.

An Edison Chronology
(to January 1901)

11 February 1847
Thomas Alva Edison is born at Milan, Ohio.

1847-1854
Lives in Milan.

1854-1863
Lives in Port Huron, Michigan.

1859-1862
Works as a newsboy and candy butcher on the trains of the Grand Trunk Railroad.

1863-1867
Works as an operator in telegraph offices in various Midwestern cities and conducts experiments with telegraph apparatus.

1868
Works as an operator at the Western Union Telegraph Company's main office in Boston and receives support from local entrepreneurs for his electrical inventions.

1869
Devotes himself full time to inventing and to pursuing various telegraph enterprises.

May-June 1873
Tests his automatic telegraph system in England.

Summer 1874
Invents quadruplex telegraph, ownership of which is disputed by Western Union and Jay Gould's Atlantic and Pacific Telegraph Company.

1875
Conducts experiments that lead to the development of the electric pen and autographic press.

1876
Has the Menlo Park laboratory constructed under the supervision of his father, Samuel.

Winter 1877
Begins experiments with carbon telephone transmitters.

Summer 1877
Begins work on the phonograph.

Winter-Spring 1878
Gains world-wide renown for inventing the phonograph.

15 November 1878
The Edison Electric Light Company is incorporated.

17 February 1879
William Kennedy Laurie Dickson writes Edison asking for a job.

22 October 1879
Edison conducts the first successful experiment with a high-resistance carbon filament.

1 October 1880
Begins the commercial production of electric lamps at the Edison Lamp Works in Menlo Park.

Winter 1881
Organizes the Edison Electric Lamp Company, the Edison Machine Works and other companies to manufacture lamps, generators, conductors, and other components for his electric lighting system.

4 September 1882
Opens the Pearl Street central station in the Wall Street district of New York.

November 1882
Closes his Menlo Park laboratory and establishes a laboratory on the top floor of the Bergmann and Company factory in New York City.

March-April 1883
Dickson again seeks employment by Edison and this time succeeds.

January 1886
Edison purchases Glenmont, his home in Llewellyn Park, New Jersey.

24 February 1886
Edison marries Mina Miller at Akron, Ohio.

18 April 1886
W.K.L. Dickson (age 26) marries Lucy Agnes Archer, 14 years his senior.

October 1886
Edison begins experiments on an improved phonograph.

10 October 1887
Organizes the Edison Phonograph Company.

Early December 1887
The Edison Laboratory opens at West Orange, New Jersey.

25 February 1888 (Saturday)
Eadweard Muybridge exhibits his zoopraxiscope at the Orange Music Hall (Orange, N.J.).

27 February 1888
Muybridge meets with Edison at his laboratory and discusses combining his zoopraxiscope with Edison's phonograph.

8 October 1888
Edison executes the first of his four major caveats for the kinetoscope and kinetograph, his motion picture system.

Ca. 24 October 1888
Dickson becomes head of the ore-milling department, one of Edison principal areas of interest in this period. In the next months he engages in some occasional work on the kinetoscope project as well.

February 1889
Edison opens an account for kinetoscope experiments in the Edison Laboratory books. The charge for the first month is $103.52.

3 February 1889
Edison executes the second of his four motion picture caveats.

24 April 1889
The Edison General Electric Company is organized.

20 May 1889
Edison executes the third of his major motion picture caveats.

Late June 1889
Dickson and Charles A. Brown are officially assigned to the kinetoscope project. They devote most of the summer to this project.

3 August 1889
Edison travels to Europe with his wife Mina. He attends the Paris Exposition and meets with Etienne-Jules Marey.

September-October 1889
The Photographic Building is constructed at the Edison Laboratory, West Orange. Many of the Edison motion picture experiments are conducted here.

6 October 1889
Edison returns to the United States. Apparently sees the results of Dickson's efforts with motion picture cylinders.

2 November 1889
Edison executes his fourth motion picture caveat, reflecting insights he had gained in his meeting with Marey.

21 November 1889
Dickson orders 6 strips of film, 3/4" wide and 54-feet long from the Eastman Company. These are said to be for astronomical experiments.

December 1889
Edison organizes the Edison Manufacturing Company as an unincorporated enterprise.

Late 1889 to March 1890
Dickson experiments with the tachyscope of Ottomar Anschütz.

1890

18 March 1890
William Friese-Greene writes Thomas Edison about his motion picture work.

October-November 1890
Edison assigns William Heise to the kinetoscope project.

Week ending 27 November 1890
G. Sacco Albanese is employed to pose for kinetoscope subjects. These may be last of the cylinder experiments:

*[Monkeyshines, no. 1]	1
√[Monkeyshines, no. 2]	2
√[Monkeyshines, no. 3]	3

1891

By May 1891
Work is completed on the experimental kinetograph which uses a horizontal-feed mechanism to move a 3/4" strand of film past the camera lens.

May-June 1891
Dickson and Heise shoot a series of films on the experimental, horizontal-feed kinetograph:

√[Dickson Greeting]	4
[Duncan and Another, Blacksmith Shop]	5
[Monkey and Another, Boxing]	6
[Duncan or Devonald with Muslin Cloud]	7
√[Duncan Smoking]	8
√[Newark Athlete]	9
√[Men Boxing]	10

20 May 1891
Women from the Federation of Women's Clubs visit Mina Edison at Glenmont. Afterwards they go down

to the Edison Laboratory and view *Dickson Greeting.*

27 May 1891
Thomas Edison shows the press *Dickson Greeting* in the experimental kinetoscope.

June 1891
Work begins on a full-scale, commercially viable motion picture system.

23-29 July 1891
Dickson goes to Rochester, New York, and negotiates with the Eastman Co., manufacturer of celluloid film, and with the Gundlach, and Bausch and Lomb optical companies for materials.

24 August 1891
Edison files three applications covering his motion picture system with the U.S. Patents Office.

1892

Spring-Summer 1892
Dickson and Heise build a vertical-feed, motion picture camera using 1 and 1/2" film and take at least one film:
[Man on Parallel Bars] 11

By October 1892
Dickson and Heise further refine the kinetograph camera, adopting a gauge and format that will be subsequently standardized. The film is now 1 and 9/16" wide. Dickson and Heise shoot at least four motion picture subjects:
√*Boxing* 12
√*Fencing* 13
√*Wrestling* 14
√*A Hand Shake* 15

31 October 1892
Alfred O. Tate writes Edison about introducing the kinetoscope at the World's Columbian Exposition in Chicago.

December 1892
Construction begins on the Black Maria motion picture studio at the Edison Laboratory, West Orange.

1893

February 1893
Construction on the Black Maria studio is completed.

4 February 1893
Dickson goes to Fort Myers, Florida to recover from a "serious illness," possibly a nervous breakdown.

25-27 April 1893
Dickson returns to the Edison Laboratory and resumes work on motion pictures, possibly producing two films immediately after his return.

Blacksmithing Scene 16
√*Horse Shoeing* 17

9 May 1893
The kinetoscope is shown at the Brooklyn Institute of Arts and Sciences by George Hopkins. This is its first public exhibition.

26 June 1893
Edison contracts with James Egan to manufacture 25 kinetoscopes.

16 August 1893
The Library of Congress receives sample kinetoscope records from Dickson, which are to be copyrighted in his name. The fee remains unpaid for almost two months. Upon its receipt on 6 October 1893, the copyright is finally registered. The subject of the film is unknown.

August-September 1893
Edison joins members of the Miller family for a visit to Chicago during the Columbian Exposition.

The Barber Shop 18

Summer 1893
The bank panic of 1893 and the ensuing depression result in the discharge of numerous "old hands" and the suspension of many activities at the laboratory.

1894

Early January 1894
Dickson and Heise take one or more short films for publicity purposes:
Edison Kinetoscopic Record of a Sneeze 19
[Fred Ott Holding a Bird] 20

January-March 1894
Production on an experimental or informal basis continues:
[Athlete with Wand] 21
√*[Unsuccessful Somersault]* 22
√*[Successful Somersault]* 23
[Men on Parallel Bars] 24
[Boxing Match] 25

6 March 1894
Commercial production of motion picture subjects officially begins with Eugen Sandow's performance in the Black Maria. Dickson and Heise continue to serve as the key members of Edison's production team.

1 April 1894

Edison shifts motion picture activities out of his laboratory with expenses totalling $24,118.04 for the development of the kinetograph-kinetoscope system. Motion pictures are subsequently pursued as a commercial enterprise through the Edison Manufactur-ing Company.

1 April 1894

William Gilmore becomes vice-president and gener-al manager of the Edison Manufacturing Company.

14 April 1894

Edison's motion pictures have their commercial debut at a kinetoscope parlor at 1155 Broadway, near Herald Square in New York City. The parlor is launched by the Kinetoscope Company, which is owned by Alfred O. Tate, the Holland Brothers and others who had been involved in Edison's phono-graph activities.

16 May 1894

Otway Latham deposits $1,000 with the Edison Manufacturing Company toward the purchase of 10 kinetoscopes. Latham wants to show boxing films; the idea of building a large capacity kinetoscope, which could show one abbreviated round of approxi-mately 150 feet of film, results. Such pictures will be shown by the Kinetoscope Exhibiting Company on an exclusive basis.

17 or 18 May 1894

A second kinetoscope parlor opens at the Masonic Temple, 148 State Street, Chicago, with 10 kineto-scopes.

1 June 1894

A third kinetoscope parlor opens in San Francisco at Peter Bacigalupi's phonograph parlor, 946 Market Street.

14 June 1894

Mike Leonard and Jack Cushing spar for six rounds before the kinetograph.

25 July 1894

Juan A. Caicedo visits the Edison Laboratory and performs outdoors on the slack wire.

18 August 1894

Raff & Gammon, as managers of the Kinetoscope Company, acquire the North American rights to exploit the kinetoscope from Edison. Only the spe-cial over-sized kinetoscopes designed for the exhibi-tion of fight films are excluded. Before this date kin-etoscopes were being sold to showmen and entre-preneurs on an ad-hoc, disorganized basis.

21 August 1894

The North American Phonograph Company enters receivership; Newark attorney John R. Hardin is appointed receiver.

3 September 1894

Edison assigns Maguire & Baucus the rights to manage his kinetoscope in Europe as long as they do so to his satisfaction. This territory will be expanded to include Asia and South America.

3 September 1894

James Corbett, the world heavyweight boxing cham-pion, appears in the play "Gentleman Jack" at the American Theatre in New York City.

7 September 1894

Corbett spars before the kinetograph with Peter Courtney.

10 September 1894

Maguire & Baucus incorporate the Continental Commerce Company as the business entity to han-dle their international motion picture interests.

11 September 1894

A grand jury in Newark is asked to decide if the law against prize fighting had been violated when the Corbett-Courtney Fight was shot. The all-male jury declines to indict anyone involved, including Edison.

[Glenroy Brothers, no. 1]   55

20 September 1894

Dickson and Heise film several scenes of rat baiting at the Black Maria:

Rat Killing   56
[Rats and Terrier, no. 2]   57
[Rats and Terrier, no. 3]   58
[Rats and Weasel]   59

[Glenroy Brothers, no. 2]   60

24 September 1894

William "Buffalo Bill" Cody and members of his wild west show visit West Orange and performed before the camera. They were accompanied by facial expressionist George Layman:

√*Buffalo Bill*   61
*Sioux Ghost Dance   62
Indian War Council   63
*Buffalo Dance   64
"The Man of A Thousand Faces"   65

26 September 1894

The Englehart Sisters duel before the kinetograph:

Lady Fencers (With Foils)   66
Lady Fencers (With Broadswords)   67

*Hornbacker-Murphy Fight   68
Danse du Ventre   69

6 October 1894

A diverse group of performers visit the Edison Laboratory and are kinetographed:

√*Walton and Slavin*   70
*The Pickaninnies   71
*Pedro Esquirel and Dionecio Gonzales   72
√√*Vincente Ore Passo*   73
Sheik Hadji Tahar   74
*Hadj Cheriff   75
Glenroy Bros., Boxers   76
*Glenroy Bros., [no. 2]   77

10 October 1894

Alexander Black's Picture Play, "Miss Jerry" has its debut at Mr. James L. Breese's studio, in West Sixteenth street, New York City. Edison's name is evoked in a *New York Herald* review.

*Luis Martinetti   78

16 October 1894

Two cowboys, who had been with Buffalo Bill's Wild West, come to West Orange to ride bucking bronchos for Edison's camera:

*Bucking Broncho   79
[Lasso Exhibition]   80

17 October 1894

First foreign kinetoscope parlor opens on Oxford Street in London.

17 October 1894

Ivan Tschernoff and his dogs perform before Edison's camera:

Skirt Dance Dog   81
√*Summersault Dog*   82

Human Pyramid   83
Sword Combat   84
Toyou Kichi   85

1 November 1894

Annie Oakley, trapezist Alcide Capitaine and cast members from the British musical comedy *A Gaiety Girl* travel to West Orange and appear before the kinetograph:

*Annie Oakley   86
√*Mlle. Capitaine*   87
Pas Seul, no. 1   88
Pas Seul, no. 2   89
√*The Carnival Dance*   90

*Imperial Japanese Dance   91
Oriental Dance   92
The Rixfords, [no. 1]   93
The Rixfords, [no. 2]   94
√*Opium Den*   95
*Chinese Laundry Scene   96
√*[Robetta and Doretto, no. 3]*   97
Elsie Jones, no. 1   98
Elsie Jones, no. 2   99
Topack and Steele   100

√*Finale of 1st Act, Hoyt's "Milk White Flag"*   101
*Band Drill   102
Trio Dance   103
The Tramp–Milk White Flag   104
The Widder   105

*Fire Rescue Scene   106
John W. Wilson and Bertha Waring   107
Fancy Club Swinger   108
[Dogs Fighting]   109

1895

8 January 1895

Dickson informs Raff & Gammon that many of their negatives have been ruined during the printing process. They will soon begin to make replacements.

20 January 1895

Magurie & Baucus open a kinetoscope parlor in Mex-ico City. President General Diaz and his wife attend the reception.

23 January 1895

Dickson and Heise film "Champion All-Round Athlete of the World" Duncan Ross and Lieut. Hartung fighting with swords on horseback.

22 March 1895

Louis Lumière demonstrates the Lumière cinémato-graphe at the Society for the Encouragement of National Industry in Paris. La sortie des ouvriers de l'usine Lumière is shown.

22 March 1895

Robert Paul writes to Edison, sending a sample of his own filmmaking efforts and offering to collabo-rate with the American inventor on a commercial basis. Edison will decline.

25 March 1895

C. Francis Jenkins and Thomas Armat sign a part-nership agreement to develop a "stereopticon phan-toscope"—an instrument that could project Edison motion pictures.

2 April 1895

Dickson resigns his position at the Edison Laboratory.

21 April 1895

Using their panoptikon/eidoloscope projector, the

Lathams project motion pictures for the press at their offices, 35 Frankfort Street, New York City.

9 May 1895

Barnum and Bailey's Circus gives a show at Orange, N.J. Some of its performers travel to the Black Maria and appear before the kinetograph:

10-19 May 1895

Heise films several scenes from David Henderson's burlesque Aladdin, Jr.:

20 May 1895

The Lathams exhibit films on the eidoloscope in a storefront theater at 156 Broadway, New York City.

28 August 1895

Armat and Jenkins submit a patent application for their phantoscope motion picture projector to the U.S. Patents Office.

28 August 1895

Raff & Gammon employee Alfred Clark begins supervising the production of Edison motion picture subjects.

6 September 1895

The Lumières submit a patent application for their cinématographe to the U.S. Patents Office. It arrives too late.

7 September 1895

Jenkins finally solves the mechanical problems that had prevented the phantoscope from functioning as a viable projector.

Late September to early October 1895
The phantoscope debuts in a specially-built motion picture theater at the Cotton States Exposition in Atlanta. While running the show, Armat makes contact with Raff & Gammon. Jenkins spends time with the Lathams.

15 October 1895
A fire breaks out in Hagenback's Arena on the Midway, destroying that show and badly damaging the phantoscope exhibition.

November 1895
Armat and Jenkins have a falling out and pursue separate commercial ventures.

Early December 1895
Frank Gammon of Raff & Gammon visits Thomas Armat's office and sees the phantoscope in operation. Raff & Gammon begin to negotiate for Armat's rights to the invention, unaware of Jenkins's role and involvement.

18 December 1895
C. Francis Jenkins shows the phantoscope at the Franklin Institute, Philadelphia.

1896

January 1896
Thomas Edison begins experimenting with x-rays.

15 January 1896
Raff & Gammon meet with Edison and discuss the possibility of marketing the phantoscope in conjunction with Edison's motion pictures. Edison agrees. The Edison Manufacturing Company is also to manufacture the projectors.

16 January 1896
Raff & Gammon send a signed contract for the phantoscope to Thomas Armat.

February
Raff & Gammon, in consultation with Armat, rename the phantoscope. It is now called the vitascope.

24 March 1896
Film production at the Black Maria resumes to meet the expected demand for new subjects:

27 March 1896
A private screening of the vitascope is held for

Thomas Edison at his laboratory.

3 April 1896
A press screening for the vitascope is held at the Edison Laboratory, West Orange. Edison plays the role of vitascope inventor.

10 April 1896
Raff & Gammon arrange to hire James H. White, who soon assumes a key role in the production of Edison films under Raff & Gammon auspices.

23 April 1896
The vitascope has its commercial debut at Koster & Bial's Music Hall, New York City, and runs for 16 weeks.

6 May 1896
Edison's new portable camera is ready for use.

11 May 1896
The eidoloscope, sporting the addition of an intermittent mechanism, opens at Hammerstein's Olympia Music Hall, New York City.

11 May 1896
James White and William Heise use the new portable camera to shoot films in New York City:

18 May 1896
The vitascope opens at Keith's New Theater in Boston and runs for 12 weeks.

25 May 1896
The vitascope opens at Keith's Bijou in Philadelphia and runs for nine weeks.

Ca. 26 May 1896
White and Heise take Edison's portable camera on a filming trip through Pennsylvania, Ohio and New York.

18-23 June 1896
White and Heise film outdoor scenes in Brooklyn and Coney Island:

27 June 1896
Press screening for Lumière cinématographe held in New York City.

27 June 1896
White and Heise film a bicycle parade celebrating the opening of a new pathway to Coney Island:

29 June 1896
Lumière cinématographe opens at Keith's Union Square Theatre in New York City and runs for 23 weeks.

27 July 1896
The second Lumière cinématographe in the United States opens at Keith's New Theatre in Philadelphia.

15 August 1896
Edison's vitascope ends its 16-week run at Koster & Bial's Music Hall.

15 August 1896
White and Heise film the Seventh Annual Baby Parade at Asbury Park, N.J.:

28 August 1896
Steamer "St. Louis" arrives in New York Harbor with Chinese Viceroy Li Hung Chang on board:

7 September 1896
The American Mutoscope Company's exhibition service, featuring large-format films and the biograph projector, has its comercial debut in Pittsburgh, Pa.

13 September 1896
The vitascope reopens in New York City at Proctor's Pleasure Palace and 23rd Street Theatre and runs at each house for eight weeks.

13-19 September 1896
Melodrama star Robert Bruce Mantell possibly performs scenes from his plays before the kinetograph at the Black Maria:

Mid to late October 1896
James H. White leaves Raff & Gammon after being hired to head the Edison Manufacturing Company's Kinetograph Department. Thomas A. Edison begins a new policy of copyrighting most of his company's films at the Library of Congress.

31 October 1896
White and Heise film a political demonstration favoring "sound money" and Republican presidential candidate William McKinley:

3 November 1896
McKinley elected President of the United States.

November 1896
The Edison Home Phonograph—an inexpensive, spring motor driven phonograph—is introduced.

14 November 1896
White and Heise film the local Newark fire department in a series scenes:

30 November 1896
Edison's own motion picture projector, the projectoscope, is premiered at the Bijou Theater in Harrisburg, Pennsylvania.

Ca. 30 November 1896
White, Heise and two assistants embark on a filming trip through Pennsylvania to Niagara Falls and Buffalo, New York. They will shoot films with the cooperation of, and for the benefit of, the Lehigh Valley Rail-road:

By 21 December 1896
Edison personnel have resumed filming at the Black Maria:

23 December 1896
Films of the Black Diamond Express, Buffalo and Niagara Falls are shown to Lehigh Valley Railroad officials visiting the Edison Laboratory.

24-25 December 1896
White and Heise spend Christmas Eve and Christmas Day filming views in Harrisburg, Pennsylvania—for exhibition on the Edison projectoscope at the local Bijou Theater:

28 December 1896
The biograph opens at Keith's Bijou Theatre in Philadelphia, beginning a relationship between the

American Mutoscope Company (later the American Mutoscope & Biograph Company) and the Keith organization that will last for approximately 10 years.

1897

January 1897
White and Heise travel to the Washington, D.C., area in preparation for filming the McKinley Inaugural:

16 February 1897
Maguire & Baucus distribute a preliminary circular advertising the Edison Projecting Kinetoscope for a cost of $100.

5 March 1897
White and Heise take films of President William McKinley's Inauguration in Washington, D.C.:

17 March 1897
Robert Fitzsimmons knocks out James Corbett and becomes the heavyweight boxing champion. It is filmed by the Veriscope Company.

4 April 1897
White and Heise film at Grace Church on Easter Sunday.

April 1897
White and Heise film Barnum & Bailey's Circus in New York City, where it is performing at Madison Square Garden:

27 April 1897
White and Heise film the ceremonies dedicating Grant's Tomb on Riverside Drive, New York City:

29 April 1897
James Corbett and William Brady sue Thomas A. Edison in the U.S. Circuit Court in Trenton, N.J., for exploiting films of the Corbett-Courtney Fight, without paying royalties called for in their contract with the Kinetoscope Exhibiting Company.

June 1897
White and Heise embark on a filming trip that takes

them to Haines Falls (N.Y.), Buffalo, Cleveland, and Chicago. Edison copyrights these and subsequent subjects as paper prints, which ensures that most Edison production survive in motion picture form.

22 June 1897

White and Heise film horse races at Sheepshead Bay Race Track, Coney Island, N.Y.:

July 1897

The Kinetograph Department makes advertising films for clients:

17-25 July 1897

James White and a new cameraman, Frederick W. Blechynden, take a number of films in and around Yellowstone National Park. They are on the early stages of a filming trip that will last approximately 10 months and take them to California, Colorado, Mexico, China, Japan and Hawaii.

6-9 August 1897

White and Blechynden shoot scenes in Seattle, Washington, related to the Alaskan Gold Rush:

12-14 August 1897

William Heise films the Monmouth County Horse Show at Long Branch, N.J.:

31 August 1897

Edison is granted a patent on its motion picture camera, patent no. 589,168.

September 1897

Heise films members of Waite's Comedy Company at the Black Maria:

14 September 1897

Edison employee Julius Manger is arrested for stealing kinetoscope films.

July-August 1897

White and Blechynden film on the Southern Pacific Railroad:

22 August 1897

White and Blechynden arrive in San Francisco. They shoot several films at the Sutro Baths:

2 September 1897

White and Blechynden film the S. S. "Coptic" departing San Francisco for China:

9 September 1897

White and Blechynden film a military athletic tournament at the Presidio military base in San Francisco:

September 1897
White and Blechynden film the U.S. Life Saving Service in San Francisco:

3-8 October 1897
White and Blechynden film scenes related to the Festival of Mountain and Plain at Denver, Col.:

8 October 1897
William Heise remains based in West Orange, N.J., and takes scenes for the local ambulance fund:

October 1897
White and Blechynden travel through Colorado and New Mexico, taking films:

25 November 1897
Heise films a local unit of the New Jersey National Guard on Thanksgiving morning:

November-December 1897
White and Blechynden undertake a filmmaking expedition through Mexico:

Spring-Summer 1897
Walter W. Freeman, Charles Hurd and Charles Webster film and photograph the Passion Play and related scenes in Horice, Bohemia (the present day Czech Reupblic).

7 December 1897
Thomas A. Edison sues Charles Webster and Edmund Kuhn of the International Film Company, and Maguire & Baucus, Ltd. for patent infringement. They don't contest the suits.

17 December 1897
Frank Guth films the execution of William Carr in Liberty, Mo.

December 1897 to January 1898
Richard Hollaman of the Eden Musee produces a version of the Passion Play in New York City. It is shot by William Paley:

20 December 1897
White and Blechynden arrive in San Diego and begin taking films in southern California:

1898

1 January 1898
White and Blechynden film the Ninth Annual Tournament of Roses parade in Pasadena, California:

22 January 1898
White and Blechynden shoot the launching of the Japanese warship "Chitose" at San Francisco:

24 January 1898
White and Blechynden film a parade commemorating the 50th anniversary of the discovery of gold in California:

February 1898
William Paley films another stage performance for Richard Hollaman at the Eden Musee:

1-3 February 1898
Heise films a number of winter scenes in and around Orange, N.J.:

3 February 1898
White and Blechynden leave San Francisco for Hong Kong via Yokohama, Japan on the S.S. "Coptic." On February 11th, they encounter a typhoon that damages the ship.

15 February 1898
U.S. Battleship "Maine" is sunk in Havana Harbor, Cuba.

6 March 1898
S.S. "Coptic" arrives in Hong Kong, with White and Blechynden on board.

6-10 April 1898
White and Blechynden film scenes in Shanghai:

14 April 1898
White and Blechynden, on board the S.S. "Gaelic," arrive in Yokohama.

March 1898
Heise films a number of scenes in Northern New Jersey and in the Black Maria:

Parade of Buffalo Bill's Wild West Show, no. 1 583
Parade of Buffalo Bill's Wild West Show, no. 2 584

Mid-May to early June 1898
Paley takes films of U.S. troops in Tampa:
Blanket-Tossing a New Recruit 585
Soldiers Washing Dishes 586
Wagon Supply Train En Route 587
9th and 13th U.S. Infantry at Battalion Drill 588
Trained Cavalry Horses 589

8 June 1898
Paley films U.S. troops embarking onto transports for the invasion of Cuba:
*Roosevelt's Rough Riders
Embarking for Santiago* 590
Cuban Volunteers Embarking 591
*71st New York Volunteers
Embarking for Santiago* 592
Loading Horses on Transport 593
Transport Ships at Port Tampa 594

22 June 1898
U.S. troops land at Daiquiri, Cuba. Paley films disembarking troops.

U.S. Troops Landing at Daiquiri, Cuba 595
Mules Swimming Ashore at Daiquiri, Cuba 596
Packing Ammunition on Mules, Cuba 597

Major General Shafter 598
*Pack Mules with Ammunition
on the Santiago Trail, Cuba* 599
*Troops Making Military
Road in Front of Santiago* 600

June 1898 to mid-July 1898
Heise takes films in the Black Maria:
The Burglar, [no. 2] 601
The Telephone, [no. 2] 602

Fake Beggar 603
Shooting Captured Insurgents 604
Cuban Ambush 605

12 July 1898
Thomas Edison sues J. Stuart Blackton and Albert E. Smith for patent and copyright infringement.

17 July 1898
U.S. troops occupy Santiago.

2 August 1898
Blackton and Smith become Edison licensees.

20 August 1898
Three Edison camera crews take films of the Great Naval Parade in the Hudson River:
Excursion Boats, Naval Parade 606

Police Boats Escorting Naval Parade 607
The Fleet Steaming up the North River 608
Victorious Squadron Firing Salute 609
Reviewing the "Texas" at Grant's Tomb 610
U.S. Cruiser "Brooklyn," Naval Parade 611
U.S. Battleship "Oregon" 612
Observation Train Following Parade 613
The "Massachusetts," Naval Parade 614
Close View of the "Brooklyn," Naval Parade 615
The "Texas," Naval Parade 616
The "Glen Island" Accompanying Parade 617
Admiral Sampson on Board the Flagship 618
Statue of Liberty 619

Merry-Go-Round 620
Farmer Kissing the Lean Girl 621

August-October 1898
Blackton and Smith take films for use with their vitagraph exhibition service and subsequently turn the films over to Edison for distribution, as per their licensing agreement:
The Vanishing Lady 622
The Burglar on the Roof 623
Elopement on Horseback 624
The Cavalier's Dream 625
Little Mischief 626
Family Troubles 627

Up-to-Date Cakewalk 628
Race Track Scene 629
Betting Field 630

September 1898
White and Heise shoot a number of productions in the Black Maria:
Ella Lola, a la Trilby 631
Turkish Dance, Ella Lola 632
Balloon Ascension, Marionettes 633
Dancing Chinaman, Marionettes 634
Skeleton Dance, Marionettes 635

20-30 September 1898
White and Heise film returning New Jersey troops:
Advance Guard, Return of New Jersey Troops 636
Return of 2nd Regiment of New Jersey 637

1 October 1898
An Edison camera crew films parading troops in Brooklyn, N.Y.:
Return of Troop C, Brooklyn 638
Parade of Marines, U.S. Cruiser "Brooklyn" 639

October 1898
William Heise leaves the Edison Manufacturing Company and withdraws from filmmaking.

The Burglar in the Bed Chamber 640
The Tramp in the Kitchen 641

1899

1 January 1899

Spain turns Havana over to American occupying forces. An Edison cameraman films the events:

January 1899

Blackton and Smith shoot a group of films that are more or less quickly turned over to the Edison Manufacturing Company.

January 1899

James White uses the local National Guard to re-enact heroic moments from the Spanish-American War.

17 March 1899

Fire destroys the Windsor Hotel, New York City. Edison filmmakers shoot films related to the event.

16 April 1899

New Yorkers honor the U.S. cruiser "Raleigh," which fought in the Battle of Manila Bay. Due to poor weather, the Edison camera crew cannot film the event.

17 April 1899

Edison crew take several scenes of the "Raleigh":

May 1899

James White shoots "reenactments" of American troops fighting Filipino insurgents:

1 June 1899

An Edison camera crew films the New York Police parade:

7 June 1899

Blackton and Smith shoot James J. Jeffries, challenger for the World Heavyweight Boxing Champion-ship, at Asbury Park, N.J.:

8 June 1899

Thomas Crahan and Robert K. Bonine leave West Orange to take films in Alaska and the Yukon.

9 June 1899

Jeffries defeats Robert Fitzsimmons in 11 rounds and becomes the new champion. Blackton and Smith attempt to film the fight at the Coney Island Athletic Club. The lighting system fails and the negatives are useless:

19 June 1899

American Vitagraph (owned by Blackton, Smith,

and William T. Rock) begins to show films at Tony Pastor's Theatre, where its exhibition service will become a permanent feature.

Reproduction of the Jeffries-Fitzsimmons Fight 696

Mesmerist and Country Couple	697
Strange Adventure of a New York Drummer	698
The Bibulous Clothier	699
A Fair Exchange is No Robbery	700

Panoramic View,	
Horseshoe Curve from Penna. Ltd	701
Panoramic View,	
Horseshoe Curve, Pa. Ltd, no. 2	702
A Ride Through	
Pack Saddle Mountains, Penna. R.R.	703
Running Through	
Gallitzen Tunnel, Penna., R.R.	704

8 July 1899
An Edison camera crew, probably Blackton and Smith, film a tune-up race for the America's Cup:

Trial Race, "Columbia" and "Defender," [no. 1]	705
Trial Race, "Columbia" and "Defender," no. 2	706

A Quiet Little Smoke	707
[The Prentice Trio]	708

July-August 1899
Thomas Crahan and Robert K. Bonine take films and lantern slides of the Gold Rush in Alaska and the Yukon:

Panoramic View of the White Pass Railroad	709
White Horse Rapids	710
Miles Canyon Tramway	711
Pack Train on Chilcoot Pass	712
Packers on the Trail	713
Burro Pack Train on Main Street, Dawson City	714
Rocking Gold in the Klondike	715
Washing Gold on 20 Above Hunker, Klondike	716

Boston Horseless Fire Department	717

New Brooklyn to New York	
via Brooklyn Bridge, no. 1	718
New Brooklyn to New York	
via Brooklyn Bridge, no. 2	719

The Early Morning Attack	720
Colonel Funstan Swimming the Bagbag River	721
Fun in Camp	722
Trick Bears	723

June to mid-September 1899
James White, probably in association with the Eaves Shadowgraph Company of New York, makes a group of films designed to be exhibited in careful synchronization with songs:

Love and War	724
The Astor Tramp	725
Tenderloin at Night	726

Late August-to early September 1899
James White films at Paul Boyton's Shoot the Chutes pond, Coney Island:

The Diving Horse	727
Shoot the Chutes Series	728

5 September 1899
Admiral George Dewey stops off in Gibraltar on his way to the United States:

Admiral Dewey Landing at Gibraltar	729

27 September 1899
Admiral George Dewey arrives in New York Harbor where he is to be greeted by a series of celebrations. The Edison company covers these events with as many as eight different camera crews:

Admiral Dewey's First Step on American Shore 730

Police Boats and Pleasure	
Craft on Way to "Olympia"	731
Admiral Dewey Receiving the	
Washington and New York Committees	732
Admiral Dewey Taking Leave of the Washing-	
ton Committee on the U.S. Cruiser "Olympia"	733
Panoramic View of	
"Olympia" in New York Harbor	734
Panoramic View of Cruiser "Olympia"	734.1

29 September 1899
Warships participate in the Dewey Naval Parade, New York Harbor:

U.S. Cruiser "Olympia" Leading Naval Parade	735
Flagship "Olympia" and	
Cruiser "New York" in Naval Parade	736
Panoramic View of Floral Float "Olympia"	737
Panorama at Grant's	
Tomb, Dewey Naval Procession	738

30 September 1899
Military units participate in the Dewey Land Parade, New York City:

Presentation of Loving	
Cup at City Hall, New York	739
Admiral Dewey and Mayor	
Van Wyck Going Down Riverside Drive	740
Admiral Dewey Leading Land Parade, [no. 1]	741
Admiral Dewey Leading Land Parade, no. 2	742
Mounted Police, Sousa's	
Band and Sailors of "Olympia"	743
Admiral Dewey Passing Catholic Club Stand	744
Dewey's Arrival at Triumphal Arch	745
U.S. Marines in Dewey Land Parade	746
West Point Cadets	747
Battery K Siege Guns	748
Governor Roosevelt and Staff	749

1900

Faust and Marguerite 786
The Magician 787
Ching Ling Foo Outdone 788
The Kiss 789

21 February 1900

An Edison cameraman films troops departing for South Africa at Halifax, Nova Scotia:

Second Canadian Contingent Leaving Halifax 790
Snowballing Scene 791
Panoramic View of the Bay of Fundy 792

28 February 1900

An Edison camera crew films a devastating fire in Newark, N.J.:

Great Newark Fire 793

Ca. March 1900

An unidentified Edison affiliate produces a group of magic films:

Clown Dining at the Infernal Palace 794
An Artist's Dream 795
The Mystic Swing 796
Uncle Josh in a Spooky Hotel 797
Uncle Josh's Nightmare 798

Off for the Fox Hunt 799

11 April 1900

James White films local National Guard units re-enacting scenes from the Boer War. In an accident, White is seriously wounded:

Boers Bringing in British Prisoners 800
Capture of Boer Battery by British 801
Capture of Boer Battery 802
Charge of Boer Cavalry, [no. 1] 803
Charge of Boer Cavalry, [no. 2] 804

12 April 1900

The American Mutoscope & Biograph Company pays Thomas A. Edison $2,500 for the option to purchase his motion picture interests for $500,000. When funding for the sale falls through, Edison will decide to hold on to the business rather than sell it.

15-20 April 1900

White, having recovered from his wounds, films local National Guard units re-enacting additional Boer War scenes. Mason Mitchell helps with the direction:

Battle of Mafeking 805
English Lancers Charging 806
Red Cross Ambulance on the Battlefield 807
Boer Commissary Train Treking 808

April-May 1900

White films scenes at the Naval Station in Newport, R.I.:

Panoramic View of Newport 809
Discharging a Whitehead Torpedo 810

Exploding a Whitehead Torpedo 811
Torpedo Boat "Morris" Running 812

5 May 1900

The Edison Manufacturing Company is incorporated, though the motion picture business is excluded from this new entity for the time being.

5 May 1900

Paley films a demonstration by supporters of horse-drawn transportation:

Roaddrivers' Association Parade 813
Racing on N.Y. Speedway May 5, 1900 814

Panorama of Gorge Railway 815
Niagara Falls from the Brink of the Horseshoe 816
New Black Diamond Express 817

May 1900

James White works with Alfred T. Schauffler and the New York City Board of Education to take sound films of school-day activities for exhibition at the Paris Exposition of 1900.

A Ride Through the Ghetto 818
School Assembly, Foreign Children 819
Dismissal to the Class Rooms 820
Kindergarten games 821
Recess Games, Boys 822
Recess Games, Girls 823
A Workshop in Full Operation 824
Classroom Gymnastics 825
Grace Hoop Gymnastic Drill 826
Rapid Dismissal to the Street 827
Ball Games. Football, etc. 828
Assembly in an Uptown School 829
Rhythmic Ball Drill to Music 830
Cooking Class in Operation 831
Marching Salute to the Flag 832
Indian Club Swinging, High School Girls 833

28 May 1900

White films an eclipse of the sun at Virginia Beach, Va.:

[Eclipse] 834

High Diving by A. C. Holden 835
Watermelon Contest 836
Bombardment of Taku Forts 837

19-27 June 1900

White, on his way to Europe, films an ocean storm aboard the "Kaiserin Maria Theresia":

A Storm at Sea 838

29 June 1900

Edison associates and the Board of Education of the City of New York screen a program of films and phonograph recordings synchronously for the first time at the Paris Exposition.

5 July 1900
An Edison cameraman films a devastating fire in Bayonne, N.J.:
*Burning of the Standard
   Oil Tanks, Bayonne, N.J.*   839

July 1900
White produces numerous films of the Paris Exposition. Many are shot using a new, fluid panning mechanism:
Champs Elysees   840
Palace of Electricity   841
Panorama of Eiffel Tower   842
Panorama of Place de L'Opera   843
Scene from the Elevator Ascending Eiffel Tower   844
Champs de Mars   845
Paris Exposition from the Trocadero Palace   846
Eiffel Tower from Trocadero Palace   847
Esplanade des Invalides   848
*Panorama of the Paris
   Exposition from the Seine*   849
Panorama of the Moving Boardwalk   850
Panorama from the Moving Boardwalk   851
Scene in the Swiss Village   852
Swiss Village, no. 2   853
Panoramic View of the Champs Elysees   854
Panoramic View of the Place de la Concorde   855
Annual French Military Carousal   856
*Breaking up of the Crowd at
   Military Review at Longchamps*   857
Scene on the Boulevard DeCapucines   858
*Street Scene at Place
   de la Concorde, Paris, France*   859
Arrival of Train at Paris Exposition   860

23 July 1900
White or an Edison-affiliated filmmaker shoots scenes in Oberammergau, Germany:
*Train Loaded with Tourists
   Arriving at Oberammergau*   861
*Opening of the Great
   Amphitheatre Door for the Intermission*   862
Street Scene in Oberammergau   863
Anton Lang's House   864

Piccadilly Circus, London, England   865
Royal Exchange, London, England   866

28 July 1900
White films aboard the S.S. "New York" on his return voyage to the United States:
Tug-o-War on Board an Ocean Steamer   867

July-August 1900
Eberhard Schneider takes films in Germany and Switzerland; these pictures are subsequently marketed by the Edison Manufacturing Company:
*Johannisfest Marchen Gruppen of the Leg-
   ends and Fairy Tales of the Past Centuries*   868

Great Fire Engine Scene in Breslau, Germany   869
Fire Drills at Breslau, Germany   870
Breslau Fire Department in Action   871
Market Day in Breslau, Germany   872
The Great Corpus Christi Procession in Breslau   873
Military Maneuvers of the German Army   874
A German Cuirassier Regiment   875
Ammunition Wagons Arriving on the Battlefield   876
*Red Cross of the German
   Army on the Battlefield*   877
Opening of Bismarck's Mausoleum   878
*Great Waterfall of the Rhein
   at Shaffhausen, Germany [sic]*   879
*View of the Rhein Falls
   from the Centre of the Rapids*   880
*Climbing Snowclad
   Mountains in Switzerland*   881

January-August 1900
Blackton and Smith take films, which they will later turn over to the Edison firm for distribution:
Leaping Dogs at Gentry's Circus   882
How the Professor Fooled the Burglars   883
Baby's Meal   884
*Harry Thompson's
   Immitations of Sousa*   885
Such a Headache   886
The Mysterious Cafe   887
*The Mischievous Clerks; or
   How the Office Was Wrecked*   888
Miniature Railway   889

July-August 1900
Blackton and Smith take films in Martha's Vineyard, while on a working vacation. These are turned over to Edison for sales purposes.
Children Bathing   890
Hooligan and the Summer Boarders   891
Hooligan in Central Park   892
Hooligan at the Seashore   893
Hooligan Has Troubles with the Cook   894
Hooligan Takes His Annual Bath   895
Hooligan Causes a Sensation   896
Hooligan's Narrow Escape   897

28 August 1900
An Edison cameraman films the U.S.S. "Alabama" off Cape Cod:
Trial Run of the New Battleship "Alabama"   898

Girls Frolic at the Seashore   899
The Fisherman and the Bathers   900

August-September 1900
An Edison camera crew films many scenics with a panning mechanism used at the Paris Exposition:
Circular Panoramic View of Niagara Falls   901
Circular Panorama of the American Falls   902
Circular Panorama of Mauch Chunk, Penna.   903

Circular Panorama of Atlantic City, N.J. 904
Panoramic View of the
    Capitol, Washington, D.C. 905
Panoramic View of the
    White House, Washington, D.C. 906
A Composite Picture of the
    Principal Buildings in Washington, D.C. 907

8 September 1900
Galveston, Texas, is hit by a devastating hurricane and flood.

10 September 1900
Blackton and Smith submit a proposal to Edison asking for the reinstatement of their license. It is accepted but they are not formally reinstated until October 10th.

11-19 September 1900
Albert E. Smith takes films of devastated Galveston:
*Searching Ruins on
    Broadway, Galveston, for Dead Bodies* 908
Bird's Eye View of Dock Front, Galveston 909
Launching of a Stranded Schooner 910
Panorama of East Galveston 911
Panorama of Galveston Power House 912
Panorama of Orphans' Home, Galveston 913
*Panorama of Wreckage of
    of Water Front, Galveston* 914
Panoramic View of Tremont Hotel, Galveston 915

29 October 1900
An Edison camera crew films the aftermath of a fire and explosion in downtown, New York City:
Firemen Fighting the Tarrant Fire 916
The Falling Walls at the Tarrant Explosion 917
Searching the Ruins of the Tarrant Fire 918

September to early November
Blackton and Smith make a series of comedies and magic films:
The Congress of Nations 919
Hooligan Assists the Magician 920
The Enchanted Drawing 921
Maude's Naughty Little Brother 922
The Clown and the Alchemist 923

September-November 1900
James White returns to Newport, R.I., to film scenes at the Naval Training School:
*Naval Apprentices at Sail Drill
    on Historic Ship "Constellation"* 924

*Gun Drill by Naval Cadets
    at Newport Training School* 925
*Gymnasium Exercises and
    Drill at Newport Training School* 926
Naval Sham Battle at Newport 927
Sham Battle on Land by Cadets
    at Newport Naval Training School 928

October 1900
The Edison Manufacturing Company rents the top floor and roof of a building at 41 East 21st Street for $150 per month. The site is to be the home of its new motion picture studio.

Sound Money Parade, New York, Nov. 3, 1900 929

6 November 1900
William McKinley is re-elected President of the United States.

29 November 1900
Edwin S. Porter is hired by the Edison Manufacturing Company to improve the design of its motion picture equipment.

November-December 1900
Blackton and Smith take a series of films that are not turned over to Edison until late the following year:
The Boston Fire Boat in Action 930
*Panoramic View of Boston
    Subway from an Electric Car* 931
The Artist's Dilemma 932

November 1900 to early January 1901
James white supervises the production of several short comedies:
Grandma and the Bad Boys 933
A Wringing Good Joke 934

Love in a Hammock 935
Love's Ardor Suddenly Cooled 936

10 January 1901
Edison cancels Blackton and Smith's license.

12 January 1901
The Hinkle Iron Company informs the Edison Manu-facturing Company that it has completed construction on the new glass-enclosed, roof-top studio at 41 East 21st Street. The studio, which allows for year-round filming, replaces the Black Maria.

Allen, Robert C. *Vaudeville and Film, 1895-1915: A Study in Media Interaction.* Ph.D. diss., University of Iowa, 1977. New York: Arno Press, 1980.

Allen, Robert C., and Douglas Gomery. *Film History: Theory and Practice.* New York: Alfred A. Knopf, 1985.

Barnes, John. *The Beginnings of the Cinema in England.* New York: Barnes and Noble, 1976.

———. *The Rise of the Cinema in Great Britain: Jubilee Year 1897.* London: Bishopgate Press, 1983.

———. *1898: The Rise of the Photoplay.* London: Bishopgate Press, 1983.

———. *Filming the Boer War.* London: Bishopgate Press, 1992.

Berton, Pierre. *The Klondike Fever: The Life and Death of the Last Great Gold Rush.* New York: Alfred A. Knopf, 1958.

Bottomore, Stephen. "Joseph Rosenthal." *Sight and Sound* 52, no. 3 (Summer 1983): 152-153.

———. "The Most Glorious Profession." *Sight and Sound* 52, no. 4 (Autumn 1983): 260-265.

———. *I Want to See This Annie Mattygraph: A Cartoon History of the Coming of the Movies.* Pordenone, Italy: Le Giornate del Cinema Muto, 1995.

Breard, Sylvester Quinn. *A History of Motion Pictures in New Orleans, 1896-1908.* M.A. thesis, Louisiana State University, 1951. Published on microfiche in *Historical Journal of Film, Radio and Television* 15, no. 4 (Fall 1995).

Brogan, Hugh, and Charles Mosley. *American Presidential Families.* New York: Macmillan, 1993.

Burch, Noël. "Porter or Ambivalence." *Screen* 19, no. 4 (Winter 1978-79): 91-105.

———. *Life to Those Shadows.* Berkeley: University of California Press, 1990.

California for Health, Pleasure and Profit: Why You Should Go There. San Francisco: Passenger Department of the Southern Pacific Company, [189-?].

Catskill Mountains. Roundout, N.Y.: Passenger Department, Ulster & Delaware R.R., 1892.

Chapman, David L. *Sandow the Magnificent: Eugen Sandow and the Beginnings of Bodybuilding.* Urbana: University of Illinois Press, 1994.

Charney, Leo, and Vanessa Schwartz, eds. *Cinema and the Invention of Modern Life.* Berkeley: University of California Press, 1995.

Cherchi Usai, Paolo. *Burning Passions: An Introduction to the Study of Silent Cinema.* London: British Film Institute, 1994.

Cinema 1900-1906: An Analytical Study, 2 vols. Brussels: FIAF, 1982. Vol. 1: *Brighton Symposium, 1978.* Vol. 2: *Analytical Filmography (Fiction Films), 1900-1906.*

Cohen-Stratyner, Barbara Naomi. *Biographical Dictionary of Dance.* New York: Schirmer Books, 1982.

Continental Phonograph Kinetoscope Company. *Kinetoscenes.* [March 1895].

Cosandey, Roland; André Gaudreault; and Tom Gunning, eds. *An Invention of the Devil?: Religion and Early Cinema.* Lausanne: Éditions Payot, 1992.

Cosandey, Roland, and François Albera, eds. *Images Across Borders, 1896-1918: Internationality in World Cinema: Representations, Markets, Influences, and Reception.* Lausanne: Éditions Payot, 1995.

Couvares, Frank, ed. *Cinema and Censorship.* Washington, D.C.: Smithsonian Institution Press, 1996.

Cripps, Thomas. *Slow Fade to Black: The Negro in American Film, 1900-1942.* London: Oxford University Press, 1977.

Dagrada, Elena. *Bibliographie internationale du cinéma des premiers temps.* 2d ed. Domitor, 1995.

Dean, Frank. *Will Rogers Rope Tricks.* Colorado Springs: Western Horseman, 1969.

Deutelbaum, Marshall A., ed. *"Image": On the Art and Evolution of the Film.* New York: Dover, 1979.

Dickson, W.K. Laurie. "A Brief History of the Kinetograph, the Kinetoscope and the Kinetophonograph." *Journal of the Society of Motion Picture Engineers,* December 1933: 444.

Dickson, W.K.L., and Antonia Dickson. *The Life and Inventions of Thomas Alva Edison.* New York: Thomas Y. Crowell, 1894.

———. *A History of the Kinetograph, Kinetoscope, and Kineto-Phonograph.* 1895. Reprint, New York: Arno, 1970.

Dictionary of American Biography. 11 vols. New York: Scribner's Sons, 1927-1958.

Dorsey, George A. *Indians of the Southwest.* Passenger Department, Atchison, Topeka & Santa Fe Railway System, 1903.

Eckhardt, Joseph P., and Linda Kowall. *Peddlar of Dreams: Siegmund Lubin and the Creation of the Motion Picture Industry 1896-1916.* Philadelphia: National Museum of American Jewish History, 1984.

Edison Manufacturing Company. *Edison Films.* Orange, N.J., 15 March 1898.

————. *War Extra: Edison Films*. Orange, N.J., 20 May 1898.

————. *Edison Films*. Orange, N.J., March 1900.

————. *Edison Films*. Orange, N.J., July 1901.

————. *Edison Films*. Orange, N.J., September 1902.

"Edison's Kinetograph and Cosmical Telephone." *Scientific American*, 20 June 1891: 393.

"Edison and the Kinetoscope." *Photographic Times*, 6 April 1894: 209-212.

"Edison's Invention of the Kineto-Phonograph." *Century Magazine*, June 1894: 206-214.

Elsaesser, Thomas, ed. *Early Cinema: Space, Frame, Narrative*. London: BFI Publishing, 1990.

Falk Jr., Byron A., and Valerie R. Falk. *Personal Name Index to "The New York Times Index," 1851-1974*. 22 vols. Verdi, Nevada: Roxbury Data Interface, 1976-1983.

Fell, John L. *Film and the Narrative Tradition*. Norman: University of Oklahoma Press, 1974.

————, ed. *Film Before Griffith*. Berkeley: University of California Press, 1983.

Filmlexicon degli Autori e delle Opere. Roma: Edizioni di Bianco e Nero, 1967.

"First Public Exhibition of Edison's Kinetograph." *Scientific American*, 20 May 1893, 310.

Fox, Richard Wightman, and T. Jackson Lears, eds. *The Culture of Consumption: Critical Essays in American History, 1880-1980*. New York: Pantheon, 1983.

Frazer, John. *Artificially Arranged Scenes: The Films of Georges Méliès*. Boston: G.K. Hall, 1979.

Gartenberg, Jon. "Camera Movement in Edison and Biograph Films, 1900-1906." *Cinema Journal* 19 (Spring 1980): 1-16.

Gaudreault, André. "Detours in Film Narrative: The Development of Cross-Cutting." *Cinema Journal* 19 (Fall 1979): 39-59.

————. "Un Cinéma sans foi ni loi." *Iris* 2 (Spring 1984): 2-4.

Gaudreault, André; Germain Lacasse; and Jean-Pierre Sirois-Trahan. *Au Pays des ennemis du Cinéma: Pour une nouvelle histoire des débuts du cinéma au Québec*. Quebec: Nuit Blanche, 1996.

Girard, Marv "Slim." *Makin' Circles with a Rope: The Lore of the Lasso Wizards*. Francestown, N.H.: Marshall Jones Company, 1985.

Gunning, Tom. "The Cinema of Attraction[s]." *Wide Angle* 8, no. 3-4 (1986). Revised version in Thomas Elsaesser, ed. *Early Cinema*.

————. "An Aesthetic of Astonishment: Early Film and the (In)credulous Spectator." *Art & Text*, Fall 1989. Reprinted in Linda Williams, ed. *Viewing Positions: Ways of Viewing Films*. New Brunswick, N.J.: Rutgers University Press, 1994.

————. *D.W. Griffith and the Origins of American Narrative Film: The Early Years at Biograph*. Urbana: University of Illinois Press, 1991.

————. "Now You See it, Now You Don't: The Temporality of the Cinema of Attractions." *Velvet Light Trap* 32 (Fall 1993): 3-12.

Hammond, Paul. *Marvellous Méliès*. New York: St. Martin's Press, 1975.

Hansen, Miriam. *Babel and Babylon: Spectatorship in American Silent Film*. Cambridge: Harvard University Press, 1991.

Hanson, Patricia King, executive editor. *The American Film Institute Catalog of Motion Pictures Produced in the United States: Feature Films, 1911-1920*. Berkeley: University of California Press, 1988.

Harper's Young People 15 (22 May 1894): 500.

Harris, Neil. *Humbug: The Art of P.T. Barnum*. Boston: Little Brown and Company, 1973.

————. *Cultural Excursions: Marketing Appetites and Cultural Tastes in Modern America*. Chicago: University of Chicago Press, 1990.

Hendricks, Gordon. "A New Look at an Old Sneeze." *Film Culture* 22/23 (1961): 90-95.

————. *The Edison Motion Picture Myth*. Berkeley: University of California Press, 1961. Reprint, New York: Arno, 1972.

————. *Beginnings of the Biograph: The Story of the Invention of the Mutoscope and the Biograph and Their Supplying Camera*. 1964. Reprint, New York: Arno, 1972.

————. *The Kinetoscope: America's First Commercially Successful Motion Picture Exhibitor*. New York: The Beginnings of the American Film, 1966. Reprint, New York: Arno, 1972.

————. *Eadweard Muybridge: The Father of the Motion Picture*. London: Secker and Warburg, 1975.

Hepworth, Cecil. *Animated Photography: The ABC of the Cinematograph*. 1900. Reprint, New York: Arno, 1970.

Hepworth, Thomas Cradock. *The Book of the Lantern*. 1899. Reprint, New York: Arno, 1978.

Herbert, Stephen, and Luke McKernan. *Who's Who in Victorian Cinema: A World Survey*. London: BFI Publishing, 1996.

Higgins, C.A. *To California and Back*. Chicago: Passenger Department, Santa Fe Route, February 1900.

Higham, John. *Writing American History: Essays on Modern Scholarship*. Bloomington: Indiana University Press, 1970.

Holli, Melvin G. and Peter D'A. Jones. *Biographical Dictionary of American Mayors, 1820-1980*. Westport, Ct.: Greenwood Press, 1981.

Hopwood, Henry V. *Living Pictures*. 1899. Reprint, New York: Arno, 1970.

Horn, Maurice, ed. *World Encyclopedia of Comics*. New York: Chelsea House Publishers, 1976.

Horwitz, Rita and Harriet Harrison. *The George Kleine Collection of Early Motion Pictures in the Library of Congress: A Catalog*. Washington, D.C.: Library of Congress, 1980.

"Injured in Sham Battle." *Philadelphia Ledger,* 12 April 1900.

Isenberg, Michael T. *John L. Sullivan and His America.* Urbana: University of Illinois Press, 1988.

Jacobs, Lewis. *The Rise of the American Film.* New York: Harcourt, Brace, 1939.

Jeffrey, Thomas E. et al. *Thomas A. Edison Papers: A Selective Microfilm Edition.* Part I (1850-1878); Part II (1878-1886); Part III (1886-1898). Frederick, Maryland: University Publications of America, 1985-1994.

Jeffrey, Thomas E. et al. *A Guide to "Thomas A. Edison Papers: A Selective Microfilm Edition, Part III (1887-1898)."* Bethesda: University Publications of America, 1994.

Jenkins, C. Francis. *Picture Ribbons.* Washington, D.C.: H.L. McQueen, 1897.

———. *Animated Pictures.* Washington, D.C.: 1898.

Jenkins, C. Francis, and Oscar B. Depue. *Handbook for Motion Picture and Stereopticon Operators.* Washington, D.C.: Knega, 1908.

Jenkins, Reese V. *Images and Enterprise: Technology and the American Photographic Industry, 1839-1925.* Baltimore: Johns Hopkins, 1975.

———. "Elements of Style: Continuities in Edison's Thinking." *Annals of the New York Academy of Sciences* 424 (1984): 149-162.

Jenkins, Reese V. et al. *The Papers of Thomas A. Edison.* Vol. 1. *The Making of an Inventor, February 1847-June 1873.* Baltimore: Johns Hopkins University Press, 1989.

Jenkins, Reese V., Robert A. Rosenberg et al. *The Papers of Thomas A. Edison.* Vol. 2. *From Workshop to Laboratory, June 1873-March 1876.* Baltimore: Johns Hopkins University Press, 1991.

Johannsen, Albert. *The House of Beadle and Adams and Its Dime and Nickel Novels: The Story of a Vanished Literature.* Norman: University of Oklahoma, 1950.

Josephson, Matthew. *Edison.* New York: McGraw-Hill, 1959.

Karp, Ivan, and Steven D. Lavine, eds. *Exhibiting Cultures: The Poetics and Politics of Museum Display.* Washington, D.C.: Smithsonian Institution Press, 1991.

Kasson, John. *Amusing the Million: Coney Island at the turn of the Century.* New York: Hill & Wang, 1978.

Kelkres, Gene G. "A Forgotten First: The Armat-Jenkins Partnership and the Atlanta Projection." *Quarterly Review of Film Studies* 9 (Winter 1984): 45-58.

"The Kinetograph." *Frank Leslie's Weekly,* 5 April 1894: 223-226.

"The Kineto-Phonograph." *The Electrical World,* 16 June 1894: 799.

The Kinetoscope Company. *Edison's Latest Wonders: The Kinetograph, The Kinetoscope.* [October 1894].

———. *Bulletin No. 1.* [December 1894].

———. *Bulletin No. 2.* January 1895.

———. *Price List of Films.* [May 1895].

Koga, Futoshi, ed. *Lumière: Les Lumières et le Japon.* Tokyo: Asahi Shimbun, 1995.

Lathrop, George Parsons. "Edison's Kinetograph." *Harper's Weekly,* 13 June 1891: 446.

Levy, David. "Edwin S. Porter and the Origins of the American Narrative Film, 1894-1907." Ph.D. diss., McGill University, 1983.

Leyda, Jay, and Charles Musser, eds. *Before Hollywood: Turn of the Century Film from American Archives.* New York: American Federation of the Arts, 1986.

Liesegang, Franz Paul. *Dates and Sources: A Contribution to the History of the Art of Projection and to Cinematography.* London: The Magic Lantern Society of Great Britain, 1986.

Low, Rachael, and Roger Manvell. *The History of the British Film, 1896-1906.* London: George Allen and Unwin, 1948.

Macgowan, Kenneth. *Behind the Screen.* New York: Delacorte Press, 1965.

Maguire & Baucus, Limited. *Edison Films for Projecting Machines and Kinetoscopes, Supplementary Catalog.* 20 January 1897.

———. *Edison Perfected Projecting Kinetoscope or "Projectoscope."* '97 Model. 16 February 1897.

———. *Edison and International Photographic Films for Use on the Edison Projecting Kinetoscope and Other Animated Picture Machines.* April 1897.

———. *Fall Catalogue. Lumiere Films, Edison Films, International Films.* 1897.

Maguire & Co., F.Z. *Catalogue.* [March 1898].

Maguire, Thomas. "The Kinetograph." *Frank Leslie's Weekly,* 5 April 1894: 223-226.

Mannoni, Laurent. *Le grand art de la lumière et de l'ombre: archéologie du cinéma.* With an introduction by David Robinson. Paris: Éditions Nathan, 1994.

Mannoni, Laurent; Donata Pesenti Campagnoni; and David Robinson. *Light and Movement: Incunabula of the Motion Picture, 1420-1896.* Pordenone, Italy: Le Giornate del Cinema Muto, 1995.

Mapp, Edward. *Directory of Blacks in the Performing Arts.* 2nd edition. Metuchen, N.J.: Scarecrow Press, 1990.

Mercer, Adam G., editor and compiler. *Sandow on Physical Training.* New York: J. Selwin Tait & Sons, 1894.

Mesguich, Félix. *Tours de manivelle: Souvenirs d'un chasseur d'images.* Paris: Bernard Grassett, 1933.

Millard, André. *Edison and the Business of Innovation.* Baltimore: John Hopkins Press, 1990.

Mitry, Jean. *Histoire du cinema.* Vol. 1. Paris: Éditions universitaires, 1967.

Musser, Charles. "American Vitagraph: 1897-1901."

Cinema Journal 22 (Spring 1983): 4-46.

———. *The Emergence of Cinema: The American Screen to 1907.* New York: Scribner, 1990.

———. *Before the Nickelodeon: Edwin S. Porter and the Edison Manufacturing Company.* Berkeley: University of California Press, 1991.

———. "Passions and the Passion Play: Theater, Film and Religion, 1880-1900." *Film History* 5, no. 4 (1993): 419-456.

Musser, Charles et al. *Motion Picture Catalogs by American Producers and Distributors, 1894-1908: A Microfilm Edition.* Frederick, Maryland: University Publications of America, 1985.

———. *A Guide to "Motion Picture Catalogs by American Producers and Distributors, 1894-1908: A Microfilm Edition."* Frederick, Maryland: University Publications of America, 1985.

Musser, Charles, with Carol Nelson. *High Class Moving Pictures: Lyman Howe and the Traveling Exhibitor.* Princeton, N.J.: Princeton University Press, 1991.

National Cyclopædia of American Biography. 64 vols. New York: James T. White, 1892-1984.

Nelson, Kenneth. "A Compilation of information About Robert Kates Bonine , 1862-1923, with an Examination of His Early Years in Photography and Film." M.A. thesis, Rochester Institute of Technology, 1987.

New York Times Index: Prior News Series (1851-1912). 15 vols. (1966-1974).

New York Times Index: Current News Series (1913-1995). 83 vols.

Niver, Kemp R. *Motion Pictures from the Library of Congress Paper Print Collection: 1894-1912.* Berkeley: University of California Press, 1967.

Niver, Kemp R. with Bebe Bergsten. *The First Twenty Years: A Segment of Film History.* Los Angeles: Locare Research Group, 1968.

———, eds. *Biograph Bulletins, 1896-1908.* Los Angeles: Locare Research Group, 1971.

———. *Klaw and Erlanger Present Famous Plays in Pictures.* Los Angeles: Locare Research Group, 1976.

———. *Early Motion Pictures: The Paper Print Collection in the Library of Congress.* Washington, D.C.: Library of Congress, 1985.

Odell, George C.D. *Annals of the New York Stage.* 15 vols. (1927-1949). New York: Ams Press, 1970.

Ohio Phonograph Co. *The Edison Kinetoscope: Price List.* August 1895.

Passenger Department of the Denver and Rio Grande R.R. *Around the Circle: One Thousand Miles Through the Rocky Mountains, Being a Description of a Trip Over the Passes and Through the Canons of Colorado.* 14th ed. 1895. Denver: Smith-Brooks Printing Co., 1903.

Peiss, Kathy. *Cheap Amusements: Working Women and Leisure in Turn of the Century New York.* Philadelphia: Temple University Press, 1986.

Phillips, Barnet. "The Record of a Sneeze." *Harper's Weekly,* 24 March 1894: 280.

Pratt, George. *Spellbound in Darkness: A History of the Silent Film.* Greenwich, Ct: New York Graphic Society, 1966.

Prescott, F.M. *Catalogue of New Films.* 1899.

"Punch and the Kinetograph." *Illustrated American,* 20 June 1891: 224.

Ramsaye, Terry. *A Million and One Nights.* New York: Simon and Schuster, 1926.

Rittaud-Hutinet, Jacques. *Auguste et Louis Lumière: Les 1000 premiers films.* Paris: Philippe Sers Éditeur, 1990.

Rosenzweig, Roy. *Eight Hours for What We Will: Workers and Leisure in an Industrial City, 1870-1920.* Cambridge: Cambridge University Press, 1983.

Sadie, Stanley, ed. *The New Grove Dictionary of Opera.* New York: Macmillan, 1992.

Sadoul, Georges. *Histoire generale du cinéma.* Vol. 1. *L'invention du cinéma, 1832-1897.* Vol. 2. *Les pionniers du cinéma: De Méliès a Pathé, 1897-1909.* Paris: Éditions Denoël, 1947-1948.

———. *Louis Lumière.* Paris: Éditions Seghers, 1964.

Sandow, Eugen. "How to Preserve Health and Attain Strength." *Cosmopolitan,* June 1894.

———. *Strength and How to Obtain It.* London: Gale & Polden, 1897.

———. *Body Building or Man in the Making.* London: Gale & Polden, [1904].

———. *The Construction and Reconstruction of the Human Body.* London: John Bale, Sons & Co., 1907.

Salt, Barry. *Film Style and Technology: History and Analysis.* London: Starword, 1983.

Savada, Elias. compiler. *The American Film Institute Catalog of Motion Pictures Produced in the United States. Film Beginnings 1893-1910: A Work in Progress.* Metuchen, N.J.: Scarecrow Press, 1995.

Sayers, Isabelle S. *Annie Oakley and Buffalo Bill's Wild West Show.* New York: Dover Publications, 1981.

Schmitt, Robert C. "Movies in Hawaii, 1897-1932." *Hawaiian Journal of History* 1 (1967).

Seguin-Vergara, Jean-Claude. "La légende Promio (1868-1926)." *1895,* no. 11 (March 1992): 94-100.

Sklar, Robert. *Movie-Made America.* New York: Random House, 1975.

Slide, Anthony. *Early American Cinema.* New York: A.S. Barnes, 1970.

Slide, Anthony with Alan Gevison. *The Big V: A History of the Vitagraph Company.* 2d ed. Metuchen, N.J.: Scarecrow Press, 1987.

Smith, Albert C. with Phil A. Koury. *Two Reels and a Crank.* Garden City, N.Y.: Doubleday, 1952.

Sobel, Robert and John Raimo. *Biographical Dictionary of the Governors of the United States, 1789-*

1978. 2 vols. Westport, Ct.: Merkler Books, 1978.

Sollors, Werner. *Beyond Ethnicity.* New York: Oxford University Press.

Spehr, Paul C. *The Movies Begin: Making Movies in New Jersey, 1887-1920.* Newark, N.J.: Newark Museum and Morgan and Morgan, 1977.

———. "Edison Films in the Library of Congress." In Iris Newsom, ed. *Wonderful Inventions: Motion Pictures, Broadcasting, and Recorded Sound at the Library of Congress.* Washington, D.C.: Library Congress, 1985.

Stabla, Zdenek. *Queries Concerning the Horice Passion Film.* Prague: The Film Institute, 1971.

Staiger, Janet. "Combination and Litigation: Structures of US Film Distribution, 1891-1917." *Cinema Journal* 23, no. 2 (Winter 1984): 41-72.

Sweetser, M.F. and Ford, Simeon. *How to Know New York City.* 11th ed. New York: J.J. Little & Co., 1895.

Susman, Warren. *Culture as History.* New York: Pantheon, 1984.

Tate, Alfred O. *Edison's Open Door.* New York: Dutton & Company, 1938.

Toulet, Emmanuelle. *Bibliographie internationale du cinéma des premiers temps.* Québec: Domitor, 1987.

———. *Cinématographe, invention du siècle.* Paris: Gallimard, 1988.

Trachtenberg, Alan. *The Incorporation of America : Culture and Society in the Gilded Age.* New York: Hill & Wang, 1982.

———. "Conceivable Aliens." *The Yale Review* 82, no. 4 (October 1994): 42-64.

Trimble, Marian Blackton. *J. Stuart Blackton: A Personal Biography by His Daughter.* Metuchen, N.J.: Scarecrow Press, 1985.

Tsivian, Yuri. *Early Cinema in Russia and Its Cultural Reception.* Translated by Alan Bodger. With a foreword by Tom Gunning. London: Routledge, 1994.

———. "The Rorschach Test for Cultures: On Some Parallels between Early Film Reception in Russia and the United States." *Yale Journal of Criticism* 7, no. 2 (1995): 177-188.

Van Loan's Catskill Mountain Guide with Bird's-Eye View, Maps and Choice Illustrations. New York: Rogers & Sherwood, 1890.

Vardac, A. Nicholas. *Stage to Screen: Theatrical Methods from Garrick to Griffith.* Cambridge, Ma.: Harvard University Press, 1949.

Variety Obituaries, 1905-1986. 11 vols. New York: Garland Publishing, 1989.

Vazzana, Eugene Michael. *Silent Film Necrology: Births and Deaths of Over 9000 Performers, Directors, Producers and Other Filmmakers of the SIlent Era, Through 1993.* Jefferson, N.C.: McFarland & Co., 1995.

Waller, Gregory A. *Main Street Amusements: Movies and Commercial Entertainments in a Southern City, 1896-1930.* Washington, D.C.: Smithsonian Institution Press, 1995.

Walls, Howard Lamarr. *Motion Pictures, 1894-1912.* Washington, D.C.: Library of Congress, 1953.

Webster's New Biographical Dictionary. Springfield, Ma.: Merriam-Webster, 1983.

Wheeler, Olin D. *Wonderland '96: Picturing the Country, the Cities, the Resorts, the Game Found Along the Northern Pacific Railroad.* St. Paul: Northern Pacific Railroad, 1896.

White-Hensen, Wendy, and Veronica M. Gillespie. *The Theodore Roosevelt Association Film Collection.* Washington, D.C.: Library of Congress, 1986.

Who Was Who. Vols. 1-4. Chicago: Marquis—Who's Who Incorporated, 1966-1968.

Williams, Alan. *Republic of Images.* Cambridge, Ma.: Harvard University Press, 1992.

Wilson, James Grant, and John Fiske, eds. *Appleton's Cyclopedia of American Biography.* New York: Appleton, 1888.

"Wizard Edison's Kinetograph." *New York World,* 18 March 1894: 21.

"The World Awheel." *Munsey's Magazine,* May 1896: 155.

Trade periodicals

Moving Picture World (1907-1917)

New York Clipper (1893-1909)

New York Dramatic Mirror (1890-1909)

The Phonogram (1891-1893)

The Phonoscope (1896-1900)

Photographic Times (1894-1900)

Variety (1905-1980)

Views and Film Index (1906-1910)

Daily and weekly newspapers

Arcadian (Halifax, Nova Scotia) Recorder (1900)

Asbury Park (N.J.) Daily Journal (1895-1900)

Asbury Park (N.J.) Daily Press (1895-1900)

Atlantic City (N.J.) Daily Union (1896-1900)

Baltimore Sun (1894-1905)

Boston Herald (1894-1907)

Brooklyn Eagle (1891-1907)

Buffalo Courier-Record (1896-1897)

Chicago Inter-Ocean (1895-1901)

Chicago Tribune (1896-1907)

Cincinnati Commercial Tribune (1896-1900)

Denver Post (1896-1897)

L'Évenement (Montreal, Canada) (1899)

Harrisburg (Pa.) Daily Telegraph (1896-1897)

Harrisburg (Pa.) Patriot (1896-1897)

Hartford (Ct.) Courant (1896-1900)

Hawaiian (Honolulu) Gazette (1898)

Helena (Montana) Herald (1897)

Hong Kong Weekly Press and China Overland Mail (1898)

Japan Weekly Mail (1898)

The Klondike (Dawson, Yukon Territory) Nugget (1899)
Montreal Gazette (1899)
New Haven (Ct.) Evening Register (1896-1905)
New Haven (Ct.) Journal-Courier (1896-1905)
New Orleans Picayune (1896-1905)
New York Evening World (1894-1896)
New York Herald (1891-1924)
New York Journal and Advertiser (1896-1906)
New York Mail and Express (1896-1900)
New York Sun (1891-1900)
New York Times (1875-1980)
New York Tribune (1894-1904)
New York World (1891-1900)
Newark (N.J.) Daily Advertiser (1891-1900)
Newark (N.J.) Evening News (1896-1900)
North China Herald (1898)

Orange (N.J.) Chronicle (1888-1907)
Orange (N.J.) Journal (1888-1907)
Philadelphia Record (1895-1906)
Pittsburgh Dispatch (1896)
Providence Journal (1896-1906)
Rochester (N.Y.) Democrat and Chronicle (1896-1900)
San Diego Sun (1897-1898)
San Diego Union (1897-1898)
San Francisco Chronicle (1894-1900)
San Francisco Examiner (1894-1904)
Scranton (Pa.) Times (1896-1900)
Seattle (Wa.) Intelligencer (1897-1898)
Seattle (Wa.) Times (1897-1899)
Washington Evening Star (1894-1906)
Washington Post (1896-1920)
Wilkes-Barre (Pa.) Leader (1896-1900)

Featuring performers, production personnel, people appearing in
the films, people who are the subject of these films as well as
organizations and corporations associated with the films.

Burglars: 579, 601, 623, 640, 883. *See also* Criminals; Tramps

Burlesque: 41, 42, 52, 60, 70, 76, 77, 81, 100

Burlesque–performances: 123, 135, 136, 137, 427. *See also* Danse du ventre; Musicals–performances; Vaudeville–performances

Businessmen: 236, 237, 776

Camels: 174

Canals: 459, 460

Canyons: 371, 435, 436, 711

Carpenters: 228

Carriages and carts: 248, 249, 274, 275, 365, 366, 380, 381, 382, 384, 402, 403, 405, 420, 470, 471, 534, 700, 813, 814, 840, 872. *See also* Sleighs and sledges; Urban transportation

Catholicism: 461, 463, 744, 873

Cats: 41

Catskill Mountains (N.Y.): 348, 349

Cattle: 357, 445, 446

Cattle drives: 437

Cattle–marking: 438, 444

Cavalry: 210, 261, 287, 293, 295, 306, 307, 308, 327, 328, 333, 335, 455, 554, 555, 583, 584, 589, 590, 593, 638, 800, 803, 804, 805, 806, 808, 856, 875. *See also* Armies (subdivided by country); Horses

Ceremonies: 739, 752. *See also* Funerals; Parades; Speeches, adresses, etc.

Charities: 202

Chemical laboratories: 344

Chickens: 243, 346, 785

Child rearing: 225, 245, 626, 707, 884, 922. *See also* Family; Infants

Children: 51, 157, 204, 232, 243, 310, 342, 347, 417, 439, 450, 486, 519, 520 570, 571, 620, 627, 722, 819, 820, 821, 822, 823, 889, 892, 890. *See also* Boy; Family; Girls; Infants

China–Foreign Relations–United States: 208, 209, 210

China–History–Boxer Rebellion: 837, 919

Chinese: 95, 96, 97, 210, 508, 510, 511, 512, 919

Chinese Americans: 397, 398, 399, 421, 487

Christmas: 281

Church buildings: 304, 309, 458, 493, 855. *See also* Convents

Cigarettes: 311, 362, 648. *See also* Tobacco

Cigars: 580, 891

Circus animals: 36, 41, 42, 81, 82, 320, 321, 322, 323, 324, 722, 727, 882

Circus performers: 129, 130, 131, 132, 133, 134, 319

Circuses. *See* Circus animals; Circus performers

City and town life: 362.1

City and town life–Austro-Hungary: 461

City and town life–Brooklyn: 171, 178

City and town life–Chicago: 354

City and town life–China: 502, 503, 508, 509, 510, 511, 513, 514

City and town life–Dawson City, Canada: 714

City and town life–Germany: 861, 862, 863, 864, 872, 873

City and town life–Harrisburg (Penn.): 278, 279, 280, 281

City and town life–Honolulu: 572

City and town life–Japan: 518, 519, 520, 521, 522, 523, 524

City and town life–London: 865, 866

City and town life–Los Angeles: 470

City and town life–Mauch Chunk (Jim Thorpe, Pa.): 903

City and town life–Mexico: 450, 451, 452, 453, 456, 457, 458, 459, 460

City and town life–New York: 157, 158, 159, 168, 169, 170, 188, 214, 215, 216, 217, 218, 219, 248, 249, 291, 292, 549, 550, 603, 643, 772, 773, 818

City and town life–Newark: 246

City and town life–Orange: 220, 425, 426, 494, 548

City and town life–Paris: 840, 841, 843, 844, 845, 846, 848, 849, 851, 854, 855, 857, 858, 859, 860

City and town life–San Diego: 464

City and town life–San Francisco: 397

City and town life–Seattle: 378

City and town life–Washington, D.C.: 288, 305, 905, 906, 907

Clerks: 776, 888

Clowns: 119, 794, 923, 932

Coaches. *See* Carriages and carts; Urban transportation

Coal: 353, 501, 517, 540, 545, 546, 579, 601

Coasting: 492, 493

Cockfighting: 27, 53, 276

Construction equipment: 289

Contests. *See* Aquatic sports; Boxing; Contests–food; Sports; Wrestling

Contests–food: 207, 428, 836

Convents: 268. *See also* Church buildings

Convict labor: 452

Cooking. *See* Kitchens

Corn-husking: 341

Cossacks: 584

Country clubs: 273, 274, 275

Courtship: 155, 185, 225, 313, 341, 621, 624, 642, 678, 724, 899, 922, 935, 936

Cowboys: 79, 80, 149, 418, 437, 438, 444, 445, 446

Cows: 286, 853. *See also* Cattle

Criminals: 346, 397, 452, 726. *See also* Burglars, Tramps

Cubans: 563, 564, 565, 599, 604, 605, 646

Dancing: 28, 33, 38, 43, 48, 49, 50, 51, 62, 64, 69, 71, 81, 88, 89, 90, 91, 92, 98, 99, 103, 107, 116, 117, 118, 120, 121, 122, 123, 125, 129, 130, 132, 133, 134, 136, 138, 139, 140, 141, 144, 145, 146, 147, 152, 153, 156, 179, 180, 181, 186, 198, 212, 213, 239, 241, 285, 320, 339, 340, 385, 387, 388, 390, 391, 422, 423, 427, 431, 432, 628, 631, 632, 659, 669, 852

Danse du ventre: 69, 92, 134, 138, 153, 186, 239, 241, 320

Dentistry: 113, 550

Devil: 625, 786, 794, 795, 796

Rats: 56, 57, 58, 59

Refugees: 563, 564

Religious ceremonies: 461, 873

Rescues: 253

Revues–performances: 71, 120, 121, 122. *See also* Musicals–performances

Rickshaw men: 513, 514, 515, 518, 521

Rifles and rifle practice: 61, 74, 86, 672. *See also* Gatling guns

Rivalries: 796. *See also* Contests; Dueling; Politics, practical; Sports

Riverboats: 511, 849. *See also* Steamships

Rivers: 227, 314, 315, 316, 317, 318, 437, 701, 702, 710, 815, 817, 849, 903

Rivers–China: 507, 510

Roads–construction: 600

Rocky Mountains: 435, 436. *See also* Mountains

Ruins: 908, 909, 910, 911, 912, 913, 914, 915. *See also* Fire ruins

Russians: 919

Sail boats. *See* Yachts and yachting; Yacht racing

Samoan Islanders: 129

Sampans: 510, 525

Santa Clara Pueblo Indians from Espanola, N.Mex: 422, 423, 439

Schools: 311, 439, 823

Schools–Exercises and recreations: 819, 820, 821, 822, 823, 825, 826, 827, 828, 829, 830, 831, 832, 833, 924, 925, 926, 927, 928

Scots: 33, 123

Sea gulls: 269, 484

Sea lions: 415

Seashore: 177, 189, 190, 191, 206, 244, 404, 408, 409, 410, 411, 412, 413, 414, 415, 467, 526, 890, 893, 899, 900

Secret Societies: 161

Secretaries: 236, 237

Seesaws: 581

Servants: 777

Sexual harassment: 312, 641, 891, 892

Sham battles: 876, 927, 928. *See also* Battles

Shaving: 18, 111, 784. *See also* Babershops

Sheep: 356

Ships: 507, 575, 576, 577, 909, 924. *See also* Boats and boating; Navies (subdivided by country); Riverboats; Steamships; Transports; Yachts and yachting

Ships–launching: 480, 481, 482, 910

Shipyards: 480, 481, 482, 483

Shoes: 362.1

Shooting. *See* Rifles and rifle practice

Signs: 896

Sleds: 492, 493

Sleighs and sledges: 280, 292, 494, 643, 665, 713

Sneeze: 19

Snow storms: 548

Snowballing: 493, 791

Soap bubbles: 342

Social elites: 197, 248, 249, 274, 275, 291, 292, 380, 381, 382, 383, 384, 388, 420, 456, 725, 799, 813, 814. *See also* Working classes

Solar eclipses: 834

Soldiers: 678, 724. *See also* Armies (subdivided by country)

South African War (1899-1902): 763, 764, 790, 800, 801, 802, 803, 804, 805, 806, 807, 808

South Americans: 46, 47

Spain–Colonies (Cuba): 536, 537

Spaniards: 28, 78, 146, 147, 604, 605. *See also* Armies–Spain

Spanish-American War: 529, 530, 531, 532, 533, 534, 535, 536, 537, 538, 539, 540, 541, 542, 543, 544, 545, 546, 547, 552, 553, 554, 555, 556, 557, 558, 559, 560, 561, 562, 563, 564, 565, 574, 575, 576, 577, 585, 586, 587, 588, 589, 590, 591, 592, 593, 594, 595, 596, 597, 598, 599, 600, 604, 605, 606, 607, 608, 609, 610, 611, 612, 613, 614, 615, 616, 617, 618, 619, 636, 637, 638, 639, 644, 645, 646, 647, 651, 652, 653, 654, 655, 682, 683, 690, 691, 724, 729, 730, 731, 732, 733, 734, 734.1, 735, 736, 737, 738, 739, 740, 741, 742, 743, 744, 745, 746, 747, 748, 749, 750, 751, 752, 753, 772. *See also* Philippines–History–Insurrection (1899-1901)

Speeches, addresses, etc.: 233, 294, 325, 326, 752

Speed records: 211

Sports: 9, 10, 11, 12, 13, 14, 21, 22, 23, 24, 25, 29, 39, 40, 54, 66, 67, 68, 115, 192, 193, 406, 407, 454, 582, 695, 696, 765, 766, 770, 771, 828, 833 *See also* Baseball; Boxing; Football; Gymnastics; etc.

Sri Lankans: 133

Stables: 247, 425

Steam: 289

Steamships: 166, 202, 203, 208, 211, 373, 374, 375, 376, 376.1, 377, 398, 399, 400, 496, 497, 498, 499, 500, 501, 508, 512, 516, 517, 566, 567, 568, 569, 570, 571, 573, 617, 684, 711, 731, 838, 867

Stenographers: 776

Stevedores: 501, 508, 517, 545, 546

Stockyards: 350, 355, 356, 357

Stores: 362.1, 502, 519, 549

Storms: 244, 496, 497, 498, 499, 500, 526, 792, 838. *See also* Floods

Storytelling: 765

Street Cleaners: 160

Street music and musicians: 34, 35

Streets–maintenance and repair: 188, 452. *See also* Roads–construction

Strong men: 26, 26.1, 26.2, 126, 127, 128

Students. *See* Schools

Suburban Handicap: 176, 359

Subways: 931. *See also* Urban transportation

Sun: 834

Susquehanna River: 314, 316, 317, 701, 702, 817

Swimming pools: 197, 345, 392, 393, 394, 516, 835

Swiss: 852, 853

Swiss Alps: 881

Location Index

Archive Holdings

Big Fights, Inc.: 40, 54

CaOOANF (David Flaherty Collection, National Film Archive, Ottawa, Ontario, Canada): 64, 143, 187, 224, 228, 243, 244, 246, 257, 262, 272, 274, 281, 302, 309, 312, 317, 339, 346, 351, 360, 361

CL-UC (UCLA Film and Television Archive, Los Angeles, California): 20, 774

CLAc (Ray Phillips Collection, Academy of Motion Picture Arts and Sciences, Los Angeles, California): 18, 26, 37, 40, 41, 46, 62, 64, 71, 72, 75, 77, 78, 86, 91, 102, 106, 111, 125, 152, 171, 173, 183, 206, 225, 243, 245, 247, 258, 260, 273, 280, 311, 341, 343, 344, 346, 362.1, 392, 455, 476, 480, 493, 527, 559, 585, 595, 599, 603, 621

DLC (Library of Congress, Washington, D.C.): 4, 9, 125, 626

DLC-AFI (American Film Institute Collection, Library of Congress, Washington, D.C.): 139, 239, 391, 626

DLC-Hendricks (Collection Hendricks, Library of Congress, Washington, D.C.): 19, 21, 26, 28, 41, 46, 54, 62, 64, 75, 77, 78, 79, 86, 91, 96, 102, 106, 115, 134, 139, 142, 152, 155, 158, 173, 183, 224, 225, 243, 245, 247, 252, 258, 259, 262, 280, 284

DLC-pp (Paper Print Collection, Library of Congress, District of Columbia): 348, 349, 350, 351, 352, 353, 354, 355, 356, 357, 358, 359, 360, 361, 362, 363, 365, 366, 368, 369, 370, 371, 372, 373, 374, 375, 376, 377, 378, 379, 380, 381, 382, 383, 384, 385, 386, 387, 388, 389, 390, 391, 392, 393, 394, 395, 396, 397, 398, 399, 400, 401, 402, 403, 404, 405, 406, 407, 408, 409, 410, 411, 412, 413, 414, 415, 416, 417, 418, 419, 420, 421, 422, 423, 424, 425, 426, 427, 428, 429, 430, 431, 432, 433, 434, 435, 436, 437, 438, 439, 440, 441, 442, 443, 444, 445, 446, 447, 448, 449, 450451, 452, 453, 454, 455, 456, 457, 458, 459, 460, 464, 466, 467, 468, 469, 470, 471, 472, 473, 474, 475, 476, 477, 478, 479, 480, 481, 482, 483, 484, 485, 486, 487, 488, 489, 490, 492, 493, 494, 495, 496, 497, 498, 499, 500, 501, 502, 503, 504, 505, 506, 507, 508, 509, 510, 511, 512, 513, 514, 515, 516, 517, 518, 519, 520, 521, 522, 523, 524, 525, 526, 527, 528, 529, 530, 531, 532, 533, 534, 535, 536, 537, 538, 539, 540, 541, 542, 543, 544, 545, 546, 547, 548, 551, 552, 553, 554, 555, 556, 557, 558, 559, 560, 561, 562, 563, 564, 565, 566, 567, 568, 569, 570, 571, 572, 573, 574, 575, 576, 577, 578, 579, 580, 581, 582, 583, 584, 585, 586, 587, 588, 589, 590, 591, 592, 593, 594, 595, 596, 597, 598, 599, 600, 601, 602, 603, 604, 605, 606, 607, 608, 609, 610, 611, 612, 613, 614, 615, 616, 617, 618, 619, 620, 621, 622, 623, 624, 625, 631, 632, 633, 634, 635, 636, 637, 638, 639, 640, 641, 642, 643, 645, 646, 647, 648, 649, 650, 658, 659, 660, 661, 662, 663, 664, 665, 667, 671, 672, 673, 677, 678, 679, 680, 681, 682, 683, 684, 685, 686, 687, 688, 689, 690, 691, 692, 697, 698, 699, 700, 701, 702, 703, 704, 708, 709, 710, 711, 712, 713, 715, 716717, 718, 719, 720, 721, 722, 723, 724, 725, 726, 729, 730, 733, 735, 736, 738, 739, 741, 744, 745, 746, 747, 748, 750, 751, 752, 753, 754, 755, 756, 757, 758, 759, 760, 761, 762, 763, 764, 766, 767, 768, 769, 777, 779, 783, 784, 785, 786, 787, 789, 794, 795, 796, 797, 799, 800, 801, 802, 803, 804, 805, 806, 807, 808, 809, 810, 811, 814, 816, 834, 835, 837, 838, 839, 840, 841, 842, 843, 844, 845, 847, 848, 849, 850, 851, 852, 853, 854, 855, 856, 882, 885, 887, 890, 908, 909, 910, 911, 912, 913, 914, 915, 919, 920, 921, 922, 923, 924, 925, 926, 927, 931, 932, 933, 934, 935

DLC-Roosevelt (Theodore Roosevelt Association Film Collection, Library of Congress, Washington, D.C.): 595, 599, 600

DNA (National Archives, Washington, D.C.): 1, 28, 206, 343, 344, 362.1, 549

FrBaADF (Archives du film, CNC, Bois d'Arcy, France): 21, 26, 41, 47, 62, 64, 72, 75, 86

Killiam (Paul Killiam, New York, N.Y.): 226

NjWOE (Edison National Historic Site, West Orange, N.J.): 1, 2, 3, 4, 8, 9, 10

NNMoMA (Museum of Modern Art, New York, N.Y.): 9, 16, 18, 21, 26, 41, 48, 54, 62, 64, 68, 75, 86, 96, 125, 140, 142, 144, 155, 185, 186, 199, 207, 243, 245, 247, 252, 255, 276, 291, 316, 344, 443, 492, 498, 577, 676, 896

NR-GE (George Eastman House, Rochester, New York): 78, 79, 91, 102, 106, 115, 134, 152, 171, 173, 183, 206, 224, 225, 234, 243, 245, 247, 255, 258, 260, 262, 280, 341, 343, 344, 346, 362.1, 392, 445, 455, 463, 476, 480, 493, 527, 549, 559, 563, 585, 595, 599, 600, 603, 609, 621, 656, 861, 862, 863, 864

UkLNFA (National Film Archive, London, United Kingdom): 40, 71, 111, 139, 316

The Biography of the Motion Picture Camera (directed by Roger Leenhardt, 1946), a documentary made in 35mm film, contains the following films: *[Athlete with Wand]* (entry no. 21); *Sandow* (26); *Boxing Cats* (41); *Buffalo Dance* (64); *Hadji Cheriff* (75); *Annie Oakley* (86). Copies are at NNMoMA and elsewhere.

DATE DUE

Le Giornate del Cinema Muto
c/o La Cineteca del Friuli
Via Osoppo, 26
33013 Gemona (UD) Italy

Many thanks
from Le Giornate to
Sara Londero and Marina Mottin

Copy Editor
Piera Patat

Design
Cyberstudio
Giulio Calderini, Carmen Marchese

Printed by
Arti Grafiche Friulane
October 1997

Photograph Credits

Academy of Motion Picture Arts and Sciences, Los Angeles, California (CLAc): entry nos. 144 (courtesy Ray Phillips), 171, 206, 343, 599, unidentified film no. 4.

American Museum of the Moving Image: entry no. 77.

Archives du Film, Bois d'Arcy, France (FrBaADF): entry nos. 46, 62, 64, 72, unidentified film no. 2.

Bison Film Archive (Marc Wanamaker): ill. p. 538.

David L. Chapman: entry no. 126.

Edison National Historic Site (NjWOE): entry nos. 1, 2, 3, 4, 8, 9, 10, 19, 123, 273, 896; ills. p. 70, 87, 118, 167, 178, 272, 361, 573.

Film Preservation Associates (David Shepard): entry nos. 20 and 65 (courtesy of Ray Phillips).

George Eastman House (NR-GE): entry nos. 79, 102, 106, 115, 152, 171, 173, 224, 234, 254, 258, 260, 280, 362.1, 392, 445, 463, 476, 493, 527, 563, 599, 603, 609, 621, 861, 862, 863, 864, unidentified film no. 7.

Charles Hummel Collection: entry nos. 30, 31, 34, 36, 38, 61, 70, 73, 81, 87, 90, 95, 101, 107; ills. p. 127, 136.

Library of Congress (DLC): entry nos. 54, 78, 139, 239, 241, 242, 243, 246, 250, 252, 253, 255, 259, 267, 269, 270, 276, 278, 279, 281, 283, 284, 285, 286, 287, 288, 289, 293, 294, 295, 296, 297, 298, 299, 300, 301, 303, 304, 305, 306, 307, 308, 309, 312, 313, 314, 315, 316, 317, 318, 319, 323, 324, 325, 326, 327, 328, 329, 330, 331, 332, 333, 334, 335, 336, 337, 338, 339, 340, 341, 342, 344, 345, 346, 347, 348, 349, 350, 351, 352, 353, 354, 355, 356, 357, 358, 359, 360, 361, 362, 363, 365, 366, 368, 369, 370, 371, 372, 373, 374, 375, 376, 377, 378, 379, 380, 381, 382, 383, 384, 385, 386, 387, 388, 389, 390, 391, 393, 394, 395, 396, 397, 398, 399, 400, 401, 402, 403, 404, 405, 406, 407, 408, 409, 410, 411, 412, 413, 414, 415, 416, 417, 418, 419, 420, 421, 422, 423, 424, 425, 426, 427, 428, 429, 430, 431, 432, 433, 434, 435, 436, 437, 438, 439, 440, 441, 442, 443, 444, 446, 447, 448, 449, 450, 41, 452, 454, 455, 456, 457, 458, 459, 460, 464, 466, 467, 468, 469, 470, 471, 472, 473, 474, 475, 477, 478, 479, 480, 481, 482, 483, 484, 485, 486, 487, 488, 489, 490, 492, 494, 495, 496, 497, 498, 499, 500, 501, 502, 503, 504, 505, 506, 507, 508, 509, 510, 511, 512, 513, 514, 515, 516, 517, 518, 519, 520, 521, 522, 523, 524, 525, 526, 528, 529, 530, 531, 532, 533, 534, 535, 536, 537, 538, 539, 540, 541, 542, 543, 544, 545, 546, 547, 548, 551, 552, 553, 554, 555, 556, 557, 558, 559, 560, 562, 564, 565, 566, 567, 568, 569, 570, 571, 572, 573, 574, 575, 576, 577, 578, 579, 580, 581, 582, 583, 584, 585, 586, 587, 588, 589, 590, 591, 592, 593, 594, 595, 596, 598, 600, 601, 602, 604, 605, 606, 607, 608, 610, 611, 612, 613, 614, 615, 616, 617, 618, 619, 620, 621, 622, 623, 624, 625, 626, 631, 632, 633, 634, 635, 636, 637, 638, 639, 640, 641, 642, 643, 645, 646, 647, 648, 649, 650, 658, 659, 660, 661, 662, 663, 664, 665, 667, 671, 672, 673, 677, 679, 680, 681, 682, 683, 684, 685, 686, 687, 688, 689, 690, 691, 692, 697, 698, 699, 700, 702, 703, 703, 704, 708, 709, 710, 711, 712, 713, 715, 716, 717, 718, 719, 720, 721, 722, 723, 724, 725, 726, 727, 728, 729, 731, 732, 735, 737, 738, 742, 744, 747, 748, 749, 750, 751, 753, 754, 755, 756, 757, 758, 759, 760, 761, 762, 763, 764, 766, 767, 769, 776, 777, 780, 784, 785, 786, 787, 788, 790, 795, 796, 797, 798, 800, 801, 802, 803, 804, 805, 806, 807, 808, 809, 810, 811, 812, 815, 817, 835, 836, 837, 838, 839, 840, 841, 842, 843, 844, 845, 847, 848, 849, 850, 851, 852, 853, 854, 855, 856, 882, 885, 887, 890, 908, 909, 910, 911, 912, 913, 914, 915, 919, 920, 921, 922, 923, 924, 925, 926, 927, 931, 932, 933, 934, 935, unidentified film no. 1 and 5. (Note: A large number of the above photographs were taken by Patrick Loughney; others were taken by the author.)

Museum of Modern Art (NNMoMA) / Film Still Archive: entry no. 132; ill. p. 291; **Film and Video Archive**: entry nos. 16, 18, 21, 26, 41, 52, 68, 75, 86, 91, 96, 125, 140, 155, 158, 159, 186, 196, 199, 207, 225, 245, 247, 265, unidentified film no. 6.

National Film and Television Archive, British Film Institute (UkLNFA): entry nos: 37, 40, 71, 110, 111, 139, 258.

National Film Archive, Canada (CaOOANF): entry nos. 143, 187, 228, 244, 257, 262, 272, 302, 351, 361.

National Film Archive, Washington, D.C. (DNA): entry no. 28.

New York Public Library (NN): entry nos. 105 (courtesy Ray Phillips), 129, 130, 133 (courtesy of Gordon Hendricks Collection, Smithsonian Institution), 182.

Ray Phillips Collection: entry nos. 33, 105, unidentified film no. 3.

Smithsonian Institution: entry nos. 12, 13, 14, 15, 26.1 (Hendricks Collection).

UCLA Film and Television Archive (CL-UC): entry no. 774.

University of Washington, Library: ill. p. 516.

Cover: Edison's Black Maria motion picture studio (March 1894). Hand tinted by Elizabeth Lennard.